CW01502444

Please send this book
to my brother in law
Mr Tom Moorwood
181 Brocklhurst Hill.
Fulwood
Sheffield X
(England)

Sheffield

from the Attercliffe Road

Hallamshire.

THE HISTORY AND TOPOGRAPHY

OF THE PARISH OF

SHEFFIELD

IN THE COUNTY OF YORK:

WITH

HISTORICAL AND DESCRIPTIVE NOTICES

OF THE PARISHES OF ECCLESFIELD, HANSWORTH, TREETON, AND WHISTON,
AND OF THE CHAPELRY OF BRADFIELD.

o

BY JOSEPH HUNTER,

AN HONORARY MEMBER OF THE SOCIETY OF ANTIQUARIES OF NEWCASTLE-UPON-TYNE.

'*Locis etiam ipsis montuosis delectamur, et sylvestribus, in quibus diutius commorati sumus.*'—Cic.

LONDON:

PRINTED FOR THE AUTHOR, BY RICHARD AND ARTHUR TAYLOR, SHOE-LANE:
PUBLISHED BY LACKINGTON, HUGHES, HARDING, MAVOR, AND JONES,
FINSBURY-SQUARE.

1819.

SOLA VIRTUS INVICTA

TO HIS GRACE

BERNARD-EDWARD DUKE OF NORFOLK,

EARL MARSHAL, AND HEREDITARY MARSHAL OF ENGLAND,

&c. &c. &c.

THE LINEAL DESCENDANT AND ILLUSTRIOUS REPRESENTATIVE

OF THOSE NOBLE FAMILIES WHO IN DIRECT SUCCESSION

HAVE BEEN FOR MORE THAN SEVEN CENTURIES THE

LORDS AND PATRONS OF THIS DISTRICT,

THE FOLLOWING ATTEMPT AT RECOVERING ITS HISTORY AND ANTIQUITIES,

AND AT DESCRIBING ITS PRESENT STATE,

IS WITH ALL DEFERENCE INSCRIBED

BY

HIS GRACE'S MOST OBLIGED

AND MOST OBEDIENT HUMBLE SERVANT,

THE AUTHOR.

LIST OF SUBSCRIBERS.

LARGE PAPER.

His MAJESTY's Library.
His Grace the DUKE of NORFOLK.

BEDFORD, William, esq. Byrches-green, Warwickshire.
Black, Mr. W., Norwich.
Britton, John, esq. F.S.A. Tavistock-place, London.
Broadley, H., esq. Hull.
Broadley, J., esq. F.S.A. Kirk-Ella, Yorkshire.
Burbeary, Mr., Sheffield.
Cockburn, Sir William, bart. Bath.
Company of Cutlers, Sheffield.
Crosse, J., esq. F.S.A. Hull.
Frend, William, esq. London.
Girdler, Mrs. Sarah.
Hayward, Francis, M.D. Bath.
Hibbert, George, esq. Clapham-common.
Hoare, Sir Richard Colt, bart. F.R.S. &c. Stourhead.
Hoult, Mr. John, Wadsley-bridge.
Lloyd, W. H., esq. London.
Mole, Thomas E., esq. Poplars, near Birmingham.
Nightingale, William Edward, esq. Lea, Derbyshire.

North, J. P., esq. London.
Parker, Adamson, esq. Longley, near Sheffield.
Radclyffe, William, esq. F.S.A. Rouge-croix pursuivant.
Rawson, Thomas, esq. Wardsend, near Sheffield.
Read, John, esq. Norton-house, near Sheffield.
Rennie, John, esq. F.R. & A.S. London.
Rimington, John, esq. Hillsborough, near Sheffield.
Russell, W. G., esq. Moseley, Worcestershire.
Sheffield Subscription Library.
Shore, Samuel, esq. Meersbrook, near Sheffield.
Sitwell, Sir George, bart. Renishaw, Derbyshire.
Staniforth, W., esq. Sheffield.
Taylor, George Watson, esq. M.P. London.
Wilson, Henry, esq. Aldermanbury, London.
Wilson, William, esq. Aldermanbury, London.
Wilson, Mr. W., Sheffield.
York, Library of Manchester College.

SMALL PAPER.

ANDOVER, Right Honourable Lord Viscount.
Alderson, Rev. William, Aston.
Aspland, Rev. Robert, Hackney.
Astley, Rev. Richard, Halifax.
Badger, Mr. Thomas, solicitor, Rotherham.
Bagshaw, Sir W. C., The Oaks, Derbyshire.
Bagshaw, Mrs., Banner-cross.
Baker, George, esq. Northampton.
Barber, Mr. Enoch, Sheffield.
Barlow, Messrs. J. and T., Sheffield.
Barratt, Mr., bookseller, Bath.
Barry, Henry, esq. Bath.
Basnett, Mr. C. H., Bath.
Beilby, Mr. Thomas, bookseller, Birmingham.
Beldon, Joseph, esq. Temple.
Bishop, Mr. E. L., Sharrow-lane, Sheffield.
Blakelock, Mr. Ralph, Sheffield.
Bliss, Rev. Philip, LL.B., St. John's college Oxford.
Booth, Mr., bookseller, Duke-street, London.
Bosville, Rev. Thomas, Ravenfield-park. (Two copies.)
Bower, Henry, esq. Tickhill.
Bradford Public Library.
Bramhall, Mr. J. S., Sheffield.
Brammall, Mr. Daniel, Sheaf-house.
Brammall, Mr. Thomas, Heeley.
Bransby, Rev. J. H., Dudley.
Bright, B. H., esq.
Bright, Richard, esq. Ham-Green, Bristol.
Brittain, Mr. Verdon, Sheffield. (Two copies.)
Broadbent, Mr. J. W., Sheffield.

Broadhurst, Rev. T., Bath.
Brookfield, Mr., solicitor, Sheffield.
Broomhead, Mr. Richard, Revel-grange.
Brownell, Mr. Peter, Sheffield.
Burnell, Peter Pegge, esq. Winkburn, Notts.
Burrell, William, esq. Broom-park, Northumberland.
Christie, John, esq. Hackney Wick.
Clement, Mrs., Swainswick, near Bath.
Clifford, Sir Thomas, bart. Tixall.
Collings, Mr., bookseller, Bath.
Crawford, Stewart, M.D. Bath.
Creswick, Mr. Nathaniel, Sheffield.
Cruttenden, E. H., esq. Bath.
Dawson, C. H., esq. Royd's-hall.
Deakin, Mr. Thomas, Sheffield.
Dealtry, Rev. William, Wigginton, near York.
Douce, W. H., esq. Bath.
Dunn, Mr. Thomas, Sheffield.
Eadon, Mr. John, Sheffield.
Edmunds, F. O., esq. Worsborough.
Eyre, Rev. Mr. Archdeacon.
Falconer, Rev. Thomas, Bath.
Favell, Mr. John, Sheffield.
Fox, Mr. Godfrey, Sheffield.
Furniss, Mr. J. B., Sheffield.
Galway, Right Honourable Dowager Viscountess.
Gales, Miss, Sheffield.
Gilbert-Cooper, John, esq. Thurgarton Priory, Notts.
Greaves, G. B., esq. Page-hall.
Gunning, Miss E., Swainswick, near Bath.

b

Gurney, Mr. Joseph, Sheffield.
Hadfield, Mr. Samuel, Sheffield.
Halifax Public Library.
Hall, John, esq. Epping-Forest.
Hamper, William, esq. Birmingham.
Harting, John, esq. London.
Hayward, William, esq. London.
Heywood, Mrs. Nathaniel, Manchester.
Heywood, Benjamin, esq. Manchester.
Hodgson, Rowland, esq. Sheffield.
Hodgson, Mr. William, Sheffield.
Hollis, John, esq. High Wycombe, Bucks.
Holme, Edward, M.D. Manchester.
Hoole, Mr. W., Crooks.
Housman, John, esq. Farm, near Sheffield.
Howse, H. E., esq. Lyncomb, near Bath.
Hudson, Mr. Joseph, Sheffield.
Hunter, Mr. Michael, Sheffield.
Inchbald, Rev. P., LL.D. Eastfield, near Doncaster.
Jackson, Mr. Henry, Sheffield.
Kay, Mr. Robert, Bolton.
Kentish, Rev. John, Birmingham.
Kesteven, Mr., London.
Kesteven, Mr. Thomas, London.
Key, Mrs. H. G., Herne-hill, near London.
Lambert, James, esq. London.
Lawson, Mrs., Boroughbridge-hall.
Lawson, Marmaduke, esq. M.P. Boroughbridge-hall.
Lloyd, Gamaliel, esq. London.
Lucas, Mr. Samuel, Sheffield.
Lysons, Rev. D., F.R. & A.S. Rodmarton, Gloucestershire.
M'Coy, Mr. Edward, Kennington, near London.
Manchester, King-Street Library.
Manchester, Portico Library.
Markland, J. H., esq. F.S.A. Temple.
Marshall, John, esq. Headingley, near Leeds.
Mason, Thomas, esq. Upper-house, near Bradford.
Maude, Francis, esq. F.S.A.
Milner, John, esq. Attercliffe.
Montgomery, Mr. James, Sheffield.
Moseley Book Association, Worcestershire.
Newbould, Mr. William, Broomhill.
Newbould, Mr. Samuel, Bridgefield.
Newcastle-upon-Tyne Antiquarian Society.
Newcastle-upon-Tyne Literary and Philosophical Society.
Nicholson, Mr. W., Shire-green.
Nowill, Mr. Joseph, London.
Nunn, Mr., bookseller, London. (Two copies.)
Oates, Mr. Charles, High-house.
Oates, Mrs., Bath.
Oates, Edward, esq. Weetwood, near Leeds.
Oates, Joseph, esq. Weetwood, near Leeds.
Overend, Mr. Hall, Sheffield.
Oxford, New College Library.
Palfreyman, Mr. Luke jun., Sheffield.
Parker, Miss E. Shiercliffe.
Parker, Rev. Francis, Sheffield.
Parker, Mr. Holy, Sheffield.
Parker, Hugh, esq. Woodthorpe.
Parker, Samuel Walker, esq. Newcastle-upon-Tyne.
Parker, Mr. William, Sheffield.
Percival, Mrs., Bath.
Philipps, Rev. N., D.D. Sheffield.
Philips, Robert, esq. The Park, near Manchester.
Piper, Rev. H. H., Norton.
Preston, Rev. M. jun.
Radcliffe, Sir Joseph, bart. Milnes-bridge-house.
Radford, Rev. Thomas, Sheffield.
Rawson, John, esq. West Don House, Sheffield.
Rawson, Thomas, esq. Wardsend.

Read, John, esq. Norton-house.
Read, Joseph, esq. Wincobank.
Revill, Mr. Samuel, Sheffield.
Robberds, Rev. J. G., Manchester.
Roberts, Mr. Jacob, Sheffield.
Roberts, Mr. Samuel, Park-grange, near Sheffield. (Two copies.)
Robinson, Rev. Robert, Whittington.
Robinson, Mr. T. H., Manchester.
Rodgers, Mr. John, Sheffield.
Sanderson, Mr. Thomas, Sheffield.
Sayle, Benjamin, esq. Brightside.
Settle, Mr. John, Sheffield.
Shearwood, Mr. John, solicitor, Sheffield.
Sheffield, Library of the Upper Chapel.
Shore, Samuel, esq. Norton-hall.
Shore, Sydney, esq. Norton-hall.
Shore, William, esq. Tapton.
Shore, Miss Mary, Tapton.
Silcock, Mr. W., The Edge.
Smith, Mr. Ebenezer, Chesterfield.
Smith, Rev. George, Sheffield.
Smith, Mr. Samuel, Carwood.
Sorby, Mr. John, Orgrave.
Spencer, General, Bramley-grange.
Staniforth, Samuel, esq. Darnall.
Sterndale, Mrs., Sheffield.
Stovin, J. S., esq., Newbold, near Chesterfield.
Surtees, Robert, esq. Mainsforth, Durham.
Sutton, Rev. Thomas, Vicar of Sheffield.
Sykes, Godfrey, esq. London.
Taylor, Mr. Richard, F.L.S. London.
Thompson, Mr., solicitor, Sheffield.
Thomson, John, M.D., Halifax.
Tillotson, Mr. George, Sheffield.
Tinker, Mr. S., Leeds.
Todd, Mr. W., Sheffield.
Turner, Dawson, esq. F.R.A. & L.S. Yarmouth.
Turner, Robert, esq. Sheffield.
Turner, William, esq. Dublin.
Upcott, Mr. William, London Institution.
Upham, Mr. John, bookseller, Bath.
Vale, Rev. W. H., Sheffield.
Wake, Mr. B. J., solicitor, Sheffield.
Walker, Samuel, esq. Aldwark.
Walker, Miss, Masborough-house.
Ward, S. B. esq. Mount-Pleasant.
Ward, Mr. T. A., Park-house.
Watson, Holland, esq. Congleton.
Watson, Rev. Thomas, Bath.
Wellbeloved, Rev. C., York.
Wheat, Mr., solicitor, Sheffield.
Whitley, Mr. Nathaniel jun., bookseller, Halifax.
Winn, Charles, esq. Nostell, Yorkshire.
Winn, Sir Edmund Mark, bart. Ackton, Yorkshire.
Wilson, Charles, esq. London.
Wilson, Mr. James, solicitor, Sheffield.
Wilson, Mr. Joseph, West-brook.
Wilson, William, esq. Finsbury-square, London.
Wood, Mr. Abraham, Bury, Lancashire.
Wood, G. W., esq. Platt, near Manchester.
Woollen, Mr. George, Sheffield.
Wright, Rev. Godfrey, Bradford.
Wright, Rev. P., Stannington.
Wybergh, Thomas, esq.
York Subscription Library.
Younge, Mr. Charles, Brincliffe Edge.
Younge, Mr. George, Sheffield.
Younge, W., M.D., Sheffield.

PREFACE.

THE ground which is here broken up owes little to the labours of any former topographer. The very name of Hallamshire is scarcely known beyond the limits of the district in which it is in *customary* use; and though the name of Sheffield is familiar to most persons into whose hands this volume will come, still it is presumed that the history and true character of the place and its inhabitants are but imperfectly, if at all understood.

Many parts of the county of York have had their history and antiquities ably illustrated; but no survey of any of the many districts into which that large county may for topographical purposes be so conveniently distributed, has comprehended any portion of the territory to which this volume relates. All that the public has seen respecting Sheffield and the district of which it is the little capital, has been in Tours, Descriptions, Directories, and Magazines; and the accounts there given have been little more than republications of the notice of the town of Sheffield in the old *Magna Britannia*, with the errors faithfully copied, but some of the information suppressed which was contained even in so scanty an article.

If, therefore, it be found that the soil on which I have laboured does not bring forth fruit of the richest and most delicious flavour, from its produce the reader will not, it is hoped, turn away disgusted at having again offered to him that which had already palled upon his taste.

Some things which had before appeared I have been compelled to reprint. But in general the contents of this volume are now for the first time submitted to the public. And even in the matter which is transcribed from manuscript authorities, or from printed books as rare as manuscripts, it will in general be seen that something is brought to bear on the subject from other sources of information. This applies more particularly to the pedigrees. It will not be found that any of them are merely copies from the visitation-books or other collections of Yorkshire genealogies; but that throughout them fresh information is interwoven, and that where the subject seemed to require it, the line has been continued from the time of the visitations to the present period.

But while it is a subject of some satisfaction to the author, that he is not presenting to the public only that of which the public was already in possession; so is he not without his apprehensions when he recollects that he has been treading where none had gone before him. Gladly would he have hailed the friendly light afforded by a learned and judicious antiquary that dispersed even a small portion of the gloom which hangs over all our Ante-Norman history: happy would he have been to have met with conclusions ably drawn from the few documents we possess respecting the events of the eleventh century, when such an important revolution was effected in the affairs of Hallamshire. But all preceding antiquaries seem to have stood aloof from this district; and it is in vain that I have searched for any incidental notice, or casual expression, of any of those writers who have entered on extensive investigations of our national antiquities, which might have betrayed the impression produced on their minds by the few but weighty evidences pertaining to the earlier periods of our history.

In doubtful matters, however, I have preferred to state different and opposing opinions, together with the evidence from which the conclusion, whatever it may be, must be deduced, to the mere statement of my own opinion when that opinion wanted the support of other authority. And if from documents which are here presented to the public, or from other evidences that have escaped my researches, any other person shall find that fresh light may be thrown on facts in the earlier and darker periods of our history, no one will more sincerely rejoice than I; for no one can feel a more honest and ardent zeal for the illustration of every point in our history, and for placing the whole on the firm and immoveable basis of present appearances and authentic record.

The collection of materials for this work was begun at a very early period of the author's life. It was among the amusements of childhood, and the chief pleasures of his youth. He has gone on increasing his store. He has spared neither time, nor labour, nor expense. He has been so fortunate as to meet with many persons who were both willing and able to assist him in his inquiries. That still other evidence exists that might be made to bear on the subject of this volume he is not disposed to deny. But if something yet remains behind, it will be allowed that much is here brought together. And he can truly say that what evidence has been presented to him he has faithfully used, and faithfully exhibited.

In the arrangement of the matter contained in this volume, no direction has been followed but that which the subject itself appeared to give. It was my original intention to confine myself to the parish of Sheffield, and to introduce what was to be told of the parishes which as to their history were in so many important particulars identified with it, in the form of notes, or in occasional digressions in the body of the work. On more mature consideration the present plan has been adopted; but I entreat the reader to bear in mind, that what is related of those parishes is rather to be regarded in the light of detached notices than of a regular and connected topographical account. And I regret that my present situation at so great a distance from the subject of my labours and the sources of information, has prevented me from adding to what I had formerly collected concerning those parishes, more especially in reference to the earth-works at Bradfield, the church notes at Treeton and Ecclesfield, and to the Court Rolls and other documents in the office of the Duke of Norfolk's auditor at Sheffield.

While the volume is not deficient of matter which bears upon the general history of this great kingdom, yet it undoubtedly contains much that will appear of interest only to those who have some natural connection with the places or persons described; and even of those who have this natural connection, there may be some to whom it may appear that the pages contain too much of genealogical matter, as they are not of the few who, in the words of old Gervase Holles, ' are listening after the memory of their ancestors.' But this must be the case with every topographical work which is composed upon the same scale of extent with those which have obtained from the public the full meed of approbation. In all such works there must be parts that appear to be addressed to local and even individual interests. Topography that descends not to these minutiæ, is wanting of its very nerves and sinews; it is a mere skeleton, or rather a phantom and a shadow.

More time has elapsed since the announcement of this work than was expected. For this some apology seems to be required. That apology must be a plain statement of the circumstances which have occasioned the delay. The many engagements of that admirable artist Mr. Blore, who has lent his assistance to the embellishment of the work, prevented him from paying so early an attention to the preparation of the drawings as it was his earnest wish to have paid. Much time has since been necessarily consumed in the tedious processes of etching and engraving, much of which has been ably performed by the skilful delineator himself, and the rest by eminent artists under his superintendance and direction. The engravings at once do credit to the accuracy of Mr. Blore's delineations, to his exact knowledge of the principles of his art, and to his taste and intimate acquaintance with every thing pertaining to the pictorial embellishment of a topographical work.

It remains only that I make a grateful record of the assistance which has been afforded to the author in the collection of the materials of the present volume.

And first I must most gratefully acknowledge the essential service rendered to this work by His Grace the Duke of Norfolk, who with the most obliging condescension was not only pleased to allow that the volume should be to him inscribed, but to direct that the Court Rolls of the Manor of Sheffield and other papers relating to His Grace's paramount interest in the district which is the subject of these pages, should be laid open for my use. Nor must I omit to acknowledge the civility of Mr. Harting, Mr. Housman, and Mr. Burbeary, in giving effect to His Grace's intention.

Next I must express thus publicly my obligations to one of the worthiest and most friendly men living, Mr. William Wilson, one of the twelve capital burgesses of the town and parish of Sheffield, who with the utmost confidence has allowed me at all times freedom of access to the collections made by his much respected father, the late John Wilson esquire of Broomhead. Of those collections and the collector I have spoken at page 276 of the present work. To them this volume owes much of whatever claim it may have on the public attention, and I beg leave once more to repeat my thanks to the worthy possessor for the opportunities he has so often afforded me of consulting and transcribing from them.

Mr. Wilson was in correspondence with many of the antiquaries of his time. John-Charles Brooke esquire, Somerset herald at arms, whose premature death was the severest blow which the cause of Yorkshire topography ever received, was his friend and frequent correspondent. He communicated to Mr. Wilson from time to time the pedigrees of the gentry of Hallamshire which were entered at the visitations of the heralds, or which by any other means found their way into that noble depository of genealogical and topographical information the College of Arms. Other interesting and useful notices from the same depository I owe to the unwearied kindness of that true lover and warm encourager of all topographical and genealogical inquiries, William Radclyffe esquire, the present Rouge-croix pursuivant at arms, who has manifested a zealous concern for the completeness of this work, by communicating whatever he had observed in the collections of former antiquaries that pertained to this subject, or that his own labours had redeemed from the dust and darkness of antiquity.

To the mediation of Mr. Radclyffe with the late Richard Henry Beaumont esquire, I owe that valuable series of original letters in which is contained the correspondence which passed between Sir William Savile and Major Beaumont while the latter was in command at Sheffield castle, in the time of the civil dissensions of the seventeenth century. And at the request of the same gentleman, Edmund Lodge esquire, Lancaster herald at arms, indulged me with the use of his abstracts of such of the Talbot letters as did not appear to him to possess sufficient general interest to be entitled to admission into his valuable ' Illustrations of British History, &c.,' to whom I beg leave thus to present my most respectful thanks.

The Reverend Daniel Lysons of Rodmarton in the county of Gloucester, a veteran topographer, has obliged the author by some valuable communications; and the unsolicited kindness of his brother the late Samuel Lysons esquire, keeper of the records in the Tower, has left me no reason to suppose that in the vast store of historical documents which were under his care are any remaining that would throw further light on the descent of property, or any other part of the history of the parish of Sheffield.

To Henry Ellis esquire of the British Museum I am indebted for a ready access to the treasures of that great national depositary.

c

The Reverend Philip Bliss of Saint John's College in Oxford has my most cordial thanks for much valuable assistance which his residence at Oxford has enabled him to afford; and I beg to present my respectful acknowledgements to the Reverend Bulkeley Bandinel, keeper of the Bodleian Library, who was pleased to give every facility to my own researches, as well in the multifarious collections of Dodsworth, as in the collections for the county of York which passed to that library from the hands of Mr. Gough.

To the Reverend Thomas Sutton vicar of Sheffield I must offer my best thanks for some valuable information respecting the ecclesiastical affairs of the parish; and I recollect with pleasure that I have in frequent conversations with the Reverend Edward Goodwin, late curate of Attercliffe, received information that has been of considerable use in the compilation of this work. My friends William Shore esquire of Tapton, and John Read esquire of Norton-house, will please to accept my best acknowledgements, the former for the valuable communications with which he has favoured the author respecting the hospital in Sheffield which was founded by the family of Hollis; and the latter for much information respecting the River Don Company, a prompt attention to every inquiry, and a zealous promotion in every possible way of the success of this work. And lastly my much valued friend Mr. Thomas Asline Ward of Park-house will accept my best thanks, for many useful communications which the public offices he has held in his native town have enabled him to supply.

To the various friends who have interested themselves in procuring that attention to the prospectus of this volume, which was a necessary preliminary to engaging in a publication that must of course involve its author in considerable expense, I shall forbear to do more than make this general acknowledgement, lest by omitting any name I might incur a suspicion of not duly appreciating services that have been rendered:—but one is now no more; and in a mixed feeling of pleasure and of sadness, I add the name of the Reverend George Smith, M.A. curate of Ecclesall and assistant-minister in the parish-church of Sheffield, by whom I was at first encouraged to arrange in this form the materials which had been collected, and whose friendly assistance was in every way most zealously afforded till he was able to counsel and act no more. The recollection of the long experienced friendship of such a man is dear to me; and I dismiss the work with less satisfaction than would have been the case, could I now present it to the hand of him who watched its progress, who would have pardoned its defects, and looked with an indulgent and partial eye upon its merits.

BATH, August, 1819.

TABLE OF CONTENTS.

Hiſtory of Sheffield.

Topographical Survey of the Pariſh of Sheffield.

Out-Parts of Hallamſhire.

LIST OF PLATES.

History of Sheffield.

CHAPTER I.

Introductory Matter.—General Description.

IN every part of an old country like England are found some traces of its former inhabitants: for men who have lived in a state of social union do not all pass away without leaving behind them some token of their existence. When these remains betray a state of splendour now no longer existing, men are naturally disposed to inquire into the causes and process of a change so remarkable; and to ask for the names, characters, and histories of the distinguished dead of whose former power and consequence those remains are still speaking. In works of the highest antiquity the parish of Sheffield is not rich; but though now principally known as a commercial district, and as possessing a monopoly of one great article of our national manufactures, we shall have to consider it under quite a different character, when it was the seat and favourite residence of a race of ancient nobility by whose history it becomes connected with the general history of this great kingdom,—men who were called to the councils of princes, or displayed their prowess in the tented field, while they exercised an almost unlimited authority among a tenantry whose habitations surrounded their castle-walls. The traces of those times are now few, and fast obliterating. Buildings for commercial purposes occupy the site of the baronial hall: the parks and chases are inclosed; the summer-mansion is become a gray and mouldering ruin; and even their very monuments, erected to bear their memories and their effigies to a remote posterity, threaten that ere long they will

'—— bowe and kneel, and fall down flat
To kisse those heaps which now they have in trust.'

Only their charity is still green, and promises to preserve the memory of the TALBOT race, when all other tokens of their residence at Sheffield shall have passed away.

The parish of Sheffield is of great extent. It stretches above ten miles in length, and its average breadth may be taken at three miles. Its area is rather more than twenty-two thousand acres. It contains many populous villages and hamlets, and one large market-

town, where stands the church, and which gives its name to the parish. In 1811, the number of its inhabitants exceeded fifty-three thousand. This was more than the whole population of Rutland, Westmorland, or Huntingdonshire. It far exceeded the number of inhabitants in many of the Swiss cantons, and of itself would form a sovereignty which many a foreign prince might envy. It was about $\frac{1}{111}$ of the whole return for England and Wales.

The distance of the parish of Sheffield from the eastern and western seas is nearly equal; and although it is further from the most northern point of Scotland than from the southern coast of England, yet a line which might be drawn nearly straight from Liverpool to Hull passing through Sheffield would divide the island into two nearly equal portions. It lies on the eastern side of that high and mountainous tract which Dodsworth, who rarely hazards such a remark, says may be called the English Apennines; 'because the rain-water which there falleth sheddeth from sea to sea[1].' The ridge of this tract lies nearly in the direction from north to south. The mountains of Westmorland, Craven, and the Peak belong to it, and it is finally lost to the south in the moorlands of Staffordshire. Sheffield lies rather at the foot of these hills than among them:

'—— qua se subducere colles
Incipiunt, mollique jugum demittere clivo
Usque ad aquam.'

The town at least stands at the point of union of many streams then become not inconsiderable, which have their rise amongst those hills, and where the hills are fast subsiding into that fine level champaign country which extends to Doncaster and beyond it.

It is in a country like this that we look for the *beautiful* in landscape. The grander and more august features of nature are to be sought in regions decidedly mountainous; and are contemplated with more complete satisfaction, where the artificial creations of man have not intruded to break the harmony of the scene. But the softer graces of landscape are to be

[1] Description of the course of the Don. Dods. MSS. in Bibl. Bodl. vol. CLX. f. 19 b. So Camden: and so long before his time, in the 7th Iter of Richard of Cirencester, *Alpes Penino.*

chiefly found in a district uneven but not mountainous, and may be contemplated with not less pleasure because among them are to be found some of the works of human hands. Close and well-wooded valleys, with streams glittering along them, and the bare scar occasionally peeping through the foliage : hills appearing from behind other hills of nearly equal altitude, some bearing fine masses of wood, and others studded with cheerful villas: views of wonderful extent embracing variety of objects, some of which are associated with events of historical importance :—these are what the vicinity of Sheffield presents to the lovers of picturesque beauty, and which never fail to arrest the attention of the passing traveller. It need not however be concealed, as it cannot be denied, that the great increase of its population and the extension of its commerce have done too much in injuring the beauty of the near, and the effect of the distant landscape. Still, however, there are many parts where the country retains much of its primæval character, and where the few low and picturesque buildings erected for commercial purposes rather harmonize with than deform the scene. This is well known to those lovers of nature who have traced to their sources those two mountain-streams the Porter and the Riveling, the banks of which in many places present some of the rarer and more beautiful picturesque combinations. The Don,

the most considerable of the Sheffield rivers, flows along the most populous parts of the parish. But few of the *streams which run among these hills* can bear away the palm for picturesque beauty from this river, and in that part of its course immediately before it enters the parish of Sheffield ; I mean in the neighbourhood of Wharncliffe Chase, where the hills are finely clothed with native woods, and rise boldly, though not abruptly, from its banks, till they place the visitor.on an elevation from which he may command a prospect rich, varied, extensive, and beautiful as eye can behold. On one of the highest peaks of these hills is a lodge built in the time of King Henry VIII. by Sir Thomas Wortley, for his pleasure to hear the harts bell, as an inscription perfectly unique in its kind, cut on the face of the solid rock, informs us. In this house Lady Mary Wortley Montague spent much of the first two or three years of her married life, the earliest and the happiest. Here was born that singular and romantic character her son. She is therefore, perhaps, not a wholly unexceptionable witness : but when she had seen with the eye of a poet and enthusiast, most of the fine landscape of Europe, writing from Avignon, she speaks of a little belvedere which she had constructed in the neighbourhood of that city, as commanding the finest land-prospect she had ever seen, *except Wharncliffe*[1].

<hr/>

[1] See her correspondence published by Mr. Dallaway, vol. iii. p. 277. Wharncliffe is five miles from the town of Sheffield to the north. It is partly a forest, and partly a deer-park. It is still a member of the great estate of the Wortley family, and is now the property of James Archibald Stuart Wortley, esquire. Its *sea of wood*, and its command of a prospect of almost unrivalled extent and magnificence render it one of the most grand and imposing scenes imaginable. If in the midst of such truly magnificent scenery the mind can turn to objects so insignificant, three seats may be discovered cut in the solid rock, *utroque sedilia saxo*, and probably intended to accommodate those who sought to enjoy this enchanting scenery. Near to them, and also cut on the living rock, or on what is technically called a ground-fast stone, is the inscription noticed in the text. For more than two centuries it was exposed to every blast that blew ; but having been originally cut in a fine bold character, it is still legible, and it has long been protected from any further injury from the weather by a small shed built over it by the late Mr. Edward Wortley-Montague. Little care was taken by any previous preparation of the stone itself to fit it to receive the inscription, and it is quite consistent with the romantic character of the inscription itself, to suppose that Sir Thomas was content with such a superficies as nature presented to him. Some of the letters have nearly perished, but the following may probably be taken as the true reading. The lines are of unequal length, accommodated to the irregular form of the stone.

<blockquote>
Pray for the faule of
Thomas Wryttelay knyght
for the hynges bode to Edward
the forthe Wychard therd Ware the vii. ? Enrc viii.
bans faules God perdon weche
Thomas cawsyd a loge to be made
hon this crag ne mydos of
Wanclife for his plefur to her the
hartes bel in the pere of owr
Rorb a thousand rccrc y.
</blockquote>

The unique singularity of this inscription attracted at nearly the same period the attention of two very popular writers of our own age ; the one the most elegant of all our topographers, the other the most topographic of all our poets, Dr. Whitaker and Mr. Walter Scott :—And may not the wild search after *written mountains* in the deserts of Arabia, by the last of the Wortley-Montagues, be traced to impressions received from this written rock on which his infancy was eradled?

Sir Thomas Wortley was high-sheriff of the county of York in the 6th and 17th years of Henry VII. and a man of principal power and consequence in his neighbourhood. In the pedigrees of this great family he is said to have allied himself in marriage with two of the principal houses in the North of England, the Fitz Williams and the Pilkingtons : but some curious particulars of the old knight's domestic history are to be found in the Bodleian. He did not long enjoy his pleasure in this lodge, for his will was proved on the 12th of March 1514-5, in which he gives directions that his body should be interred at Hemsworth. This was for some time the usual burying-place of the family, but some of them were buried in the chapel at Wortley. In that chapel was an old monumental stone, the inscription of which has not been preserved by any of our earlier collectors of church notes, and of which Mr. Wilson could read only these words Prai for the unhaunted fpirit af.... a departure from the

usual simplicity of such inscriptions, bespeaking, if I am not mistaken, the hand which inscribed the rock in Wharncliffe.

The amusing account which Taylor the Water-Poet has given of his visit to this place, I the rather transcribe because it is contained in one of his rarest tracts, published after the collection of his works in a folio volume. Its title is ' Part of this Summer's Travels, or News from Hell, Hull, and Hallifax, from York, Linne, Leicester, Chester, &c. with many pleasant passages worthy your observation and reading. By John Taylor. Imprinted by J. O. 12mo. It appears that he returned from his tour on the 20th of September 1639.

' From Leeds I went to Wakefield, where, if the valiant Pinder had been living, I would have play'd Don Quixot's part and challenged him ; but being it was so happy that he was dead, I passed the towne in peace to Barnsley and so to Wortley, to Sir Francis Wortleyes ancient house. The entertainment which himselfe, his good lady, and his most faire and hopefull daughter gave mee there, as I never did or can deserve, so I never shall be able to requite. To talke of meat, drinke, money, and free welcome for horse and man, it were but a meer fooling for me to begin, because then I should hardly finde the way. Therefore, to his worship my humble thanks remembered, and everlasting happinesse wished both to him and all that is his; yet I cannot forbeare to write a little of the further favour of this noble knight. Upon the 14th of September afternoon, he took horse with mee, and his lady and daughter in their coach, with some other servants on horseback : where three miles we rode over rocks and cloud-kissing mountains, one of them so high that in a cleere day a man may from the top thereof see both the minsters or cathedral churches, York and Lincolne, neere 60 miles off us ; and as it is to be supposed that when the Devil did looke over Lincolne as the proverb is, that he stood upon that mountain or neer it ; Sir Francis brought me to a lodge, the place is called Wharncliffe, where the keeper dwells who is his man, and keeps all this woody, rocky, stony, vast wildderness under him, for there are many deere there, and the keeper were an asse if he would want venison, having so good a master.

' Close to the said lodge is a stone, in burthen at least a hundred cart loads, the top of it is four square by nature and about 12 yards compasse. It hath three seats in the fourme of chaires, made by art as it were in the front of the rocke, wherein three persons may easily sit, and have a view and goodly prospect over large woods, townes, cornfields, fruitfull and pleasant pastures, valleyes, rivers, deares, neat, sheep, and all things needfull for the life of man ; coutayned in thousands of acres, and all for the better part, belonging to that noble knight's ancestors and himself. Behinde the stone is a large inscription engraven, where in an old character is described the ancient memory of the Wortleys, (the progenitors of Sir Francis now living) for some hundreds of years, who were lords and owners of the said lands and demaynes, which hee now holds as their right heire. About a bow-shoot from thence (by the descent of as many rings of a ladder) his worship brought mee to a cave or vault in a rocke; wherin was a table with seats and turfe cushions round, and in a hole in the same rock was three barrels of nappy liquor. Thither the keeper brought a good red deere pye, cold roast mutton, and an excellent shooing-horn of hanged Martinmas biefe: which cheer no man living would think such a place could afford: so after some merry passages and repast, we returned home.'—pp. 24, 25, 26.

Wharncliffe is the scene of the old ballad of ' The Dragon of Wantley,'

The forms into which large masses of building are accidentally thrown, sometimes are picturesque when contemplated at such a distance as to exclude observation of their component parts. The town of Sheffield occupies a piece of rising ground between its two principal rivers. Dirty and comparatively mean within, it presents a striking object from many points on the surrounding hills, and especially from Meersbrook, whence it is seen backed by the dark masses of wood which rest on Pits-Moor and Wincobank. To this effect the domes of two of the churches much contribute, and the spire of the parish-church rising above them both with protecting maternity.

Such a district as that in which Sheffield stands must abound in water. Where there are hills there will be streams. Beside the Carbrook, the Limb-Dyke, and the Meersbrook, rivulets which mark the eastern, western, and southern limits of the parish, there are five streams which flow through it, and the waters of all are united at the town : the Porter, Riveling, Loxley, Sheaf, and Don. The first of these rises near Fullwood-head, and after a short but beautiful course adds its waters embrowned by passing through the roots of the mountain-heath to those of the Sheaf, a little before that river pays its tribute to the Don. The Riveling rises in the high ground about two miles to the south of Ughill in a wild and open country; and affording in its course a boundary-line for the adjacent parishes of Sheffield and Ecclesfield, joins the Loxley near Mousehole Forge, and is conveyed by it to the Don. But a small portion of the course of the Loxley is within the parish of Sheffield. It rises near the village of Bradfield, and flows along a thinly-peopled country, which in the memory of man was wholly uninclosed and uncultivated, called Loxley-Chase; a district which seems to have the fairest pretensions to be the Locksley of our old ballads, where was born that redoubtable hero Robin Hood. The remains of a house in which it was pretended he was born were formerly pointed out in a small wood in Loxley called Bar-wood, and a well of fine clear water rising near the bed of the river has been called from time immemorial Robin Hood's Well. This well is included within the grounds at Cliff-Rocher, a place not inaptly named by its late proprietor Little-Matlock, as it bears no mean resemblance to some parts of the beautiful valley of Matlock in Derbyshire. The walks which that gentleman cut in the boldest part of the cliff, and along a natural terrace extending to that part of Stannington in which are the chapel and minister's house, were thrown open to the public, and much frequented during several summers by the people of Sheffield. Such places afford a cheap, healthful, and innocent amusement, and it is desirable that every town, but especially every manufacturing town, should possess them. The name of this public benefactor is inscribed on the wall of a house of refreshment which he erected near these grounds.

Anno Christi M. DCC. XC. IX.
Thomas et Martha Halliday
sine liberis, ætate provecti, necnon jam nunc morituri,
has construxerunt ædes.
Sic vos non vobis mellificatis apes.

He also placed over the door of a substantial mansion these lines of our English Virgil, strictly applicable to the scenery, and which may now call forth a sigh of regret from the gratified and grateful visitant, who recollects that the votive prayer has not been answered.

' ———— Nec vos dulcissima mundi
  Nomina, vos montes, cataractæ, pascua, sylvæ,
  Rupes atque cavernæ, animâ remunente relinquam.'

The three already mentioned are precipitous, shallow, rapid, noisy streams. The Sheaf on the contrary steals silently along its low channel, approaching the town to which it has given name by a less perceptible fall. It comes from that close and woody valley in which stood the Abbey of Beauchief, a religious house which we shall soon find to have had an important interest in the parish of Sheffield; and to its contemplative inhabitants has doubtless many times afforded opportunities of indulging in the favourite amusement of monastic life, angling. It can however assume a different character. When swoln by rains, or by a sudden melting of the snow on the moors to the west of the town, (a much more frequent occasion of floods in the Sheffield rivers,) it has been known not only to fill its deep channel, but to overflow its banks, and lay waste the works of man. In the year 1768 it carried down the houses which form the north side of Talbot's Hospital, when five of the pensioners lost their lives. Branches of hazel, a tree with which the vale of Beauchief abounds, are sometimes found deeply embedded in the earth near the course of this river, which seem to have been brought down ages ago, at the time of some extraordinary flood. Harrison, who writes with the impression of the event fresh upon his memory, speaks of the sudden rising of the Don at the time of Aske's rebellion, which prevented the two armies from coming to an engagement, as if it were little less than something miraculous, as no rain had fallen in the neighbourhood of Doncaster[1]. This flood evidently had its rise in this and the other tributary streams above Sheffield. The uncertain character of the Sheaf is even noticed in an instrument of as early date as the time of Edward I. In the charter by which Sir Ralph de Ecclesall gave his mill and other possessions to the monks of Beauchief, who covenant in return to find him a priest for his chapel at Ecclesall, it is stipulated on the part of the monks, that in case of high floods, or snow they should be excused from sending a canon to Ecclesall, and allowed to celebrate the due masses in their own church at Beauchief[2]. In the angle which the Sheaf makes with the Don at their junction, stood the ancient castle of Sheffield.

The Don is the most considerable of the rivers which

—and a clift in the rocks is now called the Dragon's Den. The age and the subject-matter of this puzzling old ballad have much perplexed the investigators of our popular antiquities, and collecters of our national poetry. Its date is fixed to a period before the Reformation by the mention of More of More-hall, who cuts so conspicuous a figure in it ; that family becoming extinct in the time of Edward VI. : and the true key to its subject I have no doubt is to be found in the tradition of the neighbourhood respecting Sir Thomas Wortley, which I shall present to the reader as it was committed to writing by a Yorkshire clergyman, Mr. Oliver Heywood of Coley, near Halifax, a hundred and fifty years ago.
* Sir Francis Wortley's great grandfather being a man of a great estate was owner of a towne near unto him, onely there were some freeholders in it, with whom he wrangled and sued untill he had beggared them and cast them out of their inheritance, and so the town was wholly his, which he pulled quite downe and laid the buildings and town-fields even as a common ; wherein his main design was to keep deer: and made a lodge to which he came at the time of the year and lay there, taking great delight to hear the deer bell. But it came to passe that before he dyed he belled like a deer and was distracted. Some rubbish there may be seen of the town : it is upon a great moore betwixt Peniston and Sheffield.'

[1] Description of Britain, prefixed to Holinshead's Chronicle, vol. i. p. 166. 4to edition.

[2] Dr. Pegge's Historical Account of Beauchief Abbey, p. 149.

enter the parish of Sheffield; and as of right its due, the name is continued to their united waters in their progress towards the ocean. The name of this river is said by the learned Camden to be formed out of an old British word signifying a low deep channel; but Whitaker, with more probability, brings it from the British D-Avon, *the water*[1]. Milton, who had perhaps never seen it, describes it not very appropriately by the epithet gulphy, 'gulphie Dun.' More accurately Harrison, 'the swift Done,' who praises it for the fertility of its banks: 'The fine grasse which groweth upon the banks thereof is so fine and batable, that there goeth a proverb upon the same, so oft as a man will commend his pasture, to say that there is no better feed on Done banke.' That accurate old topographer then describes its rise in Yorkshire *among the Peak hills*, a name not then confined to that part of the mountainous chain which is within the county of Derby. The head of the principal brooklet which forms this river is about four miles above Peniston, and near the springs of the Mersey. Taking a south-eastern direction, and serving for several miles to mark the boundary of the wapentake of Strafford and Tickhill, and receiving as it passes along many little currents from the west, it enters the parish of Sheffield at Wardsend, after a course of about fifteen miles. 'Then goeth it,' says Harrison, 'by Waddeslaie-wood to Waddeslaie-bridge, and at Alverton [Owlerton] receiveth the Badfield [Bradfield] water. Then passeth it to Crokes, and so to Sheffeld castell (by east whereof it receiveth a brooke from by south that commeth through Sheffeld parke.) Then proceedeth it to Westford-bridge, Briksie [Brightside] bridge, and south-west of Tinslie receiveth the Cowley stream,' &c.[2] Harrison is more minute than Dodsworth, who half a century later drew up similar accounts of the courses of our Yorkshire rivers. But I shall not follow him further, and only observe, that when it has received the waters of the Sheaf at the town of Sheffield, it suddenly changes its direction, turning to the north-east, and proceeds towards Rotherham and Doncaster: but neither 'yielding plenti of salmon all the waie as it passes,' as in the time of Harrison, nor shaded with alders and yew-trees as it is described by Camden. The waters of the Don no longer find their way to the Aire by the old channel, but are conveyed along an artificial cut called the Dutch river, made by Sir Cornelius Vermuyden and other Flemings in the time of Charles I. to the Ouse, which pours them into the Humber, the great æstuary which receives all the waters that flow down the eastern side of the hills which compose the English Apennines.

The river Don is we have seen not unknown to song. Drayton thus describes it:—

' Thou first of all my floods, whose banks doe bound my south
And offrest up thy streame to mightie Humber's mouth,
Of ewe and clining elme, that crown'd with many a spray,
From thy cleare fountaine first through many a mead doest play,
Till Rother, whence the name of Rotheram first begun,
At that her christened towne doth loose her in my Don,
Which proud of her recourse, tow'rds Doncaster doth drive
Her great'st and chiefest towne, the name that doth derive
From Don's neere bordering banks, when holding on her race,
She dancing in and out, indenteth Hatfield Chase,
Whose bravery hourly adds new honors to her banke:
When Sherwood sends her in slow Iddle, that made ranke

With her profuse excesse, shee largely it bestowes
On Marshland, whose awolne wombe with such abundance flowes,
As that her batning brest, her fatlings sooner feeds,
And with more lavish waste, then oft the grasier needs:
Whose soil, as some report, that be her Borderers note,
With th' water under earth undoubtedly doth flote:
For when the waters rise, it risen doth remaine
High whilst the floods are high, and when they fall againe,
It falleth: but at last when as my lively Don
Along by Marshland's side, her lusty course hath runne,
The little wandering Went, wonne by the loud report
Of the magnifique state and height of Humber's Court,
Drawes on to meet with Don, at her approach to Aire[1].'

Another tribute from the Muses is paid to this river in a Latin poem entitled ' *Reliquiæ Eboracenses.*' The author of this work was Dr. Heneage Dering, dean of Ripon. What is published is only part of what the ingenious author designed, which was nothing less than to present the principal events in the history of Yorkshire, and to celebrate the principal places within its circuit, in Latin hexameters. He desisted from his undertaking when he had completed three books which relate to Roman affairs. The Don is made to relate the great war which the Brigantes waged with the invaders, and, in conformity with Camden's description, he is depicted

' *Cinctus arundinibus crinem, et frondibus alni.*'

Sheffield is feigned with due regard to historic probability to be the place from which the Brigantes were supplied with arms: and her industrious artisans are represented hanging up before them armour taken from the foe, as patterns by which to fabricate their own.

' *Mille ardet Sephilæa focis. Fornace liquescit*
  Montibus effossi vicinis massa metalli ;
  Et longe resonat glomeratis ictibus incus :
  Nec limæ aut cotis cessat labor. Insuper arma
  Ante oculos fabri ponunt Romana ; notantque
  Mutandum siquid ; seu sint exempla sequenda.'

When father Don has concluded his narrative, he invites the hero of the poem and his companion to an entertainment he was about to give in his hall to his brother rivers: and much of a poetic imagination is discovered in the description of the hall and its icy ornaments. What principally engaged the attention of the visitors were certain vases of crystal, each containing the perfect image of some celebrated personage who had been born or had lived upon this river's banks. They recognise the founders of the nobility of Wentworth and Osborne, and a more eminent character of earlier times

' —— *Gallorum terror*, Sephilæius *heros*'

the great John Talbot first earl of Shrewsbury. This work is little known. The classical reader will find that he needs not the aid of local attachment to receive much pleasure from its perusal.

Salmon, which was formerly plentiful in the Don, is now rarely found there. Sometimes a solitary fish is caught, and in the month of August 1756, a very fine one was taken at Broomhead-mill, on one of the tributary streams nine or ten miles above Sheffield. They seek waters where they are less disturbed by works, and weirs, and barges. The Don about Sheffield is now chiefly noted for chub, and the Riveling for trout.

[1] *History of Manchester*, vol. i. p. 220.　　　[a] *Description of Britain*, before quoted.　[2] *Poly-Olbion*, p. 140.

None of the Sheffield streams are navigable within the parish. The navigation of the river Don commences at Tinsley. But these streams are of more importance to the commerce of Sheffield in another way than they could possibly have been had their waters been so deep and their course so unobstructed as to have been fitted for the purposes of navigation. It is to one striking peculiarity in them that Sheffield in a great measure owes its present consequence as a manufacturing place, the frequent occurrence of their *falls*. These falls are the very life of its manufactures, presenting an easily available strong motive power to works where the demand of power is necessarily large. The falls occur upon these streams about twice in each mile, and there is scarcely an instance of their not being made available to move the ponderous hammer, or to turn the quick revolving grindstone. The works erected on the rivers are however exposed to the inconvenience of having an unequal supply of water, and the attention of ingenious men has been often directed to the possibility of equalizing the supply by the construction of reservoirs near the sources of the streams. Nothing has, however, yet been done. This circumstance, combined with the great increase in the manufactures of Sheffield in the last thirty years, has led to the introduction of the more uniform powers of the steam-engine. But still the mills erected on the rivers keep their ground; and it is the opinion of experienced men, that no advantage which the steam-engine may possess in the uniformity of its operations can counterbalance the greater expense which is required in their application, when the demand for power is so extensive as in many branches of the Sheffield manufactures. The philanthropist who has witnessed the wretched accommodations which the mills erected on the rivers in general afforded to the workmen employed in them, and the ill effect both upon their comfort and morals which is the consequence of their many unemployed hours, will excuse the large addition which the introduction of the steam-engine has made to the ancient smoke of Sheffield, and wish that the use of them might become more general. It is due to the worthy proprietors of the water-mills to state that considerable improvement has of late taken place in the accommodation of the persons employed in them; but their low, damp condition admits of no remedy.

Sheffield possesses the advantage of having many copious springs of pure water rising in the midst of the town. Some of these are less abundant than formerly, the consequence it is supposed of the excavations of the coal-miners under the town. Indeed, since the construction of the reservoirs on Crooks-moor, and the regular supply which has been received from thence, the private springs have been too much neglected: an evil which at no very distant period may be felt more sensibly than at present, when the demand is every day increasing, and the means of answering it growing less. As might be expected where the ore of iron is abundant, some of these springs are slightly chalybeate.

The position of towns generally depends upon accidental circumstances. But had it been foreseen to what extent the town of Sheffield would reach, and what would hereafter be the peculiar employment of its inhabitants, throughout the whole vicinage it is hard to say what more suitable situation could have been chosen for it. Placed at the junction of the two principal streams, it is very central to the various works erected on the rivers. A situation comparatively low gives it the advantage of a regular supply of water for domestic purposes from the neighbouring hills. Occupying a piece of rising ground sloping to the rivers, peculiar advantages are afforded, of which it is to be wished that the inhabitants had more availed themselves, for the cleanliness of the streets and passages. In such a situation there can be few parts of the town that are not visited by fresh breezes from the country. There is no street in Sheffield from which the country may not be seen. But the town is not now confined to the rising ground between the Sheaf and the Don. It has climbed the opposite hills; it has stretched itself along their banks; and it accompanies them in their united progress towards Rotherham.

The air is unquestionably salubrious. Epidemical diseases are rare: nor has it been found that effects injurious to the health of the inhabitants have proceeded from those sooty vapours, the product of the manufactories, with which the air is but too commonly loaded. The climate is cold, but there appears to be something of the extravagant in this passage of a courtier's letter to the earl of Shrewsbury, written in the reign of James I. ' I trust by this time your Lo. is safe and well arrived at Sheffield, and yet that yow finde it had bin as good to have followed your frend's perswasions, and not have undertaken a walke this time of the yeare *half way to the North Pole*, &c.[1]' A few facts on this subject may serve for comparison in times hereafter, in the absence of more accurate meteorological observations. It is thought an unusually early harvest if the corn is brought home before the cutler's feast, which is held in the first week of September. About once in three years the river Don, above the town, is sufficiently frozen to admit for a day at least of the diversion of skaiting, and sometimes for a longer period. Snow falls as late as the months of April and May, and even then in considerable quantities. It is not unusual to see it lying undissolved and universally diffused for the space of a fortnight or three weeks : and in remote parts of the parish, where they were sheltered from the beams of the sun, patches of the snow are sometimes to be found in the month of May, which had fallen in the November preceding.

There seems every reason to believe that the average of health in this kingdom, and consequently of life, has greatly advanced in the last two centuries. We find in 1554 the inhabitants of Sheffield representing to the queen that the fourteen hamlets within the parish were never void of plagues and other evil diseases, which they attribute to the great number of poor and impotent persons inhabiting them. What these diseases were is not very clear, for by *plagues* we need not understand that dreadful epidemic known by the name of the plague. Of this disorder, the reproach of medicine and the scourge of our ancestors, the parish of Sheffield has been kept remarkably free. I shall here throw together a few notes respecting it, to avoid recurring to the subject in a future page of this work. In 1563 the garrison of New Haven (now called Havre de Grace) introduced the infection anew into this kingdom. In London the disorder raged for many weeks

[1] Lodge's *Illustrations of British History, &c.* vol. iii. p. 309.

C

with great violence. It was conveyed into Yorkshire: and what melancholy spectacles it occasioned may be collected from this sad entry in the parish register of Almonbury, a village near Huddersfield. ' 1563 Sep. *Henricus Beamount de Lockwodde sep. erat* VII°, *sub occasu solis. Peste seu plaga mortuus est, ideoque per uxorem et puellulam sepultus erat, quæ eum ad tumulum super equi dorsum adferebant*[1].' It does not appear that the infection at this time extended itself to Sheffield: but in the next year, when the plague was stayed, and a day of public thanksgiving was appointed, the church-burgesses of Sheffield paid xx[d] for ' a boke called Thankesgevyn for the plage, and the salter in Englysche.' Five years after it made its appearance at Sheffield, and we have these entries concerning it in the same accompts:

	s.
Paid for the kepinge of Hawle wyffe, suspected for the plage . . . . }	IIII.
To Anthonie Hibbert towards his losse in the plage tyme . . . . }	IIII.
Paid to Edward Pavye for servinge Hibbert during the tyme he kept in his house . }	II.

Pavye was the parish-clerk; and he was employed to carry provisions to the poor infected Hibbert, who it appears received a compensation out of the Burgesses' Fund, for the restraint to which for the general good he had been forced to submit. We find mention of this man again in some public accompts in reference to this disorder. ' Delivered to Anthony Hibbert the VIII day of May 1570, because he had been at Colts of Rotheram, where they dyed of the plagge XII[d].' In 1585 the plague was at Doncaster. For three weeks the town of Sheffield was watched to prevent any communication with the infected place; and we find no trace of the appearance of the disorder at Sheffield. Even in the years 1586 and 1587, when London was so terribly afflicted, and the neighbouring town of Chesterfield was so fatally attacked by it, Sheffield seems to have escaped. So also in 1603, when it was at Brimmington: and in 1609, when William Townsend the curate of Holmesfield in the adjoining parish of Dronfield died of it. In 1633 the complaint again visited Yorkshire, and a contribution was made at Sheffield ' for the reliefe of the poor in the infected townes of Thorne, Hatefield, and Birstall.' Thus in those times of peculiar distress, the parishes bore one anothers burdens. In the summer of 1666, when the attention of the whole neighbourhood was directed towards the little village of Eyam in the Peak, then rapidly depopulating through the prevalence of this dreadful distemper, the alarm extended itself into the parish of Sheffield. In the constables' accompts of that period occur these entries: ' Charges about keeping people from Fullwood Spaw in the tyme that the sickness was att Eam.' ' For watching one that fell sick.' The vigilance of the earl of Devonshire and the care of Mr. Mompesson the rector of Eyam, aided by Mr. Thomas Stanley[c] a nonconformist minister, who continued to reside among his afflicted friends, accompanied by the divine blessing succeeded in preventing the spread of the contagion. This was the last appearance of the plague properly so called amongst us.

There have been few instances of extraordinary longevity at Sheffield. The most remarkable is that of William Congreve, who is stated on his grave in the parish church-yard to have been a hundred and eleven years eight months old at the time of his death in 1754. This has an appearance of particularity, one characteristic of truth. But there is always ground for much reasonable scepticism in accounts of such uncommon longevity. They generally depend upon the testimony of an interested party: and they always pertain to persons in that class of society in which it is most difficult to obtain authentic and indisputable records of birth or baptism. Nothing sets the credulity of the country in a more striking point of view than the credit which seems to be universally given to the fables of Parr and Jenkins, to prove whose incredible number of days we have not even the evidence we should reasonably require to establish a fact little removed from common experience. But on this point we are perhaps glad to be deceived: as Louis XIV. found no flattery more acceptable than when his courtiers related instances of longevity much greater than his own. Mr. Wilson took some pains to investigate the case of Congreve, but could not find that it rested on any thing but the vague reports of the people at Bolsover where he was born. In the year 1810 when a society was established at Sheffield for the express purpose of relieving the aged female poor, out of 341 who applied, thirty-nine were eighty years old and upwards, and only one had passed the age of ninety. In the parish-register we find,

1708, Mar. 7. buried William Hunt, aged 102 years.
1739, Jan. 3. —— Mary Bradberry, widow, aged 105.
1794, —— Aaron Rodger, aged 101.

---

[1].This is one of many curious entries in the register of Almonbury, which for the first century and a half is enriched with historical and biographical notices.
[c] The name of this gentleman has been too much disjoined from the history of the plague at Eyam. ' When he could not serve his people publickly, some (yet alive) will testifie, how helpful he was to 'em in private, especially when the sickness (by way of eminency so called, I mean the pestilence) prevailed in that town, he continuing with 'em, when as it is written, 259 persons of ripe age and 58 children were cut off thereby. When some who might have been better employed, moved the then noble earl of Devonshire, lord lieutenant, to remove him out of the town, I am told by the credible that he said, It was more reasonable that the whole country should in more than words testifie their thankfulness to him, who, together with his care of the town, had taken such care, as no one else did, to prevent the infection of the towns adjacent.' *De Spiritualibus Pecci*, by W. Bagshaw, minister of the Gospel, p. 64 : a small volume, but interesting from the air of simplicity and truth which pervades it, printed in 1702, for Nevill Simmons, bookseller in Sheffield. Mr. Bagshaw had been one of the assistant-ministers of Sheffield, and curate of Attercliffe. Mr. Stanley was born at Duckmanton, educated at Staveley and Chesterfield; was for some time curate to the elder Cart, rector of Hansworth; then curate of Dore; afterwards of Ashford, and settled at Eyam in 1644. Here he gave way to the old incumbent after the Restoration. He died in 1670. See more of his character in the work above cited, and in Calamy's *Account of the ejected and silenced Ministers*,

p. 179. I hope I may be excused for departing in a note so far from the immediate subject of this work as to introduce an unpublished monumental inscription for one of the family of Mr. Mompesson, the rector of Eyam, who continued in the faithful discharge of his pastoral duties to his much suffering people through the whole of so trying a season. It is to be found in the church of Barnborough, twelve miles from Sheffield.

H. S. E.
Alicia
uxor charissima Georgii Mompesson
rectoris hujus ecclesiæ :
prudens plane fœmina
juxta ac pia ;
æternitati matura.
Effare
luctum istius diei memorabilem,
quo, procedente funere,
longævus parens octogenario major,
maritus, undecim liberi
(omnes quos pepererat) certatim plangebant
obsequentissimam filiam,
fidissimam conjugem,
æquissimam matrem.
Obiit 16 Octob. Anno æt. 47
ac conjugii 27. Dni 1716.

There is one very numerous class of workmen at Sheffield which it is feared can furnish no names to any lists of the aged. There is no grinder of cutlery who has been constantly employed at his business, and has numbered sixty years. This melancholy fact demands immediate attention to its cause.

Nearly the whole of the parish of Sheffield is now inclosed and cultivated. There is much old inclosure. The Park, which contains above 2000 acres, was divided into farms about the commencement of the eighteenth century. Previously to that period this fine tract of land surrounding their summer mansion, called the Manour, and reaching to the castle of Sheffield, had been reserved for the pleasure of the lord. There is also much land, especially in the western parts of the parish, which is newly inclosed. The soil upon coal strata is said to be not very favourable to the views of the agriculturist. But the peculiar manufacture of the town and neighbourhood affords him an excellent manure not easily to be procured in other parts of the kingdom, in the shavings and useless fragments of the bones and horns. Lime is also within his reach at a small expense. Less attention seems to have been paid to the modern improvements in agriculture here than in other parts of the kingdom. This will commonly be the case where the farms are not large, and where few gentlemen are found cultivating estates of their own. The farms rarely exceed two hundred acres, and are for the most part held on leases for term of years. They are mostly in tillage. There is comparatively little meadow land. No cheese is made. The town is principally supplied with that necessary article milk, from the farms in Derbyshire. It is brought in barrels on horseback by boys, whose irregular and boisterous behaviour upon the roads became such a public annoyance, that a clause has been lately introduced into an act of parliament for their restraint and summary punishment. Much of the land in the immediate vicinity of the town is let to the manufacturers for gardens. These afford the proprietors some profit, together with an amusement the most varied, innocent and cheerful, and no doubt contribute much to the general health of the town.

The neighbourhood of Sheffield abounds in wood: within the parish are three woods of considerable extent, the Old or Shiercliffe Park, Wincobank-wood, and Ecclesall-wood, the last of which is the property of earl Fitzwilliam. The other two are on the great estate of his grace the duke of Norfolk, whose woodward is said to have the oversight of about twenty-five hundred acres of wood in the immediate neighbourhood of Sheffield. In 1719 an exact survey was taken of the woods belonging to the duke of Norfolk, when it was found that there were

25 woods in Ecclesfield	.	1380 acres.
7 in Bradfield	. . . .	240
2 in Hansworth	. . .	200
2 in Treeton	. . . .	96
2 in Whiston	. . .	240
14 in Sheffield	. . . .	429

making a total of 2585 acres. The Wortley family had about the same extent in Wharncliffe and its neighbourhood.

The woods now remaining are but small remnants of our ancient forest-vesture. The whole of Fullwood and Upper-Hallam was once a pasturable forest, *sylva pascua;* and the Park, which owing to its present want of foliage presents from many points a bare and unpleasing appearance, once abounded in forest-trees of the noblest growth. Mr. John Harrison, a person who in 1637 made a minute survey of the Manors of Sheffield, Cowley, and Ecclesfield, for the earl of Arundel, speaks of the stately timber which was then growing in Sheffield Park; but his admiration was most excited by what he observed in Riveling-Chase. 'The Haugh-Park is full of excellent timber of very great length, and very straight, and many of them of great bigness, being about sixty foot in length before you come to a knott, insomuch that it hath been said by travellers, that they have not seen such timber in Christendome.' In another place he describes them as ' growing out of such a rocher of stone, that you would hardly think there were earth enough to nourish the roots.' In this there is nothing extraordinary. Some of the largest trees in Europe are found in parts of the Alps where there is very little soil, which have struck their roots in fissures of the rock. We have also in Evelyn accounts of the noble timber with which the hills about Sheffield were once graced. He was informed by the duke of Norfolk's auditor, Mr. John Halton, that in the Park alone there were not fewer than a thousand trees, worth at least six thousand pounds, another thousand worth four thousand pounds, and so on in proportion[1]. In these were probably included the trees which formed the stately avenue of walnuts which led from the gate of the Park next the town to the principal entrance of the Manour, ' a living gallery of aged trees.' Uniting their branches aloft, they formed an arched roof through which neither sun nor shower could penetrate. So at least I have heard them described, for their memory is still fragrant. Four generations have passed away since this avenue was destroyed: but still it is remembered as the sylvan pride of the neighbourhood, and its fall is mentioned with regret by the people whose ancestors walked under its shade. The changed appearance of the Park must excite the regret of all : except the few trees about the farm-houses just sufficient to give them the character of so many ' elmy granges,' and two or three small copses where the unevenness of the ground forbade the approach of the plough, a tree is scarcely to be found throughout this once well-wooded part of the parish. The close of the seventeenth century saw the work of destruction completed[2].

[1] *Sykes*, edited by Dr. Hunter, 1801, 4to. vol. ii. pp. 206, 211, 212.
[2] Clay-wood occupied a piece of ground very unfavourable to the views of the agriculturist. For a long time it was spared. Reasons were however at length found for its destruction, and some ingenuity was shown in the means used to reconcile the inhabitants of Sheffield to the loss of one of their fairest ornaments. ' I have often congratulated myself,' says a friend of the author to whom he has been indebted for some most valuable hints, ' that I recollect the Clay-wood. Those only who do can form a just idea of its amphitheatrical pride, stretching down to the very brink of the Sheaf that flowed at its base, and rising upwards to the lofty summit that overhangs the eastern side of the town: the long line of hill on which the Manour stood just intervening between the topmost boughs and the horizon. When rising in all its consummate pomp, and robed in its leafy honours, well might the vale deserve the lovely comparison which Miss Seward's classic muse appropriates :

  ' And Sheffield, smoke-involved; dim where she stands
  Circled by lofty mountains, which condense
  Her dark and spiral wreaths to drizzling rains
  Frequent and sullied ; as the neighbouring hills
  Ope their deep veins, and feed her cavern'd flames.
  No aërial forms on Sheffield's arid moor
  E'er wove the floral crowns, or smiling stretch'd
  The shelly sceptre ;—there no poet roved
  To catch bright inspirations. Blush, ah blush,

To the botanist or the naturalist the parish of Sheffield appears to present few features of peculiar attraction. Its hedges are adorned with great variety of plants and flowers; but few it is supposed of much rarity. The ivy-leafed bell-flower (*Campanula hederacea*) and the rose-bay willow-herb (*Epilobium angustifolium*), Ray, the naturalist, says he found in the rocks and meadows near Sheffield[1]. He became well acquainted with the neighbourhood by visiting his friend and fellow-student in natural history Mr. Francis Jessop of Broomhall. Mr. Jessop communicated to Willughby, for his *Ornithologia*, accounts of some rare birds which he had observed in his own neighbourhood. In the western parts of the parish, the sportsman, if not prevented by the recent inclosures, may meet with the partridge, pheasant, and red moorgame; and sometimes, but very rarely, with the black species.

The parish of Sheffield is rich in its mineral productions, and especially in the three mineral bodies most important to man,—iron, coal, and stone.

The iron ore is found in many parts of the parish at the depth of about fifty or sixty feet. It was doubtless the presence of the raw material which first led the inhabitants of this district to manufactures of iron. But these mines are now comparatively of small importance to the staple branches of the Sheffield manufactures: for steel is what is principally wanted; and whether from any inferiority in the ore itself, or from any difference in the original smelting and preparation, the native iron of this neighbourhood is not found to bear the process of conversion into steel so well as the iron imported from abroad. The use of charcoal for the smelting of iron ore was one great cause of the destruction of so many of our ancient forests. Evelyn has beautifully observed that 'Nature has thought fit to produce this wasting ore more plentifully in woodlands than any other ground, and to enrich our forests to their own destruction.' Nor can he withhold his ' *Diræ*, a deep execration of iron-mills, and ironmasters also, *quos ego*—' How would he have rejoiced to have witnessed the day when the coke of pit-coal became substituted for the charcoal in this consuming process! Of the iron used at Sheffield in the state of iron, a large proportion is now brought from a distance[2].

Below the iron lies the bed of coal. The mean depth is about 120 yards, and the thickness of the bed from three to five feet. This bed is the principal source of that large supply of fuel which the manufactures of Sheffield demand: and has been so from an early pe-

riod. Leland writing in the time of Henry VIII. says, ' Halamshire hath plenti of woodde, yet ther is burnid much se-cole,' by which he means the native coal of the neighbourhood, such as was brought to London, his native place, by sea[3]. The pits were lately in the hands of the duke of Norfolk, the great land-owner of the neighbourhood, but are now under lease to a private company. The mouth of the principal excavation is within the town of Sheffield, in the Ponds near the Sheaf. In that part of the bed which lies under Darnall, layers of pure and perfect charcoal are found so intermixed with the bright coal, as to render it almost certain that they are parts of the same original substance, which by some accident have escaped a part of the process by which coal was produced. It is supposed that appearances in these pits must decide the much controverted question, and prove coal to have had a vegetable origin.

The town of Sheffield is described by writers of the seventeenth century as built entirely of stone. A few of the old stone buildings remain: but brick, as being the much cheaper material, is now chiefly in use for dwelling-houses and manufactories. It seems to have been first introduced at the beginning of the last century. The Upper-chapel in Norfolk-street was the first public building of brick; and this, as if the architect was suspicious of the durability of his material, has its corners of stone. The parish had, however, one fine specimen of brick masonry of two centuries earlier date. This was the turreted gateway at the Manour; erected at the same period, and probably by the same architect, with the archbishop's brick-college at Rotherham, the red appearance of which among buildings of stone gave occasion to a well-known Yorkshire proverb. The stone was got from quarries within the parish, which still yield it of a hard and durable nature for superior dwelling-houses and public buildings. The beautiful stone of which the Infirmary is built came from quarries in Loxley. The parish also possesses within itself good stone for common slating, so that the use of thatch is little known. Quarries at Brincliffe-edge formerly furnished the manufacturers with grinding-stones; but for this necessary article they are now chiefly indebted to the quarries at Wickersley, nine miles from the town.

Thus has nature been bountiful to the parish of Sheffield: not by bestowing upon it the most delicious fruits, double harvests, or perpetual summer, but the means and materials of all durable and substantial comforts, so placed that they serve as stimulants to

---

Thou venal genius of these outraged groves,
And thy apostate head with thy soil'd wings
Veil! who hast thus thy beauteous charge resign'd
To habitants ill-suited; hast allow'd
Their rattling forges, and their hammers' din,
And hoarse rude throats, to fright the gentle train,
Dryads and fair-hair'd Naiades;—the song
Once loud as sweet of the wild woodland choir
To silence;—disenchant the Poet's spell,
And to a gloomy Erebus transform
The destined rival of Tempean vales.'—*Works*, ii. 318.

By ' Sheffield's arid moor,' the writer means the east-moors, which may be said to rise in the parish of Sheffield, but which belong rather to the county of Derby. ' The beautiful lines on Bole-hill trees which stand upon this very moor, written by Sheffield's own poet, Montgomery,' show that there inspiration has been caught, and ' promptly and happily would Miss Seward have borne her testimony to their excellence, had not the preceding lines been written before his strain arose to give Sheffield a name among the sons of song.

About the same period Sheffield was despoiled of another sylvan ornament, Broomhall Spring. It was a grove of oaks without underwood, and stood on the spot now occupied by Wilkinson Street.

[1] Gibson's Camden,—Rare plants in Yorkshire.
[2] Foreign iron was in use at Sheffield more than two centuries and a half ago. In the accompts of the Church Burgesses occur these entries under the year 1557.
Paid to Rob.t More for one stone and q.ter of Danske yron xx:11.d
Paid to y.e same Rob.t for x lib. of Spanysche yron xv
It was wanted by the burgesses for a structure which was erected in the parish-churches at Easter, called the Sepulchre-house. We may collect from these entries the relative value of Spanish iron to that which was imported from the Baltic. It was as 7 to 6: the hundred of Spanish iron costing by retail 14 shillings, of Danish 12.
[3] *Itin.* vol. v. f. 94. Yet he sometimes uses the phrase earth coal: ' though betwixt Cawood and Rotheram be good plenti of wood, yet the people burne much yerth cole, by cawse hit is plentifully found there, and sold good chepe.' *Itin.* vol. v. f. 102. Sea-coal was the common term for fossil coal, especially in those parts of England which are not on the coal-strata. So Dame Quickly to Falstaff, ' Thou didst swear to me upon a parcel-gilt goblet, sitting in my Dolphin chamber, at the round table, by a sea-coal fire, on Wednesday in Whitsun week, when the prince broke thy head for likening his father to a singing man of Windsor.'—2 Hen. IV. ii. 1.

labour. And accordingly her sons are an active, acute, and hardy race, patient of toil, unwillingly submitting to unnecessary restraints, aware of the advantages of their situation, proud of the reputation they have obtained for her, attached to their birth-place, and wherever they go remembering with more than common affection the tall graceful spire that surmounts the town, the woodland heights around it, and the streams which glitter along its devious valleys. Even the very sound of its waters poured over their broken weirs or the slow-moving wheel, the hiss of the grinding-stone, and the noise of the forge are grateful in recollection on the ear of the genuine son of what is fondly called 'Old Sheffield.'

The parish of Sheffield is in the diocese of York, the archdeaconry of the west riding, and the deanery of Doncaster. It makes part of that noble English province, the county of York, but it is so situated that its southern boundary coincides with the southern boundary of the county. The adjoining parishes of Norton and Dronfield are in the county of Derby. It is in the west-riding. This riding, or as the word was anciently written tri-hing, bespeaking at once its etymology, is subdivided into nine wapentakes. The origin of this word, which corresponds to the hundred of the more southern counties, is not quite so evident; but Thoresby, after the old glossarist to Matthew Paris, who himself quotes from Hoveden, has given the following account[1]. 'When a person received the government of a wapentake, at the appointed time and usual place, the elder sort met him; and when he was got off his horse rose up to him: then he held up his spear and took security of all present, according to custom: whoever came touched his spear with theirs, and by this touching of armour were confirmed in one common interest: and thus from pæpnu (weapons), and tac (a touch), or taccane (to confirm), they were called Wapentakes[2].' Sheffield stands in what is now called the wapentake of Strafford and Tickhill, but in times before the Conquest, of Stratford or Strafford only. Whence arose the change in its appellation does not clearly appear. But possibly when the castle of Tickhill became annexed to the crown, certain townships owing service there might be relieved from the ordinary burthens of the hundred. Accordingly in the *Nomina Villarum* of the 9th of Edward II. the manors in the wapentake of Strafford are enumerated apart from a list of about an equal number which are said to be *in libertate de Tykhill*[3]. When these became again united, Tickhill might be joined with Strafford in the designation of the wapentake. Sheffield is among the places in Strafford. This name is derived from Strafford-Sands, near Mexborough, on the Don, about eleven miles from Sheffield. There doubtless, nearly in the central point, and where the ford over the river gave facilities for the meeting of persons from every part of the district, the public assemblies of the hundred were anciently held. When Thomas lord Wentworth was about to be made an earl, he chose to take his title from this

wapentake, in which his ancestors had resided for many centuries in a state of high respectability. The upper and lower divisions of the wapentake are those north and south of the Don.

The parish of Sheffield is unknown as one of the ecclesiastical subdivisions of the diocese of York before the Norman conquest. In which of the great Saxon parishes it was included, it may not be easy satisfactorily to explain. But as there was a church at Treeton before the time of the Domesday survey, it is not improbable that the south-eastern parts, together with Hansworth, might acknowledge a dependance upon that place; while the western parts, with Ecclesfield and Bradfield, might pertain to the Saxon churches of Hope and Tankersley.

It was not till after the Normans began to find themselves secure in the possession of their newly-acquired English property, that the owners of this district erected in these parts four churches, assigning to each of them for its parish, a suitable portion of their estate. They seem to have been judiciously placed: one at the vill of Ecclesfield, to which was assigned the manor of Ecclesfield, which had been in the hands of six Saxon proprietors, or rather the six independent manors which are mentioned in the Domesday survey under the general name of Ecclesfelt. Another they placed at Bradfield, near some ancient military earth-works, to which they assigned that part of a very spacious manor called the Manor of Hallun, or Hallam, which lay north of the Riveling, together with Haldworth, and some other places which lay included within the manor of Hallam, but had obtained a certain degree of independence upon it. A third they placed in the old Saxon manor of Hansworth; and a fourth at the vill of Sheffield, near their own castle, assigning as its parish the three small manors of Grimesthorpe, Attercliffe, and Sheffield, together with all that part of the vast manor of Hallam, which lay to the south of the Riveling.

The parish of Sheffield thus comprises three entire Saxon manors, together with a very material portion of a fourth: and it appears that Attercliffe and Sheffield had in times not long before the Conquest been regarded as integral portions of the rich, populous, and extensive manor of Hallam. The townships which now bear those names are probably correct representatives of what those manors anciently consisted: while in the part of the parish which lies north of the Don we have the Saxon manor of Grimesthorpe. All the remainder of the parish belonged to Hallam. After the Conquest, these four manors, together with many other large estates in the counties of York and Nottingham, came into the hands of one proprietor, and from thenceforth they were regarded as forming but one entire manor, which was called the Manor of Sheffield, there being the castle, the mansion of the lord. But within two centuries after the Conquest, large tracts of this territory were granted out to individual proprietors, who claimed to exercise certain privileges which are supposed to be manorial, a practice which was restrained by the act of 18 Edw. I. known by the

[1] See also *Wapentachium* in Kennet's Glossary, and pæpen-getace in Lye's Saxon Dictionary.
[2] *Ducatus Leodiensis*, p. 84. Thoresby corrects in this place the learned editor of the laws of Edward the Confessor for supposing Ewerwick-shire to be Warwickshire, when speaking on the subject of wapentakes. It is remarkable that Sir Henry Savile, himself a Yorkshireman, in his edition of Hoveden, and in the section *De Wapentagio*, f. 346. b. has printed *Warwichshire* where it is plain that *Yorkshire* was the county intended.
[3] *Harl. MS.* 6281 is a copy of this *Nomina Villarum*.

D

name of *Quia emptores:* and hence arose those smaller manors which are now acknowledged within the parish of Sheffield. The most considerable of these is that fertile and populous district called Ecclesall-Byerlow, which was held by an ancient knightly family bearing the name of de Ecclesall, and their successors the barons Scrope, of the castle and manor of Sheffield by knight-service; and in the Feodary's accompts of the estate of John earl of Shrewsbury, 30 Henry VI., it is estimated at two knight's fees, value x*l.* This manor passed through the families of Strelley and Bright (in a manner which will be fully shown hereafter) to its present noble owner, the right honourable Earl Fitz-William. The estate of Shiercliffe, a part of the old manor of Grimesthorpe, was also held of the castle and manor of Sheffield by the family of Mounteney, descended of the blood of the Lovetots, who had a hall and park there, claiming and enjoying certain manorial privileges. This is now unknown as a separate manor, being extinguished, or rather absorbed into the greater manor out of which it originally proceeded, when purchased of the heirs of Mounteney, in the time of Elizabeth, by George earl of Shrewsbury. The little manor of Darnall, now the property of General Spencer, seems to have been a part of the old manor of Attercliffe; and the manor of Owlerton belonging to Lady Burgoyne extends over a small portion of the parish of Sheffield. None of these manors are noticed in the *Nomina Villarum* of the 9th of Edward II. That record speaks only of the manor of Sheffield, then held by Thomas de Fournyvayle, to whom it had descended from his ancestors the Lovetots. Of this feudal chieftain, his grace BERNARD-EDWARD DUKE of NORFOLK and EARL-MARSHAL of ENGLAND is the lineal descendant and representative. He enjoys the manor of Sheffield, and with it an immense estate, through an unbroken line of splendid ancestry, Lovetots, Furnivals, Nevils, Talbots, and Howards, reaching to the first century after the Conquest. The chiefs of this proud line had during four or five centuries their principal residence at the castle of Sheffield.

To an inquisition after the death of Thomas lord Furnival, 39 Edward III., is appended a list of forty-three places, which are said to be ' *Membra Castri de Sheffield*[1].' It presents a curious *Nomina Villarum* of the neighbourhood.

Richmond	Wodhouse	Capell
Heghlegh	Stanyford	Bernes
Hallum	Longeley	Wodsetes
Fullwode	Shirclif	Whitley
Morwod	Nepesend	Birlay
Stanyngton	Brighous	Bradfield
Walkelay	Erputes	Treton
Hop' Thorp	Orgesthorp	Orgrave
Waddesley	Skynnerthorp	Darnale ✓
Ollerton	Grykesherth	Catcliff
Stanyngton	Grymesthorp	Brynesford
Morwood	Attercliff ✓	Whitstan
Birlay	Darnale ✓	Totewick
Werlsend	Bilhagh	Aston
Souchagh	Northumley	

Sheffield is the little capital of a district familiarly known by the name of Hallamshire. Shire is *share:* a portion of territory shared or appropriated to some city, town, or castle. It does not always imply that there is any peculiar jurisdiction prevailing: for we find many instances in the northern parts of England in which the term is loosely applied to tracts of country merely, as it seems, because lying near some place of ancient note. Thus in the county of York we have North-Allertonshire, and Sowerbyshire; and the country about Massam, an old seat of the barons Scrope, is familiarly called Massamshire. But in the term Hallamshire we have this peculiarity, that for the last seven centuries at least there has been no considerable vill of the name of Hallam; nor indeed any distinct knot of houses to which that name belonged; the Hallum in the preceding list, like its neighbour Fullwode, describing probably (as at present) not a village but a wide-extended and thinly-peopled district. It is as if the name of Yorkshire existed, while there was no remain of the ancient and famous city of York.

In this we have a proof of the ancient consequence of the Saxon manor of Hallam, of which a large portion was assigned to the parish-church of Sheffield. Though as a distinct manor it passed away soon after the Conquest; though the vill from which it derived its name, and the *aula* which gave dignity to it perished at a very remote æra, still the name survived, and even became extended to districts which never made a part of the manor. But the hall of a Saxon thane of the very first rank would naturally command respect, which would perpetuate the name of the place in which it had stood, when that place and the *aula* itself had passed away.

The extent of territory to which the term Hallamshire is properly applicable has been frequently the subject of discussion. In this undefined and uncertain state will the limits of all districts be found to be, which depend more on popular opinion, than on any peculiar jurisdiction or authority prevailing throughout them. In its most restricted sense it would seem proper to confine it to what constituted the Saxon manor of Hallam; and in this case it would comprehend only the three western townships of the parish of Sheffield, together with that part of the chapelry or parish of Bradfield which is within the present manor of Sheffield. In a sense rather less restricted, it would comprehend together with the manor of Hallam the two smaller Saxon manors of Attercliffe and Sheffield, which by the Norman surveyors are said to have been *inland in Hallum*, portions of the manor of Hallam. It would then include all that part of the parish of Sheffield which lies on the right bank of the Don, with Bradfield. And the first use of the term, which is in a charter of Richard de Lovetot in the reign of Henry II., seems to be in one of these restricted senses. But in the hundred-rolls of the time of Edward I., North-Ecclesfield is mentioned as being included within Hallamshire[2]: and in a confirmation by Edward III. of a grant to Nicholas a younger son of Thomas lord Furnival, of 10*l.* rent issuing out of Hallamshire[3], it

---

[1] Preserved in a volume of Topographical Collections made by a topographer of whom little is known, named Jakes. It was once the property of Burton the historian of Leicestershire, whose hand occasionally appears in it; and afterwards of his relations the Burtons of Hallowes in the parish of Dronfield. It is now in the library of my venerable friend, the reverend Edward Goodwin of Sheffield.—So it was when this note was written; but its worthy possessor has since closed a life of eighty-five years.

[2] *Rotuli Hundredorum*, f. 109.

[3] Evidences, Norfolk-house. Yorkshire Bundle, L. No. 2.

is expressly noted that Sheffield, Bradfield, Ecclesfield, and Hansworth are included under the term.
Our next authority is Leland, who says, 'Halamshire
beginneth a ii. mile from Rotheram. Sheffield iii. miles
from Rotheram, wher the lord of Shreusbyre's castle
is, the chefe market towne of Halamshire.' And Halamshire goith one way vi. or vii. miles above Sheffilde
by west, yet as I here say, another way the next village
to Sheffilde is in Derbyshire. Al Halamshire go to
the sessions of York and is counted as a membre of
Yorkshire. Æglesfild and Bradfeld ii townelettes or
villages long to one paroche chirche. So by this
meanes (as I was enstructed) ther be but iii. paroches
in Halamshire that is of name, and a great chapelle[1].'
The three parishes of which he speaks are evidently
Sheffield, Ecclesfield, and Hansworth; with the chapelry of Bradfield. The bailiff of Hallamshire now
executes his office in all the manors near Sheffield
which belong to the lord.

There is also a jurisdiction now prevailing throughout Hallamshire created by an act of the 21 James I.
incorporating the cutlers and other workers in iron
who resided in this neighbourhood. The framers of
that act, aware of the difficulty of settling precisely the
limits of Hallamshire, gave power to the officers of
the company not only throughout that district, but
every where *within six miles compass of the same*, that
no persons inhabiting this neighbourhood might
escape the wholesome regulations of the statute.

The parishes which adjoin to Sheffield are on the
north Ecclesfield, and especially that part of it which
forms the township of Stannington, a part of the great
chapelry of Bradfield: on the west the chapelry of
Dore in the parish of Dronfield: on the south Beauchief, Norton, and Hansworth: and on the east the
chapelry of Tinsley, supposed to be a member of the
parish of Rotherham.

From this it is separated by the Carbrook, one of
its minor streams; except that near the junction of this
brooklet with the Don, the parish of Sheffield is supposed to extend itself a little beyond. On the west it
is bounded by the Limb-dyke, and on the north by the
Riveling. For part of its southern boundary it has
the Sheaf, and the Meersbrook or boundary-brook now
separating the counties of York and Derby, but heretofore performing a much more important office,
marking the separation between Northumbria and
Mercia, and doubtless also between Maxima and Flavia Cæsarienses. Where natural boundaries like these
can be obtained, it is desirable that men should avail
themselves of them, to mark out the artificial divisions
they have created. These remain unchanged amidst
all the changes which war or commerce may occasion.
But in a cultivated and populous country, and where
the residents have a personal interest in keeping parochial and manorial claims within their just limits, it
seldom happens that the true line of boundary is for-

gotten. Not so in an uninclosed and thinly-peopled
country. There is perpetual danger lest the ancient
land-marks should cease to discharge their useful office. To this inconvenience the lords of the manor
of Sheffield have been always peculiarly exposed on
the side towards Hathersage in Derbyshire, where their
manorial rights extended beyond the limits of the
parish of Sheffield. In that extreme part, the process
of cultivation is now but just commencing. To preserve the recollection of the extent of their rights in
that direction, the old lords of Sheffield were accustomed to summon their tenantry and neighbours to
periodical perambulations, at which the principal gentry
of the vicinage, and sometimes the lord himself, were
present. The party usually set out from Whiteley-
wood, and passing by Ringing-law and Stanedge,
finished their tour at the North-Wain-stones. Notes
were made of the state of the different land-marks, and
of the more material parts of the evidence given by the
aged inhabitants. Records of their perambulations
for the years 1574, 1656, 1705, 1719, and 1722, still
exist. That of 1574, as the earliest and most minute,
may not improperly be introduced in this place. It
carries us back, by the recollections of the men who
were then the patriarchs of the neighbourhood, into
the *olden tyme*, the days of our Edwards and Henries[2].

'A boundary or breefe note of all the meres and
boundes of Hallamshire, betweene Whiteley wood and
a place called the Waynstones: namely betweene the
lordes landes of Hallamshire and the lords landes of
Ecclessall and Hathersedge. Gone over and viewed
and seene the sixt day of August Anno Dni one thousand fyve hundreth seaventy and fower, by these men
whose names are here underwritten.

'Viz[t]. Anthony Blythe of Birchett, gent. James Tur-
ner, bealife of Sheffeld, William Dickinson, William
Upton, Thurstone Kirke, William Harrise, George
Skargell, Adam Gill, Ralphe Morton, Gregorie Revell,
William Fox, William Greaves, Robert Mitchell,
Thomas Smith, John Barnsley, John Shemeld, Robert
Burrowes, Robert Morton, Robert Greaves, Robert
Waynwright, Richard Rawson, Robert Hawkesworth,
Henry Hawksworth, John Mariott, Thomas Fisher,
John Ramskarr, Robert Hawkesworth junior, Thomas
Hawkesworth, Richard Awsecliffe, and Richard Ro-
berts, the writer hereof, wth othe[r] more wch men did
meete the right hon[ble] lord George the earle of Shrews-
burie the day and year abovesaid.

'*Whiteley-wood.*—First one ewe-tree standing upon
my lordes land called the Benett-field is thought to
bæe a meere betwæene my lord and the lord of Ecclessall, and soe upward to a place called Stowperstocke.
This evidence is given and shewed by one John Stone
of Whiteley-wood aforesaid, beeing of the age of sixty,
yeares and above; as hee hath heard his elders say the
same.

'*Stowperstocke.*—Alsoe from the said ewe-tree to

---

[1] *Itin.* vol. v. f. 94.
[2] The improvements in the art of surveying render these perambulations less necessary than heretofore. An excellent map of the parish of
Sheffield (on the scale of three inches and a quarter to a mile) was engraved by Carey, from the surveys of the Fairbanks, in 1795. The elder
Fairbank had previously, namely in 1771, published a plan of the town,
and the two younger in 1809 favoured the public with a two-sheet map
of the town and environs, on the noble scale of an inch to every hundred
yards. The oldest engraved plan of the town is supposed to be that published in 1732, by Ralph Gosling, who made some small collections for
the history of Sheffield. The Bucks engraved a view of the town, taken
from the Park-hill, about 1740; and Oughtibridge another, taken from

Pye-bank, about ten years before. Thomas Oughtibridge was a Yorkshire
artist of no extraordinary merit, but his engravings are valuable as giving
representations of objects no longer existing. He was nephew to the
reverend Abraham de la Pryme, F.R.S. and friend of Thoresby, of the
benefit of whose scientific and topographical inquiries the world was
deprived by his death at an early age. The de la Prymes came from
Ypres at the time of the great drainage of the Level, and settled themselves at or near Hatfield. Oughtibridge died there in 1753, and is buried
in the church of Hatfield. David Martin, a draughtsman of some merit,
engraved in a hard style six views of scenery in the environs; and a
port-folio might be filled with the engravings which from time to time
have appeared of scenery and public buildings in and near Sheffield.

a stone called Stowperstocke, wch the aforesaid John Stone tooke away, and thereof made a pig-trough; and hee hath promised to sett it there againe: for hee once before about sixteene yeares agoe tooke it away, and one ould Roger Barnsley who was of the age of 80 yeares and above, did complaine upon him, and said hee had not done well in takeing it away, because it was a meere betweene my lord and the lord of Ecclessall: and the. said John Stone upon Barnsley's complaint did bring it againe, and there it remained tenn yeares; and att the said tenn yeares end, hee took it againe, but now hee hath or will sett it there againe as it ought to bee.

'*Ringinglawe.*—Also from the said stone called Stowperstocke to a great heape of stones called Ringinglawe; from wch one Thomas Lee had taken and led away a greate sort of stones: beeing by one sicke or brook which parts Derbyshire and Hallamshire.

'*Burbadge.*—Also the said sicke or ditch leading or goeing from Ringinglawe to a place called Burbadge heade, wch is a meere betweene my lord of Hallamshire and the heires of Padley lord of Hathersedge.

'*Hurklingedge.*—Also from the said Burbadge heade to a certeine place called Hurklingedge, being a meere betweene my lord and the lordshipp of Hathersedge.

'*Stanage.*—Also from the said Hurklingedge soe forward after the rocke to Stanage wch is a meere betweene the said lordshipps.

'*Broderacke.*—Alsoe from Stanage after the same rocke to a place called the Broade Rake, wch is also a meere betweene the said lordshipps of Hallamshire and Hathersedge.

'*Seavenstones.*—Also from the Broade Rake straight downwards to a place where certeine stones are sett upon the ends and haveing markes upon them called the Seavenstones; wch ould and antient men say that the same is the meere betweene my lord and the lord of Hathersedge.

'*Wainstones.*—Also from the said Seavenstones straight over the brooke or sicke there, to a place called the Wainstones, being distant, by estimation, three quarters of a mile.

'*North-wainstones.*—Also from the said Wainstones straight on after the banke or edge to a place or certeine stones called North-wainstones. John Mariott of Ugghill being of the age of 70 yeares and above, doth say that a certeine contraversie betweene my lords father and Mr. Fitchherbert about the common or pasture called Mosker, in soe much that both their councells did meete there upon a day appointed wth diverse ould and antient men on both partyes; in soe much that the men of Derbyshire brought there wth them an ould man of the age of fyve score yeares or thereabouts called Beetson, dwelling in Darwend, to declare and speake what hee did knowe therein: and beeing further charged by my lordes councell to speake the truth and nothing but the truth as hee would take it upon his contience, did say that there was in his time a cottage house builded in Moskarr, and a man dwelling in it named , who was behind wth his rent; and that then the said lord of Hallamshire did send his officers to distreane for the said rent; and the same officer tooke att the same time a black horse a distresse, untill the rent was paid. Richard Bacon and Henry Hawkesworth and diverse

others doe affirm this to bee true.—Robert Hawkesworth being of the age of 60 yeares or thereabouts saith, that hee hath heard his father say that the lord of Hathersedge had inclosed certeine closes in Moskarr, and these the tenants and free houlders of Hawkesworth-head did pull upp and cast downe the same, for my lord of Hallamshire: and since the same was never inclosed.'

To this may be subjoined the tracing of another boundary line of the manor of Sheffield, through a tract of country formerly little more populous.

'The boundarys or mears betweene the lordshipps of Sheffeld and Wadesley; as the same was agreed, upon the division, beginneth at a certain place called Ashen Carr in Locksley, and goeth from thence to an oak called Mear Oak, and so along to a place called Rough Edge: and from the said Rough Edge to a stone called the Landed Stone. From thence to Wonsmore-cross, and so on to two stones called Dun Cow and Calf upon the plain there. From thence to a place called Cockwell hill, and so forward to a ditch called Rumbling Clough; and from thence straight to a well called Oak-well, and by the water issuing and running from the said well to a place called Otabridge into the water there.'

The parish of Sheffield is divided into six townships or constabularies, each providing for its own poor. The Park, the greater part of the town of Sheffield, and a small piece of ground lying north of the town, form the township of Sheffield. The part of the parish which lies on the left bank of the Don is the township of Brightside-Byerlow. The triangular piece of land of which the river Don and the line of the park-wall are two sides, and the eastern boundary of the parish the third, forms the township of Attercliffe-cum-Darnall. The rest of the parish was anciently but one township, known by the name of Hallam-cum-Ecclesall; but that was subdivided about the latter end of the seventeenth century into the three townships of Ecclesall, Hallam-upper, and Hallam-nether.—These three townships form the *chapelry* of Ecclesall, and the township of Attercliffe-cum-Darnall the *chapelry* of Attercliffe. The rest of the parish is under the immediate spiritual superintendency of one clergyman, the vicar: but his duties are eased by an institution, peculiar as far as appears to the parish of Sheffield. There are attached to the parish church three clergymen, under the description of assistant-ministers, and whose office it is to be helpers to the vicar in the performance of all sacerdotal offices throughout the parish. One of these is nominated by the vicar to each of the rural chapelries. There are also two chapels of ease within the town, St. Paul's and St. James's, and a chapel attached to Talbot's hospital. The parliamentary commissioners who in 1650 made an ecclesiastical survey of the whole kingdom, recommended that Attercliffe and Ecclesall should be detached from Sheffield, and form two new independent parishes.

In the old county-rate books, these townships are assessed according to the following proportions:

Sheffield	0*l.* 5*s.*	3*d.*
Hallam-cum-Ecclesall	0 3	2½
Attercliffe-cum-Darnall	0 1	9
Brightside-Byerlow	0 1	2

In 1623 when an assessment was laid on the west-riding, in lieu of that ancient tax in kind, the furnishing cattle for the king's household, the assessment was,

Sheffield	0*l*.	9*s*.	11¼*d*.
Hallam-cum-Ecclesall .	0	6	0½
Attercliffe-cum-Darnall .	0	3	3¾
Brightside-Byerlow .	0	2	2½

At the funeral of one James Rawson on Holy-Thursday, 1603, a dole of four pounds to the poor of the parish of Sheffield was distributed thus, by his son Hugh Rawson of Norwood. One half was given equally between Hallam and Attercliffe, Brightside had a mark, and Sheffield what remained. These serve to show the relative population and wealth of the four old divisions of the parish. What follows will show their comparative extent, and their population at three recent periods. The first table is the return made to the deputy-clerk of the peace for the information of the Board of Agriculture about the year 1797[1]. The second exhibits the number of inhabitants male and female according to the parliamentary census of 1801 and 1811.

	Houses.	Acres.
Sheffield	7351	3436¼[2]
Ecclesall-Byerlow . .	1071	4180
Brightside-Byerlow . .	822	2680
Attercliffe-cum-Darnall .	500[3]	1336¼
Upper-Hallam	105	8836
Nether-Hallam . . .	188	1902
	10,037	22,371

1801.

Townships.	Males.	Females.	Total.
Sheffield Town and Park .	15,483	15,831	31,314
Ecclesall-Byerlow . . .	2,675	2,687	5,362
Brightside-Byerlow . .	2,028	2,002	4,030
Attercliffe-cum-Darnall . .	1,222	1,059	2,281
Hallam-nether	1,041	933	1,974
Hallam-upper	439	355	794
Totals	22,888	22,867	45,755

1811.

Townships.	Males.	Females.	Total.
Sheffield Town and Park .	17,387	18,453	35,840
Ecclesall-Byerlow	3,190	3,379	6,569
Brightside-Byerlow	2,462	2,437	4,899
Attercliffe-cum-Darnall . .	1,436	1,237	2,673
Hallam-nether	1,233	1,151	2,384
Hallam-upper	453	413	866
Totals	26,161	27,070	53,231

In reference to the last table it is to be observed, that there was so much jealousy prevailing lest the census of 1801 was made in view of some projected military arrangement, that it is supposed many names of males were purposely withheld. This was a feeling by no means confined to the parish of Sheffield, and may serve in part to account for the prodigious excess which appears in the census of 1811. Such has been the increase of building in all parts of the parish of Sheffield, that it requires no power of divination to predict that if an enumeration be made in 1821, as it is hoped there will, an excess still more extraordinary will be disclosed.

It is also to be observed, that in the above table the population of the *township* is not to be taken as representing the population of the *town* of Sheffield. It includes the inhabitants of the several homesteads in the Park, some of which are at the distance of two or three miles from the town: while all those persons are excluded from it whose houses stand on the left bank of the Don, or to the west of Coal-pit-lane in Ecclesall-Byerlow: but these houses are obviously integral parts of the town. On the whole, in the enumeration of 1811, we may perhaps regard 40,000 as being inhabitants of the town of Sheffield, and the remaining 13,231 as being residents of the out-hamlets.

An enumeration of the parish was made in 1736 by order of the town-burgesses, preparatory to presenting a petition to parliament to make Saint Paul's church parochial[4]; when it appeared that there were in

	Families.	Individuals.
The township of Sheffield .	2152	9695
Brightside-Byerlow . . .	211	983
Attercliffe-cum-Darnall . .	245	1075
Ecclesall and the two Hallams	503	2352
	3111	14105

I shall subjoin from the parish-register a table showing the number of marriages, baptisms, and burials at the parish-church and the chapels under it, for each ten years from the commencement of the register in 1561. During the last century there have been many baptisms and burials at the different places of worship for dissenters, which have not come into the parish-register.

Years.	Marr.	Baptisms.	Burials.
1561 to 1570 inclusive	234	1085	712
1571 — 1580	275	955	721
1581 — 1590	340	1245	959
1591 — 1600	459	1364	1323
1601 — 1610	417	1475	1049
1611 — 1620	469	1699	1359
1621 — 1630	532	1884	1606
1631 — 1640	564	2130	2194
1641 — 1650	410	2126	2276
1651 — 1660	475	1698	1888
1661 — 1670	585	2086	2266
1671 — 1680	537	2240	2387
1681 — 1690	540	2595	2856
1691 — 1700	688	2221	2856
1701 — 1710	942	3033	2613
1711 — 1720	991	3304	2765
1721 — 1730	1212	3874	3828
1731 — 1740	1361	4635	3878
1741 — 1750	1584	5904	5232
1751 — 1760	1833	7036	6270
1761 — 1770	2551	8885	7547
1771 — 1780	2962	10697	9898
1781 — 1790	3863	13851	11849
1791 — 1800	4277	16152	13139
1801 — 1810	5031	17760	13384

Years.	Marr.	Baptisms.			Burials.		
		Males.	Females.	Total.	Males.	Femal.	Total.
1811	563	1020	906	1926	740	719	1459
1812	541	984	905	1889	638	623	1261
1813	580	922	895	1817	606	604	1210
1814	618	924	885	1809	616	609	1225
1815	773	1139	1088	2227	900	761	1661
1816	713	1105	1066	2171	710	632	1342
1817	573	1107	1060	2167	840	726	1566

[1] From the Appendix to *Brown's General View of the Agriculture of the West Riding*, 8vo. 1799, pp. 118, 119.

[2] 700 of these are said to be occupied by the town of Sheffield.

[3] In this number the uninhabited houses were not included.

[4] From the MSS. of the late Thomas Short, M.D., to whom the reader is indebted for the earlier part of the register accounts.

Anno 1817.	Baptisms.		Burials.	
	Males.	Females.	Males.	Females.
Parish church	1047	1006	566	500
St. Paul's . .		3	140	119
St. James's . .			17	20
Attercliffe . .	31	31	61	37
Ecclesall . .	29	20	56	50

From 1801 to 1810 inclusive, the number of marriages among the Quakers was 19; of baptisms among various descriptions of dissidents, and births among the Quakers 1179; of burials among all descriptions of dissidents 306. Few, if any of them, were entered in the parish-register.

CHAPTER II.

An Inquiry into the early State and remote History of the Parish of Sheffield.

WHERE is now collected a numerous and active population was anciently a deep solitude, the silence of which was broken only by our rivers pouring their waters in natural cascades through the woodland scenery.

Who was the first to raise the axe amongst the forests of HALLAMSHIRE, or who first established himself and his family in one of its romantic valleys, it is in vain now to attempt to recover. England boasts to have more and better early native historians than any other country of what may be called modern Europe: and yet we are seldom able to fix, with certainty, the æra of the foundation of our cities and towns; much obscurity rests upon the ancient topographical divisions of our country, and even upon many important points of its general polity and history.

Direct historical evidence is wholly wanting: and if from a few existing remains of the ante-Norman period of our history, and by deduction from the view given of this district by the Domesday surveyors, we are able to trace out a few circumstances of its early state and history, this is all we must expect. And even in this I must crave the reader's indulgence, that he will bear in mind that the ground about to be broken up has not hitherto been touched by any preceding topographer, and that he will allow me to commence my historical labours in the humble form of an inquirer.

The division of the dioceses into the small parishes as they at present appear, is not to be referred to any particular æra. It was evidently not the work of one period, but of many: the more ancient parochial divisions being again subdivided and new-moulded, whenever the lord of a manor was rich enough or devout enough to found a church on his domain.

This, we have already had occasion to observe, appears not to have been done at Sheffield till some time after the Norman conquest. The light of Christianity very early visited the vale of the Don, and shone with no ordinary splendour at Doncaster, one of the *villæ regiæ* of King Edwin. But it seems to have travelled slowly towards the source of that river: and if we may trust the argument from the silence of Domes-

day, there was no church in the Saxon times in any part of what now forms the parish of Sheffield. But by one of its earliest Norman proprietors a church was erected close to the vill of the manor of Sheffield: and when they came to apportion their estates to the several churches they erected, to the church of Sheffield they assigned as its *parœcia* the manor in which it stood, the adjoining manors of Attercliffe and Grimesthorp, and that part of the very spacious manor of Hallam which lay south of the Riveling. The other moiety of that manor was appropriated to the church built about the same period at Bradfield.

It is therefore in what we can collect concerning these four Saxon manors that we are to look for the history of the territory which now forms the parish of Sheffield: and the first point to which our attention may be directed is their geographical situation, and the several tribes, provinces, or kingdoms, to which in remote ages they may have belonged.

These lands lay upon the confines of the territories possessed by two tribes of native Britons, the Brigantes and Coritani. When for the purposes of government the Romans divided the island into several provinces, they lay on the confines of Maxima Cæsariensis and Flavia Cæsariensis: and when a few centuries later the Saxons had obtained possession of Britain, the inhabitants of these regions found themselves placed in an unenviable situation on the borders of the two rival kingdoms of Northumbria (or rather Deira) and Mercia. When the heptarchy or octarchy became one sovereignty under Egbert, these manors made a part of the county of York.

But to say that these lands lay on the confines of Flavia and Maxima, of Mercia and Deira, is not all that may be expected. The precise line of boundary of these ancient divisions of Britain seems still open to discussion, after all the attention that has been paid to it by Pegge, Whitaker, and others. The Roman geographers contain nothing decisive on this point, and the older monkish historians are content to speak of the Humber and the Mersey as separating the two districts. Higden, comparatively indeed a modern, says, when speaking of the boundary of Northumbria, ' *Ab austro flumen Humbræ descendendo versus occidentem* per fines comitatuum Nottingamiæ et Derbeiæ *usque ad flumen de Merseæ*[1].' Mr. Whitaker contends[2] in opposition to Higden, that the line of the Don was the boundary, a decision which would place the greater part of the parish of Sheffield within Flavia and Mercia. But his authorities do not seem to bear him out. For Greasborough, where he places the *Ad Fines* of Richard of Cirencester, is not on the Don: and whatever authority we may be inclined to allow to the monk's Itinerary, it is obvious that the words ' *ibi intras Maximam Cæsariensem*,' which occur at Danum in the fourth Iter, if not one of his interpolations, may be understood to mean that Danum was the first station in Maxima, and near the confines. Danum, moreover, the modern Doncaster, the Campodonum of Bede, was decidedly a Northumbrian town, and yet it stood on the south bank of the Don. On the whole, the question seems to resolve itself into a balance of probabilities—where in one scale we have the convenience of having the line of demarcation so fixed and notorious as would be the course of such a river as the Don, and in the other what may be called the prescriptive claim of the present Yorkshire boundary. There seems no good reason for the addition of that extensive tract of country which lies south of the Don to a county which without it was disproportionately large, except that its inhabitants had previously enjoyed a community of interests with their more northern neighbours: so that to me the latter scale seems to preponderate ; and we must regard the whole of the territory which forms the parish of Sheffield as having been included within the Roman province of Maxima and the Saxon kingdom of Deira.

The manor of Hallam is not without vestiges of its Brigantian population. A celt was preserved with much veneration in the cabinet of Mr. Wilson, which had been discovered near his mansion of Broomhead. In the same neighbourhood is a British *tumulus* or barrow, now known by the name of the Apron-full-of-stones. That vast trench called the Bar-dike, in the same northern part of the manor of Hallam, of which the precise æra and the purpose of its formation are alike involved in the deepest obscurity, may probably be referred to a period before the arrival of the Romans: and so also the Canyers, a range of conical hills stretching about a mile in length, if indeed that stupendous work has been raised by other hands than those divine. Few districts in this kingdom present traces more prominently developed of our primæval ancestry than the northern moiety of the manor of Hallam: and it seems no improbable conjecture that population here began to spread itself from the north. But no remains which belong to the British period are to be found in that part of the manor of Hallam which lies south of the Riveling, the part which falls more immediately within the limits of the present work.

Neither in Ptolemy, the Notitia, nor the geographer of Ravenna, have we any notice of a Roman station which can on circumstances of strong probability be placed within the parish of Sheffield. The discovery of the Roman tablets in Riveling renders it, however, highly probable that very soon after the Romans brought this island under their dominion, a municipal colony of Roman legionaries became settled within the manor of Hallam. Of this more hereafter. In the map of Roman roads in Yorkshire given in the Eboracum, one is laid down through the midst of the parish of Sheffield,—on what authority does not appear, for it is certain that no traces of it are now discoverable. The eighteenth Iter of Richard of Cirencester skirted, if it did not enter, the parish of Sheffield. This is a road not laid down in Antonine's Itinerary. It extended across the island from York to Southampton. It passed through Castleford near Pontefract, and at the distance of eighteen miles from that station it encountered another called Ad Fines, which by the learned translator of Richard's curious work, and the equally learned author of a late dissertation on the course of the Roman roads in Derbyshire[3], has been removed from Greasborough, where Stukeley and Whitaker had placed it, and fixed at Templeborough, on the Don. Here is a very fine rectangular camp indisputably Roman. But it is a curious fact, and one which well deserves the attention of those who are disposed to pursue the inquiry into the age of the Itinerary, preserved or compiled by the monk of Cirencester, that about a mile lower than Templeborough, on the stream of the Don, is the town of Rotherham, or Roderham, whose British name Yr Odar, *terminus*, is obviously reflected in the Roman name of this station, Ad Fines.

The name of the next station to Ad Fines is lost; but the road probably passed through or near Chesterfield, and so to Little Chester, near Derby. There has been so much cultivation in the country between Rotherham or Templeborough and Chesterfield, that it is perhaps unreasonable to expect to find any remains of the ancient high-way. The road between those places now lies through the town and parish of Sheffield; but the line of the Roman iter is rather to be sought on the south side of the Don, than on the present road which twice crosses that river, though it is evident from the name of the bridge at Attercliffe that there was formerly a ford at that place, and the Lady's-bridge at Sheffield is one of very high antiquity.

Traces of castrametation, which are supposed to be Roman, are to be found among the trees and thick bushes with which the hill of Wincobank is covered. This camp was of an irregular form approaching to the circle, and from it was commanded a view of the country for many miles around. In situation, form, and extent it closely resembles the encampment on the hill of Little-Salisbury, near the city of Bath. A bank extending from this place eastward, called the Roman ridge, was probably a cross iter made for the convenience of the garrison at this place, and joined the great road already mentioned from York to Southampton.

It is a prevalent opinion at Sheffield, that the area of the present parish church-yard was anciently a camp of the Romans. It is well-known that such situations were sometimes chosen for the erection of Christian temples; and the name of a street which passes under the walls of the cemetery on the north side, Campo-

[1] *Polychronicon. De regnis, regnorumque limitibus.*
[2] *History of Manchester*, vol. i. p. 66.

[3] Lysons's *Magna Britannia*.—Derbyshire, p. ccxi.

lane, may seem to give some countenance to the opinion. I have also heard that urns containing ashes as of some human body that had been burnt, were found several years ago on digging in the neighbourhood of Bank-street. Neither from this place nor from Wincobank has our *Numismata Romana* been enriched; but we must remember that in the burial-ground of a populous parish every particle of earth must have been many times dug over and sifted long before men began to give attention to matters of antiquarianism, or thought of preserving for the information of a more curious posterity, the remains of ancient date which chance submitted to their notice: nor in a situation so surrounded by buildings may we expect to find at this day any evident traces of the vallum and the foss.

Exaggerated as may be the accounts of Gildas and others of the sufferings of Britain when the Roman garrisons were withdrawn, there seems no reason to doubt that there followed times of great distress, and that the oppressions of the Saxons were not less severe than those of the Picts and Scots they were called in to remove. In the general calamity the inhabitants of these regions lying in the very centre of the island must have participated: and afterwards in the contentions of Northumbria and Mercia they must, from their frontier situation, have been peculiarly exposed to the calamities of war. Those two noble military earth-works called Castle-hill and Bailey-hill, both very near to the village of Bradfield, are evidently in their whole construction Saxon, and were doubtless thrown up for the defence of the kingdom of Northumbria. Tradition speaks loudly of the defeat and death of an invading king who came from the south, bearing a raven in his standard, amongst the hills on the north of Bradfield. History, however, affords us here no certain light; since neither in the Saxon annals nor in our own Northumbrian Bede are any events recorded that can on decisive evidence be referred, as to their scene, to the territory which now composes either the manor or parish of Sheffield.

Nor is the want of such notices in our general historians made up to us by information afforded by Saxon charters, or other evidences of a more private nature. The name of Dalen occurs in that curious topographical relic the Testament of Wulfric Spott[1], made in the time of King Ethelred, and it has been by some supposed to represent our Hallam, in Domesday written Hallun. And had the name occurred among the lands bequeathed to Morcar,—namely, Hackenthorpe, Beighton, Mosborough, Eckington, and other places in the northern parts of Derbyshire,—the trifling variation in the orthography would not have forbid us

to regard it as the Hallam of this neighbourhood. But occurring amongst those lands which are given to the abbey of Burton, a religious house which never appears to have had any connexion with Hallamshire, and in the midst of a long list of places which are neither in the county of York, nor in the parts of Derbyshire adjacent to Sheffield,—since there are other places of the name, there seems to be no good reason for giving the preference to the Yorkshire Hallam. A very learned and skilful topographer has suggested that the Halen, Ramesleage, and Sciplea, which occur together in this Saxon charter, are Hales-Owen, Romsley, and Shipley, neighbouring places in the counties of Salop and Worcester[2].

The earliest record in which we find any notice of the four manors which contributed to the formation of the parish of Sheffield is the Domesday Survey, made by order of William the Conqueror in the fourteenth year of his reign. The information which is there given respecting them, though short, will be found minute and curious, and to supply ground on which we may proceed to further inquiries into the state of this neighbourhood in times long before the arrival of the Normans.

TERRA ROGERII DE BVSLI.

Ⓜ In *GRIMESHOV* hb Vlfac . III . caȓ tȓe ꓒ dim̂ ad gȓd. ubi . II.[3] caȓ posš. ꝫꝫ. Nc̃ Roḡ ht ibi . I. caȓ ꓒ . III. uilł ꓒ . III. borđ cũ . I . caȓ. Silua pasł . III. qrenł tg. ꓒ II. lat̂. T.R.E. uat. XL. sol' m°. XX. sol'.

Ⓜ In *HALLVN* cũ XVI. bereuuitis sunt . XXIX. carucate tȓæ ad gȓd. Ibi hb Wallef com̂ aulã. Ibi posš. ꝫꝫ. xx. caruce. Hanc trã ht Roḡ de Iudita comitissa. Ipse ibi . II . caȓ. ꓒ XXX.III. uilł hntes XII. caȓ ꓒ dim̂. Ibi . VIII. ac̃ pti. Silua pasł IIII. lev̂ lḡ. ꓒ IIII. lat̂. Tot̂ Ⓜ x. lev̂ lḡ. ꓒ VIII. lat̂. T. R. E. ual' VIII. marc̃ argenti. m°.XL. sol'.

Ⓜ In *ATECLIVE* ꓒ *ESCAFELD* hb Suuen . V. caȓ tȓe ad gȓd. ubi posš. ꝫꝫ . III. caȓ. H̃ tȓa dȓ fuisse inland in *HALLVN*[4].

In what appears to be a recapitulation of the Yorkshire survey, we have this further notice of them:

Iud' comitissa.		ead' co.		ead' co.
In Hallun . XXIX. caȓ.		In Atecliue . III. c̃.		In Scafeld . III. caȓ[5].

The sense of the whole may be expressed in more modern language thus:

In Grimeshov, Grimshaw, Grimesthorpe, the modern Brightside-Byerlow[6], one manor, Ulfac had three

---

[1] Published in the *Monasticon*, vol. i. p. 266—269.

[2] See a letter to the re-editor of the *Monasticon Anglicanum*, Gent. Mag. vol. lxxxvi. part I. p. 134. In addition to what is there advanced to prove that the Walesho of Walric's charter was not, as Dugdale conjectured, Walsal in Staffordshire, but rather Wales in Yorkshire, may be mentioned that Morcar is named as a former Saxon lord of Wales in Domesday-book. I suspect the Morligtune of the charter to be a place in the wapentake of Strafford, surveyed in Domesday under the name of Mereiton. The manor had four berewites at the time of the Norman survey, but I am unable to fix its precise situation.

[3] This numeral occurs in Wilson's transcript of Domesday-book for Yorkshire, but is not found in the printed copies.

[4] It may be expected that I should describe the grounds on which I have assumed that the Grimeshov of Domesday-book is the modern Grimesthorpe, and the district in which that village stands, now called

[5] Id. f. 320 a.   [6] Id. f. 379 b.

Brightside-Byerlow. I consider the point established by the combined effect of these considerations. 1. If not here, we have no account at all of this district, which we can hardly suppose to have been lying wastc, when all the country around was cultivated and inhabited. 2. Grimeshov is in the wapentake of Strafford, and there is no place within that wapentake the name of which has a nearer affinity to Grimeshov than Grimesthorpe, the one meaning only the wood and the other the village of Grim or Grime some very early possessor. 3. It occurs in that part of the survey where we might expect to find Grimesthorpe, namely, immediately after the neighbouring manors of Brinsford, Tinsley, Orgrave, Newhall, Hooton and Denaby, are somewhat remote, there is an obvious reason for introducing them in that particular part of the survey, in their having had Ulfac the Saxon owner of Grimeshov for one of their proprietors before the Conquest. 4. Ulfac was one of the six Saxon proprietors of Ecclesfield which adjoins to Grimesthorpe. And lastly, the

carucates and a half of land that were rated to the taxes, about three hundred and fifty acres, and there might be about two ploughs. Now Roger de Busli has there one carucate; and three *villani*, villains, a superior order of tenantry, and as many *bordarii*, borderers, cottagers, an inferior class, have one carucate. There is a pasturable wood three quaranteens[1] in length, and two broad. In the time of Edward the Confessor it was valued at forty shillings, now at twenty.

In Hallun, Hallam, one manor with its sixteen hamlets, are twenty-nine carucates, about three thousand acres, that were rated to the taxes. There Earl Waltheof had an *aula*, hall, court. There may have been about twenty ploughs. This land Roger de Busli holds of the Countess Judith. He has himself there two carucates; and thirty-three villani hold twelve carucates and a half. There are eight acres of meadow, and a pasturable wood, four leuæ in length and four in breadth. The whole manor is ten leuæ in length and eight broad. In the time of Edward the Confessor it was valued at eight marks of silver; now at forty shillings.

In Ateclive and Escafeld, Attercliffe and Sheffield, two manors, Sweyn had five carucates of land, five hundred acres, that were rated to the taxes. There may have been about three ploughs. This land is said to have been inland, demesne land of the manor of Hallam.

So far the Survey. In the recapitulation these two smaller manors are represented as of equal extent, each comprising three rated carucates. Hence it appears that this part of the survey was not made with the most scrupulous accuracy. The orthography of the latter name also varies, and approaches nearer to the present mode of writing it, Scafeld. We have also an important fact which is not expressly noticed in the survey, though perhaps it might have been inferred from it, namely, that Attercliffe and Sheffield, as well as Hallam, were held by de Busli of the Countess Judith.

Whatever this district may have suffered from civil contest or foreign invasion, we have here the description of a rich, flourishing, and populous country: less prosperous than it had been in the peaceable times of the Confessor, but still more thickly studded with villages, and with more land inclosed and in tillage than were the manors in general by which it was surrounded. To assist the reader in forming a just idea of the state of the parish of Sheffield in times before and at the Conquest, we shall now proceed to analyse the information contained in this noble record.

I. First in every point of view stands the curious fact, that within the manor of Hallam arose the aula of a Saxon earl.

Few of these aulæ are mentioned in Domesday-book; and where they do appear they are commonly found in the manors possessed by the prime Saxon nobility. Only one other is found in the wapentake of Strafford. It was at Laughton en le Morthen, where its foundations may still be traced, and its Saxon proprietor was Edwin earl of Mercia. They were the courts and the places of residence of the persons to whom they belonged, and doubtless as much superior to any ordinary

manor-house as is the mansion of a modern nobleman to the edifices which now bear that name. They were to the prime nobility what the *aula regia* of writers of a somewhat later period was to the king.

To form a just conception of the ante-Norman topography of the parish of Sheffield we must first fix our attention on this edifice; since wherever it stood, there was doubtless the central point of cultivation and refinement.

In our pursuit of this inquiry we shall be engaged at the same time in the search after the long-lost vill which gave its name to the manor of Hallam, and which has come down to us in the familiar term Hallamshire. For I hold it certain that the manor of Hallam must have had a vill which bore the same name, and that where the vill of Hallam stood, there was the aula of its Saxon lord. Indeed it seems not improbable that the very name of Hallam is derived from this aula, which is only the Latin representative of the old Saxon word hall.

But in what precise point of the manor of Hallam stood a hall not unbefitting the dignity of Waltheof earl of Northumberland, Huntingdon, and Northampton, the representative of a line of Saxon and Saxo-Danish thanes, and the near relative of the Conqueror, is a question of which it is more easy to discern the importance to the right understanding the Saxon topography of this district, than to return to it an answer which shall be proof against all objections.

As far as hath yet been discovered, there is only one place throughout the whole of what at any period pertained to the manor of Hallam, where is to be found any stone foundation work that can be supposed to have ever supported such an edifice as the aula of Earl Waltheof. This is on the Castle-hill at the junction of the Sheaf with the Don in the town of Sheffield. On this 'guarded mount' rose the hall of the Norman lords of Hallamshire. They had their residence here at least as early as the time of Henry II., and the first of the two castellated mansions which occupied in succession this well chosen spot, seems to commend itself, with strong circumstances of probability as having been the aula of the Saxon lords of Hallam. Not the weakest of its pretensions lies in the fact which the Domesday survey further discloses; that in the times when the manors of Sheffield and Attercliffe made part of Hallam, they were accounted *inland*, that is demesne land, or land in the lord's own possession. Such parts of the estate we might naturally expect to find in the immediate vicinity of the mansion.

To regard the first Norman castle of Sheffield as having been the Saxon aula of the manor of Hallam is an hypothesis not liable to the objection which presses strongly against any other, that we want such evident tokens of its existence as we find at Laughton of the similar edifice of Earl Edwin. This hypothesis also accounts most satisfactorily for the superiority which we shall find the vill of Sheffield enjoying through the whole of Hallamshire in the first century after the Conquest. But against this supposition the words of Domesday are express. We might indeed, by a sacrifice of the attention and accuracy of the surveyors, reconcile the words of Domesday to this hypothesis. But,

<hr/>

redeemed land bears about the same proportion to the whole here as in Attercliffe and Sheffield, while in the wood of three quaranteens by two we may recognise the modern Wincobank.

[1] This measure is uncertain; as is also the *leua* mentioned in the next article. The former is usually translated furlong, and the latter mile; but Blomefield says the latter was two miles.

F

as the record at present stands, we are compelled to look in that part of the district which formed the manor of Hallam after the two smaller manors of Attercliffe and Sheffield had been severed from it, for the aula of Earl Waltheof.

Tradition guides us, and where we have no better guide we may be allowed to follow her, if we proceed with cautious steps, to the banks of the Riveling, the stream which once divided the manor of Hallam into two nearly equal portions. In a tone unusually loud she has long called our attention to the sloping banks of that rivulet, however now deserted, and according to our ideas less adapted for human habitation than many other places in the neighbourhood, as having once been the seat of a numerous and busy people inhabiting the vill which gave its name to the manor. In a tone equally loud she speaks of the utter ruin of the place as an act of signal vengeance by the incensed Norman conqueror, who is represented as having left not one stone upon another, but in the sublime language of holy writ to have swept it from the earth with the besom of destruction.

What passes current in the world as a tradition is often nothing more than an hypothesis: and it is difficult to distinguish between a genuine tradition delivered down through a long series of generations, and a supposition or conjecture founded on presumptions and probabilities first propounded to the world and introduced to general currency at a period very little remote. So that the credit which is due to a rumour purporting to be a tradition will be greater when the apparent probabilities are the weakest. And certainly there is nothing in the site which is pointed out in the rumour of the neighbourhood as that of the vill, or, as that rumour styles it, the city of Hallam, which may be supposed to have led any recent inhabitant of those parts to have proposed a conjecture which in process of time has assumed the form and character of a genuine tradition. Its only pretensions lie in circumstances that were not likely to present themselves in this connexion to a common observer, and in a discovery which was made in this place within the last fifty or sixty years.

The name of Haugh-park, which is on the Riveling, is not only evidently Saxon, but it betokens proximity to some considerable mansion, while it is certain that none such has existed near it since the time of the Conqueror. The place to which this tradition points is very central to the whole manor of Hallam, as that manor was in its earliest days before it was dismembered of Attercliffe and Sheffield. We also find the name of Hallam still adhering to the country on the south side of the Riveling and down to its very banks, while it has disappeared from every other part of the extensive district which once bore the name, except as it is retained in the name of Hallamshire.

These are, it is allowed, but weak presumptions, and they would avail little to fix the aula and vill of Hallam

to the site proposed, had we not another reason for looking to that point as one at least of the old centres of population and civilization in this neighbourhood.

In the month of April 1761, a countryman, one Edward Nichols, ploughing a piece of common land called the Lawns, on the Stannington side of the Riveling, discovered two thin plates of copper about six inches by five, both bearing inscriptions of which the greatest portion was perfectly legible. The inscription was in substance the same on both tablets; but one was in a more rude and barbarous character than the other, and that was broken into small fragments. On the back of the broken tablet were about a dozen names in two rows, but so defaced that only three could be made out—

> VRBANI
> SEVERI
> PARATI.

These were thought to be the names of the soldiers of whose manumission and enrolment among citizens of Rome these tablets were the record.

The inscription, as far as it could be recovered on the more perfect plate.

IMP CAESAR DIVI TRA..NI PARTHICI F DIVI NER
VAE.....................HADRIANVS AVG PONTIF
MAXIM TRIBVNVS..........VIII COS III PRO COS
QVI TIBE O...................T VERINALI SVI ET
.........................Ī HISPA II VRETIQV RV
............................R........ET PETRIAN
.........................HISP ET Ī FRISIA VETĪ
M SALIN ET Ī SVNVC ET Ī VANG ᴹ ET Ī BAE Ī ASIOR
ET Ī DELM ET Ī AQVIT ET Ī MENAR ET I VIP TRAIANA
VG CR ET II IDAN S DRI · RETI SAT QV ET I TVN
GR ET II LING ET II ASTVR ET II DONGON ET II NERV
ET III BRAC AVGVSTANOR ET III NE MET VI NERV
QVAE SVNT IN BRITANN SVB PRETORIÓ NEPOTE
QVIN ET VICENTI VRIBVS T   RITIS DIMISSIS
HON MISSIONE QVOR NOMINI SVBSCRIPTA SVN

IPSIS LIBERIS POSTERIS Q EORVM CIVITATEM
DEDT ET CONVBIVM CVM VXORIBVS QVAS TVNC
HABVISSENT CVM EST CIVITAS DATAVI SI
QVIS EA RESSENT CVM EIS QVAS POSTEA DVXIS
SENT DVMTAXAT SINGVLI SINGVLAS
    D XVI
C IVLIO GALLO C VALERIO SEVERO COS
COH Ī SVNATOR..................CVI PRAEST
AVLVNTVS   CLAVDIANVS
     EXPEDITE
      ALBANI   NV CŌ
SCRIPTVM ET RECOGNITVM EX TABVLA
EA QVAE FIXA EST ROMAE IN MVRO PA
TEMPLVM DIVI   RO   MINIS

Several of these manumission plates have been found in other parts of Europe, but these are supposed to have been the first which presented themselves from beneath the British soil. How the discovery affected the antiquaries of the time; and to whom we are indebted for having introduced them to public notice, may be seen in the note below[1]. Several inscriptions of nearly the same purport are engraved in Gruter, and by a comparison with these some of the lacunæ in the Hallamshire plate may be supplied. There was evidently a technical form observed. First appear the emperor's titles: then the names of the soldiers and their commanders, with the services they had performed; the privileges granted to them; the date of the day, month, and consulship; the name of the person soliciting the favour, and the authentication of the copy. The reader may find an elaborate dissertation upon these plates, principally collected from the Marquis Maffei's observations in his ' *Galliæ Antiquitates selectæ*,' in Gough's edition of the Britannia[1]. After the unsuccessful attempts of some of our best antiquaries to clear up all the difficulties of this inscription, I am not ashamed of publishing not a version, but an abstract of what appears to be its purport.—The Emperor Hadrian in the consulship of C. Julius Gallus and C. Valerius Severus (two consuls it has been observed unknown to the Fasti consulares), grants to certain strangers who had served in the Roman armies, and been honourably dismissed the service, the privileges of Roman citizenship; which he extends also to the wives of those already married, and to the first wife who might be taken by the unmarried, to their children and pc terity, with all the benefits of the *jus connubium*.

These tablets then were the charter of a number of discharged Roman legionaries. It was granted to them at the conclusion of their term of military service, and when they were about to exchange a wandering for a settled, a military for an agricultural life. It was also evidently granted to them in pursuance of the policy introduced by Agricola, and adopted by his successors, of drawing away the native Britons to serve in distant parts of the world, and encouraging strangers brought hither in the Roman armies to settle themselves in the conquered country, and to connect themselves in marriage with the daughters of Britain. These very tablets were that public authenticated act and record to which these veterans, their wives, their children, and their remote posterity must have had to appeal in all questions affecting their rights as citizens of Rome, a character to which material privileges were annexed. A curious question therefore presents itself, namely, how it has happened that a document so intimately connected with the dearest civil rights of a considerable body of men, should have been deposited in the remote solitude in which it has lately been found. Has it been placed there by some officious possessor with a view to puzzle and mislead some future antiquary?—Has it been dropped by accident by some casual passenger?—Or shall we suppose that a document so important to them, so material to the protection of their civil rights, went with those to whom the privileges were granted where they went, rested where they rested, was affixed to the wall of some building, as indeed the plates have evident marks that they once were; and that therefore on the sloping side of the hill declining to the Riveling, a situation often chosen by the Romans for their towns, where they were found, there a colony of Roman *emeriti* settled themselves in the time of Hadrian?

This may seem a bold conclusion from the fact of a solitary remain of this people, though of so prominent a character, having been discovered in this place. But I venture to predict that it will not always be a solitary remain of that enlightened and all-conquering people; and I would suggest to those who have it in their power to pursue the inquiry, whether they might not

your neighbourhood had made it out; I therefore waited for the pleasure of receiving his remarks, which if you please to send, you shall be troubled with my remarks thereon. I never could get an answer from Mr. Pegge, and I have never seen Lord Willoughby since I sent him the inscription. I am glad to hear that Mr. Pegge will turn his thoughts to the subject of the Druids; though Stukeley and Borlase have taken much pains with it, we want a further elucidation of it.' August 14, 1762, Mr. Watson was in Lancashire, and having just seen Lord Willoughby takes the earliest opportunity of acquainting Mr. Wilson with what he had learned from his lordship respecting the inscription. ' It seems my information was the first any member had received of it ; but so great was the alarm which it gave, that it caused a very full meeting of the society, who all agreed that it was the most curious thing of the kind which had ever been discovered in England : and as I had given his lordship very full instructions how to come at it, no pains were spared, nor interest neglected to obtain it, which at last was effected, and it is now in the possession of the Society of Antiquaries. Mr. Pegge, it seems, made several apologies before he parted with it, and at last resigned it with reluctance. I had the thanks of the society ordered by their communication, which I wish could consistently with their rules have been directed to you, *as the whole merit of its being known is certainly your own*: but from my letter which was read to the society every member would know who was the real discoverer of it. What I am now mentioning is not a point of small consequence; as you perhaps may think yourself, when I have told you that in the president's own opinion it is the finest remain of English antiquity that ever was offered to the society since his lordship became a member of it. It never was known till now what provision was made for the soldiers' wives in Britain by the imperial rescripts, and this is a law of Hadrian's for that very purpose, and the first that ever was found. It is remarkable that one of the sentences on these tables is to be found in the Corpus Juris, or body of laws belonging to the Romans. I cannot at present send you a reading of this great curiosity, as the matter is yet *sub judice*. Dr. Taylor, one of the best antiquaries in England, has undertaken to write a dissertation upon it, when his manner of reading it will appear : but what is remarkable, I hear he cannot make out so much as you have done, which causes me to suspect that the plates have received some damage since they were in your hands. They will be engraved after some time with an explanation, advice of which you may expect from me as soon as I know myself. You are requested to make further search after the Roman ways and camps in your neighbourhood, as the finding of these plates makes it very probable that there was something Roman at or near the place where they lay.' In another letter, dated 25 June, 1763, he informs Mr. Wilson that Dr. Taylor was not yet able to satisfy himself. In the next year he has received no further intelligence respecting the plate. He informs Mr. Wilson that he had had a long correspondence with Mr. Pegge on the nature of the Halifax gibbet-law ; had sent Mr. Pegge drawings of druidical remains near Halifax, but found he had no intention of entering upon the subject. Writing from Ripponden, 5 January, 1766, to Mr. Wilson, ever inquisitive after the true reading and explanation of his plate, he has nothing further to communicate respecting it. Had been transcribing old deeds relating to Kirkleghes, one of which was a charter of Edward III. in the 47th of his reign, granting license to the prioress and convent to acquire lands to a certain value; on the back of which was written, ' *Orate pro Elizabetha de Staynton quondam priorissa de Kirkelese, quia in tempore illius ista carta fuit adquisita*.' His History of Halifax had been interrupted, owing to the duke of Bridgewater having employed him to draw up an historical account of certain manors belonging to him in Lancashire; and to his having been engaged by a gentleman of distinction in Cheshire [Sir George Warren] to settle a difficulty in his pedigree of the utmost consequence to him. ' This affair,' says Mr. Watson, ' is so difficult, and at the same time so important, that I lay out all my time and attention upon it.' In another letter dated Barnsley, 11 Oct. 1768, he informs Mr. Wilson that he proposed to spend the ensuing winter in forwarding his History of Halifax, and in writing an account of his own family which he had begun. He had also thoughts of drawing up a short review of all the printed books relating to English history and antiquities, with an account of their merits, and different editions: was engaged to put in order the writings at Kirklese belonging to Sir George Armitage. Sir George Warren had some intention of publishing the account he had drawn up of the house of Warren; and was informed that Etherington, a bookseller of York, had some thoughts of reprinting Thoresby's Topography of Leeds, except the Museum, with such improvements as can be made in it. The History of Manchester, by his friend Mr. Whitaker, he says, is in great forwardness. It will be a learned performance. Concludes with thanking Mr. Wilson for some dissertations in the Gentleman's Magazine. Writing from Stockport, 12 Aug. 1775, he informs Mr. Wilson that he was preparing for the press his History of the House of Warren, and on the 26th July following, that he was much employed upon that subject, but was paying attention also to his intended History of Cheshire.

I cannot find that Dr. Taylor made any progress in his comment on this inscription. An engraving of it is to be found in Gough's edition of the *Britannia*. A part of the plate with the inscription in the *barbarous* character was in the hands of Mr. Wilson. It was found near a large ground-fast stone.

[1] Vol. iii. p. 28—31.

be well repaid for some extended researches beneath the soil where this noble document was discovered: for it is not to be supposed that it can have been conveyed by chance into that wild and desolate solitude.

That the Romans in the time of Hadrian had some transactions within what afterwards formed the manor of Hallam is rendered probable by the discovery of two coins, one of the Emperor Trajan, which was found near the village of Bradfield, the other of Hadrian himself found near Broomhead, about the time when the Riveling plate was awakened from its long repose. The legend on the reverse of Hadrian's coin though not uncommon deserves our notice, FIDES PVBLICA; as if intended to impress upon the minds of the chartered legionaries that they might rely upon the plighted faith of Rome.

If the above conclusion be admitted, how much light is reflected from these tablets upon the first planting of Hallamshire.—The Emperor Hadrian, in the second century of the Christian æra having in person peaceably settled this remote dependence on the Roman power, discharges his veteran legionaries, men collected from all parts of the world where the arms of Rome had extended themselves. To some he grants the much coveted privilege of Roman citizenship, and as an encouragement to them to ally themselves in marriage with the daughters of the country they had conquered, he extends the same privileges to their wives and offspring. A party of those who are thus endowed settle themselves a small colony on the banks of the Riveling, allured perhaps by the representations of some petty Cartismandua attached to her native soil and woodland stream, and who made a settlement in that place the price of her charms to the Roman veteran. We may regard them as having been the first to introduce among the native Britons of this neighbourhood some of the arts of social life which they had learned in their intercourse with the Romans. Then first perhaps our mines of iron were explored, and attention began to be paid to the other mineral riches of this district. Where they fixed their abode would be the metropolis of the neighbourhood, which in later times would become the vill giving name to the great manor of Hallam, and there we might expect to see arise the aula of its Saxon lord.

The two great objections to this opinion are, that we have no notice of any Roman station in this position; and that as far as appears there are no vestigia at the point in question of human habitation, and especially of a building so prominent as must have been the aula of the Saxon thane. But every year brings to light stations of that people, who spread themselves over the whole country before unnoticed and unknown. While I write this, a gentleman is pursuing most successfully investigations of a Roman station on the Fossroad a few miles from Bath, which has been noticed by neither ancient nor modern topographers. And on the other hand, how many names of Roman stations in Britain are preserved by Ptolemy and the Ravenna geographer, which the most acute investigators of the Roman antiquities of Britain have failed to appropriate!—With respect to the second point, the objection presses with equal force against every other part of the Domesday manor of Hallam. Where I would ask must we look for the foundations or any trace of the Saxon aula? And yet the information is direct and conclusive that *some where* within the manor of Hallam, Earl Waltheof had his aula.

The tradition of the neighbourhood professes to account for their disappearance. It tells us that as the resistance of the people of Hallam to the Norman conqueror was most pertinacious, so his vengeance was most signal. But supposing that the place was only partially destroyed, in one of his vengeful expeditions against the unsubdued spirits of the people north of Trent; since Sheffield became immediately after the Conquest the seat of the Norman lord of this district, there was little temptation to rebuild its broken walls, and seven centuries of time may have completed the obliteration which the incensed conqueror had begun.

Local traditions must always be received with great caution when they remove a difficulty. But the tradition that the vill of Hallam was destroyed in an act of fury in the incensed conqueror is not by any means destitute of the support of written evidence. The historians of the reign of William have in few instances descended to the notice of particular acts of atrocious abuse of power of which he was guilty, but have wrapped up his conduct during his northern expeditions in general expressions, while they seem to have wanted words to express adequately the desolation and misery he occasioned. If we would ascertain the misery he brought upon the northern parts of our island a little more in detail, we must look in the pages of Domesday:—we may there track the destroyer in his progress. As to this particular neighbourhood, he seems to have entered the county of York at Wales, and he laid that little obscure manor entirely waste. Advancing northward, the line of his march seems to have been through Ulley, Brampton, Wickersley, Brinsford, Swinton, and Wentworth. All the neighbouring manors show in the depreciation of their value that they suffered more or less. But on these places the weight of the storm seems to have rested; for though rich and flourishing in the days of the Confessor, they were returned by the Domesday surveyors as being utterly wasted and therefore of no annual value. It was but the skirts of the storm which at this time, eleven years before the composition of Domesday-book, rested upon Hallam; but that manor, which in the time of the Confessor had been valued at eight marks of silver, was then worth only forty shillings.

The extent of the wanton ravages committed by the North-man in the neighbourhood of Hallam may be further collected from an expression in a charter of the year 1161. This charter defines the rights of the lords of Sheffield and the monks of Saint Wandrille in the manor of Ecclesfield; and reference is made in it to the state of the hedges as they were anciently before they were burnt, ' *sicut sepes antiquitùs ante combustionem fuerunt* [1].'

Now though we have no express record of the destruction of the vill of Hallam or its aula, these evidences, together with the concurring tradition, with the subsequent rise of Sheffield, their former existence and their now total disappearance, seem altogether to render the fact of their destruction by the Norman invader a point of probability not far removed from certainty.

---

[1] Dods. MSS. in Bibl. Bodl. vol. cxviii. f. 74.

II. The second point to which our attention is drawn, by the brief but comprehensive notices of Domesday, is, that before the Conquest there were several villages dispersed through the manor of Hallam. The *berewitæ* of that record were knots of houses dependent on the chief vill of the manor, and of these the manor of Hallam contained sixteen. It is much to be regretted that the compilers of the Domesday survey have in this instance made an exception to their usual practice, and omitted to give the names of the berewitæ by which the vill of Hallam was surrounded. Sheffield and Attercliffe, originally among the berewitæ of Hallam, had been severed from it before the time of the survey; and Haldworth, Ughill, Onesacre, and some other places in the chapelry of Bradfield, are not counted among the berewitæ of the manor of Hallam, being as it seems separated, like Sheffield and Attercliffe, from that manor, of which from their situation within it we must suppose that they had once made a part. If we add these together, we shall find a total of distinct villages or hamlets on the right bank of the Don, little if at all exceeded by their number at any later period, or as they at present appear. The topographer in every part of the kingdom finds that the germ of almost all our towns and villages was deposited in the times preceding the Conquest.

III. In these hamlets resided that considerable agricultural population which Domesday informs us was collected on our four manors. In the manor of Hallam three thousand acres had been redeemed and brought into cultivation: in Attercliffe three hundred, in Sheffield three hundred, and in Grimesthorpe three hundred and fifty; making a total of little less than four thousand arable acres. In the rude state in which the art of agriculture was at the period before us, these would probably furnish employment to not fewer than three hundred persons, of whom thirty-six are particularly noticed as being of that class of tenantry called *villani*, a respectable class, the predecessors of our modern copy-holders and free-holders. These with their families might make up an agricultural population of about one thousand four hundred persons.

To these must be added others who were engaged in the useful and necessary arts of life.

But when we consider the mineral riches of the district, we can hardly hesitate to believe that to these another numerous class is to be added. Bede in the eighth century mentions iron among the mineral productions of this island[1]: and the remarkable fact, that in the midst of a mass of scoria, the refuse of some ancient bloomery near Bradford, was found a deposit of Roman coins[2], seems to leave it indisputable that the iron-mines of Yorkshire were explored by its Roman inhabitants. No where did the ore present itself more obviously by tinting with its beautiful ochre the beds of the streamlets in its vicinity, no where did it lie nearer to the surface, no where could there be greater facilities for subjecting the ore to the processes necessary to extract from it its metal, than in the forests through which the Don poured its waters. Many beds of scoria, of the kind just mentioned, are found in various parts of the parish of Sheffield, where

there is now no tradition nor any record of works of iron ever having existed. They are found even in the park which for many centuries past has been peculiarly appropriated to the pleasure of the lord. Over most of them the soil has so accumulated as to form a very thick crust, in which trees of ancient growth are at this moment flourishing. The probabilities are therefore strong, that before the Norman invasion, and that even while the Romans had possession of the island, the iron-mines of Sheffield afforded employment to a considerable number of persons; some to draw the ore from its bed, others to extract from it the metal, and a third class employed in fabricating weapons, implements of husbandry, or domestic utensils.

The silence of Domesday affords no presumption against the validity of this conclusion. Miners or artificers of any class rarely came under the notice of the compilers of that survey. In the lead districts of Derbyshire we have no notice of the persons employed in mining or in smelting the ore, although mention is made of the quantity of lead which the owners of some particular manors were to render to the king. Domesday must therefore be considered as neutral in this question: and in almost the very next in chronological order of the records from which we obtain our knowledge of the early state of this neighbourhood, about the year 1160, we have notice of pretty extensive iron-works established at Kimberworth by the monks of Kirkstead[3].

To the other inhabitants of the territory now forming the parish of Sheffield we may therefore with some confidence add a mixed multitude, a rude and intractable people, whose occupations were in working the iron-mines, or preparing for useful purposes the metal which was extracted from them.

To attempt to estimate their numbers would be merely wild conjecture; and it must be remembered, that of the agricultural population above mentioned, a considerable proportion must be presumed to have inhabited those berewitæ of the manor of Hallam which stood north of the Riveling, and therefore never came within the limits of the parish of Sheffield.

IV. At the time of the Domesday survey a very extensive tract of the manor of Hallam was covered with wood: but the wood was pasturable, that is, sufficiently free from underwood to be fit for the pasturage of cattle. Deer also, we shall soon find, ran in the woods of Hallamshire within the first century after the Conquest. The pasturable wood of Domesday probably occupied that part of the parish now called Fullwood, spreading itself on the one hand towards Ecclesall and on the other to the vale of the Riveling.

The exact meaning of the word *pratum*, as used by the Domesday surveyors, is not very clear. Such small patches as the eight acres which are stated to have been in Hallam, are noticed in most of the northern manors.

V. Four centuries had elapsed since Paulinus the apostle of Northumbria had built a Christian church in the town of Doncaster[4]. Still neither *ecclesia* nor *presbyter* are noticed at Hallam, or in the other manors which contributed to form the parish of Sheffield. This is the more remarkable, since so many less con-

[1] *Eccl. Hist.* lib. i. cap. 1.
[2] See Dr. Richardson's Letter to Hearne.—Leland, vol. ix. as quoted in Whitaker's *History of Manchester*, vol. i. p. 300.
[3] *Mon. Ang.* vol. i. p. 811.
[4] Beda, *Eccl. Hist.* lib. ii. cap. 14.

G

siderable manors in the neighbourhood were furnished with churches, as Hope, Tankersley, Treeton, Aston, and Rotherham.

VI. Lastly, the notices which the Domesday survey contains of this district bring us acquainted with some of its ante-Norman proprietors, or chief lords. Immediately before the change of property occasioned by the successful invasion of the Normans, the 'land which now forms the parish of Sheffield acknowledged three Saxon lords, Ulfac, Sweyn, and earl Waltheof.

Ulfac was the lord of Grimesthorpe. He, or at least a person of the same name, had also a share of the manors of Newhall, Hooton, Denaby, Mexborough, Adwick-upon-Dearne, and Ecclesfield, so that he was a great landed proprietor in the wapentake of Strafford. He may have had a mansion at Grimesthorpe, that being the only manor in this wapentake of which the sole proprietorship was in him. We hear nothing of him after the Conquest; so that it is probable he followed the fortunes of his neighbour Harold, to whom belonged Conisborough, and was stripped of all his possessions by the Conqueror.

Sweyn met another fate. Beside Sheffield and Attercliffe this person had very large estates in the wapentakes of Strafford and Staincross. Those in the former were given to Roger de Busli and Aubrey de Coci, those in the latter to Ilbert de Laci: but it appears that this person was living at the time of the compilation of Domesday-book, and that he then held Kexborough and Dodworth, both near Barnsley, of De Laci. It seems also that he was allowed to retain some part of his possessions in the wapentake of Strafford; for we find Adam Fitz-Sweyn,[1] his son, a great baron in Yorkshire, in the time of Henry I. giving to the priory of Monk-Bretton, of which he was founder, the church of Cadeby[1], one of the places in the wapentake of Strafford of which Sweyn was returned Saxon owner. The Fitz-Sweyns were a great baronial house, one of the few that had decidedly a Saxon or Saxo-Danish origin: but after a few generations they ended in female heiresses; nor does it appear that they ever recovered any part of the interest which their progenitor had enjoyed at Sheffield.

Earl Waltheof was a man of pre-eminent note in his times. He was the son of Siward the Dane, the same Siward who led the armies of the Confessor against Macbeth, the usurper of the throne of Scotland. His mother was the daughter and heir of Aldred the Saxon earl of Northumberland, chief of a family in whom that honour and office, for in those times it was both, was in a manner hereditary. It was doubtless in consequence of this descent that he enjoyed the aula and the lands of Hallam. Through his mother, Waltheof inherited a feud with the family of Carl the son of Thurebrand. Uctred the father of his grandfather Aldred was assassinated by Thurebrand as he sought the court of Canute. Thurebrand fell by the hand of Aldred; and justice being satisfied, the families made an alliance. Carl the son of Thurebrand received Aldred into his house with every show of hospitality, but alluring him into a secret place he there treacherously slew him. Many years after, the children of Carl fell by the hands of Waltheof, as they were carousing at Settrington on the wolds of Yorkshire. Such was the man who, when he could no longer maintain the liberties of his country against the strangers from Normandy, consented to become the subject and relative of the Conqueror, taking to wife the king's niece, and receiving with her the three earldoms of Northumberland, Huntingdon, and Northampton, beside being allowed to retain his former possessions. But it is not to be supposed that such a man as this would be easy in submission to a foreign yoke, or could bear the insolence of the Normans, and the daily oppression of his friends. He conspired with Ralph de Waer against the life of the king, and suffered death at Winchester anno 1075. His decapitated trunk was treated with every possible indignity: but having lain for some time in the cross way where it was buried, it was removed to Croyland Abbey in Lincolnshire, there honourably sepulchred, and, if we may believe the monkish historians, miracles were wrought at his tomb[2].

Such was the unhappy fate of the last Saxon lord of the manor of Hallam; and perhaps we may discern in it something to add strength to the opinion that the aula and vill of Hallam fell beneath the vengeance of an incensed conqueror. His widow, being the king's near kinswoman and not at all participant in his treason, was allowed to retain her husband's lands; and hence it is that the name of the countess Judith so often appears in the pages of Domesday: and hence it is that we find it in the account there given of the manor of Hallam.

This lady was the daughter of Lambert earl of Lens in Artois, by Maud his wife, countess of Albemarle, who was half-sister to the Conqueror, being daughter of his mother Arlotta by her husband Helewyne de Comitis Villâ. Historians have made free with her memory. She is left by them under strong circumstances of suspicion that she was treacherous to her lord. And Ingulphus, the monk of Croyland, her contemporary, scruples not to describe her by the execrable appellation, *impiissima Jezebel*. This is the more extraordinary, as she was a benefactor to the religious house of Saint Wandrille, or Fontenelle, in Normandy, to which she formerly had belonged[3]. I conjecture in the absence of positive evidence, that it was to her that the same monastery owed the interest it acquired in the tythes of Sheffield and Ecclesfield. The countess Judith fell into disgrace with the king when she refused to accept in second nuptials a Norman knight named Simon Saint Liz 'because he was lame of a leg.' The king we are told was so incensed at her refusal that he seized upon many of her lands, and she herself was glad to find protection from his fury in the fens of Ely. Saint Liz was advised to take her eldest daughter to wife; and the king made her the principal heir to the possessions of her family, giving with her, beside many lands, the earldom of Northampton, one of those which had been enjoyed by her father Waltheof. This he possessed during life: but on his decease it passed to David, son of Malcolm III. king of Scotland, who married his widow in the days of Henry I. This David became king of Scotland, and died in 1153.

The only lands in the wapentake of Strafford of which the countess Judith is returned owner in the

[1] *Mon. Ebor.* p. 93.   [2] Dugdale's *Baronage*, vol. i. p. 55, &c., where much more may be read concerning Waltheof and his progenitors.   [3] Bridges's *History of Northamptonshire*, p. 410.

Domesday survey, are the manors of Hallam, Atter-cliffe, and Sheffield. Even these manors are enumerated under the general head of *Terra Rogerii de Busli*, and he is said to hold them of the countess Judith. What was the precise relation which subsisted between the countess and De Busli, or what and whether any interest her family continued to enjoy in Hallamshire after the date of the Domesday survey, it seems impossible now to recover. But the recollection that the Norman proprietors of this district had held their lands of a superior the representative of its Saxon lords, was not extinct so late as the time of Edward III.: for by inquisition taken after the death of Thomas lord Furnival, it was found that his ancestors had held the castle and manor of Sheffield *of a certain king of Scotland*, by the service of rendering two white greyhounds yearly[1], perhaps the identical service by which De Busli held them of the countess Judith.

On the whole then it may appear, from the scanty evidence which time has preserved for us relating to the period before the arrival in England of the Normans, if not a point of historic certainty yet one of historic probability, that early in the second century of the Christian æra a few discharged Roman legionaries, part of the army of Hadrian, settled themselves a small community on the banks of the Riveling: that what was originally only a few cottages became at length a place of no inconsiderable extent, and the little metropolis of a very spacious manor: that, population continuing to increase, some of the inhabitants removed themselves to a small distance, clearing other portions of the soil, and laying the foundation of those numerous villages which the Domesday survey recognises in the manor of Hallam: that in later times a Saxon chieftain established his aula near to the vill of Hallam; and that they both fell together under the vengeance of the Norman conqueror: that Sheffield was originally one of the berewitæ of the manor of Hallam; but that before the Conquest it had obtained a degree of independence, had a different proprietor, and was the little capital of a very small manor to which it gave name. And it will afterwards appear that Hallam never recovered from the blow struck by the Conqueror; but that when the neighbourhood became new modelled under its Norman proprietors, Sheffield gave name to an extensive parish, and a still more extensive manor: there was the castle of its lord, and there the centre of population.

PEDIGREE of the ancient LORDS of HALLAMSHIRE.

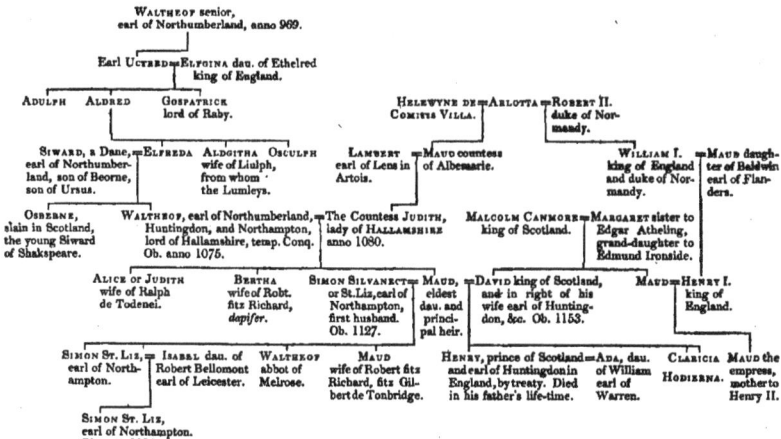

[1] Dods. MSS. E. 135 a. Harl. 801. Sheffield.

CHAPTER III.

Sheffield under De Busli and De Lovetot.

AT the time of the great Norman survey the whole wapentake of Strafford was in the hands of seven proprietors, except a very few manors which were still *Terra Tainorum Regis*. The earl of Warren had Conisborough and its numerous dependencies: Walter d'Eincourt had Wombwell and Rawmarsh: Aubrey de Coci had Hickleton and Cadeby: and Geffery Aiselyn or Hanselyn, Brampton and Cantley. William de Percy had several manors, but by far the largest portion was included in the fees of the earl of Morton and Roger de Busli. These were all persons who had accompanied the duke of Normandy in his successful invasion of England.

Grimesthorpe, Hallam, Attercliffe, and Sheffield are described in Domesday-book as being *Terra Rogerii de Busli*. But the latter three were held as before mentioned by the countess Judith, and on that account are placed last in the enumeration of his Yorkshire possessions, except one manor which seems to have been omitted by mistake in the earlier part of the catalogue.

The whole number of manors included within his fee have been found to amount to forty-six in Yorkshire, eighty-six in Nottinghamshire, besides many in Derbyshire, Leicestershire, and Devonshire[1].

In the immediate vicinity of Sheffield, he had Orgrave, Brinsford, Tinsley, Greasborough, Kimberworth, Ecclesfield, Wadsley, Haldworth, and Ughill, in the county of York; Beighton, Norton, and Dore, in the county of Derby. Of the other manors adjacent to Sheffield, Rotherham, Hansworth, Treeton, and Whiston, were the earl of Morton's, who was uncle to the countess Judith. Dronfield was *Terra Regis*; and Hathersage, with its hamlets, was part of the possessions of Ralph Fitz-Hubert, to whom also belonged Eckington and Barlborough.

First among De Busli's Yorkshire possessions, in the Domesday survey, is placed Laughton. On that fine elevation, from which he could command a view of no inconsiderable portion of his northern fee, he doubtless for a time resided in the aula left by the dispossessed earl Edwin. But he soon built for himself another residence on the Norman model, near the ancient town of Tickhill, the only place in the wapentake of Strafford which is returned in the Domesday survey as containing that description of persons called *burgenses*, and which from thenceforth became the head of his fee. The following pedigree is from Thoroton.

PEDIGREE of De Busli[2].

ARMS.—Gules one bezant[3].

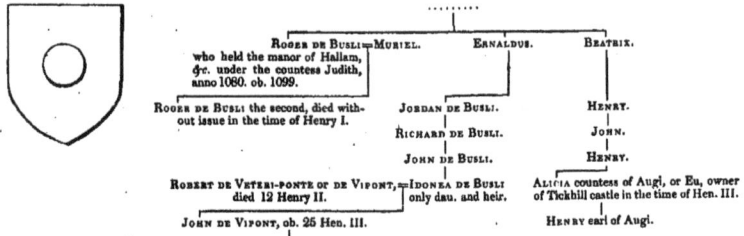

ISABEL DE VIPONT, elder of the two daughters and co-heirs, married 52 Hen. III. to Roger son and heir of Roger lord Clifford, who had in her right large possessions in the wapentake of Strafford and Tickhill.

IDONEA DE VIPONT, younger of the two daughters and co-heirs, married 1st Roger de Leyburne, and 2dly John de Crumbewell, who had in her right the manor of Kimberworth.

But when we find districts exceeding many counties in extent belonging to one person, it is obvious that his ownership is not to be regarded by us in the same light with the proprietorship of a modern land-owner. It seems to have been little more than a nominal possession which De Busli enjoyed at Sheffield. We find

---

[1] *Magna Britannia.*—Yorkshire, p. 516. But Thoroton, much nearer the truth, says he had a hundred and seventy manors in the county of Nottingham alone.—*History of Nottinghamshire*, p. 2.

[2] From Thoroton.—Notts. p. 2.

[3] On the authority of a memorandum by Dodsworth. MSS. in Bibl. Bodl. vol. clx. f. 17 a.

not the slightest trace of his connexion with the place, except that it is enumerated under the general head of *Terra Rogerii de Busli*, in the Domesday survey. Nor do we find, as in the case of many other places which were parts of the same fee, that in later times a dependence on the castle of Tickhill and its lords was confessed by any small annual payment. Sheffield was never reckoned among the towns in the liberty of Tickhill; but is uniformly spoken of in the inquisitions as held of the king *in capite*.

Of all the places in the immediate vicinity of Sheffield which formed the *terra* of their ancestor, Kimberworth is the only manor in which I have found the family of De Busli exercising acts of ownership. About the year 1160, Richard de Busli, with the consent of Emma his wife and of his heirs, granted to the monks of Kirkstead in Lincolnshire sufficient land in that manor for the erection of four iron-works, *forgias*, two for smelting the ore, and two *ad fabricandum*, for forming it into bars, with liberty to dig the ore in any part of the manor[1]. Kimberworth passed to the great heiress of the house of De Busli, Idonea wife of Robert de Vipont, in the time of King John; but long before that period Sheffield and many other estates which had been reckoned amongst the *terra* of Roger de Busli had become the property of the house of De Lovetot.

By what means, or at what time, the family of De Lovetot acquired their interest in Hallamshire does not appear on the face of any record. But early in the reign of Henry I. we find William de Lovetot possessed of Hallam, Attercliffe, Sheffield, Grimesthorpe, Greasborough, and other places in the county of York, which in the time of the Conqueror were included within the Busli fee, and also of Worksop, and many other manors in the county of Nottingham, which had previously been enumerated among the possessions of the same family. He also had acquired interests in Hansworth, Treeton, and Whiston, and other places which at the time of the Domesday survey were of the fee of Robert earl of Morton.

Little attention has been paid by our genealogists to the origin of the potent house of De Lovetot, and to the means by which they who were before barons of Huntingdonshire acquired their great interest in the north. Dugdale begins his account of the family with the above-mentioned William de Lovetot, following the metrical chronicle of Worksop, and the deeds in the Monasticon which relate to that religious house: nor does it appear on what authority Brooke, the Somerset herald, in a splendid pedigree of the lords of Worksop, which he drew up for Edward duke of Norfolk, represents this William as the son of a John de Lovetot. Thoroton has an unsuccessful conjecture, that the interest which the Lovetots obtained in the north was by the marriage of William with the daughter and heir of the Roger who is mentioned in the Domesday survey of Worksop, and whom he supposes to be a *homo* or tenant of Roger de Busli; while in fact the Roger whose name so often occurs in the survey of De Busli's fee was not any subinfeuded person of that name, but the lord-paramount himself. Nor is any stress to be laid on the deference which appears to be paid to the wife of this William de Lovetot in

the foundation-charter of the monastery of Worksop. The donations made to that house are said to have been ' *concessione et consideratione Emmæ uxoris;*' but such clauses are usual in charters of that age and nature, and it immediately follows that the deed was executed with the like consent of his sons.

I was once of opinion, that the Ricardus Surdus of Domesday-book was the direct ancestor of the house of De Lovetot, and would still submit that opinion to the censure of the better informed reader. He was one of the two persons between whom the fee of the earl of Morton was divided as immediately subinfeuded by him, at the time of the Domesday survey. The other was Nigellus Fossard, a name well known to our genealogists as lord of Doncaster, and progenitor of the Mauleys of that place; but this Ricardus who held as large a share of the Morton fee has been unaccountably passed over in silence by our genealogists and topographers, though his name is so intimately connected with the early history of so many manors in Yorkshire. Now some of the manors which he held in the southern part of Yorkshire we find soon after his decease in the hands of William de Lovetot, and between most of those which he held in that part of the county and the house of De Lovetot there was some connexion. Those manors were—

Hutton-Paynel	Whiston	Wales
Bilham	Hansworth	Ulley
Todwick	Treeton	Brampton
Houghton	Aughton	Pilley
Thurnscoe	Aston	Tankersley
		Wortley.

This opinion acquires some confirmation from a record of the age of Edward I. copied by Dodsworth from the original in the archives of Saint Mary's tower in York[2]. That record contains an account of the progeny of the three daughters of Simon son of Thorne, a Saxon proprietor of Todwick, one of the manors held by Ricardus under the earl of Morton. It relates that the second of them was given by the Conqueror in marriage to Ralph Tortemayns, armiger to Dom. Lovetoft, and that the youngest, Cassandra, was married to William de Saint Paul by the same Dom. Lovetoft. This marriage must have been solemnized about the time of the compilation of Domesday-book, and it seems to identify the Dominus Lovetoft of the record with the Ricardus Surdus of the survey. It must not however be concealed that Ricardus held many other manors in parts of the county of York very remote from those where the known possessions of the De Lovetots lay.

Like all our old surnames the name of Lovetot is found with great variety of orthography: Lovetoft, Luvetoft, Lovetot, &c. Arms the same in figure, but differing in tincture, appear in ancient authorities purporting to be the insignia of this family. In one of the windows of the parish-church of Sheffield, in the time of Dodsworth, they appeared a lion rampant parti per fess gules and sable on a silver field. The same lion on a field of gold was used as the insignia of the house of Worksop, till another was adopted formed out of the arms of a later patron Thomas Nevil lord Furnival. In a primer which was executed in the time of Edward III. for Joan de Mounteney, a

[1] *Mon. Ang.* vol. i. p. 811.   [2] *Mon. Ang.* vol. i. p. 838.

H

descendant of the Lovetots, the lion appears with the colours inverted on a field of or: and amongst the painted glass with which the windows of the church of Ecclesfield were once so richly adorned, the arms of Lovetot appeared thus—Parti per fess or and gules, a lion rampant parti per fess sable and argent. There can be no doubt that while all agreed in retaining the

same figure, it was borne in different tinctures by different members of the family.

The Lovetots became extinct at Sheffield as early as the reign of Henry II. The vouchers for the following pedigree may be found in the Monasticon, where the charters of this great family are remarkably clear in point of genealogy.

PEDIGREE of DE LOVETOT, LORDS of HALLAMSHIRE.

ARMS.—Argent, a lion rampant parti per fess gules and sable.

RICARDUS SURDUS, living 1080.

WILLIAM DE LOVETOT, =EMMA. lord of Hallamshire temp. Hen. I. and founder of the monastery of Worksop.

RICHARD DE LOVETOT, =CECILIA. lord of Hallamshire temp. reg. Steph. living 1161.

NIGEL DE LOVETOT=MARGARET. had large possessions in Huntingdonshire.

HENRY DE LOVETOT, HUGH DE LOVETOT, witnesses to deeds of the two Richards.

WILLIAM DE LOVETOT,=MAUD, dau. of Walter Fitz the second, lord of Hallamshire. Dead before the 27 Hen. II. anno 1181.

Robert, of the noble house of Clare. Survived, and was aged 24 years 27 Hen. II

RICHARD DE LOVETOT, next heir male to William. Confirmed the donations of his family to Worksop, and died without issue.

NIGEL DE LOVETOT, heir to his brother.

ROGER DE LOVETOT. ROBERT DE LOVETOT. WILLIAM DE LOVETOT.

GERARD DE FURNIVAL,=MAUD DE LOVETOT, lord of Hallamshire in right of his wife.

only dau. and heir, aged 7 an. 27 Hen. II. Living 33 Hen. III.

ROGER DE LOVETOT, sheriff of Nottingham and Derby shires, and governor of Bolsover castle.

RICHARD. NIGEL. RALPH. WILLIAM.

From the time when the De Lovetots obtained their interest in Hallamshire may be dated the superiority which the vill of Sheffield acquired, and has ever since maintained, through the whole district which has at any period borne that name. For that place they chose among all their Yorkshire possessions in which to fix their usual residence, and they seem to have sought in other ways to advance its consequence. From this time we hear no longer of the manor of Hallam, but that spacious and once consequential manor becomes annexed to Sheffield, which is indeed always spoken of as the head of the whole barony of De Lovetot.

It is by no means certain whether the original castle of Sheffield was built by the first of the De Lovetots, or that he found one erected on that most convenient site by Sweyn the dispossessed Saxon lord, or some of his progenitors. On this point we have neither remains nor record to guide our inquiries. It has indeed been disputed whether there was any castle at Sheffield, the residence of its lords, before the charter of Henry III. in the 54th of his reign, hereafter to be mentioned. But while it is in the highest degree improbable that at the head of the barony should be no mansion of the baron, we have two records which distinctly recognise its existence in times long before the 54th of Henry III.

A deed without date, but certainly before that time, preserved by Dodsworth, recites that Nicholas de Bolonia hath given to Nicholas the son of Roger de Colston, *pro homagio et servitio*, one toft in Sefeld, next adjoining the gate of the valley of the castle of the same vill[1].

The return made by Ralph Murdac, sheriff of Derbyshire, of receipts and disbursements concerning the wardship of Maud de Lovetot in the 30 and 34 Hen. II. contains these entries :—

In custamento claudendi castellum de Sedfeld vii. lib. per brevem regis.

In custodia castelli de Saffeld de ipso honore [i. e. *de honore Willielmi de Lovetot*] *et i. serviente 4l. 10s. per breve regis.*

This record is still remaining in the Court of the Exchequer, and these are among several extracts made from it by Madox, to prove his point, that Thomas de Furnival was in fact a baron, and that the castle of Sheffield was the head of his barony, although a jury in the country had delivered on an inquest for that purpose a contrary verdict[2].

The feudal chieftain of the time of our early Norman kings in his baronial hall presents not at all times an object which can be contemplated with perfect satisfaction by those who regard power but as a trust to be administered for the general good. With authority little restricted by law or usage, he had the power of oppressing as well as benefiting the population by which he was surrounded, and many doubtless were the hearts which power so excessive seduced. It is gratifying when we find those who could overcome its seductive influence. And such seem to have been the family of De Lovetot. But few of their transactions are come down to us, but none which leave any blot upon their memory, and some which show that they had a just and humane regard for the welfare of those whom the arrangements of Providence had made more immediately dependent on them.

One of their first cares was to plant churches on their domains. It was natural that one of these should be placed at the vill of Sheffield, not far from their own mansion: and the spaciousness of the edifice shows at once the liberality of the mind of its founders, and that it was no inconsiderable population which it was intended to accommodate.

[1] Dods. MSS. n. n. 12 b. Harl. 801. Sheffield.

[2] *History of the Exchequer*, p. 370.

The better to secure the regular performance of religious services in the churches which they erected, they were, according to the prevailing custom of the times, attached to certain monastic establishments. The church of Ecclesfield was given to Saint Wandrille, a foreign religious house which seems to have had considerable interest in Hallamshire before the time of the De Lovetots, and which had established a small colony in the vill of Ecclesfield. Those of Bradfield and Sheffield were annexed to the priory of their own foundation at Worksop. From the brotherhood of that house one was deputed to reside at Sheffield as the vicar, till the suppression of religious houses by Henry VIII.

The tythe of the parish of Sheffield at this period was, according to primitive custom, divided into three parts; but these three parts were not appropriated according to the intentions of those by whom the tything system was introduced; for two thirds went to the monks of Saint Wandrille, from whom, as far as appears, the inhabitants of Sheffield received no services in return; and the remaining third to the monks of Worksop, who were allowed to make what bargain they pleased with the officiating clerk.

Sheffield owed to the house of De Lovetot the establishment of an hospital for its sick, *infirmis*. This hospital stood on a little eminence on the east side of the town, still called the Spital-hill, and continued to afford its relief to the poor of Sheffield till the eighth Henry swept away so many institutions of our forefathers, the beneficial with the useless and the pernicious, in undistinguishing fury. It was dedicated to Saint Leonard, and the charter of its foundation will be found to afford us further insight into the state of the town in the first century after the Conquest.

Sciant tam presentes quam futuri quod ego Willielmus de Lu- vet' dedi concessi et hac presenti carta confirmavi in puram et perpetuam eleemosinam pro anima mea et animabus patris et matris mee et ancessorum meorum infirmis de Se- feldia terram quam Roger .... tenuit juxta pontem Done et victum illorum in molendino de Sefeldia. T. his: Rob. de Sum'vill, Henrico fil. Godardi, Petro fil. Ade, Rob. fil. Pag'. Rob. fil. Erturi, Rob. de Luvet¹.

The original charter on a small slip of parchment, with some remains of the seal appendant, is in the custody of Mr. John Harting, the duke of Norfolk's auditor. The gift of a corrody shows that the Lovetots had by this time established their mill at Sheffield; and it further appears from this charter, that the inhabitants had obtained the accommodation of a bridge over the Don. So that the town seems in the time of the De Lovetots to have possessed every thing essential to the comfortable residence of a considerable population, a church, a corn-mill, an hospital, a bridge where one was most wanted, to which may be added the protection which the castle of the lord afforded,

and the benign influence of the family which resided in it. To these we may add, on probable grounds, a market: for it is certain that there was a market at Sheffield before the grant of Edward I. to Thomas lord Furnival; for in the ninth of that reign, fifteen years before the date of the grant, he claimed certain immunities at Sheffield, as being always appendant to a market.

The inhabitants of the town of Sheffield at this period were probably for the most part small artificers, or persons who had certain services to perform at the castle. In the surrounding country, such parts of the old inclosures as were not retained in the lord's own hand were held by small copyholders, none of whom rose above the rank of the mere farmer. It is not till the De Lovetots have passed off the stage, that we find families within the parish aspiring to imitate, if not to rival, the chief at his castle of Sheffield.

Some idea of the extent of the town in the time of the De Lovetots may be formed from the position of the parish-church. The site chosen for such an edifice would be close to the town, but not actually within it. A few straggling huts and smithies forming an irregular street extending from the castle and bridge to the church gate, with a few houses lying towards the town-mill, and perhaps a branch stretching in a south-west direction, forming what is now called the Fargate in respect of its distance from the castle, seem to have formed the whole town of Sheffield. The parsonage house would then be a country residence, commanding a beautiful view of the woody hills to the north of the town, and separated from the other buildings by the extent of a spacious churchyard.

In a charter of the next century we find mention of land ' *extra barram de Sheffeld²*.' This may imply that small wickets were erected at the principal avenues to the town, for the purpose of collecting toll from strangers resorting to the market. The memory of these seems to be perpetuated in the name of one of our streets, the West Bar.

Two or three other transactions of these ancient lords of Hallamshire, in the immediate vicinity of Sheffield, claim a notice in this place.

The cell which the monks of Saint Wandrille had established at Ecclesfield was dissolved when Richard II. began, what Henry V. completed, to detach from the foreign monasteries their English dependencies. Out of the fabric of this cell or priory, as it is called, was constructed the house called Ecclesfield-Hall, where in the time of Dodsworth Mr. William Shiercliffe was residing. Into the hands of this gentleman had fallen some of the deeds of the house of Saint Wandrille, one of which containing some curious information on the early state of Hallamshire is now for the first time published from Dodsworth's copy in the

¹ Witnesses to the charters of the old barons were always persons of principal note in the neighbourhood in which they were executed, and especially to those which, like this, were of a public nature. Robert de Sumerville, whose name appears first, is called, in a charter of Maud de Lovetot, ' *quondam miles meus*,' Mon. Ang. ii. 51. He and his father of the same name witnessed the confirmation granted by Richard de Lovetot to the monks of Worksop, id. ii. 50. Nigel Fitz Godard also attested that confirmation. The names of Robert Fitz Payne and Robert de Luvet appear among the witnesses to the confirmation of Richard son of Nigel de Lovetot, of all the donations to Worksop made by his ancestors and kindred, id. ii. 51. The Fitz Paynes were a branch of the Vescis, lords of Rotherham and of many other places. Roger Fitz

Arthur gave the monks of Kirkstead a bovate of land in Hansworth-Woodhouse, id. i. 807. And as to the only remaining name, Peter Fitz Adam, the seal of one of his family was found in a field near Chesterfield, in March 1799, presenting a fleur de lis rudely shaped, and this inscription around it ✠ S. DIOTE VXORIS ADE. The Fitz Adams seem to have resided at Staveley; for in the Harl. MS. 1806, f. 18 b. is a very old draft of arms which are said to be ' *Arms Ade de Staveley*.' They are like those on the seal, barry of eight gules and argent, a fleur de lis sable.—The witnesses to this charter seem to have been persons contemporary with the second rather than the first William de Lovetot.
² Deed of Robert de Ecclesall, in Dodsworth's Extracts from the Rockley Evidences. MSS. in Bibl. Bodl. vol. cxxxix.

Bodleian[1]. It has suffered something in the transcription. It contains the first use I have met with of the term Hallamshire.

IHVS Notum sit universis sanctæ ecclesiæ filiis, tam presentibus quam futuris, hanc esse conventionem inter Dominum Abbatem Rogerum et Conventum Sancti Wandragesili, et Ricardum de Louvetot; quod essarta autem a parte dextera viæ quæ ducit de Sefeld ad Eglesfeld usque Blacaburna, remanent quiete Ecclesiæ Sancti Wandragesili sicut sepes antiquitus ante combustionem fuerunt: et essarta a parte sinistra predictæ viæ remanent Ricardo de Louvetot quiete sicuti sepes antiquitus ante combustionem fuerunt: et boscum sicut via vadit de ecclesia de Eglesfeld usque Burleiestan, ad sinistram, alium de Burleia usque ad essarta de Wereldesend ad sinistram, sit in communione sicut antiquitus fuit. Preterea ab essartis de Wereldesenda a capite collis alium ejusdem collis usque Burleistan et de Burleistan tota via usque Uhtinabrigga in bosco usque Douni per terminos predictos habet Dominus Abbas et homines sui pasturam pecoribus suis a festivitate Sancti Hilarii usque Pascha, sine cornu, et cane, et securi; et a Pascha usque ad festum Sanctæ Mariæ in Augusto, mortuum boscum sine vasto. Et porci dominici monachorum cum porcis Ricardi habebunt pascuagium. Ricardus vero in augmentum elemosynæ de omni venacione sua de Halumsira monachis de Eglesfeld decimum concedit. Hanc quoque conventionem concessit Willielmus heres et filius ejusdem Ricardi. Testibus hiis a parte monachorum Domino Gilberto Abbate de Koard, Roberto Maylard, Rogero Bovett, et Alano filio fratris ejus, Alberto janitore, Godfrido coco, Radulpho camerario, Hugone milite, Ricardo filio Fulci. Ex parte vero Domini Ricardi de Louvetot, Willielmo Faixo, Waltero de Haier, Rogero filio ejus, Rogero filio Roberti, Rogero de   Radulpho filio Uhtred. Factum est hoc cyrographum anno ab incarnatione Domini millesimo centesimo sexagesimo primo: anno vero regis Henrici junioris septimo.

     Hoc signum Domini Ricardi de Louvetot ✠
     Hoc signo Willielmi heredis sui   ✠
Hoc cyrographum factum est apud Sanctum Wandragesilum.

In that retired part of the parish of Ecclesfield where it adjoins the manor of Kimberworth, a religious solitary took up his abode. His example seems to have been followed by others, till at length a hermitage became established in this place, which was dedicated to Saint John the Baptist, for obvious reasons the patron of the desert-religionist. The first William de Lovetot settled certain lands upon the hermitage and its inhabitant, and to this gift his son Richard made a small addition. In his time the hermitage lost its inhabitant, and Richard gave it with all its appurtenances to the monks of Kirkstead, 'for his own health, that of William his son, Cecilia his wife, and others[2].' The monks of this Lincolnshire house having now obtained considerable interests in these parts found it expedient to erect a grange for the residence of their tenant or bailiff, who had the oversight of these outlying lands and iron-works. This grange, called Thundercliffe or Synocliffe-grange, was bought by one of the family of Rokeby at the Dissolution, and passing through the hands of several families, the Wombwells, Shiercliffes, and Greens, in quick succession, became the property of the right honourable the earl of Effingham, who took down the old grange and erected near its site a commodious and handsome mansion, to which the old name is still adhering.

The most splendid act of piety performed by these ancient lords of Hallamshire was the foundation and endowment of a monastery at Worksop for canons regular of the order of Saint Augustine, under the superintendence of a prior. We have a metrical chronicle of the founders and benefactors of this house, composed in the reign of Edward IV. by one of its own monks named Pigot. He assigns the third year of Henry I. as the date of its foundation, and in this he has been followed by Dugdale and Thoroton. But the date is suspicious. It does not appear that William and Emma de Lovetot had children of an age to give any consent to the deed of their parents so early as 1103: and Alexander bishop of Lincoln, who witnessed the first endowment, did not enter on his see before the 25th year of Henry I. The spacious and noble church of this monastery with its two towers at the west end still remains entire, but has suffered much in its minuter decorations. Here the funeral obsequies of the early lords of Hallamshire were performed, and here their bodies one by one were returned to the earth out of which they were taken. Before the Reformation might be seen a fine series of their monuments ranged on each side the choir, immediately before the altar, and in the Lady chapel, commencing with the founder and ending with the third earl of Shrewsbury, in the time of Edward IV., but not without some intermissions. What a noble study for the monumental architecture of this kingdom! What a deep impression must they have communicated of the existence of heroes of former days! The nameless and mutilated effigies in an obscure corner of this church, all that remain of the once splendid series, can now only affect the pensive mind with thoughts on the transitoriness of human glory, and the vanity of sepulchral distinctions.

The last of the male line of the Lovetots, lords of Hallamshire, died between the 22d and 27th years of the reign of Henry II. He left an only daughter, named Matilda, or Maud, then of very tender age. This lady was heir to his large possessions, and through her mother nearly allied to the great house of Clare.

The right of the chief lords to dispose in marriage the heiresses of those who held lands of them is one of the most indefensible points of the feudal system. It may have had its convenience in regard to the superiors, but what did the tenant gain by it; and in a well regulated community all general political institutions will be directed to the benefit of the more numerous class. In this instance a thousand objections arising out of some of the most sacred feelings of human nature immediately present themselves, which no reasons of expediency or policy ought ever to have been allowed to countervail. The wardship of the great heiress of Hallamshire fell to Henry II. Extreme tenderness of age was not always thought to present a sufficient reason for the crown to forgo the advantages which accrued from the exercise of this right. But Henry seems to have left it to his son and successor Richard to select the person to whom her hand should be given, and therefore to appoint to what new family the fair lordship of Sheffield should devolve. As might be expected, he chose the son of one of his companions in arms: and Maud de Lovetot was bestowed on Gerard de Furnival, a young Nor-

[1] Dods. MSS. vol. cxvii. f. 74.   [2] Mon. Ang. vol. i. p. 808.

man knight, son of another Gerard de Furnival, who was with the king at the siege of Acre.

It does not appear whether Richard intended to exact or remit the usual relief: but we find his successor King John, ever a needy prince, agreeing with the elder De Furnival, that he will take the homage of his son for the lands which had been William de Lovetot's, on condition of receiving four hundred marks of silver. This sum was never paid: for not long after happened the great fight under the walls of Mirabel. To the success which that day attended the arms of King John the valour of De Furnival contributed. In the battle and pursuit two hundred knights were made prisoners. One of them, whose name was Conan de Leon, fell into the hands of De Furnival. This prisoner he rendered to the king, having in return a remission of his homage-fine[1]; so that the Furnivals may be said to have established their interest at Sheffield by the surrender of a French knight of Prince Arthur's party taken by their ancestor at the great battle of Mirabel.

Still, however, they were not unexposed to contests respecting these estates. From the crown itself to the lowest of those who held lands of it, the rights of heirs male and of heirs general were offering perpetual occasions of controversy and discord. While the eldest branch of De Lovetot thus ended in a female heiress, there was another branch still existing, sprung from the first William by his younger son Nigel. When the father of Maud died, the rights of this branch were vested in Richard de Lovetot, who seems to have acquiesced in the transit of the great property of the family to his cousin, her husband, and her issue. Not so his younger brother and heir Nigel. In the Pipe Rolls of the 9th of King John there is much respecting the controversies between this Nigel and De Furnival. In that year Gerard de Furnival gave a thousand pounds and fifteen palfreys to the king, that he might quietly enjoy those lands to which Nigel de Lovetot made claim against him[2]. But though thus the best part of the inheritance passed from the name of Lovetot, the family of this Nigel continued to reside in the county of Nottingham, for several generations, in a state of respectability and splendour.

Gerard de Furnival was also early in the reign of King John engaged in legal discussions with a family which bore the name of De Ecclesfield touching certain rights which he claimed in that parish[3].

[1] Thoroton, 4to edit. vol. iii. p. 387.
[2] Id.
[3] Dods. Extracts from Fines 7 Joh. Harl. 801. Ecclesfield. Reference has already been several times made to these manuscripts; and as the name of Dodsworth must hereafter often occur in these pages, I shall here throw together a few notices of the life, pursuits, and collections of this eminent antiquary.

ROGER DODSWORTH, a name never to be mentioned but with respect, was descended of an ancient Yorkshire family, whose genealogy may be found among the Holmes's Manuscripts in the British Museum. Harl. 1987, f. 20 a. His great grandfather, Peter Dodsworth of Mashan, is there said to be a younger brother of Thomas Dodsworth of Thornton-Watlas esquire; and it is related of Simon Dodsworth, his grandfather, who was of Settrington, that he was present at the battle of Musselborough. His father Matthew Dodsworth was a younger son, bachelor of laws and chancellor to Toby Matthew, archbishop of York.—He was born at Newton-Grange, in the parish of Saint Oswald in Rydale, on the 24th day of July 1585. Part of his education he received in Archbishop Hutton's Grammar-school at Warton, under Myles Dawson, who was afterwards vicar of Bolton. Vic. Leod. p. 141. It does not appear that he was of either university, or that he was brought up to any profession; but rather that early in life he began to devote himself to those researches which, however gratifying to himself and beneficial to the public, would tend but little to the advancement of his fortunes. Ever witness for him that great national work the MONASTICON ANGLICANUM, the labour of which, Sir William Dugdale would have been the first to allow, rested principally on his coadjutor Dodsworth. But of the collections of an industrious antiquary it is usually but a very small portion that finds its way to the public through means of the press. A still more extraordinary proof of Dodsworth's indefatigable spirit is to be found in the manuscript collections in his own hand, now amongst the mighty treasures of the Bodleian library. They consist of church-notes, letters, pedigrees, charters, and many other matters of great topographical importance, which, together with some original documents preserved by him, were formerly stitched in a hundred and sixty-two volumes. Several of these volumes are now bound together, but the old numbering has been preserved. The *Catalogus Manuscriptorum Anglicanorum* presents but an imperfect view of their multifarious contents, and the student in Yorkshire antiquities may be cautioned against relying upon the abstract of them as far as they relate to certain wapentakes and certain families in the county of York, which is to be found in the Harleian collection of Manuscripts, 793—804. A complete digest of their contents, as far as they relate to the county of York, upon the plan of the Harleian abstract, would be a work of singular utility to those engaged in illustrating its general history. Dodsworth's church-notes were taken before the Civil Wars: and his abstracts of evidences while many old Yorkshire families were living upon the estates of their progenitors, and who are now extinct, and their papers dispersed. His abstracts of those in possession of Sir Francis Wortley of Wortley, and Mr. Rockley of Rockley, are very copious: and to Mr. William Shiercliffe of Ecclesfield-hall, and Mr. Thomas Mounteney of Wheatley near Doncaster, both representatives of ancient Hallamshire families, he makes acknowledgements of their kindness in assisting him with charters and records from their collections. His extracts from the Scrope charters contain many useful notes respecting Ecclesall.—The world was deprived of the services of this most laborious and useful person as the Monasticon was going through the press, in August 1654. He lies in the church of Rufford in Lancashire. His wife was Holcroft, daughter of Robert Hesketh esquire of that place, who is not the only female of that family connected with the literary history of this country. He had three daughters, Cassandra, Eleanor, and Mary; and one son named Robert, who was in the church, as was also a brother of the antiquary, named Edward, who had the living of Badsworth, and appeared at Dugdale's visitation of Yorkshire anno 1666, when he had a son named Matthew and several daughters.

In the *Fasti Oxonienses* may be found more respecting the Dodsworth collections; and as every thing connected with their history will have a value in the sight of the genuine lover of the topography of Yorkshire, I shall add that Fuller refers to them as being in his time 'at Yorkhouse, in the library of the Lord Fairfax.'—Worthies of Yorkshire, p. 201.

CHAPTER IV.

Sheffield under the Barons Furnival.

THE marriage of Maud de Lovetot with Gerard de Furnival transferred Sheffield and her other great estates in the counties of York and Nottingham to another family, who continued to enjoy them till it ended in a female heiress named Joan de Furnival in the time of Richard II. Dating the term of their possession from the grant of full livery of her lands to Gerard de Furnival, by King John, in the fifth year of his reign, they were lords of Hallamshire a hundred and eighty years.

The name of FURNIVAL was derived from a place in Normandy called Fernefal[1]. This was their hereditary seat; but it seems to have been deserted by them when they had acquired the houses and lands of the De Lovetots. Indeed not only at the Conquest, but for the first century and half after their dukes became kings of England, the Normans showed a great willingness to abandon their hereditary seats and to settle in this island.

The arms of Furnival appear without any variation in many places where their estates lay; Argent a bend between six martlets gules: and are so described in that best authority for the hereditary insignia of the ancient baronage of England, the Roll of Caerlaverok, anno 1300. These arms with a border of gules are used by the society of Furnival's Inn. For the crest our only authority is a tricking in one of Dodsworth's manuscripts[2], which appears to be intended for a copy from some original remaining in his time in the church of Sheffield. Brooke has introduced it among the embellishments of his superb pedigree of the lords of Worksop, and in the accompanying description he calls it, what perhaps the reader would not easily have discovered it to be, a horse's helmet. The engraver has well succeeded in representing the rude tricking by the hand of Dodsworth, who unfortunately was no draughtsman.

The shield in the lower part of the opposite page contains the arms of Sir Thomas Nevil knight, as they appear on the monument of his lady in the church of Barlborough;—Gules a saltier argent, charged with a martlet sable, impaling Furnival. The escutcheon of pretence is a modern artifice. The martlet which he adopted as the peculiar distinction of his branch of the great family of Nevil was obviously borrowed from the arms of the heiress whom he married.

Several members of the house of Furnival were summoned to parliament among the barons of the realm. The genealogy and history of this family have employed the pens of several eminent antiquaries. Sir William Dugdale has of course entered upon the subject in his general view of the Baronage of England[3], a work abounding in the most valuable information, and far less inaccurate than a first attempt of the kind might reasonably be expected, where one object was to recall many half-perished names, and to arrange them in exact genealogical order, a work of which none can comprehend the nicety and the difficulty but those who have actually made the experiment. Dodsworth and Vincent, Dugdale's great masters, have left in manuscript, sketches of the genealogy of this house[4]; but like Dugdale they seem to have been led into error by paying too implicit deference to the rhyming chronicles of Worksop. Thoroton[5] has shown an independence upon them, and, having the use of records which had not fallen under the inspection of Dugdale, has approached much more nearly to the truth than his learned contemporary. Of more modern antiquaries, Mr. Gough has illustrated his description of the remains of the Furnival monuments at Worksop with a pedigree[6]; and Dr. Pegge has given another, in which he differs from all preceding genealogists in his 'Historical Account of the Abbey of Beauchief[7],' to which they were valuable benefactors. I venture to offer the following as the true genealogy of this great house. It is compiled on an attentive consideration of the authorities on which the several writers before mentioned have proceeded, and of a few charters and incidental notices of the family which had not presented themselves to former genealogists. Still, however, there is much to be done before the pedigree, in all its ramifications, can be said to be complete, and established on indisputable evidence. The evidence for each step in the pedigree, as it is here given, will be found either explicitly or implicitly stated in the annexed commentary. I would gladly have added the name of one of our earliest poets, Richard de Furnival. It may be here observed, that there are fewer early charters than might have been expected in the archives of the present noble lord of Hallamshire, relating to his grace's Yorkshire possessions.

[1] Pigot's Metrical Chronicle.
[2] Dods. MSS. in Bibl. Bodl. vol. cxxxvii. f. 1.
[3] Vol. i. p. 725—728.

[4] Dods. MSS. in Bibl. Bodl. vol. xxiii. and Vincent's MSS. in Col. Arm.
[5] Nottinghamshire, vol. iii. p. 387, &c. 4to edit.
[6] Sepulchral Monuments, vol. i. p. 184.   [7] p. 153, &c.

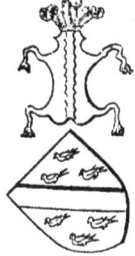

PEDIGREE of DE FURNIVAL, LORDS of HALLAMSHIRE.

ARMS.—Argent a bend between six martlets gules.
CREST.—A horse's helmet argent, with a plume of three feathers or.

GERARD DE FURNIVAL, a Norman knight in the time of Richard I. ═ ANDEL, or Andeluga. This lady was commemorated among the benefactors both at Worksop and Beauchief.

GERARD DE FURNIVAL, lord of Sheffield and Hallamshire in right of his wife. Died at Jerusalem 3 Hen. III. anno 1219. M. Paris. ═ MAUD DE LOVETOT, lady of Hallamshire, only dau. and heiress of William de Lovetot, aged 7 anno 27 Hen. II. Was living in the 33 Hen. III. anno 1249.

GALFRIDUS DE FURNIVAL. He is mentioned in a charter of his brother to the house of Worksop.

THOMAS DE FURNIVAL, eldest son and heir, was slain in Palestine in the lifetime of his mother, after the 22d of Henry III. anno 1237.

GERARD DE FURNIVAL, second son. Had the lordship of Munden-Furnival in Hertfordshire. Living 49 Hen. III. when he was in rebellion. Buried at Worksop.

WILLIAM DE FURNIVAL, third and youngest son. Had lands at Rotherham by gift of William de Vesci, which descended to his nephew Thomas, on his death without leaving issue, before 44 Hen. III. 1260. ═ ALBA or Ada.

ALICE. See Thoroton, Whittingham's and was living 52 Henry III. 1268.

------ Wife of Arnold de Mounteney, from whom descended the family of that name at Shiercliffe in the parish of Sheffield.

-----Wife of Ralph de Ecclesall.

GERARD DE FURNIVAL, lord of Hallamshire. Died, leaving no issue, and gave his body to Worksop. ═ MAUD, sister and co-heir of Richard Fitz-John, son of John Fitz-Geffery, justice of Ireland.

WILLIAM BEAUCHAMP, earl of Warwick, second husband. Died 26 Edw. I. anno 1298.

THOMAS DE FURNIVAL, lord of Hallamshire, as heir to his brother. Founder of the second castle of Sheffield, 54 Hen. III. anno 1270. Dead before 7 Edw. I. anno 1279. ═ BERTHA, survived, and was Edw. I. anno 1279.

-----Wife of Roger, son of William de Mowbray.

JOAN, first wife, dau. of Hugh Le Despenser, and sister to the elder Spencer, favourite of Edw. II. ═ THOMAS Lord FURNIVAL, lord to parliament as a baron of the realm from the 22 Edward I. anno 1294 to the 6 Edw. III. anno 1332, in which year he died on the morrow of the Purification. ═ ELIZABETH, second wife, dau. of Sir Peter de Montfort, of Beldesert castle in the county of Warwick. Survived her husband many years, and dying anno 28 Edw. III. 1354, had sepulture in Christ-church Oxford, where her tomb still remains.

WILLIAM MONTACUTE, first husband; son and heir of Simon de Montacute, Seneschal of Gascony, and governor of the Isle of Oleron.

BERTHA, wife of Ralph Bigod, third son of Hugh Bigod, earl of Norfolk.

THOMAS Lord FURNIVAL, lord of Hallamshire, succeeded his father as son and heir, and aged 40, anno 1332. Married die Sabbati in festo Sancti Matthæi apostoli circa ann. 1318. Died at Sheffield, pridie Id. Octob. anno 1339, and was buried in the Abbey of Beauchief. ═ JOAN, eldest dau. and co-heir of Theobald de Verdon, a great baron in Staffordshire, by Maud his wife, dau. of Edmund Lord Mortimer. Born in Aug. 1304. Died in child-bed 6 Non. Oct. anno 1334, and was laid with her ancestors in the church of Croxden-abbey.

WILLIAM DE MONTACUTE, first husband, died before consummation.

MAUD, wife of John Lord Marmion, who was aged 30 an. 16 Edw. II.

CATHERINE, wife of William de Thweng, a baron in Yorkshire anno 18 Edw. II.

ELEANOR, wife of Peter de Mauley the fourth, lord of Doncaster, &c.

These marriages appear in Dugdale in his accounts of the families of Marmion, Thweng, and Mauley. The ladies are said to be daughters of a Thomas Lord Furnival, and were probably daughters of the Thomas who died in 1332.

THOMAS Lord FURNIVAL, called the Hasty : lord of Hallamshire, succeeded his father as son and heir. Was aged about 17 anno 13 Edw. III. 1338. At the battle of Cressy, anno 20 Edw. III. 1341. Died without issue anno 39 Edw. III. 1366. ═ JOAN, dau. and heir of Sir Thomas de Mounteney knight, lord of Swinton, Scoles, Cowley, Shiercliffe, &c. Died anno 19 Rich. II. 1396, leaving a son, whom she calls John de Mounteney.

WILLIAM Lord FURNIVAL, brother and heir of Thos. last lord of Hallamshire of this house. Born in the castle of Alton in Staffordshire, his mother's inheritance, 10 Kal. Sep. anno 1326. Died without male issue 12 April 1383. ═ THOMASINE, dau. and heir of Dagworth, who had great possessions in Norfolk and Essex. Died 10 Hen. IV. anno 1408.

NICHOLAS DE FURNIVAL, third son. Born on the day of the Epiphany 1328. Living 10 Edw. III. anno 1336.

MARGARET, born on the vigil of the Circumcision 1320, and baptized by the abbots of Croxden and Rouceater.

JOAN, wife of Thos. Bosvile, of Cavil in Yorkshire. They have a monument in the church of Eastrington, E. R. Yorkshire.

JOAN DE FURNIVAL, sole dau. and heir, anno 6 Richard II. 1383, and then aged 14 years and more. ═ Sir THOMAS NEVIL Lord Furnival, and, in right of his wife, lord of Sheffield and Hallamshire. A younger brother of Ralph Nevil, first earl of Westmoreland. Died anno 8 Hen. IV. 1406, and was buried at Worksop.

ANKERET, second wife, dau. and heir of John Lord Strange, of Blackmere near Whitchurch.

═ RICHARD Lord TALBOT, first husband.

JOHN TALBOT, first earl of Shrewsbury, a younger son of Richard Lord Talbot and Ankeret Le Strange his wife, lord of Sheffield in right of his wife, and summoned to parliament by the style of John Talbot of Hallamshire. ═ MAUD DE NEVIL, Lady Furnival, only issue of the first marriage. Anno 10 Hen. IV. 1408, found heir to her grandmother Thomasine de Furnival, then aged 17 years, and married to John Talbot.

JOAN DE NEVIL, co-heir to her father, aged about 3 years anno 1406. She married Sir Hugh de Cokesey, and according to some authorities Hamo de Belknap.

Historical and genealogical commentary.

The first Gerard de Furnival was known in the north of England. His name appears among the witnesses of the grant made by his son to Kirkstead, of the moiety of his mill at Hansworth-Woodhouse, ' G. De Furnival, pater[1].' To this deed he subscribed along with Osmond an abbot, Theobald monk of Roche-abbey, Henry prior of Worksop; in which the order is remarkable, a monk of Roche having precedence of the prior of Worksop. Then comes the name of Gerard de Furnival, and afterwards brother Alan de Boles, Robert de Sumerville, Roger de Hair, Thomas de Rainevill, and two others, all persons of chief account in the southern parts of Yorkshire.

The family name of Andel, or Andeluga, has not been transmitted to us. Dr. Pegge supposed that he was the first to add her name to the family pedigree, but it appears in Thoroton. This lady was happy in the prayers of the monks both of Beauchief and Worksop. It was for her soul's health, and that of his brother Galfridus de Furnival, that the second Gerard gave the monks of Worksop pasture for forty cows in his park near that place. Her commemoration at Beauchief was made on the 20th day of January in each year[2].

Gerard de Furnival the second attached himself to the interests of King John. In the memorable years 1214 and 1215 he was with his sovereign, and was one of those knights who were sent from Oxford to treat with Robert de Roos and other chiefs of the barons in arms. When this negotiation had failed of its object, and the barons were besieging the tower of London, into which the king had thrown himself, he was one to whom letters were sent by the confederates threatening to destroy the castles and ravage the estates of those of their order who still adhered to the king[3]. Soon after this he and his lady had a warrant from the king to reside in the castle of Bolsover. This looks as if it had not been an empty menace; and the clause in the patent, that it was 'for the better preservation of the peace of those parts,' may have been introduced to cover the humiliating fact, that the king had been unable to protect his faithful subject and ally in the possession of his own mansion. It is by no means improbable that the original castle of Sheffield, if it escaped the general destruction of such edifices in the latter years of Henry II., fell at this time.

There is a tradition that King John once visited Sheffield. It assumes a colour of probability from the known fact of the attachment of De Furnival to his cause. But there are more traditionary accounts of visits from John than from any other of our earlier monarchs. Tradition is seldom very exact in delivering down its charge: and some things which belong to his royal namesake the king of France are received as appertaining to our own monarch of that name. Thus a house in which King John of France was for some time confined at Somerton, the ancient capital of Somersetshire, is shown to strangers as having been honoured, if honoured it may be called, by the presence of our own sovereign of the name of John.—

Very soon after the death of his prince, De Furnival joined in one of the expeditions to Palestine. He closed a short but turbulent life at Jerusalem anno 1219: but he did not

' Like a true knight of Christ sleep round his Saviour's tomb,'

for his body being brought to Europe was entombed at Ebrard in Normandy[4].

MAUD DE LOVETOT his wife survived her husband many years, and died very aged in the latter days of Henry III. In her widowhood she constantly used her maiden name. By that name she is mentioned in the records of the diocese of York in 1237, when she presented Sir Robert de Doncaster to the rectory of Whiston[5]. We find other instances of that control over the family property being exercised by this lady, which shows that during her life a large portion of the Lovetot fee was vested in her. This great heiress seems to have lived in much pomp and felicity, only unfortunate in seeing her sons go to the grave before her. In the pedigree three sons and as many daughters are stated as her offspring. The sons are mentioned by the rhyming chronicler of Worksop, and by all our genealogists; and their names, and the relation in which they stood to each other, are sufficiently established by evidence to render their situation in the pedigree indisputable.—For first we find Thomas de Furnival the head of the family in the 21 Henry III.[6]; in the next year he had a grant of the wardship of William de Mowbray, son of Roger, together with his marriage, to the intent that he might take to wife the daughter of De Furnival; and in the succeeding generation Gerard and Thomas de Furnival describe themselves as being sons of Thomas de Furnival[7].—Secondly, in respect of Gerard: it is in reference to this son that the husband of Maud de Lovetot is called *Gerardus primus* in the obituary of the house of Beauchief; and all our genealogists agree in bringing the junior house of Furnival of Munden in Hertfordshire from this second son of the house of Sheffield.—And thirdly, William de Furnival is mentioned in the pleas of juries and assize at York, 52 Henry III. as son of Maud de Lovetot[8]; and again as uncle to Thomas de Furnival in the next generation in a deed of John de Vesci to the monks of Rufford, ' cum homagio et servitio Thomæ de Furnivall et hæredum suorum de terris et tenementis quæ predictus Willielmus de Vesci pater meus dedit Willielmo de Furnivall avunculo ipsius Thomæ in Roderham, &c.[9]'

The daughters have not before had their place in any pedigree of this family. The marriage with De Ecclesall is left doubtful. There are strong presumptions, but no positive proof. The connexion at this period between the houses of Mounteney and Furnival is affirmed in the received pedigrees of the former family, often erroneous enough, and attested by a series of armorial impalements which were once to be seen in a window of the church of Ecclesfield. But the best proof is a charter which Gascoigne had perused, of 51 Henry III., wherein Sir Robert de Mounteney is described as *nepos*, that is, grandson of Maud de Lovetot[10].

[1] Mon. Ang. vol. i. p. 807.
[2] Pegge's Historical Account of Beauchief Abbey.—I shall not think it necessary to make a reference to Pegge, Thoroton, or Dugdale, for every fact which is stated on their authority.
[3] Mat. Paris, p. 177.
[4] Metrical Chronicle of Worksop.
[5] Torre's MSS. in Bibl. Dec. et Cap. Ebor.
[6] Rymer, vol. i. p. 377.
[7] Thoroton.
[8] Dods. MSS. f.f. 73. Harl. 801. f. 103 a.
[9] Mon. Ang. vol. i. p. 836.
[10] Dods. MSS. in Bibl. Bodl. vol. xc. f. 140.

Maud de Lovetot, like her husband, was a benefactor to several religious houses. In the 33 Henry III. anno 1249, after great controversies between her and Walter prior of Worksop, she signed a general confirmation of all the gifts that had been made by her ancestors to the monks of that house. The baronage had by this time begun to find that in the monastic bodies which they had so amply endowed in the first century and a half after the Conquest, they must expect to find not humble and grateful dependents, but audacious and 'formidable rivals. They did not, however, neglect to pay their benefactors in the cheap coin of commemorative masses, and it was the good fortune of the wife as of the mother of Gerard de Furnival to have the prayers of the religious long after her decease, in the churches of Beauchief and Worksop. In the obituary of the former of these two houses, of which Dr. Pegge has made such excellent use, we find the name of this lady coupled with notice of a small donation which she had made to it at Sheffield. ' *Kal. Julii: Co. Dñc Matildis Lovetot uxoris Dñi Gerardi Furnivall primi, Dñe de Halumschire que dedit nobis unam marcam de annuo redd' ad pietanciam de molendino suo in Sheffield percipiend' in die sanctorum Dionysii sociorumque ejus* [9 *Oct.*] *ad sustentand' unum solempne servicium pro animabus Dñi Gerardi mariti sui* [*et sue*] *sicut patet per cartam suam inde nobis factam*[1].'

We have little information concerning Thomas de Furnival the eldest son. Part of not a long life was spent in the pursuit of one of those wild and profitless enterprises by which men in those days made proof of their allegiance to Christ and zeal in the Christian profession. He fell by the hands of the Saracens, probably in the great slaughter of the Christian host near Damietta. His brother and companion Gerard buried the body, and returned to his native land. There is a romantic story connected with this event.—When the mother heard the melancholy tidings, her sorrow is said to have been excessive. Her mind dwelt not more on the loss she had sustained of her eldest hope, than on the shameful fact, that he whose life had been sacrificed to Christian zeal should lie in ground that was cursed by the step of the infidel. This cause of grief was however removable; and with true filial piety the younger son is said to have undertaken once more a journey to the East, and from thence to have brought away what could be collected of the beloved corse. With proper Christian solemnities she had it honourably interred in the church of Worksop, and placed over it a superb monument adorned with precious stones, and especially with a noble carbuncle.— The reader will naturally ask where is the evidence for this remarkable story. We are so accustomed to contemplate the characters of the persons who lived in those remote ages through the medium of their legal transactions, which does not often allow of our discerning any of the finer and discriminative traits of character, that the mind receives, with perhaps an excessive degree of incredulity, any anecdote in which private sentiment and individual feeling are displayed.

But the individuals of the human species were always marked by peculiar temperaments, and distinguished not more by their features than by different degrees of taste, knowledge, and affection. The credit of this story depends upon the tradition of the house of Worksop committed to writing in the time of Edward IV. by one who had the monument daily before his eyes. The verses of Pigot may not improperly close our account of the great heiress of Hallamshire, in the days of the first of the Plantagenets.

' Good Molde was buryed most principal;
  Above Sir Thomas Nevill afore the hye autere;
For a good doer most worthy of all
  That indued this place; and her husband insere :
  To reherse what she did, dyvers things sere,
As expressed is afore, it wolde take long space:
Bot in Heaven therfore we trust is there place.

When Sir Thomas was slayne for Christes sake,
  His broder came home, Gerard agayne;
And that Molde ther moder grevously gan take
  That his bones emong hethen should be lane;
  And made him retorne without more disdeyne
Againe to the holy land, and his bones home brought;
As it was Goddes will, that him dere boght.

Then tumulate here in Nottinghamshire
  At Wyrksoppe, the north side of the mynster,
With his helme on his hede will enquere
  With precious stones sometyme that were set sere,
  And a noble carbuncle on him doth lie bere
On his hede; to see they may who so will,
Of my writing witness for to fulfill[2].'

The two younger sons of Maud de Lovetot were also buried at Worksop. Alda, or Ada, the wife of William de Furnival, is said by many genealogists to have been the youngest daughter and co-heir of Richard Gernons (second son of Ranulph earl of Chester) by Joan de Morville his wife, youngest daughter and coheir of Hugh de Morville, a great baron in the north. And with this agrees what Dugdale relates of her, that she had in dowry the manor of Ayketon and others in the county of Cumberland, where the inheritance of the De Morvilles principally lay. Some genealogists state, that William de Furnival had a daughter named Helewyn, who was the wife of Eustace Bailliol. William de Furnival died before 44 Henry III., and some years after his decease great suits at law arose between Alda his widow and Thomas de Furnival the nephew of William, respecting interests in Hansworth and Whiston. ' In the pleas of juries and assize at York, the day after Saint Hilary anno 52 Hen. III., the assize came to know (I quote from the translator and abridger of Dodsworth[3]) if Thomas de Furnival have unjustly disseised Alda who was the wife of William de Furnival of her free tenement, &c.—And she complains that he disseised her of the manor of Whiston, with the appurtenances (except the advowson of the church) and of the same manor, and of the third part of the manor of Hansworth, with the appurtenances (except the advowson of the church) of the said manor.—And Thomas says that the king hath given him by charter all the lands and tenements in Whiston and Hansworth, which were of the fore-

---

[1] Pegge.
[2] The rhyming chronicles of Worksop consist of twenty-nine such stanzas as these. They are published entire in the Monasticon, vol. ii. p. 937—939, from an ancient parchment manuscript in possession of the Talbots of Grafton. A clerk of the same name with the author was presented to the rectory of Hansworth in 1318. We may observe in the

above extract an evident proof that the word *minster* was not exclusively applied to a cathedral church, or even to a church having prebendal stalls, in the days of Rowley, which were the days of Pigot. I know not that these verses have ever been referred to in the Chatterton controversy.
[3] Harl. MSS. 801. f. 103 a.

K

said William de Furnival, sometime husband to the said Alda.—Alda saith that Maud de Lovetot after the death of the foresaid William de Furnival her husband, who died without heirs, granted to the foresaid Alda all the manor of Whiston, except the advowson of the church of the same manor, and the manor of Gresthorp, with all the appurtenances, for the dower which belonged to the same Alda of the manors of Grengley, Whiston, and Gresthorp, in the county of Nottingham; and proffers a certain writing made between the same Maud and Alda, which witnesseth the same. She saith also that the foresaid Thomas afterwards confirmed the grant made by the foresaid Maud, by a certain writing of his which she produceth in these words:—' Be it known to all, &c. that on the Sunday next before the feast of Saint Gregory, in the 44th year of the reign of king Henry son of king John, it is thus agreed between Thomas de Furnival of the one part, and Alda sometime wife of William de Furnival of the other part; to wit, that the said Thomas hath granted to the said Alda for her life to hold the manor of Whiston, with its perquisites, as it is endowed by Maud de Lovetot, and for this grant the said Alda hath quit claimed to the said Thomas all the right which she had in the name of dower in the advowson of the church of Hansworth.'

Gerard and William de Furnival are thus noticed in the rhyming chronicle of Worksop.

' Sir Gerard on the south side under a merbill stone
  Near St. Peter's chappell is beryed also;
And Sir William ther brother both flesh and bone
  In our Lady chappell was beryed even tho
  In the midst of the chappell, good Molde a little fro;
Wyf to first Sir John [Gerard] Furnivall that was:
Which foresaid Sir William was gretely endued with grace,

For five candells perpetuall in that chappell
  He ordeyned to brynne before our Lady:
And myche more he ordeyn'd as we herd tell,
  As his auncestrie afore had done worthely:
  And there lyeth tumulate full worshippfull [y]
All in free stone, and on him is write
These verses here that thus are indite.
  Ne memorans palle, similie currisque calle
  De Fournvaille pro Willielmo rogo psalle.'

Such were the narrow views of the ' cloistered priest.' He can find no better proof the ' grace' with which Sir William was endowed than that he had given money to find five candles perpetually burning before the image of the Virgin: as he could find no topic on which to expatiate when he had occasion to mention a daughter of the noble and literate house of Ormond, but that she numbered among her ancestors Gilbert Becket, father to the blessed martyr Thomas. Most incorrectly has he copied the monkish epitaph. It may still be read, the letters printed in italics only excepted, the most perfect memorial of the ancient lords of Hallamshire now at Worksop.

' Me memorans palle: simili curris quia *calle*
  De Fournivalle, pro Willielmo rogo psalle[1].'

Dr. Pegge had restored the true reading[2]: but I cannot agree with him when he would transfer the inscription to a later William de Furnival. The Langobardic characters in which it is written had fallen out of use in the time of Richard II.: and Pigot might

have personally known the second William, and could scarcely mistake about his sepulchre.

The name of the wife of the first Thomas de Furnival has not been transmitted to us: but beside the daughter to whom the heir of Mowbray was contracted, he had other female issue, and the two sons Gerard and Thomas whose names appear in the pedigree. Gerard was the elder, and succeeded to the inheritance. But he did not long enjoy it; for before the close of the reign of Henry III. Hallamshire was become the inheritance of another Thomas de Furnival, whom some pedigrees represent to have been his son, but others more correctly his brother and heir. For Gerard himself died without issue, as appears by the inquisition taken after the death of Maud countess of Warwick his widow, 26 Edward I., whose son and heir was found to be Guy earl of Warwick, then aged twenty-six years and more; which he would not have been, had his mother borne children to De Furnival[3]. This further appears by the words of certain charters to the house of Worksop. Gerard de Furnival, by the description of Gerard son and heir of Thomas de Furnival, gave with his body the third part of the mills of Bradfield with the suit of his men of the soke of Bradfield to that monastery: and Thomas, son and heir of Thomas de Furnival, confirmed the gift of his brother[3]. The transactions of these two brothers are not numerous, and the one most important to our subject is, that Thomas obtained a charter to erect a castle at Sheffield.

The wife of Gerard de Furnival has had her name preserved in the evidences of the potent house of Beauchamp, to which in her second marriage she became allied. But while the Christian name Bertha of the wife of Thomas de Furnival appears in many charters, we have no positive authority to show from what family she derived her descent. But it appeared on inquisition taken after the death of her son Thomas lord Furnival, that he held the moiety of the town of Brassington, which had been given to one of his ancestors in frank marriage with his daughter by a certain earl of Derby[4]. Hence a collector of the earlier part of the last century, Mr. Vincent Eyre of Dronfield-Woodhouse, in his account of the family of Furnival, represents Bertha the wife of Thomas as a daughter of William Ferrars the seventh earl of Derby. It may be so, for Bertha was a family name among the Ferrarses; but no connexion between the houses of Ferrars and Furnival appears in the laborious comments of Vincent on the work of Brooke. Whoever she was, she survived her husband, and had considerable endowments in Bradfield. In the fine collection of family-evidences which descended with the estate of Broomhead to its late proprietor John Wilson esquire, the oldest was a deed without date of Thomas son of Thomas de Furnival, by which he conveys to John Wilson de Bromhead forty-six acres of land in Wightwistle, &c. for a rent of sixpence yearly to himself, and four shillings to his mother the Lady Bertha de Furnival, ' Diæ Brette de Furnivall,' yearly during her life, to revert on her death to the said Thomas and his heirs. To this deed is appended a seal of greenish wax, exhibiting the arms of Furnival on a lozenge shield perfectly plain, and this inscription surrounding it, s. THOME DE

[1] See an engraving of it in Gough's *Sepulchral Monuments*, vol. l. p. 182.   [2] Pegge.   [3] Thoreton.   [4] Thoroton.

FVRNIVAL. In her widowhood this lady confirmed for the health of her soul, and of the souls of Sir Thomas de Furnival her late husband and of Sir Gerard his brother, further corroboration of this part of the pedigree, four pounds to be received from her mill at Bradfield during her life[1]. Dugdale refers to Fines 54 Henry III. to show that this lady took Ralph Bigod to her second husband. But Brooke, apparently with the consent of Vincent his corrector[2], represents Bertha wife of Ralph Bigod as daughter, not widow, of Thomas de Furnival: and probably with good reason, for under the description of Dame Bertha de Furnival she was interred in the Grey Friars at Dunwich, a house founded by Richard Fitz-John, brother to her sister-in-law Maud countess of Warwick[3].

The next Thomas de Furnival is the first of the family whom we find to have been summoned to parliament among the barons of the realm: and as the family now advanced in consequence, so the accounts of them are more clear and explicit, and fewer discrepancies are found among what has been published respecting them. This Thomas was the great hero of his line: allied by marriage to two of the most potent families in the kingdom, the Spencers and Monta-cutes, and often summoned to attend the king in parliament and in his wars. He held the lordship of Sheffield between fifty and sixty years, and we shall find that he was no inconsiderable benefactor to his tenantry in the town and its vicinity. His second wife had for her dowry some of the best parts of the Furnival estates; namely, the manors of Worksop, Eyam, Stony-Middleton, Hathersage, and Whiston, with its appurtenances in Aston, Todwick, Treeton, Ullay, Brampton, Catcliffe, and Orgrave. At the time of her marriage she was widow of one of the great house of Montacute. 'For this lady,' says Dugdale, 'there is yet standing a beautiful monument of marble with her portraiture thereon cut to the life, on the north side of the quire of Christ's church in Oxford (heretofore the conventual church of St. Frideswide's monastery there): where there was afterwards a chantry of two secular priests founded to celebrate divine service daily for her soul, and for the souls of William de Montacute[4]' and many other persons her friends and relatives, among whom, however, are found none of the family of Furnival, except her husband Lord Thomas. Her life was extended to the 28th year of Edward III., when the lands which had formed her splendid dowry reverted to the family of Furnival, and became the inheritance of Thomas lord Furnival called the Hasty, grandson by his former marriage, and then aged thirty years and upwards. The monument of this lady is still to be seen in its original situation in Christ Church, Oxford, probably little changed since the time of Dugdale. 'She is represented lying on an altar tomb in a richly embroidered robe and mantle which have been highly coloured. The two ends, and that side of the monument which is exposed to view, are decorated with shields of arms and small statues in niches; but neither the arms nor the statues seem intended to remind us of the house of Furnival.

By the marriage in the next generation with the principal heiress of the baronial house of Verdon, the family of Furnival became enriched with large possessions in the county of Stafford. Among these was the castle of Alveton, now called Alton, the seat of the right honourable the earl of Shrewsbury, premier earl of England, and a lineal descendant from this great heiress. By this marriage the family of Furnival was brought into close connexion with the abbey of Croxden or Crokesden, of which the Verdons were founders and hereditary patrons. It seems to have been thought part of the duty of the monks to keep registers of the births, marriages, and deaths in the families of their benefactors. The chronicles of Croxden have supplied several names and dates in the pedigree[5]. The first marriage of the heiress of Verdon with a Montacute has been often stated, but it is at least of questionable authenticity. She married De Furnival at thirteen[6]; and died in child-bed on the 6th of the nones of October, anno 1334, aged thirty years and two months; and was interred with great pomp in the abbey-church of Croxden, before the high altar, betwixt Nicholas de Verdon son to the founder and John de Verdon her great grandfather. The funeral service was conducted by Richard Shepesheved, abbot of Croxden, assisted by a goodly company of abbots and priors; namely, the abbots of Burton, Curnbermere, Dieulacres, Hilton, and Beauchief, and the priors of Worksop and Ecclesfield[7]. It required considerable time to make due preparation for so high a solemnity: and such time was allowed, for her funeral was deferred to the 7th of the ides of January. But this was short, compared with the interval between the death and interment of her husband. He survived her only five years, dying on the pridie Id. Oct. anno 1339, in the castle of Sheffield, and was interred by the abbot of Croxden, at Beauchief, on the Monday within the octaves of the Ascension of our Lord[8].

Vincent adds to the issue of this marriage given in the pedigree a son who bore the name of Theobald, and died in his infancy. The two sons Thomas and William succeeded to the inheritance of their family. Of Nicholas their brother all that is known is that in the 10th Edward III. anno 1336, when he was eight years old, he had a confirmation from the king of 10l. annual rent issuing out of Hallamshire[9]. It was from this Nicholas that one Milborne, a notorious forger of pedigrees, claimed to descend, when he wished to show himself allied to the house of Shrewsbury[10].

The wife of the next Lord Furnival of the name of Thomas, whom Pigot has distinguished from the other Thomases of his line by the epithet Hasty, does not appear in Dugdale's or Thoroton's genealogy. I have restored her to her place in the pedigree, on the authority of an inquisition abstracted by Dodsworth, which recites that Thomas de Mounteney knight died anno 24 Edward III. seised of Swinton and Scoles, and that Joan wife of Thomas de Furnival was his only daughter and heir[11]; and also upon the authority of one of her own deeds, of which a copy is preserved in one of Dugdale's manuscripts in the Col-

[1] Thoroton. [2] Discoveries of Errors, p. 339.
[3] Weever, 721. [4] Baronage. [5] Mon. Ang. vol. i. p. 913.
[6] Baronage, vol. i. p. 474, compared with the account of the Furnivals.
[7] Mon. Ang. vol. i. p. 913, and Baronage, vol. i. p. 474.

[8] Mon. Ang. vol. i. p. 914.
[9] Norfolk Evidences.—Yorkshire Bundle L. No. 2.
[10] See Harl. MSS. 154. f. 26. and 2218. f. 74.
[11] Dods. MSS. H. H. 7. Harl. 801. Scoles.

lege of Arms, which recites that Joán Mounteney, daughter and heir of Thomas Mounteney, ' *quondam uxor Thomiæ Furnivall chivalier*,' gives her manor of Bulcotes, &c. to her son John Mounteney. We shall hear more of this lady when we come to speak of Shiercliffe, which was part of her inheritance.

William lord Furnival, who succeeded the last of those who bore the name of Thomas as brother and heir, acquired considerable possessions in Norfolk and Essex by his marriage with the heiress of the ancient house of Dagworth. But it is remarkable that among the quarterings marshalled by the old heralds for her descendants the arms of her family are never included. On the face of Vincent's pedigree it is stated that ' *Margareta filia Thomasiæ de Furnivall nupta fuit Willielmo Playce per Thomam de Hatfield Episc. Dunelmi.*' Perhaps she had another husband. Joan was her only daughter by Furnival, and so found by inquisition aged fourteen years and upwards at the death of her father.

We must now resume our history.

About the time when De Furnival married the heiress of De Lovetot, considerable changes seem to have taken place at Sheffield. That entire proprietorship which the Lovetots enjoyed in Hallamshire, broken only by the claim of the church on the tenth of the produce, did not descend to the Furnivals. Before Maud de Lovetot had passed off the stage, we find two other families had sprung up within the parish, possessing extensive influence, large estates, and manorial privileges, as subinfeudations of the great baron of Sheffield castle; the De Ecclesalls and the De Mounteneys.

The former sprung from one Radulphus, who first appears as witness to a charter of Gerard de Furnival in the time of King John. He took the name of De Ecclesall from his principal estate. He and his family held their lands of the castle and manor of Sheffield by military service: but they had their own court and copyholders, their own hall, park, and chapel, exhibiting on their patrimonial hill a miniature representation of the state which was observed at the castle below.

Shiercliffe-hall in Brightside-Byerlow was a seat of the family of De Mounteney, who had also a moated mansion of a still more ancient date at Cowley in the parish of Ecclesfield, which seems to have descended to them from the great house of De Reneville. They were of equal or perhaps superior rank to the De Ecclesalls, and like them obtained the king's license to convert part of their estate near Shiercliffe into a park.

The precise time when these two important alienations from the great estate of the barons of Hallamshire was made does not appear: but it was evidently about the time when the Furnivals came into possession: nor whether they were gifts in certain respects free except as imposing an obligation of attendance on the chief lord when called to serve the king in his wars, or granted for a certain compensation in money. The necessities of the first De Furnival must have been great. A thousand pounds was an immense sum to be raised by a baron of the time of King John: and

to support the charge of a journey to Palestine, the precious metals were indispensable. It is by no means improbable that he would avail himself of so obvious a means of supply as the alienation of portions of his domain. To this means we know that many of the crusaders' had recourse, and that thus very material changes were produced [1]. But it is perhaps more consonant to the usages of the times to suppose that these estates were given in frank marriage with daughters of the baron of Sheffield. We have already had occasion to show that a claim of descent through females of the ancient lords of Sheffield is set up by our old genealogists for both the Ecclesalls and Mounteneys, and in respect of the latter family on the best authority. In those times, when money was so exceedingly rare, nothing was more common than for the great landed proprietors to portion their daughters with parts of the domain to be held by their husband and posterity on military service; as nothing was more natural than that the baron when called to perform his quota of military service should prefer to be surrounded rather by those who were connected with him by the ties of kindredship, than by strangers.

In token of their dependency upon De Furnival, and that they might be known in the field as those who fought under his banner, the Ecclesalls and Mounteneys were accustomed to bear the same figure on their shields which was exhibited on the shield of De Furnival. The Ecclesalls bore the same charge in gold upon a sable field, and the Mounteneys on a field of gules.

Two other families shared with them the honour and the danger of leading the men of Hallamshire under the banners of De Furnival, when he was called to appear in the field: the De Wadsleys and the De Wortleys; and like the two already mentioned they also assumed the arms of De Furnival as their hereditary insignia, with the difference of three escallop shells, and three bezants on the bend. The De Wadsleys first appear about the time of Henry III. possessing a hall, a park, and manorial rights in the district from which they derived their name. They also held of the castle and manor of Sheffield; and their estates which lay on the edge of the parish of Sheffield descended by a female heiress in the time of Henry VII. to the house of Everingham of Stainborough, which in a few generations became reduced, and their estate was sold. The eldest male line of De Wortley continued at that place till the time of Charles II.

The founder of the abbey of Beauchief was Robert Fitz Ranulph de Alfreton, lord of Norton and of many other places in the county of Derby. He laid the foundation in the year 1183, and the work was completed about the time when De Furnival married the heiress of De Lovetot. This was doubtless a work contemplated with no little satisfaction by the people of Sheffield, who, while they saw its walls rising on the very borders of their parish, anticipated that they should have the opportunity of being edified by the devotion and manner of life of a description of persons to whose support in a distant country which few of them had ever visited, a large portion of the produce of their

---

[1] We may detect Gerard de Furnival making one such bargain: for in the evidences of the Wortley family which Dodsworth perused was a charter of his, by which he conveyed to William de Berri and his heirs twenty acres of land in the soke of Ecclesfield for five marks of silver, and an annual payment of three shillings. Dods. MSS. in Bibl. Bodl. vol. lxi. f. 41. If he sold other lands upon the same terms, he must have parted with not less than five thousand three hundred and thirty-two acres to raise his fine of a thousand pounds.

labour was annually devoted. They might now also look to enjoy those advantages of religious instruction and consolation, and of the orderly performance of the rites of their religion, which the proximity of a monastic establishment afforded. Not to mention that there were crumbs falling from the well spread board, that were thankfully accepted by the neighbouring poor. This house, therefore, soon became popular among its neighbours at Sheffield.

Several small benefactions were made to it at Sheffield. The donation of the second Ralph de Ecclesall must have been peculiarly acceptable to the monks. He gave them his corn-mill on the Sheaf, near the site of the monastery, at the place now called Millhouses, or in our northern dialect Milnehouses. But to this valuable donation was annexed the condition, that they should find him a canon to perform daily service in a domestic chapel which he erected near his mansion[1]. The gift of Gerard de Furnival was equally kind and judicious. The wealth of the monasteries consisted for the most part in cattle. In his extensive pasturable woods of Fullwood and Riveling he had the means of affording pasturage with little detriment to his estate. Those woods, and especially the former, lay not very remote from Beauchief. He gave them liberty to turn thirty cows into his forest of Fullwood with their young under three years old, and an acre of land on which to erect booths for their winter retreat[2]. But his son Thomas de Furnival was much more liberal. He gave them his grange of Fullwood and all lands pertaining to it, and common of pasture throughout the whole of Fullwood and Riveling for all their cattle except goats[3]: no uncommon exception in grants of common of pasture in woodlands.

Nor were the monks of Beauchief the only religious community whose cattle were allowed to run with the cattle and deer of the lord in the chases of Hallamshire. It was a grant not unworthy the acceptance of the prior of the more distant monastery of Worksop, that he might pasture forty cows with their young under three years old in the forest of Riveling[4]. With this grant Gerard de Furnival gave him also an oxgang of land in Stannington, doubtless for the same purpose that the acre in Fullwood had been given to the abbot of Beauchief.

In the time of the second Thomas de Furnival, and in the latter years of the reign of Henry III., a charter was obtained from the king for the erection of a castle at Sheffield. It ran in these terms, according as it is recited in the answers to the *quo warranto* of the next reign.

Henricus Dei gratia Rex Angliæ &c.—Omnibus &c. salutem. Sciatis quod concessimus pro nobis et heredibus nostris dilecto et fideli nostro Thomæ de Furnivall, quod apud manerium suum de Sheffeld in com. Ebor. quod castrum lapideum construere firmare et kernellare, et castrum illud sic constructum firmatum et kernellatum sibi et heredibus suis tenere possit imperpetuum. T. meipso apud Westm. xxii die Julii anno regni nostri liiii[o].

Sir William Dugdale had either a more correct copy of this charter, or he understood the terms of it in a manner rather at variance with what appears to be their first and obvious meaning. Speaking of this Thomas de Furnival, he says that he obtained a char-

ter 54 Henry III. *to make a castle of his manor-house at Sheffield*[5]. It was however in pursuance of this charter that the ruins of the ancient castle of Sheffield were re-edified, or that a castle was raised from its foundations on the site of the one more ancient, which had perished a few years before.

The castles of our ancient barons were too often, it is to be feared, scenes of tyranny and illegal outrage. The first notice we have of this new building is a complaint that Ranulph de Atton seneschal to Thomas de Furnival had taken and confined in it one Thomas of the Green, Robert of the Green, Roger Mody, Ralph son of Hugh de Sheffield, and other persons, on what pretence does not appear, and had afterwards permitted them to depart, taking from the two Greens a mark each, from Mody four shillings, and the like sum from Ralph the son of Hugh[6].

In the castle was a chapel. We find an agreement entered into between Thomas de Furnival and the prior and convent of Worksop, that they should find him two chaplains and a clerk to administer divine service in this chapel, to whom he engages to pay five marks yearly[7]. Domestic chapels like this it is supposed rarely contained the ashes of their founders, and it is probably still rarer to find the fierce but devout baron of this age willing to repose in any but consecrated ground. Yet if we may believe an anonymous collector of notices pertaining to the history of Sheffield, which he committed to writing in the year 1707, within this chapel, or at least within the castle, the body of the founder was deposited. That writer tells us that when the castle was demolished after the Civil Wars a large, flat stone was found on which these words were engraven:

> I Lord Furnival
> I built this castle-hall
> And under this wall
> Within this tomb was my burial.

Obviously not accurately transcribed. He further informs us that the stone coffin in which the body lay, was in his time used as a watering-trough at the manour-farm. And unquestionably such a stone coffin as was used for the interment of persons of consequence at the period in question is now to be seen there: but of the cover no tidings are to be heard, nor could Mr. Wilson gain any information respecting it when seventy years ago he made strict inquiry into this singular circumstance. Such a coffin as that now to be found at the manour might have been brought from some other place, as several have been discovered in the neighbourhood, at Beauchief, Bradfield, and Ecclesfield. But on the whole it seems more probable that such a stone did once exist, than that any person should have fabricated so singular a piece of ancient rhyme.

The founder of the castle died very soon after it was completed; and was succeeded by a son of his own name, to whom Sheffield and its neighbourhood have more obligations than to any individual of the house of Furnival. He was the true patriot: not more intent on establishing on a firm basis the rights of the baronage of England, than on raising the character and consequence of the class below, on whom after all

---

[1] Pegge.   [2] Id.   [3] Id.
[4] *Mon. Ang.* vol. ii. p. 55.
[5] *Baronage.*

[6] *Rotuli Hundredorum temp. Edw. I.* f. 110.
[7] Dodsworth's Extracts from Abp. Greenfield's Register, 2d part, fol. 87. Harl. 801. Sheffeld Castle.

a country must principally depend for its security and prosperity. Such characters ought not to be passed over with that slight notice which a peerage would bestow upon them.

Born to a noble estate, and of a family which boasted its connexion with some of the prime nobility of the realm, he advanced its consequence by his own splendid alliances. While his near connexion with the house of Despenser saved him from the error of joining the standard of rebellion when it was raised by the popular Thomas earl of Lancaster, into which so many of the northern nobility fell, he had the address to escape the ruin in which that house was soon after involved. In those times of vicissitude he seems to have been uniformly safe and prosperous, as he was always prudent, liberal, valiant.

How he demeaned himself in the wars of his time may be collected from the Roll of Caerlaverok, a curious heraldric poem relating to the expedition against Scotland of the year 1300. Thus speaks the worthy herald and poet:

     ' Ouec eus fu achiminer
     Li beau Thomas de Fourneual :
     Ki kant seoit sur le cheual
     Ne sembloit home ke someille.
     Sis merlos et beude vermeille
     Portoit en la baniere blanche[1].'

His services were principally required on the northern border: but he was appointed by King Edward I. captain-general and lieutenant of the counties of Nottingham and Derby. He had summons to parliament from the 22d of that king through the whole reign of his successor, and till the 6th of Edward III., in which year he died, having for some time sat in parliament with his son and heir.

To this person the inhabitants of Sheffield owed their emancipation from a state of vassalage; the regular establishment among them of a municipal court with trial by jury; a market and fair; and the inhabitants of some of the out hamlets several important privileges. But we will speak of his transactions in this neighbourhood in the order of time.

In the 9th of Edward I., being then of full age, and doing his homage, he had livery of all the lands which had descended to him from his father.

In the same year he was called to prove his right to those lands, and to certain immunities pertaining to the possession of them. It was in that year that the writs of *quo warranto* were generally issued under the authority of parliament; and the responses which De Furnival made to the questions which were proposed to him, throw some light upon the state of Sheffield at a period of which we have but few memoranda.

It being demanded of him by what right he claimed to have gallows, waif, and free warren in his manor of Sheffield, he replied, that he claimed to have gallows and free warren by the same warrant by which he and all his ancestors from the conquest of England had

possessed them: but as to waif, he said that he claimed nothing of the kind, but remitted that entirely to the king. Being asked by what warrant he refused to permit the bailiffs of the king to enter his lands of Hallamshire to execute their office, he replied, that he and all his ancestors from the conquest of England had used this liberty, that when any bailiff of the king had any duty to perform within the barony of Hallamshire, their own bailiff undertook the execution of it, and made return to the king's bailiff, who only entered the said barony in default of their own officers doing their duty. To the demand by what warrant he withheld from our lord the king his homage and service for his barony of Hallamshire, he seems not to have returned any answer: but when required to show by what authority he had made strong and embattled, ' *firmavit et kernellavit*,' a certain castle at Sheffield, he produced the late king's charter granted to his father. And lastly, when it was demanded of him by what warrant he claimed to have pleas of withernam, pillory, the assize of bread and beer, the regulation of measures, and to have his lands in the county of York free from suit, he replied, that he made no claim to pleas of withernam; that he had a pillory at Sheffield, and the assize of bread, because these are things always belonging to a market; that he claimed assize of beer, because the lords of every other town in the county had the like: as to the regulation of measures, that was a thing he never claimed, but only the custody of the standard, which he received at the hands of the king's marshal or his bailiffs: and as to being acquitted of his suit for his lands of Hallamshire, he claimed it because neither he nor any of his ancestors from the conquest of England had ever made it.

These pleas were held before John de Vallibus and his fellows, justices-itinerant, at York, in the octaves of Saint Hilary *anno nono Edvardi I.* And the abstract given above is of what purports to be an office-copy of the original record among Ragman's Rolls, made by Fauconbergh in 1660[2].

One effect of the proceedings under the *quo warranto* act of Edward I. seems to have been to introduce greater regularity into the proceedings of the manor-courts. The court-rolls of the manor of Sheffield begin in the early part of this reign.

On the 12th of November 1296, Thomas lord Furnival obtained from the king a charter under the great seal of England, for a market every week on Tuesday, at his manor of Sheffield, and a fair every year during three days, namely, on the vigil, day, and morrow of the Holy Trinity, unless such market and fair should be to the detriment of the neighbouring markets and fairs: which we may conclude they were not, as the market and fair have continued to the present time, except that the latter is held on the Tuesday after Trinity Sunday. Another fair, by what charter granted it does not appear, has been long held on the 28th of November, but before the alteration of the style on the 17th[3].

[1] See the whole of the poem in the *Antiquarian Repertory*, vol. ii. p. 107, &c. The above quotation is from Glover's transcript, made by him, with great care from what he supposed to be the original roll, a manuscript in the Cotton Library. It differs in several passages from the copy in *A. R.*
[2] In the collection of John Wilson, esq.
[3] A proclamation for Sheffield fair, 1634 :—
Thomas earle of Arundell and Surrey, earle marshall and prime earle of England, lord Howard, lord Fitz-Alan, lord Maltravers, lord Mowbray, lord Segrave, lord Bruse and Clun, knight of the most noble order of

the Garter, and one of his Maties most honorable privie counsell, straitly chargeth and commaundeth in the name of our most high and mighty prince and our dread soveraigne lord Charles by the grace of God of England, Scotland, France, and Ireland, Kinge, defender of the faith, &c.—That no person or persons do breake his Maties peace, or weare any harnesse or other unlawfull weapons within the preeincts of this fayre and markett already begunne, or duringe the continuance thereof (wch we now proclayme to hold till to morrow att night) other then such persons as are appointed by the steward of this fayre for the

The procuring these privileges was quickly followed by a more important charter given by De Furnival himself.

In laying before the reader a copy of what is familiarly called Furnival's grant, and which has long been venerated as the Magna Charta of the town, the only liberty which has been taken with it, is to restore the words which in the original are contracted. To represent accurately all the marks and abbreviations used by our old scribes, is a work for the engraver rather than the letter-founder. The original is in the custody of the town-burgesses of Sheffield.

Omnibus Christi fidelibus hoc presens scriptum visuris vel audituris, Thomas de Furnivall tertius[1], filius et heres Domini Thomæ de Furnivall salutem in Domino sempiternam. Noveritis me dimisisse concessisse et feudi firmam dedisse, omnibus liberis tenentibus meis de villa de Schefeld et eorum heredibus, omnia tofta terras et tenementa quæ de me tenent in villa predicta de Schefeld. Tenendis et habendis de me et heredibus meis, predictis tenentibus et eorum heredibus, cum omnibus pertinenciis suis, predictis toftis terris et tenementis infra villam de Scheffeld et extra pertinentibus, in feudo et hereditate, libere quiete bene et in pace inperpetuum; ita quod libera warranna mea per predictos tenentes non impediatur, nec in aliqua perturbetur. Reddendo inde annuatim mihi et heredibus meis predicti tenentes et eorum heredes sexaginta et octo solidos, novem denarios et quadrantem argenti, ad duos anni terminos, scilicet medietatem ad natale Domini, et medietatem ad nativitatem beati Johannis Baptistæ, pro omnibus serviciis et demandis. Salvis mihi et heredibus meis fideliter escaetis et sectis curiæ meæ de tenentibus predictis. Preterea volo et concedo quod curia dictæ villæ de Schefeld de tenentibus meis predictis teneatur infra predictam villam, de tribus septimanis in tres septimanas, per ballivis meis, sicut ac tenus usitatum est tempore antecessorum meorum. Et si ita contingeret quod dicti tenentes mei vel aliquis eorum super transgressione aliqua in dicta curia mea sint amerciandi, volo et concedo pro me et heredibus meis quod amerciantur per pares suos et hoc secundum qualitatem delicti. Ad hæc volo et concedo pro me et heredibus meis, quod dicti tenentes et eorum heredes tam enentes quam vendentes sint quieti per totum Hallumschire ubicunque ex omni exactione et petitione tolneti sicut illi solebant tempore antecessorum meorum inperpetuum. Et ego predictus Thomas et heredes mei hæc omnia predicta cum pertinenciis predictis sicut predictum est, predictis tenentibus meis et eorum heredibus contra omnes gentes warantizabimus inperpetuum. In cujus rei testimonium presenti scripto ad modum sirographi confecto, sigilla partium alternatim sunt apposita. Hiis testibus, Domino Roberto de Ecclesale Domino Edmundo Foliot militibus, Thoma de Schefeld Thoma de Munteney Roberto de Wadislay Radulpho de Wadislay Thoma de Furneus Willielmo de Darnale Roberto le Breton tunc senescallo de Hallumschire et aliis. Datum apud Schefeld quarto Idus Augusti anno Dñi M°CC nonagesimo septimo.

The objects comprehended in this charter are *first* the abolition of those base and uncertain services by which the inhabitants of the town of Sheffield held

their tenements of the lord: and the substitution in their stead of a fixed annual payment in money. The sum agreed upon was three pounds eight shillings and ninepence farthing, which continued to be paid many years after by the inhabitants of Sheffield under the description of the Burgery-rents. Of this the churchburgesses formerly paid 7s. 2d. annually for burgagetenures which had fallen into their hands. The sum to be demanded of each individual tenement was originally very small; and after a time when money was so much depreciated, the collection of it seems to have been discontinued. It is not at present paid. But as late as the year 1662 a jury was sworn to inquire what houses in the town were of the old burgery, and what proportion of the burgery-rent rested upon them; who made return of about four hundred dwellings[2].

When Sheffield became in consequence of this charter a free borough, the question naturally arises why it was not summoned to send its representatives to the House of Commons, as were other boroughs of less consideration than itself. And the answer seems to be this; that it might be considered as virtually represented by its lord, who was regularly summoned to take his seat in the House of Peers. To such a circumstance we may probably trace other instances of the want of representation in the House of Commons, of which so many populous towns are now inclined to complain.

Secondly: the charter provides for the due administration of public municipal justice, by declaring that the court-baron should be held at Sheffield every three weeks, as it had formerly been by the lord's officers; and that the amercements which it might be necessary to impose should be laid *per pares*, by a jury of the tenants, and should not be arbitrary or extravagant, but in proportion to the measure of the offence.

And *lastly*, that the inhabitants of Sheffield should be free from all exaction of toll throughout the whole circuit of Hallamshire, whether they were vendors or purchasers.

This charter was executed by the lord Furnival at Sheffield, on the tenth of August 1297. All the persons of rank in the immediate vicinity were assembled to witness the execution, namely,

Sir Robert de Ecclesall, knight,
Sir Edmund Foliot, knight,
Thomas de Sheffield[3],
Thomas de Mounteney,
Robert de Wadsley,
Ralph de Wadsley,
Thomas de Fourness,
William de Darnall,
and Robert le Breton, at that time seneschal of Hallamshire.

The seal affixed to the original charter is of reddish-

---

gardinge therof and for the maintenance of his Maties peace, upon paine of such punishm^t as to such offence shall appertayne. And that no person do buy or sell any cattell or merchandize forth of the accustomed lymitts of this fayre or markett, or withdraw any toll or duty due for the same, as they will answere the same att theire perills. And if any person or persons be affraide of any bodily harme, or bee wronged in buyinge or sellinge, or have any cause of action for any contract or other matter happeninge within the precincts of this fayre, let them repaire to his hono^{rs} officers here present (who have the government thereof) and they shall have such remedy by action or otherwise as to justice shall appertaine.

[1] That is Thomas de Furnival the third. It was not unusual for the barons to adopt this regal style when there were several of the same

family who bore the same Christian name. Thus in the De Mauley family, who were so attached to the name of Peter, we find Peter de Mauley the fourth, and Peter de Mauley the fifth, in a charter: Miller's *Doncaster*, App. p. ii.

[2] Verdict in the collection of John Wilson, esquire.

[3] The name of De Sheffield often occurs among the witnesses to Lovetot and Furnival charters. There are many instances of local surnames being assumed where the parties enjoyed no manorial rights in the place from which they took their name: and there can be little doubt that this is one such instance, as also that from these De Sheffields sprung the family of that name ennobled by the titles of Mulgrave and Buckinghamshire, whose first appearance in Lincolnshire seems to have been about the time of Henry III.

brown wax, and presents the arms of Furnival on a shield, within a circle of radii.

But while the lord Furnival was thus conferring favours on his neighbours in the *town* of Sheffield, he did not forget his tenantry in the remote parts of the parish, nor even those who resided in the extreme parts of Hallamshire. By his charter, without date, he granted to Thomas son of William de Stannington, and to all the men of Stannington, Morewood, Hallam, and Fullwood, herbage and foliage throughout the whole of his forest of Riveling as it lies in length and breadth between Malen-bridge, Belhag, and Whiteley-wood, of the one part, and a place called Stanedge and the common way which leads from Sheffield towards Darwent on the other. He gave them liberty to turn in their cattle, and to gather green and dry wood; valuable privileges: and they in return were to pay him and his heirs four pounds of silver yearly, by half-yearly payments, at Pentecost and the feast of Saint Martin. To this charter were witnesses

> Elias de Midhope,
> Thomas de Mounteney,
> Ralph de Sheffield, clerk,
> Henry de Spina,
> Robert de Bernes,
> Adam de Bosco,
> William Feorest, armiger,

and others. It is remarked by Mr. Wilson in 1741, that each of the four places mentioned in this charter paid twenty shillings, though the forest was then cut down, and all privileges under the charter lost.

To the inhabitants of Ughill, Nether-Bradfield, Thornset, and Hawksworth, within the chapelry of Bradfield and manor of Sheffield, he granted common of pasture on the moors between Ughill-brook, Gwentree-sicke, the way which leadeth from Hope towards Sheffield, Broadake, Sevenstones in Holderon, and Wainstones on the Water of Agden, with a reserved rent of four marks. To the inhabitants of Wightwistle he granted the like privileges on their own moors: and the rights long claimed and enjoyed in Loxley-chase by the inhabitants in its vicinity are to be traced to grants made by the same chief of the house of Furnival; so that he may properly be distinguished from the other persons of his name, by the appellation of *Thomas lord Furnival the great grantor*.

In the latter part of his life we find him entering into an extensive agreement with the monks of Worksop, by which amongst other things he commuted the payment of tythe from his manor of Sheffield into annual money-rent. This deed was executed at Nottingham on the Thursday after the feast of Saint Augustine in 1328[1].

He died on the day after the feast of the Purification in 1332: and I apprehend that this is the Thomas lord Furnival who was buried in the church of the bare-foot Friars at Doncaster[2].

The name of Furnival continued at Sheffield fifty years after the death of the great grantor; but we find no material transactions of that family which had a tendency to improve or to change the condition of their tenantry and neighbours. The son of the great grantor yielded up his last breath in his castle of Sheffield, and was succeeded by a son of his own name, who is described by Pigot as a

> ' —— sterne and right hasty man,
> The hasty Fournivall.'

He was with Edward III. in his wars in France, and particularly at Cressy. While he was in France the rectory of Whiston became void, and a clerk was presented by the attornies of Thomas lord Furnival[3]. Hence it appears that the great barons of those times were accustomed to put their estates in commission when absent on military service. Thoroton says that in the 17th of Edward III. he had an *ad quod damnum* for settling the castle and manor of Sheffield to the use of himself and Margaret his wife, which, if there has been no error in the transcription, shows that he had another wife beside the heir of Mounteney, whose name was Joan. He died in the 39th of Edw. III. anno 1366; and leaving no issue, William lord Furnival was found to be his brother and heir.

The jury summoned on the inquisition taken after his death found, *inter alia*, that he died seised of the castle and lordship of Sheffield with its members and appurtenances, which were held of the king *in capite*, as of his crown by homage and fealty only, as one knight's fee, and by the service of rendering yearly to the king and his heirs on the feast of the nativity of Saint John the Baptist two white *greyhounds*—not *hares*, as some have represented the condition of the tenure. Jakes's manuscript already referred to contains an abstract of part of this inquisition, and there the word appears thus, *Lepor'*: but the critical eye of Dr. Pegge soon discovered that the word as it now appears was the alteration of some injudicious person, for that originally it had been *Lep'ar'*, a usual contracted form of the word *Leporarias*, greyhounds, hounds used in hunting the hare[4]. Such services were by no means uncommon.

William the last lord Furnival died on the 12th of April 1383; and in the inquisition taken after his death we find that he died seised of a messuage and garden in Oldborne, Holborn, in Middlesex, where now stands Furnival's Inn, and which was the town-residence of this noble family[5].

Joan lady Furnival, his only daughter and heir, carried the great estates of her family to the house of Nevil. Soon after her father's decease she married Sir Thomas Nevil, a younger brother of Ralph Nevil who was created earl of Westmorland, and he was immediately summoned to parliament by her title of Furnival.

This nobleman was much engaged in the public affairs of his time, especially on the northern border. He seems to have taken part with Bolingbroke against Richard II., for in the first of Henry IV. he was constituted warden of Annandale and constable of the castle of Lochmaban. But in the fifth of that reign when parliament granted the king two-fifteenths, as if jealous of the intentions of the monarch, they voted that Thomas lord Furnival should receive the money, and lay it out in the king's wars. By his will, which bears date March 12, 1406, he bequeathed his body to be buried in the church of the priory of Worksop without any great pomp. He gave the king his best

---

[1] Thoroton.   [2] Chronicles of Worksop.
[3] Torre's Catalogue of the Rectors of Whiston.

[4] See Beckwith's edition of Blount's *Fragmenta Antiquitatis*; and *Gent. Mag.* vol. xxxiv. p. 329.   [5] Stowe, 390.

cup of gold with a cover: to the fabrick of the steeple at Worksop forty pounds: to John Talbot and Maud his wife his best bed with all the furniture thereto: and appointed that his feoffees of certain lands at Worksop should cause his obit to be solemnly kept every year in the priory church of Worksop, with placebo and dirige, and mass of requiem by note, on the morrow. And the same year he departed this life, and was buried according to the directions of his will, a noble tomb of alabaster being afterwards erected over his remains[1].

In the 9th of Richard II. this Thomas Nevil lord Furnival obtained a confirmation of the grant made by Edward I. of a fair and market at Sheffield[2]. Why such a confirmation was necessary does not appear.

The monument of Joan lady Furnival wife of Thomas Nevil lord Furnival is now to be seen, where we should little expect to find it, in the church of Barlborough. By the side of the communion table may be seen the effigies of a young woman in alabaster without any inscription, who is beyond doubt their early heiress of Hallamshire. For in the church notes of a collector for the county of Derby, made about the year 1707, as is supposed by Francis Bassano, a herald painter of Derby, we find a copy of part of an inscription which in his time was legible round the verge of the tomb.

' 𝕳𝖎𝖈 𝖏𝖆𝖈𝖊𝖙 ..... 𝕵𝖔𝖍𝖆𝖓𝖓𝖆 𝖋𝖎𝖑 ..... 𝖍𝖆𝖊𝖗 ..... 𝖂𝖎𝖑𝖑𝖎𝖊𝖑-𝖒𝖎 𝕱𝖔𝖚𝖗𝖓𝖎𝖛𝖆𝖑 .... 𝕿𝖍𝖔 ....'

This is sufficient to identify the statue without the aid of the arms, which were more perfect at that time than at present. In the dexter chief corner was the saltier, the arms of Nevil, and in the sinister those of Furnival, while at the feet the two coats were impaled on an escutcheon supported by two talbots collared and belled[3].

She was certainly buried at Worksop. But it is not difficult to account for the appearance of her monument in this village-church. Barlborough is about seven miles from Worksop, and it might be removed thither at the time when the havock was committed among the monuments at Worksop: or perhaps a few years after the Reformation, Judge Rodes, who was seneschal to the earl of Shrewsbury, might obtain the family's permission to remove this, the most perfect of the monuments, from the ruined church at Worksop, to grace the church of Barlborough his newly acquired estate and residence.

She had an only daughter and heir named Maud, who married John Talbot afterwards earl of Shrewsbury. Thus the great inheritance of the Furnivals accrued to that noble family.

> Dame Johane is beryed aboven the hye quere,
>   Next Thomas Nevill that was her husband;
> In alabaster an ymage Sir Thomas right nere
>   As he is tumulate on her right hand.
> And by her daughter Molde we understand
>   Went out the Fournivalls as by their name,
>   As Lovetofts by Dame Molde afore did the same.

We now therefore dismiss them, and in the next chapter shall have to speak of the lordship of Sheffield passing into the hands of a still greater family.

CHAPTER V.

Sheffield under the first five Earls of Shrewsbury.

BEFORE the close of the fourteenth century and before the ancient family of Furnival had become extinct, the artificers of Sheffield had obtained a certain reputation for one article which still continues to be regarded as the staple manufacture of the place. For thus writes our old poet Chaucer, describing the accoutrements and appearance of a miller in the days of Edward III.

> A Shefeld thwytel bare he in his hose,
> Ronde was his face and camysed was his nose.
> *The Reve's Tale.*

A thwytel or whittle, a word not quite gone out of use, was a knife, such as was carried about the person so late as the time of Charles I.[4] by those whose quality did not entitle them to the distinction of a sword. The establishment of this reputation we may pro-bably attribute, in part at least, to the protection and encouragement which Thomas lord Furnival the great grantor seems to have been disposed to extend to his tenantry in Hallamshire: and the fourteenth century was a period when the importance of our commerce and manufactures was beginning to be well understood.

Where great capitals are not employed, great fortunes cannot be made. But there are two facts in the history of Sheffield at the period at which we are arrived, which seem to show that there were persons at Sheffield even in these times who had found the benefit of successful commerce. By the voluntary contributions of the inhabitants three priests were maintained, whose office it was to assist the vicar in the performance of his duties: and property to no incon-

---

[1] Dugdale.
[2] Evidences at Norfolk-house. Yorkshire Bundle X. No. 1.
[3] See Lysons's *Magna Britannia*, vol. v. p. ccxxvii.
[4] Fuller. Worthies of Yorkshire, p. 188.

M

siderable extent had been given by divers of the inhabitants to be appropriated to public purposes, such
as the building and repairing of bridges, the making
of commodious high-ways, and the relief of the poor.
Such donations always bespeak a state of comparative
affluence.

We have no testimony contemporary with that of
Chaucer to the existence of the cutlery manufactory,
or indeed of any other manufactory at Sheffield. But
there can be little doubt that the artificers of this
neighbourhood did not confine themselves to the knife
alone, but that shears, sickles, scythes, and other edged
instruments of steel, for the making of which equal
opportunities were presented, formed at this period,
as they certainly did not long after, articles of manufacture in the smithies and wheels of Hallamshire.
Of the manufacture of arms at Sheffield we have no
direct information. All the articles enumerated in
the ordinances for the government of the cutlers of
Hallamshire, and in the later act of incorporation,
are instruments of peace. And yet in an age when
there was so large a demand for weapons of that description which could be conveniently made along
with what are known to have been among the manufactures of Sheffield, it is probable enough that her
artists might be employed in their fabrication. The
sheafs of arrows which form the device on the seal of
the church-burgesses of Sheffield have been thought to
afford a presumptive argument that the pile or arrow-
head was among the early manufactures of the place.
But I incline rather to regard that device as nothing
more than a rebus on the name of the town, Sheaffield. Perhaps a better presumptive argument of Sheffield having enjoyed a share in the manufacture of
weapons of offence may be collected from the fact,
that Sir John Cut was of a Sheffield family, and probably a native of the place, who had the office of
master of the ordnance in the Tower in the reign of
Henry VII.[1]

It would depose feebly in favour of the literary character of the place at the period of which we are
speaking, could it be proved that the sword of the renowned JOHN TALBOT EARL OF SHREWSBURY was
manufactured in his forges at Sheffield. It was found
in the river Dordon near Bourdeaux, many years after
the death of him who wielded it, bearing this barbarous inscription:

> Sum Talboti M.IIII.C.XLIII.
> pro vincere inimico meo[2].

The sword performed, however, chivalrous deeds when
wielded by his strenuous arm: and few characters claim
more unmixed admiration from those who delight to contemplate deeds of valour and feats of military achievement than this hero, who by his marriage with Maud
the daughter and heir of Thomas Nevil lord Furnival

acquired the lordship of Hallamshire and other great
estates of inheritance. This is the man whom our
great dramatic bard, to whom the ancient families of
England are indebted for having embalmed everlast-
ingly the memory of so many of their progenitors, thus
introduces to the reader at the beginning of one of his
histories:

> '——Valiant Talbot above human thought
> Enacted wonders with his sword and lance:
> Hundreds he sent to hell, and none durst stand him:
> Here there and every where enraged he flew:
> The French exclaimed The Devil was in arms.
> All the whole army stood agazed on him.
> His soldiers spying his undaunted spirit,
> A Talbot! a Talbot! cried out amain,
> And rush'd into the bowels of the battle.'

Into the origin, the antiquity, or even the earlier
history, of the great house of Talbot it is not necessary,
had I the means, to enter in this place into an elaborate investigation. It has claimed the attention of
many of our genealogists. Suffice it to observe that
the inheritance of the great family of Furnival lost
nothing of its consequence by its transference to this
chief of another noble house. Its present representative the right honourable the earl of Shrewsbury is one
of those peers, now become few in number, who can
advance an undisputed and indisputable claim to a
descent in the male line from a person of some distinction contemporary with the Conqueror. Nor has
the family come behind the chief of our nobility in
the splendour of its alliances, or in the honours it has
claimed and received from successive monarchs. Before it became enriched by the marriage with the
heiress of Hallamshire, it had acquired considerable
possessions by marriage with one of the co-heiresses
of the house of Comyn, who brought with her also at
least the heraldrical distinctions of the houses of Valence and Montchensy. The mother of the first earl of
Shrewsbury was also an heiress of one of the baronial
houses of Strange; and at an earlier period the family
had formed an alliance with a daughter of one of the
royal tribes of Wales, whose hereditary insignia they
assumed, relinquishing their own. In the person of
Sir Gilbert Talbot, the elder brother of the first earl
of Shrewsbury, the family had allied itself with the
blood royal of England. Seven earls of this house,
whose descent, families, and alliances the following
table exhibits, enjoyed the lordship of Hallamshire,
and had their usual residence at Sheffield-castle.

Having nothing to add but what is already before
the public to the earlier descents of the family, I have
given them as they stand in an elaborate pedigree compiled by Glover in 1596 for Gilbert earl of Shrewsbury, earl marshal. The genealogical reader may be
glad of the opportunity of comparing them with the
received accounts of the family.

---

[1] See Lodge's *Illustrations of British History*, &c. vol. i. p. 24, &c.
And for the connexion of the Cuts or Cuttes with Sheffield, see the Visitation of London anno 1634. Harl. MSS. 1476, f. 100. In 1434 John
Cutte senior of Fulwood gave to Richard Hugbgate, bailiff of Sheffield,
and his heirs, a messuage in Sheffield lying between the messuage of
the blessed Virgin east and the messuage of the lord west, and south
upon the king's highway; as appears by the deed in the possession of

the church-burgesses of Sheffield. In their collection of evidences appears also the name of one William Cutte 1420. In the same Visitation-
book we find William Isaacson of Sheffield, a name extinct before the
commencement of the parish-register, whose grandson Henry Isaacson,
amanuensis to bishop Andrews, was the learned author of an elaborate
work on Chronology, f. 73. See also *Fasti Oxon.* i. 828.
[2] Camden's *Remains*, 4to. 1629, p. 328.

PEDIGREE of TALBOT EARL of SHREWSBURY.

ARMS.—Gules, a lion rampant within a border engrailed or.
CREST.—On a chapeau gules turned up ermine a lion statant, tail extended, or.
SUPPORTERS.—Two talbots argent.   MOTTO.—Prest d'accomplir.

Sir RICHARD TALBOT knt.

GILBERT TALBOT
ob. 22 Aug. 5 Steph.

Sir RICHARD TALBOT knt.

Sir GILBERT TALBOT knight
ob. 14 Hen. III.

Sir RICHARD TALBOT knt.═ALICE, dau. of Alan Basset baron of Wi-
combe, relict of Hugh de Montacute.

Sir GILBERT TALBOT═GUEDOLINE, dau.   RICHARD TALBOT,
knt. ob. 2 Ed. I. │ of Rhese ap Griffin.   bishop of London elect.

Sir RICHARD TALBOT ═ SARAH, sister of William
knight.   Beauchamp earl of Warwick.

THOMAS TALBOT,   Sir GILBERT TALBOT═ ----   RICHARD TALBOT═JOAN, dau. and co-heir
a clerk. Ob. 14 Oct. lord Talbot. Ob. 24   of Richard's castle, in │ of Hugh de Mortimer
36 Edw. III.   Feb. 20 Edw. III.   right of his wife. │ of Richard's castle.

RICHARD TALBOT═ELIZABETH, second dau. and   JOHN TALBOT═JULIAN, dau. of
ob. 22 Oct. 30 Edw. III. │ co-heir of John Comyn of Bade-   of Richard's │ Roger lord Grey
nach. Ob. 20 Nov. 48 Edw. III. castle. │ of Ruthyn.

GILBERT lord TALBOT═PETRONELLA, dau. of James   JOAN, wife of
ob. 24 April 10 Ric. II. │ earl of Ormond. Ob. 23 Apr.   Sir Nicholas
42 Edw. III.   Poynings knt.

RICHARD lord TALBOT═ANKARET, dau. of John lord Strange of Blackmere, aunt═THOMAS NEVIL═JOAN FURNIVAL, first wife,
aged 26 anno 1387. Ob. │ and heir of Elizabeth countess of Nottingham. Survived lord FURNIVAL, │ only dau. and heir of Wil-
8 Sep. 20 Ric. II.   both her husbands, and died 13 May, 1 Hen. V. 2d husband. │ liam lord Furnival.

JOAN, first wife,	GILBERT, lord	BEATRIX,	MAUD NEVIL,	JOHN TALBOT	MARGARET BEAUCHAMP,	Sir THOMAS TALBOT	ELIZABETH,
dau. and co-heir of	TALBOT and	second wife,	lady FURNI-	lord Talbot, Fur-	second wife, dau. and co-	ob. s. p. 7 Hen. V.	wife of Sir
Thomas of Wood-	Strange of	dau. of John	VAL, first wife,	nival & Strange.	heir of Richard earl of	RICHARD TALBOT,	Thomas
stock, duke of	Blackmere.	King of Por-	lady of Hal-	Created earl of	Warwick. Died 14 June	archbishop of	Barre¹ knt.
Gloucester, young-	Died without	tugal.	lamshire.	Shrewsbury 19	7 Edw. IV. Buried in	Dublin.	MARY, wife
est son of King	male issue 19			Henry VI. Slain	the cathedral church of	Sir WILLIAM TAL-	of Sir Thos.
Edward III.	Oct. 6 Hen. V.			at Chatillon 20	St. Paul, London.	BOT.	Green knt.
				July 1453.			

ANKARET TALBOT,	JOHN, 2d earl of Shrews-	ELIZABETH BUTLER,	Sir CHRISTOPHER TALBOT	JOHN TALBOT═JOAN,	ELIZABETH, wife
only dau. and heir.	bury and knight of the	dau. of James earl of	of Treeton, knt. Slain	viscount Lisle. │ dau. and	of John Mowbray
Died 13 Dec. 1421	Garter. Slain at the battle	Ormond. Ob. 11 Sep.	with his brother at North-	Slain with his │ heir of	duke of Norfolk.
in the 4th year of	of Northampton 10 June	13 Edw. III. anno	ampton.	father at Cha- │ Thomas	ELEANOR, wife of
her age.	1460, and was buried at	1473.	THOMAS TALBOT	tillon. │ Chedder.	lord Sudeley².
	Worksop.		died young.		

JOHN, 3d earl of Shrews-	CATHERINE STAFFORD,	Sir JAMES TALBOT	Sir GILBERT TALBOT	CHRISTOPHER TALBOT	ANN, wife	MARGARET,
bury, born 1448. Died at	dau. of Humphry duke	second son. Died	of Grafton, K.G. third	archdeacon of Chester.	of Sir Henry	wife of Thos.
Coventry 2 June 13 Edw.	of Buckingham. Ob.	11 Sep. 11 Edw.	son, from whom de-	Sir HUMPHRY TALBOT	Vernon of	Chaworth,
IV. and was buried at	26 Dec. 16 Edw. IV.	IV.	scends the present	knight, fifth son.	Haddon	son and heir
Worksop.			earl of Shrewsbury.		knight.	of Sir Wil-
						liam Cha-
						worth knt.

ANN, first wife, dau. of William	GEORGE, 4th earl of Shrewsbury and	ELIZABETH, second wife,	THOMAS TALBOT	ANN TALBOT,
lord Hastings by Catherine his	knight of the Garter. Aged five at the	dau. and co-heir of Sir	died young.	said to have
wife, sister to Richard Nevil the	time of his father's death anno 1473.	Richard Walden of Erith		married Tho-
great earl of Warwick. Buried	Died at Winfield-manor 26 July 1538,	in Kent knight. Died in		mas Butler
at Sheffield.	and was buried in the chapel built by	1567. Buried at Erith.		lord Sudeley.
	himself in the church of Sheffield.			

a   *b*

a   *b*

Generation 1

| HENRY TALBOT eldest son. Died young. Buried in the priory of Calk in Derbyshire. | =MARY, first wife, dau. of Thomas lord Dacre of Gilesland. Died 4 Kal. Apr. 1538. Buried at Sheffield. | =FRANCIS, 5th earl of Shrewsbury and knight of the Garter. Born in Sheffield-castle anno 1500. Died at Sheffield-manour 21 Sep. 1560, and on the 21st of October following was honourably interred at Sheffield. | =GRACE, second wife, dau. of Robert Shakerley of Holme co. Cestr. esq. | JOHN TALBOT. JOHN TALBOT. Both died young. WILLIAM TALBOT, marshal of Ireland. Buried at Sheffield. RICHARD TALBOT. | ANN TALBOT. MARGARET, wife of Henry earl of Cumberland. DOROTHY TALBOT. MARY, wife of Henry earl of Northumberland. ELIZABETH, wife of William lord Dacre of Gillesland. | JOHN TALBOT died young. ANN, wife first of Peter Compton, esq. secondly of William earl of Pembroke. |

Generation 2

| GERTRUDE MANNERS, first wife, dau. of Thos. earl of Rutland. Buried at Sheffield 16 Jan. 1566-7. | =GEORGE, 6th earl of Shrewsbury and knight of the Garter. Died at Sheffield-manour on Wednesday 18th Nov. 1590, and was laid in the family-vault at Sheffield. | =ELIZABETH, second wife, dau. of John Hardwick of Hardwick co. Derby esq. sister and co-heir of James Hardwick of the same place. She was wife first of Robert Barlow of Barlow near Dronfield, esq. 2dly of Sir William Cavendish of Chatsworth, knight, 3dly of Sir William Saint-Loe, knight, and died the widow of George earl of Shrewsbury on 13 Feb. 1607. Buried at Derby. | THOMAS TALBOT, second son, died unmarried. | ANN, wife 1st of John lord Bray, and 2dly of Thomas lord Wharton. |

Generation 3

| FRANCIS lord Talbot, eldest son and heir apparent. Died without issue in his father's lifetime, and was buried at Sheffield 3 Sep.1582. | =ANN HERBERT, dau. of William earl of Pembroke. | GILBERT, 7th earl of Shrewsbury, and knight of the Garter. Born 1553. Died without male issue 8 May 1616, at his house in Broad-st. London, and was laid with his ancestors at Sheffield on the 13th of August following. | =MARY, dau. of Sir William Cavendish of Chatsworth knt. by Elizabeth his wife, afterwards countess of Shrewsbury. Married at Sheffield 9 Feb. 1567-8. Buried there 14th Ap. 1632. | =EDWARD, 8th earl of Shrewsbury. Bapt. at Sheffield 25 Feb. 1561. Died without issue 8 Feb. 1617, (when the title of earl of Shrewsbury, &c. went to a distant branch of the family,) and was buried in Westminster-abbey. | JANE, eldest dau. and co-heir of Cuthbert lord Ogle. The other co-heir married Sir Chas. Cavendish of Welbeck knight. | HENRY TALBOT, of Burton-abbey co. of York esq. fourth son. Bapt. at Sheffield 8 Octob. 1562, and was buried there 14 Feb. 1595-6. | =ELIZABETH, dau. of Sir William Rayner of Overton-co. Hunt. Married 2dly Thos. Holcroft esq. | THOMAS TALBOT died an infant. CATHERINE, wife of William ... broke. MARY, wife of Sir George Savile of Thornhill knt. GRACE, wife of Henry Cavendish esq. eldest son of Sir William Cavendish of Chatsworth knight. |

Generation 4

| GEORGE TALBOT bapt. at Sheffield 10 Feb. 1574-5. Buried there 12 Aug. 1577. | JOHN TALBOT bapt. at Hansworth 2 July 1583. Died young. | MARY TALBOT, eldest dau. and co-heir, married at Sheffield 4 Nov. 1604 to William Herbert earl of Pembroke, and died without issue. | ELIZABETH TALBOT, second dau. and co-heir, wife of Henry Grey earl of Kent, and died without issue in Oct. 1651. | ALETHEA TALBOT, youngest dau. and co-heir, married Thos. Howard earl of Arundel and Surrey, to whom she brought Sheffield and other great estates. | GERTRUDE TALBOT, elder dau. and co-heir, wife of Robert Pierrepoint earl of Kingston. | MARY TALBOT, younger dau. and co-heir, wife of Sir William Armine of Osgodby bart. |

JOHN FIRST, EARL of SHREWSBURY.

The life of this great earl has been often written. Nevertheless it seems as if this work would be imperfect were no account given of the high employments and eminent services of this illustrious lord of Hallamshire.

There are different accounts of the time of his birth, and consequently of his age when he was slain in France. Our best authority seems to be the inquisition taken after the death of his father. That inquisition recites that Richard earl Talbot died in 1396, when his eldest son Gilbert was thirteen years of age. John Talbot could not therefore have been born before 1384, nor could he have completed his seventieth year when he fell near Bourdeaux.

As before related, his mother took to her second husband Thomas Nevil lord Furnival: and John Talbot was doubtless from his earliest years the destined spouse of that nobleman's only daughter by a former wife. Pigot informs us that at sixteen he was sent by his father-in-law on business of importance into Ireland, which was afterwards the scene of many of his public services, and that he acquitted himself 'full manfully.' Lord Furnival died in 1406, when he had been for some time married to the heiress of Hallamshire.

The first instance of Talbot's exercising controul over her Yorkshire possessions occurs in 1410. In that year he presented William Newton to the rectory of Hansworth, who on the 13th of January 1412 was instituted to the rectory of Treeton on the same presentation. That was an age of pluralities, but this was not an instance; for on the 6th of May following John de Aston was instituted to the vacant church of Hansworth[3].

In 1410 he had summons to parliament among the barons by the style of John Talbot lord Furnival, and afterwards by the plainer description of John Talbot of Hallamshire.

Anno 1412 he was appointed lord justice of Ireland. In the next year, which was the first of Henry V., he was a prisoner in the Tower. He was soon released, and made lord lieutenant of Ireland. He was in that country from 1414 to 1419, and gained much reputation by his skilful management of the difficult affairs of that island.

His next public services were in France. But he came rather to share in the triumph than to bear the fatigue. He was not at Agincourt, but bore a part in the siege of some towns which held out against the

---

[1] Sir Thomas Barre.—A knight of this name was interred in the church of Hatfield near Doncaster; probably this brother-in-law of the Shrewsbury. The inscription which was on his monument is a curious specimen of the epitaphial style of the fourteenth and fifteenth centuries.

> Were ley of boddy of Cho. Barr knnpgbt
> Whe biffenfinb the frupnt npgbt
> Of could moneth of Defember
> Us wel we remember
> Gns thufanb fare hunbrib & npn,
> When ye be bcb e faib in grafe
> As ye bafe bon fo fai ye bafe

> O prep for me te brtgenr's fon
> Us A hafe for manp bun
> Nat A map cam ....
> A ben for ....

See Church Notes at Hatfield made before the Reformation, vol. ix. f. 151. of Warburton's Yorkshire Collections. Lansdown MSS. in the British Museum.

[2] This was the lady whose supposed marriage with Edward IV. was alleged by Richard III. as rendering his contract with Elizabeth Grey void. The marriage of Lady Eleanor Butler with that young and pleasure-loving monarch is still among the dubia historica.

[3] Torre's Catalogue of Incumbents.

English, and in 1420 he entered Paris with King Henry in triumph.

In 1419 his elder brother Gilbert lord Talbot died without male issue, whose only daughter and heiress dying two years after in the fourth year of her age, he succeeded to the hereditary honours and possessions of his family.

Henry V. died in 1422, and the new reign opened upon him with fresh honours. He was admitted into the order of the Garter, and enjoyed the special favour of John duke of Bedford regent of France.

In the year 1423 we find a petition exhibited in parliament against the lord Talbot, Sir William Talbot his brother, Hugh Cokesey, and many others of lord Talbot's retinue, from the inhabitants of the hundred of Wormlow in the county of Hereford, complaining of many and divers extortions, oppressions, murders, homicides, '*forciblez et torcenouses ousters de lour terres et tenementz, en amoevauntz ent lour femmes et lovr enfauntz*' by them committed, and praying that they may be bound to keep the peace towards the petitioner. till such time as a commission of oyer and terminer could be sent down among them[1]. And in 1425 we find him entering into a bond of a hundred marks to keep the peace towards Hugh Wenlock[2].

In that year he was again made lord justice of Ireland: but having in the last year of the reign of Henry V. made his name terrible to the French by his valorous deeds, his services were again required in that quarter, and in 1428 the command was intrusted to him of the whole English army then in France[3]. Here he had no common enemy with whom to contend: and the Maid of Orleans was in the field when at Patay his army was routed, and he himself taken prisoner. This was in 1429.

Instantly every engine was set to work to effect his release. 'Unreasonable and importable raunceon' was demanded. Of course his freeholders and tenants would be called upon for the usual aid; but there seems to have been something of the nature of a private subscription through the kingdom, for the redemption of a captive who was thought so great a national loss. ' 1429 Tho. Paynell, mayor. Hit is to have in mynd that for the rawnsome of the lorde Talbote the gode men of the citie of Coventrie followyng hav gyven to his rawnsome with all ther gode hertes.' To this in some public accompts of the city of Coventry is appended a list of twenty-seven persons, with the sums subscribed by each, amounting in the whole to thirteen pounds six shillings and eightpence[4]. And the duke of Gloucester sent instructions to the duke of Bedford regent of France, that if a French knight, Sir William Barbazan, could be released without offence to the duke of Burgundy, he should be offered in exchange for the lord Talbot; and if that offer was not accepted, as much should be obtained for his ransom as possible, and that sum given to the lord Talbot towards the sum demanded for his release[5]. He was not however set at liberty till 1432 or 1433, when he was exchanged for Ambrose de Lore and a large sum of money. His detention at this period

saved him from any participation in the least justifiable act of the administration of his friend the regent,—the putting to death a young, beautiful, and patriotic female on charges the most vague and unfounded.

He was no sooner released than he was in arms. He joined the duke of Bedford at Paris, and he showed himself the most active and able of the English generals in the campaigns of several successive years. Partial successes and general losses were what the English gained in the protracted struggle. On the 20th of May 1442 his services of many years were rewarded by a patent for the title of earl of Shrewsbury; a title which he chose in consequence of having a considerable estate within the county of Salop, and of a descent from the Montgomerys, ancient earls of that town.

Anno 1446 he was again lord lieutenant of Ireland, and had the title of earl of Wexford and Waterford.

But he soon returned to France, where the affairs of the English were fast declining. The duke of Burgundy had left our interest. We had few towns remaining. Our army small. Even the valour and the name of Talbot could do little. He surrendered to the king of France, and engaged not to bear arms against him for a year. It has escaped preceding biographers of this great English captain, that William of Worcester says he employed part of that interval in a journey to Rome[6].

His next public services were in Guienne. There the English made their last struggle to retain possession of France. In that struggle Talbot lost his life. The battle was fought at Châtillon on the Dordon. He contended with unequal numbers, and fell on the 20th day of July 1453, his son John Talbot dying with him.

One can scarcely read the accounts of the long and finally unsuccessful war which the English waged in France during the minority of Henry VI., without observing how unfortunate for England was the success which attended our arms on the field of Agincourt. A defeat at that period would in all probability have decided the contest: while success could produce only the effects which did ensue, a prodigious waste of human life and human comfort, and a temporary occupation of a neighbouring kingdom in defiance at once of the claims of legitimacy and the wishes of the people. There is a tradition, or a rumour which pretends to the character of a tradition, on which I should place more reliance were there less of *apparent* probability attending it. It is said that the small army with which the earl landed at Bourdeaux contained many men who were raised among his tenantry at Sheffield and its neighbourhood; and that these formed the body-guard of their aged and valiant chief; and were so entirely cut off, that throughout the circuit of Hallamshire there was not a family which had not a private grief originating in the disaster of that fatal day which filled the castle of Sheffield with the tones of loud lamentation.

Anstis has collected from some contemporary chronicle a very picturesque circumstance. After the battle, the earl's herald went to seek the body of his

---

[1] Rolls of Parliament, vol. iv. p. 254.
[2] Id. vol. iv. p. 275.
[3] The original patent, bearing date 6 Henry VI. is now among the Evidences at Norfolk-house. Patents, Bundle A. No. 1. The style of

his office was 'Governor and lieutenant-general of the kingdom of France and dutchy of Normandy.'
[4] *Gent. Mag.* vol. lxi. p. 999. [5] Rolls of Parliament, vol. iv. p. 338.
[6] Annales. Anno 1449. Hearne's *Liber Niger*, p. 469.

N

master: and when he found it he kissed it, and broke out into these compassionate and dutiful expressions: 'Alas! it is you: I pray God pardon all your misdoings. I have been your officer of arms forty years or more. It is time I should surrender it to you.' And while the tears trickled plentifully down his cheek, he disrobed himself of his coat of arms and flung it over his master's body.

The earl made his will at Portsmouth on the first of·September 1452, just before he embarked. He directed that his body should be interred in the parish-church to which Blackmere (his mother's estate of inheritance) belonged, Whitchurch in Shropshire, on the right side of the chancel; and that a chapel of our Lady and Saint George should be made, and a college be founded of the annual value of forty pounds. Or else to be buried in the college of Warwick, in the new chapel there, which Richard earl of Warwick his father-in-law had lately founded, 'should he ever attain as he ought the honour of Warwick.'

The title of Warwick was reserved for the house of Nevil. The earl's body was buried in France; and many years after was brought to England by his grandson Sir Gilbert Talbot, and laid according to his directions in the church of Whitchurch. He also placed there a monument bearing his effigies, of which but a small portion has outlasted the frequent reparations and indeed re-edification of the church. Of the inscription no trace remains.

Orate pro anima prænobilis Domini, Domini Johannis Talbot, quondam Comitis Salopiæ, Domini Furnival, Domini Verdon, Domini Strange de Blackmere, et Marescalli Franciæ: Qui obiit in bello apud Burdews VII. Julii M.CCCC.LIII.

Pigot's verses seem to rise with the subject:

.' Which Sir John Talbote, first Sir John Fournivall,
    Was moste worthie warriour we rede of all.

For by his knighthode and his chivalrye
    A knight of the Garter first he was made;
And of king Henry, first erle Scrovesberye.
    To which Sir John his sone succession hade,
    And his noble successors now therto sade:
God give them good speede in their progresse,
And Heaven at their ende, both more and lesse.

The live to report of this foresaid lorde
    How manly he was, and full chivalrose;
What deedes that he did I cannot by worde
    Make rehersal by meter ne prose;
    How manly, how true, and how famose
In Ireland, France, Normandy, Gyon and Gascone,
His pere so long renyng I rede of none.

When he was no more but XVI. yere of age
    By Sir Thomas Nevill Lord Fournivall
He was sent to Ireland, and there right sage
    He quyt him full manfully in that land over all:
    Both castles and townes he gat there royall.
Lord Fournivall was [he] by the said Nevills daughter,
And after Lord Talbot by his progenitor.

Which while he reigned was most knight
    That was in the realme here many yere,
Most dughty of hand and fereseest in fight,
    Most drede of all other with French men of werre
In Ireland, France, Gyon; whose soule God absolve
And bringe to that blyss that will not dissolve.'

Pigot was not a man to confer immortality. But in the divine language of Shakspeare he must live for ever. 'How would it have joyed brave Talbot,' exclaims Nash, 'the terror of the French, to thinke that after he had lyen two hundred yeare in his toomb, he should triumph again on the stage; and have his bones new embalmed with the tears of ten thousand spectators at least, who in the tragedian that represents his person, imagine they behold him fresh bleeding[1].'

There is a portrait of this noble earl in the gallery at Castle-Ashby the seat of the marquis of Northampton, and also of his second lady the Lady Margaret Beau-champ. These were engraved for Pennant's Journey from Chester to London. There is another portrait resembling this in the College of Arms, which is supposed to have formerly hung near the monument of his countess in the old cathedral church of St. Paul's London. Mr. Lodge had this engraved for his Illustrations of British History, &c. The descendants of the second marriage of the earl inherited honours through their mother, a co-heir of the house of·Beauchamp.

By an inquisition taken after the death of this great earl, it was found that he died seised, inter alia, of the castle and manor of Sheffield, and the manors of Treeton and Whiston in the county of York; and that John earl of Shrewsbury was his son and heir, and then forty years old and upwards.

JOHN SECOND EARL of SHREWSBURY.

The second earl of Shrewsbury was a less conspicuous character than his father: but his life was scarcely less disturbed by the turmoil of that unsettled age. We scarcely hear of him but in reference to some military exploit. He was knighted at Leicester in 1426, and was with his father both in France and Ireland. In the 35th of Henry VI. anno 1456, he was made lord treasurer of England. This was while the contentions of the two rival houses were at their height. To the house of Lancaster he was ever a faithful adherent, and he lost his life in its cause; being slain at the battle of Northampton on the 10th of July 1460, having been seven years earl. At the same time perished his brother Sir Christopher Talbot who resided at Treeton, and of whom we have this notice in the Clause Rolls 20 Henry VI.: that he and others recognise they owe to Geffery Lowther esquire two hundred pounds, upon condition of paying forty-four pounds yearly issuing out of the manors of Hansworth, Bramley, and Attercliffe, and out of lands in Treeton, Harthill, and Woodhall in the county of York, and of six acres of meadow in Beighton in the county of Derby, and out of the office of the bailywick of Stain-cross in the county of York[2]. This person, who is perhaps the original of the monumental effigies in the church of Treeton, commonly called 'earl Gilbert,' is thus mentioned in one of the Paston Letters. 'Moreou[r] there is j kome in to Enlond a knyght out of Spayne, wyth a kercheff of plesunce i wrapped aboute hys arme, the qwych knyght wyl renne a cours wyth a sharpe spere for his sou'eyn lady sake qwom other S[r] Ric Wodvyle or S[r] Xpofore Talbot shall delyv' to

---

[1] ' Pierce Penilesse his Supplication to the Diuell,' 4to, 1592, as quoted in the Essay on the Learning of Shakspeare, p. 88, 3d edit. 1789.

I have omitted one short parenthesis which much injures the effect of this fine passage.   [2] Dods. MSS. M. 14. Harl. 801. Bramley.

the wyrchip of Englond and of hem selff be Goddes grace[1].'

The earl was interred at Worksop; and on his monument was the following inscription, which probably was not inscribed till the adherents of the house of Lancaster saw the crown placed upon the head of the earl of Richmond.

Sepulchrum magnanimi atque præpotentis Domini, Domini Johannis de Talbot comitis Salopiæ secundi, ex regio sanguine ducentis originem. Qui Henrico regi fidissimus, bello apud Northamptoniam gesto, ante signa strenue pugnans, honesta morte occidit die decimo Julii Anno Domini nostri Jesu Christi 1460: cujus animæ propitietur Deus. Amen.

Salopiæ comitis lapis hic tegit ossa Johannis,
    Cui nihil antiquius quam fuit alma fides:
Hic ut serviret regi tormenta subivit
    Intrepidus ferri, sanguineamque necem:
Ergo licet parvum condat sua viscera saxum,
    Virtus Angligenum lustrat in omne solum.

The widow of this earl[2], who was a daughter of the earl of Ormond, one of the few learned peers of his age, had a strong interest in Hallamshire. She had in dowry the castle and lordship of Sheffield with its members, and also the manors of Southal, Bradfield, Ecclesfield, Hallifield, Granow, Whiston, and Treeton, (so they are enumerated by Dugdale from an inquisition,) certain property at Rotherham, and the house in London called Furnival's Inn. These she enjoyed during the greater portion of the life of her son, dying on the Saturday next following the nativity of the Blessed Virgin, 13 Edw. IV. anno 1473.

JOHN THIRD EARL of SHREWSBURY.

The third earl was born on the vigil of Saint Lucy virgin and martyr, according to the good old mode of dating, in the year 1448: and if we may believe the register of Worksop, his birth was not unattended by prodigies: for in the hour of his birth a certain simple canon of that house heard a voice which said—

*Gloria in excelsis
Deo et angelis[3].*

He was a very different character from his father and grandfather. He was more devoted to literature and the muses, than to politics and arms. A French poem composed by him and addressed to Margaret of Anjou gives him a claim to rank with the noble authors[4]. Leland, who knew those that knew him, calls him rather contemptuously ' a good symple manne:' but neither living, dying, nor after death had he reason to envy the hero whose name was used to still the babes of France, and on whose steps 'lean famine, quartering steel, and climbing fire,' were ever attendant. But in those days perfect neutrality was impossible. When scarcely fourteen he was at the second battle of Saint Albans, and was knighted by Prince Edward. Soon

after a quarrel arising among his own party, he ' loged hym at y[e] hospitall of Seynt James besides the Mews be the lord Cromwells desire for his sauf gurd[5].' He was not attainted with the other Lancastrian lords, and in 1465, though much under age, had livery of his lands. In 1470 the attachment of the Talbots to the house of Lancaster was again manifested, and he appeared with the earl of Warwick in favour of King Henry. When the opposite party finally prevailed, he was admitted by King Edward to some employments more honourable than important; but he did not hold them long, for he died at Coventry where he was on a journey, on the Saturday next after the feast of Saint John the Baptist anno 1473, aged twenty-five: ' *non sine suspicione veneni*,' says Leland ; a remark probably unworthy any regard. The remains of this earl thus cut off *florente ævo*, and who would probably have presented claims upon the admiration of posterity of a less dubious character than those of his more renowned grandfather, had his life been extended through the peaceable reign of the seventh Henry, were interred in the Lady-chapel at Worksop, but no mention is made of any monument having been erected to perpetuate his memory. By Catherine his wife, daughter of Humphry Stafford duke of Buckingham, who fell at Northampton, and sister to that Henry duke of Buckingham who was beheaded at Salisbury in the time of Richard III., he had two sons; George who succeeded him, and Thomas who died young. Dugdale and after him most of our later genealogists add a daughter who married Thomas Boteler lord Sudeley. No such match appears in Glover's pedigree, nor is any Thomas Boteler lord Sudeley to be found in Dugdale's own account of that family, contemporary with a daughter of the third earl of Shrewsbury.

' This John,' saith Leland, ' had emong his brethren one caullid Gilbert Talbot, after a knight of fame .... James his brother dyed of strips taken at Northampton feelde; but he cam first to Shiffenol in Shrobbshire a 2 miles from Tonge, where the erles of Shrobbesburye had a manar place of tymbar and a parke. Syr Christopher persone of Whitechurche was the 4. Sir Humfrey Talbot knyght was the 5. He usyd Calays. Anne sistar to the aforesayde 5 britherne by the erle was maried to Sir Henry Verney of Thonge, where she is buried in the college wth hir husband. Margaret dowghtar to the erle and sistar to the aforesayde 5 brithern was wyfe to Chawort a gentleman of Derbyshire[6].'

Sir Gilbert Talbot was governor of Calais, a knight of the Garter, and much trusted and employed by Henry VII. and Henry VIII. He continued the line of Talbot, and his descendants became earls of Shrewsbury when the male issue of his eldest brother the

[1] Paston Letters, vol. i. p. 6.
[2] There is a singular self-contradiction in the Baronage relating to a supposed first marriage of the second earl of Shrewsbury. In the text he is said to have taken to his first wife Catherine one of the daughters and heirs of Sir Edward Burnell, son of Hugh lord Burnell: but in the accompanying sheet-pedigree ' *Catherina filia et hæres Tho. Burnel mil.*' From the text Collins has copied, and after him many others. But Dugdale in his account of the Burnells takes no notice of any such marriage. He tells us, on the authority of good record, that Sir Edward Burnell died in the life-time of his father, leaving issue three daughters, who were heirs to their grandfather Hugh lord Burnell ; namely, Joyce wife of Thomas Erdington junior, aged 24, Margery wife of Edmund Hungerford, and Catherine aged 14 anno 8 Henry IV., which Catherine afterwards married Sir John Radcliffe knight.—*Baronage*, ii. p. 62. This

Sir John Radcliffe was her husband in the life-time of the earl of Shrewsbury. Glover's pedigree takes no notice of any first wife of the earl; neither do Mill, Brooke, nor Vincent.
[3] *Mon. Ang.* vol. ii. p. 939. ' *Iste Dominus Johannes Talbot comes Salopiæ tertius, natus fuit in vigiliâ S. Luciæ virginis et martyris, anno Domini millesimo quadringentesimo quadragesimo octavo. In horâ cujus ortûs nativitatisque, quidam simplex canonicus audivit vocem per aures suas procedentem et dicentem, Gloria in excelsis, Deo et angelis.*'
[4] A copy of it was in possession of Mr. Horace Walpole, who designed to publish it in his *Miscellaneous Antiquities*. See *Monthly Magazine* for July 1798.
[5] Paston Letters, vol. i. p. 110.
[6] Itinerary, vol. vii. p. 9.

third earl became extinct. From him the present earl of Shrewsbury derives his descent.—We should I suppose in the above extract from Leland, for Northampton read Tewksbury. Sir James Talbot was not more than eight years old when the battle of Northampton was fought. He was the last sacrifice which the family made to their zeal for the Lancastrian succession. Glover says she died on the 2d of September 11 Edw. IV. We have no account of him in Dugdale or the Peerages.—Sir Humphry Talbot, who is styled marshal of Calais, had a confirmation from Richard III. of an annuity of forty pounds during the nonage of George earl of Shrewsbury, and also a license for shipping a hundred tuns of wine[1].—Sir Henry Vernon was of Haddon as well as of Tong, the fine old seat of the dukes of Rutland, near Bakewell in Derbyshire. William of Worcester has preserved the memory of one of those private feuds so common at the period of which we are speaking, in which one of the Vernons lost his life:—'*Anno* 1467 *mense Novembris factum est horribile murdrum in quadam parte juxta Derby, ubi gentes domini de Grey Codnore interfecerunt Vernone armigerum, pro quâ causâ et aliis, dominus rex ordinavit unum oiere et determinere in comitatu Derby. Circa regem favebant dominum Grey: et Dux Clarentiæ favebat dominum comitem Salopie et Vernone*[2].'

In the long contentions between the houses of York and Lancaster it does not appear from our historians that Hallamshire was the scene of any military operations. Yet we must suppose that the castle of Sheffield, built for defence, and commanding a considerable tract of country, must have been held by its Lancastrian possessors as a fortress for King Henry. The old annalist just quoted mentions a skirmish at Worksop, in which a party of Yorkists were cut off by the army of the duke of Somerset in December 1460[3], a few days before the battle of Wakefield: and the following letter relating to these times and this neighbourhood will be perused with interest. The person whom the writer calls ' my lorde' was John Mowbray duke of Norfolk, who married a daughter of the first Talbot earl of Shrewsbury. The place called Estrefeld is probably Chesterfield.

'To my Cosyn J. Paston

THE king camme to Granth'm and ther taried thoresday all day and ther was headed Sᵣ Thom's Dalalaunde and on John Neille a greate Capteyn and upon yᵉ monday next aftᵣ yᵃᵗ at Dancastr and yᵉʳ was headed Sᵣ Robert Wellys and a nother greate Capteyn and yᵃⁿ yᵉ king hadde warde yᵃᵗ the Duk of Clarence and yᵉ Erle of Warwick was att Esterfeld xx mile from Dancastre And uppou yᵉ Tewesday att ix of yᵉ bell yᵉ king toke yᵉ feld and mustered his people and itt was seid yᵃᵗ wer neuᵗ seyn in Inglond so many goodly men and so well arreiyed in a feld and my Lord was whorsshupfully accompanyed no Lord yᵉʳ so well wherfor yᵉ king gaffe my Lord a greate

thanke and yᵃⁿ the Duk of Clarence and yᵉ Erle of Warwik harde yᵃᵗ yᵉ king was comyng to yᵉᵐ warde in contynent yᵉʳʸ dep'ted and wente to Manchestᵣ' in Lancasshire hopyng to have hadde helpe and socour of yᵉ Lord Stanley butt in concluciõn yᵉʳ yᵉʳʸ hadde litill favor as itt was enformed yᵉ king and so men sayn yᵉʳʸ wente westward and som men demen to London And whan yᵉ king harde yᵉʳʸ wer dep'ted and gon he went to York and came yeder yᵉ Thoresday next aft'r and yᵉʳ camme into hym all yᵉ Gentilmen of yᵉ Shire and uppon our Lady day made Percy Erle of Northumb'land and he yᵃᵗ was Erle affore Markeys Muntakew and yᵉ king is p'posed to come southwarde God send hym god spede.

Writen yᵉ xxvij day of March.   for trowyth[4].'

GEORGE FOURTH EARL OF SHREWSBURY.

This nobleman was born at Shiffnal in 1468[5], and was only four years of age at the death of his father. Including his minority he was lord of Sheffield and Hallamshire seventy years.

He was in ward to William lord Hastings, with whose name is almost invariably connected the epithets ' amiable and unfortunate:' and not without reason; for his life was sacrificed to the jealousy of a bad man, and in his whole deportment true nobility was exhibited tempered with gentleness[6]. A marriage was usually the consequence of a wardship. Lord Hastings made his will on the 21st of June 1480; in which he directs that in case the earl his ward, who had married Ann his daughter, should die before the marriage was consummated, Thomas Talbot, brother of the said earl, should take her to wife, if the law of the church would allow[7]. The wardship of the young earl was continued to the widow of lord Hastings. This lady was sister to Richard Nevil earl of Warwick, ' that setter-up and puller-down of kings,' and by her last will gave to her ward and son-in-law then of full age ' a cope of cloth of gold of white damaske, with torpheus of cloth of gold and velvet upon velvet. Also a vestment of purpure velvet with a crucifix and image of Saint Peter and Saint John embroidered.'. She also left to my lady of Shrewsbury ' a cope with lillyes embroidered, and that oon with the image of the Trinity, with a frontaill for an altar[8].'

When the earl of Richmond appeared at the head of a considerable body of troops, the hereditary attachment of the house of Talbot to the Lancastrian succession again manifested itself; and Sir Gilbert Talbot, uncle to the young earl, met him at Newport with a large force principally raised among the family tenantry[9], was with him at Bosworth, and contributed mainly to decide the fortune of the day. The young earl appeared himself in person at the battle of Stoke, and in 5 Hen. VII. had a command in the small army which was sent in aid of Maximilian the emperor against Charles king of France.

Times of tranquillity succeeded[10]: and availing him-

[1] Harl. MSS. 433. 611 & 1005.
[2] Annales, Hearne's *Liber Niger, &c.* p. 512.
[3] William of Worcester. Hearne's *Liber Niger, &c.* p. 484.
[4] Paston Letters, vol. ii. p. 36—38. The date is 1470.
[5] Leland's *Itinerary*, vol. vii. p. 9.
[6] Sir John Fenn justly observes, that we have a proof of the amiable and humane disposition of lord Hastings in the following passage of one of his letters to his lieutenant-governors of Calais. ' And I preye you to reco'msunde me to my lady Howard, my lady Bourgchier and all othr' ladies and gentilwomen of the saide towne. And in like wise to the Mayr' Lieuten' and felaship of the staple, *my felawes the souldeo's* and all othr' suche as ye shal seme gode. And oure Lord sende you yo' desirs.' Paston Letters, No. liii.
[7] *Baronage*, vol. i. p. 585.
[8] Harl. MSS. 4774. f. 54—59.

[9] Speed, p. 931.
[10] There was however a formidable insurrection in Yorkshire in 1489, two years after the battle of Stoke. The earl of Northumberland was assaulted and put to death at his house called Cock-lodge near Thirske. The rebels then marched southward under the command of Sir John Egremont and John a Chambre. They were met by the king's army under the command of the earl of Surrey, the earl of Shrewsbury, and others, and dispersed. The king followed in person, and hung John a Chambre and twelve others; Sir John Egremont escaping to the duchess of Burgundy. It is, I apprehend, a point unsettled in the history and topography of Yorkshire, *where* the royal and the rebel army encountered. In the *History of Pontefract*, p. 140, the encounter is said to have taken place at Ackworth. But it appears that the fight at Ackworth was not till the year after the suppression of Egremont's rising; and in another Yorkshire insurrection of which I have met with no notice either in our

self of his overflowing coffers, the usual consequence of a long minority, the earl indulged to a great extent in what seems to have been his favourite amusement—building. Hitherto the lords of Hallamshire had no mansion at Sheffield but the castle, or at most only a small lodge in their park. The castle though spacious, magnificent, and strong, was not, on several accounts, the most desirable of residences in times of perfect peace. This earl therefore made great additions to the lodge in the centre of his park, about two miles from the castle and the town of Sheffield, or raised there from its foundations a noble country-residence, a work which he completed early in the reign of Henry VIII. This edifice was sometimes called the Lodge, and sometimes Sheffield-manour, a name which its ruins (spread over two or three acres of ground) still bear. The site he chose for it was airy and elevated, and its towers rising above the woods in which it was embosomed, commanded a glorious prospect of the well cultivated and inhabited country around, a great portion of which acknowledged him for its lord. The town of Sheffield was not in sight; and unintersected as was the park in those days by any public road, it must have been most conveniently situated as a place for retirement and repose. It was furnished in a style of magnificence correspondent to the rank of its noble inhabitant[1], and seems to have been always a favourite residence of this earl, and, afterwards of others of his family. Some drew here their first breath, and some their last.

Early in the reign of Henry VIII., the earl being then a knight of the Garter was named of the privy-council, and made lord-steward of the household. In 1513 he commanded the van of the English army at the siege of Therouenne. In 1516 he was residing at Sheffield; and we find him in one of his letters complaining of a sickness in his family 'both here,' that is at the manour, 'and in the town[2].' In the next year he was appointed to attend on Margaret queen of Scotland, the king's sister, and to conduct her on her return home from York to Newborough. In the same year his cousin-german the duke of Buckingham proposed to strengthen the alliance between the houses of Talbot and Stafford by a double marriage; a proposal which was negatived by the earl[3], who had soon after the mortification of being nominated one of the peers who were to try that much injured nobleman. He fell, as is well known, a victim to the intrigues of Wolsey. In June 1520 the earl of Shrewsbury was present at the memorable interview between the kings of England and France in the *Champ de drap d'or; and in the fourteenth of Henry VIII., being then lieutenant-general of the north, he made some inroads into Scotland.

Wolsey was at this time in the zenith of his power. It is impossible to walk in the quadrangles of Christ-church, and not feel respect for the man to whose love of learning so princely an establishment owes its origin. But he was ever capricious, haughty, and insolent, carrying himself proudly to the ancient nobility, whom if he could not reconcile to his elevation, he might have soothed into neutrality by a more conciliatory behaviour. But Wolsey was not one of those who possessed of the substance can despise the shadow of authority. He was perpetually offering petty insults to the nobility, and indeed to every man whose hopes or fears led him into his presence. Most amusing is the exhibition which Sir Thomas Allen, one of the earl of Shrewsbury's chaplains, draws of the cardinal's behaviour to suitors.

'Please it yo[r] Lordship to be adv'tised, upon Mondey was

---

general or local historians. This arose in the west, the former in the north. Perhaps the only memorial of the second Yorkshire insurrection in the reign of Henry VII. is to be found in the curious and exact account of the life of the above-mentioned earl of Surrey, which was 'depensuld upon a table, and fixed to his funerall monument' at Thetford in Norfolk. When it is related that he was sent by the king to suppress those rebels by whom the earl of Northumberland was slain, it is added, 'And for the synguler truste that the kynge had to the seid erle, and the activyte that he saw in hym, he lefte hym in the north, and made hym hys Lyvetenaunt generall from Trent northward, and warden of the est and myddle marches of Englond, ageynst Scotlond, and justice of the forests from Trent northward, and there he contynued x yeres; and kepte the countrey in peace with policy, and many paynes takyng withoute which yt wold nat have been, for that the countrey had ben so lately ponyshed, and nat withoute desert, And thus he dide the hoole tyme of x yere, savyng in the second yere of his beyng, ther was an insurrection in the west part of the countrey, with whome the seid erle with the helpe of the kyngs true subgetts fought in the feld, and subdued them at Abworth besides Pomfrett; And besides dyvers of them that were slayne in the feld he toke the capytaynes and put them to execucion, and the residue he sued to the kyngs highnes for ther pardones, whiche he obteyned, and wanne therby the favor of the countrey.' Weever's *Ancient Funerall Monuments*, p. 835.

[1] We find him expending no less than two hundred and forty crowns of the sun for hangings to be bought at Tournay, doubtless for this house, 1516. Letter of the Earl to Sir Thomas Allen. Lodge's *Illustrations of British History*, &c. i. 14.—We are now arrived within the range of a series of the correspondence of the earls of Shrewsbury. And here it seems necessary that we should anticipate, in order to give the reader some account of a large collection of letters of which much use will be made in the remainder of the present, and the whole of the next chapter.—When the castle of Sheffield was dismantled and destroyed after the Civil Wars, the papers in the muniment-room were removed to the manour, where an inhabitant was still kept up, and which was occasionally visited by its noble owner. There they lay for some years exposed to much injury from wet, and the depredations of mice, those tiny but potent foes of antiquarianism. In this state they were found by Dr. Nathaniel Johnston, a physician of Pontefract and a very diligent student and collector. He made a report of their state to Henry Howard earl of Norwich, who had the management of the affairs of the family during the incapacity of Thomas duke of Norfolk, and who immediately entered upon measures for their better preservation. The business was

committed to the care of Dr. Johnston, who put in order and bound in fifteen volumes about six thousand original letters of the 4th, 5th, 6th, and 7th earls of Shrewsbury, and their families. These volumes the earl at the suggestion of Dr. Johnston presented to the College of Arms, and in the library of that learned body they still remain. This was done between the years 1671 and 1677. Many papers which were at that time thought of inferior importance, Dr. Johnston was allowed to retain for his own use: and having made copies of those which were deposited in the Herald's College, from the whole he compiled a history of the Lovetots, Furnivals, and Talbots, which he seems to have had the intention of giving to the public. He speaks of it as being finished and in four volumes, in a dedication designed for the work to the marquis of Halifax, dated 8 February 1693-4, which is preserved in Harl. MSS. No. 6158. It appears from Gough's *Anecdotes of British Topography* that Dr. Johnston's account of the Talbots came into the library of that gentleman, but it did not find its way with others of Mr. Gough's manuscripts into the Bodleian. By far the greatest portion of Dr. Johnston's collection of Talbot papers, original and transcribed, came into the possession of Richard Frank of Campsal, esquire, and it is supposed that they are now in the library at Campsal.

It remains to take some notice of the use which has been made of the collection of letters preserved in the Heralds College. Of these it appears that Hopkinson of Loft-house, a friend of Dr. Johnston and like him a diligent collector of Yorkshire history, made many transcripts; and possibly also from other papers which are not included in those volumes. These transcripts are now in the library of Miss Currer.—Strype was allowed to take copies of many of them, of which he has made great use in his historical works.—And lastly, Edmund Lodge esquire, Lancaster herald-at-arms, published many of the most interesting and important, in a work which is one of the most valuable contributions that has been made to our collection of original documents relating to the age of the Tudors since the publication of the Burleigh Papers: *Illustrations of British History, Biography, and Manners*, &c., 3 volumes, quarto, 1791. —This is the collection to which frequent reference will now be made under the description of TALBOT PAPERS; and thus much it seemed proper to state respecting them in this place. But in respect of those letters which are published in the *Illustrations*, I shall content myself with referring to that work, which in the material point of accuracy of transcription equals, if it does not surpass, every thing of the kind that has hitherto been given to the public.

[2] Lodge, vol. i. p. 15.

[3] Talbot Papers, vol. P. f. 11.

O

ſevenyght laſt paſt *I del*^d yor l^{re}, w^t the examinacōns, to my Lord Cardinall at Gilford, whereas he cōmandit me to wayte upon hym to the Court, and I ſhulde have p'ceps on them. The ſame tyme I ſhewed unto hym they wer but poor men, and did the treſpas of inocency, & of no malice, pretending to have byn their ryth   I followed hym to the Court, & ther gaffe attendāce, & could have no anſuer. Upon Friday laſt he cam from thens to Hampton Court, wher he lyeth: the *day* after I beſogth is G'ce I mygth knowe his pleaſure: I could have no anſuer *then.* Upon Mondey laſt, as he walked in the p'ke at Hampton Court, I beſogth hym I mygth knowe if he wold comand me any ſyrvyce; he was not *pleaſed* w^t me that I ſpeke to hym: The Sondey before I de-liv'ed the l^{re} unto him wiche Raufe Leche brogth; I can have no anſuer to noder of bothe. He that ſhalbe a ſut^r unto hym may have no oder beſynes but giff attendaunce upon his plea-ſure: He that ſhall ſo do is nedefull to be a wyſer man ner I am. I ſaw no better remedy, but com w^tout anſuer to p'ſue ſuche *thinges* yn London as yor Lordſhip cōmands to be don, except I wold have *don* as my Lord Dacre's s'rvand dothe; wiche cam w^t l^{res} for the Kyng is G'ce v moneths ſens, and yet have no anſuer; and anoder, s'vand of the *Dep.* of Cales, yn like wiſe, wiche cam befor he rode to Walayngh'm: I her that he anſuered them, If ye be not content to tary my leſer dep't when ye wyll. This is trouthe, I had lev^r yor Lord-ſhip cōmandit me to   then to delyv^r unto hym l^{res}, & bryng anſuer of the ſame. When he walkes in the p'ke he woll ſuffr no ſutor to com nye unto hym, but cōmands hym a way as far as a man woll ſhoote an arro^t.'

Pride goeth before deſtruction. In the year 1530 the natural re-action of ſuch behaviour manifeſted it-ſelf: and the cardinal's ruin was completed. Sheffield was peculiarly a witneſs of his humiliation. The earl of Northumberland, the earl of Shrewſbury's ſon-in-law, a nobleman whom he had injured in the niceſt point, was ſent to arreſt the cardinal at Cawood, and had inſtructions to deliver him into the cuſtody of the earl of Shrewſbury. They left Cawood on Sunday November 6, and came that evening to Pontefract; the next day to Doncaſter; and on Tueſday Novem-ber 8 arrived at Sheffield. He was received not at the caſtle, but at the manour, with all poſſible courte-ouſneſs, the earl, his counteſs, and the whole houſe-hold ſtanding without the gates to give him welcome: and nothing was wanting on the earl's part to induce the cardinal to regard himſelf as a voluntary gueſt rather than a priſoner. He remained at Sheffield ſix-teen or eighteen days in a ſtate of deep dejection. Of the occurrences of thoſe days, and the firſt ſymptoms of that diſorder of which he died at Leiceſter on the fourth day after he left Sheffield, we have a minute and curious account in the memoirs of the cardinal's life, left as a teſtimony of gratitude and affection by George Cavendiſh, his gentleman-uſher. It would be to do injuſtice to the writer's ſimple, lively, and affecting narrative, to attempt to clothe his facts in other lan-guage than his own. I have followed the manuſcript of Cavendiſh's work which is in the library of the dean and chapter of York.

'The next daye my Lorde removed towarde Dan-keſter, and came into the towne by torchelight; the which was his deſier becauſe of the people. Yet not-withſtandinge the people wer aſſembled, and cried out, 'God ſave your grace, God ſave your grace, my good Lorde Cardinall;' runninge before him with candles in their handes; who cauſed me to ride by his ſide, to ſhadowe him from the people, and yet they perceaved him, and lamented his misfortune, curſinge his accuſors.

And thus they brought him to the Blacke Fryers with-in the whiche he was lodged. And the next daye we removed and rode to Sheffeilde parke; where my Lorde of Shrewſburye laye within the lodge, the people all the waye thetherwarde ſtill lamentinge him, cryinge as they did before. And when we came into the parke of Sheffeilde, nighe to the lodge, my Lorde of Shrewſ-burye with my Ladie, and a traine of gentlewomen and all other his gentlemen and ſervaunts, ſtode with-out the gates to attend my Lordes cominge to receave him. At whoſe alightinge the earle receaved him with muche honour and embraced my Lorde ſayeinge theſe wordes: 'My Lorde,' quoth he, 'your grace is moſte hartelye welcome unto me, and I ame glade to ſee you here in my poore lodge, where I have longe deſiered to ſee you, and muche more gladder if ye hadd come after another ſorte.' 'Ah my gentle Lorde of Shrewſ-burie,' q^d my Lorde, 'I hartelie thanke youe, And al-though I have cauſe to lament, yet as a faithfull harte maye I doe reioyce, that my chaunce is to come into the cuſtodie of ſo noble a perſon, whoſe approved honour and wiſdome hath alwaies bene right well knowne to all noble eſtats. And S^r howeſoever myne accuſers have uſed their accuſacōns againſte me, this I knowe, and ſo before your Lordſhipp and all the worlde I doe proteſte, that my deameano^r and proceed-inge have allwaies bene bothe iuſte and loyall towardes my ſov'raigne and leige Lorde, of whoſe uſage in his graces affaiers your Lordſhipp hathe hadd good ex-perience. And even accordinge to my truthe, ſo I beſeeche God help me.' 'I doubt not,' q^d my Lorde of Shrewſburie, 'of your truthe; therefore my Lorde be of good chere and feare not, for I am nothinge ſorrye, but y^t I have not wherewith to entertayne you accord-inge to my good will, and to your honour, but ſuche as I have yow ſhalbe wellcome to it; for I will not re-ceave you as a priſoner, but as my goode Lorde, and the kinges trewe and faithfull ſubiecte. And S^r here is my wife come to ſalute you;' whome my Lorde kiſſed, with his capp in his hande, bare headed, and all the other gentlewomen; [and] toke the earles ſer-vaunts by the hande as well gentlemen as yeomen. This done theſe twoe lordes went into the lodge arme in arme, and ſo conducted my Lorde to a faire gallerey where was in the further ende thereof a goodlie tower with lodgings where my Lorde was lodged. There was alſo in the mideſte of the ſame gallery, a travers of ſarconett drawne ſo y^t the one ende thereof was pre-ſerved for my Lorde and the other for the earle. Then departed from my Lorde all the great number of gen-tlemen and other that conducted him thither. And my Lorde beinge thus with my Lorde of Shrewesburie continewed there eighteen dayes after, upon whome my Lorde of Shrewesburye appoynted divers worthie gen-tlemen to attende continuallie, to forſee y^t he ſhoulde lacke nothinge y^t he woulde deſier, beinge ſerved in his owne chamber at dinner and ſupper, as honorablie and with as manye dayntie diſhes, as he hadd in his owne howſe, cōmonlye beinge at libertye. And once everie daye my Lorde of Shrewesburey woulde repaire unto him, and cōmon with him ſittinge upon a benche in a great windowe in the gallerey. And althougbe that my ſaide earle of Shrewesburie woulde right hartelye comforte him, yet woulde he lament ſo petiouſlie y^t

it woulde make my Lorde of Shrewsburie to be verie heavie for his grefe. 'S' saide he 'I have and do dailye receave letters from the kinge, cōmaundinge me to entertayne you as one y' he highlie favoreth and loveth, whereby I doe perceave ye doe lament more then ye have cause to doe. And though ye be accused (as I truste) wrongefullie, yet the kinge cane doe no lesse, but pute yow to your triall, the whiche is more for the satisfyinge of some persons, then for anye mistruste that he hathe in your traitorous doings.' 'Alas my Lorde,' q^d my Lorde Cardinall, 'is it not a pitious cause y' anie man shoulde so wrongefullie accuse me unto the kinge and not to come to my aunswere before his grace; for I ame well assured my Lorde that there is no man alive y' loketh in this face of myne, who is hable to accuse me. It greveth me verye muche that the kinge shoulde have anye suche opinion in me, to thincke that I woulde be fauls or conspire anie evill to his person, who may well consider that I have no assured frend in all the worlde, but onlye his grace, that if I shoulde goe aboute to betraye my sov'raigne Lorde and prince in whome is all my truste and confidence before all other, all men might iustlie thincke and saye, that I lacked both grace witt and descreacōn. Nay nay my Lorde I would rather adventur to shed my harte bloude in his defence, as I ame bounde bothe for my allegiance and for my save-garde, for he is my staffe that supporteth me, and the walle that defendeth me againste all these my corrupt enemyes, and all other who knowe me, and my diligent proceedings in all his affaires and doynges muche better then anye of them. Therefore to conclude, it is not to be thought that ever I woulde maliciouslie or trayterouslie travell or wishe anie hurte or damage, to his roial person or imperiall dignitye, but as I saide before defende it with the sheddinge of my verye harte bloude, and if it were but onlie for myne owne defence, to preserve my estate and simple life, the which my enemyes thincke, I doe so muche esteme, haveinge none other refuge to flie to, for protection and defence, but onlye under the shadowe of his wynge. Alas my Lorde I was in a good estate nowe, and lived quietlie, beinge right well contented with the same, but myne enemyes, who never slepe, both continuallie studie, both slepinge and wakinge to ridde me out of there waye, perceavinge the contentacōn of my minde, doubted that if I lived, there maliciousnes and crewell dealinge should growe at lengthe to there shame rebooke and open sclander; and therefore woulde prevent the same with sheadinge of my bloude; but from God that knoweth the secrets of their harts and all others, it can not be hidd nor yet unrewarded, when he shall see oportunitye. And my good Lorde if ye woulde shew yo^w so muche my frende as to requier the kinges maiestie, that my accusers may come before my face in his presence, and there that I may make aunswere, I doubt not, but you shoulde see me acquite my self of all their malicious accusours and utterlye confounde them—for they shall never be hable to prove by any due proba-cōn, that ever I offended ye kinge in thought, worde or deede.—Therefore I desier you and most hartelye requier your good L: to be a meane for me, y' I may aunswere unto my accusors before the kinges ma^{tie}: The case is his, and if there accusacōns wer trew then shoulde it touche him more ernestlie, wherefore it wer convenient, y' he should heare it his owne self, but I

feare me that they intende to dispache me, rather then I should come before his presence, for they be well assured and verye certayne that my truthe should vanquishe all there accusacōns and untrew surmises, which is the speciall cause that maketh me'so earnestlye desier to make my aunswere before the kinges ma^{tie}. The losse of goodes, the sclaunder of my name, nor yet all my troble greveth me anye thinge so muche as the losse of the kinges favour and that he should have in me suche an opinion withowt desier of untruthe, that have with suche travell and payne served the kinge so iustlie, so paynfullie and with so good an harte, to his profite and honour at all tymes.—And against the truthe of my doinges there accusacōns proved by me uniu:te shoulde do me more pleasure and good then the obteyninge of muche treasure, as I doubt not to doe, if the case might be indifferentlie harde, Nowe my good Lorde weighe my reasonable request and lett charitye and truthe move your harte with pitye to helpe me in all this my truthe, wherein you shall take no manner of rebuke or sclander by the grace of God.' ' Well then' (saide my Lorde of Shrewesburie) 'I will write to the Kinge in your behalf declaringe to him by my le.ters howe ye lament his indignacōn, and displeasure, and also what request ye make for the triall of your truthe towardes his highnes.' And after divers other cōmunicacōns as they wer accustomed dailie to have, they departed a sonder, remayninge there thus with my Lorde the space of a fortnight, and havinge goodly intertaynement, and often desiered by the earle to kill-a doe or harte in his parke there, who allwaies utterlie refused to take anie pleasure, either in huntinge or other wise, but applied his prayers continuallie, with great devocōn; so that it came to passe at a certeyne tyme as he sat at his dinner in his owne chamber, havinge at his bourdes end the same daye (as he coustomablie hadd everie daye) a messe of gentlemen and chapleyns to kepe him companye; towardes the end of his dinner, when he was come to eatinge of his fruts, I perceaved his coloure often to chaunge, whereby I iudged him not to be in good healthe. With that I leaned over the table and speakinge softlye unto him saide, ' S^r me semes your grace is not well at ease:' to whome he aunswered and saide with a loude voice; ' for soth no more I ame, for I ame' q^d he ' taken sodenlye withe a thinge aboute my stornacke, that lieth there alonge as coulde as a wetstone, whiche is no more but wynde; therefore I praye you take upp the table, and make a shorte dinner:' and that done resorted shortlie againe. And after the meat was caried out of the chamber, into the gallerye, whereas the wayters dyned, and everie man set, I rose up, and forsoke my dinner and came into the chamber unto my Lorde, where I founde him still sittinge verie evill at ease: notwithstandinge he was cōminge with them at the bourdes ende, whome he had cōmaunded to sitt still—And as sone as I was entered the chamber, he desiered me to goe to the poticarie, and enquier of him if he hadd anie thinge that woulde breake winde upwarde. Then went I to the earle, and shewed him what state my Lorde was in, and what he desiered: with that my Lorde of Shrewesburye caused incontinent the apoticarie to be called before him, and at his cominge he demaunded of him if he hadd enye thinge that woulde breake winde upwarde in a mans bodie; and he aunswered that he had suche gere: ' then ' q^d my Lorde 'fetch me some;' then departed the apoticarie and brought with him a white confection in a fayer paper and shewed it unto my Lorde, and cõmaunded me to give him the assaie thereof before him; and so I did, and I toke the same and brought it to my Lorde, where also I toke the assaye myself and then delivered it unto my Lorde, who receaved it up all at once into his mouthe. But imediatelie after he had receaved the same, suerlie he avoided muche winde exceedinglie upwarde. 'Lo,' quothe he, 'ye maye se that it was but wynde, and nowe I ame well eased, I thanke God,' and so rose from the table and went to his prayers, as he used everie daye after dinner. And that done there came unto him suche a laske, that it caused him to go to his stoole; and beinge there my Lorde of Shrewsburie sent for me, and at my repaire to him, he saide, 'forasmuch as I have alwaies perceaved you to be a mane in whome my Lorde your m' hathe great affiaunce, and also knowinge you to be an honest man,' with manye wordes more of cõmendacõn and praise then becomes me here to reherse, saide, 'It is so that my Lorde your m' hathe often desired me to write to the Kinge, that he mighte come before his presence to aunswere to his accusacõns, and even so have I done —and this daye have I received letters from the Kinges grace by S' Will'ᵐ Kingston, [Lieutenant of the Tower ¹,] whereby I perceave yᵗ the Kinge hath in him a good opinion, and upon my request he hath sent for him by the same S' Will'ᵐ to come unto him, who is in his chamber. Wherefore nowe is the tyme come that my Lorde hath often [desired] to trie himself, (I trust) much to his honour, and it shalbe the best iourney that ever he made in all his life. Wherefore nowe woulde I have yowe to playe the parte of a wise man, to breake this matter wittelie unto him, in suche sorte that he maye take it quietlye, and in good parte, for he is ever so full of sorowe and heavines at my beinge with him, yᵗ I feare me he will take it in evill parte and then dothe he not well; for I assuer you (and so shew him) that the Kinge is his good lorde, and hath given me most worthie thankes for his intertaynment, desieringe and cõmaundinge me so to continew, not doubting but that he will right noblie acquite himself towardes his highnes. Therefore goe your waies to him and perswade with him, that I maye finde him in a goode quiet, at my cominge, for I will not tarie longe after you.' 'S',' qᵈ I, 'if it please your L. I shall endevour me to the best of my power to accomplishe your Lordshipes cõmaundment. But Sir I doubt when I shall name Mr Kingston to him, that he will mistruste that all is not well, because that Mr Kinston is constable of the Tower, and captayne of the garde, having with him as I understand twenty-four of the guard to attend upon him.' 'Marye it is truthe' quothe the Earle, 'what therefore, allthoughe he be constable of the Tower, he is the most metest man for his wisedom and discretion to be sent about anie suche meassage: and for the guarde, it is of none other purpose, but onelie to defende him againste them that woulde intend him any evill either in worde or deed; and they be all for the most parte suche of his olde servaunts as the Kinge toke of late into his service, to the intent that they should attend uppon him most iustlie, knowinge best howe to serve him.' 'Well S''

saide I, 'I shall doe what I cane,' and so departed from him towardes my Lorde. And as I repaired unto him I found him sittinge at the upper end of the gallerye upon a chest, withe his staffe and his beades in his handes. And espieinge me cominge from the Earle, demaunded of me what newes: 'for sothe' qᵈ I 'the best newes that ever came to you, if your grace cane take it well;' 'I praye God it be,' (qᵈ he) 'what is yt:' 'forsoothe S'' saide I 'my Lorde of Shrewesburye, perceavinge by your often cõmunicacõn with him that ye wer all wayes desierous to come before the Kinges Maᵗⁱᵉ, as your most assured frende hath traveled with his letters unto the Kinge, that he hath sent for you by Mr Kingston and 24 of the guarde to conduct yow to his highnes.' 'Maister Kingston' (qᵈ he) rehearsinge his name once or twise, and with that clapped his hande on his thighe, and gave a great sighe. 'S' (qᵈ I) 'if your grace woulde or coulde take all thinges in good parte, it should be much better for you. Content your self for Godes sake and thincke that God and your frendes have wrought for you accordinge to your owne desier. Did not ye alwayes wishe that ye might clere your self before the Kinge, and nowe that God and your self hath brought your desier to passe ye will not take it thankefullie. Yf you consider your truthe and loyaltie unto our sov'raigne Lorde, agaynst the whiche your enemyes cãnot prevaile, the Kinge beinge your good Lorde, as he is. Ye knowe well the Kinge cane do no lesse then he doth to you, beinge to his highnes accused of some haynous cryme, but cause yow to be brought to your triall, and there to receave, accordinge to your merits; the whiche his highnes trusteth (and sayeth no les) but that you shall prove your self a juste man to his Maᵗⁱᵉ; wherein ye have more cause to reioyce, then thus to lament, or mistruste the favourable ministracõn of due iustice: for I assure you, your enemyes be more affraide of you, then you of them, and doubt in yoʷ so muche, that they wishe that thinge, that they shall never (I truste) bringe to passe, with all their witts, the Kinge as I saide before, beinge your indifferent [iudge] and your earnest friend. And to prove that he so is, see ye not how he hath sent gentle Mr Kingston to honour yoᵘ with as muche honour as was due to yow in your highe estate, and to convey yow by suche easie journeyes as yow will cõmaunde him to doe, and that yow shall have all your desiers and requests by the waye in everie place to your graces contentacõn and good cheere: wherefore S' I humblie beseeche your grace, to imprint all theise perswasions and manye other like in your graces highe discretion, and be of good cheere: wherewith ye shall comforte your self and geve all your frendes and servants good hope of your good speed.' 'Well well,' then qᵈ he, 'I perceave more then ye cane imagine, or doe knowe, experience of oulde hath taught me.' And therewith he rose upp and went into his chamber, and went to the stoole, the laxe trobled him so sore; and when he hadd done, he came out againe; And imediatlye after my Lorde of Shrewsburie came into the gallerie unto him, with whome my Lorde mett, and then sittinge downe there upon a benche in a great baye windowe the earle asked him, howe he did, and he most lamentablye (as he was accustomed to doe) aunswered him, and thanked him for his gentle entertaynment. 'S', (quoth the Earle)' if ye remember ye have often wished to come before the Kinge to make your aunswere, and I perceavinge your often desier and request, as one that beareth yow good will have written especiallie unto the Kinge in that behalf, makinge him privie also of your lamentable sorowe y, ye inwardlye have receaved for his displeasure, who acceptethe of all your doinges therein as frendes be accustomed to doe in suche cases; wherefore I woulde advise you to plucke upp your harte, and be not agast for your enimyes, who I assure yow be more in doubte of yow, then ye woulde thinke; perceavinge y' the Kinge is mynded to have the hearinge of your case before his owne person. Nowe S', if ye can be of good cheere, I doubt not but this journey, whiche ye shall take up unto his highnes, shalbe muche to your avauncement and overthrowe of your enemyes. The Kinge hath sent for you by y' worshippfull knight Mr Kingston, and with him 14 of your olde servaunts nowe of the guarde, to defend you against your enemyes to the intent that you maye safelie come unto his ma^tie.' 'S' ' (q^d my L.) 'I trowe that Mr. Kingston is constable of the Tower:' 'Yea, what of that' (quoth the Earle): 'I assure yo^w he is elected by the Kinge for one of your frendes, and for a descrett gentleman, most worthie to take upon him the save guarde and conduct of your person, which without faile the Kinge moste esteemeth, and secretlie beareth a speciall favour farr other wise then yow doe take it.' 'Well S' (q^d my Lorde), 'as God will so be it: I ame subiect to fortune, and to fortune I submit my self, beinge a trew man, redie to accept suche chaunces as shall followe, and there an ende. S', I praie you where is Mr. Kingston?' 'Marye' (quoth the Earle) 'if ye will, I will send for him, who woulde most gladlie see you.' 'I praye you then' (q^d my Lorde) 'send for him.' At whose messuage he came, and assone as my Lorde espied hime cominge at the galleries ende, he made haste to encounter him. Mr. Kingston came towardes him with muche reverence, and at his comeinge he kneeled doune unto him, and saluted him in the Kinges behalf, whome my Lorde bareheaded offred to take up, but he still refused. Then quoth my Lorde, 'Mr. Kingston, I praye yow to stande upp and leve your kneleinge unto me, for I ame but a wretche replet with misierie, not estemeinge my self but as a vile abiecte utterlie caste awaye without deserte, as God knoweth; and therefore good Mr. Kingston stand upp, or I will knele doune by you,' whome he woulde not leve, untill he stodd upp. Then spake Mr. Kingston and saide with humble reverence: 'S', the Kinges ma^tie hath him cō̄mended unto you.' 'I thanke his highnes' (quoth my Lorde) 'I truste he be in good health and merie.' 'Yea without doubt' (quoth Mr. Kingston): 'And he cō̄maunded me to saye unto you, that yo^w should assure yourself that he beareth yo^w as muche good will and favour as ever he did, and willeth you to be of good chere. And where reporte hath bene made unto hime, that ye shoulde cō̄mit against his royall ma^tie certayne haynous crimes, which he thinketh perfectlye to be untrewe, yett for the mynistracō̄n of justice in suche cases requisite, he can doe no lesse then to send for you to your triall, mistrustinge nothinge your truthe nor wisdome, but that yee shalbe hable to acquite

your self of all complaynts and accusacions exhibited against yo^w, and to take your iourney to him at your owne pleasure; cō̄maundinge me to be attendaunt upon yow, with ministracō̄n of due reverence and to see your person preserved against all inconveniencies that maye ensue: and to ellect all suche your olde servaunts, nowe his, to serve you by the waye, who have moste experience of your diet. Therefore S' I beseeche yow to be of good cheere, and when it shalbe your owne pleasure to take your iourney I shalbe readie to geve attendaunce.' 'Mr. Kingston' (q^d my L.) 'I thanke yow for your good newes. And S' hereof assuer your self, y: if I were as hable and lustie as I have bene but of late, I wolde not faile to ride with yo^w in post: but S' I ame diseased with a fluxe, that maketh me verie weake. But Mr. Kingston, all the comfortable wordes that ye have spoken unto me, be spoken but for a purpose, to bringe me into a fooles paradise. I knowe what is provided for me; notwithstandinge I thanke you for your good will and paynes taken about me: and I shall with all speed make me redie to ride with you to morowe.' And then they fell into other cō̄municacō̄n, both the Earle and Mr. Kingston with my Lorde, whoe cō̄maunded me to foresee and provide that all thinges might be redie to departe the morowe after. Then caused I all thinges to be trussed up and made in a readines, as fast as they coulde convenientlie. When night came that wee shoulde goe to beade, my Lorde waxed verie sicke with the laxe, the which caused him still continuallie from tyme to tyme to goe to the stole, all that night, in so muche that from the tyme that it tooke him, unto the next morneinge, he hadd fiftie stooles: so that he was that daye verie weake. His matter that he voyded was wonderous blacke, the which the phisicō̄n called *coloure, adustine:* And when he perceaved it, he saide to me that if hee hadd not some helpe shortlie, he shall die. With that I caused one Doctor Nicholas a D^r of Phisicke beinge with my Lorde of Shrewesburie to looke upon the grosse matter that he avoided; upon sight whereof he determined howe he shoulde not live foure or five dayes: yet notwithstandinge he woulde have ridden with Mr. Kingston that same daye, if my Lorde of Shrewesburie hadd not ben. Therefore in consideracō̄n of his infirmetye, they caused him to tarie all that daye, And the next daye he toke his iourney with Mr. Kingston and them of the garde. And assone as they espied him, consideringe that he was their ould M', and in suche estate, lamented his misfortune with weepinge eyes; whome my Lorde toke by the handes, and many tymes as he rode by the waye he would talke nowe withe one, nowe with another, untill he came to a house of my Lorde of Shrewesburyes, called Hardwicke-hall [1], where he laye all night verie evill at ease. The next daye he rode to Nottingh'm and there lodged that night more sicke, and the next daye he rode to Leycester-Abbey; and by the waye he waxed so sicke that he hadd almost fallen from his mule: So that it was night befor he came to the Abbey of Leycester, whome at the cō̄minge in at the gate, the abbot with all his covent mett him with divers torches light, whome they right honourablie receaved and welcomed with great reverence: To whome my L. saide 'Father Abbote, I ame come hether to leve my bones amonge

---

[1] Not Hardwick in Derbyshire, but Hardwick-upon-Line in Nottinghamshire. See *Who wrote Cavendish's Life of Wolsey?* 4to, 1814, p. 18.

P

you:' ridinge so still untill he came to the stayers of his chamber, where he alighted from his mule; and then Master Kingstone tooke him by the arme, and led him up the stairs; who tould me afterwardes, he never felt so heavy a burden in all his life. And as sone as he was in his chamber, he went incontinent to his bed, very sick. This was upon Satterday at nighte: and then continued he sicker and sicker.'

The year 1536 is memorable for the suppression of the lesser monasteries. This measure occasioned a very formidable insurrection in the northern part of England. The earl of Shrewsbury was the first to present a decided opposition to the tumultuous proceedings: and in his character of lieutenant of the north soon raised an army without any express permission from the king, a step not without its hazard in the days of so suspicious and arbitrary a monarch as Henry VIII. Perhaps he was not without his fears, but they were soon quieted by a grateful letter from Cromwell. The insurgents were met at Doncaster by the earl of Shrewsbury and the duke of Norfolk, and dispersed without a battle. Several of the chiefs were executed, and their estates confiscated: a sad blow to the ancient gentry of the county of York.

This was the last public service of the earl, who was now far advanced into the vale of years. He was a devout man; and while he thus contributed his assistance to suppress those who attempted to resist the king's authority, he anticipated, probably not without painful apprehensions, the approaching downfall of those religious establishments of a higher order which the suppression of those of inferior consequence portended. He looked to Worksop: and it has been supposed that it was in the anticipation of what proved to be the fact, that with the dissolution of that house would come the destruction of the memorials of his buried ancestors, that he determined to provide for himself and his family an humbler but more secure resting-place in the parish-church of Sheffield. It seems, however, as if that intention existed before there were any indications of the approaching storm: for as early as 1510 a near relative of the earl was buried in that church, and Ann his first countess, whose remains were interred at Sheffield, cannot have been alive much later than 1520[1]. The sepulchral chapel of the Shrewsbury family in the church of Sheffield was therefore, in all probability, prepared about the time when the fourth earl built or enlarged the lodge in the park. The only document relating to it in the Talbot papers is an undated letter from one of the earl's chaplains.

'To my Lord

PLEASITH it yoᵣ Lordshipe to knowe of yoᵣ chapell at Sheffeld the forwardnes their of: the masons hath takyn downe the wall to the grond and now is preparing the ground and the ston to sett. Owre Lord send us oᵣ stone frome the roche for the waye is very ille wᵗ us to carre ston: not wᵗ stonding for my part I shall doo the best that shall ly in my lytill power by the grace of oᵣ Lord.

My Lorde the mason hathe promysith to have the chapell upe redy to cover a fore Astᵗ by gods grace: where for it may please yoᵣ Lordshipe to remembᵣ owr carpentry for the ruffe of the sayd chapell, and yowr Lordshipe to fyne me money

for the same carpentry and for the mason at owr ladys daye in lente, yff yᵉ be absent for I have relcᵈ of Mastᵣys grace VLi;

Fordᵣ iffe it shall please yoᵣ Lordshipe to adv'tised I have to my brother a preist as I am, the wicht now synghith in Barkshier: and hath downe all thys x. yere & more, & muche desireth to come unto hys native contre to be abydef yff God wolld sende hyme some smal living to rest upon. In so muche it myght please yoᵣ hono'bill lordshipe at the instance of Almighty God to accept hym at yoᵣ cōmandement in the service that Sᵣ Gervice had, for the tyme yoᵣ Lordshipe shalbe surly perfite of hys demenar and condicions, wher of I trust yoᵣ Lordshipe wylbe very well contentit; and that in lyke case I for my parte some tymes might have some helpe in yoᵣ Lordships besenes, soo that howthe he and I may have a case to praye to Almighty God for yoᵣ hon' long to coutinew in great felicite, wᵗ prosperous helth at hys plesure. Writyn at Sheffield the   daye of Februarii wᵗ the reude hand of yoᵣ powr bedman to hys lettyll power,

Sᵣ Thomas Selvestᵣ prest[2].'

The earl made his will on the 21st of August 1537. He directed that his body should be laid in the parish-church of Sheffield near Ann his first wife; without any ceremonies but *dirige* on the eve, three masses and a sermon on the morrow: and that twenty-five poor men should have black gowns who were to carry torches at his funeral. Not more than a hundred black gowns were to be given to his servants, besides the gowns to his wife's gentlewomen. He directed also, that a tomb of marble should be set over his grave with three images thereon; namely, one of himself in his mantle of the Garter, another of his deceased wife in her robes, and a third of his wife then living. He further willed that a thousand priests should receive sixpence each to say *placebo* and *dirige* and mass for his soul and all Christian souls: and that twenty-five marks should be distributed in penny-dole to such poor people as should be present at his burial, to pray for his soul. He also provided that three priests for the space of twenty years next after his decease should sing for his soul; two of them at the parish-church of Sheffield at the altar where the lady Ann his first wife lay interred, and the other in the chapel of our blessed Lady of the bridge in Sheffield, each of them to have eight marks yearly during that time.

This 'noble, wise, and prudent' earl, as a contemporary describes him, departed this life at Winfield-manour in Derbyshire, on the 26th of July 1538, and his funeral was solemnized at Sheffield on the 27th of March following.

In one of the Holmes's manuscripts in the Harleian library we have an account of his funeral by a contemporary hand[3].

'THE 26 of July anno regis Hen. 8 xxx. departed out of this world the right noble & puissant Geo. Earle of Shrewesbury & Lo. Talbott Furnivall Verdon & Strange of Blackemoore & high stuarde of the kings most honorable houshold, &c.

27 of March, This noble Earle was removed from Wynfeild to Sheffeild wᵗʰ many wo. men & tall yomen,& the same night his dirige solemplye done, & his body honorably buryed.

The morrowe after his masses solempnely song; first one of the trenitie, another of oᵣ lady, and the thurd of Requiem. Sᵣ John Talbott chef mourner.

Sᵣ Henry Sayvell, Sᵣ Henry Sackeveile, Sᵣ Henry Sutton, Sᵣ Nicho. Sterley knightes, Mᵣ John Talbott sonne to Sᵣ John Talbott, Mr Wᵐ Vernone, wo. esqᵣˢ.

---

[1] For Henry Compton the earl's grandson by the daughter of his second marriage was born 16 February 1537-8. Collins, edit. 1779, vol. iii. p. 178.

[2] Talbot Papers, vol. P. f. 5.
[3] Harl. MSS. 2076. f. 4.

There was first gentlemen in gownes and hoods.
Item 200 yomen in blacke coats.
First the ....
Then the Quier.
John Will bare the standard.
. After that certeine gentlemen :
After them certeyn chaplayns :
John Persall bare the banner of his armes.
Then next Chester and Carlill the Kings herchaughts at armes.
Then the corps.
Tho. Ashelay bare the banner of the trenitie on the right syde at the heade.
Tho. Lee bare the banner of oᵣ ladye on the leafte syde.
Tho. Eaton bare the banner of Sᵗ Georg on the right side at the feete.
Assistants ; Anthony Nevell, John Bassett, Ryc. Greuall, John Leyke.
Then the mourners, & after them the trayne.
The said Geo. Lord of Shrewsbury had Lady Anne marryed to Compton—Frauncis now Lo. had issue Georg now Lo. Talbott, Mᵣ Tho. Talbott, and my Lady Anne, children to the said Lo. Frauncis, Earle that now is.'

FRANCIS FIFTH EARL of SHREWSBURY.

. This earl was born in the castle of Sheffield in 1500, and was lately left a widower when he succeeded to the rank and estates of his ancestors. Henry VIII. gave him this character, 'He is a gentle gentilman, wise and of good coorage :' but Lloyd concludes a laboured and empty panegyric with declaring of him that 'he was at once the chiefest counsellour and the most eminent scholar of his age[1].'
He sat in the house of peers during the life of his father, whom he succeeded in the appointment of lieutenant-general of the north. This occasioned him to have much concern in the border-wars. He had also several other minor appointments under the crown, and among the rest that of surveyor-general of the royal chase of Hatfield. When Henry VIII. took his progress into Yorkshire in 1541, it was his intention to have visited the old palace at Hatfield, in which were born those two princes William one of the sons of Edward III., and Henry the eldest son of Richard duke of York his great-grandfather[2]; and to have taken the diversion of hunting in the chase. Before the king left London the earl of Southampton, Sir William Fitz William, a younger son of the house of Aldwark, wrote to the earl of Shrewsbury that he should have twenty bucks provided at Hatfield against the king's coming, and sent him warrants for that number to the keeper of the chase of Hatfield. To this the earl replied in a letter dated Sheffield 6 July, that he would provide for the king's pleasure, but would spare to use the warrants and make up the number of bucks from his own park at Sheffield. He also desired that the king might be moved to see his poor house at Winfield when he came through Nottinghamshire. This invitation the king declined, and entered the county of York at Bawtrey, where the earl of Shrewsbury met him with a considerable retinue[3].
We find this earl one of the thirteen mourners at the funeral of Henry VIII., and afterwards one of the commissioners appointed to examine the grand serjeantry claims at the coronation of Edward VI. In

the first year of the new reign he was nominated lord-lieutenant of the counties of York, Lancaster, Chester, Derby, Nottingham, Stafford and Salop. On the 21st of May 1551 the earl arrived in London from the north, to meet the French ambassador who came to treat of a marriage for King Edward. He came in company with the earl of Derby, and was attended by a hundred and forty horsemen, and 'afore him forty velvet-coats and chains, and all wearing his own livery[4].' He was in London at the time of the young king's death, 1553, at whose funeral he was chief mourner. His name is subscribed to an order of council of Queen Jane dated six days after the death of King Edward: but he soon turned about, and seven days after was concerned in the proclamation of Queen Mary. This has not passed without censure, but he shares it in common with the chief persons of the age. The duke of Northumberland left London a month too soon.
His religious bias appears in his acceptance of the commission in the first year of Queen Mary to inquire by what authority Bonner had been deprived of the bishoprick of London. He had an office at the queen's coronation, and was in high favour at her court. He availed himself of his interest there to do an act of kindness, not to say of justice, to his tenantry and neighbours at Sheffield. In the late reign they had been deprived of certain public property, under pretence that the uses to which the income from it had been appropriated came within the scope of the act 1 Edward VI. for the suppression of chantries, colleges, and guilds. Of this he obtained for them restitution, and at the same time a royal patent declaring the future uses of the income of that property, and constituting a body corporate for its management and better protection. He returned home with the high appointment of president of the council of the north. This court was instituted by Henry VIII. soon after the suppression of Aske's rebellion. It sat at York. Its powers were ample: and as might be expected where was no trial by jury there were many complaints of abuses in it. The earl of Strafford was the last president, and it was not revived after the Restoration. In 1554 he sat on the memorable trial of Sir Nicholas Throgmorton at Guildhall. We find him attending in that year with other noblemen on cardinal Pole from Gravesend to London. On his barge was carved the talbot, the family badge. He bore King Philip's cap of maintenance to the parliament-house; and in the summer of the next year we find him engaged in the celebration of the obsequies of the queen of Spain grandmother to King Philip, at Saint Paul's.
. Though this earl did not cordially approve of the measures of the Reformists, he did not object to avail himself of the opportunity which those measures afforded for recovering portions of the ancient estate of his family which had been given by his predecessors to different religious foundations. He had two extensive grants of abbey-lands, one in the 33 Henry VIII., the other in the 6 Edward VI. In the former were included the grange of Fullwood, and all the interest which the canons of Beauchief had enjoyed in

[1] State-Worthies, p. 533.
[2] William of Worcester. Annales, anno 1441. Hearne's *Liber Niger*, p. 461. See also p. 462. It has happened unfortunately for Hatfield in the wapentake of Strafford and Tickhill that there is another place of

the same name in the county of Herts : *tulit aliter honorem.*
[3] Talbot Papers, vol. P. f. 77. and Warburton's *Yorkshire Collections,* vol. ix. f. 34 a. Lansdown MSS. in the British Museum.
[4] Strype's *Ecclesiastical Memorials,* vol. ii. p. 272.

that part of the parish of Sheffield: in the second, the reversion, after the death of his sister Mary countess of Northumberland, of that part of the tythe of Sheffield which had heretofore belonged to the abbey of Saint Wandrille, and lately to the Carthusian monastery of Saint Ann near the city of Coventry. It will appear to have been the earl's intention to have procured at the same time the advowson of the parish-church of Sheffield, which on so many accounts it was desirable he should possess. But that as well as a share of the tythe of Sheffield passed at this period into the hands of one of his principal agents Robert Swyft of Broomhall esquire.

In 1558 the earl willingly concurred in the accession of Elizabeth, who admitted him of her privy-council, and continued him in the office of lord-president of the north. But he did not cordially agree in all the measures that were adopted in the beginning of her reign for the completion of the unfinished and interrupted work of Reformation. On the 18th of March 1559 he voted against the bill for restoring the supremacy of the English church to the sovereign; one temporal lord only, the lord Montacute, and ten bishops voting with him. But on the 22d when the bill came amended from the Commons he gave it his support[1]. This is the true state of the case on a point in which the conduct of the earl has been heretofore somewhat misrepresented. Soon after he was named in the great ecclesiastical commission for the northern parts; but his health was then become infirm, and he died very soon after at Sheffield manour.

The second lady of this earl is thus described in the sheet pedigree of the Talbot family in the Baronage, ' Gracia uxor Rob. Shakerley Ar.' by a slip of the pen as should appear, whence in opposition to all the best authorities she has been described as widow, not daughter, of Robert Shakerley who was a gentleman of an ancient and respectable family in the county of Derby. A visitation-book of that county 1569 adds that she had a former husband named Francis Carless. It has been said, I know not on what authority, that she was not always the mistress of the castle she inhabited. She was however a sensible, well-educated woman, as appears by her letters in the Talbot Papers. She died in August 1558; and the earl had nearly concluded a treaty of marriage with the widow of Sir Thomas Pope founder of Trinity college Oxford, when he was called away by death[2].

He was laid in the vault prepared by his father at Sheffield. His funeral was splendid. The account of the ceremonies observed, though it is long, and has before been published[3], is too curious and too nearly connected with our subject to be here omitted: and with it the present chapter may be brought to a close.

THE solemn Funeral of FRANCIS TALBOT E. of SHREWSBURY at Sheffield in Com. Ebor. Oct. 21, 1560.

' 1. The proceedings at Sheffield antecedent to the funeral.

1. The right paissant Francis late Earl of Shrewsbury, Lord Talbot, Furnival, Verdon and Strange of Blackmore, kt & companion of the noble order of the Garter, deceased out of this transitory world on Saterday, the 28 of September in the morning at his manor of Sheffield, anno MDLX.

2. (Whereupon) after the said noble body was dead and cold, he was opened, cered (that is wrapped in cerecloth) and coffined. And then it was set in a chappell within the said house, called the manor of Sheffeild (a mile from the towne of Sheffeild.)

3. The said chappell was hanged with black cloth, and garnished with scutchins of his armes within the garter. And some, of his armes, and his (two) wives impaled.

4. (His first wife) was daughter to the Lord Dacres (Thomas) and sister to the Lord Dacres that now is, William. His second wife was daughter of Mr. Shackerly.

5. In the middle of the said chappell stood the corps, and a talbott set over two trussels, and covered with a pall of cloth of gold, with a cross of white sattin. And over the same six scutcheons of buckerham in mettall.

6. And in the chappell was said every day service in English during the time that the course did there abide. Which remained there the space of XXIIII. days, till all things were ready for the interment.

7. Item, after the earles departure, the lord George, now earle (being his son and heir) sent for Garter king of armes to order the funeral. So he sent downe Loncaster herauld, to cause the herse to be made, and to see the church and house garnished, with all other things that were necessary, till Garter went downe.

II. The manner of the furniture of the church, herse, and castle.

1. Item, the body of the church in the towne of Sheffeild (where the corps was buried) was hanged with black cloth and garnished with scutcheons. (As was) also the quire where the herse stood.

2. The herse stood in the midst, four square. Twelve feet in length, and (twelve) in breadth; having a close roofe, with hatchments; rounding from the top, by the square, to the four corners. And over the top of the middle principall stood two great scutcheons of paste paper (the arms thereon) within the garter. And round about the said top were set pensills. And beneath the said top to the four posts downwards, was covered round with black cloth. And in every place of the square stood four scutcheons of paper in metall. And over the hatchment were set pensills along them: over the tops of the four principall posts, stood four scutcheons of paistepaper. And round about the said square went a bredth of black velvett. And to all the nether edge of the said velvett was fastened a valance of sarscenett, written with letters of gould Sic transit gloria mundi. The valance was fringed with a fringe of black silk a quarter deep. Over which were fastened scutcheons in metall, garnished above with pencills. The four posts of the herse were covered with black velvett; and on every post two scutcheons of buckerham in metall. And on the top of every post four pensills. And under (it, viz on the) floor of the herse was a maiestie of sarscenett, with arms of the same. And the nether part of the said herse and both sides, were covered with black cloth.

3. And without that raile went another rail; which was hanged with black alsoe; and both garnished with scutcheons.

4. And betweene the two railes stood nine stools and cushions, which were covered with fine black cloath.

5. And on the south side of the quire was a chappell, in the which chappell lay buried the ancestors of the said earl; which chappell was hanged with black and furnished with scutcheons. In which chappell was buried the said earl.

6. Item, the castle stands in the town of Sheffeild, and the said castle was hanged and garnished in this manner. First, the porch, goeing into the hall, and the hall also, was hanged with black cloath, and garnished with scutcheons of arms.

7. Then the way from the hall to the great chamber was hanged in like manner.

8. The great chamber was hanged from the top to the ground with broad cloath, and garnished with scutcheons of buckeram in mettall.

9. The castle, church and herse being thus garnished and in all readiness, the course was secretly brought from the said manor to the castle; and there remained 'till Monday the XXI. of October. On which day,

[1] See Strype.
[2] Lodge, vol. i. p. xiv.

[3] Peck's Desiderata Curiosa, p. 252, &c. from a manuscript formerly the property of Peter Le Neve, esquire.

III. *The manner of proceeding to the church with the corps,*
was thus :

1. The conductors, with black staves, in coates.
2. The poor, two and two, in gownes.
3. The quire singing, in surplices.
4. The standard, born by Mr. Thomas Eton in his long gown and a hood on his head.
5. Then all the gentlemen, two and two, in long gownes, with hoods on their shoulders.
6. Then all the chaplains of the defunct.
7. Then all esquires, as the gentlemen (two and two).
8. Then the steward, treasurer and controuler, with white staves, in their gownes.
9. Then the banner of armes, born by Sir Thomas Cockayne, in his long gowne, his hood on his head.
10. Then Lancaster herald in his longe gowne, and his hood on his head; his coat of arms on his back: bearing the elm and crest.
11. Then Chester herald, bearing the target.
12. Then Garter, principall king of armes, bearing the coate. And on his left hand, a gentleman usher.
13. Then the corps; four banners with four impalements.
14. After the corps, the chief mourner (the earl of Shrewsbury) his trayne borne by a gentleman usher.
15. The Lord Talbot, and
16. The Lord Darcy of the north.
17. Sir Thomas Gargrave, and
18. Sir George Vernon.
19. Sir William Vavasor, and
20. Sir Gervase Clifton.
21. Sir John Neville, and
22. Mr. Ed. Saville.
23. After them yeomen two and two.
24. In this order they proceeded to the church, in at the west door, and so up to the hearse, where the corps was set ; and on the same, the hatchment. Then the standard and the banners were held, one (at the head, and one) at the feet, without the railes. And after that, the mourners were placed, viz. the chief mourner at the head; and on each side, four others.
25. All things in order and every man in his place, Chester herald pronounced his stile in manner following:

‘ Laud and praise be given to Allmighty God, for that it
‘ hath pleased him of his infinite goodness, to call out of this
‘ transitory life unto his eternal glory, the high, noble and
‘ puissant Francis late earl of Shrewsbury, Lord Talbot, Fur-
‘ nivall, Verdon and Strange of Blackmore ; knight and com-
‘ panion of the most noble order of the Garter, lord president
‘ of the councill of the north, and justice of all the forests and
‘ chases from the Trent northwards.’

26. After the said praise, the service began. That is to say a psalm was sung in English. After which the priest began the communion, and said the epistle and gospell. After the go-spell the quire sung another psalme in prick-song. Which continued all the time of the offering.

IV. *The order of the offering.*

1. After the priest had .... him, the mourners stood up in the herse, and the chief mourner came forth, having before (him) certayne gentlemen, the officers of the houshold, and the officer of armes, and the other mourners following him, two and two.
2. (In this manner the chief mourner) went up and offered. Unto whom the Lord Darcy making (a) reverence, gave a purse of goulde for the offeringe. The which chief mourner had a cussion and a carpet laid by a gentleman usher, for him to kneele on. And after (that the gentleman usher) returned to the herse, and by him Garter principal king of arms.
3. Then Lancaster herauld, standing within the railes of the herse, delivered, unto the lord Talbot and the Lord Darcy, the book coat of arms. Who having Garter before them, of-fered the same to the priest; and he, with reverence, gave the same to the earl. And he gave the same to Garter, who laid it by, on a board set for that purpose. Then the said two Lords departed to the herse again.
4. Then the said Lancaster delivered the sword to Sir

Thomas Gargrave and Sir George Vernon, who, with Chester herald before them, offered the same in like manner aforesaid.
5. Then Lancaster delivered the target to Sir William Va-vasor and Sir Gervis Clifton, who offered the same as afore-said.
6. Then Sir John North [Neville] and Mr. Saville offered the helm and crest, having Lancaster herald before them in manner as aforesaid.
7. Then the Earl came down to the herse. And after a while, went up and offered himself, with Garter before him ; having neither traine borne up or cushion, or carpet to kneel on : and after returned.
8. Then the Lord Darcy and Lord Talbot offered money, having an officer of armes before them.
9. Then the other mourners offered money in the like man-ner, two after two; having at every time an officer of armes before them.
10. After the mourners had offered, then the four assistants (offered) having Chester (herald) before them.
11. Then offered all gentlemen, two and two ; having be-fore them Lancaster herald.
12. After them all the yeomen. And,
13. The offering done, the sermon begun, made by Dr. Dod, whose anthem was, *Beati mortui qui in Domino moriuntur.* During the sermon, the mourners were placed in the herse againe.
14. The sermon proceeded to the end. Then the minister of the church came downe, with the quire singing to the herse. And after certaine prayers said, the eight gentlemen took up the corps, and went to the grave with the same. And after certaine prayers said, the corps was put into the vault.
15. Then the officers of the household, and the gentlemen ushers, with the porters, broke their staves ; and soe departed home to the castle to

V. *The dinner.*

1. At the castle was prepared a great dinner, that is to say, there was served from the dressors (besides my lord's services from his own board, which were three messes of meat) cccxx. mess, to all manner of people who seemed honest ; having to every mess, eight dishes ; that is to say, two boyled mess, four roast, and two baked meats : whereof one was venison. For there was killed for the same feast, fifty does and twenty nine red deere.
2. And after dinner, the reversion of all the said meate was given to the poore, with dole of two pence a piece; with bread and drink great plenty.
3. And after the same dinner, every man was honourably contented for his pains.

Thus endeth the interment of the right noble Francis Earle of Shrewsbury.

VI. *The names of all them, who bore office at this interment.*

Banner bearer. Sir Thomas Cockaine.
Standard bearer. Sir Thomas Eton.
The four assistants. 1. Nicholas Longford. 2. Francis Curzon. 3. Francis Rolleston. 4. Godfrey Foljambe.
The eight who bore the banner rolls. 1. Peter Freschevill. 2. Arthur Copley. 3. Alexander Nevill. 4. Francis Bailey. 5. John Dod. 6. Francis Aston. 7. George Massey. 8. George Scaldfeild.
Gentlemen ushers. 1. Francis Moore. 2. Edward Vernon.
Traine bearers. 1. Thomas Gascoigne. 2. John Talbot.
Officers of the household. 1. William Talbot steward. 2. Robert Shackerley treasurer. 3. Thomas Sutton controuler.
Yeomen ushers. 1. Edward Ashfield. 2. Thomas Etton.
Conductors. 1. William Massen. 2. Edward Wright.
The six who bore the corps. 1. Richard Morton. 2. William Francis. 3. William Tendal. 4. Thomas Vernon. 5. John Booth. 6. John Rodes.

VII. *Rewards given to the officers of arms, for their pains at*
the said interment. £ s. d.

1. To Garter, principall king of arms . . . 20 0 0
2. To Chester herauld 10 0 0
3. To Lancaster herald 10 0 0

a

	£	s.	d.
4. Item, the herse with all things appertaining, and the pall	0	0	0
5. And to Mr. Garter, and clerk	2		

VIII. The painters charge.

	£	s.	d.
1. For a great banner of his arms	5	0	0
2. For a standard	4	6	8
3. Item, Clerk of arms	1	10	0
4. Item, a hand of steele, viz. a gantlet	1	0	0
5. Item, a crest	0	10	0
6. Item, a sword	0	13	4
7. Item, a target	0	13	4

	£	s.	d.
8. Item, for mantle	1	3	4
9. Item, for 8 banner rolls	5	13	4
10. For 10 doz. of pensills	5	0	0
11. For 4 doz. of scutcheons of buckerham	4	16	0
12. For 6 doz. of scutcheons, paper and metal	6	0	0
13. For 6 doz. of scutcheons, paper and colours	4	8	0
14. For 6 great scutcheons	3	0	0
15. For one great brass	0	3	4
16. For one small brass	0	2	0
17. For the painter, for his charges riding downe	1	6	8

CHAPTER VI.

George the fifth Earl of Shrewsbury.—Refidence at Sheffield of Mary Queen of Scots.—Gilbert the feventh Earl of Shrewsbury.

THE earls of Shrewsbury had several other houses in the northern parts of England; namely, at Rufford, Worksop, and Winfield; but at their two mansions in and near the town of Sheffield, the castle and the manour, they for the most part resided during the reigns of the Tudors: and the establishment which they maintained there rivalled the extent and splendour of a monarch's.

Of this we have had some proof in the account which has just been given of the magnificent funeral obsequies of the late earl, and of the retinue by which he was accompanied when he undertook a journey to the court;—how different from the half dozen postillions and as many outriders which a nobleman of these times finds sufficient for the maintenance of his dignity! We shall have other proofs in the ensuing chapter. Sir George Wheeler says he had heard that 'in times no longer ago than King Charles I. many noblemen's and gentlemen's houses in the country were like academies where gentlemen and women of lesser fortunes came for education with those of the family[1]:' meaning, I suppose, that they might share in the instruction which was provided for the younger part of the family, and when passed the age of childhood live in a state of easy dependence. In the list of persons who attended at the funeral of earl Francis are many of the best account in the vicinity, some of whom lived or had lived in this state of semi-servitude with the deceased earl. One name must not be passed over.

SIR THOMAS COCKAINE who bore the standard was the chief of the family of that name at Ashbourne in Derbyshire. He was an author. His treatise on hunting is one of the rarer tracts of the Elizabethan age. It was printed in quarto, with a well-cut figure of a talbot-dog in the title page, in 1591, when the knight

was pretty far advanced in years. In a handsome dedication to Gilbert earl of Shrewsbury, a great lover of field-sports, he acknowledges his obligations to that noble family, and especially to his grandfather earl Francis, in whose house he says that he had spent his youth. I wish I could add that this small volume contains any notices of the style of living there, or of the hunting-parties in which doubtless the old knight had joined in his youth in the earl's chases of Fullwood and Riveling. But Cockaine, though on the whole an amusing writer, is not so pleasing a gossip as a writer on a kindred sport, Izaac Walton.

A still rarer tract by another author, whose connexion with the noble family at Sheffield gives him a claim to notice in this place, is ' The Arbour of Amitie; wherin is comprized pleasant poems, and pretie poesies, set foorth by THOMAS HOWELL gentleman, anno 1568. Imprinted at London by Henry Denham, dwelling in Pater Noster Rowe, at the signe of the Starre.' In the title page of this small and extremely rare volume, the Bodleian copy being the only one known, is also the wood-cut of a talbot-dog, with these lines, alluding to the unspotted loyalty of the Talbot family, aptly represented by the generous attachment and fidelity of the dog.

   ' The Talbot true that is
      and still hath so remaynde,
   Lost never noblenesse
      by sprincke of spot distaynde:
   On such a fixed fayth
   This trustie Talbot stayth.'

The poems in this volume are chiefly amatory: and the author appears to have been of the retinue of Lady Ann Herbert, a daughter of William earl of Pembroke, who married Francis lord Talbot the eldest son

---

[1] Protestant Monastery, 1698, p. 158, as quoted by Dr. Wordsworth in his Ecclesiastical Biography. This custom might be illustrated from the inscription on the monument of Sampson Meverel in the church of Tidswell, where we have a detail of the life of an esquire of the age of Henry VI. Wolsey's household it is well known was composed of gentlemen of family, and even young noblemen. This custom may be further illustrated, if necessary, from the letters annexed to the present chapter.

and heir apparent of the sixth earl about 1562[1]. To that ' ryght noble and most vertuous lady' the volume is inscribed in two dedications, prose and verse; and the writer claims to be able to bear witness to her worthiness, ' being in her daylie presence.'—There is another work by the same author, of whose history little is known, entitled ' Thomas Howell's Devices for his owne exercise, and his friends pleasure,' 1581; and Ritson ascribes to him a translation of the story of Narcissus from Ovid, ' with a moral thereunto,' 1560[2].

RICHARD ROBINSON ' seruant in housholde to the right-honorable earle of Shrowsbury' dates from ' Sheffield castle 19 Maie 1574' the preface to a metrical work entitled ' The Rewarde of Wickednesse, discoursing the sundrye monstrous abuses of wicked and ungodly worldlings: in suche sort set downe and written as the same have beene dyversly practised in the persones of popes, harlots, proude princes, tyrauntes, Romish byshoppes and others. With a lively description of their severall faltes and finall destruction. Verye profitable for all sorte of estates to reade and looke upon. Newly compiled by &c. A dreame most pitiful and to be dreaded:

' Of things that be straunge
　　Who loueth to reede
In this booke let him raunge
　　His fancie to feede.'

The colophon, ' Imprinted at London in Pawles churche yarde by William Williamson,' with the date 1573 wrought in the ornament. It is in octavo, and extends to signature Q 3.

This prolix title-page ushers to us a work not unlike the Mirror for Magistrates. The author feigns that in a dream after a Christmas revel he is conducted to the realms of Pluto, and admitted to witness the sufferings of the damned. There he sees Helen, Tarquin, Medea, Tantalus, Vetronius Turinus, Heliogabalus, the two judges who slandered Susanna, Pope Joan, Midas, and Rosamond who murdered her husband Albonius of Ravenna. He finds preparation making for the reception of another distinguished person expected from the realms above, who turns out to be bishop Bonner. After a sight of all this misery, he is regaled with a view of Mount Parnassus, on which many of the ancient poets are enjoying themselves, to whose company a few moderns are admitted, as Chaucer, Skelton, Lydgate, Wager, Heywood, and Barnabe Googe.

This is also a work of very rare occurrence. The only copy which I have seen had lost its preface: but from that it seems may be collected, what gives a higher degree of interest to a volume which of itself is sufficiently curious, that the author was ' one of the domestic centinels who were employed at Sheffield castle to guard the ill-fated queen of Scots, and that his night watches produced this metrical composition[3].'

It may be submitted to the collectors of the biography of early English poets, whether his employment as a centinel be fatal to the supposition that the author of the Rewarde of Wickednesse was a Doctor Robinson, who about the period in question was tutor to the earl of Shrewsbury's two younger sons Edward and Henry, and who was afterwards recommended by the earl to succeed Wickham in the deanery of Lincoln[4]. The work shows an extent and variety of reading that can hardly be expected from one of the ordinary servants of the earl; it has commendatory verses addressed to the author by his friend Richard Smith a clerk; and it exhibits throughout, strong symptoms of the *odium theologicum*, e. g.

' Then after a while upon a stage full hye
An yll faste yoman a blacke trumpet blew:
And when silence was made, hee proclaymed a crye
In the name of Pluto for tydings most true.
　　(Quoth he) Bloodie Boner the butcher comes here,
　　That hath furnisht our kitchin this many a yere.
Moreover (quoth hee) it is Pluto's high pleasure,
That all men prepare in the best sort they can,
Sith he is to Pluto and Proserpine such treasure,
To receyve him amonge us as becomes such a man:
　　You know what his service hath bene heretofore,
　　Looke to your dueties, what needes any more?'

I conceive the author of this work to have been a different person from his namesake and contemporary, a citizen of London, author of various small tracts, some of which are noticed by Warton[5].

It appears from these notices that the earl of Shrewsbury of the time of Elizabeth collected about him some of the *viri mercuriales* of the time. It also appears from the following letter, that though he has been suspected of an attachment to the then rising Puritan party in the church[6], he allowed himself to be entertained by the representation of stage-plays in one of the great halls of the castle of Sheffield[7].

' Nos Domini nostri comediatores, gratulationes ad te nostras, summa cum gratiarum actione, presentamus; inter alia, in nos tua beneficia sæpius illata, hoc imprimis in memoriam reducentes, quòd traiediam hanc nostram (quà cũ sancti Georgii festum hoc celebravimus) satis sane venustam et laudatam, necessariis implementis procuraveris: quà quidem actione, summa nobis (licet indignus) accidit cõmendatio. Audientes enim et non intelligentes, jestura et forma; intelligentes vero, res ipsa, tantâ affecit oblectatione, ut quidam non inferioris conditionis homines, nos instanter aliquod simile quam breviter postumus, exercitare et ostendere postulant. Unde fit, ut tuam rursus opem petere cogimur, rogantes ut librum aliquem brevem, novum, iucundũ, venustum, lepidũ, hillarem, scurrosum, nebulosum, rabulosum, et omnimodis carniñciis, latrociniis, et lenociniis refertum, perscrutare et ad nos mittere digneris: quà in re dicunt quod Wilsonus[8] quidam Leycestrii comitis servus (fidibus pollens) multum vult et potest facere, precipue si Morgani nostri nomine tantùm pos · tules. Valeas præcor. Sheff. xxv. Aprill 1581.

　　　　　　　　　　　tuus dum sit
　　　　　　　　　　　　　THO. BAYLY.

Yf my brother Wᵐ be at the court, I pray yoᵘ cõmend me to him; and chyde him for that he will not take paines to

---

[1] The earl of Shrewsbury writes to the Master of the Rolls with proposals for the marriage of his son to the daughter of the earl of Pembroke. Talbot Papers, P 393. And on the 6th Dec. 1561 Sir Gilbert Gerard writes to Sir William Cecil, that the earl of Pembroke has accepted the offer. Id. 403. It was the brother of this lady who married Mary the favourite sister of Sir Philip Sidney : ' Sidney's sister, Pembroke's mother.'

[2] For more respecting this author and his works the reader is referred to *The British Bibliographer*, vol. i. p. 105; and *Censura Literaria*, second edit. vol. i. p. 255—261.

[3] See *The British Bibliographer*, vol. i. p. 109. See also Warton, and *Censura Literaria*, second edit. vol. vi. p. 38—43.

[4] See a letter from the earl of Shrewsbury to lord Burghley, dated Sheffield castle 12 April 1584. Talbot Papers, G 245. There is in the same collection a letter of Robinson's to the earl on the misconduct and blasphemous doctrines of the dean of Lincoln, H. 303.

[5] *History of English Poetry*, vol. iii. p. 391, &c.

[6] See his article in *A chronological account of eminent persons*, 1534—1695, in 3 volumes folio. MS. in the library of the late Dr. Daniel Williams, in Red-cross-street, London.　[7] Talbot Papers, vol. G, f. 74.

[8] Perhaps Robert Wilson, who has a brief notice in Langbaine.

write to me. And tell R. Rotherford that yf he want any money, he knoweth where I dwell. I have sent him tokens by this berar.

To my very lovinge frend Mr Thomas Bawdewine
at Couldharbar in London.'

Another author of the Elizabethan age patronized by the earl of Shrewsbury was John Jones, bachelor of medicine. He is said by Wood to be 'a Welchman born, or at least of Welch extract[1].' I apprehend he was the son or some near relation of one Morgan Jones, who under the description of ' *servus prænobilis Georgii comitis Salopiæ*' is registered among the persons interred at Sheffield, 27 June 1587; and who is probably the Morgan mentioned in the above letter. Dr. Jones was the author of several tracts enumerated by Wood, but is chiefly memorable for having written the first treatise on the waters of Buxton. His volume is entitled ' The benefit of the auncient Bathes of Buckstones, which cureth most greevous sicknesses, never before published: compiled by John Jones, phisition. At the King's Mede nigh Darby, Anno salutis 1572.' The author dedicates it to George earl of Shrewsbury, by whom ' the bathes of Buckstone be beneficially edified.' The property of the spring was in the house of Talbot as early as the 39 Henry VI.[2], but it was left for the sixth earl of Shrewsbury, early in the reign of Elizabeth, to erect a capital mansion near it for the reception of strangers who then began to resort thither from distant parts of the kingdom. At this house the chief nobility of the age were entertained by the earl, and here the queen of Scots lived when she was allowed to avail herself of the benefit of these waters for her painful and complicated disorders. There is an engraving of the house in Speed's map of the county. It was taken down in 1670 by the earl of Devonshire, to whose family it had passed from the earls of Shrewsbury. This truly noble and charitable earl did not neglect to provide also accommodation for poor persons who might wish to resort to these healing waters[3].

We may add to what Wood has collected concerning Dr. Jones, that he seems to have undertaken the cure of souls. The two professions were often united. There was another instance in Yorkshire at the same period. Timothy Bright, M.D. had the two rectories of Methley and Berwick in Elmet. John Johnes, M.D. was instituted to the rectory of Treeton 9 Oct. 1581, on the presentation of George earl of Shrewsbury, and held the living till his death in 1600, when Osmond Boorn, S.T.B. succeeded him. A daughter of Dr. Jones married John Machon, of Machon-bank in the parish of Sheffield, one of the assistant ministers, afterwards beneficed in Warwickshire.

The multifarious bequests in the will of Arthur Wilson, a younger son of the Broomhead family, bring us acquainted with the names of many persons who like himself were retainers in the household of the earl of Shrewsbury, early in the reign of Elizabeth.

' IN the name of God Amen. the x. day of June the yere of o' Lord God M. CCCCC. LVII, I Arthure Wilson, seke in body but of good and perfecte remembrance, do make and ordeyne this my last will and testament in man' and forme following. First and before all other thinges, I give and bequeth my soull to God Almighty the maker of the same and to the blessed Virgin Marie and to all the holy company of Heven; and my body to be buried in Sheffelde churche as nere to the bodyes of my brethren as can be. Also I will my said body to be brought furthe of my holl goods w' a dirige and a masse w' other thinges necessarie at the discretion of my supervisors whom I put in trust. It. I give unto my honorable lady, my gelding. It. to Mastres Margerie, an old aungell. It. to Mastres Frances Talbot, an old angel. It. to Mastres Anne Dakers, a frenche crowne. It. to Isabel Eyre, v'. It. to Mastres Anne Graven', a frenche crowne. It. to Anne Deye, IIII'. It. to Mr. Sandfurth, x'. It. to Mr. Dotton, Mr. V'nam and Mr. Whitmore, to every on of them, IIII'. It. to Ambrose Swynbanke, v'. It. to W'" Bowman, a velvet coif [and] a payre of hosecloth w' lyning for the same. It. to Mr. Dodde, IIII'. It. I give to W'" Crosland the best of all my apparell; that is to say, my best jaket, doblet, shirte, hose, chose, cappe, hat and cloke. It. I give to Sir Thomas Bedall my Ladies chaplayne, v'. It. to Jeffray Blith, III'. It. to Robert Cooke and John, either of them, II'. It. I give and bequeth unto Ric. Crosland my sister son, my sword. It. to John his brother, II'. IIII'. It. to Philipe Croks, II'. It. to Mr. Bekket, v'. It. to Nycolas Eyre, II'. It. to Cuthbert my servant, IIII'. It. to the II. yong gentlemen that waits upon Mr. Talbot, either of them, XII'. It. to Homfray, XII'. It. to Ric. Horner, my grene cote, a paire of white hose and a shirte. It. to vi. boys; that is to wit, Roberte Daill, W'" Wilcocke, Edmunde   , Alexander Bothe, W'"-Burners, Davyd Blithe, every on of them vi'. It. to George Crosland II'. It. to Raynold Crosland, an ewe and a lambe. It. I give to Edward Greves and his wife and ther children, VII. ewes and VII. lambes and on wether. It. to X'pofer my brother, xx'. It. to Eliz. his doughter, an ewe and a lambe. It. to George Wilson my brother, x'. It. to Thomas Barber and his wif my syster, II. bulloks. It. to the III. doughters of John Crosland, III. ewe hoggs. It. to John Crosland, a russet jaket. It. I give to III. sones of my brother George, that is to say Charles, Thomas, and Francis, eche of them, a shepe. It. to Thomas Wilson my brother son, II. shepe. It. to John Hodgson, a pare of my best chose and a good shirt. It. to W'" Lambe, II'. It. to Henry Grace, xvi'. It. to George Bedlington, xx'. It. to John Horner, xvi'. It. to Thomas Horner, xII'. It. to Sir Alexander Bowthe, x'. It. to my Ladyes Winser II. men and II. maides, IIII'. It. I give to Elizabeth Preste, all suche houshold stuf as she hath of myne, except wayngere, and a jacke w'be I give to Edward Greves my brother in lawe. It. I give to George Crosland my sister son, my blacke nag. Also whereas my nevye X'pofer Wilson doth owe unto me IIII'LI., the on half therof dewe to be paid at Whitsonday next, and the other half at the fest of Sainte Martyn in winter next ensuyng, I give unto the same X'pofer XL'. of the same soni' to be abated and allowed at the said II. days by even portions. Also wheras the said X'pofer Wilson my nevie dothe owe unto me xIII'LI. vi'. viii'd. dewe to be paid at the feast of the Invention of the holie crosse next enauyng the date herof, I give unto the same X'pofer IIII'LI. of the same soni'. Also I do ordeyn and constitute my welbeloved in Christ Thomas Barbar my brother in lawe, to be my true and lawfull attorney to execute and prove the last will and testament of John Wilson my brother, and to se that his child have all suche goods as shall appeare by the will of the said John : to whom I give and grante all my holl power and autoritie concernyng the said last will and testament. The residewe of all my goods not bequethed, my detts paid, and legacies, and funerall expenses performed, I give and bequeth it unto the proper use of Elyn my doughter. Also I ordayn and make Thomas Barbar of West Den and X'pofer Wilson my brother, my true and lawfull executors of this my present last will and testament, for the behofe of the said Elen my doughter, to receyve and take all suche as shalbe knowen to be myne. And I will that Thomas Barbar have the rule and

---

[1] *Athenæ Oxon.* 1721, vol. i. p. 181.   [2] See Blore's *History of the Manor and Manor-house of South Winfield,* p. 42.
[3] Those to whom Jones's work is not accessible, and who may wish for more information on the state of the bath of Buxton in the time of Elizabeth, are referred to Dr. Short's *History of Mineral Waters,* &c. p. 37—42; the *Censura Literaria,* second edit. vol. v. p. 333—340; and Lysons's *Magna Britannia,* vol. v. p. 34—39, where many very curious and entertaining particulars are collected.

governance of my said doughter and all her goods. Also I desire X‾pofer Wilson of Bromehed, and John Waynwright of Bolstarston, to be the supervisors herof, and to se this my pre-.sent last will and testament truly executed, performed and fulfilled in every behalf: and I will that either of them have vī⁴. vⅢ⁴. for their paynestakinge. Ther being witnesses, Sir Alexander Bowth, X‾pofer Stansfeld, Wilⁿ Bowman, Ambrose Swynbanke, Wilⁿ Crosland and George Crosland.'

The lady Windsor, who is here mentioned as residing with a small establishment at Sheffield, was niece to earl Francis, being daughter of his sister Elizabeth who married William lord Dacre, a nobleman well known in our border-history. Her husband Sir Thomas Windsor K.B. was son and heir-apparent of William lord Windsor, and died in his father's lifetime without male issue in 1552. She died at Sheffield, and was buried there the 26th of Jan. 1561[1]. Mrs. Anne Dacre, who is also mentioned in the will, was probably her sister, or at least a near relative. Leonard Dacre, who made an unsuccessful attempt to release the queen of Scots from the custody of his relative the earl of Shrewsbury, was her brother; and Magdalen lady Montacute her sister, whose life by Richard Smith, bishop of Chalcedon, in a style of high-flown panegyric was printed at Rome anno 1609[2].

The lady Bray, another near connexion of the house of Talbot, seems to have resided at Sheffield in the interval between the death of her first husband and her second matrimonial connexion. This lady was the only daughter of earl Francis, and married John lord Bray the last of his ancient line. This nobleman engaged in an ill-concerted rebellion against Queen Mary. It was quickly suppressed, and he narrowly escaped capital punishment. His lady acquired great credit by her exertions to procure his pardon. ' Yf it be not for yoʳ Lᵗˢ sake, and the sewte of his wyffe,' says Robert Swyft of Broomhall in a letter to the earl her father,' ' [he is] moste lyke to suffer: and what he shall do God knowethe, but my Ladye do handell her selfie in her sewtes, as well to men as to women, as she is bothe more côended and lamented then all other sewtters is; yea insomuche that the Quene, upone the reporte wᶜʰ she hathe herd of her L. wᵗʰin this two dayes gave her a gret praysse, and earnestlye said that God sent oft tymes to good women evill husbands[3].' He died not long after in consequence of wounds received at Saint Quintin. On the 18th of November 1561, the lady Bray his widow was married at Sheffield to Thomas lord Wharton, a nobleman of great power and influence in the north[4]. Him she survived, and in her second widowhood resided at Helaugh near York, a beautiful retired village where

the Whartons had a house. She adhered to the old profession of religion: and so obnoxious were her *popish practices*, as he termed them, to the archbishop, that he chose to admonish her. But it was without effect; and we find him complaining, that ' she would neither conform herself, neither yet her family. Her stout obstinacy gave an ill example, and bred great hurt in that country, and would make others undutiful[5].' She continued in the same faith, and probably the same practice, to the last: for in her will, which bears date the 12th of March 1582, she gives her soul to God Almighty, *Saint Mary and all Saints*, her body to be buried in the parish-church of Helaugh in the quire where her late good lord and husband the lord Wharton doth lie[6]; and where (it may now be added) there is a noble altar monument to their memories. Few wills in this form were proved at York in the reign of Elizabeth.

GEORGE THE SIXTH EARL of SHREWSBURY,

who in the second year of the reign of Elizabeth succeeded to the great estates of his family, served in his youth in the border-wars. He was of the queen's privy council, and admitted by her into the order of the Garter. In 1565 he was made lieutenant-general for the counties of York, Nottingham, and Derby. He was also chief justice in Eyre of the forests north of Trent, and, after the execution of Thomas duke of Norfolk, earl marshal of England[7], an office which he discharged by deputy[8].

He had not been long in possession of the family-property, before he was engaged in a serious dispute with the freeholders and copyholders of Hallamshire. Lords of manors had in early times been accustomed to receive what were called aids or benevolences from their tenants in cases of extraordinary emergency; such as when they were taken prisoner by the public enemy, when the heir was to be made a knight, or the eldest daughter to be portioned in marriage. What were originally voluntary offerings came at length through long usage to be claimed as a right[9]. The custom which had formerly existed at Sheffield had been allowed to grow obsolete: so that when the earl demanded an aid, being about to marry his eldest daughter to the earl of Pembroke, the tenants demurred. But the Lord was resolute. ' Where I perceave by yoʳ letters the frutles and unadvised answers of my freeholders within Hallomshire and other places, touchinge theire releefe, or lawfull ayde, which they ought to paye unto me at the mariage of my dowghter; I have thereof no little mervaile, considering that at theire handes I do desire no more then of right they

[1] Parish-register.
[2] Anthony Wood says that he had not been able to procure a sight of this curious biographical tract, when he wrote the life of its author. *Ath. Ox.* edit. 1692, vol. ii. p. 115. There 'is a copy of it in the library of the late Dr. Daniel Williams, O. 2300. Magdalen Dacre was born in 1538; at thirteen sent to the old countess of Bedford to be educated a Catholic; was one of the brightest ornaments of the court of Queen Mary; solicited by lord Arundel, but gave her hand to the lord Montacute: had many children, of whom three or four survived. She continued a firm friend to the Catholic interest in England, when those who espoused it were exposed to the most odious persecution. Among the Catholic divines whom she patronized, is particularly mentioned Thomas More, great-grandson to the chancellor. Battell in Sussex was her usual place of residence during her long widowhood: and there she died in the odour of sanctity on the 8th of April 1608. The work contains many anecdotes of the nobility of the times.
[3] Lodge, vol. i. p. 217.
[4] Parish-register.

[5] Strype's *Annals*, &c. vol. ii. p. 633.
[6] Torre's *Testamentary Burials.*
[7] His patent for this office may be found in West's *Symboleography*, a book of law-precedents. Its author, William West esquire, was a lawyer in high reputation who resided at Rotherham, whence the dedication to chief justice Anderson is dated. He was seneschal of the manor-court of the earl of Shrewsbury. His posterity flourished at Firbeck for a few generations. Lewis West of Wales esquire, son and heir of Sir William West, was his near relation. Most of the circumstances of the death of Lewis West, who was assaulted and murdered at Aughton as he was on his way to the fair at Rotherham, as they are related in a contemporary ballad, may be verified by historical records. To the same hand we probably owe the metrical account of the feud between the Beaumonts and the Ellands, and perhaps also the ' Dragon of Wantley.'
[8] The earl of Leicester was for some time his deputy. But we find him to be released from so troublesome an office. Talbot Papers, F. 17.
[9] Blackstone. Book ii. chap. 5.

R

owe, and but that which the lawes of this realme dothe
bothe gyve me and will compell them to paye, as all
my lerned counsaile have fully resolved withe me:
Wherof thoroughout all Shropshire, and other places
where my lands do lye, I have not beene so aunswered
as most neerest home, albeit the case thorough longe
sufferance, be growne to as greate doubte emonge
them, as where you have beene. Wherfore I woll you
declare unto suche as you shall think most expedyent
of them, that I am determyned by lawe to constrayne
those obstynate persons to paye that which by faire
meanes I have demaunded, and wold thankfullye have
recyved at their hands; which being declared, you
maye staye yo' further dealing with them, and you
shall eftsons heare from me therein, which ye shall
verie shortlye.....From Cold herbar, the xx. of Marche
1562¹.'

The refractory tenants soon after submitted, as appears by the following paper.

'Com. Ebor. }   A brieve note of the benevolence receyved
Nott. et Derb. } by Edwarde Hatefylde of my Lorde's offices
and tenants within the said counties, geven unto his
Lordshepe towardes the mariage of the Lady Katherne,
his eldist doughter, anno Regin. Dñe Elizabethe reg-
nie quinto; as particulerlie appereth by a booke made
'of the same. 1563.

Sothey, 23l. 16s. 6d.—Bradfeld, 20l. 10s. 8d.—Eccles-
feld, 23l. 8s. 7d.—Sheffeld, 22l. 4s.—Sheffeld parke, 8l. 7s. 2d.
—Whiston, 16l. 19s. 2d.—Treton et aliis, 18l. 8s. 1d.—Terr.
foren. 35l. 8s. 3d.—Chesterfeld, 11l. 9s. 6d.—Dronfyld Gyld,
11l. 13s. 1d.—Totley, xxxvi. v11ᵈ.—Pleſley, 4l. 13s. 10d.
—Gleydleys, lxxiii¹. 1111ᵈ.—Rotherham, 26l. 5s. 4d.—Kymbreworth, 23l. 11s. 8d.—Bolsterston, 25l. 17s.—Workesop,
cum membr. 28l. 12s. 8d.—Rufford, et aliis, nihil.—Spon-
don, nihil.—Wynfeld, et aliis, nihil.—Cryche, et aliis, nihil.
—Kerbywodhous, nihil.—Chauntre de Monyst. Longsdon,
and Helmdon, Pyllesbury and Croukeston, 14l. 2s. 1d.²'

These claims were abolished immediately after the
Restoration, by statute 12 Charles II.

In 1565 a treaty was on foot for a third connexion
between the houses of Dacre and Talbot. It was
agreed in the August of this year that the son and heir
of lord Dacre³ should take to wife the lady Grace Talbot, daughter to the earl: but in the succeeding January the young man died, and the lady was soon after
married to a Cavendish.

In the next year the earl lost his countess, who had
been lady Gertrude Manners, a daughter of Thomas
the first earl of Rutland of that house. She brought
him a numerous progeny, among whom were four
sons, Francis, Gilbert, Edward, and Henry, whose
names will often appear in the ensuing pages, besides
a younger son Thomas unnoticed in the peerages,
who died in his infancy, and was buried at Sheffield⁴.
She was laid in the vault at Sheffield, the first of three
countesses who were laid in that cemetery within the
space of fifteen years. No monument was erected for
her; but Howell before mentioned gave her this epitaph, which probably once hung near her grave:

'An epitaph made uppon the death of the R' Hon.
the Lady Gartrid, late countesse of Shrewisburie.

She of grace the garlande gay
in goodly giftes did weare,

Whose flowrs do now in children wise
of Talbot's line appeare.

Of Rutland's race she noblie sprang,
and linkt with peerlesse pearle
of Shrewisburie who bare the name
a noble worthy earle.

Whom she hath left behinde among
the blessed branches fine,
The working imps that sprang of them
As of a vertuous vine.'

The earl did not long remain a widower. At Chatsworth, about eighteen miles from Sheffield, resided
the lady Saint Loe, then lately become a widow. She
was the daughter of John Hardwick esquire, a private
gentleman of the county of Derby, who lived upon the
ancestorial property from which his name was derived,
near the town of Mansfield. She was one of many
daughters who married with the superior gentry of
the county, but she far outstripped the rest in the
splendour of her alliances. Her first husband was
Robert Barlow esquire, the son and heir-apparent of
Arthur Barlow, of Barlow near Dronfield, by a sister
of Sir John Chaworth of Wyverton. But he died very
young. In 1547 she married Sir William Cavendish,
a gentleman of the county of Suffolk, one of the principal persons employed by Henry VIII. in the suppression of the monasteries, and who was enriched by
many grants of abbey-lands. The marriage ceremony
was performed at Brodgate in Leicestershire, a seat of
the marquis of Dorset: and we find the duke and
duchess of Suffolk, the marchioness of Northampton,
the marquis of Winchester, the earls of Shrewsbury,
Pembroke, and Warwick, Gardiner bishop of Winchester, ladies Jane and Catherine Grey, and even the
queen's majesty herself among the sponsors at the
baptisms of her children⁵. Sir William Cavendish,
probably at her request, settled himself in the county
of Derby. He bought Chatsworth of the Leeches who
were nearly allied to his lady, and other places of other
people. He began to build at Chatsworth, but he left
the work to be finished by his widow, who was employed upon it many years after his decease on the 25th
of October 1557. Lady Cavendish took to her third
husband Sir William Saint Loe, a gentleman of an
ancient knightly family in the county of Somerset,
who was captain of the guard to queen Elizabeth.
When not in attendance upon the court this gentleman resided at Chatsworth. She obtained an un-
bounded influence over him; and his family charged
her, probably not without reason, of making an im-
proper use of her influence. She is said to have been
a woman of great wit and beauty. It is certain that
she was a woman of much address, had a mind ad-
mirably fitted for business, very ambitious, and withal
over-bearing, selfish, proud, treacherous, and unfeeling: one object she pursued through a long life—to
amass wealth and to aggrandize her family. To this
she seems to have sacrificed every principle of honour
or affection; and to have completely succeeded.

In an evil hour the earl of Shrewsbury made proposals of marriage. Before she would consent to be
raised to the bed of the first peer of the realm, she stipulated that he should give his daughter to her eldest

¹ Lodge, vol. i. p. 347—349.
² Id. vol. i. p. 348.
³ See Talbot Papers, vol. P. f. 489—497; and Lodge, vol. i. p. 361.
This young man, who was elder brother to the George lord Dacre who

was killed in the riding-house at Thetford, is not mentioned in the published accounts of the family of Dacre. ⁴ Parish-register.
⁵ See Sir William Cavendish's Funeral Certificate. Guthrie's *Peerage*,
vol. i. p. 304—306.

son, and that Gilbert Talbot his second son (the eldest being already married) should espouse her youngest daughter. These double nuptials were solemnized at Sheffield on the 9th of February 1567-8[1].

At the time of her marriage she had three sons and as many daughters. Her eldest daughter was married to Sir Henry Pierrepoint. The youngest thus married to Gilbert Talbot was not quite twelve years old. The other daughter we shall find afterwards married to the earl of Lenox. Her eldest son Henry Cavendish who married the lady Grace Talbot had by her no issue. Her second son was in the latter part of his life created earl of Devonshire: and her youngest son Sir Charles Cavendish was father to William the first duke of Newcastle.

When or where the marriage ceremony between the earl and lady Saint Loe was performed has not been ascertained: but on the 26th of June 1568 Thomas Younge, archbishop of York, a friend of the earl, yielded up his last breath at Sheffield[2].

Queen Elizabeth was pleased to interest herself greatly in the marriages of her nobility, and she did not scruple to express her approbation or disapprobation in very round terms. It was probably with much satisfaction that the new countess received the following letter from a friend and near relation about court, which is here published from the original in the collection of Mr. Wilson.

'MAY yt please you to undearstand, that Mr. Wyngfeld hath delevered your veneson to the Quenes Magesté, with my lords most humbill cōmeñcyons, and your La. with humbill thanks frome both your honors for her henes grayt goodnes. [I] assure your La. of my fayth, her Magisty did talke one longe owre with Mr. Wyngfeld of my Lorde and you so carefully, that as God ys my juge, I thynke your honors have no frende levynge that coulde have consederacyon, nor more show love and grayt afficyon. Yn the end she asked when my Lord ment to come to the court: he answared he knew not: then sayd she ' I am assured yf she myght have her owne wyll she woulde not be longe before she would se me.' Then sayd she ' I have bene glade to se my Lady Sayntloa, but now more dyssirous to se my Lady Shrewsbury.' ' I hope,' sayd she, 'my Lady hath knowne my good opennon of her ; and thus muche I assure you, there ys no Lady yn thys land that I beter love and lyke.' Mr. Batteman can more at large declare unto your honour. And so with most humbill cōmendicyons to my very good Lorde, I weshe to you both as the Quens Magūty doth disire ; and so take my leave yn humbill wyse. Frome Senjons the xxi. of October. Your honors to cōmeand
To my Lady. E. WYNGFELDE.'

Soon after the date of this letter the earl was in London: and there he learned that a severe duty was prepared for him by his sovereign. His loyalty was about to be put to extreme trial; for to him Elizabeth had determined to commit the custody of the young and engaging, the oppressed and unhappy queen of Scotland, who in this year had been forced by dissentions at home to throw herself on the protection of her kinswoman the queen of England.

With the name of this lady, whose melancholy story thus becomes for about twelve years a part of the annals of Sheffield, are associated beauty, rank, talents, learning, varied accomplishments, and unparalleled misfortunes, which raise an interest for her that gives importance to even the most trivial circumstances.

The principal and public events of her varied life have found many pens to detail them: and the policies of the courts of England, Scotland, and France respecting her, have been investigated with much success. The story of her heroic death, in which she appears with all the majesty of a martyr, has been often told with all its heart-rending circumstances. But little has been said of the occurrences of those years which passed while she was immured in Shrewsbury's strong castle of Sheffield: nor has any attempt been made to give a connected view of her private history during the long period of her captivity. This I am led by my subject to attempt. From her own correspondence, that of her keeper and his family, and the dispatches of Elizabeth's ministry and their agents, I shall endeavour to pick out the circumstances of her domestic and private history during the period of her incarceration. The events were not numerous. Hers was the monotonous life of a prisoner, varied for the most part only by temporary changes of residence, by transitions from health to sickness, by attempts to release her which served to keep hope alive, and by occasional visits from the agents of that power by which she was kept in an illegal bondage, to whom she made unavailing demands of justice, while she bore its long delay with a sedateness of mind calculated to seduce one into a persuasion of her innocence. A few letters hitherto unpublished, which have supplied some new particulars, will be found in the collection at the end of this chapter.

1568.

It was on the 17th of May that, escaping from the castle of Lochleven, the queen of Scotland landed on the shores of England, at Workington in Cumberland. She immediately addressed a respectful letter to Elizabeth, in which she explained the hard necessity by which she was compelled to leave her own kingdom and to seek an asylum in hers. The queen immediately sent Sir Francis Knollys to attend upon her, and Mary soon found that she was not so much a guest as a prisoner.

The council strongly advised Elizabeth against making any attempt to restore the fugitive to her throne; and it seems that they also counselled her against permitting Mary to proceed either to France or Spain. When they added to such pernicious counsel that it was unfit she should be at large in England, it only remained that she should here be placed in confinement.

A colourable pretext was speedily devised. Lord Darnley was a native of England and a near relative of Elizabeth. It was pretended to be inconsistent with the honour of the queen of England to countenance one who lay under strong suspicions of having been privy to his murder, till she had cleared herself of the foul imputation. A court was speedily formed for hearing this great question. It met at York : and while the proceedings were pending, Mary was in the custody of the lord Scrope, warden of the West Marches, who kept her at his castle of Bolton.

The anxiety which Elizabeth expressed in her conversation with Wingfield to know when the earl would be at court, and the apparent wish to ingratiate herself with the new countess, renders it probable that she had

---

[1] Parish-register.

[2] Monumental inscription in his cathedral church.

conceived the design of transferring Mary to the care of Shrewsbury as early as the October of this year. She knew how to prepare the way for any request she had to make. In the month of November, at a private audience, Elizabeth told the earl that 'er it were longe he shuld well perseve she dyd so trust him as she dyd few.' Shrewsbury says the queen would not tell him in what manner she intended to afford him an opportunity of manifesting his loyalty, but he doubts it will be in committing to him the custody of the Scottish queen : for it was at that time determined to remove her more into the interior of the kingdom: and it was rumoured about court that Sir Henry Gate, a member of the council in the north, and one Vaughan, who was his friend and relative, were making application for the dangerous trust. In another letter of the 13th of December, Shrewsbury tells his lady, ' Now it is sarten the Scotes quene cumes to Tutburye to my charge.'

In the choice of Shrewsbury for this delicate and trying appointment, Elizabeth evinced her usual judgement. He was a nobleman of the very first rank, and high in character as well as station. There was therefore an appearance of respect to Mary in the choice of such a one to be her keeper. He had several houses, or rather castles, in the interior of the kingdom, in any of which she might be kept with little danger of either a forcible abduction or a secret escape. His immense property enabled the earl to serve her with fewer demands upon her treasury than others would make : and he had a spirit neither to be over-awed nor corrupted. The loyalty of the house of Talbot which had passed into a proverb, and which was carried by no one to a more chivalrous extent than by the sixth earl, was a pledge to her for his fidelity and zeal in her service. Sixteen years of faithful service approved her choice. He even bore with uncommon fortitude and humility the supernumerary hardships which his tyrannical mistress thought proper to impose upon him while engaged in this service, the painful anxiety attending which he complains in a melancholy letter to Burghley nearly brought him to his grave.

1569.

The order of council for the removal of the queen of Scots from Bolton to Tutbury bears date the 20th of January. She travelled southward unwillingly. She passed through Rotherham on the 31st of January[1], and arrived at Tutbury on the 2d of February. There the earl and countess of Shrewsbury were ready to receive her.

The castle of Tutbury was held by Shrewsbury of the crown as part of the duchy of Lancaster. Here she remained several months: and one of the most interesting memorials which remain of her is a letter written by White, a servant of Elizabeth, to Sir William Cecil, in which he gives some account of her person, habits, and pursuits during the time of this her first residence at Tutbury[2]. This man being on his way to Ireland on business relating to the county of Wexford, had occasion to consult Shrewsbury on some point in his commission, and for this purpose waited on him at Tutbury. When Mary understood that a servant of the queen was at the castle, she de-

sired he might be introduced to her. After some discourse respecting Elizabeth, Mary took part in a religious service, which White observes was performed in English, and then renewed the conversation. White acquitted himself, according to his own account, like a true courtier: spoke of the virtues of his mistress; of her kindness to Mary; and of the cause she had for thankfulness that she was arrived in such a place of security. All his remarks 'she veray gentilly accepted, and confessed that indede she had greate cause to thanke God for sparing of hir, and greate cause likewise to thanke hir guid syster for this kindly using of hir: as for contentation in this hir present estate she would not require at Gods hands, but only pacience whiche she humbly prayd him to give hir.

'I asked hir grace sence the wether did cutt of all exercises abrode, howe she passed the tyme within : She sayd, that all the day she wrought with hir nydill, and that the diversitie of the colors made the worke seme lesse tedious, and contynued so long at it till veray payn made hir to give over; and with that layd hir hand upon hir left syde, and complayned of an old grief newely increased there. Upon this occasion she entred into a pretty disputable comparison betwene karving, painting, and working with the nydill, affirming painting in hir awne opinion for the moste comendable qualitie. I aunswered hir grace, I coulde skill of neither of theme, but that I have redd *Pictura* to be *veritas falsa*. With this she closed up hir talke, and bydding me farewell, retyred to hir prevay chamber.

'But if I (whiche in the sight of God beare the quenes majestie a naturall love besyde my bounden dutie) might give advise, there shulde veray few subjects in this land have accesse to, or conferens with this lady. For besyd that she is a goodly personadge (and yet in trouthe not comparable to our souverain) she hathe withall an alluring grace, a pretty Scottishe speche, and a serching witt clowded with myldnes: Fame might move some to releve hir, and glory joyned to gayn might stir others to adventure moche for hir sake. Then joy is a lively infective sens, and cariethe many perswasions to the hart, whiche rulethe all the rest. Myn awne affection by seeing the quenes majestie our souverain is dowbled, and therby I gesse what sight might worke in others. Hir heare of it self is black and yett Mr. Knolls told me that she weares heare of sundry colors[2].'

White further acquaints Cecil that lord and lady Levenstone, both protestants, were the only persons of note with her. She had a household of fifty persons. Shrewsbury was very careful of his charge, but the queen overwatched all persons in the house, for it was one o'clock every night before she went to bed. She disliked being placed so near the earl of Huntingdon, because he pretended some right to the crown; and except that she was now so much nearer to Elizabeth, she should have much preferred to have remained at Bolton. Above all things she desired to have an audience of the queen.—This letter bears date the 26th of February. The suggestion of this courtly sycophant was acted upon, and orders were soon after issued that none should have access to Mary but by special permission[3].

About the month of June the earl removed with

[1] Burghley Papers, published by Haynes, p. 507.   [2] Id. p. 509—512.   [3] Lodge, vol. ii. p. 13.

his charge to Winfield-manour, where they remained for some months. It was at this period that Leonard Dacre, a near relative of Shrewsbury, made an unsuccessful attempt to release her. In August the earl received a sharp reprimand for having projected, if not accomplished, a journey of a few miles to Buxton, the queen being persuaded that his charge required all his time and attention[1]. At the end of that month a letter from Leicester and Cecil conveyed the queen's permission that he might remove with the queen of Scots to 'his howse at Sheffeld:' it was to be done with ' no open pompe nor assembly of strangers, but circumspectly and quietly[2].' Either this permission was revoked, or Shrewsbury changed his purpose, for in the month of September he returned with his prisoner to Tutbury[3].

Shrewsbury had pleaded his state of health as an excuse for leaving his charge, and availing himself of the waters of Buxton. Elizabeth, with the suspicion incident to a consciousness of the want of integrity, availed herself of this plea, as an excuse for placing in his house another nobleman professedly as a guard upon Mary, but really as a spy upon Shrewsbury. The nobleman appointed to this ungracious office was the earl of Huntingdon, whom Mary most disliked and dreaded[4]. This was a cruel step, and was probably intended to mortify her, for she made no secret of her dislike of Huntingdon: and it came attended with another vexatious order;—her train was to be reduced to thirty persons. To this succeeded instructions to her keepers, that as before she had not been permitted to see any persons without express permission, so now she was neither to send nor receive messages without the privity of her keepers[5]. These changes were made in consequence of the discovery of Dacre's attempt, and of the views respecting her of Thomas duke of Norfolk. ' Harum nuptiarum rumor,' says Camden, ' per mulierculas aulicas quæ statim amatoria sagaciter odorantur, ad reginæ aures clarius pervenit[6].' ' The Q. Ma[ty],' says Cecil in a letter to Shrewsbury, ' is entred into no small offence with the intention that she thynketh hath bene to devise of a mariadge with the Scottish Quene[7].' This discovery much increased Elizabeth's solicitude about the safe keeping of her prisoner: so that when Huntingdon expressed his dislike of an employment which obliged him to reside in another person's house, and entreated that he might be wholly discharged of it, or allowed to remove the queen to his own house at Ashby, she was peremptorily refused, and another nobleman added to the guard[8]. This was Walter viscount Hereford afterwards earl of Essex. But he was soon relieved. It was no employment for a Devereux.

Mary's friends were chiefly in the north of England. Her story was there better known. Her residence amongst them had attached some to her interest: and in the north there was a stronger feeling of attachment to the old profession of religion (which it was understood Mary would restore) than in other parts of the kingdom. Towards the close of this year many of the gentry of the north openly declared their intention to liberate her and under the conduct of the earls of Northumberland and Westmorland marched to

York. Shrewsbury and Huntingdon were directed to remove with their charge from Tutbury to Coventry. That being a walled town was capable of sustaining a siege. But what had been ill concerted was quickly suppressed, and in the month of January the queen of Scots was again at Tutbury[9].

1570.

She remained in Staffordshire till May or June, when she was taken to Chatsworth, perhaps spending a short time at Winfield-manour in her way. The severity of her confinement was now a little relaxed. Her own ambassador the bishop of Ross, and the ambassador of the king of France her brother-in-law, had pleaded warmly with Elizabeth for some indulgences to her captive. The latter, however, received a short reply from the queen in one of his conferences, if we may trust the intelligence of Fitz-William, a person employed by the countess of Shrewsbury (to whom he was distantly related) to collect and transmit the news of the day at a time when the convenience of modern newspapers was unknown. ' Thei say Mush[r] Rambo-liet hathe donne the Frenche kinges message for the libertie of the Scotishe quene, and that she might enioye her owne realme, and to govern it, and to se the bringing up of her owne childe. The quenes ma[jtie] answered, that she marweled the king wolde troble himself in matters so farre from him, having so muche to do at home: as for the matters betwene her syster of Scotland and her, thei wolde agree well inough; he shold not nid to care for it.[·] And so it is thoughte as yet he shall not come to the speche of the quene of Scotland, and much lesse to goo into Scotland[10].' While she was at Chatsworth Beton died, one of her attendants, of the family of cardinal Beton. He was interred in the church of Edensor, and in his monumental inscription, which still remains, is called her ' prægustator,' an officer in royal households, of whom there is such frequent mention in the ballads and romance-histories of the middle ages. The vigilance of her keeper disappointed a scheme laid for her release by two sons of the earl of Derby and a gentleman of the county of Derby named Hall[11]: and at Chatsworth at the period before us was held the first of that series of personal negotiations by which hope was kept alive in the breast of the sufferer, and a colouring of reason and propriety given to a series of acts of oppression and barbarity. Cecil and Mildmay were at Chatsworth on this business in the month of October.

The earl of Huntingdon had been released from his disagreeable employment when the queen was removed from Tutbury. And it seems to have been concerted between Shrewsbury and the two ministers of Elizabeth, that Mary should be removed to Sheffield. Accordingly Cecil on his return to the court, having first expressed his thanks to the earl for the honourable entertainment he and his colleague had received at Chatsworth, and having passed some compliments on the good service which he and his countess were rendering to their sovereign, proceeds thus : ' Now for the removing of y[e] quene, hir Ma[ty] sayd at the first that

[1] Lodge, vol. ii. p. 19.
[2] Haynes, p. 532.
[3] Haynes, p. 526.
[4] Id. vol. ii. p. 20.
[5] Lodge, vol. ii. p. 21.
[6] Annales, &c. 8vo. p. 161.
[7] Lodge, vol. ii. p. 23.
[8] [9] Haynes, p. 532, 575.
[10] From the original letter in Wilson's Collections.
[11] Jebb's Life of the Queen of Scots, p. 226, &c.

5

she trusted so to make an end in short tyme y[t] your L. shuld be shortly acq'ted of hir; nevertheless when I told hir Ma[ty] that yow cold not long indure your howshold there, for lack of fewell and other thyngs, and y[t] I thought Tutbury not so fitt a place as it was supposed, but y[t] Sheffeld was y[e] metest, hir Ma[ty] sayd she wold thynk of it, and w[i]in few dayes gyve me knolledg: Only I see hir Ma[ty] loth to have y[t] Q. to be often removed, supposyng that therby she cometh to new acqueyntance; but to that I sayd yo[r] L. cold remove hir w[t]out callyng any to yow but your owne. Uppon motiō made by me, at the B. of Rosse's request, the Q. Ma[ty] is pleased y[t] your L. shall, whan yow see tymes mete, suffer y[e] Quene to take y[e] ayre about your howss on horssback, so your L. be in cōpany; and therein I am sure your L. will have good respect to your owne company, to be suer and trusty; and not to pass frō your howss above one or twoo myle, except it be on y[e] moores: for I never feare any other practise of strangers as long as ther be no corruptiō amongst your owne[1].' This letter was written on the 26th of October, and it was soon followed by another containing the queen's permission that he might remove with his charge to Sheffield-castle. The precise date of the entrance of the royal captive within those walls which so long inclosed her is not to be collected from any of the documents before me. But it was a little before Christmas 1570[2]. Shrewsbury had then been more than two years absent from home.

1571.

The train of the queen of Scots when she first became an inmate of the castle of Sheffield consisted of thirty persons, beside a few supernumeraries allowed by the kindness of the earl. They were chiefly French and Scots, as indeed their names bespeak[3].

My Lady Leinstoun, dame of honor to the queues Ma[ie].	Archibald Betoun.
M'rez Leinstoun.	Thomas Archebald.
M'rez Setoun.	D— Chiffland.
Maistresse Brusse.	Guyon l'Oyselon.
M'rez Courcelles.	Andro Matreson.
M'rez Kennett.	Estien Hauet, escuyer.
My Lord Leinstoun.	Martin Huet, m're cooke.
M[rs] Betoun, m[r] howshold.	Piere Madard, potiger.
M[rs] Leinstoun, gentilman servāt.	Jhan de Boyes, pastilar.
	M[r] Brusse, gentilmā to my Lord Leinstoun.
M[rs] Castel, physition.	Nicoll Fichar, s[e]rvant to my Lady Leinstoun.
M[r] Raullet, secretaire.	
Bastien, page.	Jhon Dumfrys, servant to Maistresse Setoun.
Balthazar Huylly.	
James Lander.	William Blake, servant to Maistresse Courcelles, to serve in absence of Florence.
Gilbert Courll.	
William Douglas.	
Jaquece de Saulie.	

The supernumeraries allowed by the earl were, according to the same check-roll,

Cristilie Hog, Bastiene's wyff.
Ellen Bog, the M[r] cookes wyff.
Cristiane Grame, my Lady Leinstoun's gentilwoman.
Jannet Lindesay, M'rez Setoun's gentil woman.
Jannette Spetelle.

Robert Hamiltoun, to bere fyre and water to the quene's cuysaine.
Robert Ladel, the quenes lacquay.
Gilbert Bonnar, horskeippar.
Francoys, to serve M[rs] Castel, the phesitien.

For her safe keeping the earl took into his employ forty extraordinary servants, selected from amongst his tenantry, who kept watch day and night at the castle.

The orders for the government of the queen's household were most strict. They are here given from the original minute in the Cotton library[4].

'To the M[r] of the Scotts Queenes houshould Mr. Beton.

First,—That all your people w[ch] apperttayneth to the Queen shall depart from the Queen's chamber or chambers to their own lodging at ix. of the clock at night, winter and summer, whatsoever he or she; either to their lodging within the house or without in the towne, and there to remain till the next day at vi. of the clock.

Item,—That none of the Queen's people shall at no time wear his sword neither within the house, nor when her Grace rydeth or goeth abroade : unless the Master of the Household himself to weare a sword and no more without my special license.

Item,—That there shall none of the Queen's people carry any bow or shaftes, at no tyme, neither to the field nor to the butts, unless it be foure or fyve, and no more, being in the Queen's companye.

Item,—That none of the Queen's people shall ryde or go at no tyme abroad out of the house or towne without my special license : and if he or they so doth, they or he shall come no more in at the gates, neither in the towne, whatsoever he or she or they be.

Item,—That you or some of the Queen's chamber, when her Grace will walke abroad, shall advertyse the officiar of my warde who shall declare the messuage to me one houer before she goeth forth.

Item,—That none of the Queen's people whatsoever he or they be, not once offer at no tyme to come forth of their chamber or lodging when anie alarum is given by night or daie, whether they be in the Queen's chambers or in their chambers within the house, or without in the towne. And yf he or they keepe not their chambers or lodging wheresoever that be, he or they shall stande at their perill for deathe.

At Shefeild the 26th daie of April, 1571, per me
SHREWSBURIE.'

The strictness of these orders was sufficient to satisfy even the jealousy of Elizabeth. 'The Q. Ma[ty],' says Burghley (lately made a peer), 'lyketh well of all your ordres, and can be content y[t] (if your self shall be so content) the nōbre above 30 permitted to be wth that quene by your L. shall remayne[5].' The precautions used for her safe keeping were not, however, unnecessary: for it came out at the time of Norfolk's second arrest, that at Easter in this year Sir Henry Percy had nearly succeeded in a scheme to deliver her, the plan being frustrated only by an unexpected change of her apartments[6]. It then also appeared that notwithstanding all the precautions which had been used, Norfolk had contrived to keep up a frequent correspondence with Mary. Of the duke's arrest, and the proceedings which ensued, we have a curious account from the pen of Fitz William, whose letter and one of the queen of Scots of this year may be found amongst the original correspondence at the end of this chapter.

[1] Lodge, vol. ii. p. 50.
[2] The earliest notices of her residence at Sheffield are perhaps those draughts of letters to the queen, the earl of Leicester, and Cecil, sent by the bishop of Ross, in the Cotton library Caligula C ii. No. 3. They are dated Sheffield December 20, 1570. In the same volume are instructions of the same date to the bishops of Ross and Galloway, and lord Livingstone. No. 214.
[3] Lodge, vol. ii. p. 52.
[4] Caligula C iii. No. 21.
[5] Lodge, vol. ii. p. 55.
[6] Id. vol. ii. p. 60.

But a letter of Shrewsbury's hitherto unpublished should be read in this place, as it shows us the extreme rigour of her confinement in the time following the arrest of Norfolk, and lets us into an acquaintance with the feelings of Shrewsbury towards his royal prisoner[1]. He seems to have allowed his sense of what he conceived a public duty to have stifled too much the sentiments of compassion, to which his heart seems on other occasions to have been no stranger. Notices of the ill state of health to which her confinement had reduced her are to be found in all her letters of this year, together with most pressing solicitations that she might be allowed to clear herself of all the matters laid to her charge, and regain her liberty.

' To the right honorable and my very good Lord my Lord of Burghley, one of the Lls of her Maties privy councell.

My very good L. After I had dispeched this berer, this quene made eftsones great complaynt unto me of her sickly estat, and that she loked verily to perishe thereby : aud used diverse melancholy words that yt is ment yt shuld so com to passe w^tout helpe of medicine, aud all because I was not redy to send up her Phisician's l'res unto yor L. which in dede I refused, for that I perceved her principall drifte was and is to have some libertie out of these gates, which in nowise I will consent unto, bicause I see no small perill therin. Notwithstanding lest she shuld think that the Quenes Ma^ie had c̃ommanded me to denye her suche reasonable meanes as might save her life by order of phisick, I thought yt not amysse upon her said complaint and instaunce to send up the said l'res hereinclosed to be considered on as shall stand w^t the Quenes Ma^ies pleasur. But truly I wold be very lothe that any libertie or exercise shuld be graunted unto her or any of hers out of these gates, for fear of many daungers nedeles to be remembred unto yor L. I do suffer her to walk upon the leads here in open ayre [and] in my large dining chamber, and also in this court yard so as both I myself or my wife be alwaies in her company, for avoiding all others talk either to her self or any of hers : And suer watch is kep̃t w^tin and w^tout the walles both night and day, and shall so c̃otynue God willing so long as I shall have the charge. Thus I commit yor good L. unto God. From Shefeld Castle this xiith of December 1571.

Postscript. I cannot perceyve that she is in any present perill of sicknes. If any ensue I will not faile to advertise the same unto your L. w^t all diligence, but I must here eftsones advertise yor L. that I am utterly against any further libertie unto her.
                    Yo^r L. ever assured
                          G. Shrewsbury.'

1572.

At the opening of this year we find Shrewsbury in London, presiding as lord high steward at the trial of Thomas duke of Norfolk. It was for him to pronounce the sentence of death on that high-minded nobleman. This we are informed he could not do but with weeping eyes. But he did not at that moment foresee how close a union their families would form in the persons of a grandchild of each, and that his castle where the cause of Norfolk's misfortunes was confined would become the inheritance that that very duke's descendant in the fourth degree, when the name of Talbot would have passed away. Execution of the sentence did not follow till the second of June.

In the absence of Shrewsbury the custody of the queen of Scots was committed to Sir Ralph Sadler, one of the most trusty of the servants of Elizabeth. In a letter to lord Burghley from Sheffield the 9th of January, he relates a conversation he had just held

with Mary[2]: and every fourth or fifth day during the short period he was in trust he remitted exact accounts of the queen's demeanour, and reported all he could collect of her private sentiments. In one of his letters he gives Burghley an account of the manner in which she received the news of Norfolk's condemnation[3]. But he disliked his employment. On the last day of that month he presses earnestly for his release[4], and soon after he was relieved by the return of Shrewsbury to his charge.

Three letters in cypher of the queen of Scots, which the earl discovered hid under a stone soon after his return, were sent to Burghley[5]. This and some other things of the same nature led to a visit of expostulation from the Lord De la War, Sir Ralph Sadler, Dr. Wilson, and Mr. Bromley, under the name of a treaty[6]. They were succeeded by a more welcome visitant, the marechal de Jos who brought money from France[7]. On that country was her principal dependence for income. She had a large dowry as widow of Francis II. Even this special messenger from a sovereign prince, himself a man of rank and honour, was not allowed to have any conversation with the queen, except in the presence of her keeper, who in a letter to Burghley at this period expresses his firm determination that no person should be allowed to enter his castle-gates, but those who had express authority from her majesty.

A small indulgence was intended her in the course of this summer. In a letter to Lord Burghley of the 26th of August, Shrewsbury mentions his intention of removing her for five or six days to the manour, while her apartments at the castle, which were become 'unklenly,' were thoroughly washed[8]. In the same letter he strongly advises against an indulgence which Elizabeth intended to allow his prisoner—a change in her servants. It seems indeed, under all the circumstances, that such a change could not with propriety have been allowed.

Before this letter was delivered to Lord Burghley he received most appalling intelligence from another quarter. The massacre of Saint Bartholomew filled the Protestants everywhere with terror and dismay. In the height of the alarm Shrewsbury added thirty soldiers to the ordinary guard of Mary; and would allow her on no pretence to go without the gates[9]. He caused all the neighbouring woods to be searched, and other places where it was possible that any friends of Mary might have secreted themselves. These additional restraints, the interruption of her correspondence, the neglect with which all her letters to Elizabeth were now treated, and perhaps a persuasion of the impolicy of the measure just adopted by her friend and brother-in-law Charles IX., all concurred to afflict her. ' She is w^tin a few dayes,' says Shrewsbury with provoking indifference, 'become more malincholy than of long before, and complenes of hur wronges and imprisonmente. I am sure her malyncoly and grefe is grettar than she in words uttars; and yett, rather than contynew this impresonment, she styckes not to saye she wyll gyve hur boddy, hur sonne and cuntry for lybarté[10].' It was not the least of her misfortunes that at these seasons of strong excitement,

[1] Cotton MSS. Caligula C iii. 84.   [3] Id. No. 43.
[2] Id. 78.   [4] Id. 79.
[5] Lodge, vol. ii. p. 64.

[4] Jebb's Life of the Queen of Scots, p. 246.
[7] Lodge, vol. ii. p. 65.   [8] Id. vol. ii. p. 68.
[9] Id. vol. ii. p. 77.   [10] Id. vol. ii. p. 82.

Shrewsbury, under instructions from above, was prompt to observe and quick to report every unguarded expression she might use. Nay, with a meanness unworthy even the disciple of that Machiavellian policy under which the statesmen of those ages acted, my Lord Burghley scruples not to convey his mistress's instructions, that Shrewsbury should 'tempt hir pacience to provoke hir to answer some what:' Mr. Lodge, with correct feeling, observes, 'What a frightful addition is this to the horrors of Mary's prison[1]!'

1573.

Early in this year there were floating rumours about court of an attempt being made, or at least meditated, to release her. To calm the ever active fears of Elizabeth, the earl wrote to her majesty a letter containing the strongest assurances of his fidelity and continued vigilance. 'I have hur sure inoughe,' he says, with an air of savage triumph remote I trust from his natural disposition, 'and shall kepe hur forthe cumyng at yo[r] Ma[tie]s cōmandemēt, ether quyke or ded, what soevar she or anny for hur inventes for the contraré; and as I have no doute at all of hur stelynge away from me, so if anny forsabull attempte be gyven for hur, the gretest perrell is sure to be hur's[2].'—Was his castle then to be stained with the blood of this much-injured woman? to be the scene of a midnight murder!— From this profanation it was however spared, and the disgrace, but little palliated by the forms without the reality of justice, fell on Fotheringhay.

The scheme of removing her for a short time from the castle to the manour in the autumn of the last year seems to have been frustrated by the unexpected intelligence from France. But in the spring of this year it is certain that she was for a few days at the manour; a change which gave occasion to a remarkable conversation between Dr. Wilson one of the secretaries, and Gilbert Talbot the earl's second son, who reported it to his father in a letter dated the eleventh of May. 'Towe dayes since, Doctor Wilson told me he hard say that yo[r] Lo. with yo[r] charge was removed to Shefeld Lodge, and asked me whether it was so or not: I answered I hard so also; that you were gone thither of force till the castle could be clenged: And further, he willed to know whether yo[r] L. did so by y[e] consent of y[e] counsell, or not; I sayde I knew not that, but I was certayne yo[r] Lo. did it uppon good grounde. I earnestly desyred him, of all frendshipp, to tell me whether he had harde any thing to y[e] contrary; which he sware he never did, but asked because, he sayd, once that lady should have bene conveyghed from that house. Then I told him what great hede and care you had to hir safe keping; especially beyng there that good numbers of men, continually armed, watched hir day and nyght, and both under hir windowes, over her chamber, and of every syde hir; so that, unles she could transforme hirself to a flee or a mouse, it was unpossible that she should scape;' &c.[3] The scheme for releasing her while at the manour to which the secretary refers, was probably that of Sir Henry Percy before mentioned. In the ruins of Sheffield-manour a window is called by her name, out of which it is traditionally reported that she escaped from the custody of Shrewsbury.

The effect of the closer confinement in which she had been kept since the August of the preceding year was still further to impair her health. The waters of Buxton were at that time in high reputation; and by the mediation of the French ambassador she prevailed in obtaining permission to visit them. She charged Shrewsbury with obstructing the gracious intentions of Elizabeth[4]: but at length they went together, all strangers being first ordered to depart, and none being suffered to come there during her stay.

Some portion of the autumn of this year she spent at Chatsworth: but in November we find her returned to her dreary abode in the castle of Sheffield, in which month she gave an honourable testimonial to one of her most trusted servants the bishop of Ross, and discharged him from her service[5].

The duty which the sovereign had imposed upon him rendered the earl of Shrewsbury obnoxious to dangers of various descriptions. If he was less rigorous than his instructions allowed, he incurred the displeasure of Elizabeth: if he exceeded them, or even acted up to their full tenour, he was making himself odious to Mary, who though today his prisoner might tomorrow be his queen. Mary's right to the succession on the demise of Elizabeth was indisputable, or at least not likely to be disputed. Of this she took care sometimes to remind him: and in one of the many personal altercations which they seem to have had together, she threatened that *she would remember him at another day*[6], and this at a time when Elizabeth's state of health gave some disquiet to those who had been most open or most active in the injurious treatment of her presumptive heir. He had seen, too, of what a queen of England was capable, in the public execution of so potent and popular a nobleman as the duke of Norfolk, on at the best but a poorly supported charge of treason. His whole conduct, however, shows that he preferred erring on the side of rigour, and considered zeal and fidelity in the service of his sovereign as his first and only duty. What was then his surprise, when in the December of this year he learned from his son Gilbert Talbot, that Elizabeth had intimated to him she had reason to suppose that his father was a secret favourer of the queen of Scots, and had discussed and openly maintained her right to the succession! This suspicion in the mind of Elizabeth he naturally traced to some machination of Mary or her friends, who might thus be endeavouring to effect her removal to the custody of some guardian less watchful than he. So he earnestly presses upon Elizabeth to consider it: and in a long exculpatory letter, dated Sheffield-castle 29th of December 1573, he declares in the most unqualified terms the falsehood of the accusation, the strictness with which he had ever sought to discharge his high trust, and his desire that he might not be permitted to live to see the day when it could properly be made a question to whom the crown of England should devolve[7].

1574.

The rumours which had awakened the suspicions of Elizabeth were at length traced to their authors, who were found to be two chaplains of the earl, Corker and Howarth, the former of whom enjoyed under his pa-

[1] Lodge, vol. ii. p. 72.   [3] Id. vol. ii. p. 96.   [5] Lodge, vol. ii. p. 114.   [6] Murdin, p. 273.
[2] Id. vol. ii. p. 101.   [4] Id. vol. ii. p. 110.   [7] Murdin, p. 273.

tronage the livings of Rotherham and Hansworth, and who were punished for the scandal[1]. This affair increased Shrewsbury's weariness of an office which was a continual source of anxiety, which consumed the whole of his time, and brought to him neither profit nor honour. He also found that the ill-paid stipend which he received from the Exchequer was by no means adequate to the expense which the residence of the queen and her suite occasioned him. His own state of health was at this time so precarious that we find him laying before lord Burghley, in a letter of the February in this year, a plan for the safe custody of the queen in the event of his death[2]. He therefore made earnest suit at the beginning of this year for his release[3]; but his services were become too valuable to suffer his reasonable request to be complied with.

On the thirtieth of August Mary lost one of her most valuable servants, Rollet her French secretary. He was buried at Sheffield on the fourth of September[4]. His death was a great grief to her. Shrewsbury immediately took possession of his papers, not without strong remonstrances from the queen. A few letters from the pope, the Spanish ambassador, and the cardinal of Lorraine were found, but nothing which appeared of importance[5]. He was succeeded by the perfidious Naue, who continued with her almost to the last[6].

But the year 1574 is chiefly memorable in the history of Mary's captivity for a marriage between one of her nearest relations and a daughter of the countess of Shrewsbury. This was Charles Stuart earl of Lenox, younger brother to her husband Darnley, and nearly related to herself, in blood. This young man spent a few days at Rufford, one of the seats of the earl of Shrewsbury, along with his mother the old countess of Lenox, and on a few days acquaintance made a love-match with the only unmarried daughter of Sir William Cavendish. ' Yt was delte in sodenly,' says Shrewsbury in an exculpatory letter to Elizabeth, who looked upon these nuptials with an eye of more than common jealousy, ' and wythowt my knowledge: but as I dare undertake and insure to your Ma^{te}, for my wyfe, she, fyndyng hyr dawghter dysapoynted of yong Bartè, where she hoped; and that th'oder yong gentylman was inclyned to love wyth a few day's acquyntans, dyd hyr best to further her daughter to thys matche; wythout havyng therin any other intent or respect than wyth reverent dutie towards your Ma^{te} she owght[7].' A more full account of the origin of the acquaintance which led to these nuptials is given in a letter of Shrewsbury to Burghley. The truth was, that the countess of Shrewsbury had long been looking out for a splendid alliance for her daughter, and eagerly embraced the offer which this young noble-

man, probably inconsiderately, had made: 'There is feu nobillmen's sonns in England,' says Shrewsbury, ' that she hath not praid me to dele forre, at one tyme or other; so did I for my lord Rutland, with my lord Sussex, for my lord Wharton, and sondry others: and now this cumes unloked for without thankes to me[8].' Elizabeth was,-as was probably anticipated, much displeased. The two countesses of Shrewsbury and Lenox were for a time placed under restraint. But her displeasure was the most severely directed towards the young couple, (neither of them twenty,) nor could the mediation of powerful friends on both sides avail entirely to subdue it. What was most unreasonable considering the terms on which the queen of Scots was with the whole Lenox family, she was charged with having been concerned in bringing about this alliance. The only issue was one daughter, the lady Arbella Stuart, who was left an orphan at about four years of age, and whose melancholy history forms so interesting a feature in the reign of James I.

1575.

The attention of Elizabeth seems to have been ever directed upon the castle of Sheffield. She had her spies who sent her immediate intelligence of every thing that happened there, and every change of every kind excited the most lively apprehensions. Hers looks more like the jealousy of conscious guilt than an honest watchfulness for the public good. In the month of February the wife of Gilbert Talbot was delivered of a son and heir in the castle: and Elizabeth immediately conveyed her ' mislykings' to the earl, on account of the repair of women and strangers which this event would occasion. The earl with all due humility implores forgiveness, but assures his constant correspondent the lord Burghley, that ' the mydwyfe excepted, none such have, or doo at any tyme cum w'in her syght; and at the fyrst to avoyd such resorte, I myselfe w^h 11. of my cheldren chrystenyd the chyld9.' In the same letter he mentions that the walls of his old castle had been shaken by an earthquake. Two or three shocks were felt in this island in the reign of Elizabeth. The apartments occupied by the queen of Scots were those most shaken by it; and she was much alarmed. ' My L. wher ther hath bene often brutes of this ladès escape from me; the xxvi. of Febrary last ther cam an erthequake, whyche so sunke chefely hur chambar, as I doubted more hur faleng than hur goinge, she was so aferde: but God be thanked, she is forth cumyng; and *grantè it may be a forwarnyng unto hur*.' Thus easy is it to moralize for another. The warning was rather addressed to the land of her oppressors, and to the earl in particular, that he should no longer lend the hall of his ancestors to such an act of protracted injustice and cruelty.

---

[1] Strype's *Annals, &c.* vol. ii. p. 251—253.
[2] Talbot Papers, vol. P, f. 673.   [3] Lodge, vol. ii. p. 118.
[4] '1574 Sep. 4. Sep. Petrus Roollett, Gallos.' Parish-register.
[5] Lodge, vol. ii. p. 119.
[6] This man conducted Mary's correspondence with Babington, and afterwards betrayed her. On the day of her execution she is reported to have said, ' I die for Naue; must I be sacrificed, and Naue be saved!' The history or the blood of such a man is perhaps not worth inquiring after; but I add this note for the purpose of stating that there lived a family in and about Sheffield who bore the name of Naue, or as they wrote it Nawe, retaining however the French pronunciation, who not improbably sprang from this secretary of the unfortunate princess. The first of this name I have found is a Thomas Nawe, who in 1578 was married at Sheffield to Alice Hoyle. The next a Henry Nawe, of Little Norton, cloth-worker, whose son (of the same name) was admitted to his

freedom in the company of cutlers in Hallamshire in 1646. Henry Nawe junior lived at Beauchief, and had a son to whom he gave the name of Lewis, as it may seem in memory of their French extraction. The last of the name was a maiden lady, grand-daughter of Lewis Nawe, who died at Sheffield in 1803.
[7] Lodge, vol. ii. p. 123.
[8] Cotton Papers, Caligula C iii. This letter is dated from Sheffield, 5 Nov. 1574. I have used the copy of it in Dr. Leonard Howard's *Collection of Lettere*, 4to, 1753, p. 235—237, which in many parts is very imperfect, a fault which those who are acquainted with the singularly imperfect formation of his written characters in which the sixth earl of Shrewsbury indulged himself will be willing to excuse. Mr. Lodge deserves great praise for his skill in decyphering the letters of this earl.
[9] Lodge, vol. ii. p. 128. The baptism of this child is recorded in the parish-register.

T

In this year a new vexation presented itself to the queen of Scots. During the summer, commissioners from the French court, accompanied by Beale an English secretary, were at Sheffield, treating with her respecting the exchange of the duchy of Touraine, which she held as dowager to Francis II. These negotiations were not conducted much to her satisfaction. It is melancholy to hear her complain as she does in one of her unpublished letters appended to this chapter, ' You may well enough imagine the situation I am in, and whether I have need of any further rough treatment.' Her friend and early companion Charles IX. was dead; and the new court not so favourably disposed to her as the old had been. She yielded a reluctant assent to the proposals which were made her. Her duchy was given to Alençon, and she received in exchange the county of Vermandaise, with the lands and bailiwicks of Senley and Vetry[1].

There is a letter of Mary's of this year dated at Sheffield the third of August, to Dr. Allan then at Doway, expressing piety and resignation, and declaring her intentions, if ever in her power, to restore the Catholic religion in this island[2]. And it was probably in the suite of this embassage that the friend of Caussin the jesuit obtained admission to her, to whom she gave a diamond-ring, and a table-book in which she had written various memoranda. This person, Caussin tells us, used to declare that ' it was impossible to see this excellent person without rapture and celestial joy[3].' The jesuit's life of her is throughout most extravagantly encomiastic. It is not necessary to suppose her guilty of the more heinous offences laid to her charge, of which however there is too pregnant proof, to discover that the life of this princess does not uniformly exhibit all the severer virtues, and is not exactly that which a wise man would choose to hold up to general imitation.

1576. 1577. 1578. 1579. 1580.

These years are almost barren of incidents in the life of the queen of Scots. Her enemies seem to have succeeded in what she perceived was their object—that it should scarcely be remembered that such a woman existed[4]. Her days were passed in close and mysterious seclusion. Even the family of her keeper were not allowed access to her. Francis lord Talbot, the earl's eldest son, once acquainted Elizabeth, ever inquisitive about his father's charge, that he had not seen her for many years past[5]. Needle-work seems to have been her principal amusement: and in this art specimens of her skill are still shown in the houses which belonged to her keeper and his countess.

In the spring of 1576 she was allowed to visit Buxton: and it was Elizabeth's intention that she should

not have returned to Sheffield, but have gone again to Tutbury. But on Shrewsbury's representation of the unfitness of that place to receive her, he was allowed to return with his charge to Sheffield[6].

Soon after Easter 1577, we find the countess of Shrewsbury endeavouring to engage her husband to spend the summer at her favourite house at Chatsworth[7]. Her letter is in a singular style of mingled affection and peremptoriness, and may be considered as one of the first overt-acts of that hostility of which more striking proofs appeared in the next year, and which embittered the remainder of the earl's life. The countess was then building at Chatsworth. She was persuaded that Elizabeth's consent might be obtained: and in a postscript uses this strange expression, ' Lette me here how you, your charge *and love* dothe, and comende me I pray you.' The earl either could not obtain permission, or did not choose to comply at first with this request, but in the September following it does appear that he was at Chatsworth[8]. The earls of Leicester and Warwick and lord Burghley spent part of the same summer at Buxton, and were much gratified by the attentions they received from Shrewsbury, who was himself there for some time, having the gout in his hand. But on intelligence from the court of rumours of the queen of Scots' escape, he hastened back to his charge[9].

A will of the queen of Scots is dated at Sheffield-manour in the month of August of this year[10].

Beside the most uncomfortable altercations with his wife, Shrewsbury was engaged at this time in vexatious disputes with his tenants in Glossop-dale. Never prince presumed more upon the loyalty of a subject than Elizabeth did on that of Shrewsbury. She took up the cause of his refractory tenants[11]: and we find the earl complaining in a letter to Burghley of a petty injury he had received at her hands, in a lease being privately granted to Charles Wharton and others, of lands lying near Sheffield-castle which had been long held by himself and his ancestors[12]. She even ventured upon reducing his allowance, which at first was not adequate to his expenses, and in the best of times was very irregularly paid. The earl justly observes, that this was a poor return for twelve years faithful and anxious service[13].

In the spring of 1580 he applied for permission to remove with his charge to Chatsworth; but Elizabeth was resolutely bent against it, and Burghley advised the earl not to press his suit[14]. Mary, however, by the mediation of foreign ambassadors, prevailed for permission to pay another visit to the healing waters of Buxton[15]. The journey must in those days have been a perilous one. It was performed on horseback. Mary was an excellent horse-woman, but when mounting

[1] Robertson's *History of Scotland*, vol. ii. App. No. vi.
[2] Cotton MSS. Caligula C ix. 230.
[3] Caussin's *Holy Court—Life of the Queen of Scots*.
[4] See one of her own letters at the end of this chapter.
[5] Lodge, vol. ii. p. 226.
[6] Id. vol. ii. p. 149.   [7] Id. vol. ii. p. 167.
[8] Lodge, vol. ii. p. 164. This visit must have been of short duration. She was at Sheffield on the 22d of August, when she wrote to Beton desiring information, and recommending great caution and secrecy. Cotton MSS. Caligula C ix. 235. Naue her secretary writes to his brother from Sheffield the 31st of August 1577, acquainting him that the queen intended to discharge one of her agents in France, and advising him to apply for the office. Id. 241. Again, the earl of Shrewsbury writes to Lord Burghley from Sheffield the 7th of November, desiring that neither Godfrey Foljambe nor Ralph Sacheverel may be appointed sheriff of

Derbyshire (Talbot Papers, F, 229); and the next day to the same, desiring that the wine which he has received at Rouen in exchange for lead, may be landed at Hull without paying the custom, being for his own use. Id. P, 859.
[9] Strype's *Annals*, vol. ii. p. 502.
[10] Robertson's *History of Scotland*, vol. ii. App. No. xi.
[11] Lodge, vol. ii. p. 219.
[12] Talbot Papers, vol. P, f. 1005.
[13] Lodge, vol. ii. p. 236.
[14] Id. vol. ii. p. 236. The earl made his request at an unfortunate time. Elizabeth had just received information from France, that ' the papistes and the Scottishe byshoppes praised the earle of Shrewsburye to be a highe friend of the quene of Scotts.' See Howard's *Collection of Letters*, p. 376.
[15] Lodge, vol. ii. p. 239.

for this journey she fell and injured her back. As before, no strangers were permitted to remain or arrive during her stay: nor was she allowed to leave her apartments, except to go to the bath which she used once or twice every day. She arrived at Buxton, in company with the earl, on the 28th of July[1], and after a week's stay returned to Sheffield.

1581.

This was a year of sickness. Mary has drawn an affecting picture of her situation in a letter to Castelnau the French ambassador:—without fresh air, not allowed necessary exercise, and become so weak in her lower extremities, that she was obliged to be carried by her servants when she would pass from room to room. She had also to complain of the mean manner in which her table was served, and notices in severe terms the entertainment which was provided for her on Easter-day. When she complained of it to Shrewsbury, he bluntly replied, that it was as well as his allowance enabled him to afford[2]. Perhaps he wished to engage her interest in his suit for the regular payment of his allowance, and the continuance of it upon the original plan. But Elizabeth instead of listening to so reasonable a request intimated to him, that she was informed he had lately been making purchases of land, and that she thought it unnecessary to attend to such applications from a man who thus showed that he was overflowing with riches. These were not golden days. Such treatment prepares one to find some of the chief of the nobility joining in the next century with the commonalty in enforcing the claims of political justice against the arbitrary power of the ancient monarchy of England.

In the summer of this year she was again at Chatsworth[3], and there is some reason to believe also visited Buxton.

In November she was engaged in another of those fruitless negotiations which contributed indeed to diversify the scene, but which also prevented her mind from assuming that placid, acquiescent frame which is generally induced by suffering long continued and hopeless. Beale, who was employed on this occasion, writing to Walsingham gives nearly the same account of her condition as she herself had given in her letter to Castelnau. She was then confined to her bed: and in one of her conferences with Beale she earnestly desired that Elizabeth would pity her distressed state; and if she were not willing to make trial of her affection and duty, yet that she would be pleased to send some physicians and chirurgeons to consult with those she had about her. In another conversation she told Beale, that 'though she was not old in years, she found herself old in body, that her hair was turned grey, and that she should soon have another husband[4].' She was then eight-and-thirty.

1582.

Such was the state of Mary's mind when her sister-in-law the countess of Lenox died. This was, perhaps, another victim to the unrelenting spirit of Elizabeth. Her remains were laid in the Talbots' vault at Sheffield on the twenty-first day of January[5]; and doubtless the queen of Scotland heard from her gloomy apartments in the castle, the knell of her young and unfortunate kinswoman, with a secret wish that she was also going to that place where the wicked must cease from troubling.

The negotiations of the last year were continued through the whole of the present: and Mary is said to have shown better judgement in the conduct of them than she did on similar occasions. The particulars may be found in her historians.

Shrewsbury during this period was making earnest solicitation for some reward from Elizabeth for his constant service in this arduous employment. But when he found that nothing was to be obtained either by letters or the mediation of friends, he determined to vary the object of his request, and to ask leave to wait in person on his sovereign[6]. He had now been ten years absent from the court. There were demurs to his reasonable request, but at length the queen's leave was obtained; and for the custody of the queen of Scots Mr. Wortley of Wortley was selected, who had married one of the daughters of the old servant of the Shrewsbury family, Robert Swyft of Broomhall. He is described in a letter to Walsingham as being 'one of the councell at York, a gentylman bothe wyse and of very good credytt in the country[7].' The earl intended to set forth about the eleventh of September, with a company of twenty gentlemen and as many yeomen, beside their servants, and his horsekeepers[8]. His agent in London was to send him down a fine velvet foot-cloth, and a pair of double gilt stirrops for the journey, which was to be performed in four days, setting out from Winfield-manour, and going by way of Leicester[9]. But though every preparation was made the journey did not take place. Francis lord Talbot, the earl's eldest son, died at Belvoir-castle the latter end of August, and on the third of September was laid with his ancestors in the vault at Sheffield. But we find the earl assigning another reason for postponing a journey which he had been so desirous of taking. In a letter to Baldwin his confidential agent, of the fourteenth of September, he says that he fears to come to London because the plague was so prevalent there[10]. But there was some secret reason. Elizabeth at this time conceived new and strange jealousies of this her trusty servant. On the subject of these suspicions there is a long and melancholy letter from Shrewsbury to Walsingham, written at Hansworth, where on the edge of Sheffield park he had lately built a small mansion[11], to which in the latter and darker period of his life he

---

[1] Lodge, vol. ii. p. 239.   [2] Id. vol. ii. p. 253.
[3] Cotton MSS. Caligula C ix. No. 1.
[4] Beale's original letters to Walsingham from Sheffield while employed in the negotiations, are to be found in the British Museum. Harl. MSS. 289.
[5] Parish-register.
[6] Lodge, vol. ii. p. 279.   [7] Id. vol. ii. p. 281.
[8] Id. vol. ii. p. 284.
[9] Talbot Papers, vol. G, f. 179.
[11] That the house at Hansworth was built by this earl I gather from these circumstances. In 1577 the earl writes to Burghley, who was then

at Buxton, and sends him the plan of a lodge which he was building. Talbot Papers, P 837. In May 1580 Francis lord Talbot reports a conversation which he had held with Elizabeth, in which he told her that he had lately been at Sheffield, and that the earl his father had accompanied him in his journey southward to a house which he was building. Lodge, vol. ii. p. 226. This small mansion, of which very little now remains, was the boudoir of the family. It derives some claim to celebrity as having been the house in which was born that eminent commander William Cavendish first duke of Newcastle, a fact not noticed in the memoirs of his life, but established by the entry of his baptism in the parish-register of Hansworth.

was fond of retiring. There is genuine pathos in this passage of the letter. ' I am by byrthe, & so lefte from all my auncestors, a trew loyall subjecte, & in y[t] will I ever lyve & dye, & lyve I may (if it so please the Lord God) to doe her Matie sum seryyce; & therfore I hope she will not leave me to ruyne my selfe wth the thoughtes of my expresse calamityes, so y[t] very shortely I may becum in cace therw[th] never after to be able to doe ether pryñce or cuntrey service[1].' What awakened the queen's jealousy at this particular juncture, and what was the precise nature of the suspicions she was led to entertain, must, I apprehend, ever remain in some degree uncertain. But it appears to me that the strongest light is reflected upon Shrewsbury's desponding and mysterious letter from one of the queen of Scots found among the Burghley papers, and published by Murdin, but not without a note on the suspicions which have been entertained and expressed of its genuineness[2]. A most extraordinary composition indeed it is, whether we regard the subject-matter, the character and relative situation of the parties between whom it is supposed to have passed, or the unguarded conduct it exposes of a woman of an understanding so masculine as the countess of Shrewsbury. At the same time it corresponds so exactly with authentic memorials of this period, its reference to minute circumstances in the Shrewsbury family is so exact without appearing the effect of design, and above all it explains so satisfactorily the disgrace of the earl at this period, that I feel myself compelled to add a testimony to its genuineness, but to assign its date, not with Murdin to 1586, but to the August or September of 1582. The queen of Scots owed nothing to the house of Shrewsbury; and for their sakes had no reason to withhold herself from revealing any expressions they might have used in a moment of heat and irritation, if by so doing she could hope to gain the confidence of Elizabeth. But how she could expect any other result from such a communication than that the dislike of Elizabeth towards her would become the more inveterate, I leave to those who are concerned to vindicate Mary's understanding, as well as her immaculate purity, to explain.

The month of June and part of July was spent at Buxton[3]: and as this was her last visit, it might be at this time that she wrote with her diamond pencil on the window, the distich which has been so often quoted, though sometimes inaccurately, if we may believe Fuller, who tells us he had the glass in his hand, and read it thus[4]—

' Buxtona, quæ calidæ celebraris nomine Lymphæ,
Forte mihi posthac non adeunda, Vale.'

1583.

The greatest part of this year was spent at Sheffield; and in the early part of it she was engaged in negotiations with Sir Walter Mildmay and Mr. Beale[5]. But she was allowed to visit Shrewsbury's seat at Worksop; for we find the earl, in a letter to Baldwin of the third of November of this year, denying that

while she was at Worksop she had been permitted to walk in Sherwood forest[6].

1584.

At length the time arrived when Shrewsbury was to be relieved from the severe and dangerous duty which his sovereign had imposed upon him. In the month of August a commission was made out to Sir Ralph Sadler to take the charge of the queen of Scots, Shrewsbury being then expected at court. Sir John Somers was to be joined with him in the charge[7].

On the eighteenth of August, Sir Ralph left his house at Standon in Hertfordshire, and on Tuesday the twenty-fifth of August arrived at Sheffield. He found the household in the midst of preparation for a removal to Winfield, Shrewsbury having received permission to take the queen thither, a few days before. Sadler prevailed with the earl to delay the journey a few days till he could have communication with the court, to which he represented how much fitter a place Sheffield was than Winfield for the custody of the great prisoner. He alleged that he could keep her better at Sheffield with sixty men than with three hundred at Winfield, and that it was there much more easy to procure provisions.

It was finally determined that she should be removed to Winfield: and on Thursday the third day of September 1584 she quitted the castle of Sheffield to return no more.

Most interesting and affecting is the account given by Sadler and Somers of her conversation with them as they journeyed together from Sheffield to Winfield. She was all duty and obedience to Elizabeth; wished in every way to conciliate her favour; assigned various reasons why it was not to be supposed that, neglected as she was by all the courts of Europe, she should now wish to withdraw herself from the protection of Elizabeth; but wished much for. liberty, and complained of her long imprisonment, ' having spent her yeres from twenty-four to past forty, and by combre and impotency become old in body[8].'

At Winfield she was kept under the same restraints as at Sheffield. On the sixth of September the earl of Shrewsbury took his leave, and the next morning set out for London. On the fifteenth, the court being at Oatlands, he took his seat as a privy counsellor at the board, when a minute was entered on the journals expressive of her majesty's entire satisfaction with the manner in which he had discharged his important trust[9].

Shrewsbury availed himself of the opportunity now afforded him to solicit his entire discharge. His plea was most reasonable. He had served long and well, to the sacrifice of his time, his ease, and his liberty. He was now advanced to that period of life when men most require and love freedom and repose. Within the last two or three years his infirmities had much increased; and the divided state of his family seemed to demand all his attention. The family differences Elizabeth had sought in vain to reconcile. The death without issue of Francis lord Talbot, by conveying the

[1] Lodge, vol. ii. p. 289.   [4] Murdin, p. 558—560.
[2] Lodge, vol. ii. p. 271.
[3] Church History, p. 181 of the fourth series of pages.
[5] Cotton MSS. Caligula C ix. 28.
[6] Talbot Papers, vol. G, f. 225.

[7] Sadler Papers, vol. ii. published by Arthur Clifford esquire, where, among much curious information respecting this period of Mary's history, is a second set of orders which Sadler found established by the earl at Sheffield, for the government of her guard.
[8] Id. vol. ii. p. 385—391.   [9] Lodge, vol. ii. p. 296—299.

right of inheritance to his second son, who it may be remembered was married to one of the daughters of his countess, not less violent, insolent, and brutal than her mother[1], had given the family of his countess a preponderance in his house which was fatal to its stability and peace. Elizabeth yielded to his importunity, and the office of Sadler and Somers was changed from one that was temporary to a permanent employment.

Here then closes the connexion of Sheffield with the story of this ill-fated woman. What follows, and she lived not long, was a series of oppressions from which she found no shelter, till she sunk into the grave. On the thirteenth of January 1585 she left Winfield for her old prison at Tutbury. There the lord Saint-John was to be her keeper, but he soon procured his discharge. On the seventeenth of April Sir Amias Paulet relieved Sadler from an employment of which he was most weary. He is said, how truly I know not, to have been the most unfeeling of her keepers. In the beginning of 1586 she was removed from Tutbury to Chartley, and from thence in the September following to Fotheringhay. It is with regret I read a letter from Shrewsbury to Burghley urging execution of the sentence pronounced against her[2]; and perceive his name in the list of those who were present at the solemn and mournful spectacle which the great hall of Fotheringhay exhibited on the eighth of February 1587. She was buried in the cathedral church of Peterborough.

And now having brought her to her grave, we shall there leave her awaiting the great day which will clear up all the mysteries of her sad story, and when every merciful allowance will be made for the infelicities of that situation in life in which it had pleased Providence to place her.

She was in England exactly eighteen years, eight months, and twenty-two days. The following table will exhibit at one view, what proportion of this time was spent at different places where she resided. I suppose the whole term of her residence in England to be divided into a hundred parts.

1 in Cumberland.
2 at Coventry, Worksop, and in her journeys.
2 at Fotheringhay.
3 at Chartley.
3 at Bolton.
4 at Winfield.
4 at Buxton.
7 at Chatsworth.
12 at Tutbury.
62 at Sheffield.

Strange were the rumours afloat in London respecting the earl of Shrewsbury and his conduct to the queen of Scots, at the time of his discharge. The curious reader is referred to the ecclesiastical memorialist of those times, Strype[3]. This and other business detained him in London during the whole of the winter, nor did he return to Sheffield till the end of July 1585. How he was received by his tenantry and neighbours will best appear by the following letter of Gilbert Dickenson, one of his superior domestics, now

first published from the original among the Talbot papers[4].

'To my Lorde,

MAY yt please yo' good Lo. to understande that dyveres honneste men have herde of yo' Lo. comming home, & wold have come to mete yo' Lo. but that I have stayed them untyll I heare fardyer of yo' Lo' pleasure : & theare is suche running from howse to howse to tell that yo' Lo. dyd ly at Winfeld all night, & every one preparing to mete yo' L. yo' Lo. shold come into the cuntry with suche loufe as never dyd man in England, wich is a gryetter comfort to hus then any worldley rycheas. & for muittones, beufes, & lames shall note be wauttiug ; nor any thing wich can be got God willing. Thuis I sease for truibling yo' L any further at this tyme. Dated at Sheffeld this xxviii[th] of July 158 [5].

Poste cryptium; if yo' Lo. thincke good the shall cum no fuirdyer then a myle be onde Chasterfeld to me yo' Lo: & I have sente one hether for muittones.

Yo' Lo. moste humbyell & obedyent sarvante tyll deathe,
GILBARD DICKENSON.'

The acclamations with which his return to the seat of his ancestors was greeted, met with little that was answerable to them in the heart of Shrewsbury. He had no affectionate family there to welcome him, and on whom, fatigued with public cares, he might throw himself in his declining age and infirm state. Most part of his time he spent at his small and quiet mansion of Hansworth[6]. It was at this period of his life that he built for himself the sumptuous monument in the church of Sheffield. Its long inscription, the work of Fox the martyrologist[7], will be found in its proper place, but not without the date of his decease, which he is said to have foretold that his heirs would neglect to supply[8].

George the sixth earl of Shrewsbury died at Sheffield-manour on Wednesday the eighteenth day of November 1590, at seven in the morning. His funeral was on the tenth of January, and then more sumptuously performed than 'was ever to any afore in these countrys: and the assembly to see the same was marvellous both of nobility, gentry and country folks, and poor folks without number.' So says a contemporary, and probably a spectator from whose hand this is copied[9]. Three persons lost their lives by the fall of two trees that were burned down at this funeral. So it stands in the accompts of the burgesses of Sheffield. Piers archbishop of York signified his intention of preaching on this occasion[10]. There is no full account of the proceedings of the day, like that left of his father's funeral; but some interesting particulars may be collected from the following extract of a letter from one Francis Needham to Gilbert then become earl of Shrewsbury[11].

' IT. maie please yo' L. since mi last I're Mr. Alexander Rateliffe imparted unto me a clause in yo' L. I'res concerning Melborne, and required me from yo' L. to give him such light and assistance as I coulde in the matter of the funerall.......... For the other parte, for that the nowe officers at armes are verie weeke in their knowledge of matters appertayning to their charge, (Somersett the most learned amongst them being deade) I have entreated Thomas Milles somtime Mr. Randolphs servant, who was his heir, to lett me have a view of his bookes & papers for such things as I thought might serve yo' L. at this season : and have collected into a booke matters

---

[1] Lodge, Introd. p. xviii.   [2] Murdin, p. 572.
[3] *Annals*, vol. iii. p. 217.   [4] Talbot Papers, vol. G, f. 88.
[5] In his haste the writer omitted the last figure.
[6] Harl. MSS. 4782, is a book of accompts of the weekly expenses of the earl's household at Hansworth in the years 1588 and 1589.

[7] Harl. MSS. 374, where is the first draught of the inscription in Fox's own hand.   [8] Lodge, Introd. p. xvii.
[9] Arthur Mower of Woodseats near Chesterfield, gent.
[10] Talbot Papers, vol. I, f. 100.
[11] Id. vol. H, f. 203.

U

as well of this subiect, as other material observacõns, which yo' L. shall receive by this bearer; and ame to besech yo' L., that when you shall have no longer use thereof, the funeralls finished, it may be retorned unto me againe, for that I mean God willing to add divers other matters of like nature unto it, when any come to my hands.

After such time as Mr. Ratliff & I had ben w'th Mr. Garter and conferred w'th him for his demaunds and proportions, whereof yo' L. hath ben advertised by Mr. Ratliffes l'res, we desered he woulde sett downe the particularities of everie sortes of stuffe for the hearse and painters work, and for their owne fes; w'ch we desered to have, aswell that yo' L. might know wher upon their demaunds were grounded, as that we might see whether he demaunded more than was allowed by others in like cases: and there upon conferred it with the billes and allowances made at the Erle of Derbies funerall, and therby see what might be rebated, as yo' L. maie perceive hy that noote inclosed w'th'in the booke: for by that composition in grosse they gott xx. or xxx. Li at the E. of Rutlands funeralls which might have been saved, and in the Sco. Q. funerall 150Li..........

Mr. Garter and we stande in som debat whether it were [more] honorable to have the funeralls perfourmed on horsback from the Mannor, or one fote from the Castle: consideriug there in state to be helde; and one the other side, it hath ben allwaies the use that noble personages are to be buried from their principall houses: & in truth it ought to be donn on horseback; but herein are two things to be considered, the charge, and conveniency in respect to the lodging and dynner; in w'ch respect the Castle is the fittest: and to perform it from thence on horsback would be somewhat troublesome, being so neare the church where they could hardly be ranged in order. But under correction, if it were to be sorted as the corps might only be carried in the chariott, and the principall mourners or states to ride with the officers of Arms and gent. of the horse, it wolde .... horses trapped with black, it maie be performed w'th full estate in everie respect; for it shoulde then be seen 25 horse a sufficient number for state, the church being so nere: and for the charges it will be donn w'th xxx. Li and the chariott to be covered w'th velvet compassed, w'ch maye be gained out of the officers composition. But it may please yo' L. to order the whole to yo' own best liking.'

It is sometimes matter of surprise how the nobility of the Elizabethan age supported their numerous and extensive establishments. But their estates were immense. A view of those possessed by this earl of Shrewsbury may be found in the appendix to the history of his manor of South-Winfield, taken from his inquisition *post mortem*. A memorandum is preserved among the Talbot papers[1] of an offer that was made to him by his sons in 1586, during the height of the family troubles, to become farmers-general of his estate. They proposed that he should retain the castle, lodge, and park of Sheffield, together with the house and domain of Hansworth, and that for the rest they should pay him annually ten thousand pounds. The rough estimate of the property then made was,

In Yorkshire	. .	3000*l.* per annum,
Nottinghamshire		1500
Derbyshire	. .	2000
Shropshire	. .	2000
Staffordshire	.	500
Herefordshire	.	800
Oxfordshire	.	200
Cheshire	. .	70

But this could not be the whole, as he had consider-

able property in London, at Chelsea, and in Wiltshire, Leicestershire, and Gloucestershire.

GILBERT SEVENTH EARL of SHREWSBURY.

Gilbert the seventh earl was born on the 20th of November 1553[2]; and before he was fifteen was married to Mary Cavendish, daughter of Sir William Cavendish of Chatsworth, whose widow was on the point of becoming the second wife of his father earl George. He was after his marriage sent with one of his brothers for education to the university of Padua[3]; and on his return was elected to represent the county of Derby in parliament, till his elder brother Francis lord Talbot dying without issue, he became the heir apparent to the earldom of Shrewsbury, and was called up to the house of peers by the title of lord Talbot. In 1590 he succeeded to the honours and estates of the family, and was soon after admitted into the order of the Garter. The profuse mode of his living, rather than the superiority of his talents, or the peculiar eminence of the stations he attained, has obtained for him the title of the great and glorious earl of Shrewsbury[4].

By a will executed on the 24th of June before his decease, the late earl appointed his two younger sons, Edward and Henry Talbot, his executors. They renounced the executorship, and Elizabeth countess of Shrewsbury relict of the late earl claimed and was allowed to administer. But these letters were revoked, and administration *de novo* granted to his successor in the earldom. Then followed violent dissentions between the new earl and the widow of his father and mother of his wife. This was as it ought to be. During the life of the old earl they had leagued together against his peace and independence: and the hostility of these two persons, which with slight intervals continued till the death of one closed the scene, (if it may not even be said to have survived her in the provisions of her testamentary disposition,) combines with countless other instances to teach the great moral lesson, that no dependence is to be placed upon the continued attachment or services of a person who may have once for the sake of another been prevailed upon to violate any of the obligations of virtue or honour. Such persons usually become, when once the tie of interest is dissolved, the bitterest as they are the most dangerous of enemies. In the fair and open path of integrity and honour, peace and security only are to be found. The *mens conscia recti*, as it is essential to internal peace, so is it also among the best defences against any unreasonable and unjust demands of others. In the disputes respecting this executorship and afterwards, it is to be feared the town of Pontefract lost the benefit of a liberal and judicious bequest made to it by the late earl.

Not with the relict only, but with almost every member of this distracted and divided family was the new earl at open variance, almost before his father was cold in his tomb. Irritated by the unreasonable pretensions of his second countess, and by the audacious conduct of her daughter the wife of Gilbert, the old

---

[1] Talbot Papers, vol. G, f. 335.

[2] A miscellaneous manuscript volume, Harl. 4990, folio 58, contains an account of the births of all the children of Robert Waterhouse of Shibden, in the parish of Halifax, esquire, in the father's own hand. His sixth son William was born at Kynsley the 4th of July 1590, and died on the 22d of November, ' commonly called the Queen's day then next,

following: and the day after that, being the 23 day of November, died George earl of Shrewsbury, *Gilbert his heir being 38*, 20 *November next after, as he himself told me.*

[3] In a letter to his father dated Padua, Nov. 4, 1570, he mentions their arrival, and promises to be diligent in his studies. Talbot Papers, vol. P, f. 571.

[4] Isaac Walton in his *Life of Saunderson.*

earl made settlements of those parts of the family-property which were in his power, little to the satis-faction of his successor and his lady[1]. Melancholy is the picture of fraternal discord which the annals of the noble house of Shrewsbury at this period present. Jealousies and suspicions of the most dreadful nature were afloat. In one of the miscellaneous volumes of the Harleian collection of manuscripts is a sheet con-taining probabilities, arguments and reasons that Ed-ward Talbot conspired against the life of the earl his brother[2]. Wood the earl's physician was supposed to be leagued with him; and his death was to be effected by subtle poison conveyed in a pair of perfumed gloves. In the Talbot papers we have a correspondence be-tween these two sons of the same mother, in which Edward Talbot, without any compromise of what is called honour, parries the determination of earl Gil-bert to meet him in the field[3]. But on this painful subject I am not ambitious of the honour of throwing more light. When such dreadful passions were agita-ting the inhabitant of the castle, how happy the indus-trious artisan whose hammer was clinking near it!

He was also at variance with his youngest brother Henry Talbot[4]: with lady Talbot widow of his elder brother lord Francis[5]: with the house of Manners his mother's family[6]: with his neighbour Mr. Wortley of Wortley[7]: and his dispute with the Stanhopes of Not-tinghamshire, arising in a very trifling cause, was pur-sued by both parties with such precipitation and violence, that it was rendered impossible for the neighbouring gentry to preserve neutrality. Abundance of particu-lars concerning this affair are to be found in the Talbot Papers[8], and also among the Harleian Collections[9]. He was on ill terms with his tenantry. The matters in dispute came before the queen; and in 1593 or 1594 the lord keeper wrote to the earl signifying her majesty's displeasure with his conduct, and advising him to ease his tenants of their hardships, in order to give her majesty satisfaction[10]. In 1595 he suffered a suspension of the queen's favour, and an imprison-ment of some continuance—for what cause does not appear. A letter of Lord Buckhurst's of the 23d of July of that year signifies to the lord keeper that ' my Lord of Shrewsbury shall be kept to remain at his own home[11]:' and on the first of October following, that most entertaining court-gossip Rowland Whyte, writ-ing to Sir Robert Sidney, says, ' My lord Shrosbery is not yet suffred to come to court, nor to have great resort unto hym. His lady hath attended these 4 daies at my lord Lumley's lodging to see the quene; and hath made my lord of Essex, my ladyes Warwick, Leighton, and Skidmer, her meanes to prepare her way, and as yet they prevaile not: in the meane tyme her mynd doth somtyme ease yt self with teares[12].' In 1596, his youngest brother Henry Talbot died at the age of thirty-three, and was laid with his family in the vault at Sheffield. He had been settled by his father on an estate at Burton-grange.

It was in the same year that Elizabeth employed

the earl in a public service, more of ceremony than real business. He was sent on an embassy to Henry IV. of France to invest him with the order of the Garter, to receive from him an oath for the observance of the treaty lately made between the two kingdoms, and to present Sir Anthony Mildmay, who was to remain ambassador in ordinary. The earl met the king at Rouen, and in the church of St. Ouen (still a magni-ficent fabrick after all the spoliations of modern times) he was invested with the order in the presence of the chief nobility of France. The earl engaged the good opinion of the king. Sir Thomas Edmunds speaking of that prince, in a letter to the earl of Shrewsbury, says, ' he did much desier to conserve yo' L.' acquaint-ance and love, and that yo' L.' honorable disposition and good carriage, wch he doth particulerlie affect, doe make yo' L. much recommended, wth other qually-ties[13].' While the earl stayed at Dieppe to refresh after having been driven about in the channel by con-trary winds, he took his favourite diversion of hunting: and soon after his return home we find him sending to the king of France, as a present, ' 12 faire cowple of hownds, a faire running horse, a gentleman with it, a huntsman and a boy, very well apparelled[14].' Sir An-thony Mildmay wrote to the earl that the king was much pleased with the hounds, and that the French nobility were *ravished* by Holland's performance on the horn[15].

The earl sat upon the trial of the earl of Essex in 1600. On the queen's death in 1603 he signed the proclamation in which King James was named as her successor; and he entertained that monarch at his house at Worksop when on his journey from Edin-burgh to take possession of the English throne. Some letters relating to this period will be found in the ap-pendix to this long chapter, to one of which I beg leave more particularly to direct the reader's attention, as it contains perhaps the most direct proof that has hitherto appeared, that the representative of lady Catherine Grey did not quietly acquiesce in the contravention of his claim, and the transference of the sceptre to the representative of lady Margaret Tudor.

The earl of Shrewsbury was continued in the office of privy counsellor by King James: but except the chief justiceship in eyre of the forests north of Trent, he had neither honours nor employment from the new court. His time was for the most part spent in the country. His name still lives in the floating traditions of Hal-lamshire: and to ' Earl Gilbert' by popular report belong all the deeds of all the house of Shrewsbury, and even some transactions, of his remoter ancestors the Furnivals.

In 1606 the lady Alethea Talbot, youngest daughter and co-heir of the earl of Shrewsbury, was married to a nobleman of high character and principles, Thomas Howard earl of Arundel and Surrey[16]. This is a ma-terial circumstance in the history of Hallamshire, this marriage transferring that fine lordship to the noble family in whom it still is vested. It appears that as

---

[1] Camden gives her this character, *rebus turbandis nata*. Annals, 1618, June 5. In one of her letters to her mother she speaks in these terms of the old earl, ' Your La.' may perceve my Lo. of S. is no changling unles it be from evell to worse:' and her conduct to him was in every way so disrespectful, that we find him towards the close of his life offering to see his son, but prohibiting his daughter-in-law from coming within his doors.

[2] Harl. MSS. 4836, f. 325.   [3] Lodge, vol. iii. p. 50—55.
[4] Talbot Papers, vol. H, f. 345.   [5] Id. vol. O, f. 49.

[6] Talbot Papers, vol. H, f. 189.
[7] Harl. vol. H, f. 523: a letter from Sir Richard Wortley to Edward Tal-bot, dated Wortley 25 Jan. 1592, in which he explains at great length the motives of his disagreement with the earl.
[8] Id. vol. H.   [9] Harl. MSS. 6996, 6996.
[10] Harl. MSS. 6996, f. 92.   [11] Id. 6997, f. 35.
[12] Sidney Papers.   [13] Lodge, vol. iii. p. 92.
[14] Sidney Papers. Letter of Rowl. Whyte, 14 May 1597.
[15] Talbot Papers, vol. M, f. 42.   [16] Id. vol. L, f. 61.

early as April 1604 the overtures for this match had been made by Sir John Hobart[1].

On the 13th of February 1608 died the old countess of Shrewsbury, at her seat at Hardwick. Here she spent the years of her fourth widowhood in abundant wealth and splendour, feared by many, beloved by none, flattered by some, and courted by a numerous train of children, grandchildren, and great-grand-children. Among the elegies of Sampson, a poet of the times, is one to her memory: and she has had a bishop and an archbishop to celebrate her praise; Tobie Matthew archbishop of York, who preached at her funeral from Solomon's description of a virtuous woman, and White Kennet bishop of Peterborough, who about a century after in the same church pronounced a splendid panegyric on a true patriot, her great-grandson, William duke of Devonshire. The application which the archbishop made of Solomon's character of a virtuous woman afforded the preacher an opportunity of entering largely into her character. The sermon was in existence long after the archbishop's decease[2], and probably it may be now recoverable. That Massinger had his eye upon her when he drew the character of Sir Giles Overreach I dare not affirm: but they were lordships in *Derbyshire* and *Nottinghamshire* which he got into his hands; and he *kept himself out of the commission of the peace*, being content rather to manage those who were in it. She also was of no very illustrious birth, but bent upon making her children ' *honourable, right honourable.*' There seems to be more than an accidental coincidence.

The death of this lady brought down into the north her grand-daughter the lady Arbella Stuart; which I notice merely for the purpose of stating, that this interesting and much injured young woman paid a visit at the same time to her noble relation at Sheffield-castle[3], and when doubtless she would visit the grave of the mother, whose misfortunes she inherited, in the church of Sheffield; nor would she forget that she was on the spot where her royal aunt had passed so many years of her long captivity. It is extraordinary that this victim of a too near alliance to the crown should have obtained so little of the public sympathy. Beautiful, (if we may trust her portrait in the gallery at Long-Leat,) sensible and sprightly as the remains of her correspondence testify, there were no dark shades in her character to disturb the feeling of admiration and respect. Without the king's permission she gave herself in marriage to Mr. William Seymour, grandson to the earl of Hertford. When it was discovered, they were both closely imprisoned. By the assistance of her aunt the countess of Shrewsbury she effected her escape. At the same time Mr. Seymour escaped from the Tower. They attempted to proceed to France. He succeeded, but she was retaken in Calais road. She was placed under a stricter guard, and died a lunatic on the 27th of September 1615. The countess of Shrewsbury was two years in confinement on account of this affair.

On the eighth of May 1616, Gilbert earl of Shrewsbury, the last male of the family of Talbot who possessed the castle of Sheffield and its surrounding dependencies, departed this life at his house in Broadstreet, London; and was laid in the vault at Sheffield, according to the directions contained in his last will and testament executed only four days before his death.

The funeral obsequies were performed in a suitable style of magnificence; but no monument was ever erected to his memory. The chapel did not afford space for another befitting his quality. The hospital erected at Sheffield by one of his descendants, in conformity to the directions contained in his will, may be considered as his best monument. Nor ought it to be forgotten that he was ever the patron of learning and of learned men. The university of Cambridge can speak of his munificence. He encouraged with all his influence the scheme for erecting a college at Ripon for the northern parts of England: and he was the patron of Augustine Vincent, the most exact of all our genealogists.

Copy of the last Will and Testament of GILBERT EARL of SHREWSBURY.

' IN the name of God, Amen. I Gilbert Earl of Shrewsbury having by God's good favour attained to the age of three score and two yeares and more; and finding my bodie weakened with sicknes and infirmitie, but being of good and perfect memorie, I give God thankes for it, doe ordain and make this my laste will and testamente in forme following. Fyrst I committ my sowle into the handes of Almightie God, hopinge to be saved by the abundant mercie and goodness of Almightie God, thoroughe the deathe and passion of Jesus Christ my onlie medentor, redeamor and most blessed Saviour. My bodie I comitt to the earthe and requier the same to lie interred in Sheffeilde churche where my graundfather, father, mother and elder brother lye buried : and my funeralle to be performed in such sort as befitts my rank and calling. All my goodes, jewelles, plate, utensiles, howsholde stuffe, iron, leade, woll, debtes owing me, arrearages of rents, leases, and chattelles of what kinde soever whereof I am or during my life shall be possessed or intituled unto, or whereof any other is interessed to my use, or in trust for me at my disposition :-and all and singuler the mannors, landes, tenementes and hereditaments wherof I my selfe am seized of any estate of inheritance in fee simple, in possession, remainder or reversion immediatlie depending uppon anie estate for life, lyves or yeares or wherof anie other or others is or are seized in fee to my use or in trust at my disposition (the manors, lands, tenements, and hereditaments late in the possession of my late brother Henrie Talbot esquier deceased, and of Henrie Cavendishe esquier or either of them in the counties of Derbie and Stafforde excepted and foreprized) I devise and bequeathe to my executors in this my last will and testament named, their heires and assignes for and towardes the performaunce of my funeralles and the speedie payment and discharge of my debtes in a schedule hereunto annexed by me subscribed mentioned and expressed ; and all other my juste and due debtes and full performaunce of my legacies in this my will or in the schedule thereunto annexed, limitted and bequeathed. And after my funeralles and debtes and legacies paide and discharged, I further will and devise the surplusage therof remaininge (yf anie be) to my executors, their heires, executors and assignes. Item I will and appointe an hospitall to be founded at Sheffeilde for perpetuall maintenaunce of twentie poore personnes, and to be called The Hospital of Gilbert Erle of Shrewsbury ; and the same to be endowed with such revenues and possessions as my executors–shall thincke fitt, not beinge under two hundred poundes a yeare. Item I give to my gratiouse Soveraigne in remembraunce of my dewtie a cupp of gold of two hundred poundes value : and to the Queene's Maiestie a cupp of gould of the same value : and to the Prince Charles a cupp of goulde of one hundred poundes value. Item I give and devise to my deere and beloved daughters eche of them a cup of goulde of an hundred poundes value. Item to their lordes and hus-

---

[1] Talbot Papers, vol. K, f. 248.   [2] Biog. Brit. p. 1203.   [3] Harl. MSS. 6986, f. 44.

bandes my sonnes in lawe, to each of them a cup of goulde of an hundred poundes value. Item to my foure grandchildren the sonnes of my daughter Arundell eche of them a cup of goulde of an hundred poundes value. Item to my Executors herein named a cupp of goulde of an hundred poundes a peice. Item I will and devise for a legacie to my servaunte Thomas Cooke one annuitie or yearlie rente of threescore poundes a yeare to be paide unto him yearelie during his naturall life at the feastes of the Annuntiation of the blessed Virgine Marie and Sainte Michaell the Archangell by equall portions, to be yssuing and goinge out of all my fee simple landes, tenementes and hereditaments aforesaide with full libertie to distraine for the nonpaiment of the same in anie of the saide landes, tenementes and hereditaments, and in anie of the saide leases. Item I will and devise to my servant William Hamonde one annuitie or yearelie rent of an hundred poundes by yeare to be paide unto him duringe his naturall lyfe at the feastes aforesaide, to be yssuinge and goinge out of my fee simple landes, tenementes and hereditamentes, with like libertie of dystresse in anie the saide landes, tenementes and hereditamentes, and in anie the saide leases. And of this my last will and testament I ordaine and make my honorable and worthie frend Sr Ralph Wynwood knight principalle secretarie to the Kinges most excellent Maiestie and my loving nephewe Sr William Cavendish knight, my Executors. In witness whereof I have hereunto subscribed my name and sett my seale, and published it as my last will and testament this fourth daie of Maie, in the yeares of the reign of our Soveraign Lorde Kinge James of England, Fraunce and Ireland the fowerteenth, and of Scotland the nyne and forteth. GILB. SHREWSBURY.

Signed, sealed and published in the
presence of Edwarde Cooke.
George Moore.
Proved at London before Sir John Bennet 14 May 1616 [1].'

' THE Proceedings of the Funerall of the right honorable GILBERT E. of SALOP at SHEFFEILD on Mondaye the 12th of August 1616 [2].

4 conductors with staves.
Pore men in gownes, 128.
Yeamen in coates.
Yeamen in cloakes.
Gent.' and Esq.' servants.
Knights and Baronetts servants.
The standard borne by Sr John Bentley.
A horse lead, covered with black cloath.
Sr William Cavendishes men.
Sr Charles Cavendishes men.
Mr. Seamor's men.
Mr. Solicitor's men.
Mr. Attorney generall his men.
The Lo. chiefe Baron's men.
The Lo. Hobert's men.
The Lo. Cooke's men.
Mr. Secretary Wynwood's men.
The Lo. Burleigh and Lo. Compton's men.
The Lo. Norris and Lo. Mordant's men.
The Lo. Willoughby and Lo. Darcve's men.

The Lo. Clifford and Lo. Ruthyn's men.
The Lo. Maltrevers' men.
Musick and singing men.
The penon borne by Sr John Savile.
The 2d horse lead.
The Viscount Lisle his servants.
E. of Montgomery & E. of Southampton's servants.
E. of Rutland and E. of Comberland's servants.
E. of Kent and E. of Arundell's servants.
The Lo. Chamberlayne his servants.
The Archb. of York his servants.
The banor of the order borne by Sr Robt Swift.
3d horse ledd.
The defunct's servants, reteynors.
The defunct's houshold servants.
Esq. being frends in cloakes.
The defunct's officers in gownes, as Clarke of the kitchin, receavours and auditors.
The defunct's solicitors and councell at law.
Secretaryes.
Chaplayns to the defunct, not being doctors.
Doctors of phisicke.
Archbish. of York's chaplaynes.
Knights.
Baronets.
Judges.
A gent. bare heded cariinge a cushion of black vellvett.
VI. trumpetts.
The tresorer, steward and comptroller all close mornors bearinge their white staves.
Earles' younger sonnes.
Barons.
The Lo. Compton and Willoughby.
Earles' elder sonnes.
The Lo. Maltrevors.
The great Banner borne by Sr Tho. Fairfax.
The 4th horse led, being the horse of honor, trapped with black velvett, led by the Gent. of the horse.
The Archbish. of York preacher. His gentleman usher before him barehed: and his traine borne.
Blewmantle—Healme and creast.
Roug cross—Sword.   }officers of armes.
Richmond—Targe.
One gentleman usher, a close mornor went with Richmond herald.
VI. assistants to the bodye, vidz.

Sir Ralf Winwood.	The representation borne by 6 gentlemen.	Sr Willm Cavendish.
Mr. Seamor.		Sr Geo. Mannors.
Sr Geo. Savile.		Sr Willm Herbert.

VI. bearers of the canopye. vidz. Baronets.

Sr Fran. Leake.	Sr Geo. Booth.
Sr Gervase Clifton.	Sr Tho. Wentworth.
Sr Geo. Greisley.	Sr Willm Kniveton.

VI. Esq. for the Bannerolles vidz.
Mr. Trentham and Mr. Turner.

---

[1] The office of executor to an embarrassed man is not a very enviable one: and in the Duchess's Life of William Duke of Newcastle, who was one of the earl's executors, we meet with the following curious passage respecting his executorship. Some allowance must probably be made for the partiality of the biographer, and the disposition to harmless exaggeration which prevails throughout her curious and interesting narrative. 'His father, Sir Charles Cavendish, had lent his brother-in-law Gilbert earl of Shrewsbury 16000l., for which, although afterward before his death he settled 2000l. a year upon him; yet he having enjoyed the said money for many years without paying any use for it, it might have been improved to my lord's better advantage, had it been in his father's own hands, he being a person of great prudence in managing his estate; and though the said earl of Shrewsbury made my lord his executor, yet my lord was so far from making any advantage of that trust, even in what the law allowed him, that he lost 17000l. by it; and afterwards delivered up his trust to William earl of Pembroke, and Thomas earl of Arundel: and since his return into England, upon the desire of Henry Howard, second son to the late earl of Arundel, and heir-apparent (by reason of his eldest brother's distemper), he resigned his trust and interest to him, which certainly is a very difficult business, and yet questionable whether it may be lawfully done or not. But such was my lord's love to the family of the Shrewsburies that he would rather wrong himself than it.

' To mention some lawful advantages which my lord might have made by the said trust, it may be noted in the first place, that the earl of Shrewsbury's estate was let in long leases, which by the law fell to the executor. Next, that after some debts and legacies were paid out of those lands, which were set out for that purpose, they were setled so that they fell to my lord. Thirdly, seven hundred pounds a year was left as a gift to my lord's brother, Sir Charles Cavendish, in case the countess of Kent, second daughter to the said earl of Shrewsbury, had no children. But my lord never made any advantage for himself, of all these, neither was he inquisitive whether the said countess of Kent cut off the entail of that land, although she never had a child; for my lord's nature is so generous that he hates to be mercenary, and never minds his own profit or interest in any trust or employment, more than the good and benefit of him that entrusts and employs him.' Life of William Duke of Newcastle, by Margaret Duchess of Newcastle, p. 122—124.

[2] Harl. MSS. 1368, lettered 'Saint George's Funeral Process &c.' f. 35—39.

x

Mr. Talbot and Mr. Gerv. Markham.
Mr. Holcroft and Mr. Jones.
   Garter—Coat of Armes.
A gentleman usher before the chiefe mourner bareheded.
The E. of Pembroke, chief mourner : his traine borne by
his page.
E. of Arundell and E. of Kent
E. of Montgomery and Visc. Lisle
Lo. Ruthyn and L. Clifford
Lo. Darcy and Lo. Mordant
  All the Earles' and Viscounts' traynes borne.

The Mannor of the offringe.

Mr. Garter goeth up with the chief mourner and his 8 as-
sistantes. The chiefe mourner only offreth, and soe retorne
all to there places againe.
Mr. Garter goeth up with the chiefe mourner againe who
then offreth for himselfe, and then staieth there to receave the
hatchm[u], which are brought up with the VIII. assistants as
followeth.
Richmond. E. of Arundell and Kent — Coate of armes.
Roug cross. E. of Montgom'y & Visc[l] Lisle—The Sword.
Blewmantle. Lo. Ruthin & Lo. Clifford—The Targe.
Rich. Lo. Darcy & Lo. Mordant. Helme and creaste.
Roug. the great banner by him that caried it.
Blew. the 2 bannerolls by them that bare them.
Rich. 2 other bannerolls by them that bare them.
Roug. the 2 last bannerolls by them that bare them.

Blew. the banner of the order.
Rich. the penon.
Rong. the standard.
All these thinges beinge offred up, the chief mornor is brought
downe to his place againe. Mr. Garter and all the assistants
with the rest offer as followeth.
Garter. The Archbishop.
Garter. The E. of Arundel and E. of Kent.
Rich. The E. of Montgom'y and Visc. Lisle.
Roug. Lo. Ruthyn and Lo. Clifford.
Blew. Lo. Darcy and Lo. Mordant.
Rich. Lo. Maltrevers and Lo. Willoughby.
Roug. Mr. Hen. Howard and Lo. Compton.
Garter. The VI. assistants of the body.
Rich. The Baronetts that bare the canopye.
Roug. He that bare the great bannor.
Blew. The VI. that carried the bannerolls.
Rich. He that caried the banner of the order.
Roug. He that caried the penon.
Blew. He that caried the standart.
Rich. The Baronetts.
    The Knights.
Garter. The steward, treasuror, and comptroller, who after
they had offred cam downe within the hearse and brake
their staves.
Then Mr. Garter came to the feete of the hearse, and with
a lowd voice p'claimed the stile of the defunct.
                       Finis.'

ORIGINAL CORRESPONDENCE

ILLUSTRATIVE OF THE PRECEDING CHAPTER AND OF THE HISTORY AND MANNERS OF THE ELIZABETHAN AGE.

The originals of most of the following letters are in the collection of manuscripts made by the late John Wilson, esq. Reference is made to the depositary which contains it, when the original is to be found elsewhere.

Epistolæ magis in proximo et ad vivum negotia solent representare, quam vel annales, vel vitæ.—BACON.

Lady CAVENDISH to FRANCIS WHITFIELD. 1552.

FRANCYS, I have spoken w[t] your mayster for the dyltes or
bordes that you wrete to me of; and he ys contente that you
shall take some for your nesecytè by the apountemente of
Neusante, so that you take seche as wyll do hyme no sarvese
aboute hys byldynge at Chattysworthe. I pray you loke well
to all thynges at Chattysworthe tyll my aunte's comynge
whome, whyche I hope shalbe shortely: and yn the meane
tyme cause Broushawe to loke to the smethes, and all other
thynges at Penteryge. Lete the weivar make bere for me
fourthew[t], for my owne drynkyng and your mayster ; and se
that I have good store of ytt, for yf I lacke ether good bere or
charcole or wode I wyll blame nobody so meche as I wyll do
you. Cause the flore yn my bede chamber to be made even,
ether w[t] plaster, claye or lyme : and al the wyndoues were the
glasse ys broken to be mended : and al the chambers to be
made as close and warme as you cane. I here that my syster
Jane' cane not have thynges that ys nedefoulle for hare to have
amoungste you : yf ytt be trewe, you lacke a great of honystè
as well as dyscrecyon to deny hare any thynge that she hathe
a mynde to, beynge yn case as she hathe bene. I wolde be
lothe to have any stranger so yoused yn my howse; and then
assure your selfe I cane not lyke ytt, to have my syster so
yousede. Lyke as I wolde not have any superfleuetè or waste
of any thynge, so lyke wyse wolde I have hare to have that
whyche ys nedefoulle and nesesary. At my comynge whome
I shal knowe more, and then I wyll thy'k as I shall have cause.
I wolde have you to geve to my mydwyffe frome me, and frome

my boye Wylle, and to my   norse frome me and my boye,
as hereafter foloweth : fyrste to the mydwyfe frome me tene
shyllynges, and frome Wylle fyve shyllynges : to the norse
frome me fyve shyllynges, and frome my boye III[s] fore pence :
so that yn the wolle you mouste geve to them twenty thre
shyllynges and fore pence. Make my syster Jane prevye of
ytt, and then paye ytt to them fourthew[t]. Yf you have no
other money, take so meche of the rente at Penteryge. Tyll
my systar Jane that I wyll geve my dowter somethynge at my
comynge whome : and prayinge you not to fayle to se all
thynges done accordyngely, I bede you farewell. Frome London the XIIII. of November. Your mystrys
                  ELIZABETHE CAVENDYSH.
Tyll James Crompe that I have resavyed the fyve ponde and
IX[s] that he sente me by Heue Alsope.
   To my sarvante Francys Wytfeld
     geve thys at Chattysworthe.

The Countess of NORTHUMBERLAND to Lady CAVENDISH.

AFTER my verey hertie comendacōns unto your Ladiship :
and whereas one of your sarvants hathe taken & pounded certayne cattell of one Nycholas Alesson's the beyrer herof,
of a percell of grounde w[ch] he hathe taken of one John Cow-
per be the lycence of Mayster Wennesley your L.' steward at
Pentryche, wherefor these shall be most hertyly to desyre you
to [be] favorable unto the said Nycholas Alesson that he may
have his cattell delyvered furthe of the pounde, and he may
occupye the ground w[ch] he hathe layd furthe his money for ;

---

[1] Jane Hardwick, afterwards wife of Godfrey Bosvile of Gunthwaite, esq.

and the rather at this my request. And thus I bid you most hertylye farewell. From Wormhall the xxvɪɪth day of Maii.

Your lovyng frende
M. NORTHUMBERLAND.

To the right worshipfull and my
verey lovyng frende my Ladie
Candache geve this.

Lady SAINT-LOE to JAMES CROMPE.

CROMPE, I do undearstande by your leters that Wortli sayth he will departe at our Ladeday next. I wyll that you shall have hym bunden yn an oblygacyon to avoyde at the same day, for sure I wyll troste no mor to hy⁵ promes. And were he doth tell you that he ys any peny behind for work done to Mr Cavendysh or me, he doth lye lyke a false knave: for I am moste sure he did never make any thynge for me but ɪɪ. vaynes to stande upon the huse. I do very wel lyke your sende-ynges sawyers to Pentrege and Medoplecke, for that will fur-der my workes: and so I pray you yn any other thynga that will be a helpe to my byldeynge, let it be don. And for Tomas Mason, yf you can here were he ys, I would very gladely he were at Chattesworth. I wyl let you know by my next leters what worke Thomas Mason shall hegine one furate, when he doth come. And as for the other mason wyche Sur James towld you of, yf he wyll not aplye hys worke, you know he ys no mete mane for me; and the mason's work wyche I have to do ys not muche, and Tomas Mason will very well over see that worke. I perseve Sur James' ys muche myslyked for hys relegyn: but I thenke hys wisdom ys suche that he will make smale acounte of thatt mater. I woulde have you to tell my aunte Lenecker ² that I woulde have the letell garden weche ys by the newe howse made a garden thys yere. I care not wether she bestow any grate coste thereof; but to sowe yt w^t al kynde of earbes and flowres, and some pece of yt w^t malos. I have sende you hv thys carerer ɪɪɪ. bundeles of gar-den sedes all wreten w^t Willem Marchyngton's hande ; and by the next you shall know how to youse them yn every pynte. Frome the Courte the vɪɪɪ. of March

Your mystres
E. SEYNTLO.

To James Crompe.

Sir GEORGE PIERREPOINT to Lady SAINT-LOE.

RIGHT wurshipfull and my verreye good Ladye : after my hertiest man' I comende me to your good Ladishippe : even so preye you I meye be to good Mr. Sentloe : most hertelye thanckinge you booth for your great paynes taken wth me at Holme, acceptinge ev'ye thinge (thoughe it were nev' so rewd-lye handlyde) in suche gentill sorte as ye dyde; wch doeth aud will cause me to love you the better whiell I lyve yf I were abill to doo you other pleass' or service: and the rather because I understand that your Ladishipe hathe not forgotten my sewte to you at your goinge awaye as spe'allye to make Mr. Sack-vile & Mr. Attorneye my frends in the matt' betwene Mr. Whalleye ande me w'in he doethe me playne wronge (as I take it in my concyence) onelye to repe trouble, & unquyett me. But I trust somoche in God's helpe, and partlye by your Ladi-shipe's good means, and contynewance of your goodnes to-wards me, that he shall not ov'throwe me in my rightiose cause. And touchinge suche cominication as was betwene us at Holme, yf your Ladishipe & the gentillwoman your dought' lyke o' beye uppon sight as well as I & my wife lyke the yong gen-tillwoman, I will not shrincke one worde from y' I said or promised; by the grace of God who preserve your Ladishipe and my M' your husbande longe together in wealthe, healthe and prosperytie to his pleasure, and your gentill hert's desyer. Frome my porer house at Woodhouse the ɪɪɪɪth of November 1561 : by the rewde lustie hande of your goode Ladishipe's assuredlye allwaye to comaunde

GEORGE PUREPOUNTE.

To the right worshipfull and my
singuler goode Ladye, my Ladye
Sentloo at London this be dd.

---

¹ Foljambe, I presume. The family suffered much for their attach-ment to the old profession.

² Marcella, daughter of Thomas Leake of Hasland and sister to Eliza-beth Leake, who was mother to the writer of this letter, married George Lynacre, a Derbyshire gentleman, and seems in her widowhood to have

---

Sir WILLIAM SAINT-LOE to Lady SAINT-LOE.

My owne, more dearar to me then I am to myseylff, thow schallt understande thatt ytt ys no smale fear nor greyff unto me off thye well doyng then I schowlde presentlye se what I dowgst, nott onelye for that my contynuall nyghtlye dreams besyde my absens hath trobelyd me, butt also cheyflye, for that Hughe Alsope kan nott sarttefye me in whatt estate thow nor thyne ys, whome I tendar more then I do Wyllyam Seyntlo. Therefore I pray the a⁵ thow doest love me, lett me schortlye heare from the, for the qnvetyng off my unquyetyd mynde, howe thy owne swete seylff wyth all thyne doeth; trustyng schortlye to be emongst yow. All thye frends here saluteth the. Harrye Skypwyth desyred me to make the aud no other pryvè that he ys sure off maestres Neyll, wyth whome he ys by thys tyme¹. He hath sentt x. thowsand thancks unto thye seylff for the same : sche hath openyd all thyngs unto hym. To morowe Syr Rychard Sackfelde and I ryde to London togy-ther ; upon Saturdaye nextt we returne hyther agayne. The quene yesterdaye her owne seylff rydeng upon the waye craved my horse; unto home I gave hym, resevyng openlye for the same manye goodlye wordes. Thus wysschyng myseylff wyth thye seylff, I bedde the my owne good sarvantte and cheyff oversear off my worckes moate harttelye farewell : by thyne who ys holye and onelye thyne, ye and for all thyne whyle lyff lastyth. Frome Wynsor the fowerth off Septembar by thye ryghtt worschypfull good maistar and moste honest husbande maestar Syr WYLLYAM SEYNTLO esquyer.

Còmendde me to my mother aud to all mye brothers and systars there, nott forgettyng Francke wyth the reste off my chyldren and thyne. The Amnar saluteth the, and sayeth no jenttlemens chyldren in Ingland schalbe be bettar welcum nor bettar loked unto then owre boyes. Ones agayne, farewell good honest swete.

My seylff or Greyves schalbe the nextt messynger.

To my owne deur wyff att
Chatsworth delyver thys.

Sir WILLIAM SAINT-LOE to Lady SAINT-LOE.

My happe ys evvll my tyme worse spentte; for that my re-warde as yett ys nothyng more then fayer wordes wyth the lyke promysys. Take all in good parte; and yff I schould understande the contrarye, yt wolde troble me more then my pen schall expresse. I have leave to cum and wayte upon the, I and my brother Clement wyth towe or thre good felloes more : had beyn wyth the by thys daye yff ytt hadde nott beyn for owre checkar mattar, the whyche I wyll nott leave over rawlye. I will forbeare the anseryng off all partycularytès in thy last lettar wryten unto me, for that God wyllyng I wyll thys nextt weke be the messyngar my seylff. Maestar Man kame home the nyghtt before the date hereoff. He puttyth me in great hope off the mattar yow wote off. Thus trustyng that God provydeth for us al thyngs for the beste, I ende; com-myttyng the and all thyne whyche ar myne unto hys blessyd wyll and ordenans. Farewell my owne sweete Besse. From Maester Man's howse in Redecrosse strete, the xɪɪth of Octo-bar, by hym who dareth not so nere hys còmyng home to terme the as thow artt : yet thyen

WILLIAM SEYNTLO.

My cosyn Clarcke saluteth the, who was by me at the wry-tyng hereoff.

To my owne good wyff att
Chatsworth delyvar thys.

Sir WILLIAM SAINT-LOE to Lady SAINT-LOE.

My honest swete Chatesworth : I lyke the wekelye pryce off my hyred cowrte stuff so evyll thatt upon Thursdaye nextt I wyll send ytt home agayne, att whiche daye the weke endyth. I praye yow cawse soche stuff as Mowsall left packt in a schete to be browght hythar by the nextt carryar: there be hand towels and other thyngs therein thatt I must occupye when I schall lye at Whytehawll. My men hath neyther schurtt nor eynye other thyng to schyft them untyll thatt cum. Trust

---

been domesticated with Lady Saint-Loe.

² Henry Skipwith, esq. fourth son of Sir William Skipwith, married Jane daughter of Francis Hall, surveyor of the works at Calais to Henry VIII., relict of Francis Neele of Leicestershire. See Harl. MSS. 1436, p. 44.

noen off yowre men to ryde eynye yowre howsyd horsys, butt onelye Jhames Cromp or Wyllyam Marchyngton; butt neyther off them wythoute good cawse serve spedelye to be doen. For nags there be enow abowte the howse to serve other purposys. One handfull off otes to everye one off the geldyngs att a wateryng wylbe suffycyent so they be not laboryd. Yow must cawse sum to overse the horsakepar for thatt he ys verye well learnyd in loyteryng.

The Quene hath fownde greatt fawt wyth my long absens, sayeng sche wolde talck wyth me farder, and that sche wolde well chyde me. Whereunto I anseryd thatt when her hyghnes understode the trawth and the cawse sche wolde nott be offendyd. Whereunto sche sayed ' Verye well, very well.' Howbeytt hand of hers dyd I not kysse.

The Lorde Kepar hath promysed me faythfullye to be att boeth dayes heryng; and that yff eyther lawe or consyens be on my syde I schall have ytt to my contentasyon. Vawghan ys cum unto towne, butt nott yett Bagott. Stevyns and we schall go thoro on Frydaye nextt, at whyche tyme hys brothar wylbe here, who hath dysbursed sevyn hunderyed off the xii. hunderyed pownds. I have had exstreme payne in my teeth sythens Sondaye dynar. Thus with akeng teeth I end, prayng the lyveng to preserve the and all thyen. Wrytan att London, ageynst my wyll where I am yff other wayes owre mattars myght well be endyd, thys xxiiiith off October :

Yowre loveng husband wyth akeng hartt untyll we mete,
　　　　　　　　　　WYLLYAM SEYNTLO.

Yff yow thynck good, lease yowre fyssehyng in Dove unto Agard. We are the losers by sufferyng hytt as we have doen.

To my loveng wyff at Chatesworth
yeve these wyth spede.

THOMAS Earl of ORMOND to Sir WILLIAM SAINT-LOE.

ALTHOWGH I have alredy wrytten to you good Syr Wylliam Sentlo by my ma͞n Nicolas Tobyn, yet for that you showld tak the more occasiou to wryt, I have thowght good to send you thease few liues of comendations, mervayling that sins my coming into this land I never reseved comendations from you. I pray you let me not think thowgh I be owt of syght that I shalbe owt of mynd. If wyshes wold help I showld be there wyth you; which I wold thynk a happy plase, both for that I showld enioy the syght of the quene's maiesty, and also have the company of you and other my frends, wythout which no man can have contentasió as I think. But seing my fortune is to be heare, I wold God wold put in the quene's head to mak you tred a boge hear ons agayn. Sir the newes of this contrey I refer to this bearer my man. My lord of Sussex is syk of an ague. And as tuching any thing that I may do heare for you or any of yours, I wol rest to yow most assured; as knoweth God who send you as well to do, as I wold wysh myself. From Dublyng, the xxviii. of January. I pray you let me be bartely comended to your sister, if a man may presume to send co͞mendasions into the privy chamber.

　　　　　　　　Your assured fre͞d
　　　　　　　　　　THOMAS ORMO͞DE.

To my veray loveng frend Syr
Wylliam Sentlo Capten of the
quen's maietyis gard.

The Earl of SHREWSBURY to Sir WILLIAM CECIL[1].

AFTER my verie hartie co͞mendaco͞ns. Having occasion at this time to remember sundrye of my verie good Lords and others wth redd deere and venison, I thought in that p'te I could not (thoughe the matter be but small) omytt the remembraunce of so deer & assured a freende as I have at all tymes found you, praying you to accepte vi. pasties w^{che} I send you by this berer as a token of my good will,

　　- having not in theese partes any better noveltyes to send yowe.

I have latelie w^{thin} my liberties apprehended an offend^r of rare kinde in this cuntry, a coyner, whose cunnyng was so slight & his bullion so bare, his stampes & yrons also wanting good workmanship, as in my town of Sheffeld at the first of his utterance, this newe founde myntor was 　　　; whom for his good will & pains takinge in that behalf I have as he

was well worthie sent him to the Quenes Maties gaole at Yorke; & all his woorkinge tooles also to hir Ma^{ts} counsaile theere, to bare recorde of his well doinge, where I doubte not but he shall receave accordinge to his demerits. And to the ende you may the better undrestande th'apperyence & good skill of this workman, I have heerinclosed sente you towe peces of his doinge wch you may at youre pleas͞ eyther shewe unto hir Ma^{tis} or otherwise as yow shall thinke convenyente. And so for this tyme I comende you to the protection of Almighty God, who send you aswell to do as I wolde myself. From Sheffelde Lodge the xiith of October 1563.

　　　　　Your assured lovinge freende
　　　　　　　　　　G. SHROWESBURY.

To my welbiloved freende Sr Will͞m
Cecyll knight principall secretarye
of the Quenes most excellent Matie.

WILLIAM CAVENDISH to Mrs. LINACRE.

GOOD aunt Linacre, after my heartie commendacoons; trusting y^t you are in good health ; these may be to let you understand y^t all we here be in health thanks be to God. I sent for Georg from Ely about ye myddest of January by cause I and Mr. Taylor thought it good for divers causes so to doe. He hath profited very well at Ely, and now he is at Cambridg he shall not lose his time. I trust I shall make suche meanes shortly y^t he shall not put you to so muche cost as he hath done, as you shall here more of by ye next bearer. He in whose chamber Georg was at his first going to Ely went from thence before michaelmas, so y^t I was faine to loke him a nother tutor the time he taried there, which would not looke unto him wth out he were considered for it. He had his chamber and lodging at ye first given him, but so I could not get him for michaelmas q'ter. Georg left one of his shets and his bolster at Ely. I writ for theme divers times since his co͞ming to Cambridg, but I cannot get theme: they say on of his chamber fellows did run away wth them, and sell them ; but how so ever it is I can not get them. I would desire you to send him a shete and a litle pillow, and now he is at Cambridg I shall looke to them. I have sent you the bill of his charges from michelmas to Christmas, wch is xlvi^s i^d: so y^t wth those ii. q'ters expenses I sent you before, iii^{li} x^d remayneth of that v^{li} I received last from you. I pray you send me mony for Christmas q'ter, wch now is allmost redy to be payed for. So having nothing els to let you understand of, I co͞mit you to God. From Clare Hall ye xxiiith of February.

　　　　　　Your loving nephew
To his verie loving Aunt M^{rs}　　WILLM. CAVENDYSH.
Linacre at Chatsworth.

Michaelmas Quarter 1568.

	s.	d.
Imprimis vi. yards of friese to make him a goune after xv^d. the yard	vii^s.	vi^d.
It. a yard and half of ruset to make him a pair of hose xx^d. ye yard	ii.	vi.
It. making of his goune		xii.
It. a yard of white lining for his hose		xvi.
It. for making his hose		viii.
It. given to Norman ye waterman for his coming and going from Ely by water		xii.
It. his co͞mons a weeke at Cambridge		xvi.
It. a cap		ix.
It. iij yards & half clothe for sherts	ii.	
It. washing		xii.
It. a quarter of clothe for collers for his sherts		v.
It. a pair of shoes		ix.
It. making of his sherts		vi.
It. his co͞mons and sising *a festo Michaelis ad nativitatem Dei*	xx.	
It. his chamber at Ely and to on for to loke to him there	ii.	vi.
It. for fier this winter at Ely		xx.
It. candles ij. pound		vi.
It. paper & ink		ii.
It. mending of his jerkin, doblet and hose		vi.
Sum of this q'ter	xlvi.	i.

The Earl of SHREWSBURY to the Countess of SHREWSBURY.
1568.

My dere none. Havenge resevyd your lettar offe the furste of Decembar whyche came in very good gyme, els hadd I sente oune of thes few remainyng wth me to have brought me worde of your helthe, whych I douted offe for that I harde nott from you offe all this tyme tyll now, whyche drove me in dumpes, but now relyved agen by your wryting unto me. I thank you swete none for your podengs & venyson. The podengs have I bestoud in this wyes : dosen to my Lade Cobbam, & as many to my L. Stuard & unto my L. of Leystere; & the rest I have resarved to my selfe to ete in my chambar. The venyson is yett at London, but I have sente for it heddar.

I p'seve Nedd Talbott hathe bene syke, & now paste dangar. I thank God I have sych anone that is so carfull ovar me & myne. God send me soone home to posesse my gretest joye: if you thynke it is you, you are not desevyd.

I wyll not forgett to dele wth the M^r of the Rolles for younge Knyfton. He semes to be myche my frende, & is now in de-lyng betwext Denenge & me, for the lees of Abbott Stoke, agreed apen by me & Tamworth he shuld so doo. He holdes it at a thousande markes; & the M^r of the Rolles hathe dreven it to v^c pounds, whych me thynks to myche for syche a lees, yett because it lyes so as I am informyd amongs Gyl-bards lands, I have made my steward to offar iiii^c pounds, & to gett day tyll the next terem, because I wold have your ad-vyse therin.

& for that I lyve in hope to be wth you before you can re-terne answar agen, you shall undarstande that this present Mondaye in the mornynge fyndeng the quene in the garden at good lesar, I gave hur Magest^e thanks that she hadd so lytell regard to the clamorous pepull of Bolsor in my absens. She declared unto me what evel speche was against me; my nereness & state in house kepyng, & as mych as was told hur, whych she nowyes beleved, wth as good words as I cold wyshe; declaring that er it were longe I shuld well perseve she dyd so trust me as she dyd few. She wold nott tell me wherein, but doute it was aboute the custody of the Scotes Quene. Her is pryvate spech that Gates & Vah^n shuld make sute to have hur, but this day I perseve it is altered. I thynk before Sondaye thes mattars wyll com to som passe, that we shall know how long our abode shalbe; but how so evar it faules out, I wyll not fele but be wth you before Kyrsomas, orr els you shall com to me.

The plage is dispersed far abrode in London, so that the Quene kepes hur Kyrsomas her, & goeth nott to Grenwych as it was mente. My Lade Cobam your dere frende wyshes your presence here : she loves you well. I tell hur I have the cause to love hur best, for that she wyshed me so well to speede as I dyd : & as the pene wrytes so the harte thynks, that offe all erthely joyes that hath happenyd unto me, I thanke God chefest for you : for wth you I have all joye & contentasyon of mynde, & w^thoute you dethe is mor plesante to me than lyfe if I thought I shulde long be from you; & therefore good wyfe doo as I wyll doo, hope shortely of our metenge, & fare-well dere swete none. From Hamton courte this Monday at mydnyght, for it is every nyght so late before I goo to my bedd, being at playe in the preve chambar at Premyro, wher I have loste almost a hundereth pounds, & laked my slepe.

Your fethefull husbande tyll dethe
G. SHREWSBURY.

Wyfe tell my doughter Maule that I am nott plesed wth hur that she hath nott wryten to me wth hur systar; yett wyll I not forget hur & the reste, & pray to God to bless them all.

To my wyfe the Countes of Shrowes-
bury at Tutbury geve this.

The Earl of SHREWSBURY to the Countess of SHREWSBURY.
1568.

My dere none. I have reseved your lettar off the viii. of Decembar, wherin apereth your desyre for my soune cum-mynge. What my desyre is thereunto I refarre the same to your construcsyon. If I shuld so jugge of tyme, me thynks tyme longar synste my cumminge heddar w^thoute you my only

---

joye, than I dyd synaste I maryed you : suche is faythefull af-fecsyon, whyche I nevar tasted so deply off before. This day orre to morow we shall know grete lyklyoddes of our despache. I thynke it wylbe Kyrsomas Even before I shall aryve at Tut-bury. Thyngs faules out very evell agenst the Scotes Quene. What she shall doo yett it is nott resolved off.

As it chanses, I am gladde that I am here: for if I were nott I were lyke to have most p't off my leses graunted ovar my hedde ; there is suche sute for leses in revarsyon off the Duché. My p'k that I have in kepynge called Morley p'k is graunted in revarsyon for xxx. yers, wherin I have made some ature. My good nebur hath a promes off it, I mene Stanoppe; but I shall make it dere the havinge offe it, & if I canne gett it put in I am aboute to gett a frende offe myne to put the forrest of the Peke in his boke. I have offered a thousande pounds for a lees in revarsyon for xxx. yeres. I must pay Denenge v^cLi. for his lees of Stoke. How money wylbe hadd for thes mattars insure you I know nott. I wyll make suche menes to Mr. Myldmay for the staye of Tutburye tyth, as I will nott be prevented; for it is hye tyme, for ther was nevar such styfeinge & prancinge for leses in revarsyon, as be now at this prysente.

My L. Stuard hathe bene syk, & in dangar, but now well. My L. Shefeld is departed this lyfe ; & my L. Pagett juste aftar. Your blak man is in helthe.

Your faithfull husbaunde tyll my ende
G. SHREWSBURY.

From the court this Mondaye the xiii. of Decembar. Now it is sarten the Scotes Quene cumes to Tutburye to my charge. In what ordar I cannott aserten you.

To my wyfe the Contés offe Shrowes-
bury at Tutbury geve this.

MARY Queen of SCOTS to ————[1]. 1569.

MON Cousin m'estant permis maintenant ce que iauois il i a long temps desiray, cestoit de fayre mon deuoir vers le roy et la reyne et tous Messieurs mes bons amys et parans, du nombre desquels ie vous ay tousiours tenu et trouvez des prin-sipaulx, ie nay voullu faillir de vous fayre ce mot pour vous, prier de donner credit a ce porteur, qui vous declarera l'oca-sion de son voiasge et lestait de mes affayres, tant issi quen mon malheurheulx pays. Et pourceque ie le connois fidelle, et doubte quel inconueniant pourroit venir aux lettres, ie ne les feray plus longues ayus meremetant pur lui avous fayre ample discours du tout ; ie vous priray me fayre part de vos nouuelles, que ie prie a dieu ettre tousiours aussi bonnes queles scauriez souhayter: et apres vous auuoir besay les meins ie feray fiu. De Winkfeild ce ix. de Juing

votre bie affectionne et bonne Cousine
MARIE.

Sir RICHARD CAVENDISH to the Countess of SHREWSBURY.

PLEASETH yt your Ladyshypp, that as I acknowledge my selfe wholy indettyd unto you, as well for your wonted cur-tesye to my selfe, as your honorable l'res in the behalfe of my brother to Mr. Gerard, so have I nowe an humble sute unto yow, wherof I crave such acceptation as your L. may conve-nyently admytt : wch ys thys ; that where my brother (havyng hys oldest daughter aboute the age of xviii. yeares) ys very desyrous for a tyme to place hyr in servyce w^h your L. (by reason of such honorable report as he hath receeyved of yow) so yt would please your L. the rather at my humble sute to re-ceyve hyr into your servyce : trustyng at yf you vouchsave so to doo, neyther the condytyons of the mayden, neyther hir parents mayntenance of hyr in your servyce, shall move your L. forthynk your curtesye in thys behalfe. Thus comendyng my humble servyce both to my Lord and your L. I shall not cease to pray for your glad prosperytie. Fro Grymston haule in Suffolke thys xii^th July 1570.

Your Ladyshypp's humble to commande
RYCHARD CAVENDYSHE.

To the ryght honorable hys syn-
guler good Lady, the Countes
of Shrewsburye.

---

[1] Probably the Duke de Nemours. In vol. 9126. MSS. in the Royal Library at Paris.

MARY Queen of SCOTS to the Duchess de NEVERS[1]. 1570.

MA Cousine, mayant mon ambassadeur leuesque de Glascou faict entendre la memoire quauiez encores de nostre encienne amitie, et besoing quauies de vous enquerir de mes nouuelles, ie nay voullu faillir par ce [porteur] vous en mercier, et vous tesmoigner le grand contentement que jen ay receu ce .... iray donques que nostre premiere inteligence soit entre nous renouuellee, et me faisant part de voz nouuelles, maymer, comme ie vous promets de faire vers vous. Et pour ceste fois nayant plus grand [sujet] ni vous ennuiray de plus longue lettre, que pour vous prier fayre mes affectionnees recommendations a mon Cousiu vostre Mons' de Nevers; et en prenant vostre part, ie priray dieu qui vous doint ma Cousine en sante, longue et heureuse vie. De Schefild ce dernier Desembrier,

Vostre plus affectionne Cousine, et encienne amye,
A ma Cousine Madame la   MARIE.
Duchesse de Neuers.

HUGH FITZ WILLIAM to the Countess of SHREWSBURY.

[After some foreign intelligence.]

THE Lordes of the Kinge's syde continue still in their consultation at Edenburgh, and the Lordes of the Quene's syd be in the Earle of Argile's contrys, and sturreth not.

My Lord of Sussex hath discharged of late xvi[c] men; and the reste is lyke to be discharged shortlye. And thei say he laborethe to be dispatched both of his levetenantshipp, and also of his presidentshipp: and hath a grante so to do, w[t] favor of the Quene's Ma[tie].

The Earle of Linaux hathe writen to his wyfe y[t] the King his son hath the printe of a lion on his syde.

The Duke of Norfolk hathe set out a submission in writing; and hath declared his perfite seale in the Quene's Ma[tie'] religion; and hathe utterly renunced the mariage w[t] the Scotishe Quene, and how to subpresse the rebells. It hathe come to divers men's handes, but yet I have not sene it.

There is divers of the Rebells endited at Norwich at this last assize; and v. of them be loked for to come to the Tower shortly, and for the rebellion this time twel monethe thereabowte, be condemned to perpetuall prison, w[t] the losse of landes and goodes.

Sr Thomas Cornewalles and his son in lawe Mr. Kytson be at libertie, by cawse thei be cötented to come to the devyne service.

There hathe been seditious bills hurled in the courte, and at Northampton at the assizes, and in other places; for wch cause, besides the proclamations made in that behalf, the counsell hathe directed their I'res in to the contryes for the ponishing of suche lewde dealing. And thus w[t] my mpost humble cömendacöns, I take my leave of your honorable good L. wishing unto my Lord and you and to my frende all helthe to Godes pleasure. Scribeled at London the xxviii[th] of July 1570.

Your honorable good L.' ever to comande during lyfe,
         HUGH FITZ WILLIAM.

To the right honorable ...... of
Shrewesbury .... Chates-
worthe .... wheare.

HENRY CAVENDISH to the Countess of SHREWSBURY.

MAYE yt please your honor, I thought yt good to let your La: understande of a mysfortune that happened in my howse. On Thursday at nyght last at supper, II. of my men fell owt abowte some tryflynge worde, and to all theyr fellows judgement that harde theyr jangelynge, wear made good frends agayne, and went and laye togeether that nyghte, for they had byn bedfellows of longe before, and loved one thother very well, as every boddye tooke yt in the howse :—On Fryday mornynge very early by breake of daye, they wente foorthe, by name Swenerto' and Langeford, w[t] II.'swords a peece, as the sequele after showed; and in the fyelds faughte together, and in fyghte Swenerto' shlewe Langeford, to my great greyfe booth for the sodeyne deathe of the one, and for the utter dystructyon of the tother, whom I loved very well. Good Madam, let yt not trowble you in any thynge: we ar mortall,

and borne to many and strange adventures; and thearfore must temper our mynds to bear shuch burthens as shall be by God layd on our shoulders. My greattest greyffe, and so I iudge yt wyll be some trowble to your La. that yt shoulde happen in my howse—Alas madâ what coulde I dooe w[h] yt; altogether not once suspectynge any thynge betwyxte them. I have been ryghte sorofull for yt, and yt hath trowbled and vexed me, more then in reason yt should have donne a wyse man. I would to God I could forget that theyr never had byn any shuch matter. Upon the faite donne I sent for Mr. Adderley, and used hys counsell in al thyngs. Swenerto' fledde presently, and ys pursued but not yet harde of. Thus humbly cravynge your La: dayly blessynge I end, more then sadde to trowble your La. thus longe w[t] thys sorrofull matter. Tut: thys present Saturday.

Your La.' most bounden humble and obedyent sonne,
To my Lady.   HENRY CAVENDYSHE.
Returne thys.

My juwell thys Saterday at nyght I resavyed thys later, meche to my greffe for the myshap. Yett was ever lyke that Swenertone shulde comete some great faute: he was a vane lewd feloue, Fare well my dear harte.

Your faythefoull wyffe,
       E. SHROUESBURY.

HUGH FITZ WILLIAM to the Countess of SHREWSBURY.

AFTER my due and moost humble cömendacöns unto yor honorable good L. May it please the same t'understande, that I cänot lerne the certaynetie of all the causes of thoccasions that the Duke was comitted to the Tower; but thei any one was for sending mony to relive the Lordes of the Scotish Quene's syde, as by mony and I'res intercepted it may appeare: for the Scotishe Quene as thei say sent the Duke a I're of her owne hand at good lengthe, requiring him to send ayde to her frendes in Scotland, or ells thei were hable to holde out no longer: wheare upon presently he sent VI.'L. in golde w[t] a I're to the Scotishe Quene, an other to the Lordes of Scotland of her syde, and an other to Banister, all his doer in the northe, to conveaye the same, the w[ch] was broughte to a marchant man to conveye w[t] speede in the name of   The marchant aunswered that he wolde receive it beare, and cause it to be payed imediatly there: but that colde not be, but to be conveyed as it was sealed up. The marchant marveling at the earnestnes of Hieforde, and after he was gonne feling the waight of the bagge being very hevy, brooke the sealee and opened the bagge, and found the I'res and the golde, wheare w[t] being very muche a fearde, came to the court. and showed the bagge and the I'res: wheare upon .my Cosen Skipwithe was sent to the Duke that no man sholde talk w[t] him but in his hearing, and Hicforde his secretary was sent to the Tower on Saterday at the night ; and on Sonday in the mor'ing was examined by S[r] Thomas Smythe and Mr Doctor Wilson, and his examinations sent to the court ; and there upon Sr Raufe Sadler was sent to the Duke, and came thither by IX. of the clocke in the morning and discharged his howseholde, and continued w[t] him till he went to the Tower ; and imediately after Sr Raufes cöming according to Hicfords confession thei did searche for their sifer ; and he did appointe a wronge place and [they] found it not; but there thei found the Scotishe Quene's I're, wheareupon the Duke was had to the Tower. And Hicforde came from the Tower to the Cherter howse, and founde the sifer in the rowfe amongest the tyle stones, which discovered the hole matter. The laste weeke the Duke sent to the Quene, that if her Ma[tie] wolde sende to him my Lord of Burley, he wolde declare the hole matter: and whan he came, he wolde nauther say nor writte, but denyed probable thinges. And the same day came into the Tower Banister his man, and there was examined, and stowtely denyed matters layed to his charge; in so muche as Hicfordes examinations was sent to the Duke, and Hieforde was broughte face to face before Banister, who was racked on Twysday last; and Barker was going to the rack, and upon his confession was stayed. Yesterday S[t] Thomas Wrothe, M[r] Osburne and others was sente tto' the Charter howse to take an inventary of all his goodes; and the daing is that the Duke took up on interest xxᶜLi, but thei cānot fynde wheare above vıᶜL. hathe biue bestowed of it. His doing is so evident and playne to undermyne oᵗ mooat soverayne lady, that if he scape deathe, yett never imprisonment as longe as she lyvethe : but suerly he will hardly escape that is to be layed to charge.

Thei say the Quene wilbe at my Lorde of Burlye's howse besides Waltam on Sonday nexte, wheare my Lord of Oxford shall marry Mʳˢ Anne Sicelle his doughter.

Chippine Vitellus is cōme in to Flanders agayne out of the Spanishe court : and hathe given him the contie of Holstroughte in the Lowe contryes. And the Duke de Medena Seli is cōming by sea wᵗ a xxx. sale, whereof is vɪɪɪ. men of warre.

Thei say the Turke dothe muche harme bothe by sea and land: and good newes of good conclusion is looked for out of Fraunce by the nexte messenger of the consumation of the mariages: but there is nothing spoken of the Quenes Matᶦᵉˢ mariage.

He that murdered the Earle of Linaux and he that let thennemyes in at the posterne gate be both executed.

And thus leaving all my matters to determyne of the Almightie God that seethe the wronges that is donne me who wᵗ his mightie power will revenge my cause when it shall please him, I moost humbly take my leave of yoʳ honorable good L. wishing my Lord and you all helthe wᵗ thencrease of honor to Godes pleasure. Scribeld at London the xxıᵗʰ of September 1571. I cānot lerne Banister's confession upon the racke as yet ; but he was put to the racke for the denying of moost manifeste trothes at the first.

Your honorable good L. ever to cōmande during lyfe

HUGH FITZ WILLIAM.

*To the right honorable ...... tes of
Shrewsbury .... at Chattes-
worthe .... wheare.*

ROBERT Earl of LEICESTER to the Earl of SHREWSBURY.
1571.

My veary good L. I am right gladd to fynd that good & frendly acceptacōn at your hands dayly of my good wyll toward you ;—wᶜʰ you shall not fynd no way slack at my hands whearin I can doe you honor or pleasure: for I have alway had yᵗ good affectyon to you that my deayer hath byn to shew yt by all good meanes I might. And being your pore kinsman as I am, & of your house, you must think ther can not be a greater comfort to me then to se your L. prosper every way.— And as in respect of such allyance by nature I was bound so to wyshe unto you all good, so I assure your L. the erneat zeall you have & doe shew toward God in matters of trew religione, and the faythfull care and dewty I have seene you shew in the servyce of your prince & cuntrey, doth farr more bynd me to you, & to seke all meanes I may to acknowledge yt. And your L. doth se how God himself wyll prosper them that unfainedly professe his cause, and he wyll not se them undefended in the myddest of greatest dangers, as hit hath appered myraculously ever toward this our gracious sofferaine by the sinyster & mysterious devyces many ways attempted agenst her, & only over thrown by the mighty hand of God— And no dowbt for his cause sake, & his mercy sake, he wyll styll & longe preserve her and mainteyn such also as zelously love him & faythfully serve her. Your L. seeth how he putteth into her hart dayly more & more to conceave ryghtly of you. And I know yᵗ your L. hath no small cause to reioyse at her good opinion of you. God send your L. alway grace to deserve yt of her, as I doubt nothing at all therof. I suppose we shall se your L. hear, or yt be long; & therfore I wyll trouble you the lesse at this tyme; but praying my most harty cōmendacōns to be del to my good Lady your wyffe : & so God kepe & blysse you both. In hast this xɪɪɪ. of Dec.

Your L. assured and faythfull kinsman

R. LEYCESTER.

Yᵉ Spanishe Embassatʳ ys comanded to depᵗ yᵉ realm furthwᵗʰ. Some unkindnes wyll followe, but better yᵗ than to suffer his lewd practyses at home.

*To yᵉ right honorable my veary good
L. & cousē therle of Shrewsburye
one of her Maᵗᵗᵉˢ prevy councell.*

The Earl of SHREWSBURY to the Countess of SHREWSBURY.

My dere none, beinge here aryved at Wyngfeld late yeastarnyght from Rofford thou wery in toilinge aboute, yett thynkinge you wold be desyrous to her from me, screbled thes few lynes to lett you understand I was in helth & wyshed you anyghts wᵗ me. I pyked out a very good tyme, for synst my cōmyng from home, I nevar hadde lettars but thes this mornynge from Gylbard, whyche I sende you. I mynd tomorrow, God wyllinge, to be wᵗ you at Chatsworth : & in the mene tyme as occurentes ē to me you shalbe partakar of them. I thanke you, swete none, for your bakeu capon, & chefest of all for remembering of me. It wylbe late to morrow before my comynge to Chatsworth, vɪɪ. or vɪɪɪ. of the clock at the soneste : & so fare well, my trew none. This xxvɪɪɪᵗʰ June.

Your fathefull husband

To my wyfe the countes of   G. SHREWSBURY.
Shrewsbury.

The Earl of SHREWSBURY to the Countess of SHREWSBURY.

My dere none, I see how carfull you are of my helthe whych if I were syke wold relyve me agen. I reseved a lettar from Gylbord sent by Nykls Clark. You maye see the tyme aproches nere that a new alarom wylbe gyven me. When you have redd his lettar I pray you wryt to me agen, for I mynd of Monday to wryt by Antony Barlow: he wyll be gladd of the pursyvanteshepp if he can gett it : he shall have my good wyll therein. If you wyll wryt upp, he may safly delyvar it, therfor I pray you fele nott, but send me your advyse consarnyng this mattar. Fare well my only joye. This Saturday. I pray you kepe promes: you sed you wold be wᵗ me wᵗin a fortnyght at the furthest: therefor lett me her from you when I shall send for you your horses my swet harte.

Your fathefull husband most assured,

G. SHREWSBURY.

The Earl of SHREWSBURY to the Countess of SHREWSBURY.
1573.

My dere none : of all joys I have undar God the gretest is your selfe : to thynke that I posses so fathefull, & onne that I know loves me so drᵗ, is all & the gretest comforte that this yerth can gyve. Therefore God gyve me grace to be thankfull to him for his goodnes showed unto me, a vyle synare.

And where you advyse in your lettar you wylled me to whych I dyd that I shold nott be   to this lade nothyng of the mattar: my stomake was so full, I asked hur in quyck mānar, ' wheʳ she wrytt any letters to any hur frends that I wold stand in hur tytell.' She afyrms of her honor she hathe nott. But how so evar it is she hathe wrytten therein, I may safly answar I make small acount therof.

I thanke you my swet harte that you are so wylling to cō when I wyll. Therefore dere harte sende me word how I myght send for you : & tyll I may have your compeny, I shall thinke longe my only joye: & therefore apoyᵗe a day : & in the mene tyme I shall content me wᵗ your wyll ; & longe dayly for your cumynge. I your letters con very well ; & I lyk them so well they could nott be amended ; & have sent them upp to Gylbard. I have wrytten to him how happy he is to have syche a mothar as you are. Farewell only joye. This Tuesday evenyng.

Your fathefull one

To my wyf.   G. SHREWSBURY.

WALTER DEVEREUX Earl of ESSEX to the Earl of SHREWSBURY.

My verie good Lord, because I have now disposed my garrisons for this winter season, maynie gentlemen of my companie are desirus to repose them selfs in England ; some for weriness of those travells and hazards that the cuntrey yeldith; other uppō better respects, as the bearer Mʳ Candishe; who I assuer your L. hath   bene so redy and willing to take paines as I cold not look for more of eny privat or mᵉ ceniary soldier. Therefore I cannot but give hym his due cōmendacōn desiring your L. and my Lady to accept of his returne as of one licensed and cōmended by me : and in very dead amonge all those that now leve this place, I know not one whose return shall be more acceptable, or for whome I can be better persuaded to do good.

Towching the service undertaken here, I leve to his report and for the successe I find more difficulty to traine the gentelmen of our nacōn to endure paines meet for soldiers then to bring to good effect the journey I have in hand, wherin I see no doubt at all thoughe the begyning have bene somewhat untoward. And so recomending the bearer unto your L. I bid you most hartely well to fare. Frō Knockfergus the 23 of Octob. 1573.   Your L.' assured frend and kinsman

                          W. ESSEX.

To the right honorable my verie good Lord the Erle of Shrowes-burie Erle Marshall of England & of her Matⁱᵉ privy counsell.

Lord TALBOT to the Earl of SHREWSBURY.

RYGHT honorable my hu̇ble deautie remē'bred: mea̔y it please your Lo.: I have steayed writinge because I hoped to have hard su̇thing of Corker; but I can here nothinge. I have dealt wᵗʰ my Lord tresorer and my Lord of Lecester boueth, but I can not learne of them anie thinge that he hathe seayed of late, or done; he remeaneth still in close prison in the Flete. The Quenes mᵃᵗⁱᵉ hathe spoken to me, and tould me of your Lo.' letter wᶜʰ I brought; and howe well shee did accept it; wᵗʰ manie other comfortable wourds: but no thinge of anie matter. The matter of Corker is alŏst forgotten here; here is nothinge but of King Philipe crīinge dounne in to Flanders; and preparinge the Quen's navè to seay; but whether my Lord Admiraule goueth himselfe or no it is not given out for serteayne as yet. The quene matie gouethe of Saterdeay cum senight to Havering of the bower and their remeaneth tyle shee begins hir progres wᶜʰ is to Bristo; the gests he not drauen, but shee is deter̄ined for sertean to gowe to Bristo. This is all wᶜʰ is wourthie writinge; but as matter shall happen here I wyll God willinge advertes your Lo: accordinge to my deautie. Thus with my deaylie prear to Almightie God for your Lo.' longe life wᵗʰ much healthe, I hu̇blie tacke my leave: cravinge your Lo:' delie blessinge. Fro the couert at Grinwege this xᵗʰ of Meay 1574.

       Your Lo:' lovinge and moste obedient sonne

                   FRANCIS TALBOTT.

Lord TALBOT to the Earl of SHREWSBURY. 1574.

RYGHT honorable my hu̇ble deautie remē'bred. Meay it please your Lo: I have sent you here inclosed suche adver-tismens as latlie is came oote of France. Oute of Scotlande this is the newes: that Sʳ George Carye and Sʳ Harrie Leaye and Capteāe Reade goinge to yowe the castell were almost sleane wᵗʰ a grente pease oute of the castell. The are so fraee wᵗʰin as it is thoucht the castle wyll be taken verie shortlie wᵗʰoute ane grente trouble. There is some taulcke of a progres to Bristo; but by reason of the unsesonableues of the yeare, ther is greate meanes made for hure not goinge of so longe a progres: but 'hure Maᵗⁱ'ˢ greate desire is to gowe to Bristo. Mʳ Hattouu be reason of his greate syckenes is mindeℓl to gowe to the Spawe for the better recoverie of his healthe. All your Lo.' frinds do well here. My Lord treasurer and my Lord of Lecester do deaylie aseke for your Lo. and howe you have your healthe this springe. This is all that is at this tyme wourthie writinge: wherfore for this tyme I hu̇blie tacke my leave, cravinge your Lo.' delie blessinge. Frō the couert this xxⁱⁱⁱᵗʰ of May.

       Your Lo,' lovinge and obedient sonne

                   FRANCIS TALBOTT.

GILBERT TALBOT to the Countess of SHREWSBURY.

MY moste hu̇b̄le duty remembred unto your good La: To fulfyll your La.' cōmandement, & in discharge of my duty by wryting, rather then for any matter of importance that I can learne, I herewᵗʰ trouble your La.—Her maᵗⁱᵉ styrreth litell abrode, and since the stay of the navy to sea, here hathe bene all thinges very quieat; and almoste no other taulke but of this late proclamation for apparell, wᶜʰ is thought shall be very severely executed both here at the cowrte, & at London. I have wrytten to my Lorde of the brute yᵗ is here of his beyng sick agayne, wᶜʰ I nothing doubte but yᵗ it is utterly untrew:

howbeit because I never harde from my L. nor yoʳ La. since I came up, I cannot chuse but be sumwhat trobled, & yet I consyder the liké hathe bene often reported moste faloely, and without cause, as I beseche God this be. My lady Cobbam asketh daly how your La. dothe, and yesterday prayed me, the next tyme I wryt, to doe her very hartie cōmendacōns unto your La. saynge openly she remayneth unto your La. as she was wonte, as unto her deereste frend. My La. Lenox hathe not bene at the cowrte since I came. On Wednesday next I trust (God willing) to goe hence towards Goderidge; and shortely after to be at Sheffeld. And so most hu̇bly cravé'g your La.' blessing, wᵗ my wonted prayer, for your honor and most perfite helthe lounge to continew. From the cowrte at Grenewidg this xxvⁱⁱⁱᵗʰ June 1574.

       Your La.' most hu̇ble and obedient sun

                   GILBERT TALBOTT.

To my Lady.

I receaved a l're from my lorde since this l're was sealed, & then I had no tyme by this messenger to wryte agane unto your La. wᶜʰ came in a comfortable season unto me.

The Countess of PEMBROKE to the Countess of SHREWSBURY.

I AM loathe to lett passe any fitt messenger wᵗʰout visiting your La. wᵗʰ my l'res: and being desirous to heare of your health, do the oftener send to enquier of the same. At this present, I am to crave your furtheraunce bothe to my Lo. my father, (whom least I should any waies displease, ame loathe my selfe to move) and to this bearer my brother Savile, who dothe referr his consent till he knowe my Lo.' pleasure therein, that they will agree that my sister Marie who is no smale comforte unto me, maie staie here to goo this sommer into Walles wᵗʰ me. Hereiu your La. shall verie muche pleasure me: wherof, as sondrie other your courtesies, you shall find I will never be unmyndfull. Thus with my humble deutie remembred, wᵗʰ like cōmendacōns to your La. do even so take my leave. Ramesburie this xxⁱⁱⁱᵗʰ of Marche 1574.

       Your La.' assured loving daughter

To my La. my mother.   K. PEMBROK.

ANN Lady TALBOT to the Countess of SHREWSBURY. 1575.

GOOD Madame, I am to crave pardon of you for not wryte-inge by my Lorde's man Harry Grace. The cause I wylled hym to declare to your La. whych was the extremity that my ayster of Pembroke was in at that tyme; whych hath contenued tell Theursdaye laste. Sethensse that daye she hath ben out of her soundynge, but not able to stand or goe. Her greatest gryf is nowe want of slepe, and not able to away wyth the syght of meat: but consederynge her estat befor we thynke our selfes hapy of thys change, hopeing that better wyll followe shortely. The Quynes Maᵗʸ hath ben here wyth her twyas; very latt both tymes. The last tyme yt was x. of the cloke at nyght or ever her Maᵗʸ whentte hensse, being so great a myste as ther were dyveres of the barges and boottes that wayted of her loste ther wayes, and landed in wronge plases: but thankes be to God her Maᵗʸ came well home wythout colde or feare. For the holdyng of the Prograce, I am sure your La. hereth: for my part I can wryt noe sertaynté, but as I am in all other matters as I have alwayes professed and as dewtye doth bynd me, ready at your La.' cōmandement; and in any thynge I maye showe yt ether at thys tyme or when occassyon serveth, yf I be not as wyllynge therto as any chylde of your owne, then lett me be condemned accordynge to my desertes: otherwyse I humbly crave your La.' good openyon of me not to decrease, rememberynge your La.' cōmandement here to for, to wryt to you as often as I coulde, whych nowe in thys plase I shall have [better] meanes then I have had in the country, and ther upon pressumyng to lengthen my letter upon any occassyon although I cou't thys of my ayster very evell uewes, yet consederynge her recovery, I hope my long scryblynge wyll the lesse trouble your La. And so wyth my moste humble dewty to my Lorde and your La. I humbly take my leve. From Baynardes Castell the vⁱⁱⁱ. of Maye.

       Your La.' assured loveing daughter to cōmande

                   ANNE TALBOT.

My shyster of Pembroke hath wylled me to rem̄ber her humble dewty to my Lorde and you, wyth desyre of hys dayly blessynge. Assoone as she is able she wyll dowe yt her selfe.

To theryght honorable and my as-
sured good Lady and moother
the Countes of Shrowsbery.

GILBERT TALBOT to the Countess of SHREWSBURY.

My duty most hu͞bly remembred unto your good La. By wrytinge of my Lord's letter, I becum ignorante what to wryte to your La. unlesse I shoulde declare the same over agayne, and I make none other accoumpte, but when I wryte to one it is to bothe. This bearer Mr. Tyndall was at Hack'ey, where he founde them their well. And I truste very shortely that the dreggs of all misconstructions will be wyped away, that their abode their after this sorte wilbe altered. I studyed according-inge unto my duty to have do͞une what in me lay, if neede hadd bene, to have answered thos leude fellowes of the Peake that came hither, themselves knew not wher aboute, only drawne by doultishe perswasions of like, to travell hither; & by sum of their owne confessions, promised their sute shoulde be favored & preferred by the Bowes at the cowrte, whos dis-honest and folishe deling breedeth a doble shame to them-selves. And those pore ignorante fellowes y͞t came, are con-tented to returne agayne as they came; as I thinke John Knyveton hathe more at large advertised your La. The crea-dits of S͏ᵗ Jerrome and his brother is farr lesse in all other syghts then in their owne vayne imaginations, who by their lokes are very like to deseave straungers. I harde S͏ᵗ Jerrome say his towe brothers Edwarde & Roberte are in Fraunce: but sum think y͏ᵗ they are still in Inglande. It may be it was spoken to th'ende y͏ᵗ I shoulde here it, for I was taulking w͏ᵗʰ an other, harde by him, when he spake it. (My sister Pen-broke is now growne meetely strounge agayne, and paste all daunger: her ma͏ᵗⁱᵉ sendeth to her continually. She hathe prayed me to doe her hu͞ble and very hartie co͞mendaco͞uns unto your La. Of other things I hu͞bly crave pardone of your La. because of my L.' l're. I truste not to tarry here passing a weeke, but woulde be gladd before my co͞minge to under-stande sum sertayntie of the progresse, wherof I am in great doubte. And thus I moste humbly crave your La.' daly bless-inge, & pray to God for your La.' lounge continuance in all hon͏ʳ & perfyte healthe. From Shrewsbury place this XIIII͏ᵗʰ of May 1575.

Your La.' moste hu͞ble and obedient lovinge sun,
To my Lady. GILBERT TALBOTT.

The Countess of LENOX to the Countess of SHREWSBURY.

My humbl duty remembred: beseching your La. of your dsly blesinge: presuming of your mother like affeccyon to-wards me your childe that trusts I have not so evell deserved as your La. hath made shewe, by your lett͏ʳˢ to others, whych maketh me dotful that your La. hath ben informed som great untruth of me or elce I had well hoped that for som smal trifels I shuld not have continued in your displeasur so longe a time. And I myght be so bould as to crave at your La.' hands that it wold pleas you to exteme shuch falce bruts as your La. hath hard reported of me as lightly as you have don when others wer in the like cas, I shuld thinke myself much the more bounde to your La. I besech you make my harty co͞mandacions to my aunt. I take my leave in humble wyse. Hacknay xxv. of July.

Your La.' humbl and obed͏ᵗⁿᵗ doughter,
To the ryght honorabl the E. LENOX.
Countys of Shrewsbury
my very good mother.

MARY Queen of SCOTS to the Duke de NEVERS. 1575[1].

MON Cousin, i'ay resceu vostre honeste et courtoyse lettre,

aunesque tres grand contentement, pour le tesmoignaage que me donner par iscelle, que mes longues aduersites n'ont eu le pouuoir de vous oster la boune voulonte en la quelle i'auuois tousiours fait estast de vous trouuer, de fayre pour moy, ou loccasion seu presenteroit comme pour l'une de voz meilleures parentes et amyes. Et tant senfant que ie veuille nesglinger une telle offre de vous, que ie vous priray mettre amy a pre-sent en l'affaire de mon duche de Thourayne, le quel on me veut oster; et me donner et a mes gens fauueur et conseill pour acsepter l'eschange qui me sera offert, a ce que ie n'i fasse si grande perte. Vous pouuez assez considerer l'estast auquel ie suis, et si i'ay besoing d'estre rudement traitee. Par de la, ie ne vous endiray aultre chose, si non que ie vous prie m'ifayre office de bon amy: et mon Ambassadeur vous pourra informer du reste. Quant a ma saute, ce porteur vous en pourra dire, qui me fera cesser de vous importuner dauuantasge si non apres m'ettre recommandee de bien bon cueur a vottre bonne grace, priant Dieu quil vous doint mon Cuusin en sante, longue et heureuse vie. De Schefild ce penultiesme de Juillet,

Vostre bien affectionnee et bonne Cousine,
A mon Cousine Monsieur MARIE.
Duc de Nevers.

MARY Queen of SCOTS to the Duchess de NEMOURS[2].

MA tante, il i a long temps que ie ne me suis ramantire a votre bonne grace; non pour ne desirer di ettre continuee, mays pour ettre de si pres rescherchee, que lon fayt trouuer mauays la grosseur de mes paquets, et le nombre de mes lettres; di-sant que i ecris a trop de gens, que ie n'ay que fayre d'auuoir tant d'inteligence; si esse quilz ne se font pas prier d'ouurir tout, et en retenir ce quil leur en plaist. Mays a mon advis, il leur fassche de ce que lon ce forment, que ie suis encores en ce monde. Si esse que tant que ie y seray, vous aurez puis-sance sur moy, et pourrez fayre estast de la bonne voulonte d'une pouvre princesse, captiue et en adversite, centant que de niepce qu'avez eu ce monde; ce que ie vous supplie fayre, et me despartir quelques fojs de voz bonnes nouuelles, et de celles de mon oncle Monsieur de Nemours, a qui ie vous priray me permetre de me recommander issi bien affection'eem', et a tous voz enfans mes cousins: et vous ayant bese les mayns ie pri-ray Dieu vous donner ma tante en sante tres heureuse et longue vie. De Schefild ce VI. de Nouuembre.

Votre bien affectionnee & obeissante bonne niepce,
A ma tante Madame de MARIE.
Nemours[3].

MARY Queen of SCOTS to the Duchess de NEMOURS[4].

MA tante, si auriez iamays pance autrement si non que ie serois tres ayse d'entendre de voz bonnes nouuelles, et que ie fusse continuee en vostre bonne grace, vous m'auriez fait grand tort, pour l'honneur et le respect que ie vous doibs, et veux porter toute ma vie: et ie vous supplie dors en auuant faire telle estime de moy, et que ce me sera tres grand plesir d'entendre de vottre bon portement, et de celui de mon Cou-sin Mousieur de Nemours, et de voz petits enfans mes cou-sins[5], que ie tiens aussi chers comme propres freres de mes cousin de Guise. Vous porries aysement iusger si les pauvres prisoniers sont ayse de s'entre oubliez de leurs ensiennes amys et parents, bien qu'ilz ne leur soit permis ecrire a toutes occa-sions, comme ils vouldroient bien: et mesmes a present que ie suis pressee d'escrire dauuant le partement du Sieur de la Mothe de Londres, ie ne vous diray donc autre chose, si non que auuesques me mayns, ie porte part de ceulx qu'auner. Par de la dieu y veuille metre fin, et ie metray a la presence, apres vous auuoir bayse les meins a mon Cousin Mon͏ʳ de Ne-mour, et a vous; et vous avoir prie de montrer toute fauueur a ce porteur, pour l'amour de moy: et ie priray dieu qu'il vous dont ma tante, tres longue et heurheuse vie. De Chefild ce

---

[1] No. 8702. MSS. in the Royal Library at Paris, f. 122.
[2] Id. f. 123. It is not easy to collect the date of this letter or the next. I place them here, as they plainly belong to the darker periods of her captivity.
[3] Ann of Este, daughter of Henry duke of Ferrara. This lady was first married to Francis duke of Guise who was brother to the queen of Scots' mother. He died in 1563: and in 1566 she took to her second husband James duke of Nemours. She lived till the 7th of May 1607.

[4] No. 9126. MSS. in the Royal Library at Paris.
[5] The mother of the duke de Nemours was of the house of Valois, and he was consequently related to the queen of Scots. She was Charlotte of Orleans daughter of Lewis duke of Longueville. James 2d duke of Nemours was born in 1531, and died 15 June 1585. He was therefore spared the pain of witnessing the tragical termination of his near rela-tive's life.

xii. de Januier, vottre tres obeissante et affectionnee bonne niepce,   MARIE.

A ma tante Madame la Duchesse
de Nemours.

GILBERT TALBOT to the Countess of SHREWSBURY. 1575.

My duty moste humbly remembred unto your good La.— Here is no thinge that I can advertise your La. of. Yester-day Ratclyfe my brother Savill's man came from London wth a l're to my L. from his m^r, of my L. of Pembroke and my sister's departure from London on Thursday laste. Their hole companie is aboute xxx. persons. The Q.' mat^{ie} hathe lente them one of her beste shippes, throughly furnished to carry them to Andwerpe, and hathe apoynted Mr. Willm Gorge the captayne therof. My brother Saville and my sister hathe earnestly desyred me to excuse them for not wryting now unto your La., and to gyve you most hu'ble thankes for the further-ing of my L.' liberallitie unto them; whereof at large I wrytt unto them. Howbeit Mr Alderman Osburne to whom my L. earnestly directed his l'res to gyve them creadite for one hu'dreth markes and he wolde repay the same at Michellmas, woulde not lende them any more then fyvetie poundes, & that not in presente money, but by a byll of exchange to be re-ceaved in Andwerpe, for wch he muste pay for the exchange, interest; wherin, in myne opinion he hathe litell deserved the good turnes y^t my L. dothe unto him, & hindered them of my L.' gyfte. My L. is continually pestered wth his wonted busynes; and is very often in exceeding collor of sleyghte oc-casion; a great greife to them y^t loves him to se him hurte himselfe so muche. He now speketh nothing of my goyng to house, & I fere would be contented wth scilence to passe it over: but I have great hope in your La. at your cu'minge, and in all my life I never longed for any thing so muche as to be from hence; truly Madame I rather wishe my sealfe a plowman then here to contynewe. My L. myndeth to send me to Killingworth, when her ma^{tie} cōmeth thither. Your La.' pretty fellow is a rvghte honeste man every way. I truste your La. thinketh so, besyde his owne desertes, by father & moe-ther: who doe all moste hu'bly crave your La.' blessing; and pray for your La.' lounge healthe in all hon' & happines. Sh. this presente Wednesday. My Lorde is now goyng to Tan-kareslay to courslæ; I here not of any that dothe mete him there. Your La.' moste hu'ble and obedient loving son,

To my Lady.   GILBERT TALBOT.

GILBERT TALBOT to the Countess of SHREWSBURY.

My duty moste hu'bly remembred unto your honor.

My Lorde lefte me heare behind him when he wente to Worsop on Wednesday; for that Perence and the workme' were not then redy to goe toward Gotherydge: but I hastened them so muche that yesterday they wente early. There is gone wth Perence, Loe, Swyfte, and one other; they meane to consyther what may be donne of the oulde weare; & if they see no possibilitie of recoverie therof this winter, then to vewe ye new place y^t is spoken of, and get all thinges in redines that presently uppon my cōmynge thither it may goe in hande. Madame where it hathe pleased your La. to bestow of us a greate deale of furniture towards house, we can but by our prayers for your La. shew ourselfes dutifull as well for this as all other your La.' continuall benefytts towards us, whereof we can never fayle so lounge as it shall please God to conti-new his grace towards us. Presently after your Lu.' departure from hence, my L. apoynted him of the wardrop to delyver us the tester and curtaynes of the oulde groene & redde bedd of velvett and satten y^t your La. did see; and the clothe bedd tester & curtaynes y^t we now lye in, and ii. very ould counter-poynts of tapestry; and forbad him to delyver y^t bed of cloth of gould & tauney velvet y^t your La. sawe. That wch your La. hathe geven us is more worth then all that is at Gothe-rydg, or here of my L.' bestowing. On Wednesday y^t my L. wente hence, Cooks brought in a peace of housewyfe's clothe nothing deere of xii. pence ye yarde & so was holden; w^{ch}

Cookes tould my L. woulde very well serve my wyfe to make sheetes, bore clothes & such lyke: wch my L. at the fyrst yealded unto, & bade him carry it to Steale to measure, into the uttre chambre, and he sayde he thought it very deeare of that pryce, and theruppon my L. refused to buy it: wch was no otherwise then the demall of ye plate your La. called for. But whether the man or the plate be more in faulte I stande doubtefull. I pray God when he will, to amende both.

Tyt Tymperley came ye^sternyght. It apereth by a note y^t came wth the stuffe y^t there is suche thinges comme as Nico-las Steward wrytt for, as thredd & silke or such like; but it is lapped amonge so many other roulles of the lyke, and nothing wrytten on the backs yde, y^t we can not tell wch is for your La. from other folkes'. If therefore my cosen Jane will wryte what your La. sente for, we shall sende them : they appeare to be but small thinges : I thinke my Lorde will be heare to-morow at nyght; and about Twesday I thinke we shall set forwarde. Thus I beseche your La. moste hu'bly of your bles-sing to your lyttell fellow and myselfe, who is very very well, thankes be to God : not forgetting my prayer to God for your La. in all hon' to your hart's desyre. Sheffeld this Fryday xiiith of Octobre 1575.

Your La.' moste hu'ble and obedient loving sun,

To my Lady.   GILBERT TALBOTT.

MARY Queen of SCOTS to M. D'HUMIERES[1]. 1576.

MONSIEUR d'Humieres, despuis la mort du feu roy Monsig-neur votre bon maystre, ie n'ay jamays peu auuoir inteligence de vottre estast, que despuis peu de temps, eusa que Rallay mena esclursie, et questies encores en bonne sante, de quoy luy auvoit assure vottre bon frere monsieur de Baieulx, qui s'estoit tant enquis alors de mes nouuelles, ce qui ma men se presentent si bonne occasion, du retour du presidant de Tours mon Chansellier, de luy commander en soustienne vous aller visiter de ma part, et porter la presente, et vous fayre enten-dre comme mon douayre m'estant oste en Tourayne, ie suis pour recompance, renvoiee ettre votre voisine, que repance n'auriez malagreable vea l'ansiene conoissance entre nous, et ce que i'ay eu l'honneur de vous etre en respect de feu roy vottre maytre ; despuis la mort duquel, il me semble n'auuoir trouue amitie in conoissance en ses nouuelles courts, que l'en-droit de ceulx qui estoient des siens, qui sont quasi tous se-pares a present. Et pour le fayre court, ie n'eusse sceu auuoir voisin duquel ie feusse plus contente, comme ce porteur vou dira ; auquel ie vous prie donner credit comme feriez a moy mesmes : et ou il aura besoing de votre fauueur et conseill pour mon service, l'enarder, comme ma fiance est en vou : et que par son moien dors en amant i'auray de voz nouuelles, et vous des miennes. Et pour ne fayre tort a sa sufisance, ie fini-ray par mes affectionnees recommendations a vous et a votre famme, priant Dieu vous donner Monsieur d'Humieres, en sante tres heureuse et longue vie. De Schefild le xxvi. de May,   Vottre meilleure et plus assuree ensienne amye,

A Monsieur d'Humieres.   MARIE.

MARY Queen of SCOTS to the Duchess de NEMOURS[2].

MA tante i'ay este bien marrie d'entendre par mon Chan-selier present porteur, qu'a son partement esties malade : sans cela i'eusse espere que m'eussiez desparti de voz bonnes nou-uelles, et de celles de mon Cousin Monsieur de Nemours. Mays ie vous supplie que ce soit pour la premiere commodite qu'aurez ; et ce pendant me continuez tousiours en voz bonnes graces, comme celle qui vous respecte et desire obeir comme bonne niepce ; sur quoy ie vous priray donner credit a ce por-teur, qui par mesme moyen vous pourra randre bon compte de noz nouuelles issi, et spesiallement de ma santay, qui des-puis un an et plus a este assez mauuaise, mays commence un peu a s'amander: et pour ne vous ennuier sans meilleur sub-iect, ie priray dieu vous donner ma tante, en saute, tres heur-heuse et longue vie. De Schefild ce xxvi. de May,

Vottre tres obeissante et affectionnee bonne niepce,

A ma tante Madame la Duchesse   MARIE.
de Nemours.

---

[1] In a volume entitled 'Memoires du Regne du Roy Henry III.' No. 8715 of MSS. in the Royal Library at Paris, f. 76.
[2] In a volume entitled 'Diuerses Lettres de la Reyne d'Escosse Marie

Stuart vefue du Roy Francois IIe, et de la Reyne Marguerite a Mesdames les Duchesses de Guise et de Nemours, et autres.' No. 9126. MSS. in the Royal Library at Paris.

GILBERT TALBOT to the Earl and Countess of SHREWSBURY. 1577.

My duty ec. This morninge early I delyvered your L.' paequet to my L. of Lec. who uppon redynge therof sayde, he wolde wryte to your L. by a poste y' is here, & willed me to sende away your lackey. I asked him how longe he thoughte to tarry here, and prayed him to tarry as longe as myght be. And he sayde he knew not whether to goe to Chatesworth on Tweaday or Wednesday or Thirsday cum sevennyghte, but thone of thos three dayes w'thoute fayle. There came sum score of fowle hither on Saterday w'ch served here very well yesterday, & will do thes III. or 4 dayes. Sir Hughe Chamley sente hither to my L. of Lec. a very fatte beiffe, w'ch my L. of Leo. badd me goe doune to see, and to take him to use as I lysted; but I toulde him I was suer your L. wolde be angry if I toke him; yet for all this, he wolde force me to take him: and so I kepe him here in the towne tyll I know your L.' pleasure what shalbe donne w'th him; he wolde serve very well for Chatesworthe. Balye thynketh y' they will tarry II. or III. dayes at Chatesworthe: There is no worde yet come from my L. of Huntington & my La. whether they will meete my L. of Lec. at Chatesworthe or not; if they doe (as he hathe wrytten very earnestly to them) I thynke he will not cum to Ashebye, but goe the nexte way to Kyllingworthe & there tarry but II. or III. dayes only. My L. of Rutlande by reason of the fowle after noone yesterday, lay here all the last nyght, in y'e chamber where S'r Henry Lea lodged. I shewed the Pre of my La. Lennoxe your daughter to my L. of Lec. who sayde that he thoughte it were farre better for him to deferr her sutes to her ma'tie, till his owne cū'minge to the courte, then otherwyse to wryte to her before; for y' he thynkethe her ma'tie will suppose his l're if he sholde wryte, were but at your La.' requeste, & so by another l're wolde streyghte answere it agayne, & so it doe no great good : but at his metynge your La. he will (he saythe) advyse in what sorte your La. shall wryte to the Q.' ma'tie, w'ch he will carry unto her, and then be as earneste a solisitor therin as ever he was for any thing in his lyfe, & he doubtethe not to prevayle to your La.' contentacōn. Tomorrow my L. of Lec. menethe to goe to Sir Peres a Leyes to mete w'th my L. of Darbye, if the wether be any whytt fayre. And thus moste hū'blie cravinge your Lo.' blessinge w'th my wonted prayer for your longe continuans in all honor & moste perfyte healthe & longe lyfe I sease. At Buxtons in haste this presente Munday before noone.

Your ho.' moste hū'ble & obedyent son,
G. TALBOTT.

The Lords doe pray your L. to remember theyr case knyves.
To my L. and my La.

RICHARD TOPCLYFFE to the Countess of SHREWSBURY.

WE did yesternight cume to Rieote my Lo. Norices, where lait did arryve the countesses of Bedforde and Cumberl. and therie of Cumberl. the L. Wharton and his wife. The fatte erle cumeth this day, my L. of Lec' benge departed towarde the coort, to Sir Tho. Gresham's XXXIIII. myles hence (wherby you may perceave of his healthe) onely a lytell trubled w'th a byele drawen to a heade in the calfe of the legge, w'ch maketh hym use his lytter. The countesse kept hym over longe wayking, asking hym if Buxstone sent sownde men haltinge home. Butt I never dyd heare hym cōmende the place nor the interteign' halfe so muche: and did aware that he wished he had tarried III. wieks longer w'th his chardge of v'cL. but saiethe he, it hathe, and would have coste my friends deeply. His L. wished her ma'ty would progresse to Grafton & Killingworthe upon whiche condicyon he would see Buxstone this somer ageyn. But the next yeare is thretenyd that iorney. I can send your La. no more unpleasant newes butt that his Lo. hathe said w'th me in vowes that he will be as tender over your Lorde and yourselfe, and bothe yours, as over his owne healthe: and my Lo. is very cayrfull over his too younge cossens M'r Ed. and M'r Hen. to have them placed in Oxforde, wishinge that he may fynde of his kindered to worke his good will uppon, as he hathe done hethertoo of meny unthankfull

[1] This phrase is best explained by a passage in Bishop Latimer's 6th sermon preached before King Edward VI. ' Howe God is dyshonored

persons. Good mad. furder you my good Lo. your husb.' dispocycyon that way for your sone Char. My Lo. will bringe his owlde deadenfews unto a newe lyffe: and therew'th I end ; in very humble sort. The IX. of July 1577.

Your La.' ever at cōmandem't,
RYC. TOPCLYFFE.

The phizicions and all other for the beste worke of the well, that my Lo. is trubled w'th a byele, and so hymself thinkethe.
To the ryght honor : my singular good La. the Countesse of Shrewsbury.

GILBERT TALBOT to the Countess of SHREWSBURY. 1577.

My duty m. hū' rem. I truste your La. will pardone me in wrytinge playnely & truly, altho' it be bothe blū'tely and tediously. I mett my L. at Bolsor yesterday aboute one of the clocke; who at the very fyrste was rather desyrous to heare from hence, then to inquyre of Kyllingworthe. Quothe he, ' Gilbert, what taulke had my wyfe w'th you ?' ' Marry, my L.' quothe I, ' it hathe pleased her to taulke w'th me once or twyse ' synce my cū'minge, but the matter she moste spake of, is no ' smale discomforte for me to understande.' Then was he very desyrouse & bade me tell him what. I began, ' Truly, Ser, w'th ' as greved a mynde as ever I sawe woman in mylyfe, she toulde ' me your L. was vehemently offended w'th her, in suche sorte, ' and w'th so many wordes & shewes in your angre of evell will ' towards her, as therby your La. sayde you colde not but ' stande doubtefull that all his wonted love & affection is ' cleane turned to the contrarye; for your La. further sayde, ' you had geven him no cause at all to be offended. You ' hearinge that your imbroderers weare kepte oute of the Lodge ' from theyre bedds by John Dykenson's cōmandem't sayde to ' my L. thes words in the morninge, " Nowe did you gyve cō- " mandem' y' the imbroderers shoulde be kepte oute of the " Lodge?" and my L. answered " No." " Then," quothe ' your La. " they weare kepte from theyr bedds there yester- " nyghte : and he that did so aynde Jo. Dyckenson had geven " y' expresse cōmandm't." W'ch my L. sayde was a lye.' And' he sayde it was utterly untrewe. And so I wolde have gone on to have toulde the reste ; howe your La. willed him to inquyre whether they weare not in this manner kepte oute or no ; his proceedinge into vehem't coller & harde speches : but he cutt me of, sayinge it was to no purpose to heare any resaytall of this matter, for if he lysted he sayde he cold remember cruell speches your La. used to him, w'ch weare such as, quothe he, ' I was forced to tell her, she scolded lyk one y' ' came from the Banke'.' ' Then, Gilbert,' sayd he, ' judge you ' whether I had cause or not. Well,' quothe he, ' I will speke ' no more of this matter : but she hathe suche a sorte of var- ' lets aboute her as never restethe carryinge of tales :' & then uttered cruell words agaynst Owen chetely and the imbroderers, over lounge to troble your La. w'th. So beyng alyghted from his horsse all this whyle, sayde, ' Lett us gett upp and be ' goynge ; and I shall have ynoughe to doe when I cum home.' Then quothe I, ' I thynke my La. be at Chatesworthe by this ' tyme.' ' What,' quothe he, ' is she gone from Sheffeld ?' I answered, ' By IX. of the eloke.' ' Whereuppon he seemed to marvayle greatly, & sayde ' is her malice suche she wolde not ' tarrye on nyght for my cū'minge?' I answered y' your La. toulde me that he was contented at your fyrste cōming you sholde goe as yesterday: w'ch he forsware he never harde of. ' Then,' quothe I, ' my La. further toulde me that when your ' L. was contented for her departure that day, he sayde y' he ' had busynes in the Peake and wolde shortely cum thither, & ' lye at Chatesworthe.' Quothe he, ' her goynge away thus ' geveth me smale cause to cum to Chatesworthe,' but answered not whether he sayde so or not. But I assure your La. before God, he was & is greatly offended w'th your goyng hence yesterday.

After he had seene all his grounds aboute Bolsor, and was comen into the way homewards, he began w'th me agayne, sayinge y' all the house myghte deserne your La.' stomoke agaynste him by your departure before his cū'minge. I an-

by whoredom in thys cytie of London. Yea the Bancke when it stode, was never so commune.'

awered besyde yᵗ I sayde before, yᵗ your La. sayde you had very gret & earnest busynes as well at Chatesworthe for your thynges there, as to dele wᵗʰ sertayne freeholders for Ser Thomas Stanhope: but he allowed not of any reson or cause, but was exceedinge angrye for the same. Whereuppon I spake at large wᶜʰ I beseech your La. to pardon my tediousnes in repetall therof, or at lest yᵉ most therof. Quoth I, ' I pray ' your L. gyve me leave to tell you playnely what I gathered ' by my Lady. I see she is so greaved & vexed in mynde as ' I proteste to God I never sawe any woman more in my lyfe : ' and after she had toulde me howe wᵗʰoute any cause at all ' your L. uttered moste cruell & bytter speches agaynste her, ' when she all the whyle never uttered any undutyfull worde, ' and had particularly imparted the whole matter, she playnely ' declared unto me that she thoughte your L.' harte was wᵗʰ- ' drawn from her, and all your affection & love to hate & evell ' wille :' sayinge yᵗ you toke it as your crosse yᵗ so contrary to your deservinges he adiudged of you, applinge the manyfolde shewes wᶜʰ you so infynitely have made profe; & so forgott no earnest protestacōns yᵗ your La. pleased to utter to me of your deere affection and love to him bothe in healthe & syck- nes, takinge it uppon your soule yᵗ you have wysshed his greives weare on yourselfe to disburthen & quyte him of [them.] And quothe I, ' My L. when she toulde me of this ' her deere love towards you, and now howe your L. had re- ' quyted her, she was in suche perplexitie as I never sawe wo- ' man :' and concluded, yᵗ your La.' speche was yᵗ now you know he thoughte hī selfe moste happye when you were ab- sente from him, and most unhappye when you weare wᵗʰ him. And at this, I assure your La. he melted; and altho I can not say his very words weare yᵗ he had iniured & wronged you; yet bothe by his countenance & words it playnelie shewed the same; and answered : ' I know,' quothe he, ' her love hathe ' bene great to me: and myne hathe bene & is as great to her: ' for what can a man doe more for his wyfe then I have done, ' and daly doe for her?' and so reckoned at large, your La. may thynke wᵗʰ the moste, what he had geven & bestowed. Wherunto I coulde not otherwise replye then thus. Quothe I, ' My L. she weare to blame if she consydered not thes thynges: ' but I gather playnely by her speche to me yᵗ she thynkethe ' notwᵗʰstandinge that your harte is hardened agayneste her, ' as I have once or twyse alredy toulde your Lordship, and yᵗ ' you love them yᵗ love not her, and beleave thos aboute you ' wᶜʰ hatethe her.' And at your departure I sayde your La. toulde me that you verely thoughte my L. was gladder of your ab- sence then presence. Wherin I assure your La. he depely protested the contrary: & sayde ' Gilbert you know the con- ' trarye ; and how often I have curced the buyldinge at Chates- ' worthe, for wante of her companye : but, (quothe he) you ' see she carethe not for my companie by her goynge away. I ' wolde not have done so to her for vᶜLi.' But after this he taulked not muche ; but I know it pynched him, & in my conscyence I thynke so; but what effecks will follow God knoweth.

I will wryte agayne to your La. what I fynde by him this day; for yesternighte havinge not talked wᵗʰ any but my selfe, I know that his harte desyred reconsyliation if he wyste wᶜʰ way to brynge it to passe. The lyvyng God grante it, and make his harte turne to your comforte in all thynges.

To morrow he will send me to Darby aboute Sʳ Thoˢ Stan- hop's matter. I moste humbly beseche your La.' blessinge to me & myne. George reioyced so greatly yesturnyghte at my L.' cū minge home, as I colde not have beleved if I had not seene it. Sunday at ix. of the clocke. For God's sake Maddame pardone my very tedyouse & evellfavored scryblinge.

Your La.' moste hūble and obedient lovinge sun,
GILBERT TALBOTT.

The hastie l'res from Sʳ John Cunstable was to advertise yᵗ there are ii. Scotts yᵗ travell wᵗʰ lynen cloths to sell, yᵗ gave l'res of importance to this Quene: thʼone of them is brother to Curle. My L. Hūtington' l're was refusall of land yᵗ my L. offred him to sell.

GILBERT and MARY TALBOT to the Countess of SHREWSBURY.

MY duty moste hūblie remᵐ R. Hoˢ. my moste sinḡler good

La. This day my L. intendethe to goe to Worsopp; to morow to Rufford; and on Saterday hither agayne. He was not so inquysatyve of me touchinge your La. synce my laste beyng at Chatesworthe, as he was the tyme before; only he hathe asked me divers tymes when I thought your La. wolde be heare: wherto I have answered sume tymes that your La. was so evell at ease wᵗʰ the reume, as you knew not when God wolde make you able; other tymes, that I thought when your La. were well, you wolde desyre respett to stay for sum monethes, if he wolde gyve you leave: for you assuredly thought my L. was better pleased wᵗʰ your absence then pre- sence. Wherunto he replyed very ernestly the contrarye, in suche sorte as he hathe done heretofore, when I have toulde him the lyke. I found occasion to tell him that your La. mente not to houlde Owen as your growme any longer, seynge it was his pleasure to be so offended wᵗʰ him: howbeit (I sayde) your La. toulde me that you knew not what offence he hadd cōmytted, nor other by him at all then that he was a symple trewe man; & yᵗ you wolde be glad to understand sumthynge to lay to his charge, when you sholde turne him oute of your servise. But he answered no other then that it was his wille for dyvers causes yᵗ he wolde not utter. Further I sayde your La. toulde me you mente to take sum wyse fellow to your growme, yᵗ sholde not be so symple as Owen was, but one yᵗ had bene in servise heretofore, and knew what were fytte & belonged for him to doo in yᵗ service. (Quoth he) ' I beleave ' she will take none of my puttinge to her.' Synce yᵗ tyme he gave no occasyon of speche of your La. and indeede I have not bene very muche wᵗʰ him these iiii. or v. dayes, for he hadd muche busynes with others. He is nothing so merrye in my jugemᵗ as he was the laste weeke, but I assure your La. I know not any cause at all : nor other thynge I know worthye your La.' knowledge at this present: therefore wᵗʰ moste hūble desyre of your La.' blessinge to me & myne, and our prayer for your La.' continuance in all honᵗ, moste perfyte helthe & felicitie I cease. Sheffield this present Thursday 1 August 1577.

Your La.' moste hūble and obedyent lovinge chyldren,
GILBERT TALBOTT. M. TALBOTT.,

George is very well I thanke God: he drynkethe every day to La. Grandmother; rydethe to her often, but yet wᵗʰin the courte : and if he have any spyse, I tell him La. Grandmother is cōme & will see him; wᶜʰ he then will either quyckly hyde or quyckly eate : and then askes where La. Danmode is.

GEORGE SKARGELLE to the Earl of SHREWSBURY[1].

MAY yt plese your honnar to understand, that yowr L.' howse is quyet & well, God be pressed ; & the Quene ys sarvet wᵗʰ her vetteles & welle plesed for thes ii. dayes. Farther to lete yowr L. understand yᵗ yesterday a boutt iii. of clock, I went downe to yᵉ gardens at Castelle to se wat ster ther wase of yowr L.' fockes, & ther wasse at dyese Mʳ Andelbe, Thor- stone Howlle, John Roger, George Rolland, & Wᵐ Cravene for money; and James Neckes & other whear in the gardene wᶜʰ did not pley wyell I tared: & thene I went upe into the towne to se wat ther wase ther; and at John Sheldones in a parlar Wᵐ Clemanes & iii. other wasse at cardes for money, & wen they saw me they gave over: & so then presentlye I mett wᵗʰ ii. Glossope dale mene, wᶜʰ wold not know me speek to me ; & my harte was folle to se the stowttenes of theyme. I sayd to theyme the tyme had bene they wold have knowene me, & the tyme might be the wold now me agene & thene I retorned to yᵉ Manar agene. Herynge ther wasse x. of theame of Glossopdall comene frome Londone, devyued wᵗʰ myselve to go wᵗʰ a prevè watch; to yᵉ end yᵉ strangers might know alltho yowr L. wasse away, & the Baylley, yet yowr L. had leafte wateche in the contry: & I send Dyck Kepper a nother wey, & I tock wᵗ me Ralphe Martene, Cra- vene & others, as   barar hear of cane lett your L. under- stand by tolcke, & serched bothe bregges to se the watche, & coled at James Holdsworthes as well as at other hosses, be cosse the Glossop dalle men ley ther, that they might know no strangers cold be in the towne of Sheffelde, bott yowr L.' of- fesares by yowr L.' comondment wasse prevè who they wasse. And thus for trobellynge yowr L. to moche, I tack my leve for this tyme, tresting yowr L. wille note be a fended, be cosse I ded do yt of my selve wᵗʰowt your L.' comondmḗnt. Sheffeld Logge this.vIII. of May 1579 at xII. of yᵉ clocke at nowne.

Yowr L.' moste humbell sarvand telle dethe,

To my Lord.   GEORGE SKARGELLE.

The Earl of SHREWSBURY to THOMAS BALDWIN[1].

Bawdewine

I HAVE receved your severall l'res and some   & some torches by yᵉ carrier wᶜʰ was delivered unto the Baylie of Sheffeld. I have litle to say for this tyme, but wishe that as good order may be taken for my shippe as may be. And for my L. Mountegle, I am sory for his deth; & shall geve order for the looking to Brierley as well as I can. I would have you to bye me a yard of scarlett of fowre nobles a yard.   I care not so muche for the fyn̄es thereof, so that yt be of a good dye: your other scarlet was too deare; and send the same downe as sooue as you can. And yf you can gett any fyne oyle of roses that is very pure & good, send me some downe; or any other fyne cooling oyle for my feete to have in store. I am glad to heare that hir Maᵗⁱᵉ hath suche gratious liking for my sonnes Edward & Harrye wᶜʰ is my gret comfort. God blesse them. And yf the parliament nowe continew, (as I perceve by Mʳ Secretary yt doth) I thinke yt were good they staye their iourney untill yt be towards newyeres tyde or afterwards; so may you dispatche all things the better in the meane tyme, & go wᵗʰ them the better your selfe; but I would have you to come to me before to perfecte all things. And in the meane while, take such order that they be not idle nor loose their learning in any wise. And so for this tyme I ende. Sheffeld this xxᵗʰ of November 1580.   Your L. & Mʳ,

G. SHREWSBURY.

To my servant Thomᵃ Bawde-
wyne at Shrewsbury house,
London.

MARY Queen of SCOTS to ELIZABETH Queen of ENGLAND. 1583[a].

MA Dame ma bonne soeur, l'ay guarde si longue silence non pour paresse ou fautte de desir de vous rammentenoir moy & mes affaires, ou de voŭs fayre ouuerture qui vous fut si agreable que le puisse, par ce moyen recouurir quelque part en vottre bonne grace; mays par crointe de vous importuner, ne voiant aucun de mes lettres auuoyr cest heur de meriter responce de vous; come souuent ie lay ecrit a monssieur de la Mothe, ambassadeur du Roy monssieur mon bon frere, le priant fayre tant pour moy que de m'advertir de ce que ie pourroys eviter ou amander en mes dittes lettres, pour les vous, fayre trouuer dignes aumoigns de quelque favourable responce. Mays il ne m'a donnay aucune luimere en ce la sinon toutes les foys qu'il ma ecrit. Il me promet beaucoup de vottre bon naturel vers moy, me conseillant lenfayre prouve de reschief & vous solissiter par mes lettres auvoir memoyre de moy : ce qui est cause que ie me suis enhardie de vous fayre la presente. Par la quelle ie vous suppliray de me donner response a mes requestes precedantes & accelles que monssieur de la Mothe vous a faytes de ma part, ou bien me fayre entendre comme ie me debray gouverner pour obtenir plus amiable traitment de vous, atendant que dieu vous inspire a mettre fin a mes longs ou que je puisse auvoyr subject de vous donner occasion de m'estimer vottre oublisge & affectionnée amye, aussi bien comme ie vous suis prosche parente; & pour ne vous priant madame qua ce coup ie ne me puisse doüilloir que monssieur de la Mothe m'ayt fait entreprenare en vain de recommancer mon accoustum façon de vous ecrire, mays que j'aye plus tôst oecation par vottre gracieuse & desiree responce de le remarcier de son bon advis & concevoir quelque esperance que vous escriuuent plus amplement une autre foys, ie ne troueray plus vottre oreille sourde a mes offres & resquestes : de quoy vous auuoir bese les mayns, ie feray humble supplication. Adieu & qu'il vous doint madame en sante tres heurheuse & longue vie. De Chefild ce xvI. de ianvier,

Vottre tres affectionnée bonne soeur & cousine,

A la Royne d'angleterre madame   MARIE R.
ma bonne soeur & cousine.

[1] Talbot Papers, vol. G, f. 51.

GILBERT and MARY TALBOT to the Countess of SHREWSBURY. 1583.

Mʏ bounden duty, duty &c.—On Fryday at nyghte my L. sente to me to be wᵗʰ him the nexte morninge erly. I came to Worsop aboute IX. a clock, & founde the II. erles together, but saw them not tyll dynn' was on the table. After ordinary greetynge at the borde, my L. spekynge of Welbeck, my L. of Rutlange sayde he was s̄uer my L. wold pay for it, & 'so,' qᵗ he, 'you promised me yesternight,' wᶜʰ my L. denyed ; but sayde my L. 'Your L. was exceeding ernest wᵗʰ me so to doe;' wherat they were bothe very merry; and he styll was ernest wᵗʰ my L. therin, but he laughed it of   After dynn' my L. caled me to him into his chamber, & tolde me a longe tale of the cause of his metynge wᵗʰ that lord; theffecte in substance was to contynewe frendshipp wᵗʰ him ; & recyted many resons that he had to truste him better then any noble man ; & sayde that I had lyke cause to doe so, bothe in respect of kyndred, & yᵗ he lovethe me exceedinge well : & sware by God he was never more ernestly delte wᵗʰ then he had bene by him synce his cū'minge, for me ; bothe to be good to me in present & hereafter : & bad me take knowledge therof & gyve him thankes, & yᵗ in any case I sholde goe to Newarke to him. And before he had ended all that it seemed he wolde have sayde, he was caled away by the others beynge reddy to goe done to horsse. So when I came oute I brefely gave him thanks for yᵗ my L. had tolde me; & he wysshed he were able to doe me any pleasure, desyred me to cum to Newarke, & he wolde tell me more, & non lyvynge be better welloum : & so we parted. Then rode I sum parte of my L.' way wᵗʰ him. He tolde me yᵗ the cause he wolde not have me carry my wyfe to London was, for yᵗ he thoughte your La. wolde goe upp to London, & then wolde my wyfe ioyne wᵗ̶ʰ you in exclaiminge agaynste him, & so make him to judge the worsse of me, wᵗʰ much to yᵗ effecte. I alledged the nessessitie of my wyve's estate: how ill I colde lyve here wᵗʰoute any provisions; but he cutt me of, saynge he loked owrely for leve to goe upp, & after he had bene there himselfe, I mighte carry her if I wolde, & if I did before, he colde not thynke I loved him : & for her helthe, he sayd fisitians myghte be sente for, tho he bare the charges; & wolde not suffer me to speke a worde more therof, but bad me now doe it if I wolde. Then he tolde me that Lewis beynge at Newarke, Hercules Foliambe telde him, yᵗ he harde my L. had c̄omanded me to putt away my wyfe; & caled Lewis, & he affyrmed it, & so my L. willed me to charge Folliambe therwᵗʰ & make him brynge oute his autor. Then he tolde me that the matters was harde betwyxte your La. & him : yᵗ Sir W. M. & the Mʳ of the Rolles was wholly on your syde, & wolde have sett done an order clene agaynste him; but yᵗ the L. chefe Justyce wolde not therto consent, but stuck to him as frendly as ever man did. He wolde hun' & love him for it whylste he lyved; and yᵗ the order was deferred tyll Thursday laste; and that this laste weeke he had founde oute & sente upp all the pay books wrytten by Ryc. Cooke, of all mann' of conveances whatsoever, wherby there appered that Knyveton & Cooke delt the most trecherously wᵗʰ him yᵗ ever any men had done; but recyted not wherin, savynge that he hathe not Hardwyk & the West cuntrey lands wᵗʰoute impechm' of waste, as he wolde be sworne his meninge was. Further yᵗ W. Candishe he sayde was not 'asshamed to demande xvIII. hundred pounds for   & made suche a matter of yᵗ, as was never harde ; wherof he spake so oute of purpos, as it were in vayne to wryte it. Then c̄omended H. Candishe excedingly for mayntayninge his hon', wᶜʰ he sayde he sholde fare the better for; & tolde yᵗ dyvers noble men had of late answered for him very stoutly, espetially yᵉ erle of Cumberland. Then tolde yᵗ Bentall herynge how evell he was spoken of at London, & for yᵗ your La. had caled him traytor, he desyred leve to goe upp, ether to be clered or condemned: & yᵗ he had wrytten by him to my L. Tresurer, & my L. of Lester yᵗ he myghte be thorroly tryed, & have as he had deserved. As for his knowledge of him, he wrote he had founde him the trueste & faythfullest servante yᵗ ever he hadd. He sayde Bentall rather choste to goe upp of himselfe then to be sente for : and that he had bene twise examined before my L. Tresurer & my L. of Lester, & had sped well, & so wolde

[a] Cotton MSS. Caligula B viii. f. 329.

2 A

doe he hoped. Thes are all the spetiall poyntes yᵗ I can remember he spake. I began many tymes to tell him my greffes, & to open my estate, but he wolde not suffer me to speek, but sayde he loved me beste of all his chyldren, & yᵗ I had never geven him cause of offence but in tarryinge so longe at Chatesworthe; wᶜʰ thynge he also wolde not suffer me to answer, but sayde it was paste, & he wolde not here more therof. He apoynted me to mete him at Wynkefeld to morrow at nyghte touching the cause wᵗʰ the purveors, wᶜʰ is apoynted at   chappell the nexte day heynge Sⁱⁿ Mathew's day.

When I was parted wᵗʰ my L. I mett Style wᵗʰ the stuffe. The secrete he tolde me of th'estate of my L.' boddy was yᵗ swellinge wᶜʰ he sayde he thoughte none but himselfe did know: but when I tolde him where it was, he marvayled yᵗ I knew it. He tolde me yᵗ Bentall perswaded my L. yᵗ he was able to doo him suche servis above as he never had done him, and to discover the secretes of all thynges, espetially by his brother yᵗ serves my L. of Lestor: but Steele sayd he verely thoughte he sholde he layde upp in pryson. He sayde he talked wᵗʰ Curle all the day before he wente, & all yᵗ morninge, but I colde gett oute no partycular thynge of him besydes his contynual familiaritie wᵗʰ all the Scotts. He sayd ther is not any aboute my L. but Strynger, but sekethe my undoynge.

I am in hope to mete Mʳ Seriante Roods at Wynkefeld. Herineclosed is a note for your La. to reede. The remaynder of Rufford & Langeford is assuredly in my bro. H. Candishe, as the other lands yᵗ are unrevocable are.

I desyre to know whether your La. thynkethe that her Matⁱᵉ will be offended wᵗʰ my goynge to Newarke to yᵗ erle or not, considerynge what speches she used to me of him. If it be not in yᵗ respecte, I thynke it is very nessessary I goe thither, seeynge yᵗ he hathe used so good offyces for me to my L. My L. sayde to one yᵗ my L. of Lester was Bentall's gret frend. God prosper your La. in all thyngs. We moste huᵐblie besechie your La.' blessinge to us all.

         G. TALBOTT. MARY TALBOTT.

HENRY CAVENDISH to the Countess of SHREWSBURY.

MAYE yt please your honor, I receyved a lettar from your La. by my brother Wyllm: and whearas your La. wrytes yt ys sayed wᵗ you that I am gonne onely up to Londo⁻ to playe at dyse, the sayer or speaker of yt in tyme wyll be asshamed of hys occupacyon, and   be noted cõmonly for false, or els bewar how he crepeth into every man's judgement and mynde wheare he ys not made pryvye, nor caulde to counsell. For me I lyttle regarde reports, nor studdy to please every mã⁻. I have attayned to please those I seeke if I please your La. for others I lyttle esteme to please thear fantasyes, and wyll lesse every daye, knowyng I am as free borne as any other, and therefore thynke I dooe well yf I please myselfe; wᶜʰ by God's grace I wyll assuredly shortely dooe, and showe whearfore my cõmynge up was, neyther to playe at dyce, to seeke ease and dallyance, or for any other vayne delyghte, but to seeke vyrtù, and honor in armes, wᶜʰ by hys lycence that yeldes all thyngs I am resolute to fulloe, knowynge nottwᵗʰstandynge that yt wyll be yll spoken of, and letted by my frends, not for my good, but for envy. But by that meanes I shall staye some babelyng tounges from talkynge of my playe and cause them to sharpen thear wytts to devyse some other great faulte in me; more I thynke in my conscyens to trowehle your honor the⁻ to mend any yll in me, ys ther dryffte. My studdy ys to please your La. and so I end⁻vour my selfe dayly; and for my playe your La. shall hear, yf you hear the trewthe, shall be altered, and I gyven to other playe, that many myslyke, though most fytte for a gentlemã⁻. Thus humbly cravynge your La.' dayly blessynge I end, prayynge to God to send your ho. longe lyffe and good healthe. Coleherbert the vⁱᵗʰ of November.

Your La.' most bounde⁻ humble and obedyent sonne,

         HENRY CAVENDYSHE.

NICHOLAS KYNNERSLEY to the Countess of SHREWSBURY.

THE nyght aftʳ John was come wᵗ mi lettʳ Ezabeth told me yᵗ Gylberd Dickenson came to hur in yᵉ bechwase, & axed yff your ho. were here; & she answered 'No.' And he axed when you went aweay, &⁻ [she] sed 'Yesterday.' He axed

when you wold com agyne; she answered 'Shortly as she⁻ thowght.' And lat at nyght there came a boye from Sheffelde in a grene cote, & talked wᵗ them in yᵉ stable, & sed he moste goe very yerly in yᵉ mornyng to Sheffield agyn. Whatt the meanyng be thes questyons & yᵉ lackey comyng so late & goyng so yerly in yᵉ mornyng, I knowe not, except yt be to bryng me Lo. worde of your absence here, & so yᵗ he myght com upon yᵉ soden & fynd you a way. So I leve yt to your ho.' wysdom to conseder of yt as you thynke beste; bot I thynke good you were there. Mʳ Knyveton ryd by to day to Sheffeld as I was told, & called not as I   told wᵗ I mervell off. Me La. Arbella at vⁱⁱⁱ. of yᵉ clocke this nyght was mery, & eats hur meat well; bot she went not to yᵉ scolle yᵉˢ vⁱ. days: therfore I wold be glad off your La.' comyng, yff there were no other mattʳ bot yᵗ. So I beseke yᵉ Allmyghty preserve your La. in helthe, & send you soune a good & comfortable end of all your great trobles & greffs. Wynfeld this Twysday yᵉ v. of Novembar at vⁱⁱⁱ. of yᵉ clocke at nyght 1588.

Your ho.' moste dewtyfull bound obedyent sarvant,

         NYCHOLAS KYNNSLAY.

*To yᵉ ryght ho. me syngular good
La. & Mⁱˢ yᵉ Countess of Salop gyf this wᵗ speed.*

Sir FRANCIS WILLOUGHBY to the Countess of SHREWSBURY.

URGENT occasyon hâth made me bolde to write unto your Ladieshippe at this instant; my wife hath beene longe sicke, and for the recoverie of her health is at Buckstones, wheare having receaved noe helpe is growne to suche weakenesse, that nowe beinge desyrous to retorne home is not able to adventure the iorneye eyther on horsebacke or in a coache. Whearfore I am humblie to desyre your Ladieshippe to lende her your horse-litter and furniture, that by your Ladishippes good meanes she may saeflie goe home. Thus hopinge of your Ladieshippe's favour in this, bothe I and my wife in anye service we cann, rest readie at your Ladieshippes comandemẽt: desyringe God to have your honour alwayes in his protection. At Buckstones this xxvⁱᵗʰ of Aprill 1589.

Your honour's to commaunde,

         FRA. WYLLUGHBY.

*To the right honorable my verie
good Ladie the Countesse of
Shrewsburie give thease.*

GILBERT and MARY TALBOT to the Countess of SHREWSBURY. 1589.

OUR bounden duty moste humblie remembred. In lyke humblenes we render your La. thanke for your lytter; the laste tho the leste of your infinite goodnesses towards us & ours. We are safely comme hither to Dunstable (we thank God) this Shrofe Munday at nyghte: and now, for yᵗ the fowle way is paste, we thynk beste to returne your La.' lytter agen from hense.

Suche newes as on the Quene's hye wayes we have mett wᵗʰ, your La. shall nowe understand. Fyrst that her Matⁱᵉ (royally in person) was at the parlamᵗ house the fyrste day of this parlamᵗ: where Sʳjante Snagge was admytted for the Speker of the nether house. My Lorde of Darby is Lord Steward duringe this cession. That yesterday one tolde a man of myne that as yet nothynge of any moment hathe bene touched in the nether house, nether any expectacõn yᵗ any gret matters wilbe handeled, but yᵗ it will shortely ende. That a day or two before the parlamᵗ began, the Lᵈ Chane⁻, the Lᵈ Thesʳ wᵗʰ ı. or ıı. more of the prevy counsell, and Mʳ Auturnea & Mʳ Solicitor were wᵗʰ th'erle of Arundell in the Towre: synce wᶜʰ tyme ther hathe bene no suche speche of his arraynemᵗ, as there was before. This is all the Queene's hye wayes hatha afforded us of newes. Yet further we here that all your Ladishypp's   are very well. And thus in haste, most humblie beseeching your La.' blessinge to us & all ours who pray evermore to the moste hieate spedely to graunte unto your La. all contentmᵗ wᵗʰ longe lyffe, we humblye seace, till our nexte l'res wᶜʰ shall not be longe,

Your La.' most humble & obedient lovinge chyldren,

         GILB. TALBOTT. MARY TALBOTT.

We have desired your La.' leter men to bringe a leter to your La. from Beakewod wher Mrs Markhame's ernest intrety mad us to leve her tell the returne ther of. I besech the all mighty to send your La. my La. Arbell and the rest of your La' a most hapi long life.

To my Lady.

GILBERT and MARY TALBOT to the Countess of SHREWSBURY.

OUR bounden dutyes moste humblie remembred. In lyke hu'ble mann^r gevinge your La. thankes for your l're wch lately we receved, whereby we understand that wch beste contenteth us, the good health of your La. wth all yours there.

Touchynge our busynes here, we can not yet (by any possible meanes) procure the dispatch therof, but are styll delayed wth daly promis: and particularly for the offyces. I lately understandinge that the Erle of Essex meante to renew his sute to her ma^{tie} for Tutbury, I toulde him that I was very sorry my happ was to be crossed therin by any, seynge the same offyce hadd contynued in the hands of my auncestors this two hundred yeres paste: muche more by suche a one as his Lp. was, of whom I never deserved otherwysse then well; and who I was ryghte sorry sholde use so great discurtesy to me &c.: wth muche more to the lyke effecte. When I hadd ended he answered that it lyinge so very nere his chefe house & in his owne cuntrey, he hadd moved her ma^{tie} therin more then a yere synce, who did dyrectly promis him that she wolde make stay therof for him, and not graunte it to any other: wch promis he sayde he was fully purposed to have now renewed to her ma$^{tie's}$ memory; nevertheless so muche he respected my house, and so great good affection he bearethe to me as he was contented both to surcease his sute for himselfe, and to further me therin all that he coulde: wch I colde not but take very thankfully at his hands. And thus muche I have imparted bothe to my Ld Trer. and to Mr Secretary, and they have declared the same to her ma^{tie}, so as there is now no scrupell at all that I can lerne, & yet my bylls are unsigned, and put of from day to day. I assure myselfe that before this l're shall cum to your La.' hands, you shall have harde of the wycked murther of the Frenche kynge. In this mann^r: a freare of a new order wch this kynge himselfe erected, caled the order of Dominick, desyred to have private accesse to his owne person, for matters tendynge hylye to his hon^r & servyce. And beynge admytted he delivered unto the Kynge a l're importynga an offer of one of the chefe gates of Paris to be at the Kynge's c$\bar{o}$mandem^t: but before the sayde l're was fully redd, that cruell varlett (wth a longe sharpe poynted knyfe y^t he hadd in his wyde sleve for y^t purpose) stabbed the Kynge into y^e syde therwth. Yete the K. havynge sum glympse of the knyfe stroke it sumwhat doune wth his arme, wherby it pierced not so depe into his boddy, but y^t ther was hope of his recovery. The Kynge himselfe wrested that knyfe oute of the vyllane's hande: (sum sayes he pulled it oute of his owne boddy) but certayne it is, that the K. stabbed the varlett two or three tymes into the face & hedd therewth, & so by thos y^t were nerest the Kynge he was instantly slayne in ye place: The K. immediately sente for the K. of Navar to him, who was incamped nere unto him, wth many others of the nobilitie: And after he hadd hadd sum private speeh wth the K. of Navarre, he desyred all thos noble men ther presente to receve him for theyr Kynge and no other; wch they all faythfully vowed to do. And they all (wth that Kynge) did also vow to be revenged of the Kynge's dethe. Sum thynke it is not a freare indeede who did this wycked acte, but sum other person who determininge to sell his lyffe in y^t revenge, did so apparell himselfe to th'ende therby to procure accesse. Uppon this newes my Lo. Chancellor who was then at Holdenby at the marryage of his nephew was sente for upp agen wth all spede: And this nyghte he will be at London. He purposed to have tarryed ther x. or xii. dayes longer. Here they will resolve what course is fytteste to be taken for the K. of Navar's ayde, so sone as they shall be agen advertised how the nobilitie & people are bent towards him. All thyngs here are after the wonted manner. Thus moste humblie besechynge your La.' blessynge wth our wonted prayers for your moste happy longe lyffe in all comfortes; and our prayers to God to prosper my Lady Arbell, and to blesse our lyttell ones, & to rewarde your

La. for your gret goodnes to them, we humblie seace. This fyrst of July 1589.

Your La.' moste humble and obedient lovynge chyldren,

GILB. TALBOTT. MARY TALBOTT.

Meny good wordes I continewally receve and promis of as much as I can desire; but nothing performed for your La.' ease; nothing done. How my Lo.' reversion of his ofesis standes this letter will advertis your La. and for Welbeke it is much mor bacward then it semed to be at our coming up. We will labor still by all good menes, and leve the succes to God, who in short time may make greter alteration when we lest loke for it. God turne all to the best. Here is a brut, but I know not of what credit, that Foler shalbe the Q.' leger imbasitor in Scotland. The Q. axed me very carfully for my La. Arbell the last day; God bless her wth all his good blessinges, & geve your La. that and all other comfortes.

To my Lady.

ROBERT Earl of ESSEX to the Countess Dowager of SHREWSBURY.

MADAM, this bearer Christopher Hannam hath a good while belonged unto me, and now desireth to be entertayned in service by you. That your La. meaneth to receave one in the place of a gent. usher I understand by my good frend Sr John Wingfield, who hath made choyse of this man to be preferred to your service, and moved me for my consent therto. Wherin I am so far from dissenting, that for manie respects I have great lyking of it. First for his owne sake, that he shall be placed with so honorable a ladie: then for my selfe, y^t it is my happe to have a man worthie to be preferred to your La. and I hope when you have made proofe of his service, he will deserve my comendac$\bar{o}$n; and your La.' good lyking. The iudgment of my La. of Kent and Sr John Wingfield who have thowght him meete for your service might well suffice for his credite; yet I thowght it not enough to give him leave, unlesse I added therto these l'res in his c$\bar{o}$mendac$\bar{o}$n, wch I do wishe may so farre stand him in steede, as that for my sake his service may be somwhat the more acceptable unto your La. So I committ your La. to God's protection. From the Courte the 23 of Marche 1590.

Your La'ps to do your service,

R. ESSEX.

To the ryghte honorable the Countes of
Shrewesberey dowger this be dd.

WILLIAM Lord COBHAM to the Countess Dowager of SHREWSBURY.

MY honorable good Lady. I understand from my cosin Jo^n Manners, that you ar well pleased searche should be made in certeine grownds of yours, for such black stone as I stand in present neade of for my buildings. For your La.' greate courtesees towards me in this, I yelde you my humble thancks: and wth my service I wyll requite yt yf yt lye in my smale power: as knoweth the Almightie God. And so I humblie take my leave. From the cowrt at Richmond this xxviith of Februarie 1595.

Your La^{ps} at comandm^t,

W. COBHAM.

To the right honorable the Countesse
of Shrewslurie dowger at Hard-
wicke.

Lady GRACE CAVENDISH to the Countess Dowager of SHREWSBURY.

I MOST humbly thanke your La. for your leter from Mr Cavendysah whyeh I have returned by thys berer. It is the greatest comfort can cum to me to hear he is so well passed so far of his longe and dangerus iurnay, at the end wher of I trust in God he is by thys tym: for by a nott he left wyth me at hys goinge, of hys days iurnays (wherin he hath altered but on day as appeareth by hys letters) he was at Constantinople the xx. of thys month; from whych I besech Almyghty God send hym short and safe return to your ladyshyp's comfort, and myn chefly. Thus most humbly craveinge pardon for my bould wrytinge thus much unto your honor of hys iurnay, whych can not on day escape me wythout account of hys iurnays, I humbly take my leve, wyth lyke desier of your La.' dayly blessinge, and my prayer for your La.' helth and comfort. From Dowbridge hoult thys 27 of June.

Your La.' most humble and obedyent daughter,

To my Lady.   GRACE CAVENDYSSHE.

Lady GRACE CAVENDISH to Mrs. KNIVETON.

GOOD aunt, M' Cavendysshe hath sent hear inclosed a letter to my honorable good La. whych he desireth you to delyver. It is a autt he hath to her honor, whych I trust she wyll not be offended wyth hym for. I have presumed to send her honor ii. fatt capons whych ar not so good as I desier the wer, but I hope to have better shortly, now wee have corn in the barne: and a hundred of wardens, the best frute our cuntrey wyll afford thys year; whych good aunt delyver to her honor wyth my most humble duty, and lyke desier of her honor's dayly blessinge; thyukeinge my selfe most bound for her honor's bounty ever to me, whych I cau no wàys deserve, but wyth my prayers for her ho.' helth and happynes in all thynks. Good aunt thus most lovyngly to my awet nephew and nece, to whom I have sent a dosin wardins. And thus wyth my harty cômendations to yourselfe, I take my leve. Tutbury thys x. of October.

Your assurede lovinge nece,

GRACE CAVENDYSSHE'.

*To my .... re aunt M*ʳ*ˢ*
.... eton: geve ....

JOHN MANNERS (afterwards Sir JOHN MANNERS) to WILLIAM CAVENDISH (afterwards Earl of DEVONSHIRE).

Sʳ

THE cheefe cause of my writyng unto you att thys tyme is to understand from yow how my honorable good Lady your mother doth, my Lady Orabella, and your selfe, and all at Hardwyck: for it now is a good whiel since I was their; yet the last night I lay forth of myne owne howse was in Hardwick: for i am become an eveill travailler this wynter tyme.

Sʳ I am bold also to acqwainte you wᵗʰ a supplication to the Quen's Maᵗⁱᵉ, and a l're to my L. Anderson, for the procuring of the pardons of Hollyngworth and Stafford wᶜʰ wear condem͠ed for the burglary in Glossopdaile. Sondry gentlemen have ioyned wᵗʰ me theirin, and if you like theirof, then and it may please you to putt to your hand, I wyll hartely thancke you therfor. My undersherif is not yet côme down from London that I heer of; but I have sent woord that he doe satisfy your request in that baching Bawberye wᶜʰ you sent me woord of, by your sarvant Lent. And this beeing all wᶜʰ I have to troble you wᵗʰ at this tyme, wᵗʰ remembrance of my duty to my Lady, and most lovyng comendacôns unto your selfe, I leave to the Almightye's blessed protection. From Haddon this vi. day of Decemb' 1598.

Your assured lovyng frend,

JOHN MANNERS.

I pray you send me woord whoe is sheriff, for I doe not yet heer therof.

To the right worshipᵘ my verie lovinge
frend Mᵣ William Cavendish esquire
give this at Hardwicke.

W. WYNGFIELD to the Earl of SHREWSBURY².

RIGHT honorable, I have procured diverse parcells of sundry sortes of oares, whyche they that gathered them thoughte them to be lyklyest to have gould or silver in them. If any of them prove well, the whyche brought them unto me knew wher they had them, and can fetche more at any tyme, if neede requyre. I sent Richarde Browen, Bayliffe of Barley, to Mʳ Robert Eyre to knowe where the goulden hill or banke was, whych your honor writ of, that search myght be made for gould mettall there. Mʳ Eyre sayd he knewe none such hill or bancke, but poore people in the contrey founde certayne peeces of such lyke mettall, wherof he brought some unto your Lordship: & some Mʳ Eyre sent to Manchester to be tryed their, & that was founde nothynge worth. I have sent the oare left at Sheffeld Lodge wrapped in a lynnen clothe & a paper in the same cloth wherin is written ' The oare left at Sheffeld Lodge.' This oare is in the top of the bagge above all the rest. Thus praying to God to preserve your Lordship in health, wealth & happines, I most humbly take my leave. Sheffeld xv. of Aprill 1600.   Your servant,

To the right honorable th'earle   W. WYNGFELD.
of Shrewsbury.

Lady DOROTHY STAFFORD to the Countess Dowager of SHREWSBURY.

RIGHTE honorable and my verie good Ladie. I have according to the purporte of your honoᵇˡᵉ letters presented your Laᵖ'ˢ newe yeresgifte, togeather wᵗʰ my Ladie Arbella's, to the Queene's Maᵗⁱᵉ; whoe hathe verie graciously accepted thereof, and taken an especiall likeing to that of my La. Arbella's. It pleased her Maᵗⁱᵉ to tell mee that whereas in certaine former letters of your Laᵖ'ʸ, your desire was that her Maᵗⁱᵉ would have that respecte of my La. Arbella that she mighte be carefullie bestowed to her Maᵗⁱᵉ'ˢ good likeing, that according to the contents of those letters, her Maᵗⁱᵉ tould mee that shee would be carefull of her, and wᵗʰall hathe retorned a token to my La. Arbella; wᶜʰ is not so good as I could wish it, nor so good as her Laᵖ deserveth, in respecte of the rarenes of that wᶜʰᵉ she sente unto her Maᵗⁱᵉ. But I beseeche you, good Maddam, seing it pleased her Maᵗⁱᵉ to saie so muche unto mee touching her care of my La. Arbella, that your Laᵖ will vouchesafe mee so muche favoᵣ as to keepe it to your selfe, not makeing anie other acquainted wᵗʰ it, but rather repose the truste in mee, for to take my opportunitie for the putting her Maᵗⁱᵉ in mynde thereof, wᶜʰ I will doe as carefullie as I can. And thus being alwaies bownd to your Laᵖ for your honoᵇˡᵉ kindenesses toward mee, I humbly cômett your Laᵖ to the safe protection of Almightie God. From Westminster this xiiiᵗʰ of Januarie 1600.   Your Laᵖ'ˢ moste bounden

DOROTHIE STAFFORD'.

To the right honorable my verie good
Ladie the Countesse of Shrews-
burie Dowager.

JOHN MANNERS to the Countess Dowager of SHREWSBURY.

GOOD Madam, I was very glad of the receipt of your La.' l're, and chefly for that I doe understand theirby that you be in good helth, wᶜʰ I pray Almighty God long for to contynew. Towching your La.' request in the behalf of Sʳ Edward Dyer, this much may please you to understand, I received a l're from the Erl of Shrew. by young Sellers, desiring me to take order for the safe keping of Mʳ Beresford's goods in Mʳ Dyer' right, because the said Mʳ Berisford had made him his executor. Wheirupon I did presently send tow of my servants unto Birchearer, wᶜʰ is wᵗʰin tow mylles of me, and their left tow men to looke unto his howse and cattail he hath their, who doe their parts honestly, for thei have fownd a good porcion of wool that was

---

¹ The writer of these two letters was the daughter of George earl of Shrewsbury, who married Henry Cavendish, the eldest son of Sir William Cavendish and the countess of Shrewsbury. Her husband, to whom she seems to have been an affectionate and faithful wife, is the ancestor of the Cavendishes of Dovebridge, now represented by lord Waterpark.
² Talbot Papers, vol. K, f. 5.
³ There is a good account of this lady on her monument in St. Margaret's church, Westminster.
⁴ Here lyeth the Lady Dorothy Stafford, wife and widow of Sir William Stafford knight, daughter to Henry Lord Stafford, the son of Edward the last Duke of Buckingham. Her mother was Ursula daughter to the Countess of Salisbury the only daughter to George Duke of Cla-

rence, brother to King Edward the 4ᵗʰ.
⁴ She continued a true widow from the age of 27 till her death. She served Queen Elizabeth 40 years, lying in the bed-chamber; esteemed of her, loved of all, doing good all she could to every body, never hurted any, a continual remembrancer of the suits of the poor. As she lived a religious life in great reputation of honour and virtue in the world, so she ended in continual fervent meditations and hearty prayer to God: at which instant (as all her life) so after her death she gave liberally to the poor, and died aged 78, Sept. 22, 1604.
⁴ In whose memory, Sir Edward Stafford her son hath caused this memorial of her to be in the same form and place as she herself long since required him.'

hydde in a rocke: And their I appointe them to remain, and have sett sealles upon the lockes wheir any goods be, and have charged them to have good care also that their be no sheepe nor cattail purloyned owt of the pastures: so as I have no doubt all things their shalbe in saftey untill I heer forther. Their is at Byrcheover a great quantitè of lead, wooll, sheep, and some cattail, but his *money* (wch he is thought not to be wthowt) platte, and stuffe is at Denkly, whither Mr Harpir had sent befor the receitt of my l're to take order. Mr Dyer

I am well knowen unto, but being your La.' frend I will carrye the better either in this or any other service you may please to cõmande me. And so I pray God Almighty long to preserve your good La. From Haddon this xx. day of Decemb^r 1602.

Your La.' most humbly to cõmande,
JOHN MANNERS.

To the right honorable and my singuler
good Lady the Countesse of Shrewes-
bury at Hardwyke.

JAMES I.

FRANCES PIERREPOINT to the Countess Dowager of SHREWS-BURY. 1603.

MAY yt please your honour, Sur Jhon Halles eam post from London uppon Tuesday last, and yesterday went towards Barwike, wher he dothe heare be on of the Kinge's chamber, that his Ma^{ts} woll be on Satterday nexeste; and ther stay until he hath settled the parts ther aboutes. Also he sayeth that al thingee in the southeren partes procede peaceably: only my Lord Beauchamp is sayd to mak some assemblyes, which he hopeth wil soddenly dissholfe into smoke, his forse beyng feble to make hede agenst so grayt an unyon. So geveynge your honour most humble thankes for your moste honourable and continuall bounty to me, and most humbli cravyng your La.' blessinge, I humblie tak my leve; beseeching the Almighti to send you long lyfe, al comfort and happines. This present Friday,

Your Ladyship's humble and obedyent dauter,
F. PIERREPONT.

Mr Pierrepoint remembers his humble duti to your honour.
To my Lady.

GEORGE Earl of CUMBERLAND to the Countess Dowager of SHREWSBURY. 1603.

GOOD Madam, pardon my thus longe silence, havynge beene sence my cu'myng from you soe trobled wth preparyng for his Mai.' cummynge to this ruinated place, that I have had nether leasure nor fitt meane till nowe; when I dooe as I will ever acknowledge my selfe soe much bound to you for your many favors, that I protest you shall ever cõmand me, and would be as glad of any cause wherin I myght shewe it as of any fortune that could happen to me; wch I praye you hould your selfe assured of. I will not now troble your La. wth wrytyng answere to the speech that passed betwyxt hus concernyng my doughter, nor wth a further sute that I am forced to macke to you, but refer all to this berer, whom I pray your La. truste. He is the man that I most dooe'. Soe wyshyng your La. all happynes I rest ever to be cõmanded by you,

CUMBERLAND.

To the right honorable and my verie
good Lady, the Countess Dowager
of Shrewesbury these dd.

The Earl of SHREWSBURY to JOHN HARPUR Esquire².

Mr HARPUR, yt maye be I shalbe verie shortly in the cuntrie, & perhaps may be soe happie as to entertaine the Kinge our sov'aigne at Worsupp. I would entreate you to lett all

---

my good frends in Derbyshire & Staffordshyre know so much, to the end that I may have theire companie against such tyme as his Matie shall come thither. I know not how soone. If yt soe hap as I shall know w^{thin} a few daies the certaintie; but then yt wilbe to late for your horses or anie thinge else to be prepared, unlesse you prepare them presently upon the receipt hereof. All things heere are well, & nothinge byt unitie & good agreement. God continue yt. Amen. Amen.

At my chamber in Whytehalle pallace this 30th of Marche, beinge Wednesdaie at night, in verie great hast, 1603.

Your frend moste assured,
GILB. SHREWSBURY.

I will not refuse anie fatt capons & hennes, partridges, or the lyke, yf the Kinge come to mee. G. SH.

To my verie good frend Mr John Harpur,
Esq. at Swarston. dd.

EDWARD TALBOT (afterwards Earl of SHREWSBURY) to the Countess Dowager of SHREWSBURY.

MY duty most humbly remembred to your ho^r. May please you be advertised that yesterday beinge Fryday I receyved a l're from my servant Towars from London, wherin he writeth that he hath not as yet any answere from my sister Grace of the l're wch I writt unto hir wch your ho^r knoweth of, but said y^t she would writ unto me an answere, but as yet hath not. And he writeth further that she delivered the l're to my brother hir husband, who he himself did see read it, and he saith that it semeth by his speaches that he did well accept therof, and thanked me for my remembrance, and wished he had bene ther before my comminge downe, and intreated my man in his next l're to commiend him kindly unto me. After whiche his speaches, my sister spake privately unto him, and as he writeth said these wordes, wch he thought should not have proceded from hir: wch were these, 'Assure my brother, I am and ever wilbe as sorry to doe any thing that may be eyther hurtfull to him, or the house whereof I came, as any sister or woman in the world, except great and extreame necessity doth inforce me thereunto; wch nowe God knowes is much, and we are hardly delt with, both by my ould Lady and my Lord:' adding furth' y^t I should assure my self that assoone as my Lord did move any such matter unto hir, as she professed as yet he hath not done, I should knowe of it: which answere accordinge to my l're dated from Newarke, he made acquainted to Mr Willäm Cavendishe, who returned him this speech, 'Assure yourself she will not doe it without a great some of money;' which my Lord can not give, without they will take ther payment in wordes, and that will pay no debtes, nor releive ther present want. But they are wise enoughe for that, and if my sister should, yet the recovery will not be good unlesse your ho^r consent therunto, wch I hoope you never will. And this is all he advertiseth in those matters.—But he writeth that the Earle's jewells and platt are laid to pawne; and that ther is as many sutern every day at his chamber, as at the most noble men in the court, but they come onlye to crave their debtes. Alsoe ther is not any thinge done by the Earle in Parliament, nor like to be that he can learne. Thus with my wife's most bounden duty and my owne unto your ho. most humbly cravinge your blessinge to us bothe, doe most humbly and hartely beseech the continuance of your honorable favour, with the like humble thankes for your most honb^{le} bounty towardes us. Soe wishinge you most long and happy yeares, doe humbly take my leave. Bothell the XIIth of Maye 1604.

Your honr's most humble and faithfully affected sonne to be commanded, EDW. TALBOTT.

To the right ho^{ble} and my very good
Lady and mother in lawe the Lady
Elizabeth Countesse of Shrewsbury
dowager : at Hardwicke dd.

---

¹ The young lady mentioned in this letter was Ann only daughter & heiress of the earl of Cumberland. The negotiation was not brought to a successful issue, and by two marriages she became countess of Dorset, Pembroke, and Montgomery. It appears by a letter from Sir John Harpur to the Earl of Shrewsbury, that a double marriage was about this time projected between the families of Clifford and Cavendish. Talbot Papers, M 308.

² From a copy made by Mr. Wilson from an original, on which was this

note, which shews that it was circulated among the gentlemen of Derbyshire, and doubtless contributed to collect that noble appearance of gentry who waited upon Kinge James at Worksop.

' I received this letter from my cosine Harpur, that you gentlemen may see yt, & consider of yt ; & wthall I understand by him that Mr Henry Cavandish answered the noblemen to his credite, wch I am glad of, & those that love him. JOHN CURZON.

WILLIAM KNYVETON to MRS. KNYVETON.

GOOD mother, though I have no newes worth yᵉ writinge to you att this tyme, yet I could not forbeare to signifie my dutie unto you, havinge so convenient a messenger. The endinge of yᵉ parliamᵗ is yet vere uncertaine. The sicknes is thought to encrease verie little in yᵉ cittie, but more in divers parts of the countrie, especially north ward. Yesterday ther was sent from the Duke of Florence certaine presents to yᵉ Kinge, Queene & Prince: to yᵉ Kinge II. fine horses wᵇ exseedinge riche furnetuers, II. verie fayre moyles wᵇ a litter: & to the Queene II. moyles & a litter: & to yᵉ Prince a verie fayre chayre. Yt is thought yᵉ Kinge of Denmark's brother wilbe heere shortly, but to what end I yet heare not. The La. Arbella & my cosen Wᵐ Cavendishe are well, thanks be to God. Mʳ Diott of Lychfeild hath married on Thursdaie last a riche widowe: she was yᵉ widowe of one Sheffeld a lawiar, & is sister to yᵉ Lady Wortley¹ whom yt is thought Sʳ John Harpur shall marrie, and yt is said yᵉ Erle of Shr. is a meanes for him. So most humbly cravinge your blessinge wᵗʰ my dayly prayer to God for yᵉ long & happie continuance of my ho. good lady in healthe, honor & all happines, I humbly take my leave & rest,   Your most obedient lovinge sonne,

27 Maii 1604.   Wᵐ KNYVETON².

The La. Arbella willed me to cōmend hir verie kindly unto you. She telles me she hath written to my ho. good lady by this bearer. Touchinge yᵉ Erle, I heare no more then as I last writte you. He stands in his old state for ought I heare & no better.

To my very lovinge mother Mⁱˢ Knyveton att Hardwicke dd.

Sir JOHN MANNERS to the Countess Dowager of SHREWS-BURY.

GOOD Madam, I received a very kynd l're from your La. by my sonne George's servant, which was much to my comforte to understand therby your honorable and naturall affection for the birth of this child, whom I pray God Almighty to blesse and prosper wᵗʰ all good giftes, yf it be his wyll. And because my sonne now doth waite upon your La. him self to know your pleaseur about the christenyng, I rekon it a part of my duty to geve your La. most humble thankes for the honourable favours shewed both to me and myne, wᵉʰ I have many waies received from your good La. I wold indeed have bene parsonally at the christenyng my self, but that I fynd my body not ablle well to travaill. And so ready to be cōmanded by your La. to my small porcion of power, I pray God Almighty evermore to preserve you in all honour and felicytie. From Haddon this XVIIIᵗʰ day of June 1604².

Your good La.' humbly allwaies to cōmand,

JOHN MANNERS.

To the right honoʳable my singuler good Ladie the Countesse of Shrewsburie Dowager at Hardwick.

WILLIAM CAVENDISH to the Countess Dowager of SHREWS-BURY.

MY humble dewtie presented to your Laᵖ &c. I trust in God to wayt on your Laᵖ very shortly, wᵉʰ of long I have desired to doe. Yt is thought the parlemᵗ will end of Saterday & wᵗʰin three or IIII. dayes after I mean to sett out of towne. His Maᵗⁱᵉ IIII. dayes since hath bene moved by my La. Arbell for me: who promiseth as afore, at the next call wᵉʰ is thought wilbe at Michelmas terme, at the next session of parlemᵗ⁴. I have no further to advertise your Laᵖ then I have alredy. And so wᵗʰ my dayly prayer to yᵉ Almightie to graunt your Laᵖ long & happy lyfe wᵇ all honor & comfort, I most hu'bly ceass, most hu'bly beseching your Laᵖ's dayly blessing. Frō Londō this Wedensday the IIIIᵗʰ of July 1604.

Your Ladyship's most humble & most bound sonn,

W. CAVENDYSSHE.

The Erle of Penbrok's mariag is deferred for III. monethes: stayed by great persons as I credibly here.

To my Lady at Hardwyck.

WILLIAM CAVENDISH to the Countess Dowager of SHREWS-BURY.

MY bounden dewtie most humbly reme'bred to your Laᵖ. Having bene but one night in towne, I can advertize your Laᵖ of litle. My La. Penbroke, Monday last, went as far as the Erle of Kent's, to have mett hir father, where she reseved letters from Rufford yᵗ the Erle of Shrowsbury was not abell to travell : som say yᵗ about a moneth hence he purposeth to be in towne.

Yt is sayd yᵗ the Duke of Holstˢ, my La. Arbell, & my Lady Marqueste shall christen the Q. Maᵗⁱᵉˢ daughter; but wᵉʰ of yᵉ Lady Marquesses I know not. For your Laᵖ's matters I shall plie them ernestly, both to quite your Laᵖ of suite; and yᵗ I may yᵉ soner wayt of you. The Quene of Spayne is lately brought a bed of a sonne. The Spanish imbassador here for ioy made many fireworks in the street before his howse, & cast gold & silver amongst the peple to yᵉ vclue of ccᴸⁱ. Cardinall of Medices unkell to the Duke of Florence is chosen Pope: yt is thought he will faver the French more than the Spanyard. And so most humbly beseching your Laᵖ's blessing, I most humbly ceass, wᵗʰ my dayly prayer to yᵉ Almightie to graunt your Laᵖ a long & happy lyfe. Frō London the XXIIIᵗʰ of Aprill 1605.

Your Ladyship's most humble and most bound sonn,

W. CAVENDYSSHE.

GEORGE CHAWORTH to the Countess Dowager of SHREWS-BURY.

MOST honorable Madam. These are to desyre your honor's pardoˢ for the last letters I sent you, because I made that speede with them (that they might give your hoʳ the fyrst intelligens of the arraignments)⁶ that I could not in so short tyme make them fytt for your honor's readeing or heareing. As I have alwaye deservedly esteemed your honor my best patron, so I must now in all humiletye beseech your hoʳ ever gratiousnes to shew yourselfe espetially to me in protecting in vucsafing to laye your honor's cōmand on my unnkell George Chaworth to stand my frend & speake for me to my unnkell Henerye Chaworth, for that now he ys determined to settell his estate, he would please to favor me as Sʳ George Chaworth dyd, and

¹ Relict of Sir Richard Wortley of Wortley, knight. The match with Sir John Harpur did not take place : but in 1605 she married William Cavendish, and became countess of Devonshire.

² Afterwards Sir William Knyveton of Myrcaston, bart., brother to Saint-Loe Knyveton, the antiquary.

³ The infant whose baptism is the subject of this letter was John eldest son of Sir George Manners of Haddon, and grandson to Sir John Manners the writer. By his mother who was a Pierrepoint, he was great-grandson to the old countess of Shrewsbury. In 1641, by the extinction of the male line in the eldest branch of his family, he became earl of Rutland, and was progenitor of his Grace the duke of Rutland, now the owner of the fine old mansion at Haddon, from whence this and some others of these letters were written.

⁴ This refers to his introduction into the peerage. In May 1605 he was created Baron Cavendish of Hardwick, and in August 1618, earl of Devonshire. He was the second and favourite son.

⁵ Brother to the queen.

⁶ Of the persons concerned in the Gun-powder plot. The earl of Shrewsbury was very unjustly subjected to suspicion of having been concerned in that affair. Among the Talbot Papers is to be found an examination of one John Dakin concerning certain slanderous speeches used by John Clay of Criche in Derbyshire, gentleman, tending to accuse the earl of some concern in the Gunpowder treason, M 380. His countress had certainly an attachment to the old profession. In the same collection is a letter from John Parker (probably of Norton-Lees) to the earl, in which he recites a conversation between Sir John Manners and Sir Peter Frechevile of Staveley respecting his countess's attachment to Popery: 27 June 1606, M 342. And W. Bellenden writes to the comtess from London 12 Feb. 1608, a letter which accompanied a present of reliques, namely, a part of the cross and measures of the length and breadth of the body of St. Mary Magdalene from St. Maxence in Provence. O 127. The earl seems to have taken an interest in the theological questions of the day. We find him writing an angry letter to Sir William Bowes of Walton near Chesterfield, a great favourer of Puritans and Puritanism, in answer to his objections against some book put forth by the universities. Sheffeld Jan. 3, 1602, Talbot Papers, K 89. He steered a middle course between Popery and Puritanism. Dr. Boys, one of King James's translators of the Scriptures, was for a short time his chaplain. He tells us that the earl had always some young promising divine from the University of Cambridge staying in his house. See *Life of Boys* in the *Desiderata Curiosa*.

not take awaye the goodnes of his will to me, but rather to mend then cross yt, as I heare he goeth about. I have written to Mr Timothey to informe your honor what my unnkell Henerye meaneth to doe against me, and whearein my unnkell George maye pleasure me; for I assure your honor my unnkell Henerye was accustomed, and I beleeve will yet be wholly guided by him : therefore I much build upon your honor's effecting his love for me.—I beseech your hor pardon this exceeding rudenes and bouldnes in me. I doubt yt wilbe much offensive, for that I knowe your hor hath many wayghtie and worthye affayres of your owne that be over troblesome unto your honor : but I beseech your honor, impute this to the best, which ys that I flye unto your honor as to my protectress and defender. And so I beseech God to send your hor freedome from all trobles, & to heape uppon you manye yeares of joye and blesednes. From the Court this 13th of Februarye 1605.

Your honor's most bounden,

GEORGE CHAWORTH.

To the r. honorable my espetiall good
Ladye the Countess Dowager of
Shrewsburye give this at Hardwick.

Dr. JAMES MONTAGUE (afterwards Bishop of BATH and WELLS) to the Countess Dowager of SHREWSBURY.

MY most honorable good La. This bearer my uncle Lassels hath promised me to deliver this lettre unto your honor. I think my Lo. Candish acquaynteth you with all the parlament newes. It is a very joyfull matter to see how well the Kinge, his Lords and Comons doe agree togeether in one this parliament: and all agaynst the papistes. The Kinge offered his Meditations to the house, as his Matie called them: the Lords they drue a bill, and the Commons an other ; and these 3 bills wer all on in effect, to have some severe execution uppon the preests and recusants. For the late executions of the traytors I am suer your honor hath hard how they died. Ther was but 2 of the 8 that would freely confesse ther fact to be a sinne agaynst God. It is thought that the Lords shall not be arrayned, but only brought into the Starre-chamber. Ther are diverse Jesuites and preests lately taken: on specialle man that is the Provinciall of the Jesuites, and hath his hand farre in this action, which they call Garnett or Walley. The Kinge is very glad of his apprehension, for he is the most dangerous man to this state that liveth. His Matie goeth comonly to Hampton Court at the beginninge of the weeke, and tarrieth ther till the latter end of the weeke. I am alwayes with his Matie in these iurneys, which maketh mee that I can not write so often to your honor as I would.

Thus with my humble duty to your honor, I take my leave. Court, this 20 of Februarye 1605.

Your honor's most faythfull frend,

JAMES MOUNTAGU.

To the most honorable La. the Countesse
of Shrewsbury dowager, these.

JAMES HUDSON to the Lady ARBELLA STUART.

Right honorable & my very good Lady,

It mae pleas your grace,

THIS bearer is the power man named Richard Lasaye, upon whome your grace hath ben so long desyrus to showe sume part of your honorable piettye & charetty, whome by chance this dae I mett in the streits : & becaws your grace hath dyverss tymes sent to me to inqwyre of hime, I have taken this boldness to signeffye thus much to your grace by wrytting : & so praing God to presserve your grace, I humble taek my leave, & ever remayne,

Your grassis most humble to comand wth service,
London this 24 of
February 1605.

JA. HUDSON.

To the right honourable & my very
singullar good Lady my Lady
Arrebella hir grace dd. at the
Courtt.

Dr. JAMES MONTAGUE to the Countess Dowager of SHREWSBURY.

MY most honorable good La, uppon occasion of my con-

tinuall followinge of his Matie in his iorneys, I have ben longer silent then I should have ben. The newes heer is all in parlament busines. The matter of religion, to compell every man to the Comunion hath much trobled them: but now they are agreed that all shall come to the Comunion, within the space of 2 yeares, or else they shalbe in the nature of Recusants. For the matter of Purveance, the Kinge is very desierous for the ease of the subiect to have a composition, and to pay a yearely soom of monny, and to be freed from the Purveor : but as yet the lower house will not heare of any composition, for that they feare they can have no assurance from the Kinge, and then they should boeth give ther monny, and be trobled with the Kinge's takers to. It is thought the parlament is like to continew yet a good while; for they must part with on subsidy more, and 2 fiveteens, or else this is nothinge that they have don. The Provinciall of the Jesuites Garnet, who is in the Tower will prove a notorious traytor, and to have had his hand in all these treasons, and a principall man that caused them to take armes when the powder plott fayled. The Earle of Northumberland will goe cleere in this matter. His lady is permitted to come to him, and ther is expectance of his liberty shortly. But with the rest of the Lords it will goe hard. Ther be many traytors sent doune into ther severall counties wher the dwelt to be executed ther, and some more arraynments are expected heere.

The Kinge of France hath raysed a great army, and is reddy to goe into the feeld ; but no man knoweth whither, or agaynst whom : but as it is thought agaynst the Duke of Brittayne, who is at a place called Seydan toward Germany ; but he maketh all his neyghbors afrayd.

Our Queene and mistresse groweth bigg, and looketh her about the latter end of May. The Court will tarry heere at White Hall till Easter, and then to Greenwich, wher the Queene purposeth to lye in.

Thus havinge no other matter at this time to troble your honor withall, with my humble duty I take my leve, beseechinge the Lord to keepe your honor longe in healthe and prosperity. From the court this 7 of March 1605.

Your honor's most assured and faythfull poore frend,

JAMES MOUNTAGU.

To the most honorable La. the Countesse
of Shrewsbury dowager at Hardwike.

The Earl of RUTLAND to the Countess Dowager of SHREWSBURY.

Madame;

I was gladde to heare of your La.' good health by my cosen Mr Edward Talbott, whoe also holdeth himself much bounde for your honourable kindenes and favoures when hee was wth yow, wch wee his kinsemen cannot but acknowledge with much thankefullnes : desiriage your honourable contynuance of your good favours and love towards him, wherein you shall bynde mee especially above the rest to a thankfull acknowledgement thereof, and to remayne

Your La.' humbly to command,

Belvoire, 13 Octobe' 1606.

RUTLAND.

To the righte honourable Lady, the
Lady Countesse Dowager of
Shrewesbury dd. dd.

WILLIAM KNYVETON to the Countess Dowager of SHREWSBURY.

MAY yt pleas your Lap to understand that we heare heere for certayne that upon Thursdaie & Fridaye last att night, divers of the cittie of Lyncolne, & other such unruly persons thereabouts, have throwen open certayne inclosures of Sr Thomas Mountson's, & Sr Thomas Dallyson's neere Lyncolne. The Kinge hath divrs tymes spoken of some lawe to be made agaynst Inclosers, but ther is yet nothinge done therein. The parliamte sittes still, but hath very little to doe. Yt is now agreed that Sr Thomas Fleminge who is Lo. Chief Baron shalbe Lo. Chief Justice of England; and Justice Tanfeild shalbe in his place, & S'geante Crookes shall succeed him. His Matie intends a progresse (notwthstandinge all these stirres) into the Ile of Wight, but the jests are not yet sett downe. Yt is sayd he will goe wthin these xiiii. or xv. dayes to Theobalds, & lye there some smalle tyme, & then begin the progresse. The Lo. Treasurer is comme to his howse heere agayne, who had bin in the countrie for a tyme very discontented, I thinke partely wth some message the Kinge sent him aft' he had refused to paie money to ye Lo. Hey, wch his Matie had given him¹, & partely also because the great sute for Sr Richard Levison's lands is passed agaynst Sr George Curzon our countraieman, whose daughter & heire the Lo. Buckhurst's sonne hath married. His Matie aft' some displeasinge messages sent ye Lo. Treasorer a dyamond, & wished he might live so longe as that ringe would continue; wch they say revived my Lo. Tri̇er agayne. Thus being bould to troble your ho. wth these small matt^{rs}, wch are the certaynest newes that I can att this tyme write to your ho. wth my dayly prayer to God for your La^p's longe lyfe wth the continuance of health, increase of honor & all happinesse to your La^p & all yours, I most humbly take my leave, & rest

     Your La^p's ev^t most humbly to be cõmaunded,
22^d Junii 1607.   Wm KNYVETON.
To the r. honorable and my approved
  good Lady the Countesse dowager of
  Shrewsbury att Hardwicke.

THOMAS Earl of ARUNDEL to the Countess Dowager of
         SHREWSBURY. 1607.

MADAM, as soone as ever God out of his greate goodnes had blessed us with a sonne, wee all resolued to have bin sutors unto your La. that you would vouchsafe to have bin his godmother. But it hath pleased the Queenes Matie (oute of her especiall favor) to interpose her selfe, farre contrary to oure expectation (seeing it hath neuer till this time beene seene or knowne that the King's M^{tie} and the Queene haue christened any childe together) wch must at this time stay the proceedings in oure firste desire; unlesse eyther the unusualnes in like cases, or some other accidente may divert the Queene from her intente: which if it doe happne then wee will advertise your La^p thereof by poaste, and will earnestly goe forward in oure humble suite. In the meane time, my wife & my selfe beseech your La^p that you will make us both with our little one, happy, by the continuance of your La^p's good wishes, and daily blessinge: and cease not our continuall prayers to God for your La^p's longe health and happines. And so I reste,

     Your La^p's louinge & dutifull son to cõmande,
Arundell house, this   ARUNDELL.
  27th of June.
To my most honorable and worthy grand-
  mother the Countesse of Shrewsbury at
  Hardwicke.

The Countess of SHREWSBURY to the Countess Dowager of
         SHREWSBURY. 1607.

MY duty most humbly remembered, w^t like humbel thankes for your La.' fayre and wellwrought Armen, wch God willing I will kepe as a gret juel both in respect of your La. and of her from hom your La. had it. Ther can nothing be wrought in metell w^t more life. I am very glad to here that your La.' helth is beter, and that the payn in your hepe declineth. I will dayly pray that your La.' health, and all other trew comfortes may increase. Yesterday the Q. removed to her howes at Thebales, and of Friday com seven nightes, the K. the Q. and my Lo. Chamberlayn doth, God willing, cresin the letell infant at Arandall howes: the cresining must be at Whit hall⁴. I am sure your La. hath hard long er this from Aran-

dall howes, wher I thanke God, all is well; but sume pavn in my bed hath kept me from thence these 3 or 4 dayes. My Lo. of Arandall is at Thebals, wch my Lo. of Salesbury doth not other wayes youse as his own then my Lo. Lumlay hath daune None such sence his exchang w^t the Q. wch your La. will imagine wil gretly leson both his care and his charge. So agayn w^t my prayers for your La.' most hapi long life and most humbel desire of your La.' dayly blesing to me and all mine, I humbly take my leve this viii. of July.

     Your La.' most humbell and obedient daughter,
               MA. SHROWSBURY.
The Ermen was as well brought up as was posibell. It shall li by my daughter of Arandall the day of the cresning, but no longer.
To my Lady.

The Countess of SHREWSBURY to the Countess Dowager of
         SHREWSBURY.

MY duty most humbly remembered: I thenke it longe sence I hard of your La. and therfore send this bearer to bring us word of your La.' good health, and to pray to the hiest to send your La. a hapy new yer, and mayny of them. I have mad bould to present your La. w^t this quishion, wch is mad iust by the pateron of my daughter of Arandal's bed, and I   and do beseech your La. to yous it every day at your prayer to leane of it, which I pray God you may doe w^t all comfort. My Lo. desires me to reme'ber his duty to your La. and so humbly beseching your La.' blesing to us all, in like humbel maner I will take my leve w^t the prayrs of us all to the hiest for your La.' longe life.

     Your La.' most humbel and obedient daughter,
At Shefild Loge, this   MA. SHROWSBURY.
  30 of Desember.
To my Lady.

The Earl of SHREWSBURY to HENRY BUTLER².

HARRY Butler, Tell Richard the cooke y^t I wold have him stay at Sheffeld till I come thither, wch shall be, God willing, tomorrow at nyght. Tell Moorhouse that my Lady Arabella will be at Sheffeld some day this week, as I verily thinke. Fyshe ynough muste be watered; for ther will be an extrame great number in the hall every day. Fatt beefe & fatt muttons muste be hadd, & the heife in tyme killed & powdered. Fatt capons provided & reserved till then, & every thing else that either Richard or Moorehouse can provyde or think usefull: & Wyngfeld's best advise to be had and followed. So in extreme hast I end.

Send away this l're to be safely delivered to Leygh spedely, whersoever he be, for it requyreth gret hast. Send this other l're to Sr Charles⁴ this day also.

  At Tankyrsley this Wednesday 29 Aug. 1609.
                    G. SH.

The Earl of NORTHUMBERLAND to Sir HENRY SLINGSBY.

COUSIN Slingisbie, nowe my landes in Yorkshier are survaied, and the most of them letten, I desier to have this sömer Courtes of Survaie holden in everie mannor, for the better manifestinge of my estate hereafter: and for that purpose I have granted out a cõmission to divers gentlemen in ye contrie my friendes, to ioine wth my officers in ye busines; amongest the which I have used yow for one: desiring that if your occasions will permitt yow, yow will take the paines to sitt and ioine with them, wherein I shall thincke my self beholding to

---

¹ Here is a curious historical anecdote. Lord Hay was one of James's Scotch favourites. The virtuous lord treasurer was Thomas Sackvile earl of Dorset. He survived this uncourtly act but a short time, dying suddenly at the council-table in April 1608.

² The child was named James after his royal godfather. He was the eldest son of the earl of Arundel and lady Alethea Talbot, bore the title of Lord Mowbray and Maltravers, and died in the life-time of his father.

³ Talbot Papers, vol. M, f. 679.

⁴ Sir Charles Cavendish, youngest of the three sons of Sir William Cavendish and the Countess of Shrewsbury; the intimate friend and almost inseparable companion of Gilbert earl of Shrewsbury. His eldest son, who bore the name of his father, was buried at Sheffield on the 25th of April 1594,

and his second son William was born in the earl's house at Hansworth. This was the Duke of Newcastle of the Civil Wars. There is a curious passage relating to the youth of Sir Charles in a letter of George earl of Shrewsbury to his second countess, from Sheffield the 7th of June 1575. 'And seinge I am constreyned to absent my sunne Gilbord, I wyll provyd forr him & his wyf, which I will use your advise therin, & surely I wold have you provyd for Charls your sun; he is seely ledd to foll̇y: for w^tin 11. nyght after you went from me, his man Morton intysed his master, 'Blyth, & my armorer to go a atelyng in to Staly parke in the nyght: & I wold wysh you to advise him from those doinges, lest som myshappe myght c̈ thereby, to his harme & your grefe.'

yow. The time and place they shall acquaints yow with. And so in hast with my harty cōmendations I rest

Your true freind and cousin,
The 26 of Julie 1613. NORTHUMBERLAND'.
To my very loving freind and cousin Sʳ
Henry Slingisby, knight, geve these.

Lady ARBELLA SEYMOUR to ――――².

Sʳ—THOUGH you be almost a stranger to me, but onely by sight, yet the good opinion I generally heare to be held of your worth, together wᵗ the great interest you have in my Lo. of Northampton's favour, makes me thus farre presume of your willingnesse to do a poore afflicted gentlewoman that good office (if in no other respect, yet because I am a Christian) as to further me wᵗ your best indevors to his Lo. that it will please him to helpe me out of this great distresse and misery, and regaine me his Maᵗˢ favor, which is my chiefest desire. Whearin his Lo. may do a deede acceptable to God, and honorable to himselfe, and I shall be infinitely bound to his Lo. and beholden to you, who now till I receve some comfort from his Maᵗʸ rest The most sorrowful creature living,
ARBELLA SEYMAURE.

LORDS of the COUNCIL to GEORGE LASSELS and FRANCIS COOKE ³.
AFTER our very hartie cōmend. Whereas directions were formerly given by his Maᵗˢ comaundiment for the sealing uppe

and sending hither to London of certeyne evidences and writings remayning in the Castle and Mannor of Sheaffield [and] at the Mannor house of Worsoppe some tymes belonging unto Gilbᵗ late Earle of Shrewsbury: and that informacōn is nowe made unto us, that one Swifte⁴, servant to the lady Marie Countes Dowager of Shrewsbury haveing notice of the afforesaid directions, did secretly convey away greate nombers of those writings and evidences out of the Castle of Sheaffeld, and delivered the same to a sister of his, the wife of one Mʳ Bossevile of Gunthwaite, willing her for the better conceyling therof, to locke them uppe in her owne trunckes, whear it is cōceyved they are still remayning. Theis shalbe therfore to will and requier you to make your ymediat repaire unto the house of Mʳ Bossevile afforesaid, and taking the assistance of any of his Maᵗˢ publicke officers (if you shall fynde cause) to make diligent search there, for the said writings and evidences. And such as you shall fynde there of that kinde, to see safely sealed uppe, and sent forthwᵗʰ to Shrewsbury house in Broad-Strete, to the end they may be viewed and disposed of, according as his Maᵗⁱᵉ shall please to cōmaunde. And so we bid you hartely fairewell. From Whitehall this 28ᵗʰ of June 1619.

Your loving frends,
G. CANT. HEN. SOUTHAMPTON.
G. CALVERT. JO. DIGBY.
EDW. COOKE. ROBERT NAWNTON.
HEN. CAREWE. JULIUS CESAR.
To our loveing freinds Geo. Lassels
and Fr. Cooke, esqrs.

CHAPTER VII.

Removal of the Lords of the Manor.—The Civil Wars.

'To strangers now descends the heapy store,
The race forgotten, and the name no more.'

FEW places present a more striking contrast between what they were and what they now are than Sheffield. In the times of which we have been speaking the parish presented the peculiar and almost anomalous appearance of a thriving manufacturing town, the centre of a manufacturing district, and at the same time the seat of a rich and noble family surrounded by their spacious domain. It is not to be supposed that these can long co-exist in the same place. The lord can ill bear the too close proximity to the dirt and smoke of a manufactory: and it is as little suitable to the genius of commerce that it shall be impeded in its exertions by inclosures made for the pleasure of the lord. The individuals of the house of Talbot seem to have been much attached to their hereditary seats at Sheffield; and the struggle might have been longer maintained;—we might have still seen among our hills and valleys not the faded but the perfect glories of feudal magnificence: but for the event which has just been related—the death of Gilbert the seventh earl of

Shrewsbury without male issue. This event gave an easy victory to the spirit of commerce.

Three times had the barony of Hallamshire passed to female heiresses: and as often had the husbands to whom they united themselves chosen to settle on the barony. But the daughters of the earl of Shrewsbury were married to the prime of the English nobility, and it was not to be expected that any of them would desert their hereditary seats to maintain a divided authority at Sheffield.

But what had been the work of centuries was not in a day brought to that state of ruin in which it now appears.—In the present chapter we shall endeavour to trace out the departing steps of the spirit of feudalism as they slowly retired; and in the course of it shall speak of the civil contentions of the seventeenth century, as far as they affected this neighbourhood, which accelerated, if they may not be said to have effected, the utter demolition of her strongest hold—the ancient castle of Sheffield.

Among the vainest of mortal expectations is the hope of perpetuating a family. In the eighteenth year

---

¹ Written from the Tower, where the earl had been confined, since 1605, for a supposed connexion with the Gunpowder treason.
² From the original, Cotton MSS. Vesp. F iii.
³ From a copy in the Wilson collections.

⁴ He was afterwards a knight, (Sir Francis Swift,) and married Elizabeth Grevile, a daughter of Sir Edward of Harrold-park in Essex; another of whose daughters, Margaret Grevile, was the wife of Godfrey Bosvile of Gunthwaite, esq. Hence arose the relationship mentioned in this letter.

of the reign of Elizabeth the house of Shrewsbury consisted of the earl, four sons, and one grandson. In forty years all these had passed away, nor was any male issue left by them to take their estate and honours.

Edward the eighth earl survived his brother earl Gilbert about a year: and on his death the title of Shrewsbury passed to a very distant relative, George Talbot of Grafton in Worcestershire, esquire, the descendant in the fourth degree of Sir Gilbert Talbot, K.G. third son of John the second earl of Shrewsbury. This branch of the family had flourished in the midland counties in great respectability. Their marriages had been with the superior gentry of those parts. An intercourse had been maintained with the heads of the family at Sheffield. Among the Talbot Papers is a letter from Frances the widow of John Talbot of Grafton to Francis earl of Shrewsbury, dated the 25th of May 1558, in which was inclosed twenty-two pounds, (no inconsiderable sum in those days,) to buy apparel for her daughter who was domesticated with the earl[1]: and in 1591 John Talbot of Grafton wrote to Gilbert earl of Shrewsbury to engage him to become a trustee for estates which he meant to settle on his son John Talbot, then about to marry[2]. To the possessions of this part of the family earl Edward made some material additions, the better to enable them to support the high rank to which they were unexpectedly called.

Of the eldest line of Talbot there remained therefore only certain female heiresses, amongst whom and their descendants the ample possessions of the family were for the most part divided.

The earls Gilbert and Edward had three sisters, only one of whom left issue. She was the wife of Sir George Savile of Thornhill, knight and baronet. Her descendants inherited a part of the Talbot property, in virtue of settlements made by her father earl George. It was thus that Rufford came to the house of Savile.

Henry Talbot, the youngest son of earl George, was settled by his father at Burton-grange. He left only two daughters. Gertrude the elder married Robert Pierrepoint the first earl of Kingston, and from her descended his successors in the earldom. Mary lady Armine the younger daughter lived many years at Burton-grange, 'according to her rank, in the decency of a plentiful estate.' She had no children; and like lady Elizabeth Hastings, half a century later in the same county, employed a noble income in well-directed acts of beneficence. Some particulars of her life together with her portrait may be found in the biographical collections of Samuel Clark[3]. She lived till 1675.

But it was to the three daughters of earl Gilbert that the largest share of the family inheritance descended, together with the ancient baronies: and the earl had the satisfaction of seeing them married to husbands every way befitting their rank and quality.

The eldest was LADY MARY TALBOT. On the 4th of November 1604, after many delays and much difficulty in arranging the settlements, the nuptials were celebrated at Sheffield of this lady with William Herbert third earl of Pembroke of that house. This was the fifth matrimonial connexion which had been formed within a century and a half between the families of Talbot and Herbert, and it is remarkable that they were all unfruitful: for this marriage may be said to have been so, the countess having only one child or two born 'some eighteen years after her marriage,' (as the duchess of Newcastle informs us[4],) and who died in infancy. Lord Clarendon has drawn the character of this nobleman with his usual strength and precision[5]. His lady survived a connexion which does not seem to have been a happy one; and in her widowhood, Philip earl of Pembroke and Montgomery brother and successor to her husband had the control, and in fact the benefit, of her share of the Talbot property. Hence it is that we find the name of that nobleman connected with the history of the manors and rectories of the Talbot family in the middle of the seventeenth century.

The second was LADY ELIZABETH TALBOT. The date of her marriage is fixed to the latter end of the reign of Elizabeth by a very remarkable letter in the Talbot Papers[6]. Her lord was Henry Grey for a while Lord Ruthyn, but afterwards earl of Kent. She also died without issue. The name of this lady has found a place in catalogues of royal and noble authors, for a book of receipts with which her ladyship favoured the world. But her employment of Butler[7] and her patronage of Selden connect her more worthily with the literary history of her age. She died in 1651.

LADY ALETHEA TALBOT was the earl's youngest daughter. Queen Elizabeth was her godmother; and gave her a name till then unknown to the baptismal vocabulary of England, as Vincent informs us, ' out of her maiestie's true consideration and judgement of that worthy family, which was ever true to the state: .... Αληθεια signifying in our English, veritie or truth[8].' I have somewhere read that offence was taken at the name as savouring too strongly of heathenism. She came not behind her sisters in the splendour of her alliance; having for her husband Thomas Howard earl of Arundel and Surrey, earl marshal of England, the only son of Philip earl of Arundel who died in prison in the reign of Elizabeth[9], and grandson of Thomas duke of Norfolk who fell a sacrifice to the jealousy of Elizabeth respecting Mary queen of Scots. But the earl of Arundel is not to be estimated by his birth, his honours, or his offices. He had personal merit of no common order. High-souled and high-principled, he presented in an effeminate court a pattern of primitive nobility: a true lover of the arts, he was the encourager of those who professed them: taking the lead among his countrymen in the admiration of the works of ancient art, he spared neither pains nor expense to submit specimens of it to those who could not visit the countries which produced them. An unpleasing likeness, but a very striking portrait, is drawn of him by Clarendon[10], and the particulars of his life may be read at large in the historical discourses of Sir Edward Walker. While he drew the best part of that income which he so nobly employed, from the estates of his

[1] Talbot Papers, vol. O, f. 20.   [2] Id. vol. I, f. 129.
[3] The Lives of sundry eminent Persons in this latter Age, 1683, part ii. p 192.   [4] The Life of William Duke of Newcastle, p. 210.
[5] The History of the Rebellion, vol. i. p. 56.   [6] Lodge, vol. iii. p. 141.
[7] Ath. Ox. vol. ii. col. 326.   [8] Discoveric of Errours, p. 470.
[9] The lady of Philip earl of Arundel was a co-heir of the house of Dacre, which had frequently intermarried with the house of Talbot. Hence the earl of Arundel and lady Alethea Talbot were related in blood before marriage.—I shall take the opportunity which this note affords, of re-

marking that the elegiac stanzas published in the *Illustrations of British History*, &c. iii. 357, from a copy in the hand-writing of Ann countess of Arundel, which have obtained for that lady a place in the last collection of royal and noble authors, formed a popular poem in the time of Elizabeth or her successor. In the *Collection of Old Ballads*, 3 vols. 12mo, 1723—1738, is a poem very nearly resembling it, entitled, 'A servant's sorrow for his late royal mistress Queen Anne, who deceased at Hamptoncourt the 2d of May 1618. To the Tune of *In sad and ashey weeds*,' iii. 139.   [10] History of the Rebellion, vol. i. p. 55.

wife's inheritance, (as he gratefully acknowledged in his last will,) neither he nor his lady did much to change in any respect the posture of affairs at Sheffield. I shall therefore only further relate concerning him, that on the breaking out of the Civil Wars, he retired to his favourite Italy, and died at Padua on the 4th of October 1646. His lady survived about seven years, and died abroad on the 24th of May 1654.

On the 22d of May, 3 Charles I. anno 1627, by indenture of four parts between these three co-heiresses and their lords of the first, second, and third parts, and Sir Edward Leech and John Dix of the fourth part, it was covenanted that the three earls and their ladies should levy a fine to the said Leech and Dix and the heirs of the said Leech of the castle of Sheffeild, the manors of Sheffeild, Colley, Kimberworth, Waddesley, Worrall, Whiston, Treaton, Rotherham, and Dinnington; and the rectories of Sheffeild, Tickhill, and Rotherham: the manor of Worksopp, the parke of Worksoppe, the rectory of Harworth, and all priviledges happening or renewing in the townes, parishes, hamletts and feilds of Sheffeild, Ecclesfeild, Tickhill, Colley, Kimberworth, Waddesley, Worrall, Addercliffe, Whiston, Treaton, Rotherham, Dinnington, Gresbrooke, Masbrooke, Tinslowe, Catcliffe, Brinsford, Orgrave, Dalton, Morthing, Bradmarshe, Brasingthorpe, Over-Whiston, Gilthwaite, Braincroft, Braywell, Steed, Ronfeild, Todwicke, Ainston, Gledleyes, in the county of Yorke: and in Worksopp and the neither towne of Worksoppe, Gateford, Giltonwells, Woodsetts, Harworth, Shireoakes, Kilton, Ratcliffe, Steetley, Darfold, and the Lathes and in Harworth in the county of Nottingham—To the use of the earl of Pembroke and his lady for their lives and the longer liver of them, with several remainders over: remainder to Henry lord Maltravers for life, remainder to Thomas Howard esquire for life, remainder to the first son of the said Thomas and the heirs male of his body, with like remainder to every other son of the said Thomas and their heirs male successively: remainder to the younger sons in succession of the said Lord Maltravers father to the said Thomas and the heirs male of the body of every such sons successively, with several remainders over, remainder to the heirs of Alethea countess of Arundel in fee:—Which fine was accordingly levied in Trinity term 3 Charles I.[1]

During the lives of the three co-heirs, the courts for the manor of Sheffield were held in the joint names of the earls of Pembroke and Arundel: and the proceeds of the estate seem to have been shared among them. We find instances of all the parties exercising control over the property. But in 1654 all the daughters of earl Gilbert being dead, as were their husbands, the countesses of Pembroke and of Kent having left no issue, and therefore all the early remainders created by the before-recited covenant being extinguished, Henry earl of Arundel eldest son and heir of lady Alethea Talbot being also deceased, Thomas Howard esquire, then become earl of Arundel, entered into the undivided possession of the castle and manor of Sheffield. Soon after the return of Charles II. he was restored to the title of duke of Norfolk forfeited by his ancestor, with divers collateral remainders: but the management of his property was committed to his brother Henry Howard earl of Norwich, who in 1677,

on the death of his brother without issue, became the sixth duke of Norfolk of the family of Howard. He died in 1684, leaving his estate and title to his eldest son Henry the seventh duke of Norfolk, a protestant. To complete the view of the descent of the manor of Sheffield, although a little out of place, it may be added that the protestant duke of Norfolk was succeeded by his nephew Thomas the eighth duke, who dying without issue in 1732, his title and estate descended to his brother Edward duke of Norfolk, who died on the 20th day of September 1777 at the age of ninety-one.

The eighth duke of Norfolk by his last will and testament entailed the castle and manor of Sheffield, &c. on the Graystoke and Glossop branch of his family, in failure of issue male from his brothers Edward and Philip, intending that they should accompany the title of duke of Norfolk. This settlement it pleased Duke Edward to renew and confirm, when he had lost his two nephews the sons of Philip Howard esquire of Buckenham in Norfolk, who died in the prime of life, and was himself childless. And accordingly by indentures of lease and release of eight parts, bearing date the 10th and 11th of July 1767, he settled the castle and manor of Sheffield, as the estate continued to be described, on himself for life, remainder to the first and other sons of his own body, remainder to Charles Howard of Graystoke the younger esquire (passing over his father who was then living and who enjoyed the title of duke of Norfolk for some years), remainder to the younger sons of Charles Howard of Graystoke the elder and their heirs: remainder to Henry Howard then of Sheffield esquire, remainder to Bernard-Edward Howard, first son of the said Henry Howard esq., and his issue male: remainder to Henry-Thomas Howard second son of the said Henry and his issue male, remainder to the child (if a male) of which Juliana wife of the said Henry Howard was then enceinte, remainder to any other sons of the said Henry Howard and their heirs.

In virtue of this settlement, on the death of Edward duke of Norfolk, Charles Howard of Graystoke the younger, then become earl of Surrey, his father still living, became owner of the castle and manor of Sheffield with its appurtenances, which he enjoyed till his decease in 1815, when, in pursuance of the before-recited settlement, Bernard-Edward Howard esquire then become duke of Norfolk succeeded to this ancient inheritance of his family; and the barony of Hallamshire had once more the satisfaction of acknowledging as its lord a nobleman who drew his first breath within its precincts.

The following genealogy is confined to those of the illustrious house of HOWARD who were descended from lady Alethea Talbot the heiress of Hallamshire. The Suffolk, Carlisle, and Effingham branches sprung from the parent stock before the time of Thomas earl of Arundel. The descendants of Sir William Howard the unfortunate viscount Stafford are here omitted, as they had no connexion with Sheffield, and I had no inclination to swell the volume unnecessarily with matter which has already been laid before the public. For the same reason the descent of Thomas earl of Arundel is omitted, though his line of splendid ancestry is peculiarly attractive to the genealogist.

---

[1] See ' The title of the castle, mannor, &c. of Sheffeild in Com. Ebor. and severall other mannors in the said county late parcell of possession of Gilbert earle of Shrewsbury,' among Rawlinson's Manuscripts in the Bodleian.

PEDIGREE of the Illustrious Family of HOWARD DUKE of NORFOLK,

From the time when it became connected with Hallamshire.

ARMS.—Four grand quarters, 1. HOWARD. Gules on a bend between 6 cross-crosslets fitchée argent, an inescutcheon or charged with a demi-lion rampant pierced through the mouth with an arrow, within a double tressure florée counterflorée gules.

    2. PLANTAGENET. Gules 3 lions passant guardant in pale or, a label of 3 points argent.

    3. WARREN. Checkie or and azure.

    4. MOWBRAY. Gules a lion rampant argent.

    Behind the whole two marshal's staves in saltier or, enamelled at each end sable.

CREST.—On a chapeau gules turned up ermine a lion statant guardant or, gorged with a ducal coronet argent.

SUPPORTERS.—On the dexter side a lion argent, and on the sinister a horse of the same holding a slip of oak fructed proper.

MOTTO.—Sola virtus invicta.

THOMAS HOWARD, earl of Arundel, Surrey, and Norfolk, &c., descended in the seventh degree from John Howard, created duke of Norfolk anno 1483. Restored in 1603 to all the honours lost by the attainder of his father Philip earl of Arundel. Installed knight of the Garter 13 May 1611 : Earl marshal of England 29 Aug. 1621 : Earl of Norfolk 6 June 1641. Died 4 Oct. 1646, and was buried with his ancestors at Arundel in Sussex.
= Lady ALETHEA TALBOT, heiress of Hallamshire, youngest of the three daughters and co-heirs of Gilbert earl of Shrewsbury, and the only one who left issue. She died on the 24th of May 1654.

Sir JAMES HOWARD K.B. commonly called Lord Mowbray and Maltravers, eldest son and heir apparent. Died at Ghent, his father still living.	HENRY-FREDERICK, earl of Arundel &c. summoned to parliament by the title of Lord Mowbray 21 Mar. 1639. Died at his house in the Strand, London, 7 Apr.1652, and was buried at Arundel. = Lady ELIZABETH STUART, daughter of Esme duke of Lenox.	THOMAS HOWARD, died unmarried.	GILBERT HOWARD, died unmarried.	CHARLES HOWARD, died unmarried.	Sir WILLIAM HOWARD, K.B. and viscount Stafford, so created 11 Nov. 1646, having married Mary sister and heir of Henry Stafford Lord Stafford. Beheaded 29 Dec. 1678.

THOMAS, fifth duke of Norfolk of the family of Howard, to which title he was restored by act of parliament 13 Chas. II.¹ lord of Hallamshire. Died at Padua, unmarried, 1 Dec. 1677.	Lady ANN SOMERSET, first wife, dau. of Edward marquis of Worcester and sister to Henry first duke of Beaufort. = HENRY, sixth duke of Norfolk, lord of Hallamshire. Created baron Howard of Castle-Rising and earl of Norwich, and in 1672 earl marshal and hereditary earl marshal of England. Died at Arundel-house, London, 11 Jan. 1684, and was buried at Arundel. = JANE, second wife, dau. of Robert Bickerton, son of Jas. Bickerton lord of Cash in Ireland. She survived the duke, took to her second husband col. Thomas Maxwell, and died at the Holmes near Rotherham 28 Aug. 1693.	PHILIP HOWARD, third son, commonly called Cardinal of Norfolk. Born at Arundelhouse anno 1629. Died at Rome 16 June1694.	CHARLES HOWARD, fourthson. Bernard HOWARD, 8th son. Of whom hereafter, as ancestors of the second and third house of Howard of Norfolk.	ESME HOWARD, ninth and youngest son. Died 14 June 1728, aged 82, and was bur. in the churchyard of St. Pancras, Middlesex, as were also his wife Margaret, and an only dau. and heir named Elizabeth Howard.	TALBOT HOWARD. EDWARD HOWARD. FRANCIS HOWARD. 5th, 6th, and 7th sons, all died unmarried.	CATHERINE, wife of John Digby of Gothurst co. Bucks, esq., son and heir of Sir Kenelm Digby. ELIZABETH, wife first of col. Alexander Macdonald, secondly of Sir Bartholomew Russel. ANN, died in her infancy.

HENRY, seventh duke of Norfolk, lord of Hallamshire. The protestant duke.K.G. Born 11 January 1653-4. Died without issue at his house in St. James's-square, London, 2 April 1701, and was buried at Arundel. = Lady MARY MORDAUNT, dau. and sole heir of Henry earl of Peterborough, married in 1677. Divorced in 1700, and took to her second husband Sir John Germain. She died at Luswick St. Peters co. Northampton, 16 Oct. 1705.	THOMAS HOWARD, of Worksop,esq., second son. Accompanied James II. to France: was with that king in Ireland, and lost in his passage from that country to Brest on the 9th of Novem. 1689.	= ELIZABETH-MARIA, only dau. and heir of Sir John SavileofCopley co. York, baronet.Died 10 Dec.1732, and was bur. at Arundel.	ANN-ALETHEA, died in her infancy. ELIZABETH, wife of George marquis of Huntley,afterwards duke of Gordon. FRANCES, wife of the marquis Valperaizo, a Spanish nobleman².	GEORGE HOWARD, married Arabella dau. &. sole heir of Sir Edward Allen of Hatfield-Peverel co. Essex, relict of Francis Thompson of Humbleton co. York, esq. and died without issue 6th Mar. 1720-1.	JAMES HOWARD, drowned at Sutton-wash, 12 Aug. 1702. Never married.	FREDERICK-HENRY HOWARD, of the Holmes near Rotherham, a posthumous child. Married Catherine dau. of Sir Francis Blake, of the county of Oxford, knight, relict of Sir Richard Kennedy of Ireland, bart. and dying without issue 16 March 1726-7, left the Holmes, the manor of Rotherham and other property, to the Effingham branch of the family of Howard.	JOHN HOWARD, died in his infancy. CATHERINE. ANN. ELIZABETH, Both nuns in Flanders. PHILIPPA wife of Ralph Standish of Standish co. Lanc. esq.

a

THOMAS, eighth duke of Norfolk, lord of Hallamshire. Born 11 Dec. 1683. Died without issue at Norfolk-house, 23 Dec. 1732, and was buried at Arundel.	=MARY, dau. and heir of Sir Nicholas Sherburn of Stonyhurst co. Lanc. bart. Married 2dly to Peregrine Widderington, esq. brother to lord Widderington. Died 25 Sept. 1754, and was buried at Mitton.	EDWARD, ninth duke of Norfolk, lord of Hallamshire, third son of lord Thomas Howard. Died without issue 20 Sept. 1777, at the age of 91, and was laid with his ancestors at Arundel.	=MARY, dau. and co-heir of Edw. Blount of Blagdon, esq. third son of Sir Geo. Blount of Sodington, baronet. Died 27 May 1773, and was buried at Arundel.	HENRY HOWARD, second son. Died without issue 22 Nov. 1720 aged 36, and was bur. at Arundel². RICHARD HOWARD, 4th son, called Abbot Howard. Died at Rome 1722⁴.	WINIFRED, first wife, dau. of Thomas Stonor of Watlington-park, co. Oxon. esq.	=PHILIP HOWARD, fifth and youngest son, of Buckenham co. Norfolk. Died 23 January 1750, and was bur. at Arundel.	=HENRIETTA, second wife, sister of Mary Blount duchess of Norfolk, widow of Peter Proli esq. of Antwerp. Died 26 Mar. 1782.	MARY, only dau. wife of Walter Aston of Forfar.

THOMAS HOWARD, presumptive heir to Edward duke of Norfolk. Died unmarried 11th Jan. 1763, aged 34, and was bur. at Arundel.	WILLIAM Lord STOURTON.	=WINIFRED HOWARD, married 11 Oct. 1749. Died 15th July 1753.	EDWARD HOWARD, after the death of his brother, heir presumptive to Edward duke of Norfolk. Died unmarried 7 Feb. 1767, and was buried at Arundel.	ANN HOWARD, co-heiress of the eldest line of Howard of Norfolk. Married 19 Apr. 1762. Died 16 Jan. 1787.	=ROBERT EDWARD Lord PETRE.	JULIANA-BARBARA, second wife, dau. of Henry Howard of Glossop, esq., sister of Bernard-Edward duke of Norfolk.	JAMES, fifth son. ASTON.	=Lady BARBARA TALBOT, daughter of George earl of Shrewsbury.

CHARLES, Lord STOURTON.	=MARY, dau. and co-heir of Marmaduke Lord Langdale.	ROBERT Lord PETRE.	=MARY, elder dau. of Henry Howard of Sheffield and Glossop, esq., sister to Bernard-Edward duke of Norfolk.	GEORGE = ----dau. of PETRE. Philip Howard of Corby-castle co. Cumb. esq.	ANN, wife of —Onslow, esq.	MARY ASTON, elder dau. and co-heir, married at Worksop-manour to Sir Walter Blount bart.	BARBARA ASTON, younger dau. and co-heir, married at St. James's Westminster 2 Feb. 1762 to the Hon. Thomas Clifford of Tixal co. Staff. son of Hugh lord Clifford of Chudleigh.

WILLIAM, now Lord STOURTON.	=CATHERINE, dau. of Thomas Weld of Lulworth-castle co. Dors. esq.	CHARLES LANGDALE esq. and other children.	EDWARD, now Lord PETRE.	=FRANCES, dau. of Sir Richard Bedingfield of Oxborough co. Norfolk, bart.	ROBERT PETRE and other children.	Sir WALTER BLOUNT bart. and other children.	Sir THOMAS CLIFFORD of Tixal bart. and other children.

¹ This act, so important to the house of Howard, contains very extensive remainders, viz.
1. to the heirs male of Thomas earl of Arundel.
2. the heirs male of Henry late earl of Arundel.
3. the heirs male of Thomas earl of Arundel son of Philip earl of Arundel.
4. the heirs male of Thomas earl of Suffolk then deceased.
5. The heirs male of Lord William Howard of Naworth.
6. Charles earl of Nottingham and his heirs male.

² Henry duke of Norfolk, father of this lady, by his will dated the 20th of Jan. 1682 gave to his daughter lady Frances marchioness Valperaizo and her child ten pounds *per mensem*, for one year next after his decease:

and in case her husband did not take her home within that time, he left the sum of 100*l.* to be employed in conveying her and her child to Madrid, where her husband resided : and committed the management of this affair to his son lord Thomas Howard.

³ In the Blount pedigrees there is mention of Henry Howard of Clun, esquire, who married Mary daughter of Sir George Blount bart. in the early part of the last century.

⁴ This is stated on the authority of a manuscript note in Mr. Gough's copy of the *Ducatus Leodiensis*, now in the Bodleian. The notes, which are not numerous, were copied by Mr. Gulstone from Thoresby's own hand.

Second House of HOWARD of NORFOLK.

CHARLES HOWARD, of Graystoke co. Cumb. esquire, fourth son of Henry-Frederick earl of Arundel. Had the estate of Graystoke by gift of his father. Died 31 March 1713, and was buried at Dorking.	=MARY, eldest dau. and co-heir of George Tattershal of Finchampstead co. Berks. esquire. Died 7 Nov. 1695. Buried at Dorking.

HENRY-CHARLES HOWARD, of Graystoke, esquire, son and heir.	=MARY, dau. and co-heir of John Aylward, esq. Died 2 Oct. 1747, and was buried at Dorking.

HENRY HOWARD, eldest son, died unmarried.	JOHN HOWARD, second son, died unmarried.	CHARLES HOWARD, tenth duke of Norfolk on the death of his cousin Edward duke of Norfolk. Born 1 Dec. 1720. Died 31 Aug. 1786.	=CATHERINE, dau. and co-heir of John Brocholes of Claughton co. Lanc. esquire. May 1739. Died 21 Nov. 1784.	MARY HOWARD, died in France unmarried.	CATHERINE HOWARD, died in France unmarried.	FRANCES HOWARD, died at Brussels unmarried in Decem. 1769.

MARY HOWARD. Born June 1742. Died at Paris Nov. 1756.	MARY-ANN, first wife, only dau. and heir of John Coppinger of Ballivolane co. Cork, esquire. Married 7 July 1767, and died 28 May following.	=CHARLES, eleventh duke of Norfolk. Lord of Hallamshire 1777 to 1815. Born 15 March 1745-6, and died without issue 16 Dec. 1815. Buried at Dorking.	=FRANCES, second wife, only dau. and heir of Charles Fitz-Roy Scudamore, esquire, of Holm-Lacy co. Hereford, by the duchess of Beaufort his wife, who was dau. and sole heir of James viscount Scudamore of the kingdom of Ireland. Married at St. George's Hanover-square 2 April 1771.

Third House of HOWARD of NORFOLK.

BERNARD HOWARD, esquire, eighth son of Henry-Frederick earl of Arundel. Died 21 Oct. 1717, and was buried at St. Pancras, Middlesex.	=CATHERINE, dau. and co-heir of George Tattershal of Finchampstead co. Berks. esquire, relict of Sir Richard Lichford of Dorking, knight. Died 8 April 1727, and was buried in the church of the English Dominicans at Brussels.

a

BERNARD HOWARD, esquire, = Hon. ANN ROPER, dau. of Christopher lord Teynham. Married 24 June 1710. Died in 1744, and was buried in the church of the English Augustines at Paris.

ELIZABETH HOWARD, a nun at Brussels. MARY HOWARD, a nun at Brussels. CATHERINE HOWARD, a nun at Brussels.

only son. Died at Winchester 22 Apr. 1735, and was buried at St. James's church near that city, in the parish of St. Cross.

BERNARD HOWARD, eldest son. Died unmarried at Buckenham in Norfolk, and was buried at Toft near that place.

HENRY HOWARD, of Sheffield and Glossop, esq. Born 9 Apr. 1713. Died at Glossop 11 Nov. 1787, and was laid with his noble ancestors in the Shrewsbury vault at Sheffield. = JULIANA, dau. of Sir William Molyneux of Wellow co. Notts. bart. Married at Wellow, 30 Oct. 1764.

THOMAS HOWARD, canon of the collegiate church of St. Peter at Doway. Died there.

CHARLES HOWARD, D.D. and superior of the seminary of St. Gregory at Paris.

ANN HOWARD, abbess of the English nuns at Paris near the Bastile.

MARY HOWARD, died young.

BERNARD-EDWARD, twelfth duke of Norfolk and earl marshal of England, to which titles he succeeded on the death of his cousin Charles the eleventh duke. Born at Sheffield 21 Nov. 1765. = Lady ELIZABETH BELASYSE, dau. and co-heir of Henry earl Fauconberg. Married 23 Apr. 1789.

Lord HENRY-THOMAS HOWARD-MOLYNEUX-HOWARD, of Thornborough-castle co. Glouc. second son : deputy-earl marshal of England : and allowed the same place, title, and precedence which he would have enjoyed had his father lived to attain the dukedom of Norfolk, October 1817. = ELIZABETH, dau. of Edward Long of Aldermaston co. Berks. esq., formerly Judge Darnall in the Admiralty-court in Jamaica. Mar. 12 Sept. 1801.

EDWARD-CHARLES HOWARD, third and youngest son : fellow of the Royal Society. Born at Sheffield 28 May 1774. Died 28 Sept. 1816. Was mar. and had issue.

MARY-BRIDGET HOWARD, born at Worksop 29 Sept. 1767. Married 13 Oct. 1785 to Robert lord Petre.

JULIANA-BARBARA HOWARD, born at Darnall 25 June 1769. Married 16 Jan. 1788 to Robert-Edward lord Petre.

HENRY-CHARLES, earl of Surrey, only child, and heir-apparent. Born 9 Aug. 1791. = Lady CHARLOTTE LEVESON-GOWER, dau. of George marquis of Stafford. Married 26 Dec. 1814.

HENRY HOWARD, son and heir-apparent.

Five daughters.

HENRY lord Fitz-Alan.   EDWARD HOWARD.

It was not to be supposed that the noble earls to whom the co-heiresses of the house of Shrewsbury were given in marriage would abandon their hereditary seats, and keep up the splendour which the castle of Sheffield in former days had exhibited. Sheffield was not a place to supplant Wilton in the affections of the earl of Pembroke: nor could it vie with Arundel, from which the chief of the house of Howard derived the most honourable of the titles which the attainders and confiscations of a former reign had spared to him. Yet neither were the parks and chases inclosed nor the mansions dismantled, nor was Sheffield entirely unvisited by its lords in the reigns of the first Stuarts. An establishment continued to be maintained both at the castle and manour, which, though but the shadow of what it had been, was sufficient to keep up in the minds of the inhabitants of this district the remembrance of glories which they once had witnessed.

From a large collection of stewards' accompts preserved by the late Mr. Wilson, the following items are collected.

1632.

' In a bill of ' Monie disbursed at Sheffeld Lodge at our hoᵇˡᵉ Lord's beinge there,' 27 Julie 1632.

To the pore	£1	0	0
To the bull-beters	1	0	0

' Dysbursed at our hoᵇˡᵉ Lo.' cominge forth of the North the 5 of Septemb. 1632.

To the pore	2	0	0
To a blind harper	0	1	0
Pᵈ by Sir William Howarth's apointmᵗ for 4 knives and 6 forks	0	18	0
Wᵐ Hinchliffe for worke donne for my Lo.' coaches	0	4	8

1633.

' Wine delivered to Sheaffeild castle when the surveiors and other gentlemen were there.

36 quarts of white wine	1	4	0
3 quarts of sack	0	3	0
1 quart of claret	0	0	8

' More delivered to the Manuor 23ᵈ Sept. 1633.

6 quarts of sherry sack	0	6	0
5 quarts of white wine	0	3	4
1 gallon of vinegar	0	2	0
3 ounces of cloves and mace	0	3	0
2 oz. of nutmegs, 1 lb. of sugar, & 1 lb. of currants	0	3	0
1 oz. of cinnamon	0	0	6

The surveyors were persons employed to superintend certain repairs at the castle which were going on in this year. Among the bills relating to them are these items.

' For repairing some breaches of the walls upon the river of Dunne, by Raven-poole and other places, and other necessary repaires within the castle : viz. xxxvi. dayes at xᵈ. per diem. Item for lyme x. loads at 13ᵈ the load.

The glazyers worke at Sheaffeild castle, for repayreing and makeing newe of glase, at two pence halfepenny the foote. The newe building cometh to 669 foote. The castle cometh to 1046 foote. There is 49 casements saldering into the iron casements at 3ᵈ. a peice.'

In another bill:

' Foure cases of knyfes ii. dosen in everie case, from John Rawson, xxxˢ. a case.'

Beer was brewed at the manour, and sent by way of Hull to London. A person named Matabdes Hollis was the agent at Hull. A bill of this person for fish dated May 1633, ' when my Lord was at Worksop and Sheffield,' amounts to vi. x. v. In this accompt were ten salmons which cost ii. ix. vi.

Another bill is indorsed

' Francis Baker, gardener, his bill for garden seeds sowne at the Manner newe garden.'

1634.

In the accompts of this year :

' A bill of charges for bringinge of the water-works to Sheffield castell.

Item unto the iiii. almes-women	£4	0	0

1636.

Lord Maltravers was at the manour in August.

' For wine to the castle for the commissioners

Aprill the 3ᵈ till the 7ᵗʰ	0	15	3
At the assembly quest a pint of canare and a quart of claret	0	1	2
At the great leet, 1 quart of sherry, and 1 pint of canare, 1 bottle of claret and 1 quart of white wine and sugar	0	3	6
For moweing and makeing all the haye in the Rowlee for the deare, mylne-horses, &c.	3	18	5

Paid to Edward Ratcliffe and his partners for cuttinge and riveing old roots and other old wood into cords, and setting them up in the lawnds, nunnrie, and other places, beinge in number 465 cords at 11^s. . 111^d.

Paid for leading four loads of hay from the Rowlee to the great stable at the castle, for my Lo.' use there: v1^s.

Item to be allowed for moneys disbursed aboute the newe cole myne on the Parke hill topp and there-aboute, more then the profits of the coales there came to this last yeare £8 19 6

A bill for making the coach way betwixt Hallam head and the Gate-house 2 16 2

1637.

Among the bills of this year is one from Nicholas Hicke 'for makeinge of Sheth bridge.' Ten men were employed upon the work about 16 or 17 days: 'A bill of charges for mossing and ridginge the armourie:' ' Palinge the Castle-orchards :' ' Worke done for Sheffield castle about the decayed building.' ' A paire of knives bought of Mr. Rowland Revel for my ladie, 15^s.'

1639.

' A bill of expences attending the sickness and buriall of Mr. Robert Browne.

Mr Doctor Rooe for his pains and attendance 4 days £4 0 0
The apothecary 2 0 0
Coffen 0 7 0
To Richard Wordsworth for 10 yeards of black to cover the eorpse 1 3 4
Grave making and Church dues 0 5 0
To the ringers 0 10 0

Brown was one of the Lord's commissioners, and died at the castle or manour. Doctor Rooe or Roe came from Doncaster. There was probably no physician then residing at Sheffield. He travelled it appears, as was indeed usual in those times, attended by his apothecary.

1641.

' For beare and tobacco that was given to them that watcht

by apointment of the comitianers, and for wormewood beare, 111^s.'

1642.

'Charges of sendinge venison to London for my Lo. Arundall.

Paid for a dozen earthen potts to bake venison in, to send to London £1 12 0
Item paid for butter for fillinge the potts with the venison 1 12 0
Item paid more for butter for fillinge the potts at the second bakeinge 1 12 0
Item paid Rich. Wadsworth for spice, for season-inge the venison 2 2 10
John Hemmingway for the carriage of x11. potts of venison to London 2 7 0
Item paid for canvass to tye upon the heads of the potts 0 3 7
                                                        9 8 7

' The 12th of July 1642. A bill of charges for the caredge of the 4 wheele peeces from the castle of Sheaffeld to Donc-kaster, and theire furniture:

Imprimis paid to Mr Housley Freeman for his draught for caredghe of them and the wheeles and stockes 0 11 0
Item paid to James Twibell for carying of another of them 0 11 0
Item paid to Henry Smith for carying of another of them 0 11 0
Item paid to James Oxspringe for caryinge of another and bringinge 4 muskets hom againe to Sheaffeld castle 0 12 0
Item paid to Law. Smith for taking of the wheeles & going to Donckaster with them 0 2 6
                                                        2 7 6

1644. ' For packinge and cayringe 4 packes of writings from castle to the manner 0 3 2
1646. Received at Sheffield winter fair, the other fair beinge lost by reason of a great presse of soul-diers theare then 1 5 0

We are now arrived within the sound of those wars which interrupted the peace that England had so long enjoyed, and were the occasion of infinite natural and moral evil, though they issued in the establishment of our free and envied constitution, and in placing on the British throne for its protection, first a prince of the house of Orange and afterwards the august family of Brunswick. For however the truth may be disguised, there is no essential difference between the opposition which was made to Charles I., and that which in later times was presented to his son: and had King James II. been successful in his war in Ireland, and had by force of arms regained possession of his throne, we might have had another Clarendon to have given us the history of another rebellion. In both instances there was much of private resentment and unworthy passion interfering with the great public principle on which the parties proceeded: there were some men who (as is the case in all unsettled times) sought to benefit themselves by engaging in the contest; and both parties showed too little willingness to come to a just accommodation when the sword had once been unsheathed. But the substantial question on which the parties were at issue, both in the time of Charles I. and of James II., was whether the ancient constitution of England had not left the crown in possession of certain prerogatives the exercise of which was incompatible with the safety and welfare of the subject. The powers of the ancient monarchy of England had been usurped in dark and barbarous ages by military chief-

tains, or voluntarily conceded to answer particular purposes, which purposes no longer existed. In the early part of the reign of Charles I. the controversy might be said to have begun, when the people by their representatives in parliament called for the reduction of the royal prerogative. The king heard with impatience requests which seemed to him to strike at the very root of all his authority: and at last, weary with the importunity of his parliament, he listened to those counsellors who advised him to assemble that body no more. For eleven years England had no parliament. This of itself—to every man who wished not that his life and fortunes should be at the mercy of a single person—must have shown that the power of the crown to summon or to suspend the summoning of parliament required some regulation. But without a parliamentary grant even in those days, the king was unable to defray the expenses of the state, much more to take any active part in the contentions of the continent. To supply himself with money, King Charles had recourse to the expedient of reviving obsolete powers of the crown, by which tyrannical princes in former times had enriched themselves at the expense of their subjects. Again was evidence afforded of the necessity of curtailing the royal prerogative. Precedents were to be found for most of the king's measures; perhaps for all of them. But the times were changed, and just notions of civil liberty and the rights of the subject were pretty widely diffused. Nor indeed was it a difficult thing, to convince most men that there could be no good and sufficient reason for calling upon all the gentry of the kingdom to take upon themselves the honour of knighthood[1]; or to give subsidies under the name of loans at a time when there was no pretence of danger from abroad. The ship-money was at least of doubtful obligation, and at a time when men were become impatient of the acknowledged prerogative, it was not to be expected that they would acquiesce in the revival of those claims which, if they had ever existed as rights of the crown, had long become obsolete. Accordingly when the king's necessities at last obliged him to call parliament together, the two parties found themselves at issue on some of the most important questions of civil policy, which it was hardly to be expected could be decided but by the sword.

There is commonly a more lively attention to political questions in a manufacturing than in an agricultural district. If the state of closer contact into which persons who are engaged in the same manufacture are brought, generate some evils, it produces also a quicker circulation of information, and a more ardent feeling of common interest. We accordingly find Sheffield and its neighbourhood represented by the royalists as being actively disaffected: while the parliamentarian writers describe the same feelings and the same conduct by other terms. But other things combined to produce this state of the public mind at Sheffield. There was at that period a numerous party in the kingdom who with an increase of civil liberty wished also for a change in the ecclesiastical constitution of the country. They thought that the Reformers had not gone far enough; that many ceremonies were retained which became not the simplicity of the gospel, and for which they contended that there was no Scripture warrant. Many went so far as to think that a church-government similar to that which was adopted in Scotland and by some reformed churches abroad, was more accordant with the apostolical form than the existing hierarchy; while others were for abolishing church government altogether, and leaving every congregation to manage its own concerns. The soundness of the principles on which the Presbyterians and Independents of those times acted is much more problematical than that of the doctrines of political freedom for which others contended, and which were indeed no more than

were a few years afterwards acknowledged by the estates of the realm to be fundamental principles of the British constitution, when the nation's controversy with the house of Stuart was brought to its final issue. The *religious* as well as the *political* feeling was active at Sheffield. It was fostered by two puritanical vicars in succession, Toller and Bright, to whose zeal the parish owed its chapels of Ecclesall and Attercliffe: and it appeared in operation, while it provided at the same time materials for its future support and extension in the election in 1628 of Mr. Stanley Gower to be an assistant-minister, and first curate of the newly erected chapel of Attercliffe, a presbyterian divine of great zeal and influence, afterwards a preacher before the house of commons, and a member of the assembly of divines at Westminster. Of the three most opulent families within the parish,—the Jessops of Broomhall were at that time represented by a minor, while the Brights of Carbrook, and the Spencers of Attercliffe were decided parliamentarians. The house of Howard had not an influence sufficient to counterbalance that of the two last-mentioned families aided by what was the general feeling: and the house of Wentworth, though represented by the prime minister himself, had not at the period before us acquired much influence among its neighbours at Sheffield.

In the accompts of the constables of Sheffield from June 1641 to June 1642 we have these entries, 'notes of preparation,' for the approaching convulsion.

'For charges about gathering subsidies, and pole money, and about the Protestacōn £1 6 1
For watching and warding at the castle . . 2 7 6
Spent when the justices were at the castle . . 0 2 8
Spent about Mr. Symson's businesse who was sent
from the house of cōmons 0 5 0

This last entry may relate to the measures taken by the House for embodying the militia in the different counties, one of their first steps when the king, having made an unsuccessful attempt to gain possession of Hull, prepared to reduce it by force.

In June or July 1642, the lord Mowbray and Maltravers was at the manour. Under his direction four wheel pieces with their furniture were sent to Doncaster for the king's use, from the castle of Sheffield: and from Beverley, where he was with the king, he trans-

---

[1] This expedient is happily burlesqued in the following poem, published from an original in a small volume of old poetry in the Wilson collections.

Verses on account of King Charles the First raising money by knighthood, 1630.

Come all you farmers out of the country,
    Carters, plowmen, hedgers and all,
Tom, Dick, and Bill, Ralph, Roger and Humphry,
    Leave off your gestures rusticall;
Bidd all your home spunne fashions adew,
And sute your selves in the fashions new.
    Honor invites you to delights,
    Come to the Court, and be all made knights.

He that hath forty pound
    Shalbe promoted from the plough,
His wife shall take the wall of her grannum,
    Honor is soe dog cheape now.
Though thou hast neither good birth nor breeding,
If thou hast money, be sure there is speeding.
    Honor invites, &c.

Knighthood in ancient time was an honor
    Which the best spiritts did not disdaine,
But now it is used in such a base manner
    That it is no credit but rather a staine.
Tush its no matter what people do say,
The name of a knight a whole village will sway.
    Honor invites, &c.

Shepherds leave singing your pastoral sonnetts
    And to learn compliments shew your endeavors;
Cast off for ever your tenpenny bonnetts
    And cover your coxcombs with three pound bearers.
Sell cart and waggons, new coaches to buy,
And then 'Good your worship,' the vulgar will cry.
    Honor invites, &c.

And being then to worship advanced,
    Keepe all your tenants in awe with a frowne,
And let your rents be yerely enhansed
    To buy your great ladyes new fashioned gowne.
Jugg, Cis, and Nell shalbe all Ladified,
Instead of carts, they in coaches shall ryde.
    Honor invites, &c.

Whatever you do, have a care of expences,
    In hospitality do not exceede,
Great store of followers belongs unto princes,
    A coachman and footman is all that you neede.
And still observe this, let your servants meat lacke,
And keepe gay apparell upon your wives back.
    Honor invites, &c.

Now to conclude, and shutt up my sonnett,
    Leave of the cart, whipp, hedge-bill and flaile:
This is my counsell, thinke well upon it,
    Knighthood and Honor are now putt to saile.
Then make haste quickly, and lett out your farmes
And take my advise in blazing your armes.
    Honor invites, &c.

mitted an order to the persons whom he left in trust at Sheffield-castle, to deliver such arms as could be spared to the Lord Savile for the king's use[1].

The other party were not idle. Supported by Sir John Gell who was in force in Derbyshire, they succeeded in gaining military possession of the castle and town, about which they cast up entrenchments.

The most active person at Sheffield on the side of the parliament was John Bright of Carbrook esquire, the son and heir of Stephen Bright of the same place, one of the persons of whom the forced loans had been demanded[2], and who died just at the commencement of the war. Young, active, ardent—to him the direction of the efforts of his party at Sheffield seems to have been committed till he joined Sir Thomas Fairfax, in whose army he soon rose to the rank of colonel.

On the twenty-fifth of August 1642, the royal standard was erected at Nottingham. To William Cavendish earl and afterwards marquis and duke of Newcastle, whose name has before appeared in these pages, the king committed the command of his forces, and the general military conduct of his affairs in the northern counties. Those of the parliament were placed under the command of the Lord Fairfax and his gallant son.

One of the first acts of open hostility in the neighbourhood of Sheffield was an attack upon the house of Sir Edward Rodes, a zealous parliamentarian, at Great Houghton. This was made by captain Grey, a Northumberland gentleman, at the head of three hundred dragoons. Instantly the whole of the western part of the wapentake was in arms. Rotheram-moor was the place of rendezvous. 'Though to this worthy knight,' say the Diurnals in an article from York dated September 19, 1642, 'it is a sad accident, yet it has put courage into our West-riding; for on a sudden 1500 men were in arms to take these cavaliers on their march; but they got notice of it, and escaped by night to Mansfield in Nottinghamshire.' Lord Fairfax, Sir John Savile of Lupset, and Sir William Lister of Thornton-in-Craven, are so moved at this, that it will prove advantageous to the country; for they will have 5000 men armed in a few days, and have sent to Sir John Hotham for 1000 foot, one troop of horse,

twelve barrels of powder, one ton of match, and other necessaries; being resolved to have satisfaction out of the malignants of the county, or die for it. The suffering these Northumberland rogues to pass through the county hath taught us wit, and it is resolved no more shall come this way.' Such was the spirit of bitterness in which the contest was begun.

When the earl of Newcastle marched into Yorkshire with his army consisting of about 8000 men, he found the people so generally attached to the parliamentarian cause that the king's friends had for the most part retired for protection into York. Not without encountering opposition he reached York: and finding that place already well defended he advanced southward, placing garrisons at Tadcaster, Pontefract, and other places. Leeds and Wakefield, where garrisons had been placed by the Fairfaxes, soon surrendered to the earl, who making Wakefield the head-quarters of his army, continued to advance southward with a strong body of troops. 'Receiving intelligence,' says his duchess, the entertaining memorialist of his life, ' that in two market-towns south-west from Wakefield, viz. Rotheram and Sheffield, the enemie was very busie to raise forces against his majesty, and had fortified them both about four miles distant from each other, hoping thereby to give protection and encouragement to all those parts of the country which were populous, rich and rebellious; he thought it necessary to use his best endeavours to blast those their wicked designs in the bud; and thereupon took a resolution in April 1643, to march with part of his army from Wakefield into the mentioned parts, attended with a convenient train of artillery and ammunition, leaving the greatest part of it at Wakefield with the remainder of his army under the care and conduct of his general of the horse, and major-general of the army...My Lord first marched to Rotheram, and finding that the enemy had placed a garrison of soldiers in that town, and fortified it, he drew up his army in the morning against the town, and summoned it: but they refusing to yield, my Lord fell to work with his cannon and musket, and within a short time took it by storm, and entered the town that very night[3]. Some enemies of note that were found therein were taken prisoners; and as for the

---

[1] ' A coppey of an order for the delivery of armes att Sheffeild Castle from my Lord.

Thes are to desire you according to his Maieste's co^mand & warrant under his hand, to take an especiall care that all the armes in Sheffeild Castle (excepting sum to be left for defence and securitie of the plase) be saflie delivered unto the Lord Savill, or to his assignee, together with an exact list of the said armes, whereof you are to keepe a coppy ; for all which this shall be your warrant, together with the receipt of the same under the Lord Savill's hand, for his Maiestie's use. From Beverley 29 July 1642.

I doe likewise desire you should assist all you may the carryage of thes armes to such plases as you shall bee directed.

To Mr Webster, Mr Bright, Kellam Homer, & Rawson, and to all & everie of them, or to any other whom it may concerne.

This is a trewe coppie of a warant from the Lord Mobrie Maltravers under his owne hand.'

Arms were not only to be found in all the old castles of those times, but each township had a few articles which were public property. We have the following inventory of arms belonging to the township of Sheffield anno 1615. 3 corslets, 8 headpieces, 4 musketts, 1 caliever, 9 swords and 3 girdles, and hangers, 4 muskett rests, 5 bandilieroes, 5 pikes, 5 flaxes, 5 tuch-boxes, & 2 paire of bullett moodes. And of old armour, 8 daggers & 8 girdles, 3 corsletts, 3 headpieces and 2 old calivers.   [2] Rushworth, vol. i. p. 193.

[3] John Shaw, M.A., born at Sickhouse in the chapelry of Bradfield, was at that time vicar of Rotherham. He left an account of his life and times, which has never been published ; but a good abstract of it may be found in Calamy's *Account of the ejected and silenced Ministers*, p. 823. He was in Rotherham when it was taken by the earl of Newcastle, and a person at that time particularly obnoxious.

Among the rare tracts relating to this period of our history is a sermon preached by this Mr. Shaw at Hull, whither he removed from Rotherham, entitled ' The three kingdoms' case: or their sad calamities : together with their cause and cure, with some very remarkable passages of Providence, worthy of generall observation.' 4to 1646. It is dedicated ' To the Christian and wel-affected reader, especially to my worthy and loving friends, both the inhabitants within the town and county of Kingston-upon-Hull, and also the parishoners of Bradfield in the west-riding of Yorkshire.' In this dedication he gives the following account of the taking of Rotherham, and his own particular adventures at the time.

' To conclude let me for the same end acquaint you, the inhabitants of Bradfield, with another instance, though of a lower ranke, viz. the mervailous delivery of a minister of Christ's gospel, born in your parish, wherein you may still see God's hand ; learn to trust and praise him more: 'tis this, when the earl of Newcastle besieged Rotherham in May 1643, at last the town wanting powder (which was taken at Gainsborough, as it was bringing to them) and some houses being on fire by the enemies grunadoes, the town was forced to entertaine a parley with the earl, who after some shamefull repulse and losse assured them under his hand, that upon laying down their arms they should have their estates, lives and liberties safe; but as soon as he entered, fined, imprisoned, plundered many, and as it seems had a speciall intent to ruine the minister of the place aforesaid; yet, first, the minister went through the midst of the town (then so throng'd) undiscerned by any ; secondly, he hid himself in a vault of a house not inhabited (after he heard of the enemies base unfaithfulnesse and cruelty) which house the enemy (pulling downe the works about the towne) came into, and kept as their main guard night and day, and lay close by him (which thing he neither did nor could suspect before hand;) thirdly, the enemy proclaimed him traitor by a cryer throughout the town, yea, and all others traitors also who know-

common soldiers, which were by the enemy forced from their allegiance, he shewed such clemency to them, that very many willingly took up arms for his majesty's service, and proved very faithful and loyal subjects, and good soldiers.

'After my Lord had stayed two or three dayes there, and order'd those parts, he marched with his army to Sheffield, another market-town of large extent, in which there was an ancient castle; which when the enemies forces that kept the town came to hear of, being terrified with the fame of my Lord's hitherto victorious army, they fled away from thence into Derbyshire, and left both town and castle (without any blow) to my Lord's mercy; and though the people in the town were most of them rebelliously affected, yet my Lord so prudently ordered the business, that within a short time he reduced most of them to their allegiance by love, and the rest by fear, and recruited his army dayly; he put a garrison of soldiers into the castle, and fortified it in all respects, and constituted a gentleman of quality, Sir Will. Savil kᵗ and bar. governour both of the castle, town and country; and finding near that place some iron-works, he gave present order for the casting of iron-cannon for his garrisons, and for the making of other instruments and engines of war¹.'

It seems to have been the earl of Newcastle's intention to have marched into Derbyshire against Sir John Gell, who was there in considerable strength. But he had miscalculated on the force at Wakefield, or on the power which might be brought against it. While he was at Sheffield he received information that Sir Thomas Fairfax, having strengthened his small army from the several garrisons in the western parts of the county, had fallen upon his head-quarters, taken nearly all the troops he had left there, together with his general of horse the lord Goring, and his whole magazine. This disaster compelled the earl to adopt new counsels, for it was no less than the moiety of his army which he had lost, and he immediately fell back upon York.

Traces of the earl of Newcastle at Sheffield we find in the destruction by his soldiers of much of the park-paling, and the burning of the castle-barns: in the protections which he granted to some of the neighbouring gentry: in the removal from their places of

two of the assistant-ministers Mr. Toller and Mr. Rawson: and in the garrison which he placed at the castle. The commission of Sir William Savile purports that he was appointed 'governor and commander in chief of the towne and castle of Sheffield, as also of all the forces horse and foot now appointed for that garrison, or hereafter to be sent thither for defence of the same.' It was dated the 9th of May 1643.

Thus was Sir William Savile appointed to maintain as a military post the hall of his ancestors—for he was a grandson of the sixth earl of Shrewsbury. The watchman was to take his perpetual stand on its towers; and its spacious courts were to echo the measured step of the sentinel, or the noisy cabals and rude brawls of a soldiery. Sir William Savile had had some experience in military affairs, for he had served under his relative the earl of Arundel in his expedition against the Scots in 1639, and was enthusiastically devoted to the royal cause. But he did not remain long at Sheffield. The services of such a man were too valuable to be wasted on a petty fortress. We have the two following memorials of him during his abode at Sheffield.

To Sir WILLIAM SAVILE, Baronet.

FORASMUCH as there is and will be dayly occasion during the abode of this part of the army here, for posthorses for conveying of paquets and other services from Sheffelde to diverse places upon occasion: These are therefore to authorize you to direct the warrants to the constables near adjoyning to bring in from tyme to tyme soe many able and sufficient horses or mares as you shall think requisite for the said service, together with sufficient hay and provender for them for three dayes. Given under my hand the xv. day of May 1643.

W. NEWCASTLE.

'WHERAS we are informed that the inhabitants of the chapelry of Bradfeld have made their severall compositions for and towards the maintenance of his Maᵗⁱᵉ'ˢ armie, and since that tyme have some of their goodes taken from them: wee theirfore authorize and require them to take theire goods wheresoever they shall fynde them: and this our warrant shall be their discharge. Fayle yee not herein as you will answer the contrary. Given under our handes at Sheffeld this 18 of May 1643. WILLᴹ SAVILE.

RALFE .. RUSBIE.

MARMADUKE LANGDALE.

When Sir William Savile left Sheffield he appointed

ing of him, brought him not in to them within 24 hours; in the aforesaid house the souldiers seekingth im most diligently, thrust their swords betwixt the boards frequently, yet neither found nor hurt him; fourthly, at last they looked up to a vault above their heads (which lay visibly open to view, by the space of three yards and more, where himself and his man lay indeed) and swore that he was there, whereupon they instantly ran up the stairs (which they kept) broke open the door (entring to the vault which they saw, and where he was) found it lockt, and the key in the door in the inside, sought him five severall times, the great windowes all open round about, he and his man lying on their sides could have taken hold on them, yet never found either of them (no cause but that Jer. 36. 26.) fifthly, he having layen there on the stones most part of three days and nights, viz. from Thursday May 4, 1643 (when the town was taken) till Saturday evening May 6, could not stir, scarce cough or spet, lest he should be heard, and no friend, meat, drink or relief could come at him (the enemy keeping the town, that house and stairs to the vault) he resolved that night rather than starve, to goe down and yeeld himself to their cruell mercies (for he might hear them swear his death with many dammees) presently that very afternoon they went away (he cannot to this day learn any reason why) for they came thither again the next day, and staid there constantly long after, as if they had meant (as indeed the good and wise God did) to give him just a-fit time and space to get safe away, for neither before nor after could he get away thence, nor longer stay there; sixthly, when he was come down the stairs from the vault, though the enemy he found removed, yet were the doors lockt; but the enemy had caused a carpenter to pull up two boards of the floor to seek for him in a hollow place underneath, and left them unnalied down again; through which space (as if they had ment to have made him a way forth) he got out: seventhly, when he came forth by that

hollow aforesaid, he came through the midst of the town again to his house undiscerned; and as he was stepping into the hall (not knowing now who lived there or in any other house) there were seven cavaliers billeted (having formerly plundered him sufficiently) amongst whom he was just stepping, had not a friend of his pulled him by the shoulder into another room next the hall: eighthly, yet durst he not tarry there, but got to a vault in another house, and lay upon an earthen floor the remainder of three weeks in the midst among them, yet never got cold, nor was the least sick, no not so much as usually before: ninthly, after this he got safe to Manchester, and after some cumbers, is safely returned to his native country; for all which, he entreats his friendly neighbours, and readers, that praise may be returned to the only wise God, and sole and lively confidence put in him for ever and ever.'

This is transcribed from the copy of Shaw's sermon in volume 254 of the small quartos of the collection of pamphlets published in the time of the Civil Wars, given by his present majesty to the British Museum. I am not aware that it has ever been publicly noticed to whom we are indebted for having taken such pains to collect and preserve the fugitive productions of that important period. Volume 100 of the small quartos has evidently been soiled by a fall into the mud. It fell from the hands of the unhappy Charles. It had been lent to his majesty much against the inclination of the proprietor. This fact is noticed in a manuscript note on the third leaf, which is subscribed Geo. Thomason. He was probably the bookseller, whose name appears in the title-page of the 'Histoire de l'entree de la reyne mere du roy &c.' republished by Mr. Gough. 'A Londres par Jean Raworth pour George Thomason et Octavien Pullen, a la rose, au cimitiere de Sainct Paul. 1639.'

¹ Life of William Duke of Newcastle, 33—35.

Thomas Beaumont esquire deputy-governor of the castle and town. This gentleman was of the ancient family of Beaumont of Whitley near Huddersfield, and led a hundred-and-twenty trained men of the county of York in the regiment which Sir William Savile commanded under the earl of Arundel. Much of the correspondence between Sir William Savile and Major Beaumont during the time that the latter was residing at Sheffield has been preserved. In these letters, which were collected from amongst his family-papers by the late Richard Henry Beaumont esquire, and deposited by him in the Bodleian library, we have a full account of the Sheffield garrison. The letters of Sir William Savile breathe much of the high-toned and heroic spirit which animated the supporters of the royal cause.

To render the letters which follow more intelligible, it may be proper to introduce them with a very brief notice of the state of affairs in Yorkshire during the time of Major Beaumont's command at Sheffield. In the latter six months of 1643 the affairs of the king in the north were prosperous. The earl of Newcastle soon recovered possession of Wakefield, and dislodged all the parliamentarian garrisons in the west-riding. Lord Fairfax and his son Sir Thomas Fairfax threw themselves into Hull, the only town which the parliamentarians possessed in the whole county.

But early in the ensuing spring the tide turned. An army of sixteen thousand men advanced from Scotland under the command of the earl of Leven. The earl of Newcastle, then made a marquis, marched northward to meet and oppose them. This relieved the Fairfaxes, who immediately advanced upon York, making a successful attack upon the royal garrison at Selby by the way. They effected a junction with the Scotch army at Wetherby. The earl of Manchester with a considerable force also marched upon York from the south. The marquis of Newcastle retired into that city.

While York was besieged by three considerable armies, Prince Rupert advanced from Lancashire to its relief. By his persuasions the marquis of Newcastle was induced to march out of York, and give battle to the besiegers. They fought on Marston-moor, about six miles from York on the north, and the royalist army suffered a complete defeat. This battle, which was decisive of the king's affairs in the north, was fought on the 2d of July 1644. York surrendered; and the marquis of Newcastle precipitately left the kingdom.

LETTERS addressed to Major THOMAS BEAUMONT while Lieutenant-governor of Sheffield-castle.

Sir WILLIAM SAVILE to Major BEAUMONT.

Sir,

I FORMERLY writte to you about Capt. Ditchfield, and the rest of the officers of Coll. Throgmorton's regiment. I now write again by him that you will further him all you can, & if he have use of them, I pray you let him have some dragoones.

I exspect an account of Ancient Oxley, why he then came away from Medley for & here that he ran away, and that his soldiers would have stayed him, & he offered to pistoll them.

For bullets I pray be still diligent, and for Mʳ Spencer[1], if he pay 133l. 6s. 8d. sett him at liberty.

[1] Of Attercliffe. One of the charges against Sherland Adams rector of Treeton, removed by the parliamentary commissioners, was, that he had caused the house of lieut.-col. Spencer of Attercliffe to be plundered by the king's party, and the colonel to be imprisoned, who had

I am glad to heare you have so good a hart of the businesse, and if I had not thought itt stronge, you may assure yourself I would never have left you theare, I beinge

Your faithfull friend & servant,

WIL. SAVILE.

Pontefratt
29th May 1643.

Sir WILLIAM SAVILE to Major BEAUMONT.

Sʳ

I RECEVED your letter by this bearer: & for the newes of Sʳ Raph Hopton itt is very true: he hath overthrown all the Western forces, taken 2000 prisoners, 16 piece of cannon, and done many wonderfull things[2]; & Coll. Ledgerd is killed at Briggs, & that towne taken by Coll. Cavendish, & 500 men killed and taken. All people are fortunate but wee : yett as long as Sheffield castle houldieth out, I think myself happy. For the mach you write for, I shall shortly send you some : but I put you in mind once more to use your snaphance peices to keepe century with. That will save our mach. For Wᵐ Savile, if you would be quite of him, send him to me. I am glad to heare you goe on so well with your work: and I assure you I will see no man shall be a looser by itt. For pay of officers, I have no time to say more then this; lett every one be pleased: & for Capt. Waterhouse, I pray you supply his wantes : & send me by the next a list of how many you are, both officers and soldiers, and others. Remember me kindly to all my freinds with you: & I always remaine

Your faithfull friend & servant,

WIL. SAVILE.

30th May 1643,
Tadcaster.

Your commission is as mine: which is to do what you have a mind to, for the good service.

Sir WILLIAM SAVILE to Major BEAUMONT.

Sʳ Tadcaster 3 June 1643.

I RECEVED your letter dated yesterday: & for the writings that are Mʳ Spencer's I am williuge he have them restored: but I beare nothing of an assessement I wished you to make; whearin by assesinge all about you att easy suᵐes weekely (as some of the richest of all, ten shillings weekely, & some but six or twelve pence weekly, & so all sumes betweene them to forenamed) a competent sume of mony might be got upp for the weekly entertainment of the officers & soldiers in the castle. For the bulletts that are alreddy made, if you think the way be safe, send them to the castle att Pontefratt, & write to the governor there to keepe them for me: & I have att Pontefratt Castle, that is for your house, twenty firkins of butter. I have mach to, but itt will not be at Pontefratt untill tomorrow night att the soonest. For gunpowder I shall not be unmindfull of you, but however be carefull : & for provision of fish I have sent to Scarbrough for as much as will serve you one day in a weeke for a yeare. For Wᵐ Savile I will examine him about that you write, he beinge now at York. For Capt. Markham he is not to have any pay, nor his dragoons. I wonder much he should exspect any. I make no question but he will behave himselfe well & carefully, & if he dos so, he may easyly believe I will be carefull of him. For Sir Fran. Wortley itt is heare said that he is confined in his house. Whither he is or no, you must not suffer Shefield Castle to suffer, if you can helpe itt. I have looked over the list you sent me, & think that a troop of dragoons may very well be spared, & thearfore I could wish you could devise a way to gett fifty of them horsed. If Mʳ Bright, my Lord of Arrendel's balife, have any lead, sease of itt, carry itt into the castle, & if you can find any delinquents that have not compounded, serve them so to. Lay out intelligence to see if you can learn of any packet that came from London to Manchester : such a prize would do well. If you send your providore or his deputy unto Marshland, that country affordeth att this present great store of provition, malt & meale especially ; & gett 100 hogsheads of beare brewed at least, & when any

afterwards 350l. to pay for his release. See Ardron's Ploughman's Vindication.

[2] The battle of Stratton in Cornwall, in which the earl of Stamford was routed. It was fought on the 16th of May.

sendeth for provition into the toune of Shefield or neare theare-about, do you superseade the warrantes under your hande, & I will make it out, & let your providors be diligent every way.

Lett every one about Sheffield continue to be carefull, for theare is the harte of

Your most faithfull freind & servant,
　　　　　　　　WIL. SAVILE.

I shall desiare to heare what becometh of Sir Francis Wortley, & how the case standeth with him & his forces.

I would know whether you have provided yourself of a chirurgion. There is one att Barnesley that will searve your turne. Send for him, & if he will not cume I will provide you.

If you will send to my tenant Sutton, who doth live either at South Wingfield or Sherland in Darbyshire, send a woman with your letter, & Sutton will either go to my wife, or find a messenger.

For my noble friend Ser. Ma. Beaumont deputy
governor of the toune and castle of Shefeild.
Let the bearer passe, this 3 June 1643 with
this lettere & tow more.　Wil. Savile.

Sir WILLIAM SAVILE to Major BEAUMONT.

S[r]　　　　　　　　Pontefratt 7th June 1643.

For M[ris] Bright[1], she hath made such way for herselfe, as I must entreate you to spare her for three weeks, against which time I hope she will provide you some money. But in the mean time send to M[rs] Westby att Gilthwait for 150*l.*, & be sure she do not outrun you, & have 100*l.* at least.

I have receved your letter, & Capt. Hemsworth's by the bearer: & for the messinger you write of, I doubt not but you have him before now with you, & I hope for a returne from you this night of his message. However send a load of bullets tomorrow, & some 12 at least to guard itt. In my oppinion itt had beene better way to have sett downe every man perticularly what he should have payd; but that would have beene more labor. I like well of the course you have taken: only this, the impotition that is layed uppon any towne must not excuse for the general assessment: & such townes as I make a score against, is not convenient for you to medle with att present. But for the Derbysher tounes make them pay soundly, & take as greate compase as you like yourselves; but let no man know what you receve, & something must be weekely taken out of the souldiers pay to allow them shoes & clothes withall. You are to send to Wood of the Worldesend[2], & who is to pay you ten pounde in ben leather. For Edward Hill of whom you write, make him pay what you think fitt : & for Wood att whom Gen. King lay, if he have payed him money, wee must not medle: else make him pay. In haste I rest　　　　Your most assured friend & servant,
　　　　　　　　WIL. SAVILE.

My service to all my friends.

Sir WILLIAM SAVILE to Major BEAUMONT.

S[r]　　　　　　　　Heath 21 June 1643.

In the firste place I must intreate you to make James Syll send by the next messenger what monies he hath leavied of the great assesment, and whether any constables refuse to pay or noe, that course may be taken with them. I desire likewise by the next to have returned me a mapp of the castle, and also a new survey of what victuals are now in itt. Your letter by this bearer I recieved, and for matters of money, I have 30*l.* of yours which I received in goold of M[r] Denison. I pray you take it againe of James Syll, out of my particular monies; and bee sure you want not any money nether for yourself nor your freinds, soe long as any roundhead hath either fingers or toas left, within tenn myles of the castle.

For those goods that you have left, if your wife plesse to send them to Pontefratt Castle, they shall bee there with some of mine. I will send to your wife today, and know how she meanes to dispose of herselfe and children, wherein I shall doe her the best service I cann, and send you word of her resolu-

[1] Of Carbrook.
[2] Wardsend.
[3] i. e. more than sufficient to defray the expenses of the garrison, &c.

cōns. I have received the bulletts according as you write, and shall hereafter desire you to send me the sizes as well as the number of the bullets. Wee are now upon our march towards Leeds, and I hoope hastily to send you good news. For all other things in your letter, I shall take care: & once againe entreate you to plunder as many goods as to make yourself a savor[3]. So in haste I am

Your faithfull freind & servant,
　　　　　　　　WIL. SAVILE.

Send a particular of what moneyes are paid. If you have a mind to send home, the way will bee cleare tomorrow.

Sir WILLIAM SAVILE to Major BEAUMONT.

Sir,　　　　　　　　8th of July 1643.

In return of your letter of the 6th instant, I will write to Sir Fran. Wortley to discharge George Sanderson. For your cozen Armitage of whom you write, he is assesed 100*l.*, & that being payed he will be no further troubled; if you would have me doe any more, write and itt shall be done. I like all very well, onely I would have you send boldly into Bradfield parish & there abouts; & I think if the tow companies that are to march, stay theare this night, itt is best, & you may send the dragoons with them : & then when the foot marcheth to Hallifax, the dragoons may bring in some that refuse to pay. If you have a mind ....

[The remainder of this letter is destroyed.]

Sir WILLIAM SAVILE to Major BEAUMONT.

　　　　　　　　8th of July 1643.

You are to send my own company & Capt. Maude's company presently to Halifax, theare to receave further orders from the Major Gen. or him that commandeth in cheif. They are shortly to return to the castle. Send Sir Fran. Wortley word of your march, for feare you give him alarm, & lett the companies march presently, but no coulors. Send one before to the commander in chief, one hour or tow before you come near Halifax, to receave orders for quarters. Capt. Maud is to cōmand these men.　　　　WIL. SAVILE.

To Major Beamount att
Shefield castle.

Sir WILLIAM SAVILE to Major BEAUMONT.

Sir,　　　　　　　　18th July 1643.

I received your letter dated yesterday, & have acquainted Gen. King with itt : & he hath given order to me to send to Coll. Betton who is now at Doncaster to come to Shefield & ly theare, if you have any hopes of doing any goode of the enemy. I pray you thearefore from time to time, give notice to Coll. Betton, if any newes happen to you that may be of advantage to us : & send this enclosed to him & I know he will be reddy to assist you in all thinges. So in hast I rest

Your faithfull friend & servant,
　　　　　　　　WILL. SAVILE.

I will be att Shefeild shortly.
Seale the enclosed, & send them away.

Sir FRANCIS MACKWORTH and another to Major BEAUMONT.

Major Beamont,

Wee desire you will take care that the assessment which is to be paied within Bradfeild parish be furthwith levyed and collected: for there is a necessitye for the money towards payment of the soldyers. And if the goods of those which refuse to pay will not extend to make satisfaction, that you will take order that the profitts of their lands may be disposed of towards payment thereof, or otherwise to apprehend their persons if they cann be found. Wherein we hope you will not faile. Soe wee rest. From Hallifax the XIX. of August 1643.

Your affectyonate freinds,
　　　　　　　　FRAN. MACKWORTH.

To our very good freind Major　...............
Beamont at Sheffeild castle,
theise.

Both parties had necessarily recourse to severe and harsh measures to raise the sums required by their numerous garrisons as well as by the moveable force.

Sir Ingram Hopton to Major Beaumont.

Sir,

I have by my Collonel's appointment sent to your castle one Barcker, the verriest knave in our cuntry. He cannot be used to ill; and with this carracter leave him to you, not douting but you will lay that charge upon the mart[ial] that he will be kept safe. I doe intend to se yow as I goe into Lincolnshire, and to be merry with yourself and the rest of my friends with you for one day. And soe I remaine

Your faithfull freind and servant,

Leathley   In. Hopton[1].
this 26th of August.

For his much honored freind Major Beaumont, Deputie governor of Shefeild Castle, these.

Sir Francis Mackworth to Major Beaumont.

Sr

By an especiall order from his Excellency these are to desire you to send mee a catalogue of the names of your prisoners with theire offences for which they stand cŏmitted: and lykewise the tyme of theire imprisonment: and so neare as vou can the vallue of theire estates both real and personall. Hereof I pray faile not:

Your servant to cŏmand,

Hallifax 9 September,   Fran. Mackworth.
1643.

To my much honored freind Leiften[t] Colonell Beumont at Shefeild, or the Command[r] in chiefe there, these.

Sir William Savile to Major Beaumont.

Sr   Cottinham 7ber 22th 1643.

Itt is his Ex.' pleasure to release Cornett Hill. I pray you thearfore if the man & woman I writt for in my last be not cumed from you, to send him alonge with them. If thay be cume away, then I pray send Cornett Hill to Pontefratt Castle to Sr John Redmond, and write to him that Sr Tho. Glemham's desiare is that he be kept att Pontefratt till further orders. So in hast I rest

Your faithfull freind & ....,

Wil. Savile.

Sir William Savile to Major Beaumont.

Sr   Cottenham 7ber 22th 1643.

I received your letter of the 17th instant together with a muster of Capt. Horsfall's troope: & I doe desiare him that he will march forthwith with his troope into Lincolnshire to the regiment, & lett him send one trooper to the regiment to give them notise of his cuminge. I desiare he speedily march with his troope, because theare are but few Capt. with my regiment of horse: & lett Capt. Horsfall carry with him his muster-roll sined by yourself & Capt. Himsworth, & the comisaryes deputy at Lincon will make itt upp.

Sr, for Lt Coll. Shawcrosse wife if you can conveniently gett her, take her prisoner, & wee will treat of the rest of the businesse. For other businesse I shall trouble you no more att present. Always remaininge

Your faithfull friend & servant,

Wil. Savile.

Sir William Savile to Major Beaumont[2].

I pray you remember me to all my freuds with you. Scout well, and lay out for intelligence, and if you heare any thing that in the least concerns the army, send speedy [information] therof to Mr Rolston his Exc[ye]'s secretary. Soe soone as the armye is past by you, send an officer to me withe a note of such things as you want: and I shall doe my best to procure them, and send them to you by him. I pray you remember me to my wife, and tell her I desire to have her company here, and the sooner she comes the better. Yours,

Wil. Savile.

[1] He fell in the expedition into Lincolnshire, of which he speaks in this letter: slain at Winceby fight on the 6th of October 1643.
[2] This appears to be a postscript to the preceding letter.
[3] This letter is added to this interesting series from the orignal in the

Sir William Savile to Major Beaumont.

Sir,

Wee have here at Yorke received intelligence that one Thomas Sheircliffe a Londoner, and a man very like to be disaffected to his Majesty & his service, is very lately removed hence to Rotheram to one Robert Sheircliffe his father in Briggate there. I shall desire you to send for him speedily, & examine him; & except he cann cleare himself by very authentique evidence, reteyne him prisoner with you. The presumptions again him are these: He brings a letter from a femynine rebell in London, whose husband died in the parliament service .... sculking here without knowne occasion, departed heare uppon first notice of him, & is to retorne to London speedily. Theis things sumd upp togeather (in my sence) amount to a stronge evidence against him. His liberty or imprisonment is left to your discretion. Whereof I beseech you would at your next leasure give accompt to

Yorke   Your serv[t],
29th Oct. 1643.   Wil. Savile.

[Sir William Savile to Major Beaumont.

Sr

I heare that Gell and Fairfax are ioyned together, & now aboute Nottingham. I shall therfore entreate yow to be very carefull, and lett foure of the centories att least have there matches continually lighted and be in readines for any enimy, which by God's blessing (I hope) will never hurt yow. If his Exc. should by chance come to that towne with his armye, be very carefull during his aboade y[t] all the guards doe there duties as well by day as night, & lett them all use match during that time. And I desire yow to invite Bassett and other officers as yow thincke fitt to dinner and supper with yow. For sending into Bradfeld parish for the present I thinke itt not convenient. If my Lord come to Sheafeild, lett none of my men quarter in the towne, for feare of hindring his quarter; and if the castle chance to be beseegd, keepe it to the uttermost, as yow love him that is

Your most faithfull frend & servant,

York 9ber the 2, 1643.   Wil. Savile[1].]

Sir William Savile to Major Beaumont.

Sir,   York 5th 9ber 1643.

In returne of yours yesterday for the which I returne you thankes, & desiare you as any thinge hapneth, to give notise both to the army and me: & for the assesses, lett the cuntry pay freely: for whatever they pay to the castle shall be allowed; & I will befriend all the tounes that pay to the castle. If my wife be with you, I pray tell her I would be glad to see her; & that I am at Sir Rob. Ingram's house. I pray tell Capt. Hemsworth I have received his letter, & have no time to write to him, but I wish all to be carefull, which I know you will all be. I have taken order to send you more pouder & mach speedily. For the oxen I lately sent you, I pray you kill them presently, for you may be taken of a sudden. Goe on with all thinges, & never yield till all the pouder be spent, & make use of the peices that hang upp in the dininge roome. If they be well handled, they are of good use. Lay out for inteligence. Send as occation offreth. In hast I rest

Your faithfull frend & servant,

Wil. Savile.

If you be hesiedged, I will make them warme lodgings. My true love to all with you.   Wil. Savile.

For his Majesties service.
To Major Beamount at Shefield Castle.
Hast, hast, post hast. Wil. Savile.
Doncaster y[e] 6th af past 4 in the afternoon.   Tho. Hay.

Lord Eythin to Major Beaumont.

Sr

I receaved your letter yesternicht, and returns ynw thanks

Wilson collections. In the November of this year, the earl of Newcastle marched from York to Chesterfield, where he remained for some time, and no doubt passed, as was expected, through Sheffield.

for your intelligence. I intreat you to lett me heir of Sr Thomas Fearfax, wch way he bends his troupps, that we meay weat upon him. If yoù wrytt or send, send it by Rotheram. I remayne   Your servant,

Doncaster   EYTHIN[1].

the 10th of 9ber 1643.

At 10 a klok in the morninge.

For the commander in cheif of Sheaffeild.
Hast, hast, post hast. Eythin.

Sir WILLIAM SAVILE to Major BEAUMONT.

Sr   Yorke 10th of 9ber 1643.

IN returne of your letter of yesterday, I have written to Sir Edward Osborne. I hope before this time you have receved the 10 barrelles of pouder and mach: & when you receve orders to be heare the next weeke to cume to the cōmittee, if your occasion will suffer you, I should be glad to see you. However I would have Cap. Franck cume   for I would speake with you. For the letter brought by Wm Watson, I have alreddy answered itt: but for the assesment, you must send for itt till such time as the other way be setled. For Cap. Hemsworth's letter, I shall save myselfe the labor of writinge to him, Sam. Savile goinge so soone. I rest

Your faithfull friend & servant,
WIL. SAVILE.

Sir WILLIAM SAVILE to Major BEAUMONT.

Sr   York 27th 9ber 1643.

I HAVE not hard any thinge since this businesse began that I am so much displeased with, as the puttinge downe the table at Sheffeild Castle. Let me entreate you to rejoyse, & sett upp the table againe. I am tould that the men att the Woodhead have left that place: if so I desaire a good party may speedely be sent into those partes, & if possible lett some be feched in that may make you merry this winter: & now when the army is neare, I desire that you may make use of the time. I would have Cap. Hemsworth cume to this toune to speake with   Your faithfull friend & servant,

WIL. SAVILE.

I desiare to have my love remembred to you all; & tell Sam. Savile that I desiare him to go on with the pistoll worke, with speede, & take money out of that 500l. left in James Sill's hands.   Yours,   W. S.

... yow send me woord what you heare of Heathcote: and yf   Bluden be neare you, send him to me.

WIL. SAVILE.

Willm Greaves parson of Brelaford was taken prisoner neare Tutburie Castle by Sr John Gell's forces, and is now deteyned in Derbie. It is desired that he might be exchanged for Mr Nicholas Heathcoat, now prisoner in Sheffield Castle.

Sir WILLIAM SAVILE to Major BEAUMONT.

Sr   York Jan. 3, 1643.

I PRAY you lett Major Monckton have forty men out of the bow companies now in Sheffield Castle: that is twenty men out of my Majors cumpany, & twenty out of your company: & Lt Broune to go with them, & to staye theare till furder orders, which will be (I think) some ten dayes.

I receaved your letter dated yesterday, & desiare you to send the shott as is desiared.

[The remainder of this letter is destroyed.]

Sir WILLIAM SAVILE to Major BEAUMONT.

Sr   Yorke 19th Jan. 1643.

I AM glad to heare that you are all well. I desiare to heare from you by the next how the mortar piece & her equipage doeth goe forward, & whither the 300 bandeleroes be reddy, or delivered to Sr Fran. Mackworth; for they want bandeleroes mightely heare: & how many pistolls are made: as likewise how Cutbert hath found the hopyard at Rufford, which the sooner it is gathered, the more for the profitt.

Your most faithfull freind & servant,
WIL. SAVILE.

I desiare to know how many bandeleroes can be gotten reddy by Fryday sennight. I have (I think) a cōmodity of wine. I must send some to Shefield. My love to all my freinds with you.   Yn   W. S.

The Marquis of NEWCASTLE to Major BEAUMONT.

Sr

I CANNOT expresse ye sorrow I have for the losse of your noble Colonell; both in respect of his Maties service, & my owne particular: but since it has pleased God to call him from us, you may be pleased to take notice that I intend to take the governmt of Sheffield Castle & that garryson into my owne hands, & to imploy you as you have formerly beene in that charge: & therefore I doe hereby desire your care in ye execution of all things thereunto belonging, as comander in cheef there: hereby requiring you to receave orders from mee, ye Lord Lieutenant Generall, or such other comanders in cheif of ye army as shall have authority from mee to comand you, & none else. And for the 100 men you were comanded to send to Doncaster, I pray you faile not upon sight hereof to send 20 more to make up them already sent 100: and so in assurance thereof I remaine

Yorke   Your very affectionate freind,
24th Jan. 1643.   W. NEWCASTLE.

To my very worthy frind Serjeant Major
Thomas Beaumont, att Sheffeild, these.
For his Matis especiall affairs. Hast, hast,
post hast. W. Newcastle.

The Marquis of NEWCASTLE to Major BEAUMONT.

Sr

I PERCEAVE by your l're that you writt to my secretary, that Sheffield is taxed at 30l. for the charge of the workes at Doncaster. And because I find that the sume for the raysing those works was to be imposed equally upon the divisions of Tickbill and Strafford, and that the limitts of your garrison could not possibly bee exempted from that charge, in respect every part of these divisions are allotted to one garrison or another, and that those parts of the countrey receave equal protection from that garrson, I see no occasion why one part must be spared more than another, and therefore you must be content to subscribe thereunto.

For bulletts and grenades, I pray you deliver from time to time so many as Colonell Belasyse commander in cheif shall send you warrant for.

For the troops wch are quartered within the townes allotted to your garrison, if they be quarter'd by the Commander in cheif, or the Lieutenant Generall of the horse, my order to remove them will crosse theirs, wch I conceave not fitt: but if you please to have a little patience, I presume the greatest part of the horse there will be drawne away into other quarters within a few dayes, wch will serve your turue without an order therein. And so presenting my service to you I remaine

Your very affectionate frind & serveyut,
Newcastle   W. NEWCASTLE.
13o Feb. 1643.

To my very worthy freind Major Beaumont,
Governor of Sheffeild Castle, theise.

Jo. WATKINSON to Major BEAUMONT.

Worthy freind,

YOU may perceive by the coppy of his Extrs letter, & this note both hereinclosed, that his Lordship desireth these quantitys of iron shott to be sent to him to Newcastle, with what speed may bee. I must intreat you to send to Mr Clarke of Doncaster all these severall sorts of shott; & wt you want of any kind of them, to get the shott-makers at the forge to make that quantity to be sent to his Excy, & the like quantity to remaine in our stores. I pray them to be made with what possible speed you can. Especially them which is to be sent to Newcastle: & send them to Mr Clarke of Doncaster, to whome I have writt to speed them hither. Choll. Bellasyse doth much wonder that the eight hundreth bandeleers & the swords which he spoke to Mr Sam. Savile for, that they are

---

[1] Better known in the history of these wars as General King.—He was lieutenaut-general under the earl of Newcastle.

not come. If they be not sent away, I pray send them presently, for he hath great occasion to use them: not having further at present, but that I am

Your truly affectionate freind & servant,
Yorke   Jo. WATKINSON.
the 18ᵗʰ Feb. 1643.
To his much honored freind Major Beamont
at Sheifeild, these dd.

The next letter is in a different strain.

The Earl of MANCHESTER to Major BEAUMONT.

Sir,

BEING in these partes by cõmand of the Parliament, to reduce such places as yet refuse obedience to their commaundes, I have sent you this summons that you deliver to mee the Castle of Sheffeild now in your possession, with the armes, ordnaunce and ãmunition therin. In the performance whereof you may expect all civilitie becoming a gentleman of your quality. If you make any doubt of my performance, if you will come or send any one to mee at Doncaster, you shall receive full satisfaction therin. I desire your speedy answer, and rest

Your servant,   E. MANCHESTER.

Sʳ

I SHALL desire you to send unto me Steephen Lawrence, a trooper of my army, now prisoner in your Castle, and I shall send unto you one of the like quallitie. I rest

Doncaster   Your servant,
the 27ᵗʰ of July 1644.   E. MANCHESTER.

Major-General CRAWFORD to Major BEAUMONT.

Sʳ

I AM sent by the Earle of Manchester to reduce this place you hold, and therfor send you yet a sũmons, though my trumpett was shott att, against the lawes of armes, the other day. You may easily perceive I desire not the effusion of blood, otherwise I should have spared myself this labour. If you think good to surrender it, you may expect all fair respects befitting a gentleman and souldiers: otherwise you must expect those extremities which they have that refuse mercy. I desire your answere within one houre, & rest

Sheffield,   Your servant,
August 4ᵗʰ 1644.   L. CRAWFORD.

The writer of this letter was Major-general Crawford, who was sent by the Earl of Manchester to reduce Sheffield-castle and other garrisons in the neighbourhood. We shall take our account of the siege from Vicars's Parliamentary Chronicle[1].

' After this, this noble and victorious general the virtuous and valourous Earl of Manchester advanced farther, and sent out a party of his army (consisting of about one thousand two hundred foot, and a regiment of horse, commanded by Major Generall Crawford and Colonell Pickering, two of their biggest peices of ordnance) to take in Sheffeild-castle, a strong hold in Yorkshire, wherein were a troop of horse and two hundred foot, strongly fortifyed with a broad and deep trench of eighteen foot deep, and water in it, a strong brest-work pallizadoed, a wall round of two yards thick, eight peices of iron-ordnance, and two morter-peices. Our forces being come neer this castle[2], sent them three great shot, which did execution in the castle, after which they sent a summons to the castle, who shot three times at the trumpeter, two of which shots came very neer, and hardly mist him: and they flourishing their swords cryed out, ' they would have no other parley.' Whereupon ours advanced into the town, and there quartered that night, in which night and next day they raised two batteries within

threescore yards of the enemies outworks, whereon our ordnance fell to play upon them, and did as much execution on the walls as peices of their bignesse could doe; the greatest being but a demi-culverin. And after about foure and twenty houres playing and plying thus with their ordnance, and finding it would protract too much time to be thus battering with their peices, they resolved to send to my Lord Fairfax for the Queen's pocket-pistoll and a whole culverin, which accordingly were soon brought thither and presently mounted: and the next morning betimes, after their comming, those three began to play, which did very great execution upon one side of the castle, and brought the strong walls thereof down into the trenches, and made a perfect breach. And the noble Major-Generall having prepared all things in a readinesse for storming the castle, both faggots, ladders, and other accommodations thereunto, & digested the form of storming by a councell of warre, it was resolved to send another summons to the castle, which produced a present treaty between three gentlemen sent out of the castle, and three like men of our party, who speedily concluded the surrender of the castle upon fair articles. Wee took in this castle foure hundred armes, besides the great gunnes aforementioned, twelve barrels of powder, much match, twenty tuns of great iron shot, about foure hundred pounds worth of corn, beef, bacon, cheese and other provisions; all which and many other things (except a hundred muskets, and a morter-peice, which were brought away) were left in the castle for supply thereof, the country thereabout giving my Lord's soldiers five hundred pound among them for their good service against the place.'

Articles of agreement between the commanders authorized by Major-General Crawford, and Major Thomas Beaumont, Governor of Sheffield Castle, for surrendering the same to the right honourable the Earl of Manchester.

ART. I. The Castle, with all the fire-arms, ordnance and ammunition, all their furniture of war, and all their provisions (except what is in the following articles) to be delivered to Major-General Crawford tomorrow, by three o'clock in the afternoon, being the 11ᵗʰ of this instant August, without any diminution or embezzlement.

ART. II. That the Governor and all other officers shall march out of the castle upon the delivery thereof, with their drums and colours, and each his own horse saddled, sword and pistol, to Pomfret Castle, or wheresoever they please, with a sufficient convoy or pass, for their security; the common soldiers to their own home, or where they please.

ART. III. That all officers and soldiers, marching out on this agreement, shall have liberty to carry with them their wives, children, and servants, with their own goods, properly belonging to them, and shall have all convenient accomodation for carrying the same away.

ART. IV. That the Lady Savile, and her children and family, with her own proper goods, shall and may pass with coaches, horses, and waggons to Thornhill, or elswhere, with a sufficient guard, befitting her quallity; and without injury to any of their persons, or plundering any of their goods or otherwise. She, they, or any of them, to go or stay at their own pleasure, until she or they be in a condition to remove themselves.

ART. V. That the Gentlemen in the Castle being no soldiers, shall march out with each his own horse saddled, sword and pistol: and shall have liberty to remove their goods, and to live in their own houses, or elsewhere, without molestation; they conforming to the ordinances of Parliament. And they

<hr>

[1] *The burning bush not consumed, &c.* Lond. 1646. 4to, p. 7.
[2] In a short manuscript account of this expedition of Major-general Crawford in a contemporary hand, and formerly in the possession of

Miss Chaloner or Chalner of Darnall, it is said that when he was on the road to Sheffield, ' Rotherham Street ends were so blockt up that it required some time to take it.'

shall have protection of the Earls of Manchester and Leven. And all officers and soldiers, who chuse to lay down their arms, shall have the same protection.

ART. VI. That the governor, officers, soldiers, gentlemen, and all others who are by this agreement to carry their own goods with them, shall have a week's time for removing the same; and in the mean time they are to be in the castle, and secure from embezzlement. And this article is to be understood of all such goods as are at present within the castle, or under the absolute command thereof.

ART. VII. That Kellam Homer[1], now living in the Castle, shall have liberty to remove his goods into the town, or elsewhere, without molestation.

ART. VIII. That the governor, officers, gentlemen, and all other persons, shall (according to the articles above mentioned) march out without injury or molestation.

ART. IX. That hostages, such as Major Crawford shall approve, shall be delivered by the governor, upon signing the articles for delivery of the castle, and safe return of the envoy; which hostages shall be returned safe, upon the performance thereof, unto such place as they desire.

Signed by us, Commissioners authorized by
Major Crawford, at Sheffield, this 11th of
August 1644.   J. PICKERING.
                                 MARK GRIMSTON.
                                 WILLIAM HAMILTON.
Signed by us, Commissioners authorized by
Major Beaumont, governor of Sheffield
Castle, this 11th of August 1644.
                                 GABRIEL HEMSWORTH[2].
                                 SAM. SAVILL.
                                 THOS. ROBINSON.

The Lady Savile, whose personal security is guaranteed by one of these articles, was the relict of Sir William Savile, late governor of the castle. She was a daughter of Thomas lord Coventry some time lord keeper of the great seal, and a favourer of the royal cause equally active and zealous. 'This gallant lady,' says Dr. Peter Barwick in the life of his brother Dr. John Barwick, dean of St. Paul's[3], 'famous even for her warlike actions beyond her sex, had been besieged by the rebels in Sheffield Castle, which they battered on all sides by great guns, tho' she was big with child, and had so little regard for her sex, that in that condition they refused a midwife she had sent for, the liberty of going to her. Yet this unheard-of barbarity was so far from moving her that she resolved to perish rather than surrender the castle. But the walls being every where full of cracks with age, and ready to fall, the soldiers of the garrison began to mutiny, not so much concerned for their own danger, as for the lamentable condition of this noble lady so near the time of her falling in labour; for she was brought to bed the night after the castle was surrendered.' Thus the distress of these sad times visited even the tenderer sex.

Another person of note who was in the castle at the time of its surrender was Sir John Kaye, of Woodsome, baronet, an active partisan of the royal cause. To him as well as to Major Beaumont the governor, Major-General Crawford granted passports to proceed to their respective homes, on an engagement from them not to bear arms against the Parliament[4]. As

for Major Beaumont, he retired to Whitley, and after the Restoration was knighted by King Charles II. with his own sword, 27 June 1660. He died on the 30th of May 1668, and was buried at Kirk-Heaton.

In the register of burials for the parish of Sheffield occur the following entries:

1644. June 5. Maria fil. Thom. Beaumont Ar.
      Aug. 8. Mr Stringwidge.
      Aug. 10. Erasmus Sands, gen.
              Miles.
          11. Miles.
          15. Duo Milites.

And in the accompts of the constables of Sheffield for this year, we find entries of expenses for providing for the troops of Sir Charles Lucas, Lord Goring, Colonels Eyre and Milward, and Major-General Crawford, while they lay at Sheffield.

Crawford and his party immediately advanced against Staveley-hall, which had been fortified by its owner, the lord Freschvile, and was held for the king; and then dislodged the garrisons of Bolsover-castle and Winfield-manour. Every thing in the north now went against the king. After the defeat on Marston-moor, the war might be said to cease in the north, except that Pontefract-castle long held out, and in the almost romantic exertions of its little valiant garrison furnished a noble subject for the historic muse. The hasty and vain expedition of Lord Digby from Welbeck to join the marquis of Montrose, of which a most animated account is given by the noble historian of these times, served also to keep alive the hopes of the royal party, and to display the zeal of its partisans. Colonel John Bright was left by Crawford governor of Sheffield-castle; but he was soon called to take upon himself a more important command, being appointed military governor of the city of York. His successor at Sheffield was Captain Edward Gill, the head of an old Sheffield family, who in the reign of Elizabeth had removed themselves from the smoke of the town to the fresher and purer air of Norton. He was governor here in 1645 and 1646.

A few documents relating to his government are here printed from the originals in the Wilson collections.

Straford and Tickill.

WHEREAS I have receiv'd an order from Mr John Ellis, These are to will and require you the cunstables of the severall townes hereunder written yt you assiesse, colect and gather the three munths last assessment and areares of the former six munths according to your former wart upon Munday next at Rotharm or Tusday next at Sheffeild unto Mr John Ellis: likewise that you keepe stronge watch and ward, that all such persons as shall repeire from Newworke or any other place infected, be restrained and kept in some convenient place remote from company for a convenient time. Faile you not herein at perill. Middlewood the 12   THOMAS WANEWRIGHT.
        May 1646.
To the Constables of Darfield, Wombwell,
   Hoyland, Wentworth, Ecclesfield, Brad-
   field, and to every of them.

[1] This person was a steward or other superior domestic of the owners of the castle of Sheffield.
[2] A major of foot who died in the time of the war: fellow-soldier and near relative of Major Beaumont. His mother was Susan Beaumont aunt to the governor, and his father of the same name with himself was second son of Stephen Hemsworth of Great Purston near Kippax. Harl. MS. 4630.
[3] p. 112.
[4] Sir John Kaye's passport was in these terms: 'These are to desire all officers and sould[rs] imployed for the service of the King and Parliam[t]

to permitte and suffer the bearer hereof Sr John Key quietlie to passe from hence wth his servants and goods whatsoever, to his owne house at Woodsome, and their to reside wthout any of your letts or molestacons: hee the said Sr John Key and his servants and everie of them conforminge themselves to all ordinances of Parliam', and demeaninge themselves as becometh good subiects. Given under my hand at Sheaffeild this 13th day of August 1644.   L. CRAWFURD.
From the original in the Wilson collections, amongst many papers relating to the compositions and other transactions of the Kayes in the time of the Civil Wars.

Post scriptum—If the moneyes be not in pay at this time and place abovesaid, he will send shoulders presently which will be a greater chardge to the contrye: so he writes in his order.

WHEREAS I was forced to send Nicholas Spateman both to Yorke and Southwell when ye Scots weare last in Bradfeild and Ecclesfeild, and besides ye charges and paynes of Nicholas Spateman was forced to present Leef general Leisley wth a case of kneves and a sword wch cost 3l., for y^e ease of y^e sayd towneships only, I shall therefore desire y^t Bradfeild would disburse to Nicho. Spateman 3l., and Ecclesfeild 1l. 10s., for y^e discharge of y^e forsayd expences.   By me

EDW. GILL.

To y^e Constables of Bradfeild & Ecclesfield.
Sep^t 28th 1646.

___

To the CONSTABLES and INHABITANTS of BRADFEILD.

WHERAS I have received order to quarter 45 soldiers and officers in your towneship this month of Novemb^r and because it is so far distant from ther duty I shall intreate you doe as other places have don, to pay to each soulior 4^d per diem, to pay for this month's quarter; and if money com from Yorke I shall pay it againe. Howsoever I will promis to take them away at the month's end, and to send them to quarter w^t you at any time if their residense wth you may be serviceable to keepe others out.   EDW. GILL.
Sheffield Castle No. 6th 1646.

___

RICHARD BACON,

I HAVE stayed y^e writ, in hope you will pay this money unto y^t Martiall. If you doe not, I must goe on, and shall not be so easily taken of.   Your lo. frend,

ED. GILL.

___

ROB. GREAVES,

I PRAY according to your word, pay unto Martial Bullock the arear of quarter, for it must needes be payd.

ED. GILL.

___

RICHARD BACON,

I WISH & entreat you to come downe about five of the clock this day in the afternoone, & to send word to Sugworth for him to come wth yow (& to Barker howse if you thinke fit) & to meet ether at our Lane head, or in our towne; & call of Ralph Greve.

Sheffeld souldiers were at my house yesterday about what wee will do, & will be certified ether what will be doue & by whom, or otherwayes. And so I rest

Your freind to use,
JOHN MARYOTT.

___

THIS is to require you upon sight herof to apprehe'd y^e persons under written, and bring them, wth y^e names of those y^t harbour them, unto Sheffeild Castle of Saterday nexte. Faile not as you will answer a counsell of warre to be held for y^t purpose.   EDW. GILL.
To y^e Constables of Bradfield.
Edw. Senior.
James Clarke.
Rich. Slithe.
Joseph Goddard.
Richard Stich.
George Hoyland.

___

RECEIVED of Bradfeild of Rich. Bacon for provision in y^e month of No^r for this garrison to y^e valeue of 10l. 2s.
EDW. GILL.

___

To the CONSTABELS of BRIGHTSIDE BIERLEY and BRADFELD and to everey of them.

WHERRAS I have receaved a leter from Robert Bradforth, harbinger, he havinge rec^d c̄mand from the right honorabell the Earle of Penbrough for providing of sartan horses for his

___

[1] Journals of the House of Commons.

Magest's & the Commisinor's use, to goe from Rotheram to Mansfeld: as allso what hay, straw, provender, veales, motons, torkeys, capones, piges, & wild fowle or other provesion that youe can get: & you are desired to bring them in to the howse of Willm Watsone at Rotheram, of Weddensday next by 10 of the clock in the fore nowne. For what yowe soe deliver yowe are to rec. satisfacion for the same, & I doe desire youa to give me acownt in youre prosedings hearein. Given under my hand at Rotheram the 8th of Feabruary 1646.

THOMAS WAINEWRIGHT.
To the Constables of Bricteside Bierley—
one horse. Bradfeild—sixe horesses.

Not only was the castle of Sheffield thus taken military possession of, but the estates by which it was surrounded were seized by parliamentary commissioners. The heads of the house of Howard were adherents of the king, and before the close of the war had retired to the continent. A lease was granted by the commissioners to two persons named Philips and Holland, of the manors of Sheffield, Rotherham, Cowley, Kimberworth, Wadsley, Worral, Whiston, Treeton, Dinnington, &c. They also ordered that 30l. per annum should be paid out of them to Midhope chapel, and 20l. to the minister at Barnsley, which was afterwards increased to 40l. per annum. When the tenants refused to pay their rents to Philips and Holland, the sequestrators appointed persons to assist them in collecting their rents. But this state of things did not continue long: for on the 24th of November 1648, the house of commons voted, that the earl of Arundel should be admitted to the composition of his estate for 6000l., in regard he had suffered losses by the parliament forces; and that the 6000l. should be paid for the use of the navy.

On the 30th of April 1646, a resolution passed the house of commons that the castle of Sheffield should be made untenable: and on the 13th of July in the next year another resolution passed for the sleighting and demolishing of it[1]. We are indebted to Mr. Wilson for having preserved the following notices of proceedings in consequence of these orders of the house.

WHERRAS by vertue of an order from the C̄mittee of the Militia of the county of York, Sheffeld Castle is to bee sleighted and demolished by the country people in this devision : And where the Lordes officers have undertaken att their owne charges to demolish the same, and to save the country from that burthen, wee doe therefore require & charge all and every person & persons that they doe not att any time take or carry awaie from the said Castle any tymber, leade, stones, or any other materialls whatsoever w^thout the consent, leave & approbac̄on of the said Lordes officers; as they will answerr the same att their perills.

Given under our handes the 27th Feb. 1648. Wm BLYTHE[2].
JOHN CROOKE.

___

May 30th 1649. This day I, Andrew Carter, having vewed the remaning part of Sheffeld Castle now standing, being impart teanable, that the enemy may both rong the state & towne:

But acording to my judgment, to mak the said bilding unservesable for warr, and to be imployed for an hoespatall is as foloeth.

Imprimes: the new bilding uppon the south-west part for to be raced down, nex towards the towne.

2^ly the bildings one the south part, fowre windowes to bee maid; betwene each buttra one : in lainkth eaight foot, and in hith eaight foot: And they to bee but three foot and a halfe from the ground. Likewise three windowes more to bee maid out of the second story, of six foot in breadth, & eaight foot in hith: all to be towards the towne.

[2] Of Norton-Lees—a captain in the parliament service.

3ly the ould tower wher the stabls ar: ther to be one window maid be looe from one port hole or loope hole to the other: from the grownd table upward to the port hooles.

4ly all the battlements for to bee not above one foot and a halfe.

This I conceve it will mak it as untenable as other ordenary gentle mene's howses.   AND. CARTER.

AN accompt of demollishing Sheffeild Castle, Januarie the 23 A° 1648.

Materialls of the Castle sould as followeth.

	£	s	d
To Nic. Atkinson, the slate of the hall	1	10	0
Wm Birley, 6 stones	0	1	0
Henry Bulles, 1 dore	0	1	10
Nat. Creswick, for certaine seelinge	0	10	0
John Crooke, for the Territ	5	10	0
Itm 2 bad dores, 2 pieces of wood & one dore, for the schoole	0	10	0
Nic. Atkinson, for slate of the ould backehouse	1	13	4
Edw. Wood, 2 table planckes in the hall 1 frame & a piece of a plancke	0	16	0
Wm Saunder, for ye litle kichen	3	0	0
Nic. Hicke et socios, for all the materialls of the ould kitchenn, savinge lead. Itm to be joyned to that bargen the wood of the round tower	36	0	0
Wm Ward, one table, 2 litle bords	0	3	0
Itm one dore	0	2	8
John Crooke, 2 pieces & 1 plancke	0	3	4
Leonard Wood, 2 dresser tables in ye ould kitchen	0	10	0
Edwd Wood, 2 planckes & one clogge	0	10	0
Wid. Butler & Rob. Twigge, for all the timbr of the ould backe-house	15	0	0

Sept. 10, 1649.

	£	s	d
Wm Birle, 2 sparrs	0	2	0
Mr Stones, the plaster over the ould kitchin	1	0	0
Edwd Wood, a table in ye sentrie house	0	8	0
Rob. Serjison, for certaine ould wood & a doorsted	1	6	8
Rob. Alline, 4 plancks	0	12	0
Thos Rawson, for window-shutts	0	1	0
Nic. Hyckes, for all the tymber of the square tower	14	10	0
Thos Rawson, for ye seelinge over ye gate	2	10	0
Sam. Staniforth, for a table	0	10	0
Edwd Ellise & Jane Staniforth, for certain stone steps & pavers	1	5	0
Edwd Saunderson, for pavers of ye senterie house	0	8	0
Itm for pavers & steps of ye halle	1	0	0
Thos Lee, for halfe a foother of sheete lead	6	0	0
Robt Serjison, for the roofe timbr of the halle	5	10	0
Edwd Wood, one litle stone windows	0	4	0
Joseph Capper, one butteris of stone	1	0	0
Itm more, for certaine stone taken by him forth of ye Castle diches			
Edwd Brewell & R. Paramower, for one butteress	1	0	0
Edwd Brewell, for topstone & other stone not agreed for			
Nichs Hicks, for certaine timber & bords	1	10	0
Tho. Rawson, for an iron grate	0	2	0
Robt Offerton, a stone trough	0	6	8
Nic. Hick, for the roofe over Middelton's chamber	6	0	0
John Dale, for 2 flores in Nic. Spademan's chamb.	3	0	0
Itm for certain roods of ashler unmeasured, & stone steps	0	10	0
Cap. Blithe, for bords & plaister	3	0	0
John Crooke, for bords	3	0	0
Edwd Wood, for the stone of a square room at the halle-end	1	10	0
John Crooke, for barrs of iron & 2 dores	0	7	0
John Dalle & J. Crooke, 2 particõns 30s.			
Rob. Twigge, for a certaine piece of a stone walle	1	5	0
Wm Walton, for 8 joysts	1	0	0
John Crooke, for certaine iron	0	6	0
Jane Staniforth, for wood	3	0	0
Alex. Nodder, a lead	1	10	0
Itm for certaine stone			

	£	s	d
Rob. Brelsforth, 3 somertrees & 8 great joysts	2	4	0
Colonell Bright, 2 flores & 10 great joysts	8	0	0
Nic. Hicke, 10 great joysts	1	6	8
I had of Makine, for top stones & 2 planckes	0	7	0
Thos Wright, for stone	1	5	0
Thos Rawson for 62 stone of sheet lead.			
To ye Manner, one load of bords.			
Wm Cooke & Wm Scargell, for 6 roods of ashler	1	2	0
Wm Cooke, for 2c of lead	1	2	0
Mr Green for 8 stone of lead	0	12	6
John Pallmer & Ja. Staniforth, for 18c ould iron	10	0	0
Rob. Offerton, for lead	1	0	0
John Staniforth, for 4 roods of ashler, 2 dores, 7 pavers, a stone trough, a stone harth			
Rob. Dent, for stones			
Henry Swift, for certain stones			
Geo. Hall had 5 loads of stones			
Hen. Webster had stones also			
John Crooke, for 24 yards of top stones	0	6	0
Rob. Skargell, 14 stones & a half	0	15	0
John Pearson, 15 stone for the use of the Manner			
Wm Birke, for 6 stone & dim. of lead	0	9	0
Nic. Atkinsonne, the stone of the newe breach [bridge] at Castle	4	10	0
Skers, for the wood in the stables	2	5	0
Tho. Skargell, for 4 loads of broken timber from the Parke			
For 20 loads of stones at the Castle			
For a lead pipe that weigheth — stones			

Disbursements 27 of Januarie 1648, aboute makinge the Castle of Sheffeild untenable.

	£	s	d
Paid to 31 workemen, paniars, baskets, ropes, candells, lockes, and other things, as it doth appeare by the note of particulars	7	9	4
Februarie the 3 Aº 1648. Itm pd more to workmen & other severall expences, ut patet per bill	5	19	4
Shors, for dimollishinge all the walle after the water side, & spent at yr bargen makinge	8	10	0
10th Pd more that week	2	19	3
17th Pd more that weeke	2	13	2
24th Pd more that weeke	5	18	0
March the 3d Aº 1648. Pd more this weeke	4	13	6
Let Mic. Wright a walle at thend of the hall to dimollish, & pd	1	13	4
Itm pd Shors for dimollishinge the halle	7	0	0
Itm pd Shors, more for dimollishinge a peece next to Nic. Hicke part, to the towne	2	5	0
Itm pd Shors more for dimollishinge the round of either side ye gate-house	9	1	6
Mich. Wright for dimollishinge ye end of the chappell, & one piller	1	11	0
Hobsons for dimollishinge a wall next the Dungan	6	3	4
John Pearson, plumer, & 2 workmen for worke donne at the Castle	0	13	6
Pd Shores for the dimollishinge of the Castle, accordinge to Mair Carters, for the stone worke	10	0	0
Julie the 7, 1649. Pd Ric. Claitonn carpenter for latinge at Castle	0	11	0
My chargs at Castle in waitinge, & spent aboute the saftie of the lead et ali'	0	13	2
Spent & paid for chargs of wainge up of 20 foothers of lead at Bowtrie, of 2 men, & given to the porters	0	13	6
John Pearson, plumer, for worke done by him & 2 others at Castle	0	10	0
Constantine Noble and Davie Price, for carreinge stones forth of the chamber	0	5	0
Claiton & 3 men & the plumer, for worke donne at Castle, upon bill	0	16	6
For waitinge to the materialls at Castle certaine weekes pd to ye plumer	0	10	0
Richard Claitonn for makinge the wood worke to keepe up the Castle, ye walles beinge let doune March ye 10, 1648. Pd more to severall workmen at Castle & for my chargs for waitinge theare	10	0	0
	6	17	0

17ᵗʰ Pᵈ more to severall workmen for 2 weeks worke donne at Castle £7 12 2

Itm pᵈ Shors for dimollishinge a stere case with certain other peices of walles 0 15 0

The chargs of bringinge Maiʳ Carter from Yorke to vewe the Castle 5 15 0

Pᵈ to Tho. Skargell, for horsmeate, mansmeate & drinke, he beeinge theare 2 daies with his attendance 1 14 6

Aprell the 7, Aᵒ 1649. Pᵈ to severall workmen for that weeke, & for other necessaries, ut patet 5 1 2

14ᵗʰ Paid more for that weeks worke, ut patet 6 5 4

21, Pᵈ more the 21ᵗʰ of Aprell as it doth apeare 4 8 7

28, Pᵈ more the severall workmen, the 28 of Aprell as it doth apeare by yᵉ particulars . 2 17 10

May the 5, 1649. Pᵈ more to the workmen for this weeke 3 0 2

Shores for dimollishinge the crosse walles . . 1 12 6

Pᵈ more the 11ᵗʰ of May to severall workmen . 4 1 8

Edwᵈ Maikine for 16 days worke at Castle . . 0 18 8

To 3 Shors for everie one of them 6 dˢ worke . 1 1 0

For cutinge wood to smilt yᵉ lead 0 13 4

For leadinge the wood forth of yᵉ parke to yᵉ Castle 1 0 0

John Pearson for castinge yᵉ 41 foo. & 3 pigs . 10 7 6

Robᵗ Rawson for waitinge upon yᵉ castinge of the lead, when I could not be theare 0 6 0

My chargs & expences of waitinge of the smilting a fortnet 1 16 0

Pᵈ at severall times to workmen, for takinge up the lead pipes in yᵉ parke & yᵉ orchards . . . 4 14 9

Itm pᵈ for yᵉ cariage of all the pips to yᵉ Manner 1 10 0

John Pearson for hellpinge to loade the pipes . 0 8 8

For the cariage of 41 foo. & 3 pigs of lead to Bawtrie' at 13ˢ pʳ foo. 26 13 0

Spent in ridinge aboute 2 dayes to hire the lead carringe to Bawtrie 0 5 6

Spent in goinge 2 severall times to Bawtrie to get yᵉ lead weighed 0 16 0

To the porters to drinke 2 severall times . . . 0 3 4

To Tho. Rawson for his paines of waitinge to the workmen, & his men to watch upon the night, beeinge there night and daie for a certaine time Octob. the 13, Aᵒ 1649. Pᵈ for 2 dozeon of baskets for yᵉ Castle 2 0 0

baskets for yᵉ Castle 0 4 0

Itm pᵈ the Shores for 5 dˢ worke 0 5 0

Imanewell Halltoun his chargs to Bawtrie aboute yᵉ leade 0 3 6

20ᵗʰ John, Homfrie, & Robt. Shores everie one of them 2 dˢ at 14ᵈ. per diem . . . 0 7 0

30ᵗʰ John Shore, 8 dˢ at 14ᵈ. per diem . . 0 9 4

Homfr. Shore 8 dˢ at 14ᵈ. per diem . . . 0 9 4

Rob. Shore 8 dˢ at 14ᵈ. per diem . . . 0 9 4

Nov. the 10, Aᵒ 1649. John, Homfr. & Rob. Shore for 2 dˢ worke everie one of them . 0 7 0

14ᵗʰ Rich. Claitonn, his sonne, & Edwᵈ Maikine for worke donne by them in cutinge the timber from the walle at Castell, for the fallinge of an oute walle 0 3 6

Tho. Rawson & 3 witnesses yʳ chargs to goe to Justice Wintworth to bynd to yᵉ secions them that stole yᵉ lead at Castle, lyinge forth one night 0 13 6

For watchinge for findinge the theeves, aboute findinge the lead 1 10 0

For dimollishinge of the last dimollishmᵗ . . 1 13 4

Shores more, aboute wallinge up the dores, carri-

inge in the . . . . ., & other worke aboute the Castle, donne by them £0 18 6

Tho. Skargell for 2 dˢ leadinge wood to yᵉ Castle - to melt yᵉ lead into pigges . . . . . .

Mʳ Phillips of Bautrie for weighinge up 41 foothers of lead 1 10 9

Pᵈ Shore that waiteth upon the Castle for coles to keepe a fire theare upon nights 0 1 6

For 3 Shores, 3 dˢ worke when the tennants came in to fill the carts 0 3 6

Spent & paid to 3 men & upon myselfe, lyinge forth one night to waite an oportunitie to search for lead 0 5 0

To 3 Shors for getinge up ould pips at Castle . 0 4 0

To 3 Shors for waitinge to yᵉ Castle 8 weekes, & lyinge there 0 10 0

For coles to yᵉ Castle to make a fire in theire chamb. 0 5 0

For candles 0 2 6

Pᵈ 3 Shores for goinge to yᵉ secions to witnesse against them that stole lead from the Castle . 0 12 0

Tho. Rawson for goinge to yᵉ secions 0 10 0

Januarie the 30, Aᵒ 1649. Pᵈ spent aboute yᵉ entertainment of Maior Carter, hee cominge to vewe the Castell aboute yᵉ dimollishmᵗ . 2 17 9

To 3 Shores for brekinge a windowe at Castle yᵗ Mair Carter did direct to breake through, & for yᵉ waitinge to yᵉ Castle 10 weeks 1 0 0

After all this work of destruction, still sufficient of the old castle remained to encourage its owner to entertain the idea that it might still be used by him as an occasional residence: and the earl of Arundel soon after he had compounded for his estate issued the following order to his agents at Sheffield:

'Mʳ GRIFFITH, John Staniforth and Robert Rawson, I doe hereby require you and every of you to take course and order that the roomths of Sheffeild Castle remayneinge standeinge and not pulled downe be presently well and sufficiently repaired and amended wᵗʰ glasse-windowes, and such other necessary reparations as are needfull, soe that the same be made a fitteing habitation: and to fence the foldsteades and yardes thereto belonging wᵗʰ gates and other materialls. And herein I desire you to take the direction of Mʳ James Webster the elder, or his assignes. And for your disbursments & charges laid forth for & about the same, they shalbe allowed upon your, and every or any of your accompts. And this shalbe your warrant in my behalfe for soe doeing. Given under my hand this fift daye of January Anno Dni 1649.

ARUNDELL & SURRKY.'

Indorsed. 'My Lord's warrant for repairinge the roomes at Sheffield Castle undemolished².'

But it was now too late. Nothing effectual was done, or perhaps could be done. Its ruined walls were never built up again. No establishment was ever afterwards maintained at the castle. The scheme for converting it into an hospital to carry into effect the gracious intentions of the earl of Shrewsbury was abandoned: and from this period the once proud castle of Sheffield was but a heap of shapeless ruins, every year doing something to complete the destruction which the axe of violence had begun. It is to be regretted that when every thing had been done for the

---

¹ This quantity of lead, it appears by other accompts, was bought by Mr. Andrew Morewood, who paid for it 500l.

² I shall subjoin certain documents relating to the management of these estates at this period and a little later.

JOHN STANIFORTH,

Mʏ Lady the Countesse of Arundel died as we are certainly informed the xxiiiiᵗʰ day of May last, according to our English accompt; wherefore I pray you take care that no wood or trees or timber be felled, cut, or carried of the lands at Sheffeild, Rotherham, or in Hallamshire, wᶜʰ were heretofore the lands of the said Countesse, other then what was fallen

before the said xxiiiiᵗʰ day of May for the use of the Iron workes; and that you keepe an exact accompt of all such corn wood, as was uncarried away of the lands before her death.

London 6 June 1654.   Your loving freind,

FAB. PHILIPPS.

WHEREAS some persons pretendinge an interest to the goods and chattells of Allathela late Countesse of Arundell deceased, doe by writinge of notes &c. somon and sollicite the tennants of this Lordshipp of Sheffeild for the payinge of theire arreares of rent, not mencruinge

satisfaction of political jealousy, the rest was not left to time, the *slow* destroyer; and that we still might have been allowed to trace out the foundations at least of that suite of apartments where the royal captive pined away the years of her long seclusion; of the hall where the honoured chieftain of former days held his wassel, or the chapel in which he prayed: and that Sheffield, like its neighbour Pontefract, might still have had its ruined towers to attract, delay, and delight the curious traveller. But an active and industrious manufacturing population makes few sacrifices to taste; and does not long endure the near neighbourhood of plots of ground not occupied by what immediately concerns itself. Its noble owners residing at a distance and rarely visiting Sheffield extended not over it their protection: so that a few vaults are all which now remain to bear witness that such an edifice once stood on what is still however called The Castle-hill.

Still the Manour existed: an edifice less extensive, less splendid, but sufficient to display the magnificent spirit of those by whom it was erected and inhabited. This place had suffered nothing in the late contentions. It does not appear that either party had thought of placing a garrison in it, or that it was ever even a military post: and the Park, the spacious and noble park, which spread around it was still uninclosed. This house was a habitable residence forty or fifty years after the castle had perished. It was occasionally visited by its noble owner; and an agent of the family constantly resided there. In the accompts of the constables of Sheffield under the year 1662 occurs this entry, of which I have met with no satisfactory explanation, ' Charges about a scandall concerning Frenchmen being at Sheffeld Mannor,' immediately following an entry to this effect, ' Charges of souldiers that came to search for armes.' When Sir William Dugdale held his visitation at Sheffield in 1666, he found Mr. Francis Radcliffe residing at the manour, an agent of the Norfolk family, who led him through the half-deserted rooms in which he noted the heraldric insignia of its former possessors still remaining in the windows. It was in this house in 1671 that Dr. Johnston made that collection of letters of the Talbot family to which such frequent reference has been made. I have conversed with those who had heard from persons who had witnessed it, that the duke of Norfolk of the reign of King William and his sister-in-law the Lady Howard used to attend public service at the church at Sheffield, and that the appearance of their carriages on the Park-hill top was the signal to the ringers to begin their final peal. The son of Lady Howard, Thomas duke of Norfolk, in 1706 gave the order for the dismantling of this house and the dispersion of its furniture. In some of the old houses in the neighbourhood are preserved a few heavier and more durable articles of furniture which are traditionally reported to have come from Sheffield manour. In the inventory of its furniture preserved among the Talbot papers no notice is taken of any family-portraits or other paintings either here or at the castle: but if it contained any they were probably removed to Worksop-manour, the only one of the Shrewsbury mansions in the north of England which the dukes of Norfolk maintained, where they would perish in the fire of the 20th of October 1761. When the manour ceased to be the residence of the agents of the Norfolk family, for them and the occasional residence of the duke himself a house was built in the town of Sheffield. This, which stood in the Far-Gate and was commonly known by the name of the Lord's house, has been lately taken down.

When there was no longer any mansion there was no longer any necessity for a park. At the time when the manour was abandoned, the park was divided into farms, and distributed among about twenty tenants.

The native forests of Hallamshire then also felt the power of the spirit of innovation. The most unsparing falls were ordered in every part of the domain. The fine avenues of the park were wholly destroyed, and Fullwood and Riveling rich in native forest trees were deprived of all their ancient sylvan honours.

The fall at this period of two venerable oaks must have been viewed with sensations of more than ordinary regret. Their wonderful magnitude made them the pride of the forest; and their age, having outlasted many generations and some races of the chiefs whose estate they had adorned, themselves still flourishing and vigorous, commanded for them a respect not unallied to the religious feeling. They stood in different parts of the domain: the one on the conduit plain within Sheffield park. Evelyn was informed that this oak stretched its arms on all sides to the distance of forty-five feet or more from the trunk; and was therefore capable of affording shelter to above two hundred horsemen. The other stood, as Evelyn informs us, ' at the upper end of Riveling,' perhaps on the very spot where the towers of the Saxon Waltheof had appeared before they felt the power of an unpitying conqueror. Either for its gigantic appearance or owing to some tradition respecting it not now to be recovered, it had acquired the name of the Lord's Oak. Its bole was twelve yards in girth, exceeding the famous Greendale oak in Welbeck park by three feet: and when it was cut down its top or branches yielded not less than twenty-one cords of wood. This king of the forests was felled in 1690.

The reader owes the pleasure he will receive from the following elegant stanzas of which this sylvan monument is the subject, to a friend of the author who bears a truly filial heart towards the land of his birth, and who has in them beautifully touched upon some of the earlier fortunes of this district.

THE LORD'S OAK.

In all their pride still wave the Wharncliffe's woods,
Still o'er their bowers the summer dews descend,
In freshness flow the Don's translucent floods
High o'er whose banks the rifted rocks ascend;
Still all his hidden brooklets rippling wend
Through mossy banks, and murmur as they flow
Where pensile flowers like bashful virgins bend
To see their beauties in the waves below
That kiss their perfumed lips, and in their blushes glow.

But in the Riveling's solitary vale
Where all seems dead and silent save the stream,
Where no tree waves its branches in the gale,
Nor scarce a blossom woos the summer beam ;
The pilgrim pauses, as the wandering dream
Of time-sepulchred years o'er memory's plain
Slowly returns.....Pursuing still the theme,
He marks the spot where once in grandeur stood
The lordly Oak, sole monarch of the solitude.

Amidst the silende and the loneliness
Of that dark valley where no leaf appears,
He stood the sovereign of the wilderness,
And flourish'd greenly, and without compeers
In strength and beauty, and adorn'd by years:
The earth his footstool—Heaven his canopy—
No Druid's rites he saw, no victim's tears;
But widely there his giant arm unfurl'd
His green and bloodless banner o'er a peaceful world.

Planted by him who waved the vengeful sword
Of conquering William's desolating ire,
A wrath the Saxon long in vain deplored,
Amidst thy city's ruins, HALLAMSHIRE.
And so it grew unscathed by wind or fire,
The red deer's shelter, and the falcon's nest:
Long waved it there, ev'n when the hoary sire
Told how the hand for ages had been blent
th kindred dust that rear'd that sylvan monument.

Where roll'd the confluent rivers at their base
Frowning and dark that chieftain's towers arose,
Th' embattled strength of SHEFFIELD's earlier days,
Pride of his friends and terror of his foes:
Through many a summer's sun and winter's snows
There waved his banner....Long those towers withstood
All that time, war, or tempest could oppose;
Till red Rebellion rear'd his standard there,
Then desolation follow'd through each future year.

In later times rose those baronial Halls
Where once the lights of feudal grandeur shone;
Amidst whose courts the winding serpent crawls,
And makes her nest within the broken throne
Where lordlings sat.—Those bowers are now o'erthrown
Where gentle hands once gather'd freshest flowers
To garland brows that should have worn a crown.
Vanish'd are these, the victims of decay,
His Oak alone remain'd, when they were pass'd away.

Ask ye what fell'd the pride of Riveling's vale?
Ask ye what laid its leafy monarch low?
'Twas not the angry spirit of the gale—
'Twas not the bolt of Heaven that dealt the blow—
Nor slow decay (though full of years)—ah no!
There is a power more fatal far than these—
See where the vale's sad Genius striking low
His viewless harp, mourns its dark loneliness—
Ask there that power's fell name,—he'll say 'twas Avarice.

Peace to his shade who rear'd that goodly tree,
The once proud Castle, and the mouldering Hall—
Green let the memory of the chieftain be,
And honour'd still the name of FURNIVAL.
Let History's faithful hand withdraw the pall
That time has thrown upon the good and brave—
—And let the Muse that still deplores its fall
The sacred page exultingly invoke
That bids it flourish still, the Lord's majestic Oak.

WILLIAM HANDLEY STERNDALE.

CHAPTER VIII.

Modern History of Sheffield.

'BY a survaie of the towne of Sheffeld made the
second daie of Januarie 1615 by twenty four
of the most sufficient inhabitants there, it appeareth
that there are in the towne of Sheffeld 2207 people:
of which there are

725 which are not able to live without the charity of
their neighbours. These are all begging poore.
100 householders which relieve others. These (though
the best sorte) are but poore artificers: among
them there is not one which can keep a teame
on his own land, and not above tenn who have
grounds of their owne that will keepe a cow.
160 householders, not able to relieve others. These
are such (though they beg not) as are not able
to abide the storme of one fortnight's sickness,
but would be thereby driven to beggary.

1222 children and servants of the said householders:
the greatest part of which are such as live of
small wages, and are constrained to worke sore,
to provide them necessaries.'

Such was the state of the town of Sheffield at the
commencement of the seventeenth century! Copies
of this curious document are in many hands; and it
may be that the survey was made with reference to the
charitable intentions of Gilbert earl of Shrewsbury.
There is enough in it to move his compassion; and
the munificent provision which he made. for twenty
of the old and poor inhabitants was doubtless hailed
by such a population as a gift worthy to entitle him to
what indeed he has obtained, an affectionate and grateful remembrance.

But the question arises, how it had happened that

the town of Sheffield was in that state of poverty which the survey discloses: how it had happened that it had rather fallen back than advanced in consequence in the course of the two preceding centuries: and why we find not among its population the merchant, the substantial burgher, such as was to be found at Doncaster and York, and in many other English towns now far below Sheffield in commercial importance. That such a question is to be proposed at the outset of our inquiry into its modern history is the more extraordinary, when we recollect that the immediate vicinity of Sheffield possesses natural advantages of a superior order to those which perhaps any other spot in this island can boast, for that peculiar species of manufacture which has fixed itself there; that it had acquired an extended reputation for those manufactures as early as the reign of Edward III.; and that the princes of the house of Tudor had shown at all times a generous concern for the protection of commerce and the encouragement of those engaged in it.

I shall briefly state what may have been among the reasons.

And, first, the difficulty with which extensive capital can be made available in the Sheffield manufactures; and correspondent to this, the ease with which the operative mechanic can establish himself as an independent manufacturer. The class of journeymen was not wholly unknown; but they were few when compared with the whole number of persons engaged in the trade, which was for the most part carried on by small masters labouring themselves, surrounded by their children and apprentices. Workmen, it is probable, could not have been obtained to fill any extensive manufactory, and to work under the eye and direction and for the profit of one master. The personal attention which in such a state of things was required from the master, was incompatible with any spirited exertions in seeking out the best markets; and the manufacturers of Sheffield, like those of Salisbury at present, (where some portion of the cutlery manufacture still remains,) were content to wait at home for the arrival of the casual purchaser.

The only large commercial concerns connected with the trade of Sheffield were the furnaces and forges in which the iron was prepared for the use of the manufacturer. It was from these works that the fortunes which were made at Sheffield in the seventeenth and early part of the eighteenth centuries were acquired, by gentlemen who were known by the name of ironmasters. But these in the times before the accession of the Stuarts to the throne of England had not contributed to enrich Sheffield: for as they were originally built by the noble lords of the manor, so the works were carried on for their benefit, till the breaking up of their domestic establishment at the castle. The grinding-wheels were also erected on the streams by the lords of the manor; but they seem in these early periods to have been leased out to certain of the manufacturers.

The occupation of so large a portion of the surrounding country, by the parks, chases, and various inclosures of the lords, was another cause of the poverty which the survey describes. There were no wealthy families of gentry inhabiting the parish of Sheffield,

and therefore closely connected with the town, who might supply a deficiency of capital, or engage themselves either in the commerce of Sheffield or in schemes which tended to the advancement of its commercial consequence. In point of fact, when Sir Henry Saint-George held his visitation of the county of York in 1612, there was in the parish only one family, (the Jessops of Broomhall,) who entered their pedigree. And for the same reason it was impossible for a person who had become at all enriched by commerce, and was desirous of establishing himself in the vicinity of the town,—so that while he enjoyed the pleasures of rural occupations he could also pay some attention to his commercial engagements,—to establish himself in the parish of Sheffield. Such persons were compelled to remove themselves wholly from the vicinage.

Sheffield enjoyed not in these times that almost entire monopoly it possesses at present of the staple article of its manufactures—the knife. We had an import trade in that article till the time of Queen Elizabeth; and knyves of Almayne, knyves of France, knyves of Collayne, are among the articles enumerated in the Custom-house rate-books of the time of Henry VIII.[1] Queen Elizabeth in the fifth of her reign laid some restrictions on this import trade[2], but more as it seems with a view to encourage the London manufacturers than those in the country. London was at that time the principal mart for the finer species of cutlery: but beside London, Salisbury, Woodstock, and Godalming were rivals with Sheffield in this department of our national manufactures. We may conclude that the artisans of Sheffield attempted at least to produce the finer kinds of wares, from the present which the earl of Shrewsbury made to his friend Lord Burghley, of 'a case of Hallomshire whittells, beinge suche fruictes as his pore cuntrey afforded with fame throughout the realm[3]:' but it is probable that the manufactures rather consisted of the coarser and inferior kinds; the knives, as Fuller expresses it, which were ' for common use of the country people[4],' and which excited his surprise when he saw them offered at the low price of one penny.

And, lastly, the rules to which the Sheffield manufacturers were in those times subjected, were little calculated to encourage a spirit of commercial enterprise, or to put it in the power of the manufacturers to avail themselves to their full extent of the natural advantages which their situation presented. In the times of which we are speaking, the superintendance of the artificers formed a part of the business of the court-leet of the manor. A jury of cutlers was empannelled with the other juries, whose office it was to assign marks to the different manufacturers wherewith to distinguish their respective wares, to enroll indentures of apprenticeship, and to levy the fines to which persons became subject who wrought in opposition to certain regulations which were agreed upon by the whole fellowship of cutlers, and sanctioned by the lord of the manor. In the court-rolls of the manor of Sheffield of the 7th of Elizabeth these regulations are recited at length: and again more fully in 1590. An abstract of them will show how far they were calculated to give full scope to any spirit of commercial enterprise, and will also throw no inconsiderable light

---

[1] See the Rates, &c. 1545, lately republished in *The British Bibliographer.* [2] Stow, p. 1038.

[3] Lodge, vol. ii. p. 414. [4] *Worthies of England.*—Yorkshire, p. 188.

upon the state of the town and its manufactures in the reign of Elizabeth.

'The actes and ordinaunces made and agreed uppon the firste daye of September, in the twoe and thirteth yere of the reigne of oure Soveraigne Ladye Elizabeth, by the grace of God Quene of England, Fraunce and Ireland, Defendor of the Faithe &c. Aswell by all the hole fellowshippe and company of cutlers and makers of knyves w^thin the Lordshippe of Hallomshire in the countye of Yorke, whose names are particularlye expressed in a sedule hereunto annexed, As alsoe by th'assente of the righte honorable George Erle of Shrewsburye, Lorde and owner of the said Lordshippe of Hallomshire, for the better relief and comodytie of the porer sorte of the said felowshippe.'

The first article makes the strange provision, that no person engaged in the said manufactures, either as a master, servant, or apprentice, shall perform any 'worke apperteyninge to the said scyence or mysterye of cutlers' for eight and twenty days next ensuing the eighth day of August in each year; nor from Christmas to the twenty-third day of January; but shall apply themselves to other labours, 'upon payne of forfeyture for everye offence founde and presented by twelve men of the same felowshippe of the some of twentye shillinges to the use of the said earle his heirs and assignes, to be levyed as other his fines and amercyaments w^thin the said lordshippe have beene accustomed.' 2. No person to exercise the said trade who had not served an apprenticeship of seven years, or been instructed by his father for that term. Penalty forty shillings. 3. No person to have more than one apprentice in his service at one time, nor engage another till the former be in his last year, nor take any for a less term than seven years. Penalty forty shillings. 4. No person occupying any wheel for the grinding of knives to allow of any work being done there during the holiday months. Penalty as before. 5. No occupier of a wheel to suffer any person to grind or glace any knives there who does not reside within the lordship and liberties; on the same penalty. 6. No person to be suffered to exercise the trade who has not sufficiently learned it within the said lordship. Penalty as before. 7. No person to strike any mark upon his wares, but that which is assigned him in the lord's court. Penalty ten shillings. 8. No hafter shall haft any knives for any chapman, hardware-man, or dagger-maker, or other person not dwelling within the liberties. Penalty twenty shillings. 9. Nor shall knife blades be sold to any person not dwelling in the liberties. Penalty six shillings and eightpence. 10. No journeyman to be employed under the age of twenty, except such as shall be allowed by the jury, or who have been apprentices or taught by their fathers. Penalty forty shillings. 11. No person who has not served an apprenticeship or been instructed by his father, to set up in the trade, except he first pay to 'the jury or twelfe men of the cutler's occupation for the time being,' five pounds, the one half for the earl's use, the other half for the poor of the said corporation, to be distributed by the jury. Penalty forty shillings. 12. Every apprentice to be presented to the jury within one year, and the indentures to be sealed before them. At the expiration of the term each apprentice to bring his indentures to the jury, and to subscribe the rules here established. Penalty ten shillings. 13. All persons summoned to serve upon the jury, to appear on pain of forfeiting six shillings and eight-pence. 14.

Each juryman to appear when summoned by the foreman, to settle questions touching these ordinances; on the like penalty. The 15th article gives power to the jury, with the concurrence of the lord or his 'learned steward' for the time being, to make fresh regulations. 16. At the great court of the earl holden at Sheffield in Easter week, twelve men of the said scyence and mystery, to be nominated by the earl or his learned steward, to inquire into offences, and to punish offenders. The last article declares, that if these ordinances do not prove so beneficial as is expected to the poorer sort, the earl may make them or any of them void.

There is something amiable in the spirit of attention to the condition of the poor in which these regulations are conceived: and when we consider how slowly the best established truths in political œconomy make their way even in more enlightened times, we need not be surprised that two centuries ago it was not perceived that by giving a wider scope to the spirit of commercial enterprise, and by an encouragement which in its immediate operation was directed to the class of those to whom the epithet *poor* could not be applied,—but who in those times at Sheffield were the rich,—the most efficient and valuable assistance would be rendered to the poorer members of society. We may observe in them also a laudable attention to the maintenance of that reputation which the manufactures of Hallamshire had obtained; and I wish I could add that the records of the manor-court did not present instances in which in some of their best points these ordinances were violated. The cutler's jury were frequently called on to levy the penalties for unworkmanly wares; and this, combined with some other circumstances, led to the first great alteration in the state of the modern town of Sheffield; the incorporating of its manufacturing population.

The powers of a lord of a manor in his court-leet are somewhat undefined. That he should interfere with the internal concerns of a manufacturing neighbourhood was a right founded only upon usage: and it is not improbable that among a people who have always been impatient of acquiescence in authorities that were questionable, there were some,—some among the fair dealers and some among the fraudulent manufacturers, —who were disposed to call in question the expediency and the authority of the ordinances. As long as there was the personal presence of the lord to support them, it might be easy to maintain their authority; but when that influence was withdrawn, it would become more necessary to place the ordinances upon a new and less questionable basis. As early as March 1621, only four years after the death of Gilbert earl of Shrewsbury, a bill was presented to parliament entitled, 'for the good order and government of the cutlers in Hallamshire:' but we find no further notice of it in the journals after it had been read the first time. On the 25th of March 1624, Sir John Savile presented a second bill to the house of commons; and this on the 3d of April was committed to the said Sir John Savile, the burgesses for York, Cumberland, Northumberland, Derby, and Nottingham, Mr. Bankes and Mr. Darcy. On the 12th, Mr. Brooke reported on the bill; the alterations were twice read, and it was ordered to be engrossed. It passed the commons on the 23d; and as we hear no more of it in their journals, it probably received as a whole the sanction of the lords.

The act is entitled, ' An act for the good order and government of the makers of knives, sickles, shears, scissors, and other cutlery wares in Hallamshire, in the county of York, and parts near adjoining:' and in its preamble is set forth, that whereas the greatest part of the inhabitants of those parts consist of persons engaged in the different departments of the cutlery manufacture, and that by their industry and labour they have not only gained the reputation of great skill and dexterity in the said faculty, but have relieved and maintained their families, and have been enabled to set on work many poor men inhabiting thereabout, who have very small means or maintenance of living, other than by their hard daily labour as workmen to the said cutlers, and have made knives of the best edge, wherewith they served the most part of this kingdom and other foreign countries; untill now of late that divers persons using the same profession in and about the said lordship and liberty, and within six miles compass of the same, not being subject to any rule, government, or search of any others of skill in those manufactures, have refused to submit themselves to any order, ordinance, or search, but every workman has taken liberty to himself to take as many apprentices and for what term of years he pleases; whereby and by the multitude of workmen the whole trade and the exact skill formerly exercised therein is like in a short time to be overthrown: by means of which want of government and search, the said workmen holding themselves free and exempt from all search and correction, are thereby emboldened, and do make much deceitful and unworkmanly wares, and sell the same in divers parts of the kingdom, to the great deceit of his majesty's subjects, and scandal of the Cutlers in that lordship and liberty, and disgrace and hindrance of the sale of cutlery and iron and steel wares there made, and to the great impoverishment, ruin and overthrow of multitudes of poor people; which offenders not being subject under any oversight, survey or authority, do pass unpunished for their offences, abuses and misdemeanors.—For the remedy whereof it is enacted, that all persons engaged in those manufactures within the aforesaid limits shall form one body politic, perpetual and incorporate, of one master, two wardens, six searchers, twenty-four assistants, and the rest commonalty of the said company of cutlers of the lordship of Hallamshire: that the existing master, wardens, searchers, and assistants, shall choose their successors every year on the feast day of Saint Bartholomew: that *Robert Sorsby* be the first master, and continue in office till the feast of Saint Bartholomew next ensuing the passing of the act, and for one whole year after: that *Godfrey Birley* and *John Rawson* be the first wardens; *William Warter, William Creswick, Thomas Philipot, Robert Wilkinson* of Hills, *John Dungworth,* and *John Webster,* be the first searchers; and that *William Webster, Thomas Creswick* sen., *George Smedley, James Creswick, Robert Stacy, Edward Creswick, Thomas Wright* sen., *Henry Dyson, George Wilkinson, Lawrence Pearson* sen., *George Barnsley, Edmund Swift, Robert Carr, Robert Barnsley, William Wylde, Richard Jackson, Lawrence Pearson* jun., *Thomas Smyth, Thomas Crofts, Thomas Milward, George Dam, Thomas Pearson, Thomas Parkyn,* and *Thomas Haworth,* be the first four-and-twenty assistants: that in case of the death, or

removal for just cause, of any officer of the company, those who remain may elect a successor; and that all the officers shall make oath for the proper discharge of their respective duties.—It is further enacted, that it shall be lawful for the said officers or the greater part of them, to make such laws, acts, ordinances and constitutions as to them shall appear good and wholesome, profitable, honest and necessary for the good order, rule and government of all the members of the said company, their apprentices and servants, and to levy reasonable penalties on those who neglect to observe them, the money so raised to be given to the poor of the said corporation. There is some relaxation of the strictness of the former ordinances in relation to apprentices, the members of the corporation being allowed to take a second apprentice when the first has served five years, nor is the employment of sons of freemen to interfere with the master's right to take apprentices; but none are to be taken for a shorter term than seven years, nor for a term which will expire before the apprentice shall have attained the age of twenty-one. All persons engaged in the said businesses to make the edge of all steel instruments manufactured by them of steel and steel only, and to strike on their wares such mark, and such only, as should be assigned to them by the officers of the company, on certain penalties, which and all penalties imposed in virtue of this act may be recovered in any of his majesty's courts at Westminster, or in any court of record in the counties of York or Derby.

Thus was the government of the persons engaged in the staple business of the neighbourhood placed upon a firm and permanent basis. How far the establishment of any restrictive corporate laws is a benefit to any branch of commerce has been made a question; and how far Hallamshire has benefited by those provided for her artisans. But we cannot peruse the act without perceiving how very little the legislature of King James's time chose to interfere with the internal concerns of the persons incorporated by this act, going a very little way beyond the establishment of a company of thirty-three persons, all interested in the prosperity of the trade, and themselves subject to any regulations they might think it expedient to propose, and not holding their situations for life, but giving way in part at least to others at the expiration of the year. Such persons could not be supposed to have an interest distinct from that of the great body of the manufacturers, nor would they propose any restrictive measures which in their judgement were not called for by the circumstances of the times. Three hundred and sixty persons immediately enrolled themselves members of the company, and by their proper officers proceeded to enact such laws as at that time appeared to be convenient and necessary. They passed a law that all persons should serve the offices to which they were regularly chosen, should attend necessary meetings, and answer summonses. To the six searchers power was given to enter dwelling-houses where they had reason to suppose that deceitful wares were concealed. The restrictions on taking apprentices, already sufficiently rigid, were made yet more so. The members of the body were prohibited from working for strangers, or selling to them unfinished wares. Two-pence annually was required from every member of the corporation under the description of mark-rent. To the officers of the company were added a clerk and a beadle. Eighty-one freemen were admitted in the second year, thirty-four in the third, and thirty was from that time the average of new members till the Civil Wars.

It will be observed, that the powers of the corporate officers extend not only throughout Hallamshire, but, every where within six miles compass of the same. This arose from the difficulty which has always existed of ascertaining the precise limits of that district. The manufacture of one article mentioned in the preamble to the act, sickles, has scarcely at any time been found within any supposed limits of Hallamshire. It was then as now confined for the most part to Ridgway, Troway, and Norton, villages in the county of Derby. It was also doubtless the intention of the framers of the act, that all persons within the limits who were engaged in the manufacture of any species of iron instruments should be comprehended under it. But it was for some time a question, whether the makers of scythes, and still more whether the makers of files, were subject to the control of the company. It was settled that they were members of the corporation. The company had at first no property. But the lords of the manor having given up to them the little advantage they derived from the amercements laid by the cutlers' jury, and a certain income being derived from the fees on indentures, admissions to the freedom of the corporation, and the mark-rents, the company were enabled to build a hall, which was erected on the site of some old burgage houses of the town of Sheffield opposite the south side of the parish church. This was accomplished in 1638.

The early part of the seventeenth century was distinguished by the accomplishment of three important public works, of which a more convenient opportunity of speaking in detail will occur hereafter; namely, the establishment of a grammar-school, the renewal of public worship in the old chapel of Ecclesall, and the foundation in 1629 of a chapel at Attercliffe. The remainder of the century presents us with nothing material in the history of the town that has not been already given in the preceding chapter. I shall subjoin a few *memorabilia minora* of this century, in extracts from the accompts of the town's-trustees of Sheffield, made by the late Mr. Vincent Eyre.

	£	s	d
1647. Paid to Thomas Skargell for beef, mutton and lambe, for a present for the Lord of Arundell	4	10	0
1656. To two trumpeters at the proclamation of the Lord Protector	0	10	0
To Edw. Berry and four other musitians at that time	1	0	0
To the ringers and others	1	9	0
1658. For wine which was sent when the townsmen went to visit the Lord of Arundel	1	1	0
1661. Spent by the townsmen when the King was proclaimed	8	13	4
1673. Paid for ringing and drink &c. when word came of my Lord's being Earl Marshall	1	8	0
1680. Paid M⁻ Pegg for wine sent to the Earl of Arundel	0	18	0
To Stephen Allen for a veale and mutton to send to him	1	8	6
Paid the ringers for ringing when the Duke of Norfolk was over	0	3	0
1700. Paid M⁻ Renny the first payment towards building the Town-hall	50	0	0

This building stood at the south-east corner of the parish churchyard; and was used for public meetings of the inhabitants, the holding of the quarter-sessions, and of the manor-courts. Below the hall were prisons for the occasional reception of the accused and the convicted.

To the above may be added from the parish-register:

'Paid November the 22th, 1666, by M⁻ John Lee to John Wynch by order of the Lord Mayor of London, the summe of twentie-seaven pounds and tenn shillings, being collected in the towne and parish of Sheffeld towards the reliefe of those persons who have beene greate sufferers by the late sad fire within the city of London.'

In the constables' accompts 1673—1675:

	£	s	d
Charges expended about the insurrection about measures, and the sessions for the same	5	8	2¼
Charges about the train band soldiers to Doncaster to meet the Duke of Buckingham	2	6	10

And lastly, in the year 1682, the town was thrown into great alarm by an attempt made by Sir Simon Degge and Thomas Eyre, esquire, to bring Sheffield within the scope of the Peverel-court, an obsolete court then lately revived in the county of Derby. The officers of the corporation and the inhabitants at large as with one voice joined in a petition to the Duke of Norfolk, entreating him to use his authority and influence against what they considered an innovation and grievance. The project was relinquished, for which indeed there could originally have been small or rather no pretence.

A comparison of the number of marriages in the first decennary of the seventeenth century, and the corresponding period of the eighteenth will show that there had been a great increase in the population of the parish of Sheffield between the two periods. In the former there were 417, in the latter decennary 942. Early in the eighteenth century we find the persons employed in the incorporated trades of Hallamshire estimated by one of themselves at six thousand. It was supposed that there were about that time several thousand persons more in and about Sheffield engaged in different departments of the iron-trade not within the scope of the corporate laws, such as 'smiths, anvil-makers, edge-tool-makers, and nailors[1].' The goods manufactured amounted in value *communibus annis* to above 100,000*l.*, and of these it was supposed that about one half were exported. Fifteen hundred tons of Hallamshire manufactures were sent every year from Sheffield to Doncaster, along ways which are described in the pamphlet quoted below as almost impassable, to be forwarded by water to Hull. But still there were no capitalists engaged in the Sheffield manufactures. The only commercial concerns which when considered individually could be called large, were the forges and other works for preparing the raw material for the use of the manufacturer. There were no correspondencies opened with houses on the continent. The exports were chiefly made by London merchants, who had their agents residing at Sheffield under the denomination of factors, whose office it was to receive, or as it was called to take in, for their superiors the goods of the petty manufacturers. The merchant, that is a person wholly un

---

[1] See a rare pamphlet, entitled, The Methods proposed for making the river Dunn navigable, and the objections to it answered, &c. 4to, 1723, p. 13, 14.

connected with the manufacture of the article in which he deals, and concerned only with its dispersion, was still unknown among the residents of Sheffield. Even the home-consumption was principally supplied by means of the London houses, the manufacturers of Sheffield scarcely doing more than sending small ventures to Chester, Bristol, and some other places at the time of their annual fairs.

The want of a due mixture of persons well-educated and of a superior situation in life, rendered Sheffield at this period less distinguished by the elegancies and refinements of social life than by feelings of independence and rugged honesty, by hospitality, and a rude and boisterous conviviality. There were no assemblies. There was no theatre. The principal amusements of the place were the sports at the Castle bowling-green, and social meetings at the taverns. A very small number of books kept in the vestry of the parish church was the only library. In the public buildings—the town-hall, the boys' charity-school, and the Dissenters' chapel, erected about this time—there was not the least attention paid to architectural decoration. The dwelling-houses were plain substantial buildings, with here and there in front a carving of the heraldric insignia of the London incorporated cutlers, which those of Sheffield have appropriated to themselves: and the house in the Far-gate was perhaps a solitary instance, which exhibited the old and excellent adage over its door, ' Qui nemini bonus est sibi pessimus.'

The severe labour required in some departments of the Sheffield manufactures, which is now eased by improvements in the machinery employed, is said to have occasioned an unusual number of cases of distorted limbs.

There was little communication between Sheffield and the neighbouring towns. Few persons travelled for amusement along roads that were adapted rather to the use of the pack-horses, who pursued their weekly journey to the metropolis by Heeley and Newfield-green, than to the light vehicle, or even to the stage-waggon, which was first established on the road about the beginning of the century by one Wright of Mansfield.

The town at the commencement of the eighteenth century consisted of the following streets, lanes, and passages.

High Street.	Campo Lane.
Far-Gate.	Hartshead.
Balm Green.	Snig Hill.
Hollin Lane or Blind Lane.	Irish Cross.
Red Croft.	New Hall Street[1].
Town-head Street.	Mill Sands.
Pinfold Lane.	The Under Water.
Church Lane.	The Isle.
Ratten Row.	Water Lane.
Broad Lane.	Castle Green.
West Bar.	Castle Green Head.
West Bar Green.	Castle Fold.
Scargell Croft.	Castle Hill.
Fig-tree Lane or New Street.	Wain Gate.
	Bull Stake.

Dixon Lane.	Pudding Lane[2] or King Street.
Shude Hill.	
The Ponds.	True Love's Gutter.
Jehu Lane.	

The display of a new spirit of enterprise and improvement at Sheffield may be referred to about the year 1720; and one of its first efforts was the improvement of the navigation of the river Don.

There were at that period many persons at Sheffield who were aware that one great impediment to the extension of the commerce of the town was the difficulty of communication with the capital, and with the two ports of Liverpool and Hull. The inhabitants of Lancashire were making great improvements in the navigation of the river Mersey; and there was a project much canvassed at Sheffield of making an excellent carriage-road over the East-moors to the first wharf constructed on that river. But the attention of the people of Sheffield was naturally more immediately turned to their own river; and it was soon found to be both practicable and expedient to make the stream which was so serviceable to the manufacturers in the preparation of their wares, the means also of conveying them, when finished, to a distant market.

The earliest record concerning the navigation of the river Don is a petition presented to parliament in the 20th year of King Henry VI. A.D. 1442. The commons of the counties of York, Lincoln, Nottingham, and Derby, presented to the king, to wit, that ' ther is, and of longe tyme hath been an usuall and a commune passage fro dyvers and many parties of the said countees, unto the citees of York, Hull, Hedon, Holdernes, Beverley, Barton and Grymesby, and so forth, by the hie see, by the costes, unto London and elles where, with all maner of shippes charged with wolle, leed, stone, tymbre, vitaille, fewaille, and many othir marchandises, by a streme called the Dike, in the counte of York, that daiely ebbith and floweth; over whiche streem ys made a brigge of tymbre called Turn-brigg, in the parisshe of Snayth in the same counte, so lowe, so ner the streem, so narrowe and so strayte in the archees, that ther is, and of long tyme hath been, a right perilous passage, and ofte tymes perisshinge of dyvers shippes; and atte every tyme of creteyne and abundaunce of water, ther may no shippees passe under the seid brigge, by the space of half a yere or more,' to the great injury and inconvenience of the neighbourhood, as well as to the diminishing of the king's revenue: The petitioners therefore pray the parliament to beseech the king to grant, with the concurrence of parliament, license to any persons of the said counties, to take down the said bridge, and build another with a moveable leaf in the centre for the passage of vessels, to prohibit persons from stopping the course of the stream by stones, or piles, or ' any othir disceyte,' and to confirm to the shipmen passing along the said river the right they had of old time enjoyed, of having towing paths on the banks of the said river. Which petition was accordingly presented by parliament, and was granted by the king in all points[3]:

At this period the river Dike or Don was not navigable higher than Stainford, where was the wharf

---

[1] So called from the first Dissenters' chapel which stood in this part of the town on the site of Hollis's Hospital, and was known by the name of the New Hall.

[2] For the meaning of this name see Stow's London, p. 212.
[3] Rolls of Parliament, A.D. 1442, 20 Hen. VI. vol. v. p. 44.

for the merchants of Doncaster, and in general for the inhabitants of the higher parts of the valley. King Edward III. granted a charter for a market and fair at Stainford, at the particular request of his son Edmund duke of York, to whom he had given the town amongst other property that had belonged to the earls of Warren[1]. Only some smaller craft were accustomed to come up the river as high as Doncaster at particular seasons of the year, and occasionally vessels of a greater burthen.

It does not appear that any thing was done for the improvement of the navigation of the river till the inhabitants of Sheffield began to turn their attention to it as opening for them an easy communication with the port of Hull, and from thence with London. The manufacturing population of Sheffield acting by their corporate officers, engaged the concurrence of the corporation of Doncaster, and in the years 1721 and 1722 a digested scheme was laid before the public. It was by this scheme proposed, that the river should be made navigable for vessels of thirty tons burthen as high as Doncaster, and from Doncaster to Sheffield for vessels of twenty tons. It was proposed that the corporation of Doncaster should undertake the performance of the former part of the scheme, and that the latter should be effected by the company of cutlers of Hallamshire.

Such was the first design. The scheme met, as was probably foreseen, with much opposition. The country gentlemen whose estates lay contiguous to the river saw nothing in it but an unwelcome intrusion, and were not convinced, or affected not to be so, by the arguments of its promoters, of the general benefit which would result from it. It was in vain that they alleged that thus the Sheffield manufactures would be brought more cheaply to market; that encouragement would be given to what must be allowed to be an important branch of our national manufactures—the iron-trade of Sheffield; that a more easy conveyance would thus be obtained for the lead produced in the lead-districts of Derbyshire, and also for mill-stones, with which useful article it appears that the midland and southern counties of England were chiefly supplied from quarries five miles from Sheffield; that thus would be opened a more ready means of conveyance for the marble and rotten-stone of the Peak and the cheese and butter of Cheshire to London and other places; and that the owners of estates on its banks, instead of suffering any detriment from the measure, would receive a material advantage in the opportunity which would be afforded of bringing to them lime and coal at so cheap a rate. All these and divers other benefits to be expected from the measure, are set forth in the pamphlet lately quoted, but they failed to make any favourable impression on the minds of the original opposers of the measure.

By degrees, however, these reasons, together with some concessions on the part of the projectors to meet individual interests, brought off some of those persons whose opposition was most dreaded, and particularly Lord Frederick Howard, whose estates near Rotherham were supposed to lie most obnoxious to injury. But it was not till 1726 that a bill for the purpose was presented to parliament. On the 11th day of March

it was read a first time in the house of commons. The bill was contested in all its stages. Many of the neighbouring country gentlemen opposed it with great earnestness; and the inhabitants of Bawtry and Gainsborough, who thought that their interests would be affected by it, petitioned parliament in opposition to it. But the public advantage was too evident, and was so forcibly represented by Mr. Samuel Shore and Mr. John Smith, the two deputies from Sheffield appointed to watch the progress of the bill, in the committees of the house, and in personal conversations with members, that the bill passed the commons on the 16th of April, and the lords on the 6th of May following[2]. One of the Sheffield deputies left London before the fate of the bill was quite decided: the other was met at Mansfield by a large party of gentlemen from Sheffield, and made a sort of triumphant entry into the town whose interest he was thought to have very essentially promoted.

A part of the original design had, however, been abandoned. The act now passed only empowered the company of cutlers of Hallamshire to make the river navigable from a place called Holm-stile in Doncaster to the utmost extent of Tinsley westward, that is to within three miles of the town of Sheffield; and gave them power to improve and keep in repair the high-way from Sheffield to Tinsley. This part of the original project was probably the more willingly abandoned, as it appears from the map published with the original scheme, that the works upon the river between Tinsley and Sheffield were thought to present an insuperable objection to the rendering that part of the stream fit for the passage of vessels; and it was proposed that a canal should be cut from the forge at Brightside to pass on the left bank of the river and to join the stream at the Walk-mill, a project which must have been attended with a great expense, if indeed it were at all practicable in the hands of the engineers of that early period.

The corporation of Doncaster obtained the necessary powers for the improvement of the river below that town, namely, from Holm-stile to Wilsick-house in the parish of Barnby-Don, by an act passed in the next session of parliament.

But in works so extensive as this, to reconcile private interests and to procure acts of parliament is not all that is to be done. Unexpected difficulties arose; and in 1732 the two corporations were glad to relieve themselves from powers which they had taken so much pains to acquire. It was now proposed that they should consolidate their interests, and transfer them in a hundred and fifty shares to private individuals. They applied to parliament to sanction this arrangement; and in that year an act was passed transferring the powers already granted to the two corporations to them, who were incorporated under the name of 'The company of proprietors of the navigation of the river Don.' In 1739 the company obtained a fourth act, which empowered them to improve the navigation of the river from Wilsick-house to Fishlake-Ferry.—Under these several acts of parliament, the river Don was made fit for the passage of barges of considerable burthen from Tinsley to Fishlake, from

[1] De la Pryme's Collections, amongst Warburton's MSS. in the Lansdown Library, vol. ix. f. 53.

[2] The dates and some other particulars are from the private correspondence of Mr. Smith.

whence there was a constant communication open with the Humber, to the great benefit of the town and commerce of Sheffield, and eventually of those who had embarked in what for many years was thought a hazardous and unpromising undertaking.

The reader may be gratified by a list of the original adventurers.

Shares.		Shares.	
6	Cutlers Company.	1	Francis Sitwell.
10	Corporation of Doncaster.	1	William Brookes.
10	Town's Trustees of Shef-	1	Benjamin Roberts jun.
	field.	2	Benjamin Greaves.
1	James Crawshaw senior.	2	Joseph Steer.
2	Samuel Shore senior.	2	Thomas Buck.
3	John Brown.	1	John Allen.
2	Thomas Heaton.	2	Nicholas Broadbent.
2	John Smith.	2	Thomas Wilson.
2	Samuel Shore junior.	1	Joseph Turner.
1	Lydia Shore.	1	John Dickson.
2	John Battie.	2	John Roebuck.
2	John Gell.	1	Jonathan Moore.
2	Thomas Middleton.	1	Joshua Matthewman.
4	William Parkin.	1	Thomas Cawton.
2	Trustees of Hollis's Hos-	1	John Morton.
	pital.	4	George Bradshaw.
1	William Sitwell.	2	William Dickson.
1	William Wildman.	3	Thomas Rayney.
1	Charles Wright.	1	John Cowley.
1	James Crawshaw junior.	1	Richard Fayram.
1	Ann Parkin.	1	John Smith.
2	Richard Goodwin.	1	Ann Heaton.
1	Elizabeth Drake.	1	William Mawhood.
2	Christopher Robinson.	3	John Arthur.
6	William Steer.	1	Richard Whitaker.
4	John Dossie.	1	John Beale.
8	John Balguy.	1	Thomas Cooper.
1	John Drake.	1	John Nodder.
5	Samuel Staniforth.	1	George Steer.
3	John Fell.	8	Henry Broadhead.
1	Elias Wadsworth.	2	Thomas Hardcastle.
1	Matthew Charlton.	2	John Newsom.
1	Thomas Short.	1	Charles Arthur.
1	John Ellison.	5	Richard Ellison.
1	William Lyon.		

Another proof of the public spirit which began to manifest itself in the reign of George I. was the erection of Saint Paul's church, a spacious and handsome edifice which was built in 1720, though not opened for public worship till 1740.

The year 1742 is memorable in the history of Sheffield for the introduction of a new manufacture which has become a formidable rival to the ancient and staple manufactures of the neighbourhood, or rather an effective auxiliary in advancing the town of Sheffield to the rank it now holds among the commercial towns of this great empire.

It was in that year that Mr. Thomas Bolsover, an ingenious mechanic, when employed to repair the handle of a knife which was composed partly of silver and partly of copper, was struck with the possibility of uniting the two metals so as to form a cheap substance, which should present only an exterior of silver, and which might therefore be used in the manufacture of various articles in which silver had before been solely employed. He began a manufacture of articles made of this material, but confined himself to buttons,

snuff-boxes, and other light and small articles. Like many other first inventors he probably did not see the full value of his discovery, and it was reserved for another member of the corporation of cutlers of Sheffield, Mr. Joseph Hancock, to show to what other uses the copper plated in this new method might be applied, and how successfully it was possible to imitate the finest and most richly embossed plate. He employed it in the manufacture of candlesticks, tea-pots, waiters, and most of the old decorations of the side-board, which previously to his time had been formed only of wrought silver. The importance of the discovery now began to be fully understood; various companies were formed; workmen were easily procured from among the ingenious mechanics of Sheffield; while the streams in the neighbourhood furnished opportunities for erecting mills for the rolling out the metals. Birmingham early obtained a share in this lucrative manufacture; but the honour of the invention belongs to Sheffield, as it is supposed to stand unrivalled in the extent to which the manufacture is carried, and the elegance and durability of its productions.

This naturally introduced a share in the manufacture of silver-plate: and for the encouragement of this manufacture an act was passed in 1773, by which the persons engaged in it were relieved from the necessity of sending every article to London, and an assay office was established in the town, which was opened on the 20th of September 1773[1].

Sheffield has also (as a consequence of the introduction of the manufacture of articles plated with silver) obtained a very considerable share of an important branch of our national commerce—the refining of the precious metals and the separating them from other substances to which they were accidentally united. This business was first introduced and carried to a great extent by Mr. John Read, who settled at Sheffield about the year 1765.

That small but useful article the button was among the articles of Sheffield manufacture in the seventeenth century: and it formed a very considerable branch of the trade of the town soon after the discovery made by Mr. Bolsover.

And last and least, but not wholly to be passed over, the beautiful forms of many of the articles manufactured in the plated metal have been imitated in a kind of pewter, called Britannia metal, in which there has been for many years an extensive home and export trade.

The advance of the rebels in 1745 had no other effect upon Sheffield but to produce a temporary panic. About the year 1758 the extensive lead-works on the Porter were begun: the first public brewery was established: and a silk-mill was erected near the Don, the machinery of which was soon after applied to the spinning of cotton. But the cotton-trade has made no great progress at Sheffield, being confined to the single factory which was first erected; enlarged indeed, when rising from its ashes after two successive conflagrations.

It was not till near the beginning of the reign of his present majesty that any great improvement was

---

[1] I have been favoured with the following account of the quantity of wrought plate assayed at this office at various periods.

	lb.	oz.	dwt.
In the year ending 30th of June 1775	3010	10	9
30th of June 1781	2569	11	5

	lb.	oz.	dwt.
In the year ending 30th of June 1790	3079	4	1
30th of June 1801	3848	6	12
30th of June 1811	3882	1	4
30th of June 1818	6214	8	11

manifested in the taste and manners of the inhabitants of Sheffield, or in the management of their greatly increased commerce. No communication had been established with the metropolis by means of coaches. The roads on many sides of the town were rough and inconvenient. No fresh depository of books had been proposed. Between 1740 and 1760 several attempts had been made to establish a weekly newspaper, but without success; and the public were disposed to acquiesce in an arrangement of Ward's, to circulate in Sheffield on the Monday the Northampton Mercury which was printed in that town on the Saturday. From the year 1733 the assemblies were held in two rooms of the boys charity school, where the company enjoyed conversation or the mazy dance by light, not of wax, which beamed from sconces of tin. The manufacturers were still their own merchants; superintending one day the detail of their manufactory, and perhaps themselves taking a part in the manual operations which were going on there, and another engaged in negotiations with a distant purchaser. There was little communication with the gentry of the surrounding neighbourhood, who rarely visited Sheffield except at the annual feast given by the company of cutlers.

But the trade, the population, and the buildings of the town continued regularly to advance: and in the first ten years of the present reign very material changes for the better were to be observed at Sheffield. Some of the persons whose fathers had been manufacturers, established themselves in the character of merchants and general dealers in the long list of articles made at Sheffield. They employed considerable capitals, and opened extensive correspondencies immediately with houses on the continent and in America. Few were the instances in which these undertakings were not successful; and the town soon began to experience the benefit of a direct commerce with distant countries, in the erection of warehouses on a scale that had never before been witnessed; in the projection and formation of new streets; in the villas which were seen arising in the vicinity of the town; and in the introduction of some of the refinements and elegancies of social life. The roads were improved. A regular and quick communication with the metropolis was formed. A bank was established. A subscription library was opened on the plan of one formed a short time before at Leeds: and in 1762 a handsome suite of rooms was prepared for balls and assemblies, to which was soon after annexed a theatre, with scenery and decorations not inferior to those of any provincial theatre.

From the blow which it received by the American war, Sheffield seemed to rise with renovated strength. The town had the good fortune to find in the earl of Surrey (the late duke of Norfolk), who in 1777 became owner of the vast interest which his family enjoyed at Sheffield, a nobleman who was disposed to encourage its growth and prosperity. The extension of our towns has seldom proceeded according to any previously concerted plan, but by the caprice or convenience of the individual proprietors of the soil. Such was the case at Sheffield. As its commerce was extended, and population increased, streets were lengthened, and new ones added in every direction, without the least attention to uniformity and order. The ways and passages which had been left by our fore-

fathers, and the ground which had been set apart by them for places of public concourse, were ill adapted to the convenience of a population exceeding the ancient population of Sheffield in a six-fold proportion. This inconvenience was more peculiarly felt in and about the market-place, which remained in its old situation within a stone's-throw of the castle. About the time of the conclusion of the American war, when commerce began to revive, the principal inhabitants of the town joined in a petition to the earl of Surrey, owner of the market, that he would take measures for the improvement of the market-place and the adjacent passages; with which his lordship was graciously pleased to comply: and in 1784 he applied to parliament, and obtained an act under which he was empowered to purchase various private interests in that part of the town in which the market was held, to take down the ancient stalls and other buildings pertaining to the market, and to destroy the old slaughter-houses which were then most offensively situated in the very centre of the town, and close to the butchers' shambles. He was also empowered to erect another market-place on the same site, and to widen the adjacent streets: the whole of the improvements to be conducted under the inspection and subject to the regulation of the principal inhabitants, who were nominated in the act commissioners for that purpose. The earl was further authorized to remove the market for live cattle from the Bull-stake, (now called the Hay-market,) where it had been usually held, to some more convenient situation. Eleven thousand pounds for these purposes the earl was empowered to raise by way of mortgage on the shops and standings in the new market-place about to be erected: and a clause was introduced into the act, enabling him to dispose of certain small chief-rents, rents-service, rents-seck, and rents called Fridleys, which were payable to him as lord of the manor out of certain copyhold and freehold estates within Hallamshire, being parcel of the castle, honour, manor, or lordship of Sheffield, or of any other manor or lordship which belonged to him, applying the purchase-money to the projected improvements. As all the purchases under the powers contained in the act were to be completed in three years, the business was entered upon immediately, and the new shambles were opened on the 31st of August 1786. The whole was conducted with much satisfaction to the public. A handsome and exceedingly convenient market-place was obtained, together with a readier communication between the upper and lower parts of the town through New-market-street, and the streets on each side of the shambles: the great obstruction in that great public thoroughfare the Bull-stake on the days when the market was held was removed, and a convenient place set apart for the beast-market in the Wicker: and those great but necessary nuisances the slaughter-houses were placed in the best situation possible, close to the waters of Don.

For these improvements the town was in a great measure indebted to Vincent Eyre, esquire, the principal agent for the earl of Surrey in the management of his Yorkshire estates. That gentleman, perceiving also a disposition that the town should extend itself over Alsop-fields, which were the sole property of the earl, lying between Norfolk-street and the Sheaf, caused regular plans to be drawn of that part of the estate, to which adherence was required in the building-leases which from time to time the earl was induced to grant. To these streets, now among the best parts of the town, Mr. Eyre gave names for the most part taken from the family-names and titles of the noble proprietor of the soil.

About the same period the vicar of Sheffield obtained an act of parliament for the improvement of the glebe-land belonging to the vicarage. Under the powers contained in this act, the new church of Saint James was erected, and much improvement made in that part of the town which lies near the vicarage on the west side of the parish-church: and also in Church-street, opposite the south side of the church, by the sacrifice of a small portion of the church-yard, which, from feelings not dishonourable to the parties interested, was not effected with the same universal satisfaction that attended the other improvements of the town.

The great increase in the population of Sheffield caused a proportionably increased demand for a supply of that most necessary article in life—water. That small ancient reservoir, which many of my readers must remember, called Barker-pool, is probably to be referred to the early part of the fifteenth century [1]. This was doubtless a first attempt at supplying the deficiency of the springs, of which two, one in the Ponds and the other called Bower-spring, were of principal note. And no further means of supply seem to have been thought of till 1697, when Mr. Peter Whalley, an engineer of Nottingham, applied to the duke of Norfolk for a lease of about a rood of land near the Lady's bridge, then in the occupation of Mr. William Sitwell, and also for a lease of that part of the river Don which lies between Lady's bridge and Cawton's weir. This he obtained, together with a lease of a piece of waste ground near Barker-pool, forty feet long by thirty in breadth, and license to break up the streets in the town, being part of the lord's waste, for the purpose of laying down his pipes. It was his intention to erect an engine near the river, by which he could force up the river-water to the reservoir near Barker-pool, whence it was to be distributed in pipes through the town. In this scheme he was supported by the full concurrence of the inhabitants of Sheffield; but Mr. Whalley died when he had made small progress in the undertaking. The design was then taken up by five public-spirited inhabitants of Sheffield, Mr. Chapel, Mr. Lee, Mr. Drake, Mr. Turie, and Mr. Waterhouse, who obtained a lease of the same premises with the same powers. What progress they made, or what success attended their scheme, is not certainly known; but it is evident that it was seriously engaged in, for an engine-house was built, which appears in Oughtibridge's View of the town, and probably also a reservoir was constructed. But the project was soon abandoned: and in 1713 Messrs. Goodwin and Littlewood obtained from the lord of the manor a grant of the privilege of laying pipes through the commons, highways, and waste-grounds of the manor, for the purpose of conveying water from the springs and dams near the White-house. In 1737

Messrs. Matthewman and Battie obtained a share in this concern, and in 1742 the whole of it fell into their hands. These gentlemen, perceiving that the supply was still inadequate, and that the resources at the White-house seemed by no means likely to meet the yearly increasing demands of the town, turned their attention to the deep valley on Crook's-moor, which separates the townships of Sheffield and Nether Hallam, where the sides of the hills abounded with fresh springs, and it seemed possible to pin up the water in reservoirs at a small expense. They immediately set about the work; and from the reservoirs here constructed and the works at the White-house the town received a supply nearly adequate to its demands. But as it continued rapidly to increase, in 1782 Mr. Joseph Matthewman (son to the former) and three other gentlemen who were become equal and joint proprietors of the work undertook to enlarge their scheme; and for their better encouragement the earl of Surrey granted them a lease for ninety-nine years, of the privileges they had before enjoyed for shorter terms, at an uncertain annual rent varying according to the success of the adventure. This company formed a new reservoir near the White-house for the supply of the west part of the town, and another capacious one a little higher in the Crook's-moor valley than those already existing there. This reservoir was completed in February 1785, is spread over four acres of ground, and is computed to contain when full 300,000 hogsheads. Five much smaller reservoirs have since been constructed in the two valleys above the grand reservoir, and it seems that no addition can now be made to the supply which is derived from this quarter. From the grand reservoir the water is conveyed, in pipes of $4\frac{1}{2}$ inches bore, a distance of eleven hundred yards, to what is called the Working-dam at Porto-Bello; from thence to a stone cistern in Division-street, which contains about seven hundred hogsheads, from whence the water is distributed by pipes to all parts of the town [2].

It has been before observed, that one of the peculiar advantages which Sheffield possesses for the manufacture in which it has attained so deserved a reputation, lies in the frequent *falls* on its rivers, which supply a powerful motive agent available at a comparatively small expense: and also that great inconvenience is experienced from the inequality of the supply of water; there being often a superabundance in the winter, and a long deficiency in the summer months. At this period, when the spirit of useful improvement was abroad at Sheffield, the public attention was much directed to the practicability of providing a remedy for this inconvenience. I have now before me the brief but instructive Report made by Mr. William Jessop of Newark, an experienced engineer, who in the year 1785 was employed to make an actual survey to ascertain the possibility of equalizing the supply of water to the various works erected on the Sheffield rivers. He seems to have entertained doubts of complete success, but was persuaded much might be done. He gives up as nearly hopeless any attempts on the Sheaf, the Riveling, and the Loxley. The Don and the Por-

---

[1] Mr. Wilson notes having seen a deed of 12 Hen. VI. in which the name of Barker of Balm in Sheffield occurs. The walled-in pool which was destroyed about 1793, seems to have been that made by Robert Rollinson, a mercer in Sheffield, who died in 1631, aged 91.

[2] Most of these particulars are taken from a MS. memoir on the means by which Sheffield has been supplied with water for domestic purposes, by the late Mr. Joseph Matthewman.

ter alone he thinks practicable. And with respect to the former, he recommends that a reservoir for the surplus water which falls in the winter months be constructed at a place called Deadman's-ford, a few miles above Penistone, on the south side of the Don, where he conceives it would be possible to pin up thirty acres of water, which might average in depth three yards. A similar reservoir of twelve acres he conceives might be formed on Denby-common near Ingburchworth, and eight smaller ones in other places on the Don or its branches, where upon an average may be had about four acres of water, two yards deep. —As a reservoir for the Porter, he points out the White-moss, a bog of about sixty-five acres, the sides of which he is confident will be found water-tight, and that the only objection to the scheme must lie in the difficulty of procuring water. But he proceeds to show that this difficulty is not so great as at first may appear, for that a considerable supply of water may be expected from the bowels of the earth, as many coal-pits in that neighbourhood had failed of success in consequence of wanting a vent for the water; and secondly, that the sloping sides of those wild uncultivated hills contain springs not large enough to force themselves a channel, and therefore dissipating over a large surface waters which might easily-be drawn to the reservoir by drains, the expense of which would not exceed fifteen pounds per mile.

In summing up the information contained in his report, Mr. Jessop calculates that ten cubic feet of water in each second, in addition to what the Don affords in the driest times, would be sufficient for the works.

	Cubic yards.
30 acres of water at Deadman's-ford, 3 yards deep	435,600
12 acres on Denby-common, 4 yards deep . .	232,320
6 out of the 8 lesser reservoirs, 24 acres, at 2 yards deep	232,320
	900,240

Thus would be provided a supply for 56 days of 12 hours each, at 10 cubic feet each second, for the works on the Don. Half that quantity Mr. Jessop thinks would be sufficient for the Porter, which would be afforded for more than six weeks by the 314,600 cubic yards of water to be reserved at the White-moss.

His estimate of the expense follows.

Head at Deadman's-ford, with catch water drains, &c.	£1500
Head on Denby-common	600
Six lesser places	1500
	3600
White-moss reservoir, with drains, &c.	1000

This scheme was less successful than others which had been proposed. A meeting was held at Sheffield on the 8th of November 1785, of persons more immediately interested in the subject, among whom it was the general opinion, that the report afforded sufficient grounds for prosecuting further inquiries. The subject has been often since discussed, but nothing done: and it seems that the introduction of the steam-engine renders the project of much less obvious utility.

In the year 1791 the court-baron of the manor of Ecclesall was revived by earl Fitz William, after having lain dormant many years. A gaol was erected by private subscription on land given for the purpose by his lordship.

In the same year an act was passed for inclosing the common fields in the townships of Upper and Nether Hallam, which occasioned some commotions, but they soon subsided.

The provisions of the act 21 James I., by which the cutlers inhabiting Hallamshire were constituted one body corporate, remained unaltered till the year 1791. In that year an act was passed introducing some changes into the constitution of the body, of which the most material were, that twelve of the existing officers of the corporation should give way every year to twelve others, to be chosen out of twenty-four persons nominated by the master-manufacturers, who were to meet for the purpose of nominating them on the first Monday in August in each year: that any number of boys, the sons of freemen, might be taken as apprentices by members of the corporation, but that of children of non-freemen only one was to be held as an apprentice who was in the first three years of his term: that no person should be allowed to exercise any of the incorporated trades who was not a freeman, but that freemen might employ persons who were not freemen in new inventions, and that any person might obtain the freedom of the corporation on paying to the funds of the body twenty pounds: and lastly, that the accompts of the corporation should be printed for public use.

An increase of the proportional number of the necessitous poor is the universal concomitant of the extension of manufactures. The inhabitants of the township of Sheffield had seen their manufactures and commerce increasing year by year; but they had also witnessed a correspondent rapid increase of their poor-rates, which in the year 1750 were considerably less than four hundred pounds, while that sum and more has since been paid to the out-poor only in a single week. In the course of the year 1791 the heads of a bill for the employment and better relief of the poor, founded on the successful experiment which had been made at Shrewsbury, were presented to a public meeting; and after a warm discussion finally rejected.

Neither the promoters of the scheme nor those who opposed it could justly be charged with having any other view than on the one hand to improve the condition of the poor, and on the other to afford some relief to those from whom the funds for their support were to be drawn. The only question was about the means; some being of opinion that the proposed house of industry offered no benefits which did not appear to belong equally to the system which was established and in operation. Least of all could the wealthier part of the population of Sheffield, at the period at which we are now arrived, be justly chargeable with a want of a benevolent concern for the welfare of their poor neighbours. At no period indeed has there appeared any want of a proper attention to every call of humanity, and least of all in 1792. To the school for the support and education of poor boys had been added, a few years before, another for the reception of girls; and in 1792 a scheme for the erection of an hospital or infirmary upon the most extensive scale, for the benefit of the sick and poor, was laid before the public, and patronized by a subscription, which, taking every circumstance into the account, may justly be called unparalleled.

It soon, however, appeared that the friends of hu-

manity had chosen the lucky moment to lay the project before a liberal public. The war of the year 1793
gave such a check to the commerce of Sheffield as occasioned gloom and dismay to overspread every class
of its population. Much discontent was the consequence. The measures of government were very freely
canvassed in the associations which had lately been
formed in connexion with the Corresponding Society
as it was called of London; and at various public
meetings for the purpose of petitioning for peace, or for
a mode of electing members of the house of commons
which should give to that house more of the character of an elected and representative body, very in-
flammatory harangues were sometimes delivered, which
others represented as being worse than they really
were, and Sheffield lay for some time under the most
vehement suspicions of being infected with principles
decidedly revolutionary. But on the other hand, those
who approved of the principles and views on which
we had entered into the war with France, were eager
in adopting every means by which they could manifest
their approbation of the measure. A state of painful
disunion was the consequence. Suspicion, distrust,
and hatred took place for a time of that friendly and
unanimous spirit, and that absence of bigotry, religious or political, which in better times had honourably
distinguished the inhabitants of Sheffield. Accidental
circumstances contributed to inflame political jealousies; and on one melancholy occasion a volunteer
corps, which had been raised in the town, were drawn
out in the streets, when two of their townsmen were
killed by a discharge of musketry.

This volunteer corps of infantry was formed in the
month of April 1794. It consisted of 490 men, who
were reduced to 351 in 1802, when it was disbanded.
The late right honourable the earl of Effingham was
the colonel. Many of the gentlemen of Sheffield and
its neighbourhood joined the regiment of cavalry which
was raised at the same period in the southern parts of
the west-riding.

On the renewal of the war in 1803, and the alarm
of an invasion, a much more numerous body of men
offered their services as a volunteer corps of infantry,
and were accepted. The questions of domestic politics were at this period lost sight of in an apprehension
of common danger, and persons of all parties rallied
round the throne. It happened to the volunteer regi-
ments in this part of the kingdom, that they had an opportunity of signalizing their loyalty and spirit under an
apprehension of real danger. Beacons were placed in
every part of the west-riding, to give early notice of an
expected descent upon the coast. The determined and
enthusiastic spirit with which the Sheffield volunteer
corps appeared on the parade, and marched towards
the appointed place of rendezvous, when on the morning of Thursday the fifteenth of August 1805 a neighbouring beacon gave the signal, can never be forgotten by those who witnessed it, and afforded a triumphant refutation of the suspicions which were propa-
gated by the maligners of the volunteer system of defence. A troop of cavalry was raised at the same period
at Sheffield and its immediate neighbourhood, and the
two neighbouring villages of Norton and Ecclesfield
made a tender of volunteer service which was accepted. All these volunteer corps have been represented as not inferior in discipline to any which were

raised in that time of danger. They continued em-
bodied till the termination of the war.

In the year 1802, the first of a series of acts of parliament was passed, which, though of a private nature
in the first instance, are of great importance in the
history of the town and parish of Sheffield. Since the
grant which had been made by Thomas lord Furnival
to his free tenants, no material alienations had been
made from the great estate enjoyed by the lords of the
manor. George the sixth earl of Shrewsbury had even
added to that estate by his extensive purchases in
Brightside Byerlow. The settlements and entails of the
family had precluded sales in more modern times, had
the successive chiefs of the house of Howard been disposed to make such alienations. In 1802, on the petition of Charles duke of Norfolk; Bernard-Edward
Howard, esquire, on behalf of himself and his infant
son; Henry-Thomas Howard, esquire, on behalf of
himself and his infant son; and Edward-Charles Howard, esquire, an act was passed ' for vesting several
messuages and hereditaments in Sheffield, and divers
detached parts of the settled estates of the most noble
Charles duke of Norfolk, in trustees upon trust to sell,
and for laying out the monies in the purchase of more
convenient estates and otherwise.' This was followed
by another in 1805, and a third in 1810, since which
time a fourth act has been passed, in one or other of
which a considerable portion of the most improved
parts of the estates of the lord of the manor have been
included. The sales under these acts have been conducted with every liberality towards the tenants and
occupiers of the lands, on the part of his grace's agents.
The purchases have for the most part been made by
residents within the town and parish, and will eventually tend to the enriching of the town, as they have
of course produced a great accession to the list of
freeholders in the parish of Sheffield.

In the 29th year of George II. an act of parliament
was passed, by which the proceedings in personal actions in the courts-baron of Sheffield and Ecclesall
were regulated. This act having proved in some respects inefficient and inconvenient, it was repealed by
another act, which received the royal assent on the
18th of June 1808. By this act certain persons are
appointed commissioners for hearing and determining
causes in which the property in question does not exceed in value five pounds, and for administering summary justice between the parties. There are no peculiar features in its constitution by which it is distinguishable from the other courts of request, which have
superseded the old courts-baron in other manors where
the population has increased in the degree that it has
increased at Sheffield. In the same year the old town-
hall of Sheffield was taken down, and another erected
much more commodious, in that part of the town called
the Hay-market. In this hall are held the meetings of
the commissioners, the sessions of the justices of the
peace, and any public assemblies for accidental purposes.

This municipal regulation naturally turned the
thoughts of the inhabitants of Sheffield to other improvements. The want of a regular and more effective police had been long evident in the imperfect
manner in which the streets were cleansed and lighted,
and the total absence of any public provision for the
watching of the town. It was foreseen that it could

not always be expected that Sheffield would be so fortunate as at present it is, in finding in the neighbouring justices of the peace gentlemen who would undertake the laborious duties of police magistrates in the midst of such a population, and whose exertions, patient, unremitted and judicious, are above all praise. Difficulties, however, presented themselves which were too formidable to be at that time overcome: and it was not till 1818 that a bill was passed for the more effectual watching, cleansing, and lighting the town; in which however there was no provision for a police-magistrate, at the particular suggestion it has been understood of the gentlemen in the neighbourhood of Sheffield who are in the public commission of the peace.

The clauses in the act of incorporation restricting the persons comprehended under the act from increasing at pleasure the number of their apprentices, and preventing persons who were not freemen from being employed in the corporate trades, having been found inconvenient, and ill adapted to the rapid growth of the manufactures and commerce of the town, a slight relaxation of them was made by statute in 1801; but in 1814 a much more important change was made. By an act which was passed in that year, liberty of engaging in any of the incorporated trades, either as masters or journeymen, was extended to all persons, whether sons of freemen or strangers, whether they had served an apprenticeship or no, and whether they had had a mark assigned them by the officers of the company or no, any where within the limits of Hallamshire.

In the next year, 1815, a very important point was gained by the persons interested in the foreign commerce of Sheffield. The company of proprietors of the river Don navigation had made many important improvements in the navigation of the river. In 1793 an act had been obtained for making a navigable canal from the river to the town of Barnsley, with many collateral cuts; and in the same year, another for a canal from the Don at Stainforth to join the Trent at or near Keadby. But still the town of Sheffield was suffering under the inconvenience of having the wharf upon its own river at the distance of three miles. Many attempts had from time to time been made to procure the concurrence of all the parties interested, in a plan for a canal from Sheffield to the wharf at Tinsley. This was accomplished in 1815; the money required for the purpose was easily raised, and on the 7th of June in that year the royal assent was given to an act incorporating the subscribers to the scheme, by the name of 'The company of proprietors of the Sheffield canal,' and giving them the power to make and maintain a navigable cut from the west part of the Castle orchards, adjoining the town of Sheffield, to the navigable part of the river at Tinsley. This useful work is now proceeding, and the time is near at hand when the merchants of Sheffield will possess the convenience of direct water-communication with the German ocean.

At no period, perhaps, has more of public spirit manifested itself at Sheffield than since the revival of its commerce after the depression of 1816. In the session of parliament of 1818, three bills were introduced connected with the town and trade of Sheffield, two of which were passed into law. The first and most

material was the act for the better watching, cleansing, and lighting the town; in which also some other regulations are contained of minor consequence, but tending to the health and comfort of the inhabitants. —A plan was proposed for introducing the gas-light, and immediately a capital of forty thousand pounds was raised for the purpose, and the subscribers incorporated by act of parliament.—A third bill was not so fortunate. To the ancient manufactures of Sheffield had been added many years ago various iron articles, such as grates, ovens, &c. which were cast in foundries. In the same manner various small articles were cast, such as the blades of knives, scissors, and, other things which had formerly been made solely of hammered steel; and it was found that the articles of this kind made of the cast-iron would receive a polish from the grinder nearly equal to that of the hammered articles, and which might at least deceive an unpractised eye. The danger to the established reputation of Sheffield arising out of this practice was soon perceived: and application was made to parliament not to prohibit the continuance of the manufacture, but to oblige the makers of these articles to affix some mark, by which they might be distinguished by every purchaser from those made of hammered steel the genuine production of the long approved forges of Hallamshire. The principle of the bill was approved in both houses, but some of the minor details remained unsettled when parliament was dissolved.— The old gaol of the manor of Sheffield, which stood in King-street, has been taken down, and the plot of ground which it occupied has been set apart as an enlargement of the Market-place: a large building in Scotland-street, originally erected for a dwelling-house and merchant's warehouse, having been purchased by his grace the duke of Norfolk for the reception of prisoners.—And lastly, a society has been lately formed, who have in view the formation of a public library upon a scale correspondent to the size and opulence of the town. Hitherto the town has been satisfied with the slowly accumulating stores of the old subscription library, which seemed to resist every attempt which was made for its improvement, and with the scanty supply which could be obtained by bookassociations. In this point the traveller on the continent of Europe is forced at every stage to make comparisons to the disadvantage of our native country. We seem however to be rousing ourselves. Liverpool and Manchester have led the way; and it is hoped that the time is now arrived when the enlightened and liberal inhabitants of the town and neighbourhood of Sheffield will have within their reach a store of works in every department of literature for their own consultation and reference, and to encourage an attention to matters of literature and science in a future generation.

It is with unfeigned satisfaction that I conclude the general history, and proceed to some details of a more minute description at a period of so much prosperity. May the future historian of this place have to record future and equally valuable improvements; and may the great Giver of all good influence all hearts to a grateful sense of his kindness, and to a disposition to imitate the past generations in their patient industry, incorruptible integrity, and exemplary benevolence.

CHAPTER IX.

Ecclesiastical Affairs.

'DONATIONEM etiam et concessionem quas Willielmus de Lovetot fecit præfatis canonicis [de Worksop] de molendino et vivario et dimidiâ alneti de Holmker, et de illâ portione in ecclesiâ de Schefeld quam Radulphus et Willielmus sacerdotes in illâ habuerunt; videlicet de omnibus decimis plenarie tertiam partem in omnibus, cum terris ad eandem ecclesiam pertinentibus, et oblationibus et obventionibus altaris, sicuti præfati sacerdotes eas unquam melius habuerunt[1].'

' Præterea concedo et confirmo Deo et ecclesiæ Sanctæ Mariæ et Sancti Cuthberti de Wyrksopa, illam portionem in ecclesiâ de Sheffeld, quam Radulphus et Willielmus sacerdotes in illâ ecclesiâ personaliter habuerint ex concessione et præsentatione antecessorum meorum: videlicet de omnibus decimis tertiam partem plenarie in omnibus, cum terris ad eandem ecclesiam pertinentibus, et oblationibus et obventionibus altaris, sicut præfati sacerdotes eas unquam melius habuerunt[2].'

These passages are to be found in two charters in the *Monasticon*; one a grant by Henry III. in the ninth of his reign *pro immunitate tolneti* to the monks of Worksop; the other a confirmation by Maud de Lovetot in her free widowhood, of all the donations made by her ancestors to the monks of that house. We may draw from them the following conclusions:

I. That there was a church at Sheffield as early as the reign of Henry II.; for William de Lovetot, by whom it was given to the house of his grandfather's foundation at Worksop, was dead before the twenty-seventh of that king's reign.

II. We may infer from the expression *antecessorum meorum*, that it was not this William de Lovetot the father of Maud, but some predecessor or predecessors who had endowed the church of Sheffield with one-third of the whole tythe of the parish, had annexed to it a portion of glebe, and had allowed the priest to receive towards his sustentation the oblations and obventions. Hence the foundation of the church is to be carried higher than the time of the second William de Lovetot: and as it appears also that two priests named Ralph and William had enjoyed the living before the church was annexed to Worksop, we may with high probability refer the foundation of a church at Sheffield to the first William de Lovetot in the time of Henry I., the same person who erected and splendidly endowed the monastery of Worksop.

III. It appears that the whole of what on the foundation of a church at Sheffield had been set apart for the support of the officiating priest was given to the monks of Worksop, without, as far as appears, exacting from them an engagement for any specific stipend or support for the vicar whom they presented to take the cure of souls in the parish.

IV. It is evident that only one-third of the tythe of Sheffield was settled upon the church, and given with it to the monks of Worksop.

What was become of the other two-thirds?

The taxation of ecclesiastical benefices made by authority of Pope Nicholas in the time of Edward I. enables us to answer that question.

' Abbas S. Wandregesilii tenet maner. de Ecclesfield et Walneleghes, tenementa in Bradfield et eccl. de Sheffield.' And again in the list of benefices in the deanery of Doncaster:

Ecclesia de Ecclesfield cum duabus partibus ecclesiæ de Schefeld	£106 13 4
Porcio prioris de Worksop in ecclesiâ de Schefeld	10 0 0

To the abbot of Saint Wandragesilius, then, the remaining two-thirds of the tythe of Sheffield belonged.

Saint Wandragesilius, Saint Wandrille, or Fontenelle, is, or rather was, a Benedictine convent in Normandy, situated near the banks of the Seine, about six or seven leagues from Rouen. It was founded in the earliest period of the French monarchy by the saint of that name, who was a near relative to King Pepin, and constable to Dagobert. By the desire of his friends he married a lady of noble birth; but they separated by mutual consent on the day of the ceremony, and took religious habits in different monasteries. After removing for some time from place to place, a great lord gave Saint Wandrille a beautiful piece of ground near the Seine for the purpose of erecting a monastery; and Batilda, queen of France, made him large gifts for the support of monks who resorted to him from all quarters to the number of three hundred. Saint Wandrille presided over his monastery till his death in the year of Christ 685, on the 22d day of July, the day consecrated to his memory in the Roman Catholic calendar. Such is his legend extracted from Ribadeneira.

This house suffered much from the Normans when they settled in the north of France: but after a while it became popular among them, and in 1033 the church which had been burnt was rebuilt[3]. This was thirty-three years before the great emigration from Normandy to Britain. Many of the chiefs who attended the duke of Normandy in his expedition, brought with them an attachment to this religious house, and were scarcely warm in their new possessions when they endowed it with tythe in England and even entire manors. The abbot of Saint Wandrille

---

[1] *Mon. Ang.* vol. ii. p. 55.   [2] *Id.* vol. ii. p. 50.   [3] *History of the Alien Priories.*

was no small proprietor at the time of the Domesday survey.

Amongst the benefactors to this foreign monastery was the countess Judith, widow of earl Waltheof and owner of the manor of Hallam. This lady endowed Saint Wandrille with a part of the manor of Boughton in Northamptonshire; and it may be submitted as no improbable conjecture, that it was to this lady rather than to one of the De Lovetots that the monastery owed its great interest in Hallamshire.

We have already had occasion to observe that the monks of Saint Wandrille placed a small colony at Ecclesfield; and in the time of Dodsworth the effigies of the saint was to be seen in one of the windows of the fine church at that place.

This foreign house continued to enjoy its two-thirds of the whole tythe of Sheffield till the time of Edward III. or Richard II. Those princes began what Henry V. completed to detach from the foreign monasteries their English possessions. Richard II. in the ninth of his reign transferred to the Carthusian convent of Saint Ann without the walls of Coventry, which he had lately founded, all the interest which the house of Saint Wandrille had enjoyed in this neighbourhood, ' *et jam in manu nostrâ virtute cujusdam recuperationis inde in curiâ Domini Edwardi nuper regis Angliæ avi nostri per ipsum exstit*,' &c.[1] In the possession of this house they continued about a hundred and fifty years. Thomas Ricard, the prior of the Carthusians of Coventry, inscribed his name in one of the windows of the church of Ecclesfield when they were restored so magnificently with painted glass at the beginning of the sixteenth century. Among Dodsworth's papers is a commission from that convent directed to John Mounteney of Shiercliffe, to collect certain arrears of tythe of corn and other things in the parishes of Ecclesfield, Bradfield, and Sheffield[2]. And in the return which was made by the commissioners for a general ecclesiastical survey in the 26th of Henry VIII., the rectory of Sheffield is said to belong to the monastery or house called the Charter-house at Coventry.

We have thus brought down the history of the greater moiety of the tythe of Sheffield, or of what was called the rectory, to the period of the Reformation. It was then taken possession of by the Crown, together with other property belonging to the monastic establishments. On the 13th of April 3 Edward VI., under the description of ' *totam illam rectoriam et ecclesiam nostram de Sheffelde cum suis juribus membris et pertinenciis universis in comitatu nostro Ebor. nuper prioratui Carthusi juxta civitatem Coventrie tunc dissoluto dudum spectantes*,' it was granted to Mary countess-dowager of Northumberland, together with much other property of the like description. This lady was a daughter of George the fourth earl of Shrewsbury; and the unthrifty character of her husband rendered such a grant as this peculiarly acceptable.

Three years after, namely on the 10th of July 6 Edward VI., the seal of the court of Augmentation was affixed to a most extensive grant of abbey-lands made

to Francis earl of Shrewsbury, brother to the countess of Northumberland. Amongst much other property, the reversion of the grant which had been made to the countess for life of the rectories of Sheffield, Ecclesfield, Bradfield, Cantley, Tickhill, Kirkby in Malhamdale, Rothwell, &c. is given to the said earl: ' *ac etiam advocationes, donationes, præsentationes, liberas dispositiones, et jura patronat. vicariarum prædictarum ecclesiarum de Sheffelde, Ecclesfelde, Bradfelde, Cantley, Kirkby, Rothwell, Tickhill*,' &c. to be held by the said Francis and his heirs for ever *in capite* and by the twentieth part of a knight's fee, paying for the said rectories, after the death of the said countess of Northumberland, two hundred pounds a year into the court of Augmentation[3].

The countess of Northumberland died at an advanced age in 1572, and was laid in the vault at Sheffield amongst her ancestors and kindred. The son and heir of Francis, George the sixth earl of Shrewsbury then entered into the enjoyment of this comprehensive grant: and the rectory being thus reunited with the manor has attended it in its descent to its present noble owner. In the endowment on Queen Henrietta-Maria in 1626, is 126*l.* per annum issuing out of the reserved rents of the rectories of Bradfield, Sheffield, Ecclesfield, and Tickhill[4].

When two-thirds of the whole tythe of Sheffield were given to the foreign house, there remained one-third, which together with the manse and croft, the oblations and obventions, would have formed an excellent provision for the officiating clergyman. This two priests enjoyed, whose names Radulphus and Willielmus appear in the two instruments lately quoted, and are there it is probable alone preserved.

But the second William de Lovetot thought proper to transfer this portion of the tythe to the house of Worksop, and to leave to the monks of that house the power of nominating a vicar. In the possession of that house it continued till the Reformation.

At the Reformation this portion of the tythe of Sheffield was assigned over by the Crown to different purchasers.

In the 36th year of Henry VIII. Robert Swyft of Broomhall, esquire, and his brother William Swyft had a valuable grant of abbey-property[5]. In this grant is included the third part of the tythe of Ecclesall, Heeley, and Hallam; that is, of the whole of that portion of the parish of Sheffield which now forms the three townships of Ecclesall and the two Hallams. This tythe at the time of the grant was in the tenure of Thomas Stocks. This has been since held by the Jessops descended of Robert Swyft, from whom it passed to their co-heirs the Wilkinsons and Gells.

The third part of the tythe of Attercliffe in the 14th of Elizabeth was in the possession of William Wentworth, who on the 24th of April in that year executed a deed of sale of this portion to one Richard Fenton[6], by whom or by his assigns it was conveyed to the lords of the manor of Sheffield, to whom it belonged in the seventeenth century.

With respect to the remainder of this third part, there is an indenture made the 16th of November,

[1] Pat. 9 Ric. II. part. 2. m. 30. in *Mon. Ang.* vol. i. p. 965.
[2] Dods. MSS. B. 152 a. in Harl. MSS. 801. Sheffield.
[3] From a copy of the original record in the Rolls chapel among the Norfolk Evidences.
[4] Rymer's *Fœd.* vol. xviii. p. 693. pat. 2 Car. i. p. 4. n. 3.
[5] Pat. 36 Hen. VIII. A 8—189 in Col. Arm. From Brooke's Collections.
[6] Evidences. Norfolk-House.—Yorkshire Bundle L. 24.

18 Elizabeth, between Roger Manners[1] esquire of the body to the queen on the first part, and Gilbert Talbot esquire son of George earl of Shrewsbury on the other part; whereby in consideration of 856l. 13s. 4d. by the said Talbot to the said Manners paid, Manners conveys to him *inter alia* Tasker-field and Peny-croft in Sheffield, and all that portion of tythe of corn and grain called the third sheaf of the tythe corn of Sheffield town within the parish of Sheffield, then or late in the tenure of Richard Roberts: and all that portion of tythe with the appurtenances yearly growing, coming, and renewing in Brixard [Brightside] Bierlow in the parish of Sheffield, then or late in the tenure of John Bullows: and the third part of all the tythes of corn and grain yearly growing, coming, renewing, and happening in Sheffield aforesaid, with their appurtenances then or late in the tenure of George Swift; and all profits, commodities, emoluments, and hereditaments to the premises in Sheffield aforesaid belonging, with all their rights and appurtenances: which premises in Sheffield aforesaid did belong to the late dissolved monastery of Worksop, and were parcel of the possessions of the same: all which had been granted by Queen Elizabeth, by letters patent under the great seal dated the 27th of April in the 18th year of her reign, to the said Roger Manners, to be held of the queen as of her manor of East Greenwich, paying annually for the third sheaf eighteen shillings, for Brightside tythe thirty-one shillings, and for the third part of Sheffield tythe thirteen shillings and four-pence[2].

In the year 1639 that part of the tythe of Sheffield which belonged to the representatives of the Talbot family was leased as follows:

Robert Saursbie, the tythe-corn of Sheffield	£38	0	0
William Spencer and John Wilson, the tythe-corn of Attercliffe-cum-Darnall	38	0	0
John Staniforth and William Unwin, the tythe-corn of Ecclesall	50	0	0
The tythe of Brightside-Byerlow was let for	115	0	0
The tythe of Heeley	3	0	0
The tythe of the upper part of Hallam	30	0	0
The tythe of the nether part of Hallam	50	0	0

Leases have from time to time been granted of different portions of the tythe of Sheffield: but in later times the more eligible plan has been adopted of leasing out the tythe to the tenant of the soil.

It will be observed that it was not only what is called the greater tythe, but two-thirds also of the small tythe which was given to the monks of Saint Wandrille, and that came to the house of Shrewsbury. Having remained in the hands of the lords of the manor till the close of the last century, this two-thirds of the small tythe of Sheffield was purchased of the late duke of Norfolk by the Reverend Mr. Wilkinson, and annexed by him to the vicarage, charged with a payment of ten pounds *per annum* to the infirmary for ever.

It was usual for the diocesan to interfere with the impropriators of the benefices in behalf of the vicars who had to perform the sacerdotal offices in the parish churches: and we accordingly find that in the adjoining parish of Ecclesfield, William Greenfield, arch-

bishop of York, in 1310 settled the provision that was to be made for the vicar by the abbot and convent of Saint Wandragesilius. But no such ordination was made at Sheffield. If the attempt was made, it was probably frustrated by a papal bull: for with respect to their Nottinghamshire livings, the house at Worksop obtained from Pope Alexander III. in 1161, a bull which provided that the vicars appointed to those benefices should be answerable to the bishops for the cure of souls, but to the priory for the profits of the living[3]. To suppose that the protection of this bull extended to their rights in Sheffield, or that one of similar powers was obtained respecting it, seems most satisfactorily to account for the fact that in the records of the diocese of York is found no memorial of an ancient ordination of a vicarage at Sheffield. Such an instrument enabled the monks of Worksop to make hard bargains, if they were so inclined, with the priests whom they presented to their numerous benefices. It cannot be said that they dealt in an illiberal manner with the clerk whom they presented to serve the church of Sheffield. At the Reformation the profits of the vicarage were found to consist in

A house and croft, value per annum	£0	10	0
Tythe of wool and lambs	1	16	0
Oblations	6	18	0
Easter-book	4	0	0
Minute and privy tythes	0	2	8
	£13	6	8[4]

Out of this sum, the vicar had to pay to the archbishop for synodals, four shillings, and to the archdeacon for procurations, seven shillings and sixpence, leaving a clear income of 12l. 15s. 2d. or the vicarage-house and croft, and twenty-four times their value in yearly income. At the same period the income of the three assistant-ministers was but seventeen pounds.

It was evidently the intention of the earl of Shrewsbury to have possessed himself of the right of presenting a vicar to the church of Sheffield, where he was rector, where his household and himself attended on the public ministration of holy ordinances, and where was the place in which the remains of his buried ancestors reposed. And in the grant of the 6 Edward VI. the advowson and presentation of the church of Sheffield are expressly conveyed to him. This seems to have been done under a misunderstanding of the *jus patronatum* being annexed to that largest portion of the tythe which belonged to the Carthusians of Coventry. But however that might be, it is certain that a grant of the advowson had been made several years before to the two Swyfts, Robert and William, namely by letters patent bearing date the 15th of May 1544, 36 Henry VIII., the same grant which conveyed to them their share of the tythe of Sheffield[5]. They had not an opportunity of presenting till the reign of Elizabeth, when William Swyft exercised the right. It passed along with the Broomhall estate to the respectable family of Jessop, descended of one of their co-heirs; and on the decease of William Jessop, esq. in 1734, without male issue, his four daughters and

[1] Of Uffington, co. Linc. a younger son of Thomas first earl of Rutland and and uncle to Gilbert Talbot.
[2] From an abstract of the indenture among the Norfolk Evidences.
[3] *Mon. Ang.* vol. ii. p. 53.
[4] From the return in the general ecclesiastical survey, 26 Henry VIII. now in the Augmentation-office: obligingly communicated to the author by the Rev. Thomas Sutton.
[5] From the collections of John Reynolds, gent., of Plaistow.

co-heirs agreed upon exercising the right of present-ing to the vicarage of Sheffield in rotation. Two of them died unmarried: the other two married into the families of Wilkinson and Gell. The Rev. James Wilkinson, vicar of Sheffield, last survivor of the children of Andrew Wilkinson and Barbara Jessop, gave by will his share in the presentation to Elizabeth-Barbara wife of the Reverend Marmaduke Lawson, who now enjoys it alternately with Philip Gell, esquire, of Hopton in the county of Derby.

As the profits of the vicarage were found at the dissolution of the priory of Worksop, they were suffered to continue: so that a recent terrier differs little from that already given.

'A perfect terrier and account of all the glebe-lands, houses, &c. belonging to the vicarage of Sheffield.

Imp. a house where the vicar dwells with a stable and croft, containing about an acre of land.

Item, the ground-rent of some houses amounting to the sum of thirteen pounds, eleven shillings, a year.

Item, a third part of the small tythes [to which is now to be added the other two-thirds settled on the living by Mr. Wilkinson, charged with the payment to the infirmary.]

Item, one pound, ten shillings, paid yearly for the manor-house of Sheffield.

Item, all the usual surplice-fees.

Item, twenty shillings a year left by Mr. Hill late of Sheffield, payable out of some lands near Attercliffe forge.

Item, all offerings due at Easter.

Item, tythe corn of some land called Chennel-Ings, Shemeld's lands, and Clark-farm, containing about nineteen acres.

Item, the interest of fifteen pounds left to the vicar of Sheffield by the last will and testament of Dr. Waterhouse late of Sheffield, deceased.'

In the return made to the parliamentary commissioners, anno 1649, the profits of the vicarage are estimated at twenty-two pounds per annum. In 1688 the whole income of the vicar was about ninety pounds per annum, including certain gratuitous payments. Archbishop Sharpe writing at the beginning of the last century says that the vicarage is valued in his books at 75l. a year, and may be worth 80l. In 1786 the vicar obtained an act of parliament enabling him to grant building-leases of the glebe-land by which the income is considerably improved. The great increase of population has contributed to advance the profits of the living, while the patronage of the two chapels of ease within the town, and the share in the patronage of the rural chapelries, render it a most respectable piece of preferment, as it is also one which brings with it many, various, and laborious duties. It has been the good fortune of the parish of Sheffield to find in those who have sustained the character of its vicar gentlemen by whom those duties have been well discharged: and to the present very worthy incumbent the parish is much indebted for a warm interest in its concerns, and especially for a zealous promotion of schemes which have for their object the instruction or the general benefit of its poorer inhabitants.

And in this he ever found willing and active coadjutors in the three clergymen (two of whom have lately finished their earthly labours) who when he entered on the vicarage filled the respectable office of ASSISTANT-MINISTERS. Of the origin of an institution which provides for the parishioners of Sheffield the services of three clergymen, who derive no authority from the vicar, but officiate conjointly with him in the performance of all sacerdotal duties, we are now to speak:

and we shall find that while it was placed upon its present footing only by a charter of the first year of Queen Mary, its history is to be traced into times long before the Reformation.

The documents from which our account of this institution is to be drawn are first, a petition to the crown from the inhabitants of Sheffield, praying for the restoration of certain lands of which they had been deprived by the commissioners under the act of the 1 Edward VI. for the suppression of colleges, chantries, guilds, &c. Secondly, the patent which was granted at the time of the restoration of those lands, specifying the uses to which the profits of them were to be annually devoted. And thirdly, certain deeds which remain among the evidences of the church-burgesses of Sheffield, a body corporate created by the aforesaid patent.

Neither the petition nor the patent has before been published.

To the Quene our moste drad Soveraynge.

IN moste lamentable wyse shewythe and côplaynythe unto your ma^{tie} your trew faithfull and obedyent subiects Robert Swyft and Wm Taylor of the parishe of Sheffeld in the countie of Yorke and for and in the names of all other thenhabytance of the said parish, that wher your said orators together with others of the said parishe stand and be lawfullye seasyde in ther demaine as of fee, of and in certen lands tenem^{ts} and burgages set lyinge and beynge in the towne and parishe of Sheffeld aforesaid to the yerlye valew of xxvii^{td} and also of and in one messuage with appurtenances called the George set lyinge and beinge in the Olde Chaunge in your Grac's cytye of London w^{che} were gyven and assigued by dyvers persones of longe tyme paste to and for the reparacôn and amendm^t of severall brygs and wayes w^{in} the said parishe of Sheffeld; and to the reparacôn of the churche ther and to the releffe of the moste nedye and indegent persones inhabytynge w^{in} the said parishe. The issues and proffets of all and singuler w^{che} premisses were yerlye by the churchegraves of the said parishe for the tyme beynge receyved and converted to the uses before remembred, unto abowte xiiii^{th} yeres laste paste the inhabitaunts of the said parishe were enforced and côstrayned for ye ther said parishe was verey grett and populus haveyonge w^{in} the same xiiii. hamletts w^{che} for the moste parte are never woyd of plags and other evell deseases by reason of the gret nomber of poore and impotent persones inhabytynge w^{in} the same to imparte and yerlye bestawe sume porchon of the reveneues of the said premises to and for the fyndynge of iii. prestes w^{in} the said churche to helpe and assyste the vycare there as well in the vysytacôn of the said dissessed persones w^{in} the said parishe from tyme to tyme as in the mynistracôn of devyne service and other sacrant^{ts} w^{in} the said churche. In w^{che} forme the same côtynued untyll the makynge of the statute for dissolucôn of colegges and chauntrees. And for as moche as the cômissioners appoynted for surveye of the said colygges and chauntres perceyvid that the inhabytants of the said parishe had in some one yere before the makynge of the said statute gyven and bestowed of the issues and profetts of the said premisses amongste the iii. severall prests the sume of xvii^{td} over and besyds ix^s. iiii^d. for an obyte, the said inhabytaunts wete côpelled to certyfye before the said cômisyoners the said yerly rent of xvii^{td}. ix^s. iiii^d. and accordynlye have ever synez answered and paid the same unto your m^{tie}'s receyvor of your grace's revenewes in the said countie of Yorke. Yet nevertheless one Henrye Bayleye of London skynner of his moste covetus and ungodlye myude sekynge onlye his owne pryvate gayne and lucre hathe exebyted in your highnes courte of Augmentacôn a surmissyd informacôn côserninge the said lands wherby he hathe côtynually vexed and disquieted your said subiects and parishoners by the space of ii. hole yeres now laste paste and yet côtynuythe the same to ther gret losse and impoverishment onles your hyghnes' accostomed clemencye and pytye be herin shewed. And for as moche moste drade soverayne ladye as the premisses were not gyven to the fyndynge of any preste or prestes to have cõtynuance for ever bot were fownde by the said parishoners of the said parishe of Sheffeld do thiuk that the same were not w'in the cõpasse of the estatute, so that your Grace is not justelye intituled to suche rent as was imployed in forme abovesaid to the fyndynge of the same prestes. And for that moste gracyous Ladye as the vycare of the said churche is not able w'owte assystens to serve the cure, and to mynister the Sacraments and other devyne services w'in the said parishe for the cõsyderacõn afore alegged ; and also for that your highnes hathe no profett nor benyfytte by the said rent by reason the same is paid furthe agen by the hands of your grace's receyvors unto the said III. prestes for the yerlye pencõns now goynge abrode at their lybertye, the churche beynge unserved to the gret discomefoorthe of the said inhabitaunce by reason of y' gret decaye of suche moste godlye service as heretofore hathe beyne used w'in the said churche: Yt may therfor please your moste exilent ma'n in the advancement of God's glorye and his devyne service to restore unto your said orators the said rent to be imployed and bestowed as heretofore it hathe beyne, your said orators dischargeinge your hyghnes of the said penchons ; and your said subiects and all other the inhabitaunts of the said parishe and their posteryties shall have moste iuste cause for this charytable dede to pray unto God for the preservation of your moste royall estate longe to rayne and cõtynewe.

The queen having taken this petition into her gracious consideration, directed her warrant to William Marquis of Winchester, Lord High Treasurer, Sir John Baker knight, chancellor of the exchequer, and the other officers of that court, to prepare letters patent accordingly, which are as follows:

MARIA Dei gratia Angliæ, Franciæ et Hiberniæ regina Fidei Defensor Omnibus ad quos presentes litteræ nostræ pervenerint, Salutem. Cum dilecti subditi nostri, Burgen-

Recital of the Church-Estates.

ses et inhabitantes villæ et parochiæ nostræ de Sheffelde in comitatu nostro Eboraci, a tempore cujus contrarii memoria hominum non existit, seisiti fuerunt et extiterunt in dominico suo ut de feodo, de et in uno annuali redditu octodecim denariorum exeunti de uno messuagio sive tenemento in Attercliff infra parochiam de Sheffelde præd. modo vel nuper Radulphi Bawnford; ac de et in uno alio annuali redditu duorum solidorum exeunti de uno messuagio in Parva Sheffelde infra parochiam de Sheffelde præd. modo vel nuper Roberti Tailour; ac de et in uno alio annuali redditu viginti unius denariorum exeunti de uno messuagio vocato Stele Bank in Sheffelde præd. modo vel nuper heredum Stele; ac de et in uno alio annuali redditu quatnor-decim solidorum exeunti de uno messuagio in Sheffelde præd. vocato Graie-Stoues nuper heredum Christopheri Eyre; ac de et in uno alio annuali redditu viginti unius denariorum exeunti de uno messuagio in Attercliffe præd. nuper Willielmi Staniforth; ac de et in tribus messuagiis ac terris et tenementis cum pertinentiis in Attercliff præd. modo in seperalibus tenuris Richardi Savage, Hugonis Person, et Willielmi Wood; ac de et in uno messuagio ac terris et tenementis cum pertinentiis in Darnal infra parochiam de Sheffelde præd. modo vel nuper in tenura Richardi Burrows; ac de et in uno cottagio et uno crofto terræ cum pertinentiis jacentibus apud le Brushes in Sheffelde præd. modo in tenura Rowlandi Archdale; ac de et in duobus cottagiis et duobus croftis terræ cum pertinentiis in Olherton iufra parochiam de Sheffeld præd. modo vel nuper in seperalibus tenuris Thomæ Michell et Nicholai Fox; ac de et in uno cottagio et duobus clausis terræ et prati in Walkeley infra parochiam de Sheffield præd. modo in tenura Willielmi Hale; ac de et in uno messuagio et quatuor clausis terræ et prati cum pertinentiis in Halome infra parochiam de Sheffield præd. modo in tenura uxoris Sele viduæ; ac de et in diversis clausis terris et pratis in parochia [de] Sheffield præd. in tenura Johannis Parker vel assignatorum suorum; ac de et in quatuor messuagiis et terris ac tenementis eisdem pertinentibus in Sheffeld præd. modo vel nuper in seperalibus tenuris Alexandri Clarke, Willielmi Partington, Roberti Heptenstall, et Thomæ Michell; ac de et in uno hor-

reo tribus cottagiis et uno crofto vocato Pincencroft Len, cum pertinentiis in Sheffeld præd. modo in tenura Humfredi Stafford vel assignorum suorum; ac de et in uno prato cum pertinentiis in Sheffeld præd. in tenura Willielmi Borrows; ac de et in viginti et quiuque cottagiis ac omnibus gardinis et croftis terræ cum pertinentiis eisdem cottagiis pertinentibus in Sheffeld præd. modo vel nuper in seperalibus tenuris Willielmi Burley, Thomæ Trippit, Egidii Greave, Willielmi Trickett, Thomæ Bland, Richardi Barley, Willielmi Walton, Henrici Ashley, Thomæ Fox, Alexandri Smith, Viduæ Hinchlif, Galfridi Fulforth, Laurencii Bowre, Richardi Lethom, Rodgeri Birley, Jacobi Taylour, Radulphi Drake, Richardi Lome, Thomæ Arthure, Johannis White, Thomæ Clayton, Willielmi Trippet, Thomæ Wilson, Henrici Damme, et uxoris Gladwine viduæ vel assignatorum suorum; ac de et in uno clauso terræ et prati cum pertinentiis in Sheffield prædict. Radulphi Hollinhead; ac de et in tribus croftis terræ cum pertinentiis in Sheffield prædict. modo vel nuper in seperalibus tenuris Willielmi Spooner, Aliciæ Jackson viduæ, et Willielmi Hibline; ac de et in duobus messuagiis sive tenementis ac terris et pratis eisdem pertinentibus, cum pertinentiis in Sheffield prædict. modo vel nuper in seperalibus tenuris Hugonis Hawke et Jacobi Slatter; ac de et in uno clauso terræ et hosci vocato Lady-Spring, et duobus croftis vocatis Malkin Crofts in Heeley in parochia de Sheffield prædict. modo vel nuper in seperalibus tenuris Thomæ Blith et Jacobi Tailour; ac de et in uno clauso terræ et certis terris in campis de Sheffield prædict. modo in seperalibus tenuris Willielmi Glete et Thomæ Lewes; ac de et in uno clauso terræ et prati vocato Red-Hill cum pertinentiis in Sheffield prædict. modo in occupatione Roberti Bowre; ac de et in uno crofto et diversis terris pratis et pasturis cum pertinentiis in Aughton infra parochiam de Aston in dicto comitatu nostro Eboraci in tenura sive occupatione Georgii West generosi, vel assignatorum suorum; ac de et in duobus messuagiis et tenementis cum pertinentiis situatis et existentibus in le Old Change in parochia Sancti Augustini infra civitatem nostram London, modo vel nuper in seperalibus tenuris sive occupationibus Rowlandi Sheppard et Willielmi Willoughby. Quæ quidem omnia et singula prædicta mes-

How Burgesses became seized; by grants and for what uses.

suagia et cottagia, crofta, prata, terræ, tenementa et cetera præmissa per diversos annos elapsos præfatis Burgensibus et Inhabitantibus de Sheffield et heredibus successoribus suis per diversas personas dat. conces. legat. et assignat. fuerunt ad usus et intentiones, quod iidem Burgenses et Inhabitantes villæ prædictæ pro tempore existentes omnia et singula exit. redditus et proficua premissorum, annuatim et de tempore in tempus converterent et inpenderent, tam ad reparationem ecclesiæ parochialis de Sheffield

1st. Repairs of the church.

præd. ac pontium et communim viarum et

2d. Bridges and ways.

passag. infra parochiam prædict. quam ad sustentationem et relevamen pauperum et indigentium Inhabitantium infra parochiam

3d. Relief of the poor.

prædict. Et ad eosdem pios usus et intentiones prædicti Burgenses et Inhabitantes

So applied,

villæ de Sheffield prædict. pro tempore existentes, omnia redditus et proficua premissorum per tempus prædict. impendebant et convertebant, usque circa tricessimum annum regni precarissimi patris nostri

till 30th Hen. VIII-

nuper regis Henrici Octavi; ad quod quidem

when three priests were appointed and maintained by voluntary gifts. After-

tempus tam populorum quam parochianorum prædict. piæ elargissiones elemosin. ceterisque modis et viis (quibus tres presby-

wards part of the said rents were ap-

teri celebrantes et ministrantes in ecclesia parochiali prædict. sustentabantur) ita paula-

plied to support the

tim decrescebant, frigebant, et penitus de-

said priests, viz.

minut. et extinct. extiterunt; uti prædict.

16l. 10s. per ann.

Burgenses et Inhabitantes villæ et parochiæ prædict. pro tempore existentes cum percell. redituum et proficuorum premissorum præd. tres presbyteros in ecclesia parochiali prædict. sustentari, vidiaque et stipendia eorundem presbyterorum extenden. ad sexdecim libras et decem solidos per annum annuatim persolvere necessario cogerentur: ac unum lampadem ardentem in ecclesia parochiali

Also a lamp

prædict. et unum anniversarium in eadem

19s. a year.

ecclesia annuatim inveniebant et sustinebant,

16 10 Priests.

ac novem decem solidos in sustentationis ex-

17   9 paid in all.

ñensis eorundem lampadis et anniversarii annuatim expende-
bant; in quorum quidem stipendiorum persolutione, ac lampadis et anniversarii sustentatione, dicti Burgenses et Inhabitantes dictæ villæ de Sheffield perseverabant et continuabant
usque confectionem cujusdem actus parlia-
By statute of chan-
tries 1 Edward VI.
said rents were for-
feited to the crown,
viz. 17l. 9s. 4d.
menti in anno regni precarissimi fratris nostri nuper regis Edwardi Sexti primo facti et
editi de diversis collegiis canteriis et gildis
dissolvend. et determinand. virtute et co-
lore cujus quidem actus, prædict. Burgenses et Inhabitantes
coacti fuerunt reddere et annuatim solvere ad usum prædict.
fratris nostri de exit. proficuis et reventionibus premissorum
pro redditibus et proficuis prædictor. premissorum sic per eos
pro stipendiis dictorum trium presbyterorum, ac pro sustentatione prædict. lampadis et anniversarii annuatim expendit.
quendam annualem redditum septemdecim librarum novem
solidorum et quatuor denariorum. Nichilominus ex eorundem
tempore diversos quæstiones et ambiguitates
Doubts as to title
of premises aris-
ing;
de jure et titulo premissorum mot. et ort.
fuerunt (videlicet) utrum prædict. messuagia, cottagia, et cetera premissa, aut prædict.
redditus septemdecim librarum novem solidorum et quatuor
denariorum per predict. Burgenses et Inhabitantes ad usus prædict. in forma prædict. annuatim expendit. aut neutra eorundem ad manus prædict. fratris nostri aut ad manus nostras,
ratione vel pretextu dicti actus parliamenti devenire debuerunt.
NOS igitur premissa consideran. et intelli-
Queen Mary for
divers considera-
tions,
gen. predict. villam et parochiam de Sheffield
spaciosas et largas in se continere circuitus
et distanc. ac tant. populorum turba, tam-
toque parochianorum numero suffert. et replet. esse, ut vicarius dictæ ecclesiæ parochialis de Sheffield sine aliorum presbyterorum presidio et   sacramenta et sacramentalia
ac alia divina servitia in ecclesia prædict. et parochianis prædict. ministrar. minime possit aut valeat, Nec non volentes et
intenden. prædict. quæstiones et ambiguitates de jure et titulo
premissorum penitus tollere et delere et amovere, ac sacramenta et alia divina ministeria ad Dei Omnipotentis gloriam
in ecclesia parochiali prædict. et parochianis prædict. deinceps
de tempore in tempus imperpetuum ministrari et celebrari
prout temporibus retroactis (videlicet tempore precharissimi
patris nostri et aliorum progenitorum nostrorum regum Angliæ)
ante hac usitat. et consuet. fuit ac etiam ut hæc nostra inten-
tio plenum et debitum capere et sortire valeat effectum, pre-
dilectus consanguineus et consiliar. noster Franciscus comes
on request of the
earl of Salop, and
said burgesses,
Salop, ac dicti dilecti subditi nostri Burgenses et Inhabitantes villæ et parochiæ de Sheffield prædict. nobis benigne et humiliter sup-
plicaverunt ut nos eosdem Burgenses et Inhabitantes in unum corpus corporat. et politicum per nomen
Duodecem Capital. Burgenses Communitat. villæ et parochiæ
prædict. facere creare erigere et stabilire dignaremur perpetuis temporibus futuris duratur. eosdemque Duodecim Capitales Burgenses ac Communitatem et successores suos, personas habiles et leges capaces ad recipiendum et perquiren-
dum eis et successoribus suis infra parochiam de Sheffield
prædict. terras tenementa et hereditamenta in formis sequen.
et ad usus et intentiones infra scriptum facere et creare etiam
dignare valemus. SCIATIS igitur quod nos supplicationibus
grants for herself
her heirs and suc-
cessors.
prædict. benigne auscultan. et inclinan. de
gracia nostra speciali ac ex certa scientia et
mero motu nostris, nec non pro consideratione prædict. et addict. benignam humilem
et specialem petitionem dicti prædilecti consanguinei et con-
siliarii nostri Francisci comitis Salop. et dictor. dilectorum
subditorum nostror. Burgen. et Inhabitan. villæ et parochiæ
de Sheffield prædict. voluimus, ordinavimus, constituimus,
decrevimus, et concessimus, ac per presentes pro nobis here-
Incorporates the
said Burgesses a
body.
dibus et successoribus nostris volumus, ordinamus, determinamus, constituimus, quod
dicti Burgenses et Inhabitantes villæ et parochiæ de Sheffield prædict. sint et erunt in-
corporat. per nomen Duodecem Capitalium Burgensium et
Communitat. villæ et parochiæ de Sheffield in Com. Ebor. in
re facta et nomine imperpetuum; et quod iidem Duodecem
Burgen. et Communitas de cetero sint et erunt unum corpus
corporat. et politicum perpetuis futuris temporibus duratur,

ipsosque Duodecim Capitales Burgenses et Communitas dictæ
villæ et parochiæ de Sheffield unum corpus corporatum et politicum de se realiter et ad plenum creamus, erigimus, ordinamus, facimus, constituimus, declaramus et incorporamus per
presentes; habeantque successionem perpetuam et per idem
nomen et sub eodem nomine placitare et implacitari, ac de-
fendere et defendi, respondere et responderi valeant et possint
in omnibus curiis et locis nostris, ac heredum et successorum
nostrorum, ac in omnibus aliis curiis et locis quibuscunque
in omnibus et singulis actionibus, sect. querel. caus. et demand. realibus personalibus seu mixtis quibuscunque. Quodque
iidem Duodecim Capitales Burgenses et
Common seal.
Communitas et successores sui habeant et
habebunt commune Sigillum ad demissiones faciend. et alia
quæcunque agend. tractand. et sigilland. prædict. messuagia,
cottagia, terras, tenementa, et cetera premissa, aut aliqua
hereditamenta sua quæcunque tangen. sive concernen. Nec
non quod prædict. duodecim capitales burgenses et communitas per nomen Duodecem Capitalium Burgens. et Communitat.
villæ et parochiæ de Sheffield prædict. sint et erunt personæ
habiles et in lege capaces ad capiend. et recipiend. sibi et
successoribus suis imperpetuum messuagia, terras, tenementa
et hereditamenta et cetera premissa supradict. cum eorum
pertinentiis univers. Et ut ea omnia et singula suum debitum
sortire valeant effectum, de gratia nostra speciali ac ex certa
scientia et mero motu nostris assignavimus, nominavimus,
fecimus et ordinavimus, ac per presentes pro nobis, heredibus
et successoribus nostris nominamus, facimus, et ordinamus
dilectos nobis Robertum Swift armigerum, Hugonem Smith,
Richardum Fenton, Willielmum Taylour,
First Burgesses.
Robertum Moore, Willielmum Walton, Robertum Smith, Hugonem Chawner, Willielmum Borowes,
Johannem Holland, Thomam Mitchell, et Thomam Parker de
Attercliff, Inhabitantes villæ et parochiæ de Sheffield prædict.
fore et esse primos Duodecim Principales Burgenses villæ et
parochiæ prædict. AC ETIAM volumus, ac pro
When a Burgess
dies or is removed,
rest of Burgesses
or major part with-
in one month to
elect another.
nobis, heredibus et successoribus nostris per
presentes concedimus prefata Duodecim Capitalibus Burgens. villæ et parochiæ de Sheffield predict. successoribus suis, quod quo-
tiens et quandocunque contigerit aliquem
predict. Duodecim Capitalium Burgens. obire vel ab officio suo
Capitalis Burgens. eorundem villæ et parochiæ pro aliqua causa
rationabili amoveri, quod tunc et totiens bene liceat et licebit
aliis Capital. Burgens. superviven. et remanen. aut majori parte
eorundem, cum et quando eis placuit et expediens videbitur
infra unum mensem proximum sequen. mortem seu amotionem hujus modi Capitalis Burgens. nominare, eligere et assignare alium de prædict. Inhabitantibus villæ sive parochiæ
prædict. magis discretiorum et proborum virorum fore et esse
Capital. Burgensis villæ et parochiæ de Sheffield prædict.
Qui quidem elect. et nominat. a tempore hujus modi elect.
erit unus Capital. Burgens. villæ et parochiæ prædict. durante
vita sua. ET ULTERIUS de ampliori gratia nostra, ac ex certa
scientia et mero motu nostris dedimus et concessimus, ac
per presentes pro nobis, heredibus, et suc-
Grant of said here-
ditaments.
cessoribus nostris, damus et concedimus prefatis Duodecim Capitalibus Burgens. et
Communitati villæ et parochiæ de Sheffield prædict. omnia
singula prædict. messuagia, cottagia, gardina, terras, tenementa, prata, pascuas, pastur. redditus, reventiones, hereditamenta et cetera omnia et singular. premissa cum eorum pertinentiis universa in dicta villa et parochia de Sheffield prædict. ac predict. tofta, terras, tenementa, prata, pasturas, et
hereditamenta cum pertinentiis in Aughton prædict. in prædict. parochia de Aston in dicto comitatu nostro Ebor. ac
prædict. duo messuagia et tenementa cum pertinentiis scituat.
et existen. in le Olde Change in parochia Sancti Augustini
infra dictam civitatem nostram London. Necnon prædict. annualem redditum septemdecem librarum novem solidorum et
quatuor denariorum per prædict. Burgenses et Inhabitantes
villæ et parochiæ de Sheffield prædict. dicto fratri nostro nuper regi Edwardo Sexto ut prefertur annuatim solut. ac reven-
tionem et reventiones prædictorum messuagiorum, terrarum,
tenementorum, reddituum et ceterorum premissorum cum
eorum pertinentiis universis, ac reddit. et annualia proficua
ñuecunque super quibuscunque demissionibus seu concessioni-

bus premissorum aut alicujus inde parcell. fact. reservat. ac omnes singulos boscos, subboscos, et arbores nostras quascunque de in vel super premiss. vel aliqua inde parcella crescen. sive existen. ac totum jus, titulum, statum et interesse nostra quecunque de et in omnibus et singulis premissis et qualibet inde parcella habendum et tenendum et gaudendum prædict. messuagia, cottagia, terras, tenementa, prata, pascuas, pasturas, redditus, revensiones, boscos, subboscos, ac cetera omnia et singula premissa; ac totum jus, statum, titulum et interesse nostra de et in eisdem cum suis pertinentiis universis, prefat. Duodecim Capitalibus Burgensibus et Communitati villæ et parochiæ de Sheffield prædict. et successoribus suis im-

To hold to the said 12 Burgesses to the uses following:

perpetuum; ad usum et intentionem, quod iidem Capitales Burgenses, Communitas, et successores sui cum parcell. reddit. et profi-

1. To support 3 priests.

cuis premissorum invenient et invenire faciant de tempore in tempus imperpetuum tres capellanos sive presbyteros ad celebrand. et ministrand. divina ser-

Their duty.

vitiæ et ministeria ac sacramenta et sacramentalia aliaque ad divinum cultum necessaria in ecclesia parochiali de Sheffield præd. et parochia ibidem. Quos quidem tres presbyteros volumus esse assistentes et auxiliantes de tempore in tempus imperpetuum vicario ecclesiæ parochialis de Sheffield prædict. pro tempore existen. in celebrat. et ministerio sacramentorum et sacramentalium, et in omnibus aliis ad divinum cultum necessar. in ecclesia parochiali prædict. et parochianis ejusdem ministrand. Nec non ad usum et intentionem quod prædict. Duodecim Principal. Burgenses et Communitas dictæ villæ et parochiæ de Sheffield successores sui totum remanen. de reddit. et profic. premissorum pre-

II. Surplus applied to
1. Repairs of the church.
2. Bridges and ways.
3. Poor inhabitants.

ter et ultra sependia necessaria et convenientia vad. et stipend. præd. trium presbyterorum et capellanorum de tempore in tempus capellanorum pro tempore existen. vertant et impend. ad reparationem ecclesiæ parochialis de Sheffield prædict. ac pontium et communium viarum, ac pauperum et indigen. inhabitan. infra eandem parochiam,

Power to purchase to the yearly value of 20l. for same uses.

Et ulterius, de alteriori gracia nostra, licenciam damus et concedimus pro nobis, heredibus, et successoribus nostris per presentes prefatis Burgensibus et Communitati villæ et parochiæ de Sheffield prædict. et successoribus suis, quod ipsi et successores sui perquirere et capere valeant et possint sibi et successoribus suis terras tenementa et hereditamenta infra parochiam de Sheffield prædict. clari annui valoris viginti librarum ad usus et intentiones prædict. dummodo eadem terræ et tenementa de nobis non teneantur in capite, nec per servitium militare, nec de aliquo alio per servitium militare, et etiam cum licentia dominii sive dominorum de quo vel de quibus hujus modi terr. et tenementa tenta fuerunt; statut. de terris et tenementis ad manum mortuam non ponend. aut aliquo alio actu, statuto sive ordinatione inde in contrarium fact. sive edit. in aliquo non obstante.

On the death or removal of an assistant, Burgesses or major part to elect another in 6 weeks.

Et insuper per presentes volumus et concedimus quod quoties et quandocumque contigerit aliquem prædict. trium capellanorum pro tempore existen. obire, sive aliqua de causa a ministratione præd. amoveri, quod tunc et toties bene liceat et licebit prædict. Duodecim Capital. Burgens. et successoribus suis, aut majori parti eorundem, cum et quando eis placuerit et expediens videbitur infra sex hebdomadas proximas sequen. mortem seu amotionem hujusmodi capellani nominare et assignare alium capellanum fore unum dictorum trium capellanorum in villa de Sheffield prædict. qui quidem capellanus sic electus erit unus dictorum trium capellanorum ad ministran. ibidem sacramenta et sacramentalia alia faciend. et exequend. prout ceteri duo capellani ibidem facient, seu facere debent. Proviso semper, ac volumus et ordinamus per

Burgesses' release from annuities to 3 priests.

presentes, et prædict. Duodecim Capitales Burgenses et Communitas prædict. villæ et parochiæ de Sheffield prædict. concedunt pro se et successoribus suis, quod iidem Burgenses et Communitas, et successores sui nos, heredes et successores nostros annuatim et de tempore in tempus de cetero

a festo Annuntiationis beatæ Mariæ virginis ultimo præterito acquietabunt, exonerabunt aut deinceps conservabunt de seperalibus pensionibus et annuitat. subsequen. ac presbyter. nuper celebrant. et servient. in ecclesia parochiali prædict. per prædict. nuper fratrem nostrum nuper regem Edwardum Sextum nuper dat. et concess. videlicet, de quadam annuali pensione sive annuali redditu sex librarum, tresdecim solidorum et quatuor denariorum cuidam Alexandro Bothe clerico dat. et concess. durante vita sua. Ac de una alia pensione quinque librarum cuidam Richardo Beock clerico dat. et concess. durante vita sua. Ac de una alia pensione quinque librarum cuidam Willielmo Hall durante vita sua dat. et concess.

viz. to				
A. Booth	6	13	4	
R. Bewick	5	0	0	
W. Hall	5	0	0	
	£16	13	4	

Et ulterius damus ac certa scientia et mero motu nostris per presentes, concedimus prefatis Duodecim Capitalibus Burgensibus et Communitati villæ et parochiæ de Sheffield prædict. omnia et singula exitus redditus reventiones et proficua prædictorum messuagiorum terrarum tenementorum et prædict. redditus septemdecim librarum novem solidorum et quatuor denariorum ac ceterorum premissorum cum eorum pertinentiis universis a dicto festo Annuntiationis beatæ Mariæ virginis ultimo preterito hujusque provenien. sive crescen. habend. eisdem Duodecim Principal. Burgens. et Communitati ex dono nostro absque compo̅to seu aliquo alio proinde nobis heredibus vel successoribus nostris quoquomodo reddend. solvend. vel faciend. Eo quod expressa mentio vero valore annuo aut certitudine premissorum sive eorum alicujus aut de aliis donis sive concessionibus per nos vel per aliquem progenitor. nostrorum prefatis Duodecim Principal. Burgens. et Communitati ante hæc tempora fact. in presentibus minime fact. existit. aut aliquo statuto actu ordinatione provisione sive restrictione inde in contrarium fact. edit. ordinat. seu provi. aut aliqua alia re causa vel materia quecumque in aliquo non obstan. In cujus rei testimonium has litteras nostras fieri facimus patentes. Teste me ipsa apud Westmon. octavo die Junii anno regni nostri primo.

Queen's grant of said lands and rent of 17l. 9s. 4d. to the burgesses for ever.

From these authentic documents it appears that in times long before the reign of Henry VIII. the inhabitants of Sheffield had found the necessity of engaging the services of more than one clergyman in their large and populous parish, and had accordingly by means of voluntary contributions, supported three priests who had been accustomed to assist the vicar in the ministration of all divine ordinances. This fact deposes very favourably to the serious and religious spirit of our ancestors, and I am not acquainted with any similar instance in the northern parts of England, except that in the church of Laughton-en-le-Morthen, formerly a place of more consequence than it is at present, there was a stipendiary priest maintained 'by the devotions of the parishioners,' as it is stated in Archbishop Holgate's return of the chantries within his diocese[1]. The unsettled and uncertain state into which the ecclesiastical affairs of this kingdom were thrown by Henry VIII. occasioned in the parish of Sheffield a failure of the contributions by which the priests were maintained, and in the thirtieth year of that king's reign it is alleged that these contributions were wholly withdrawn. The three priests had, it is probable, been of real use to the inhabitants, and there were not wanting those who had a just value for their services. These persons diverted to their support the produce of certain lands, which had been given by various benefactors at different periods for public uses, such as the reparation of the bridges and highways, and also of the parish-church, and for the relief of the poor: and if we might rely upon the

---

[1] Dods. MSS. in Bibl. Bodl. vol. xcii. f. 143, &c.

allegations in the petition and preamble of the patent, for these *only:* but it will soon appear that the donors of some portions of the public lands contemplated the appropriation of the income arising from them to other purposes. This fund was under the control of the vicar and church-graves or *church-maisters,* a term not yet quite extinct, and applied to the church-wardens. Out of the produce of these lands the three assistants were maintained from the 30th of Henry VIII. to the 1st of Edward VI. a period of eight years.

When the commissioners under the statute for the suppression of colleges, &c. visited Sheffield, they found the three priests enjoying an income from this fund : and choosing to consider them in the light of chantry-priests, they seized upon that portion of the public lands from which their income was derived, and, confiscated it to the use of the crown. These lands remained in the possession of the crown during the whole reign of Edward VI. Whatever remonstrances or petitions might have been presented against what appeared to the inhabitants of Sheffield to be an extension of the act beyond what was the intention of its framers, they were of no avail. The earl of Shrewsbury, the fast friend of the town, had little interest in the court of King Edward.

Early in the new reign the subject was revived, and the petition of the inhabitants was so well seconded by the earl that the lands in question were restored, and the queen granted the patent which has been already recited.

By this patent, the burgesses and inhabitants, *burgenses et inhabitantes,* of the town and parish of Sheffield are declared to be one body politic and corporate, by the name of TWELVE CAPITAL BURGESSES AND COMMONALTY OF THE TOWN AND PARISH OF SHEFFIELD, with power to acquire lands, plead, and be impleaded, &c. and to have and use a common seal: twelve gentlemen of the town and parish are nominated the first twelve capital burgesses, with power to fill vacancies which may occur by death or removal : to the twelve burgesses and commonalty the premises in question are assigned over in trust for the uses and intents following :

I. To find and maintain with necessary and convenient wages and stipend three chaplains or presbyters to celebrate divine ordinances in the parish-church of Sheffield as helpers to the vicar.

II. To repair the parish-church, bridges, and common-ways.

III. To assist the poor and needy inhabitants.

And lastly, as to the material and permanent provisions of the patent, the right of election of the three presbyters is declared to be in the twelve capital burgesses only, who are required to proceed to election within six weeks of the death or amoval of any of the three priests.

This patent was executed at Westminster on the eighth day of June 1554, and the burgesses without delay procured a seal to be cut, choosing for its device the ancient rebus the two sheafs of arrows in saltier between two pheons, and this inscription SIGIL-LVM . VILLÆ . DE . SHEFFELDE . ANNO. 1554.

The patent, clear and express in settling the uses of the trust, is not equally so in defining the duties of the three presbyters, or the respective rights and duties of the twelve capital burgesses, and the com-

monalty. Hence dissentions have in former times arisen in the parish; but it seems to be now understood that it is the duty of the assistant-ministers to take an equal share with the vicar in the performance of sacerdotal offices in and out of the church. The question was once proposed to counsel on the part of the commonalty of Sheffield 'Whether seven of the twelve burgesses, five being against it, may not be of force to make leases, &c., and how many of the commonalty are requisite: and if the greater part of the burgery be divided from the greater part of the commonalty, what is then to be done:' which Mr. Serjeant Hutton, an eminent legal authority in the time of James I. answered by advising that twenty-four persons should be elected out of the whole body of the commonalty as a common council to act in concert with the burgesses in granting leases and in the performance of other acts relating to the property. This was never done, and the commonalty gradually withdrew from taking any part in the management of the property, remitting that entirely to the twelve burgesses, with whom by the patent rested the sole nomination of the three presbyters.

To the credit of the body, and to the honour of the individuals in whose hands this trust, so important to the best interests of the inhabitants of Sheffield, has been placed, let it be observed, that it has been uniformly administered with a due regard to the benefit of those for whom they were placed in trust. Unlike other small corporate bodies, at whose disposal church-preferment has been placed, here no private inclination, no personal or family interest has intruded to divert them from paying an honourable and Christian-like regard to the interest of that part of the church of Christ for which they stand intrusted. They seem to have resisted the temptation before which many mighty have fallen of regarding trustee property in the light of private property, and of administering it not so much for the benefit of those for whom they are placed in trust as for their own. May they ever pursue this honourable course! And though to place in the same church three clergymen possessing a co-ordinate authority with the vicar appears contrary to the monarchical spirit of the English establishment, yet it may be observed, that the experiment seems here to have succeeded, no unedifying rivalries and contentions having sprung up among them, but all striving together in the work and labour of love.

The stipend which has appeared to the burgesses 'necessary and convenient' has remarkably varied: and if we suppose their minds in this point to be uniform, the variation would afford an excellent illustration of the change in the value of money during a period of two centuries and a half. In the time of Henry VIII. it was seventeen pounds, which was divided among the three priests in the proportion of seven, five and five. During the remainder of that century each had about seven or eight pounds *per annum.* This stipend was advanced to ten, twelve, and more in the reign of James I. Early in that reign Mr. Robert Rollinson bequeathed two houses in Sheffield to the burgesses in trust for the use of two of the ministers. In 1619 there were contentions between the burgesses and the commonalty respecting the sum proper to be allowed to the three ministers. The matter in dispute was referred to the arbitration of Francis

Coke and George Lascelles, esquires, who decided that Mr. Towne, one of the ministers, should have forty marks yearly, and his house-rent freed if it exceeded not fifty shillings; that a second, to succeed to a place then vacant, should have twenty marks yearly, and his house-rent freed, but not to exceed forty shillings; and that Mr. Dawson should have ten pounds yearly, and for house-rent a sum not exceeding forty shillings. The award goes on to recite the bequest of Mr. Rollinson, which was not to take effect till after the death of his widow. The arbitrators direct that whenever she died, two of the ministers should 'rest satisfied with the said two houses,' a hard decision, if the houses in Fig-Tree-lane which are here intended were not more desirable residences two centuries ago than they are at present. The arbitrators then direct, that, to meet the additional demand on their fund, which the new arrangement would occasion, the property of the trust should be so improved as to produce a hundred pounds a year; which was immediately done. A few years later, the parliamentary commissioners made return that 'There be three assistant-ministers belonging to the said church, viz. Mr. Bridges, Mr. Metcalfe, and Mr. Bagshawe, all able and painefull preachers, who have for their salarye fortye marks apiece.' At the close of the century each had forty pounds, and their income has since been more than quintupled.

The two chapels of Ecclesall and Attercliffe, of which we shall speak more at large in the account of those townships, have been considered as appendages to the office of assistant-minister at Sheffield.

The rents of the property at different periods have been,

          anno 1570 . . . . £36   16   11
               1595   49   7   8
               1620 100   5   3
               1736 250   14   3

And they are now supposed to yield a clear yearly income of above 1000l.

Notwithstanding it is alleged in the petition, that the lands which were seized by King Edward's commissioners were given for secular uses and the repair of the church, it does appear that some part of them at least had been assigned to the church-graves for other purposes, and might without any inpropriety have been brought within the scope of the act. To prove this point, as well as to bring the reader acquainted with certain altars and services which were in the parish-church of Sheffield before the Reformation, a few notices of evidences in possession of the church-burgesses, and extracts from them, are here inserted.

Anno 1320. A grant from Adam Drake of Attercliffe to the service of the Virgin Mary in the church of Sheffield, of a rood and half of land in a field at Attercliffe called Leyland.

Anno 1333. A grant from John del Wodd.del Brome to John de Elcliffe chaplayne, of land in Sheffield lying in Balne.

Anno 1366. Release from Robert Raunkell and Hugh de Tibbshelff to Adam Sumpner, Henry de Tapton, and William de Wood, keepers of the service of the blessed Mary in the church of the blessed Peter at Sheffield, and their successors, of all his right and claim in a toft in Sheffield lying between the toft of

John de Walkmylnes on the east, the toft of William Colt on the west, and towards the church of Sheffield on the north. The witnesses to this deed are John del Wood, John Mountenay, John Cutler, Richard Stubbe, John de Walkemylne and others, and it was executed at Sheffield on the Sunday next after the feast of Saint Lucy the virgin.

Anno 1417. Grant from John Stube of Sheffield to Robert Challoner of the same place, of half a toft in Sheffield lying in length between Water-lane on the west, &c., paying yearly to the Lord de Furnival three-pence as the manner is in the said town of the tenements held in burgage.

Anno 1499. Lease from William Taylor and other greves or church-maisters of Sheffield to Geffery Buttery of Sheffield, one of the said greves or church-maisters, of four tenements in Sheffield, beneath the Yrish-cross, and all other such lands and tenements as the said Geffery hath held of the said church-maisters in the fields of Sheffield aforesaid, to hold for forty years at thirty-three shillings and four-pence yearly rent.

Anno 1498. May 10. Deed of feoffment whereby William Hyne of Sheffield grants and confirms to John Plesaince vicar of Sheffield, Geffery Butterey, William Tailour, and Thomas Challoneur three tenements, with one house called a smeethy house, in Sheffield, lying in Water-lane, to hold to the said feoffees, their heirs and assigns for ever.

Anno 1498. May 12. An Indenture of three parts, between the said William Hyne of the one part, the said John Plesaince of the second part, the said Buttery, Tailour, and Challoneur of the third part, reciting the said deed of feoffment; and that the south tenement was then lett for seven shillings a year, the middle tenement with the said smeethy for ten shillings a year, and the north tenement next the water for six shillings a year. Whereby it was agreed that the said Plesaince, Buttery, Tailour, and Challoneur, and their heirs should for ever stand and be enfeoffed of the said premises to the use of the said William Hyne for his life; and after his decease that the said feoffees and their heirs should immediately suffer the four church-maisters of Sheffield and their successors to receive the rents of the said tenements, and thereof yearly *to pay to the priest of Saint Catherine saying mass in the said church* for the time being, seven shillings at Whitsuntide for the better support and augmentation of the service thereof, called Saint Catherine's service.—Also the said four church-maisters shall take the rent of the said middlemost tenement with the said smeethy, and with nine shillings coming from the said rent, the said four church-maisters should cause the Devote Obit or yearly Day Diridge and Masse of Requiem yearly to be kept and celebrated in the said church on the first day of February, or within seven days next after for ever, for the souls of the said William Hyne and Phillis his wife, of Thomas Hyne and Jennet his wife, of John Whitebrede and Isabel his wife, (fathers and mothers of the said William and Phillis his wife,) and of all Christian souls. And if it should happen that any part of the said nine shillings should not be spent on the day of the said Obit, about the said Diridge, Mass of Requiem, waste of tape about the herse, and other ceremonies, then the said four church-maisters should divide and distribute the said money so unspent amongst the poor people for the health of the soul of the said William Hyne and of the souls aforesaid. Also the said church-maisters should on the day of the said Obit divide amongst them of the profits of the said middlemost tenement and smeethy, twelve pence to the intent that they should be at the Diridge and Mass of Requiem, and pray for the soul of the said William Hyne and for the souls aforesaid.—Also the said church-maisters should take the profits of the said north tenement to maintain, uphold, and sustain as well yearly fermes of the other two tenements, as the yearly reparation of the same three tenements, smeethy and other premises for ever; to the intent that the said seven shillings limitted to the augmentation of St. Catherine's service, the nine shillings limitted for keeping the said Obit, and the twelve pence appointed to the said church-maisters should be yearly for ever paid, the said three tenements duly repaired, and the good and virtuous mind of the said William Hyne performed. But in case the said several limitations should not be truly performed in form aforesaid, then the said feoffees should stand and be enfeoffed of the said premises to the use of the freeholders of Sheffield called the burgesses, and should suffer the said burgesses to take the profits of the said premises, and dispose thereof in mending of bridges, causeys and highways most defective and within one mile of Sheffield: and in other deeds of charity as they shall think most meritorious, for the health of the said William Hyne and the souls aforesaid.

Anno 1501. May 1. Declaration of trust by Felice [Phillis] late wife of William Hyne of Sheffield, and daughter and heir of John Whitebrede sometime before citizen and fishmonger of London, reciting a deed of the 12th of Henry VII. whereby she had enfeoffed Geoffery Buttery, Robert Parker, William Taylour and Thomas Challoner, of a tenement in the Old Change London, and declaring that the said feoffment was in trust for the said Felice for life, and after her decease in trust to make sale of the said tenement, and dispose of the money thereby arising in buying a cross of silver and gilt, with the image of the crucifix, of our Lady, and Saint John, thereunto annexed, and other such ornaments as the said feoffees shall think most needful and meritorious: and the said cross to be used in the parish church of Saint Peter of Sheffield, and there to remain for ever, to the intent that the said Felice and her said late husband, and father and mother, might be the better remembered and prayed for, in the said church and parish.

Anno 1508. Release from William Staniford son of John, son of Richard, to Robert Hudson bailiff of Sheffield, and others, of one yearly rent of twenty-one pence issuing out of lands and tenements in Attercliffe, which were Adam Copley's; to be received out of the said lands and tenements to the use of God, the blessed Mary, and the sustentation of the light or guild of the blessed virgin Mary in the parish-church of Sheffield, according to the form and effect of the deed of donation made by the said Adam Copley deceased.

Two things are particularly deserving notice in these extracts: first, that it is evident there were at least two chantries, that of the blessed Virgin and that of Saint Catherine, in the church of Sheffield: an additional proof, if more were wanting, of the incompleteness of archbishop Holgate's return of chantries, published by Stevens from Dodsworth's collections, in which there is no mention of any in the parish-church of Sheffield. And secondly, that the church of Sheffield was dedicated to Saint Peter, as Torre represents it, although it has been usual to call it the church of the Holy Trinity, and one of the fairs of Sheffield was held on the eve, day, and morrow of that high festival. At present the name of Saint Peter's seems to be gaining ground upon the other.

I shall subjoin a collection of extracts from the old accompt-books of this public trust, illustrative at once of the objects to which the income has been heretofore applied, and of the ecclesiastical history of this parish at a most interesting period [1].

'A remembrance that I Thomas Bray dyd geve thys boke to the Churche there to remayne as a presydent for the takinge of the reconynges from tyme to tyme, and to th'entent that yt may be a testamoney how the rents belonginge to the xii. capitall burgesses of the towne and parish of Sheffelde be spent; as shall appere w'yn this boke. An° Dñi 1557.

1557. Itm p to Mr Robt Swifte as apperyth by a quyttaunce of his owne towards ye losinge of one oblygacyon, wch certin of ye paryshe stande bounden to paye, in parte of payment of a more some p^d and dysbursed by hym aboute the obteynynge of the same lands	VI. XIII. IIII.
Itm p^d to Edwarde Parye for his wages being Clerke of ye paryshe church of Sheffield; and granted hym of newe at thys same reconynge VI^s. VIII^d. in toto, the sum of	XIII. IIII.
Itm p^d to the same Edwarde for whaschinge of the churche clothes, and candyls . . .	III. IIII.
Itm p^d to Thomas Barten for makynge of a candyllstycke of wodde before ye Crucifix . .	VI.
Itm p^d to my Lorde's rent gatherer for ye towne rent, of ye lands belonginge to the Capital Burgery	VII. II.
Itm p^d to Sr Rycharde Bewcke for a paynteyd clothe	VIII.
1558. Itm p^d for a clothe to ye Sepulcers house côteynynge XII. yards at VIII^d. ye yerd . . .	VIII.
Itm p^d to Hugh Paynter for payntynge ye Sepulcre clothe	IIII.
Itm p^d for settiuge uppe of ye Resurecôn . .	VII.

These entries relate to ceremonies observed in catholic times in the parish-churches, about the time of Easter. The performance of them was discontinued early in the reign of Elizabeth, so that the good people of Sheffield might as well have been content in 1558 with their old sepulchre-house, and its faded appendages. Whoever wishes for further information concerning these ceremonies may consult *Ecclesiastical Biography*, vol. i. p. 485, and *Anecdotes of Painting*, 12mo edit., vol. i. p. 76.

Rec^d of Mr Baylyf of Sheff. viz. Hughe Smythe for his father and mother, and Richard Fenton's, theyr graves at VI. VIII. a grave	XX.
Paide to Sr Willm Kynge for ane arnest peny .	IIII.
1559. Itm paid to Sr Rycherde Bewcke for his wags for one yere endyt at Wytt-sondaye last	V. X.
Itm p^d to Ralph Hollynshead for wodde for the cômunyon table	VI.

This was in pursuance of orders from above. It was

---

[1] These extracts as well as the notes from the charters above given were made by Mr. Wilson.

directed that the altars in all the churches should be taken down, and the stones of which they were composed, applied to some common purpose. A moveable table for the celebration of the Lord's Supper was to be provided. The burgesses of Sheffield seem to have been in more haste to procure the table than to take down the altars. The work of Reformation went on but slowly in the northern counties. We shall find other instances of tardy compliance with the queen's injunctions.

At the name of *Ralph Hollynshead*, the spirit of every true antiquary is stirred within him. Who was he?—I fear no more than an humble carpenter. But surely our Hollinshead was of the kindred of his illustrious namesake and contemporary, who was a north-countryman. His will however, the best resource of a genealogist, throws no light on his extraction or alliances. It was made at Sheffield on the 25th of June 1581, when he was 'sick in body.' He desires to be buried in the church-yard of Sheffield; mentions his wife Elizabeth, to whom he leaves a lease of certain lands, and a son Laurence Hollynshead, alias Mellor, who is made joint-executor with his widow. It was proved at York.

> Itm p[d] to the ryngers y[t] dyd rynge for S[r] Thomas Twell, at the receyvynge of certen stuf gevyn by hym to the church, wth p[d] to the prestes and clerke for deyrge   XVI.
> Itm p[d] for the costs and chargs for feching S[r] Thomas Twell will from Blythe   II.
> 1560. Itm paid the xxviii[th] daie of October for powling downe of the awters   IIII. IIII.

In pursuance of the queen's injunctions. We may observe that it is *awters* in the plural. Beside the great altar, there was one in the Shrewsbury-chapel, and probably each of the guilds of St. Mary and St. Catherine had its altar.

> Item paid for a surplesse for Edward Pavye   IIII. VI.
> Paid to John Howe the Organe maker for a full aquytance the some of   X.
> Item gevyn to Sir Willm Howton for a gods peny beinge hyred to serve the parysche and to have xx. nobles by yere   XIII.ob.
> Itm there was lost by the falle of y[e] money in theyr hands   xx.ob.

'There is like to be a calling-downe of the base money, I understande, very shortely; and the Queen's Ma[te] hathe sworne that the daye and tyme shall be kepte secrete to herself, and that fewe besyds shall knowe; so as the very tyme whensoever it chaunceth, will be so shorte and sodeyne that men are like to have small warninge of the matter, I doubte not but your L. will foresee and provyde, for one[1].' Strype is very diffuse upon this subject. 'Rumours of it run from one market-day to another, and the markets rose, and provisions grew dear. This unseasonably prevented the Queen's determination, so that she was fain in the midst of these bruits to issue out a proclamation to stay them. But neither could this remedy it; the same rumours being before hand universally spread into men's heads by sinister means. And another sort took hold of these rumours out of covetousness: and so the prices of all things were universally enhanced, that were to be sold for money. Piti-

ful hereby was the condition of the meaner sort of people, as labourers in husbandry, handicrafts men, serving-men, soldiers, and others living by wages or pensions, who must buy their victuals and sustenance with money: these were miserably oppressed with unreasonable prices and dearth. This moved the Queen; and for the remedying hereof, she thought fit to delay no longer putting her intent into execution. And so she reduced the moneys of her realm to such a true standard, as should never hereafter be changed or altered[2].

> 1561. Itm p[d] to a waller for mending y[e] church yerde wall   XV. IX.
> 1562. Itm delivered to a churche warden and y[e] constable, to the conveyinge of George Hoode to y[e] justice   X.
> Itm p[d] y[e] xv[th] of February for y[e] tenne cō-mandements & other boks   II. VI.
> Itm p[d] to Laurence Okes for a bell rope and an organe rope   III. IIII.
> Itm paide to W[m] Dickenson for a locke, and mendinge of y[e] clocke   III. IIII.
> 1564. Itm payde to Roberte Sponer for the se-conde parte of the homelyes   V.
> Itm gevyn to Roberte Spooner for his costs to Doncaster for y[e] boke of homyleyes   X.
> Itm p[d] for the paraphrases of Erasmus in En-glysche and the Quene's Iniunctyones   XV. IIII.
> Itm lyme to stoppe the fonte taken by Pavye   IIII.
> 1565. Payd to Hewghe Sponner the xxiiii[th] day of December for mending the bybell   II. VIII.
> Payd for felling and hewing III. loade tymber that was gotten in owre Lade Spryng, to make ladders for the churche, and for leadinge y[e] same, wth ale   III. I.
> Payd to Robert Hobson and his man for 3 days, for working, and making the formes that childer sytt on, at xvi[d]. the day, & for one day, he & his tow men at II[s]., with ale   VIII. IX.
> Payd for eges, and gathering blood to make morther   XII.
> Payd to Willm Goodroyd of Darbye for his paynes for comyng to loke on owre church, to have whytlymed hyt, and to have sete on the screpture; toward his charges in money xvi[d]., & for his dyner IIII[d].
> 1566. Itm p[d] to Benyt Bridges the xxix[th] daye of May, for whytlymynge the churche, and wryt-ynge the scryptures   XXXIX. X.
> Itm p[d] to Roberte Swyft the xIIII[th] daye of April for makynge the cōmunion-table   V.
> Itm gevyn towards the makynge of Bryght-syde Brydge   XXVI. VIII.
> Itm gevyn towards the makynge of Hygheley Brydge   XX.
> 1567. Itm p[d] for the dyner of the XII. Burg. and ale after, the recc'nynge day   IIII. XI.
> Itm p[d] to M[r] Yonge the scole M[r] for the ac-complyment of his wage at Chrystynmas   IX. VIII.
> Itm for hempe to stoppe the fonte   IIII.
> Itm p[d] for the boke of the articles   IIII.
> 1568. Itm gevyn to Thomas Tryppytt for goyng to London wyth a younge wenche   V.
> Itm gevyn by thassent of the sayde Burges. to the buyldynge of Ollerton Brydge   XX.
> Itm payd for the Burgesses dyner, the recōn-inge daye wth drynke for neybours   V. IIII.
> Itm gevyn to M[r] Yonge for the obtey'inge of a lycense to kepe the scole   X.
> Itm gevyn to the pore people of the towne and parysche   XX.

---

[1] Letter of Francis Allen to the earl of Shrewsbury, 3 Sep. 1560. Lodge, i. 345.   [2] Annals, vol. i. p. 265.

Drawn by I. Mair

Engraved by S. Noble

1569. Itm payde for Mʳ Hudson the Deyn's dyner, and his mans, and Pavye's the xxiiiiᵗʰ day Feb. . . xvi.
Itm payde for a boxe to put the synginge breade in . . . . iiii.
Itm payde to John Tymp'ley for bryngynge of the newe byble from London . . . . . . xxi.
Itm payde for the same byble, a Cōmunyon boke and a salter . . . . xxxii.
Itm paide for Mʳ Juell's boke the xviiiᵗʰ of August . . . . vi. vi.
To Wᵐ Fytharber, a pore man . . . . . v.
1570. Itm pᵈ the xiiiiᵗʰ daye of August for cloth to sett pore Lancelott daughter to service at London . . . . v.
Itm pᵈ for iiii. songe bookes of Jeneveies psalmes . . . . iii.
1571. Itm payd the xv. daye of Februarii for a saulter for the churche in meter . . . . . ii. iiii.
Item payd to pore seke peyple at the co-maundement of the Capitall Burgesses, &c. . . xi. iiii.
Distributed amonst the pore of every Byer-lawe in yᵉ towne and parysh . . . . . . iii. x.
1572. Itm for a quarte of wyne for yᵉ cōmunyon upon Whytson Sondaye . . . . iiii.
Itm payd and dysbursed by Willm Taylear, the costes and chardgs in suete of lawe for and con-cerninge the lands in Litle Sheffeld, aboute the tryall of the same; as appeareth by his bylls shewed before the sayd Burgesses and others at this same reconyng . . . . xv. xii. viii.
Note that Fraunces Swyfte who dyed in the yeare of our Lorde God 1572, dyd bequeath by his last wyll and testament to the xii. Capitall Burgesses one howse wᵗʰ the apurtenances in the tenure and occupacōn of one Thomas Byrley, cutler, neyghe unto the Barker Powle, after the naturall deathe of his two sisters.
1573. The recōninge of Richarde Jessope gent. and Johne Moselaye, Collectors of the land ap-pertay'inge to the xii. Capytall Burgesses of the towne and paryshe of Sheaffeld and the com-mons of the same, taken and made the xiiiᵗʰ daye of November anno 1573, for one year, endyd at Pentycoste año pred' before the righte honorable Lorde George Erle of Shrewsbury and all the Burgesses wᵗʰ many inhabytants of the sayd towne and parische as followeth, &c.
Itm pᵈ at the buryinge of Rodger Sikes the Aqua Vita man . . . . xx.
Itm paid to Robert Andertone at the settinge forthe of his ii. children to London . . . . v.
To yᵉ pore of yᵉ towne and parishe of Sheffeld v. vi. viii.
Itm gyven to Willᵐ Lee a poore scholler in Sheaffeld towards the settynge him to the Uni-versytie of Chambrydge, and buyinge him bookes and other furnyture. [which money was after-wards returned.] . . . . xiii. iiii.
1568. Itm paid to John Sheldon on the viii. daye of Marche for Thomas Yowles sone, set-tinge forthe to servis.—Firste for iii. yeards and a halfe russett friese iiiˢ. Itm paid for a yearde of carsaie for the said Yowlle's boye xxiiᵈ. Item paid for a yeard lyñen clothe to make hym a doblet xᵈ. Item paid for a yearde of canvase to lyne the said dublet, and a dossyne-buttons for the same viiᵈ. Item paid for a shirt clothe and a coller for the said boye xviᵈ. Item paid for halfe a yearde of whytte pleyne clothe for the said boye viiᵈ. Item paide for a paire of showes for the said boye xᵈ. Item for his aparel makinge xiiiiᵈ.
Item paid the iiii. daie of June to Adame Gylles men for makeinge the great belleclapper . xvi.
1570. The xxiiii. daye of Januarye.—Stuffe sold by the Chyrch wardens, and tymber at the takinge doune of the loftes in chirche, as heare-after followethe:
One lofte on the north side sold.
One stayre of the south side.
One deyse in the rood quire.
Itm solde to George Tynker the crosse stones xiiᵈ.
Itm paid for pullinge doune the crosse in the Chirch yeard iiiiᵈ.

These entries relate to the destruction of the rood-loft and the church-yard cross, which was done in obedience to injunctions of the queen in furtherance of the work of Reformation. The rood-loft at the east end of the nave contained a representation in large of the crucifixion. We have this pleasant passage concerning it in Sir John Ferne's *Lacie's No-bilitie*, 4to, 1586. Columella the husbandman says, 'When maister Paradin began his speech of the Crosse, he wakened me. I remember well, when it stood in the upper end of our church body, and had a trim loft for it, with a curten drawne before it to keepe it warme: yea, zur, zutch was the time then, that we borrell folke were taught, there was a God upon it, and we must creepe many a time, and make offerings of egges to it for our sinnes, but I thinke verelye the priest did eate them up, &c.—but in deede zur, the crosse was in that tyme a God, and yet I marvell where he hath left his Godhead, vor in those dayes, we leawd and unlearned people durst not pass by it in the Church yarde, without bending of a knee, now these paltryes (God save our good Queene and her wise Lords) been taken away[1].'

A Remembrance that Sʳ Willm Howton was hyred in the presence of the holle paryshe by the xii. Capytall Burgesses the viᵗʰ daye of November Anno Dñi 1560 and had gevyn to hym xiiiᵈ. ob.
A Remembrance that Sʳ Wᵐ Broune was hyred in the pre-sence of the holle parysh by the xii. Capitall Burgesses, the xiiiiᵗʰ day of November Anno Dñi 1564, to come at Easter next at the furthest, and gevyn hym xiiᵈ.

THE PARISH CHURCH.

The church of Saint Peter is a rectangular build-ing having neither porch nor chapel protruding beyond the buttresses. Its length from east to west is about 240 feet, and its breadth about 130. A tower and spire rise near the centre of the building. Originally, like most of our churches that were erected for the use of a considerable population, it was in the form of a cross, the tower and spire rising at the intersection of the two limbs. In the original design were included side-ailes both on the north and south, above which rose the nave with a range of clerestory windows. Per-haps the first change in its form was produced by the erection of the Shrewsbury chapel which now forms the south-east angle of the building. Since that period there have been many changes and many re-edifica-tions, till nothing remains of the original fabric except the massy pillars that support the tower, and the whole has assumed a form which never belonged to the an-cient churches of this country, a parallelogram con-tained by walls of equal altitude.
The church sustained some damage in the great storm of 1703. The chancel soon after underwent a thorough repair under the direction of Lady Howard, widow of Lord Thomas Howard, and guardian to her son Thomas duke of Norfolk, whose initials appear

[1] P. 99.

in several places on the east wall. Where stand the present vestry and burgesses room was formerly an engine-house, and it was put in its present state in 1777. But the great renovation of this edifice has been the work of the present century. The pewing was very irregular and inconvenient. In this point the archdeacon at his visitation in 1800 signified to the church-wardens his intention of enforcing a speedy reform. This was supposed to present a favourable opportunity for a general repair of the fabric: and accordingly at a meeting of the inhabitants held in the chancel on the 3rd of November in that year, the Reverend George Smith in the chair, the expense of the new pewing was taken upon themselves by individuals who claimed seats in the church, the church-burgesses at the same time signifying their intention to undertake the whole charge of repairing the fabric. Some delays occurred in carrying the resolutions into effect, and it was not till Sunday the 6th of October 1805 that the church was re-opened for public worship, the nave, that is the whole of that part of it west of the tower, having been rebuilt from the foundations.

On entering by the principal door we are now therefore presented with a view of a spacious, lofty, and well-pewed church, capable of accommodating from two thousand five hundred to three thousand persons, which number it is supposed usually attended the late Sunday evening services. Here are no fantastical or ostentatious ornaments, but nothing seems to be wanting for the decent performance of all the sacred ordinances, and for the comfort of the parishioners while attending divine ministrations. It may seem too fastidious to say that the shields might be dispensed with that are placed between the arches on each side of the nave, or if they were placed at all might have been made to present some memorial of former benefactors of the parish, or of those persons whose achievements and monumental memorials it was thought expedient to remove and to destroy. A much stronger objection will however lie against an innovation which totally destroys the unity of the edifice, and which was never supposed by those who gave consent to it to be more than a temporary measure. The arches which separate the nave from the chancel have been filled with brick-work, leaving only a communication through a small door, so that all view of the altar is intercepted from the part of the church appropriated to public worship. I must also be permitted to record a strong protest against the unsparing abolition of every memorial of our ancestors, whose buried remains had consecrated in a peculiar manner that part of the church to the feelings of many worshippers within it: a system which having completed its work in the body of the church, so that not a line or a trace remains, is now making an alarming progress in the chancel itself. When I last visited the church in 1817, the two finest brasses it contained, those of Lady Elizabeth Butler and of Stephen Bright of Carbrook, a man eminent in his day and generation, and whose liberal donations to the church might have saved his name from violation, had been recently torn from the stones to which they had been attached, and were lying amongst a mass of rubbish in the vestry.

'Si pia majorum violas monumenta, viator
Ultrices Furias experiere brevi.'

In contemplation of the ruin which was then impending, in December 1800 I made an accurate transcript of all the monumental memorials which could then be found within the church: but I had reason to regret that this had not been done sooner, as the inscriptions more than half obliterated were almost as numerous as those which were perfect, and the marks where monumental brasses had been torn away showed that at least as many were lost as were suffered to remain. I have since had the more reason to regret it, on discovering that Dodsworth's church notes at Sheffield were few; that little was added to them by Dugdale; and that Wilson, though he copied some, left much the greater portion of them unnoticed. Other antiquaries who have visited the church of Sheffield have for the most part contented themselves with attending only to the Shrewsbury chapel.

Many of these inscriptions were only names and dates useful to the genealogist, but little interesting to those not immediately connected with the parties commemorated. I shall give at length those inscriptions only which appear on any account remarkable, interspersed in a general view of this little plot considered as the cemetery where rest the *proceres* of our neighbourhood.

But first it may be proper to pay respect to an humble but very worthy person, whose remains lay in the church-porch, the appropriate place of interment according to ancient usage of those who held the lowest office in the church. An oval slab was placed against the wall of the porch by his son, who was a clergyman, bearing the following inscription. When the porch was destroyed in 1790, the slab was thrown unregarded into the Shrewsbury chapel.

Near this place lyeth the body of
WILLIAM ELLIS,
a man who in the midst of a corrupt age
retained
in spite of custom and example
a primeval severity of life,
tempered with the gentlest manners and most
humane disposition.
His singular probity, joined with a steady
undeviating zeal for virtue and religion,
gained him
the character of an honest man
and good Christian.
He was clerk to this church forty years, in which
he approved himself both knowing and
faithful.
Also Elizabeth his virtuous and prudent wife,
and three children.

He } dyed { Sep. 11, } 1743, aged { 69.
She }   { May 3, }   { 75.
This stone hath filial piety
erected to the memory of the
best of parents.

The south aile was almost exclusively devoted to the interments of members of the numerous and once opulent family of the name of Bright, especially of those who had lived at Whirlow-hall, Graystones, and Brincliffe-Edge, all in Ecclesall-Byerlow. Among them lay 'Hellen wife of Thomas Borton esquire,' 1656, who was by birth a Bright, and married into the family of Burton of Dronfield, lords of that manor, and possessing considerable property there. Near the porch-door lay 'John Crooke cutler, church and schoole burges,' 1669, father to the assistant-minister of that name, and 'Elizabeth wife of Robert

Littlewood,' 1738. At the east end of this aile was commemorated Montague Wortley, 1780, who spent a long life at Sheffield in obscure circumstances, though descended of the Wortleys of Barnsley, heirs male of the ancient house of Wortley of Wortley, a descent which he did not forget to commemorate by engraving the arms of that house upon the stone which he placed over the remains of his first wife in the yard adjoining[1]. In the same part of the church were memorials of the names of Marshall, Walton, Asline, and Broomhead, and near the centre door was a large and handsome plate on which had been engraved a long inscription, from which nothing more could be recovered than that the person intended to be commemorated had borne the name of Pearson, and died in 1694.

In the north aile were memorials of the family of Mr. Humpton formerly assistant-minister, also of the names of Hall and Stead. In this aile lay Mr. Christopher Broomhead and Sarah his wife, a venerable couple, he dying in 1729 aged 80, and she in 1732 aged 84. They are worthy of remembrance as having been maternal ancestors of the literate family of Balguy, whose connexion with Sheffield is elsewhere recorded, and having also married another daughter to the Reverend Christopher Robinson M.A. rector of Welby, a writer in defence of revelation, whose widow and son were commemorated on the same flag. The above-mentioned Christopher Broomhead was son to Henry Broomhead of Fullwood. Not far from them lay many members of the family of Battie, very respectable inhabitants of Sheffield in the last century, and their representatives the Smiths, for whom there were several handsome brasses which it is said were preserved by their descendant Thomas Smith of Dunstone-hall near Chesterfield, esquire, when this part of the church was stripped of its monumental memorails[2]. Near to these were the names of Dawson, and Handley, namely, the family of Richard Handley of Sheffield, apothecary, 1680 and 1691.

In the middle aile were memorials of Lambert[3],

and Barnsley of Gothard-hill; and advancing towards the pulpit a brass plate pointed out the place of interment of Thomas Short, M.D. and other members of his family[4]. Near this another plate contained the name of John Creswick, 1779, and next to that was a crowded plate on which were recorded the names and ages of the several members of a worthy family well-known and respected at Sheffield, the Waterhouses, a branch of the family of that name which had considerable property in the chapelry of Bradfield. The names of Gascoigne, Farbeck, Webster of Owlerton, and his heirs the Brights and Ryalses of the same place, next occurred, and an imperfect inscription recording the interment of Elizabeth daughter of Robert Ashton, esquire, by Mary his wife, daughter of Robert Hall of Stumperlow, gentleman. Near the spot where the pulpit now stands was a stone fairly inlaid with brass, and two plates, one of arms, and the other containing the inscription below—

Arms quarterly 1 and 4, MURRAY;—Azure, 3 mullets argent within a double tressure flowered and counterflowered or. 2 and 3, STRATHBOLGY ;—Paly of six pieces or and sable, quartering STUART, or, a fess checkie argent and azure. On an escutcheon of pretence, Quarterly 1 and 4, DALTON; —Gules, semée of cross croslets a lion rampant argent. 2 and 3, BRIGHT ;—Parti per pale azure and gules, a bend or between 2 mullets argent.

' Here lies the body of the right hon^{ble} Lady JOHN MURRAY, who departed this life at London the twenty-first day of May 1765, aged thirty-three, near the remains of her mother Mrs. Dalton, daughter of the late John Bright, esq. of Chesterfield.'

The arms were repeated on an achievement.

Near this place were interred many members of the family of Burton of Royd's-mill and Sheffield, a junior branch of the Burtons of Dronfield: and stones bearing the names of Spooner, Hellewell, Sutcliffe, Hawley, and Yeomans filled up the space from the pulpit to the entrance of the chancel.

In the aile running from south to north, between the nave and chancel, were inscriptions mentioning the interment of William Dalby, 1765, Richard Sea-

---

[1] The Wortleys of Barnsley made some unsuccessful attempts to recover the ancient inheritance of their family when it was passed by will of the last baronet to an illegitimate daughter. All hope of recovering the property having ceased, Richard Wortley of Barnsley, gentleman, was content to place two sons, Montague and Francis, as apprentices to cutlers at Sheffield. The indentures of the former were enrolled in 1709, of the latter in 1710. I wish I could add that they retrieved by successful commerce the fortunes of their ancestry.

[2] Mary wife of John Battie, of Sheffield, gent. died 1708, aged 24. John Battie gent. 1747, aged 64. Margaret his second wife, 1744, aged 61. William Battie, 1774, aged 63. Margaret Battie, 1773, aged 60. Ann Battie, 1776, aged 59. Mary Battie, 1790, aged 71. Ann Smith, 1772, aged 14. Thomas Smith, 1774, aged 49. John Battie gent. 1789, aged 79. Susan Smith, 1797, aged 73. William Smith of the city of Norwich, brother to Thomas Smith, 1801, aged 72.—The issue of Thomas Smith and Susan his wife (formerly Battie) was one son, the late Thomas Smith of Dunstone-hall, esq., and a daughter wife of the Reverend Alexander Mackenzie, curate of St. Paul's.

[3] Joseph Lambert, son to the Reverend Mr. Lambert, vicar of Waggon in Holderness, 1742, aged 23.

[4] ' In memory of Thomas Short of this town M.D., who departed this life Nov. 28, 1772. Mary his wife, who died Dec. 19, 1762. Mary their daughter, Dec. 3, 1753. Elizanet Anderton wid^w their daughter, who died May 16, 1798.'

A more convenient opportunity may not be presented of introducing a notice chiefly bibliographical of Dr. Thomas Short. He was a native of Scotland, but settled at Sheffield early in life, where he soon fell into considerable practice not only in the town but among the gentlemen of the surrounding country. I apprehend the date of his settlement at Sheffield may be fixed at or near 1725. In 1732 he married Miss Mary Parkin, or Parkins, sister of William Parkins, of Mortemley, esquire, by whom he had two sons and two daughters. In 1762 he lost his wife, and soon after retired to Rotherham, where he died on the 28th of November 1772.

Works.

1734. The natural, experimental, and medicinal history of the mineral waters of Derbyshire, Lincolnshire, and Yorkshire, particularly those of Scarborough, &c. 4to. dedicated to Sir Hans Sloane, president, and to the council and fellows of the Royal Society.

1739. A dissertation upon Tea, explaining its nature and virtues by many new experiments, &c. Dedicated to Thomas Lord Malton. A second edition was published in 1753, 4to.

1740. An essay towards a natural, experimental and medicinal history of the principal mineral waters of Cumberland, Northumberland, Westmorland, Bishoprick of Durham, Lancashire, Cheshire, Staffordshire, Shropshire, Worcestershire, Gloucestershire, Warwickshire, Northamptonshire, Leicestershire, and Nottinghamshire, &c. 4to. This forms a second volume of Short's Mineral waters.

1746. Medicina Britannica: or a treatise on such physical plants as are generally found in the fields or gardens of Great Britain, &c. 8vo.

1750. Observations natural, moral, civil, political, and medicinal, on city, town, and country bills of mortality, &c. 8vo.

1765. A general treatise on various cold mineral waters in England, but more particularly those at Harrowgate, Thorp-arch, &c. 8vo.

1766. A general treatise on the different sorts of cold mineral waters in England, &c. 8vo.

1767. A comparative history of the increase and decrease of mankind in England and several countries abroad, &c. 4to.

This list, with his ' Rational discourse on the inward uses of water,' &c., and a few communications in the Philosophical Transactions, is supposed to contain the whole of Dr. Short's publications.

Before the time of Dr. Short there had been at Sheffield Dr. Morton, Dr. Waterhouse, Dr. Lee, and Dr. Pearson. About the time of the decline of Dr. Short's practice, Dr. James, the inventor of the fever-powder, settled at Sheffield, but without much success. Dr. Buchan also tried Sheffield, and it was during his residence here that he composed the popular book his ' Domestic Medicine.'

man of London, esquire, Jonathan Hall of Dovehouse, 1778, and the plates of the family of Fell of Attercliffe-forge.

'Here lye the remains of JOHN FELL of Attercliffe-forge, gent. who died April 30th 1724, aged 58 years. Ellen his wife died Jan. 7th 1724, aged 60 years. Also two sons and three daughters, viz.

Ann ⎫ ⎧ Feb. 18th 1700,⎫ ⎧ one year.
William ⎪ died ⎧ May 2[d] 1713, ⎪ aged ⎧ 19 ⎫
Thomas ⎬ ⎨ Dec. 14th 1726, ⎬ ⎨ 28 ⎬ years.
Mary ⎭ ⎩ Jan. 9th 1727, ⎭ ⎩ 23 ⎭

Eliz: the wife of Gam[l] Milner of Atter: died Jan. 18th 1736, aged 32 years.'

'Here lyeth the body of ALICE the wife of JOHN FELL the younger of Attercliffe-forge, gent. and daughter of Rich[d] Bagshaw, of Castleton, esq. She died Aug. 8th 1737, aged 27 years. John his son and of Elizabeth his second wife died the 15th of April 1743 in the first year of his age.'

'Here lyeth the body of JOHN FELL, esq. of Attercliffe-forge, who died May 17th 1762, aged 66 years. Elizabeth his second wife ob[t] 29th Jany 1795 æt. 85.'

In the body of the church were hung two achievements which were placed there after the death of the last Mr. and Mrs. Fell, viz.

FELL;—Argent, 3 lozenges in fess between as many mullets of eight points pierced azure; impaling LAUGHTON—Quarterly per fess indented or and argent.

Near to the plates of the Fells was a stone bearing the name of Rebecca Waterhouse, 1708, who was also commemorated in an inscription by her husband on a board affixed to the wall above her grave. She was the first wife of John Waterhouse, of Sheffield, M.D. and her interment on the 30th day of January probably led to the bequest of Dr. Waterhouse of fifteen shillings per annum for a sermon to be preached in the parish-church on that day[1]. A little to the north lay John Bordman, 'from Sheffield mannor,' 1641; Elizabeth wife of Mr. Gardiner, 1686; and Elizabeth wife of Christopher Cowley, gentleman, 1752. Here also were several memorials of the name of Sorsbie, viz. Elizabeth wife of Malin Sorsbie, 1676; Elizabeth wife of Robert Sorsbie, 1690; Robert Sorsbie, gentleman, 1754, and others partly defaced. Of this family was the first master-cutler of Hallamshire; Robert Sorsbie, D.D., who was precentor of York; and Malin Sorsbie, D.D., of Ryton in the bishoprick of Durham.

THE CHANCEL.

Close to the door on the south side, and affixed to the wall, was formerly a brass with an inscription commemorating a person who is supposed to have been the executioner of King Charles I., but with better reason to have been the translator of the *Vindiciæ contra Tyrannos*.

'Hic jacet
GULIELMUS WALKER, qui variis durante nupero interregno muniis arduis, sub Mercurii non Martis vexillo laudabiliter functus, redeunte rege Carolo Secundo, in prædiolum paternum templo huic vicinum, se lubens subduxit: ubi cum Mathematices aliarumque scientiarum studio, per multos annos otia posuisset; tandem fatis cessit decimo quarto die Novembris, Anno Dom. 1700.'

Near this door are also several plates with inscriptions of the family of Bamforth, of the High-house in

Nether-Hallam, namely, of George Bamforth, who died 1677, aged 76; his son of the same name, who died 1701, aged 75; Margaret daughter of Mr. George Bamforth, who died 1709, aged 21; and George Bamforth esquire, of the High-house, the last male heir of his family. For this gentleman, who was cut off in the prime of life, of whom on better authority than his epitaph it may be said that he promised to become a most useful and respectable member of society, there is a monument placed against the south wall near the spot where his remains are interred.

'Near this place lyeth the body of
GEORGE BAMFORTH,
late of High-house near Sheffield, esq.
a gentleman distinguished by an amiable disposition,
a public spirit, and strict integrity,
generous, humane and just to all.
By his death,
which was early and much regretted,
his wife lost an affectionate husband,
his acquaintance a warm friend,
his servants a kind master,
and society an useful member.
He married
Margaret daughter of William Bamford,
of Bamford in the county of Lancaster, esq.
but dying without issue
he was the last male heir of his family.
His relict Margaret Bamforth
as a testimony of conjugal love
has dedicated this monument to his memory.
He died May 31st 1739, aged 29 years.

Along with the Bamforth inscriptions on the floor are other memorials of persons connected with that family, viz. Samuel Turner of Sheffield, mercer, 1791, and others of his family; and John Burton of Bramley-hall, in the parish of Hansworth, esquire, who died the 8th of November 1772, aged 32. On his plate are engraven these arms, viz.

Quarterly 1 and 4, BURTON;—Azure, a crescent argent within an orle of etoils and a border or. 2 and 3, BAMFORTH;—Argent, a fess ingrailed gules; impaling LAW—Sable, on a chevron between 3 wolfs' heads erased argent as many pellets.

In this part of the chancel are also on the floor memorials of John Bourne, 'surgeon to the most noble the Marquis of Rockingham,' 1777; and Thomas Bromley, 1786, 'who was nearly allied to the above John Bourne, and particularly noticed in that gentleman's will:' and against the wall, of Francis Barlow of Sheffield, gentleman, 1689, and Catherine his wife, 1687, and the Reverend Robert Turie.

'Adjacent in the yard is a tomb erected with R. T. inscribed thereon, under which lyeth the body of Robert Turie, late assistant-minister of this church: buried July the 7th 1720.
The 26th Psalm, verse the 8th. Lord, I have loved the habitation of thy house, and the place where thine honour dwelleth.
The 84th Psalm, verse the 4th. Blessed are they that dwell in thy house, they will be always praising thee.
Verse the 10th. I had rather be a door-keeper in the house of my God than to dwell in the tents of ungodliness.'

A neat marble tablet placed against the brick-work which fills up one of the arches that separate the chancel from the nave bears the following inscription.

---

[1] This lady's maiden name was Shippen, and she was the widow of Bower when she married Dr. Waterhouse, at Silkstone, 16 Nov. 1695. Dr. Waterhouse has no memorial, but he was buried at Sheffield 15 Aug. 1714. He left a widow, who was Mary eldest daughter and co-

heir of John Cart, M.D. of Manchester, where he was in high reputation as a physician, son to John Cart, rector of Hansworth. She took to her second husband James Walker of Manchester.

' In memory of MARY the wife of
the Rev⁴ THOMAS SUTTON, vicar of this parish,
who died April 19ᵗʰ 1814,
aged 23 years.
If we believe that Jesus died and rose again, even so them
also which sleep in Jesus will God bring with him.'

In this portion of the chancel are also memorials of
Captain Gervas Harestaff, 1696; Thomas Bretland,
1696; Jane the wife of Robert Turner of Sheffield,
and daughter of William Jennings of York, 1786;
and many of the family of Nevil Simmons, 1707—
1790.

Against one of the pillars of the chancel a plate:

' Here lies interred the remains of the Rev⁴ Mʳ JOHN DOS-
SIE, late vicar of this church, and also governor and preacher
at the hospital for poor men and women, erected by Gilbert
Talbot Earl of Shrewsbury; the first of which preferments he
enjoyed near 41 years, and the latter 50 years: and departed
this life the 24ᵗʰ of Decʳ 1753, aged 77 years. Also of ELIZA-
BETH late wife of the said John Dossie, who departed this life
the 7ᵗʰ of May 1752, aged 67 years. And of MARGARET,
3⁴ daughter of the said John Dossie by the said Elizabeth his
wife, who departed this life the 10 day of January 1747, aged
23 years.'

On another plate:

' Also of Jⁿᵒ DOSSIE, gent. eldest son of the said John Dossie, who departed this life the 12ᵗʰ day of May 1754, aged
45 years.'

Much of this part of the chancel is appropriated to
the interment of the family of Spencer, formerly of
Attercliffe-hall, and now of Bramley-grange, in the
parish of Braithwell, lords of the manor of Darnall.
There are brasses or inscriptions on the floor for the
following members of this family:

William Spencer of Attercliffe-hall, gent., 1649.

Joseph fifth son of William Spencer of Attercliffe,
gentleman, 1651.

Thomas fifth son of William Spencer, esquire, 1654.

The seventh son of William Spencer of Attercliffe,
esquire, 1657.

Faith daughter of William Spencer of Attercliffe,
esquire, and wife of Samuel Child of Leeds, gent. and
merchant-draper, 1666.

William eldest son of William Spencer, gentleman,
1673.

John Spencer, gentleman, 1679.

William Spencer of Attercliffe, gentleman, 1686.

Arms.—SPENCER .... a fess ermine between six sea-mews'
heads erased ..... impaling WESTBY .... on a chevron
..... 3 cinquefoils ....

Nearly in the centre of the chancel and opposite to
the communion-table was the fine brass of the father
of Sir John Bright baronet, with another plate on the
same flag exhibiting the arms which were granted to
him who sleeps below.

BRIGHT—a bend between two mullets ....

' Here lieth interred the body of STEPHEN BRIGHT, of Carbrooke, gent. who died the sixt of June 1642, in the sixtieth
yeare of his age. Also JOANNA his first wife, with two of their
sonnes, THOMAS and STEPHEN, and their three daughters,
MARY wife of William Jessop, esq. RUTH wife of Edward Gill,
gent., and SARAH was here buried.'

At a little distance from this lay another daughter
of Stephen Bright.

' Here lieth interred MARTHA late wife of William Lister,
of Thornton in the county of Yorke, esquire, sixt daughter of

Stephen Bright of Carbrooke, gent., buried the ninth day of
Septembʳ 1663, in the 24ᵗʰ yeare of her age.'

Arms.—LISTER ; Ermine on a fess .... 3 mullets .... impaling BRIGHT as before.

Inscriptions in this part of the chancel for John
Turner of Sheffield, merchant, 1796; and James his
son, 1784; Martha Armitage, 1756; Margaret wife of
Mr. William Watson, 1778; Sarah wife of Vigors
Harvey esquire, 1793; William Watson of Hagg-
house, 1791. William son of William Watson, the
first born of twenty-three children and the last survivor, who died in 1793, aged 74. For this gentleman
there is a small marble monument.

' Here lie the remains of
WILLIAM WATSON gent.
of Shirtcliff-hall,
who died July 22, 1793, aged 74 years.
He was a dutiful son and a good Christian,
charitable to the needy,
a father to the fatherless and widow,
and a friend and well-wisher to all men.
Here also lie the remains of
SARAH HARVEY his sister,
wife of Vigors Harvey, esq.
who died April 18, 1793, aged 65 years.'

' Sacred to the memory of
JOHN PARSONS, esq. of Sheffield,
who died Dec. 25ᵗʰ 1814, aged 70 years.
Also of
MARY PARSONS his sister,
who died September 30ᵗʰ 1815, aged 68 years,
and who
from an affectionate regard to her brother's memory bequeathed 1500l. to be invested in the
public funds; the interest or dividends thereof
to be annually distributed among 48 aged,
infirm, and poor silver platers: and 2l.
to a clergyman duly appointed, for
preaching a sermon on the anniversary of St. John the Evan-
gelist, for ever.'

Inscriptions on the floor, where lie Mary Sitwell
1751, and her two daughters Mary Sitwell 1733, and
Catherine Hurt 1754. Also Jonathan Hurt of Sheffield, mercer, 1731, and many of his children. Near
to these lie Joshua Laughton of Brincliffe-edge, gent.
1703; Thomas Warburton, 1742; and Sarah Warburton wife to Thomas Warburton late of Wakefield,
and daughter to Richard Stanley esquire of Crundall
in Hampshire, who died 19th Oct. 1727, aged 47.

Brass for William Plessington esquire, 1652.

Memorials of the interment of Sarah wife of Samuel
Bates 1788, and others of the family; Thomas Eyre
1679, Frances wife of John Eyre of Sheffield-manour
1686, John Ellison 1698, and others of that name.

On a brass plate:

' Here lyeth the body of ANTH. SAYLES, late of this parish,
apothecary, who departed this life July 23, 1712, in the 32
year of his age. He was the last male of that ancient family
of Sayles of Laughton le Morthing, in which church lyeth interred his father, grandfather, great grandfather, &c. with
their wifes and children.'

Other inscriptions commemorate Frances his wife
1710, and Sarah his daughter 1709.

On the same stone are commemorated Robert
Blackburne gentleman, of Bate-green in the chapelry
of Bradfield, 1727; Mrs. Winifred Pole, daughter of
Francis Pole of Rark-hall esquire, 1731; Elizabeth

2 P

relict of John Fox, 1757; Benjamin Blackburne of Alderman's-head in the parish of Peniston, gentleman, 1736; and Michael son of John and Elizabeth Fox, 1758.

On another, Arthur Palmor gentleman, 1723; Bridget his wife, 1736; Anne wife of William Lyon, surgeon, 1739.

On a third, still further towards the north wall, the names of Wood and Pearson, Fenton and Roebuck.

Near these, a stone covers the remains of Benjamin Steer of Sheffield, mercer, 1746, and several of his family and connexions; Alice his relict, 1758; Mary daughter of Mr. George Walker, Jane wife of Dennis Brown surgeon, 1747; Sarah Serjeantson Browne 1763, Dennis Browne 1767, John Elam 1770.

Brasses for several of the name of Nodder, viz. John Nodder of Sheffield, gentleman, 1732; Deborah his wife 1740, John Nodder 1772, and several children of Isaac Nodder 1744—1766.

At the north end of the chancel was the burial-place of the Jessops of Broomhall, the patrons of the church. Many of them are here interred: but whether the successive generations of this family have paid little attention to that point; whether the memorials which they erected have been removed by some illicit hand; or whether they are only concealed by some useless pewing and wainscoting to be discovered a century hence for the gratification of some more fortunate topographer, I pretend not to say; but their only monumental memorial was erected pursuant to the will of his widow, for the last male of the family, William Jessop of Broomhall esquire, whose several employments, marriage, and issue are thus set forth.

> 'Here lie the bodies of
> WILLIAM JESSOP,
> of Broomhall, esq.
> and
> the Honᵇˡᵉ MARY JESSOP his wife,
> daughter of James Lord Darcy,
> of Navan in the kingdom of Ireland;
> which William Jessop
> was treasurer and commissioner of the
> Alienation Office,
> one of his Maᵗⁱᵉˢ Judges of Chester, &c.
> and 9 times chosen member of
> parliament for Aldborough
> in this county.
> He had
> by his said wife one son, who on the death
> of his grandfather the Lord Darcy
> succeeded him in his estate and title,
> but died in the life-time of his father:
> and four daughters,
> BARBARA married to Andrew Wilkinson, esq.
> of Boroughbridge,
> ISABEL married to John Gell, esq.
> of Hopton in the county of Derby,
> and BETHIA and MARY.
> The said William Jessop died
> Novʳ 15ᵗʰ 1734, anⁿᵒ ætat. 70.
> The Honᵇˡᵉ MARY JESSOP,
> June 17ᵗʰ 1737, æt. 66.

Arms.—Quarterly 1 and 4, JESSOP; Barry of 6 argent and azure, on each piece of the first 3 mullets gules. 2 and 3, SWYFT; Or, a chevron barry nebulée argent and azure between 3 roebucks courant proper.

On an escutcheon of pretence—

DARCY;—Azure, semée of cross-crosslets and 3 cinquefoils argent ;—the whole impaling DARCY.

Not far from this monument is another, a well-merited tribute of public respect to the Judge's grand-son, the Reverend James Wilkinson, vicar of Sheffield. The bust, which is a striking resemblance, was the work of Francis Leggitt Chantrey esquire, R.A. & F.R.S. whose birth will hereafter give celebrity to Norton his native village, and whose extraordinary powers were first noticed and fostered by gentlemen in the neighbourhood of the place of his nativity. It was his first work. He had never before this commission offered or attempted to chisel marble: and when he undertook it, had no more certainty of being able to complete it, than that self-confidence with which true genius, though modest as his, never fails to be inspired. It bears the following inscription:

> 'This monument
> was erected by a subscription
> of the nobility, gentry, clergy and others,
> to the memory of
> the Reverend JAMES WILKINSON, A.M.
> vicar of Sheffield, prebendary of Ripon,
> and one of his majesty's justices of the peace
> for the west and north ridings of Yorkshire,
> whose life had been preeminently distinguished
> by unaffected piety, inflexible integrity,
> and unwearied zeal in the service of the public
> during a period of half a century.
> He died the 18th of January 1805, aged 74 years.'

A few more sepulchral memorials remain to be noticed, within that part of the chancel which is separated by the long railing before the altar.

Here are the memorials of the Ratcliffes of Sheffield-manour, viz. of Francis 1685, Anne his daughter 1677, and Mary wife of Luke Ogle 1684. Also of several children of William Simpson gentleman 1664—1669. Abigail wife of William Gardiner, assistant-minister, 1666: Christopher Cowley of Sheffield, gentleman, 1753; Lydia wife of Thomas Chapell, gentleman, 1666; Thomas Chapell 1693; Robert Chapell esquire 1736; John Harrison 1746; and Mary his wife 1766.

Here also lies Sarah relict of John Balguy 1766, near her sister Mrs. Elizabeth Drake.

'M.S. ROB. DRAKE, Apoth. qui obiit Junii 17° 1723° ætat. 33°. Juxta virum requiescit ELIZABETHA DRAKE Roberti uxor, cui per annos plusquam 42 feliciter superstes, vita demum funesta est 28° die Nov. A.D. 1765, æt. suæ 83°.'

Dodsworth transcribed these two inscriptions in the body of the church, which were not remaining in 1800.

'HELLEN wife of John Payin gentleman at 25 years of age dyed on the 9th of October in the yeare of our Lord. 1613, is here entombed where from she expects a resurrection.'

'MARGARET wife of Thomas Horner was buried the 23 day of Decʳ 1599.'

The two following he copied in the church-yard:

'Under this stone is placed and buryed the body of Mr. ROBERT HOLLAND, vicar of Sheffield, the 24 August 1597.'

'MARGARETA ux. Georgii Yonge, et parvulus ejus filius sub hoc cippo teguntur, unde expectant resurrectionem a mortuis, et demum vitam eternam. Amen. Peperit partus cæsulam mortis. Anno Dñi 1617.'

To the brasses no longer remaining must now be added that of Lady Elizabeth Butler, after having been for three centuries firmly united to the massy paviour under which her remains repose. The removal of this memorial is not the only violence that has been committed upon this sepulchre. It should appear from

Drawn & Engraved by E. Blore

Monument of the Revᵈ James Wilkinson, M.A. Vicar of Sheffield,
in the Parish Church of Sheffield.

page 176.

Published June 1ˢᵗ 1818 by the Revᵈ J. Hunter Bath.

p 147

Drawn by E.Blore.   Engraved by C.Arlap.

Chapel and Monuments of the Shrewsbury Family
in St Peter's Church, Sheffield.

Published Jan.y 1 1819 by the Rev.d J.Hunter Bath

the rough state of the superficies of this stone, that it was formerly nearly if not entirely covered with ornamented brass. Dodsworth describes it as ' a marble stone fairly inlaid with brasse:' and when Sir William Dugdale visited the church there were some armorial insignia upon it which guide us with greater certainty than the inscription itself to the individual who is here interred, and of whom, though allied to so many illustrious houses, we have no notice in the Peerages.

'bere lyeth Elizabeth, doughter of Thomas erle of Ormond, and of Lore his wyf, Comtyne wyf to the Lorde Mountjope, whiche Elizabeth deceased the xx. day of februarp the yere of our Lord M ccccc x. on whose soule Jhu haue mercp men[1].

The arms which Dugdale found on this monument were,

BUTLER .... a chief indented ..... and BUTLER impaling BERKLEY of Beverstone .... a chevron between 10 crosses pattee .... quartering .... 3 fleur de lis.....

It remains that we inquire who this lady was; for in vain should we search in the books where we might

most reasonably expect information; and secondly, how it has happened that she has found interment at Sheffield.

Thomas Butler the seventh earl of Ormond succeeded to that dignity on the reversal of an attainder in the first parliament of Henry VII. He married Anne daughter and heir of Sir Richard Hankford, by whom he had two daughters, who survived him and became his heirs: the one married Sir James Saint Leger, and the other Sir William Boleyn. So far the Peerages. But this inscription and the arms place beyond controversy what Anstis in his 'Order of the Garter' has stated, that the seventh earl of Ormond married a second wife, namely, Lora daughter of Sir Edward Berkley of Beverstone, knight, widow 1st of John Blount Lord Mountjoy, and 2dly of Sir Thomas Montgomery, K.G. No other issue of this marriage is known; and the lady here interred must have died in her early youth. Her father died in August 1515, very rich and very aged. Her father's sister was the wife of John Talbot second earl of Shrewsbury.

JAMES BUTLER, 4th earl of Ormond.	= JOAN, dau. of Gerald earl of Kildare.						
ELIZABETH, wife of John Talbot earl of Shrewsbury.	JAMES, 5th earl of Ormond.	JOHN, 6th earl of Ormond.	ANNE, 1st wife, daughter of Sir Richard Hankford.	= THOMAS BUTLER, seventh earl of Ormond. Will dated 31st July 1515.	= LORA, 2d wife, daughter of Sir Edward Berkley.	= JOHN BLOUNT, Lord Mountjoy, 1st husband, aged 30, 15 Edw. IV. ob. 1 Hen. VII.	= Sir THOMAS MONTGOMERY, K.G. 2d husb.

ANN BUTLER, wife of Sir James Saint Leger.	Sir WILLIAM BOLEYN.	= MARGARET BUTLER.		ELIZABETH BUTLER, died 20th Feb. 1510, buried at Sheffield.	LORA BLOUNT, died 6 Feb. 1480, and was buried at Fulham. [Weever, p. 526.]
		THOMAS BOLEYN, = ELIZABETH, daughter of earl of Wiltshire.	Thomas duke of Norfolk.		

Lady ANNE BOLEYN.

THE SHREWSBURY CHAPEL.

This sepulchral chapel of the Talbot family was founded by George the fourth earl of Shrewsbury in the time of Henry VIII. It occupies the south-east corner of the church. The outer walls of the church form its south and east sides, while within it is screened off from the rest of the church by substantial oak railing and wainscot. In the beautiful engraving of this chapel, the artist has supposed the screen on the north side removed. It is rectangular, and about twenty-five feet by seventeen. On the north side it is also separated from that part of the chancel where stands the communion-table by a stone arch enriched with coat-armour, which overshadows the tomb of the founder and his wives. The earth beneath is excavated for a vault. It was from the first intended as a sepulchral chapel; but it appears from the founder's will that there was an altar here, the *piscina* of which indeed still remains near the foot of the sixth earl's effigies.

In the east window was a grand shield of the arms and quarterings of the founder, surrounded by the Garter, *viz.*

1, MONTGOMERY—Azure, a lion rampant and border or. 2, TALBOT—Gules, a lion rampant and border engrailed or. 3, OLD TALBOT—Bendy of ten pieces argent and gules. 4, VALENCE—Barry of 10 argent and azure, an orle of martlets gules. 5, NEVIL—Gules, a saltier argent charged with a martlet of the field. 6, FURNIVAL—Argent, a bend between 6 martlets gules. 7, VERDON—Or, a fret gules.

8, STRANGE—Argent, 2 lions passant in pale gules. 9, LOVETOT—Argent, a lion rampant parti per fess gules and sable.

On each side of this great shield were two smaller shields containing the arms of the same earl impaling those of his two wives, *viz.*

HASTINGS—Argent, a maunch sable. WALDEN—Or, on a bend gules cotised azure, between 6 martlets of the second three wings argent.

The heraldric ornaments, having been originally on so frail a material as glass, have perished.

The monument of the founder is an altar tomb with spiral columns at the four corners, and upon it cumbent effigies of the earl and his two countesses, It stands in a recess beneath the arch, and three of its sides are concealed by the wainscot and the upright shafts which support the arch. The side exposed to view presents three rose compartments, and in the centre of each a shield of arms in brass. That in the centre contained the six principal quarterings of the earl, *viz.* Montgomery, Talbot, Nevil, Furnival, Verdon, and Strange. That on the dexter the same impaling Hastings, and that on the sinister the same impaling Walden. The tomb has been robbed of the last. The effigies are in marble, and in the best style of the age: the work it is probable of some Italian artist, whose name I once hoped to have recovered from some notice of him in the Talbot papers. The earl is represented with his coronet and in the robes of the order of the Garter, his feet resting on a talbot, and his hands

[1] It is plainly so in the original—a mistake of the engraver for Amen.

joined as in prayer. There is a character given to the countenance which leaves no room to doubt that it is intended to be a portrait. On a close vest beneath his robe are embroidered the six principal quarterings of his house. On the dress of the two ladies who lie beside him are also heraldrical devices. Their hands are joined as in prayer, and at their feet are angels supporting plain shields.

The inscription is engraven on a ledge of brass running round the monument. The reader will not fail to remark in the exquisite engraving of this monument, the peculiarity of certain characters in the inscription which seems to show that the artist, whoever he was, was not unacquainted with the remains of classical antiquity. The author of it was premature in writing ' *Hic quoque jacent corpora Dominæ Annæ et Elizabethæ;* ' for the latter, who survived till 1567, chose to lie in her own country in the church of Erith in Kent, where is a monument to her memory.

Nearly in the centre of this chapel stands an altar tomb without inscription or effigies: so that the only guide to the period of its erection, and to the person in whose honour it was erected, are the shields of arms with which the sides are adorned.

On the west end is a shield of sixteen quarterings, *viz.*

1, TALBOT. 2, MONTGOMERY. 3, OLD TALBOT. 4, COMYN .... 3 garbs within a double tressure flowered and counterflowered .... 5, VALENCE. 6, MONTCHENSY .... 3 inescutcheons barry of 6 vaire and .... 7, MARSHALL .... a bend lozengy .... 8, STRONGBOW .... on a chief .... 3 crosses pattee fitché .... 9, MAC MOROUGH .... 3 garbs .... 10, STRANGE. 11, NEVIL. 12, FURNIVAL. 13, VERDON. 14, LACY .... a fess .... 15, LOVETOT. 16, TALBOT.

The whole within the Garter, with two talbots for the supporters—Crest, a lion statant on a chapeau. Motto, *Prest d'accomplir.*

At the east end,

TALBOT quartering FURNIVAL, VERDON, and STRANGE, and impaling MANNERS .... 2 bars .... a chief quarterly 1 and 4 .... 2 fleurs de lis .... 2 and 3 .... a lion passant guardant .....

On the north side two shields,

TALBOT quartering as before and with a label of three points, impaling HERBERT parti per pale .... and .... 3 lions rampant .... a border componée. TALBOT quartering as before, impaling OGLE ..... a fess between 3 crescents .... quartering BERTRAM .... an orle ....

On the south side two shields,

TALBOT quartering as before, impaling CAVENDISH .... 3 bucks' heads caboshed .... a crescent for difference. TALBOT quartering as before, impaling a plain shield.

Now these are plainly the armorial insignia of George the sixth earl of Shrewsbury, his first countess, and their four sons. The marriage of Edward Talbot with Ogle did not take place till after the 27th day of September 1583, the day on which the articles of marriage were signed. Hence the monument was not erected before that date. Again Henry Talbot the earl's youngest son was unmarried, as appears by the femme side in his shield being left blank. I cannot fix precisely the period of his marriage, but it was in or about the year 1587, which brings the time for the erection

of this tomb within a small compass. But none of the Talbots died within that period. It seems therefore that this might be the first design of the sixth earl for a monument for himself, abandoned for one of an entirely different form and structure, or perhaps intended by him as a memorial of his son and heir apparent Francis Lord Talbot, who was interred at Sheffield in September 1582.

Against the south wall is the monument of George the sixth earl of Shrewsbury, erected by himself in distrust of his executors. It is in the style which prevailed at the latter end of the reign of Elizabeth, when ornaments borrowed from Italian or classical architecture began to be mingled with the appropriate subjects and ornaments of early English sepulchral architecture. The earl is represented lying on a sarcophagus in plate armour, and with a truncheon in his hand, bare-headed, his helmet standing beside him. Before the injury which the features sustained a very few years ago, the face bore a striking resemblance to the portrait of this earl engraved by Mr. Lodge in the second volume of his Illustrations, &c. The truncheon has been broken off. At his feet the talbot. On the wall immediately above the effigies is a plain slab which contains the long inscription given below, surrounded by a border composed of shields of arms and military trophies alternately. The shields exhibited matches of the earl's ancestry, but most of them have perished. Above is a grand shield of the arms and quarterings of the earl within the Garter, *viz.* Talbot, old Talbot, Comyn, Valence, Montchensy, Montgomery, Strange, Nevil, Furnival, Lovetot, Verdon, and Lacy, with crest, supporters, and motto; and the whole surmounted by a lion sejant affrontée. The whole was once richly painted and gilt.

Some parts of the inscription are become illegible. It was the composition of John Fox the Martyrologist, whose first draught of it with various corrections and alterations in his own hand now remains among his papers in the Harleian library[1]. He has executed his task as if the subject of his encomium was really numbered with the dead. Fox died three years before the earl.

In presenting this inscription to the reader it may be proper to state that the best authority has been followed, namely, a copy taken therefrom when it was new set up, among the collections of Mr. Wilson, compared with the monument itself in part, where the inscription is still legible.

' Christo opt. max. et posteritati sacrum.

IN spem certam[2] futuræ resurrectionis, illustriss. conditur hic heros Georgius Salopiæ Comes, sui nobilissimi generis longâ serie a Normanorum conquestu derivati, nullâq. unquam perfidiæ labeculâ aspersi, Comitum ordine sextus, summus regni Mariscallus, a Talboto, Furnivall, Verdun, Lovetoft, Extraneoq. de Blackmere, honoribus amplissimis, Dominus insuper et Baro nuncupatus : Garteriani quoq. equestris ordinis sane præclarissimi, sodalis dignissimus : Francisci Comitis unicus qui supererat filius et successor, omniumq. virtutum ex asse hæres.

Qui quantum pacis belliq. artibus, omnibusq. corporis atq. animi dotibus eximiis eniti potuit, id omne, secundùm pietatem in Deum, uni patriæ, ejusq. principibus impendere sole-

---

Drawn & Etched by E. Blore.

Front View of the Monument of
George, the fourth Earl of Shrewsbury and his two Countesses,
in St. Peter's Church, Sheffield.

Page 175

bat. Ut qui Mariæ reginæ temporibus, in Northumbriensis Comitis succursum, a patre tum superstite ac belli duce primario, cum tribus armatorum millibus, ad Louvicum in Scotiam ire jussus, strenue summâq. cum laude bellicam illam præfecturam administrarat. Pariq. cum laude, et non minore successu, paulo post Beruvicum hosti in occursum missus, quingentorum cataphractorum equitum cohorte stipatus fuit, concomitantibus Barone Graeio, strenuo equite Drureio, aliisq. rei militaris scientiâ peritissimi belliq. principatum tum gerente Westmario Comite.

Deinde regnante Elizabethâ Anglorum gemmâ, cum Scotórum Regina Maria prælio domi superata, in Angliam compulsa esset, atq. apud Scotici limitis præfectum primum diverteret, donec in utriusq. regni perniciem, magna moliri est comperta, huic illustri Comiti tutius custodienda traditur, anno M.D.LXVIII. Quem penes honorifice ac splendide satis usq. annum M.D.LXXXIIII. per tria amplius lustra, hospitata, non sine magnâ ipsius hospitis impensâ, curâq. anxiâ vix exprimendâ. Qui, divinâ providentiâ gubernante, in causâ tam arduâ, cujus magnitudo gravissima utilitas publica fuit, tam laudate ac feliciter se gessit, eum virum fidelem non minus quam providum atq. prudentem, ipsa Invidia judicare debet. Quamq. semper ab omni suspicione perfidiæ fuerat alienus, illud declarat, quod licet a malevolis propter suspectam cum captivâ reginâ familiaritatem sæpius male audiret, cum tamen ejusdem reginæ cansa ex senatûs regni consultu a proceribus in arce Fodringhaiensi cognoscenda esset, inter magnates qui reatus sui in testimonium ac vindictam admittendi erant, hunc nobiliss. Comitem ser* Regina Elizabetha unum esse voluit; illumq. post judicium latum, ejusdem sententiæ transactorem constituit; dato ad hoc diplomate regio, magno sigillo Angliæ communito.

Ita vir iste genere clarus, publicis bene gestis magistratibus clarior, domi ac foris clariss. illustriss. erga principem et patriam fidei et summi apud omnes honoris, quem ad fatalem maturæ senectutis horam, sine fortunæ ludibrio perduxerat, æterno numini spiritum a quo acceperat, firmâ in Xtum fide placide et tranquille reddidit XVIII. mensis Novembris anno Redemptoris Xti M.D.XC.

Ex priore conjuge, D. Gertrude, Thomæ Rotolandiæ Comitis nata, utriusq. sexus prolem suscepit egregiam: Franciscum scilicet primogenitum, eo superstite, e vivis sublatum: Gilbertum hæredem futurum; Eduardum; Henricum; Catherinam Herberti regulo copulatam, ac sine sobole extinctam: Mariam Georgio Savillo equiti disponsam: et Graceam Henrico Cavendichi equitis hæredi, nuptam.

In the old copy which is here followed, the date of the earl's death is not given. In the superscription it is added that 'the date could not be placed, but he departed this life 18 Nov. 1590.' Dugdale informs us, that in his time the date was wanting, and that the earl prophetically foretold that his executors would not take care to supply it[1]. Perhaps it was added on public notice being taken of the omission in the Baronage.

These monuments have sustained less injury than might have been expected in the course of so many years, and in the heart of a populous town. The screen by which they have been protected has not however saved the effigies on the founder's tomb from the hands of boys, if not of 'children of a larger growth,' who have been ambitious of inscribing the initials of their names on the marble[2]. It is to be wished that they were kept more free from dust, which is allowed to accumulate upon them year after year. But there is a

more serious consideration respecting one at least of these memorials of past grandeur. The ferrugineous matter which veins the marble of which the sarcophagus and other parts of the monument of the sixth earl are composed is gradually mouldering away, to the imminent danger of the whole fabrick.

Prolix as is the epitaph on the sixth earl already given, there was another not less so in English verse painted upon a board, and hung near his tomb. Of this no traces now remain, but Dodsworth has preserved a copy[3]: It is more an elegy than an epitaph.

'AN Epitaph upon the death of the noble Lord GEORGE Earle of SHROWSBURYE who departed this mortall life the yere of our Lord God 1590, buried the eighteenth day of November.

Such as desire to live when fatall threed is spunne,
Syth mans life is short ther course they must runne;
  That fame and worthy acts and vertues maie commend
  Unto posterities that live unto the end.

Else everie worthy deed full soone awaie shall weare,
Then shall they live as though they neer lived heare :
  What difference shall be 'twixt great and meanest man,
  When of there famouse deedes noe booke ought record can.

What booteth titles great of honour soe to have,
Or Cressus goulden store, when they lie in there grave :
  More worth a thousand fold they famouse for to bee
  For vertues and noble acts then all the rest to thee.

What moved hath this peere himselfe to indevor
By his deserts to advance of his house the honour;
  Whose fame I am to weake, in verse well to expresse;
  Aide me therefore my Muse to show his worthinesse.

Of this house the heralds say in England there hath bene
Great Lords and Barons bould yere Normans did it wynne :
  Whose daughter and his heire, Talbott of Normandie-
  Did take unto her mate; a man of like degree :

And of this progeny Barons by name sixteene,
And Earles in number six of great renowne have beene.
  There matches often were with great nobility,
  As planely doth appeare at large by Pettegree.

To speake of such as these, there valor in the field,
And of there worthy acts adventred with spere and sheild
  Which have bene heretofore, I leave to each ther due
  To yeald long time it craves : the story who will vewe

Maie hereby understand there acts of Chivalrie'
Which fame with blast of trump hath blowne both far and nye.
  And he that sleepeth now within this stately tombe,
  Of both these Talbots race by right descent is come :

George Earle of Shrowsbury, Washford and Waterford,
Erle Marshall of England, Talbot of Goodridge, Lord
  Verdon of Altoun, Furnivall of Sheffield,
  Lord Luftot of Worksopp, Lord Crumbwell of Wingfield,

Lord Strange of the Blackmeere, and Justice by North Trent
Of forests and chases, a councellor, President
  Unto his soveraine Quene &c. for his loyalty
  Knight of the Garter, eke these titles all had hee :

Which solemnly proclamed by heralds that daie
When was his funerall ; with honour every day.
  Lefetenant of Stafford and Darbyshire also
  In days most dangerouse he was assigned tho.

A mighty man he was, in wealth he did abound,
Of all his howse therein the like was never found :

---

[1] *Baronage.* His relict Elizabeth countess of Shrewsbury, who is completely passed over in the epitaph, built her own monument in the church of Derby, in like distrust of her heirs.

[2] From this practice some of our finest monuments have suffered. A French writer has these lively remarks : ' Deux milles barbares environ ont porté une main temeraire sur ce chef-d'œuvre; [la statue du François 1er] ils ont gravé leurs noms, avec une pointe, sur les parties les plus interessantes . . . . Alexandre Syts est le dernier qui s'est gravé ;

illustre comme Erostrate, il a quitté la ville de Gand pour ajouter son nom au nombre de ceux que je viens de citer. Amis des arts, permettez moi d'imprimer sur cette liste le cachet de l'ignorance et de l'infamie. Conservateurs, qui avez dans vos mains les belles statues de la Grèce, voilez la statue d'Apollon, si jamais un Alexandre Syts osait souiller son sanctuaire.' Le Noir ' *Musée impérial,*' p. 224.

[3] Dods. MSS. in Bibl. Bodl. vol. clx. f. 127.

He fast was to his freind, and heavy to his foe;
He lived soe direct that none could worke him woe.

The poore mans plaint to here his eares would alwaise bend,
And them in there cause against there foes defend.
Five hundred pound he gave for ever to remaine
To Chesterfield to help poor tradesmen without gaine.

Of courage he was stoote noe injury would beare,
No subject in this land in whome he stood in feare.
　Great was this Talbots strength, if he to prove had list,
　More power he could have raised than each man could have
　　wisht.

But ever he lay full his country to defend,
And never did oppresse whereby he might offend.
　Marie Queen of Scots then vanquished att home
　In battill, unto us for succor first did come:

When she by seaventeen yeares abode with this great peer,
Untill against her realme to worke she did conspire
　Great things; whereof by Lords thrice tenn and six of name,
　She tainted was at last and suffered for the same.

Soe great a trust as this so long was never seene,
A subject for to be a keeper of a Queene.
　To scape out of his hands by divers waiss she sought;
　But still he did prevent the waies that she had wrought:

For wisely he did see what perill might have been
If she had scapt away, to realme or cake to Queene:
　Wherefore he showed himselfe most carefull for to be,
　Soe great a charge to keepe with all fidelity.

Whereby he hath preserved his name of soe great renowne;
The Talbot ever true and faithfull to the crowne.
　But yet for all his wealth his honour and his fame,
　Loe where he lies in earth from whence at first he came.

For each thing bearing life in time it shall decay,
And nothing so sure as death, uncertaine is the day:
　He spareth noe degree, but with his sythe in hand
　He mowes downe all the grasse, his force none can withstand.

Such as applye themselves uprightly for to live,
When they yeald up there breath it never doth them greive:
　But such as have no care of baile nor blisse at all,
　They never have regard what things on them befall.

Such men live in this world as though they should not dye,
And as the dreadfull Hell was nought else but a lye:
　But sure the day will come when each accompt must yeald,
　Before the fearfull judge when noe man shall them shield.

Wherefore while time there is let us for mercy crave,
That after wee goe hence a blessed place may have.
　In peace thou worthy wight rest here till Christ shall come
　Upon all flesh to give his censure and his doome,
　And then with joyfull voice Lord call him unto thee,
　Where he may ever dwell with them that blessed be.'

On the 27th day of June 1809, in company with
Mr. V. H. Eyre and Mr. John Greaves, I explored
the vault beneath the Shrewsbury chapel which had
been closed since the year 1787. By eight or nine
steps from the chancel we descended to an upright
door which we found so decayed that it fell from its
bolt and hinges on a very slight force being applied to
it. We were then admitted into a room about ten
feet square and six feet in height, its stone roof supported by a rough hewn pillar rising in the centre. We
found only two coffins lying on tressels; that on the
right contained the body of Gilbert earl of Shrewsbury, while on the left lay another with the following
inscription on a brass plate:

　　　　　HENRY HOWARD, Esq.
　　　　　　　of Glossop,
　　　　　　obᵗ 11 Nov. 1787,
　　　　　　　ætatis 74.

The coffin of the earl of Shrewsbury was of oak, and
on a brass plate affixed to it was engraven an inscription which Dodsworth copied from the lead in which
the body in his time was folded. It was placed in its
present oaken case in 1778, when this part of the
church was much repaired by the earl of Surrey.

'The body of GILBERT earl of Shrewsbury Washford and
Waterford, high seneschal of Ireland, Lord Talbot, Comyn of
Badenagh, Montchensie, Strange of Blackmere, Gifford of
Brimsfield, Clifford of Corsam, Furnival, Verdon, and Lufe-
tote, knight of the Garter, privy councellor to his Maᵗᶦᵉ, Justice in Eyre from Trent northward, who died the seventh day
of May A.D. 1616, aged 64.'

Formerly more of the coffins were in sight; for
Thoresby, who collected every thing, had preserved in
his museum 'A shred of the velvet pall now wholly
divested of its blackness by lying many years over the
countess of Shrewsbury's coffin in the vault at Sheffield[1].' This coffin and others deposited here are probably walled up in that part of the vault which lies under the founder's tomb.

A catalogue of the persons interred here.

Ann countess of Shrewsbury, daughter of Lord
　Hastings.
1538. Mary Lady Talbot first wife of Francis earl of
　Shrewsbury.
1538. George fourth earl of Shrewsbury.
　　　William Talbot marshal of Ireland his fifth son.
1560. Francis earl of Shrewsbury.
1565. Thomas Talbot an infant son of the 6th earl.
1566. Gertrude countess of Shrewsbury.
1572. Mary countess of Northumberland.
1573. George Pierrepoint, an infant; probably son of
　Henry Pierrepoint, of Holme-Pierrepoint, by Fran-
　ces Cavendish daughter to the countess of Shrews-
　bury.
1577. George Talbot, an infant son of Gilbert after-
　wards earl of Shrewsbury.
1581. Elizabeth countess of Lenox.
1582. Francis Lord Talbot.
1590. George sixth earl of Shrewsbury.
1594. Charles son of Sir Charles Cavendish, and elder
　brother to William afterwards duke of Newcastle.
1595. Henry Talbot, brother to Gilbert earl of Shrews-
　bury.
1616. Gilbert earl of Shrewsbury.
1632. Mary countess of Shrewsbury.
1787. Henry Howard, esquire.

Mr. Sherburn (an agent of the Norfolk family at
Sheffield, a distant relation of Mary duchess of Norfolk,) and his lady are said to have been both laid in
this vault.

In the church as it was pewed before the late alterations, or rather renovation, was a closet called the
Lord's Closet, where the earls of Shrewsbury and their
family used to sit to attend divine service, and another
for their household. There was also a loft called Mr.
Jessop's loft, the seat of the patron of the church.

The windows of the present church are all modern,
and have no painted glass. Not a trace remains of
the ancient ornaments of its windows. When Dodsworth saw it in 1620, he took account of the following

[1] *Ducatus Leodiensis*, p. 484.

In the first window on the north side, divers kneeling, and this inscription:

'Pray ye for the soules of Geffry Butry' and Robert Butry and Joan his wife.
Randal Pigot, knight.
Thomas Butry, chaplayne.'

In the second window:

'Pray ye for the soules of HUGH COKE¹ and for the soules of AGNES ELLEN and JONE his wives.

Arms, quarterly FURNIVALL and NEVIL.

In the third window:

'Pray ye for the soules of JOHN HORNER and AGNES ....'

In the east window of the chancel:

Arms;—TALBOT quartering STRANGE—The arms of the first earl of Shrewsbury.

In other windows of the church:

Azure 3 dragons' heads erased or, quartering argent 3 boars passant in pale sable.
MOUNTENEY;—Gules, a bend between 6 martlets or.

Azure, a bend between 6 martlets or.
TALBOT impaling BEAUCHAMP;—Gules, a fess between 6 cross crosslets or. The arms of the first earl of Shrewsbury and his second countess.
RUDDE;—Vert, 3 fishes hauriant argent.

Between the Shrewsbury chapel and the vestry is the communion-table, with a painting of the Last Supper, by Nathaniel Tucker, an artist who resided at Sheffield, and left portraits of the principal inhabitants between 1765 and 1780; and on the wall, memorials of various benefactions which have been made to the poor. The old capacious stone font, (prepared to receive the whole body of the infant, according to the ancient practice of the English church,) which stood near the west door, has long disappeared, and given place to the present marble bason which stands near the communion-table. Not far removed from it is a relic of the old church, the three wooden stalls in which the priest and his two assistants sat at the celebration of mass.

Drawn & Etched by E.Blore.

Published, Jan¹ 1ˢᵗ 1819, by the Rev.ᵈ J. Hunter, Bath.

The vestry and a room over it in which the church-burgesses meet for the transaction of their business, occupy the north-east corner of the church. In the vestry are about two hundred volumes of books, which were given by different benefactors as the beginning of a parochial library in 1707 and a little after. We look in vain amongst them for any volume of the least curiosity.

The parish register is a record of the baptisms, marriages, and burials of the whole parish, and is of course now become very voluminous. Of the register, if any

was kept in pursuance of Cromwell's injunction in 1534, no traces remain. The first volume of the register contains from 1560 to 1634, and is in fine preservation. The second ends in 1652, the third in 1686, the fourth in 1702, the fifth in 1719. It has been in general well kept, and in this parish, as in many others, the oldest registers are the best. More care was formerly taken in the preparation of the ink, and in the selection of able scribes. The scrawl of an ignorant parish-clerk was not formerly admitted into a register, by the evidence of which very important in-

¹ This person, who was one of the three priests of Sheffield, lived in the time of Henry VII.

² Probably a mistake of the copyist for Cokesey, and the same Hugh de Cokesey who married Joan daughter and co-heir of Sir Thomas Nevil Lord Furnival.

terests might one day be determined. It is much to be regretted that the form of registering burials prescribed by the late act of parliament on this subject is not more discriminative.

There was an organ in this church in the time of Queen Elizabeth, but it was silenced by the puritan spirit which prevailed in the parish in the middle of the seventeenth century, nor was another erected till the period of the late great repairs of the church.

Here are a set of chimes and a peal of ten bells. They were placed in the tower in the year 1799, when the old peal of eight was removed. There was a scheme or placing the old peal in Saint Paul's. The third bell was the gift of the Cutlers' Company in 1688, the fourth of Gilbert earl of Shrewsbury and Mary his countess in 1606. They were all re-cast in 1745. On a supernumerary bell vulgarly called the Tom Tinker was the date 1588.

The public duty at the parish-church is taken week by week by the vicar and his three assistants. They also took their turns on Sundays at the chapels of Ecclesall and Attercliffe, till the curacy of Attercliffe was separated from the office of assistant-minister. The occasional duty there was performed by their respective curates. There are two sermons each Sunday, prayers every evening; and morning prayers on Wednesdays, Fridays, and all saints' days throughout the year. A Wednesday evening lecture was voluntarily undertaken in December 1815 by all the clergymen residing in the parish, and is still continued.

Much inconvenience having been found to arise from the irregularity as to time with which bodies were brought to the church for interment, the following petition was presented to the archbishop of York, signed by the vicar, assistant-ministers, church-wardens, and seventy-three respectable inhabitants.

' To the most reverend father in God William by Divine Providence Lord Archbishop of York, primate of England and Metropolitane.

May it please your grace,

Whereas a custom hath prevailed amongst the inhabitants of the town and parish of Sheffield of bringing their dead to be buried at unseasonable hours, to the great inconvenience of the minister that is obliged to attend, and of other persons that are invited to such funerals; we whose names are underwritten humbly beg that your Grace would please to discharge the vicar and assistant-ministers of the town and parish aforesaid from burying any corpse after four o'clock in the afternoon, except for every such corpse as shall be buried after that hour, the friends of the deceased will pay into the church-wardens' hands for the time being the sum of twenty shillings to

be disposed of in such manner as the vicar and church-wardens shall think fit; and we as in duty bound shall ever pray, &c.'

To which his Grace was pleased to return the following answer.

' I DO hereby consent to the prayer of this petition, and do order the vicar of Sheffield to publish the petition, together with this my cousent to the prayer of it in the parish church of Sheffield.   Witness my hand,
February the 16th 1722.   W. EBOR.

The wish of our forefathers *to be brought honestly to the earth* still continues to influence all ranks. By the usual conditions of the benefit societies, the sum of eight pounds is to be paid to the friends of deceased members towards the expenses of the funeral. At the interment of the poorest, all the friends and neighbours are invited, each of whom deposits a shilling, and receives a coarse cake made for the occasion. Biscuits, remains of ' the funeral baked meats,' are given with the usual mourning by the higher ranks; and the old custom of hanging up garlands of paper in the church after the interment of young unmarried women, is not wholly discontinued. On the glove, which always is suspended within the garland, are written the name and age of the party commemorated by these frail memorials. Since the introduction of Methodism the ancient and indeed primitive custom has been revived of accompanying the body to its long home with ' dirges due.'

The fee customarily paid on opening a grave in the body of the church was six shillings and eight-pence, but since the late repairs no interments have been permitted in that part of the church. The fee on interments in the chancel is ten shillings. The church stands in a spacious area which has been used as a burial-ground from time immemorial. Till within the last century there were few interments on the north side of the church. This ground, though spacious, is much too confined for so populous a parish, even with all the relief it has obtained by the allotment of other pieces of ground for the same purpose at Saint Paul's and Saint James's, and of others for the use of different descriptions of Dissenters. The two rural chapels of Ecclesall and Attercliffe stand in very spacious burying-grounds.

On the 16th day of July 1817 his grace the archbishop of York consecrated a large piece of ground on the west of the town, to be used hereafter as a place of interment.

A Catalogue of the VICARS of SHEFFIELD.

Vicarii.	Patroni.	Temp. Instit.	Vac. per
Frater Johes Twistleton	Prior et Convent. de Worksop	4 Kal. Nov. 1309.	
—— Johes de Sheffeld	. . . iidem . . .	3 Kal. Mar. 1314.	
—— Rogerus de Walsingham or Walkeringham	. . . iidem . . .	26 Apr. 1315.	
—— Willielmus de Retford	. . . iidem . . .	7 Kal. Jun. 1316.	Resig.
—— Johes de Byby, Ryby, or Dryby	. . . iidem . . .	6 Kal. Jul. 1338.	Death.
—— Johes Hanclev, Stancley, or Stalkley	. . . iidem . . .	4 Oct. or Dec. 1368.	Resig.
—— Rogerus de Upton, afterwards Prior of Worksop	. . . iidem . . .	27 Oct. 1375.	Resig. or Priv.
—— Johes Someley or Stanley	. . . iidem . . .	26 Oct. 1387.	Resig.
—— Rogerus de Upton	. . . iidem . . .	16 Nov. 1390.	Resig.
—— Henricus de Bromeley	. . . iidem . . .	18 Dec. 1397.	Death.
—— Johes de Scheffield	. . . iidem . . .	24 Aug. 1401.	Resig.
—— Robertus de Toowell or Trowell	. . . iidem . . .	13 or 17 Sep. 1412.	Death.
—— Johes de Leghston	. . . iidem . . .	1 Feb. 1418.	Resig.
—— Ricardus de Wyrksop	. . . iidem . . .	2 Jan. 1434 or 1437.	Resig.
—— Johes Howe	. . . iidem . . .	15 Aug. 1452.	Death.
—— Willielmus Burne	. . . iidem . . .	10 May 1458.	Death or Resig.
—— Willielmus Bolton	. . . iidem . . .	18 Aug. 1459.	
—— Willielmus Symondson	. . . iidem . . .	. . . . . .	Resig.
—— Johes Plesaunce	. . . iidem . . .	11 Sep. 1482.	Death.
—— Thomas Cundall	. . . iidem . . .	22 Sep. 1501.	Death.
—— Thomas Stokks	. . . iidem . . .	2 Mar. 1512.	Resig.
—— Thomas Wode	. . . iidem . . .	30 Jul. 1519.	Death.
—— Robertus Gawthorpe	. . . iidem . . .	23 Jan. 1534.	Death.
—— Ricardus Hayward	Willielmus Swyft, gen.	6 Mar. 1558-9.	Death.
Dominus Johes Atkyn [1]	Ricardus Jessop	25 Jul. 1567.	Death.
—— Robertus Holland	Ricard. Jessop et Anna ux. ejus	27 Oct. 1569.	Death.
Thomas Toller	Willielmus Jessop, arm.	23 or 24 Feb. 1597.	Death or Resig.
John Bright, A.M.	Willielmus Jessop, arm. de Scofton	20 Aug. 1635.	Resig. or Cess.
Edward Browne	By the powers then in being	23 April 1643.	Cess.
Thomas Birbeck	. . the same . .	1644.	Resig. or Eject.
James Fisher	. . the same . .	1654.	Resig.
Edward Browne	. . restored . .	1662.	Eject.
John Lobley, A.M.	Jane Jessop, widow	5 Mar. 1662.	Cession.
Charles Wilson, A.M.	Francis Jessop, esquire	6 Oct. 1681.	Cess. or Resig.
Nathan Drake, A.M.	Willm Jessop of Broomhall, esq.	1 Oct. 1695.	Resig.
John Dossie	. . . idem . . .	15 May or 20 June 1713.	Cession.
James Wilkinson, A.M.	Andrew Wilkinson of Boroughbridge, esq.	23 Sep. 1754.	Death.
Thomas Sutton, A.M.	Philip Gell of Hopton, esq.	30 March 1805.	Death.

With the early names in this catalogue there are no circumstances of character or history handed down to us. We may remark a quick succession in the vicarage in the times before the Reformation; twenty-three incumbents in the space of two hundred and fifty years. They were all canons of Worksop. Upton, one of them, became prior of his house. Gawthorpe, who held the living in the changeful times of the Reformation, seems to have been a man of complying habits. He entered upon his preferment in the time of Henry VIII., enjoyed it in the Protestant reign of Edward; did not resign when Mary was restoring the old system: and died possessed of it in the first year of Elizabeth.

Of the later vicars, a few biographical notices may be acceptable.

Robert Holland. Take his character from his diocesan the venerable Edwin Sandys.

' My honorable good Lorde,

At my laste beinge wth you, I moved yor L. in behalfe of Mr Hollande vicar of Sheffilde; yor aunswere was so honorable that I thought my self muche beholden to yor L. for it. And I learne that synce he hath reaped frute thereof: yf it

would please yor L. to bestowe upon him a small benefice neare adioyninge now fallen wherof yor L. is patrone, as yow might be sure of his faithfull and diligent service so in myne opinion yow should do a greate good to that people in givinge them a preachinge pastor. I have many other things to imparte unto yor L. but another tyme will serve better. Thus I comende yor good L. to the good direction of Godd's holy spirite. Byshopthorpe this x^th of March 1578.

Yo^r L.' in Christ most assured,
E. EBOR.[2]

To the ryght honorable my very good Lord the Earle of Shrewsbury [1].

Such letters of recommendation were not uncommon from the bishops to patrons of livings. The benefice then vacant was Whiston, to which Mr. Holland was instituted on the 18th day of March, only eight days after the date of this letter, on the presentation of the earl of Shrewsbury. He continued to reside at Sheffield, and dying there on the 21st day of August 1597, was buried nearly opposite the great window on the south side of his parish church. His grave stone, which Dodsworth saw, was removed, probably by some of his descendants, for he had a numerous family, and another laid down, which two hundred and twenty years after his decease continues to point out the

[1] He was also rector of Whiston.—Buried at Sheffield 22 Sep. 1568.
[2] Talbot Papers, F 299.

2 R

spot in the church-yard where this early vicar was interred.

Thomas Toller, whom Dr. Calamy (writing, it is probable, from the information of Ralph Thoresby of Leeds,) calls 'the worthy Mr. Towler[1].' He seems to have been a man more than commonly earnest in the important work in which he was engaged: and to have been held in much esteem by his parishioners. He resigned the vicarage in 1635, and stepped into the assistant-minister's place, then void by the resignation

of Mr. Bright, previous to his entering upon the possession of the vicarage. Mr. Toller died in July 1644, having been an officiating clergyman in the parish forty-six years.

I know of nothing published by Mr. Toller; but there remain in manuscript poetical paraphrases of the Lord's Prayer and the Apostles' Creed, by his hand. As probably they are the only remaining specimens of his genius and style of thinking, the shorter of the two may be here laid before the reader.

THE PERPETUAL SACRIFICE.

1	If any in distresse desire to gather Trewe comforte, let him seeke it of	Our Father :
2	For wee of hope and helpe are all bereaven, Except thou ayde us Lorde	which art in Heaven :
3	For thou doest ayde us, therefore for the same Wee prayse thee singing	hallowed bee'thi name.
4	Of all our miseries, caste up the su'me; Shewe us the joyes, and let	Thi kingdom come.
5	Thou doest dispose of us, even from our birth; What can wee wishe—	Thi will be done in earthe.
6	Thine is the earth; as are the planetts seaven, Thi name be blessed heere,	as it is in Heaven,
7	Nothing is ours, eyther to use or paye, But what thou gevest Lord;	Give us this daye
8	Wherwith to cloath us, wherwith to feede; For without thee, wee wante	our daylie breade.
9	But wante no faults, no daye without sinne passes; Pardon us good Lorde,	and forgeve us our trespasses
10	No man from syning free did ever lyve; Forgeve us Lorde our synnes,	as wee forgeve.
11	If we forgeve not one another, thou disdaynist us : We pardon	them that trespasse against us.
12	Forgive us what is paste, a newe path treade us : Direct us alwayes in thi faith,	and leade us
13	As thine owne people, and thi chosen nacion Into all trewth; but	not into temptacion.
14	Thou that of all good graces art the gever, Suffer us not to wander,	but us delyver
15	Us from the daungers of the worlde, the fleshe and the Devill So shalt thou free all us	from all evill.
16	To these petycions let all church and leymen, With one consent of harte and voyce, saye to it	Amen.

John Bright, Mr. Toller's successor, was born at Bradway in the parish of Norton, in 1594, but his father Thomas Bright settled himself soon after at Carbrook. Stephen Bright of that place was elder brother to the vicar, and Colonel John Bright (afterward Sir John Bright) was his nephew. He was an assistant-minister for some time before he became vicar. Mr. Jessop the patron married one of his nieces, sister to Colonel Bright. He died in April 1643, and was buried at Sheffield.

At the time of his decease, the ecclesiastical constitution of the country was in a state of great disorder. In that very month, the earl of Newcastle was at Sheffield with his army; and soon after, by what authority does not appear, was put into the vacant vicarage *Mr. Edward Browne*, a warm partisan of the royal cause. In the parish-register occur these entries : ' 1643-4 Jan. 7, Mr Barney knowled the great bell for Mr Browne his possession into the vicarage of Sheffeild, being his proxit.'—And again, ' 1643-4, Mar.'23, Edwardus Browne, vicarius, inductus fuit in realentem, actualem et corporalem possessionem vicariæ de Sheffield. Thornam Barney, clericum.' His name occurs as vicar in July 1644, but the next month brought

a change of the times. The royalist garrison of the castle surrendered, and the royalist vicar was displaced. His name is mentioned in Walker's Sufferings of the Clergy, as well as that of his friend Mr. Barney, but without any particulars. When the vicarage of Sheffield was vacant by the non-subscription of Mr. Fisher, under the Act of Uniformity, Mr. Browne returned and entered upon the living. What was the nature of the title he set up, or whether he was opposed by the patrons, I cannot say; but he ceded the living before the 30th of October 1662, when he was instituted on the presentation of the Crown to the rectory of Crofton, near Wakefield, then void by the non-subscription of Francis Burley, an ejected minister, who has escaped the notice of Dr. Calamy[2]. Upon this living Mr. Browne resided till his death in 1687.

Thomas Birbeck was chosen an assistant-minister in 1635, and appointed vicar of Sheffield in 1644, by the parliamentarians. He was son to Edward Birbeck, or Burbeck, bachelor of divinity, a Puritan divine, chaplain to that religious nobleman John lord Darcy of Aston, and rector of Staveley, where this his son was born. In 1648 he left Sheffield, and went to reside at the pleasant and valuable rectory of Ack-

[1] *Account of the Ejected and Silenced Ministers*, p. 785.
[2] Perhaps he conformed: as I find no notice of him in the MS. diaries of Mr. Oliver Heywood, which are full of notices of his ejected and silenced brethren in the west riding of Yorkshire.

worth, near Pontefract. This preferment he held till the Restoration, when Dr. Bradley, the displaced incumbent, returned. Mr. Birbeck then came to reside among his old friends at Sheffield. He preached frequently amongst them, and did much good. Dr. Calamy gives him this character. ' He was a very worthy divine, and solid substantial preacher, one of a cheerful spirit,'—no common subject of encomium on the divines who come within the scope of Dr. Calamy's observation,—' but much affected with the stone.' He escaped from the pangs of that disorder on the 8th of July 1674, and was interred in the church-yard of Sheffield. The wife of Mr. Birbeck was sister to Mr. James Creswiek, who was also a Puritan divine, ejected from the living of Freshwater in the isle of Wight, a native of Sheffield. An interesting memoir of this gentleman is given by Dr. Calamy. He suffered less than many of his brethren when the Act of Uniformity compelled him to leave his living, for he had a good fortune, and with part of it purchased the manor of Beghall, near Ferrybridge, upon which he lived handsomely, and married his only daughter (for whom he wrote a book of fatherly counsel published after his decease) into the respectable family of Farrer of Ewood.

Of Mr. Fisher, the next vicar, a more favourable opportunity of speaking will occur in the next chapter.

John Lobley. He entered upon the vicarage in trying times. Many of his parishioners adhered to the Non-conformist ministers, and among them were some of the best quality. He conducted himself with great temper and moderation, and is by no means to be supposed to have lent his assistance in the violent measures which were pursued towards his predecessor. He was sometimes disturbed by the Quakers. While in the discharge of his duty in the parish-church, his ears are said to have received this rough salutation from one of that body, ' Thou false teacher, come down.' When he had been eighteen years vicar, he resigned, and was presented to the vicarage of Chesterfield. At that town he died in May 1694.

Charles Wilson was born at Broomhead-hall, second son and eventually heir to Christopher Wilson of that place, once a great favourite of the earl of Strafford, but after his death, a captain in the parliament service. His mother, the daughter of a clergyman, is said by family tradition to have been a very discreet, excellent woman. On the 2d of February 1658-9, being then twenty-seven years of age, he was presented by Edward Montague earl of Manchester, one of whose chaplains he was, to the living of Kimbolton in Huntingdonshire. He conformed at the Restoration, and in 1673 and 1674 had a troublesome suit at law with Robert earl of Manchester, his patron's son, in which however he had the advantage. Next year he resigned Kimbolton, and was immediately presented to the rectory of Babworth in Nottinghamshire, by Ann Wortley alias Newcomen, the daughter and heir of Sir Francis Wortley, of Wortley, baronet. In 1681 he resigned that living in favour of Richard Wilson, his younger brother's son, and in the October of that year was instituted by Richard Sterne, archbishop of York, to the vicarage of Sheffield. Here he was useful and popular. In 1684 the church-burgesses thought proper to augment his income out of their fund. In 1692 he obtained a considerable addition to his property, by the death of his brother Reginald Wilson, of the island of Jamaica, who perished in the earthquake that destroyed Port-Royal. In 1695 he came to the resolution of devoting the remainder of his life to retirement; and refusing to place a curate at Sheffield, to which he was solicited, withdrew to his paternal inheritance at Broomhead. In that remote and wild solitude, almost inaccessible in those days during several months of the year, the last eight years of his life were spent; and in that hall of his forefathers where his first breath was drawn, there he drew his last, in September 1703, and was gathered to his fathers of more than twelve generations in the church of Bradfield, leaving behind him the character of one who had ' fought a good fight, and finished his course with joy.'

Nathan Drake held the vicarage seventeen years, namely, from 1695 to 1713. He was of a family which has given many of its sons to the church and literature. Not to mention any later members of this worthy family, there were Dr. Richard Drake, precentor of Sarum, who published Bishop Andrews' Greek Devotions; Dr. Samuel Drake, vicar of Pontefract, author of a Life of his tutor and friend Mr. Clieveland; another Dr. Samuel Drake, who was rector of Treeton, who published a beautiful edition of Parker's Antiq. Britan.; and Mr. Francis Drake, F.S.A. whose History of York ranks high among our topographical works. Most of these were friends as well as relations of the vicar of Sheffield, who before he settled there had the living of Market-Weighton in the east-riding. He printed a Sermon against Bribery, which was delivered in the cathedral at York, when he was chaplain to his friend and neighbour Mr. Ingleby Daniel, of Beswick, sheriff of the county. In 1697 he published a Sermon delivered in his own parish church of Sheffield, against the use of false weights and measures. Archbishop Sharp gave him the prebend of Bilton in the cathedral church of York, 1703; and ten years after, he left Sheffield on being presented to the rectory of Kirkby-Overblows. There he died in April 1729, retaining that regard for his former parishioners at Sheffield, which is commonly to be found in the breasts of those who have known them well, even after a long separation.

The space of more than ninety-one years from the removal of Mr. Drake was filled by only two incumbents, Mr. Dossie and Mr. Wilkinson. The former a very respectable parish-priest, the latter something more and better: a Dares, ' αφνειος, αμυμων,' and though not a priest of Vulcan, yet a priest among the sons of Vulcan. His death, at the age of 74, was considered as the greatest public loss the town of Sheffield had been known to sustain, and all were inclined to hail him ' *Father of the town of Sheffield, and its neighbourhood.*' To the influence arising from his office were added the influence which the possession of magistracy gives; the influence of a noble income, and of hereditary respect, for he was the representative of the family of the Jessops of Broomhall, and resided in the house of his forefathers; and the influence of the most gentlemanly address, combined with a tall and graceful person, which could not fail of commanding respect. ' Whether we regard him,' said a contemporary and friend, ' as a divine labouring by his example as well as precept to inculcate the great and sacred truths of revealed religion; or as a magistrate executing those laws of his country which were framed by the legislature for the protection of every thing valuable in society, and with a most patient attention to every minute particular from every person, but more particularly from the poor, the ignorant, and unprotected, to enable him to administer justice with the most scrupulous impartiality, but at the same time to blend it with mercy, whenever it was in his power;—whether we consider him as a friend ever ready with his purse, as well as with his advice or interest, to do any good or generous act;—or as a great public character commanding respect by a dignity in person and manners rarely to be met with, who was deservedly looked up to and consulted upon every occurring occasion, whether for the relief of the poor, the defence of his country, the protection of every useful institution, the encouragement of merit in any situation, or of any plan calculated in any way to improve or benefit society in general, but more particularly the town and neighbourhood of Sheffield:—whether we contemplate him in any or all of the above points of view, there will be abundant reason to admire the excellence of his understanding, the integrity of his conduct, and the zeal which he displayed in accomplishing all his purposes.'

Such was Mr. Wilkinson. The fourth of seven sons of Andrew Wilkinson, of Boroughbridge, esquire, many years member of parliament for Aldborough, and principal store-keeper of the ordnance, he was early designed for the church, and received a most excellent classical education under Mr. Clarke of Beverley school. From under his care he was removed to Clare-Hall in Cambridge, and was admitted to the degree of B.A. in 1752, and M.A. 1754. Sheffield, the family living, becoming vacant in 1753, it was reserved for Mr. Wilkinson, till he was of age to take it. This and a prebend in the collegiate church of Ripon was all the preferment he enjoyed, nor did he seek or wish for more. At Sheffield he had sufficient scope for the exercise of his benevolence, and of that desire of usefulness which entered so largely into his moral constitution. He undertook very early in life the office of a magistrate for the west and north ridings, the duties of which, as he executed them, were most laborious. In the latter part of his life he enjoyed great affluence, all his brothers having gone before him. He then spent a portion of his time at his family mansion at Boroughbridge, but much the largest portion was still passed at his favourite and quiet retreat near Sheffield. At Boroughbridge he died after a long and painful illness, on Friday the 18th of January 1805, and was buried in the church of that town, where a handsome monument was erected to his memory by his relative and executor, the late Reverend Marmaduke Lawson, bearing this inscription:

Sacred
to the memory of the Revd JAMES WILKINSON, A.M.
fourth and last surviving son of Andrew Wilkinson, esquire.
He held the vicarage of Sheffield fifty years, and for
nearly the same length of time
discharged the duties of a magistrate;
for the execution of which important trusts
extensive and accurate knowledge, uncommon discernment,
superior talents, and conciliating manners
eminently qualified him.
He was candid, modest, unassuming, yet of steady courage:
uninfluenced by selfish views, he ever firmly persevered in the
path of duty.
His piety was sincere, and without ostentation,
his benevolence diffusive, active, unwearied.
What wonder that one in whom
so many great and amiable qualities
were united, whilst living should be revered, and when dead,
be regretted as a public loss!
He departed this life January 18th 1805, in the
75th year of his age.

Mr. Wilkinson published only one sermon: a plain, unaffected, interesting discourse delivered in Saint Paul's church, on the day when first the Infirmary, that noble monument of the liberality of the passing generation of inhabitants of Sheffield and its vicinity, was opened for the reception of patients. He entered not into religious controversies; but in theology, he was of the school of Clarke, Balguy, and the rational divines of the former half of the last century.

The inhabitants of Sheffield, who had benefited so largely by his public and private services, were not unmindful of what was due to the memory of Mr. Wilkinson. There was one day of public mourning: an engraving was executed from the portrait which had been painted some years before by desire of the Company of Cutlers, and hung in their hall: the hand of Chantrey, as we have seen, was called to give his features to marble for a monument to be erected at the public expense in the parish-church: and impressed upon a medallion in copper, the features of his countenance will be perused by far distant generations. The good should be had in everlasting remembrance.

It has been said that the vicarage of Sheffield was intended for a near relative of Mr. Wilkinson, who has since gained literary honours on the plain of Troy. His mind took another turn.

Drawn & Engraved by John Shury

A Catalogue of the ASSISTANT-MINISTERS of SHEFFIELD.

1554. Sir Alexander Booth.	1554. Sir Richard Bewick.	1554. Sir William Hall.
1558. Sir William Kynge.	1568. Sir Robert Beane.	1560. Sir William Hutton.
1564. Sir James Amgill.	1573. Sir George Hancock.	1562. William Swift.
1572. Richard Roberts.	1594. Sir John Hill.	1567. Sir Henry Bowckcock.
1599. - - Bower.	1596. John Machon.	1569. Sir William Kynge.
1602. ―― Beete.	1605. ―― Hobman.	1570. John Baure.
1606. William Watson.	1607. ―― Payne.	1593. Sir William Sampson.
1619. ―― Dodson.	1609. ―― Hancock.	1609. Daniel Turven.
1620. ―― Northorpe.	1616. ―― Northorpe.	1615. ―― Wood.
1621. Edward Hunt.	1618. Edward Dawson.	1618. John Towne.
1629. Thomas Rawson.	1635. Thomas Barney.	1628. Stanley Gower.
1649. William Bagshaw.	1635. Thomas Birbeck.	1635. John Bright.
1652. William Parsons.	1647. ―― Metcalfe.	1636. Thomas Toller.
1656. Edward Prime.	1651. ―― Bankes.	1644 ―― Moseley.
1662. William Gardiner.	1652. ―― Leighton.	1645. Hugh Everard.
1689 Samuel Leech.	1657. John Crooke.	1646. John Bridges.
1694. Samuel Hunmore.	1658. ―― Hoole.	1656. Matthew Bloom.
1694. William Williams.	1658. William Stone.	1662. Cuthbert Browne.
1695. Robert Turie.	1661. Rowland Hancock.	1673. Thomas Woodsen.
1720. William Humpton.	1662. Thomas Barney, restored.	1673. Daniel Leech.
1752. John Dickenson.	1667. Peter Watkinson.	1708. George Lee.
1766. John Downes.	1670. John Thompson.	1719. Benjamin Ferrand.
1774. Edward Goodwin.	1708. Thomas Read.	1729. Isaac Hemmingway.
1817. Edward Goodwin.	1719. John Baines.	1731. Robert Tempest.
	1760. George Bayliffe.	1755. John Smith.
	1804. George Smith.	1776. Matthew Preston.
	1817. William-Humphry Vale.	

This catalogue has been for the most part compiled from the accompts of the church-burgesses, by whom the assistants are elected and their stipends paid. We shall meet with many of the names hereafter amongst the curates of the rural chapels, or the masters of the grammar-school.

ST. PAUL'S CHURCH.

Till the year 1720, the parish-church and a small chapel at the hospital were the only places of worship belonging to the Establishment in the town of Sheffield. The great increase of the population had rendered it highly necessary that another should be erected; and in the reign of Queen Anne such a project was entertained, much canvassed, and some steps taken to carry it into effect.

But the difficulties were great.—It appears to be a defect in the English ecclesiastical constitution, that it possesses not a power of ready accommodation to the changes in point of populousness which are perpetually taking place in a commercial country. But many of the difficulties seemed to be removed when an individual came forward with the liberal offer of a thousand pounds towards the erection of the building, and a settlement of thirty pounds per annum for the support of a minister.

This person was *Mr. Robert Downes*, a goldsmith in Sheffield: and stimulated by his example, other well disposed persons in the town and neighbourhood added their contributions; and a piece of ground was purchased adjoining the town, called Shaw's-close or Oxley-croft, and on the 2d of October 1719 the archbishop of York granted a commission to the duke of Devonshire, the marquis of Caermarthen, the earls of Scarsdale, Sandwich, Strafford, and Kinnoul, Lord Downe, the honourable Thomas Wentworth, Sir Arthur Kaye bart., Thomas Wentworth junior esq., William Jessop esq., John Bright esq., George Bamforth esq., Robert Chappel esq., Robert Turie clerk, George Lee, John Bright, and twenty other of the principal

inhabitants of Sheffield, to erect thereon a chapel-of-ease to the parish-church of Sheffield, the patronage of which was to be vested in Robert Downes and his heirs.

On the 28th day of May 1720 the first stone was laid, and in the course of a year the church was so far finished as to be ready to receive a congregation.

It was then discovered that a very important preliminary had not been finally settled: namely, in whom the right of presentation should be vested: the patron of the parish-church, the vicar, and Mr. Downes, each preferring a claim.

This occasioned great heats and animosities, great disappointment to the subscribers, and great inconvenience to the inhabitants of Sheffield, who had the mortification of seeing a noble edifice raised for their accommodation standing year after year wholly unoccupied and useless. Representations were made to the archbishop; but pending the difference among the parties above mentioned, he did not feel himself prepared to grant them relief.

At length, on the first of May 1739, Mr. Robert Downes presented himself before the justices of the peace at their sessions then held at Pontefract, and certified the building under the Act of Toleration, as a meeting-house for Protestant Dissenters, and a certificate was accordingly granted. On the 12th of May following the ground and building upon it were regularly conveyed by Robert Downes of Sheffield, goldsmith, Joseph Downes of Manchester, clerk, William Humpton of Fullwood, clerk, and ――― Wilkinson of Hilcoats in the county of Derby, gentleman; to Francis Sitwell, John Hussey, John Ellison, Benjamin Steer, Christopher Cowley, William Hawley, Matthew Lambert, John Redfearne, William Hildreth, Thomas Warburton, Joseph Kenyon, and Gilbert Dixon, as trustees, to allow the said Robert Downes and his heirs to appoint a Dissenting-minister to perform divine service in the said building till the license of the archbishop could be procured:—the necessity which was

2 s

universally felt for another place of worship in Sheffield being declared to be the reason, and that it was to be used by Dissenters only till such time as it was regularly set apart for the service of the church of England: the persons above named, and their successors to be chosen on each vacancy by themselves, together with the master-cutler for the time being, to be the trustees: which deed was registered at Wakefield on the 15th day of May.

This strong measure brought the affairs to a crisis; and in the next session of parliament an act was passed in which it is declared that the building or chapel erected in Shaw's-close, or Oxley-croft, shall after the consecration thereof be a perpetual cure and benefice, and be deemed a chapel-of-ease to the parish-church of Sheffield, and that John Downes clerk shall be the first perpetual curate: for providing a maintenance for the curate, Joseph Bright esquire, Thomas Wright, Francis Sitwell, and seventeen other gentlemen, inhabitants of the town and parish of Sheffield, together with the master-cutler for the time being, are empowered to let the seats in the said chapel, upon such terms that they be not less than four shillings each upon an average; and out of the proceeds are to pay thirty pounds per annum to the Reverend John Dossie, so long as he continues vicar of Sheffield, and the remainder to John Downes, so long as he shall remain curate of the said chapel: but after the death or removal of the said John Downes, forty-eight pounds per annum shall be paid out of the said seat-rents to Joseph Downes of Manchester, and his heirs for ever, the remainder to the curate for the time being. The nomination of the curate is given to the vicar of Sheffield for the time being, and his duty is declared to be the same with that of the curates of the other chapelries within the parish. The act further declares what share of the surplice-fees of this chapel shall go to the vicar, empowers the trustees to elect successors whenever they are reduced to twelve, and to choose a warden out of themselves on Easter Tuesday in each year: and declares further that the chapel shall be for ever under the jurisdiction of the archbishop of York.

On the 22d of May 1740, it was opened for public worship, and on Sunday the 16th of November was consecrated by Dr. Martin Benson bishop of Gloucester, commissioned for that purpose by Lancelot archbishop of York.

The chapel was built by Platts of Rotherham, and is a spacious and handsome Grecian structure. The dome was not added till 1769, when there was a subscription for the purpose among the gentry and inhabitants of the town and neighbourhood. In 1772, the Corinthian capitals within the chapel were finished. Mr. Francis Sitwell gave the clock, and it has a fine-toned organ built by Snetzler.

In the ailes of this church are many memorials of persons who have been interred within its walls. And on the walls are four monuments, on one of which is the following inscription:

Juxta hanc columnam
placide quiescit REBECCA fidelissima conjux
Gulielmi Hildreth
et sororis filia Roberti Downes
hujus ecclesiæ præcipui fundatoris.
Quæ obiit 12. Aug. ætat. 65.
anno Salutis 1760.

The others are for Benjamin Withers 1770, Roger Wilson 1774, and William Birks 1783.

CURATES OF ST. PAUL'S.

John Downes, M.A. nephew to Robert Downes. He was once intended for the law, but took orders, and was the first minister of St. Paul's. He left Sheffield in 1745, when he was presented to the rectory of St. Michael, Wood-street, London. He was also lecturer at St. Mary-le-Bow. Here he continued till his death about 1760.

Works.—*An Apology for Public Worship, and the Consecration of Churches*, a sermon preached at St. Paul's Chapel in Sheffield, 16 Nov. 1740, the day of its consecration.
A Sermon preached before the Company of Cutlers at Sheffield, 8vo, 1742.
A Popish prince the pest of a Protestant people, a sermon, 4to, 1745.
A Defence of set or prescribed Forms of Prayer, 1746.
Sermons, one volume, 8vo, 1761.

Henry Downes, of St John's College Cambridge, B.A. 1743, succeeded his father in his curacy, which he held along with the mastership of Talbot's Hospital, and after 1768 with the vicarage of Ecclesfield. He died the first of July 1775.

Thomas Radford, of St. John's College Cambridge, B.A. 1770, M.A. 1774, held this curacy till 1789, when he resigned, on being appointed curate of St. James's.

Alexander Mackenzie, M.A. chaplain to the earl of Eglinton, succeeded Mr. Radford, and after a highly respectable discharge of his public duties in this chapel died in London on the 30th day of October 1816, at the age of 61, and was interred in the chapel amidst the tears of his congregation. In the beautiful monument just erected to his memory, Sheffield has another specimen of the work of her own artist—Chantrey.

This monument
was erected by the voluntary subscription of the
congregation of St. Paul's Church,
as a tribute of affectionate regard, to the memory of
their most excellent pastor,
the Rev. ALEXANDER MACKENZIE;
who for twenty-eight years
performed the duties of his ministry,
with truly Christian benevolence, exemplary zeal, and
eminent ability.
He died in London on the 30th of October 1816,
aged 62 years, and was here interred.

The Reverend *Thomas Cotterell*, M.A. curate of Lane-End in Staffordshire, and late fellow of St. John's College Cambridge, succeeded Mr. Mackenzie.

ST. JAMES'S CHURCH.

The town still continuing to increase, it was found that the churches already provided were not sufficient for the accommodation of the inhabitants. As early as the year 1768, there was a scheme on foot, and indeed almost matured, for the erection of another church, the patronage of which it was proposed to vest in the Company of Cutlers, by an act of parliament similar in its provisions to the act obtained for Saint Paul's. It appears by a sheet of the conditions now before me, that 550*l.* were subscribed; and that a meeting of the inhabitants was to be held on the 14th day of October in that year, to adopt measures for soliciting further subscriptions, and to consult on the propriety of immediately presenting a bill to parliament. For some reason which does not now appear, the scheme was dropped.

Still the object was not lost sight of; and in the act which was obtained in 1786 for the improvement of the vicarage estate, the vicar was empowered, with the consent of the archbishop, to set apart a portion of his glebe for the purpose of erecting another church, or chapel-of-ease to the parish-church of Sheffield, upon such terms as the vicar for the time being might think expedient.

In 1788, the public availed themselves of the permission, encouraged by the vicar, who contributed liberally to the proposed undertaking, and a chapel was erected on part of the Vicarage-croft, at an expense of somewhat more than 3000*l.* which was raised in shares of fifty pounds, each of which entitled the subscriber to a pew as a freehold inheritance. By the conditions, the minister was to be appointed by the vicar for the time being, the fees to the vicar were to be the same as those paid at St. Paul's, and a rent-charge of 20*l.* a year was fixed upon the church to the vicar of Sheffield for ever.

On the 5th of August 1789 it was consecrated, by William archbishop of York; and from much respect to the then vicar of Sheffield, who had much promoted the undertaking, it was dedicated to St. James.

In 1797 the east window was taken down, and replaced by a painted one executed by Peckitt of York, on which is represented the crucifixion of our Lord.

The Reverend *Thomas Radford* accepted the curacy, resigning at the same time the curacy of Saint Paul's: and here he continued his labours till his much-lamented death on Sunday November 10, 1816, having exercised his ministerial office in the town of his birth for the space of forty-one years, loved and respected. He was also rector of Hardmead in Berkshire, and vicar of Mexborough with which is united Ravenfield, where he was interred. His congregation at Sheffield, unwilling to be without some memorial of their deceased pastor, placed a tablet to his memory in the chapel of St. James, bearing this inscription:

Sacred to the memory
of the
Revd THOMAS RADFORD, M.A.
first minister of this church, to which he was licensed A.D.1788.
After an affectionate discharge of his
ministerial duties during 46 years
he was called to give an account of his stewardship
in the 69th year of his age,
A.D. 1816.
Reader! thou art a steward:—art thou faithful?
This frail memorial, a tribute of affection and regret,
was erected by the seat-holders.

The Reverend *Thomas Best*, M.A. of Chipping-Campden in Gloucestershire, was presented to the perpetual curacy of St. James in January 1817.

CHAPTER X.

Societies of Dissenters.

A LARGE proportion of the inhabitants of Sheffield are dissenters from the Establishment: and a history of the parish would be incomplete in which no notice was taken of the several societies into which they are distributed. Within the town are fourteen edifices which were originally erected and still are used by them as places of worship. Many of them are capable of containing large congregations, and are commodious if not handsome structures. The Dissenters, copying their Puritan ancestors, discard the use of ornament from the buildings erected for divine worship. Perhaps they carry this point too far.

The Upper Chapel . . . . . Presbyterian.

The Nether Chapel . . .
Queen Street Chapel . . .
Howard Street Chapel . . }Independent.
Garden Street Chapel . .
Lee Croft Chapel . . . .
Coal-pit Lane Chapel . .

Town-head Chapel . . . . . Baptist.

Norfolk Street Chapel . . .
Carver Street Chapel . . }Methodist.
Bridge-houses Chapel . .

Scotland Street Chapel . . { Methodist of the new connexion.

The Quakers' Meeting.
The Roman Catholic Chapel.

Of these, only the first two have stood their century: the rest have been erected within the last forty or fifty years, and they are all filled with devout and serious worshippers. What are the causes or what may be the remote consequences of the great increase of separatists, is a problem at this time extremely interesting, but of difficult solution. This however may be observed, that as far as *principle* is concerned,—and who can doubt that there is much of principle, just or mistaken, engaged in this affair,—it cannot be considered as a subject of lamentation by those who look only to the interests of religion. For whether it is that a man feel himself more edified, and think that the motives to virtue and godliness are more strengthened by an attendance on religious services such as the church of England has not prescribed, and by the public discourses of ministers who cannot come within her pale, and on that account frequent the meeting-house rather than the church; or whether he feel himself bound to contend for the point that each congregation shall choose its own minister and manage all its concerns free from any foreign interference; or with others, has found or supposes he has found, that the articles and liturgy of the church of England describe views of the Christian system different from those which he collects from the Scriptures, which are the principal avowed reasons for dissent:—that numbers should on these grounds have embraced dissent with all its disqualifications cannot be regarded as an unfavourable sign of the times; since it plainly shows that there is amongst us a real regard to religion, and that we in this island are not in that state of apathy and religious formality into which most other countries are sunk, where the spirit of persecution has effectually succeeded in putting down all classes of religionists except that which happened to obtain the patronage of the civil authorities.

The Roman Catholics ought not perhaps to have been placed in this chapter. They are not a numerous body at Sheffield; but it is supposed that they are increasing. In 1767, according to a list delivered to the archbishop of York, there were in the whole 319 persons of that communion, among whom we find two priests, Mr. John Lodge and Mr. William Winter, and also the names of Henry Howard esquire, Mrs. Julia Howard his wife, and their two sons Bernard and Henry, then in their infancy. They met for worship in a large room behind what was called the Lord's-house, and the duke of Norfolk allowed an annual stipend to the officiating priest. They have since purchased a piece of ground near the site of their former place of worship, and erected on it a neat and handsome chapel which was opened in 1816.

Of the Quakers and Methodists mention will be made hereafter. For the origin of the other classes of Dissenters we must look back to the reign of King Charles II.

Where much of the puritan spirit had prevailed before and during the Civil Wars, there we may expect to find the separatists numerous from the ecclesiastical establishment as it was settled on the return of Charles II. The vicar of Sheffield and the three assistant-ministers, the only clergymen at that time connected with the parish of Sheffield, could not comply with the terms of conformity, and resigned their preferments. They were not without that countenance which numbers are supposed to give, for the names are preserved of nearly two thousand clergymen, who in August 1662 withdrew themselves from the church.

These men had doubtless their faults and weaknesses. They cavilled about trifles. They were credulous about possessions. Their piety was for the most part of a severe and gloomy character. The frequency and the tedious length of their religious exercises give great reason to suppose that many of them confounded the instrumental means with the ends of religion. Their notions of religious liberty were of the most confined description. It was from the mighty mind of Locke that light on this great point first diffused itself generally among an English public. But they had real, in-wrought piety: a deep sense of the importance of their pastoral office: many of them were persons of extensive reading and real learning; and their conduct was unimpeachably correct. It was the great boast of their friends, that the enemy had nothing to object against them saving in matters of their God. The sincerity of their religious profession was brought to the severest test. And for their early and steady opposition to the political doctrines contained in the Act of Uniformity, they deserve the gratitude of all men who think the Revolution a blessing, and who are thankful for the mild and equitable rule of the illustrious house of Brunswick.

It was natural for those who had attended the ministrations of the ejected clergy and who thought with them, to wish for a continuance of that instruction and consolation which they had been accustomed to receive. Many of the more opulent laity contributed to the support of the destitute ministers, or received them into their houses; and they in their turn ceased not to exercise their ministerial functions. It was soon perceived that if no means were adopted to prevent it, the Non-conformist body would be cast into societies, and thus acquire a form and consistence which might make it formidable. Many severe laws were passed. The ejected ministers were prohibited from residing in any corporate town, or in any place where they had been settled before the Restoration; and it was made highly penal in them to conduct any religious service except in their own families. Trained as they had been to the office of the ministry, thinking it the most important in which any man could engage, and feeling it to be their duty to continue in the discharge of their pastoral offices, the Non-conformist ministers could no more comply with this law than could their ancestors in the time of Queen Mary with the enactments of the legislature intended to stop the progress of protestantism: and though such sights as were exhibited in her days would hardly have been tolerated in those of Charles II., yet the prisons throughout the kingdom were crowded with the ejected clergy, many of whom died within their walls.—But we must attend more particularly to what immediately concerns the parish of Sheffield.

The names of the assistant-ministers ejected were Edward Prime, Matthew Bloom, and Rowland Hancock. The vicar was James Fisher.

Mr. Prime had been an assistant-minister about eight years. Of his life we have these particulars. He was born at Weston, perhaps Wheston, in Derbyshire, and educated at the grammar-school of Chesterfield. He was afterwards of Christ College Cambridge. On leaving the university he became tutor in the family of Thomas Westby of Ravenfield esquire, who was an active justice of the peace during the interregnum. He was minister of Baslow in his native county, when he was chosen by the burgesses into the office of assistant-minister at Sheffield. After his ejectment he was more fortunate than many of his brethren. He escaped the operation of the severer laws against Non-conformists. When the times would allow he established a fortnight lecture at Sheffield, preaching more frequently at Attercliffe. He continued his lecture till he was disabled by age and infirmities. He lived till 1707, and preached, as his custom was, on Saint Bartholomew's-day in that year, the anniversary of his ejectment, taking for his text the words of Joshua, '*And now behold the Lord hath kept me alive these forty and five years.*' He died on the 26th day of April following, and was interred in the parish church-yard of Sheffield, the last of six of the ejected ministers whose remains were laid in that wide cemetery[1], and one of the last survivors of the whole number. A high character for piety and worth is given of him by the biographer of the ejected clergy[2], and by his son-in-law Mr. Robert Fern of Wirksworth, in a published funeral sermon delivered on occasion of his death.

Mr. Bloom was born at Brotherton, a village near Ferrybridge. He was of Magdalen College Cambridge, and elected an assistant-minister in 1655. He was also curate of Attercliffe; and to him was owing the formation of the old society of Dissenters in that populous hamlet. He had recourse to a secular employment for the support of himself and family. Having suffered an imprisonment in the castle of York, he died suddenly at Sir William Ellis's house at Wyham in Lincolnshire, on the 13th of April 1686[3].

The first appearance of Mr. Hancock at Sheffield is as under-master of the grammar-school. About 1651 or 1652 he was presented to the vicarage of Ecclesfield by no better authority than *the powers then in being*, which he resigned in 1660 to Mr. Wright the old incumbent. On the 22d of April 1661, the burgesses elected him into the place of one of the assistant-ministers. Some doubts seem to have been entertained of the legality of his election; for at a meeting of the burgesses held at the church on the 11th of June 1662,—present Sir John Bright bart., William Spencer esquire, Francis Jessop esquire, Henry Bright gentleman, and others, beside some of the commonalty,—it was resolved, ' that as for matter of title, Mr. Hancock now is an assistant, the burgesses will be ready to maintain.' But on the 14th of August following a counter resolution was passed; namely, that Mr. Barney, who had been removed during the Civil Wars, ' is and shall be from henceforth elected and chosen an assistant in the roome and stead of Mr. Rowland Hancock.' Ten days after, the Act of Uniformity put an end to these dissentions.

Mr. Hancock continued to reside in the neighbourhood of Sheffield till the act was passed by which the non-conformist ministers were required to remove to the distance of at least five miles from the places in which they had exercised their ministry. He was received by Mr. Sylvanus Rich, a gentleman of an ancient family at Bull-house near Peniston, and a generous patron of the ejected ministers. When the severity of the statutes was a little relaxed in 1672, he returned to his own house at Shiercliffe-hall, and preached there as the circumstances of the times would allow, and also at Brook-side, a very retired place in the cha-

pelry of Bradfield. He died at Shiercliffe-hall on the 14th of April 1685, and was buried at Sheffield on the 17th, leaving the character of 'a very pious man, of excellent natural parts, and tolerable learning, though he had not been bred at the University. His sermons were succinct, methodical, elaborate[4].' He was for a time in the castle of York[5]. He left no son; but in the descendants and present representatives of his daughters we may see fulfilled the Scripture promise, that *the children of the just shall be blessed after them.*

As Shiercliffe-hall Mr. Hancock collected a few of his neighbours, who formed a small church on the independent model; but it had no existence after his decease, the members of it joining themselves to the congregations at Sheffield and Attercliffe. Mr. Bloom was joined with him in the pastoral office. The following account of the formation of this church is copied from a record made at the time; and it may probably be taken as a specimen of the mode in which other independent churches in other parts of the kingdom were first formed.

' A REGISTER of the Members and Transactions of the Church of Christ under the Guidance of Rowland Hancock of Sherclif-hall, and Matthew Bloome of Attercliffe, Ministers of the Gospell.

On the eight and twentieth day of July Anno Dñi 1676 was a meeting held at Shercliff-hall, when after a sermon preached by Mr. Bloome and solemne prayer to God to direct us in and prepare us for our following work, the following rules and preface to them was read in the assembly.

God haveing by his good providence so ordered it that Rowland Hancock and Matthew Bloome, ministers of the gospell, have been called to, and for some yeares persevered in the exercise of their ministry near to each other, whereby they and their respective auditories have had, and if the Lord please may still have, opportunities of joyning together in religious exercises: And whereas they have not enjoyed the sacrament of the Lord's Supper in any fixed way, to the great grief and trouble of themselves and diverse of their Christian friends: they the said ministers have now, after earnest seeking of God and at the desire of some of their hearers, and with the advice and approbation of divers of their brethren of the ministry, agreed with each other and with several of their auditors into one congregation or church, for the enjoyment of the Lord's Supper, and all other ordinances of Jesus Christ, according to the rules and in the way and manner hereafter expressed: viz.

1. That the said ministers, with such of their families and neighbours as have formerly communicated in the Lord's Supper, and are knowne to and approved by them, and express their desires to join with them according to the rules hereafter mentioned, doe all meet together upon the 28 day of July next at Shorclif-hall; and then and there with fasting and prayer give up themselves to the Lord and to one another, to walk together in Church communion according to the gospell: —the said Rowland Hancock and Matthew Bloome to take the oversight of the said people, and they to own the said R. Hancock and Mr. Bloome as their ministers.

2. That the Lord's Day next following, the sacrament of the Lord's Supper be administered to the persons so united as aforesaid; and from time to time upon every seventh Sabbath, unless there be some reasonable cause to change the days.

3. That the said ministers from that time meet together

[1] These six are:
1674. Thomas Birbeck.   1685. Rowland Hancock.
1678. Robert Durant.   1697. Nathaniel Baxter.
1680. Richard Taylor.   1708. Edward Prime.
The following ministers silenced by the Act of Uniformity were natives of Sheffield:
John Crooke son of John Crooke.
William Pell son of William Pell.
James Creswick son of James Creswick.
Samuel Bayes son of Richard Bayes.
Of all these persons some account may be found in Calamy.

[2] *Account of the Ejected or Silenced Ministers, &c.* by Dr. Edmund Calamy, p. 787.
[3] Id. p. 787.
[4] Id. p. 787.
[5] This fact is stated by Dr. Calamy, and confirmed by the MS. diary of Mr. Oliver Heywood, another ejected minister. ' 1668 May 31, Mr. Copley of Batley took Mr. Hancock at Allerthorp near Wakefield, and hath sent him and two others prisoners to York castle. This adds to the mercy that I escaped their hands.'

as often as conveniently they can and occasion shall require, upon week days, for ordering the affairs of the congregation, and to confer with such as shall offer themselves to join in communion with the said church, and that in all cases of moment and public concerne, the juste satisfaction and concurrence of the people be duly regarded.

4. That such only be admitted into communion with the said church, as do make a credible profession of the Christian religion; that is to say, do evidence themselves to have a competent knowledge of the fundamental doctrines of Christianity, and to be sound in the faith, and of an unblamable and holy life.

5. That all such as never before communicated in the Lord's Supper, shall before their admission to communion with the said church, solemnly own their baptismall covenant at a publick meeting of the said church.

6. That in judging of the knowledge, faith, and conversations of such as shall offer themselves to be admitted into communion with the said church, regard shall be had to the rules laid down by the late assembly of divines at Westminster, in their forms of Church government published in the yeare 1648.

7. That we shall not exclude any as ignorant whom we can discern (by the utmost condescention to their capacities) to understand the fundamentall doctrines of Christianity, though by reason of bashfulness, want of literature or the like, they be not able to express their knowledge in a cleare and distinct manner. Nor shall we insist upon the way of question and answer, with any person that hath already given or hereafter shall give us good satisfaction of their knowledge by other wayes.

8. That where persons have been formerly guilty of scandalous sins, we shall not refuse communion with them, if they have for a competent time credibly manifested their unfeigned repentance for the same.

9. That the names of such persons as shall seek a stated communion with the said church shall (after satisfaction given to the ministers of their knowledge and faith) be seasonably published in a public meeting of the said church, and if no sufficient exception come in against them within one whole month next after the publication of their names as aforesaid, that then such persons shall be admitted into communion with the said church: but if any just exception come in against them within the time aforesaid, that then their admission shall be deferred till they have either cleared themselves of what was objected against them, or given satisfaction some other way.

10. That for the present no person shall be admitted into communion with the said church in the Lord's Supper, who doth communicate with the parochiall assemblies in that ordinance as it is now administered there. And that all persons, especially those of the neighbourhood who shall hold communion with us, be careful to attend the ministry of the said ministers as God shall give them opportunity. And that every member of the said society shall give account whom they heare if called upon thereto. Yet it is not intended hereby to debarre any person from the occasionall hearing of other orthodox ministers, nor from the occasionall partaking of other ordinances in other congregations, where they are dispensed according to the scriptures: nor to debarre any from becoming fixed members of other congregations, when by the providence of God they shall be called thereto. Nor is it intended as any censure upon the present parochiall churches, nor on any that communicate with them; nor upon parochiall churches as such: but it is intended only to prevent such danger to persons' soules, and also such scandalls and prejudices to the said church as might accrue in regard of some present circumstances of the times and of this neighbourhood.

11. That in case any person in communion with the said church shall fall into grosse error or scandalous practice, what would have been a sufficient ground of denying admittance to that communion shall be taken as a sufficient ground of suspension from it.

12. That in regard we live in times of sad defection and strong temptations, those who are to be admitted into communion with the said church, shall before such admission evidence their serious purpose to submit themselves to the oversight and admonitions of their ministers and brethren, and to

adhere to the truthes, offices and ordinances of Christ, and to continue in fellowship with the said church notwithstanding any temptation, opposition, danger, or trouble that may occur, so long as God shall give them opportunity.

13. That considering the present state of many neighbouring parishes, such of other parishes (though remote) as cannot enjoy the sacrament of the Lord's Supper in a way satisfactory to their consciences in the places where they live, and shall desire communion with the said church, may be freely admitted according to the rules herein expressed. Yet so that if the providence of God shall hereafter vouchsafe them his ordinances in their due purity in the places where they dwell, they shall then be seriously advised and required to joyne themselves with such with whom they may cohabite.

14. That in case any stranger shall at any time desire occasionally to communicate with the said church in the Lord's Supper, he may be admitted to such communication if he be personally known to and approved by either of the ministers, or otherwise do give satisfaction to them concerning himself.

15. That both ministers and people be constantly carefull of mutuall inspection and of endeavouring to edify one another; and that authoritative admonitions be used, and proceedings thereupon made, according to the rule of the gospell, so often as occasion shall require.

16. That meetings on the week days be held by the ministers and people so often as the ministers shall judge convenient, and for such exercises as the ministers shall direct.

17. That a deacon or deacons be chosen to take care of such things as properly appertain to that office.

18. That a register be kept of all the members and transactions of the said church.

19. That these things are not designed as an exact and perpetuall rule of Church order or government, but are only expressive of our desires to do what we can in our present circumstances; and are to be observed during the continuance of our present restraint: nor is it designed hereby to make any party or schisme in the church of Christ; but as all particular churches are members of Christ's Catholique church, so we shall by God's assistance use all good means for maintaining union and communion with all other churches and Christians as God shall give us opportunity: and in all matters of weight and difficultie not before determined, we shall seek the advice and help of such as shall be willing to hold correspondence and communion with us.

20. That in case of persecution or danger we shall be willing to comply with such prudent advice as any may offer for the security of the said church, so farre as may consist with our dutie to God.

After the rules were read, and some things therein explained, it was demanded of the people thus:

Doe you all fully approve of these rules and freely consent to joyne in Church fellowship according to them? And they did all particularly manifest their approbation and consent.

Then the ministers did express themselves thus:

We do also fully approve of the said rules and freely consent to joyne in church fellowship according to them.

Then were the heads of the Christian religion read, as they are drawn up by the Assembly of Divines in the Form of Church Government aforesaid. After the reading thereof the ministers declared thus—This we are fully persuaded is the true faith of Christ revealed in the Scriptures, and in this faith we are resolved by the grace of God to live and dye, and we hope the same of you all. To which they did all manifest their assent.

Then both ministers and people did give up themselves to the Lord, particularly renewing their covenant with him in the following profession; one of the ministers pronouncing the same on the ministers' part, and one of the people on the people's part:—

'I doe heartily take the Lord to be my only God and chiefe good, and Jesus Christ to be my only Savior and Redeemer, and the Holy Ghost to be my sanctifyer: giving up myself wholly to this One God to love and obey him sincerely and perfectly, according to all his laws contained in the scriptures, and all this as long as I shall live.

'And in particular I doe consent and resolve through the strength of Christ to hold constant communion with the church of Christ in the worship of God, and to submit to the discipline and government which Christ hath ordained for his owne glory and his people's good.'

And lastly, the declarations following were made by the people thus :

' I doe seriously purpose by the grace of God to submitt myselfe to the oversight and admonitions of the ministers and brethren in this church, and to continue in fellowship with the said church according to the rules agreed upon, notwithstanding any temptation, opposition, danger or trouble that may occure, soe long as God shall give me opportunity.'

—by the ministers thus : it was pronounced by Mr. Hancock—

' I doe declare in my owne name and in the name of my brother Bloome here present, that we doe consent joyntly to take and manage the pastoral oversight of this church or congregation, and to dispense all the ordinances of Jesus Christ therein as the Lord shall give us ability and opportunity: and that it is our serious purpose to continue in fellowship with the said church according to the rules agreed upon, notwithstanding any temptation, opposition, danger or trouble that may occur, so long as God shall give us opportunity.'

The persons that then joyned in this fellowship were these whose names follow:

Rowland Hancock,	} Ministers.
Matthew Bloome,	
Mr. John Hatfield.	Robert Hoole, his brother.
Mrs. Antonina Hatfield.	William Wadsworth.
Mrs. Hancock.	Mary Wadsworth.
Mrs. Jennet Bloome.	William Marsland.
Joseph Capper.	Mary Nicholson, widow.
Joseph Nutt.	Hannah Cox.
Robert Hoole, tanner.	Margaret Parkin.
Widow Hoole.	Margaret Sharp.
William Hoole, cutler.	John Oldale.

Thirty-four other persons immediately joined themselves to this society. It had but a short existence. A misunderstanding arose between the two ministers. Of the grounds of it but an imperfect acquaintance could now be obtained were they worth inquiring into; but it was a subject of much grief to their fellow-nonconformists. It occasioned a separation, and Mr. Bloom became sole pastor of part of the church who met for worship at Attercliffe.

It is not to any of the three assistant-ministers, but to Mr. James Fisher the ejected vicar of Sheffield, that we owe the formation of the first society of Dissenters in the town of Sheffield. This respected and useful minister was settled in London in the early part of his life. He was living at Clipsham in the county of Rutland in 1640, when he took to wife Elizabeth Hatfield, sister of Anthony Hatfield of Laughton-en-le-Morthen, the head of a respectable family at that place, who had formerly their residence in Hallamshire. By this connexion Mr. Fisher became brother-in-law to Stephen Bright of Carbrook, whose name we have such frequent occasion to mention, and closely allied to most of the principal puritan families in the neighbourhood of Sheffield and Rotherham. This alliance doubtless led to his removal into Yorkshire. In 1646 he was settled on the vicarage of Sheffield, I know not by what authority, and here he continued till his ejectment in 1662 ; being, as Calamy was informed, ' an excellent preacher, and an instrument of much good in that populous town [1].' He survived his ejectment three or four years. They were years of much affliction. In the accompts of the constables for the township of Sheffield this entry appears under the year 1663: 'Charges about Mr. Fisher seekeing and carry-

ing to Yorke 1l. 17s. 6d.' This was probably in consequence of his name being introduced in the depositions of that Ralph Oates, who dealt about him firebrands and death with a remorseless heart and an unsparing and unnatural hand. When there was so much inclination to convict and execute, that Mr. Fisher was not put upon his trial may be taken as a fair presumption of his innocence. He had not been long released when he was again taken to the castle of York on vague and indefinite charges of disaffection. It was supposed to be the intention of his enemies to keep him there for the remainder of his life, but after a time he was set at liberty by the humane interference of the second Villiers duke of Buckingham. This was at a time when he could not return to his own home. The pleasant village of Hatfield near Doncaster, where resided his friend and relative Captain John Hatfield, offered him retirement and repose. But his constitution was broken, and after four or five months residence there he died in January 1665-6. This is Dr. Calamy's account: but in the manuscript diaries of that indefatigable preacher, traveller, and recorder Oliver Heywood it appears that Mr. Fisher was alive in the November of 1666, and was residing at Laughton, not at Hatfield. The passage is as follows: ' On the Monday [12th of November 1666] Mr. Wadsworth and I travelled to Rotheram, and from thence with Mr. Hancock, with whom we met at Mr. Clayton's, wee went to Mr. Hatfield's of Laughton to visit Mr. Fisher of Sheffield, who lives there, when we met with that precious gentlewoman Mrs. Martha Hatfield, concerning whom so many strange things are recorded in a book concerning her.'

The book here mentioned was published by Mr. Fisher. It passed through five editions in the author's life-time, but is now rarely to be met with. The reader may not be displeased to find in this place some account of its strange contents. The edition here described is that of 1664, the fifth with some enlargements on the former editions. Its title is, 'The Wise Virgin: or a wonderful narration of the various dispensations of God towards a childe of eleven years of age; wherein as his severity hath appeared in afflicting, so also his goodness, both in enabling her (when stricken dumb, deaf, and blinde through the prevalency of her disease) at several times to utter many glorious truths concerning Christ, Faith, and other subjects; and also in recovering her without the use of any external means, least the glory should be given to any other. To the wonderment of many that came far and near to see and hear her. With some observations in the fourth year since her recovery. She is the daughter of Mr. Anthony Hatfield gentleman, in Laughton in Yorkshire; her name is Martha Hatfield. By James Fisher, a servant of Christ, and late minister of the gospel in Sheffield.' Then follows an address, 'To all those who love our Lord Jesus Christ in sincerity, and especially my much endeared friends the parents of this childe of wonders,' subscribed 'yours (through grace) James Fisher. Sheffield, January 20, 1652-3.' Next follows another address, 'To the godly consciencious reader,' from John Firth, dated Finningley, Jan. 25, 1652. Then an address ' To the reader,' from Wa. Barnard, Church Sandal, January 28, 1652. These introduce

[1] Calamy's Account, &c. p. 785.

us to the narrative itself, which is divided into three parts, her disease, her speeches, her recovery. Her disease seems to have been an extraordinary case of catalepsy. We are told that the disease 'seized upon the organ of her senses, so that shee could neither speak, see nor hear (to the apprehension of any about her); shee could not move but as shee was born of others; and much of this time her teeth were so closed that she was not capable of receiving food, only some liquid matter they dropped in at a broken tooth, and this very little, she putting it out as fast as it was given her. Thus lay she divers months, even untill December [1652] an object of sorrow to her parents, and of astonishment to all others, capable only of their pitty not of their help.' 'During this continued paroxism she had frequently (sometimes every day) certain grand extasies, whereby (after that her body had been racked upon the wheel of convulsion) it became as stiff and expanse as that body which is seized on by death and coldness. In which extasies God did to astonishment appear: For now flowed those streams of living waters, those precious divine sentences contained in the ensuing pages &c.' Her speeches fill a hundred pages, and consist of incoherent cries and expressions, abounding with quotations from scripture, and are what might be expected from a young woman educated as the daughters of such a family as hers were, with a voluble tongue but an intellect weakened by disease. The volume contains a strong attestation to the truth of the account, of which indeed, however extraordinary in some of its parts, there seems no reason to doubt. She was visited by many persons, amongst whom were the Lady Lambert, Colonel Bright and his lady, and other persons of the best account in the neighbourhood where she resided. Her speeches were taken down from her mouth by ' a scholar by name Master John Cromwell, one related to Master Hatfield's family,' and by Mr. Edward and Mr. William Rodes, two of the sons of ' that worthy patriot Sʳ Edward Rodes.' The persons who witnessed the scene were divided in opinion, some attributing it to a good spirit and some to an evil one. But ' it was the judgment of a very judicious physician, who was sometimes with her, that her disease was natural, her speech supernatural.' In December her fits left her, when Mr. Hatfield her father sent a narrative of her recovery, which forms the third part of the work, which when read by Mr. Fisher to ' the officers and members of the church of Christ in Sheffield, who were met at a private conference, it caused many tears of joy,' and as they had before met to pray for her, so now they returned praise for her recovery. To some of the editions of this volume is prefixed an engraving in which the young woman is represented in one of her extasies, one of the rarest portraits in the English series.

It will be observed that there is mention in the above notices of this volume of a church of Christ at Sheffield, by which we are to understand that a certain portion of his parishioners had formed themselves into an independent church, of which Mr. Fisher the vicar, who is said by Calamy to have been ' congregational in his judgment,' was the pastor. These religious associations formed the nucleus of many societies of non-conformists, while others in parishes where the mini-sters had been presbyterian date their origin in times after the ejectment. This church of Mr. Fisher's remained united, nor was the flock scattered when the shepherd was smitten. Mr. Fisher was indeed obliged to remove to a distance from them: but the same storm which drove him from them sent other ministers to their assistance and comfort. Sheffield came not under the description of a corporate town. It was therefore one of the few places of any consideration in which the ejected clergy could take up their abode in the darker times of the reign of Charles II. Among the ejected ministers who at this time made Sheffield their home were Richard Taylor and Nathaniel Baxter, of whom Dr. Calamy has given a good account. The former was a native of Sheffield, and they both died and were buried there. Mr. Robert Durant was another. This gentleman had been ejected at Crowle in the county of Lincoln, and being confined in the castle of York he there became acquainted with Thomas Woolhouse esquire, of Glapwell in Derbyshire, who was also in prison on account of religion. Mr. Woolhouse was acquainted with the people at Sheffield, and recommended to them Mr. Durant as a proper successor to Mr. Fisher. He was invited to become the pastor of Mr. Fisher's church, and preached a sermon preparatory to his first administration of the Lord's Supper among them on the 17th of November 1669. Of his public services in his pastoral relation we have this account in the valuable collections of Dr. Calamy[1]. On the Sunday mornings he expounded the scriptures, and preached in the afternoon on the doctrines of the Christian religion, and every month he and his congregation kept a fast. An excellent character is given of Mr. Durant for abilities in his ministerial work, for a spirit of forbearance and love, and a gentlemanly deportment. He died on the 12th day of February 1678, aged 71, and was buried in the parish church-yard. He died generally lamented, and Mr. Lobley, the vicar of Sheffield, is reported to have said on hearing of his decease, ' And is the good old man dead? I am sorry for it. He hath carried it so very well that I wish they may get one that will tread in his steps.' A testimony honourable to both parties.

I have not been able to discover where the Dissenters of Sheffield held their public assemblies during the time of Mr. Durant's ministry. But just a month before his death they had finished a meeting-house called the New-Hall, which was either raised from its foundations, or (what I believe to have been the fact) was formed out of an edifice which bore that name. One George Saunderson of Midhope, yeoman, by his will bearing date in 1649 gave to Francis his third son a messuage in Sheffield called the New-Hall. Mr. Thomas Hollis of London, who always professed to owe much to the labours of Mr. Fisher, was a liberal contributor towards the preparation of this place of worship; and when a larger meeting-house was erected in 1700, he bought the New-Hall and converted it into alms-houses for his charity. Mr. Francis Barlow, an iron-master of considerable property, was also a liberal contributor.

Two years passed after the death of Mr. Durant before the independent church at Sheffield had another regular pastor. But on the 28th of April 1681 Mr.

---

[1] Continuation of the Account, &c., p. 599.

Timothy Jollie was solemnly ordained to the pastoral office. The diary of Mr. Oliver Heywood contains a full account of the service, in which he himself took a part: but the particulars have already been laid before the public.

Mr. Jollie was one of the sons of Mr. Thomas Jollie of Lancashire, an ejected minister, in whom appeared some of the best and of the worst parts of the Puritan character. The son was born a short time before the Restoration; and being intended by his father for the ministry among the non-conformists, he was placed in an academy conducted by Mr. Richard Frankland, in which were educated most of the non-conformist ministers of the second race in the northern counties. He afterwards pursued his studies in one of the academies near London, and was young when he took upon himself the arduous office of pastor to so large and respectable a society as were the Dissenters at Sheffield.

Soon after his settlement at Sheffield Mr. Jollie connected himself in marriage with a daughter of Mr. Fisher, the lately ejected vicar of Sheffield, who proved herself in every respect a companion suitable to him.

It will appear from what has been already stated, that the persecution of the non-conformists was relaxed in the middle of the reign of Charles II. In 1672 he granted liberty to the Dissenters to exercise their worship. This measure is represented by some writers as having been fatal to the design of compelling all the non-conformists to return within the pale of the church. Sir John Reresby, who took a very active part in the opposition to non-conformity in the neighbourhood of Sheffield, says that it was never from that time at all practicable to prevent the formation of conventicles. The attempt was however made, and in the latter years of King Charles II. the permission was withdrawn, and the gaols again filled with the poor non-conformists. Scarcely had Mr. Jollie been a year at Sheffield, when to avoid a meditated seizure of his person he left his home, and lived privately among his distant friends. In January 1683 he ventured to return. He was immediately apprehended, taken before Sir John Reresby, and committed, on a charge of holding a conventicle, to the castle of York. A fine was at the same time levied by distress upon his furniture, which compelled Mrs. Jollie, then recovering from her first confinement, to remove to the house of her brother Mr. Fisher, a medical practitioner at Sheffield. After an easy restraint of two months Mr. Jollie was allowed to return home, on recognisance to appear at the ensuing assizes. He appeared accordingly; when the court tendered him the oath for good behaviour, and he was assured that he should suffer no trouble so long as he acted conformably to it. But when he understood that in the term 'good behaviour' was included the forbearance of public preaching, he rejected the offer, and threw himself upon the court. His contumacy drew on him some reproachful expressions, and a sentence of six months imprisonment in the castle. There Mrs. Jollie soon joined him.

Every Lord's day except one Mr. Jollie preached in the prison. Many of the citizens and several of the prisoners came to hear him. He also preached on other

days: 'a privilege this,' says Mrs. Jollie, from whose hand-writing I am transcribing[1], 'which rendered his imprisonment wonderfully easy.' On the 1st of October 1683 his term expired. The family remained some days among their friends at York, and on the 10th came to Doncaster. On the 11th they went to Hatfield, where they had near relatives, and were hospitably entertained till the 24th. They then removed to Braithwell, where lived Mr. Bosville, a worthy conformist minister, and a relative of Mrs. Jollie. On the next day her cousin Hatfield of Laughton sent his coach for them, and 'on a sore snowy morning' they came to Laughton. On the 2d of November they returned to Sheffield.

When Mr. Jollie persisted in preaching, fresh warrants were issued againt him. To avoid them he fled into Lancashire: but when the violence of the storm had a little abated he ventured to return, and discoursed for several successive Sundays from those words of our Lord, ' *If any man will come after me, let him deny himself, and take up his cross daily, and follow me.*'

In 1685 he was again interrupted in the performance of his public services, and escaped the miseries of a fresh incarceration, only by the care of his friends in keeping secret the place of his concealment. In the midst of these proceedings King Charles II. died.

It cannot be supposed that the non-conformist body, in their gratitude for the relief which King James's declaration for liberty of conscience afforded them, would be over scrupulous in examining the reasons of the measure. It was enough for them that it relieved them from the oppressions to which they had been subjected, that it restored the father to his family, the pastor to his attached and grateful flock. They have been supposed to have incurred deserved reproach by the addresses of thanks which on this occasion they presented to the throne. They have been accused of sanctioning despotic measures, of having given up the cause of protestantism, and of having lent themselves to the private views of King James. The Dissenters of Sheffield were among those who addressed on this occasion. The address, conceived in respectful, grateful, but guarded terms, must have convinced the monarch that the men from whom it proceeded would lend no support to any measure which had for its object either the subversion of protestantism, or the destruction of our civil liberties.

' The humble ADDRESS of divers of your Majesties loyal and dissenting subjects in the town of Sheffield and other parts in the west riding of the county of York.

Dread Sovereign,

As we your Majesties loyal subjects cannot but have our hearts most deeply affected with those signal divine blessings of liberty, peace, and prosperity as well sacred as civil, which under your Majestie we not only at present enjoy, but are likewise assured shall be preserved to us during your Majesties reign, especially when we eye them as fruits of that most noble testimony first imprinted no doubt by the finger of God upon your royal breast, and after most freely and fully published to the view of the world in your Majesties late declaration for liberty of conscience, as your constant sense and opinion, which therefore we trust shall prove an indelible principle, viz. That conscience ought not to be constrained—so we cannot but, as in solemn duty bound, prostrate our most sincere grateful ac-

[1] In a short account of her own and her husband's troubles, written for the use of her daughter in a strain of good sense and piety which seems to justify the encomiums passed upon her in a published funeral dis-

course on occasion of her death in 1709, by William Bagshaw, minister at Stannington. The MS. was lately in possession of her descendant Mrs. Blythe of Saint James-street in Sheffield.

2 U

knowledgements of this your princely bounty and goodness at your Majesties feet, blessing from our hearts that great God by whom kings rule and princes decree justice, for directing your royal Majestie unto that truest method of government which leaves entire to God his absolute soveraignty over the souls of men, which undoubtedly will be the stability of your throne; render you truly great in the esteem of all good men, who shall reap the blessed fruits of your wisdom, justice, and moderation, and may become a noble pattern for imitation. And praying from our very souls that your Majestie, after a long and happy reign over us, in pursuance of the same great ends of rule, under the conduct of divine grace and wisdom, may be fitted and prepared for a crown that is incorruptible :

    Who are your Majesties most loyal and thankfull subjects.'

    That liberty which was granted them by the crooked policy of King James was fully confirmed to the Dissenters by an act of the legislature in the first year of King William. The object of this enactment was to relieve them from the penalties of the acts of King Charles's reign on easy conditions.

    The dissenting interest flourished at Sheffield under the ministry of Mr. Jollie. There are existing two characters of Mr. Jollie: one drawn by a gentleman who had studied under him, Dr. Benjamin Grosvenor; the other by Mr. De la Rose, his assistant in the ministry, in a splendid funeral paneygric which he pronounced from the pulpit of what is now called the Upper Chapel, after the manner of the French preachers, and in which Mr. Jollie is classed with the Bourdaloues, the Cheminaises, and the Flechiers. We have no specimen of the oratory which drew forth these commendations, except one sermon which was delivered on occasion of his father's death: nor is it known that Mr. Jollie published any thing beside, except a biographical sketch of his friend Mr. Thomas Whitaker of Leeds. Much is said by both in Mr. Jollie's praise, as a tutor and a minister. The increase of his society rendered it necessary to erect a larger place of worship: and a piece of land was purchased for that purpose between Pepper-alley and Alsop-fields, on which a meeting-house was erected in 1700, Mr. Field

Sylvester[1] laying the first stone. He and Mr. Joshua Bayes, father to the minister of that name, contracted for the purchase; and on the 25th of November 1704 they conveyed the ground and building upon it to Thomas Hollis junior, citizen and draper of London, John Browne of Sheffield gentleman[2], William Stead of the same place mercer, Samuel Shore of the same place hardwareman, William Burch, Jonathan Smith, Benjamin Kirkby, Luke Winter, Joseph Fletcher[3], all of the same place cutlers, Joseph Sanderson and Samuel Sanderson of the same place tanners, and John Crooke the younger of the same place chandler, in trust for the use of Protestant-Dissenters. This building with three galleries was intended to receive a large congregation, and indeed Mr. Jollie's was the largest in his time in the county of York. In the year 1715 Mr. Neal procured a list of the dissenting congregations throughout the kingdom, with the names of their ministers and the number of members. At that time, when about two hundred persons had withdrawn themselves, the society at the Upper Chapel consisted of 1163 persons, 75 of whom were freeholders of the county of York. Mr. Jollie's register of baptisms is in existence from May 1681 to July 1704. They average about twenty-five a year. The chapel was opened by Mr. Jollie, who on that occasion addressed the assembly from Genesis xxvi. 22.

    The state of the times compelled Mr. Richard Frankland to remove with his academy from place to place. For three or four years he resided at Attercliffe. This was found a convenient situation for the purpose; and soon after Mr. Frankland had left it, Mr. Jollie established there an academy for the education of young men designed for the dissenting ministry. Mr. Jollie maintained the reputation of his academy till his death. Some of the most useful and popular ministers among the Dissenters in the early part of the last century issued from it. He had also under his care three men who attained eminence of another kind: Saunderson, the blind professor; Bowes, the Irish chancellor; and Secker, archbishop of Canterbury[4]. 'He was a man,'

[1] This gentleman was a native of Mansfield, but spent the greatest part of his life at Sheffield. He was of the same family with Edward Sylvester the learned Grecian, for whom see *Ath. Or. i. 594*: and his sister married Lieut.-col. Etherege, a relative of Sir George Etherege the dramatic writer. Mr. Field Sylvester ' on the 11th of May 1670 was bound apprentice to Mr. Thomas Hollis, a wholesale cutler in London, whom he served eight years, during which time he went twice into France, and once into Flanders and Zealand. He served his said master at Sheffield one year for 20*l.*: but was then cast off for refusing to go to France again on hard terms, and in a time of danger. He then did business for Mr. Joshua Shepherd for about ten years, to whose care and kindness he ascribed under God his comfortable circumstances in the world. He died of an apoplexy at Hackenthorpe, on the 10th of May 1717, aged 63, and was interred at the corner of the meeting-house in Sheffield, where himself had laid the first stone.' MS. memoirs by his grandson the Rev. Field Sylvester Wadsworth. Mr. Sylvester had two daughters, Cassandra who died young, and Rebecca wife of the Rev. John Wadsworth.

[2] Father-in-law to John Sparrow of Wincobank, esquire, many years a most respectable member of the society of Dissenters meeting at the Upper Chapel; brother to Samuel Sparrow of London, merchant, author of a volume of prayers and moral essays published in 1769; and said in the title page to be by ' a merchant.'

[3] This gentleman married Mary Heathcote, a niece of Mr. Field Sylvester, being daughter of his sister Judith Sylvester, who married Ebenezer Heathcote an apothecary in Saint Giles's in the fields, London. Mr. Fletcher's eldest son, who bore the name of his maternal grandfather, was educated at the grammar-school in Sheffield, and afterwards under the Rev. John Wadsworth at Sheffield, and Mr. John Eames, F.R.S. in London. He was for some years minister of a congregation of Dissenters at Ware in Hertfordshire, from whence he removed to Coventry, where he exercised his ministry for many years in connexion with a large and flourishing society of Dissenters. There he died on the 11th of February 1763, aged 61, and was interred in the church of Saint

Michael in that city. He published ' A funeral sermon, preached at Ware 29 Dec. 1742, on occasion of the death of Mr. Rivers Dickenson of Tottenham in Middlesex ;' and in 1744, ' Sermons on several occasions by the Rev. and learned John Howe, M.A. sometime Fellow of Magdalen college, Oxford,' in two volumes 8vo, with memoirs of the life of Mr. Howe.

[4] This prelate, like many other persons who have attained stations of eminence to which at the outset of life they seemed to have no pretensions, had his enemies. One means which they adopted to show their dislike was to recall to the public observation the circumstances of his birth, baptism, education, and early connexions in the dissenting body. But it is remarkable that after all little seems to have been discovered, for it is certain that little that is clear and satisfactory has ever been laid before the public respecting that period of his life which passed before he went over to Paris to pursue his medical studies. His chaplain, who published a review of his life soon after his decease, has given us very scanty notices of the first four-and-twenty years, and has passed over unnoticed the friends of that period who had doubtless no inconsiderable influence in forming the prelate's mind to that excellence which he has so well described, and for whom it is known that the prelate himself continued to cherish no common regard. The subject may now be considered without heat, partiality, or prejudice. I shall therefore throw together a few notices of his early life, principally collected from original but authentic sources.

Thomas Secker was one of a large family in respectable but not affluent circumstances. They were a family of Dissenters, and his brother Mr. George Secker continued a Dissenter to the last, and was a member of Mr. Fletcher's congregation at Coventry mentioned in a former note. To what society the parents of Secker belonged, is not quite evident, as it is believed that there was no congregation of Dissenters very near to Sibthorp in Nottinghamshire, the place of their abode. Thomas Secker was born in 1693, and was one of the youngest children, if not the last born. While he was still in his infancy, an elder sister became the wife of Mr. Richard Milnes, a respectable tradesman at Chesterfield, father

says Dr. Grosvenor[1], 'of an excellent spirit, of great spirituality, and sweetness of temper. The orders of his house were strict and regular: and few tutors maintained them better, and with so little severity. Every thing here was systematical. But the defects in his institution as to classical learning, free philosophy, and the catholic divinity, were made amends for to those who were designed for the pulpit, by something those pupils who had any taste took from him in his public performances. He had a charming voice, flowing and of a musical sound; a natural eloquence; his elocution and gesture were such as would adorn an orator; the pathetic was sometimes so heightened with that divine enthusiasm which is peculiar to true devotion, that he

by a second marriage of Dr. Richard Milnes, a highly respected physician of that town not long since deceased. To this sister devolved much of the care of Secker's earliest years, and hence it is that we find him a pupil in the grammar-school of Chesterfield. Mr. and Mrs. Milnes were both Dissenters: and when it was the intention of his friends to devote young Secker to the ministry, it was natural that they should think of sending him to Attercliffe, where Mr. Jollie's academy was then in the height of its reputation, and only fourteen miles distant from Chesterfield. This was in 1708 or 1709. At this early period of his life there was much of the *gaieté du cœur* about him, and perhaps more of sprightliness and levity than was common among the dissenting youth of those times. Stories have floated down of foolish pranks played by the students of Mr. Jollie's academy in the time of Secker, which seem to receive some countenance from the following passage of a letter from the Rev. Thomas Cooper, a Dissenting minister at Houghton-tower in Lancashire, where he settled soon after he had left the Attercliffe academy: 'I hear T. Jollie and Bowes are gone to London, and that the mad work at Morton's has caused the tutor to have a stricter eye over his pupils. I cannot but imagine that the new set will far outstrip the old ones in all sorts of learning, and that such famous discoveries as Mr. Taylor's are every day made in order to edify the young generation. I long to hear some private news you have stirring amongst you. Pray, Sir, favour me with some remarks on the place. I hear the house is turned topsy-turvy, and a strange degeneracy there is since I and some others left it. I desire you would be pleased to send me some Psalm-tunes, and present my respects to *my son Secker*, to George, and the rest of my friends thereabouts.' This letter bears date the 8th of October 1709. It has been questioned whether Secker ever *communicated* with any congregation of Dissenters. This seems to be put beyond controversy by a list which still exists of the members of Mr. Jollie's church at Sheffield, in which the name of Thomas Secker appears along with the names of other young men students in his academy. The precise time of his residence in the family of Mr. Jollie does not appear. In 1711 he had left Attercliffe and was in London. There he was introduced to Dr. Watts, at whose suggestion he entered himself as a student for the Dissenting ministry in an academy established by Mr. Jones, a man of real learning and great abilities, at Gloucester. His letter to Dr. Watts, written soon after his admission into this academy, which has been often published, describes the objects and plan of study, and exhibits the young writer in a favourable point of view. The same satisfaction with Mr. Jones, and with his situation, he expresses in a letter written in the same month to his sister Mrs. Milnes, a copy of which is now before me. Mr. Jones was then intending to remove the academy, which had been held in a close part of the town, to a country situation, a change which Secker seems to have much approved. He speaks of his intention to spend the ensuing vacation among his friends at Chesterfield.

In this academy he spent four years, and they were four years well employed. This was the full term of a student's residence. At the conclusion of it, the regular course would have been that he entered upon the practice of his profession by undertaking the charge of some congregation of Dissenters. This however he did not do: and the silence of those who could have set the question to rest, has left a material point in his early history affected with some uncertainty, namely, whether he ever intended to take the charge of any Dissenting society. I mean only the silence of those who wrote under instructions from his grace's family; for it has been asserted over and over again by persons living in the neighbourhood of Chesterfield, who remembered him when visiting there, that he offered himself as a candidate to the small society of Dissenters in the little town of Bolsover. Mere silence on the other side, without any positive denial, can hardly be taken as a counterpoise against the concurrent testimony of several persons: and the only part of the tradition which can, I think, with any pretence of probability be set aside, is that he was a *candidate*, and not merely an occasional supply. For it appears from evidence before me that in the autumn of 1715, when he had just left Mr. Jones's academy, Secker was at Chesterfield: and it further appears from Neal's list of Dissenting congregations made in that very year, that Bolsover was then destitute of a minister, and that the congregation was under the temporary care of the Rev. Mr. Thomas, the minister at Chesterfield on whom Mr. and Mrs. Milnes attended, and who was an intimate friend of young Secker. Under these circumstances, nothing can appear more probable to those who know any thing of the usages of Dissenters, than that Secker might occasionally relieve his friend from a journey of seven or eight miles: and officiating to a vacant congregation as a young and unengaged minister, he might easily be mistaken for a candidate. Nor is any thing more probable than that, if he did aspire to a situation in every way unworthy his talents and acquirements, the members of the Bolsover congregation might be little disposed to invite him to make a permanent settlement among them. Those sprightly and agreeable manners which at this period of his life recommended him to the affectionate regards of his family and acquaintance would be no recommendation to a country society of Dissidents, in whom little of the old Puritan character was it is probable effaced, and who were unable to comprehend the value of a young man possessed of a vigorous understanding, considerable theological knowledge, and piety genuine but rational. What would be the effect of a cool reception from such people as the congregation at Bolsover must have consisted of, upon his ardent and aspiring mind, there were probably at that time those who could foresee.

He left Chesterfield in the winter of 1715-1716, and he next appears in London. He seems to have then laid aside all thoughts of engaging in the ministry among the Dissenters, but he still retained the principles religious and political which he had imbibed during his education among them. His biographer has very justly observed, that when he was a young man his letters were 'full of imagination, vivacity, and elegance.' This long note shall be further enlarged by a few extracts from a small collection of letters addressed to his brother and sister Milnes, which will be found further illustrative of his early character and history.

'London, [Jan. 1716.]

'We had a very loyal and civil mob on Thursday night with illuminations in every house, and a great number of bonfires. In one over against Bow Church they burnt the Pretender, the Pope, Earl of Marr, Duke of Ormond, and Lord Bolinbroke, in figures which they intended at first to have carried in procession with great pomp, but the King forbad it. At another I was agreeably entertained with a Concert of Warming-pans carried by gentlemen very well dressed round the fire, and played upon by others following them with white staves. A very proper sort of music, and well-received by the company. Some little disturbance there was on the other side, but very inconsiderable. Only in Cousin Brough's parish they had the impudence to toll the bell almost all day as at a funeral. It is reported here with the utmost confidence by men of note, that the Pretender is certainly under arrest for several millions by the Duke of Orleans' order in Lorrain. The town agrees very well with me, and I hope will continue to do so. Pray give my service to Mr. Thomas, and tell him alderman Ludlam is a more obstinate blind Tory than ever, and will scarce believe Marr's declaration genuine, or that there was any such thing as a rebellion in Scotland, unless it was by the Presbyterians: however, he retains his usual civility to me, and makes me very welcome.'

'London, [March 1716.]

'Now I talk of news, did you see the strange light in the skies last Tuesday night? If you had as much of it as we, I doubt not but you have monsters and prodigies enough to fill a sheet with. Here it has been improved into armies fighting, heads appearing, and what not. One good woman in Moorfields sat preaching and preparing us all for the day of judgment. Another, who had a greater turn to politics than religion, explained it against the king for not reprieving the two Lords, till another informed us it was actually done, and so spoiled the scheme. But the best conjecture I heard was, that it was Lord Derwentwater's soul marching in state out of purgatory. Since then indeed I have met with some people (who were doubtless either Presbyterians or Atheists) that imagined the whole business was only a quantity of matter, of which by reason of the hard weather the air must be prodigiously full, set on fire by the increasing heat of the sun, as is very usual in cold countries. But a profane account as this I hope you will pay little regard to . . . . . For all this summer, if my health continues, I shall not be able to stir one step except for one week to Oxford. Yet I sincerely profess, all the variety and novelty of this great city would not equal the pleasure of an entertainment with an honest, learned, good-natured friend or two at such a place as Chesterfield.'

'Dear sister, London, [July 26, 1716.]

Well, Mrs. Milnes, if you will not give me an account of your journey to Lincoln, I will give you one of my ramble to Oxford: for I can only deal with you as I do with people on the road. I first stand still, and see whether they will turn out, and if they will not I then turn out myself. You must know then, on Friday night I had been playing the good fellow, and coming home about twelve found a summons down to Brentford next day, in order to go to Windsor on Monday. I obeyed very readily, and resolved to kill two birds with one stone, and to go to Oxford at the same time. For I had just then received the news that Miss (I cannot spell that ugly name) was married beyond recovery; and travelling you know is an old remedy for desponding lovers . . . . . I left the company and went to Oxford. There I met with an honest friend I had not seen of two years before, and in him with all the pleasure I could wish for. We talked our own talk without controul, and railed at the University as freely as they do at somebody else. I hope you do not think I mean the King: for I can assure you while I was there a very considerable person said publicly, 'We had the happiest king in the world, for he was sure of the Church's prayers while he lived, and had a double right to go to heaven when he died, both as he was a cuckold, and as he was the Lord's anointed.' Nor is their respect for his friends unworthy in the least the duty they bear to him. If a man of zeal for the government does but perform the least action that is remarkable and out of the way, he is sure

[1] See a Funeral Sermon for Dr. Benjamin Grosvenor by Mr. John Barker, p. 27, 28.

would make our hearts glow with a fervour, which he kindled in the breasts even of those who endeavoured all they could not to be moved by him.' 'There have been tutors of greater learning, who have been capable of laying out a greater compass of education: but at the same time it must be acknowledged, that the relish for practical religion; that devotional spirit which was so improved by his example; that sweetness of temper and benevolent turn of mind which a soul of any thing the same make insensibly catches from such an example, are things not every where to be met with, and yet have such an influence towards our usefulness and acceptance as ministers, as cannot easily be supplied by any other qualities.' This is probably a very fair estimate of Mr. Jollie's character as a tutor, and agrees well with the representations of the state of his academy in the Life of professor Saunderson.

Mr. Jollie died on Easter-Sunday the 28th day of March 1714, and was interred in the burial ground at the Upper Chapel in Sheffield. What can now be recovered of the inscription on his tomb is as follows:

Chr. Ser. Sa.
TIMOTHEUS JOLLIE,
verbi Dei interpres eloquens
et evangelicus:
doctrinæ Christianæ fundamenta
. . . . do vir prope divinus,
verè magnus.
Philosophiam, sacramq. Theologiam
professus,
juventutis tutor felix peritus.
In ecclesia Christi Sheffieldiensi
per annos . . . .
pastorem . .'. . . vigilem fidumq. :
in cœlum migravit
5 Calend. Aprilis A.D. 1714.
ætatis suæ 56.
Christus in vità, in morte lucrum.

So large a society required the services of more than one minister. Mr. Jollie had for his assistant a young man from Mr. Frankland's academy, Mr. Jeremiah Gill, who spent several years at Sheffield before he became pastor of a congregation of Dissenters at Hull, where he died at the age of forty in 1709. A memoir

---

to see the face of his betters, and meet with a reward to the full : whereas a man of contrary principles may do what he will without the least danger of such a favour. As to the libraries, manuscripts, inscriptions, and such fine things as I saw there, an account of them will afford no great entertainment . . . . . I am just going to lose all my company. Mr. B. is going over into Flanders, and Mr. Chandler's son of the Bath [afterwards Dr. Chandler], who has lodged with me these four months, has got a place of seventy pounds a year, and is to leave us next week, as I would do the town if it was not chiefly for one reason. I have a very good opportunity of studying natural philosophy, and particularly anatomy, this winter, which I know not whether I shall ever meet with again, and therefore would willingly improve now, for it is a study of a great deal of pleasure, and may be of some use . . . . . Pray desire Mr. Milnes to let me know what I am in his debt, for I had need consider how matters stand with me whilst I live here : and besides, I must lay out twenty or thirty pounds in books this winter. I believe the lead-mines must be melted down, if they will but sell well; and then, Mrs. Milnes, your five pound comes.'

Without date.
'I have through the goodness of God pretty well recovered myself by the using of exercise, and eating little, which I continually find the best physick : for the original of all my disorder is the badness of my stomach. I have been, fifteen, or twenty pounds, it is pretty much the same to me, only sending often is more troublesome to me, and, if he has enough by him, not more convenient for him. Mr. Bowes [afterwards the Irish chancellor] is fixed in the change of his religion, notwithstanding all I could do. I wish he has not forsaken us like Demas, having loved the present world.'

Nov. 1718.
'I know not whether I have told you that I have thoughts of going to France some time in January, but am not resolved as yet.'

'Dear brother,   Calais.
I went on board at Dover last night about two o'clock : we came over against Calais by eight, but the weather being misty and dark we kept out till about two, and then landed in good health. I was very little sea-sick. We set out in the Paris coach tomorrow morning, and shall get there this day sevennight. We have been examined on one account or another at four several places, but treated with much civility. The town seems not much preferable to Chesterfield either for beauty or largeness, but fortified to the sea, and carefully guarded. I observe the soldiers are not near so well cloathed as ours. I hope I shall find the country cheap. Our passage in the coach will cost us but twenty-five shillings, and we have a bottle of Champaigne before us that would cost you perhaps seven and sixpence, and stands us but in eighteen pence. You shall hear from me as soon as I get to Paris, and if in the mean time you have occasion, you may direct to me thus : 'A Monsieur Monsieur Secker, (for in this land of ceremony one Monsieur will not serve their turn) au Caffée de Gregoire.' I find myself able to talk French among them better than I expected, but here every body talks English.'

'Dear sister,   Paris, June 13, 1719.
I am very much concerned at your illness, and the more so because it hinders you from writing to me. Your complaints will always be matter of grief to me, but the hearing them from yourself will be pleasant. Let it be a short letter, let it be ill wrote, let it be as it will—but if you have any ability to write, it will always be a joy to me to receive letters from you, and I hope some advantage to you to write to me. I have not time for a long letter now, but I was not willing to let three days more pass without giving you a fresh assurance of the part I take in all your afflictions. Would to God I could do more for you, or that I was nearer

---

to you to do what I could. Supply for me as much as you can what I ought to do, and endeavour to make yourself something more easy for my sake under all.' . . . . [Mrs. Milnes died in the November following.]

Paris, Nov. 6, 1719.
'I shall be obliged this winter, and the next year, to extraordinary expenses besides maintaining myself, which I must go through and fit myself for my business, the best I can, whatever be the event. If I had had the good fortune to have lodged only two hundred pounds in the public stocks here when I came first, I might have gained by this time four or five thousand pounds, a sum which would have set me perfectly at ease all the rest of my life. But we must never blame ourselves for not doing what nobody could foresee a probability of success in. It is true the profession of physick is a lottery too, and has perhaps as many blanks in it as any other: but it was the only way I had to dispose of myself; and supposing the worst to happen, I shall only be obliged to lead a more private life in a more private way than I needed to have done before I entered upon this adventure.'

'Dear brother,   Leyden, Dec. 20, 1720.
You will be surprised at the date of this letter; but my coming here was so very sudden, that I had no time to send you or any body word of it, nor even to see my aunt Brough, though but eight miles off. I landed but two days ago, therefore can say nothing of the country. Nor can I be certain how long I shall stay, but it will be no longer than is necessary to get a degree, which I hope may be done in two months.'

London, April 1721.
'I obtained the degree, and arrived here last Thursday.'

Exeter College Oxford, 1721.
'When I came down here about a week ago I found your letter dated Nov. 15th, though I had given express orders that all letters should be sent up to London to me. I would not have you be positive that you guess right about my affair of importance. There are more affairs than one of importance in life. Whatever it be, it is very much at a stand at present, and yet may possibly go on again . . . . . If you write to me here, where I shall stay only a fortnight longer, it is proper not to give me my title.'

London [early in 1722.]
'The uncertainty I was in about putting on a gown is over: for I was ordained by the bishop of Durham yesterday. I believe his lordship intends to take me down to his diocese next summer. If so, it shall be hard but either going or coming I will see you.'

'Dear brother,   St. James's, Dec. 21, 1734.
You have always shown so friendly a concern about every thing which related to me, that I ought to make you acquainted with the honour the King hath very unexpectedly done me, of nominating me on Thursday last to the bishoprick of Bristol. Far from making application for any thing, I had not the least suspicion the day before, that I was thought of : and indeed the account that I was pitched upon gave me uneasiness, not pleasure. For I have already as much business in the management of this parish as I know how to go through, and the income of that bishoprick is so small that it will not in less than four years time pay the present expense of coming into it. But all my friends agree that as it is thus providentially laid in my way I ought to accept of it, and, as it is a mark of his majesty's regard, to accept it thankfully. This therefore I have accordingly resolved upon, and hope God will enable me to discharge the duties of the station I am called to. If you write to me soon, make no change on the outside of your letter, nor in the inside even. I had the pleasure of seeing Mr. Clarke last week, and hearing that our friends at Chesterfield were well. I desire my humble service to them all, and am   Your loving brother,
                         THOMAS SECKER.'

of his life by Mr. Whitaker of Leeds, is to be found in the same volume which contains Mr. Jollie's account of Mr. Whitaker, a volume chiefly made up of sermons and tracts by Mr. Whitaker, published by Bradbury, a Dissenting divine of political celebrity, who was educated by Mr. Jollie at Attercliffe. Mr. Wadsworth and Mr. De la Rose were also assistants to Mr. Jollie.

In the original formation of Dissenting societies sufficient care was not taken to settle the conditions of the union, and to define the respective rights of the parties composing it. They were for the most part formed in times of distress, when the pressure from without produced a union of feeling and interest which it was not supposed would be less intense in a period of prosperity. The contrary has in many instances proved to be the fact: and at Sheffield a difference of opinion arose on the death of Mr. Jollie which produced most unpleasant results.

The congregation were greatly divided in opinion respecting the choice of a successor. A majority in what was called the *church* wished to invite Mr. De la Rose, who was Mr. Jollie's last assistant, to be the pastor. But the church at that period formed but a very small part of the congregation, which was composed of the whole non-conformist body at Sheffield, the greatest part of whom belonged to that class of Dissenters called Presbyterian; and a very large majority of the congregation, together with the trustees, were decided against the admission of Mr. De la Rose to that office. A very unpleasant state of disunion followed, which ended in about one fifth of the whole congregation at the Upper Chapel withdrawing themselves and erecting another place of worship now called the Nether Chapel, and in the settlement of Mr. John Wadsworth as pastor at the Upper Chapel, of Mr. Timothy Jollie, son to the lately deceased pastor, as his assistant.

This was Mr. Jollie's first settlement as a minister. In May or June 1720 he accepted an invitation from a society of Dissenters who met for worship in Miles's-lane, London, to become an assistant to their aged pastor Mr. Clarke. Mr. Clarke died in 1724, and Mr. Jollie succeeded him. He died in 1757. In some private memoirs of his own life, I find Mr. Jollie assigning as a reason for quitting Sheffield, that he found an indolency of temper growing upon him *from the way of living there.*

About the time of Mr. Jollie's removal from Sheffield, the small congregation of Dissenters at Attercliffe, which had been founded by Mr. Bloom, became so united to the society at Sheffield that they had the same ministers. Mr. Daniel Clark succeeded Mr. Jollie as assistant to Mr. Wadsworth, and resided at Attercliffe. This gentleman was grandson to Samuel Clark, the collector of the biography of Puritan divines. He married Mrs. Bagshaw of Hucklow, the widow of Mr. William Bagshaw of that place, and the daughter of Mr. Dunn of Attercliffe. She and her son by Mr. Bagshaw are both interred in a vault in the Upper Chapel. Mr. Clark died on the 11th of November 1724.

His successor was Mr. Benjamin Roberts [1]; on whose

death in 1740, Mr. Field Sylvester Wadsworth became assistant to his aged parent, the venerable pastor of this Christian society.

The elder Mr. Wadsworth resigned his office of pastor about Christmas 1744; but his life and usefulness ended nearly at the same period, for he lived only till the May following. His father, Mr. William Wadsworth of Attercliffe, had been imprisoned in the castle of York for violating the laws which had been made for the restraint of non-conformity. Mr. John Wadsworth had been an assistant to Mr. Jollie, but was pastor to a congregation at Rotherham when he was invited to succeed him in his pastoral office. The academy for the education of Dissenting ministers which had flourished under the care of Mr. Jollie, was continued, but not with equal celebrity, under Mr. Wadsworth. The younger Mr. Wadsworth, a man of the most amiable disposition, was assistant-minister to this society from 1740 to 1758. At the age of nineteen, in 1736, he was sent by his father to the academy at Northampton, conducted by Dr. Doddridge, where he had for his fellow-students Mr. Job Orton, and his townsman Dr. John Roebuck. Before this period the minds of the Dissenting body throughout the kingdom, but especially of the ministers, had been much directed to the Arian controversy which sprung up in the church of England about the beginning of the last century. Many amongst them received Dr. Clarke's views on the subject, and amongst these was young Wadsworth. On that account, and that account alone, he was withdrawn from the academy at Northampton, at the particular request of his learned tutor, and finished his studies for the Christian ministry under Mr. Eames. Two years were spent by him at Kibworth in Leicestershire in the exercise of his ministry, and he died at Sheffield in 1759, aged only forty-two.

Mr. Thomas Haynes succeeded the elder Mr. Wadsworth in the pastoral office. He removed with his family from Nantwich, where he had spent several years, in the spring of 1745, and closed a valuable and useful life at Sheffield on the 3d of December 1758.

It was on the resignation of the younger Mr. Wadsworth, that a minister who has obtained a large share of the public attention, and who has been excelled by few in the best graces of a Christian and a man, piety, sincerity, the zealous exertion of his talents, and a fearless avowal of his convictions, although in those convictions he might be so unfortunate as to differ from many of the good and of the wise, became a candidate for the situation of a minister of this society,—Dr. Joseph Priestley. Mr. Haynes had some share in the direction of the early studies of this eminent person, and would gladly have had his assistance. He was at that period of his life an Arian: but as under the ministry of the younger Wadsworth and Mr. Haynes the congregation had in general adopted those views, there was no objection made to him on that account. There were however in the society some whose fastidious ears were displeased with certain real or supposed imperfections in his delivery, and they rejected him to place in the situation his friend Mr. John Dickinson, who was at that time minister at Diss in Norfolk.

[1] A near relation of this gentleman, and like him a native of Sheffield, was Mr. Samuel Roberts, many years minister of a Dissenting congregation at Salisbury, who during the rebellion in 1745 published an animated discourse on the love of our country, and in 1748 a Fast-Sermon, which went through several editions. Both the Roberts's descended from a Gilbert Roberts, who was born at Sheffield in the time of Gilbert earl of Shrewsbury.

It was at this period that the connexion between the congregations at Sheffield and Attercliffe was dissolved, or rather that the congregation at the latter place became dispersed, the small remainder of it joining the congregation at Sheffield. At the same time also the distinction of pastor and assistant was laid aside: and the small society at Ronksley's chapel in Fullwood was placed under the pastoral care of the two ministers of the Upper chapel in Sheffield. On the death of Mr. Haynes, Mr. Joseph Evans was associated with Mr. Dickinson in the pastoral office, and they continued the joint pastors of this congregation and of Fullwood till the death of the latter in 1780. To him succeeded Mr. Benjamin Naylor, who settled at Sheffield at the close of an academical course which he had passed with distinguished credit in the Warrington academy. Having been minister of this society more than thirty-eight years, Mr. Evans resigned his connexion with it in 1798; but his exemplary life was continued till the last day of the year 1803. I have been prevented, by considerations which to many persons will be obvious, from enlarging on the characters of the gentlemen who have been ministers of this society: but I will not deny myself the satisfaction of saying that a fairer name than the one last mentioned adorns not these pages: single-hearted, mild, devout, and benevolent, his unblemished life was spent in the search after truth, the unwearied discharge of his pastoral duties, and the promotion of every benevolent and useful undertaking. More I need not say:

' *Quod si digna tuâ minus est mea pagina laude,*
At voluisse sat est.'

On the resignation of Mr. Evans the connexion between the societies at Sheffield and at Fullwood was dissolved, and Mr. Naylor became the sole pastor of the Sheffield congregation. He continued to sustain that character till Midsummer 1805, when to the great regret of the society with which he had been so long connected he found himself under the necessity of leaving Sheffield. His successor was the Reverend Nathaniel Philipps, D.D., who is now the popular and much esteemed pastor of this society.

The Upper Chapel is a plain square building with a vestry or conference-house, as it is sometimes called, adjoining. In the vestry is a small library. A Sunday-school is maintained by the members of this society. The ground before and behind the chapel is used as a place of interment. The practice was begun of interring within the walls, but it is now nearly a century since any bodies have been laid there. On the walls of the chapel are two monuments, one for Mr. John Rutherford, a surgeon at Sheffield. The other bears the following inscription:

H. S. E.
JOHANNES BAGSHAW,
Hochelatensis in pago Derbiensi:
religione purâ,
matrem erga superstitem pietate,
ingenii atque morum suavitate,

a cumine singulari, ac supra ætatem eruditione;
præter sui ordinis plerosque, nobilitatus.
Qui in academia Edinburgensi
(ubi artium liberalium studiosissimus
in animo magis quam corpore excolendo
se exercebat) pulmonum
eheu! tabe affectus,
in itinere ad suos,
spe gloriæ sempiternæ in Jesu reposita,
ex hac vita demigravit,
V.N. Maii A.C. M.DCC.XXI.
Æt. An. XX. M.XI.D.XVI.
Eliza Clark
mater,
Gratia Bagshaw
soror atque hæres,
filio ac fratri unico et charissimo,
H. M. M. F. C.
Perge Viator,
Macte nova virtute esto, sic itur ad astra.

Above are the arms of Bagshaw:

Or, a bugle-horn sable, garnished and stringed vert between 3 roses proper.

THE NETHER CHAPEL.

It will be recollected that on the death of Mr. Jollie, about two hundred of the congregation at the Upper Chapel withdrew themselves. These chose Mr. De la Rose (Mr. Jollie's late assistant) to be their pastor. Mr. Elias Wordsworth, a gentleman of property and great religious zeal, was one of them, and he fitted up a temporary place of worship, in which Mr. De la Rose officiated until a chapel was built, which from its situation lower in the same street has been called the Nether Chapel. Mr. De la Rose continued pastor of this society till his death on the 31st of December 1723. Mr. Robert Kelsal (his successor) after a short residence at Sheffield removed himself into Derbyshire, where he had the charge of two of those congregations which were collected from amongst the miners in the Peak by Bagshaw the ejected minister[1]. Mr. Ogle Radford, Mr. Roberts, and Mr. Smith, were ministers of this society in the interval between the removal of Mr. Kelsal and the settlement of Mr. John Pye[2], who was ordained pastor of this society on the 18th of May 1748. Mr. John Harmar, a relative of Harmar the author of the ' Illustrations of Scripture,' succeeded Mr. Pye in 1774. Mr. Harmar was an ingenious mechanic, and his machine for shearing and raising cloth has been introduced with good effect into the clothing districts. There is an engraved portrait of him. He died in connexion with this society in 1798. Mr. John Dawson succeeded Mr. Harmar, and some time after his resignation Mr. Joseph Gilbert became the minister, who was also classical tutor in the Independent Academy at Masborough. After about four years connexion with this society, in 1817 he removed to Hull: and was succeeded by the Rev. Thomas Smith, M.A.

In the burial-ground adjoining the Nether Chapel are several tombs of the family of Wordsworth, who

[1] Mr. Kelsal's epitaph on a tomb in Tidswell church-yard seems worth preserving. ' To the memory of the Rev. Robert Kelsal, who originally came from Pool-bank near Altrincham in Cheshire, and was minister of the gospel at Great Hucklow and Bradwell; which charge he fulfilled with great zeal and integrity near the space of fifty years. His life was spent in the practice of most virtues that can adorn and dignify the human mind. Of gentle manners and ingenuous conversation he was agreeable to all who had the opportunity of his acquaintance. But these were only secondary qualities; he had an unfeigned piety towards God, and was

charitable and benevolent to his fellow creatures. He was a sound scholar; well skilled in the writings of the ancients, yet free from ostentation and the love of praise. As a minister of the Gospel he had great talents, and was, as St. Paul says, an example to his flock in conversation, charity, faith, and purity. He has left an example not easy to be equalled, but must ever be admired, and we hope imitated. He died June 23, 1772, aged 73 years.'

[2] Dr. John Pye Smith of Homerton, author of several theological works, is this gentleman's nephew, and a native of Sheffield.

were originally of the parish of Peniston. Some members of the family acquired great affluence in London. They have been considerable benefactors to this society. Three sisters, the ladies of Sir Charles Kent, bart., of Harry Verelst, esquire, and of William-Henry Chauncey, esquire, were the heiresses of this family.

COAL-PIT-LANE CHAPEL.—HOWARD-STREET CHAPEL.

When Mr. Harmar was chosen minister at the Nether Chapel, a small part of the society withdrew, amongst whom was Mr. Edward Bennet, a sugar-baker, who at his own expense erected a place for worship in Coal-pit-lane. Sole founder, Mr. Bennet was also during his life the pastor of the congregation which met there. He had always a young minister of the Independent class of Dissenters residing with him to supply his place when indisposed or absent, but neither he nor the minister received any emolument. The small sums which the seat-holders paid were placed at interest till the time of Mr. Bennet's death, when he directed by will that this sum together with 250*l.* more should be paid by his executors to the church and congregation, for the purpose of building a larger place of worship, if that was preferred to remaining where they were. This liberal offer was accepted; and with the money, increased by further donations from Mr. John Bennet and other persons, the chapel in Howard-street was erected, to which the congregation removed from Coal-pit-lane in 1790. They have had a quick succession of ministers; namely, Mr. Burgess, Mr. Slatterie, Mr. Taylor, Mr. Barnard, to whom succeeded their present minister the Rev. James Mather. From 1790 to the present time the chapel in Coal-pit-lane has been occupied by different Independent societies, who seem to have met here only till some larger meeting-house was provided for them. A small congregation of Independents now use the chapel, whose minister is Mr. Parish.

LEE-CROFT CHAPEL.

About 1780, a small society of Independent Dissenters built the chapel in Lee-Croft, and invited Mr. Povah to be their minister. They soon gave up the place to a congregation of Independent Methodists, whose minister was Mr. Macnab. Some years after Mr. Macnab's decease, the Reverend Francis Dixon with a society of Independents obtained possession of the place.

GARDEN-STREET CHAPEL

was erected about the same time, by the Reverend Mr. Bristol, who preached in it for some time to a congregation of Independents. He sold it to the Wesleyan Methodists, who occupied it till the erection of their great chapel in Carver-street. It was then again occupied by a society of Independents whose minister was Mr. Bell. He was succeeded by Mr. Barlow, and he by the Reverend Mark Docker, the present minister.

QUEEN-STREET CHAPEL.

On the 20th of June 1783 a lease for 99 years was granted by the church burgesses of Sheffield to Thomas Vennor of Sheffield, gentleman, and John Read of the same place, merchant, of a piece of land situated near a new street to be called Fig-street, or Queen-street,

at the rent of 5*l.* 2*s.* per annum. A chapel was erected upon it, Mr. Vennor contributing 450*l.*, Mr. Read 350*l.*, and other persons 300*l.* or thereabouts, to defray the expense. Mr. Vennor, by will dated the 31st of March 1786, gave up what he had advanced for the benefit of the said chapel ' as long as it should continue and be regularly used as a place for the worship of Almighty God, if the minister who should perform the usual duty therein should maintain and enforce the doctrine agreeable to the first thirty-one articles of the Church of England.' Mr. Vennor died soon after, and Mr. Read the surviving lessee, by indenture bearing date the 11th of March 1794, conveyed over the premises to Joseph Read of Sheffield, refiner, Thomas Vennor of Wakefield, architect, and nine other persons, in trust to permit the portion of ground in front of the chapel to be used as a burying-place by the families of Vennor and Read, and the chapel to be devoted to the purpose expressed in Mr. Vennor's will: and in their default to be sold, and the purchase money divided among the representatives of the original subscribers, in proportion to their subscriptions. The first minister was Mr. Jehoiada Brewer. In 1796 he removed to Birmingham, when the present minister, the Reverend James Boden, settled at Sheffield.

TOWN-HEAD CHAPEL.

About 1806, the few Baptists who were scattered among the different Independent societies began to meet together at the chapel in Coal-pit-lane, and chose Mr. William Downes (one of themselves) to be their minister. After some time they determined upon the erection of a larger place of worship; and the chapel at Town-head-cross was built by them, and opened in 1814. On Mr. Downes's removal, their present minister the Reverend Mr. Jones settled amongst them.

The WESLEYAN METHODISTS were first received into Sheffield in the year 1741 by Mr. Edward Bennet, father of the gentleman of that name already mentioned. He built for them a chapel in Pinstone-lane, which was demolished in a riot on the 25th of May 1743. He built a larger and stronger meeting near the former, which, though several times attacked, was never pulled down. This building is now converted into two dwelling-houses. About the same time Mr. John Wilson, an optician, built for them another chapel, which was pulled down by a mob. The Methodist chapel in Norfolk Street was opened on the 30th of June 1780; another in the Bridge-houses about fifteen years after; and a third, large and handsome, in Carver-street in 1804. These are all supplied with ministers under the direction of the Conference. The chapel in Scotland-street was built about 1764 by Mr. Bryant, one of the persons who received ordination from a bishop of the Greek church who was in London about 1760. He preached above thirty years in this chapel. Since his death the place has been occupied by the Methodists of what is called the New Connexion. They separated from the great body of Wesleyans on a point of internal discipline. Mr. Alexander Kilham, a leader in the secession, was for some time minister here.

The QUAKERS are a numerous body at Sheffield, and have a large meeting-house and burial-ground near Bank-street.

CHAPTER XI.

The Grammar-School.

AMONG the objects to which the funds of the church-burgesses were formerly appropriated was the education of youth. In their accompts occurs this entry under the year 1573. ' Gyven to Willm Lee a poore scholler in Sheaffeld, towards the settinge him to the Universytie of Chambrydge, and buyinge him bookes and other furnyture XIII^s. IIII^d.' But it was not merely by such casual donations as this, that they promoted the important cause of education. There was a school at Sheffield before the foundation of the present grammar-school, which was especially under their patronage.

	s.
1564. Itm Mr Yonge for hys gayt to Yorke and hys lycens	x.
1567. Itm p^d to Mr Yonge the Scole M^r for the accomplyment of his wages at Chrystynmas .	IX. VIII.
Itm p^d also to the sayde Scole M^r at o^r Ladye daye	XIII. IIII.
Itm p^d also to the Scole M^r for makynge uppe his wages	XIII. IIII.
1568. Itm gevyn to Mr. Yonge for the obteyn-inge of a lycens to kepe the scole	x.
1595. Sir Wm Sampson, teaching 20 poore l. schollers	III.

At the beginning of the seventeenth century a much better provision was made for the purpose by Thomas Smith of Crowland in Lincolnshire, an attorney at law, and who is supposed to have been a native of Sheffield. He may be regarded as the founder of the present grammar-school.

By inquisition taken at Wakefield on the 4th of September 1604, by Sir John Savile knight and others, commissioners appointed under the statute 43 Elizabeth to redress the misemployment of lands given to charitable uses, it was found that Thomas Smith, of Crowland in the county of Lincoln, gentleman, made his will on the 2d day of July 1603, and that he had thereby given to the town of Sheffield thirty pounds a year so long as the world should endure, for the finding of two sufficient learned men to teach and bring up the young children there in godliness and learning, that is to say, a schoolmaster and usher, the former of whom was to receive twenty pounds *per annum*, and the latter ten pounds, to be elected by the minister and twelve of the best and most sufficient parishioners of Sheffield, and by them to be removed at pleasure. And it was further found that the said testator did direct that his executor Bartholomew Martyn should enter into bond unto Henry Lockten of Swinshead in the county of Lincoln, esquire, the supervisor of the said will, for assuring the said thirty pounds to be paid as aforesaid.

The jurors further found that the said Thomas Smith died seised of lands and hereditaments of the yearly value of 18l. and also possessed of goods and debts to the value of 904l. 15s. 8d. and that the said executor had assets sufficient in lands, goods, and chattels of the said testator, whereout to pay, discharge and satisfy the premises so given for the maintenance of the said schoolmaster and usher: and that the executor had not entered into the bond aforesaid, nor assured any lands to the said schoolmaster and usher.

Therefore the said commissioners, by virtue of the aforesaid statute and their commission under it, ordered, decreed, and judged that the said Bartholomew Martyn of Carlton in Moreland, yeoman, executor, should on or before the 2d of February then next following, lawfully, perfectly, sufficiently, and absolutely assure and convey to the governors of the Free Grammar School of Sheffield (then lately founded and incorporated by virtue and means of royal letters patent) and to their successors for ever, lands, tenements, and hereditaments, being freehold, of the then yearly value of thirty pounds for the purpose aforesaid: and that the said executor, his heirs, executors, and administrators, should be bound in 1200l. to the said governors, as well for the true entry into, and quiet enjoyment of, the said lands by the said governors and their successors for ever, against all men; as also that the said lands then were and should remain during forty years next following of the clear yearly value of thirty pounds: and that the said executor, his heirs, executors, and administrators, should pay yearly from the death of the said testator thirty pounds to the said governors till such assurance should be made as aforesaid[1].

It will be observed that Smith made his will on the 2d of July 1603, and that this inquisition was taken on the 4th of September 1604. The royal patent bears date the 4th of May 1604: so that it appears Smith died soon after he made his will, and that the inhabitants of Sheffield immediately applied to King James, requesting of him to incorporate the vicar and twelve of the principal inhabitants conformably to the tenour of the will, and to make them persons capable in law to accept donations of land. Till such a patent was granted and such a body corporate created, the executor could not safely have performed this part of the will.

The letters patent declare that the king erects, creates, founds, and establishes a school in the town of Sheffield, for the education of the youth of that town and parts adjacent, to be called ' The free grammar-school of James King of England, within the town of Sheffield, in the county of York,' to consist of

---

[1] From a minute of the decree in the duke of Norfolk's auditor's office at Sheffield.

one pedagogue or master, and one sub-pedagogue or usher, and of children and youth therein taught and instructed. For the protection of the lands and revenues of the said school, thirteen discreet and honest persons are constituted a body politic and corporate, with a common seal, under the name of 'Governors of the goods, possessions, and revenues of the free grammar school of James king of England, &c.,' the vicar being one. As vacancies occur in this body others are to be elected by the surviving governors, but the vicar of Sheffield for the time being to be one *ex officio*. In the governors is vested the right of electing the master (who must be a Master of Arts, or a Bachelor at the least) and the usher, who are to instruct the scholars in Latin and Greek letters, and are removable at the pleasure of the governors. To the governors is further given power to receive lands, to make fit and wholesome statutes touching the school, and to nominate the scholars: and lastly, it is directed, that all the profits, &c. of the lands, &c. settled on the school, shall be applied by the governors 'to the relief, sustentation, and maintenance of the master, usher, and scholars,' for the time being, and in the sustentation and reparation of the school-house and other messuages on the school estates.

It is observable how exactly this patent is made conformable to the tenour of Smith's will, although no mention whatever is made of his name; but the king takes to himself the credit of being the founder of the school, and imposes upon it his own royal name. It does not appear that his majesty did more than grant the patent: nor was that act of grace on his mere motion, but on the humble suit and petition of the inhabitants of Sheffield. And further, that there is in it no specification of any property already settled on the school.

The governors named in the patent who were nominated by the earl of Shrewsbury were:

Thomas Toller, vicar of Sheffield.

William Slack.	Hugh Rawson.	Robert Mitchel.
William Lee.	George Wilkinson.	William Rawson.
William Dickenson.	Henry Bright.	Thomas Bright.
Robert Rollinson.	John Holland.	Malin Staeye.

The lands which Smith's executor settled to these uses, pursuant to the decree before recited, were situated at Leverington in the county of Cambridge. These were afterwards sold by the governors, and lands at Wadsley purchased with the money[1].

Smith made no provision for erecting a school-house. He probably had no other object than to endow the school, which was beforetime maintained by the burgesses. In 1606 an assessment was laid on the whole parish 'towards the charges in establishing the school[2].' The sum raised was 103*l*. 18*s*. 1*d*., which appears to be a larger sum than was required for the expenses of procuring the patent and the commissioners' decree. By indenture dated the 3d of March 1619 the church-burgesses granted to the governors of the school a messuage called 'the school-house,' with the garden and croft adjoining, to be holden for 800 years at one shilling rent.

Later benefactors have been, Ann Shemeld, (whose effigies were formerly depictured in one of the windows

of the school); John Hill, who about 1637 gave 100*l*.; Mr. Francis Barlow, a name to which Sheffield has other obligations, who gave 140*l*. for the use of the school; and Mr. James Hill, an under-master, who by will 1709 gave the governors all his lands at Gilberthorpe-hill, then valued at six pounds *per annum*, for the use of the master. In 1709 a house was built for the head-master with donations from the governors and others.

The original school-house must have had an existence before the date of the patent; for we find it represented in 1644 as then in such need of repair that it was 'not habitable.' It was probably taken down soon after that date; for in 1648 the present building was erected, as appears by the date inscribed upon its portal. Part of the materials came from Sheffield castle.

The building is now very much below the level of the street in which it stands. There appears to be all that minute attention to truth and nature which is so much admired in 'The Borough,' in the following description of the humble edifice by the Reverend Dr. Inchbald, written not long after he had passed from this school to University College, Oxford.

> ' WHERE sooty tops of clacking tilts arise,
> Which heave their smoky volumes to the skies;
> Where the red furnace boils with hollow roar
> That melts to fiery wave the massy ore;
> Where chearful labour whistles o'er the wheel,
> Which smoothes to keenest edge the stubborn steel:
> 'Twas in that mart of ancient, honest fame,
> (How ancient, Fox, let Chaucer's verse proclaim,)
> 'Twas there to form aright our tender youth
> Instruction mild forth pour'd the light of truth;
> And wayward nature first was taught to bear
> The yoke of thraldom in a master's care.
> Pleased I remember, and for ever must
> Till memory's powers lie slumbering in the dust,
> The wall-encircled court that day withstood,
> Low-sunk in which our noisy prison stood:
> The low-arch'd porch of ancient Gothic date,
> The modest portal of our prison gate:
> (In piteous case disastrous to disclose,
> There oft I've seen the little lingerers pause,
> With artful head the truant tale contrive,
> To Chadwick's frown all tremblingly alive)
> The gloomy entrance with its double door,
> The scooped threshold, and the deep-worn floor,
> The row-ranged forms to glossy smoothness wore,
> With many a name all hack'd and mangled o'er:
> The high-raised wall that half shut out the day,
> And fix'd attention, while it bounded play.'

Nothing could be more exact and happy.

In 1776 a subscription was begun for the reparation of the school, when 805*l*. was raised; a part of which was expended, and the remainder placed on real security for the benefit of the school. The salary to the head-master has of late been 60*l*. a year. At present there are twenty scholars on the foundation, and about as many others who are instructed in classical literature. There are no exhibitions to the Universities, nor privileges except what belong to the natives of the county of York in general. The same twelve gentlemen are now church-burgesses and governors of the school. The seal represents a youth and the sheafs of arrows, the old insignia of Sheffield.

---

[1] Carlisle's *Concise Description of endowed Grammar-schools in England and Wales,'&c.*, vol. ii. p. 897.

[2] The particulars of this assessment (in the hand of Hugh Rawson one of the first governors) are among the Wilson collections.

2 Y

Catalogue of the HEAD-MASTERS of the GRAMMAR-
SCHOOL.

Thomas Rawson died in 1645.
1645—1648. William Younge.
     1648. Roger Stiere.
1649—1651. Peter Laufitt.
1652—1658. William Whitaker.
          Francis Potts.
1664—1696. Thomas Balguy.
1696—1699. Charles Daubuz.
          Christopher Robinson.
          William Humpton, an assistant-minister.
          John Cliffe, died in 1748.
          Thomas Marshall.
          John Smith, an assistant-minister.
1776—1809. Charles Chadwick, vicar of Tinsley. Died
          1809.
1809—1818. Joseph Wilson.
     1818. William White, A.M. Fellow of Saint John's
          college, Cambridge.

I have not met with any notice of a head-master of
the grammar-school before Rawson, though the first
time in which I have seen any notice of him as holding
this office is in 1629. In the next year he was elected
one of the assistant-ministers ; but he speaks of having
been long in this situation in the following petition,
which as well as the counter petition seems to be worth
preserving.

' To his excellency the right hon^ble Ferdinando Lord Fairfax
Lord generall of all the Northern forces.
The humble petition of Thomas Rawson, master of the free-
school at Sheffield, humbly sheweth,
THAT whereas your petitioner (havinge a longe time beene
schoole master there) was upon May 5th 1643 forced to flie
from the rage and fury of the Earle of Newcastle's army; And
so soone as seidge was laid against Sheffield castle, August 3d
1644 returned againe to his place and charge there: Yet
Robt Stacy of Owlerton, collector of the rents and profitts of
the foresaide free schoole, contrary to the patent, doth detaine
the accustomed wages of your poore petitioner meerely because hee did not teach, which was by reason of his absence
necessitated by the garrison held there against Kinge and Parliament, by which meanes your petitioner is disinabled from
maintaininge his familie which is great, and payinge such as-
sessements as are accordinge to ordinance of Parliament, for the
advancemt of the publick cause, his assessement beinge still
as great as when hee received his accustomed wages.
And whereas the said Robt Stacy in his last accounts gave
up the full and just sume of 49l. 6s. 11d. which hee the collector hath now in purse of the rents and profits belonginge to the
free schoole aforesaid, out of which your petitioner was alwaise paid his accustomed stypend—May it therefore please
your Excellency to tender the case of your poore petitioner (in
some degree or other, the case of all the well affected in the
kingdome where the enemie hath prevailed) and to enjoine the
foresaid Robert Stacy out of the foresaid sume of 49l. 6s. 11d.
belonginge to the free schoole of Sheffield to pay your petitioner
his accustomed wages accordinge as by patent he is bound to
doe dureinge the time of his necessitated absence by reason of
the garrison held there against Kinge and Parliament. And
your petitioner shall ever pray, &c.
20th 9ber 1644.'

' I DESIRE Col. Bright to cause the schoole governors to pay
the some petitioned for, or els to see the refusers be sent to
mee that they may give an accompt of their neglect.
FER. FAIRFAX.'

(Counter Petition.)

' To his excellency the Lord Fairfaxe, generall of the Northern
forces for Kinge and Parliament.
The humble petition of Robert Stacy and others, beinge
feoffees or governors of the free grammar schoole of Sheffield,
Humbly sheweth,
WHEREAS Mr Rawson school master of the said free

schoole hath shewed a command to us from your Lordship for
payment of the wages of the said schoole due in his absence
from the towne of Sheffield, and otherwise to appear before
your Honour : May it please your Honour to vouchsafe your
petitioners to present some reasons whereby they conceive they
ought not to pay the said wages to the said Mr. Rawson.
1. Your petitioners conceive the payment therof, as hee de-
mandeth, to bee a breach of their patent for the schoole, and
of the trust reposed in the feoffees, who are appoynted to pay
the wages to the schoolmaster and usher supplyinge the place.
2. The charge they were at in his absence by maintayninge
one, conformable for any thinge they know to all orders of
Parliament.
3. The great charge they shall be att in the reparation of
the schoole house, which is not habitable, and by the expresse
words of the patent, they are to repaire out of the same revenues which Mr. Rawson requireth of them—May it please
your Excellency to take the aforesaid premises into your grave
consideration, and to vouchsafe a determination thereof as you
in your wisdome shall conceive fitt. And your petitioners, as
bound, shall ever pray for your Lordship's health with increase
of much honor.
York the xxiiith of October 1644.'

' I REQUIRE the within named Robert Stacy upon sight hereof to pay unto the petitioner the some within mentioned dew
unto him, or appeare before me or such as I shall appoint to
shew cause to the contrary. FER. FAIRFAX.'

From the time of Rawson there was a quick succession of masters till Thomas Balguy accepted of the
situation in 1662. After twenty years residence at
Sheffield, he was married there on the 8th of June
1682 to a lineal descendant of Dr. Thomas Westfield
bishop of Bristol, whose name was Mrs. Sarah Hathorn-
white. The issue of this marriage was two sons,
Thomas and John, the former of whom died in his
youth.

JOHN BALGUY attained no inconsiderable eminence
as a theologian, and was engaged in several of the
controversies which were agitated among the divines
of the former half of the eighteenth century. He was
born at Sheffield on the 12th of August 1686, and
baptized on the 27th. When he was only ten years
old he lost his father, but he found an able instructor
in Mr. Daubuz, who was his father's successor in the
school at Sheffield. In 1702 he was admitted of Saint
John's College Cambridge, and took his Bachelor's
degree in 1706. In 1707 he returned to Sheffield,
where his mother still resided, and was engaged at the
grammar-school in the instruction of youth. His son
Dr. Thomas Balguy had not been able to ascertain
whether he was ever elected master. In 1708 he was
taken into the family of Mr. Banks as tutor to his son.
Mr. Banks had lived at Shiercliffe-hall, but then resided
at Scofton, having left Sheffield, where in the practice
of the law he had acquired a large property. In 1710 he
was admitted to deacon's orders, and in 1711 ordained
priest. He was introduced to the Liddell family by
his friend Mr. Banks, and resided for a time with Sir
Henry Liddell at Ravensworth-castle. Sir Henry gave
him some preferment in the county of Durham; and
soon after, namely, on the 6th day of June 1715, he
married Miss Sarah Broomhead of Sheffield, one of three
daughters of Christopher Broomhead, of the High-street
in Sheffield, who was master-cutler in 1696. Mr. Broomhead had two other daughters, one of whom married
Mr. Robert Drake, an apothecary in Sheffield, son of
the vicar of that name; and the other, Mr. Christopher
Robinson, master of the grammar-school at Sheffield,
and rector of Welby in the county of Lincoln.

After his marriage Mr. Balguy left the house of Sir Henry Liddell, but continued to reside in the neighbourhood. In 1718 he made his first appearance as a controversialist in 'Sylvius' Examination of certain Doctrines lately taught and defended by the Rev. Mr. Stebbing,' which was followed by two other tracts under the same assumed name: and in 1726 by his 'Letter to a Deist.' In 1726 he was admitted M.A., and in 1728 was collated by bishop Hoadley (whom he had defended in the tract above mentioned) to the prebend of North-Grantham in the church of Sarum. He soon afterwards obtained the vicarage of Northallerton, on which he resided to the end of his life.

A complete account of his Sermons and other publications, all of which evince great good sense and much liberality, may be found in his article in the *Biographia Britannica*, the tribute of filial affection, furnished by Dr. Thomas Balguy archdeacon of Winchester. Through life he had a delicate constitution, and he died at Harrowgate at the age of 63, on the 21st day of September 1748.

Mrs. Balguy survived her husband, and returned to the place of her birth. Her sister Mrs. Drake had continued to reside at Sheffield, and was then in twenty-fifth year of her widowhood. These two ladies lived together nearly sixteen years. Mrs. Drake died first. Dr. Balguy and Miss Drake his cousin, who constantly resided with him at Winchester, were on a visit to Mr. Cane, a clergyman who had married one of the daughters of Mrs. Drake, when they heard of her death. They hastened to Sheffield to pay the last tribute of respect to the memory of an excellent woman. 'Poor Mrs. Balguy,' says Mr. Cane in a letter written soon after his return from Sheffield, 'decays very gradually, and cannot possibly continue long; how soon the alteration may be God only knows: whenever it does happen our connexion with Sheffield will be entirely at an end[1].' Mrs. Balguy survived her sister not quite two months. The family burying-place is near the communion-table in the parish-church.

Dr. Thomas Balguy the archdeacon, and who declined the offer of a bishopric, never resided at Sheffield; but not long ago there were some alive who could remember his visits to his mother and aunt, and the eminently instructive discourses which he was accustomed to deliver on those occasions from the pulpit of the parish-church. His name appears on the table of benefactors in that church.

Of Mr. DAUBUZ, who succeeded the first Balguy in the mastership of the grammar-school and was the early tutor of John Balguy, the best account that can be collected is to be found in a note to a visitation address by Dr. Zouch, late of Sandal. He was a native of Guienne, but at twelve years of age was driven from his native country, with his only surviving parent Julia Daubuz, by the religious persecution of 1686. In 1689 he was admitted of Queen's College Cambridge, and remained in college till 1696, when he accepted the situation of head-master of the school of Sheffield. He left Sheffield in 1699 on being presented to the vicarage of Brotherton near Ferry-bridge, where he was much loved and respected. He died there on the 14th of June 1717, it is said of chagrin, in consequence of the discouragement of Dr. Bentley, who knew more

of the world than he did, to whom he mentioned his intention of publishing his elaborate commentary on the Book of Revelation. This work appeared after his decease, and receives high encomiums from Dr. Zouch and other writers on the subject of ancient prophecy. There is another work of Mr. Daubuz, which displays also great learning, entitled 'Caroli Daubuz Presbyteri et A.M. pro testimonio Flavii Josephi de Jesu Christo, libri duo: quorum priore de variâ ejus fortunâ, usuque, necnon auctoris consilio in eo conscribendo pertractatur; posteriore, vero ex stylo ac dicendo modo et sensu, ejus veritas comprobatur. Cum præfatione Johannis Ernesti Grabe: Lond. 1706. 8vo.'

CHRISTOPHER ROBINSON, M.A. the relative and friend of Mr. Balguy, was many years master of the grammar-school. Mr. Balguy thought it one of the most pleasing of the advantages which he obtained by his collation to his prebend, that it afforded him an opportunity of doing something for this worthy man and near connexion of his family. He gave him a small living which was in the gift of the prebendary,— perhaps Welby in Lincolnshire, of which place he was rector, and where he resided when he had given up the school at Sheffield. But he ever retained a pleasing recollection of the society he had found there; and he declares in a letter to one of his Sheffield connexions now before me, that he knows of no place in which such rational and chearful and innocent society is to be found as at Sheffield. Mr. Robinson published several theological treatises. 'The excellency and necessity of revelation,' eight discourses, 1733. 'The peculiar and distinguishing characters of the gospel,' 1738. 'Christianity the sole, true, and infallible rule of life,' 1739. 'The rule of life set forth sufficiently and compleatly in the Holy Scriptures,' 1740. It is probable there were others. The two Mr. Robinsons, vicars of Norton, were his near relatives.

I shall add some account of four other persons, natives of Sheffield and educated at this school, who have obtained some celebrity in the world of letters.

JOSHUA BAYES, the son of a father of the same name, who was master-cutler in 1679, and, as we have seen, a principal person among the Dissenters at Sheffield. He was born at Sheffield in 1671. His father's brother, Samuel Bayes, was for some time minister of Beauchief, but silenced by the Act of Uniformity. Joshua Bayes was placed for theological learning under Mr. Frankland at Attercliffe in 1686, and in 1694 was ordained a minister after the Presbyterian method at the first public ordination among the Dissenters in London. His life was spent in London as pastor of two congregations in succession, and he died there in 1746. He printed several sermons, and was the author of the Commentary on the Epistle to the Galatians, in that popular and useful work 'Henry's Exposition.' Either he or his son engaged in a controversy (in which Mr. Balguy took a part) on the difficult question Of the spring of action in the Deity. The tract was published in 1731, and entitled 'Divine Benevolence,' &c., in reply to Mr. Balguy's 'Divine Rectitude.' What may be the truth may never, like many other points of metaphysical inquiry, be placed beyond controversy: but there can be no doubt whether Mr. Balguy or Mr. Bayes took the side which is most consonant to the wishes and feelings of every human being. Mr. Thomas Bayes the son was also a Dissenting minister, and recommended by his mathematical attainments to the honour of being elected a Fellow of the Royal Society.

JOHN ROEBUCK, M.D. was one of many sons of John Roebuck of Sheffield, a considerable manufacturer, and born at Sheffield in 1718. His parents were Dissenters, and from the grammar-school at Sheffield they removed their son to Dr. Doddridge's academy at Northampton, then in high estimation. He had there for his fellow-students Jeremiah Dyson, afterwards well-known as an active member of the house of commons, and Dr. Mark Akenside. His friendship with both these persons continued during life.

From Northampton he removed to Edinburgh to pursue his medical studies, which he finished at Leyden, and in 1743 had his diploma from that university.

He settled at Birmingham for the practice of his profession, and met with great encouragement. As he had been distinguished for his attention and ability while a student, so now he was noted for his skill, integrity, and compassion in the discharge of the duties of his profession.

Chemistry was ever a favourite study, and at Birmingham he pursued it to extensive practical benefits: first, by the introduction of an improved method of refining gold and silver; and afterwards, by a simple and cheaper process of obtaining the sulphuric acid, for which the demand in commerce was then fast increasing. The success of the works for the producing of this article, which he established at Preston-pans in Scotland, induced him to leave Birmingham, to give up his medical profession, and to settle in Scotland.

Success in these undertakings stimulated him to engage in a more extensive concern: and aided by a capital advanced by several of his relations and friends, he established the iron-works on the banks of the river Carron in the year 1759.

In all these concerns he was successful; and was rapidly realizing a noble fortune, when he became the lessee of some extensive collieries in the neighbourhood of Edinburgh, which exhausted all his present resources, compelled him to withdraw his capital from the works which owed their origin to his knowledge and ingenuity, and finally brought ruin upon himself and many of his near connexions. In the clouded as well as the bright periods of his life Dr. Roebuck retained his spirit and good-humour; and he died after a very short confinement on the 17th of July 1794.

An excellent memoir of Dr. Roebuck, from which these particulars are collected, appears in the fourth volume of the Transactions of the Royal Society of Edinburgh, with an estimate of what he has done for Scotland. He was less known as an author than as an experimenter. The ingenious author of the memoir observes, that ' he left behind him many *works,* but few *writings.*' The few essays which he left enable us to judge of what might have been expected from his talents, knowledge, and boldness of invention, had not the active undertakings in which from an early period of life he was engaged, and the fatiguing details of business, occupied the time for study and investigation. ' A comparison of the heat of London

and Edinburgh,' read in the Royal Society of London June 29, 1775; ' Experiments on ignited bodies,' read 16th Feb. 1776; ' Observations on the ripening and filling of corn,' read in the Royal Society of Edinburgh 5th June 1784, are all the writings of his, two political pamphlets excepted, which have been published.

The younger brothers of Dr. Roebuck remained at Sheffield, and were the first merchants of that place who opened correspondencies with mercantile houses on the continent.

JAMES CAWTHORNE was a year younger than Dr. Roebuck, and his contemporary at the grammar-school. He was born at Sheffield on the 4th of November 1719, the son of Thomas Cawthorne an upholsterer and of Mary his wife, daughter of Mr. Edward Laughton of Gainsborough. At fifteen he was removed to the grammar-school at Kirby-Lonsdale, and in 1736 he was residing at Rotherham, an assistant it is supposed to the Rev. Mr. Christian, master of the grammar-school in that town. On the 8th of July 1738 he was matriculated at Clare-Hall. When he left college he was for some time assistant to Mr. Clare, who had an academy in Soho-square, and whose daughter he married. He took orders about the year 1743, and in the October of that year was elected master of the grammar-school of Tunbridge. He retained this office till his death on the 15th day of April 1761. He died in consequence of a fall from his horse. This inscription is on his monument:

' H. S. E.
JACOBUS CAWTHORNE,
scholæ Tunbridgiensis magister,
qui juventuti tam literis quam moribus instituendæ
operam magno non sine honore dedit.
Integer, comes, et omnibus carus vixit,
valde desideratus, heu citius! obiit
Apr. 15, 1761, ætat. suæ 40.
Opibus, quas multis larga manu distribuit,
fruitur et in æternum fruetur.
Soror mœsta ex grato animo hoc posuit.'

The sister by whom this monument was erected was the wife of the Rev. Edward Goodwin of Sheffield, whose memoir of Mr. Cawthorne's life and writings has supplied the particulars above given, and who published in 1771 a complete edition of Mr. Cawthorne's poetical works, which place him in no mean rank among the poets of the eighteenth century. Pope was his master; and his ' Abelard to Eloisa' may be read without disgust, after that sweet composition to which it is a sequel; and his ' Essays' have a portion of the wit and sense of his great master. He practised composition in English verse at a very early age, and in 1736, when he was only seventeen, his ' Perjured lover, or tragical adventures of Alexis and Borina,' made its appearance from Garnet's press in Sheffield, said to be by ' a young gentleman ' of that place.

EBENEZER RADCLIFFE, one of the pupils of Mr. Cliffe, had the singular honour of pronouncing the funeral oration over two of the most eminent theological scholars of the last century, Dr. Benson and Dr. Lardner. He had powers of a very superior order, and may be said to have established a permanent reputation upon works which rarely survive the occasion which produces them. He was born at Sheffield in January

1732, the son of William and Hannah Radcliffe, formerly Shemeld. From the grammar-school he was removed to the house of the Rev. Daniel Lowe of Norton, who had many young gentlemen under his care for education, and with whom he remained till he entered the academy over which Dr. Doddridge was then presiding. He spent one year at the university of Edinburgh, and settled as a minister among the Presbyterian dissenters at Boston in Lincolnshire. From this place he removed to London, where and at Walthamstow he exercised his ministry till the year 1777, when he withdrew from the profession, and retired to the enjoyment of independence and literary leisure at Walthamstow, where he died on the 17th day of October 1809.

In 1769 he married Miss Parish, the eldest daugh-

ter of Edward Clarke Parish esquire, by whom he had an only daughter, now the wife of Stephen Iveson of Blackbank, near Leeds, esq.

Mr. Radcliffe's publications were all professional: consisting of single sermons, funeral orations, and tracts. He was a frequent contributor to the 'Library,' a monthly publication, and perhaps the first attempt at establishing a magazine on a theological basis. His 'Letters to the prelates,' which were published anonymously in 1772 after the rejection of what was called the Dissenters' bill in the house of lords when it had passed the commons, are supposed to have produced their intended effect, when a few years after the disqualifications were removed, for the removal of which the Dissenters had applied in vain in 1772.

CHAPTER XII.

Charitable Institutions and Foundations.

SAINT LEONARD'S HOSPITAL.

THIS hospital was founded by William de Lovetot about the time of Henry II. Its charter has been already given [1]. The endowment he settled upon it was not large. It consisted only in the *victus* of the *infirmi* who were admitted to be its inmates, to be taken from his mill. In the four hundred years of its existence it probably received other benefactions. I have seen a receipt in 1658 for the fee-farm rent of the rectory of Sheffield and tythe sheaf of Brightside Byerlow and *Spittle-fields*. And in the accompts of the earl of Arundel's steward 1635 is this entry, 'Paid Mr. Wroe for a rent due to his majesty forth of the spittle at Sheffield for one year 0.33.4.'

But whatever property it acquired all was swept away at the Reformation: and Dodsworth, who visited Sheffield in August 1620, speaks of it only as a thing which had been. 'There hath been a spittle there on this side the bridge.'

Some efforts were, it seems, made to recover it. In the accompts of the constablery of Sheffield we find:

1639. For charges at Doncaster att y° dutchy court £0 2 2
And another time there about St. Leonard's
     spittle 0 1 6

This ancient hospital (or spittle, according to the English abbreviation,) still continues to give name to the little eminence on which it stood, Spittle-hill.

THE OLD ALMS-HOUSES.

Near the foot of the Lady's-bridge were four habitations for as many poor widows.

It is supposed that the building was formerly the chapel of the blessed Lady of the bridge.

Both the lord of the manor and the town's trustees seem to have been interested in maintaining them. There are entries in the accompts of both parties of certain repairs. The lords of the manor were accustomed to allow twenty shillings a year to each of the inmates.

They were taken down when the bridge was improved in or about 1767.

THE TOWN-TRUST.

This consists in houses, lands, shares in the river Don navigation, and other property acquired with savings out of the annual income.

Of its origin we have spoken in the chapter on the ecclesiastical affairs of the parish. The property has been accumulated by the benefactions of various individuals, amongst whom it is probable were the Furnivals, and particularly that Thomas lord Furnival who gave the town its charter. Most if not all the benefactors lived before the Reformation. The gifts were made by them not exactly for the purposes to which we apply the term *charitable*, but rather for *public* uses; generally however with a reversionary respect to the assistance of the poor, on which account this fund may not improperly be placed among our charitable foundations. The objects specifically mentioned in the most authentic document we have respecting it, are the maintaining of the Lady's-bridge, the keeping in order of Barker-pool, and the repairing of high-ways (in which will be observed a conformity with the petition of the first year of queen Mary); and to these is added, that it was given for other charitable and public uses within the town of Sheffield.

Before the Reformation this fund seems to have been managed by the vicar and church-graves, and it is on this account that we find the vicar the contracting party on the side of the town in an engagement for the building of the Lady's-bridge in the time of Henry VII. How a considerable portion of it became severed from the rest and placed at the disposal of a newly created corporate body has been already related.

Little has at any period been allowed to transpire respecting the portion which remained: and it is uncertain to whom the management of this fund was intrusted when the vicar and church-graves ceased to have the control of it, what was their number, under what authority they acted, or how in general the trust was administered. It seems however that in the year 1565, ten years after the definitive settlement of a portion of this public property to church uses, there was a kind of *new beginning* in the management of the other part of the property, when it is conjectured that a patent or a decree in chancery may have been obtained to settle the uses and the management of the property. In the quaint style of the times the oldest accompt-book in the possession of the town-trustees is entitled 'The booke aswell of the burgesses rents there, as also of the reconynge of the same, howe and after what man' the sayde rents are ymployed, as by God's grace w'in shall appere, made and begoyne in the yere of o' Lorde God M.V^c.LXV.' It further appears from this book of accompts, that the income of the property was devoted to various purposes; such as the keeping in repair the town-armour, clothing the piper or waite, providing the jurymen's dinner at the grand inquest of the manor, repairing the market-stead and the Irish cross, cleansing Barker-pool, paying coroners' fees, keeping up the public butts, the pillory, cuck-stool, &c., repairing of bridges and highways, and many other public uses of minor importance or arising out of the peculiar demands of the time.

The persons in whose hands the property was at this time vested were accustomed to grant leases sometimes under the description of 'The Burghers or major part of the Burghers of Sheffield,' sometimes of ' The Burghers or major part of the Burghers and Free tenants of Sheffield,' and sometimes under other names: and it appears that soon after the Civil Wars doubts were entertained respecting the title of the parties holding it, in which the tenants were naturally much interested. The tenants are charged with endeavouring to retain possession of the portions of the estates on which they were settled, although their leases were expired; and with refusing to enter into new covenants for the continuance of their possession; more we may hope with a view to bring the management of this property into a more orderly state, than for any private benefit or emolument of their own.

This however rendered an appeal to the court of Chancery a necessary measure, from whence issued a commission of charitable uses, and a decree was made on the sixth day of September 1681, which placed this property on the footing on which it stands at present. The preamble of the decree recites, that whereas there are certain lands and tenements at Sheffield given for the uses already mentioned, and that

these lands had been leased by certain of the inhabitants, under various names and descriptions as before, and that the rents had for sixty years and more been applied to 'the charitable uses aforesaid, and other publique and charitable uses for the aid and ease of the poore inhabitants,' until now of late that the tenants detained possession, refusing to take leases and to pay any increase of rent. The decree then goes on to state that the tenants, in number seventy-nine, had received notice of the time and place of holding the commission of inquiry; that the petition of the inhabitants of Sheffield, complaining of the misemployment and misconversion of the rents, had been considered; and that credible information had been received that all or most of the tenants were willing that the rents should be employed according to the charitable uses before specified: wherefore Thomas Rokeby, Roger Belwood, and Thomas Hezletine, esquires, and Richard Sowrey gentleman, (the commissioners in the said commission,) adjudged the said premises to thirteen inhabitants of Sheffield, namely, William Simpson, Thomas Chappell, Robert Soresby, George Lee, Francis Barlow, William Cooke, Thomas Rawson, Thomas Bretland, Joseph Shemeld, Lyonel Revel, Zachary Wilson, Joshua Bayes, and James Newson, gentlemen, and their heirs and assigns in trust for the uses aforesaid; and that such persons as now claimed any right, title, or interest in the said premises, should upon request convey and transfer them to the said thirteen gentlemen. And for the better performance of the said charitable uses it was further decreed, that whenever any three or more of the said trustees should be dead, the survivors should convey the said premises to the survivors, and to such other persons as should be nominated and appointed by the greater part of the inhabitants within the town of Sheffield, so that the estate in law of the premises should not remain in trustees under the number of ten for above the space of six months.

This decree is evidently now the authority under which the town-burgesses or town-regents, or town-collector and his assistants, (as the body is sometimes called,) hold and administer the property. And the inhabitants at large on the whole have had reason to approve of the manner in which the proceeds of the town's estate have been employed. Since the making of the decree the income of the body has been much increased, partly by the general increase of the value of real property, and partly by the success of their speculation in shares of the river Don navigation: and the fund has been relieved from the charge of maintaining Lady's-bridge, which has been thrown on the riding, and from the care of Barker-pool, which, having become a nuisance rather than a benefit to the town, has been destroyed. To the only remaining *specific* object, the repair of the highways, it was less necessary that the trustees should direct their attention, that object being attained by parliamentary provisions; so that they were left at liberty to avail themselves of the discretion allowed by that valuable and most important clause in their charter, *any other charitable and publique uses*; and out of their income of about 1200*l*. have been accustomed to subscribe liberally to the public charities, and to indulge the town without any rate with that luxury of modern times and now indispensable convenience—a general lighting. The right of the inhabitants at large to elect the persons by whom vacancies in the trust were to be supplied, was in danger of being lost. For many years it is believed there was no public election: but the attention of the inhabitants having been drawn to this point in the year 1811, by the circulation among them of the decree then obtained from the petty bag office, the last vacancies were filled by popular election in 1818. The device on the seal is the two sheafs of arrows in saltier, with the inscription SHEFFIELD FREE TENANTS. The following gentlemen are the present trustees:—

Published Jan.t 1.t 1819, by the Rev.d J. Hunter, Bath.

THE HOSPITAL OF GILBERT EARL OF SHREWSBURY.

' I will and appointe an hospitall to be founded at Sheffielde for perpetuall maintenaunce of twentie poore personnes, and to be called The Hospital of Gilbert erle of Shrewsbury: and the same to be indowed with such revennues and possessions as my executors shall think fitt, not beinge under two hundred poundes a yeare.'

There were two strong bars to the performance of this part of the will of earl Gilbert, want of assets, and the statute of mortmain.

He died in 1616, a few days after he had made the will: and the inhabitants of Sheffield would in all probability have lost the benefit of his gracious intentions, had not his heir at law and descendant in the fourth degree been a person of a liberal and noble mind.

No doubt the poor inhabitants of Sheffield looked with an earnest desire for the fulfilment of an intention which offered to so many of them a place of retreat and comfort for the declining years of life. But no steps, as far as appears, were taken to carry into effect the earl's design till after the Civil Wars, when we find a person engaged in surveying the old and ruinous castle of Sheffield, with a view to ascertain the practicability of appropriating portions of it to the purposes of an hospital: and some memoranda still exist, made under the inspection of Mr. Howard about the year 1654, which have a prospective view to the carrying into effect the intention of the earl.

In or about the year 1665 the foundations of the present hospital were laid, on ground which had formerly been a part of the orchard belonging to the castle. The buildings for twenty poor persons were nearly completed in the summer of 1666[1]. In 1673 they became inhabited by ten men and ten women, of whom one of the men was appointed governor. In that year Mr. Howard, then become earl of Norwich, made certain statutes and orders for the government of the persons in the said hospital, and touching the nomination of those who should be admitted to become its inmates.—This inscription was placed over the entrance :

The hospital of the right hon. Gilbert earl of Shrewsbury, erected and settled by the right hon. Henry earl of Norwich, earl marshal of England, great grand-child of the aforesaid earl, in pursuance of his last will and testament. Anno Domini 1673.

Keeping in view the intentions of his great-grandfather, whom he was careful in every step he took not to defraud of the honour of being accounted founder of this hospital, the earl of Norwich directed that the persons who should enjoy the benefit of it should be poor persons of good character of the town and parish of Sheffield ; and if none such could be found there, of any other place or parish where he had estates that had descended to him from Gilbert earl of Shrewsbury, chosen by himself and his heirs: that they should receive two shillings and sixpence per week for their maintenance, coals, and certain articles of dress; that they should wear blue gowns, and the master one of scarlet; that they should attend prayers read by the governor; and that the inmates should be mutually assistant, and pious, sober, and orderly in all their conduct.

On the 23d day of November 1680 the said Henry earl of Norwich, then by the death of his elder brother without issue become duke of Norfolk, conveyed certain portions of his estate to trustees for the perpetual support of the hospital: namely, the rectory of Peniston, with all the glebe lands, tythes, oblations, obventions, profits, and commodities thereunto belonging; the tythes of Cumberworth ; the rectory of Kirk-Burton, with the glebe-lands and tythes there-

unto belonging in Holm-Firth, Shepley, Thirstyland, and Shelley, or elsewhere within the said rectory; the farms and lands at Meadow-hall in the parish of Rotherham reputed or called Executory lands ; a piece of land at Ardsley near Barnsley, and other lands, cottages, and woods in the parish of Barnsley; and Jeoffry croft in the parish of Sheffield, all in the county of York: also lands in Barneley, Critch, Heage, Belperward, and Duffield, in the county of Derby. All these premises were assigned by the duke to Francis Jessop of Broomhall, esquire, Thomas Chappell senior, Cuthbert Browne of Hansworth, clerk, and William Spencer of Attercliffe, gentleman, in trust out of the proceeds thereof to keep the hospital in repair, and to provide gowns and provisions for the pensioners ; a power being reserved to the duke and the heirs of his family to add to the number of the trustees at their own discretion.

In 1693 all the original trustees being dead, and Henry duke of Norfolk being also deceased, a new trust was formed by his son of the same name, consisting of William Jessop of Broomhall, esquire, Joseph Banks of Sheffield, esquire, Robert Sorsby and Richard Bacon of Sheffield, gentlemen, with like powers as before.

To Lady Mary Howard, relict of Lord Thomas Howard who was lost in a voyage to France, the hospital owed a material improvement in its constitution. This lady during the nonage of her son Thomas duke of Norfolk, to whom she was guardian, with the advice and consent of Dr. John Sharp archbishop of York, nominated a clergyman to succeed to the lay-brother who had held the office of governor of the hospital, and made him also collector of the hospital rents. She gave also a hundred pounds towards the expense of enlarging a small chapel (which had formed a part of the original structure), by annexing to it the hall of the hospital, and of placing in it seats and pews by which several hundred persons might be accommodated

---

[1] It was during this stage of the business that the following correspondence took place :

' Sir,

His Grace the lord archb'shop of Yorke hath lately received two severall letters from the lords of his Majestye's most honorable privy councell to make certayne inqairyes concerninge all the Hospitalls within his dioces, and to give an accompt thereof to them with all possible speed, his Grace hath comitted the care hereof within the West Ridinge to his Archdeacon; who beinge informed that you have a certaine hospitall or hospitalls within your parish, hath inioyned me to writte to you, and request you in his name to returne what possible satisfaction you can to these following queeries :

1. Who was the founder of your hospitall ?
2. For how many persons there bee places in itt ?
3. Whether by the orders of the foundation they are to bee bestowd upon men or women, and how many of each sex ?
4. Whether they bee confined to persons of a certaine place or country, or bee left at large ?
5. Who are the maisters of the hospitall, or have the disposing of the void places ?
6. What yearely pention is allowed to each allmesman admitted into the hospitall ?

Further his Grace is comanded and doth require you to give notice to the maister of the hospitall or hospitalls, or others who have the disposinge of allmesmen's places in them, that it is his Majestie's expresse will and pleasure that all such places which are at present or shall become void, shall bee reserved and kept for such maimed seamen and soldiers as shall be sent unto them from his Majestie's comissioners in that behalfe appointed, to whom they are to give information of all such places as shall fall void, that they may be supplyed by such persons and none others. Your care and speedy dispatch herein will conduce to his Grace's satisfaction, that hee may accordingly give account to his Majestie and his privy counsell; that this may effectually bee don is strictly inioyned upon me, and according as you make returns itt shall bee certified to his Grace by   HEN. WATKINSON.

Yorke, August 2, 1666.'

' Mr. Staniforth,

I rec'd your copy of Mr. Watkinson's letter, and as to the 6 articles therof, I conceive they are to bee answeared all in one : viz. That the hospitall is not finished nor inhabitable: But as to particulars, you may say to the first : Gilbert Earle of Salop intended an hospitall att Sheffield by his will, after debts and legacies paid, which were many, and I question whether all bee satisfyed. To the 2d. To the number of persons it cannot bee answeared, for though 20 was intended, yet the lands are fallen much short in valew, and it may bee a question in law whether the executor of Earle Gilbert (who now is Mr. Henry Howard) ought to nominate the whole number with halfe the yearly maintenance, or the halfe number with the whole yearly maintenance.

To the 3d. If the halfe number of poore bee taken to y⁰ whole yearly maintenance, then weemen.

To the 4th. The executor hath the private directions and declarations of Earle Gilbert in that particular.

To the 5th. The maister of the hospitall is the executor himselfe above named, a person of honour, and now beyond the seas ; who att his owne chardge and out of his owne estate, and upon his owne land, hath begun not perfected a lardge building hospitall-wise: But whether this is to bee what Earl Gilbert intended, the honorable Mr. Howard himselfe must resolve the question: for it is his Honor's building upon his owne land, and not yet directed by any deed of feoffment, or otherwise, to a charitable use, and soe not within the view of Mr. Watkinson's letter, and therefore (if finished) not to bee as an hospitall, and soe I thinke noe mention need bee made therof to the Arch Deacon.

To the 6th. The answer is —nil—

These solutions to the 6 queries is but what I note downe in hast; but I would advise Mr. Ratcliffe that not a stone more were added to the hospitall att present for thes 6 or 16 reasons, untill his Honor or commissioners bee acquainted herewith. Tomorrow I am for Nottingham, and upon Twesday sevenight may bee at Sheffield.

In halst your very lo. friend,

Wingf. Ma. 16 Aug. 1666.   IM. HALTON.'

beside the people of the hospital. She also provided that the governor should read prayers twice a week in the chapel, and preach twice on the Sundays, a provision which was much approved, many persons of the parish of Sheffield resorting to the chapel to attend divine service. The income of the governor, who was Mr. John Dossie, afterwards vicar of Sheffield, was at that time thirty pounds *per annum*, with what he could further make by letting the pews. This change her son the duke of Norfolk, when he came of age, sanctioned and continued.

The next material change was an addition to the number of pensioners: and to effect this purpose, as well as to place on a permanent basis the departure from the original constitution in the appointment of a clergyman as governor, application was made to Parliament in the eleventh year of George I. 1725, and an act was passed by which the before recited estates were vested in William Jessop of Broomhall esquire, Joseph Banks esquire, William Levins of Grove in the county of Nottingham esquire, William Green of Thundercliffe in the county of York esquire, John Batty of Sheffield gentleman, Wardell-George Westby of Ravenfield in the county of York esquire, Robert Chappell of Attercliffe esquire, John Staniforth of Darnall, and John Fenton of Little-Sheffield, gentlemen, together with certain moneys that had arisen out of savings from annual income then in the hands of the said Jessop and Banks, in trust to continue the pension of two shillings and sixpence a week to the persons then in the hospital, with such other allowances of clothes, coals, &c. as had been before; and in further trust to erect additional buildings to receive such other poor persons as should be added to the then present number of hospital pensioners, of whom as many more as could be maintained out of the revenues of the hospital should be added, to be in every respect on the same footing with the others, and to be chosen like them first from the poor of Sheffield, and in default of such from the poor of other places where the estates of the duke of Norfolk inherited from the Shrewsbury family lay. The nomination of these, as of the former, to be in the said duke of Norfolk and his heirs, and, in default of their appointment for the space of six weeks after a vacancy, in the trustees.

By this act of parliament the new regulation introduced by Lady Howard was made a part of the constitution of the hospital; it being enacted that the governor should for ever be a clergyman of the church of England, and that he should perform the services before mentioned in the chapel of the hospital. His residence in the hospital is dispensed with, provided he remove to no greater distance than into the town of Sheffield, as is also the provision in the original statutes that he should be a person unmarried, and that he should wear a gown of scarlet.

Provision is made in the act of parliament for perpetuating the trust by nomination to vacancies as they occur, by the duke of Norfolk and his heirs.

The trustees are enjoined by the act to provide accommodation for not fewer than eight additional pensioners, four men and four women, and they are empowered to add hereafter to the number whenever the income from the hospital estates shall be sufficient to allow them so to do.

At Michaelmas 1763 the pension which had remained unchanged since the foundation of the hospital was advanced to three shillings and sixpence per week.

In 1768 a portion of the building was carried away by a sudden rising of the Sheaf.

On the 3d day of March 1770, Edward duke of Norfolk endowed the hospital with 1000*l*. This sum was applied under the direction of the trustees to repair the breach occasioned by the flood, and to erect a larger and more commodious chapel.

An act of parliament was obtained in the same year sanctioning the advanced income of the pensioners and giving an optional power of increasing it, and making some other minor alterations in the constitution of the hospital.

In 1793 the pensions were advanced from three shillings and sixpence to five shillings per week. The present number of pensioners is seventeen men and as many women, some of whom do not reside in the hospital. The last improvement of their income was made by the late duke of Norfolk on the 25th day of March 1812. The men now receive ten shillings a week, and the women eight shillings. According to the original constitution they are provided with coals; and have a blue gown and two linen shirts every other year, and a purple gown every seventh year. Instead of the badge which was to be worn according to the original statutes, a button is used bearing the figure of a talbot-dog.

CATALOGUE OF GOVERNORS.

1708—1753. John Dossie, vicar of Sheffield.
           Henry Downes, curate of Saint Paul's and vicar of Ecclesfield.
           William Downes, rector of Harworth.

The governor of this hospital was endowed with the income of three hundred pounds, and of a share of an estate at Neepsend by the last will of Mr. William Birley of Throgmorton-street, London, in 1715.

HOLLIS'S HOSPITAL AND SCHOOL.

To the family of Hollis, which was enriched by commerce and raised into general notice by the munificence with which the last Mr. Thomas Hollis encouraged the arts and supported the principles of civil and religious liberty in which he had been educated, Sheffield has many obligations.

Thomas Hollis, the founder of the family, was born at Rotherham, and baptized there on the 4th of September 1634. His father (of the same name) was by trade a smith, and his mother was sister to Mr. John Ramsker or Ramscar, a cutler of Sheffield, whose concerns seem to have been more extensive than those of most of his contemporaries in that business[1]; as while he manufactured his goods in Sheffield, he had a shop

---

[1] Mr. Ramsker was one of those tradesmen who in the time of the Commonwealth and of Charles II. issued their farthing tokens. Like the rest, it is wretched both in design and execution. On one side the name of the issuer encircles the dagger in saltier of the Cutlers' Company, and on the other the initials of his name, with the place of issuing and the date, 1655, which is rather early for coins of this class. I have met with five others issued at Sheffield. The issuers were Stephen Carr of Attercliffe, —— Broadbent, Robert Boughton, Robert Downes, and Zachary Wilson, whose name and that of Lionel Revel appear on the same piece. There may have been others. Later times have made large additions to the *numismata Sheffieldiensia* in copper, silver, and even a more precious metal: but the particular notice may without impropriety be deferred till they become matters of antiquarian curiosity.

in the Minories in London, where they were vended. With this uncle Thomas Hollis was placed as an apprentice, his indentures being enrolled in the books of the Cutlers' Company at Sheffield on the 25th of July 1648.

The preaching of Mr. Fisher, the vicar of Sheffield, wrought powerfully on the mind of young Hollis, and before the term of his engagement to Mr. Ramsker was expired he had experienced what is called his conversion. This indeed happened before he left Sheffield; for, having had experience of his fidelity and industry, Mr. Ramsker sent him to London, during the time of his apprenticeship, to take the management of his concern in the Minories. To the business there I suppose Hollis succeeded, for it was in the Minories that he was established as a cutler, or rather a wholesale dealer in the articles of Sheffield manufacture; and the flourishing trade and large property of which he died possessed show what may be done in a long life by regular habits, industry, and frugality. He was also the pious and devotional character. To his prayers he added alms-deeds: and this not in the questionable method of posthumous donation, but while he lived he was the friend to the aged and the poor, the encourager of works of piety, the patron of the education of the young.

He was a Dissenter of the Baptist denomination. To the erection of the first Dissenting chapel at Sheffield he was a liberal contributor, as he was also on the building of the larger chapel in 1700. In the year 1703 he purchased the former chapel, called the New Hall, together with a small house adjoining, and converted them into sixteen dwelling-houses for as many elderly women, widows of cutlers, and other persons employed in the peculiar manufactures of Sheffield, probably thinking that they had the first claim upon him to whose labours he was principally indebted for that affluence which enabled him to indulge his benevolent and liberal propensities.

At his death in 1718 no permanent provision had been made for the inmates of the hospital. He was contented with making them annual presents in money, clothing, and fuel. At his decease he desired that these might be continued, and those who survived him were willing rather to exceed than to come short of his intentions of beneficence.

In the year 1726 Thomas Hollis, son of the founder, vested the estate of Whirlow-hall, lately purchased of Sir John Statham, Brocco-hill closes, and Creswick-close, on which Hollis-street was soon after erected, together with 2000l. South-sea-annuities stock, in trustees for the benefit of the hospital and for other purposes, especially for affording assistance to the Dissenting ministers of Sheffield, Rotherham, and Doncaster, and for the support of schools at those places. The trustees in the deed named are Thomas Hollis of London, cutler, John Hollis, Thomas Hollis junior, Isaac Hollis, and Richard Solly of London, cutlers and merchants, John Browne senior, and Samuel

Shore of Sheffield, gentlemen, John Smith and Jonathan Smith of Sheffield, cutlers, William Stead mercer, Daniel Bridges hatter, John Crookes grocer, William Burch schoolmaster, and John Wadsworth minister—all of Sheffield.

In 1732 the charity was further endowed by Thomas Hollis, grandson to the founder, by gift of two shares in the river Don navigation. It has since that time been further endowed by different members of the Hollis family, with sundry houses and grounds which were contiguous to the hospital, by which means the hospital has now the benefit of a large and open area. And lastly, the well-known Thomas Hollis in 1773 gave by will 300l. By the same will he conveyed the bulk of the Hollis property to his friend and fellow-traveller Mr. Brand.

By means of these donations and of savings out of their annual income the trustees have been enabled to rebuild the hospital, and materially to improve the accommodations of its inmates.

It appears from a memorandum signed by the second Thomas Hollis in 1727, that 100l. per annum out of the proceeds of the trust estate were to be disbursed in the hospital and school annexed to it in these proportions:

	£	s	d
The sixteen widows 4l. per annum each, to be paid quarterly	64	0	0
For coals and firing amongst them	5	0	0
Gowns, one each in two years	8	0	0
To the hospitaller for reading prayers	2	0	0
To the schoolmaster and schoolmistress for teaching about fifty children to read, and their catechism	16	0	0
To a writing-master, who was to teach about forty or fifty children to write, three or four months in the year in the upper room of the oratory	5	0	0
	£100	0	0

The estates having much increased in value, the trustees have been enabled to enlarge the income of the widows and other beneficiaries. On December 21, 1812, (Saint Thomas's day, when the annual accompts are settled and the annual feast is held,) the last increase was made, and since that time the widows have received one guinea every three weeks: and the orator, who is also schoolmaster, fifteen guineas quarterly, having also a good house in the hospital yard. The minister of the Upper Chapel has since that period received 30l. per annum, the minister of the Nether Chapel 10l., Fullwood minister 20l., the ministers at Rotherham and Doncaster 20l. each, the schoolmaster at Doncaster 20l., and the schoolmaster at Rotherham 40l.

The widows in the hospital were to be and still are of cutlers, scissor-makers, file-cutters, box-makers, button-makers, and sheathers in Sheffield, and within two miles of the town, not absolutely rejecting others if proper objects.

PEDIGREE of HOLLIS of LONDON, &c.

ARMS.—Argent, on a chevron azure between 3 holly branches slipped and fructed, proper, as many wood-pigeons of the field, beaked and membered gules.

ELLEN, first wife, sister of John Ramsker of Sheffield, cutler. Married at Rotherham 28 June 1632. Died about 1646.—THOMAS HOLLIS of Rotherham, smith, buried there 4 Feb. 1663. Will proved at York 24 March 1663, and administration granted to Mary his widow.—MARY, second wife.

THOMAS HOLLIS of the Minories, London, cutler, born at Rotherham, and baptized there 4 Sep. 1634. Died in London 4 Sep. 1718, aged 84. First founder of the hospital at Sheffield.—MARY, dau. of —— Whiting of East-Ham in Essex.

JOHN HOLLIS, bap. at Rotherham 7th of May 1648. | MARY HOLLIS, bap. at Rotherham 13 Feb. 1653.

THOMAS HOLLIS of London, cutler, eldest son. Second founder of the Sheffield hospital. A governor of Saint Thomas's Hospital, London. Was twice married, but died without issue 24 Jan. 1731.

NATHANIEL HOLLIS, second son. Died in 1738.

JOHN HOLLIS of London, third son. A governor of Saint Thomas's Hospital. Died 21 Dec. 1735.—HANNAH, dau. of John Sampford of Redrith.

—— wife of —— Laddes.

THOMAS HOLLIS, only son, principal heir to his uncle. Died 14 June 1735.—— dau. of —— Scott of Wolverhampton.

ISAAC HOLLIS, of High-Wycombe, esq. eldest son. Died 8 June 1774.

SAMUEL, second son.

TIMOTHY HOLLIS, of Great Ormond-str. London, esq. third son, a benefactor to the hospital.

ELIZABETH, wife of William Ashhurst of Castle-Hedingham, co. Essex, esq.

MARY, wife of Edward Winnock of London.

HANNAH, wife of Samuel Edwards of London.

ANNE, wife of Richard Solly of London, cutler.

—— a dau. died unmarried.

THOMAS HOLLIS, of Corscombe, co. Dorset, esquire. Born in London 14 April 1720. Died unmarried 1 Jan. 1774.

JOHN HOLLIS, of High-Wycombe, esquire, only son, and only surviving male representative, 1819.

HANNAH, wife of —— Anthony of Beaconsfield.

THE BOYS' CHARITY SCHOOL.

At the north-east corner of the parish church-yard stands a school-house, where sixty boys are clothed, maintained, and educated till they are of proper age to be placed out as apprentices.

This excellent charity was begun in 1706. Mr. Drake the vicar, and Mr. Turie an assistant-minister, were the principal promoters of the design. The boys were for some time taught in a room, I suppose in the hall, at the earl of Shrewsbury's hospital, the duke of Norfolk giving 30l. annually. In 1710 the present school-house was erected: Joseph Banks of Scofton, esquire, contributing 100l., Mr. Ellis of Brampton-Bierlow, 20l., and many of the inhabitants of Sheffield subscribing according to their ability. The combination of many individuals in the establishment of a public charity may be said to have been scarcely known before the beginning of the last century. The honourable Thomas Watson-Wentworth, (grandson to the first earl of Strafford and father to the first marquis of Rockingham,) a nobleman who has monuments of his munificent and benevolent spirit in almost every village and town within a wide circuit around his hospitable mansion at Wentworth, was the first to endow the school with a permanent income. He gave 100l. to be laid out in lands.

The school has received many other benefactions and legacies. The principal of these were a bequest of 500l. from Mrs. Elizabeth Parkin in 1766, and another of 3000l. three per cent. consolidated Bank annuities, from Mr. Thomas Hanby, of which the school began to receive the benefit in 1797. Of the 3000l. stock the Company of Cutlers are trustees, and they are directed by Mr. Hanby's will to pay out of the proceeds 10l. per annum to the master of the school, 20s. to a clergyman to preach an annual commemoration-sermon, 10s. to the clerk and sexton, and 5l. for a dinner. The residue of the proceeds to be appropriated to the maintenance and education of as many children as may be, either boys or girls, in this school, who are

to be nominated by the master and two wardens of the Company of Cutlers, the passed masters, the church-burgesses, and the vicar and church-wardens for the time being: the children to be of parents who belong to the established church, and those of his own kindred to be preferred.

The gross rental of the real estate of this charity in 1814 was 283l. 15s. With this sum, the income from property of other descriptions acquired by donations and legacies, collections at the churches and other places of worship, annual subscriptions, and the yearly donation of 30l. from his grace the duke of Norfolk, fifty-four boys are maintained and educated. Six more are on Hanby's foundation.

The boys wear a blue uniform, except those who are clothed in green, supposed to be in pursuance of directions in Mrs. Parkin's will. Hanby's boys, by the express direction of his will, wear the dress of the boys of Christ's Hospital in London.

The portrait of Mr. Hanby, who is said to have been educated in this school, and whose name we shall again find as a benefactor to his native town, is preserved at the school.

A society has lately been formed consisting of young men who have been educated in this school. They meet monthly, and subscribe small sums towards its support. They call themselves, appropriately, 'The grateful Society.'

THE FREE WRITING-SCHOOL, AND BIRLEY'S CHARITY.

Near the grammar-school is another public school, under the patronage of the church and town burgesses, in which children are taught writing and accompts. This was built in 1721, in pursuance of the will of Mr. William Birley before mentioned. 'I give to the town of Sheffield, in the county of York, nine hundred pounds to purchase an annual rent or income for the uses following: viz. the income of three hundred pounds I appoint to be for encouraging writing and arithmetic, to be taught at the free-school or such proper place by a fit person, and the said income to be allowed him for it: and the income of three hundred pounds more I give towards the support of a minister to perform divine service in the chapel of the hospital, or in any other place that shall be regularly appointed to that use: and the income of the other three hundred pounds to old and indigent tradesmen or their widows. And I leave the disposing hereof to the church-burgesses, school-burgesses, and town-burgesses, desiring the money to be paid into their hands as soon as possible, or placed in some good public fund till paid.' He gave also for the same uses an estate at Neepsend, after the death of Sarah Wright of Tickhill, whom he nominated an executor along with Daniel Philips doctor of medicine, and Mr. William Parkin. The will bears date the 10th of June 1715.

I have not found that this school has received any further endowment.

BARLOW'S CHARITY.

Francis Barlow of Sheffield, gentleman, by his will dated the 6th of December 1688, and by a codicil dated the 2d of March 1689, left a charge of 8*l.* a year for six years next after his decease, and 6*l.* a year for ever after, upon certain houses lately purchased by him of Joshua Shemeld, to be paid every Christmas to the overseers of the poor of Sheffield, and to be distributed to the most needy decayed tradesmen of Sheffield.

Mr. Francis Barlow, whose name we have before had occasion to mention, was the representative of a family of that name long resident in the parish of Sheffield. The will of his great-grandfather Henry Barlow, or Barley, of Attercliffe, bears date the 16th of April 1589. He himself was baptized at Sheffield the 26th of September 1626, the son of Humphrey Barlow of Sheffield by Dorothy his wife, daughter of Gregory Sylvester of Mansfield, by Cassandra his wife, formerly Pease. Mr. Francis Barlow was one of the town-trustees, and admitted to an honorary freedom of the Company of Cutlers along with other gentlemen the 28th of August 1681. He had no issue; and by his will gave considerable estates to his nephew Thomas Barlow, son of Samuel Barlow of Leeds. This gentleman was living at Sheffield in 1691, when he had a grant of coat-armour, *viz.* Sable, two bars ermine, on a chief indented parti per pale or and argent an eagle displayed of the first. He afterwards resided for some time at Renishaw, but finally settled himself at Middlethorp near York, where he built a handsome house on the model of those of Italy which he saw in his travels.—By act of parliament 11 and 12 William III. the rent-charge on the houses at Sheffield was transferred to certain lands at Middlethorp.

SITWELL'S CHARITY.

Mr. Francis Sitwell of Sheffield, attorney, in 1740 gave 400*l.* to the Company of Cutlers, which he directed should be lent to poor cutlers in sums of 5*l.* each without interest, for six months, on a deposit of goods exceeding 5*l.* in value. This money is now lost.

PARKIN'S CHARITY.

Besides the five hundred pounds which Mrs. Elizabeth Parkin gave by will to the Boys' Charity School,

she gave another sum of five hundred pounds, of which the interest was to be distributed yearly to poor persons by the vicar, three assistant-ministers, and church-wardens.

In this benevolent lady settled the fortunes of three brothers, Thomas, William, and John Parkin, natives of Sheffield, sons of Thomas Parkin an ironmonger there, who died at the age of eighty-five in 1729. Thomas died before his father; William was a merchant in London, and fined for sheriff; and John, the father of Elizabeth Parkin, resided at Bristol. After the death of the grandfather, Mrs. Elizabeth Parkin is reported to have managed the extensive mercantile concerns with a masculine spirit and uncommon ability. In 1749 she purchased the estate of the Westby family at Ravenfield for 28,000*l.* upon which she went to reside, and died unmarried on the 9th of May 1766 at the age of 63. She gave her estate at Ravenfield to her cousin Walter Oborne esquire, with remainder over to her cousin Matthew Worgan of Wolley, in the county of Somerset, esquire, and on their decease without issue, to the late William-Parkin Bosville esquire, descended of a brother of her great-grandfather Jasper Bosville. Mr. W. P. Bosville died without issue, when the estate passed to its present proprietor the Rev. Thomas Bosville his brother. Mrs. Parkin had considerable estates in several parts of the kingdom, and other places as well as Sheffield have benefited by her liberality.

KIRKBY'S CHARITY.

Mr. John Kirkby, by his will dated the 31st day of July 1779, gave to the Rev. John Dickinson and the Rev. Joseph Evans, ministers of the Upper Chapel in Sheffield, and also to Samuel Shore of Meersbrook, esquire, Samuel Shore of Norton, esquire, and Joseph Roberts of Sheffield, merchant, the sum of 400*l.* in trust, to place it out on proper security, and to pay the income thence arising to two poor widows in such proportions as the trustees and their successors should appoint. When the trustees are reduced to three, others to be chosen by them.

SUNDAY-SCHOOLS.

These were introduced at Sheffield in 1785, and received all necessary patronage. They are found both in the town and in the more populous parts of the parish. At present there are thirteen distinct schools of this class supported by members of the Establishment, and conducted by gratuitous teachers, in which about 900 boys and 600 girls are taught. To most of the societies of Dissenters are also attached Sunday-schools. It is needless to observe that the Lancasterian or Madras system is universally introduced.

THE GIRLS' CHARITY-SCHOOL.

At the north-east corner of the church-yard stands the Girls' Charity-school. This was erected in 1786 at the expense of 1500*l.*, which was raised by the contributions of many well-disposed persons in the town and neighbourhood of Sheffield. Sixty girls are here educated, maintained, and clothed, and trained to be domestic servants. This charity has received several benefactions and legacies: but its property is still small, and it depends almost solely for its support upon its annual contributors, and congregational collections.

THE GENERAL INFIRMARY.

Sheffield—thus provided by individual munificence or the conjoint efforts of many benevolent persons with funds for the occasional relief of the necessitous, with retreats for the aged, and asylums for the destitute youth of both sexes—still wanted a house to which those might retire in whom the evils of poverty were aggravated by the inflictions of disease, and receive the benefit of pure air, wholesome diet, freedom from domestic cares, and medical assistance. The inhabitants of this neighbourhood, ever ready to attend to the call of humanity, answered an anonymous invitation by a numerous attendance at the Town-Hall, on Monday the 23d of April 1792.

The reverend James Wilkinson, the late respected vicar of Sheffield, took the chair. Many gentlemen were present whose zeal in every good cause was well understood, but the proceedings at first were languid: the magnitude of the undertaking seemed to appall every one; and there was some appearance of an intention to disperse without coming to any definitive determination on the subject, when the countenance of the late Mr. Richard Swallow caught the eye of a gentleman who sat near the chair, and who intimated to the vicar his persuasion that Mr. Swallow had some important communication to make. This determined the chairman to propose a subscription, and he himself headed the list with a donation of 200l. Dr. Browne immediately followed with the same sum; when Mr. Swallow informed the meeting that he was commissioned by his friend and the great and general friend of humanity, Mrs. Fell of New Hall, to offer 1000l.

towards the good work, to which he immediately added 200l. from himself. The subscription list now filled with extraordinary rapidity. In a very short time the contributions amounted to 15,000l. to which 2000l. more were added, and a legacy of 500l. from the late Francis Hurt Sitwell esquire in addition to the same sum given by him in the original subscription, before the building was roofed. This sum is spoken of in the reports relating to the charity as *unparalleled*: and when it is recollected that the Infirmary of Sheffield lying on the confines of its county, and having therefore none of the attractive features of a county institution, and though its doors were to be open to the sick and lame poor of all nations, obviously intended more immediately for the benefit of the poor of one particular place, supported too, as for the most part it was, by persons who resided or had an interest in that particular neighbourhood, it will not probably be easy to find a public charity which does more honour to the founders of it.

Some time was lost before the committee to whom was confided the management of the concerns of the infant charity, could meet with ground that appeared eligible as a site for such a building as was contemplated. They at length pitched upon a situation about half a mile from the town, on the north-west side, possessing most if not all the requisites for the purpose. It belonged to his grace the duke of Norfolk, who with the utmost readiness consented to an exchange, directing his agents to lean to the interests of the charity in every doubtful point. Mr. Rawsthorne was chosen to conduct the building through its several stages; and the first stone was laid on Wednesday the 4th of September 1793 by Mr. Swallow as deputy of Mrs. Fell; and on Wednesday the 4th of October 1797 it was opened for the reception of patients.

The building is of stone got in the neighbourhood: and while its extent and prosperity do the utmost credit to the persons to whom it owes its existence, so do the simplicity and beauty of the exterior, no less than the convenient internal arrangement, to the ingenious architect by whom it was planned. Secured from the annoyance of manufactures and the too near approach of other buildings, by the purchase of about thirty-one acres of the land which surrounds it, it stands a conspicuous and beautiful object from two of the principal approaches to the town.

To persons suffering from accidents its doors are always open: to the sick, on the recommendation of subscribers. Mr. Ernest the house surgeon and apothecary, who has annually received the cordial thanks of the subscribers for the able and assiduous manner in which he has discharged the duties of his important office, has undertaken also the superintendence of a Jennerian institution connected with this establishment. This was begun in 1802, and to June 1815, 12,904 persons had been inoculated with the vaccine lymph. The total number of in-patients and out-patients up to the same period was 16,247. Between June 1814 and June 1815, the number of persons admitted as in-patients was 424, out-patients 720. 45 in-patients and 69 out-patients were admitted on sudden accidents.

Nearly the whole of the sum originally subscribed was expended in the purchase of the land and the erection of the building. The annual expenses are defrayed out of benefactions and legacies, and by annual contributions. In the list of benefactors one deserves particular notice. ' A gentleman who desires his name may not be known, by Messrs. Thos. Coutts and Co. bankers in London, 6337l. 2s. 10d.' The same bountiful hand presented at the same time two of the like sums (being the proceeds of the sale of 30,000l. three per cent. stock) to the infirmaries at Nottingham and Derby.

This institution owed much at its commencement to the active spirit and ability of Dr. Browne, a gentleman who devoted considerable talents to the interest of the town, and whose death on the 10th of April 1810 was felt by all as a common loss; a feeling testified by the unusual tribute of a public mourning. He was chairman of the weekly board of governors till his death. His successor was the Rev. Thomas Radford; to whom succeeded the present chairman, the Rev. Thomas Sutton.

HANBY'S CHARITY.

Mr. Thomas Hanby by his last will and testament dated on the 12th of January 1782 gave to his late partner [in the house of Sitwell, Tappenden, and Hanby, in Foster-lane, London] John Tappenden esq. and James Mitchell esquire, and the survivor of them, 10,000l. three per cent. consolidated bank annuities stock, upon trust to pay the annual dividends arising therefrom to his wife: and on her decease to transfer 8000l. of it to the Company of Cutlers, upon trust to employ the proceeds of 3000l. in the education and

maintenance of children in the boys' charity school as before mentioned, and to lay out the proceeds of the remaining 5000l. for the benefit of poor housekeepers in the parish of Sheffield, members of the church of England, of sober life and conversation, and of fifty years of age, and upwards, of whom two-thirds are to be men, and one-third women: each of whom is to receive on the 29th day of July (the testator's birthday) twenty shillings in money, a black hat and a blue cloth coat or cloak: the nomination to be in the master and two wardens of the Company of Cutlers for the time being, the past-masters, the church-burgesses, the vicar and church-wardens for the time being; the kindred of the testator always to have the preference, few of whom have hitherto applied. The number to be limited only by the extent of the dividends.

Mr. Hanby died on Christmas-day 1786, and Mrs. Hanby, who was sister to Caslon the letter-founder, on the 15th of January 1797.

HUDSON'S CHARITY.

Mr. Joseph Hudson of London, hardwareman, left by will 200l. to be laid out at interest, and out of the proceeds to pay ten shillings each to sixteen of the most indigent file-makers in the town of Sheffield. This charity is in the patronage of the Cutlers' Company.

SICK-CLUBS, AND THE FEMALE BENEFIT SOCIETY.

Benefit-societies or Sick-clubs were introduced very early among the mechanics of Sheffield. It may be worth recording that these most meritorious and useful associations were first established at Sheffield in 1728 by John Hancock, a scissor-smith, who had witnessed something of the kind in Ireland. So it is said in a pamphlet on the state of the poor in Sheffield published in 1774. But in a list of these societies which was circulated about twenty years ago, the oldest then existing was represented as established on the 20th of September 1720. Three then in being originated in 1732, and five more which were founded before 1750. Nothing but great forbearance on the part of claimants on the funds of these societies could have continued their existence for so long a time, founded as they were at first on insufficient information, and with a liberality which it was impossible to sustain without the assistance of honorary members, to which at the first formation of these societies the persons who joined them did not look. Every thing connected with these institutions is highly creditable to the character of the inferior classes of the town of Sheffield. They evince the presence of foresight, and the willingness (so hard to be produced in any class of society) of forgoing a present good for a remote and contingent advantage. The sums paid from the stock of the societies have been immense. From the fifty-two which existed in 1786, there were paid in that year 3670l. 15s. 7½d. to sick members. There is a provision not only for the time of sickness, but for the bringing decently to the earth the remains of those who have been members. And when it has happened, as unfortunately in many instances it has happened, that the too great liberality of the plan has led to the dissolution of one of these societies, those which maintained their ground have voluntarily received the aged, sick, and expensive members of the decayed society, bringing with them only the little pittance which belonged to them on the division of what remained of their own funds. Such acts of genuine humanity require no eulogium.—There are at present about 50 men's and 8 women's benefit-societies. The contribution is for the most part 1s. 3d. per month. And the allowance when sick 10s. per week, for some weeks, and afterwards 5s. per week so long as the incapacity for labour continues: and finally 8l. to the family on the death of a member, or 2l. to any married member on the death of his wife, and 6l. to his family on his own decease. Well-managed as they are, it certainly may be a question with the more opulent part of the community, whether they present not the opportunity of doing more certain good with the less risk of diminishing the spirit of frugality and of providence, than schemes which propose to improve the condition of the poor in which the beneficiaries are merely passive.

The first woman's society of this kind is that called by way of eminence 'THE FEMALE BENEFIT SOCIETY.' It was founded in 1795, and the mixture of honorary and benefited members formed from the first a part of the plan. It owes much of its success to the attention, care, and zeal of an enlightened and benevolent lady, Miss Cheney, who will excuse the liberty taken in introducing her name on this occasion. The adaptation of the claims to the contributions has been founded on juster data: and every thing promises to make this a permanent as it is a most valuable part of the plans devised by the humane and liberal for limiting the misery and increasing the comforts of the poor of Sheffield. In July 1818 the property of this society was rather more than 1500l. The number of honorary members was 145, of benefited 574.

I cannot conclude this section without observing, that some excellent remarks on the structure and management of such associations as this, may be found in a pamphlet published in 1805, by Mrs. Cappe of York, entitled ' Observations on Charity Schools, Female Friendly Societies, &c.'

SOCIETY FOR BETTERING THE CONDITION OF THE POOR.

This society of great exertions, but small pretensions, was founded in the spring of 1803. It owes its origin to a few individuals, principally of the society of Quakers. It is the peculiar feature of this institution that its members visit the poor at their own houses, and thus become intimately acquainted with their character and their wants. They propose premiums for frugality and foresight, by inviting the poor to make small deposits of money which are returned to them with a large increase in articles of clothing. They supply the peculiar wants of the sick. They act as a puerperal charity. They support schools for children and adults: and, though last not least worthy the imitation of others, they pay particular attention to the cleanliness of the houses of those persons with whom in their

visits they become acquainted. It was in conversation among the members of this society that the scheme for establishing a court of requests in Sheffield for the recovery of small debts originated. This society, small and inconsiderable at first, soon gained the public confidence: and when in the years 1809 and 1812 money was collected at Sheffield for the relief of the peculiar distress which then prevailed, a considerable portion of what was collected was placed under the management of the committee of this society. But a still more remarkable proof of the public confidence was exhibited in the memorable winter of 1816-1817[1]. At that period of deep and universal distress, the sum of 2857l. was subscribed at Sheffield for the relief of the poor. This large sum, together with 500l. which was sent from the London association for the relief of the manufacturing districts, was placed at the disposal of this society, with a confidence which the result showed was not misplaced.

With this society is connected the school known by the name of THE SCHOOL OF INDUSTRY.

There are two other societies similar in plan and operation with this, called The Benevolent and The Compassionate Societies.

SOCIETY FOR SUPERSEDING THE NECESSITY OF CLIMBING BOYS.

In the year 1803 a letter signed ' Pity' appeared in The Iris, or Sheffield Advertiser, which under the direction of its amiable proprietor has been always open to every appeal in behalf of humanity, as well as to every suggestion for the improvement in any way of the town which he has chosen for his residence. Its object was to invite the attention of the public to the situation of that wretched class of beings the children employed in the service of the master chimney-sweepers. It proceeded from the humane and enlightened mind of Mr. T. A. Ward of Park-house, a gentleman to whom his native town has already many obligations. It was immediately answered by Mr. Samuel Roberts of Park-grange, and the formation of this society was the consequence. They began by the introduction of machinery adapted to the purpose for which the children had been employed, and succeeded to a certain extent in obtaining for it the approbation of the inhabitants. But many were unwilling to change their old practice; and more were lukewarm in their support. But the society did not confine itself to what might be done at Sheffield. Mr. Roberts in particular laboured to procure a more extended attention to the subject, and the circulation of his ' Tales of the Poor' has in more than one instance been the means of inciting the humane in other places to the attempt of obtaining the utter abolition of the practice. The Sheffield society has been the means of bringing this subject under the consideration of parliament: and it is hoped that in a future session such enactments may be made as will

[1] As a proof of the peculiar and aggravated distress of that period, the following is a statement of the casual poor relieved by the overseers, weekly, from 30th of November 1816 to the 1st of March 1817, for the township of Sheffield only:

			No. of Families.				Amount paid.					No. of Families.				Amount paid.
1816.	Nov. 30.	. . .	840	. . .	£328		1817.	Jan. 18.	. . .	1430	. . .	£487
	Dec. 7.	. . .	906	. . .	362			25.	. . .	1383	. . .	464
	14.	. . .	1100	. . .	400			Feb. 1.	. . .	1353	. . .	461
	21.	. . .	1197	. . .	403			8.	. . .	1281	. . .	424
	28.	. . .	1260	. . .	437			15.	. . .	1247	. . .	413
1817.	Jan. 4.	. . .	1417	. . .	506			22.	. . .	1208	. . .	393
	11.	. . .	1504	. . .	509			Mar. 1.	. . .	1201	. . .	377

secure the young and defenceless from the possibility of being engaged in an employment so injurious, so dangerous, and so degrading.

SOCIETY FOR THE RELIEF OF THE AGED.

The office of overseer of the poor of Sheffield, burthensome as it is in so populous a township, has always been held by the inhabitants, and the duties of it performed in person. Here has been no hired and permanent overseer; but whatever advantage a township may obtain in the more easy detection of imposture by the employment of the same person year after year in the office, is gained by having a permanent vestry clerk as an assessor with the overseers. One advantage, and a great one it is, arising from gentlemen performing personally the duties of this office, has been, that it has led the minds of several persons to a more attentive consideration of the state of the poor and the best means of improving it, which has been pursued after the year of their engagement has expired. It was in the year in which he served the office that the mind of Mr. Roberts, whom we have just had occasion to mention, was first peculiarly turned to this subject. To him we owe much valuable information on the state of the poor in Sheffield, communicated through various channels, as well as many useful suggestions for its improvement. And to him we owe the establishment of a society which has for its object to pay attention to those poor and necessitous persons who have reached an advanced period of life; many of whom have received much valuable assistance and real comfort from the attentions of members of this society, and the relief which the liberality of the public has put it into their power to afford. At present their attention is confined to the case of aged females.

LANCASTERIAN SCHOOL.

In 1809 Joseph Lancaster delivered a lecture at Sheffield, on the new mode of instruction practised in the Borough School. Here, as in almost every other large town, the subject was immediately taken up, and in a few months a school consisting of nearly a thousand boys, under the superintendance of a single master, was in full and perfect operation. A large building in the West Bar Green, which had formerly been used as an iron-work, was engaged for the use of the school; and there it continues to be held, supported by the voluntary contributions of persons of all descriptions. In 1815 a Lancasterian school for girls was founded.

THE NATIONAL DISTRICT SOCIETY'S SCHOOLS.

These are of a few years later origin than the Lancasterian school. Five hundred boys and as many girls are here educated. The building is in Carver-street; and there is an auxiliary one in Garden-street containing 120 girls. These schools are said to present a complete model of the Madras system of education, and to be not inferior in number or discipline to any similar establishment in the kingdom. The scholars in these schools attend divine service at some of the churches in the town twice every Sunday.

PARSONS'S CHARITY.

Mrs. Mary Parsons, sister and heir of Mr. John Parsons, a gentleman who had acquired considerable property in the silver-plated manufactory of Sheffield, gave by will 1500l. to be invested in the public funds, the interest or dividends thereof to be annually distributed among forty-eight aged, infirm, and poor silver-platers, and 2l. to a clergyman for preaching a sermon on the anniversary of Saint John the Baptist for ever. She died on the 30th of September 1815.

To these may be added a few minor donations taken from the table of benefactors in the parish-church.

1621. Mr. Robert Rollinson of Sheffield, mercer, gave by will 20s. per annum to the church, 40s. to the Cutlers' Company, 10l. to the workhouse, and 10l. to the free-school.—So it is stated on the table of benefactors. This was the person who gave the two houses for the assistant-ministers, which I find in Burton's notes from Torre's collections he *built* for the purpose; and that he also ' bought thirty buckets, and hooks to hang them on in the church, made a large pool to contain water at the head of the town, and gave lands to the school.' Barker-pool existed before this time. He probably enlarged and otherwise improved it.

1657. John Crook settled 3l. yearly for the maintenance of a woman to teach poor children to read.

1699. Mr. Richard Boughton by his will charged his lands called Gill Carr with the payment of 5l. per annum for the use of poor cutlers and scissor-smiths.

1727. Mr. Francis Greaves gave to the churchwardens 30l., the interest to be given to such poor persons as have no pension from the town, every Christmas eve for ever.

The last thirty years have thus been fruitful of schemes devised by the humane and liberal for combating ignorance and misery in whatever form they may appear. Nor have the inhabitants of Sheffield showed themselves on any occasion regardless of those applicants, of whatever country or whatever class, who seemed to present a reasonable claim on the liberality of the British public. The Hibernian Society, the Society for the Conversion of the Jews, the Missionary Societies, the Bible Societies, (whether those connected with the Establishment or supported indifferently by members of the Establishment and others,) have found. no more zealous supporters than at this place in the higher, the middle, and the lower ranks of life. It remains only to add that Sheffield has its HUMANE SOCIETY, which is supported in a manner quite adequate to its confined demands: societies for the distribution of moral and religious tracts; and a bank for savings. So that it may be truly said, that there are few cases of want or misery for which relief is not provided ; and that Sheffield, populous but poor in comparison with many other places, is rich in the good works of charity.

We now proceed to some further notices of the parish of Sheffield, arranged according to proximity of situation, and not to the order of time.

𝕿opographical 𝕾urbey of the 𝕻arish of 𝕾heffield.

THE parish of Sheffield is divided into six townships:—

SHEFFIELD,	UPPER-HALLAM,	BRIGHTSIDE-BYERLOW,
ECCLESALL-BYERLOW,	NETHER-HALLAM,	ATTERCLIFFE-CUM-DARNALL.

I.

𝕿he 𝕿ownship of 𝕾heffield.

THE Park, the Park-hill, the greatest part of the town of Sheffield, and a small portion of the parish lying north-west of the town, comprehending the villages of Porto-Bello and Leavy-Greave, and reaching to the brow of the hill that overhangs the reservoirs on Crooks-moor, form the township of Sheffield. From that brow the boundary is an irregular line which passes beyond the infirmary to the Don opposite to Neepsend. To this may be added a small tract lying along the Don near the Castle-hill which was formerly orchards and other appendages of the castle. The whole of this township lies on the right bank of the Don, and its area is 3436¼ acres. In 1811 the persons male and female inhabiting this district amounted to 35,840.

A century ago the whole town of Sheffield lay within the township. But the formation of new streets has extended it on the south into the township of Ecclesall-Byerlow, and even united to it the hamlet of Little Sheffield lying in that township. Much building on the left bank of the Don in the township of Brightside-Byerlow must now be considered as part of the town of Sheffield.

The Park contained, according to Harrison's survey made in 1637, 2461 acres 3 roods and 11 perches, all within a ring-fence of eight miles. This is still the entire property of his grace the duke of Norfolk, no part of it having been included in the late acts for the sale of portions of the Yorkshire estates of the family. There were two principal entrances to the park: one at the place still called the Park-gate, near the hospital and opposite to the castle; the other opened upon Gleadleys-moor. The Sheaf flowed through the park. The ancient foot-path from Sheffield to the White-house, and from thence to Heeley,

passed under the paling. Near Newfield-green is some old walling that seems to have been a part of the ancient inclosure. It would appear from the manner in which it is laid down in the old maps of Yorkshire, that the park extended beyond the limits of the parish of Sheffield towards Gleadleys and Hansworth. The boundary of the township of Attercliffe-cum-Darnall we may safely assume as its ancient limits on that side.

This was the park of the lords of the manor of Sheffield. It was a park by prescription. At least no royal charter can now be produced for converting this fine tract of land to the purposes of a park. If it be the tract to which the Domesday surveyors point, when they tell us that the manors of Attercliffe and Sheffield were once demesne-land of the manor of Hallam, it may claim an antiquity to which few such inclosures can make pretensions. The grant of Richard de Lovetot to the monks of Ecclesfield, of the tythe of his venison in Hallamshire, shows that as early as the time of King Stephen deer were running in the woods of Sheffield, and probably in this very inclosure. While the Furnivals and Talbots maintained their state at Sheffield-castle, it was used for their pleasure and the more immediate supply of their table. Dodsworth has preserved the memory of a singular and indeed a savage custom of which this park was formerly the scene. In the topographical notes which he made at Sheffield in 1620, he writes that ' the late Gilbert earl of Shrewsbury was wont on every yeare on a certayne day to have many bucks lodged in a meadow near the towne side about a mile in compasse, to which place repaired allmost all the apron-men of the parish, and had liberty to kill and carry away as many as they could with their hands; and did kill some tymes twenty, and had money given them for wine by the Earle[1].'

---

[1] Dods. MSS. in Bibl. Bodl. vol. clx. f. 132 b. The singularity of this custom awakened Dodsworth's curiosity. He wished to make further inquiry into its origin and continuance, but nothing more is found among his papers. May not the Cutlers' venison feast in September have grown out of this custom ?

When the mansions at Sheffield became deserted, it was an object of less consequence to keep up the stock of deer: but when Harrison's survey was made, there were still a thousand fallow-deer in the park, and ' of deer of antler, two hundred.'

In 1692, Henry duke of Norfolk was engaged in legal discussions with the inhabitants of Hansworth, the Intake and Gleadleys, respecting the right of road through the park to the market at Sheffield. He filed a bill in Chancery against Burrowes Trippett gentleman and others deforciants. A commission issued to William Jessop esquire, Thomas Barlow, Joseph Banks, and Richard Bacon, gentlemen, to receive and record evidence that could be given by several aged inhabitants of these parts; who on the 14th day of January in that year took the depositions following, which throw some light upon the state of this part of the parish, while yet it was, what now it is only in name—a park.

David Lee of Attercliffe, aged 80 years, deposed that he had known the road in question through the park seventy years: that previously to the Civil Wars no persons passed without asking leave at Samuel Newbolt's house, that being the gate next Gleadleys-moor. The other gate next the town of Sheffield was generally open, because it was the way from the town to the coal-mines in the park which belonged to the owner of the park. But still the road before the Civil Wars was known to be only a road on sufferance, and he had known the London carriers pay money for liberty to pass that way.

When he was asked if he knew another road by the hospital along the top of the park-hill to the Intake, and so into the road from Sheffield to London, he answered that it was only a private way to the manour, till about seventy years before, it came to be much used.

He further deposed that Shear-bridge was the only way into the park; that it was built and repaired by the lords, and that the roads through the park were also maintained at their expense.

John Barber of Sheffield-park, aged 76, knew the road in question, and that it was always considered to be a private road. He remembered that ' John Wilson was desirous to come that way with his wain and cart, and was forced several years together to come by Newfield-green and Heeley to Sheffield, though the same was much about, and worst way by a great deal; and though he used all endeavours to come through the park by the way aforesaid.' And further said, ' that he, this deponent, thirty years or thereabouts before the death of James Wardley, this deponent's uncle, (who died about thirty years since, and who had for fifty years before his death been a keeper and lived in the said Sheffield-park) lived and remained with him the said James, who was ninety-five years old when he died. And he, this deponent, was educated with him the said James Wardley; and saith that the said James Wardley often and frequently told this deponent that there was no highway through the said park, but only a way of sufferance: and that Gilbert earl of Shrewsbury, who was owner of the said park, and to whom the said James was keeper therein, did not only use to turn cart-loads and carriages, but also gentlemen and saddle-horses; and that the common highway from Sheffield to Gleadleys-moor, and so on to London, was by Little Sheffield, Heeley, and Newfield-

green, which appeared to be very ancient way, being worne very deep.'

Of the other road to the Intake he said that it was only a private path to the manour, and that at the end was a gate which was always kept locked.

Nathan Garlicke of Heeley, cutler, aged 60, deposed that the ancient high road from Sheffield to London was by Newfield-green; that he had seen carriers and pack-horses go that way; and that his father, who was eighty years of age at the time of his death, always said the same.

Robert Simon of Gleadleys, joiner, aged 60, had taken coal-pits on lease, and sold the coal to John Wilson, who charged his servants not to go through the park, lest he should be sued as a trespasser.

Thomas Lee of Sheffield, dyer, aged 47, deposed that he ' knoweth a certain pretended highway leading from Sheffield town to Gleadleys-moor, by and through the Low Oaks and Samuel Newbolt's house, and that he hath known the same as long since as ever he can remember; and that he was born and brought up, and ever since, and still lives hard by the park-gate leading from Sheffield town, and on the said way. And that as long as he can remember, he has several days and times been present at that park-gate leading from Sheffield town end to both the ways through the park, and seen one Thomas Fox and yeoman Eyre, upon the account of the owner of the said park, stand several days and times, and keep the said park-gate chained up, and make passengers pay money, or not suffer them to come that way. And this deponent hath seen several persons, and on several days and times, pay money for coming that way; and saith that he the better remembered the same, for that the said keepers of the said gate, when they had got any little quantity of money of persons for coming that way, used to send for ale out of it, and this deponent hath a great many times sat by them, and drunk with them of the said ale.'—He further said that he had been lessee of the farm at the Low Oaks, and about eight years before had obtained a verdict on an action for trespass against one George Wright who had gone that way.

Ralph Hunter of Sheffield, husbandman, aged 60, was present at the trial between the last deponent and George Wright of Mansfield, carrier. The great way by the Low Oaks was stopped about twenty years before. Remembered Shear-bridge being of wood, and that it was built of stone about thirty years ago by the lord.

Nicholas Shiercliffe of Sheffield, cutler, aged 86, deposed that he had known the road seventy-five years, and that ' before the unhappy Civil Wars broke out, the gate of the said park next Gleadleys-moor was by order of the owner of the said park four times every year stopped up, to prevent the same being claimed as a highway; and that several times he hath seen the same chained up, and the carriers' pack-horses, carts, and carriages stopped from going that way without asking leave, or paying something.' He also deposed, that the ancient highway leading from Sheffield to the north-east part of Hansworth parish was through Attercliffe and Darnall, and to the south-east part of the said parish through Little Sheffield, Heeley, and Newfield-green, and so to London.

Richard Abdy of Sheffield, cutler, aged 82, deposed,

Drawn & Engraved by E Finden

_ Remains of Sheffield Manor.

Page 222.

Published Oct 1 1819 by Rodwell & Martin Bond Street

that ' he and his master going on the said way with a stithy of iron about sixty years ago, found the gate at the house, now in Newbolt's possession, locked up, and his master made him, this deponent, climb over the said gate to ask leave at the said house, which he did, and upon asking leave they were suffered to pass1.'

Other persons deposed to the same effect on several of the points comprised in what is above abstracted. There is now one turnpike high-road from Sheffield to Worksop and Mansfield passing through the park and dividing it into two nearly equal portions.

At the time of Harrison's survey much of the park was let as open pasture land: and at that time or soon after coal-pits and iron-stone-pits were opened within its precincts. When it was divided into farms, small buildings which had been erected in different parts of it as lodges for the keepers were converted into farm-houses, and others were erected. The farms are both arable and pasture. This is the least populous part of the parish. But on the west side of it several houses have been erected within the last thirty years by mer-chants of Sheffield, allured by the beauty of the situa-tion and its contiguity to the town.

We have already had occasion to observe that the park, now so destitute of timber, once abounded in forest-trees of the noblest growth. Some were indi-genous, but others planted, probably by the fourth earl of Shrewsbury when he built a country residence in this park, at the beginning of the sixteenth cen-tury, called Sheffield Manour2, and sometimes Sheffield Lodge. The general *style* seems to have been long straight avenues of oaks and walnuts, pointing to-wards the manour which stood nearly in the centre of the park.

' The scite of Sheffield lodge,' says Harrison, who lived when the edifice was entire, ' standing on a hill in the midst of the park, being fairly built with stone and timber, with an inward court and an outward court, two gardens, and three yeards, containeth 4 acres, 1 rood, 15 perches.' It were to be wished that he had left us a more circumstantial detail of this edifice, and that Sir William Dugdale, who examined it thirty years later, had not contented himself with delineating the few armorial decorations of its great gallery. It is in the dilapidated and grey remains of this vast edifice, and in its weed-grown courts, that the spirit of feudal magnificence which once inhabited this district seems still to linger. It is only here and among the monu-mental effigies of its noble inhabitants, that sensible objects compel us to look back to a time when a state of society existed at Sheffield essentially different from that which now prevails there. Here the mind cannot resist impressions from the days which are passed. We recall the chieftain of the age of the eighth Henry living here in the bosom of his numerous family, and unwillingly issuing forth to disperse the cloud of re--bellion which was gathered in the north: we see the fallen Wolsey treading the gallery with heavy step, or engaged in close conference with his courteous host in one of its windowed recesses, and hearing the name of Kingston with alarm, as described in the vivid nar-

rative of his faithful Cavendish; and at the window which still bears her name, may view the victim of the lawless power of Elizabeth looking for the friend who was to bring the means of descent from a height so fearful, that she might regain the liberty she loved; while the whole pile is calculated to dispose the mind to serious contemplation on the mutability of all hu-man affairs.

It is to be regretted that when the owners of this edifice were no longer concerned to uphold its fabric, they did not allow it to remain sacred to Quiet and Meditation. If it be said that the purposes of utility and benevolence are better answered by allowing some of the poorest of the poor to make their habitation in these once splendid apartments, and to build their brick cottages against and amongst the walls of the edifice, I answer that man has a mind as well as a body to be fed, and that it is amongst the higher offices of benevolence to put it into his power to imbibe high and holy sentiments. Such intrusions might have found their way into the hallowed precincts of Rievaulx or Kirkstal. Not a less numerous tenantry now pos-sess these remains, than when the mansion was entire and furnished accommodation to the earl of Shrews-bury and his long retinue. One effect of the intro-duction of this new species of inhabitants has been to render it impossible to recover the exact arrange-ment of its various apartments, or to assign the parti-cular appropriation of some which remain entire. The house which is now the residence of the tenant of the manour-farm seems to have been built at a later pe-riod than the other parts of the edifice, by earl Gil-bert. This was an outer porter's lodge. Between it and the main body of the building rose two lofty oc-tagonal towers about sixty feet apart, built of stone but cased with brick, and in later times finely mantled with ivy. Between these was the principal entrance to the court, where a noble flight of steps led to the door which opened into what was called the great gal-lery. The last of these towers fell in the great storm in the night of March the 2d 1793.

It was not the practice of our ancestors to introduce much architectural ornament in their dwelling-houses. Ornament was reserved for the public and especially for ecclesiastical edifices. There is nothing in the ruins of Sheffield-manour which as a single object presents a fine subject for the pencil, and as a whole the ruin is less picturesque than it was fifty years ago, when the twin towers were both standing. Its interest as a building arises not from the beauty of minute portions, but from the *extent* of the whole. Of the present state and appearance of the ruins the engrav-ings here given from faithful and beautiful drawings will long preserve the memory, when the ruins them-selves shall have perished: but no pencil, no pen could do justice to the magnificent panorama of distant scenery which spreads around the site of this edifice. The founder, while he took care to screen it from the winds by close and thick plantations up to its very gates, placed it on the highest point in the park. The fir-crowned heights of Norton, the sweet vale of Beau-chief, the purple moor of Totley, and the barren hills

1 From the original record of the depositions at the office of his grace the duke of Norfolk at Sheffield.
2 The Talbots were fond of giving the name of manour to their houses.

They had Worksop-manour, Winfield-manour, Brierley-manour, and Sheffield-manour.

of the Peak, the thick woods of Wharncliffe and Wentworth, the widening vale of the Don, and the hills of
Laughton and Hansworth, each distinguishable by its
spire, are all comprehended within the view from this
elevation. The manour itself, its towers and battlements appearing above the thick woods in which it
was embosomed, must have once formed a prominent
and striking object in the scenery from many points
of the surrounding country.

The armorial ornaments of the great gallery are
preserved by Sir William Dugdale in a manuscript
of exquisite beauty in the library of the College of
Arms, entitled '*Insignium, epitaphiorumque &c.
Ebor. exempla.*'

1. A talbot statant argent on a field parti per pale sable and
   gules: within the Garter.
2. The cross of Saint George within the Garter.
3. France and England quarterly within the Garter, and
   ensigned with a royal coronet.
4. The six great quarterings of Talbot, viz. Montgomery,

Talbot, Nevil, Furnival, Verdon, and Strange, impaling Hastings.
5. The same six quarterings impaling Walden.
6. France and England quarterly impaling Spain.

An inventory of 'the household stuff' here and at
the castle, as it stood in the time of Elizabeth, is preserved among the Talbot papers[1]. Fewer relics of its
former inhabitants have been found among the ruins
than might have been expected. At the public-house
(for a part of it is licensed for that purpose) are preserved a key and other trifles that have been found
here; and not long ago a small enamelled phial of neat
workmanship, and a gold coin of Philip and Mary in excellent preservation were picked up among the ruins[2].

At the manour the principal agent of the Norfolk
family resided till 1706. One of these, Mr. Francis
Ratcliffe, was living there in 1666, when Sir William
Dugdale held his visitation for the county of York in
his character of Norroy-king-at-arms. A few additions
are made below to the pedigree which he entered.

PEDIGREE of RATCLIFFE of SHEFFIELD-MANOUR and the HOLMES.

Rotherham Ratcliffe[3], == ---- dau. of ---- Cole,
of Studham, co. Bucks. | of ------ co. Bucks.
Died 1640.

Thomas Ratcliffe, eldest son and heir. Citizen of London.	Anne Allison, of == Francis Ratcliffe, of Sheffield-manour, == Anne Trapps, of Houndhill, second

Thomas Ratcliffe, eldest son and heir. Citizen of London.

Anne Allison, of Wem, co. Salop. 1st wife. Died without issue. Buried at Sheffield 9 Sep. 1656.

Francis Ratcliffe, of Sheffield-manour, gentleman, aged 44, 10 April 1666. Made his will 29 May 1678, in which he calls himself, his wife, and children, Ratcliffe alias Wratten. Was buried in the chancel of the parish-church of Sheffield, 16 July 1685.

Anne Trapps, of Houndhill, second wife, dau. of Robert Trapps Birnand enquire, son and heir of Sir Francis Trapps Birnand, of Harrowgate, knight. Married 8 July 1658. Died at Holme-Hall near Rotherham, and was bur. at Sheffield 22 Feb. 1710-11.

Henry Ratcliffe, == Mary ----	Francis Ratcliffe,	Thomas Ratcliffe,	Robert Ratcliffe,	Mary Ratcliffe,	Anne Ratcliffe,

Henry Ratcliffe, of Holme-Hall in the parish of Rotherham, gent. Bap. at Sheffield 27 Oct. 1661. Buried there 2 Feb. 1740-11.

Mary ---- Buried at Sheffield 28 Jan. 1688-9.

Francis Ratcliffe, 2d son, bap. at Sheffield 20 July 1665. Living 1678.

Thomas Ratcliffe, 3d son, bap. at Sheffield 21 April 1668. Living 1678.

Robert Ratcliffe, 4th son, of Holme-Hall, gent. bap. at Sheffield 17 October 1670. Buried there 14 June 1699.

Mary Ratcliffe, bap. at Sheffield 14 May 1659, became the wife of Luke Ogle, and dying 25 March 1684, was bur. in the parish-church of Sheffield.

Anne Ratcliffe, bap. at Sheffield 7 Dec. 1677, and was buried in the parish-church of Sheffield.

Francis Ratcliffe, of Holme-Hall, gentleman. Bap. at Rotherham 24 August 1687. By his will dated 6 March 1745-6 he gave his real estate to his friend and sole executor John Kent, of Kimberworth, gentleman; died soon after, and was buried with his family in the parish-church of Sheffield on the 1 April 1746.

The Park-hill, the abrupt ascent from the Sheaf,
is a populous suburb to Sheffield. It is chiefly inhabited by persons employed in the collieries, or engaged
in various branches of the Sheffield manufactures.
Here is a school with an endowment of thirty pounds
a year, for which a hundred children are to be taught
reading, writing, and accompts.

The hospital of Gilbert earl of Shrewsbury stands
at the foot of the hill, and close to the Sheaf. To the
chapel of this hospital many of the inhabitants of the
Park and Park-hill resort for public worship.

The passage into the town from the park is over
the Sheaf-bridge, or, as it was anciently and is now
commonly and properly called, the Shear-bridge. That
is its name: a name which may assist us in investi-

gating the etymology of the name of Sheffield, the
field not on the Sheaf but on the Shea, a word formed
from the Saxon ea, water[4], to which the f has been
corruptly added, borrowed from its adjunct field. In
the name of the bridge over this stream the letter does
not appear, but instead of it a consonant borrowed
from the word with which the name of the stream is
connected. This bridge was for a long time of wood
only. It was the private property of the lords of the
manor, and was first built of stone by the earl of Arundel in 1637. It was rebuilt in 1769. It led directly
to one entrance to the castle.

In Harrison's survey, to which we have before referred, we have this account of the castle and its appendages.

[2] The former of these is in the curious museum of Mr. William Staniforth, senior surgeon of the Sheffield general infirmary.—A considerable
hoard of silver-plate was found in the park in 1787. An imperfect description of it was published in the newspapers of the time; and from
the account given of the engraved ornaments, I should conclude that it
had been stolen from Sandbeck, and secreted here.
[3] This is the name as it stands in C. 40. MS. in Col. Arm. Sir William
Dugdale's visitation-book. I suspect it should be *Roger*. In the register
of matriculations at University College Oxford is this entry, for which

I am obliged to the reverend Philip Bliss of St. John's. 'Jun. 8. 1638.
Franc. Ratclyff, fil. Rogeri Ratclyff de London, arm. ætat. 15.' The C.
40, though a most valuable document, has not been compiled with all
the care that such a work demanded: or, if the original record was well
compiled, it has suffered something in the transcription. I would refer
those whom it may concern, as one proof, to the pedigree of Crawshaw
of Arksey near Doncaster.
[4] For this etymology of the name of the stream from which the town
takes its name, the author is indebted to a very ingenious and able ety-
mologist and antiquary.

'Sheffield Castle, very spacious, built about an inward court. On the south side an outward court yard or fould, builded round with divers houses of officers, as an armoury, barns, stables, and divers lodgings, all containing by measure . . . .

	A. R.	P.
'Sheffeild Castle, ... all containing by measure	4 0	30¼

Three orchards adjoining: the first whereof is compassed with a stone wall, and lyeth between the river called the Little Sheath on the west, and the Little Park on the east, containing . .

... and the Little Park on the east, containing	5 1	0¼

Item the second orchard called the Nursery, and lyeth near the aforesaid orchard towards the south, and a parcel of ground called the Hop-yeard towards the north, containing . . . .

... the Hop-yeard towards the north, containing	1 1	25 7/10
The third orchard near the Nursery . . .	6 0	24¾
The Hop-yeard	1 0	26 4/10
The Cock pitt yard	0 2	28 7/10
In occupation of the keeper of the castle . .	18 3	16¼

Of the foundation of the castle of Sheffield, of its inhabitants, and finally of its demolition, every thing has already been said in the historical part of the pre-sent work. It remains therefore only to say, that so total has been the destruction of it, and so completely is its site occupied by modern buildings, that the only vestiges of it are some portions of what appear to have been ancient cellars of the castle, now belonging to the hotel. It seems to have occupied the whole space between the Wain-gate, Dixon-lane, and the rivers: and to have had a communication by a drawbridge with the orchards on the right bank of the Sheaf, where now is preparing the bason of the Sheffield canal. The subterraneous connexion between this place and the Manour, a mile and a half distant, may be mentioned, to add one more to the instances of traditions so palpably absurd connected with ancient edifices.

An old half-timbered house in the Pónds was undoubtedly an appendage to the castle. Tradition says it was the laundry. It is called in the inventory before mentioned 'The hawle at the Poandes.'

The gaol or prison for the manor of Sheffield, another ancient dependance on the castle, was situated in the heart of the town on the east side of King-street. A particular description of this prison, which was examined with a scrutinizing eye by Mr. Nield in 1801, may be found in the *Gentleman's Magazine*, vol. lxxv. p. 300. It has been lately taken down.

Close to the castle was a bridge over the Don in the time of Henry II. It was built anew in the reign of Henry VII. pursuant to an agreement entered into for that purpose between Sir John Plesaunce vicar of Sheffield and William Hill master-mason.

'This Indenture berys wytness that Syr John Plesaunce vicar of Sheffeld and William Hyll of the same maister mason have bargained for the makyng a Brygge of ston undyr this fourme that follows: yat is to wytt; that the said William Hyll shall make a suffycient brigge over the watyr of Dune neghe the castell of Sheffeld, wele and suffyciently after the sight of workmen of the same crafte and gode men of the parysh. The whych shall be made v. arches embowed, IIII. jowels, and II. heedys, with sure butments at eythyr ende. Also the sayd William shall mak of his own costys all mason worke, and he shall pay for the cleusyng of the ground werk for all his partners, and his scaffyld makyng. The stoppyng of the watyr, and the makyng of centres shall be of both theyr costys equally deelyd. And the said Syr John Plesaunce shall cause all manner of stuff nedeful to the said werk to be brought to the grounde of the parysh cost, yat is to say, lyme, ston, sande, and tymber, to mak the centres of the scaffaldys and all oder thyng yat long to the werk. And the said William shall hafe for the makyng of it a c. markys to be paid like as the werke is wroght; and when the thyrd part of the brygg is fully fynyshyd, the said William shall be content and paid of xxiil. ils. iiid. And when the secound part is fynyshyd he shall bafe in likewise. Also the said William has promysed by these Indentures yatt the said werke shall goe forthe contynually and not lie undone in his defaulte, upon payn of forfetyng xls. Also the said Syr John has promysed by these Indentures also, that the aforesaid payment shall be truly kept on his behalfe, upon payne of forfetyng xls. And to all these covenants and syngler afore rehersed truly to be kept on eythyr party, the sayd Syr John and William to these Indentures enterchangeably have set theyr sealys, these beyring wytteness, Nycholas Wortley gentylman, Richard Barnbe gentylman, John Wykersley gentylman, Robert Bytry, Richard Trippett, Richard Wyott, William Jackson, and others. Gyfen at Sheffeld the xx. day of the moneth February in the ycre of the reigne of Kyng Henry the VII. after the Conquest of England the fyrst.

At the bridge was a chapel: not on the bridge as at Rotherham and Wakefield, but at its foot. Chapels were usually erected on bridges, perhaps to collect alms from passengers. Here daily service was performed; and it may be remembered that the fourth earl of Shrewsbury directed by his last will and testament, that a priest should celebrate masses for his soul in this chapel for twenty years next after his decease. He died in 1541; so that before the twenty years were expired, the statute of the 1st Edward VI. swept away both his priest and his masses. The chapel itself was converted to secular uses, and we find in accompts of the Shrewsbury family that it was used as a wool ware-house in 1572[1]. It was afterwards inhabited as an alms-house, and was finally destroyed in one of the reparations of the bridge about the middle of the last century.

The Lady's-bridge is now repaired by the west riding, according to a decision of the justices of the peace at the sessions for that riding held at Pontefract in 1689.

On part of the castle fold stands a large inn erected on a tontine scheme about the year 1783.

On the opposite side of the street stands the new Town-hall, where the court of requests, the manor-courts, the sittings of the magistrates, &c., are held.

This part of the town is now called the Hay-market, but formerly the Bull-stake, which is also the name of a street in the city of Canterbury. It is, I fear, a name little creditable to the humanity of our ancestors.

In the Market-place was formerly a market-cross. There were two other crosses in the town, the Irish cross, and the Town-head cross.

The way leading from the Market-place to the parish-church is now called the High-street: but in Gosling's plan of Sheffield, and in old writings, it is called the Prior-gate, the way by which the prior of Worksop used to approach the church with which he was so intimately connected.

In George-street, a new street connecting the High-street with Norfolk-street, is a large building originally erected for an hotel and coffee-house, which has been since used as a merchant's warehouse, and now contains the books of the Subscription-library, lately removed to this place from Surrey-street[2].

At the south-east corner of the church-yard stood the Town-hall, which was built in 1700 and taken down in 1808. The church stands in a spacious square. Among the public buildings which contribute

to form the square are the two charity-schools, the Subscription News-room, the Cutlers'-hall, and the Parsonage-house; while a view is from some points gained of the east end of Saint James's church along Saint James's-street.

The church has been already described; and indeed little remains to be said in this section, the subjects which would have claimed our attention having already been noticed in the historical part.

On the front of the Cutlers'-hall are carved the arms of the London Company of Cutlers, (with whom however the cutlers of Hallamshire have no connexion,) and their untranslatable motto ' pour parvenir a bonne foy,' which Dr. Pegge proposes to correct by reading ayez for a, and then renders to succeed in business take care to keep up your credit[3]. The device on the seal of this corporation is a saltier of two swords with this inscription on the verge, SIGILL . MA . GARDIAN . INQVISIT . ASSISTENT . ET . COM . CVTTELAR . IN . HALLAMS ᴴ ᴿ .

In the hall are portraits of the reverend James Wilkinson, and Robert Athorpe Athorpe esquire, of Dinnington, and also a bust, from the hand of Chantrey, of Dr. Browne. On the first Thursday in September a dinner is given in this hall to the nobility and gentry of the neighbourhood, and the principal inhabitants of the town, called the Cutlers' feast. I find by a memorandum in a contempory hand, that on the 7th of September 1682, John Winter being master-cutler, the noblemen and gentlemen following were present.

The Duke of Norfolk.	Sir Ralph Knight.
Lord Clifford.	Francis Jessop, esquire.
Lord Coniers.	John Gill, esquire.
Lord Castleton.	— Taylor, esquire.
Lord Lexington.	— Wombwell, esquire.
The Hon. Sydney Wortley	— Knight, esquire.
Montague.	Lord Castleton's eldest son.
Sir Henry Marwood.	Lord Coniers' two sons.
Sir William Wyvil.	

A perfect Catalogue of the MASTER-CUTLERS.

1624.	Robert Sorsby.	1645.	William Warter.
5.	John Rawson.	6.	Thomas Ludlam.
6.	William Warter.	7.	Malin Sorsby.
7.	William Webster.	8.	Robert Brelsforth.
8.	Robert Sorsby.	9.	Richard Jackson.
9.	John Webster.	1650.	George Barnesley.
1630.	William Creswick.	1.	William Birley.
1.	Robert Stacie.	2.	Thomas Bate.
2.	James Creswick.	3.	Edward Barlow.
3.	George Valliance.	4.	William Crawshaw.
4.	William Walker.	5.	Thomas Pearson.
5.	Thomas Creswick.	6.	John Webster.
6.	Richard Wilkinson.	7.	Malin Sorsby.
7.	John Crook.	8.	John Rawson.
8.	James Creswick.	9.	William Creswick.
9.	Robert Carr.	1660.	Stephen Carr.
1640.	Robert Scargell.	1.	Robert Allen.
1.	Thomas Milward.	2.	James Staniforth.
2.	Richard Slack.	3.	James Newton.
3.	Richard Bayes.	4.	John Pearson.
4.	William Pell.	5.	Thomas Jennings.

[1] The earls of Shrewsbury were great dealers in this article. In the Talbot Papers, vol. G, f. 24, is a letter from William Every, dated the 4th of June 1580, offering the earl 400l. for his wool of that year.

[2] The first librarian of the Subscription-library was Joseph Saunders, an humble coadjutor of Humphry Wanley in assisting to collect, arrange, and preserve the treasures of the Harleian library. What was Saunders's office in the splendid establishment of the Oxford family I do not know; but when in the latter part of his life he came to reside at

Sheffield he had a large collection of maps and plans of the Harley estates, for which he refused large sums that were offered him by the representatives of the family; but was at last glad to part with at a low rate. He married the daughter of one Fisher of Sheffield, one of the last persons in this neighbourhood who cultivated that fosterer of half the bad passions of the human heart—astrology.

[3] Anonymiana, Century iv. No. 94.

1666. Nathaniel Robinson.
  7. George Creswick.
  8. John Webster.
  9. Robert Sorsby.
1670. Edward Barlow.
  1. Richard Parramore.
  2. Matthew Arnold.
  3. John Sutton.
  4. Castle Shemeld.
  5. William Crawshaw.
  6. James Newton.
  7. John Pearson.
  8. Thomas Jennings.
  9. Joshua Bayes.
1680. Jonathan Webster.
  1. Robert Nicholls.
  2. John Winter.
  3. Edward Badger.
  4. William Ellis.
  5. Thomas Tooker.
  6. Benjamin Kirkby.
  7. John Webster.
  8. Robert Brelsforth.
  9. James Webster.
1690. Joseph Downes.
  1. John Webster.
  2. Thomas Johnson.
  3. John King.
  4. John Trippett.
  5. Robert Spooner.
  6. Christ' Broomhead.
  7. Richard Downes.
  8. Andrew Wade.
  9. Benjamin Pearson.
1700. Robert Savage.
  1. Richard Marsh.
  2. Ephraim Nicholls.
  3. John Pearson.
  4. Edward Sanderson.

1705. Joseph Nutt.
  6. Ezra Cawton.
  7. George Cartwright.
  8. John Downes.
  9. James Hoole.
1710. John Morton.
  1. Samuel Smith.
  2. Samuel Twible.
  3. Thomas Tooker.
  4. John Birks.
  5. William Moor.
  6. Thomas Broadhead.
  7. John Guest.
  8. Tobias Ellis.
  9. Peter Symon.
1720. James Longsden.
  1. James Crawshaw.
  2. John Smith.
  3. Jonathan Moor.
  4. Jeremy Beet.
  5. Thomas Redforth.
  6. John Tooker.
  7. Andrew Wade.
  8. Andrew Wade.
  9. Thomas Cotton.
1730. Samuel Wainwright.
  1. Thomas Wilson.
  2. John Ward.
  3. Cotton Watkin.
  4. John Osborne.
  5. Joseph Turner.
  6. Joshua Cawton.
  7. Joseph Shepherd.
  8. Joseph Kenyon.
  9. Jonathan Dixon, jun.
1740. Jonathan Dixon, sen.
  1. Richard Kent.
  2. Thomas Rose'.
  3. George Marriott.

1744. John Spooner.
  5. Joseph Leathley.
  6. Robert Dent.
  7. Edward Windle.
  8. Leonard Webster.
  9. George Smith.
1750. William Hides.
  1. Thomas Newbold.
  2. Joseph Parkin.
  3. Thomas Law.
  4. Joseph Owen.
  5. William Webster.
  6. Benjamin Withers.
  7. John Wilson.
  8. Jonathan Moor.
  9. Joseph Ibberson.
1760. William Webster.
  1. William Parker.
  2. George Graves.
  3. Joseph Hancock.
  4. Samuel Bates.
  5. Joseph Bower.
  6. William Birks.
  7. John Turner.
  8. Thomas Beeley.
  9. Jeremiah Ward.
1770. Joshua Cawton.
  1. William Trickett.
  2. Robert Owen.
  3. George Britain.
  4. Joseph Kenyon.
  5. John Winter.
  6. John Green.
  7. Samuel Norris.
  8. William Linley.
  9. Josephus Parkin.
1780. John Rowbotham '.
  1. Peter Spurr.

1782. William Fowler.
  3. Joseph Hawksley.
  4. Benjamin Broomhead.
  5. Thomas Settle.
  6. Samuel Wilson.
  7. Jonathan Watkinson.
  8. Thomas Nowel.
  9. Thomas Tillotson.
1790. Joseph Ward.
  1. George Wood.
  2. John Henfrey.
  3. Thomas Warris.
  4. Benjamin Withers.
  5. William Birks.
  6. Joseph Fletcher Smith.
  7. William Linley.
  8. Samuel Broomhead Ward.
  9. Benjamin Vickers.
1800. Samuel Newbould.
  1. Joseph Bailey.
  2. Joseph Withers.
  3. James Mekin.
  4. William Nicholson.
  5. John Eyre.
  6. John Sorby.
  7. Peter Brownell.
  8. Ebenezer Rhodes.
  9. Robert Brightmore.
1810. John Tillotson.
  1. John Eadon.
  2. James Smith.
  3. John Holt.
  4. Joseph Parkin.
  5. James Makin.
  6. Thomas Asline Ward.
  7. George Tillotson.
  8. John Fox.

II.

The Township of Ecclesall-Byerlow.

THE great antiquity of the park at Sheffield is proved by the line of its boundary forming the division of the constabularies or townships of the parish. The ground between the Porter and Sheaf, till those streams enter the park, and a tract lying north of the Porter, comprising Broom-hall and a considerable portion of Crook's-moor, form the township and manor of Ecclesall. To this must be added Lidgate and a small territory around, which on the division after the inclosure act of 1779 were assigned to Ecclesall. Great difficulty was at that time found in drawing the line of boundary between Ecclesall and Nether-Hallam. Hence its great irregularity.

The area of this township is 4180 acres. In 1796 it contained 1071 houses. In 1801 they had increased to 1114, when the population amounted to 5362 persons. The population in 1811 was 6569. Since that period there has been a great increase of buildings within this township, principally by the extension of the town of Sheffield in a western direction. Little-Sheffield, which was once a distinct hamlet of this township, is now become a part of Sheffield, and the time is not far distant when the same may be said of Highfield.

There is no village of Ecclesall. In this respect the township resembles Fullwood and Hallam, and some of the spacious townships of the parish of Halifax. The population resides for the most part in what is now the town of Sheffield, but there is a good deal of building about Sharrow-moor. The western parts

---

' He died in the year of his office, and Richard Kent served again.   ' He died, and Mr. Parkin served again.

of the township are thinly peopled for a manufacturing district.

Many of the inhabitants are engaged in agriculture; others in different branches of the Sheffield manufactures; and some are employed in a large snuff-manufactory on the Porter, the property of Messrs. Wilson. In the less populous parts of this township are several old halls or *Gentilhommeries,* as the French would call them, which have been or are residences of the principal freeholders of the manor. Of these and their inhabitants more hereafter. Several modern villas have been erected at Highfield.

The chapel is situated nearly in the centre of the township. To the chapelry of Ecclesall the two townships of Upper- and Nether-Hallam belong, each of them electing a chapel-warden. The three townships were once united.

The turnpike road from Sheffield to Chesterfield and from thence to London passes through this township; and another to Buxton and Manchester runs the whole length from east to west. The turnpike-house at Ringing-low on the moors, five miles from Sheffield, is at the extreme point of the township westward.

On that part of Crook's-moor which is within this township the races were formerly held. I can trace them no further back than the year 1713, when the town's trustees of Sheffield were ' at charges to get horses to the races.' Perhaps they were established about that time. The inclosure bill gave the death-blow to this amusement.

It will be recollected that in the return to the *Quo warranto* of the 9 Edward I., Thomas lord Furnival laid claim to the *jus furcœ* throughout Hallamshire. In this township of Ecclesall-Byerlow, but not far from the confines of Nether-Hallam, is a little eminence still called the Gibbet-hill, on which conspicuous spot doubtless the lords of Hallamshire were accustomed to erect the gallows when they were called to the exercise of this power.

Ecclesall-wood is of considerable extent, and occupies the south-west angle of the township. It is the property of the right honourable earl Fitz-William, who has a considerable estate here, who is also lord of the manor, and has his court and prison.

Of the successive proprietors of the manor I have now to speak.

Of these four thousand acres there is no express notice in Domesday-book: but they are included in the survey made of the manor of Hallam, of which sufficient notice has already been taken.

In the time of King John, about one hundred and fifty years after the Conquest, and about the time when Gerard de Furnival married the great heiress of Hallamshire Maud de Lovetot, appears one Radulphus bearing the name of De Ecclesall, and settled on this part of what had been the barony of De Lovetot. His name appears among the witnesses to a grant of Gerard de Furnival to the monks of Kirkstead[1] before the 3 Henry III. 1219. He gave lands to the neighbouring abbey of Beauchief, which was founded in his time by De Alfreton, the lord of the opposite hill of Norton, and in the abbey he was buried[2].

Next appears Sir Robert de Ecclesall, a knight, the son and heir of Ralph. He confirmed his father's grant to Beauchief[3]. In Dodsworth's notes from the Scrope charters[4] is a tricking of his seal, which was circular, and bore this inscription, s . roberti . de . heccle- sale round his shield of arms, a bend between six martlets; of which the colours, as they are given in that curious heraldric list in the *Antiquarian Repertory,* were the field of sable and the charge of gold.

Sir Robert left Ralph de Ecclesall his son and heir. He was also a knight. Before his time the family had a mansion and a small park called Joce Park. To these accommodations he added a chapel. Of its foundation and appropriation to the abbot and twelve monks of the convent of Beauchief, situated in the valley immediately below his patrimonial hill, we have this satisfactory and curious account :—that to ensure the regular performance of divine offices in his chapel, Sir Ralph de Ecclesall gave to the monks of Beauchief his mill on the Sheaf, until he should provide them with six marks annual rent some where in exchange, when the mill was to revert to him and his heirs. Out of the proceeds of the mill a canon was to be supported, and a clerk officiating daily at his chapel, and the surplus was to go to the general expenses of the convent. The canon who was to officiate in his chapel was to say the Lord's Prayer daily on leaving the chapter-house, for the soul of Sir Ralph's father, and for all departed souls. In case of great floods or snow, when probably the Sheaf would be impassable, the canons were to be excused from sending a brother to Ecclesall, and allowed to celebrate the accustomed masses in their own church. On no account were they to send a brother who should be disagreeable to him or his heirs. If the chapel should by any means fail, the convent was to find a canon or secular chaplain to celebrate in the parish-church of Sheffield: and if the convent should attempt to procure the aforesaid chantry to be removed to the abbey or elsewhere, they were to be subject to excommunication, and to lose their mill. To this deed were witnesses Sir Thomas de Furnival, Sir Ralph de Wortley, Ralph de Schefeld clerk, William Gahame, Thomas de Leys, Thomas de Wadhouse, and others. Such was the original intention: but this agreement was some time after altered; and Sir Ralph covenanted that the monks should receive the rents of his mill, and, retaining four marks, pay the residue to him and his heirs; and gave them besides, lands at Attercliffe of four marks and a half value; a toft with the houses in the town of Sheffield; and a toft and all the land which he had by inheritance in the vill and territory of Dronfield in pursuance of the aforesaid engagement. And lastly he gave them a piece of ground near the river Sheaf for the erection of a fulling-mill, with leave to turn the river if necessary, he to have one third of the profits and to bear one third of the expense[5].

Further respecting this Sir Ralph de Ecclesall I have not found, except that there was a fine levied at York, 8 Edw. I. 1280, between Thomas de Folejamb complainant and Sir Ralph de Ecclesall deforciant, of the manors of Ecclesall and Aldwark, forty shillings

---

[1] *Mon. Ang.* vol. i. p. 807. Ralph de Ecclesall is also a witness to Richard de Lovetot's confirmation to Worksop, *Id.* ii. 51. It is not improbable that he is the same person who, by the name of Radulphus filius Radulphi filii Gilberti, witnessed the elder Richard de Lovetot's grant

of the hermitage to Kirkstead, *Id.* i. 808.
[2] Pegge, p. 148.   [3] *Id.* p. 149.
[4] MSS. in Bibl. Bodl. vol. cxxxix.
[5] Pegge, p. 149.

rent in Thorp, ten shillings rent in Dalton, and eight shillings rent in Routhmareys [Rawmarsh], to be the right of the said Thomas of the gift of Ralph for life, remainder to Robert son of the said Ralph, and to Cecily daughter of the foresaid Thomas, wife of the said Robert, and to the issue of the said Robert and Cecily[1].

To Sir Ralph succeeded a second Sir Robert de Ecclesall his son. His name appears in 1297 among the witnesses to Furnival's charter to the town of Sheffield. In 1299 he released to the monks of Beauchief all claims or demands he might have of two marks rent on account of Ecclesall mill, or in any other respect[2]. In 3 Edward II. 1310, a fine was passed between Robert de Ecclesall plaintiff and Adam de Ecclesall deforciant, of the manors of Ecclesall and Aldwark, &c. to be the right of the same Robert and his heirs[3]. About the same time his name appears among the witnesses to Sir Thomas Chaworth's grant of his whole hamlet of Greenhill to the monks of Beauchief[4]. In the 12 Edward II. 1319, he had a license to impark Joce-park and his wood at Ecclesall called Hazlehurst[5],-that is the wood of hazels, a tree with which the whole vale of Beauchief still abounds. This appears as if Sir Robert de Ecclesall had a prospect of leaving heirs to succeed him in his inheritance. What changes took place in his family after this period we can only conjecture; but certain it is, that by deed executed at Nottingham in the third year of the succeeding reign, 1329, he granted to Joan de Wanton, daughter and heir of John de Wanton, sometime lord of Masham, and to Richard Welles, his manor of Ecclesall, and what he had in Ecclesall, Aldwark, Sheffield, Brom, and Crakes [Crooks], to have to the same Joan and Richard, and to the heirs of the body of the said Joan, and in default of such issue to remain to Sir Geffery le Scrope knight, and to his heirs with warranty[6]. He was an aged man at the time of executing this deed, and died before the sixteenth of Edward III. 1342; for in that year Maud countess of Ulster, who was daughter of Henry Plantagenet earl of Leicester, nephew to Edward I., settled by fine six messuages, &c. on Thomas Cok and Isabel his wife and the heirs of Thomas, after the decease of Maud, who had been the wife of Robert de Ekeleshale, and who held them for term of life[7]. With him ended the line of the old Ecclesalls lords of Ecclesall.

In pursuance of the settlement above mentioned the manor of Ecclesall passed to the great family of Scrope. Sir Henry le Scrope son of Sir Geffery le Scrope, on whom it was settled in remainder, was in possession as early as the 17 Edward III. 1343, and in his descendants in the male line it continued till the 9 Henry VIII. 1517, with some slight intermissions occasioned by the confiscations and forfeitures of those dubious times. It was not to be expected that the hall and park of a knightly family at Ecclesall, pleasant as they must have been, could seduce the barons Scrope from their ancient hereditary seats at Masham and Upsal, even if they could have borne the near neighbourhood of a family like the Talbots firmly seated at their castle of Sheffield. In point of fact we have no evidence that any members of the house of

Scrope made their abode at Ecclesall. On that account, as well as that I have little to add to what is already before the public in the Baronage, I shall pass briefly over the series of Scropes lords of Ecclesall. I would not fear to incur the imputation of overcharging these pages with genealogical matter, were I able to remove all the difficulties in their splendid but unsettled pedigree.

Sir Henry le Scrope, after a long life spent in the public service under Edward III., died in the 15 Rich. II. 1391, seised, as appears by inquisition, of the manors of Masham, Upsal, Ecclesall, &c. leaving Stephen his son and heir, then aged forty years, and a younger son William, who was created earl of Wiltshire by Richard II. and who was sacrificed by Henry IV. when he obtained possession of the crown.

Stephen lord Scrope had summons to parliament among the barons from the 1 Richard II. to the 7 Henry IV. in which year he died, seised *inter alia* of the manor of Ecclesall with its members in Sheffield and Aldwark, save that Margaret his widow held two parts of the said manor: Henry his son being his heir, and thirty years old and upwards.

This is that Henry lord Scrope of Masham whose treason is opened to him by Henry V. in a noble passage of Shakspeare's *Historie* of that king's reign. He was beheaded at Southampton, and his lands were given to Henry lord Fitz-Hugh for life. His brother Sir John Scrope obtained them again from Henry VI., and had summons to parliament as lord Scrope of Masham and Upsal. In a feodary's account of the estate of John earl Shrewsbury 30 Henry VI., now in the duke of Norfolk's auditor's office at Sheffield, this John lord Scrope is put down owner of the manor of Ecclesall, holding it of the castle and manor of Sheffield as two knights' fees valued at ten pounds, and four pounds for aids. He died on the 15th of November 34 Henry VI. 1455, seised as by inquisition of the manor of Ecclesall, &c.: Thomas his son being his next heir, and then aged twenty-six years.

Thomas lord Scrope enjoyed the manor of Ecclesall, as did his four sons, Thomas, Henry, Ralph, and Geffery, in succession. These all died leaving no male issue. On the death of Geffery lord Scrope, who was a clerk, in the 9 Henry VIII. 1517, his estates were divided among his three sisters, namely, Alice wife of Thomas Strangways, or according to others of Sir James Strangways of Whorlton-castle, knight; Mary, or according to others Margery, wife of Sir Christopher Danby of Farnley, knight; and Elizabeth wife of Sir Ralph Fitz-Randal of Spennithorne;—all in the county of York.

On the partition of the Scrope estates among these co-heirs, Ecclesall was allotted to Elizabeth Fitz-Randal. She had issue John Fitz-Randal, who died without issue, and five daughters her co-heirs, of whom the eldest became the wife of Sir Nicholas Strelley of Lindby, in the county of Nottingham, knight, who had in her right the manor of Ecclesall, but had no issue[8].

By patent dated 25 Henry VIII. 1533, the king pardoned Sir Nicholas Strelley knight, and Elizabeth his

  [1] Dods. MSS. D.D. 132 b. Harl. 801. Ecclesall.   [2] Pegge, p. 149.
  [3] Dods. MSS. G. G. 19. Harl. 801. Ecclesall.
  [4] Pegge, p. 127.
  [5] Dods. MSS. H.H.H. 114 b. Harl. 801. Ecclesall.
  [6] Dods. MSS. D.D. 136 b. Harl. 801. Ecclesall.

  [7] Thoroton, p. 6, from St. Loe Kniveton's Collections.
  [8] From the collections of J. C. Brooke esq., Somerset herald, now in the College of Arms, which have supplied many other particulars in the descent of this manor. His information was derived from the evidences of Charles marquis of Rockingham.

               3 E

wife, that they had acquired, without his license, to themselves and their heirs, of William Holgill and John Savage, the manors of Ecclesall and Wood-Lathes, and certain messuages in Ecclesall, Wood-Lathes, Sheffield, Brome, Croke and Aldwark, the advowson of the church of Fingale, and the fourth part of the manor of Spennithorne.

But whether this relates to the above-mentioned Sir Nicholas Strelley, or to his successor in this manor of the same name and rank, does not clearly appear: for on the death of Sir Nicholas of Lindby, the manor of Ecclesall passed to a distant cousin, Sir Nicholas Strelley knight, who was captain of Berwick in the first year of Edward VI. They were both descended of another Sir Nicholas Strelley of Strelley in the county of Nottingham, who lived in the reign of Henry V.

In 1537 Sir Nicholas Strelley, the captain of Berwick, obtained a grant from the crown of the site of the then lately dissolved abbey of Beauchief[1].

In 1542 we find him engaged in a dispute with the tenants of the manor of Ecclesall respecting common of pasture on a place called Row-hill, which was referred to the award of Francis earl of Shrewsbury[2].

In 1547 Sir Nicholas Strelley sold to Francis earl of Shrewsbury all his lands in the town and fields of Sheffield[3].

Sir Nicholas Strelley had by three wives a numerous issue, sons and daughters. His acquisitions at Beauchief he settled on Nicholas Strelley esquire, his second son; and further, by deed bearing date the 14th of May 38 Henry VIII. 1546, he demised the manor of Ecclesall to the said Nicholas for fourscore years: and on the 5th of February 2 Edward VI. 1548, the reversion after the expiration of the said eighty years was conveyed to the king and his heirs[4].

Sir Nicholas Strelley died on the 25th of August 1561. His son Nicholas Strelley esquire died in 1602, and was buried at Sheffield on the 26th of October in that year, where also were interred four children of his son and heir Gervase Strelley esquire, who died in their infancy. There is no other memorial of their interment at Sheffield but the entry in the parish-register: and it is singular that the family should have sought any other resting-place than the hallowed precincts of their own abbey, which the later generations have indeed used as their cemetery.

There is, or at least lately was, within the manor of Ecclesall an ordinary dwelling-house which was dignified by the title of Ecclesall-hall. It stood near the old chapel, and probably on the site of the original seat of the Ecclesalls lords of Ecclesall. I have not found any evidence of the Strelleys having resided in it; and it seems more probable that from the first of their settlement in this neighbourhood, they inhabited such part of the abbey of Beauchief as could be most easily applied to that purpose[5], till Mr. Edward Pegge, who married the heir-general of the family in the time of the Commonwealth, erected in 1671 the present mansion on a site a little removed from the abbey; which is now the property of Peter Pegge-Burnell esquire of Winkburne in the county of Nottingham, and the residence of his nephew Broughton-Benjamin Steade esquire.

By letters patent under the great seal of England, dated the 2d of December 21 James I. 1623, when the eighty years' term was nearly expired, the king granted the manor of Ecclesall from the time of the expiration of the said term to William lord Sanquaire viscount Aire, to hold for twenty-one years, in consideration of 200*l.* paid into the Exchequer by the said Lord Aire.

This was one of those beneficial leases by which the king enriched his Scottish favourites. The lease was assigned in 1634 by the lord Aire, then become earl of Dumfreize, to Edward Barker, who in the same year conveyed the moiety or half part of the manor for the unexpired term to Stephen Bright in consideration of 1500*l.*, and by indenture of the same date the other moiety in consideration of 1000*l.* redeemable on payment of 1040*l.*

In 1628, King Charles I. under the broad seal of the duchy of Lancaster granted *inter alia* the manor of Ecclesall to Edward Ditchfield, John Highlord, Humphry Clarke, and Francis Mosse, trustees appointed by the city of London, reserving a fee-farm rent of 60*l. per annum:* and on the 30th of May 1636 the said Ditchfield, Highlord, Clarke, and Mosse, granted the said manor to Stephen Bright and Thomas Sharp his trustee, in consideration of 1800*l.*

8 May 1638. By indenture of bargain and sale enrolled, the said Thomas Sharp, in consideration of ten shillings, conveys to the said Stephen Bright the manor and lordship of Ecclesaw *alias* Ecclesall, &c., to hold to the said Stephen Bright, his heirs and assigns for ever.

26 Sept. 1646. Edward Barker released to John Bright all his interest in the said manor.

The Edward Barker to whom the earl of Dumfreize assigned his lease of this manor was without doubt Edward Barker of Dore, a township of the parish of Dronfield, which adjoins to Ecclesall. He was the representative of an ancient family at that place, and the progenitor of the late General Sir Robert Barker bart. Stephen Bright was of Carbrook in the township of Attercliffe-cum-Darnall, but of a family who had long been principal freeholders of the manor of Ecclesall. The John Bright above mentioned, in whom centred all the interests created in this manor, was the colonel of that name in the Parliament army, and after the Restoration Sir John Bright baronet. A more favourable opportunity of giving the genealogy of this family will occur under Carbrook. It may be sufficient here to observe, in order to complete this account of the descent of the manor of Ecclesall, that Sir John Bright left an only daughter and heir, who married Sir Henry Liddell bart., on whose second son, John Liddell esquire, this manor and other property of Sir John's were settled, and who on the death of his grandfather took the name of Bright. His son Thomas Bright, of Badsworth near Pontefract, esquire, left an only daughter and heir named Mary, who on the 26th of February 1752 married the most noble Charles-Watson Wentworth, the second and last marquis of Rockingham, who in her right was lord of the manor of Ecclesall and owner of extensive estates there. On his decease without issue in 1782, this manor formed but a very small part of the estates which descended

---

[1] Pegge, p. 203.
[2] Brooke's Collections.
[3] Evidences at Norfolk-house. Yorkshire Bundle L. 14.
[4] Brooke's Collections.
[5] Dr. Pegge, however, supposes that no part of the abbey itself was ever used as a residence by the Strelleys, p. 211.

to his nephew the right honourable William Wentworth Fitz-William earl Fitz-William, in whom the family of Fitz-William returned to their native county after an absence of more than three centuries, to the enjoyment of far greater splendour and more abundant affluence at Wentworth, than had been enjoyed by any of their knightly ancestors in their ancient hereditary seat at Sprodborough.

To this account of the descent of the manor of Ecclesall it only remains to add a genealogy of the Strelleys of Beauchief during the time that they were in possession: to which may not improperly be added a continuation of the pedigree in a family residing on the very borders of this township, and having possessed for many years the capital mansion and freehold within this manor, Whiteley-wood.

PEDIGREE of STRELLEY of BEAUCHIEF, LORDS of the MANOR of ECCLESALL; and of their Representatives the PEGGES of BEAUCHIEF.

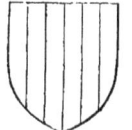

ARMS.—STRELLEY. Paly of six argent and azure.
PEGGE. Argent a chevron between three piles sable.

Sir NICHOLAS STRELLEY, knight, captain of Berwick. Ob. 3 Eliz.

NICHOLAS STRELLEY esquire, second son, settled by his father at Beauchief. Buried at Sheffield 26 Oct. 1602[1]. = BRIDDFT, dau. of Anthony Thwaites, gent. Buried at Norton 23 March 1591.

MARGERY, first wife. = GERVASE STRELLEY of Beauchief, esq., son and heir. Lord of the manor of Ecclesall. Died 6 James I. = DOROTHY, second wife, dau. of William Burnell of Winkburn, county Notts., esq. | CHARLES NORTH of Walkering-ham, esq., second husband. | ANTHONY STRELLEY of Beauchief, esq. Buried at Norton 3 Jan. 1610. | NICHOLAS STRELLEY. | URSULA, buried at Norton 26 Feb. 1589. | MARY STRELLEY, married at Norton 5 July 1604 to George Eyre, vicar of Mackworth. | BRIDGET STRELLEY, married a' Norton 22 Oct. 1585 to Dennis Beresford of Greenhill, gent.

NICHOLAS STRELLEY, son and heir apparent. Bap. a' N.rton 26th March 1597. Died in his infancy, and was buried at Sheffield 20 March 1597. | MARGERY, bur. at Sheffield 5 Aug. 1592. MARY, bap. at Sheffield 25 Sept. 1595, bur. there 10 Nov. 1596. | GERVASE STREL-LEY, bur. at Sheffield 11 March 1597. BRIDGET, bap. at Norton 28 July 1588. | ANNE STRELLEY, died unmarried 10 April 1660, aged 69, and was bur. in the abbey of Beauchief. | JANE STRELLEY, bap. at Sheffield 5 Feb. 1593. | GOODETH STREL-LEY, wife of Robert Beauchief, gent. Died in May 1665, and was buried in the church of Dronfield. | WILLIAM STRELLEY, died in 1635, and was buried at Dronfield. = GERTRUDE, dau. of Adam Eyre of Bradway in the parish of Norton, gent., (a younger son of Rowland Eyre of Hassop, esq.,) by Elizabeth his wife, dau. of Thos. Barley of Dronfield-Wood-house.

ANNE, second wife, sister of William Clark-son of Kirton, co. Notts, esq. = EDWARD PEGGE of Beauchief, esquire, son of Edward Pegge of Ash-bourn, gent., (a younger son of Humphry Pegge of Osmaston, son of Ralph Pegge of Shirley,) by Anne his wife, dau. of Henry Jackson of Stanshop, co. Staff., by Anne his wife, daughter of John Bruen. Aged 11, 1634. Aged 40, 11 Aug. 1662. High-sheriff of the county of Derby 1664. Built the hall at Beauchief 1671, and restored public worship in the church of the abbey. Died 31 Dec. 1679, and was buried in the abbey of Beauchief. = GERTRUDE STRELLEY, sole daughter and heir. Born 3 October 1631. Married at Norton 17 July 1649. | NICHOLAS STRELLEY, died young. | WILLIAM STRELLEY, buried at Norton 19 Nov. 1635.

GERVASE EDWARD. EDWARD. All died young. | STRELLEY PEGGE of Beauchief, esq. barrister-at-law, dau. of John Annesley esq., of Ballyshannon in Ireland, who survived and re-married Sir Geffary Paul. No issue. | ANNA-CATHERINA, first wife, dau. of Will. Eyre of High-ton, esq., who mar. Isabella Jessop of Broom-hall. Married at Bakewell 27 Dec. 1692. = CHRISTOPHER PEGGE of Beauchief esq., youngest son. Died 28 March 1729, aged 69, and was buried at Beauchief. = LETITIA, second wife, daugh. of Christopher Pegge of Shirley (son Ralph of Shirley) by Prudence his wife, dau. of Nathan' Bate of Little-Chester. Married at Drayton-Basset 9 Aug. 1702. Died 1748. | ELIZABETH, SARAH. CATHERINE. Died young, or unmarried. | ANNE, wife of Thomas Southby of Birdsal, co. York, esq. — MARY, wife of Thomas Tatton of Withenshaw, coun. Cestr. gent. | GERTRUDE, wife of Francis Stevenstone, coun. Derby, gent. GOODETH, wife of Robert Belt of Bossal, co. York, esq. | DOROTHY, wife of Richard Hall of Barlow-Lees in the par. of Dronfield, gent. FRANCES, wife of Paul Webster of Chesterfield, gent.

ANNE PEGGE, only issue of the first marriage, wife of Philip Foster Smith esq., of Bramhurst near Uttoxeter. | FRANCES, first wife, dau. and sole heir of Robert Revel of Carnfield, coun. Derb. esq., mar. at Brampton 22 May 1735. Died without issue. = STRELLEY PEGGE of Beauchief, esq., owner by descent of the manor of Ecclesall. High-sheriff of the county of Derby 1739. Died 7 April 1770, aged 60, and was bur. at Beauchief. = MARY, 2d wife, dau. of Peter Broughton of Lowdham, co. Notts, esquire. Died 4 August 1774, aged 52, and was bur. at Beauchief. | LETITIA, wife of Jonathan Lee of Chesterfield, gent. Died 17 June 1773, and was buried in the church of Chesterfield. | CHRISTOPHER PEGGE of Stanshop, co. Stafford, clerk, B.A. and M.A. 1740. = MARY, dau. of George Alsop by Catherine Bradenel his wife, married 1741. | EDWARD. CHRISTIANA. All died unmarried.

STRELLEY PEGGE of Beauchief, esq. eldest son and heir, barrister-at-law and groom of the privy chamber to his present majesty. Died unmarried 12 July 1774, aged 29, and was buried at Beauchief. | PETER PEGGE-BURNELL of Beauchief, esq. and now of Winkburn in the county of Notts. High-sheriff of the county of Derby 1788. Assumed the name of Burnell on becoming heir to a moiety of the estate of his distant relative — Burnell of Winkburn, esq. = MARY, dau. and co-heir of William Milnes of Aldercar-park, co. Derby, esq., by Margaret his wife, sister and heir of William Soresby of Chester-field, esq. | JONATHAN. | FRANCES LEE wife of Robert Belt of Hillsborough co. York, esquire. mar. in 1768. | MILICENT, wife of Thos. Steade of Sheffield, and Hillsborough in the parish of Ecclesfield, esq. | MARY-LETITIA PEGGE. | CHRISTOPHER. NATHANIEL. LUCINDA. CATHERINE. All died young. | CHRISTIANA, wife of the rev. Thos. Fulton.

EDWARD-BROUGHTON. JANE.

[1] The burial of this person is also registered at Norton.

We have in this family an instance which by some has been supposed rare, of the direct descendants of the original grantee possessing and residing upon the abbey-lands granted to their ancestor. What indeed could tempt the family to forsake a residence circumstanced so agreeably in every respect as Beauchief? Not to be last enumerated among the advantages of this choice spot is the preservation of so many records of the monastic establishment in its days of prosperity, and that there has arisen among the family of its modern owners an antiquary who has known how to make a judicious use of the materials for its history. The late Dr. Samuel Pegge, rector of Whittington, was descended of Humphry Pegge of Osmaston, who was cousin-german to Edward Pegge who married the heiress of Beauchief. But through his mother he had a nearer connexion with the house whose history he has so well described. She was a daughter of Francis Stevenson of Unstone by Gertrude his wife, the daughter of Edward Pegge of Beauchief esquire, and Gertrude Strelley.

The reader may find a very pleasing description of the sequestered and beautiful scenery around Beauchief in a work entitled 'Peak Scenery,' by Mr. Rhodes of Sheffield, a gentleman who in the midst of his commercial pursuits, and an active engagement in any scheme which has for its object the benefit of his place of residence, has found time to cultivate a taste for the beauties of nature and of art, which is combined with powers of description of no ordinary kind. We have had many engravings of the remains of Beauchief, and there is one in the work here referred to which will have a permanent value as being from the pencil of Chantrey.

Of what Mr. Edward Pegge did here some time after he had married the heir of Strelley, we have a circumstantial and curious account from the hand of Brailsford, a Derbyshire antiquary who lived at the beginning of the last century. 'Beauchief-hall was built by Edward Pegge, to which there is first a spacious outer green yard, from which through a large pair of well-wrought iron gates and on each side pallisadoed with iron, wee enter into a garden on the south side of the house, and on a large walk through the middle of the garden are conducted to a noble pair of stone staires of 19 greises (or steps), at the head of which entring thro' a pair of gates into a foot-pace, from which goes down staires of 9 stepps both east and west into a paved court yard, and from the same foot-pace continues our assent up as many stone stepps into a passage over a large stone arch (under which passeth a faire walk the whole front of the house) and under a balcony into the hall (the staires all of stone, and several persons may walk together in a breast up them, they are set with rails and banister of good stone worke, and so is the head end of the garden along on each side the staires) and on a fair stone over the door leading into the hall we engraven, viz.

'Eben-ezer.

Hæc domus ergo Deus stet honoris grata columna:
Nam domus et domini conditor ipse Deus.
E. P. Maii 17, 1671.

'Here is a fair prospect adorned with wood. And on the paved court before the house thro' a pair of gates

out of another garden on the east of the house into a long large walke set with firr trees, on the side of a fair close at the far end of which walk wee are in view of the ruines of Beauchiefe Abby, which is about a quarter of a mile from us, and of an extensive prospect into Yorkshire over the towne of Sheffield. In a part of this close is the swetest and clearest echo from the hall that I ever heard.

'Over a portall within the hall dores is cut on wood Pegg's arms quartering Strelley, and a fess dancittee or deep indented.

'There is also entrance into the house both east and west by stone staires of 12 greises, with balconies over the doors.

'On the ground flore of the house are 17 rooms. On the next flore with the hall, parlor and dininge roome are 7 rooms; and in the dining room is a pritty wrought chymnie piece of alabaster, and between two pillars on each side supporting a canopie is the effigies of an ancient man with a long beard, with a furr'd gown of halfe sleeves, and upon a mantle thrown over his shoulders a collar of S.S. and roses, a little book in his hand, a ruff up to his eares, and a cap upon his head, like to a judge's cap. On the outside of the said supporters or pillars is the arms of Pegge quartering Strelley's. Above this flore of rooms is another story.......

'The kitchen gardens and the stables are at a convenient distance from the house west. And here is a pritty large walled paddock for deer, well wooded, before the front of the house adjoyning to the out yards.

'The chymney piece above mentioned was given by Mr. Adrian Mundy of Quarne, whose only daughter and heir (a great fortune) was to have been married to Gervase Pegge elder brother to Christopher Pegge now of Beauchieff, but that he was snatched away by death, when he was a student of Grey's Inn.

'A remaining part of the body of Beauchieff abbey is repaired at the sole charg of Pegge of Beauchieff-hall, and that is theire burying place, and where sometimes is divine service and preaching.'

The connexion which Sir Ralph de Ecclesall established between his chapel and the monastery of Beauchief would naturally strengthen the interest which contiguity of situation gave to that house among the freeholders of his manor of Ecclesall. In the records of the monastery we accordingly find the names of many of them as benefactors, so that at the Dissolution it was no small estate that the abbey possessed in this manor.

William Fitz-Gamul of Ecclesall gave the canons a rent of 12d., which was confirmed by Hugh Hanselen of Little Sheffield[1].

William del Holyns gave a parcel of land, meadow and wood. To which deed were witnesses Roger Hanselen, Thomas de Bosco of Sheffield, Adam Cocus, and Lambertus Tinctor of the same place, with others. This was probably Mylneclyffe, as William Mercator of Sheffield quit claimed to the convent all that placea terræ called Le Mylneclyffe, which he lately held of William del Holyns. The boundaries are 'inter terram Ricardi fil. Ade Coci de Schefeld et le Botheclyfe Syke, et abuttat. ad unum caput versus occi-

[1] Pegge, 162.

dentem super nam que ducit de domo mea versus Schefeld, et ad aliud caput versus Orientem super terram predicti Ricardi.' Roger son of William de Holins released all his right and claim in that tenement which the canons had by the gift and grant of William de Holyns his father in Le Holyns, or Les Holyns, which are described as being in the soke of Eccleshall in Halumschyre[1].

Hugh Haunslen or Hanslen of Little Sheffield gave the canons of Beauchief leave to make a dam for their mill called the New Mill, in his *cultura* de Holleford, so that they might conduct the river Seheve at pleasure, and as was convenient through his alder-plot on the south part of the cultura without coming on the arable land, for the health of his and his wife Julian's soul[2].

Roger Hanslen son of Hugh gave the convent a rent of 5*s.* which Roger del Holyns was wont to pay him for a bovate of land held of him in Ecclesall, *cum wardis, releviis, et omnibus aliis eschaetis.* Robert Hanslen, another son of Hugh, gave a rent of 12*d.* which William his brother was to pay him for the land which Adam Carectarius (Carter) held in Brendeclive and his homage. William the other brother of these Hanslens gave 3*s.* rent and a bovate of land with a toft in Brendclive, which the said Adam bought and held of him[3].

Further respecting the Hanslens and their connexions Dr. Pegge found that the above-named Adam Carter infeoffed William de Brendclive in four acres of land in Brendclive; and that Robert de Engeland confirmed to Adam de Schefeld dictus Cocus, and Elena his wife, all that land which he bought of Roger son of Juliana Carter in Brendeclyfe, and 2½*d.* rent to be received of Betrice wife of Robert Hanselin for a sum of money they had given him, they paying to the canons yearly 18*d.*

Hugh sold to the canons Richard Fitz-Thoke his native *cum omnibus catallis mobilibus,* for 6*s.* He gave them also Richard le Serjeaunt *nativum suum cum tota sequela sua:* which Richard held lands of him with wood and pasture in Ecclesall.

Roger son of Peter de Bradefeld quit claimed to Robert de Engeland above mentioned a moiety of land *cum tofto, crofto et edificiis* at Brendclif, which fell to the said Roger on the death of Julian daughter of Adam Carter, his mother: Robert to pay 3*s.* yearly to the abbey. Said Robert also quit claimed to the convent his chief lords in frank almoigne 6*d.* rent in Le Brendeclyf, to be received from a toft and croft and an acre of land which he bought of his daughter Agnes in her virginity[4].

John Scheffeld, the last abbot of Beauchief and the convent, leased 1534 to Richard Jeyscock, or rather Jeyfcock, and Robert his son, and Catherine the wife of Robert and their children, one tenement, lands, meadow and pasture, within the Byerlow of Eckylsall, which tenement is called Hoolt-house, for 30 years; rent 20*s.* ' of able money, with suet of court and mylne, with a boon sycull in harvest, and a boon plough in sede tym, and a toulehin at Chrystynmas[5].'

ECCLESALL CHAPEL.

The old chapel of Ecclesall is described by those who remember it as a small and low building containing nothing of the least curiosity. It consisted of two parts, the nave and the chancel, and had on its south side three lancet-shaped windows not seven inches wide. There was a small shed at the west end which contained a bell. Mr. Wilson observes, that there was a board within it on which were carved a hand in a praying posture, and the date 1406, with the initials R. B.

The monks of Beauchief no doubt continued the daily service in this chapel, to which there was a short and pleasant walk over the fields, till the Dissolution. This service fell with the abbey, and the building remained, but no service was performed in it till 1622. In that year the inhabitants of the township, stimulated as it appears by that religious zeal which Mr. Toller the vicar of Sheffield was the means of exciting, set about restoring its dilapidated walls, and fitting it up as a place of religious worship. They laid down a floor in the chancel, erected a small wooden steeple, set up pews, a pulpit, and a communion table, and new glazed the windows. A second contribution enabled them to obtain some of the other appendages of religious worship, namely, ' a pulpit cushion with silk tassels,' a table-cloth of linen, a bason for baptizing, pewter veasels for the communion-service, a surplice, bell, and hour-glass: and finally, by the voluntary engagement of the inhabitants, the promoters of this good design were enabled to offer five pounds *per annum* as a salary to their minister. These particulars are extracted from the book of accompts kept at the time. Mr. Edward Hunt son-in-law to Mr. Toller, one of the assistant-ministers of Sheffield, was the first curate of Ecclesall.

The accommodation which this small chapel afforded was all the convenience the inhabitants possessed for public worship, except their parish-church, till the year 1788. On the 21st of January 1784, a brief for the erection of a new chapel was certified at Doncaster sessions. The estimate was 1553*l.* 4*s.* 5½*d.* The site chosen for it was a little removed from the site of the old chapel, on a spot called Carter-knoll. It was opened for public worship on the 13th of December 1788, and consecrated by William archbishop of York on the 5th of August following. The old chapel was taken down. The present is a plain neat structure. Standing on an elevated point of ground, its white walls form a pleasing object from many parts of the surrounding country. The traveller from Derbyshire who has traversed the exposed and barren ridge of the East-moors, hails it as the signal of his arrival in a richer and milder region.

An extensive piece of ground surrounding the chapel was at the same time consecrated as a place of sepulture. Many families not resident in the chapelry have here their burying-places. The practice has been begun of interring within the walls of the chapel. Mrs. Bayliffe, wife of the then curate of Ecclesall, was one of the first persons laid there. She died on the 26th of December 1801, at the age of 82, and her husband was laid beside her in 1804. The propriety of the practice has been often discussed. This at least may be urged in defence of it,—that if we seek to perpetuate the memory of our friends, or to protect their remains from future disturbance, we must seek the interior and not the exterior of the church, where few memorials, though of the most durable materials, stand their century.

A chastely ornamented tablet has been placed against the west wall of the chapel on the outside, to the memory of the Reverend George Smith, the late curate of Ecclesall. The inscription has the two faults into which writers of epitaphs are most liable to fall—triteness and diffuseness without discrimination.

> ' Near to this place
> lie the mortal remains of
> The Rev. George Smith, A.M.
> assistant-minister
> of the parish-church of Sheffield
> and curate of this chapel.
> He died 7th April A.D. 1817, aged 53.
>
> Not holy office, not the sacred vest,
> Nor prayers of wife, nor children's tears could keep
> The wearied body from this home of rest,—
> The pastor and his flock together sleep.

> But when the grave shall render up her dead,
> And all who ever breath'd on earth arise,
> The faithful shepherd then his sheep shall lead
> An humble band immortal to the skies.'

The achievement of the late lord John Murray of Banner-cross is preserved in the chapel. It presents the usual arms and quarterings of the house of Murray, with Dalton quartering Bright on an escutcheon of pretence, as before described.

The old chapel had obtained a share in Queen Anne's bounty, and the value which was then certified according to Bacon was 9*l.* 10*s.* The real income is now about 100*l.* a year. The minister has a cure of souls in a population exceeding ten thousand persons, spread over more than half the parish of Sheffield. The parliamentary commissioners in 1649 reported that there were in this chapelry three hundred families, and suggested the propriety of making it a distinct parish. What would they now say! The curate is nominated by the vicar of Sheffield, and has been usually one of the assistant-ministers.

Catalogue of the CURATES of ECCLESALL.

1622—1629.	Edward Hunt.
1629—1635.	William Dawson.
1635—1656.	Uncertain.
1656—1659.	John Crooke.
1659—1662.	Uncertain.
1662—1689.	William Gardiner.
1689—1694.	Samuel Leech.
1695—1720.	Robert Turie.
1720—1752.	William Humpton.
1752—1766.	John Dickenson.
1766—1769.	Henry Charnley.
1769—1804.	George Bayliffe.
1804—1817.	George Smith.
1817—	Matthew Preston.

JOHN CROOKE was born at Sheffield, and educated at Magdalen College Cambridge, where he had for his tutor a man of some eminence in his day, Mr. Joseph Hill. He was two-and-twenty when he became curate of Ecclesall, which he relinquished in 1659, on being presented to the perpetual curacy of Denby near Peniston. He was one of those clergymen who could not comply with the terms of the Act of Uniformity in 1662, and gave up his living. But he was more fortunate than many of his brethren, for he had a good estate left him by his father, on the income of which he lived at Wakefield till his death on the 9th of January 1687. Dr. Calamy gives him this character: ' He was a sober and stout man, very sound and orthodox, of good natural parts, active and vigorous in a good cause, and very able to defend the truth by argument!.' He married Sarah daughter of Robert Howsley of Sheffield, (who left two houses in Fig-tree-lane to the burgesses and overseers of the poor for the use of two poor widows,) widow of John Bridges of Sheffield, clerk, by whom he had Samuel, John, and Sarah. He was himself a small benefactor to his native parish, the curate of Ecclesall enjoying thirty shillings *per annum* of his gift.

ROBERT TURIE was a native of Scotland, and held this curacy along with the office of assistant-minister. He is said to have been an excellent preacher and a man of very liberal sentiments. He was a great admirer of Baxter, whom he frequently quoted in his sermons. He was a great promoter of the education of youth. To him and to Mr. Drake the vicar, Sheffield owed the establishment of the charity-school for poor boys; and to him more particularly the foundation of a public school in Brightside-Byerlow. It is said that he was once elected master of the free grammar-school, but declined the appointment. He died in 1720. The inscription to his memory in the parish church breathes an amiable spirit of piety. His piety, like that of the good centurion, was accompanied with alms-deeds. In his life and at his death he was a liberal benefactor not only to his own parish, but to the country round. A list of his bequests, which seem to have been judiciously made, may be worth preserving.

	£.	s.	d.	
To the abbey-church of Beauchief .	5	0	0	per ann.
To the church of Wales	5	0	0	——
To a school at Killamarsh . . .	2	0	0	——
To a school at Wales	2	0	0	——
To a school at Darwent	2	0	0	——
To a school at Stony-Middleton .	3	0	0	——
To the chapel at Darwent . . .	10	0	0	——
To a school at Edale	2	0	0	——
To the chapel at Edale	8	0	0	——
All his books to the minister of Bradfield.				
To the chapel at Dore	100	0	0	
To the school at Dore	40	0	0	
To the church of Stainton . . .	40	0	0	
To the school at Bamford . . .	40	0	0	
To the school at Kirkall	40	0	0	
To the poor of Sheffield	5	0	0	
To the poor of Eccleſall	2	10	0	
To the poor of Hallam	2	10	0	

JOHN DICKENSON.—In 1755, at the request of the burgesses and several of the principal inhabitants of Sheffield, he published *Two Discourses on the injustice and wickedness of false weights and measures, preached at the parish-church of Sheffield on Sunday December 15th,* 1754. Mr. Dickenson soon after removed to a distance from Sheffield, appointing Mr. Charnley his curate. This produced unpleasant altercations with the vicar and with the burgesses, which ended in Mr. Dickenson's resigning all connexion with the church of Sheffield. Mr. Charnley had the curacy of Eccleſall some time after Mr. Dickenson's resignation, but in a little time he left the parish.

GEORGE BAYLIFFE was 44 years assistant-minister, and more than 34 years curate of Eccleſall. He was born at Kirkby-Lonsdale in Westmorland, on the 25th of October 1721, educated at Sedbergh, and first settled in the neighbourhood of Sheffield in 1745, as curate to the vicar of Ecclesfield. In that situation he continued till 1760, when he was elected one of the assistant-ministers of Sheffield. He closed a useful and blameless life on the 20th of December 1804, leaving two sons, both clergymen, Thomas of Saint John's College Cambridge, B.A. 1778, who is now vicar of Rotherham, and William of Trinity College Cambridge, B.A. 1783, who is rector of Blore in Staffordshire.

One of the last public acts of the life of Mr. Wilkinson the late vicar of Sheffield, was the presentation of the Reverend GEORGE SMITH to the curacy of Eccleſall. This gentleman was the only son of the Reverend John Smith, assistant-minister, curate of Attercliffe, and master of the grammar-school, under whom he was educated. He was afterwards of Trinity

College Cambridge, where he took the degree of M.A. He had for a short time the living of Papplewick in Nottinghamshire, but finally settled in his native town as curate to Mr. Wilkinson. In January 1805 he was elected one of the assistant-ministers, and was immediately presented to the curacy of Eccleſall. On this preferment he continued till his decease on the 7th of April 1817, at the age of 53. With the rational piety of divines of the old school in the English church he joined the zeal and ardour which distinguishes the members of the new. While his parishioners were edified, instructed and delighted by his public preaching and his devout administration of the ordinances of the church, they found in him one who was ever ready to attend to their private calls and to assist them in every possible way with his advice and services. In his domestic relations he was most truly amiable, and his friends and acquaintance have long to regret the sensible, lively, and cheerful companion.

Mr. Smith's publications were:

A Sermon delivered in Attercliffe chapel on Monday February 28, 1794, *being the day appointed for a General Fast.—To which is annexed a Narrative of transactions relative to the disposal of the vicarage of Rotherham.*

A Sermon delivered in the parish-church of Sheffield to the original united lodge of Odd Fellows. July 9, 1798.

The payment of tribute a duty of strict moral obligation. A Discourse delivered in the parish-church of Sheffield on the 30th *of January* 1799.

A short peal on the new bells.

On the prevalent and increasing neglect of the holy Communion. A Sermon, to which is added an appendix containing an account of the number of communicants, at the quarterly sacrament in the parish-church of Sheffield for the last twenty years. 1799.

From which it appears that the daily average of communicants in 1780, was 182, and in 1799, 100 only. It is however to be observed that within that period the church of Saint James was opened, and the Lord's Supper was administered there.

There is no meeting-house for any description of Dissenters in this township, except the small chapel at Whiteley-wood.

Here are two schools with small endowments, one on Sharrow-moor, the other on Broad-oak Green.

In the chapel is the following, 'Memorial of charities given to the township of Eccleſall.'

'May 16, 1683. Mr. Roger Lee late of Little Sheffield by his last will gave fifty pounds to the trustees therein named, to be lent at interest or laid out in lands, and the interest or rents to be paid the first week in November yearly for ever, to twelve of the most aged decrepit poor persons in this township.

'William Crawshaw late of the same place, deceased, by his will gave ten pounds to and for the said uses.

'Nov. 15, 1719. Doctor George Lee, grandson to the said Roger Lee, (having the monies in his hands,) by his last will charged a close at Little Sheffield, called Burton-field, with the payment of three pound yearly to the said old persons for ever, in lieu of the monies above said.

'Robert Turie, clerk, deceased, in his life time gave forty pounds to be lent out at interest, or laid out in lands, and the interest or rent to be paid yearly for ever to a master to teach six poor children of Eccleſall to read English, and write.

'1731. Henry Younge of Little Sheffield gave a house and conveniences belonging to it, in the West-barr in Sheffield, in the possession of widow Revill, the yearly rent three pound twelve shillings free from all incumberances, after the decease of Matthew Abdy's wife of Sheffield aforesaid, to the poor of Ecclesall for ever.

'1729. Thomas Marshall gave forty shillings yearly for the use of a schoolmaster to teach six poor children, either boys or girls, in Upper Ecclesall, to read English; the monies charged upon a house and land called the Tenter-houses, to be paid to the churchwardens and overseers of the poor, and a school-house on Broad-oak Green, to be used for that purpose for ever, as by his last will.

'1721. John Bright of Chesterfield esq. by his last will bequeathed to the overseers of the poor of Ecclesall twenty pounds, to be laid out in lands, and the rents and profits to be yearly distributed to twenty poor housekeepers sometime the week before Christmas, with the approbation of his nearest relations living at Bannercross and the Edge.

'1729. Henry Younge late of Little Sheffield, gave bond to pay seventy pounds for the use of the poor of Ecclesall; the validity of which bond being afterwards disputed by his executor, the township agreed to accept of forty pounds in lieu thereof, which was accordingly paid by his executor.

'1747. John Bright of Chesterfield esq. son of John Bright before mentioned, gave sixty pounds to be laid out in lands, the rents and profits whereof to be expended in bread and distributed in loaves to the value of fourpence each, in the chapel of Ecclesall, at four times in the year (to wit) every first Sunday after the feast of St. Michael, the feast of the Nativity, the feast of Easter, and upon Trinity Sunday, immediately after divine service in the forenoon, to such thirty poor inhabitants of Ecclesall for the time being as shall attend divine service in the forenoon of those days during the whole time of performing the same.

'These several sums have been laid out in the purchase of a close at Ecclesall-Byerlow, near Machon-bank, called the Carr, which was conveyed to certain trustees for the several uses, intents, and purposes of the above-mentioned charities.

'1750. Mr. John Yates of Wickersley, by his will bequeathed 10l. to be laid out in land, or put out to interest by the chapel warden and overseers of the poor, and the profits arising therefrom to be distributed to the poor of Ecclesall annually for ever.'

BANNER-CROSS.

This is one of the ancient esquires' seats in the manor of Ecclesall. It stands near the chapel, and not far from the turnpike road to Manchester, from which however it is shut in by plantations, while its front presents a pleasing feature in the landscape to the traveller on the opposite hill along the road to Chesterfield. The name might tempt an antiquary to wild conjectures, especially when he stands on the base of an old stone cross still remaining, and looks along Salter (perhaps Psalter) lane, towards Sheffield. But I shall forbear.

At this place flourished one branch of the family of Bright, who have had large possessions in this western part of the parish of Sheffield, and one of whom, as we have seen, acquired the manor itself. That part of the family who resided here were among the superior yeomanry of these parts at the beginning of the seventeenth century, but they soon stepped into the rank of gentry. It does not appear that they ever presented themselves at the visitations of the heralds, or that they had ever a grant of coat-armour. They became extinct in 1748, on the death of Mr. John Bright of Chesterfield and this place, whose granddaughter and heiress Mary Dalton conveyed this es-

tate to her husband Lord John Murray, of the house of Athol. He was colonel of the 42d or Highland regiment of foot, but after his marriage spent much of his time at Banner-cross, where he made many improvements. Lady John Murray died in London on the 21st of May 1765, at the age of 33, and was interred at Sheffield. She left an only daughter, who in 1782 married William Foxlowe esquire, a younger son of Samuel Foxlowe esquire, of Staveley in the county of Derby, who obtained the royal license to take and use the surname of Murray only. He was a lieutenant-general in the army. Mrs. Murray died leaving no issue. The general purchased the interest of the Athol family in this property, and retired to this place with the intention of spending within its tranquil shades the evening of an active and honourable life. In his hands Banner-cross promised to be more than it had ever been in its best of days. With the assistance of Mr. Jeffery Wyatt, he planned and began to execute, on the site of the old house, a fine structure in the style which for want of a better term must be called Gothic. It was begun in 1817, and the work proceeded so rapidly under the eye of its master, that its pinnacles were seen rising above the woods around it in the summer of the next year; when on Saturday the 29th of August 1818, the possessor was called away by death, leaving his work to others to finish, inhabit, and enjoy.

What the house was before General Murray came to revive its ancient hospitality, is not inaptly described in the following lines of Mrs. Hofland, formerly Miss Barbara Wreaks of Sheffield. Having conducted her reader through the precincts:

'Through many a winding path of flowery shrubs
That long unprun'd and unregarded shoot;'

she enters the house—

'A gloomy mansion, where in empty state
And cobwebb'd ruin hangs a goodly list
Of pictur'd lords, and many a beauteous dame
Of Athol's princely race: for time has been
They grac'd these gloomy walls, and e'en of late
Hath Beauty's queen here shown her peerless power,
And given her mandates from a Murray's eyes.
Bereft of these, the mouldering mansion wears
In every view, the signal of decay:
Slow whispering winds creep through the chilling rooms,
The tatter'd hangings shake with every breeze:
Through the long passages, and cold dark halls,
(So fame reports,) the flimsy spirits glide
In robes of white, or sweep the narrow stairs
In all the shapes of fear-form'd misery'.'

In the church of Chesterfield are various monumental memorials for owners of this house, who resided in that town. One was alderman and mayor of Chesterfield, and high-sheriff of the county of Derby. The portrait of this gentleman is in the collection at Banner-cross. From those monuments, the parish-registers of Sheffield and Chesterfield, wills, and private information, the following pedigree, which, imperfect as it is, is perhaps the best that can now be collected, has been carefully compiled.

See *Poems by Barbara Hoole*, 12mo, Sheffield 1805, p. 95.

PEDIGREE of BRIGHT of BANNER-CROSS.

ARMS.—Parti per pale gules and azure a bend or between two mullets argent.
CREST.—On a wreath a mass of clouds and therefrom a sun issuant, all proper.

JOHN BRIGHT of Banner-cross
was seated there in the reign of Elizabeth.

ROBERT BRIGHT of Banner-cross, eldest = EMOTE PARKIN,	HENRY BRIGHT	WILLIAM BRIGHT	Other issue.
son and heir. Bap. at Sheffield 7 Oct. widow, married	of Sheffield, bap.	of Sheffield, bap.	
1593. Made his will 1 Aug. 1667, and at Sheffield 10	there 17 October	22 Mar. 1612. Liv-	
dying 6 days after, was buried in the pa- July 1633.	1602. Living	ing 1634.	
rish church-yard, Sheffield, where his	1626.		
grave-stone still remains.			

JOHN BRIGHT of Ban- = ---- dau. and	ROBERT BRIGHT of = BRIDGET, daughter	STEPHEN BRIGHT, third son,	SAMUEL BRIGHT of	SARAH.
ner-cross, gent. eldest co-heir of Tho-	Sheffield, second son, of Thomas Scargel	bap. at Sheffield 27 October	Chesterfield, apothe-	
son and heir, bap. at mas Dale of	bap. 18 April 1641. of Sheffield, by Brid-	1664.	cary, fifth son, bap.	
Sheffield 27 Apr. 1634, Whiteley-	Made his will 14 Dec. get Oagathorpe his	JAMES BRIGHT, fourth son,	at Sheffield 7 April	
buried there 11 Nov. wood in the	1670, and was buried wife. Married 2	baptized at Sheffield 11 April	1650. Bur. at Ches-	
1686. township of	at Sheffield 3 January Dec. 1663, bur. 6	1647. Both mentioned as	terfield 22 Nov.	
Ecclesall.	1671. Aug. 1668.	then alive in their father's	1682.	
		will.		

JOHN BRIGHT of Banner-cross and = MARY, daughter of	ELIZABETH, wife of	ANNE, wife	SAMUEL	JOHN	MARY BRIGHT,	RUTH BRIGHT,
Chesterfield, esq., bap. at Sheffield Richard Youle,	Jonathan Watson,	of ------	BRIGHT,	BRIGHT,	mentioned in	wife of Thomas
7 March 1658. An alderman of gent., alderman of	to whom she was	White.	died	died in	her father's will	field, to whom
Chesterfield, and mayor in 1714: Chesterfield. Died	married at Shef-	Living 9	young.	his in-	1670.	she was mar-
high-sheriff of the county of Derby 6 Dec. 1714, aged	field 13 July 1686.	Feb. 1721.		fancy.		ried 4 August
1722. Will dated 9 February 1721. 58, and was buried	Living 9 Feb. 1721.					1691.
Died 19 June 1734, aged 77 years, on the 8th in the						
and was buried on the 21st in the church of Chester-						
church of Chesterfield. field.						

JOHN BRIGHT of Banner-cross = BARBARA, 5th and young-	NICHOLAS BRIGHT = MARY, dau. of	MARY,	ANN,	ELIZABETH,	SAMUEL.
and Chesterfield, esq., eldest est dau. of Francis Jessop	of Chesterfield, Godfrey Wat-	wife of	wife of	wife of Jo-	RICHARD.
son and heir. Executor to his of Broomhall, esq., marr.	gent., second son : kinson of	Thomas	Samuel	seph Bright	ROBERT.
father's will. Died without settlement dated 1 Feb.	an executor to his Brampton,	Hinckes-	Dawson	of Graystones,	THOMAS.
male issue 3 April 1748, aged 1701. Married at Shef-	father's will. Died near Chester-	man,M.A.	of Baw-	in the town-	MARY.
68, and was buried with his fa- field 4 March 1701. Died	10 May 1732, aged field, gent.,	rector of	trey, by	ship of Ec-	SARAH.
mily in the church of Chester- 9 Jan. 1722, aged 43, and	40, and was buried married at	Matlock	whom a	clesall, esq.	All died
field. was buried in the church	in the church of Brampton 15	and vicar	son		young.
of Chesterfield.	Chesterfield. Oct. 1717. Di-	of Ches-	John		
	ed 8 Sep.1766,	terfield.	Dawson.		
	aged 68,bur.at				
	Chesterfield.				

ADIN SORESBY of = BARBARA BRIGHT, eldest dau. and	RICHARD DALTON = MARY BRIGHT, younger	----- BRIGHT,	----- BRIGHT, co-
Chesterfield, gent. co-heir apparent, bap. at Sheffield	of Sheffield, mer- dau. and co-heir appa-	co-heir, wife of	heir, wife of the
Died without issue 13 Oct. 1702, married at Chester-	chant. rent. Buried in the mid-	the rev. Mr.	rev. Joseph Saun-
16 Feb. 1722, ten field 10 April 1721. Died without	dle aile of the parish-	Greatorex.	ders curate of
months after his issue 27 March 1726, aged 24.	church of Sheffield.		Brampton.
marriage.			

BRIGHT DALTON, born 1735, only son, and made	Lord JOHN MURRAY of Banner-cross and = MARY DALTON, sole heiress to her brother's es-
heir, by his grandfather's will, to Banner-cross and	Chesterfield, in right of his wife, and of tates, born in 1732, married at Sheffield 13 Sep.
other estates of the family. He was drowned on	Pitnacre in the shire of Perth, the eldest 1758 by Dr. John Fountayne, dean of York. Died
the 3d of August 1748, four months after his	son of John duke of Athol by his second 21 May 1765, and was buried with her mother in
grandfather's decease, at the age of 13, and was	wife, the dau. of William Lord Ross of the parish-church of Sheffield.
buried at Chesterfield.	Hawkhead. Died in France 1787.

WILLIAM FOXLOWE, afterwards MURRAY, = MARY MURRAY, only dau. and heir. Died
esquire, a lieutenant-general in the army. without issue in 1803; and with her ended
Died at Banner-cross 1818. the descendants of John Bright and Barbara Jessop.

The late General Murray gave by will his estate at Banner-cross to his sister Mrs. Bagshaw, the wife of the reverend William Bagshaw, a younger son of the late Colonel Samuel Bagshaw of Ford, but by the death of all his brothers without issue the eldest representative of the eldest branch of that family. This is another point at which the family of Bagshaw touch upon Hallamshire. All the late branches have sprung from William Bagshaw of Hucklow and Abney in the Peak of Derbyshire, who appeared at Sir William Dugdale's visitation of that county in 1662, and was then 64 years of age. He had a very numerous progeny; and three of his sons were the founders of three several families of the name, all opulent and respected.

I. William Bagshaw the eldest son. He was a clergyman, and for a while an assistant-minister at Sheffield and curate of Attercliffe, where we shall have occasion to speak of him again. He had afterwards the living of Glossop, from which he was ejected by the Act of Uniformity. He then went to reside on his own estate at Ford. His son and successor, Samuel Bagshaw of Ford, was married at Sheffield on the 20th of April 1685 to Sarah Child, the daughter and co-heir of Samuel Child of Leeds by Faith his wife, a daughter of William Spencer of Attercliffe-hall, esquire. The late Colonel Bagshaw of Ford was the grandson of that marriage, and by Catherine Coldwell his wife had William, who died an infant, Samuel Bagshaw late of Ford, esquire, John Bagshaw late of the Oaks in Norton, esquire, by gift of his cousin of that place; both dead without issue: Richard, who died an infant: and William, who married the sister of General Murray.

3 G

II. John Bagshaw of Litton and Hucklow, high-sheriff of the county of Derby 1696. He was twice married. By his first wife Grace, daughter of Henry Bright of Whirlow in the manor of Ecclesall, he had William his son and heir, whose only son, and widow, the daughter of Joshua Dunn of Attercliffe, lie interred in the Upper Chapel in Sheffield. The heiress of this branch carried Hucklow to her husband Aymer Rich of Bull-house, esquire; but there were male descendants from the first-named John, by his second wife, whose line it may now be found difficult to trace.

III. From Adam Bagshaw, the youngest of the three sons, descended that part of the family who resided at Castleton and the Oaks in Norton. The Oaks came to them by the marriage of Richard Bagshaw, his second son, with Elizabeth, the daughter and heir of Henry Gill of that place, whose descent and issue will be found on a future page.

WHIRLOW- or WHORLOW-HALL.

This is another ancient freehold inheritance of the family of Bright within the manor of Ecclesall. The house, after having been in the hands of tenants for more than a century past, still bears marks of having once been the residence of a family of good account. It stands near the edge of the parish of Sheffield, and not far from the hamlet of Dore, where many of the family of Bright have resided. They were settled at Whirlow at least as early as the time of Elizabeth, and probably before that period: but they never entered any pedigree at the herald's visitations. Indeed, at the last visitation of the county of York, Henry Bright of this place was a disclaimer; that is, he consented to have it recorded that he made no pretensions to coat-armour. The subjoined pedigree is compiled from the usual authorities in these matters—parish-registers, monumental memorials, wills, and other deeds, with the assistance of a brief notice of the family by the late Dr. Pegge, in a manuscript volume of genealogical collections in the library of Samuel Shore esquire, at Norton-hall.

PEDIGREE of BRIGHT of WHIRLOW-HALL.

JOHN BRIGHT of Whirlow, yeoman. Died intestate, and was buried at Sheffield 24 April 1586.	**=AGNES** had administration of her husband's effects 3 May 1587.	

HENRY BRIGHT of Whirlow, yeoman. Made his will 4 Jan. 1614, in which he directs that his body shall be buried in the church of Sheffield. He was buried there 8 Jan. 1615, and his will was proved at York on the 27 April following.	**=ANNE,** executrix to her husband's will.	**JOHN BRIGHT,** living 1614, when he was nominated a supervisor of the will of his brother. It is probable that he is the person of the name who stands at the head of the pedigree of Bright of Banner-cross.

JOHN BRIGHT of Whirlow, eldest son and heir, baptized at Sheffield 4 Dec. 1575.	**=GRACE,** dau. of Anthony Bright of Dore, yeoman, sister to Anthony B. of Dronfield-Woodhouse. Marr. sett. dated 1600. Married at Sheffield 17 June in that year.	**THOMAS BRIGHT,** second son, had Ecclesall-hall and the Scroggs by his father's will.	**WILLIAM BRIGHT,** third and youngest surviving son, bap. at Sheffield 19 June 1590. Living 1614.	**ANNE,** wife of Anthony Bright of Dronfield-Woodhouse, to whom she was mar. 28 Jan. 1611.	**JOAN,** wife of Warren Scargell, to whom she was mar. at Sheffield 17 Jan. 1615.	**ELIZABETH,** living unmarried 1614. **HENRY, ELLEN.** All died young.

HENRY BRIGHT of Whirlow, gentleman, one of the 12 capital burgesses of Sheffield, bap. at Sheffield 17 Jan. 1602. His will bears date 1680. He died on 14 June 1684, at the age of 82, and was buried among his family in the south aile of the parish-church of Sheffield.	**=GERTRUDE RAMSCAR,** of the chapelry of Bradfield, buried at Sheffield 8 Nov. 1664.	**ELLEN BRIGHT,** mentioned in the will of her grandfather, who gives her a ewe and lamb, 1614.

HENRY BRIGHT of Whirlow, gent., bap. at Sheffield 1 Jan. 1632. Married 1655, buried at Sheffield 20 Jan. 1694.	**=ELIZABETH,** dau. of Ralph Clarke of Ashgate, in the parish of Chesterfield, gent., by Frances Blount of Eckington, his wife; sister to Cornelius Clarke of Norton-hall esquire, bur. at Sheffield 19 Dec. 1688.	**EDWARD HARRIS** of Stretton, co. Derby, first husband.	**GERTRUDE,** wife first of John son and heir of Nicholas Greaves of Shephouse in the parish of Peniston. Mar. sett. dated 29 April 1662. And secondly, of Benjamin Eyre of Edale, co. Derb.	**GRACE,** wife of John Bagshaw of Litton and Hucklow, esquire.	**ANNE,** wife of Francis Stevenson of Ounston in the parish of Dronfield, gent.	**Other children,** most of whom, if not all, died in their infancy.

BENJAMIN BRIGHT, son and heir-apparent, mentioned in his grandfather's will. Died in the life-time of his father, and was bur. at Sheffield 12 Aug. 1687.	**CORNELIUS BRIGHT,** buried at Norton 21 June 1682. Said to have been drowned in one of the ponds at Norton-hall.	**HENRY BRIGHT** of Whirlow, gent., only surviving son and heir. Bap. at Sheffield 26 April 1664. Living at Whirlow 1705.	—	**ANNE BRIGHT,** bap. at Sheffield 16 June 1661. Died unmarried, and was buried at Sheffield 4 Dec. 1680.	**HANNAH BRIGHT,** bap. at Sheffield 19 April 1663, married Revel Copley of Cold-Aston, gent., second son of John Copley of Skelbrook, near Doncaster, esq.	**GERTRUDE BRIGHT,** bap. at Sheffield 4 June 1665. Living unmarried 1680.

HENRY BRIGHT, bap. at Sheffield 18 June 1701.	**DOROTHY BRIGHT,** bap. at Sheffield 2 Sep. 1695.	**ELIZABETH BRIGHT,** bap. at Sheffield 13 March 1698, buried at Norton 14 July 1707.	**JANE BRIGHT,** bap. at Sheffield 28 July 1699.	**JOAN BRIGHT,** bap. at Sheffield 16 Nov. 1704.	**ANNE BRIGHT,** bap. at Sheffield 1 Dec. 1709.

I can carry this genealogy no further. Perhaps the last-named Henry died in his infancy. At any rate he did not succeed to the estate of his family, for his father sold Whirlow-hall and the estate around it. It passed into the hands of Sir John Statham of Tidswell, an attorney in great practice, who resold it in June 1725 to the Hollis family, for the endowment of their hospital at Sheffield, for the sum of 1900l.

The last Bright of Whirlow reduced himself and his family to want. His habits seem to have been those of low vulgarity coupled with an extravagant fondness for the chase and adventurous horsemanship. The most incredible stories of his equestrian exploits are still told by the villagers about Whirlow. There was a small public-house in Fullwood known by the name of Water Carr-hall, which was the principal scene of this wretched man's in-door dissipation. At this house he was accustomed to meet his two friends, Fox of Fullwood and Hall of Stumperlow, who were running the same low road to ruin. Here they held their revels while their estates were going to decay, and continued them till they all found themselves in the very jaws of poverty. Hall was reduced so low that, like Well-born in Massinger's play, he was refused bread at the ale-house where his property had been squandered away. This anecdote Mr. Wilson had received on good authority.

The case of these three gentlemen bears a close resemblance to that of three other persons of the same neighbourhood, of much superior rank and property, who at the same period were playing the same game on a grander scale and with the same success: Sir Gervase Cutler of Stainborough, Sir Francis Burdett of Burthwaite, and Sir William Reresby of Thribergh. The evil influence of the profligate court of Charles II. extended itself through all the gradations of society, producing vice, ruin, and misery.

But while the parent stock was thus untimely rooted up, a branch which had shot out from it still existed, and its ramifications are now extending themselves among the mechanics of Sheffield. In the course of some inquiries which I made in the year 1803 after the remains of this once considerable Hallamshire family, I found one Joseph Bright living in that obscurest of all parts of the town of Sheffield, Sands-Paviours. He was more than seventy years of age, and had all the appearance of a cutler *of the old school*, with no trace of having ever occupied a station higher than that in which he then appeared. With some degree of distrust I heard him announce himself the male representative of the former owners of Whirlow-hall, the descendant of a William Bright whose name appeared in the fragment which he produced of a settlement of the Whirlow estate on the marriage of John Bright with Grace daughter of Anthony Bright of Dore in 1600. But he was unquestionably right. I have since had the means of verifying his statement. William Bright, the third son of Henry Bright of Whirlow, on whom the estate was settled on failure of issue from his elder brother (in preference to the *second* son, who was to succeed only on failure of issue from the first and third), left Stephen Bright his son and heir, who by Ellen his wife, daughter of John and Mary Hudson of Rocher-head in Bradfield, had Joseph Bright of Ecclesall, born in 1644, grandfather to the Joseph Bright first mentioned. The old man had then living three sons and as many daughters.

In the will of the first Henry Bright of the preceding table we see something of the simplicity of early times. To his younger children and to his infantine grand-children he bequeaths part of the live stock on his estate, a ewe and a lamb to each. It was doubtless intended that they should run with the flock of the eldest son, to whom the land descended, and multiply to make fortunes for the younger children. In the ' History of Craven' are preserved some curious depositions relating to Fountain's Abbey, wherein an old man, who had been a shepherd to the abbot, says that ' when he kept the flocks, having a lambe given him the firste year.....of th'onlie increase which came

of that lambe he had threescore and thirteene good ewes when the abbaye was put downe¹.'

Beside the two families of whom an account has been already given, there have been several other persons of the name of Bright living in the style of gentry within the manor of Ecclesall, and all doubtless sprung from some common ancestor. Probably that ancestor lived at or about Dore, where the family was seated at least as early as the reign of King Henry VIII.; for Ellen daughter of Robert Bright of that place, who married Francis Sitwell of Eckington, must have been born in that king's reign. An Anthony Bright of that place, probably brother to Ellen, had a numerous issue. His great-grandson John Bright of Dore, yeoman, made his will in 1669, in which he mentions a son Stephen, and two daughters Ellen and Mary. Anthony Bright had also three daughters, namely, Ellen wife of Thomas Burton esquire of Dronfield, who in 1628 served the office of high-sheriff of the county of Derby; Grace, the wife of John Bright of Whirlow; and Elizabeth, of Nicholas Burley of the Yews in Bradfield; and a younger son named John Bright, who was living at Brincliffe-edge in the manor of Ecclesall in 1620. By Elizabeth his wife, daughter of Rowland Revel of Cold-Aston, he had a daughter Ellen, who married John Brooke of Pond near Silkston, yeoman, whose estate was afterwards possessed by his relative John Charles Brooke, esquire, a name dear to the lovers of Yorkshire topography. Elizabeth, another daughter of John Bright of Brincliffe-edge, was the wife of Richard Adwick of Almholme in the parish of Arksey, gentleman. He had also a son named Anthony Bright, who was the father of John Bright of Lees-hall and Dronfield, gentleman, who in 1682 married Anne Barker, a daughter of Francis Barker of Dore and of Lees-hall, esquire, by Anne his wife, daughter and sole heir of John Parker, of an ancient family in the parish of Norton. This Mrs. Bright was before married to John Cave of Lees-hall. Her children were John Bright of Dronfield, gentleman, living there in 1730, Anne, Mary, and Francis.

John Bright of Lees-hall sold the estate at Brincliffe-edge in 1693 to Thomas Bright of Graystones in the manor of Ecclesall, gentleman, whom he calls his brother. But as this Thomas Bright was married at the time of this purchase to a lady whose name before marriage was Elizabeth Bright, we are not warranted, in the absence of concurrent testimony, in setting down this Thomas Bright, from whom most of the existing members of this family whose descent is known are sprung, as son of Anthony, son of John Bright of Brincliffe-edge. In his will dated in 1696, this Thomas Bright calls John Bright of Banner-cross his cousin.

This Thomas Bright of Graystones, gentleman, was born a little before the Civil Wars. He was twice married: first to Barbara Froggat one of the daughters of Godfrey Froggat of Middle-Mathfield, in the county of Stafford, gentleman, by Elizabeth his wife, daughter of James Bullock of Greenhill in the parish of Norton, gentleman. She died in 1675; and he married secondly, on the 29th of September in the same year, Elizabeth Bright. Beside many daughters he had four sons, all of whom married and left issue. Two of them were the offspring of his first marriage, namely, John and Thomas, both of whom died in the lifetime of their father. Thomas left an only child of his own name, who was living in 1696, when the grandfather made his will: but I can trace him no further.

John Bright the eldest son, by Elizabeth his wife, daughter of Alexander Ashton of Whiteley-wood in Ecclesall, gentleman, left Thomas, Robert, and Barbara, all living in 1696. Thomas was of Graystones, and by Mary Webster his wife had many children; of whom Thomas was father of Paul Bright, late of Inkersell in the parish of Staveley, gentleman, who had seven sons and three daughters, most of whom are now alive. John Bright, a younger son of Thomas Bright and Mary Webster, was of Sheffield, and the father of John Bright of the same place, who by Susanna his wife, daughter of Westby Hatfield of Sheffield, mercer, fourth and youngest son of John Hatfield of Hatfield near Doncaster, esquire, had a son John-Hatfield Bright now of Sheffield.

Joseph Bright esquire, the third son of Thomas Bright, succeeded his father in the estate at Graystones. He was in the commission of the peace, and married Elizabeth daughter of John Bright of Banner-cross, esquire. I am uncertain whether this lady had not a former husband, Thomas Gladwin of Chesterfield, esquire. Mr. Bright had three sons, John, Thomas, and Joseph, of whom Thomas Bright was vicar of Ecclesfield, and also two daughters, Elizabeth wife of —— Abby, and Mary wife of John Nodder of Sheffield, gentleman. The representative of this branch of the family is the reverend James Bright of Grafton-Regis in Northamptonshire.

On James Bright, the youngest of the four sons of Thomas Bright of Graystones, the estate of Brincliffe-Edge was settled by his father's will, and there he resided till his death in 1727. He married Judith, one of the daughters of Alexander Fenton of Gleadleys, gentleman, sister to John Fenton of Little Sheffield, gentleman, who by Ann Lee his wife had Elizabeth Fenton his only daughter and heir, who was married at Sheffield on the 31st of December 1748 to John Rotheram of Dronfield, esquire, who was high-sheriff of the county of Derby in 1750. James Bright had by Judith Fenton his wife an only son Thomas Bright of Hawley-croft in Sheffield, gentleman, father of the late Mr. Thomas-Fenton Bright.

WHITELEY-WOOD.

This is another of the old hall-houses of the township of Ecclesall. It exhibits evident tokens of having been built for the residence of a family of gentry, which indeed it was. It stands sequestered in its own woods; but from the house or its immediate neighbourhood may be commanded a view of the Porter valley, and the cultivated hill of Fullwood beyond it. The many works which have been erected on the Porter are so constructed and disposed that they commonly present an agreeable and harmonized feature in the landscape, a feature almost peculiar to the neighbourhood of Sheffield: so different are the low and small buildings erected for the iron-manufactures from the huge cotton-mills with which some of the finest valleys in Yorkshire are deformed.

Thomas Dale was a considerable freeholder of the manor in the time of Charles I., and had a house here. He left two daughters his co-heirs, one of whom was married to John Bright of Banner-cross, as hath been already related; the other married Alexander Ashton, descended of the Ashtons of Shepley in the county of Lancaster, who made this place his usual residence, and probably built the present house. He was married in 1659.

PEDIGREE OF ASHTON of WHITELEY-WOOD.

! He left other children besides those mentioned in the pedigree.

The hall and estate of Whiteley-wood passed on the extinction of this family to the Pegges of Beauchief; and were sold by Mr. Strelley Pegge to that ingenious mechanician Mr. Thomas Bolsover, of whom we have already had occasion to make honourable mention. He died here on Tuesday the 13th day of September 1788, at the age of 84, leaving two daughters, Mrs. Hutton and Mrs. Mitchell. The house has since been the property and residence of Mr. William Hutton, who died in March 1818. He added considerably by purchases and inclosures to the property possessed by his grandfather.

About 1789 Mrs. Hutton and Mrs. Mitchell built a small place of worship near the house, for the convenience of persons employed in their extensive works on the Porter. The success which has attended the labours of these benevolent ladies and their successors, in the education and the religious instruction of the poor who were placed more immediately under their influence, I am happy to say, has shown that the close association which must take place in a large manufactory among the labouring classes is not incompatible with a very sound and healthful state of the public morals.

BROOM-HALL.

This respectable old mansion stands a little to the north of the Porter, and about a mile west of Sheffield. It is a low building embosomed in trees:

'———— secreta parentis
Anchisæ domus, arboribusque obtecta.'

The part of it represented in the engraving is of an age not later than the time of Henry VIII. The Jessops added to the original structure during the time it was in their possession. The modern part was built by the reverend James Wilkinson, vicar of Sheffield,

who resided in this hall of his maternal ancestors during nearly the whole period of his long incumbency. It was here that in his character of magistrate he was accustomed to administer justice with prudence and equity. In the year 1791 Broom-hall was attacked by a mob of misguided and thoughtless people, who set fire to the house and much damaged the library which had been collected by Mr. Wilkinson's great-grandfather, Francis Jessop esquire, one of the earliest members of the Royal Society.

3 H

Around it lay a beautiful estate richly cultivated, well watered, and well wooded, which descended in a right line to Mr. Wilkinson from many ancestors.

It does not appear at what time this estate was granted off by the De Ecclesalls or their successors. Among the lands settled by Sir Robert de Ecclesall (the last of his name) on Joan de Wanton, was 'what he had in Broom.' The first owners of these lands as a separate estate of whom I have found mention, were the De Wickersleys, some of whom resided here; though it may be presumed that their principal place of abode would be at the village of which they were lords and from which their hereditary name was derived, about ten miles from Broom-hall.

At that place they were very early settled. The first who used that surname was Richard Fitz-Turgis, who in the reign of King Stephen was co-founder with Richard de Busli of the neighbouring abbey of Roche[1].

Robert de Wickersley married Joanna daughter of Adam de la Roche, son of Simon de la Roche[2].

Thomas Wykersley was returned lord of the manor of Wickersley 9 Edward II. 1315, along with Jordan de Ilde and Richard de Dred[3].

By his last will and testament bearing date 20 May 1471 Roger Wickersley bequeathed his body to be buried in the chapel of Saint Mary within the church of Saint Alban at Wickersley[4]. He died four days after, and was interred according to his directions, the fine flag which covers his remains still existing, having the arms of Wickersley, a fess between three cinquefoils, at its four corners.

Nicholas Wickersley by his will dated the 3d of April 1505 bequeathed his body to be buried in the church of Wickersley on the north side. It was proved at York on the 15th of the same month[5].

John Wickersley esquire by his will dated the 3d of May 1506 bequeathed his body to be buried in the church of Sheffield[6]. This I apprehend to be the person of that name who was one of the witnesses of the covenant for building Lady's-bridge.

By deed dated at Sprodborough the 11th of April 11 Henry VIII. John Everingham clerk, at the instance of John Wickersley the younger, son and heir of John Wickersley senior esquire deceased, conveyed to George Lynacre esquire, John Knifton esquire, Nicholas Everingham and Richard Everingham, gentlemen, his manor of Wickersley with the appurtenances at Wickersley, Hoton-Lyvet, Sheffeld, Ecclesall, Halom, Bramley, Attyrcliff, Darnall, Tikhill, Kymbreworth, Tynneslowe, and Brekesherth, in the county of York, and at Haversege in the county of Derby, which the said John Everingham together with Henry and Thomas Everingham and Thomas Wickersley now deceased held of the gift of the said John Wickersley the elder, father to the first-named John Wickersley, for the performance of his last will; to hold to the said Lynacre, Knifton, Everingham, and Everingham, according to the force and intent of the said last will[7].

24 April 1528 John Wickersley, describing himself

of Broom-hall in the parish of Sheffield esquire, bequeathed his body to be buried in the parish-church of Sheffield, ' in the rode chapel, nigh the image of the same rode[8].'

About this time the family became extinct. Nicholas Wiekersley, son of John, was the last of the name. His only daughter and heiress became the wife of Robert Swyft the younger, esquire, son of another Robert Swyft, a gentleman of large possessions and excellent character who resided at Rotherham. By this marriage Robert Swyft became possessed of Wickersley, Broom-hall, and the other estates of that ancient family. He seems to have made Broom-hall his principal residence. It was conveniently situated in the near neighbourhood of the noble family at Sheffield-castle, one of whose principal agents he was. It was in the name of this Robert Swyft that the petition of the inhabitants of Sheffield for the restoration of the church-lands was presented, and his name stands first among the twelve capital burgesses named in the patent. He also obtained the tythes of Ecclesall, Heeley, and Hallam: and to him and his brother William Swyft was granted in the 36th year of Henry VIII. anno 1544 the advowson of the church of Sheffield.

On the origin of the family of Swyft who thus obtained so predominant an interest at Sheffield, our old genealogists are not agreed. The compiler of a curious collection of Yorkshire biography and genealogy which now forms part of the Harleian collection of manuscripts[9] deduces them from Durham: representing Robert Swyft the elder as son of another Robert Swyft of Aller-gill in that bishoprick, son of Anthony of the same, son of Edmund, son of John, son and heir of Sir Humphry Swyft knight, who held Aller-gill by gift of bishop Beaumont. But this account is not supported by reference to charters or other documents. A smaller but more valuable collection of Yorkshire genealogy is contained in volume 6070 of the same library of manuscripts. It is founded on the visitation of Flower and Glover in 1585, but contains many most valuable additions, evidently the work of some skilful person, and one who was aware how much more valuable is a pedigree of few descents well established, than one without reference to evidence though reaching beyond the Conquest. This compiler, whose name I wish could be retrieved, begins his pedigree of Swyft with the grandfather of the first Swyft of Broom-hall, a person residing at Rotherham, and evidently of some consideration there, having married into one of the oldest and most opulent families of the wapentake, the Annes of Frickley. He lived in the time of Henry VII. But it may be shown that even before that time the name of Swyft was common and respectable in the neighbourhood of Sheffield and Rotherham. In 1455 there was a grant from Richard Wood, bailiff of Sheffield, and William Swyft of Tinslowe, to John Hyne of Sheffield of half a toft built upon lying near Water-lane[10]. John Swyft of Tinslowe or Tinsley died intestate, and on the 10th of May 1491 Margaret his widow had license to take the mantle and the ring[11].

[1] Tanner, 637.   [2] Dods.
[3] Harl. MSS. in Mus. Brit. 6281.
[4] Dods. MSS. Harl. 801.   Wickersley.
[5] Torre's Testamentary Burials at Wickersley.
[6] Torre's Testamentary Burials at Sheffield.
[7] Evidences of the Rev. J. Wilkinson. Notes from them made by the late Thomas Blore esq.
[8] Torre's Testamentary Burials at Sheffield.
[9] No. 4656. It may be worth observing that the rough draught of this MS. is in the cathedral library at York, and in the catalogue is called Nelson's Heraldry,' xvi. D 5.
[10] Evidences of church burgesses.
[11] What this means may be collected from the following passage in Stowe. ' This Godnay in the year 1444 wedded the widow of Robert

In 1493 administration of the intestate's goods was granted by the proper authorities at York to her and her son Thomas Swyft chaplain. This Thomas Swyft became afterwards rector of Wickersley and of Burnsall, and by the description of Sir Thomas Swyft priest made his will on the 8th of February 1524. Therein he desires that his body may be buried in the church of Rotherham before the door of our Lady's quire. He gives certain sums of money to various relations, and also to the church of Rotherham and the chapel of Tinsley. He gives also to the reparation of the *gate* (that is the road) at Tinsley. To the monastery of Rufford he bequeaths a great silver salt gilt, with a cover, and to the Lord Abbot there a girdle with harness silver gilt. He gives to Robert Swyft of Rotherham a macer, a bowl, with a cover, of silver, having a roebuck upon it: and he appoints the said Robert Swyft and Robert Nevile provost of the college of Saint John at Rotherham his executors. This bequest of a silver bowl bearing the heraldric insignia of the family affords strong ground of presumption, to say no more, that the two Swyfts were nearly allied, and consequently that Robert Swyft of Rotherham could hardly have been so lately from the bishoprick of Durham.

This will further shows that the family enjoyed no inconsiderable property; and thus contributes to render disputable a position which has been generally received concerning it, on the sole authority as it seems of the Harleian manuscript 4630, that a fortunate marriage with the rich widow of a brewer in London in the time of Henry VIII. was the immediate cause of the elevation of this family above their neighbours.

By tradition in the family of Dr. Jonathan Swift dean of Saint Patrick's, his ancestors were from Yorkshire, and allied to the family of whom we are now speaking[1]. The first of his ancestors of whom we have any certain knowledge was Thomas Swift rector of Saint Andrew's Canterbury. He was born in 1535[2]. I do not despair of being able at some time hereafter to establish his relationship to the clergyman lately mentioned (his namesake) the rector of Wickersley, who died eleven years before.

Robert Swyft, the executor of Sir Thomas Swyft, married to his first wife Anne daughter of William Taylor of Sheffield. He lived to the eighty-fourth year of his age, and has a monument in the north choir of the church of Rotherham with the following inscription:

' Here under this tomb is placed & buried the bodys of Robert Swift esquire, & Anne his first wyfe, who lived many yeares in this towne of Rotherham, in vertuous fame, great wealth, & good worship. They were pittifull to the pore, and relieved them, & to their friends no lesse faithfull than bountifull: Truly they feared God, who plentifully poured his blessings uppon them. The said Anne died in the moneth of June, in the yeare of our Lord God 1539, in the 67th yeare of her age; & the said Robert departed the VIII. of August, in the yeare of our Lord God 1561, in the 84th yeare of his age: on whose soules, & all Christen soules, th' omnipotent Lord have mercy. Amen. Respice finem.'

He had two daughters and two sons. One daughter married Lionel Reresby of Thribergh esquire, from whom descended a race of baronets of that name and

place. She has a monument in the church of Thribergh on which she is called ' *celebris pia filia Swifti.*' Another married Richard Waterton, chief of that ancient house of Waterton of Walton in the parish of Sandal, but left no issue. The sons were Robert and William Swyft.

Robert married the heir of Wickersley, and was of Broom-hall. I have found his name in connexion with the parish of Sheffield first in 1532, when he had a lease from the abbot and convent of Beauchief of a messuage with all lands, feedings, and pastures, lying in Archerfield and Whitfield, for forty years, at the rent of 13s. 4d.[3] In 33 Henry VIII. 1541, Thomas Greenwood and Cecilia his wife surrendered to him by the style of ' Robert Swyft of Broom-hall, gentleman,' in the manor-court of Sheffield, certain lands called ' Stacye-house.' In 1 Edward VI. 1547, he had license to alienate two messuages called Archerfield and Whitfield with the appurtenances in Ecclesall, lately in the tenure of Robert Swyft and Thomas Rodes, and another messuage in Ecclesall in the tenure of John Bostock, to William Taylor and John Taylor and their heirs. By letters patent dated at Westminster the 15th of May 36 Henry VIII. 1544, he and his brother William Swyft had an extensive grant of abbey lands, and along with them the advowsons of Sheffield and Beighton, to be held of the king in capite by knight's service, by the twentieth part of one knight's fee. The consideration money was 532l. 6s. 10d. Again, by indenture bearing date the 31st of August 5 Edward VI. 1551, William Swyft of Beighton in the county of Derby, gentleman, releases his right and title in those lands, &c. and in others granted to them jointly by King Edward VI., to his brother Robert Swyft. To this deed is a seal appendant bearing the arms of Swyft, a chevron between three roe-bucks courant, charged with as many pheons, and on a chief the same number of escallop shells[4].

Robert Swyft of Broom-hall died before his father, and left only female issue. The eldest daughter, named Frances, married Sir Francis Leake of Sutton in the county of Derby, knight, progenitor of the Leakes earls of Scarsdale. Mary the second daughter was married at Hatfield on the 24th of January 1558, to Francis Wortley of Wortley, esquire; and Anne the youngest married Richard Jessop, son of William Jessop of Rotherham, gentleman.

On the partition of the estates of Robert Swyft among these his three daughters and co-heirs, by deed bearing date the 22d of September 1561, to Leake were assigned the manors of Wadsley, Worrall, and Wickersley; to Wortley, Beighton, Birley, and Hackenthorp, with the parsonage of Beighton and its appurtenances; and to Jessop, the estate at Broom-hall, and another at North-Lees in the parish of Hathersage in the county of Derby[5].

A large share of the Swyft property thus passed into other hands: but enough remained to enable the second son William Swyft to maintain the port and rank of an esquire at a time when that title was not so liberally conceded as at present it is. He presented

---

Large late maior, which widdow *had taken the mantell and ring* and the vow to live chaste to God tearme of her life; for the breach whereof the marriage done, they were troubled by the church, and put to penance both he and she.' London, 4to, p. 187.
[1] See the Dean's own account, printed in the appendix to his Life by Dr. Sheridan, and to Deane Swift's Essay. Though the Dean wrote on this subject, he writes in a manner which shows that he had not thought it worthy of much attention.
[2] See his Monumental Inscription from Saint Andrew's church, in the Index to the *Biographia Britannica,* word ' Swift.'
[3] Pegge, 194.
[4] From collections made by John Reynolds of Plaistow.
[5] Id.

to the vicarage of Sheffield in 1559, and the baptism of his only son and heir Sir Robert Swyft is recorded in our parish-register. He had left Beighton and was residing at Rotherham on the 20th of August 1568, when he made his will; in which he directs that a substantial honest dinner shall be provided on the day of his funeral for his worshipful and honest friends; and that every poor man, woman, and child that shall attend his funeral, shall have a dinner and a penny in silver. To his sister Mrs. Reresby he bequeaths a black gown, and directs that his wife and children shall be clothed in black ' after the ancient custom of this realm.' He desires his wife Margaret and Robert his son to solemnize a marriage between his ward Rauf Beiston esquire and either of his two unmarried daughters ' which he shall like best.' He expresses his hope that his son Robert Swyft will follow the steps of his late grandfather, and he gives to him a chain of fine gold weighing twenty-four ounces, and two rings of gold graven with his arms and cognizance. He also makes him his executor, and Sir Thomas Gargrave of Nostel, knight, supervisor, to whom he gives a sovereign, value thirty shillings. This will was proved in the archbishop's court at York.

In the person of the son the honours of the family were advanced. His mother was Margaret, daughter of Hugh Wyrral of Loversall esquire, and widow, when married to Swyft, of Thomas Ricard of Hatfield. He himself was twice married: first to Bridget, one of the daughters and co-heirs of Sir Francis Hastings, the last of that ancient name at Fenwick near Doncaster; and secondly, to Ursula, daughter of Stephen Barnham of Lewes in Sussex, (who was brother to Benedict Barnham alderman of London, a name familiar to genealogists,) and co-heir to her brother Martin Barnham esquire. In Nalson's manuscript before noticed, we have this account of him: ' Sir Robert Swyft of Rotherham and Doncaster, knight, had the title of Cavalier given him by Queen Elizabeth; was twice high-sheriff of Yorkshire, in the forty-second year of Queen Elizabeth and the sixteenth of King James; was justice of peace in the forty-first and forty-second of the said queen; was *tam Martis quam Mercurii*, a great swordsman and an elegant speaker. At a charge given by him at Doncaster, he told the grand jury that there were two governments in this nation, the one *gubernatio belli*, the other *gubernatio pacis*, the government of war, and the government of peace:—Among the Romans Cn. Pompeius *Magnus* had the government of war, but Quintus Fabius *Maximus* had the government of peace:—Now I need not tell you whether of these governments are to be preferred: I shall refer you to the positive and superlative degrees of Magnus and Maximus[1].' This Sir Robert Swyft was bow-bearer of the royal chase of Hatfield. In July 1609 he entertained Henry Prince of Wales at his house at Tristhorp, close to the chase, who had come thither for the purpose of taking the diversion of hunting[2]. He had also a house in Doncaster. ' From York,' says the lively water-poet, ' I rode to Doncaster, where my horses were well fed at the Bear, but myself found out the honourable knight Sir Robert Anstruther, at his father in lawes, the truly noble Sir Robert Swift's house, he being then high-sheriff of Yorkshire, where with their good ladies, and the right honourable the Lord Sanquhar, I was stayed two nights and one day, Sir Robert Anstruther (I thank him) not only paying for my two horses' meat, but at my departure he gave me a letter to Newark[3].' Sir Robert Swyft died at Doncaster on the 14th of March 1625, and was buried in the church of that town; but his memory long survived in the traditional stories of his contests with the deer stealers in the chase of Hatfield, and perhaps is not yet extinct.

His son Barnham Swyft was created by King Charles I. lord viscount Carlingford of the kingdom of Ireland. He enjoyed the title a very short time, and with him it became extinct. His only daughter and heir Mary Swyft was only seven months old at the time of her father's death in 1634. She was so unfortunate as to marry the thoughtless and profligate Fielding of the court of Charles II., who scattered the Swyft property to the winds.

There were seven generations of the name of Jessop at Broom-hall. The last, who was one of his majesty's justices of Chester, died in 1734, leaving only female issue. The family first became known to the heralds in 1575, when Richard Jessop, being settled on the estate which had come to him by his wife, and having three sons, and therefore a prospect that his name would be perpetuated, applied to William Flower Norroy-king-at-arms for a grant of arms and crest, who assigned him those which appear below. At the same time he entered a pedigree, in which he gave no account of his ancestry beyond his father[4]. Another was entered by his grandson Wortley Jessop at Saint George's visitation of Nottinghamshire 1614, and a third by Francis Jessop at Sir William Dugdale's visitation of the county of York 1665[5]. These official pedigrees form the basis of the annexed genealogy, in which however are many material additions from the evidences of the late reverend James Wilkinson and other indisputable authorities.

[1] F. 289.   [2] De la Pryme's Hatfield. MS. in the Lansdowne library.   [3] *Penniless Pilgrimage.* Works, folio. Lond. 1630, p. 140.

[4] Harl. MSS. 1171, f. 80 b.   [5] C. 40. in Col. Arm. f. 120.

PEDIGREE of JESSOP of BROOM-HALL.

ARMS.—Barry of 6 argent and azure, on each piece of the first 3 mullets gules.
CREST.—On a torce a turtle dove standing on an olive branch which is bent over its head all proper.
ARMS of SWYFT.—Or, a chevron barry nebulée argent and azure between 3 roe-bucks courant proper [1].

ROBERT SWYFT of Rotherham, = AGNES, daughter of
in the time of Edward IV. | Anne of Frickley.

ANNE, first wife, dau. = ROBERT SWYFT of Rotherham, = CATHERINE, second wife,
of William Taylor of | esq. Born 1477. Died 8 Aug. | dau. of Richard Bosvile
Sheffield. Died June | 1561, aged 83, and was buried | of Gunthwaite, esq. It is
1539, aged 66, buried | at Rotherham. | certain there was a second
at Rotherham. | | wife. Her name and family
| | are taken from Harl. 4630.

WILLIAM JESSOP = EMOTE, dau. of John Charlesworth	ROBERT SWYFT = ELLEN, dau. and heir of	WILLIAM SWYFT of = MARGARET, dau.
of Rotherham.	of Treeton. Her will is dated 10	of Broom-hall,	Nicholas son of John	Rotherham, esq.,	of Hugh Wyrral
	Feb. 1569; and was proved before	esquire.	Wickersley of Wickers-	second son. Died 10	of Loversal, esq.
	the dean of Doncaster 1570.		ley and Broom-hall, esq.	May 11 Eliz.

LAURENCE JESSOP,	AGNES, wife	RICHARD JESSOP of Broom-hall, gent.	ANNE SWYFT,	FRANCIS SWYFT,	MARY SWYFT,	Sir ROBERT
second son, mention-	of --- Vescy.	Presented to the vicarage of Sheffield	youngest dau. and	second son. Died	wife of Francis	SWYFT of
ed in the will of his	Mentioned in	in 1567 and 1569. Will dated 8 Oct.	wife of Sir Francis	at Sheffield	Wortley of	Rotherham
mother 1569; and	the wills of	22 Eliz. Proved before the dean of Don-	Leake of Sutton,	second son. Died	Wortley, esq.	and Doncas-
of his brother 1580.	her mother	caster 22 April 1581 by Francis Wort-	co. Derb. knight.	14 April		ter, knt.
	and brother.	ley his executor. Buried at Sheffield	being aged 27, 5	1575.		
		26 Nov. 1580.	and 6 Philip and			
			Mary. Buried at			
			Sheffield 10 Mar.			
			1567.			

MARGARET, first wife, dau. = WILLIAM JESSOP = ANNE,	2d = JANE, 3d wife, dau.	RICHARD	FRANCIS	SUSAN JES-	MARGARET, wife of Tho-
of Sir John Atherton of	of	Broom-hall,	wife, dau.	of Edward Disney.	JESSOP,	JESSOP,	SOP, buried	mas Symcocks esq., a
Atherton, co. Lanc. knight,	esq., eldest son	and heir, aged 13,	of	Survived and remar-	2d son.	3d son.	at Sheffield	justice of the peace for
by Margaret his wife, dau.	---Goodrick.	1575. Buried at	---Goodrick.	ried (at Sheffield 26	Living	Living	14 April	the counties of Notting-
and co-heir of Thomas	Living 5	Sheffield 8 Sep.	Living 5	Nov. 1635) with	1575.	1575.	1575.	ham and Somerset.
Catherall of Little Mitton,	James I.	1630.	James I.	Lionel Fanshaw of				
co. Lanc. esq. Married at				Dronfield, gent.				
Sheffield 21 Jan. 1582. Bur.								
there 26 April 1585.								

WORTLEY JESSOP, = CATHERINE, second dau. and	GEORGE JESSOP of Brancliffe, in the	MARGARET, wife of Hum-	ANNE, wife of
gent., eldest son and	co-heir of Thomas Doyley of	parish of Anston, esq., second son,	phry Savage of North-	Thomas Eyre
heir-apparent. Born 13 Apr. 1583.	London, M.D., a younger son	born at Broom-hall 29 May 1584,	Lees, in the parish of	in the parish
Marr. settlement dated 30 Jan. 5	of John Doyley of Chislehamp-	bap. at Sheffield 3 June. A barrister	Hathersage, gent., and	of Hather-
James. Made his will 13 Apr. 1615.	ton, co. Oxon. esq.—It seems	of the Middle Temple. Will dated 4	secondly of William Young	sage, esq.
He was lost at sea, and his will was	she took for her second hus-	Sep. 1651, and proved before the	gent., to whom she was	
proved in the manor-court of Mans-	band Mr. Henry Lukin, at	judges for probate of wills under the	married at Sheffield 27	
field 27 May 1617.	Worksop 22 Dec. 1618. See	keepers of the liberties of England	July 1646.	
	Ath. Ox. i. 275.	28 Sep. 1653. Buried at Sheffield 17		
		Nov. 1651.		

MARY, first wife, dau. of Stephen = WILLIAM JESSOP of Broom-hall, esquire, only son, = JANE, second wife, dau. of Sir Francis	ANNE, wife of
Bright of Carbrook, gent., sister	heir to his grandfather, aged 4, 1614. Made his will	South of Kelsterne, co. Linc., knight,	---- Wade of
to Sir John Bright bart., married	1 April 1641, and died soon after, being interred at	by Anne his wife, dau. of Anthony Irby	Nottingham.
at Sheffield 1 Feb. 1630-1, buried	Sheffield on the 15th of the same month. His will	of Whaplode in the same county, esq.	
there 13 May 1635.	was proved before the dean of Doncaster 6 August	Marr. sett. dated 4 June 1637. Buried	
	1641.	at Sheffield 18 Oct. 1675.	

WORTLEY JES-	WILLIAM JES-	ESTHER JES-	FRANCIS JESSOP of Broomhall, = BARBARA, dau. of Robert	ANNE JESSOP, bap.	WILLIAM JES-
SOP, bap. at	SOP, bap. at	SOP, bur. at	esq., and F.R.S., eldest surviv-	Eyre of High-low, and of	at Sheffield 24 June	SOP, a posthu-
Worksop 13	Worksop Oct.	Worksop 21	ing son and heir, aged 27, 16	Holme-hall, esq., son of	1640. I apprehend	mous child,
August 1633.	1634. Died	Jan. 1632-3.	Sep. 1665. Bap. at Sheffield 25	Thomas Eyre and Anne	this lady is the 'Anna	bap. at Shef-
Died young.	young.		April 1638. Made his will 10	Jessop. Marr. sett. dated	Jessop generosa,'	field 30 July
			April 1688, and was buried at	11 May 1664. Buried at	who was buried at	1641, buried
			Sheffield 3 April 1691.	Sheffield 26 Sep. 1706.	Sheffield 10 August	there 2 Oct.
					1674. Par. Reg.	1647.

WILLIAM JESSOP of Broom-hall, = The hon. MARY DARCY, dau.	FRANCIS JES-	JANE,	ELIZABETH, wife	ANNE, bo.	BARBARA,	FRANCIS.
esq., eldest son and heir, bap. at	of James Darcy of Sedbergh-	SOP, 2d son,	wife of	of Thomas Burton	30 Octob.	wife of John	RICHARD.
Sheffield 22 Feb. 1664-5. A	park, co. York, esq., (son of	M.A. and rec-	Marriot	M.A. vicar of Ha-	1674, bap.	Bright of	ANNE.
bencher of Gray's inn, one of his	James Darcy of the same	tor of Treeton	Pett of	lifax. Born 11 Oct.	at Shef-	Banner-	All died
majesty's justices of Chester and	place, 6th son of Conyers lord	bap. at Shef-	the co.	1671, baptized at	field 7 Nov.	cross and	young.
treasurer of the Alienation office;	Darcy) who was created ba-	field 19 Dec.	of Essex,	Sheffield 30th.	Died un-	Chester-	
also M.P. for Aldborough. Died	ron Darcy of Navan in the	1668. Died	esq., born	April 1700.	marr. and	field, esq.,	
at Broom-hall 15 Nov. 1734, and	kingdom of Ireland in 1721,	unmarried,	27 Nov.		was buried	baptized at	
was buried with his ancestors in	with remainder to his grand-	and was bur.	1667.		at Sheffield	Worksop 28	
the parish-church of Sheffield on	son James Jessop...Died 17	1667.	with his fami-		23 October	Apr. 1679.	
the 30th. With him ended the	June 1737, and was buried		ly at Sheffield		1740.	Married at	
male line of this family.	near her husband. Her will		25 May 1728.			Sheffield 4	
	bears date 17 May 1735.					Mar. 1701.	

a

---

[1] This figure appears upon the old monument at Rotherham; but Flower when he describes the quarterings of Wortley, copied as he says from 'a buriall escocheon standing in the Angel in Rotheram,' 1585, gives the chevron vaire. In Fairfax's book of arms Robert Swyft is said to bear Parti per pale or and vert, a chevron between 3 roe-bucks courant, as many pheons all counterchanged, on a chief azure 3 escal-

lop shells of the first. To which Edmondson adds this crest, a cubit arm habited argent charged with 2 bends azure, grasping a laurel wreath vert, encircling a martlet or. This looks much like a coat granted in the reign of Henry VIII. when the heralds thought they could never over-charge a shield with devices. The older and simpler coat has been retained by their descendants.

JAMES JESSOP Lord DARCY of Navan, only son and heir-apparent. Succeeded to the title on the death of his grandfather in 1731, and assumed the surname of Darcy by act of parliament. Died unmarried 15 June 1733, in the lifetime of his father.	ANDREW WILKINSON of Boroughbridge, esq. Member for Aldborough, and principal store-keeper of the Ordnance. Died 1784.	BARBARA JESSOP, eldest dau. and co-heir, bap. at Sheffield 20 Nov. 1697, mar. there 3 Sept. 1723, died Feb. 1768.	JOHN EYRE of Hopton in the county of Derby, esq., son of William Eyre of High-low, esq., by Catherine his wife, dau. of Sir John Gell baronet. Assumed the surname of Gell on becoming heir to his mother's inheritance.	ISABELLA JESSOP, bap. at Sheffield 30th July 1701. Married there 12 Oct. 1721. Died July 1738.	MARY JESSOP died unmarried.	BETHIA JESSOP, bap. at Sheffield 25 Dec. 1704. Died unmar. and was bur. at Sheffield Nov. 1781.
CHARLES WILKINSON of Boroughbridge, esq. LL.B. a barrister, and M.P. for Aldborough, died unmarried April 1782.	WILLIAM WILKINSON, 2d son, col. in the army, died unmar. May 1761.	ANDREW WILKINSON, of Boroughbridge, esq., 3d son, captain in the royal navy and M.P. for Aldborough, died without issue 29 May 1785.	DOROTHY, dau. of Richard Lawson alderman of York, by Barbara his wife, dau. of Thomas Burton vicar of Halifax, by Eliz. Jessop his wife.	JAMES WILKINSON, vicar of Sheffield, son, died unmarried at his seat at Boroughbridge 18 Jan. 1805, having survived all his brothers.	THOMAS WILKINSON, 5th son, capt. of engineers, died unmar. Dec. 1773.	GEORGE WILKINSON, 6th son, died in the service of the honor. E.I. company 1761, unmar.	JOHN WILKINSON, seventh and youngest son, died unmar. May 1781.

Emote Jessop, wife of William who stands at the head of the pedigree, survived her husband, and was living at Treeton when she made her will the 10th of February 1569. She directs that her body shall be buried in the churchyard of Treeton. She gives to William Jessop, Richard Jessop, Francis Jessop, and Margaret Jessop, her son's children, to be divided amongst them, 6l. 13s. 4d. to be delivered to their father: and to Richard Clarke and Nicholas Clarke his brother 20s. to be delivered to their father. She gives to her daughter Agnes 3l. 6s. 8d., and to her sister Ales Frith 20s., as also a silk hat, a petticoat, and a pair of sleeves. She wills that her farm shall remain to Laurence her son and Agnes her daughter during the term to come therein; she gives them the residue of her property, and desires her son Richard to be an overseer between them.

The will of Richard Jessop bears date the 8th of October 22 Elizabeth, whereby he gives to his son William all the household stuff at Broom-hall. It recites that the testator and Anne his wife had passed by fine all the lands at Tilne and other places to Robert Holland clerk and William Taylor in fee, which lands he by feoffment had given to Richard Cottes and John Pettinger gentlemen in fee, to the use of Richard and Francis the testator's sons, which writings he desires his trustees to ratify. Eight hundred pounds which he had out on security, he desires to go amongst his other goods to be distributed amongst all his children at the discretion of his executor. He gives to his daughter Margaret all her mother's apparel, to Mrs. Wortley a ruby that was her sister's, and to Mrs. Leake twenty shillings in gold. He wills that his brother Laurence shall continue on the farm at Treeton; mentions the wife of Laurence and his sister Agnes Vessie; makes Francis Wortley esquire sole executor.

Further respecting Richard Jessop or Jessoppe, as was the orthography of the name at this period, among the evidences at Broom-hall was a deed dated the 5th of March 4 Elizabeth, by which William Swift of Haytffeld [Hatfield] esquire conveyed to him and Anne his wife, the grange of Little Sheffield, &c. In a letter of Thomas Baldwin to the earl of Shrewsbury dated the 22d of December 1580, he says, ' I did send yowre honor ..... a boxe, in the wᶜʰ is a commission to enquire after the deathe of Jessop, wᶜʰ I do truste yowe have reseaved¹.' And again in an unpublished letter of the earl written in the next year, ' I have sent you by this berar Walthall yᵉ pursevant the inquisi-

cön for Jesoppe wᶜʰ as it semeth is unperfecte for that he is found to hould certen lands in Little Sheffeld & Ecclesall in capite, not declaringe whether by knight service or in sockage, whereby it is lyke some furder inquisicön may be made. And to come to the certaine knowledge thereof I would have you make serche for Robᵗ Swyft, his l'res patents for those lands & for ould Jesoppe office, and that so sone as maye be, & so to gett that matter to an ende for that my tyme is so shorte, Jesop being wᵗʰin one yeare of his agᵉ².'

Wortley Jessop died several years before his father. On him, his wife and issue had been settled by deed dated the 30th of January 5 James I., Broom-hall, or the manor of Broom-hall as it is described, the grange called Little Sheffield grange, and other lands, together with the advowson of the vicarage of Sheffield, to which his only son succeeded on the death of his grandfather. Wortley Jessop resided at Scofton, and there made his will on the 13th of April 1615, in which he directs that if he die within forty miles of Sheffield his body should be buried on the north side of the chancel in the church of Sheffield, near his deceased mother. He was probably at that time about to set out on the voyage in which he was wrecked and lost his life, as his grandson informed the heralds who have preserved the fact. He gives to his wife all his leases, goods, &c., except his great gilt saltseller and his little gilt saltseller, which were to be used by her and go to his heir. He directs that his brother William Boles shall have the third part of the benefit of the statute acknowledged at Lincoln to the testator by Mr. Richard Bulkey. He gives 40s. to his brother George Jessop for a ring, and 10l. to buy him a gelding. He gives to his mother 20s., to his sister Savage, his sister Anne, and his sister Cressye³ 20s. each. To his godson George Savage a double sovereign. To each of his brother Savage's children 5s. each; and to his sister Cressye's children the like. He gives 5l. to buy a silver bowl or tankard to be given to Queen's College Oxford, lest he should be thought unmindful of the great good he received in that house. He gives to Mr. Toller, vicar of Sheffield, 40s., to Mr. William Cart 40s., and entreats him to preach at his burial, and he desires his wife to continue to him the yearly contribution during his abode at Worksop. He gives to Christopher Carleil 20s., and to William Vessie 40s., with legacies to his servants and the poor of Worksop. He appoints his wife his executrix. ' Now as to my children, my little son William is

¹ Lodge, vol. ii. p. 242.   ² Talbot Papers, vol. G, f. 70.   ³ A Doyley.

well provided for if God spare him in life;' yet he desires his wife to pay to his loving father William Jessop esquire 100*l.* in a year after the testator's death, which he desires his father will bestow in the education of his said little son: and in case his wife should marry again, he desires her to pay to his brother and friend Mr. Humphry Savage of North-lees the sum of 200*l.* to be employed for the benefit of his little daughter Anne Jessop. He makes further provision for her, and gives to the said Humphry Savage five marks to buy him a ring, twenty marks to buy a gelding, and a yoke of his best oxen. This will was proved the 27th of May 1617, before George Small gentleman, steward of the manor of Mansfield in the county of Nottingham.

George Jessop of Brancliffe, esquire, the younger brother of Wortley Jessop, had eleven children by Martha his wife; namely, three sons and eight daughters. The sons were Richard, George, and Francis. Richard survived his father, but I do not find that he had issue, or was married. George was of Brancliffe, and married Dorothy, daughter of Godfrey Meynell of Langley, esquire, relict of James Dangerfield gentleman. He died without issue, and his wife surviving was married a third time to John Hutton gentleman, and dying on the 2d of May 1674, aged 51, was buried at Langley. Francis Jessop the youngest son was also of Brancliffe, and by his will bearing date in 1676 conveyed that estate to his relative and namesake Francis Jessop of Broom-hall, esquire. The daughters of George Jessop the elder, as their names appear in the wills of their father and brother, were Ann Laughton, Elizabeth wife of William Cressy, Mary Marshall, Sarah Smith, Gertrude Macqueen, Margaret, Dorothy, and Martha Jessop. There are inscriptions in the church of Anston for members of this branch of the family, of whom there is no account in the visitations.

The name of Mr. Francis Jessop is not unknown to science. He was one of the earliest members of the Royal Society, and much acquainted with the literary men of his day. Ray was his frequent guest at Broom-hall. ' *Proxima statio fuit Sheffeldia in comitatu Eboracensi. Ibi a vetere amico D. Jessop perbenevole exceptus sum, in cujus ædibus etiamnum diversor*[1].' And again, ' *Ego ex quo huc veni, partim physicis partim mathematicis studiis memet exercui; siquidem D. Jessop mathematicis imprimis delectatur, in quibus non contemnendos sanè progressus fecit*[2].' Willughby in the preface to his *Ornithologia* makes grateful mention of the assistance he had received from Mr. Jessop, ' who sent us the descriptions and cases of many rare birds, and discovered and gave us notice of many species thereabout [Broom-hall] which we knew not before to be natives of England:' and afterwards associated him with Ray, Skippon, and two other gentlemen as executors to his will.

I know of but one work of Mr. Jessop. It is a pamphlet bearing the imprimatur of Lord Carbury, president of the Royal Society, 3 November 1687, entitled ' *Propositiones Hydrostaticæ ad illustrandum Aristarchi Samii Systema destinatæ, et quædam phænomena naturæ generalia.*' To the principal treatise is annexed a letter to the honourable Francis As-

ton son and heir-apparent of Walter lord Aston on the same subject; and the whole is dedicated to Lord Clifford, son and heir of the earl of Burlington, to whose family he professes to owe many obligations, in common with every lover of nature and science. But in the Transactions of the Royal Society are several of his communications, *viz.* On Fairy-Rings, on the Damp in Mines, on a subterranean Fungus, on an unknown Mineral, and an account of a Medical Case at Sheffield, where the principal symptom was the vomiting of certain insects. The patient was attended by Mr. Fisher a surgeon in Sheffield, an intimate friend of Mr. Jessop. There was another friend of Mr. Jessop of the same name, who seems to have been a physician. He was brother to the surgeon; and both were sons of Mr. James Fisher the ejected vicar of Sheffield. William Walker of Darnall was another of his friends. Several of Mr. Jessop's letters may be found in Ray's Correspondence, which show both his love of natural history and his attachment to the severer study of the mathematics.

Mr. Jessop seems to have taken a leading part in the concerns of the parish. He was an active church-burgess, and his name stands first in a list of seven gentlemen on whom the honorary freedom of the Cutlers' Company was conferred in 1681.

He left two sons, William and Francis. The former he brought up to the law, the latter to the church. The former attained considerable eminence, as the latter would doubtless have done, possessed as he was of talents, zeal, and connexion, if his friends had not had to deplore in him eccentricities which rendered it inexpedient to place him in any high or responsible station. All the preferment he enjoyed was the rectory of Treeton, which was presented to him by Henry duke of Norfolk on the 25th of February 1692, soon after he had left Lincoln College Oxford. He closed an unhappy life in May 1728, and was buried with his ancestors in the parish church of Sheffield. He published ' The Church of England established upon scriptural and primitive foundation—in a Sermon preached in Sheffield church the twelfth day of March, in the year of our Lord 1709-10, by Francis Jessop M.A. rector of Treeton, and formerly fellow of Lincoln College in Oxon.' to which college it is inscribed in a fantastical dedication. It is possible there may be other sermons of his in print. I have seen one fairly transcribed by himself, as if for the press, entitled ' A Sermon distinguishing between religious and sinful sensuality, proving the religious man to be the greatest sensualist, and thereby confuting the best plea the sinner hath for pursuing his lusts, by Francis Jessop, M[r] of Arts, rector of Treeton, &c.,' with a dedication to the archbishop of York.

His conduct at Treeton gave occasion to this epigram.

' Hark Satyrs, bring Boanerges down ;
  A fighting priest, the bully of the gown—
  In double offices, he serves the Lord
  To fight his battles and to preach his word;
  And double praise is to his merits due,
  Who thumps the cushion and his people too.'

These lines were perhaps the retort of his neighbour Dr. Lockyer the rector of Hansworth, whose classical inscription for Lord Molesworth's dog mo-

---

[1] Letter to Martin Lister dated 7 kal. Aug. 1668. Ray's *Philosophical Letters*, published by Derham, 1718, 8vo, p. 30.

[2] Ray's *Letters*, p. 31.

nument at Edlington Mr. Jessop had shamefully but ingeniously parodied.

Mr. William Jessop the elder son of Mr. Francis Jessop is an instance of the successful combination of politics with the law. He attached himself to the interests of the Pelham family, and was a principal law adviser of the ministry in the reign of Queen Anne, in which the duke of Newcastle held the office of lord privy seal. Many of his communications at this period may be found in Harl. MSS. 2262. He was brought into parliament early in life for Aldborough, which place he represented at the time of his death. In July 1716 he was made a commissioner of the Alienation-office in the place of Mr. Cayley, and receiver-general in the place of Lord Orrery, and in 1728 second judge of Chester. He also obtained an Irish peerage for his son, a young man who after having given promise that he would do credit to his high rank was cut off by an acute distemper on the 15th of June 1733. The father upon this event retired to Broomhall, where he closed an active life on the 15th of November in the succeeding year[1].

After the death of Mr. Jessop, the estate of Broomhall was held in coparceny by his daughters and coheirs. Two of them died unmarried; and the Reverend James Wilkinson the last surviving son of the

elder of the two married daughters, by a codicil to his will bearing date the 22d of December 1801, gave to his cousin Philip Gell of Hopton, esquire, all the moiety which he then held in coparceny or in common with him of the estate at Broom-hall (except his share of the living of the vicarage of Sheffield, which he bequeathed to his relative the Reverend Marmaduke Lawson[2]) charged with the payment of all such debts and legacies as his personal estate would not extend to pay. Mr. Gell has disposed of a great part of his property here, and Broom-hall has passed by sale into the hands of Mr. John Watson of Shiercliffe-hall.

The literary spirit of this family lives in its present representatives. The name of Sir William Gell is deservedly held in the highest respect by the lovers of the remains of classical times; and Mr. Marmaduke Lawson, the eldest son of the Reverend M. Lawson, of Magdalen College Cambridge, where he was admitted A.B. in February 1816, obtained in 1812 one of Sir William Browne's medals for the best Latin ode, and in 1816 one of the chancellor's medals for the best classical exercises. In 1814 he was elected the first Pitt scholar. At the general election of 1818 Mr. Lawson was returned member of parliament for Boroughbridge.

JOHN GELL of Hopton, esq., formerly John Eyre of that place.	=ISABELLA, dau. and co-heir of WILLIAM JESSOP of Broom-hall, esquire.			
PHILIP GELL of Hopton, esquire, eldest son and heir, died in Aug. 1795. =DOROTHY, dau. and co-heir of William Milnes of Aldercar-park, esq. Survived, and married Thomas Blore esq. F.S.A.	JOHN GELL, admiral of the blue, died unmarried.	MARIA-CATHARINA. ISABELLA. TEMPERANCE.	MARY GELL, died unmarried 1791.	ANNE, wife of Hugo Meynel, esquire.
PHILIP GELL of Hopton, esquire. Living 1819. =GEORGIANA-ANNE, youngest dau. of Nicholas Nicholas (formerly Heath) of Boys-court, Kent, and Mackworth, co. Derb. esquire.	Sir WILLIAM GELL, M.A. & F.S.A.	MARY GELL,	HENRY GELL, died in his infancy.	ISABELLA GELL, died in her infancy.

MACHON-BANK.

This place was once the residence of a family who bore the name of Machon, whom we find in the visitations of the seventeenth century.

PEDIGREE of MACHON of MACHON-BANK.

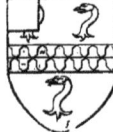

ARMS.—Gules a fess vaire between 3 swans' heads erased argent, a canton of the third.

JOHN MACHON of Machon-bank. =			
JOHN MACHON of Machon-bank and Briocliffe. Died 1602. =ELEANOR, dau. of --- Parker of Maddow- [Meadow] hall near Sheffield.			
JOHN MACHON of Magdalen-hall Oxford, M.A., vicar of Aston in the county of Warwick. Afterwards of Longdon and Ridgeley in the county of Stafford. Died in 1640 or thereabout. =ANNE, dau. of John Jones, doctor of physic, and rector of Treeton.	ROBERT MACHON, died unmarried.	RICHARD MACHON, died unmarried.	
JOHN MACHON, M.A., master of Christ's Hospital in Sherburn in the bishoprick of Durham. Aged 65, 21 August 1666. =DEBORAH, dau. of William Blackiston of York.	EDWARD MACHON =MARGARET, dau. of of Langdon, co. of John Well of Ha-Stafford. Aged 60, metwich, co. Staff. 1666.	HENRY, died unmarried.	ANNE, wife of Ambrose Holden.	MARGERY wife of Thomas Routh.

[1] Their deaths are thus announced in the obituary of the *Gentleman's Magazine* for 1733 and 1734. '1733, June—Died the Lord Darcy, only son of Judge Jessop of Lincoln's Inn Fields. About two years ago he changed his name by act of parliament to Darcy, the title and estate descended to him by his mother. The title goes to — Darcy esq., a relation, now page of honour to his majesty,' vol. iii. p. 327. '1734, Nov. Died William Jessop esquire of Yorkshire, one of the grand sessions for Chester, Montgomery, &c., one of the commissioners and receiver-general of the Alienation-office, member for Aldborough in Yorkshire, which he had represented from the first year of King George I. to this time,

and one of the benchers of Gray's Inn.' Vol. iv. p. 627.—At vol. v. p. 101, is 'An elegy sacred to the memory of William Jessop esq. &c.'—not worth transcribing.

[2] Mr. Lawson was a grandson of the judge's eldest sister Elizabeth, who married the Reverend Thomas Burton vicar of Halifax. Two daughters were the issue of that match, one of whom was Mr. Lawson's mother, the other married — Palgrave. Mr. Lawson had a sister, wife of Andrew Wilkinson, the third of the seven sons, and he himself took to wife Miss Barbara Isabella Wilkinson, by whom he left seven children, Marmaduke, Barbara, Andrew, Dorothy, James, John, and Mary.

This is the visitation pedigree. Mr. Wilson had found that a James Machon of Machon-bank died in the time of Elizabeth, leaving eight daughters his co-heirs, one of whom married —— Genn of Hullock in Holmfirth. The third John Machon was one of the assistant-ministers of Sheffield before his removal into Warwickshire. His daughter Anne was baptized at Sheffield the 2d of March 1599. His wife was the widow of Storth at the time of his marriage. See more respecting her father at page 60.

The family continued in great respectability in Durham. The master of Sherburn-hospital was deprived of his preferment in the Civil Wars, recovered it at the Restoration, and held it till his death in 1679[1]. The continuation of the pedigree may be found in Surtees's *History of Durham*, vol. i. p. 143.

MOUNT PLEASANT.

The house so called, situated at High-field in this township, is now the property and residence of Samuel Broomhead Ward esquire. It was built by Francis Hurt-Sitwell esquire, a name which has often occurred in these pages, and to which Sheffield has many obligations ; and was for some time his residence.

PEDIGREE of SITWELL of RENISHAW, &c.

ARMS.—Barry of eight or and vert, 3 lions rampant sable, with the baronet's mark.
CREST.—On a wreath or and vert, a demi-lion rampant sable holding a shield parti per pale or and vert.

FRANCIS SITWELL of Eckington, co. Derb. Buried there 9 March 1605. Will proved at Lichfield 16 May 1605. == ELLEN, dau. of Robert Bright of Dore, co. Derb. Proved her husband's will.

| GEORGE SITWELL of Eckington, bap. there 23 Sep. 1569. Bur. there 23 Apr. 1607. | MARY, dau. of Thomas Walker of Derby. Proved her husband's will in the Prerogative office, Lichfield. | FRANCIS SITWELL, bap. at Eckington 26 Aug. 1565. Was married and had issue 1605. | WILLIAM SITWELL, bapt. at Eckington 23 Oct. 1574. | GRACE, wife of Thomas Crofte, mar. at Eckington 3 Feb. 1594. | FRANCES, wife of Richard Treeton, mar. at Eckington 1 Oct. 1593, and had issue living 1605. | ALICE SITWELL, bap. ton 28 Sep. 1572. Living 1605. |

GEORGE SITWELL of Renishaw, in the parish of Eckington, esquire, son and heir. Bap. at Eckington 15 March 1600-1. High-sheriff of the county of Derby 1653. Had a grant of coat-armour from Sir Edward Walker, Garter, 1 March 1660. Appeared at Dugdale's visitation of Derbyshire 18 August 1662, when he entered his pedigree. His will bears date 20 May 1667, and he was buried in the church of Eckington 2 August 1667, where is a monument to his memory. == MARGARET, dau. of Hugh Childers of Car-house, near Doncaster, gent. Buried at Eckington 22 Jan. 1658.

| FRANCIS SITWELL of Renishaw, esq., son and heir. Bap. at Eckington 18 Jan. 1630-1. Aged 32, 18 Aug. 1662. High-sheriff of the county of Derby 1671, in which year he died, and was buried at Eckington. | CATHERINE, dau. of Henry Sacheverel of Barton and Morley, esq., by Joyce his wife, dau. and heir of Francis Mansfield. Mar. in 1656. Died 15 May 1705, aged 69, and was buried at Morley. | GEORGE SITWELL, second son. A merchant residing at Seville 1662. Of Lond. 1706, when he made his will. Died in 1708, and was interred with his wife's family in the church of Riselip, co. Midd. | ELIZABETH, daughter of Ralph Hawtrey of Riselip, esq. Died 1712. Buried at Riselip. | ROBERT SITWELL, a merchant residing at Leghorn 1662. Of London 1684, when he made his will, which was proved on 10 Sep. in that year by his wife Elizabeth. | JOHN SITWELL, living 1667. — WILLIAM SITWELL, living 1706. — HUGH. MATTHEW. MARGARET. SUSANNA. All died infants. | MARY, wife of William Revel of Ogston, co. Derby, esq., to whom she was married at Renishaw before John Spademan, esq., a justice of the peace, 17 Feb. 1656. | ELIZABETH, wife of Robert Copley of Nether-hall, in Doncaster. she was mar. 10 May 1659. |

| GEORGE SITWELL of Renishaw, esq. Born 23 Aug. Bap. 3 Sep. 1657. Will dated 17 June 1721. Bur. at Eckington 24 Feb. 1722-3. | ANNE, dau. and heir of Thomas Kent of Povey, in the parish of Dronfield, gent. Mar. at Dronfield 20th May 1680. Died before 1696. | FRANCIS SITWELL of London, merchant, 2d son. Born 28 Aug. 1669. Aged 3, 1662. Will dated 13 Oct. 1729. Bur. at Eckington 30th June 1732. | HENRY SITWELL of London, merchant, third son. Bap. 25 July 1661. Will dated 2 Dec. 1691, proved 5 July 1692 by his brother Francis. | WILLIAM SITWELL, of Sheffield, attorney-at-law, 4th son. Bap. 16 Octob. 1662. Died before 1721. | MARY, dau. of Leonard Reresby of Ecclesfield, gent., of the ancient house of Reresby of Thribergh. Bap. at Ecclesfield 21 April 1670. Married there 21 Sep. 1693. Died 31 Decem. 1751, and was buried in the parish-church of Sheffield. | JOHN, 5th son. MARY. | JOYCE, wife of Thomas Allestree of Alvaston, co. Derb. esq. Living a widow 1721. |
| | | | | | | CATHERINE. |

| FRANCIS SITWELL of Renishaw, esq., eldest son and heir. High-sheriff of the county of Derby 1745. Will dated 9 Jan. 1745. Died 20 May 1753, and was bur. at Eckington. | GEORGE SITWELL of London, merchant, 2d son. Will dated 28 Apr. 1739, proved 12th June 1746. | THOMAS SITWELL, a clergyman, and Fellow of Corpus Christi College, Oxford. Had the estate of Povey by will of his maternal grandfather, and died unmarried. Will dated 10 May 1736, proved 10 June 1737. | ALICE SITWELL, eldest dau. married at Eckington 11 March 1707-8 to William Sacheverel, of Barton and Morley, esquire, and died without issue. | ELIZABETH SITWELL, the last survivor of this branch of the family, died unmarried in 1769. |

[1] Hutchinson's *Durham*, vol. ii. p. 596.

FRANCIS SITWELL of Sheffield, attorney, eldest son, bap. there 8 Aug. 1694. Died unmarried July 1741, and was buried at Eckington, having been a considerable benefactor to the place of his birth.	WILLIAM SITWELL of London, citizen and iron-monger, 2d son. Afterwards of Renishaw, esq. Baptized at Sheffield 29 Apr. 1696. Died 18 April 1776, and on the 30th was buried at Eckington. Will dated 1 Dec. 1773, proved 21 April 1776.	HENRY SITWELL, bap. at Sheffield 26th of May 1698. Living 1721.	MARY SITWELL, bap. at Sheffield 20 Jan. 1700. Died unmarried 30 Jan. 1733-4, and was buried in the chancel of the parish-church of Sheffield.	FRANCES, first wife, dau. of Statham. Mar. at Sheffield 1 June 1719.	JONATHAN HURT of Sheffield, gent. Died 29 Dec. 1731, aged 40¹, and was buried in the chancel of the parish-church of Sheffield. Will dated 6th Nov. 1731, proved at York 18 July 1732.	CATHERINE SITWELL, second wife, baptized at Sheffield 20 Aug. 1702.
JONATHAN HURT, bap. at Sheffield 10 Nov. 1721, buried there 2 June 1723.	STATHAM HURT, bap. at Sheffield 17 April 1724, buried there 1 April 1725.	FRANCES HURT, bap. at Sheffield 11 June 1725, buried there 1 Aug. following.	MARY HURT, born 13 March 1720, bap. at Sheffield 6 April following. Married John Heaton of Sheffield, and died 21 Feb. 1753.	FRANCIS HURT-SITWELL of Sheffield, Mount-Pleasant, and Renishaw, esq. Assumed the surname and arms of Sitwell by royal sign-manual dated 7 Mar. 1777. Bap. at Sheffield 29 Apr. 1728. Died 16 Aug. 1793, and was buried at Eckington on the 31st.	MARY, dau. of the Rev. —— Warnford of York. Died 13 July 1792, and was buried in Eckington on the 27th.	CATHERINE HURT, died 23 Mar. 1730, aged 20 weeks, and was buried in the parish-church of Sheffield.
ALICE, first wife, dau. of Thomas Parke of Liverpool, esq., married at Walton 1 Aug. 1791. Died 3 May 1797, aged 31, and was bur. at Eckington.	Sir SITWELL SITWELL, of Renishaw, baronet, eldest son and heir, sometime member of parliament for West-Looe, and justice of the peace for the counties of York and Derby. Born at York in September 1769. Created a baronet of the united kingdoms by patent bearing date 3 Oct. 1808. Died at Renishaw July 1811, and was buried with his ancestors in the church of Eckington.	SARAH-CAROLINE, second wife, dau. of James Stovin of Whitgift, esq. by Theodosia his wife, dau. and co-heir of John Sparrow of Wincobank, near Sheffield, esquire. Married at Warmsworth 23 July 1798.	FRANCIS SITWELL, of Barmoor-castle, co. Northumberland, esq., 2d son, sometime M.P. for Berwick. Died in 1813.	ANNE, dau. of Sir Ilay Campbell of Succoth, baronet, sometime lord president of the Court of Session in Scotland. Married 21 Sep. 1795.	HURT SITWELL, of Thurcroft co. York, and Turney-hall co. Salop, esq., 3d son. Died at Lisbon 3 Mar. 1803.	ANNE, dau. of Simon Hardy of Huntingdon.	MARY SITWELL, only dau. mar. in 1790 to Sir William Wake, of Courteenhall, co. Northamp. bart., and died 22d Nov. 1791. Buried at Eckington.
Sir GEORGE SITWELL, of Renishaw, baronet, only son and heir. Living 1819.	SUSAN, dau. of Crawford Tait, esq. of town.	MARY-ALICE SITWELL, married at Eckington 28 Aug. 1815 to her cousin Charles Wake esq., son and heir apparent of Sir William Wake, bart., and died in 1816.	ANNE-ELIZABETH SITWELL, wife of lieut.-col. Sir Frederick Stovin, knt. commander of the most honourable order of the Bath.	CAROLINE SITWELL, born 1799. Died 16 Feb. 1800.	FRANCIS SITWELL, of Barmoor-castle, esq.	WILLIAM DEVZELL SITWELL. / SUSAN-ANNE. MARY-AMELIA. ANNE-JANE. / FRANCIS-HURT SITWELL.

TAPTON-HILL,

The pleasant seat of William Shore esquire, is in the township of Ecclesall, but near the borders of the two Hallams. It commands a delightful prospect over the Porter to the hills of Ecclesall and Norton.

The name of Shore is deservedly held in high respect at Sheffield; and is dear to every friend of civil and religious liberty, of the cause of humanity, and the best interests of mankind. It is ancient at Sheffield. In 1440 John Shore of Barnsley granted to William Shore all his lands and tenements in Sheffield². The name appears in some of the earliest pages of the parish-register; but the first who can with certainty be set down as an ancestor of the later members of this family is a John Shore who made his will in 1682, and it was proved in the archbishop's court at York on the 28th of June in that year, by Sarah Shore his widow and John Eyre of Sheffield, gentleman, the executor and executrix therein named. His eldest son Samuel Shore was an intelligent and active member of the town-trust, and much improved his property by purchases of the timber and other things when in the year 1708 the park of Sheffield was thrown into farms.

¹ This date exactly agrees with the following entry in the register of baptisms in the parish of Rotherham, ‘ 1691, Nov. 26, Jonathan son of Mr. Volantine Hurt.’

² Evidences in possession of the Church-burgesses of Sheffield.

PEDIGREE of SHORE of SHEFFIELD, MEERSBROOK, NORTON, TAPTON, &c.

ARMS.—Argent a chevron sable between 3 holly-leaves vert.
CREST.—On a wreath, a stork regardant, holding in its right claw a pebble of the sea-*shore.*

JOHN SHORE of Sheffield. = SARAH SIMS. Made his will 2 March 1682, and was buried at Sheffield 23 March following. | Died 17 July 1738, aged 90, and was buried at Sheffield on the 24th.

SAMUEL SHORE of Sheffield, merchant, born 17 May 1676. Died 1 Feb. 1751, and was buried at Sheffield. = JANE, dau. of George Sykes of Norton, co. Staff. Born 4 Sep. 1681. Married at Sheffield 7 Nov. 1700. Died 17 Aug. 1750, and was bur. at Sheffield.

SYLVANUS SHORE, = SARAH GODDARD, of the family of Holland Goddard of Cork in Ireland. second son. Born 8 July 1678. His family settled in Ireland.

ISAAC SHORE, bap. at Sheffield 3 Feb. 1681, mentioned in his father's will, but is supposed to have died young.

SAMUEL SHORE of Sheffield and Meersbrook, esq. Born 21 Aug. 1707. Retired to Meersbrook in the parish of Norton, in the county of Derby, in the latter part of his life; and died there in Sept. 1785. Buried at Sheffield. = MARGARET, dau. and heir of Robert Diggles of Liverpool, merchant. Mar. at Horbury near Wakefield, 17 Oct. 1734. Died 1 Jan. 1755, aged 41, and was bur. at Sheffield.

JOHN. SAMUEL. THOMAS. GEORGE. JOSHUA. All died young.

HANNAH. ANNE. SARAH. ELIZABETH. All died in their infancy.

ANNE SHORE, died unmarried Oct. 1755, aged 39. LYDIA SHORE, died unmarried 3 April 1777, aged 70.

JANE, wife of John Finch of Dudley, merchant, to whom she was mar. at Sheffield 21 Sept. 1732.

MARY, wife of John Milnes of Wakefield, merchant, to whom she was mar. at Sheffield 9 Feb. 1738. The present Sir Robert Shore Milnes bart. was the eldest son of this marriage.

ESTHER, wife of Robert Milnes of Wakefield, merchant, to whom she was mar. at Norton 6 Feb. 1766, and died without issue.

ROBERT-DIGGLES. GEORGE. THOMAS. JOSHUA. All died young, and unmarried.

URITH, first wife, dau. of Joseph Offley of Norton-hall, esq., lord of the manor of Norton, elder sister and co-heir of Edmund Offley of Clapham in the county of Surrey. Married at St. Margaret's Westminster 15 March 1759. Died at Norton 30 Nov. 1781. = SAMUEL SHORE of Meersbrook, esq., formerly of Norton-hall in the county of Derby, and of Clapham in the county of Surrey. Born 5 Feb. 1738. High-sheriff of the county of Derby 1761. = LYDIA, second wife, only dau. and heir of Freeman Flower of Gainsborough and Clapham, esq., mar. 3 April 1788.

JOHN SHORE, second surviving son. — MARY. — WILLIAM SHORE, third surviving son. — See below.

JANE, wife of — ANNE. ESTHER. All died young, and unmarried.

MARGARET SHORE, died at Fieldhead near Sheffield, unmar.

SARAH SHORE, living unmarried.

HANNAH, wife of Thomas Walker of Manchester, merchant.

OFFLEY SHORE, died 31 Aug. 1767, aged 7 years, and was buried at Norton.

SAMUEL SHORE of Norton-hall, esq., lord of the manor of Norton. Rebuilt the hall in 1815. = HARRIET, youngest dau. of Fitzwalter Foye esq., of Castle-hill in Buckland Newton near Sherburn, co. Dorset, and co-heir to her brother Sydney Hollis Foye esquire. Married at Buckland 13 March 1788.

BOHUN SHORE, third youngest son, of the 4th dragoons. A lieutenant-colonel in the army.

SYDNEY SHORE = ---- only dau. of Charles esq., eldest son. White of Lincoln, esq., by a daughter of Sir Francis Bernard baronet. Married at Mary-le-Bone church 6 May 1812.

OFFLEY SHORE, second son.

ELIZABETHA-MARIA. HARRIET. URITH-LYDIA. AMELIA-THEOPHILA. MARIA-THEODOSIA. OCTAVIA.

JOHN SHORE late of Sheffield, esquire, and now of Norton near Malton, in the county of York, second surviving son of Samuel Shore of Sheffield and Meersbrook. = GERTRUDE, dau. of George Binks of Sheffield, and Hall-Carr in Brightside-Byerlow, gent., married 5 August 1776.

JOHN SHORE of Sheffield, banker, eldest son. = ELIZA, dau. of Thomas Hardy of Wakefield, esq., mar. 17 March 1806.

GEORGE SHORE of Sheffield and Gainsborough, second son, died 31 Jan. 1815, aged 30. = CHARLOTTE, 4th dau. of W. A. Gordon of Exeter, esq., married at Saint Mary's Lichfield 1 Jan. 1805.

CHARLES SHORE, third son, a lieut. in the 20th regt. of Native Infantry E. I. Co.'s service, died at Prince of Wales's Island 4 August 1811.

ARTHUR SHORE of Sheffield, 4th son.

GERTRUDE, wife of Alexander Goodman of Sheffield, merchant. — MARY, wife of J. Myers esquire of Preston, co. Lanc.

WILLIAMSHORE fifth son, a capt. in the N. York Militia. — MARGARET, wife of John Jeeves of Sheffield, mer[.].

FRANCES, died unmarried.

SARAH SHORE, living unmar. — JOHN and HAROLD died in their infancy.

THOMAS. ELIZABETH. JOHN. FREDERICK. ISABELLA.

GEORGE. MATILDA. WILLIAM. HENRY. MARIA.

WILLIAM SHORE of Tapton, esquire, third surviving son of Samuel Shore of Sheffield and Meersbrook. = MARY, dau. of George Evans of Cromford near Matlock, co. Derb. Niece and heir of Peter Nightingale of Lea, in the county of Derby, esq. Married 26 Nov. 1792.

WILLIAM-EDWARD NIGHTINGALE of Lea, in the county of Derby, esquire, only son. Assumed the surname of Nightingale by the Prince Regent's sign manual bearing date 4 Feb. 1815, in pursuance of the will of his maternal uncle Peter Nightingale of Lea, esquire. = FRANCES, dau. of William Smith esquire, of Parndon in Essex, member of parliament for the city of Norwich. Married at St. Margaret's Westminster 1 June 1818.

MARY SHORE, only daughter.

ANNE SHORE, died in her infancy.

III.

The Township of Upper-Hallam.

THIS township has the largest superficies and the smallest population of the six which compose the parish of Sheffield. Its area is 8836 acres, of which 3150 were uninclosed moor-land in 1796. There were at that period only 105 houses. Much more land has since been brought into cultivation, and more houses built. In 1811, the number of inhabitants was 886. This population is rather dispersed over the township in single houses, or in long straggling hamlets, than collected in villages. This is the consequence of the state of the township in early times, when it was mostly chase and forest-land. The germ of most of our villages was deposited before the Norman Conquest.

This township lies between the Riveling on the north and the Porter on the south. Its eastern boundary line is at the distance of about two miles from Sheffield. On the west it adjoins to Derbyshire.

The manufactures of Sheffield have extended themselves less into this than into the other townships. A majority of the inhabitants are engaged in agriculture. They are distinguishable from their eastern neighbours as well by dialect as employment. There are remnants of our ancient tongue remaining amongst the rude and simple inhabitants of this remote part of the parish, which are not found and scarcely understood in the more populous parts. Both in dialect and manners they assimilate more nearly to their neighbours of the Peak than to those on the other side. This is the more remarkable, since they are cut off from their neighbours on that side by long tracts of high moorland, which till lately were crossed only by narrow bridle-ways, along which was raised at intervals a rude stone pillar or a wooden pole, while scarcely a winter passed which did not prove them to be insufficient to guide the belated traveller on his way. One of these called Stanedge-pole is still remaining, which serves the further purposes of marking the divisions of the counties of York and Derby, and showing the spot at which meet the three parishes of Hathersage, Ecclesfield, and Sheffield.

Those of the inhabitants of this township who are engaged in the cutlery manufacture, are either employed in the grinding wheels which are erected on the Riveling and the Porter, or work in small sheds attached to their dwelling-houses, bringing the produce of their labour week by week to their employers in the town.

This tract is part of the *sylva pascua* of the manor of Hallam: forest-land, but so free from underwood as to be fit for the purpose of pasturage, and indeed for the sports of the field. A considerable portion of it where the ground declines towards the Porter has the name of Fullwood, while the northern moiety declining towards the Riveling formed, together with a considerable tract of the township of Stannington, Riveling-chase. The names of Fullwood, Fullwood-Booth, the Lodge and Lodge-moor continue to speak of the ancient state and former appropriation of this part of the parish of Sheffield.

It was the property of the old lords of Sheffield, who admitted of few freeholders on this part of the domain. As the park was for their domestic use, so this was reserved by them for the pleasures of the chase. We have already had occasion to mention the grants to the monks of Beauchief of liberty to turn their cattle into the forest of Fullwood, and to erect their vaccaries, &c. At the Reformation Francis earl of Shrewsbury procured whatever interest the abbey had in Fullwood, together with other abbey property, in exchange for the manor of Farnham-Royal in Buckinghamshire. The prior of Worksop had also similar privileges in the forest of Riveling.

We have also spoken of the grant made by Thomas lord Furnival of herbage and foliage in Riveling to the inhabitants of Stannington, Morewood, Hallam, and Fullwood. This grant seems to have been the ground of dispute in after times between the lord and the residents of this district; for in the thirtieth of Elizabeth we find two yeomen, William Fox of Fullwood and Robert Mitchell of Hallam, procuring from Chancery an exemplification of the charter.

These open chases afforded fine opportunities for such marauders as Robin-Hood; who doubtless himself in proper person made some of his first essays in 'chasing the fallow-deer,' in Fullwood and Riveling, lying so near to Loxley, which beyond all competition has the fairest pretensions to be the birth-place of that noted outlaw; not sparing perchance the abbot's herds. Numerous are the places on the Derbyshire moors, close adjoining to these, which bear his name, and a spot in the church-yard of Hathersage has been pointed out from time immemorial as the grave of his most celebrated companion. For the protection of the game an officer was appointed by the lords of Sheffield. He was called the Master of the game in Hallamshire. In the time of Henry VII. this office was held by Thomas Shiercliffe, whose portrait in his forester's costume was once to be seen fairly depicted in one of the windows of the church of Ecclesfield. He had under him several keepers. Henry Wrasteler was the keeper of Riveling in the time of Shiercliffe at a salary of three halfpence a day. This man in 1505 joined with the vicar of Ecclesfield in setting up one of the windows of that church when they were so beautifully restored with painted glass. In the time of Charles I.

Laurence Hall and Thurston Morton were keepers of Fullwood, and Richard Ibbetson and William Barnsley keepers of Riveling, at a salary of two pounds a year each. Soon after that period the office became extinct. When there was no longer any thing to keep, there needed no keeper.

Gilbert earl of Shrewsbury was a passionate lover of field-sports. The chases of Hallamshire were not wide enough for his ambition, and I find him drawing an unfavourable comparison between them and the extensive levels which spread around Hatfield[1]. I shall add a few notices of his field-sports from the Talbot papers.

‘ John Talbot writes to him, then Lord Talbot, 1589, that he had bought horses and hawks for him in Ireland, I. 17.

Sir John Byron writing from London January 1590-1 offers him the use of his hawks and hounds for the season, I. 106.

The earl of Derby, 1593, sends as a present the best falcon of those which he had from the Isle of Man, I. 174.

The bishop of Meath writes from Arbrachan, 1594, with a present of goshawks, I. 194.

Lord Burghley, 1602, thanks the earl for a fat stag killed by the countess, K. 52.

Laurence Esmonds writes from Duncannon, 1608, with a present of wolf-dogs and hawks, L. 156.

Sir Thomas Fairfax writes that the prince is pleased with the earl's hounds, M. 358.

Elizabeth countess of Ormond and Ossory writes to the countess of Shrewsbury, 1608, from the Carrick, with a present of greyhounds, O. 120.’

The township of Upper-Hallam is understood to form part of the chapelry of Ecclesall. It sends a chapel-warden and bears one-fourth of the chapel repairs. Great part of it however lies very-remote from the chapel of Ecclesall, and still more distant from the parish-church, or the church of any neighbouring parish; so that the opportunities of attending public worship must have been rare to the few inhabitants of this district till 1729, when a small chapel was built in that part of it called Fullwood, in pursuance of the will of William Ronksley of Gunthwaite, gentleman, who was a native of Fullwood.

‘ And forasmuch as Fullwood the place of my nativity is very remote from church and chapel, my mind and will is, that for the conveniency of the inhabitants thereof, who are most of them dissenters from the church of England, immediately from and after my decease the interest or product of four hundred pounds shall be reserved for four or five years; and if a large and handsome chapel shall be built and finished with a pulpit and convenient seats, near unto Birksgreen, with the interest or product of the said four hundred pounds for the space of time aforesaid; from and after the time that the said chapel shall be built, seated, and finished, as is aforesaid, I give and bequeath the said four hundred pounds to and for the use of the said chapel for ever. That is to say, my mind and will is, that the yearly interest, rent, and product of the said four hundred pounds shall be paid by the order and appointment of my very much honoured and esteemed friend William Jessop of Broom-hall in the parish of Sheffield, esquire, and by the order and appointment of his heirs for ever (if so be that he and they will be so charitably kind as to take that care and trust upon them), to such dissenting minister officiating in the said chapel as shall have

been chosen and approved of by the said William Jessop or his heirs, by two half yearly payments at all times for ever. But in default of such heirs, or if he or they shall not be willing to execute or cause to be executed this my trust as aforesaid, then and in that case my will is, that the major part of the inhabitants of Fullwood aforesaid, or Upper-Hallam, shall have power and authority to choose, place, and displace their said minister, and may and shall manage the said four hundred pounds for his yearly salary as aforesaid, as feoffees or trustees for the same may and ought to do.’

The following particulars of the life of this benefactor have been preserved by Ralph Gosling.

William Ronksley was born about 1650, and educated in the Grammar-school at Sheffield. Early in life he established a small school at Hathersage, whence he removed to Bradwell, and while there drew up his *Regiæ Grammaticæ Clavis*. He was next engaged as clerk or amanuensis to Francis Jessop of Broom-hall, esquire, and while in that situation was the publisher of a sheet almanac. On Mr. Jessop's death in 1691 he was taken into the family of William Monckton of Hodroyd, esquire, a relation of Mr. Jessop, as tutor to his son. Here he applied himself very closely to his studies, and made great advances in classical knowledge. In 1707 he published ‘ An application of Lilly's Syntax,’ which Gosling calls excellent. Last of all he was taken into the family of the Bosviles of Gunthwaite, as a tutor, and in that situation he died on the 4th of January 1724. In these various employments he accumulated considerable property, which by a will dated the 29th of October 1723 he gave to his nephews John and Humphry Wardle, directing that the former should take the name of Ronksley, according to the desire of his late brother John Ronksley, subject however to many bequests to relations, and to charitable and public uses.

Jeremiah Gill was the first minister of Fullwood. He resided at Stumperlow till 1754, when a small house was erected for the minister on a piece of ground adjoining the chapel, by the benefactions of the neighbouring Dissenters. Here he died in 1758, and was interred in the chapel. From that time till 1798 it was supplied by one of the ministers of the Upper-Chapel in Sheffield. In that year the Rev. Joseph Evans resigned; and some assistance being obtained from funds intended for the support of dissenting-worship, the Rev. Joseph Ramsbotham settled here as minister, who in 1802 was succeeded by the Rev. William Whitelegg, and he in 1810 by the Rev. Mr. Elliott. He left Fullwood in 1812; and the chapel was for some time supplied by lay-preachers, and afterwards by students from the Independent academy at Masborough. The Rev. Mr. Macdonald is now the minister.

The money with which Ronksley endowed the chapel has been lost.

The same person left a small sum for the use of a school in Fullwood. ‘ Item I give and bequeath thirty pounds to be paid three years after my decease to and for the use of a school in Fullwood aforesaid for ever, for which four children of the poorer sort shall be taught to read English only, to be chosen out of Full-

[1] Vide *Gent. Mag.* vol. lxv. p. 371.

3 L

wood aforesaid by Humphry Wardle and John Wardle alias John Ronksley of Fullwood, and by their
and either of their heirs at all times for ever, and for
want of such heirs by the feoffees or trustees for the
said school for the time being, which school I would
have to be on or near Birks-green, that is near to
John Broomhead's house, if the neighbours think
good.'

About 1790 a small chapel was built on Rann-moor,
in this township, for the use of the Methodists in connexion with the Reverend John Wesley.

A mineral spring at Fullwood was once of considerable note. We have seen that it was much resorted
to in 1666, a period of alarm respecting the plague. Dr.
Short, who gives an analysis of its waters, says that ' it
was of very great note formerly, much frequented, and
vast benefit reaped from its use, in all cases wherein
light chalybeates take place[1].' He had been told that
there was once a treatise written upon it, but he could
not learn when or by whom. It was sometimes called
Fullwood-Spa, and sometimes Heaton-Spa, ' from its
benefactor,' says Dr. Short, ' the late Mr. Thomas
Heaton of Sheffield, who laid a bason, built a house
over it, and made a way to it, from his great philan-
thropy.' The doctor recommends that a bath should
be constructed near it. Whether this spring ever deserved the reputation it obtained is questionable, and
what it had obtained it has long lost.

The only mansions in this township which require
any notice are Fullwood-hall and Stumperlow-hall.

FULLWOOD-HALL.

This house was for many ages the seat of a family
of the name of Fox, who had considerable possessions
in this township and in the adjoining chapelry of Bradfield. Agnes the wife of John Fox of Fullwood is
mentioned in the court-rolls of the manor of Sheffield in the 6 Henry VI. In the same rolls we meet
with William son and heir of William Fox of Fullwood in the 28 Elizabeth. This was the person who
procured the exemplification of Furnival's grant. He
had four children, to whom he gave the names of Ulysses, Zachariah, Sophronia, and Gertrude, a curious
selection to be madeby a yeoman of Upper-Hallam.

Ulysses Fox of Fullwood, yeoman, was his son and
heir. He married Elizabeth daughter of William
Green of Smallfield in the chapelry of Bradfield, by
whom he had a son named William Fox, who was
baptized at Sheffield 12 Dec. 1613. He married Anne
daughter of John Morewood of the Oaks in Bradfield, gentleman, who survived him, and took to her
second husband Henry Balguy of the Hagg in the
parish of Hope, gentleman. To William Fox she bore
Joseph Fox of Rowlee in the parish of Hope, lead-merchant, who was a small benefactor to that parish at
his death in 1669, and George Fox of Fullwood-hall,
who in all records in which his name appears is designated ' gentleman,' and who used as the device on
his seal, the crest a bear rampant supporting a battle-
axe, with the motto round ' And let God help.' I
have not found that there was ever a grant of arms to
this family. The said George Fox married Mary
daughter of Francis Poole of Park-hall in the parish
of Barlborough, gentleman, of an ancient Catholic

family. She survived, and married a second time with
Robert Blackburn of Bate-green in the chapelry of
Bradfield, gentleman. In the parish-register of Bradfield, one of the sons of George Fox is entered as baptized ' by a Jesuit, said to be a Popish bishop, 4 April
1684.' There was a large family.

George Fox wasted his estate. He and his brother
William Fox mortgaged Fullwood-hall to Nicholas
Sylvester of Chapeltown, gentleman; and on the 4th
of September 1707 John Sylvester of Birthwaite gentleman, executor of the last will and testament of Nicholas Sylvester, and George Fox of Fullwood-hall
gentleman, surrendered in the court of the lord of the
manor of Sheffield, Fullwood-hall, &c., to John Fox
of Sheffield-park, gentleman.

It does not appear from any evidence before me
whether the new proprietor were connected in blood
with the former possessors. Mr. John Fox built a
house in Dixon-lane in Sheffield, over the front of
which he placed arms of the name of Fox, namely,
a chevron between three foxes' heads. He left no
issue, and at his death was a small benefactor to
Hollis's hospital. Fullwood-hall then became the
property of his niece Dorothy wife of James Oliver,
gentleman, (whose maiden name was Bamforth,) and
her only daughter Miss Sarah Oliver who died unmarried in 1741. Mrs. Oliver took to her second husband the Reverend William Humpton, one of the assistant-ministers of Sheffield and curate of Ecclesall.
She died in 1746, when a considerable estate became
divided among many relations, in too small portions
to each to raise any of them into the rank of gentry.
Fullwood-hall has since passed by purchase into the
hands of George-Bustard Greaves, esquire.

STUMPERLOW-HALL.

In 1593, Thomas Archdale of Stumperlow and
Matilda his wife surrendered lands there to William
Topham, alias Short, of Dronfield, mercer, who in 39
Elizabeth surrendered them to Thomas Machon, who
in 9 Charles I. is described as of Stumperlow.

These were probably the lands on which there was
afterwards a capital mansion erected, which in the
phrase of a country not very scrupulous in applying
the term is called a hall, Stumperlow-hall. It appears
to have been built about the time when Robert Hall
was first settled here, namely 1655; and was for fifty
years and more the residence of himself and his posterity. They ranked as gentry, but did not appear at the
visitations.

Robert Hall and Dorothy his wife had several children, of whom Mary married Robert Ashton of Whiteley-wood, gentleman, and Catherine, Edward Gelley
of Sheffield. He had also a son Henry Hall born in
1655, who was dead before 1716. In that year his
children Henry Hall of Leeds, merchant, John Hall,
and Anne Hare, together with his widow Sarah Hall,
surrendered in the manor court of Sheffield that capital messuage called Stumperlow-hall, &c., to Daniel
Gascoigne of Sheffield, apothecary, and John Hawksworth of Bridge-house, lead-merchant. During the
greatest part of the eighteenth century Stumperlow-
hall was the estate and residence of the family of Mr.
Hawksworth.

[1] *History of Mineral Waters*, p. 271.

IV.

The Township of Nether-Hallam.

IN the admeasurement of the parish of Sheffield communicated to Mr. Brown and published in the agricultural survey of the west riding, this township is said to consist of about 1900 acres, on which were erected 188 dwelling-houses. This was in 1796. But it seems to be under the truth; for in 1801 the number of inhabitants was 1974. Perhaps the territory of Heeley, which lies apart from the main body of the township, was not included in the communication to Mr. Brown. In 1811 the population was increased to 2384.

This township lies to the north-west of Sheffield, and adjoins Ecclesall and Upper-Hallam. The Don separates it from Brightside-Byerlow; and the Riveling and Loxley from Ecclesfield. A small portion of the ground on the left bank of the Loxley is laid down as pertaining to this township in the map of the parish of Sheffield.

The turnpike road from Sheffield to Peniston passes through this township, and along its line there has been much building in the course of the last twenty years. To a knot of new houses forming a considerable village about a mile from Sheffield on this road, has been given the name of Philadelphia.

Near to it are the horse-barracks built in 1794.

Five of the ancient hamlets or villages of the parish of Sheffield are in this township: Upperthorpe, Walkley, Owlerton, Crooks, and Heeley. They all appear in the list of *Membra castri de Sheffield* 39 Edward III. except Crooks, for the omission of which it is not easy to account. It is probable that some of them at least were among the berewites of the manor of Hallam.

A considerable majority of the inhabitants of these villages and of the whole township are employed in different branches of the Sheffield manufactures.

There is no place of public worship in any part of this township.

At the village of Crooks is a school which was founded by Ronksley, the benefactor to Fullwood.— 'Item my mind and will is, that from and after my decease the interest or product of one hundred pounds shall be paid by two half yearly payments to George Wardle for and during his natural life, and at and after the decease of the said George Wardle I give and bequeath the said one hundred pounds to and for the use of a school to be built or purchased in or near to Crooks in the parish of Sheffield for ever, for which twelve children of the poorer sort to be chosen out of Crooks aforesaid and out of the neighbourhood thereof shall be taught to read English only; and my mind and will is, that my honoured friend William Jessop of Broom-hall esquire and his heirs shall admit, place and displace both the master of the said school and the twelve children to be taught therein as aforesaid, at all times; and his heirs failing, I commit that whole trust and power to the burgesses for the free school in Sheffield for the time being.'

In 1794 a new school-house was erected by the inhabitants of Crooks and the neighbourhood.

There is also a school at Heeley with an endowment of about 14*l.* *per annum.* Mr. Thomas Chapman, who died on the 19th of June 1801 at the age of 81, was the principal benefactor.

The whole of this township is within the manor of Sheffield, except Owlerton and a small district around it which claims to be a manor of itself. The earliest lords of whom I have found notice were the Creswicks, a name numerous and respectable in the parish of Sheffield, probably derived from the small and now almost extinct hamlet of that name in the parish of Ecclesfield, and not far from Owlerton. On the 22d of October, 43 Elizabeth, 1601, a court-baron of the manor of Owlerton was held, when Thomas Creswick was the lord. This person was probably son to John Creswick of Owlerton-hall, who by that description is nominated a supervisor in the will of John Rawson of Hooper-thorpe, now Upper-thorpe, 1594. The same Thomas Creswick was also lord in 1607. But in 1652 the court was held in the name of Robert Stacie, son and heir of Malin Stacie deceased; who in 1657 signs a receipt to John Staniforth the younger for nineteen shillings and eightpence 'for a reliefe for such lands as the right ho^ble Thomas Earle of Arundel holdeth of the manor of Ollerton.' In 1666 a court baron for this manor was held, when Robert Stacie was lord, and William Simpson steward. Soon after this date it passed into another name; for in 1675 Robert Sorsby was the lord, and William Simpson steward. In 1691 the court was held in the names of Robert Sorsby and George Bamforth gentlemen, and in 1724 of George Bamforth only.

None of the persons of whom we have been speaking appeared at any of the visitations of the county of York: but the following table will serve for the illustration of the descent of this manor during the seventeenth century. It will also be found to contain some early generations of one branch of the wide-spread family of Rawson, who were principal freeholders in this township, having their abode at Upper-thorpe and Walkley. By the marriage of his ancestor Robert Rawson of Wardsend with Mary Rawson daughter of Edward Rawson of Walkley, in 1650, the present Thomas Rawson of Wardsend esquire is descended of this family, of whose descent in the male line from a long series of principal freeholders of Hallamshire I shall have hereafter to speak.

WILLIAM RAWSON of the parish=ELIZABETH, of Sheffield, tanner. Will dated 19 March 1549. Proved at York 23 April 1550. | to whom and her son James Rawson her husband devised lands at Attercliffe, Norwood, &c.

JOHN RAWSON of Hooper-thorpe, or Upper-thorpe, yeoman. Named a devisee in his father's will 1549. His own will bears date 12 June 1594, in which he directs that his body shall be buried in the church or church-yard at Sheffield. = ----- dau. of Henry Hatfield of Whitfield, in the parish of Glossop, co. Derb.

JAMES RAWSON of Norwood, in the township of Brightside-Byerlow. Named a supervisor in the will of his brother John Rawson 1594. Died 1 June 1603, leaving several sons, whose posterity continued at Norwood many years.

ANNE RAWSON, married at Sheffield 4 Nov. 1565 to John Creswick of Owlerton-hall.

ELIZABETH, wife of Francis Howsley of Sheffield, to whom she was married 11 Novemb. 1566.

CATHERINE, wife of John Parkin, who was an executor to John Rawson's will. Married 16 July 1570.

EDWARD RAWSON of Upper-thorpe yeoman, son and heir. Buried at Sheffield 15 Oct. 1597, and his will was proved at York 3 May 1598 by his two sons William and John Rawson his executors. = ELLEN BARBER, married at Sheffield 13 June 1569. Will proved at York by John Rawson her son 5 July 1604.

MARGARET, wife first of Nicholas Saunderson of Sheffield, yeoman, uncle to Dr. Robert Saunderson bishop of Lincoln; and secondly of Richard Allen of Liversedge, who was named an executor in the will of John Rawson.

JOAN, wife of Lawrence Staniforth of Darnall, yeoman, and probably in second nuptials of Thomas Shaw.

ROSE, wife first of ---Wagstaff, and secondly of Hugh Scargell of Steel-bank, to whom she was married 11 Feb. 1584.

THOMAS CRESWICK of Owlerton-hall, lord of the manor of Owlerton 1601 and 1607.

WILLIAM RAWSON of Walkley, yeoman, eldest son, bap. at Sheffield 29 Oct. 1574. Executor to the will of his father 1598, and overseer of the will of his brother John Rawson 1637. Made his will 1 Sept. 1647, and it was proved at York in May 1649. = ALICE DALE, mar. at Sheffield 9 July 1599.

JOHN RAWSON of Upper-thorpe, yeoman, second son. Executor to his father's will. Bap. at Sheffield 13 Dec. 1577. Made his will 3 Jan. 1637, and it was proved at York. = ELIZABETH, sister of Richard Boroughs of Tinsley, gentleman, mar. at Sheffield 6 October 1602.

ROBERT SORSBIE of Sheffield, cutler. The first Master of the Company of Cutlers. = CATHERINE CLAYTON, married at Sheffield 23 Oct. 1597.

EDWARD RAWSON of Walkley, who died in 1678, aged 78, leaving many children. ALICE, wife of William Creswick, and other children.

ROBERT STACIE of Owlerton-hall, (son and heir of Malin Stacie,) lord of the manor of Owlerton 1652. = MARGARET RAWSON, baptized at Sheffield 24 Aug. 1613.

EDWARD RAWSON of Upper-thorpe, yeoman, eldest son and heir, died in 1669, leaving many children.

THOMAS RAWSON, M.A. vicar of Ledsham and rector of Whiston, both in the county of York. Had lands at Brightside by his father's will. Buried at Whiston Dec. 1681, leaving a numerous issue.

ELIZABETH RAWSON, bap. at Sheffield 1 Nov. 1618, married there 14 Oct. 1635. Buried in the parish-church of Sheffield 13 March 1676. = MALIN SORSBIE of Sheffield, gentleman, buried there 8 Dec. 1680.

ROBERT SORSBIE D.D, precentor of York, &c. bap. at Sheffield 25 Mar. 1599.

ROBERT STACIE of Owlerton-hall, yeoman. Made his will 15 Jan. 1676. = MARGARET, executrix to her husband's will.

ELIZABETH STACIE.

ALICE, wife of John Revel of Whiston, gent., mar. at Sheffield 7 Sept. 1657.

ROBERT SORSBIE of Sheffield, gent., lord of the manor of Owlerton 1691, bap. at Sheffield 25 Dec. 1636. = ELIZABETH REVEL, married at Sheffield 8 June 1674.

MALIN SORSBIE D.D. of Riton in the bishopric of Durham, 1683. Bap. at Sheffield 7 Feb. 1639.

JOHN WEBSTER of Owlerton, died 24 Dec. 1727, aged 79, and was buried in the middle aile of Sheffield church. = MARY STACIE, only dau. and heir, mar. at Sheffield 14 Aug. 1687.

ROBERT SORSBIE, bap. at Sheffield 12 Jan. 1679.

MALIN SORSBIE, bap. at Sheffield 2 August 1683.

ANNE SORSBIE.

JOHN, STEPHEN, and ELIZABETH died in their infancy.

JOHN BRIGHT of Owlerton, gentleman, son and heir of Stephen Bright of Raisin-hall in Brightside-Byerlow, by Anne his wife, dau. of Thomas Bright of Gray-stones in Ecclesall-Byerlow. = ELEANOR WEBSTER, bap. at Sheffield 13 Oct. 1692, died 19 April 1748, buried with her father.

ANNE WEBSTER, bap. at Sheffield 10 June 1691.

JOHN WEBSTER, at Sheffield 13 Dec. 1688, buried there 13 Jan. 1689.

JOHN BRIGHT of Owlerton, gent., son and heir, died without issue 16 Dec. 1770, aged 39. = MARTHA EYRE of Southall-green in the parish of Ecclesfield, died 14 July 1766, aged 26.

ELEANOR BRIGHT, wife of John Ryals of Sheffield filesmith.

It remains to speak of the descent of the manor of Owlerton since 1724, when George Bamforth appears as sole lord.

This gentleman was one of a very numerous family spread over the parish of Sheffield, descended of John Bamforth who was living at Sheffield in the reign of Elizabeth. The branch to which he belonged had flourished at the High-house, a capital mansion in this township, and had become enriched by successful commerce and productive leases under the Norfolk family. They had acquired the manor of Owlerton, together with the adjacent manor of Wadsley. Just at the time when the Bamforths of the High-house were beginning to take a leading part in the concerns of the neighbourhood and of the county, they became extinct by the death of the only male heir at the age of twenty-eight.

The family made pretension to coat-armour, but it does not appear that they presented themselves at any of the visitations.

PEDIGREE of BAMFORTH of the High-house.

ARMS.—Argent a fess ingrailed gules.

JOHN BAMFORTH of Sheffield, living there in the time of Elizabeth.

GEORGE BAMFORTH of the High-house, yeoman, bap. at Sheffield 28 Feb. 1601. Made his will 14 Jan. 1675, and it was proved at York by George Bamforth his son and executor 11 May 1677. Buried in the chancel of the parish-church of Sheffield 14 April 1677. **=** WINIFRED OXSPRING, married at Sheffield 26 Jan. 1625, bur. there 16 May 1646.

ROBERT BAMFORTH, mentioned in his brother's will, with his children Mary, Sarah, Anne, and Elizabeth.

WILLIAM BAMFORTH of Darnall, mentioned in his brother's will, with his children John, William, George, Annis, Elizabeth, Mary, Sarah, Ruth, Rebecca, Martha, Hannah, and Abigail.

ANNE, wife of Henry Moore of Orgrave, gent.

MARY, wife first of Robert Brown, and secondly of ---- Rawson.

ELIZABETH, wife of George Wood.

GEORGE BAMFORTH of the High-house, gent., one of the lords of the manor of Owlerton, bap. at Sheffield 14 Aug. 1625. Admitted to his freedom in the Company of Cutlers of Hallamshire 26 March 1653. Died 21 Oct. 1701, and was buried in the chancel of the parish-church of Sheffield. **=** MARGARET, dau. of ---- D and of Dronfield, co. Derb. gent., mar. in the old chapel of Ecclesall 28 May 1683. Buried with her husband 13 July 1727.

JOHN BAMFORTH, bap. at Sheffield 8 April 1627. Not mentioned in his father's will.

ANNE, first wife, dau. and co-heir of Rowland Hancock, clerk, of Shircliffe-hall, once vicar of Ecclesfield and assistant-minister of Sheffield. Bur. at Sheffield 19 May 1717. **=** GEORGE BAMFORTH of the High-house, gent., lord of the manor of Owlerton, born 17 May 1684, bap. at Sheffield 3 June. Bur. there 28 April 1730. **=** ESTHER, second wife, dau. of William Burton of Royds-mill, gent., bap. at Sheffield 28 April 1700. Mar. her first husband at Ecclesfield 30 May 1723. Died in her third widowhood 19 Dec. 1778, and was buried in the parish-church of Sheffield. **=** ROBERT CHAPELL of Sheffield, esq., husband, a barrister-at-law. **=** PAUL MEYER esq., of Baker's-hill in Sheffield, 3d husband; second son of Sir Peter Meyer of London, knt., son of Jacob Meyer, a merchant of Hambro'.— Mr. Meyer was one of the twelve capital burgesses of Sheffield. Married there 17 Dec. 1740. Buried 28 Dec. 1743.

MARY, first wife, dau. and co-heir of Mr. Francis Mason of Crofton near Wakefield; who left a son named Paul Meyer.

MARGARET BAMFORTH, bap. at Sheffield 16 Feb. 1688. Died unmar. 11 Nov. 1709, and was buried in the chancel of the parish-church of Sheffield.

GEORGE BAMFORTH of the High-house, esq., son and heir, lord of the manors of Owlerton and Wadsley, bap. at Sheffield 8 August 1710. Died without issue 31 May 1739, and was buried on the 4 June in the parish church of Sheffield. **=** MARGARET, dau. and co-heir of William Bamford of Bamford, co. Lanc. esq., by Margaret his wife dau. of Edward Davenport of Stockport. Died in Feb. 1776. **=** JOHN SENIOR of the High-house, second husband.

WILLIAM BURTON of Royds-mill, gent., brother to Esther Burton in the line above. Buried in the parish-church of Sheffield 19 May 1764.

MARGARET BAMFORTH, sister and sole heir. Bap. at Sheffield 6 July 1711. Bur. there 11 Oct. 1749.

ANNE BAMFORTH. Bap. at Sheffield 4 Dec. 1712. Died unmar. and was bur. at Sheffield 17 April 1735.

MARY, born in 1713, and died in 1714.

MARY, born in 1715, and died in 1720.

JOHN, born died in 1716.

JOHN BURTON of Bramley-hall, in the parish of Hansworth, esq., eldest surviving son and heir. Died 8 November 1772, aged 32, and was buried in the chancel of the parish-church of Sheffield. **=** CATHERINE, dau. of John Law of Rotherham. **=** Sir RICHARD COPE baronet, second husband.

Other children. See under ROYDS-MILL in the township of Attercliffe-cum-Darnall.

CATHERINE BURTON, posthumous and only child. Lady of the manor of Owlerton, and relict of Sir Montague-Roger Burgoyne, bart. 1819.

The manor of Owlerton and the High-house were settled by the last Mr. Bamforth on his wife as part of her jointure, and she enjoyed them above six-and-thirty years, more than twenty of which she was the unacknowledged wife of Senior, who is said to have been butler to Mr. Bamforth. She resided at High-house with an unmarried sister, Mrs. Anne Bamford, who survived till February 1779. Mrs. Anne Bamford being the last surviving child and heir of William Bamford of Bamford, esquire, left that estate to William Bamford of Tarlton in Lancashire.

The High-house has since been sold to Mr. Christopher Oates of Sheffield, merchant, and is now the residence of his son Mr. Charles Oates.

The hall at Owlerton is a substantial old house, bearing marks of having seen better days. Mr. Wilson observes, that in his time the courts of the manor were kept at the hall, and that divers tenants held their lands by the service of repairing the mill-dam, and performing other works about the mill.

V.

The Township of Brightside-Byerlow.

THAT part of the parish of Sheffield which lies on the left bank of the Don is the township of Brightside-Byerlow. In the map of the parish, about ten fields on the right bank of the river near Carbrook are coloured as belonging to this township. The little stream called Blackbourn-brook divides it from the parish of Rotherham.

The area according to the survey of 1796 is 2680 acres; and there were at that time 822 houses. The population at recent periods has been found—

Anno 1782—2186.
       1786—2741.
       1801—4030.
       1811—4899.

A large proportion of the population inhabit the Wicker and the Bridge-houses, which being separated from the other buildings of the town of Sheffield only by the river, may be regarded as integral portions of the town. The communication with the Wicker is over the Lady's-bridge, and with the Bridge-houses over an iron bridge on three stone arches, which was constructed in 1795, in the same place where till that period had been only a bridge of wood. There are persons still living who remember the Don flowing through green and pleasant meadows between the Green-lane and Lady's-bridge.

The turnpike-road from Sheffield to Barnsley passes through this township. There is much new building along its line. There are several hamlets, and two ancient villages, Brightside and Grimesthorpe, which lie retired and pleasant.

A considerable part of this township bears the name of Pits-moor. This part was the latest inclosed. All the rest, except the Wicker and what was left as woodland, was brought into cultivation at a very remote period. A much greater proportion of wood is to be found in this township than in any other part of the parish of Sheffield. The most considerable are Wincobank-wood, Hall-Carr-wood, Burnt-greave, the Great Roe-wood, and the Old or Shiercliffe-park, which so beautifully clothes with a forest vesture the ground declining to the river on the west side of this township, with its near neighbour Cookwood, from which it was separated little more than a century ago. All these woods are the property of his grace the duke of Norfolk, who is also lord of the manor.

It has been already shown that in the Saxon times this part of the parish of Sheffield was the manor of

Grimshaw, and that Ulfac was the last Saxon proprietor. It afterwards passed to De Busli and De Lovetot, and from them to the present owner. A considerable portion was however granted off very early to the family of De Mounteney, who had a hall and park at Shiercliffe in this township, and who claimed manorial rights. This however reverted by purchase to the line of the original lords at a time and in a manner which will be described immediately.

Though the name of Grimshaw has disappeared, the name of Grimesthorpe, which has evidently the same origin, is still existing; and how it has happened that in the designation of the township in which it stands (for as a manor it has not had any separate existence, the copyholds being surrendered in the lord's courts for Sheffield or Ecclesfield) it should have been supplanted by its neighbour Brightside, it is not easy to explain. But a still more extraordinary circumstance connected with the name of this township is the change which has taken place in the orthography of the name of the village of Brightside, and consequently of the township. That name is probably not older than two centuries. We have seen that Harrison, the coadjutor of Holinshed, writes the word Briksie, and that in the deed of sale of its tythe in the time of Elizabeth it is written Brixard. In a list of the churchwardens of the parish of Sheffield for the year 1565, by a contemporary hand, the word is Brykehurst[1]. In a deed of John Everingham 11 Henry VIII[2] it is written Brekesherth, which seems to have been the original and true orthography, since it is also so written in a deed of Thomas de Furnival to Worksop, recited by Thoroton, in 1328. All the little villages and hamlets throughout Hallamshire gave surnames to some family having property within them; and I make no doubt that the John Brekesherd who was a plaintiff in the 15 Henry VI. respecting lands in Sheffield, Kimberworth, Tinsley, and Brinsford[3], derived his name from this village. It seems too that Grykesherth in the *membra castri de Sheffield*, which occurs between Skinnerthorp and Grimesthorp, is an error of some transcriber for Brykesherth. This is perhaps one of the most remarkable instances that can be produced of the propensity of the common people to substitute for a name the meaning of which is unknown to them, a word to which they can attach a meaning[4]; and let me add, of the acquiescence of the better informed in such a substitution.

[1] Among the Wilson Collections.
[2] Broom-hall Evidences.
[3] Dods. xxx. 37 s. Harl. 801. Tinsley.
[4] Another instance in the neighbourhood of Sheffield is Laughton en le Morthen, or Morthing, which is commonly known by the name of Lighten in the morning. There is something not inappropriate in this misnomer when used by the people of Hallamshire, who look eastward to the village of Laughton, and may often see its lofty and delicate spire beautifully defined in the early light of the morning.

By the deed just mentioned of Thomas de Furnival he gave to the monks of Worksop 5 marks yearly rent from his mills of Brekesherth.

By a decision of the justices of the peace at the sessions held at Pontefract in 1665, the repair and support of Brightside-bridge was declared to be a burden on the wapentake.

At Brightside are considerable iron-works and a paper-mill. Here is also an aluminous spring; and it appears that attempts have been made to establish an alum work, as in most of the accounts of Sheffield we are told that in the neighbourhood of the town are mines of alum.

Neither at Brightside nor in any part of this populous township is there any place of public worship, except that in the Bridge-houses is a small Methodist meeting. The inhabitants of Brightside for the most part attend the chapel at Attercliffe, and consider themselves as within that chapelry. The inhabitants of Attercliffe, Darnall, and Carbrook only, built and endowed the chapel, and joined in the petition to procure the archbishop's sanction to their undertaking.

I have nothing more to add respecting this township generally, or the village from which it derives its name. We therefore proceed to the notice of some places within the township which have claims of different kinds on our attention.

SHIERCLIFFE-HALL.

This was an ancient estate of inheritance of the family of Mounteney, descended of Sir Robert de Mounteney, grandson of Maud de Lovetot, in the time of Henry III. By marriage with an heiress of De Reneville in that reign they acquired the manor of Cowley, where Dodsworth was informed they had 'great woods and abundance of redd deare, and a stately castle-like house moated about, pulled down not long since by

the earl of Salop after he had purchased the land[1].' In the reign of Richard II. Sir John Mounteney had a license from the crown to inclose 200 acres of land, 300 acres of wood, and 20 acres of his demesne land in Shiercliffe, and to make a park of the same.' He had also a charter of free warren in all his demesne lands at Cowley, Shiercliffe, &c.[2]

In the feodary's accounts of the estate of John earl of Shrewsbury 30 Henry VI. the manor of Shiercliffe then held by Thomas Mounteney is reckoned at the fourth part of a knight's fee. The manor of Wadsley was valued at the same.

The family continued to reside at Shiercliffe and Cowley in a state of much splendour till the reign of Henry VIII., when the eldest line ended in female heiresses.

A family of this rank and consequence has not been overlooked by our genealogists. Few collections of Yorkshire genealogies are without a pedigree of them; but they are for the most part little more than copies from Hopkinson's pedigrees, which may be regarded as the *codex receptus* of Yorkshire genealogy. In his early descents Hopkinson and his copyists have followed that unknown hand which about the reign of Henry VIII. favoured so many of the gentry of the county of York with descents from the Conquest, and they have therefore admitted many things that are of little or rather no authority. The reader will be better satisfied with a pedigree of the early descents of Mounteney from the handwriting of Dodsworth, who says he had it from Richard Gascoigne, another laborious collector for Yorkshire, and who compiled it from records in the hands of Mr. West of Rotherham, the earl of Shrewsbury's seneschal for Hallamshire[3]. The later generations are from wills, deeds, the visitation-books, &c.

PEDIGREE of MOUNTENEY of SHIERCLIFFE, COWLEY, &c.

ARMS.—Gules a bend between six martlets or.

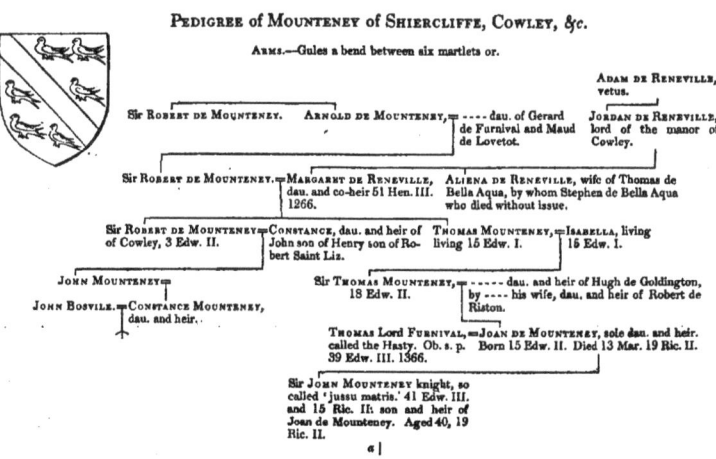

[1] Dods. MSS. in Bibl. Bodl. vol. clx. f. 17 a.
[2] Dods. MSS. M. 12 b. Harl. 801. Shiercliffe.
[3] Dods. MSS. in Bibl. Bodl. vol. xc. f. 140.

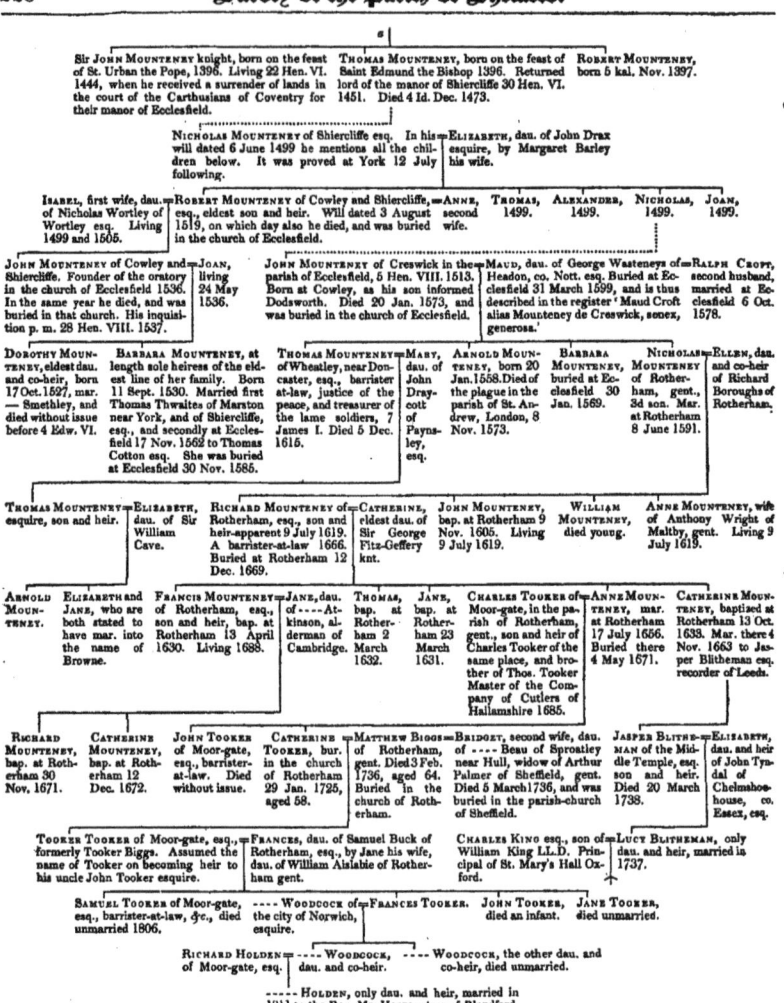

One of the most curious relics of the early Mounteneys was a missal executed by one of the illuminators of the time for Joan de Mounteney the heiress, who married Thomas lord Furnival the Hasty. Dodsworth saw it in the hands of his friend Mr. Thomas Mounteney of Wheatley[1]: but as he looked upon everything with the eye of a genealogist and herald, he has contented himself with describing the heraldric decorations, and with copying the family anniversaries with which the calendar was thickly interspersed. I wish the present notice of so interesting a relic may be the means of bringing it again into view, or of drawing from its fortunate possessor a more particular account of the miniatures with which I have no doubt it was richly adorned. In the will of her descendant Nicholas Mounteney 1499 this choice volume is made the

[1] Dods. MSS. in Bibl. Bodl. vol. cxvii. f. 18.

subject of a particular bequest ' *unum primarium cum armis meis pictis*.' The birth of the lady for whose use it was first compiled, is thus recorded on the first page: ' Nata est Johã filia Thomæ Mounteney militis in fõ Sẽi Michĩs Archangeli An° Dni 1321.' The other entries of the same nature have been used in the composition of the pedigree. They extend to the time of James I.

The impalements may be taken as some authority for the early matches of the family. They are thus described by Dodsworth.

FURNIVAL impaling LOVETOT. MOUNTENEY impaling FUR-NIVAL. MOUNTENEY impaling ermine two bars gemelles. MOUNTENEY impaling paly of six argent and azure. MOUN-TENEY alone. MOUNTENEY impaling vaire a bend componée or and ... FITZ-WILLIAM lozengy argent and gules. VIPONT azure six annulets or. MOUNTENEY alone. Gules a fess dancette between ten billets or. The same impaling azure a fess dancette between ten billets or. MOUNTENEY impaling quarterly 1 and 4. Argent two bars azure, 2 and 3, argent three chaplets gules. MOUNTENEY impaling argent three chaplets gules.

This lady Joan de Mounteney had also during the time of her coverture a seal executed of beautiful device and workmanship. Suspended from the branches of a tree on each side the trunk is a shield, one of which bears the arms of Furnival, and the other those of Mounteney. Around them is the inscription SIGIL-LVM IOHANNE DE FVRNIVALL: but in her widowhood she resumed her maiden name. It is presumed that she entered into second nuptials. This is certain, that Thomas lord Furnival her husband died without issue: yet in the deed which follows preserved by Dugdale in one of his manuscripts in the College of Arms[1] she acknowledges a son John de Mounteney, afterwards a knight, and her successor at Cowley and Shierclife, the births of whose three sons are registered in the missal.

To this deed the seal above mentioned is appendant.

' Sciant presentes et futuri, quod ego Johanna Mounteney filia et hæres Thomæ Mounteney, quondam uxor Thomæ Furnivall Chr. dedi, coņcessi &c. Johanni Mounteney filio meo manerium meum de Bulcotes cum omnibus pertinentiis in Com. Nott. Dedi etiam prædicto Johanni omnia terra et tenementa prata &c. in Rishetou juxta Rothewell in Com. Northampt. &c. ac in Swynton et Scoles in Com. Ebor. Habend' &c. præ-dicto Johanni heredibus et assignatis suis &c. Data apud Sherclyffe in Com. Ebor. in festo Sẽi Martini Episcopi in hyeme 15 Ric. 11.'

On the sixth of June 1499 Nicholas Mounteney esquire made his will. He desired that his body might be buried before the image of Saint Mary in the church at Ecclesfield, and directed that a priest should say mass for his soul for one full year after his decease. To the fabrick of the church of Ecclesfield he gave one seme of iron. To Robert his eldest son he gave all his heir looms, among which are specified, 'unum cali-cem argenti, unum mese boke, unum primarium cum arnis meis pictis, cum omnibus ornamentis capelle mee pro capellano seu presbytero meo cantanti et mis-sam celebranti.' It is not certain whether this chapel was at Cowley or Shiercliffe. To Isabel the wife of his son Robert he gave a girdle that had been used by his wife Elizabeth Mounteney; and he made his three younger sons Thomas, Alexander, and Nicholas, his

executors, who were to order for his soul's health as they thought fit. He also nominated Thomas Clerk, vicar of Ecclesfield, one of the supervisors. This will was proved at York on the 12th of July following.

Robert Mounteney succeeded as son and heir, and married a sister of Sir Thomas Wortley, of Wharn-cliffe celebrity. His portrait and that of his lady, with the arms and effigies of his ancestors from the time of Arnold de Mounteney, once appeared in the east window of the south aile of the church of Ecclesfield, placed there by him in 1505. His will bears date the 3d of August 1519, and he was buried according to the directions it contained in the church of Ecclesfield.

Fragments remain of the sepulchral stone of this Robert Mounteney, and also of that of his son and heir John Mounteney, who was interred in the same church in 1536. Their heirs probably thought that the memorials which they placed over their graves would endure for ever, when having cut the inscription deep in the stone, they filled up the letters with some pitchy or metallic substance. But there are now a far less perfect memorial of this ancient and opulent family than is another inscription in the same church boldly carved in oak, requesting prayers for the souls of Robert Mounteney and Anne his wife, and for the good estate of John Mounteney and Joan his wife, who constructed the oratory in 1536. This John Mounteney, the last of his name at Cowley and Shier-cliffe, died in the prime of life ; and a tradition is not to be wholly passed over, that he was assaulted and wounded in the church porch of Sheffield, of which wound he died; but by whom it was inflicted, or on what account, the tradition does not explain. By in-quisition taken after his death 28 Henry VIII. he was found to hold the manor of Cowley of the king as of his honour of Tickhill by knight-service; the manor of Shiercliffe, of whom or by what service the jury knew not; and the manor of Steynton of the king by knight service; and Dorothy and Barbara Mounteney were found to be his daughters and co-heirs[2].

Still two male branches of the family continued in a state of high respectability at Wheatley near Don-caster, and at Rotherham. Wheatley was sold to Sir Robert Anstruther, who re-sold it to the family of Cooke its present possessors. The name disappeared at Rotherham about the close of the seventeenth cen-tury. It may be submitted as at least probable, that the Richard Mounteney who was born at Rotherham in 1671 was the gentleman of that name who lived at Putney, where was born to him a son of the same name, afterwards one of the barons of the Exchequer in Ireland, and the learned editor of Demosthenes.

Of the two daughters and co-heirs of the oldest house, one was eight and the other five years of age at the death of the father. The elder married —— Smethley, probably of Brantingham in the county of York. She died at an early age leaving no issue. It was found by inquisition post mortem 4 Edward VI. that Dorothy Smethley held before her death the ma-nor of Shiercliffe with its appurtenances of the earl of Shrewsbury as of his castle of Sheffield by knight-service, and that Barbara Thwaites was her sister and heir[3].

Barbara Mounteney married Thomas Thwaites

[1] C. 40, f. 149 a.
[2] From a volume of Abstracts of Yorkshire Inquisitions in the library of the College of Arms, supposed to be part of Gascoigne's Collections.
[3] Id.

3 N

esquire of Marston near York. They had issue three children, Sarah and William who died young, and Anne who married William Ingleby esquire, afterwards knighted, and high-sheriff of the county of York in the 7th year of Elizabeth. She died without issue.

In Hilary term 3 Elizabeth 1561, a fine was levied in the court of King's Bench between John Ingleby and William Staveley querents, and Thomas Thwaites esquire and Barbara his wife deforciants, of the manor of Shiercliffe with its appurtenances, and 50 messuages and 20 cottages &c. in Shiercliffe, Crux, Butterthwaite, Thorpe, Cowley, Heseley, Rotherham, Bilbethorpe-hill, Ecclesfield, Scoles, and Hoyland ; the right of the said John and William of the gift of the said Thomas and Barbara, for the use of the said Thomas and Barbara and the heirs of their bodies; remainder to the heirs of the body of the said Thomas; remainder to the heirs male of William Thwaites, father of the said Thomas; remainder to the said Barbara[1].

Thomas Thwaites died in the same year, or early in the next, for on the 17th of November 1562 his widow was married at Ecclesfield to Thomas Cotton gentleman.

In 1568 there was a deed of bargain and sale of the manors of Cowley, Shiercliffe, and Hesley, from Sir Thomas Wharton and Robert Bowes esquire, to John Thwaites esquire, brother of Thomas Thwaites; and by a similar deed bearing date 1 April 14 Elizabeth 1572, the said John Thwaites conveyed the manors of Cowley and Shiercliffe to George earl of Shrewsbury[2]. This must have been a most valuable acquisition to the earl, the lands lying surrounded by his vast estates and reaching within a short distance of his park and castle. The purchase was afterwards contested, and on the 4th of September 29 Elizabeth 1587 James Thwaites son and heir of John had a verdict at York in his favour[3]. All difficulties were after a time removed, and the manors of Cowley and Shiercliffe passed along with other estates of the lords of Sheffield, subject however as to the hall at Shiercliffe and a part of the domain to a long lease granted by the Thwaiteses to the family of Boroughs. This lease expired in 1638.

Shiercliffe was now shorn of its ancient honours; and from having been a residence of a family of opulence and rank next to the great baron of Hallamshire, it became the farm of a race of yeomanry, tenants to its owner. William Boroughs the first lessee under Thwaites, in his will dated the 15th of April 1587, describes himself as of Shiercliffe-hall yeoman, and directs that his body should be buried near the north church door in Sheffield. He mentions many relations; and gives Shiercliffe-hall to his wife Margaret to continue in while she lives, and after her decease to his brother Robert Boroughs and William his son. He leaves a small sum to the poor man's box in the church of Sheffield, and twenty shillings to his neighbours of the Bridgehouses and Neepsend 'to make merrie therwith.'

Richard Boroughs of Tinsley gentleman was a disclaimer at Sir William Dugdale's visitation in 1666; but the marriages of the family had been among the superior gentry of the wapentake. Daughters had

married to Mounteney, Fretwell of Hellaby, Westby of Car-house, and Westby of Gilthwaite.

When the lease to the Boroughses was expired, we find Mr. Rowland Hancock tenant at Shiercliffe-hall. Of him we have already spoken, and of the church of non-conformists, of which he was the pastor. He left two daughters, one of whom married Mr. Barnforth of the High-house, and the other Joseph Banks esq., who resided at Shiercliffe-hall.

Of Mr. Banks, who was a man of great influence at Sheffield and its neighbourhood, we have these notices in some brief memorials of his contemporaries by a very respectable old inhabitant of this township, Mr. Thomas Handley of Hall-Carr. He was the son of a gentleman who had been an officer under Sir John Reresby in the garrison at Burlington, and who died at a very great age at the house of Mr. Banks at Scofton in Nottinghamshire. He served his clerkship with Mr. Chappell, an attorney at Sheffield in great practice. As soon as the term of his clerkship was expired he married Miss Hancock, who had a fortune of four hundred pounds. They were married at Sheffield on the 5th of August 1689. He established himself as an attorney at Sheffield, and soon got into great practice. In 1692 he was under-sheriff to Major Gill of Car-house, then high-sheriff of the county of York.

He was an agent for the dukes of Norfolk, Leeds, and Newcastle. He got a fortune rapidly.

His children were all born at Sheffield or at Shiercliffe-hall; but he left Sheffield when he had scarcely passed the middle period of life, and fixed himself at Scofton near Worksop. He sat in one parliament for Grimsby, and in another for Totness. He died on the 27th of September 1727, at the age of 62, and was buried at Reevesby in the county of Lincoln, where he had purchased a fine estate. Mr. Handley gives him this character, that he was ever true to his client, but well-paid, a pleasant and very facetious companion, and says that he never seemed to enjoy life more than when he had collected a few of his old Sheffield friends, whom he used to invite to pay him an annual visit of two or three days in his retirement at Scofton. His only daughter was the amiable and accomplished Lady Whichcote, wife of Sir Francis Whichcote of Aswarby baronet; and his son Joseph Banks of Reevesby-abbey, esquire, was member of parliament for the city of Peterborough. The last named Joseph Banks was grandfather to the present right honourable Sir Joseph Banks, knight grandcross of the order of the Bath, and baronet, a privy-counsellor, and president of the Royal Society.

The traveller on the road from Sheffield to Peniston must have observed on his right hand about a mile from Sheffield, a narrow field dividing two thick woods which evidently were once united. Near the top of this slip of green stands Shiercliffe-hall. Mr. Banks was one of the few persons of his time in the neighbourhood of Sheffield who had the convenience of a private carriage. In those days the descent down the Bridgehouse-hill was more tremendous than it still is, after all the attempts which have been made to reduce the acclivity. This was Mr. Banks's way to town. To provide himself with a safer way, he is said to have obtained leave from the duke of Norfolk to

[1] Brooke's Collection in the library of the College of Arms.   [2] Evidences at Norfolk-House, L. 21, 22.   [3] Brooke's Collections.

make the aforesaid opening through his grace's wood, which by some mistake was made wide enough for twenty carriages, and is much more appropriately used as meadow or corn land, than as a road. It carries in its name the remembrance of its original purpose, being still called in our northern dialect the Coach-gate.

In the course of the last century Shiercliffe-hall was in the hands of various tenants of the Norfolk family. Of the original edifice nothing now remains; but a good modern house has been built on or near the site, which still bears the name, and is the pleasant residence of Mr. John Watson.

Lying along the banks of the river at the foot of the hill on which stands Shiercliffe-hall are the hamlets of Neepsend and Farfield; and beyond these the rolling-mill and a large corn-mill, both beautifully situated at the foot of the woody steep called the Old Park. The rolling-mill is for the use of the manufacturers of silver plated articles, and is still in possession of a descendant of Mr. Joseph Hancock the second founder of that manufacture. The corn-mill was built in

1795, at a time of scarcity and clamour against supposed monopolists, by an extensive combination of the mechanics of Sheffield, acting in concert through the medium of their benefit societies. The foundation stone was laid with much solemnity, in the presence of the members of forty-three societies who were engaged in the scheme, and of a vast concourse of people.

In that part of the township which lies on the north of the turnpike-road over Pits-moor are the villages of Scraith and Longley, and three or four mansions that have been residences of the superior yeomanry of the neighbourhood; as Raisin-hall of the Brights, Gothard-hall of the Barnsleys, and Norwood-hall of the Rawsons.

At the Bridge-houses resided Mr. Joseph Clay, a gentleman who took an active part in all the public concerns of the parish, and who at this place closed a long and useful life in 1797. He left an only daughter now the wife of George-Bustard Greaves esquire, late lieutenant-colonel of the regiment of Sheffield volunteer infantry, whose pleasant seat, Page-hall, is on the confines of this township, but within the parish of Ecclesfield.

PEDIGREE of CLAY of the BRIDGE-HOUSES, &c.

ARMS.—GREAVES. Quarterly gules and vert an eagle displayed, holding in its beak a slip of oak fructed or.
CLAY. Argent a chevron ingrailed between three trefoils slipped sable.

ARTHUR SPEIGHT of Attercliffe, gent. Died 16 Mar. 1738, aged 58, and was buried in the chapel of Attercliffe.
= JANE, dau. of Thomas Diston of Sheffield, gent., by Jane Boughton his wife. Bap. at Sheffield 5 Mar. 1682. Mar. there 10 June 1708. Died 19 June 1743, and was buried on the 22d in the chapel at Attercliffe.

ROBERT CLAY of Chesterfield, removed from thence to Sheffield, and for some time resided at Walkley. He died in July 1737, and was buried near the east end of the parish-church of Sheffield.
= JOANNA, dau. and co-heir of John Rawson of Walkley, died 24 Feb. 1747, aged 77, and was buried with her husband.

THOMAS. JANE. JAMES. All died young, and were buried in the chapel of Attercliffe.

ANNE SPEIGHT, co-heir, bap. at Sheffield 7 Aug. 1719. Married Charles Wright of the Farm near Sheffield, gent.[1]

ELIZABETH SPEIGHT, first wife, bap. at Sheffield 21 June 1711. Died 25 Jan. 1748, and was buried in the chapel of Attercliffe.
= JOSEPH CLAY of Bridge-house, gent., baptized at Sheffield 22 Feb. 1712. Died 22 June 1797, and was buried in the chapel of Attercliffe.
= SARAH, second wife, dau. of Ralph Elmsall of Thornhill, co. York, gent. Buried in the chapel of Attercliffe.

MARGARET CLAY, wife first of ---- Chamberlaine, and 2dly of James Allot of Chrigle-stone near Wakefield and of Attercliffe, gent.

ELIZABETH CLAY, married at Sheffield 10 Jan. 1720 to William Humpton, 1734. assistant-minister of Sheffield, and curate of Ecclesall.

RAWSON CLAY of Sheffield, merchant, died 1734. Many other children, most of whom died young.

SPEIGHT and JANE died infants.

ROBERT CLAY of Attercliffe, gent., died unmarried 28 March 1786, aged 40, and was buried in the chapel of Attercliffe.
= JOHN CLAY esq., second son, died unmarried June 1796, aged 40.

JOSEPH, ELIZABETH, and ELMSALL, died infants.

GEORGE-BUSTARD GREAVES of Page-hall, esq., the only son of George Greaves late of Sheffield, merchant, by his wife, a daughter of Richard Bustard of Lutherton, co. York, gent.
= ELLEN CLAY.

JAMES ALLOTT of Attercliffe, gent., only issue 30 Aug. 1783, aged 50, and was bur. in the chapel of Attercliffe.
= ESTHER, dau. of William Burton of Royds-mill, gent., by Margaret his wife, sister and heir of George Bamforth of the High-house, esq.

GEORGE GREAVES of Healey-hall near Doncaster, esq., eldest son.

ANNA-MARIA-ROOKE, only dau. of Joseph Henley esq. of Waterperry-house, co. Oxon. Married at Waterperry 20 July 1817.

JOSEPH-EDWARD GREAVES-ELMSALL esq., second son, took the name of Elmsall by royal sign manual 26 April 1817, in grateful respect to the memory of his maternal relation William Elmsall of Brierley-manour, in the parish of Felkirk, esq.

HENRY GREAVES of Clare-hall, Cambridge.

JOHN GREAVES.

GRIMESTHORPE.

This village is pleasantly situated on the sloping side of Wincobank-hill, and close beneath the wood with which all the higher part of that eminence is covered. It has a school with a small endowment.

In the time of Queen Elizabeth Grimesthorpe was the residence of John Saunderson, who here carried

on his business of a tanner. In his will dated the 8th of June 1602, being then 'sick in body,' he gives ' to Rob.t Saunderson sonne to Rob'te Saunderson of Gilfit my brother the some of sixteen poundes and ten shillings;' to William another son forty shillings, and to Elizabeth a daughter forty shillings. To Margaret and Elizabeth, daughters of Richard Allen of

---

[1] After the death of this gentleman there came out proposals for publishing ' A Collection of Thoughts; consisting of a great variety of Reflections, Illustrations historical and allegorical, curious Anecdotes, Apothegms, Witticisms, religious Maxims, critical Observations, Characters, Essays, Odes, Elegies, Epigrams, Epitaphs, &c.—The whole being the result of very extensive and critical reading of the ancient and modern historians, philosophers, divines, poets, essayists, and other writers of distinguished abilities. By the late Mr. Charles Wright of the Farm, near Sheffield; and now printed from his own manuscript:'— but I do not find that the work was ever published.

Liversedge, each forty shillings. To Christopher Capper his servant ten pounds. To James son of Roger Hooton twenty nobles; to Jennet Hooton another daughter twenty nobles; to Margaret and Elizabeth, daughters of the said Roger, forty shillings each. To the poor man's box for the parish of Sheffield ten shillings. To his aunt Dorothy Mirfyn an annuity of thirteen shillings. The residue of his property he bequeaths to Jennet his wife, and Edward Saunderson of Sheffield tanner, to whom he commits the execution of his will, and he makes Robert Saunderson and Richard Allen supervisors.

I have been thus particular in noticing the bequests of this will, because they throw light upon the situation and circumstances of a Hallamshire family at the time of the birth in it of that eminent prelate Robert Saunderson, bishop of Lincoln, and regius professor of divinity in the university of Oxford. He was the Robert, son of Robert of Gilfit or Gilthwaite, mentioned above, and at the date of the will was fourteen years of age. A larger sum was bequeathed to him than to his brother and sister, perhaps as an encouragement to him in his studies. Thoresby, long ago, corrected an inaccuracy into which Walton and Wood were betrayed in consequence of finding the bishop's father residing at Gilthwaite, and the bishop himself passing through his grammar-studies in the school at Rotherham; and has restored to Sheffield the honour of having produced this light of the English church[1]. Mr. Wilson had heard that at the time of the birth of this son, the father resided at a house in Sheffield near the Irish-cross, which was called ' The lane-head-door.' The fact of his birth at Sheffield can hardly be disputed, when we have the entries in the parish-register not only of the baptism of this son, but of the other children of his father, who were only two, one older and one younger than the bishop.

' 1586. Sep. 21. Will'mus Sanderson fil. et hæres Rob'ti Sanderson.
1587. Sep. 20. Rob'tus Saund'son fil. Rob'ti Saund'son.
1588. Dec. 9. Elizabetha Saunderson fil. Rob'ti Saunderson.'

But the father certainly left Sheffield very soon after the last of these dates, and settled at Gilthwaite about seven miles distance from Sheffield. Gilthwaite is near to Whiston; and I conjecture that his removal to that place had some connexion with the guardianship of Thomas, son of Thomas Stringer of Whiston, gentleman, to which he was appointed on the 9th of March 1587-8. The elder Stringer was much employed by the Shrewsbury family in the management of their estates; and the fact which Walton has preserved, that the bishop's father was a sponsor along with Gilbert earl of Shrewsbury at the baptism of Gilbert Sheldon, son to a retainer of the earl, afterwards archbishop of Canterbury, favours the supposition that he might succeed Stringer in his appointment.

It is not necessary to enter at large into the particulars of a life so well known as that of Bishop Saunderson, who has a long article in the Athenæ, and of whom Walton has written in his usual interesting manner; and especially since they were only the years or rather months of infancy that he spent at his native place; nor, I regret to say, do I find his name connected in any way in after life with the town in which

his first breath was drawn. As an eminent native of the parish of Sheffield, it may however be proper to state that Saunderson passed from the grammar-school of Rotherham to Lincoln College Oxford, where he took the degree of B.A. in 1604, and was elected a Fellow of the College in 1606, having then, as Wood informs us, ' a metaphysical brain and matchless memory.' He became M.A. in 1607, and in 1611 was ordained priest. He had afterwards for a time the rectory of Wibberton in Lincolnshire. This he resigned, and in 1619 became rector of Boothby-Paynel, chaplain to Bishop Mountaine, and a prebendary in the churches of Southwell and Lincoln. On Laud's recommendation he was made one of the chaplains to King Charles I. who much delighted in his conversation. He was employed in the scheme of 1641 for rendering the book of common-prayer more acceptable to the Puritan party; and in the next year, being then D.D. and regius professor of divinity at Oxford, he was named by both houses of parliament as one to be employed in settling the affairs of the church. In the next year he was nominated one of the Assembly of Divines, but he never took a seat in that assembly. In all the attempts at reconciling the differences respecting the church, Saunderson's opinion was required: but when all failed, he was himself stripped of his professorship, and in 1648 retired to live in privacy on his rectory of Boothby. The return of the king in 1660 freed him from much injurious and oppressive treatment, and restored him to his professorship. On the 28th of October in that year he was consecrated Bishop of Lincoln. But he was then above seventy years of age, and he lived only till the 29th of January 1663. The reader may find in Wood[2] a long list of his writings, which are mostly casuistical and theological. ' All authors,' says Wood, ' especially those that are famous, do speak honourably of him.' He further tells us that in addition to his theological knowledge, the bishop was exactly versed in the history of our nation, was a complete herald and genealogist, had made a good collection of English genealogies, and also of monumental inscriptions and arms from churches and windows. These collections were, it is feared, dispersed; but it is understood that a part of them at least is in the library of Sir Joseph Banks at Reevesby-abbey. The bishop himself, as was natural, entertained a due sense of their importance and value. He thus speaks of them in his last will preserved in a miscellaneous manuscript volume in the Harleian library.

' I give to my sonn Henry all the books in my study whether printed or written, that relate to the history of England; or to heraldry; or to genealogies, foreign or domestic; together with all paper-books and loose papers of that concernment (which are very many, and would be highly valued of such as delight in that kind of study) either for himself to make use of (if his genius will incline thereto) or else to part with them to some such person as will give a good rate for them; for having used so much care and diligence as I have done to make those collections, I would not have my pains therein too much undervalued[3].'

What I have further to add relating to the bishop, is a table of his kindred, which will show how closely

[1] Duc. Leod. p. 78.   [2] Ath. Ox. vol. ii. 213—217.   [3] Harl. MSS. 7048, f. 356.

he was connected with Sheffield. He who was an ardent lover of heraldrical and genealogical subjects, and who, as we have seen, knew how to appreciate collections of that nature, ought not to be himself without such a memorial. In the earlier generations I have followed Thoroton[1], who deduces the first John from an Alexander de Bedick of the county of Durham, living in 1333.

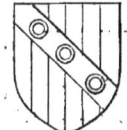

PEDIGREE of SAUNDERSON of SHEFFIELD, &c.

ARMS.—Paly of six argent and azure, on a bend sable three annulets or.

JOHN SAUNDERSON of Tickhill.

WILLIAM SAUNDERSON, eldest son. From whom descended the Saundersons of Sandbeck, peers of England and Ireland.

HENRY SAUNDERSON, ---- or JOHN, second son.

ROBERT SAUNDERSON of the Yews, in the parish of Maltby, co. York. — ---- dau. of ---- Micclethwaite of Peniston.

JOHN SAUNDERSON of Midhope, in the chapelry of Bradfield.

NICHOLAS SAUNDERSON of Gouchill.

JOHN SAUNDERSON of the Yews, eldest son.

CHRISTOPHER SAUNDERSON of Stirap, in the parish of Blythe, second son. — DYONISIA, dau. of ---- Barber of Rowlee.

HENRY SAUNDERSON, 3d and youngest son.

NICHOLAS SAUNDERSON of Sheffield, gent., elder twin with Robert. Married at Sheffield 7 Feb. 1575, and buried there 24 May 1580. — MARGARET, dau. of John Rawson of Upperthorpe.

RICHARD ALLEN of Liversedge, 2d husband, married at Sheffield 15 Oct. 1581.

ROBERT SAUNDERSON of Sheffield, Giltawaite, and Blythe, gent., 2d son. — ELIZABETH, dau. of Robert Carr of Butterthwaite in the parish of Ecclesfield.

JOHN SAUNDERSON of Grimesthorpe, tanner. Will dated 8 June 1602. Buried at Sheffield the 12th instant. — JOAN or JENNET HUDSON, married at Sheffield 29 Ing 1602. Living 1602.

EDWARD SAUNDERSON of Sheffield and Grimesthorpe, only son, bap. at Sheffield 15 Jan. 1576-7. Will dated 21 April 1617. Bur. at Sheffield the 24th inst. — ISABELLA, dau. of Nicholas Shiercliffe of Hole-house, in the parish of Ecclesfield. Mar. at Sheffield 7 Aug. 1598, buried there 2 Jan. 1613.

ANNE, first wife, dau. of Edward Gill of Lightwood in the par. of Norton, gent. formerly of Sheffield, bap. at Sheffield 25 Dec. 1581, mar. at Norton 29 Oct. 1604.

WILLIAM SAUNDERSON of Blythe-abbey, gent., eldest son and heir. Bap. Sept. 1586. — ELLEN, second wife, dau. of William Kniveton of Bradley, co. Derb. esq., widow of Roger Sturton of Sturton, esq. Vinc. Notts.

ROBERT SAUNDERSON D.D. bishop of Lincoln. Born at Sheffield 19 Sept. 1587. Consecrated bishop 28 Oct. 1660. Died 29 Jan. 1662. Buried at Buckden. — ANNE, dau. of Henry NelsonB.D. rector of Haugham, co. Linc.

ELIZABETH SAUNDERSON, married at Blythe 13 Oct. 1607 to Leonard Gill of Norton, gent.

See Zouch's edition of Walton's Lives for the children of the bishop.

NICHOLAS SAUNDERSON of Sheffield, gent., eldest son and heir, bap. at Sheffield 3 Aug. 1600. — ---- dau. of ---- Norton of Sandal-Magna, gent.

EDWARD SAUNDERSON of Sheffield, gent., 2d son, bap. at Sheffield 17 Aug. 1602. Will dated 28 May 1670. Buried at Sheffield 19 Feb. 1673.

ANNE, dau. of Francis Barlow of Sheffield.

ROBERT SAUNDERSON of Blythe, gent., slain on the king's part at Nottingham-bridge 1645. — MARY, dau. of Gervase Bosvile of Warmsworth, near Doncaster.

ELIZABETH, wife of Robert Eyre of Ragnel, gent.

MARY, wife of Robert Mellish of Blythe, gent.

ANNE, wife of James Lane.

The last named Nicholas Saunderson had several children, among whom were Mary the second wife of John Cart, rector of Hansworth, and Martha wife of Gilbert Morewood of Dronfield, gentleman. Edward the brother of Nicholas had a numerous progeny, most of whom settled at Sheffield or in its neighbourhood. There were five Saundersons lords viscount Castleton of the kingdom of Ireland, the last of whom was created baron Saunderson of Saxby in the county of Lincoln, by King George I. before his coronation; in the next year viscount Castleton of Sandbeck in the county of York, and in 1720 earl of Castleton, an English honour. But all the honours became extinct on his death without issue in 1723. He left Sandbeck and other property to his kinsman[2] Sir Thomas Lumley K.B. a younger son of Richard the first earl of Scarborough, enjoining him to take the name of Saunderson; which he did. On the death in 1739 of his elder brother Richard the second earl, Sir

Thomas Lumley Saunderson became earl of Scarborough. It may be added that Matthew Sylvester, the editor of Baxter's Memoirs of his life and times, who was for some time chaplain to Sir John Bright at Carbrook, is said by Calamy to have been a family connexion of Bishop Saunderson[3]; and that Charles Hoole, who has a notice in the *Athenæ Oxonienses*, an eminent school-master of his time, was also the bishop's relative. The family of Charles Hoole had property in this township, but it appears that he was born at Wakefield[4].

To the pedigree of Saunderson I shall add that of Gill, with which, as we have seen, there was a double connexion. It will be found to contain many additional particulars to the pedigree which was entered at Dugdale's visitation of the county of York[5]. The name is pronounced with the g soft, and is probably derived from Julian or Gillian. Gill with the hard g is a local surname derived from gill a brooklet.

[1] *Notts.* Throsby's edition, vol. iii. p. 427.
[2] This relationship was through the family of Bellasis, of which was the earl of Castleton's mother.
[3] *Account of the Ejected and Silenced Ministers*, p. 449.
[4] *Ath. Ox.* vol. ii. col. 272.
[5] C. 40, in Col. Arm. f. 196.

PEDIGREE of GILL of SHEFFIELD, NORTON, CAR-HOUSE, &c.

ARMS.—Parti per bend or and azure, three mullets of six points in bend, pierced and counterchanged.

JOHN GILL of Lightwood, in the parish of Norton.
Buried at Norton 3 Dec. 1589. He contributed 25l.
to the loan at the time of the Spanish Armada.

| FRANCIS GILL, eldest son and heir-apparent, buried at Norton 11 Sept. 1589, unmar. | WILLIAM GILL of Lightwood, 2d son, died unmar., and was buried at Norton 26 May 1598. | GEORGE GILL, of Lightwood and Hazleborough, buried at Norton 28 Sept. 1622. | EDWARD GILL of Sheffield, and afterwards of Norton. With him the pedigree in C. 40, f. 196 b. begins. Buried at Norton 2 July 1614. | IMMEN RODES, married at Sheffield 4 June 1576, buried at Norton 21 May 1597. | ADAM GILL of Sheffield, whose descendants continued there for several generations, and seem to have afterwards removed to Chesterfield. | ANNE GILL, married at Dronfield 19 June 1569 to William Blythe of Norton-Lees. |

| PHILIP GILL of Lightwood, gent., eldest son and heir, baptized at Sheffield 4 Sept. 1577. Buried at Norton 18 Oct. 1630. | DOROTHY, dau. of Robert Allott of Bentley in the parish of Elmley, co. York, gent. Buried at Norton 17 May 1646. | LEONARD GILL of Norton, gent., second son, bap. at Sheffield 22 Mar. 1579. Died 21 March 1654, and was buried in the church of Norton. | ELIZABETH, dau. of Robert Saunderson of Sheffield and Gilthwaite. Mar. at Blythe 13 Oct. 1607. | ANNE GILL, only dau. bap. at Sheffield 25 at Norton 29 Oct. 1604 to William Saunderson of Blythe. |

| RUTH, first wife, dau. of Stephen Bright of Carbrook, gent., mar. at Sheffield 23 Sept. 1633. Buried in the chancel of the parish-church of Sheffield 15 March 1635. Had an only child Elizabeth, who died an infant. | EDWARD GILL of Car-house, in the parish of Rotherham, esq., eldest son and heir. A commander in the parliament army, and sometime governor of Sheffield-castle. One of the members of parliament for the west-riding 1653. Bap. at Norton 24 Jan. 1610. Aged 56, 10 April 1667. Buried at Rotherham. | ELIZABETH, second wife, only dau. and heir of Captain Henry Westby of Car-house, (by Elizabeth his wife, dau. of Richard Boroughs of Gilthwaite,) brother of George Westby of Gilthwaite and Ravenfield, gent. Married at Rotherham 18 July 1638. Buried there 3 June 1677. | ELIZABETH GILL, bap. at Norton 26 March 1614. Mar. there 30 Oct. 1634 to William Spencer of Attercliffe-hall, esq., a lieut.-col. in the parliament-service. Buried at Norton 14 June 1636. | MARY GILL, bap. at Norton 14 April 1619. Mar. there 28 June 1641 to Rowland Morewood of the Oaks in the chapelry of Bradfield, gent., and dying on 25 Mar. 1652 was bur. in the chancel of Bradfield-church. | LEONARD, JOHN, GEORGE, and ANNE, all died in their infancy, and were bur. at Norton. |

| ELIZABETH, first wife, dau. and co-heir of Joshua Brooke of Newhouse in the parish of Huddersfield, gent. Mar. at Huddersfield 31 January 1665. Had an only child, Sarah Gill, who died unmarried. | Colonel JOHN GILL of Car-house, eldest son and heir, bap. at Rotherham 14 May 1643. Aged 23, 10 April 1666. High-sheriff of the county of York 1692. Died 24 Jan. 1705. Bur. at Rotherham. | SARAH, 2d wife, ... buried 7 Aug. 1675, no issue. — MARTHA, third wife, dau. of Joshua Horton of Sowerby, esq. Bur. at Rotherham 4 Apr. 1689. | RUTH GILL, bap. at Rotherham 4 March 1641. Married there 21 April 1664 to Joseph Stones of Himsworth and Mosborough, merchant. | ELIZABETH GILL, bap. at Rotherham 23 Aug. 1646. Mar. there 3 Feb. 1667-8 to her cousin John Morewood of Alfreton, esquire. | HENRY GILL of the Oaks in Norton, esq., 2d son, bap. at Rotherham 26 July 1654. Died 7 March 1715, and was buried in the church of Norton. | URSULA, dau. of William Drake of Bernoldswick-Cotes in Craven, esq., by Mary his wife, dau. of John Stillington of Kelfield, esq. Married at Greasborough chapel 2 Nov. 1675. Bur. in the church of Norton 23 Oct. 1689. | MARY, LEONARD, and ANNE, all died young. |

| WESTBY GILL of Car-house, esq., son and heir, bap. at Rotherham 21 March 1679. Sold his estate, and was afterwards Comptroller of the board of works. Died about 1746. | JOHN GILL, bap. at Rotherham 28 Sept. 1682. Said to have died unmarried at Chambre co. Lanc. about 1762. | ELIZABETH GILL, bap. at Rotherham 26 Nov. 1684, wife of Benjamin Gregge of Chambre co. Lanc. esq. Major in the army and high-sheriff of the county of Lancaster 1722. | MARTHA and MARY, died in their infancy, and were buried at Rotherham. | EDWARD and MARY died infants. | RICHARD BAGSHAW of Castleton, esq., and in right of his wife of the Oaks in Norton, second son of Adam Bagshaw of Wormhill, 4th son of William of Hucklow and Abney. | ELIZABETH GILL, only surviving dau. and heir, bap. at Norton 28 Dec. 1676. |

| RICHARD BAGSHAW of the Oaks in Norton, esq. Died without issue at the Oaks 19 Feb. 1776. | MARY, dau. of John Simpson of Renishaw and of Babworth, gent., son of William Simpson of Sheffield. Died 11 Jan. 1792. | WILLIAM BAGSHAW of the Oaks esq. Died unmarried June 1785. | JOHN BAGSHAW of the Oaks, esq., last surviving son. Died unmar. Nov. 1791. | ALICE BAGSHAW, wife of John Fell of Attercliffe-forge, gent., and died without issue. | ELLEN BAGSHAW, wife of William Chambers of Hull, M.D., whose grandson William Chambers Darling assumed the surname of Bagshaw, and now resides at the Oaks. Knighted in 1805, on presenting an address on the victory of Trafalgar, when high-sheriff of the county of Derby. | MARY BAGSHAW, wife of John Howarth of Manchester, gent. | ELIZABETH BAGSHAW, died at the Oaks unmarried 1778. — HENRY, URSULA, ADAM, and GILL, all died young or unmarried. |

Mr. William Simpson of Sheffield, mentioned in the preceding pedigree, was living there at the time of Sir William Dugdale's visitation, and entered his pedigree from his grandfather, who was Lancelot Simpson or Sympson of Maidstone in Kent. Samuel the son of Lancelot was of Blythe in Nottinghamshire, and it appears from other authorities was vicar of Blythe. By Faith his wife, daughter of Alexander Nevile of Wystow in Nottinghamshire, he had William Simpson of Sheffield, who married Elizabeth daughter of William Linley of Hull by Dorothy his wife, daughter and co-heir of Bryan Batson of York, sister to Francis Linley of Bowling. In 1681 the

honorary freedom of the Company of Cutlers was conferred on Mr. Simpson. He left Sheffield before his death and retired to Babworth. All his children were born at Sheffield. One of the daughters married Henry Wood of Barnsley esquire, who about the reign of William III. was the magistrate to whom the inhabitants of Hallamshire made most frequent resort. The only surviving son was John Simpson of Eckington and Babworth, who by Elizabeth his wife daughter of Francis Stringer of Sutton-upon-Lound esquire, by Elizabeth his wife daughter of Sir John Newton of Barrs-court bart., had William Simpson of Staniforth co. York, John Simpson of Stoke co. Derb.

whose only daughter and heir married Sir Henry Bridgman bart., Linley Simpson of Babworth esquire, Mrs. Fairfax of Newton-Kyme, Mrs. Bagshaw, and Mrs. Jane Simpson who died unmarried.

NEW-HALL.

On the rich alluvial meadows on the north side of the Don, the late John Fell esquire erected for his own residence a handsome brick house, with spacious gardens, to which he gave the name of New-hall. He chose to place it within the sound of those iron-forges where he and his father had acquired their wealth. These forges are perhaps the oldest in the neighbourhood. Till the time of James I. they were in the hands of the éarls of Shrewsbury, and worked for their benefit. Afterwards they were leased to Captain Copley and others. Though standing in this township they are commonly called Attercliffe-forges. The piers of an old bridge over the Don from the forge to Attercliffe were standing a few years ago, and with the abrupt declivity on the Attercliffe side of the river formed a truly picturesque scene. The present bridge near this place was built by the late Mr. Fell, and was for many years open for public use.

The first Mr. Fell was the maker of his own fortunes. He began life as a clerk to Mr. Heyford at Wortley-forge. From thence he removed to Brightside, and in the Attercliffe-forges he acquired considerable property, which his son increased, but left no child to inherit.

New-hall was for many years the residence of Mrs. Elizabeth Fell, the widow of the younger Mr. Fell. Here she spent the latter years of a long life in the practice of benevolence and the ' odour of sanctity.' She was the younger of two sisters, Miss Laughtons, of good family but small fortunes, who came to reside at Sheffield about the year 1730, for the same reasons that in more recent times persons have chosen to reside in Wales. They were soon noticed by Mrs. Elizabeth Parkin, and finally taken under her protection. One married Mr. Fell; and the other Mr. Walter Oborne, a near relative of Mrs. Parkin, to whom she gave by will her estate at Ravenfield. Mrs. Oborne left no issue. Mrs. Fell by her last will left the following sums for charitable purposes within the parish of Sheffield:

500l. to the charity school for boys in Sheffield.
500l. to the school for girls.
300l. to the Sunday school in Attercliffe.
300l. to the Sunday school in Brightside-Byerlow.
250l. the interest of which was to be distributed amongst poor widows, widowers, and old house-keepers in Brightside-Byerlow on Saint John's day for ever.

She gave New-hall to her friend Richard Swallow esquire, whose son of the same name now resides there, and is married to a sister of Hugh Parker of Woodthorpe, esquire.

PEDIGREE of FELL of ATTERCLIFFE-FORGE.

ARMS.—Argent, 3 lozenges in fess between as many mullets of 8 points, pierced azure.

WILLIAM FELL of Rotherham.	SUSANNA, dau. of John Kaye
Will dated 11 Jan. 1694.	of Nabbs, iron-master.

JOHN FELL of Attercliffe-forge, iron-master. Born in 1666. Executor to his father's will 1694. Died 30 April 1724, and was bur. in the parish-church of Sheffield.	ELLEN, sister of Gamaliel Milner of Burton-grange, gent. Died 7 Jan. 1725, aged 60, and was buried with her husband.	THOMAS FELL, living 1694, engaged with his brother at the Forge. Went abroad.	ELIZABETH FELL, 1692.	MARY FELL, wife of Thos. Rayner of Gainsborough.

ALICE, first wife, dau. of Richard Bagshaw of Castleton and the Oaks, esq. Died without issue 8 Aug. 1737, and was buried in the parish-church of Sheffield.	JOHN FELL of Attercliffe-forge and New-hall, esq. Born 6 March 1696, bap. 2 April at Sheffield. Died without issue 17 May 1762, and was buried in the parish-church of Sheffield.	ELIZABETH, second wife, sister and co-heir of Henry Laughton of Scotter, co. Linc., descended from Sir John Newton of Barrscourt near Bath, baronet. Married at Attercliffe-chapel 3 July 1740. Died at New-hall 29 Jan. 1795, and was buried in the parish-church of Sheffield.	ELLEN FELL, wife of John Ellison of Sheffield, to whom she was mar. 23 Oct. 1734.	ELIZABETH FELL, bap. NEE of Attercliffe, gent., 2d son of Gamaliel Fell, without issue 18 May 1704. Died Milner of Burton-grange, gent. at Sheffield 18 Jan. Bur. at the cha-pel of Attercliffe 1737. Bur. 4 May 1748, aged in the pa-48. rish-church of Sheffield.	GAMALIEL MIL- SUSAN, second wife, dau. of John Wilson of Broom-head, and Attercliffe-cha-pel 13 May 1742. Died 30 March 1766, aged 54.	WILLIAM, THOMAS, ANNE, and MARY, all died young or unmar.

JOHN FELL, only child, bap. at Sheffield 14 Oct. 1742. Died 15 Apr. 1743.		GAMALIEL MILNER now of Attercliffe, esq., only surviving child. One of the twelve capital burgesses of the parish of Sheffield.	SUSAN, dau. and heir of John Walton of Thurlstone in the parish of Peniston, gent.

GAMALIEL MILNER, eldest son.	dau. of Pashley of Retford.	JOHN MILNER of Attercliffe, esq., second son.	WILLIAM MILNER, third son. Died unmarried.

ROYDS-MILL.

This place is probably so called from a rood or cross that may have stood here on the road-side from Sheffield to Rotherham.

It was for two or three generations the residence of one branch of the Derbyshire and Staffordshire family of Burton. This is perhaps now the only remaining branch of the family from which sprung the historian of Leicestershire, and the still more celebrated author of The Anatomy of Melancholy. Close to the house are now the extensive refinery of Messrs. Reads and Lucas, and a mill for the rolling and slitting of iron bars. When the Burtons resided here it was a quiet rural residence. But on the other hand its inhabitants had not in those days so convenient access to their church and market. Where is now a wide and level road, much less than a century ago was a way so narrow, and kept in such ill repair, that Mr. Burton is said to have been often obliged to obtain leave from his relative Mr. Handley of Hall-Carr for his carriage to pass through Mr. Handley's inclosures.

Pedigree of Burton of Royds-mill, Sheffield, &c.

ARMS.—Azure, a crescent argent within an orle of etoils and a border or.

RICHARD BURTON of Tutbury, co.=MAUD, sister of Robert
Stafford. Ob. 9 May, 8 Hen. V. | Gibson of Tutbury.

Sir WILLIAM BURTON of Falde and | RICHARD BURTON of Chesterfield,=ANNE, dau. of Robert
Tutbury, knight. Slain at Towton- | steward to John earl of Shrews- | Barnesley of the coun-
field 1461. From whom descended | bury 12 Hen. VI. and 5 Edw. IV. | ty of York.
the Burtons of Linley. | Buried at Chesterfield.

JOHN BURTON of Totley in the parish of=ELIZABETH, dau. and co-heir
Dronfield. Living 12 Edw. IV. and 2 | of Robert Shaw of Hill, co.
Hen. VIII. Buried at Dronfield. | York.

JOHN BURTON of Totley and Dronfield.=ELIZABETH, dau. of Richard Revel of Stan-
Buried at Dronfield 1556. | nington in the chapelry of Bradfield.

THOMAS BURTON of Cartlege, in the=ALICE, dau. of John | JOHN BURTON,=JOAN, dau. of Robert Poynton
parish of Dronfield, eldest son and | holm of Cartlege, married at | second son. | of Dronfield-woodhouse. Mar-
heir. Buried at Dronfield 17 Jan. | Dronfield 27 Oct. 1556. | | ried at Dronfield 15 Nov. 1562.
1585.

THOMAS BURTON of=ELLEN, dau. of Anthony Bright of Dore, | MICHAEL BURTON of Holmesfield,=ANNE, dau. of | JOHN BURTON=ELIZABETH
Cartlege, bap. | in the parish of Dronfield. Married at | in the parish of Dronfield, esquire, | Robert Rams- | of Apperknoll | Mower of
at Dronfield 26 Jan. | Dronfield 19 May 1598. Made her will 2 | bap. 19 Nov. 1578. High-sheriff of | car of Brad- | in the parish of | Greenhill in
1567. High-sheriff | Feb. 1653, being then residing at Brin- | the county of Derby 1646. Died | field. Married | Dronfield 1634. | the parish
of the county of Der- | cliffe-edge in the parish of Sheffield, and | without issue 12 July 1656, and | at Dronfield | | of Norton.
by 1628. Died 21 | it was proved by John Bright her ne- | was buried in the chancel of Dron- | 26 Feb. 1609. |
June 1645, and was | phew and executor 6 Aug. 1656. Bur. | field church. | Buried there |
buried in the chancel | in the parish-church of Sheffield 11 | | 26 Dec. 1646. |
of Dronfield church. | May 1656.

THOMAS BURTON of Fan-=JANE, dau. of | GODFREY BURTON of | WILLIAM BURTON of=MARY, eldest dau. of George=GEORGE MILNES of Ches-
shaw-gate, in the parish | Robert Seli- | Dronfield. Married | Holmesfield, gent., | Mower of Holmesfield, gent., | terfield, iron-monger, and
of Dronfield, baptized at | oke of Dron- | Anne dau. of George | bap. at Dronfield 4 | married at Dronfield 14 July | afterwards of Dunston, 2d
Dronfield 31 May 1601. | field, gent. | Mower of Holmes- | April 1611. Died 8 | 1644. In her second widow- | husband. Buried in the
Bur. there 3 June 1643. | Mar. there | field, and had a daugh- | July 1657. Buried in | hood resided at Holme near | church of Chesterfield 8
| 28 April | ter Anne wife of Cor- | the chancel of Dron- | Chesterfield, where she made | July 1671.
| 1626. | nelius Blythe of Cold- | field church. | her will 2 June 1690. Proved
| | aston, gent. | | at Lichfield 16 Nov. 1692.

PRUDENCE, first wife,=THOMAS BURTON of=DOROTHY, second | MARY, wife | WILLIAM BURTON of Holme,= | MICHAEL BURTON,
dau. of Francis Lowe | Holmesfield and Al- | wife, dau. of Per- | of Robert | parish of Brampton, gent., 2d | died an infant.
of Owlgreave co. Derb. | dercar-park, married | cival Willoughby | Macheon, | son. Executor and principal | —
esq. Died 30 April | at Dronfield 20 April | M.D. of Derby, son | 1690. | heir to his mother. Bap. at | JOHN BURTON.
1671, aged 31. Buried | 1645. Died 9 January | of Sir Perceval | | Dronfield 21 April 1646. Bur. | —
in the church of Hea- | 1702. Buried in St.Pe- | Willoughby of Wol- | | at Chesterfield 3 May 1720. | MICHAEL BURTON.
nor. | ter's church Derby. | laton.

MICHAEL BURTON of Holmes-=MARY, third dau. and | Other | WILLIAM BURTON of Royds-=ANNE, dau. of William Fen- | MARY | ANNE
field and Wirksworth esq., son | co-heir of Henry Wig- | children. | mill, gent., son and heir. | ton of Sheffield, brother of | BURTON. | BURTON.
and heir. Born 19 Oct. 1673. | ley of Wigwall co. | | Died in Dec. 1719, and was | Alexander Fenton of Glead-
Justice of the peace and deputy | Derb. esq., by Mary | | buried in the middle aile of | leys, gent. Her sister mar-
lieutenant for the county of | his wife, sister and | | the parish-church of Shef- | ried Thomas Handley of
Derby 1711. Died 23 Dec. | co-heir of John Spade- | | field. | Hall-carr, gent.
1719, and was buried at St. | man of Rodenook, | |
Martin's in the Fields London. | esq., married 5 July | |
| 1691.

JOHN BURTON=ANNE, dau. and | WILLIAM BURTON=MARGARET, dau. of George | TIMOTHY BUR-=ELIZABETH, | ESTHER, wife 1st | WILLIAM,
of Chesterfield, | heir of Edward | of Royds-mill, 2d | Bamforth of the High- | TON of Whit- | dau. of Cor- | of George Bam- | ELIZABETH,
gent., eldest | Haslam of | son, bap. at Shef- | house, in the parish of | tington. Died | nelius Farr | forth, 2d of Ro- | ANNE,
son and heir, | Newbold near | field 25 June 1704. | Sheffield, gent., sister and | without issue | of Bolsover. | bert Chappell, | died in-
bap. at Shef- | Chesterfield. | Bur. in the parish- | heir of George Bamforth of | and was buried | | and 3d of Paul | fants.
field 12 May | | church of Sheffield | the same place, esq. Died | at Sheffield | | Meyer of Shef-
1703. | | 19 May 1764. | in Oct. 1749. | | | field, esq.

EDWARD | ANNE | GEORGE=JOHN | ELIZABETH,=WILLIAM BURTON=MARIA, 2d wife, | MICHAEL=MARTHA, | ESTHER, wife | WILLIAM,
BURTON of | and | BAMFORTH. | BURTON | first wife, | of Sheffield, sur- | dau. of --- Bill, | BURTON | dau. of -- | of James Al- | ROBERT,
Chester- | MARY. | BURTON, | of Bram- | dau. of Pe- | geon, 3d son. One | rector of Dray- | of Shef- | Living- | lott of Atter- | ANNE,
field, attor- | | eldest son, | ley-hall, | ter Hussey | of the twelve capi- | cott, co. Staff. | field, at- | ston or | cliffe, gent. | all died
ney. Married | | died with- | esq., eld- | of Atter- | tal burgesses of | by --- his wife, | torney, | Levison | — | young.
Anne Hal- | | out issue | est sur- | cliffe-forge. | Sheffield, and co- | dau. of Thomas | 4th son, | of Birm- | MARGARET,
lifax, sister | | at the Ha- | viving son. | Died with- | lord of the manor | Harrison of Dil- | co-lord of | ingham, | wife of Sam'l
to the bi- | | vannah be- | See his | out issue 24 | of Wadsley. Died | horne in the | the manor | merch'. | Turner of
shop of St. | | fore his fa- | marriage | Dec. 1768. | 24 May 1798, and | same county, by | of Wads- | | Sheffield,
Asaph, | | ther. | and issue | | was buried in the | Susan his wife, | ley. | | mercer.
and died | | | p. 225. | | middle aile of the | dau. of William
without is- | | | | | parish-church of | Beckwith of
sue 23 Apr. | | | | | Sheffield. | Thurcroft in co.
1782. | | | | | | York.

CHARLES BURTON, only | MARGARET BURTON, only | MICHAEL BURTON, | WILLIAM BURTON,
surviving son, unmarried | surviving dau., now living | in the naval service. | in the naval service.
1819. | the widow of --- Hill esq.,
| 1819.

Thomas Burton of Fanshaw-gate, who died in 1643, left three sons, Michael, Thomas, and Francis. Michael was of Mosborough, and by Anne his wife, daughter of Henry Ducket rector of Eckington, had a numerous issue. The names of his children appear on his monumental brass in the chancel of the church of Eckington.—Thomas the second son was of London and Putney, married and had issue.—Francis the youngest was lord of the manor of Dronfield, and served the office of high-sheriff of the county of Derby in 1669. He was buried at Dronfield in 1687. By his first wife Anne, a daughter of Thomas Wright of Unthank, gentleman, by Anne his wife, daughter of Thomas Shiercliffe of Whitley-hall in the parish of Ecclesfield, gentleman, he had only female issue who survived; but by Ellen his second wife, daughter and heir of Cassibelan Burton, son of William Burton of Lindley the historian of Leicestershire, he had beside others that died young, two sons, Constantine Burton, who was lost in the Bay of Ostend 1707, and Ralph Burton his son and heir, lord of the manor of Dronfield, who was killed by a fall from his horse on the East-moors between Holmesfield and Grindleford-bridge, on the 10th of August 1714.

Michael Burton of Holmesfield and Wirksworth, who died in 1719, had issue three sons, John, Michael, and Henry. Michael was of Saint John's College Cambridge, M.A., and Henry of Emanuel College in the same university. John the eldest son was also of Saint John's, and afterwards of the Inner Temple. He resided at the Hallows in the parish of Dronfield, and by Anne his wife, daughter of Joseph Rogers of Cowley in Dronfield gentleman, had two daughters, Mary who died unmarried, and Jane the wife of Philip Smelter of Goddard-hall in this township of Brightside-Byerlow, who died without issue in 1802.

From a point on the road from Royds-mill to Sheffield the general view of the town is taken that is prefixed to this work.

A small and ancient fulling-mill is still called the Walk-mill. This was a general name for mills of that description, and persons engaged in the making of cloth were anciently called Walkers. Hence that name is so common in the west riding of Yorkshire. We may add, and so respectable too, not fewer than thirty gentlemen of that name having voted at the election of a registrar for the west riding in 1809, each of whom possessed a freehold of one hundred pounds a year within the riding. In the Harl. MSS. 1174, f. 38, is a tricking of a seal of the age of Edward III. bearing as a device the shears used in clipping the wool, in the form of which there has been no improvement, with the inscription round, SIGILLVM RICARDI LE WALKER.

Hall-carr was for two or three generations the residence of a respectable family of the name of Handley; and before them of the families of Wylde and Pyrrans. Mr. Thomas Handley of this place reached the age of ninety. He was for half that period one of the twelve capital burgesses of the parish of Sheffield, and was an attentive observer of every thing that passed around him. It was the amusement of his latter years to commit his recollections of persons and affairs to writing. To him this volume owes some of its in-

terest: and it would have been far less imperfect in respect of that period which intervenes between times when we cease to expect any other than written evidence, and that to which living evidence can extend, had not Mr. Handley's papers for the most part shared the fate of minor historical and biographical collections. One of his sons settled in America, as did also a grandson; and both were friends of Washington, and assistants in the establishment of American independence.—A descendant of this village Nestor in the fourth degree, who has favoured the public with the delightful stories in ' The Panorama of Youth,' would give fresh celebrity to this place, could she be induced to apply her powers to subjects of a higher character.

THE WICKER.

A level space of ground extending from the foot of Spital-hill, or as it is sometimes called Handley-hill, to the Lady's-bridge is called the Wicker. It was once a green, and, like the village-greens in the merry times before inclosure bills were known, it was the place for the sports and pastimes and athletic exercises of the inhabitants of the town. Lying close under the outer walls, it doubtless often presented a lively and cheerful scene to the lord and lady of the castle. Here were the public butts at which the inhabitants of Sheffield were trained to archery. They were maintained at the public expense, and we find them mentioned in the town's accompts as late as the time of Charles I. It was here too that the freeholders of Hallamshire were accustomed to assemble with horse and arms at the annual muster, according to an ancient custom which it is said is noticed in some copies of the Quo warranto roll of the age of Edward I. From this assembly the Wicker was formerly called the Sembly-green; and the Court-house of the manor, perhaps the only one which stood on the green, was called the Sembly-house. Speaking of the manor of Sheffield, Harrison, in the survey before quoted, says ' I cannot here omitt a royalty that this manor hath above other manors: that is, upon every Sembly Tuesday is assembled upon Sembly-green, where the court is kept and near unto the castle, at the least 139 horsemen with horses and harness provided by the freeholders, copyholders, and other tenants, and to appear before the lord of the manor or the steward for the court to be viewed by them, and for confirming the peace of our sovereign lord the king.' Harrison has also preserved a list of the freeholders and others who were obliged by the tenure of their lands to send a man and horse on this occasion. Amongst them we find no less a personage than ' The Lord Deputy of Ireland,' the title of office at the time he wrote, 1637, of the noble owner of Wentworth, who held lands at Scoles of the earl of Arundel's manor. We find also the names of

Mr. Stephen Bright,
Mr. Richard Boroughs,
Mr. John Shaw clerk,
Sir Richard Scott knight,
Mr. Howsley Freeman,
Mr. George Westby,
Mr. Jessop,

who sent two men, and many others of the principal gentry of the vicinage. It is supposed that the full

3 P

number of these mock soldiers never appeared. In an older list than Harrison's I find the names of only ninety-six tenants who held their lands by this service. At the latter end of the seventeenth century, the number was reduced to sixty or eighty. In 1715 and 1716 a delicate regard for the feelings and wishes of a protestant government induced the lord of the manor to desire that it should be discontinued. The practice has not been resumed. Sembly Tuesday was the Tuesday after Easter-day. It was a day of merriment. The troop, some in military dresses and some in their labouring garb, must have cut a figure grotesque and ridiculous. In the museum of Mr. Wilson was preserved the dress which was worn by the man whom his father sent to this annual review, and who was always the captain for the day. They paraded the Wicker, and afterwards the principal streets of the town. One amusement of the day was probably of high antiquity. The men were accustomed to tilt on horseback against a large bag of sand suspended from the bough of a tree. He who succeeded in piercing it with his spear gained the applause of the spectators; while he who failed was fortunate or adroit if he remained seated in his saddle. There was a dinner provided for them by the lord.

I conjecture that the field near the town in which Dodsworth informs us was the annual buck-hunting, was no other than the Sembly-green.

Here too was probably the May-pole of which we find notice in the public accompts of Sheffield.

The Wicker is however no longer a place of diversion. The town has been allowed to extend itself over a great part of it, and the more open parts are occupied by the stalls in which cattle are penned on the weekly market. But the taste for athletic exercises has been long on the decline; and the simple and innocent amusements of our ancestors have given place to others of a less harmless character. The town-waits are less welcome visitants than they formerly were; and bands of mummers performing the interlude of Saint George and the King of Egypt are scarcely now to be seen, as lately they were, parading the streets at Christmas. The fine manly exercise of throwing the quoit is almost disused; and a game unknown to the southern parts of the kingdom, in which the youth of Hallamshire had acquired great skill, consisting in driving a small and hard ball called a trip to a great distance, by the blow of a stout piece of wood fixed at the end of a flexible rod, is much less enjoyed than once it was. Indeed Sheffield is now so hemmed in by inclosures that it is hard to find room for the athletic exercises of former times.

The nursery which lies along the river-side from the Wicker to the Bridge-houses was formerly garden-ground belonging to the castle.

VI.

The Township of Attercliffe-cum-Darnall.

A TRACT of country which is nearly in the form of an equilateral triangle, of the area of two square miles, is the township of Attercliffe-cum-Darnall. One side is the line of the park wall, another the course of the Don, and the third is marked by the course of a little rill called the Carbrook, which rises near Bowden-homesteads, and falls into the Don near the village which bears its name. It lies east of the town of Sheffield.

In 1811 the population of this township amounted to 2673 persons. Some are employed in agriculture; but many more in different departments of the iron-manufactures. A considerable work called the blast-furnace, for smelting and casting iron, is on the banks of the Don, and in that part of the township which is nearest to Sheffield. The spacious chimney of the principal furnace emits a perpetual flame, affording a useful light to the belated traveller on many of the roads around it. There has been much digging for coal on what was lately known as Attercliffe-common, between the villages of Attercliffe and Carbrook.

Attercliffe and Darnall are both populous villages. Carbrook is a much smaller village.

The Sheffield canal, which is now in preparation from Tinsley to Sheffield, runs through this township in a line nearly parallel with the course of the Don.

The turnpike road from Sheffield to Rotherham passes through the villages of Attercliffe and Carbrook; and there is another turnpike road through Attercliffe and Darnall to Worksop.

The bridge by which the road from Sheffield to Attercliffe crosses the Don is called Washford-bridge; and hence it should seem originated the error of the commonly accurate topographer Speed, or of his predecessor our own Saxton, in whose map appears at this spot a village with the name of Westbury. The river at this place is deep and the banks high; but notwithstanding this, the name of Washford plainly shows that there was a ford over the Don at or near this place before any bridge was erected.

We have no means of ascertaining the antiquity of

this bridge. It was repaired in the reign of James I. in pursuance of the following sessions order.

'West Red. } Generalis Sessio pacis tent. apud Rother-Comitat. Ebor. } ham die Jovis scil. 8° die Octobris anno regni Dni nri Jacobi nunc regis &c. quinto—Coram Roberto Swifte milite, Will'mo Rokeby, Johanne Mawliverye, et Carolo Ricard armigeris, justic. &c.

'Forasmuch as the bridge called Attercliffe-bridge, scituate on the river of Dunne, beinge the comon passage betweene Sheffeld and Rotheram, and so betweene Yorkshire and Darbyshire in those partes, is fallen into such ruyn and decaye that his Maties subjects cannot well passe over the same without the daunger of their lyves: and for that yt hath pleased the right honorable Gilberte earle of Shrewsburie out of his noble disposition towards the furtherance of such a good and charitable worke to bestow uppon the countrie towards the repaire therof, tymber to the vallue of xxl.; and for that a view hath been taken therof by towe of his Maties justices of peace neare thereunto, whoe doe certifie that fyftie poundes wille hardly suffice sufficientlye to repaire the same : It is therefore ordered by this courte that the saide some of fyftie pounds shalbe allowed for the repaire therof, and to bee assessed uppon the whole west rid, and by the high constables within the severall weappentacks therof furthwith levied and collected and paide over to the hand of Hughe Rawson, Peter Perrins, John Staniforth, and Nicholas Turton, whoe are appointed overseers of the workes for repaire of the same bridge; and are to dispose the same for that purpose as shalbe most fittinge and requisite for the benefite of the countrie.'

At the sessions held at Wakefield on the 17th of October 1647 an order was made to assess on the west riding the sums necessary for 'the repair of Burton-bridge, Huddersfield-bridge, Westforth-bridge, alias Attercliffe-bridge, and Cowper-bridge. They had probably been destroyed in the Civil Wars.

Hitherto it was only a bridge of wood. In 1672 it was first built of stone. An order was signed by the justices of the peace at the sessions held at Pontefract in that year to levy 150l. on the riding for that purpose. It is now considered as a riding-bridge. The present was erected about 1794.

At the sessions held at Rotherham 1659, it was determined that the burthen of keeping Brookflat-bridge over the Carbrook rested on the townships of Darnall and Hansworth; and at the sessions at Pontefract in 1665, that Brightside-bridge was to be maintained by the wapentake[1].

Attercliffe was a manor of itself before the Conquest; *inland* of the manor of Hallam. In the Domesday-survey it is written Ateclive, and it is observable that it is placed before Sheffield, 'In Ateclive and Escafeld,' as if it were the superior place. It had the same proprietor, Sweyn; and has ever since passed along with the manor of Sheffield. It is not mentioned in the *Nomina Villarum* of the 9 Edward II.; but there is notice of it as a manor distinct from Sheffield in 20 Henry VI., when Sir Christopher Talbot

of Treeton acknowledged that he and others owed Geffery Lowther esquire two hundred pounds, on condition of paying forty-four pounds yearly, issuing out of the manors of Hansworth, Bramley, and Attercliffe, and out of lands in Treeton, Harthill, and Woodhall, &c.[2]

Darnall and a small territory around it is a manor of itself.

The common-fields and waste grounds within the manors of Attercliffe and Darnall were inclosed in 1811, in pursuance of one of the most selfish inclosure acts ever passed. Before that period there was in the midst of the village of Attercliffe a spacious green, sufficient for the exercise of the inhabitants, but not of such extent as to alarm the political speculatist for the consequences of so much land lying in an unproductive state. Of this convenience the public were deprived. But the act further contained a clause declaring that it should be lawful for the commissioners 'to stop all roads not turnpike, both in the new inclosures *and old*.' This was drawing tight the cords of property to the utmost. This was in the true spirit of the monopolizing genius of modern times, which would leave the poor and the public as little as possible which they can claim as a right. The commissioners, whoever they were, acted up to the extent of their powers, and shut the public from paths which had been used from the times when first population settled on the banks of the Don, and from field-paths the most delightful which this neighbourhood or any neighbourhood could boast. It is now irremediable. Private possession will insist upon its rights, and prosecute as a trespasser the botanist, the naturalist, the contemplative man, the lover of nature, and the worshipper of the God of nature, all of whom found congenial haunts in the quiet walk which lay along the right bank of the river, and all of whom must hate the noisy, crowded, dusty, or dirty road along which they are now obliged to pass, whenever their steps tend in this direction. But this may serve as a warning to the public in other places to watch the clauses of inclosure bills, and to endeavour to obtain some little attention to the claims which they have to present. The whole of what was inclosed by this act were fifty acres of common-field, and two hundred and thirty acres of waste land.

On what was the public green is a school, which was built by subscription about 1787; and looking upon it is a handsome mansion, the residence of Gamaliel Milner esquire, one of the twelve capital burgesses of the town and parish of Sheffield, whose pedigree has been already given, from the time when the family first became resident in the parish of Sheffield.

---

[1] From a book of the bridges in the west riding, among the Wilson Collections.

[2] Dods. E. 64 a. Harl. 801. Hansworth.

ATTERCLIFFE-CHAPEL.

' A record concerning the building of Attercliffe Chappell.*

' Blessed be the Lord who hathe put into the heartes of his people to build a house unto his name.

' In the yeare of our Lord God 1629 certaine of the chiefe of the inhabitantes being by God's providence mett togeather, they had a conference about building a chappell; who afterwards made the rest of their neighbours acquainted with the motion, and finding them willing set uppon the worke.

' They let the building of the walles to Thomas Arnalde and Henry Barber, free masons, for four shillings a roode, and four pence a foote for free stone, for which worke only they had £36 2 8

' They let the roofe to Thomas Hick, carpenter, who also had for that worke 11 6 8

' John Wilson was chosen to receive the people's fre-will offering, and to pay the workmen wages.

' Michael Hylee to be an assistant to help to provide thinges necessary for the work, and Humphry Twigg to keepe the booke.

' Uppon the 15 day of July the foundation was laid; and a little before Christenmas the walls being raised to the height, the roofe was laid on: at the rearing wherof the people came so willingly and gave so liberally, that for bread and cheese and beere and ale ther was such plenty as the like had not bene before; every one had inoughe, and much was spared and sent to the poore.

' After this, the worke staid till the sommer after, except the couvering of it, and other small matters.

			£ s d
The slaters had for their worke	. . . .		5 13 4
And the wallers for the court wall and getting stone			1 19 8
At sommer, Thomas Hick and others which helped him set on to make the staules and som other thinges, who had for that worke and the dores being made before			9 14 8
The pulpit, the head, and cushion cost . .			5 13 0
Thomas Arnald with others to help him had for shooteing the walles			4 19 9
The glasse for the windowes cost			2 15 6
The land wheron the chappell is built, with the rest belonging to it cost			3 8 0
There was spent in lime for the whole worke			6 19 9
Nailes			1 5 7 ob.
Willm Hinchliffe for iron work			1 10 6
Bestowed in ale and bread on the workmen that helpd with carrige of stone and timber and lime			3 16 3
For getting of pavers and paving			2 15 10
For other things belonging to the worke . .			6 11 10

' About Michaelmass things were brought to a good forwardness. Mr. Bright and John Wilson went to the Lord Ar. Bishop of York, and having obtained his license, the 10th of October 1630, being the Sabbath-day, divine service was read and two godly sermons preached by the Rev^d Mr. Thomas Toller, vicar of Sheffield, upon the seventh of Jere-

---

ª Preserved among the Wilson Collections.

miah and eight' verse, and a liberal collection for the poor: John Wilson being church-warden.

' In the year 1633 Mr. Bright beautified the quier with sentences of Scripture at his own charge. Stone being brought to the place, he made the court-wall and gates, which cost 5*l.*

' The right honorable the earl of Arundel at the humble suite of Mr. Bright gave us stone and timber, and neighbours of other towns helped us with carriage of slate, free stone, timber, and lime. They that had draughts within us, led wall-stone and timber: many gave horse-loads of lime. Mr. Spencer and Robert Carr suffered the stone through their ground, which was a great furtherance.

' Mr. Bright procured us a bell. Mr. Willm Pleasington gave us iron to make barrs for windows. Francis Moor glazed the window next the pulpit. Christ. Capper gave us all the hair that shott the walls. Richard Pigot beautified the two pillars with his work. Mr. Bright gave a bible to the chap-pell in 1633.

' October 26th 1636, the chappell was consecrated· (and endowed the same year) on St Matthew's day.

' The endowment of 10*l. per ann.* given as follows :—

			£	s	d
Mr. Bright	.	.	5	0	0
Mr. Spencer	.	.	2	0	0
John Staniforth	.	.	0	10	0
Robert Houle	.	.	0	10	0
Michael Hyley	.	.	0	6	8
William Warter	.	.	0	6	8
Richard Rhoads	.	.	0	6	8
Robert Chappell	.	.	0	4	0
Hugh Chaloner	.	.	0	4	0
Richard Newbowne	.	.	0	4	0
John Homer	.	.	0	4	0
Edmund Swift	.	.	0	4	0

' The above laid land security for payment of the above sums.

' Ministers were maintained by the contributions which were gathered quarterly, viz. 25th March, 24th June, 29th September, and 22^d December.'

What follows was communicated to Mr. Wilson by Dr. Burton of York, the learned author of the *Monasticon Eboracense.* It purports to be an extract from Torre's manuscripts.

' Attercliffe Chapel 27 Oct. 1636, Stephen Bright of Carbrooke, gent., William Spencer of Attercliffe-hall, gent., and other the inhabitants of the town of Attercliffe, by their petition to Richard archbishop of York shewed—That within the parish of Sheffield are the villages of Atterclyff, Darnal, and Carbrook, wherein dwell many parishoners whose houses are most of them distant from the parish church two miles &*c*. by reason of the smal whide [width] cannot have room to stand in the parish church &*c*.—Therefore they the said inhabitants for the more public service of Almighty God, receiving of sacraments, marriages, churching of women, and burials, have at their own costs and charges built a chappell in the said village of Attercliffe, for them to resort thither for divine service &*c*. which they humbly pray may be dedicated. —Also farther pray that whereas there are three assistant-ministers to the vicar of Sheffield, chosen by twelve capital burgesses and commonalty of the town and parish thereof, from tyme to tyme according to a grant to them made under the great seal of England, That one of these three assistants be from time to time chosen, nominated, and commanded to the archbishop of York by the vicar of Sheffield for him to serve the said cure, which curate they do hereby promise shall have ten pounds *per ann.* settled already upon trustees in trust for that purpose, besides his stipend of fifteen pounds *per ann.* out of the church.—Whereupon the said Archbishop constituted Richard bishop of Sodor to consecrate the chapel and chapel-yard thereof; which was then done accordingly, and the chapel dedicated to the name of *Capella Jesu Christi Salvatoris infra villam de Attercliffe.*'

The ' *Tenor sententiæ consecrationis*' was to the same effect, with the usual clauses for saving the rights of the parish-church to which this is declared to be a chapel of ease; and enjoining on the persons on whose behalf the petition for a consecration was presented attendance at their parish-church at least once a year at the feast of Easter. The reason of the delegation of the bishop of Sodor, or the Isle of Man, ' *Sodorensis sive Insulæ de Man,*' is declared to be the illness of the archbishop: and the dimensions of the chapel 66 feet from east to west, 30 from north to south, with an aile 36 feet from east to west, and 9 from north to south.

The parliamentary commissioners in 1649 made the following return[2].

' Attercliffe Chappell. Wee finde neare two myles distant from its parish-church; and that it hath parochiall rights belonging to it, without a mynister, and butt tenn pounds *per. ann.* maintenance belongs it, which was given by certaine inhabitants for ever. The chappellrye consists of about two hundred and fiftye famelyes. Therefore wee thinke fitt that the said chappell of Attercliffe to be made a parish church: and the townes and places of Grymsthorpe, nether parts of Bright-side Barley in the same parish of Sheffield, be annexed and made of the same parish.'

With no more than this small endowment the chapel remained for many years; but in 1731 it had the good fortune to obtain by lot 200*l.* from the governors of Queen Anne's bounty, and in 1756 the like sum again by lot. The first two hundred pounds had never been demanded, the ministers being content with the interest which the governors allowed; but in 1760 a farm was purchased at Walton near Chesterfield, at the expense of little more than four hundred pounds, the surplus money being raised by Mr. Smith, then the curate, and·a few of his friends. This farm at the time of the purchase produced 12*l.* 10*s. per annum.*

Some further addition has been made to the minister's income by the surrender to him of the pews of the north gallery which was built in 1740 by Mr. Fell and Mr. Milner. Those gentlemen were allowed to let out the pews as a compensation for the expense they incurred in the erection. In 1793 Mrs. Fell gave up her moiety, and in 1795 the other moiety was given up by Mr. Milner. In 1779 also, by a faculty from the court of York, a gallery was erected by certain of the inhabitants at the east end, from which certain seat rents were made payable to the minister amounting to 2*l.* 17*s. per annum.*

The chapel-yard has been twice enlarged, namely, in 1754, and in 1786 when 900 square yards were added from the waste. In respect of this matter private convenience proved of public advantage. The chapel was placed at the very extremity of the village of Attercliffe that it might be near to the principal promoter of the work—Mr. Bright of Carbrook; but it was also thus placed on the very verge of the common, and thus facilities were presented for the en-

---

[1] Probably it should be the ninth. ' Will ye steal, murder, and commit adultery, and swear falsely, and burn incense unto Baal, and walk after-other gods whom ye know not; and come and stand before me in this house which is called by my name, and say We are delivered to do all these abominations?'

[2] Parliamentary surveys of church lands, commonly called Oliver's surveys, in the Archiepiscopal library at Lambeth, vol. xviii. f. 442.

largement of its cemetery, a circumstance of some consequence in so populous a district.

Of minor benefactions to the chapel may be mentioned that in 1716 Mrs. Elizabeth Grammer of Darnall gave a silver cup and salver for the communion; another salver was given in 1789 by Mrs. Fell, who about the same time gave a new bell, and soon after a barrel organ.

In 1709 Margaret Bamforth of the High-house bequeathed to the overseers for the benefit of the poor of Attercliffe-cum-Darnall ten shillings annually, being part of the rent of a close at Dronfield, which in the year 1784 was advanced to 13 shillings and 9 pence.

1720. Elizabeth Grammer bequeathed fifty pounds to the overseers of Attercliffe and Darnall, to be at interest for the benefit of the poor.

1786. William Staniforth bequeathed fifty pounds to the chapel wardens and overseers of the poor to be at interest to keep a vault and two tombs in repair in the chapel-yard; the remainder of the interest to be divided amongst the poor of Attercliffe not assisted by the poor-rates in sums not less than two shillings and sixpence to each family.

The chapel is a modest respectable building, placed on an eminence rising abruptly from the meadows near the Don, perhaps the cliff from which the village has taken a part of its name. On each side one of the door ways is a tablet affixed to the wall, which bear the following inscriptions.

<table>
<tr><td>M. S.
RACHAELIS
pientissimæ parentis
Rev^{di}
Edwardi Goodwin
quæ obiit Martii 9
anno salutis 1787,
ætat. 85.</td><td>M. S.
ELIZABETHÆ
carissimæ conjugis
Rev^{di}
Edwardi Goodwin
quæ obiit Julii 18
anno salutis 1786,
ætat. 60.</td></tr>
</table>

Within the chapel a neat marble slab has been lately placed on which is commemorated another member of this family.

Near this place
are deposited the mortal remains,
together with those of his wife and mother,
of the Revd EDWARD GOODWIN,
minister of this chapel forty-one years,
and one of the three assistant-ministers of the
parish church of Sheffield for forty-three years.
After a long life uniformly devoted
to the service of God and the good of man,
he was removed to eternal rest
on the 1st of July 1817,
in the 86th year of his age.
The memory of the just is blessed.

There have been many interments within the walls of the chapel. A brief notice of the sepulchral memorials which are, or at least lately were in the chapel, will suffice.

Anne wife of Matthew Slack of Attercliffe 1709. Mrs. Anne Bird of London 1736. Dr. Samuel Jollie 1701. Mr. Jonathan Wilson 1717. Hephzibah his wife 1741, and Jonathan his son 1754. Anne daughter of Edmund Swift of Darnall, gent., 1763. Mr. William Steer of Darnall 1726. Sarah his wife 1729. Arthur Speight of Attercliffe, gent., 1738, and others of his family, both of his own name and the name of Clay, who all appear in a pedigree before

given. Against the wall is a handsome monument for the same respectable family, bearing arms, viz.

CLAY.—Argent, a chevron ingrailed between 3 trefoils sable, quartering Sable, a cross moline argent charged with a trefoil of the field. CREST.—A pair of wings argent semee of trefoils sable.

Near to those lately mentioned are the names of Bullas, Taylor, Jackson, and at the east extremity of the middle aile lie Benjamin Ferrand, formerly the minister of this chapel, who died 27 Feb. 1728, aged 38, and Elizabeth his widow, who died 4 Dec. 1752, aged 60; and two children Benjamin and Thomas.

In the east cross aile are memorials of William Wadsworth and others of his family, of James Allott of Attercliffe and Esther his wife 1783 and 1777. And a brass plate bearing this inscription.

Hannah filia et hæres Thomæ Goodyer (Mancunii, gen.) et charissima conjux Danielis Leech, assistentis Sheffieldiæ, obiit Oct. 30, A.D. 1691. Samuel filius secundus et Collegii Lincolniensis apud Oxon. alumnus obiit Aug. 3, A.D. 1693.

But the inscription which seems most worthy to be preserved, and which sixteen years ago was nearly obliterated by the countless steps which had passed over it, and the busy feet of the catechumens whom the late venerable minister of this chapel used to assemble in the aile in the floor of which it was placed, is that of Samuel Jollie.

'Hic sitæ sunt reliquiæ Samuelis Jollie nuper Attercliffiensis, medici.

Transiere patres, simul et nos transibimus omnes,
Cæli patriam qui bene transit, habet.
Amoris et mortalitatis
posuit hoc Μνημοσυνον T. I. A.D. 1701.'

I take those to be the initials of the Reverend Timothy Jollie, who was residing at that period at Attercliffe.

CURATES of ATTERCLIFFE.

1630—1635. Stanley Gower.
1635—1642. James Bright.

1643—1648. No regular curate, but the chapel was supplied by the aged Mr. Toller who had been vicar of Sheffield, Mr. Pool, Mr. Birbeck the vicar, Mr. Rawson an assistant-minister of Sheffield, Mr. Cart rector of Hansworth, Mr. Bridges, Mr. Towne, Mr. Barney, Mr. Metcalfe, and Mr. James Fisher vicar of Sheffield.

1648—1651. William Bagshaw.
1652—   John Bridges.
1653—1662. Matthew Bloome.
1662—1673. Cuthbert Browne.
1673—1708. Daniel Leech.
1708—1719. George Lee.
1719—1729. Benjamin Ferrand.
1729—1731. Isaac Hemmingway.
1731—1755. Robert Tempest.
1755—1776. John Smith.
1776—1817. Edward Goodwin.
1817.   John Blackburne.

Mr. Stanley Gower, the first curate of Attercliffe, was a divine of no small note in his own day, though little is to be found respecting him in any of our biographical writers. I shall endeavour to collect the hitherto scattered materials of his history, and to combine them into one narrative.

He was born about 1590 and educated in Trinity College Dublin, where he had for his tutor Dr. Joshua Hoyle, who was in high repute for biblical knowledge. Hoyle was a friend of Usher, and it was probably on his recommendation that Mr. Gower was received into the family of that learned prelate in the character of domestic chaplain[1]. How long he remained with him or what occasioned the separation has not been discovered: but as early as 1619 he was come over to England and was living in the family of the first earl of Devonshire, who kept up a magnificent establishment at Chatsworth and Hardwick.

When Mr. Gower became attached to the household of the earl of Devonshire, there were two very different characters under the same patronage, Hobbes and Mr. Richard Rothwell.

This Mr. Rothwell in his youth had been one of the gayest of the gay, but had become one of the most rigid and withal one of the most superstitious and extravagant of the puritan divines. In his devotion to the ministerial work, and his labours in preaching and travelling, he emulated the apostles, but most of all the ' sons of thunder, for when he preached the law, he used to make men tremble, yea sometimes to cry out in the church, opening the depths of Satan and deceitfulness of the heart, so that he was called the rough hewer.' He would never accept of any benefice lest a restraint should be laid upon his going about from place to place to preach the gospel. He did not however decline the offer made by the earl of Devonshire to become one of his domestic chaplains.

The cool philosophy of Hobbes had no chance against such an antagonist. The preaching of Rothwell had a great effect upon the mind of Gower, who now experienced what was called the change unto godliness, and could mention ' the very sermon and point' of Mr. Rothwell to which he owed his conversion.

Mr. Gower now looked upon Mr. Rothwell as his spiritual father and paid him the reverence of a child. Mr. Rothwell on his part felt for him all the affection of a parent. They agreed never to separate. When Mr. Rothwell was invited by Lady Bowes of Walton afterwards Lady Darcy, to preach amongst the illiterate people in the neighbourhood of Barnard-castle, Mr. Gower went with him; when he settled at Mansfield and was preaching in all the country round, Mr. Gower was his constant attendant. He died in the midst of his labours in the year 1627. Mr. Gower received his last breath, nor was his regard for his memory disproportionate to his attachment while living. He gave to the world an ample memoir of Mr. Rothwell's life and character. It is pitiable to see so much real piety, so much Christian zeal, so much benevolent regard for the welfare of mankind, combined with so much extravagance, absurdity, and ignorance. With an hereditary respect for the memory of the puritan ministry of this kingdom, confirmed by an attention to their character, their principles, and their conscientious adherence to them in the midst of persecution, I have found it impossible to contemplate the full-length portrait which Mr. Gower has drawn but with a sentiment in which any feeling is predominant rather than admiration. The curious reader may find it in

' Lives of sundry modern English divines,' published in 1651 by Samuel Clark, from whence it has been transferred, with some curtailment, into Middleton's ' Biographia Evangelica.' After perusing either of these accounts the sagacious remark of Fuller in his ' Worthies of Lancashire,' when speaking of Rothwell, will please the judicious reader. Among Mr. Rothwell's distinguishing excellencies was that of being a potent exorcist, and one of the most prominent circumstances in Mr. Gower's narrative is the contest in which he was engaged with the Devil which had possessed the body of one John Fox, who lived in the neighbourhood of Nottingham. After a long conflict Mr. Rothwell prevailed and expelled this troublesome intruder, to the wonderful satisfaction of Mr. Gower, who was an eye-witness, and details all the circumstances with the most artless wondering simplicity. Mr. Gower, we shall afterwards find, had a principal share in drawing up that well-known confession of faith commonly called ' The Assembly's Catechism.' The doctrines of that confession depend not for their truth upon the authority of the men by whom it was compiled, but it would be well if those who are disposed to pay to it an implicit deference would consider by whom and what kind of men it was compiled and imposed. ' I revere the piety of the early Non-conformists,' says a philosophical writer when he had been contemplating the narrative now before us, ' nor will I yield to any man in admiration of their self-denying integrity; I have not however while reading this narrative been able to suppress the reflection how poorly divines of such taste and judgement, though competently furnished with the learning of their time, were accomplished for the arduous task on which they ventured of framing confessions and catechisms which should direct the Christian faith and order of their posterity. These surely were not the men divinely gifted to

' Enlighten climes and mould a future age[2].'

The same year in which Mr. Rothwell died, Mr. Gower was elected an assistant-minister in the church at Sheffield; and in 1630 he was nominated to the curacy of the newly-erected chapel at Attercliffe. He continued at Sheffield till the year 1635, when he was called away to a distant part of the kingdom.

Sir Robert Harley, an ancestor of the earl of Oxford, a great encourager of the puritan divines, presented Mr. Gower in that year to the rectory of Brampton-Bryan in Herefordshire. To this living Mr. Gower retired. It was welcome to him. The income of his little preferment at Sheffield had not been sufficient to meet the demands of his family, and he left Sheffield in debt. Sir Robert Harley was resident in his parish, and was a kind and liberal benefactor to him. ' He became,' says the author of the MS. life of his predecessor Pierson, ' a great blessing to Bramton and all the neighbourhood by his preaching at the monthly lectures, and by his constant observance of the Ember-fasts, to which he had the resort for many miles of a very numerous and pious auditory. The Lord's days were constantly observed by him in most excellent sermons, morning and afternoon, and catechising the

---

[1] All this is on the authority of ' The Life of Thomas Pierson, rector of Brampton Brian.' MS. in the Lansdowne library No. 761, where is a brief notice of Mr. Gower, f. 147.

[2] See an admirable article on the Life of Rothwell in ' The Monthly Repository for Theology and General Literature,' vol. vi. p. 140, &c.

youth.' He did not forget his old friends at Sheffield. Five of his letters to Mr. John Staniforth of Darnall, whom he calls his son, are preserved among the Wilson collections. The earliest is dated from Brampton-Bryan 5 April 1636, in which he speaks of distractions in the church at Sheffield, and makes many professions of gratitude and regard to his correspondent. Dec. 5, 1636, Sir Robert Harley had promised to help him out of his difficulties; owed Mr. Staniforth ten pounds for interest. June 14, 1638, Mr. Staniforth had been with the earl of Arundel at Shrewsbury, which was but twenty miles from Brampton: still owing money to Mr. Staniforth. March 24, 1638-9, sorry that he has not yet paid his debt which 'weighs much upon his thoughts:' could not pleasantly remind Sir Robert of his promise; sends a psalm-book to his little God-daughter, who he expects is by that time able to read it. His daughter Betty keeps what Mr. Staniforth had given to her 'as a relic.' Has another son, who by comparison of dates must have been the son to whom he gave the name of Humphry, and who was afterwards the learned Dr. Humphry Gower, master of St. John's College Cambridge, and Lady Margaret professor of divinity.

Few small towns suffered more in the civil wars than Brampton. Lady Harley held out the castle for seven weeks in the summer of 1643, against a large party of the royalist army when the greatest part of the town was burnt. Mr. Gower was plundered of every thing, and he particularly regrets the loss of the manuscripts of his early friend and 'magnus Apollo' Mr. Richard Rothwell.

But in that year he was called from Herefordshire to appear on a more public theatre. He was nominated in the 'Act for the calling an assembly of learned and godly divines to be consulted with by the parliament for the settlement of the government and the liturgy of the church, and for the vindicating and the clearing of the doctrine of the church of England from false aspersions and interpretations.' This was the title of the act by which the Assembly of Divines at Westminster was summoned. In the deliberations of that assembly ' he signalized himself in many respects,' says the author of the life of Pierson, ' but especially in assisting the compiling the Confession of Faith, and the larger and shorter Catechism composed by the Assembly.'

London from this period became for several years his constant residence. He had the church of Saint Martin's Ludgate. We find him concerned in several public ordinations according to the new directory[1]: and among the preachers before the House of Commons. The thanks of the house were voted to him, to be conveyed by Sir Robert Harley and Mr. Hallowes, for a sermon which he preached before the house at the monthly fast on 31 July 1644, and he published it with the quaint and absurd title ' Things now a doing: or the Churches travaile of the child of Reformation now a bearing,' Another of his sermons is in print preached before the house on 31 Dec. 1646.

Mr. Gower changed his residence once more. In 1650 he was presented to the rectories of the Holy Trinity and Saint Peter's in Dorchester, and in that town he continued to reside till his death. He died in the year of the Restoration, and thus no doubt escaped being ejected or silenced by the Act of Uniformity soon after passed.

Two of his letters which have a pleasing air of simplicity are given below from the originals[2].

Of the same school with Mr. Gower, but a more

---

[1] See Calamy's Continuation, &c. 67, 550.
[2] To theyr much respected sonne and i⁶ughter
{ John } Staniforth,
{ Mary }
at theyr howse in Darnall neare Sheffeilde in Yorkeshire.
                                        These.

Most loving sonne and daughter,

CHILDREN are the living images of theyr parents, towards whom love descendeth st'ily, and therefore easily, freely. How oft therefore our thoughts reflect upon you our deare sonne and daughter, w⁶ʰ what delight they stay upon those many objects we remember, our intima⁶e rejoycing, we have forborne to utter eyther hitherto by l' or now by any long relation; partly for that wee wanted your Genius to see whether your selves would quicken towards us, and partly also, least in so great a distance we should but begett a newe griefe to dwell upon so unpleasant a thought as our absence. Besides these, you have bene such indulgent children towards us your poore parents, and contrary to the law, or perhapps your expectation, have put your selves on the score for us, thus crowning at our parting the constancy of your first love expressed towards us at our meeting, that indigency hitherto hath raysed up that old companion of love, jealousy in our minds, least wee should not be equally reloved where wee love. All these have forced a stopp to our best servant, these paper messengers of our mind w⁶ blush not, otherwise wee pray you thinke that there can come none in that roome, nor clayme that interest in our affections w⁶ yo⁺ both doe and may: nor shall we always wee trust leave unpayd any thing but our love. The interest of our debt I have sent, and written to Nicho. Sanderson for to pay........

And now durst I be bold to pen former passages, what might we say of our suspected counsells in the 2 howses of our parlim', what of the projects, purposes in getting yo⁺ a stepmother, what of our expedition to Chester? In w⁶ passages I must needs take in my servant Robt. Rawson our fidus Achates, and W. L. our banger on. From thence to Grimsthorpe where your parlour will bring to mind ev'y thing well, but that tragicall scene at Carbrook wherein we have left the guilt on them and the griefe on ourselves. I wish when wee shall forgett the one, hee do not remember the other. I will go no farther because I know not who may oversee these lines but these cause many desires once more to see you [till] when we may satisfy ourselves w⁶ thoughts.

I pray yo⁺ now let these lines present my best wishes to our freinds at Raisin-hall, w⁶ theyr neighbo⁺ ₜ Tho. ₎ Rawson, our good host and hostess; my kind doctress; Tho. Scargel and his wife with all theyrs :

our faythfull butcher, his w'fe; Robt. Scargell, &c. I shall never have done if I particularize. therefore in general to all our quondam frends: concerning whom as we wish all happines, so wee pray you let them know we are well placed under a noble and hon⁶le patron, blessed w⁶ a sonne Robt. w⁶ bears our patrons name in Herefordshire; and being ev'y thing, if we be to our good God but thankfull. O the divisions of Reuben! the alterations in your church and churchmen since our removall! I pray God both bless the deliv'rance to mee, and sanctify the change to yo⁺. I wish I had bene a false prophet when I fortold these things among yo⁺.

My wife hath sent a lace for hir son John's coate; and I have sent yo⁺ a penny for to hang about my little god-daughter's neck. The L. bless them both, and all yours. Thus w⁶ many harty wishes pray
            Your most unchanged fa. and mother,
                                    STA. ₎ GOWER.
                                    SARAH ₎

I want my daughter to call mee up this spring in a morning: and old Tho. Scargell to drinke a draught of scurvey grass ale w⁶ mee when I am up. I pray yo⁺ tell them so.

Brompton Bryan in Herefordshire,
      5th Aprill 1636.

The second was written while they lived in London.

To theyr very lov. son Mr. Jo. Staniforth
at Durnhill neare Sheffield in Yorkeshire.
                                        These.

' Son,

FOR feare you should catch my infection and forgett to write, I have broke my use, and begun to blott paper. I was in hope my goddaughter would have bene here; and then I should have conceived some hope of seeing you at least, if not my daughter also, w⁶ would much have ioyed your long absent parents —

You writt imperfectly of placing your daughter here; we should have bene ready, and shall to do our best that way, but would gladly know what kind of place you intend her. Wear our family likely to advance hir, we should not be slack to receive her, but our plundered condition maks us keepe but one mayd, and therefore are not likely to give satisfaction eyther to you, to hir, or to ourselves, should shee come so farr to so little purpose. I hope you let hir not lose hir tyme w⁶ you, especiall hir reading and wryting: this, with a little cookery, will render hir acceptable in very good places. When you thinke hir fit for the citty, none shalbe more forward to settle hir than wee. Your old kindnesses are

sensible disciple, was one of his early successors in the curacy of Attercliffe, Mr. William Bagshaw. Of this gentleman we have a full account from the pen of his nephew Mr. John Ashe, to which few particulars are to be added.

Mr. Bagshaw was born at Litton in the parish of Tidswell. His father of the same name had much improved a small inheritance by success in the lead-mines. From his early youth he was attached to religious studies, and opposed successfully the views of his family who sought to divert his mind to some other pursuit. After a suitable education at different grammar-schools he was sent to Cambridge, and being admitted of Corpus-Christi college was under the care of Mr. Boise.

His first public labours were at Wormhill, a chapel in his native parish. He had been there but one quarter of a year when a scene of wider usefulness opened upon him. Though only in his twenty-first year he was chosen one of the assistant-ministers of Sheffield, and appointed to the curacy of Attercliffe. He was also domestic chaplain to Colonel John Bright, afterwards Sir John, and consequently we may presume resided in the hall at Carbrook. On New Year's Day 1651 he was ordained at Chesterfield after the Presbyterian manner, Immanuel Bourne, rector of Ashover, being moderator on the occasion. His orthodox confession of faith was afterwards published, with a sermon of Mr. Bagshaw's 'on Christ's purchase,' dedicated to his friends Mrs. Jane Jessop and Mrs. Elizabeth South her sister, then living at Broom-hall.

Early in 1652 Mr. Bagshaw resigned his connexion with the church of Sheffield. He settled at Glossop, 'the remotest corner of his native county,' where he laboured most assiduously in the ministry amongst a rude but attached and grateful people. A connexion mutually acceptable was dissolved by the provisions of the Act of Uniformity. Tears testified his people's gratitude and esteem.

He had an estate at Ford in the parish of Chapel-en-le-Frith. To this place he retired, exercising his ministerial functions whenever opportunity was afforded him. When some indulgence was granted to the Non-conformists in 1672 he preached more publicly; and in the uncertain and dangerous times which succeeded, as well as in the more prosperous days after the Revolution, he was most assiduous in what he conceived to be the duty to which the providence of God had appointed him; and so assiduous were his labours in instructing the people in his own neighbourhood that he obtained the appellation of ' the Apostle of the Peak.' Various societies of Dissenters in the wilder parts of Derbyshire still exist which were first collected by Mr. Bagshaw.

His last public sermon was on the death of King William. The next Sunday he was confined to his bed. To a friend who lamented that he saw him un-

able to address his friends as usual on that day, he observed ' My silence is a sermon:' and when another expressed his regret that Mr. Bagshaw could not even converse with them at any length, he said emphatically, ' I have spoken to you before.'

There are many interesting particulars of Mr. Bagshaw's useful life and peaceful death in the work before quoted; and also of his manner of conducting public services, in which was something peculiar. A list of his works may also be found too long to be here transcribed. Popular in their day, they are now forgotten. They are chiefly pieces of practical divinity, and the fame of the practical divine, like that of the physician, can hardly be expected to outlive its century. Of all his works, probably, the only one now inquired after is his little tract ' De Spiritualibus Pecci,' which contains a brief account of several clergymen and other pious persons his friends, delivered in a simple, natural, and interesting manner. It was one of the first books, if not the very first, printed for a bookseller at Sheffield.

Of Mr. Bloom we have already given an account in the eleventh chapter.

His successor in 1662 was a man of a different character, Cuthbert Browne, commonly called Dr. Browne. He came from Greasborough to Sheffield, where he was for eleven years an assistant-minister and curate of Attercliffe. He seems to have engaged more in worldly concerns than became a minister. He was lessee of the tythe-of Attercliffe under the duke of Norfolk, and had a general commission for the management of his grace's estates in and about Sheffield. Neither the procuring the commission nor his conduct under it gained him much respect. On the 3d of April 1679 he was instituted to the rectory of Hansworth on the presentation of Henry duke of Norfolk, and on the 21st of February 1680 to the rectory of Treeton on the same presentation. He had also a prebend in the cathedral church of York, and his son Obadiah Browne enjoyed the rectory of Whiston by the patronage of the Norfolk family.

In the chancel of the church of Treeton is the following inscription :

Depositum
CUTHBERTI BROWNE, E. A. P.
non ita pridem de Treaton
et Hansworth rectoris
nec non eccl* Metr* S. Petri
Ebor. prebendarii.
Ob. 6to die Febr. 1692,
æt. suæ 59mo.
Memoria justorum in benedictione.

A contemporary of Mr. Browne, whose manuscript we have before quoted, has preserved an anecdote of him too curious to be omitted—' In the beginning of the year 1691 Dr. Browne fell ill as I remember. I am told there is a law that noe glebe land shall be

---

not forgotten, though they must lye still upon the score, till God enable us to some satisfaction.

My wife, my corrector, tells me I say not well, in putting in cookery, though my simplicity thought it best ; instead of wᶜʰ you must read, sewing and starching. The newes here is nothing but expectation of the Scotch Com'issioners, wᶜ we heare are upon theyr way: then both kingdoms send propositions to the king: some of the members of the howse of commons have bene wᵗ Sir Thos. Fairfax to send some souldiers into Ireland : the Presbyterian party obey, the Independᵗ demurr, and prepare a mutinous petition, wᶜ the howse hath declared as you find by the enclosed: some of the officers are sent for; the issue is expected.

Some news more there is I shall refere you for to yᵉ bearer: if it prove true you will not receive this letter, if otherwise, it will suffice, that you hear what it should have bene. I am called upon to make an end, the bearer stays, I must therefore refere you to him, who hath letters of credence—Your knives, my wife and I thank you for. Her godson and my goddaughter we forget not to pray for . . . . You so remembrd to you both; we in haste take leave, being

Your moste affectionate parents,
STANLEY GOWER.
SARAH GOWER.

3 R

plowed after the death of the incumbent, but his friends have power to sow, and reap the succeeding cropp. When he was ill and was sensible and could speak, his only cry was Plow, plow. A great many teams were gotten, and a great deal was plowed, though I believe not so much as was designed had the doctor lived a little longer.'

Mr. Daniel Leech made an attempt to establish the right of the curate of Attercliffe to keep a register of the baptisms, marriages, and burials at his chapel apart from the parish-register. But on an appeal to the archbishop he was restrained, and ordered to render an account to the vicar of Sheffield, as appears by a memorandum in the parish-register under the year 1696.

On the death of Mr. Daniel Leech a number of persons in this chapelry joined in a petition to the church-burgesses of Sheffield, that they might have Mr. John Leech for their minister. They seem to have been mistaken in addressing the burgesses on this subject unless they had already procured the consent of the vicar. At all events their petition was unavailing, and Mr. George Lee became curate of Attercliffe. He died 25 Nov. 1719; one of the three assistant-ministers who all died within one twelvemonth.

Mr. Ferrand was vicar of Peatley-magna in Leicestershire. Mr. Tempest, one of the younger sons of Sir George Tempest of Tong, baronet, removed to Nottingham. Mr. Smith had the grammar-school. For Mr. Hemmingway there is the following inscription in the church of Rotherham:

Subtus reponuntur
ISAACI HEMMINGWAY reliquiæ
qui
olim hic, nuper Attercliffii
curam sacerdotalem egit.
Fidus erat amicus, peritus
theologus, et bonus vir.
Eum
divitiis multi, doctrina perpauculi,
virtute nulli superabant.
Decessit 3tio die Martii A.D. 1730-1,
ætatis suæ 29.

The Reverend Edward Goodwin, the late highly respectable curate of Attercliffe, was born at Barlow near Chesterfield in the year 1732 or 1733. His first settlement at Sheffield was as under-master of the grammar-school, and while in that situation he communicated an account of the town and parish of Sheffield to the Gentleman's Magazine[1]. An account of Greasborough in the same miscellany is also from his pen[2], as is also the memoir of his brother-in-law the Reverend James Cawthorne master of Tunbridge-school, whose works he collected and published in a quarto volume. To that Magazine he continued to be a contributor on various subjects, topographical, biographical, and moral, till within a short period of his death: for though he arrived at a very advanced age and through many infirmities was incapacitated for the performance of his public duties, he retained his faculties unimpaired, and in a cheerful old age exhibited a pleasing and edifying example of the effect of religious principles and the consciousness of a well spent life.

In a populous village where such men as Gower, Bagshaw, Fisher, and Bloom had been ministers, it was to be expected that the principles of Non-conformity would prevail; and accordingly the society which was formed at Shiercliffe-hall under the pastoral care of Mr. Hancock and Mr. Bloom consisted for the most part of persons from this place. After the breach between the two ministers many of the congregation adhered to Mr. Bloom, and these formed a separate society who met for worship in the village of Attercliffe where Mr. Bloom resided[3]. The congregation at first consisted of two-and-twenty persons, amongst whom appears the name of Mr. Spencer of Attercliffe-hall. About as many more were soon after added, and the society continued to increase so that in 1716 it consisted of 250 persons[4].

Mr. Bloom died in 1686; and soon after, namely, in 1691, Mr. James Wright is mentioned in the diaries of Mr. Oliver Heywood, as dissenting-minister of Attercliffe. This gentleman was of both the universities, 'performing his exercises for the degree of B.A. at one, and M.A. at the other.' He married a daughter of William Cotton of Wortley and Nether Denby ironmaster, a great patron of the Non-conformists, sister to William Cotton of the Haigh in Darton, esquire, and to Thomas Cotton an eminent dissenting minister in London. By this lady he had a son Dr. Samuel Wright, also a minister, who was born at Retford, where his father exercised his ministry many years[5]. His successor at Attercliffe was Mr. Edward Prime, one of the ejected assistants at Sheffield, who continued to officiate here till his death in 1708.

In 1716 Mr. Samuel Blythe of Norton Lees was the minister of this society, and about the same time Mr. Wilson.

This congregation was soon after taken into connexion with the Upper-chapel at Sheffield; and about 1750 it was dissolved, the small remains of it uniting themselves to the Sheffield societies of Dissenters.

About the year 1780 a small society of Dissenters was formed here, who separated from the church upon very different principles. They published a defence of the principles of their association in a pamphlet entitled 'An answer to ' a brief defence of the first article of the Church of England,' by a society of Unitarian Christians at Attercliffe near Sheffield,' 1784. The founders of this society were Mr. John Lawton, and Mr. John Spencer, an untaught but ingenious man who left what he called 'An humble attempt towards a new Pilgrim's Progress,' which was published after his death by the Reverend Astley Meanley of Stannington. The persons forming this society never had a minister settled among them, but after some time joined the Dissenters who met at the Upper-chapel in Sheffield.

[1] Vol. xxxiv. p. 157, &c.   [2] Vol. xxxiii. 531-534.
[3] In a collection of remarkable circumstances and events by Mr. O. Heywood is the following memorandum: ' On July 21, 1661, near Sheffield by the river Dun was seen a great army of white soldiers upon the earth : after them went another great multitude of horsemen all in white with white horses. 'After appearance near an hour, they all vanished away. Attested by many credible persons. Mr. Bloom formerly minister at Addercliffe near Sheffield, where the sight was seen, having examined some neighbours and living in the town, told me of it.'
[4] Neal's List of Dissenting Congregations, MS.
[5] See A Sermon on the death of Mr. Thomas Cotton, by J. Wright, D.D. 1730. Note p. 29.

In 1807 a chapel was built at Attercliffe by a sub-scription amongst Dissenters of the Independent de-nomination; and the Reverend Maurice Philips, who was a tutor in the academy at Masborough near Ro-therham, was invited to be the minister. He resigned in 1813, and the Reverend Richard Richards suc-ceeded him. A house for the minister's residence was also built by subscription.

The Wesleian Methodists have a chapel at Atter-cliffe.

When the Non-conformists were excluded from the universities, they sought to repair to themselves the inconvenience thence arising, by the foundation of academies, where what was called university learning was taught; and the many excellent theological scho-lars whom these institutions have produced, have gained for them no inconsiderable share of public ap-probation. The first of these in the north of England was established by Mr. Richard Frankland, who was in the prime of life when he was ejected from Bishop's-Auckland in Durham. Of this person an ample ac-count is to be found in Calamy[1]. He had his pupils first at Rathmel, to which place he retired after his ejectment; from thence he removed in 1674 to the neighbourhood of Kendal; from thence in 1683 |to Calton, and in 1686 he came to Attercliffe. After three years residence here he returned to Rathmel, where his academy was in high reputation till his death in 1698. He educated three hundred persons, most of whom were ministers among the Non-conformists. A list of the students in his academy is published, as an appendix to a funeral sermon for the Rev. Daniel Madox.

Soon after Mr. Frankland's removal, the Reverend Timothy Jollie, minister of the Dissenters in Sheffield, having taken the hall at Attercliffe, established an academy upon a plan similar to Mr. Frankland's, whose pupil he had been. Of him and his academy and pu-pils we have already spoken.

The hall at Attercliffe was for several generations the residence of the family of Spencer, who possessed considerable property in this manor and elsewhere,

and were themselves lords of the manor of Darnall in this township.

Respecting this family we have the following certi-ficate under the hand of George Owen, York herald, in the year 1648.

' WHEREAS William Spencer of Bramley-grange in the county of York, gentleman, hath had consultation with me concerning the bearing of his arms, being as it appears by tradition received from his ancestors, as also by the usage of the arms by his father and grandfather, and by a pedigree by him produced to be descended of a younger branch of the fa-mily of Spencer of Badby in com. Northamp. he not being able at present to make any precise proof what filial difference he ought to give (as indeed it is often the case of many younger branches of worthy families of this kingdom) for want of pre-serving and registering their genealogies and pedigrees. He in that regard hath requested my advice how he may (in the bearing of his arms) demean himself to relate to that family without prejudice to any thereby: which I have advised him to do by giving the fess wavy, and the crest being a sea-mew, to bear it on a wreath on a rock proper, as it is above depicted.'

Mr. Spencer gave an account of his family no higher than his grandfather, who was Thomas Spencer of Sheffield, with whom also the notices of this family in many public and private collections of Yorkshire genealogies commence. I am not aware that any thing has since been done to establish the point which came recommended with strong presumptions to the York herald[2]. And where Owen left it there I must be con-tent to leave it too, only observing that in the Act of Resumption, 4 Edw. IV. 1464, an exception is made in respect of a grant from the crown to a William Spen-cer of ten pounds *per annum*, to be received by him out of that one half of the church of Rotherham which belonged to the crown[3].

The first named William Spencer in the following pedigree, son of Thomas Spencer of Sheffield, made his will in 1620, describing himself of Bramley-grange, gentleman. By that will he gives to his eldest son lands at Bramley-grange, Bramley, Micklebring, Co-nisborough, Carbrook, Masborough, and Rotherham, but makes no mention of lands at Attercliffe.

Owen's pedigree may be found in Harl. MSS. 1067.

[1] *Account, &c.* 284—288.
[2] The published accounts of the great house of Spencer do not afford the means of showing the connexion of those of that name who have resided in the parish of Sheffield, and the line from which descend the dukes of Marlborough, and the earls Spencer. Nor yet with Edmund Spenser. The words of Gibbon will be long remembered: ' The nobility of the Spencers has been illustrated and enriched by the trophies of Marlborough, but I exhort them to consider the Fairy Queen as the most precious jewel of their coronet.' Spenser was indisputably of the North-amptonshire family. At this alliance he modestly hints in the dedication of ' The tears of the Muses ' to the Lady Strange, wife of Ferdinando then Lord Strange, afterwards earl of Derby, and daughter to Sir John Spencer of Althorpe; ' some private bands of affinity, which it hath pleased your ladyship to acknowledge.' Much obscurity still rests on the extraction and early history of this great poet, which is the more ex-traordinary as it is plain from several of his writings that he was a reader and lover of history and family antiquities. I conjecture that it was in studies of this nature connected with his own family that he met with the name of *Una:* for it appears that Elizabeth Lady Spenser, wife of Sir Philip Spenser, was a daughter of Robert Tiptoft; and that Sir Robert Tiptoft knight married a lady who bore the name of *Una*. These per-sons were all buried together in the Grey Friers at Ipswich. See Weever, 750.
[3] Rolls of Parliament, vol. v. p. 553.

PEDIGREE of SPENCER of ATTERCLIFFE-HALL and BRAMLEY-GRANGE.

ARMS.—Azure, a fess wavy ermine between six sea-mews' heads erased argent.
CREST.—On a wreath a rock proper and thereon a sea-mew also proper.

THOMAS SPENCER of Sheffield, ===== dau. of ---- came out of Northamptonshire. | Hatfield of Yorkshire.

| THOMAS SPENCER died without issue. | WILLIAM SPENCER of Bramley-grange, gent. Made his will 6 Jan. 1620. Bur. at Braithwell 6 June 1624. | ANNE, dau. of ---- Stanforth of Tinsley. Married at Sheffield 4 Aug. 1583. Living 1620. | ROSE SPENCER, bap. at Sheffield 6 May 1565. Mar. there 25 Oct. 1590 to Nicholas Parkin. | ROBERT and JOHN SPENcerbrothers, legatees in the will of William Spencer. | RICHARD SPENcer of Sheffield. A legatee in the will of William Spencer. |

| WILLIAM SPENCER of Attercliffe, gent., eldest son and heir. Lord of the manor of Darnall. Bap. at Sheffield 23 June 1584. Died 19 April 1649, and was buried in the chancel of the parish-church of Sheffield. == ALICE, dau. of James Mitchell of Morthing, gent. Buried at Sheffield 10 Oct. 1644. | GEORGE SPENCER of Newhall-grange, gent., second son. Had lands at Tickhill by his father's will. By his wife, the daughter of ---- Brownell, he had one son named George, and five daughters, Catherine, Alice, Anne, Mary, and Elizabeth. | THOMAS SPENCER of Hooton-Levet, in the parish of Maltby, where he had lands by his father's will: third and youngest son. He had five children, William, Thomas, John, Margaret, and Jane, from whom descended many persons of this name in the neighbourhood of Maltby. |

| ELIZABETH, first wife, dau. of Leonard Gill of Sheffield and Norton, gent. Married at Norton 30 Oct. 1634. Bur. in the church of Norton 14 June 1636, with an only dau. named Elizabeth, who died in her infancy. == WILLIAM SPENCER of Attercliffe and Bramley-grange, esq. A lieut.-colonel in the parliament army, and a justice of the peace during the Commonwealth. Bap. at Sheffield 31 January 1613. Buried there 28 Dec. 1667. == SARAH, 2d wife, dau. of Geo. Westby of Gilthwaite and Ravenfield, gent. Bur. at Sheffield 12 January 1669. | MICHAEL SPENCER of London, gent., 2d son, who by Elizabeth his wife, dau. of Richard Taylor alderman of Chesterfield, had a dau. named Elizabeth, the only survivor of their children in 1650. | JOHN SPENCER of Attercliffe, gent., third son. Mar. at Eckington 15 Feb. 1641 to Anne, dau. of Richard Taylor aforesaid, by whom he had one dau. named Anne. He was buried in the church of St. Peter at Norwich 8 Jan. 1665[1]. | ANNE SPENCER, married at Sheffield 27 August 1628 to James Bright; and after his decease to John Dawson of Misterton co. Notts. | MARGARET SPENCER, married at Sheffield 17 May 1630 to Ralph Fretwell of Hellaby near Bramley-grange, gent. | MARY SPENcer, mar. at Sheffield 21 Feb. 1655 to Andrew Morewood of the Hallows in the parish of Dronfield, gent. |

| WILLIAM SPENcer of Attercliffe, gent., son and heir. Bap. at Braithwell 20 Jan. 1641. His will was proved at York by Elizabeth his relict 11 Feb. 1691. == ELIZABETH. She is supposed to have been a Hatfield of that name at Laughton-en-le-Morthen. | JOHN SPENCER, second son, bap. July 1644. — SAMUEL SPENCER, third son, bap. 5 July 1646. Died 28 Feb. 1647. Buried in the chapel of Bramley. | SAMUEL SPENCER, fourth son, bap. Jan. 1649. Probably he settled at Worksop, where a Sam[l] Spencer gent. was living in 1687, and had a son of his own name. | JOSEPH SPENCER, THOMAS SPENCER, 5th and 6th sons, both died infants. | SARAH SPENCER, bap. at Sheffield 6 March 1638. Mar. there 15 Dec. 1664 to John Wordsworth of Swatheball near Barnsley, gent. | FAITH SPENCER, bap. at Sheffield 6 Jan. 1639. Married there 24 July 1656 to Samuel Child of the Holmes near Leeds, gent., and was buried at Sheffield 14 Jan. 1667. | HANNAH, bap. 20 Nov. 1642. | MARY, bap. 19 May 1654. Feb. 1665. |

| WILLIAM SPENCER, eldest son and heir-apparent. Born 8 Oct. 1667, bap. at Sheffield 20th. Bur. there 21 Nov. 1673. | THOMAS SPENCER of Attercliffe and Bramley-grange, gent., 2d son and heir. Bap. at Sheffield 3 April 1670. Buried there 21 June 1703. == ELIZABETH, dau. of William Fairfax of Steeton, co. York, esq., (by Catherine his wife, dau. of Robert Stapleton of Wighill, esq.) son and heir of Sir William Fairfax, who was slain at the siege of Montgomery-castle 1644. Buried at Sheffield 2 Aug. 1708. | TERTIUS SPENCER, born 8 Nov.1671. Bap. at Sheffield 12th. | QUARTUS SPENCER, born 14 July 1674. Bap. at Sheffield 20th. | QUINTUS SPENCER, born 18 Jan. 1676. Bap. at Sheffield 30th. | SEXTUS SPENCER, born 26 July 1680. Bap. at Sheffield 18th Aug. A divine. | ELIZABETH SPENCER, born 13 Jan. 1676. Bap. at Sheffield 16th. |

WILLIAM SPENCER of Bramley-grange, esq., son and heir. == MARGARET, dau. and heir of Henry Eyre of Bramley-hall, esq., by Sarah his wife, sister and co-heir of John Bolles of Thorpe-hall, co. Linc. esq. Married at Wickersley 4 Dec. 1726. Died a widow in Sept. 1745, at the age of 47, and was buried at Braithwell.

| HENRY-EYRE SPENCER, eldest son, bap. 23 Aug. 1727. Died without issue. Lost at sea. | WILLIAM SPENCER of Bramley-grange, esq., bap. 28 May 1731. Died in 1790, and was buried in the parish-church of Sheffield. == FRANCES, dau. of William Milner of Burton-grange, esq. Died at Bramley-grange 15 Sept. 1815, and was buried with her husband. | THOMAS CHARLES SPENCER, third son, bap. 7 Jan. 1735. | MARGARET SPENcer, bap. 7 Mar. 1729. Married Edward Elwick of Wakefield. | ELIZABETH SPENcer, twin with Margaret, bap. 7 March 1729. Died unmarried. | SARAH SPENCER, bap. 11 May 1733. Wife first of Thomas Foljambe of Aldwark, esq., and secondly of Edmund Hutchinson of Bath, gent., son of Simon Hutchinson of Ripon, co. York. |

| WILLIAM SPENCER of Bramley-grange, esq., eldest son and heir. Lord of the manor of Darnall, and a lieutenant-general in the army 1819. == CHARLOTTE, dau. of John Swann esq. | HENRY SPENCER, second son, Capt. in the 43d regiment. Died unmarried at Guadaloupe in May 1794. | FRANCES SPENCER. | MARGARET SPENCER. |

CARBROOK.

This village consists of a very few houses, one of which was the residence of a family of whom frequent mention has been made in this work.

In the time of Elizabeth it belonged to Richard Fenton, who sent one man and horse to the annual assembly in the Wicker. But before the close of that reign Thomas Bright, who had before that time resided at Bradway, a hamlet of the parish of Norton, was living here.

[1] His monumental inscription is preserved by Blomefield. 'Here lyeth the body of John Spencer of Attercliffe in the county of York, gent., who was the third son of William Spencer of the same towne and county, gent., who was baptized the 4th of November 1619, and here interred the 8 of January 1665'—with the arms. *Hist. of Norfolk*, ii. 635. In 1808 this inscription was not to be found. So true it is that the pages of a topographer outlast the monumental brass.

PEDIGREE of BRIGHT of CARBROOK and BADSWORTH.

ARMS.—Parti per pale azure and gules, a bend or between two mullets argent[1].
CREST.—On a wreath or and argent a sun issuing from behind clouds all proper.

THOMAS BRIGHT of Bradway in the parish of Norton, and of Carbrook, yeoman. Buried at Sheffield 28 April 1616. = JOAN ..... survived, and had administration of her husband's effects 1616.

JANE, first wife, dau. of Geo. Westby of Whaleyco Derb. gent., sister to Geo. Westby of Ravenfield and Gilthwaite, gent. Mar. at Sheffield 25 Sept. 1610. Bur. there 11 Nov. 1633. At the time of her marriage she was widow of - - - - Smales.	STEPHEN BRIGHT of Carbrook, gent. eldest son and heir. Bailiff of Hallamshire and lord of the manor of Ecclesall. Bap. at Norton 27 June 1642, and was buried in the chancel of the parish-church of Sheffield.	BARBARA, 2d wife, dau. of Ralph Hatfield of Laughton-en-le-Morthen, gent. by Margaret his wife, dau. of Robert Mirfield of Thurcroft, gent. Bap. 25 May 1614. Mar. at Laughton 4 Nov. 1635.	THOMAS WESTBY second son, died an infant.	ROBERT BRIGHT second son, died field, esq., 2d husband. A 3d son, of Sheffield, mercer, bap. the peace at Norton 24 Aug. &c. in the 1692. Died without issue, and was buried at Sheffield 18 Aug. 1653.	JOHN BRIGHT M.A. vicar of Sheffield, 4th son, bap. at Norton 7 Jan. 1594-5. Bur. at Sheffield 23 April 1643.	JOAN dau. of Smales Whaley aforesaid.	DYONISIA BRIGHT, only dau. bap. at Norton 4 Aug. 1581, mar. there on the feast-day of St. Bartholomew 1601 to John Parker of Norton-Lees, esquire. Died without issue, and was buried at Norton 26 Sept. 1604.
	ELIZABETH BRIGHT, bap. at Sheffield 12 May 1637. Bur. there 21st inst. — HANNAH BRIGHT, bap. at Sheffield 18 April 1638. Died unmar.	MARTHA BRIGHT, youngest dau. bap. at Sheffield 30 Jan. 1639-40. Married William Drake of Thornton and Middop in Craven, esq. Died without issue, and was bur. at Sheffield 9 Sept. 1663.	STEPHEN BRIGHT, eldest son, bap. at Sheffield 25 Dec. 1635. Went abroad and never returned. — JOHN BRIGHT, 2d son, bap. at Sheffield 30 Nov. 1637. Died in his infancy.	JOHN BRIGHT of Leeds, esq. One of the lords of the manor of Leeds. Bap. at Sheffield 21 Sept. 1642. Died without issue.	ELLEN, dau. of William Bagnal of Bury-hill, co. Staff. gent., widow of John Metcalf of Leeds, mercer.	RUTH BRIGHT, only dau. bap. at Sheffield 1 Nov. 1640. Heir to her brother, and mar. to Thomas Dixon esq. of Little-Woodhouse near Leeds, an alderman of that borough, and twice mayor.

THOMAS, STEPHEN, and SARAH, died in their infancy.	CATHERINE, first wife, dau. of Sir Richard Hawksworth of Hawksworth knight, relict of Will. Lister of Thornton in Craven, esq., who was slain at Tadcaster 7 Dec. 1642.	ELIZABETH second wife, dau. of Thomas Norcliffe of Langton co. York, knt.	Sir JOHN BRIGHT bart., of Carbrook and Badsworth. Lord of the manor of Ecclesall. A col. in the parliament army. Baptized at Sheffield 14 Oct. 1619. Died at Badsworth 13 Sept. 1688, and was buried there.	FRANCES, third wife, dau. of Sir Thomas Liddell of Ravensworth-castle, esq. She survived, and took to her second husband Sir John Newton of Bar's-court near Bath, bart.	SUSANNA, fourth wife, dau. of Michael Wharton of Beverley, esq. Died without issue. Thomas Vane of Raby-castle, esq.	MARY BRIGHT, bap. 8 Nov. 1614. Married there 1 Feb. 1630-1 to William Jessop of Broom-hall, esq.	RUTH BRIGHT, bap. at Sheffield 6 Feb. 1617-8. Married there 23 Sept. 1633 to Edward Gill of Carhouse, esquire.

- - - - BRIGHT, first son. Died in his infancy.	JOHN BRIGHT of Badsworth esq., son and heir-apparent, aged 6, 1666. Died without issue in the life-time of his father.	Lady LUCY MONTAGUE, dau. of Edward earl of Manchester.	Sir HENRY LIDDELL of Ravensworth-castle in the bishoprick of Durham, the third baronet of his family. Died 1 Sept. 1723, and is bur. at Kensington.	CATHERINE BRIGHT, only surviving dau. and heir. Buried at Kensington 24 Feb. 1703.	DOROTHY BRIGHT, sole issue of the second nuptials. Living 1666. Died young.

THOMAS LIDDELL, son and heir-apparent. Died before his father 1715.	JANE, dau. of James Clavering of Greencroft in Durham, esq.	JOHN LIDDELL-BRIGHT of Badsworth, esquire, second son. Assumed the name of Bright on becoming principal heir to his grandfather. Died 6 Oct. 1737.	CORDELIA CLUTTERBUCK of Hydes, co. Essex.	HENRY LIDDELL, 3d son. On whom Carbrook was settled. Died without issue.	ANNE, dau. of John Clavering of Chopwell in Durham, esq.	GEORGE and MICHAEL died unmarried.	ELIZABETH LIDDELL, wife of Robert Ellison of Hebburn in Durham.

HENRY Lord RAVENSWORTH of Ravensworth-castle, so created 29 June 1747. Died without male issue 1 Feb. 1784, when the peerage became extinct.	ANNE, only dau. of Sir Peter Delmé, married Apr. 1739. Died in June 1794, aged 81.	THOMAS LIDDELL, dau. of William Bowes of Gibside, knight.	MARGARET and CATHERINE died young.	JAMES	THOMAS BRIGHT of Badsworth, esquire. Lord of the manor of Ecclesall.	MARGARET, dau. and heir of William Norton of Sawley esq. by Margaret his wife, sister and co-heir of John Lowther of Ackworth esq. She re-married 1748 Sir John Ramsden of Byrom, bart.	CORDELIA, wife of Clifton Winington of York, M.D.	STEPHEN, JOHN, HENRY, ANNE, CATHERINE, all died young or unmarried.

AUGUSTUS-HENRY Duke of GRAFTON, first lord. Married 29 Jan. 1756.	ANNE LIDDELL, only daughter and heir.	JOHN Earl of UPPER Ossory, second lord. Died in 1818.	Sir HENRY-GEORGE LIDDELL of Ravensworth-castle, 5th baronet. Died Nov. 1791.	ELIZABETH, dau. of - - - Steel esq., of Hampstead.	MARY BRIGHT, sole dau. and heir, married 26 Feb. 1752 to the most noble CHARLES Marquis of ROCKINGHAM, and died without issue at Hillingdon-house near Uxbridge.

Sir John Bright is the only person of his family who entered a pedigree at the visitations of the heralds. He appeared before Sir William Dugdale in 1666, and gave an account to his grandfather; but such was his indifference to the subject that the grandfather appears without any designation of rank, marriage, or place of abode. He is to be found in the register of Norton. He lived at Bradway, where his son the vicar of Sheffield was born. The proximity of this village to Ecclesall and the purchase of the manor

[1] These arms and crest are what the French call armes parlant. The shield being parti per pale azure and gules, was intended to represent morning and evening, and each has its bright star. So says Sylvanus Morgan in his Armilogia, p. 148.

3 s

made by his son at least authorize a supposition that he was of the same stock from which proceeded so many families of the name in that western part of the parish; and more laborious or more fortunate inquirers may hereafter discover the connexion which existed among them. This Thomas Bright left Bradway, and spent the latter part of his life at Carbrook where he died.

Stephen Bright was much employed by the earl of Arundel in the management of his great concerns at Sheffield. He so improved his own estate, that in the 17 Charles I. he had a grant of arms from Sir John Burrough, Garter, as ' a person of 1000l. a year estate, of credit and respect in the affections of the gentry, and of extraordinary merit.' He died in 1642, just before the breaking out of the civil wars in which his son Sir John took such an interested part.

Sir John Bright was about three-and-twenty at the death of his father. We find his name subscribed to the protestation of the gentlemen of the county of York against the king's declared intention of raising forces in the county without the concurrence of parliament[1]. This was in May 1642; and when the king proceeded to take decisive measures against those who opposed him, Bright was the most active in the neighbourhood of Sheffield to raise companies for the parliament-service, and did raise several, receiving a captain's commission from the Lord Fairfax. We find him named as a commissioner for the west riding in the ordinance of parliament dated 1 April 1643, for ' sequestering the estates of notorious delinquents[2].' He thus engaged himself deeply and earnestly in the cause.

In the account of the military transactions of the times we first meet with him in the attack which was made on the head-quarters of the earl of Newcastle at Wakefield, in May 1643, when the earl was lying about Sheffield and Chesterfield with the greater part of his army. He acquitted himself in this affair to the satisfaction of his general, who soon after made him a colonel of foot. Captain John Hodgson who served under him five or six years says of him, ' He was but young when he first had the command; but he grew very valiant and prudent, and had his officers and soldiers under good conduct[3].'

Colonel Bright accompanied Sir Thomas Fairfax in his Cheshire expedition, and was commonly with him till he joined the confederated armies before York. The battle of Marston-moor soon ensued, and the royal cause in the north of England received a fatal blow. It was fought in July 1644.

Many fortresses which were garrisoned for the king surrendered to the victorious army; and amongst others the castle of Sheffield, of which colonel Bright was appointed governor; but he soon resigned the command to his brother-in-law Captain Edward Gill, seeking for himself a more important service.

On the 23d of December 1644 we have an account of an attack which he made with his regiment of horse on a party of the king's forces under Sir William Cobb in which he was successful; and in the next year he was one of the four colonels nominated by the besieging army to treat for the surrender of Pontefract-cas-

tle which had been bravely defended. It was given up on the 21st of July 1645. The castle of Scarborough surrendered on the 25th. The garrison of Skipton expecting they must next fall, dispatched their horse to Newark. A troop of colonel Bright's met with a party of them on the 28th, killed several, and took Sir Charles Howard of Naworth prisoner, together with some officers and private men.

The cause of the parliament was now every where triumphant, and negotiations began to succeed to rougher contentions. Had the politicians of the time been as enlightened and sincere as the officers were brave, the monarchy of England might have been at that period restored with those just limitations which were established at the Revolution. Colonel Bright continued to serve under Cromwell in Scotland, and at the second siege of Pontefract-castle, which the royalists had recovered by an ingenious but desperate stratagem. While this siege was going on, Sir Marmaduke Langdale appeared for the king, when Colonel Bright was sent to secure Carlisle; and soon after we find him in treaty for the surrender of Pontefract-castle, a treaty in which it must have been painful to a man of feeling to engage, when he had to require and finally to demand that six unnamed of that little brave garrison should be excepted from mercy. In 1650 he was in Cromwell's army marching into Scotland; but when it arrived at Newcastle he threw up his commission in disgust, having solicited a fortnight's leave of absence to settle his affairs at home, and been refused.

During the Commonwealth, Colonel Bright was one of the six representatives in parliament of the west riding, and an active member of various committees in the country. He was at one time governor of York, and also governor of Hull, two important stations. He served the office of high-sheriff of the county of York for two successive years, 1654 and 1655. An incident which occurred during his shrievalty, and which shows that hoaxing is not a new folly, I do not recollect to have seen noticed in any printed work. I copy from a manuscript which seems to have been part of the collections of Francis Hildyard, the York antiquary.

' 1656.—The 5 October; by virtue of a letter whereunto the hand of John Bright esquire, sheriff of Yorkshire and governor of Hull, his hand was forged and directed to the deputy governor Major Elton, who upon receipt thereof by the post sent for and secured John Lord Viscount Dunbarr, Sir Thomas Remmington, Sir Robert Hilyard, Sir Matthew Appleyard, John Anlaby, Durand Hotham esquire, Mr. Christopher Brodripp and Mr. William Dalton, at the garrison at Hull, where alsoe Capt. John Overton of the castle, and Major Waterhouse who commanded the South blockhouse at Hull, were turned out of their commands. But the high-sheriff upon notice hereof came to Hull, where he acknowledged the abuse, set the gentlemen secured at liberty in 48 hours of their restraint, and reinvested the commanders of the castle and blockhouse into their charge again. There are other gentlemen alsoe secured in other garrisons upon the same forgery, as Mr. Henry and Mr. Richard Day at York, Sir Francis Boynton, Sir Thomas Norcliffe, and Mr. Walter Paler, at Scarborough, but upon the discovery they alsoe had their enlargement.'

The turn which public affairs took was a great disappointment to those gentlemen who had engaged in the contest with the pure and honest intention of so

[1] Hurtley's *Malham*, App. p. 36.
[2] *Collection of Acts and Ordinances*, folio, 1646, p. 13.
[3] *Memoirs of Captain John Hodgson*, p. 103.

Carbrook Hall & Chimney-Piece.

limiting the royal prerogative as to give additional stability to the throne and security to the people. Colonel Bright may be presumed to have concurred in the measures for bringing about the Restoration; for we find that as early as the 16th of July 1660 he was admitted into the order of baronets, having been previously knighted. His name does not however appear among the actors on that occasion.

From this time he seems to have led a retired life; residing occasionally on his paternal inheritance at Carbrook, but more commonly at Badsworth where he had purchased a considerable estate. He was one of the twelve capital burgesses of Sheffield, and we find him occasionally present at the meetings of the body. He did not wholly give up his principles on the change of the times, and from his patronage of some of the ejected ministers we may conclude that he did not concur in the harsh measures which were adopted by the king's ministry. By four marriages into families of equal or superior rank, and of his own county, he surrounded himself with valuable connexions, and managing his estate with a just economy he passed the remainder of his days in wealth, esteem, and honour. For the last two years of his life he suffered under the tortures of the stone, a disease which in its more violent forms seems to have been more prevalent formerly than now. He was released by death on the 13th of September 1688, but a few weeks before a change, which this old parliamentarian would have been amongst the first to hail and welcome. He was honoured with a magnificent funeral at the church of Badsworth. In the sermon which Mr. Hunter delivered on the occasion a high character was given of him; and in that church a handsome monument still perpetuates his memory. The inscription being wholly genealogical, it seems unnecessary to insert it here, especially as it may be found in the *Ducatus Leodiensis*.

The only son of Sir John Bright died before him. He married the Lady Lucy Montague, daughter of Edward earl of Manchester, a marriage which does not appear in the published accounts of that noble family. There was no issue. Catherine Bright the only daughter and heiress of Sir John married Sir Henry Liddell of Ravensworth-castle in Durham, baronet, whose younger children the estates of the family were settled. Badsworth and the manor of Bright were given to John Liddell the second son, who assumed the name of Bright. This practice, so common in these times, and to which it seems we must owe the preservation of the ancient and respected surnames of this kingdom, was then rare. The name of Wortley had been taken by one of the house of Montague a little before, but I am not acquainted with another instance in the west riding of the county of York during the seventeenth century.

The estate of Carbrook was settled on the third son of Sir Henry Liddell and Dame Catherine his wife, by fine levied in 1699. This Henry Liddell esquire died without issue, and left Carbrook to his wife Anne Liddell. This lady was the daughter of John Clavering of Chopwell in Durham by Susan his wife, sister to Edward Thompson esquire, of Marston near York. By her last will and testament she bequeathed her es-

tates at Carbrook to Mrs. Mary Whetham wife of General Whetham, a daughter of the said Edward Thompson. This lady entered into possession, and by her will bearing date the 6th of March 1770 she gave this estate to Oliver Tilson of Hill-street in the parish of Saint George Hanover-square esquire, and Francis Barlow of Essex-street in the Strand esquire, in trust for the use of her son John Whetham and the heirs male of his body; in default of such issue, to her daughter Lucy-Anne Whetham for life and to her children male or female. In default of such issue, to the daughters of the said testator's son John Whetham. In default, to her god-daughter Miss Lucy Sotheron, daughter of her nephew William Sotheron of Darrington esquire, who was son of William Sotheron esquire by another daughter of the aforementioned Edward Thompson esquire, and the heirs male of her body. In default, to her niece Anne Apthorpe daughter of Stephen Apthorpe D.D. and Fellow of Eton College, by Frances his wife, another daughter of Edward Thompson of Marston, and the heirs male of her body. In default, to all and every the younger children of her nephew William Sotheron and the heirs of their bodies. In default, to the right heirs.

John Whetham of Kirklington esquire, the son of the testator, died without issue; and so also did her daughter Lucy-Anne Whetham, who became the wife of Colonel Byron. At her decease Carbrook became the property of Miss Lucy Sotheron; and Miss Apthorpe having died unmarried, the brother and sisters of Miss Lucy Sotheron, namely Admiral Frank Sotheron, Mrs. Elizabeth Sinclair, Miss Mary-Catherine Sotheron, and Mrs. Henrietta Dealtry, wife of the Rev. William Dealtry, joined in taking the legal steps necessary to bar the contingent remainders[1].

The hall at Carbrook, like the hall at Attercliffe, has been deserted by its owners for more than a century, but it still retains traces of its former consequence. It seems to have been built by Stephen Bright in the reign of James I.

DARNALL.

This village and a small territory around it claims to be a manor of itself. It is not mentioned in Domesday-book, nor in the *Nomina Villarum* 9 Edward II. In this respect it resembles Ecclesall, Owlerton, and Wadsley, other manors in the neighbourhood. Darnall is mentioned in the list of the *Membra castri de Sheffield*.

Like Ecclesall and other places, it may have been one of the early subinfeudations of the great baron of Sheffield. A William de Darnall witnessed Furnival's grant; but I have before had occasion to observe that almost every village and hamlet throughout Hallamshire had some family deriving from it their surname, and who never made pretensions to manorial rights. And respecting the family of De Darnall it may be observed, that we do not find them among the gentry of the reign of Henry III. in that curious and very complete catalogue in the Antiquarian Repertory, where the chiefs of the houses of Ecclesall, Wadsley, Wortley, and Mounteney all appear.

In the time of Elizabeth, Robert Wainwright and Nicholas Trippett were engaged in a suit at law with

[1] For these particulars the author is much indebted to his friend the Rev, William Dealtry of Wigginton near York.

Anthony Roberts, who had bought of them one moiety of the manor of Darnall[1]. By indenture bearing date the 15th of February 16 Charles I. 1641, Richard Wainwright of Dungworth in the chapelry of Bradfield conveyed one moiety of this manor to William Spencer of Attercliffe-hall gentleman, for the sum of 700*l.*[2] Whether he acquired the other moiety before or after does not appear; but he held his court-baron for this manor in 1645, and it has descended entire to his lineal heir male and representative William Spencer of Bramley-grange esquire.

Darnall is inhabited for the most part by agriculturists and persons engaged in the collieries, or the different departments of the Sheffield manufactures. An attempt was made many years ago to establish a glass manufactory, but the scheme did not succeed.

The principal freeholders of this small manor were the families of Chappell and Staniforth. From the former the wood called Chappell-wood has its name. Several of this family were in the profession of the law at Sheffield. The name has been long extinct, nor have materials for a pedigree fallen into my hands.

The Staniforths are still here; and have a capital mansion in the heart of the village, which was built in 1723 by the father of the present inhabitant. They are a rare instance of a Hallamshire family residing upon lands possessed by their ancestor of the reign of Richard II. They might be here much earlier; but from that period there is a regular succession of family evidences, establishing the following pedigree.

PEDIGREE of STANIFORTH of DARNALL, &c.

ARMS.—Erminois, on a fess wavy gules 3 lions rampant argent.

THOMAS DE STANYFORD of Darnall. Living there 13 Ric. II. and 3 Hen. IV.

WILLIAM DE STANYFORD of Darnall, 13 Ric. II. and 3 Hen. IV. Died without issue. — JOHN DE STANYFORD of Darnall, 3 and 12 Hen. IV. when he had a grant of lands from Geffery Lowther esq. — ---- sister to the wife of John Smyth. Deed of partition of lands between Stanyford and Smyth 12 Hen. IV. — RICHARD DE STANYFORD of Attercliffe, 3 Hen. IV.[3]

JOHN STANIFORTH of Darnall, son of John, 1 and 3 Hen. IV. Called *senior* in 20 Hen. VI.

JOHN STANIFORTH.

AGNES BIRLEY, first wife. Divorced 6 Aug. 1450. — JOHN STANIFORTH of Darnall, yeoman, 12 and 28 Hen. VI. and 12 Edw. IV. Will dated 1 May 1481. — MARGARET, second wife. Survived and was executrix to her husband's will. — WILLIAM STANIFORTH. Deed 4 Dec. 3 Hen. VII. respecting lands at Attercliffe.

THOMAS STANIFORTH, 1481.   RICHARD STANIFORTH, 1481.   JOAN STANIFORTH, Executrix to her father's will.   CATHERINE STANIFORTH, 1481.

THOMAS STANIFORTH = MARGARET.   JOHN STANIFORTH of Darnall, = JOAN, dau. of Roger cutler, 31 Hen. VIII.   Fretwell of Maltby.

LAURENCE STANIFORTH of Darnall. Dead before 1590.

JOHN STANIFORTH of Darnall, yeoman, son and heir, bap. at Sheffield 28 Jan. 1571[4]. Made his will 16 June 1630, and he died soon after, being interred at Sheffield 11 Oct. 1630. — JANE, dau. of Richard Lewys, sister to Samuel Lewys of Thorp-Audline co. York. Of the family of Lewys of Marr, whose pedigree may be seen in *Duc. Leod.* p. 243. Died at Carbead and was buried at Silkston 2 May 1632.   NICHOLAS STANIFORTH.   MARY STANIFORTH.

JOHN STANIFORTH of Darnall, gent., son and heir. A principal agent of the earl of Arundel. Executor to his father's will 1630. Buried 27 Aug 1661. — MARY. Survived and made her will 13 Oct. 1676. Supposed to be a dau. of Stanley Gower rector of Brampton-Bryan, &c.   WILLIAM STANIFORTH of Hull, 1630. Dead before 1 Aug. 1633.   ANNE, 1630 and 1633.   DOROTHY, wife of George Pearson, 1630 and 1633.   MARY, wife of Michael Hyley of Attercliffe, 1630 and 1633.

JOHN STANIFORTH of Darnall, gent., bap. at Sheffield 18 Sept. 1636. Married 1686. Will dated 11 March 1700, and he was bur. 12 Apr. 1704. — ELIZABETH, dau. of Thos. Wright vicar of Ecclesfield. Survived and was executrix to her husband's will. Her will dated 18 May 1715. Died 6 Dec. 1720, aged 71. — JOHN GRAMMER of Bakewell, gent., 2d husband. Married 1705. Had a son John Grammer by a former wife.   GRIFFITH STANIFORTH of Sheffield, 1676, second son.   WILLIAM STANIFORTH of Bakewell, 1676, third son.   MARK STANIFORTH of Leeds, 1676. Dead 1700. Supposed to be the person of this name who married Phœbe dau. of William Milner of Leeds, merchant. See *Duc. Leod.* p. 216.   MARY, wife of -- Dixon of Wakefield, by whom a son Staniforth Dixon, 1676.   SARAH, wife of -- Blake of Sheffield, by whom John-seph, Mary, and Charles.   RUTH, bap. at Sheffield 19 October 1651. Died 25 August 1668, and was buried in the church of Wakefield.

JOHN STANIFORTH, born 6 Feb. 1687, bap. at Sheffield 23, buried there 14 May 1697.   SAMUEL STANIFORTH of Darnall, esq. Made principal heir to his uncle John Staniforth, who directed in his last will that he should be educated under the direction of his aunt Elizabeth, at the University and Inns of Court. Bap. at Sheffield 26 Jan. 1689. Died 15 Nov. 1748, and was buried in the chapel-yard at Attercliffe. — ALETHEA, fifth dau. of Thomas Macro of Bury St. Edmunds, esquire, by Susan his wife, dau. and heir of John Cox, rector of Risby near Bury. Married at Bradfield 19 July 1722. Died 29 June 1750, aged 53, and was buried with her husband.   MARK STANIFORTH, bap. at Sheffield 12 March 1693.   WILLIAM STANIFORTH of Leeds, 1715, heir in remainder to Samuel Staniforth by will of his uncle John Staniforth.

[1] Calendar of Chancery Proceedings in the Tower.
[2] From the original conveyance among the charters in Wilson's Collections.
[3] A deed of this Richard Stanyford is important for the establishment of the first descents in the pedigree. It recites that in 3 Hen. IV. he granted to John de Staniforth his brother and John his son and the longer liver, a messuage and croft in Darnall, which he had of the feoffment of Thomas de Staniforth his father and William de Staniforth his brother, with a parcel of wood and meadow in Tinsley-park.
[4] A grant from George earl of Shrewsbury 1590 to Thomas Staniforth of Braithwell, of the custody and marriage of John son and heir of Laurence Staniforth of Darnall deceased.

a

THOMAS STANIFORTH of Liverpool, esquire.=ELIZABETH, dau. of An alderman and mayor of that borough. Bap. at Sheffield 24 April 1735. Dead. Had a grant of arms. | Charles Gore of Liverpool, merchant. | SAMUEL STANIFORTH of Darnall, esq., second son. Living unmarried 1819. | ELIZABETH, wife of John Trevers Younge of Sheffield, merchant. | MARY, wife of Thomas Younge of Sheffield, M.D. | Four sons died in their infancy.

SAMUEL STANIFORTH=--- dau. of of Liverpool, esq., son ---Little- and heir. An alder- dale, esq., man of that borough, of White- and mayor in 1813. haven. | ELIZABETH, wife of --- Hext of Cornwall, esq. | Other children died young or unmar. | JOHN, SAMUEL, and CHARLES YOUNGE, all now or late of Sheffield. | Four dau. | THOMAS YOUNGE of Sheffield, clerk, formerly of Peterhouse Cambridge. | WILLIAM YOUNGE of Sheffield M.D. One of the twelve capital burgesses of Sheffield. | ---YOUNGE, wife of William Warris of Sheffield, merchant.

Mr. John Staniforth obtained from the earl of Newcastle when he was at Sheffield in May 1643, a Protection in these terms:

'It is my expresse pleasure and command that no officers or soldiers of his Majesty's army under my command presume at any time hereafter to plunder, molest, or trouble the person, house, family, goods, or chattels of John Staniforth of Darnall in this county, without particular order and speciall warrant therein. And hereof none of them may fayle at theire perills. Given under my hand the XVIIIth day of May 1643. WIL. NEWCASTLE.'

Three or four small dwellings at Darnall are called

Mrs. Grammer's alms-houses. They were built by her to be inhabited by poor widows, to whom Mr. Staniforth of Liverpool makes a small yearly allowance in money and fuel.

The name of Staniforth has been very numerous in the parish of Sheffield; and in the township of Attercliffe-cum-Darnall there resided for several generations a family of the name, of whom it may be proper to insert two or three of the later descents. Possibly they sprung from the Richard Staniforth of Attercliffe in the preceding pedigree, but their immediate ancestors were of Wincobank in the parish of Ecclesfield.

JOHN STANIFORTH of Attercliffe, gent., son of John, son of William of the same place. Died 10 March 1765. Buried at Attercliffe. | =ELIZABETH, dau. of Henry Younge of Sheffield. Married 3 May 1715. Died 17 Jan. 1758, aged 67. Bur. at Attercliffe.

WILLIAM STANIFORTH of=MARY, only dau. and heir Sheffield, and afterwards of Cox Macro D.D. of Norof Norton near Bury St. ton and Little Haugh, co. Edmunds, esq. Born 4 Suffolk, chaplain to King Sept. 1717. Bap. 17 Oct. George I. and justice of Died 11 Nov. 1786. | the peace. Married 8 May 1767. Died without issue 16 Aug. 1775. Buried at Norton[1]. | JOHN STANI-=ANNE, dau. of FORTH of Rev. John Dos- Manchester, sie, vicar of Bap. 20 Apr. Sheffield. Sur- 1726. vived and remarried John Sherburn of Sheffield, gent. | ROBERT STANIFORTH of=CATHERINE, Manchester, third son. dau. of Rev. Bap. 7 April 1727, and John Dossie, of Little Haugh after the vicar of Shef- death of his brother Wil- field. liam Staniforth. | ANNE, wife of John Al- lott of Sheffield. | Other children died in their infancy.

JOHN PATTESON of=JANE STANIFORTH, only dau. and heir, Norwich, esquire, heir also to her uncle William Stanilate member of par- forth, from whom she inherited Norton liament for that and other property of the family of city. Macro.

JOHN STANIFORTH PATTESON, mar. Ann-Elizabeth Tasker. | ROBERT DOSSIE, capt. in the 6th regt. of foot: killed at Fort Erie in America. | ELIZABETH. | MARTHA. | CATHERINE-SOPHIA. | WILLIAM-FREDERICK.

[1] By the death of this lady without issue, the Wilsons of Broomhead and the Staniforths of Darnall became co-heirs of the name and blood of Macro, as will appear from the subjoined pedigree, which was for the most part compiled by the late Mr. Wilson, whose mother was a Macro.

THOMAS MACRO of Bury St. Edmunds,=SUSAN. several times alderman or chief magi- Died 27 April 1713, strate of Bury. Died 27 Sept. 1701, aged 88. aged 86. See Nichols's *Literary Anecdotes*, ix. 359. His will bears date 4 April 1701.

THOMAS MACRO of Bury St. Edmunds,=SUSAN, only dau. and heir of John Cox clerk, rector of Risby esquire. Five times chief magistrate of near Bury, by Susan his wife, dau. of John Alliott rector of Bury. Died 26 May 1737, aged 88, and Little Thurlow co. Suff. and sister to Anne wife of Charles Wilwas buried in the church of St. James son vicar of Sheffield. Which John Cox was grandson of Richin that town. ard Cox through of Ely.—She was born 3 Aug. 1660. Married 9 Jan. 1678. Died 29 April 1743, and was buried in St. James's church Bury. | MARY, wife of Sir --- wife of --- Cox, Isaac Rebow of by whom she had a Colchester, knt., son Thomas Cox, and M.P. for that who was beyond sea borough. Mar. in in 1701, when his Dec. 1685. grandfather made his will.

COX MACRO,D.D.=MARY, dau. of of Norton and Lit- Edward Godfrey tle Haugh co. esq. of King's-Suff. Chaplain to street Golden-King George I. square London. and justice of the Under-treasu-peace. Died in Feb. rer to his pre-or March 1767, sent majesty aged 84, and was when Prince of buried at Norton. Wales. Died 31 See *Lit. Anec.* ix. Aug. 1753, and 359. was buried at Norton. | RALPH MACRO,D.D. preacher at the Rolls and King's chaplain. Died at Bath, and was bur. there 19 Oct. 1728. | THOMAS=ELIZA-MACRO,an BETH, the Cold-stream Guards regt. of 1720; and coigne. afterwards Married a captain 1736. in General Columbine's regt. Died in 1739. | SUSAN MACRO, eldest dau. Died unmarried '24 Sept. 1730, aged 45. ELIZABETH MACRO, third dau. Died unmarried 5 Mar. 1767, aged 80. Both buried in Saint James's church Bury. | MARY MACRO, 2d dau. born 1688. Mar. her cousin John Wilson of Broomhead esquire. | ANNE MACRO, 4th dau., wife of Thomas Stewart of Whepstead co. Suff. gent., by whom she had a son Thomas S. of Bury, surgeon, and Susan. Mar. 9 Feb. 1720. Died in Sept. 1750. | ALETHEA MACRO, fifth dau. married in 1722 Sam¹ Staniforth of Darnall, and died in June 1750. | ISABELLA MACRO, sixth and youngest dau. Died unmarried 12 Sept. 1771, aged 67, and was buried in St. James's church Bury.

EDWARD MACRO of London, esquire, only son and heir-apparent. Died unmarried in his father's life-time April 1766, and was buried at St. George's Hanover square. | MARY MACRO on the death of her brother, sole heir, married 8 May 1767 to William Staniforth of Sheffield, and in her right of Norton, esquire, and died without issue 16 Aug. 1775. See *Lit. Anec.* ix. 366. | JOHN WILSON of Broomhead, esq. The antiquary. | THOMAS STANI-FORTH of Liverpool, esquire. | SAMUEL STANI-FORTH, now of Darnall.

3 T

The capital mansion of the Staniforths was built by Mr. Samuel Staniforth in the year 1723, and it is remarked by Mr. Wilson that this large house was finished in the space of one year. After the death of Mr. and Mrs. Staniforth, and the removal of their eldest son to Liverpool, it was for some time the residence of Henry Howard esquire, father to his grace the duke of Norfolk. The birth in this house of Edward Charles Howard (the youngest son of Mr. Henry Howard), a young but distinguished Fellow of the Royal Society, honourably connects it and the village in which it stands with the history of modern science and the arts.

At Darnall resided for many generations a respectable but not opulent family whose name was Chaloner or Chalner. It ended in a maiden lady who died about fifty years ago. Of this family it has been supposed was one of the two Chaloners, whose names appear in the list of persons nominated for the trial of King Charles I. What remain of the family papers throw no light upon this point, neither indeed do they on another subject which has been much canvassed in and out of the parish, connected with that tribunal.

After the Restoration there retired to this his native village a person named William Walker. He continued to reside here till the year 1700, when he died, and was buried in the parish-church of Sheffield. His monumental inscription has been already given; and from this it appears that during the time of the Commonwealth he was engaged in many civil employments, that he retired to a little paternal estate, and that he spent his time in the study of the mathematical and other sciences.—What the particular employments were in which he was engaged during the Interregnum has never been explained; but the writer of the memoirs of Thomas Hollis, who is now known to have been Archdeacon Blackburne, conjectures that he is the person to whom there is an allusion in the Apology for the Presbyterian Ministers 1649, on the charge of holding antimonarchical principles, ' the same Walker who has written the Monthly Mercuries,' and that therefore he was the translator of the *Vindiciæ contra tyrannos*, published in 1648[1]. The tradition of the village of Darnall goes to fix on Walker that his was the rash hand which smote off the head of the King. The evidence which was collected by the late Mr. Wilson and Mr. Goodwin, and laid before the public in successive communications to the *Gentleman's Magazine*[2], is thought by the writer of the Hollis memoirs to fix the deed on Walker with more certainty, than attends the evidence which would fix the bloody and evil deed on any other name. It consists of recollected confessions in his dying moments, tradition of a warrant having been sent for his apprehension, which he escaped through the connivance of Mr. Spencer of Attercliffe, joined to the fact, that in the trials of the persons who composed the court of justice, Walker was several times mentioned[3] as being the name of the man who actually struck the blow.

I shall now add two or three facts respecting him, which may hereafter assist in deciding a question which many persons doubtless will think of very small importance. After his decease most of his papers were sent to a brother named Joseph Walker, who was a bookseller in London. Some remained at Darnall and passed into the hands of his friends the family of Chalner. Very few of them relate to mathematical subjects. They show, however, a literary turn, and an inclination to topographical pursuits. There are amongst them an account of the proceedings of that detachment of the earl of Manchester's army which took the castle of Sheffield; the assessment for the support of the garrison at Sheffield castle; bills of subsidies for the township of Attercliffe-cum-Darnall; a list of the constables of the township from 1584 to 1699, and of overseers of the poor from 1626 to 1699; and extracts from the court rolls of the manor of Darnall. In the list of constables appears the name of William Walker *anno* 1650. This might be his father, who bore the name of William, or it might be the man himself.—Among the papers are also several letters of his brother Joseph Walker, in one of which he speaks of having sent a copy of Petavius. In these letters Joseph Walker enters at large into the political occurrences of the times, in which he as well as his correspondent appears to have taken a lively interest. Incidental mention is made of a Captain Ward and a Major Breman, as being intimates of William Walker.

It also appears from the records of the Company of Cutlers of Hallamshire, that in 1681 the honorary freedom of their body was conferred on Mr. Walker along with Mr. Jessop of Broomhall, and a few other persons of the first respectability in the parish; a distinction which plainly shows that at that period at least he was not living with the secresy of a man over whose head the axe of justice was suspended; and that he was not looked upon with the evil eye of political jealousy by the persons among whom his lot was cast. It is reported that he was engaged for some time in giving lectures in the mathematical sciences in Mr. Jollie's academy. A small box of Napier's bones, which was once the property of Mr. Walker, is in the museum of Mr. William Staniforth of Sheffield.

Here is, it is confessed, nothing decisive. But I should be sorry to suppose that a man of learning and science could have been guilty of such a deed; and it will be recollected how easily the village rustics might be induced to fix such a deed on a retired republican, living, it is probable, a secluded and studious life, and bearing the branded name of Walker.

We have now finished our history and survey of the parish of Sheffield; and I have to entreat the reader's further indulgence to some historical and topographical notices of four parishes and a large chapelry lying adjacent to the parish of Sheffield, which are comprehended in the *Membra castri de Sheffield*, and which are, *by repute* at least, portions of HALLAMSHIRE, and as to parts of them indisputably so, in however restricted a sense that term may be used. These parishes are ECCLESFIELD, HANSWORTH, TREETON, and WHISTON; and the chapelry, the chapelry of BRADFIELD. We may call them OUT-PARTS of HALLAMSHIRE.

---

[1] *Memoirs of Thomas Hollis*, p. 131.
[2] See *Gent. Mag.* xxxvii. 548, xxxviii. 10, &c.

[3] See ' *An exact and most impartial accompt of the indictment &c. of twenty-nine regicides*,' &c. 8vo. 1679, p. 228, 272, and 279.

Out-Parts of Hallamshire.

I.

The Parish of Ecclesfield.

THE village of Ecclesfield lies due north of the town of Sheffield, at the distance of five miles.

The great turnpike-road from Leeds to London through Sheffield passes near, and the church of Ecclesfield and parsonage-house situated on a little eminence present themselves pleasing objects to the traveller who is journeying southward. He has at the same time on the left the majestic woods of Wentworth, with the graceful Ionic column rising from amidst them erected by the late marquis of Rockingham to commemorate a political triumph in the acquittal of his friend Admiral Keppel. Wentworth-house and its woods are now what Sheffield-manour and its woods once were. May it be long before the seat of the noble house of Wentworth shall be what the seat of the house of Talbot now is!

The church or chapel of Bradfield is subordinate to the church of Ecclesfield, from which it is six miles distant. We shall speak of it and its spacious parish or chapelry in another article. We have now to attend to what forms more particularly the parish of Ecclesfield, of which the church and village are nearly at the central point. Its boundary line on the north and west coincides with the boundary of the wapentake of Strafford and Tickhill. On those sides it adjoins Tankersley and its chapelry of Wortley. On the east it has Wentworth and Rotherham, and on the south Sheffield.

The duke of Norfolk is lord of the manor, owner of the rectory, and patron of the church. He has much land and extensive woods. But there are many ancient freeholds, and houses which in the common language of the neighbourhood are dignified with the name of halls. Several of these are now deserted by their proprietors. The families in whom they descended from generation to generation have either become extinct, or have retreated to a greater distance from the smoke and other annoyances of the iron-manufactures. In the neighbourhood of Chapel-town are extensive iron-works. Some portion of the Sheffield manufactures is found here. All the nails manufactured in Hallamshire are made in this parish. The parish produces coal and iron-stone. At the village

of Ecclesfield is a cotton-factory. But still the general character is rather that of an agricultural than a manufacturing district. There have been some recent inclosures, so that there is now but little land in an unproductive state. In 1801 the parish contained 1020 houses, and 5114 inhabitants. In 1811 its inhabitants were 5834.

This is the district surveyed in Domesday-book under the name of Eclesfelt. In the Saxon times it was in the hands of six proprietors; and hence according to the nomenclature of that survey it was said to consist of or to contain six manors. But it had only four rated carucates, and there were only two villeins, and as many bordarii. There was a pasturable wood of little more than two square leuæ in extent. In the time of the Confessor it was valued at three pounds. At the time of the survey it was worth only ten shillings. The Norman had been there.

The names of the six Saxon lords were Ulfac, Elsi, Godric, Dunninc, Elmar, and Norman. Ulfac we have met before as lord of Grimesthorpe. Godric had Brinsford and Greasborough, neighbouring manors. Elsi and Norman had other property in the wapentake. Perhaps Elsicar may derive its name from this person. Roger de Busli is returned as sole Norman lord.

Very soon after the Conquest a religious house was erected at the village of Ecclesfield which was made dependent on the foreign monastery of Saint Wandrille. It was under the superintendence of a prior. Of its founder we are ignorant; but most probably it was either Roger de Busli or the Countess Judith, a known benefactor to that house. It was exhibited in parliament in the reign of King Edward III. that the church of Ecclesfield was founded by the monks of St. Wandrille three hundred years before, which fixes its foundation and also the existence of the priory at a period not long after the Conquest.

But by whomsoever it was founded, the priory of Ecclesfield acquired a predominant interest in the whole parish. When De Lovetot succeeded to the interest of De Busli in this neighbourhood, he found but a divided sovereignty at Ecclesfield. We have already given a deed by which it was intended to define the respective rights of the monks and of De Lovetot. But much seems to have been left unsettled; for from the time of King John to the seventh of Edward I. we find the lords of Hallamshire engaged in legal discussions with the monks touching this manor of Ecclesfield.

Fines 7 John. Ebor. It is commanded to the sheriff of York that he take into the hand of the lord the king the manor of Ecclesfield which belonged to Ralph de Ecclesfield, and hold it until 100 marks which the said Ralph owed to Gerard de Furnival be paid[1].

Clause. 7 John. m. 11. Ebor. The king to the sheriff of York, &c. We command you that presently upon sight of these letters you take into our hand the land of Ecclesfield with the appurtenances which Ralph de Ecclesfield holds of the monks of Saint Wandrille, whoever holds it whether the said Ralph or Robert his brother[2].

This Ralph de Ecclesfield was, I believe, a clerk. Robert was his heir; and had Thomas who had Roger who had another Thomas. This Thomas was living in the 7th of Edward I., and was deforciant respecting the manor of Ecclesfield against the abbot of Saint Wandrille plaintiff, as appears by pleas of jurats and assize of that year before John de Vallibus[3].

Again in the same year, Fine between Geffery abbot of Saint Wandrille plaintiff and Thomas de Furnival deforciant, of the manor of Ecclesfield and the advowson of the church of the same acknowledged to be the right of the said abbot and convent of Saint Wandrille[4].

It would appear as if the question was now set to rest. But in Kirkby's Inquest, and the *Nomina Villarum* 9 Edward II., Thomas de Furnival is returned lord of Ecclesfield, and at a somewhat later period this manor is settled in dower on Elizabeth countess of Shrewsbury. While on the other hand in Pope Nicholas' taxation, the abbot and convent of Saint Wandrille are said to hold the manor of Ecclesfield[5], and the courts for the manor till the Reformation were held in the name of that house, or of the successors to its interests the Carthusian monastery of Saint Anne of Coventry. To suppose that there were two manors, a lay and a rectorial manor, will scarcely remove the difficulty.

Anno 1319. License granted to the prior of Ecclesfield to absent himself from his church and monastery till the feast of Saint Martin[6].

Anno 1334. The prior of Ecclesfield was present with other abbots and priors at the solemn funeral of Joan lady Furnival in the monastery of Croxden.

Anno 1369. The king, Edward III., presented to the vicarage of Ecclesfield as holding the temporalities of this house.

Anno 1376. The commons in parliament present that the prior of Ecclesfield was forcibly ousted from the possession of the church of Ecclesfield by one Sir Henry Medbourne chaplain to the Lord Latimer, and pray that both parties may be heard[7]. This was in the last year of Edward III.

The kings of England were now making great strides towards the entire separation of the English dependences from the foreign monasteries. Richard II. found the priory of Ecclesfield and all its appurtenances in the hands of the crown, and in the 9th of his reign *anno* 1386 gave them to the newly founded Carthusian monastery of Saint Anne near the city of Coventry[8]. By such an appropriation he prevented the clamour which might have arisen from the ecclesiastics of his time.

It was in the midst of the contentions which issued in the dissolution of the priory of Ecclesfield that in all probability the treasure was secreted which was discovered in the year 1770 in the house of one Richard Wood an inhabitant of Ecclesfield. It consisted of groats and half groats of the reign of Edward III. Mr. Wilson was informed that as many were found as would have filled a peck-measure, and that they were sold *en masse* for sixty pounds.

The rectory and the manor of Ecclesfield were granted in 3 Edward VI. to Mary countess of Northumberland for life. This grant was followed by another, giving them in reversion to Francis earl of Shrewsbury and his heirs. The countess of Northumberland died in 1572, when they came to her nephew George the sixth earl, and from that period they have descended along with the manor of Sheffield. Ecclesfield-hall, in which the courts were held, was formed out of the buildings inhabited by the monks.

A considerable portion of the parish of Ecclesfield lay within the manor of Cowley. This manor is not mentioned in Domesday, nor in the *Nomina Villarum* 9 Edward II. It belonged to the house of De Reneville, who were of prime account in the west riding, and from them passed to the Mounteneys. They had a moated mansion at Cowley, which the earl of Shrewsbury destroyed when he bought the Mounteney lands in the time of Elizabeth, as hath been before related.

THE VICARAGE.

On the seventh of the ides of September 1310, William archbishop of York ordained that there should be a perpetual vicar in the church of Ecclesfield with the chapel of Bradfield, presentable by the abbot and convent of Saint Wandrille to whom it was appropriated; who should have for his portion all the small tythes, *viz.* of wool, lambs, fowls, calves, pigs, broodgeese, eggs, pigeons, line, hemp, and fruits growing in orchards and virgults within the said parish; and should have all the oblations and mortuaries whatsoever; the tythes of garbs and hay only being excepted, which should belong to the said religious entirely.

He also ordained that the said religious should within a year's time build the vicar a house near the church, to consist of a hall, two chambers, and one pantry; and a stable for two horses: and that they should assign him one acre of land at the least to be inclosed at their cost.

And as to the burthens incumbent on the church, he ordained that the said religious should, when need required, repair and rebuild the chancel both of the church and chapel, and pay procurations due to the archdeacon; and that they should also find two fit chaplains to assist the vicar in the cure; namely, one

---

[1] Dods. MSS. H.H.H. 10 a.   Harl. 801.   Ecclesfield.
[2] Id. 11 a.   [3] Id. G.G. 58.
[4] Id. G.G. 58 b.
[5] Tanner, 683.

[6] Notes from Archbishop Melton's Register, f. 137. Dods. MSS. B. 86 a. Harl. 801. Ecclesfield.
[7] Rot. Parl. vol. ii. p. 329.
[8] *Mon. Ang.* vol. i. p. 965.

in the church of Ecclesfield and the other in the chapel. The extraordinary burthens to be borne between the said religious and the vicar rateably to their respective proportions[1].

Alethea countess of Arundel endowed the vicar of Ecclesfield with a third part of the tythes of the whole parish, including Bradfield, which had come into her hands as heiress of the house of Talbot[2]. The church has had other benefactions.

The vicarage is valued in the king's books—

	£	s.	d.
First fruits	19	13	4
Tenths	1	18	4
Procurations	0	7	6
Subsidies	1	14	0

Since the Reformation the right of presenting to the vicarage has been vested in the house of Shrewsbury and their representatives; but I find William Beever of Hornthwait in the parish of Peniston, yeoman, giving by will, dated the 7th of August 1684, to John Beever his son ' all his right and title to the presentation to the vicarage of Ecclesfield.'

A CATALOGUE of the VICARS of ECCLESFIELD.

Temp. Instit.	Vicarii.	Patroni.
16 Kal. Maii 1311	Dñs Rob. de Bosce, mon. S. Wandragesili	Ab. et Co. S. Wandragesili.
2 Id. Dec. 1328	Fr. Joh. Faunel *idem*	. . . . *iidem* . . .
18 Sept. 1349	Fr. Rob. Guillelm *idem*	. . . . *iidem* . . .
29 Oct. 1369	Dñs Wil. Fulmere, pbr.	Edwardus III. rex et custos temp. pred. ab.
	William Bryan	
23 Oct. 1401	Arnaldus Wyke	Prior et Co. S. Annæ in Coventria.
3 Sept. 1411	William Dene	. . . . *iidem* . . .
5 April 1415	Arnaldus Wyke	. . . . *iidem* . . .
1 July 1424	Rob. Normanton cap.	. . . . *iidem* . . .
	Thomas Swyft	. . . . *iidem* . . .
13 Oct. 1478	Thomas Clarke cap.	. . . . *iidem* . . .
22 Mar. 1517	John Talbot, S.T.P.	. . . . *iidem* . . .
8 April 1519	Mr Wil. Holme, pbr.	. . . . *iidem* . . .
2 Oct. 1544	Car. Parsons, S.T.B.	Franciscus Comes Salopiæ.
12 Sept. 1549	John Tyas	. . . . *idem* . . .
21 Oct. 1580	Jodocus Nitzum	Georgius Comes Salopiæ.
8 Aug. 1585	Ricardus Lord	. . . . *idem* . . .
29 July 1600	Nicholas Denham, A.M.	Gilbertus Comes Salopiæ.
26 June 1628	John Newton	Willielmus Comes Pembrochiæ.
10 Dec. 1638	Thomas Wright, A.M.	Thomas Comes Arundelliæ.
	Immanuel Knutton	
	Rowland Hancock	
	Thomas Wright	
23 May 1691	Edward Mansel, ob. 27 July 1704	
27 July 1704	Thomas Bosvile, S.T.B.	Thomas Dux Norfolchiæ.
23 July 1708	Willielmus Steer, ob. 1745	Thomas Gill, gen. p.h.v. by grant from Thomas duke of Norfolk.
	Thomas Bright, ob. 23 Jan. 1768	
	Henry Downes, ob. 1775	
	James Dixon presented in 1775, chaplain to the late Marquis of Rockingham.	

The monks of Saint Wandrille, it appears, were accustomed to present one of their own body to this church, and the names lead one to suppose that the vicars of their presentation were foreigners. No striking proof of the regard of this monastic body to the interest of religion, or of this particular parish, whose spiritual wants it was theirs to supply. Holme held the livings of Whiston and Treeton along with Ecclesfield, and Tyas had also the rectory of Treeton. He was buried at Ecclesfield the 9th of October 1580. Lord appears in the court-rolls of the manor of Sheffield under circumstances which do not depose favourably to the manner in which he sustained the clerical character. Newton was vicar of Rotherham before he

settled at Ecclesfield[3]. Wright when he had enjoyed this living a few years was ejected by the parliamentary commissioners. But he left Ecclesfield not without hope of returning, addressing his parishioners in a farewell sermon from a verse of the one hundred and twenty-sixth psalm, ' *He that goeth forth and weepeth, bearing precious seed, shall doubtless come again with rejoicing, bringing his sheaves with him.*' He did return; and on the Restoration took possession of his vicarage, which he held full thirty years after, dying in February 1691 at the age of eighty. Immanuel Knutton was buried in the church of Ecclesfield the 28th of November 1655. His daughter married George Phipps the elder, of High-green in this parish, gent.

[1] Notes from Torre's MSS. made by Dr. Burton of York, the author of the *Monasticon Eboracense*.
[2] *Mag. Brit.* vi. 512.
[3] On the stone which covers his remains in the church of Ecclesfield is the following inscription :

[4] Johannes Newton vicarius hujus ecclesiæ. Vir ingenio acer, variâ linguarum et artium literaturâ instructus, moribus probus, pastor prudens, et præco diligentissimus, sub hoc lapide Domini sui adventum expectat. Obiit 8ro die Sept. An° Salutis 1638°, ætatis suæ 55^.'
How much was lost when such a man as this died!'

3 v

Of Rowland Hancock we have before spoken. Edward Mansel, 'judicious Mansel, grave and holy[1],' has a monument in the church. He was of a Northamptonshire family, and married Mrs. Saxton, a daughter of George Westby of Gilthwaite, gent. A short catechism compiled by him is still used among the descendants of his parishioners in the fifth degree. He rebuilt the parsonage-house, and left a parcel of land lying near Ecclesfield-common to the church for ever. William Steer was the eldest son of a father of both his names who resided at Darnall, and whose younger son Charles also brought up to the church had the living of Hansworth. The inscription on the monument of Mr. Steer in the church of Ecclesfield was written by the Reverend John Balguy of Northallerton. Mr. Downes was also curate of Saint Paul's in Sheffield.

Over the door of the parsonage-house is the following inscription:

'Edward Mansel vicar 1695.
Nemo soli sibi natus.
Vivat rex.
Floreat ecclesia.'

THE PARISH-CHURCH.

'The church of Ecclesfield is called by the vulgar, and that deservedly, the Minster of the Moors, being the fairest church for stone, wood, glass, and neat keeping that ever I came in of country church.' So two centuries ago said Dodsworth; and though since his time it has suffered much, especially in its windows, it is still a remarkably fine village church, and contains much that may recommend it to the attention of the antiquary.

Dodsworth, on what appears to be good authority, an appropriation by the archbishop of York, at the instance of Hugh le Despencer earl of Winchester in 1323, says that Richard de Lovetot gave the church of Ecclesfield to the abbot and monks of Saint Wandrille in the reign of Henry I.[2] We have seen that the monks claimed to be the founders of the church. That the effigies of their saint with his name in Langobardic characters, which went out of use in the reign of Henry III., appeared in one of the windows, will not decide the question between these contending authorities. He was represented as an old man holding a crosier. Fragments of this were lately to be seen, and probably are still there. The church is dedicated to St. Mary.

Ecclesfield was a wealthy parish; and at the beginning of the sixteenth century, the principal families residing within it, and other parties who were connected with it, determined to ornament the windows of

---

[1] This is the character of Mr. Mansel given by Mr. Henry Parke curate of Wentworth, his contemporary, in a poem it is believed never published, which contains amusing and characteristic sketches of the clergy and other gentlemen in his neighbourhood about the time of the Revolution. A few extracts will not be thought misplaced. The poem is entitled ' A letter to a friend in London.' Speaking of his patron the Honourable Mr. Wentworth—

94

'A gentleman of noble race
Woodhouse and Wentworth both does grace:
Believe me without artifice
He's just and affable and wise,
Discreet, accessible, and good;
Who never knew how to be proud:

100

In any business when concern'd,
Ingenious too he is and learn'd;
The best of all the *Noble coram*
For law and sense is not before him.
The EDMUNDSES both young and old

105

Their ancient way of living hold:
They serve their God and feed the poor,
None without alms depart their door:
And both in their respective station
Practise a virtue out of fashion;

110

'Tis hospitality I mean
That makes folks fat that once were lean.
Brave Colonel GILL is still the same,
A patriot of deserved fame;
Who rather than his free-born toe

115

Should e'er be pinch'd with wooden shoe,
To draw the sword is once more able
To fight for freedom and the bible
Against the popish Irish rabble.
He's noble, valiant, just, and free,
As all true Englishmen should be.

120

ADAMS the wealthy, good, and mild,
He builds his house and tills his field;
But amongst all attornies he
A miracle is sure to be
Who follows law with honesty.

125

BRIGHT to his prince will always true be,
And so will ISAAC KNIGHT and NEWBY.
Of all that do with medicines meddle,
Of all that play upon the fiddle,
WILL. BOROUGHS is the learnedst physician,
And PHILIP FLINT the chief musician.

130

WATERHOUSE goes to law with those
Who his encroachments do oppose,
And ELLIS snuffs and cracks i'th' nose.
JOHN TOWERS' face is full of pimples,
And WRIGHTSON JOHN has got the simples.

135

Having thus done with fine lay people,
We'll come to those that manage steeple.
WATTS has great parts genteel and jolly:
Judicious MANSEL's grave and holy.

140

LOCKIER is debonaire and civil,
Well read and made complete by travel.
Logician CADE is kind and gay;
And TWITTY honest as the day.
Great JESSOP is a sound divine,

145

His sense is strong and masculine.
DRAKE does in eloquence excel,
He's popular and preaches well.
Brave HARRY FARRER's bold and witty,
And though his teeth are out is pretty.

150

Cam's sacred fountain never sent forth
A scholar more refined than WENTWORTH.
Glad Barnber has its smiling JERRY
Politely learn'd and sweetly merry.
But Darfield's EATON above all

155

Is pious, prudent, liberal,
In all things apostolical;
Free of his bread and beef and liquor,
In short a venerable vicar.'

Notes.

104. Of Worsborough.   112. Colonel John Gill of Carhouse near Rotherham, son of an old parliamentarian officer. See the pedigree p. 234.   121. Of Bank-top.   126. Of Badsworth.   127. Knight of Langold; and Newby of Hutton Roberts.   130. Dr. Boroughs of Swinton.   131. A poor fiddler.   132. Of Braithwell.   134. Of Brampton.   139. Of Barns-hall. See the pedigree.   141. Rector of Hansworth and dean of Peterborough.   143. Chaplain to Mr. Wentworth.   144. Vicar of Wath.   145. Rector of Tretton.   147. Vicar of Sheffield.   149. Rector of Hemsworth.   152. Rector of Tankersley.   153. Jeremiah Cudworth rector of Barnborough.   155. Rector of Darfield.

Poor Henry Parke the author of these lines spent but an unhappy and discreditable life. He was born about 1660, and was of Christ's College Cambridge, where, according to the published list of graduates, he took a bachelor's degree in 1682. In May 1690 he was presented to the perpetual curacy of Wentworth. In 1694 he proceeded M.A. It does not appear that he had any other preferment. He died at Wentworth, and was buried in the chapel under a stone close to the reading-desk which bears this inscription:

'Here lieth a penitent sinner: the earthly remains of that reverend divine Mr. Henry Parke, 14 years and a half minister of this chapel: buried here the 10th of November 1704.

Divine and poet, take thy rest:
Thy soul we hope is with the blest.
Thou shalt not pass without a line:
Sweet was thy verse, thy preaching fine.'

His widow became housekeeper in the Wentworth family.

I am not aware that Mr. Parke published any thing except a sheet entitled ' *Lachrymæ Sacerdotis:* a Pindarick poem, occasioned by the death of that most excellent princess our late gracious sovereign Lady Mary the Second, of glorious memory. By Henry Parke curate of Wentworth in Yorkshire.' London 1695. Reprinted in the Supplement to the Harleian Miscellany, 1810. Vol. ix. p. 260.

[2] Dods. MSS. B. 89 a. Harl. 801. Ecclesfield.

this church with painted glass. There was some professor of this art in the reign of Henry VII. whose hand appears in many of the churches of the west riding.

Dodsworth saw the church when the windows so ornamented were entire. The following account of its fenestral decorations will be found to embrace all the particulars which he has preserved, or what are to be found in the beautiful manuscript *Monumenta Eboracensia* compiled under the inspection of Sir William Dugdale.

East window of the north aile. The figure of a knight kneeling, having on his surcoat the arms of Fitz-William, Lozengy argent and gules, with the sable mullet, the distinction of that branch of this right ancient family, which flourished at Aldwark, a little district near the Don, remote from the rest of the parish of Ecclesfield, but which is understood to pertain to it. Beneath the knight was this inscription:

' *Orate pro animabus Dñi Ricardi Fitz William, et Dñe Elixabethe uxoris ejus, qui hanc fenestram fieri fecerunt ; filiorum filiarumque suorum. Aº Dñi* M.CCCCO.II.'

There were also the effigies of his lady, of seven sons and as many daughters, all kneeling.

I do not find more in Dodsworth or Dugdale respecting the Fitz-William window. But while the figures and inscription have either wholly or for the most part perished, there have been spared several shields of arms, impalements of the family of Sir Richard Fitz-William, viz.

WENTWORTH, Sable, a chevron between three leopards' heads or, impaling FITZ-WILLIAM. RERESBY, Gules on a bend argent, three crosses patonce sable, impaling the same. MIRFIELD, [Vert] two lions passant argent, impaling the same. FITZ-WILLIAM of Sprodborough, without the mullet, impaling the same. FITZ-WILLIAM impaling argent, three bars gules.

There is no monumental memorial for Sir Richard Fitz-William who was buried in this church.

A window on the north side contained the figure of a knight kneeling, on his surcoat the arms of Mounteney, and beneath it this inscription:

' *Orate pro animabus Roberti de Mounteney et Isabellæ uxoris ejus, filiorum, filiarum eorum; qui istam fenestram fieri fecerunt. Aº* M.CCCCC.V.'

In this window were various shields of arms, viz.

FURNIVAL, MOUNTENEY, LOVETOT, Parti per fess or and gules, a lion rampant parti per fess sable and argent; DENICOURT, Gules, a fess dancette between ten billets or; argent, three chaplets gules; and ermine, two bars gemelles gules.

But the most superb display of the effigies and arms of the Mounteneys was in the east window of the south aile, where was a complete series of the chiefs of this house commencing with Arnold Mounteney who married the daughter of De Furnival, and extending to Robert who married the sister of Sir Thomas Wortley. Their effigies were all represented in a kneeling posture, as were also the wives, on whose mantles the arms of their respective families were depicted. They are arranged by Dodsworth in the following order:

ARNOLD MOUNTENEY : on his own surcoat the arms of MOUNTENEY; and on his lady's, MOUNTENEY impaling FURNIVAL. .... MOUNTENEY. On his lady's mantle MOUNTENEY impaling Ermine three bars gemelles gules. THOMAS MOUN-

TENEY. The impaled coat on his lady's mantle, paly of six argent and azure. THOMAS MOUNTENEY. The impalement azure, two bars nebulee argent, a bend vaire or and gules. JOHN MOUNTENEY. The impalement argent, three chaplets gules. THOMAS MOUNTENEY. The impalement ROCKLEY, Lozengy argent and gules, a fess sable. ROBERT MOUNTENEY. The impalement WORTLEY, argent, on a bend between six martlets gules three bezants.

In another window,

ROKEBY. Argent, on a chevron between three rooks sable, as many mullets of the field. ' *Alexander Rookby filius Domini Thomæ Rookeby de Rickmondshire militis, et quondam vicarius Ebor.*' Where *vicarius* may be intended for *vice comes*. ROKEBY impaling sable, a chevron ermine between three boars' heads couped or. ' *Willielmus filius et heres predicti Alex.*' ROKEBY impaling BARNBY, Or, a lion rampant sable charged with escallop shells of the field. ' *Johannes filius et heres predicti Willielmi.*' ROKEBY. ' *Thomas filius et heres predicti Johannis.*'

The Rokebys were of Thundercliffe or Synocliffe-grange.

The south window of the south quire. In this window were the effigies of Thomas Shiercliffe, the master of the game in Hallamshire. Dodsworth describes the figure as that of a man kneeling, about his neck a horn, at his side a sword; in his hand a long bow with five broad-headed arrows under his girdle; a bloodhound with collar and line near him, a book open before him. His wife also kneeling.

' *Orate pro bono statu Thomæ Schyrcliffe, et pro anima Agnetis uxoris ejus, qui hanc fenestram fieri fecerunt. Aº Mº. Dº.* VIº.'

The effigies of this person appeared in two other windows of the church; in one of which on the north side he was represented with his two wives, seven sons and four daughters, all kneeling, with this inscription:

' *Orate pro animabus Thomæ Shercliffe et Agnetis et ... uxorum ejus, qui hanc fenestram fieri fecerunt.*'

And in the other, which was on the south side of the body of the church, he was again represented in his character of a forester, with his horn, falchion, arrows, and hound, with many harts and beasts of game and fowl of warren, in various parts of the window. The figures of his wives and children were in the same window. Over his head was the word Schirclyffe, which in Dodsworth's time had been lost from the inscription.

' *Orate pro animabus .... eorum viventium filiorum filiarumque, qui hanc fenestram fieri fecerunt.*'

To the memory of this person was an inscription of a singular cast painted on a board and hung up in this church, which is here given as it is found in Dodsworth's notes.

' Here lyeth Thomas Schyrcliffe
    In Halumshire Mr of game
Who of justice, truth, love, and bounty
    Had alwayes the same.
Alexander his son and heire
    Lies here hard by,
Who languished in sorrow
    By his Mrs cruelty.
So Goddes she was,
    But of like nomination
As Prudence to the Goddesses
    Have application.
Progeny that read this
    Eschew like fate : Jehovah say amen.
Continew your posterity on earth
    And I rest in heaven,—Finis.'

A window in the great quire. The effigies of a man with twelve others in shaven crowns and white gowns all kneeling, and this inscription:

' *Orate pro Thoma Ricard priore et conventu ejus domus Stæ Annæ Carthusianæ ordinis prope Coventriam, qui istam cantariam et fenestram fieri fecerunt.*'

In the same window was the figure of Saint Wandrille; the arms also of Furnival, and gules, three bars argent, a lion rampant sable.

In other windows were the following inscriptions:

' *Orate pro animabus Thomæ Clerk vicarii ecclesiæ de Ec-clesfield et Henrici Wrastelar dudum custodis de Ryveling, qui istam fenestram fieri fecerunt. A° Dñi* M.CCCCC.V.'[1]

' *Orate pro animabus Thomæ Clerk et Willielmi patris et Isabellæ matris mei, filiorum filiarumque earum, qui hunc fenestram fieri fecerunt.*'

' *Orate pro animabus Henrici Hyncheklyff et Agnetis uxoris ejus filiorum filiarumque eorum, qui hunc fenestram fieri fecerunt.*'

' *Orate pro animabus Johannis Werth et Agnetis uxoris ejus et Willielmi Werth et Aliciæ uxoris ejus, qui hanc fene-stram fieri fecerunt.*'

' *Orate pro animabus Thomæ Parker et Elizabethæ uxoris ejus, filiorum filiarumque suorum, qui hanc fenestram fieri fecerunt.*'

In an east window are still to be seen the six principal quarterings of TALBOT within the garter, and also HASTINGS within the garter, not noticed by Dodsworth or Dugdale.

It must be to the regret of all true lovers of the remains of ancient time and ancient art, that the question is now to be proposed, at what period and by whom the church of Ecclesfield was despoiled of these beautiful and appropriate ornaments. There is not I apprehend any proof of their existence at a period later than the time of Dodsworth, who visited this church before the civil wars, for it does not appear certain that Dugdale did not in that part of his *Monumenta* copy from Dodsworth's notes. Common fame will of course ascribe the destruction to the parliamentarians, and Brooke has preserved a tradition that the church did suffer much in the civil wars, when amongst other things its old organ was destroyed. It is however but justice to the parliament of 1643 to transcribe a clause from the act of that year, ' for the suppression of divers innovations in churches and chappels, &c.,' expressly framed for the protection of such ornaments as those of the church of Ecclesfield.

' Provided that this act or any thing contained shall not extend to any image, picture, or coat of arms in glass, stone, or otherwise, in any church, chappell, church-yard or place of public prayer as aforesaid, set up or graven only for a monument of any king, prince, or noble man, or other dead person which hath not been commonly reputed or taken for a saint, but that all such pictures, images, and coats of arms may stand and continue in like manner and form as if this act had never been had nor made; any thing in this act to the contrary thereof in any wise notwithstanding.'

But after all it is less probable that a destruction almost total of ornament scattered in such rich profusion around this village church should have been accomplished since the Restoration, than that some over zealous or perhaps profoundly ignorant William Dowsing should have been here among the commissioners

under the act before us. I can hardly suppose that Immanuel Knutton, who had been intruded into the place of the exiled vicar, was a man to extend over such things any very powerful protection.

No mention is made of any chantries in this church in Archbishop Holgate's return. But there were several altars, as appears by the will of one Henry Birley of Ecclesfield, made in 1391, about the time when the priory was dissolved. He directs that his body shall be buried in the church-yard of Saint Mary at Ecclesfield, and he bequeaths to the altars of Saint Mary, Saint Catherine, Saint Nicholas, and Saint John the Baptist, and to the service of the holy cross in the said church, to each of them the sum of six shillings and eight pence[2].

The Mounteneys had a private oratory. Parts of the following inscriptions remain. The rest has been supplied from Dodsworth's notes, who saw them when entire.

' *Orate pro animabus Robarti Mountney et Annæ uxoris ejus; ac pro bono statu Johannis Mountney et Johannæ uxoris ejus, qui hoc oratorium fieri fecerunt* XXIIII. *die mencis Maii, Anno Dñi* M.CCCCC.XXX.VI.'

On two sepulchral stones:

' *Orate pro anima Roberti Mountney de Cowley armigeri, qui obiit tertio die mensis Augusti A° M°.cccc°,xix°., cujus animæ propitietur Deus.*'

' *Orate pro anima Johis Mountney de Cowley armigeri, qui obiit* 11° *die mensis Augusti A° Dñi* M°.cccc°.xxx°.vi.° *cujus animæ propitietur Deus. Amen.*'

Over the pew is painted in black letters on the wall ' Sedes domini domus antiquæ et manerii de Cowley: et . . . . id juris tenent. 1663.'

Over another pew in the body of the church; ' This stall was apoynted by the right honorable Gilbart earle of Shrewsbury for Gilbart Dickenson and his wife, 1601.'

In a pew in the south aile which belongs to the duke of Norfolk as owner of Ecclesfield-hall, are painted several of the family badges: viz. the talbot, the white lion of Mowbray, and the white horse of Arundel within the garter. 1659.

Over the seat belonging to the proprietors of Thundercliffe, ' Tota hæc sedes grangiæ de Scenocliffe est antiqua:' and on the pannels are carved in a bold but rude manner the arms of WOMBWELL . . . . a bend between six unicorns' heads . . . . impaling WENTWORTH and the same impaling ARTHINGTON . . . . a chevron between three escallop shells . . . .

Near this seat is the following sepulchral memorial. ' Here lyeth the bodyes of Nicholas Wombwel of Synoclyffe Grondge esquyre and Isabel his wife, whiche sayde Nicholas was the son of Henry Wombwell. 1571.'

The desks, chains, and some tattered fragments of books are still remaining, the donation of Edward Hatfield, a vicar whose name I am sorry to say does not appear in the list lately given. Dodsworth says that Hatfield ' gave all the fathers to the church of Ecclesfield to be chained in the said church, with this inscription, ' A book for ever to be chayned in the church of Ecclesfeild of the gift of Edward Hatefeild, somtymes vicar of the same, on whose soule, &c.' Hat-

---

[1] This inscription I have been forced to re-translate from the copyist of Dodsworth.

[2] Dods. MSS. II. 65 b. Harl. 801. Bradfield.

field had also the rectory of Treeton, and died in 1587. Wilson says that in his time there were remaining Erasmus's Paraphrases, Lyra, Bede, and many others, and that the best of them were taken away by one of the vicars.

Sir Francis Foljambe of Aldwark, baronet, in 1640 presented a bell.

In 1769 in digging near the great south porch a stone coffin was found containing the bones of a human body.

This spacious and still beautiful church abounds in monumental memorials of the principal families who have had their residence within the parish. Of these a short notice must suffice. In the north chancel are many memorials of the Greens of Thundercliffe; and in the south chancel of the Shiercliffes of Whitley-hall. Of both these families the pedigree will be given immediately. In this part of the church are also various monuments and achievements of the ancient family of Foljambe of Aldwark. The inscriptions are long and circumstantial, being what the inscriptions of such a family ought to be, a public record of its genealogy, extending from 1643 to 1759.—The family of Watts of Barnes-hall have also many sepulchral memorials; and we find also monuments of Freeman of Howsley-hall, Rawson of Wardsend, Phipps of High-green, and Parkin of Mortemley. William Parkin of that place, esquire, died without issue the 2d of May 1757, having married to his first wife Mary daughter of Lionel Copley of Sprodborough esquire, and to his second Catherine sister of Patience Warde of Hutton-Paynel esquire.

I shall add the inscription from the monument of Sir Richard Scott, which was repaired in 1749 by John Watts of Barnes-hall esquire.

'RICHARDUS SCOTT, antiqua Scotorum in agro Eboracensi familia oriundus, et in equestrem ordinem meritò scriptus, cujus inter proavos maxime eminuit summâ semper laude nominandus Thomas Scott Arch^{us} Ebor^{is} qui inter alia quamplurima munificentiæ suæ monumenta Collegium Jesuanum Rotherhami instituit, et Collegio Lincolniensi Oxonii supremam manum imposuit.

'Tali dignus prosapia, hic ipse R.S. vir fuit pietate in Deum, probitate in homines præstantissimus: cujus rei indicium est hospitium publicum in hoc oppido exstructum et pauperum usibus dicatum. Miram in societate comitatem exhibuit, perfectam in amicitiâ fidem observavit, summam in rebus gerendis peritiam exercuit. Peregrinandi studio apprime deditus transmarinis partibus peragratis eodem animo patriam revisit quo primum inde profectus et cum in Hispanæ inquisitionis laqueos incidisset ea firmitate in religionis suæ proposto perseveravit, ut nec blanditiæ constantiam ejus flectere potuerint, nec minæ convellere. Notis jucundus, suis charus, omnibus gratiosus, felicissimam vitam transegit et plurimum desideratus non improvisa morte in Hibernia extinctus est; cum clarissimi viri Thomæ Wentworth comitis Straffordiensis &c. proximam a rege potestatem ibidem exercentis comitio adjutus, gratia honoratus, favore amplificatus fuisset. Obiit Jul. 17, Anno Dñi 1638, ætat. suæ 55.

'Cujus memoriæ ab interitu vindicandæ et majorum decori juxta ejus voluntate ad posteritatem transmittendæ honorarium hoc monumentum lubens posuit mœstissima ejus privigna Catherina Norcliffe arctissimo pietatis vinculo astricta et veræ filiæ loco semper ab ipso habita.'

Sir Richard Scott is represented in armour, recumbent and his head resting on his left hand. Above is a shield of his arms, namely, Vert three roe-bucks trippant argent, attired or.—Crest on a wreath, a roe-

buck's head as in the shield, between two sprigs vert. The same arms appear on another part of the monument impaling azure a fess between three trefoils ermine.

To this may be added one other inscription which is not now to be found, but has been preserved by Dodsworth.

'Here lyeth buryed the body of William Carre, son and heir of James Carre of Southey within this parish of Ecclesfield. He was patron and proctor of the church and township of Darton. He marryed Mary one of the da. of Robert Marsh of Darton-hall, by whom he had issue George, Katherine, Mary, Charles, and Ellen, all living at the tyme of his death. He lived XXXV. yeares and VI. monthes; and he departed this lief A° D. M°. VI°. and XIII. and in the XI. year of the reigne of our Lord James by the grace of God of England, Scotland, France, and Ireland, King, &c.'

Of this family was Charles Carr D.D. bishop of Killaloe, who in 1721 was admitted heir in the manor-court of Ecclesfield to lands lately held by his brother Thomas Carr esquire deceased.

The parish-register of Ecclesfield commences in the first year of Elizabeth, but is imperfect, especially in the middle of the seventeenth century.

It remains that we notice some of the old mansions in the parish of Ecclesfield, and their former possessors. And first Barnes-hall.

BARNES-HALL.

The names of Chapel and Bernes appear in the roll of the *Membra castri de Sheffield* in the time of Edward III.

Sometime after, Bernes, called *Manerium de Bernes*, was in possession of Robert Shatton, of whom it was purchased for 140*l.* by Thomas Scott, archbishop of York, commonly called Rotherham from the place of his birth.

Archbishop Scott, though born at Rotherham, was of a family which had resided in the parish of Ecclesfield '*tempore quo non est memoria hominum*,' as he himself declares in his last will. He made large purchases in and about his native place, where he founded a college, and rebuilt or made large additions to the church. Very considerable parts of his estate he devoted to charitable and church uses.

But he did not forget his kindred after the flesh in disposing of that immense property which the high offices he held in church and state enabled him to acquire.

The following extract from his last will, which bears date at York the 6th of August 1498, will show in what manner he disposed of his manor of Bernes.

'Item volo, quod Johannes Scott consanguineus meus, cui est hereditas quanquam parva, in parochia de Ecclesfield successive descendens in eodem nomine et sanguine, a tempore quo non est memoria hominum, ut ipsa augeatur, me per gratiam meliorato, habeat sibi, et heredibus masculis de corpore suo legitime procreatis, quod emi de Roberto Shatton pro CXL. lib. Ac etiam manerium meum de Howsleys cum pertineñ. quod emi de Thoma Worteley milite pro CXX. lib. Et in defectu talium heredum, volo, quod frater suus Ricardus sub eadem lege et conditione habeat prædicta maneria. Et in defectu talium heredum, volo quod prædicta maneria revertantur rectis heredibus meis. Item volo, quod sub eadem lege et conditione prædicti Johannes et Ricardus habeant tenementum

3 x

meum vocatum Sugworth, in parochia de Bradfeld, cum omnibus pertineñ.'[1]

Then followed a race of Scotts residing at Barnes-hall. But it seems that they did not descend from either of the *consanguinei* of the archbishop, but rather that both John and Richard Scott died without issue, when this estate went according to the limitations in the archbishop's will to his right heirs, who were the descendants of George Scott his brother's son. For Richard St. George, Norroy-king-at-arms, on his visitation of the northern parts 1612, subscribed

a pedigree declaring that it 'was well proved by authenticall matters,' in which it was stated that the archbishop of York and lord chancellor of England died in May 1500, aged 76; that his brother married and had Sir Thomas and George. George had John, who had Richard Scott of Barnes-hall, who had Nicholas, who had Thomas, married to Isabel daughter to —— Alcock of London, by whom Richard, living in 1612. Sir Richard Scott founded an hospital near Barnes-hall, and endowed it with thirty pounds *per annum*.

PEDIGREE of SCOTT and WATTS[2] of BARNES-HALL.

ARMS of SCOTT.—Vert, three roe-bucks trippant argent attired or.
CREST.—On a wreath, a buck's head and neck argent attired or between two sprigs vert.

RICHARD SCOTT of Barnes-hall.⚭---- dau. of Edward Barber of Rowlee co. Derb.

NICHOLAS SCOTT of Barnes-hall. Buried at Ecclesfield 1 Aug. 1563.⚭JOHN WATTS of Muckleton, co. Salop. Died in 1601, aged about 104. Buried at Worthley.⚭ANNE SCOTT, died in 1605, aged 80.

THOMAS SCOTT of Barnes-hall, gent., buried at Ecclesfield 2 Nov. 1585. Will dated 1 Nov. 1585, proved at York 21 Dec. following.⚭ISABEL, dau. of Arthur Alcock, of St. Martin's Vintry London, dyer, aged 43, 1605.⚭RICHARD WATTS, second husband. Married at Ecclesfield 22 Sept. 1586.

ELIZABETH, first wife, dau. of Thomas Moseley alderman of York. Buried in the church of St. John, Ousebridge-end, York.⚭SIR RICHARD SCOTT of Barnes-hall, knt. Comptroller of the household to Thomas earl of Strafford, and privy-counsellor in Ireland. Died in Ireland without issue 17 July 1638.⚭---- second wife, dau. of -- Udal, and widow of Thomas Norcliffe esq. of York. | RICHARD WATTS, M.A. Fellow of Trinity College Camb. Vicar of Chesterton, and chaplain to Thomas earl of Strafford. Had Barnes-hall by gift of his half-brother Sir Richard Scott.⚭SARAH, dau. of George Beverley merchant. | GILBERT WATTS, Yorkshire Fellow of Lincoln College, Oxford, D.D. and translator of Lord Bacon's work ' *De augmentis scientiarum.*' Vide *Ath. Ox.* vol. ii. col.134. In the MS. collection of biography in the public library at Leeds, it is said that he was born at Rotherham.

SARAH WATTS, born in 1633, lived but a few days. | RICHARD WATTS, born in 1634. M.A. of Trinity college Camb. Died of the small pox. | EDWARD WATTS, born in 1636. | MARY, first wife, dau. and heir of James and Mary Bulloughs of the Edge in the parish of Ecclesfield. Married 1663. Died 1669.⚭BENJAMIN WATTS of Barnes-hall. Born in 1639. A disclaimer 1666.⚭ALICE, second wife, one of the eight daughters and co-heirs of Robert Nettleton of Thornhill-Lees, clerk. Mar. 10 Nov. 1670. | JOHN WATTS, born in 1641. Died in 1645.

RICHARD WATTS, born 1665. Died in infancy. BENJAMIN WATTS, died in infancy. | RICHARD WATTS of Barnes-hall, clerk. M.A. of Trin. col. Camb. —— JAMES WATTS, born June 1669. Died 22 Dec. 1697. Buried in the church of Ecclesfield. | ROBERT WATTS of Barnes-hall, esq. formerly of London, citizen and fishmonger. Born 26 July 1674. Died 18 Nov. 1739, and was interred in the church of Bath.⚭ELIZABETH, dau. of Charles Wynn and Salter worth co. Notts. Born 1671. Died 20 May 1727 without issue, and was buried in the Abbey-church of Bath. | BENJAMIN WATTS of London, goldsmith. Born 21 Feb. 1675. Died without issue by Elizabeth his wife dau. of Thomas Boucher of London. | FRANCIS WATTS of Coln-bridge-forge in the parish of Kirk-Heaton. Born 7th Nov. 1677. Died 15 Feb. 1737. Buried at Kirk-Heaton. | ANNE, dau. of Richard Beaumont of Whitley-hall esq., by Susanna his wife, dau. of Thomas Horton of Barkis-land esq. | JOHN WATTS of Barnes-hall. Born 21 Nov. 1683. Died 17 Aug. 1751. Buried in the church of Ecclesfield. | WILLIAM WATTS D.D. Fellow of Lincoln col. Oxford. Chaplain to Bishop lord Crew, and prebendary of Durham. Born 27 July 1686. Was married, but died without issue in 1736. | SARAH WATTS, born 26 March 1673. ALICE WATTS, born 30 Aug. 1679. Died unmarried 7 June 1748. Buried at Ecclesfield. CATHERINE WATTS, born 1 May 1681. Died unmarried 1723. Bur. at Ecclesfield.

ELIZABETH WATTS, s.p. | ALICE WATTS, s.p. | SARAH WATTS, s.p. | FRANCES WATTS, died unmarried. | Sir WILLIAM HORTON of Chadderton co. Lanc. bart. and of Barnes-hall in right of his wife. Died 25 Feb. 1774.⚭SUSANNA WATTS, only dau. and heir. Married at Tankersley.

Sir WATTS HORTON of Chadderton bart. Died in 1811, aged 58.⚭Lady HARRIET STANLEY, sister of the earl of Derby. | Sir THOMAS HORTON, bart. Second son.⚭Lady ELIZABETH STANLEY, sister to the earl of Derby. | WILLIAM HORTON, third and youngest son.

H. S. ANNE HORTON, only dau. and heir. Married at Bath 22 July 1814 to Charles Rees esq.

[1] See Hearne's *Liber Niger*, p. 677.
[2] The pedigree of Watts is little more than a copy of one in the hand-writing of the Rev. John Watson late rector of Stockport.

HOWSLEY-HALL.

Maud de Lovetot the great heiress of Hallamshire granted by deed without date to John Camerario all the lands which were Josselin de Burne's in Burne in Chapel or Chapel-town: which lands in process of time came into possession of the family of Howsley who seated themselves there, and from whom the capital messuage or seat was called Howsley-hall.

On the 21st of February 15 Henry VI. 1436, Robert Normanton vicar of Ecclesfield, Richard Pigburn of Scausby, John Skyres of Wath, Thomas Greff of Sturch-hill, and John Wilson of Wadsley, granted to John Howsley and Joan his wife for their lives all the lands &c. which they had of the gift or feoffment of the said John Howsley, within the bounds of Chapel in the parish of Ecclesfield, to hold &c. to the said John and Joan his wife, remainder to William son of John and the heirs male of his body, remainder to John brother of William, remainder to the right heirs of the father.

John Howsley appears in 1505, and Thomas Howsley in 1532.

It appears by a roll in possession of the Freeman family, that Thomas Howsley of Howsley made a tender of chief rents from Martinmas 1566 to 1577 in Ecclesfield church porch to George Talbot earl of Shrewsbury, who was then lord of Ecclesfield.

So far from the notes of the late John-Charles Brooke esquire, Somerset herald at arms.

Thomas Howsley of Howsley-hall married Alice Scott on the 14th of May 1560, who survived and in 1601 had administration granted of his estate and effects. He left two daughters his co-heirs, namely, Elizabeth who was married on the 17th of February 1583 to Gilbert Dickenson brother of Francis Dickenson of Rotherham gentleman. Gilbert Dickenson resided at Howsley-hall, as appears by a general pardon granted to him in the second year of James I. Anne Howsley the other co-heir married Gerard Freeman in 1594, who died seised of Howsley-hall in 1637, leaving Howsley Freeman his son and heir then aged thirty-six.

In 1618 Howsley Freeman married Mary daughter of Thomas Steel, and after the civil wars compounded for his estate by the sum of 156l. He had two sons, viz. Thomas Freeman who succeeded him in the possession of Howsley-hall, and Richard Freeman of the city of York. Thomas died in 1684, when Howsley Freeman gentleman was found to be his son and heir.

From this last named Howsley Freeman descended the late Howsley Freeman of Howsley-hall esquire, a captain of militia who died in 1783 without issue and intestate; when his three sisters became his heirs, namely Grace then the wife of Richard Brown of Aberford, Lydia wife of John Lambert of Leeds, and Margaret Freeman. They divided the inheritance, and chose their respective portions by lot; when Howsley-hall fell to Grace Brown, who dying without issue at Wakefield the 5th of July 1787, by deed and will gave it to Lydia Mackneth, daughter to her sister Lydia Lambert, and to her nephew John Mackneth of Wakefield clerk, husband of her said niece, enjoining him to take the name of Freeman. With this injunction he complied, and took the name of Freeman by royal sign manual bearing date the 7th of Sept. 1787.

The Freemans of this place used for arms, Azure three lozenges or. They did not appear at any of the visitations.

WHITLEY-HALL.

This house and estate was formerly the seat of a respectable family of the name of Parker, descended of a younger son of the house of Parker of Norton-Lees in the county of Derby. In a collection of Lincolnshire genealogies now in the Harleian library No. 1436, f. 71. we meet with a pedigree of the family communicated by William Parker, formerly of this place, but who had removed himself to Horncastle in the county of Lincoln. The arms were the same as those pertaining to the Parkers of Norton-Lees, viz. Gules a chevron between three leopards' heads or, with a crescent for difference. Quartered with them was Gules a tower or, and perched thereon a bird argent.

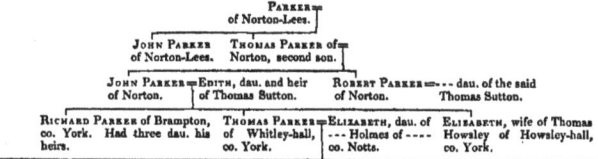

It will not escape the judicious reader that this pedigree is deficient in dates. But it must have been compiled about the time of King James I., for Richard Parker of Brampton appears in the court-rolls of the manor of Ecclesfield anno 1591, together with his three daughters, who were Agnes the wife of Thomas Shiers, Catherine mother of William Simpson then aged 14 years, and Anne who had been the wife of Godfrey Shawe, but then married to Thomas Bloome.

In 1616 Thomas Shiercliffe purchased the estate of this family, and it continued to be the residence of his descendants till their extinction by the death of Mr. John Shiercliffe in 1789 without male issue.

No name appears more frequently in the early volumes

of the court-rolls for the manor of Ecclesfield than the name of Shiercliffe; and there can be little doubt that the family were indigenous to this neighbourhood, deriving their name from Shiercliffe, where the Mounteneys had their seat, and not removing hither from Wolverhampton, as is stated in an old pedigree of the family. The arms and crest depicted below were confirmed to William Shiercliffe of Ecclesfield-hall, the friend of Dodsworth, by Richard Saint George, whose certificate is now in the possession of Miss Elizabeth Gunning of Swainswick near Bath, a co-representative of that branch of the family which resided at Whitley-hall. The arms are evidently allusive to the office

which was held by Thomas Shiercliffe in the reign of Henry VII., of master of the game to the lords of Hallamshire. The best authorities for the earlier descents of this family are a pedigree entered at the visitation of 1612, and another showing the descent of William Shiercliffe of Ecclesfield-hall from the master of the game, compiled by William Shiercliffe himself, and preserved among Mr. Wilson's collections. I have also had the assistance of a pedigree compiled by Charles Green esquire, Lancaster herald, in drawing up the following table, in which I have endeavoured to avoid stating any thing as proved which was of dubious authority.

PEDIGREE of SHIERCLIFFE of ECCLESFIELD-HALL, WHITLEY-HALL, &c.

ARMS.—Or, a fess between 3 greyhounds' heads erased sable, collars and rings gules.
CREST.—On a torce or and sable a falchion erect proper, hilt or, having a leopard's head thereon or.

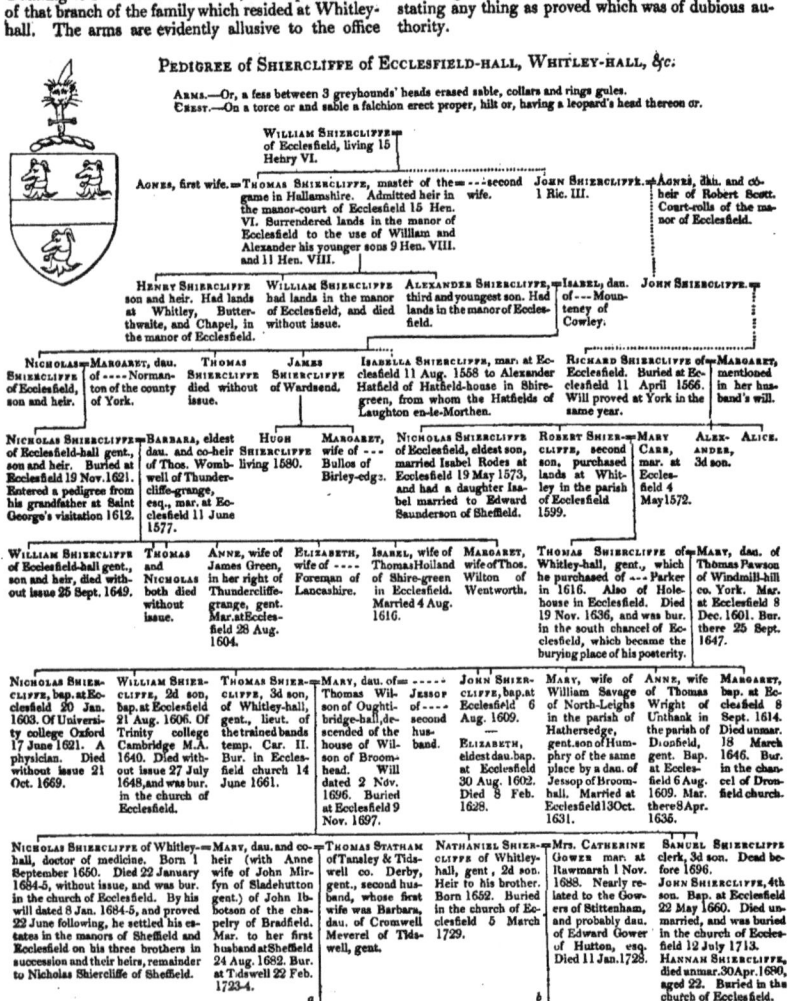

WILLIAM SHIERCLIFFE of Ecclesfield, living 15 Henry VI.

AGNES, first wife.═THOMAS SHIERCLIFFE, master of the game in Hallamshire. Admitted heir in the manor-court of Ecclesfield 15 Hen. VI. Surrendered lands in the manor of Ecclesfield to the use of William and Alexander his younger sons 9 Hen. VIII. and 11 Hen. VIII.═second wife. │ JOHN SHIERCLIFFE, 1 Ric. III. │ AGNES, dau. and coheir of Robert Scott. Court-rolls of the manor of Ecclesfield.

HENRY SHIERCLIFFE son and heir. Had lands at Whitley, Butterthwaite, and Chapel, in the manor of Ecclesfield. │ WILLIAM SHIERCLIFFE had lands in the manor of Ecclesfield, and died without issue. │ ALEXANDER SHIERCLIFFE third and youngest son. Had lands in the manor of Ecclesfield.═ISABEL, dau. of ---Mounteney of Cowley. │ JOHN SHIERCLIFFE.

NICHOLAS SHIERCLIFFE of Ecclesfield, son and heir.═MARGARET, dau. of ----Normanton of the county of York. │ THOMAS SHIERCLIFFE died without issue. │ JAMES SHIERCLIFFE of Wardsend. │ ISABELLA SHIERCLIFFE, mar. at Ecclesfield 11 Aug. 1558 to Alexander Hatfield of Hatfield-house in Shiregreen, from whom the Hatfields of Laughton en-le-Morthen. │ RICHARD SHIERCLIFFE of Ecclesfield. Buried at Ecclesfield 11 April 1566. Will proved at York in the same year.═MARGARET, mentioned in her husband's will.

NICHOLAS SHIERCLIFFE of Ecclesfield-hall gent. son and heir. Buried at Ecclesfield 19 Nov. 1621. Entered a pedigree from his grandfather at Saint George's visitation 1612.═BARBARA, eldest dau. and co-heir of Thos. Wombwell of Thundercliffe-grange, esq., mar. at Ecclesfield 11 June 1577. │ HUGH SHIERCLIFFE living 1580. │ MARGARET, wife of --- Bullos of Birley-edge. │ NICHOLAS SHIERCLIFFE of Ecclesfield, eldest son, married Isabel Rodes at Ecclesfield 19 May 1573, and had a daughter Isabel married to Edward Saunderson of Sheffield. │ ROBERT SHIERCLIFFE, second son, purchased lands at Whitley in the parish of Ecclesfield 1599.═MARY CARR, mar. at Ecclesfield 4 May 1572. │ ALEXANDER, 3d son. │ ALICE.

WILLIAM SHIERCLIFFE of Ecclesfield-hall gent., son and heir, died without issue 25 Sept. 1649. │ THOMAS and NICHOLAS both died without issue. │ ANNE, wife of James Green, in her right of Thundercliffegrange, gent. Mar. at Ecclesfield 28 Aug. 1604. │ ELIZABETH, wife of ---- Foreman of Lancashire. │ ISABEL, wife of ThomasHolland of Shire-green in Ecclesfield. Married 4 Aug. 1616. │ MARGARET, wife of Thos. Wilton of Wentworth. │ THOMAS SHIERCLIFFE of Whitley-hall, gent., which he purchased in 1616. Also of Hole-house in Ecclesfield. Died 19 Nov. 1636, and was bur. in the south chancel of Ecclesfield, which became the burying place of his posterity.═MARY, dau. of Thomas Pawson of Windmill-hill co. York. Mar. at Ecclesfield 8 Dec. 1601. Bur. there 25 Sept. 1647.

NICHOLAS SHIERCLIFFE, 2d son, bap. at Ecclesfield 20 Jan. 1603. Of University college Oxford 17 June 1621. A physician. Died without issue 21 Oct. 1669. │ WILLIAM SHIERCLIFFE, 3d son, bap. at Ecclesfield 21 Aug. 1606. Of Trinity college Cambridge M.A. 1640. Died without issue 27 July 1648, and was bur. in the church of Ecclesfield. │ THOMAS SHIERCLIFFE, of Whitley-hall, gent., lieut. of the trained bands temp. Car. II. Bur. in Ecclesfield church 14 June 1661.═MARY, dau. of ----- son of Oughtibridge-hall, descended of the house of William son of Broomhead. Will dated 2 Nov. 1696. Buried at Ecclesfield 9 Nov. 1697. │ JOHN SHIERCLIFFE, bap. at Ecclesfield 6 Aug. 1609.═JESSOP of ---- second husband. │ MARY, wife of William Savage of North-Leighs in the parish of Hathersedge, gent. son of Humphry of the same place by a dau. of Jessop of Broomhall. Married at Ecclesfield 13 Oct. 1631. │ ANNE, wife of Thomas Wright of Unthank in the parish of Dronfield, gent. Bap. 6 Aug. 1609. Mar. there 8 Apr. 1635. │ MARGARET, bap. at Ecclesfield 8 Sept. 1614. Died unmar. 18 March 1646. Bur. in the chancel of Dronfield church.

ELIZABETH, eldest dau. bap. at Ecclesfield 30 Aug. 1602. Died 8 Feb. 1628.

NICHOLAS SHIERCLIFFE of Whitley-hall, doctor of medicine. Born 1 September 1650. Died 22 January 1684-5, without issue, and was bur. in the church of Ecclesfield. By his will dated 8 Jan. 1684-5, and proved 22 June following, he settled his estates in the manors of Sheffield and Ecclesfield on his three brothers in succession and their heirs, remainder to Nicholas Shiercliffe of Sheffield.═MARY, dau. and co-heir (with Anne wife of John Mirfyn of Sladehutton gent.) of John Ibbotson of the chapelry of Bradfield. Mar. to her first husband at Sheffield 24 Aug. 1682. Bur. at Tidswell 22 Feb. 1723-4. │ THOMAS STATHAM of Tansley & Tidswell co. Derby, gent., second husband, whose first wife was Barbara, dau. of Cromwell Meverel of Tidswell, gent. │ NATHANIEL SHIERCLIFFE of Whitley-hall, gent, 2d son. Heir to his brother. Born 1652. Buried in the church of Ecclesfield 5 March 1729.═MRS. CATHERINE GOWER mar. at Rawmarsh 1 Nov. 1688. Nearly related to the Gowers of Stittenham, and probably dau. of Edward Gower of Hutton, esq. Died 11 Jan.1728. │ SAMUEL SHIERCLIFFE clerk, 3d son. Dead before 1696. │ JOHN SHIERCLIFFE, 4th son. Bap. at Ecclesfield 22 May 1660. Died unmarried, and was buried in the church of Ecclesfield 12 July 1713. HANNAH SHIERCLIFFE, died unmar. 30 Apr. 1690, aged 22. Buried in the church of Ecclesfield.

a   b

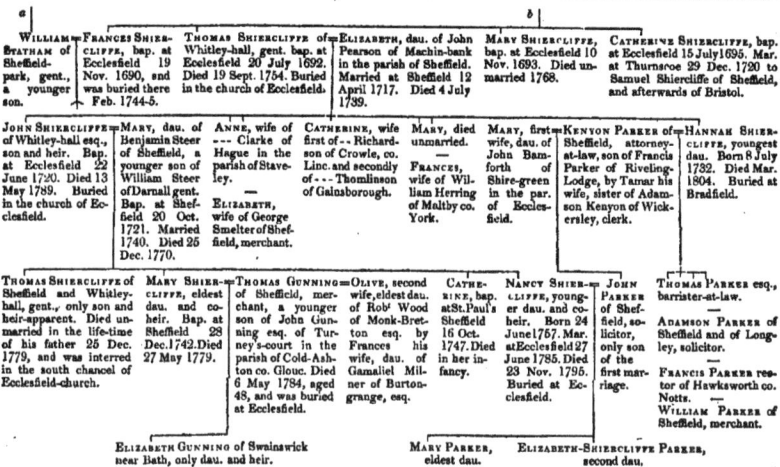

WILLIAM STATHAM of Sheffield-park, gent., a younger son. = FRANCES SHIERCLIFFE, bap. at Ecclesfield 19 Nov. 1690, and was buried there Feb. 1744-5.

THOMAS SHIERCLIFFE of Whitley-hall, gent. bap. at Ecclesfield 20 July 1692. Died 19 Sept. 1754. Buried in the church of Ecclesfield.

ELIZABETH, dau. of John Pearson of Machin-bank in the parish of Sheffield. Married at Sheffield 12 April 1717. Died 4 July 1739.

MARY SHIERCLIFFE, bap. at Ecclesfield 10 Nov. 1693. Died unmarried 1768.

CATHERINE SHIERCLIFFE, bap. at Ecclesfield 15 July1695. Mar. at Thurnsroe 29 Dec. 1720 to Samuel Shiercliffe of Sheffield, and afterwards of Bristol.

JOHN SHIERCLIFFE of Whitley-hall esq., son and heir. Bap. at Ecclesfield 22 June 1720. Died 13 May 1789. Buried in the church of Ecclesfield. = MARY, dau. of Benjamin Steer of Sheffield, a younger son of Darnall gent. Bap. at Sheffield 20 Oct. 1721. Married 1740. Died 25 Dec. 1770.

ANNE, wife of --- Clarke of Hague in the parish of Staveley. —— ELIZABETH, wife of George Smelter of Sheffield, merchant.

CATHERINE, wife of first of -- Richardson of Crowle, co. Linc. and secondly of - - Thomlinson of Gainsborough.

MARY, died unmarried. FRANCES, wife of William Herring of Maltby co. York.

MARY, first wife, dau. of John Bamforth of Shire-green in the par. of Ecclesfield. = KENYON PARKER of Sheffield, attorney-at-law, son of Francis Parker of Riveling-Lodge, by Tamar his wife, sister of Adamson Kenyon of Wickersley, clerk.

HANNAH SHIERCLIFFE, youngest dau. Born 8 July 1732. Died Mar. 1804. Buried at Bradfield.

THOMAS SHIERCLIFFE of Sheffield and Whitley-hall, gent., only son and heir-apparent. Died unmarried in the life-time of his father 25 Dec. 1779, and was interred in the south chancel of Ecclesfield-church. = MARY SHIERCLIFFE, eldest dau. and co-heir. Bap. at Sheffield 28 Dec.1742. Died 27 May 1779. = THOMAS GUNNING of Sheffield, merchant, a younger son of John Gunney's-court in the parish of Cold-Ash-ton co. Glouc. Died 6 May 1784, aged 48, and was buried at Ecclesfield. = OLIVE, second wife, eldest dau. of Robt Wood of Monk-Bretton esq. by Frances his wife, dau. of Gamaliel Milner of Burton-grange, esq.

CATHERINE, bap. atSt.Paul's Sheffield 16 Oct. 1747. Died in her infancy.

NANCY SHIERCLIFFE, young-er dau. and co-heir. Born 24 June1757. Mar. atEcclesfield 27 23 Nov. 1795. Buried at Ecclesfield. = JOHN PARKER of Sheffield, solicitor, only son of the first marriage.

THOMAS PARKER esq., barrister-at-law. ADAMSON PARKER of Sheffield and of Long-ley, solicitor. FRANCIS PARKER rector of Hawksworth co. Notts. —— WILLIAM PARKER of Sheffield, merchant.

ELIZABETH GUNNING of Swainswick near Bath, only dau. and heir.

MARY PARKER, eldest dau.

ELIZABETH-SHIERCLIFFE PARKER, second dau.

THUNDERCLIFFE or SYNOCLIFFE-GRANGE.

This house was a grange of the Cistertian abbey of Kirkstead in Lincolnshire, which had forges and other considerable property in this part of the parish of Ecclesfield and the adjoining parish of Rotherham, of the gift of De Busli and De Lovetot[1]. In the general confirmation made by King John to the monks of that house the forges of Tunnocliffe with the appurtenances are mentioned. In the 36 Henry III. the abbot of Kirkstead had free warren granted in these lands.

At the dissolution, Thomas Rokeby obtained possession of these lands. He was descended of the great family of that name in the north riding. His only daughter and heir married Henry Wombwell, son of Hugh, who was second son of Thomas Wombwell of Wombwell esquire. His descendant Thomas Womb-

well re-built or enlarged the old grange, for in the hall were his arms impaling those of Arthington, and the initials T.W. A.W. 1575. This person as well as his brother Nicholas Wombwell of Tickhill appeared at Flower's visitation of the county of York 1585, and the pedigree which he then delivered forms the basis of the earlier descents of the following table[2].

Robert Green compounded for his estate after the civil wars. He was also a benefactor at the rebuilding of the College of Arms after the great fire in 1665. His pedigree therefore appears in the Heralds' books of benefactors[3]. The arms below were granted by Richard Saint George by patent dated the 6th of October 1612 to Thomas Green of Cawthorne in the county of York, father to James Green the first of Thundercliffe.

PEDIGREE of WOMBWELL and GREEN of THUNDERCLIFFE-GRANGE.

ARMS of GREEN.—Azure, three demi-lions rampant erased erminois.
CREST.—Out of a mural coronet gules a demi-lion rampant as in the field.

HENRY WOMBWELL of Thundercliffe-grange, son and heir of Hugh Wombwell, second son of Thomas Wombwell of Wombwell, esquire. = - - - - dau. and heir of Thomas Rokeby of Thundercliffe-grange, esquire.

NICHOLAS WOMBWELL of Thundercliffe-grange, esquire, son and heir. Buried in the north chancel of Ecclesfield-church 30 May 1571. = ISABEL, dau. of Thomas Wentworth of Wentworth-Woodhouse, esquire. This lady I suppose to be the Isabel Wombwell who was buried at Rawmarsh 30 Nov. 1576.

THOMAS WOMBWELL of Thundercliffe-grange, esq. Living 1585. Bur. at Ecclesfield 2 Sept. 1592. = ISABEL, dau. of Richard Arthington of Arthington co. York, esq. Bur. at Ecclesfield 7 June 1593.

NICHOLAS WOMBWELL of Tickhill, esquire, 2d son. Living 1585. = ELIZABETH, dau. of --- Rolston, widow of Nicholas Maleverer of Letwell, esquire. Married at Ecclesfield 15 June 1573.

---

[1] See p. 28.   [2] Harl. MSS. 1394, f. 281.   [3] Vol. ii. f. 83.

3 Y

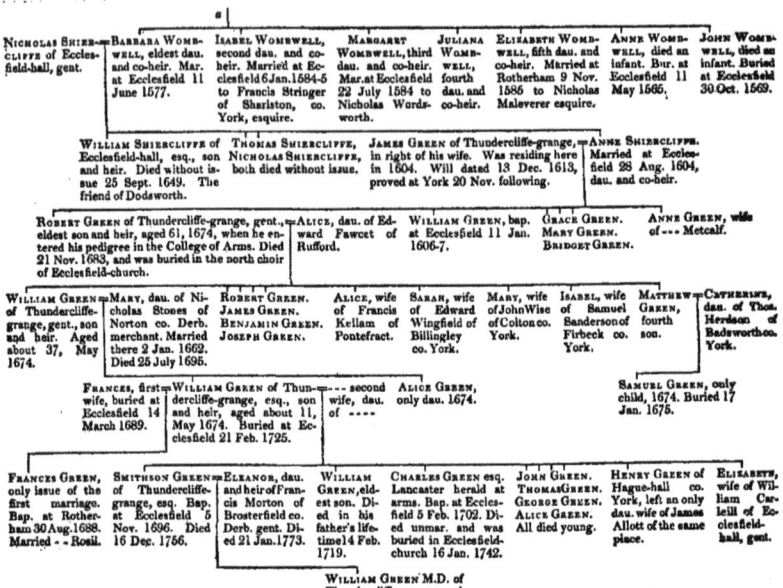

NICHOLAS SHIER=BARBARA WOMB-｜ISABEL WOMBWELL,｜MARGARET JULIANA｜ELIZABETH WOMB-｜ANNE WOMB-｜JOHN WOMB-
CLIFFE of Eccles-｜WELL, eldest dau.｜second dau. and co-｜WOMBWELL, third WOMB-｜WELL, fifth dau. and｜WELL, died an｜WELL, died an
field-hall, gent.｜and co-heir. Mar.｜heir. Married at Ec-｜dau. and co-heir. WELL,｜co-heir. Married at｜infant. Bur. at｜infant. Buried
｜at Ecclesfield 11｜clesfield 6 Jan.1584-5｜Mar.at Ecclesfield fourth｜Rotherham 9 Nov.｜Ecclesfield 11｜30 Oct. 1569.
｜June 1577.｜to Francis Stringer｜22 July 1584 to dau. and｜1585 to Nicholas｜May 1565,｜
｜｜of Sheriston, co.｜Nicholas Words- co-heir.｜Maleverer esquire.｜｜
｜｜York, esquire.｜worth.｜｜｜

WILLIAM SHIERCLIFFE of｜THOMAS SHIERCLIFFE,｜JAMES GREEN of Thundercliffe-grange,=ANNE SHIERCLIFFE.
Ecclesfield-hall, esq.,｜NICHOLAS SHIERCLIFFE,｜in right of his wife. Was residing here｜Married at Eccles-
and heir. Died without is-｜both died without issue.｜in 1604. Will dated 13 Dec. 1613,｜field 28 Aug. 1604,
sue 25 Sept. 1649. The｜｜proved at York 20 Nov. following.｜dau. and co-heir.
friend of Dodsworth.

ROBERT GREEN of Thundercliffe-grange, gent.,=ALICE, dau. of Ed-｜WILLIAM GREEN, bap.｜GRACE GREEN.｜ANNE GREEN, wife
eldest son and heir, aged 61, 1674, when he en-｜ward Fawcet of｜at Ecclesfield 11 Jan.｜MARY GREEN.｜of --- Metcalf.
tered his pedigree in the College of Arms. Died｜Rufford.｜1606-7.｜BRIDGET GREEN.
21 Nov. 1683, and was buried in the north choir
of Ecclesfield-church.

WILLIAM GREEN=MARY, dau. of Ni-｜ROBERT GREEN.｜ALICE, wife｜SARAH, wife｜MARY, wife｜ISABEL, wife｜MATTHEW=CATHERINE,
of Thundercliffe-｜cholas Stones of｜JAMES GREEN.｜of Francis｜of Edward｜of John Wise｜of Samuel｜GREEN,｜dau. of Thos.
grange, gent., son｜Norton co. Derb.｜BENJAMIN GREEN.｜Keilam of｜Wingfield of｜of Colton co.｜Sanderson of｜fourth｜Herdson of
and heir. Aged｜merchant. Married｜JOSEPH GREEN.｜Pontefract.｜Billingley｜York.｜Firbeck co.｜son.｜Badsworth co.
about 37, May｜there 2 Jan. 1662.｜｜｜co. York.｜｜York.｜｜York.
1674.｜Died 25 July 1695.

FRANCES, first=WILLIAM GREEN of Thun-=--- second｜ALICE GREEN,｜｜SAMUEL GREEN, only
wife, buried at｜dercliffe-grange, esq., son wife, dau.｜only dau. 1674.｜｜child, 1674. Buried 17
Ecclesfield 14｜and heir, aged about 11, of ----｜｜｜Jan. 1675.
March 1689.｜May 1674. Buried at Ec-
｜clesfield 21 Feb. 1725.

FRANCES GREEN,｜SMITHSON GREEN=ELEANOR, dau.｜WILLIAM｜CHARLES GREEN esq.｜JOHN GREEN.｜HENRY GREEN of｜ELIZABETH,
only issue of the｜of Thundercliffe-｜and heir of Fran-｜GREEN, eld-｜Lancaster herald at｜THOMAS GREEN.｜Hague-hall co.｜wife of Wil-
first marriage.｜grange, esq. Bap.｜cis Morton of｜est son. Di-｜arms. Bap. at Eccles-｜GEORGE GREEN.｜York, left an only｜liam Car-
Bap. at Rother-｜at Ecclesfield 5｜Brosterfield co.｜ed in his｜field 5 Feb. 1702. Di-｜ALICE GREEN.｜dau. wife of James｜leill of Ec-
ham 30 Aug.1688.｜Nov. 1696. Died｜Derb. gent. Di-｜father's life-｜ed unmar. and was｜All died young.｜Allott of the same｜clesfield-
Married - - Rosil.｜16 Dec. 1756.｜ed 21 Jan.1773.｜time 14 Feb.｜buried in Ecclesfield-｜｜place.｜hall, gent.
｜｜｜1719.｜church 16 Jan. 1742.

WILLIAM GREEN M.D. of
Thundercliffe-grange, and
other children.

Dr. Green sold Thundercliffe-grange to Mr. Hugh Mellor of Ecclesfield, who left it to his brother Mr. Thomas Mellor. Of him it was purchased by Thomas the third earl of Effingham, who had previously become possessed of the manors of Rotherham and Kimberworth, which had been left by Lord Henry Frederick Howard to the Effingham branch of the family. From him the earl also inherited the house at the Holmes near Rotherham, in which for a time he resided. The earl took down the old Thundercliffe-grange, and about the year 1777 laid the foundation of the present handsome edifice. He did not long enjoy it, and on his decease without issue it passed to his brother Richard the fourth earl of Effingham, who much improved the place and made it for many years his usual summer residence. He died in 1816.

The present mansion is said to be near the site of the old grange, but not exactly on the site. The old house was within the parish of Ecclesfield: the present is in the parish of Rotherham, where the noble owner was lord of the manor and patron of the church.

WARDSEND.

At an opposite extremity of the parish of Ecclesfield is Wardsend, an ancient place, being mentioned in the deed of De Lovetot and Saint Wandrille, where it is written Wereldsend. It is part of the duke of Norfolk's estate, but has been held under his grace's family by several generations of the family of Rawson, and is now the pleasant seat of Thomas Rawson esquire, late major-commandant of the Ecclesfield volunteers.

The direct ancestors of Mr. Rawson held Brookside in the chapelry of Bradfield, a freehold in the manor of Sheffield, from the time of Edward IV. to the 18 of Charles II. when Richard Rawson of Hatfield-house in the parish of Ecclesfield conveyed it to George Shaw, the son of Robert Shaw of Storrs. The following pedigree is compiled from the deeds of the Brookside estate, together with wills and other evidences for the later generations.

PEDIGREE of RAWSON of BROOK-SIDE and WARDSEND.

ARMS.—Quarterly sable and azure, a quadrangular castle argent, on a chief ermine three bulls' heads caboshed gules.
CREST.—On a wreath argent and sable, an eagle's head erased at the neck sable, gorged with a collar dancette and charged with two annulets interlaced in fess or.

RICHARD RAWSON.

ROBERT RAWSON son and heir 16 Edw. IV. when he claimed to hold of the lord the Brookside estate, which he surrendered 10 Hen. VII. to the use of his son Richard.

RICHARD RAWSON in 9 Hen. VIII. surrendered said lands to the use of Robert his son; and in 38 Hen. VIII. to the use of Richard his grandson, son of Robert deceased.

ROBERT RAWSON, died in his father's life-time.

RICHARD RAWSON of Dungworth-Storrs in the chapelry of Bradfield. Will dated 27 June 1591, in which he desires to be buried in the church or churchyard of Bradfield. Proved at York 30 Sept. following. = JENNET. Buried at Bradfield 20 March 1597.

RICHARD RAWSON of Brook-side, son and heir. Baptized at Bradfield 3 June 1560. Bur. there 7 May 1636. =ALICE.	ALICE, wife of William Swycket. Mar. at Bradfield 11 Feb. 1585.	ANNE, wife of John Spoone, to whom she bore Richard Spoone, founder of the chapel of Stannington.	JENNET RAWSON, died unmarried. Her will proved at York by Jennet Rawson her mother 28 Jan. 1592.	HELEN, wife of Thomas Dungworth.

ROBERT RAWSON of Brookside, yeoman, son and heir. =ALICE. Mentioned in his grandfather's will. Will dated 11 March 1662. Proved at York 1 March 1665. Buried at Bradfield 14 Sept. 1664. | Had one-third of the Brook-side estate settled on her 14 James I. Died before her husband.

RICHARD RAWSON of Brookside and Hatfield-house, eldest son. Sold Brookside. Was twice mar. and had three sons, Robert, Richard, and Thomas.	THOMAS RAWSON, 2d son. Executor to his father's will.	ROBERT RAWSON of Wardsend, third son. An executor to his father's will. Bap. at Bradfield 22 Aug. 1621. Mar. at Ecclesfield 24 Aug. 1650. Buried there 7 Feb. 1666. =MARY, dau. of Edward Rawson of Walkley in the parish of Sheffield. See her descent under the township of Nether-Hallam.	=JASPER BOSVILLE of Wardsend, first husband, a younger son of Thos. B. of Braithwell. Mar. at Ecclesfield 5 Aug. 1647. Died 15 Feb. 1649. Buried in the church of Ecclesfield.	HELEN, wife of John Beighton of Small-field in Bradfield.	ANNE, wife of Edward Adamson of the chapelry of Bradfield.	MARY, wife of Robert Eyre of Brad-field.	ALICE, wife of Christopher Dungworth Greaves.

ROBERT RAWSON, EDWARD RAWSON, JOHN RAWSON, are stated to have died without issue.	THOMAS RAWSON of Wardsend, youngest son, aged 1 year at the time of his father's death. Buried in the church of Ecclesfield 23 May 1728.	=HANNAH SWYFT, buried in the church of Ecclesfield 24 June 1714.	MARTHA RAWSON.	MARY BOSVILLE, sole dau. and heir, wife of Thomas Parkin of Sheffield.

THOMAS RAWSON of Wardsend, son and heir. Died in Sept. 1766, aged 71, and was buried in the church of Ecclesfield.	=DOUGLAS, dau. of ---Carr of the Edge and Southey, in the parish of Ecclesfield, gent. by Jane his wife, dau. of Nicholas Steade of Onesacre, gent.	JAMES RAWSON of Sheffield.	=ELIZABETH, dau. of Ezra Simon of Sheffield.	EDWARD, died young.	HANNAH, wife of ---Birks of Hansworth.	SARAH, wife of ---Elliot of Sheffield.	MARY, wife of --Vicars of Sheffield.

---first wife, dau. of John Barker of Bakewell esquire. Died 25 May 1794, and was buried in the church of Ecclesfield.	=THOMAS RAWSON of Wardsend, esq. eldest son and heir. To whom and to his brother and sister the arms above depicted were granted by patent, anno 1817.	=FRANCES, second wife, dau. of John Roe of Everton near Liverpool esq. Mar. 1797. Buried in the church of Ecclesfield.	JOHN RAWSON of West Don-house in the township of Nether-Hallam. Fellow of the Royal College of Surgeons; and one of the twelve capital burgesses of the parish of Sheffield. Died without issue 1819.	---dau. of Rev. Edward Mason of West Retford co. Notts. Married 1801.	HANNAH RAWSON of Wardsend.

We must not quit this parish, and proceed to its chapelry of Bradfield, without observing that it was the birth-place of Mr. Samuel Walker, who in the year 1746 founded those extensive iron-works at Masborough near Rotherham, which in the words of his modest epitaph ' now afford so singular an example both of the public and private benefit which may arise even from the smallest beginnings, when favoured by divine providence, and prosecuted with integrity, foresight, regularity, and an active comprehensive genius.'—The beautifully situated house and estate at Wincobank in this parish were purchased of the representatives of the late John Sparrow esquire, by one of the family of Mr. Walker, and have since been sold to Joseph Read esquire.

Brush-house, or as it was formerly written Brushes, was the favourite residence of John Booth esquire, who had been much connected with Mr. Samuel Walker in his commercial engagements. Here Mr. Booth spent the latter part of an active life in mathematical and philosophical studies, and indulging a natural and patriarchal desire prepared his own sepulchre amidst the shades his own hand had formed, in which his remains are now reposing.

Aldwark, the seat of the Clarelles, Fitz-Williams, and Foljambes, lies remote from the rest of the parish of Ecclesfield, and has never, as far as I know, been considered as making part of Hallamshire. Its long line of resident proprietors presents a fine subject to the genealogist and antiquary.

II.

The Chapelry of Bradfield.

A BLEAK, high, and mountainous tract of country lying between the Riveling and the Don, extending north-westward to the point where meet the three counties of Chester, Derby, and York, forms the chapelry of Bradfield. We have no exact admeasurement of it, but its area can scarce be less than fifty thousand acres. On the west it has the parishes of Hathersage, Hope, and Glossop in the county of Derby; on the north Peniston, on the east Tankersley and Ecclesfield, and on the south Sheffield. In 1801 it contained 763 houses and 4102 inhabitants. In 1811 the inhabitants were 4354.

Some portions of this district are among the highest grounds of the English Apennines. The waters of the Ewden and the Loxley, its two principal streams, are carried eastward by the Don to the German ocean; but some of its lesser streams are poured by the Mersey into the Irish channel.

In many parts the surface of the ground is covered with huge stones which bid defiance to all the efforts of cultivation. The soil in general is thin and poor. As long ago as the times before the Conquest there were a few small hamlets with a scanty portion of cultivated ground about them, and a few insular spots on which individuals had settled themselves and brought to submit to the plough. These descended from sire to son, and formed almost the only parts of this wide district over which till within these few years the empire of man seemed to be extended. All without the inclosures was barren, or produced only a scanty feeding of grass to the sheeep which ranged at large upon these hills. Here and there a few stunted trees were to be found; but the fern and the heath and the foxglove seemed to be the plants to which the soil was most congenial, mixed indeed with the slender wires of the bilberry, the cow-berry, or the more highly valued cranberry.

This district is now rapidly passing into the state of general cultivation; such parts I mean as are capable of being made productive. The business of inclosing was begun about thirty years ago. A country which is passing from a wild into a cultivated state has a naked and unpleasing effect; especially when, as in this instance, the new fences are all of stone.

The inhabitants are rugged as their soil. The hard and little profitable labour of clearing new ground naturally falls to the share of men little if at all removed above the rank of the operative husbandman: and the agriculturists who are tenants of the old inclosures (for the old and wealthy families are gone), or who cultivate small estates of their own, having little intercourse among themselves and less with their market-town, from which they are shut in by long and wearisome hills, are scarcely a degree above the day-labourers in intellect, in habits, or in knowledge. The Sheffield manufactures have extended to these regions. Many grinding-wheels are erected on the Riveling and the Loxley, and there are extensive iron-works on the Don near Oughtibridge. Many of the little farmers, especially those who inhabit Stannington and Worral, join with their rural employments the labour of the forge or of the wheel, hammering out the blades of razors or knives in small sheds attached to their dwelling-houses, or polishing them in the wheels on the streams below. The cutlers at Wadsley in this chapelry are supposed to present, both in their wares and the method of preparing them, no mean representation of what the state of the manufacture was two centuries ago.

Since the inclosures the state of the roads in this district has been much improved, and new roads have been made affording an easier communication with the more populous country around. There are persons still living who can remember that the journey from Stannington to the parish-church at Bradfield was not to be performed without some danger and difficulty: and the hospitality of the worthy family at Broomhead-hall has been encroached upon for a fortnight or three weeks by their friends from Sheffield, who had come to partake for a day of their Christmas festivities, and were prevented by a sudden fall of snow from regaining their homes. A new road from Sheffield to Manchester which follows the course of the Don for many miles in this chapelry is singularly picturesque and romantic. It penetrates into Lancashire by the pass at Woodhead.

In the northern parts of this chapelry are many remains of very high antiquity. Near the church of Bradfield is Bailey-hill, a Saxon camp as fair and perfect as when first constructed, save that the keep is overgrown with bushes. An elliptical area of about an acre is defended on one side by a large and steep natural bank; and on the other by an artificial agger, 110 yards long on the outside, and about 80 within. The area is further protected by a ditch accompanying the artificial agger, which runs 18 yards above it, and about 8 yards above the level of the area within. The only entrance to the area is by a narrow pass at one extremity, while the other is occupied by a circular tumulus or keep on a base of 174 yards in circumference, and rising to the height of about 27 yards. The base of this hill is surrounded by a ditch ten yards broad. The date of this work it is now impossible to ascertain: but it is obvious that so complete a work must have been formed not in haste or to serve any temporary purpose, but to be used as a constant military post: one of the frontier barriers it is probable of the kingdom of Northumberland.

At the distance of about a quarter of a mile, and on the other side of the village of Bradfield, is another earth work called The Castle-hill. This is less perfect than Bailey-hill; but the remains of a keep are visible, surrounded with a ditch except on the steep side of the hill where a ditch was not necessary, and on the slope of the hill there is an appearance of an intrenchment. The Reverend John Watson, who examined these remains and communicated his opinion respecting them to Mr. Wilson, says that he conceives Castle-hill to have been formed as an additional security to Bailey-hill, being placed on the very point from which alone Bailey-hill could be annoyed, and commanding a range of country which was not within view from Bailey-hill. The name it has always borne of Castle-hill appeared to Mr. Watson a reason for rejecting the supposition that it was raised for the purpose of attacking the garrison at Bailey-hill. It was plainly, he thought, the work of the same people who constructed the more perfect work. Near both these encampments several single pieces of Roman coin have been discovered.

Bar-dike, which is now the boundary between Broomhead-moor and Smallfield-common, Mr. Watson conceived to be a British work. It is an immense trench. He further conjectured that here the Britons may have made a stand against a body of forces coming from the side of Bradfield, and that their chief being slain in the encounter was buried under that vast carnedde on that part of Broomhead-moor which is known by the name of Roman Slack, and which is by the common people called the 'The apron full of stones.' The name of Roman Slack in Mr. Watson's opinion points out who were the party against whom the Britons were contending, though in what particular expedition he pretends not to say.

Near to Handsome-cross in the middle of Bradfield-moor is an ellipse eight yards by seven, of twelve stones, with a confused heap in the middle, which appeared to Mr. Watson to be druidical; as did also the Hurkeling-stone which is now a boundary mark between Broomhead-moor and Agden; and what he calls a small temple on the Side. Near to this are various barrows, some of which have been explored and found to have been raised over bodies which had previously been burnt. Among these tumuli was found the Celt which Mr. Wilson preserved in his museum.

The Lawns in Stannington where the Roman tables were found are near the Riveling, and about seven miles distant from Broomhead.

The chapelry of Bradfield formed the northern moiety of the Saxon manor of Hallam. But the Domesday-survey contains notices also of six small tracts designated by the term manor, that are now included within the chapelry. These are Haldworth, Ughill, Withala, Wadsley, Sceuelt, and Onesacre, of which the third and fifth are of uncertain appropriation. All these, except the two last, came with the manor of Hallam to Roger de Busli, from whom they passed to the Lovetots and their successors lords of Sheffield.

The name of Bradfield does not occur in Domes-

day-book. The village might be one of the berewitæ of the manor of Hallam. But whether what is now called Bradfield, or Nether Bradfield at a little distance from it where is an ancient stone cross, be the older vill, is not a point that is ascertained. One of the Bradfields after the Conquest gave name to the northern moiety of the manor of Hallam as a manor, as well as to the chapelry; and we find the manor of Bradfield mentioned in the *Nomina Villarum* 9 Edward II. and in other early records: but it seems to have been allowed silently to merge in the neighbouring manor of Sheffield.

That part of the produce of this district which belonged to the church was appropriated to the monks of Saint Wandrille. It passed afterwards to the Carthusians of Coventry, and was obtained by the Shrewsbury family at the Reformation.

The inhabitants of Bradfield had been accustomed to compound with the religious for their tythe. The bargain they had made Gilbert earl of Shrewsbury attempted to set aside. He was resisted by the freeholders, and on a solemn hearing of the cause the modus anciently paid was confirmed.

The same earl of Shrewsbury is charged with having attempted to deprive the inhabitants of Bradfield of certain lands which had been given at or before the Reformation for public uses. These lands he seized in 1592 and held them till 1615, in which year a decree was made by Thomas lord Ellesmere lord high chancellor in favour of the inhabitants. The decree directs that the lands in question shall be settled in the hands of ten feoffees, inhabitants of the parish or chapelry of Bradfield, to be employed by them for the repair of the church or chapel, payment of lays, taxes, and fifteenths, the relief of the poor, and such other good and charitable uses as to the inhabitants or major part of them shall seem meet and convenient. Whenever the number of feoffees should be reduced to six, four more were to be chosen to make up the number ten, and the deeds of the said lands were to be deposited in a chest for the use of the inhabitants. These lands in 1741 produced about 50*l. per annum.*

Of the profits of the rectory Alethea countess of Arundel gave one-third to the vicar of Ecclesfield for the time being. In the year 1784 the remaining two thirds were divided into four parts, one belonged to the curate of Bradfield, another to Hugh Spooner of Sheffield gentleman, and two to Francis Hurt Sitwell of Renishaw esquire.

Before the erection of the church or chapel of Bradfield the rude inhabitants of this wide district could have had few opportunities of attending the celebration of religious ordinances. The church of Ecclesfield lay very remote from them; nor were there any other churches to which they could resort without traversing long and wearisome hills, and as to many of them at least spacious and trackless heaths. On the weak authority of the *Magna Britannia* I have been led to state, when speaking of the original distribution of this district as to ecclesiastical concerns, that this church was given to Worksop, from whence it would follow that the Lovetots or the Furnivals were its founders[1]. But from what has been already said of the endowment of the vicarage of Ecclesfield on far better

[1] The donations of the Furnivals to Worksop in Bradfield were :—An oxgang of land in Stannington field, and pasturage for forty cows in

authority, it appears evidently to have been from the first a dependance on the church and priory of Ecclesfield, that is ultimately on the monastery of St. Wandrille. By the monks of Ecclesfield, or by the lay lord of the manor, or perhaps by their joint efforts, the inhabitants of this district were favoured with a church placed in the midst of them; at what precise period of time cannot now be ascertained, but probably not later than the reign of Henry II.

We have seen in the account of the endowment of the vicarage of Ecclesfield that the monks of the priory were required to find two chaplains to assist the vicar, one of whom was to officiate in this chapel of Bradfield. This was finally settled by Archbishop Melton. What they were to allow the chaplain was left to be settled in a private treaty between the parties. At the Reformation the appointment of the chaplain to the church of Bradfield became vested in the vicar of Ecclesfield for the time being, but no permanent provision seems to have been made for his support. Mr. Mansel the good vicar of Ecclesfield in the year 1700 made a representation to Archbishop Sharp of the state of this curacy, who gave twenty pounds towards the purchase of a house for the curate's residence, to which Mr. Mansel added twenty, and about thirty pounds more were raised in the neighbourhood. When a few years after the prospect of obtaining Queen Anne's bounty stimulated the exertions of the friends to religion and the church, there was a second subscription in which the honourable Thomas Watson-Wentworth was the largest contributor. The bounty was obtained; and the feoffees of the town-lands lending their assistance, a house and small piece of land at Nether-Bradfield were bought and settled on the curate for ever. Mr. Turie of Sheffield furnished the house with a library.

Mr. Wilson has remarked that in 1741 the vicar of Ecclesfield allowed the curate of Bradfield twelve pounds *per annum* and the surplice-fees.

The chapel has four wardens; two for Bradfield, one for Stannington, and one for Bolsterstone.

The number of communicants on Easter Sunday 1617 was 1141, in which surely many children must have been included.

CURATES of BRADFIELD.

1562. Sir John Webster.
1582. John Hygson.
1587. Sir Robert Tymothe or Tinmouth.
1593—1617. William Marcroft.
1617—1628. Matthew Ducket, Mr. Meredith, Mr. Rawson, Mr. Ellis, Mr. Attoy. All these names appear in this short interval of persons officiating as curates of Bradfield.
1628—1633. Matthew Booth. He resigned on being presented to the vicarage of Peniston.
1634. Godfrey Winter.
1635. William Scott.
1636—1640. John Watts.
1649—1658. Robert Chadwick. Buried here 5 Apr. 1659.
1659—1662. John Hoole. Displaced for nonconformity.
1662—1666. Thomas Goeld.
1666—1701. John Hoole. Restored, having conformed.

1701—1709. William Wills.
1710—1721. Benjamin Thompson.
1721—1725. Francis Poole.
1725—1741. Charles Steer presented by his brother William Steer vicar of Ecclesfield. He resigned on being presented to the rectory of Hansworth.
1741—1767. Christopher Butterfield.
     John Webster.
     Francis Dixon brother to James Dixon vicar of Ecclesfield.
1799—   Thomas Newton son-in-law to Mr. Dixon of Ecclesfield.

For this list we are principally indebted to Mr. Wilson, and though imperfect it is perhaps the best that can now be recovered.

THE CHURCH.

The church or chapel of Bradfield has a porch, tower, and bells, and having been new pewed about sixteen years ago is a commodious place of worship. On the rafters of the roof are a few shields of arms and badges, a bend, fretty, two chevrons, a cross pattee, a talbot, and the falcon and fetterlock. The latter seem to speak for themselves, but I cannot find that the former were borne by any families that had connexion with Hallamshire. There are also some small remains of painted glass in the windows; a lion rampant, a stag, a tree, &c. But in the time of one of the Randal Holmes there was the following mutilated inscription in the great east window[1]: 'Ora pro animabus Ric .... Ervyngham ... istam fenestram fieri fecerunt ....' under the effigies of a man and woman kneeling; in which it is evident that he has mistaken Everyngham for Ervyngham, and that therefore this window was erected after Everingham had married the heir of De Wadsley, that is about the time when so much cost was bestowed upon the embellishment in the same manner of the church of Ecclesfield.

The only monumental inscriptions worth notice are on two brass plates fixed against one of the pillars at the entrance of the chancel. On one are these arms:

MOREWOOD . . . . . a tree . . . . . . quartering
STAFFORD . . . . a chevron between three martlets . . . . .

And the draughts of a man, his wife, five sons and four daughters, all kneeling.

'Nere this place lyeth interred ye bodies of John Morewood gent. and Grace his wife, by whom he had issue 9 sonnes and 7 daughters. She dyed the 13th of July 1647, and he the 23 of Novembr following.

They both are changed, not dead: the good near dies
But they (as doth the sun) are set to rise
There bodies here, there soules in heaven attends
There blessed reuniting happy friends.'

On the other plate is this inscription in a better style:

'In memoriam Mariæ nuper uxoris Rowlandi Morewood de Okes gen.: filiæ Leonardi Gill de Norton generosi, quæ spiritum ultimum anhelavit vicesimo quarto die Martii Anno Dom. 1652 ætatis suæ 33. Ditata progenie quinque filiorum, viz. Johannis, Leonardi, Gilberti, Samuelis, et Josephi; quorum tres sc̄i. Johannes, Samuel, et Josephus sunt superstites.

Riveling, the gift of the first Gerard lord of Hallamshire; one third of the mills of Bradfield with the suit of his men of the soke of Bradfield of the gift of the second Gerard; four pounds of silver annually from the said mill of the gift of Bertha de Furnival, confirmed by her son Thomas de Furnival. They had six marks more rent from this mill, for Thomas

de Furnival confirmed to them amongst other things *twelve marks rent* from his mill at Bradfield.

[1] In a small scrap of paper in Harl. MSS. 2129. 268. in his handwriting of notes taken at Bradfield.

Quæ prius quam hine emigravit testimonium obtinuerat quod placuisset, et mortua adhuc loquitur.' Alluding to Heb. xi. 4 and 5.

The parish register commences in 1559, and has been well preserved.

A copy of the Book of Martyrs was given for the use of the parishioners to remain in this church by John Shaw clerk, afterwards vicar of Rotherham and Hull, a noted preacher during the civil wars, and who was then residing on his paternal estate at Sick-house. Henry Birley by his will before mentioned 1391 gave twenty shillings ' to the covering of the chapel of Bradfield when it happens, the same chapel to be covered in lead[1].'

At Nether Bradfield is a school founded by Mr. Thomas Marriott of Ughill about the year 1712, who endowed it with ten pounds *per annum*, for which the schoolmaster was to instruct twenty poor girls and boys.

Following the plan we have before adopted, it remains after these general notices to speak of particular places within the chapelry that present any claims on our attention. We shall begin with those which are nearest to Sheffield, and proceed from thence to the northern parts where the chapelry adjoins the parish of Peniston.

WADSLEY.

In the Domesday-survey this place is joined with Withala (perhaps Worral) and Ughill. From the latter it lies very remote. But they had the same proprietor before the Conquest, one Aldene, who in the three places had thirteen bovates of land which had been taxed and two ploughs. There was also a pasturable wood of a square leua in extent. In the time of the Confessor his property had been valued at twenty shillings, but at the time of the survey it was found to have been utterly laid waste. This Aldene had another manor at Haldworth in this chapelry, of two rated carucates and a pasturable wood of a square leua. This which had been worth twenty shillings was also lying waste. Aldene was therefore a great proprietor in this chapelry; and if he could be identified with the Saxon of his name who was a joint proprietor of Wickersley, another of the ruined manors, it would seem that he was on some account or other an object of peculiar dislike to the Norman invader.

All these places recovered themselves. Ughill, an insular spot at a cheerless distance from other human habitations, was the lonely residence of one Ellis in the time of the Furnivals, who made to him and the inhabitants of Nether Bradfield, Thornsett and Hawksworth a grant of common of pasture on their neighbouring moors. Ughill afterwards was the seat of a respectable yeomanry family of the name of Marriott, who resided there for many generations. One of them was the benefactor lately mentioned.

Wadsley had a more splendid destiny. It became the seat of a family similar in rank to the De Ecclesalls, and like them holding this estate by the name of a manor of the great baron at Sheffield-castle. Like the Ecclesalls also, they adopted for their heraldric in-

signia the arms of Furnival, charging the bend with three golden escallop shells for distinction's sake. They had at Wadsley a hall and park, and domestic chapel[2], which were not wholly destroyed in the reign of Elizabeth, but of which now only the names remain.

We shall endeavour to recover some particulars of this knightly family of Wadsley.

The first of this family with whom we meet is a Rogerus contemporary with Radulphus the first lord of Ecclesall. He was the father of Wido or Guy de Wadsley, who with his son Robert is mentioned in a confirmation deed to Beauchief without date[3].

Ralph de Ecclesall clerk granted to Roger son of Cotemoy or Costenot and his heirs one acre of land butting upon Wadsley, namely that which he held of Ralph son of Robert son of Wido de Wadsley, rendering yearly for the same to him and his heirs three pence at the feast of the Assumption of Saint Mary the Virgin, for all services, &c.[4]

This Ralph and Robert de Wadsley are probably the same persons who appear among the witnesses to Thomas lord Furnival's charter to Sheffield, 1297.

1294, 22 Edward I. Robert de Wadsley gave to Robert the son of Nicholas de Langers that land which Robert de Bethemys sometime held in Langers with one place of new inclosure lying between the said land and the moor of Wirrall on the one part, and between his land and that of Thomas de Furnival on the other, rendering to him and his heirs four shillings and one penny of silver. Dated at Wadsley on the vigil of Saint James the apostle[5].

1307, 35 Edward I. The king granted to Robert de Wadsley a market on Friday at his manor of Rotherham, and a fair there for three days, to wit, on the eve, day, and morrow of Saint John the Baptist[6].

1312, 6 Edward II. Robert son of Edmund de Wadsley gave to Robert Senur of Wortley, and to the heirs of his body, land in Wadsley and Bradfield. Dated at Wadsley on the sabbath day next after the feast of Saint Margaret. Ralph de Wadsley a witness[7].

This Robert de Wadsley was a knight, and in the same year a witness to a confirmation of Sir Thomas Chaworth to Beauchief[8].

30 Henry VI. Edo de Wadsley, probably the same name with Wido or Guy de Wadsley, held the manor of Wadsley of John earl of Shrewsbury at the fourth part of a knight's fee.

And lastly, Sir John Wadsley knight about the time of King Edward IV. left a daughter and heir named Margery, who carried this manor of Wadsley to her husband Henry Everingham of Stainborough near Barnsley, the chief of a very potent Yorkshire family. For her and for her husband was formerly the following memorial in a window of the church of Silkston, the parish in which Stainborough is situated : ' Orate pro animabus Henrici Everingham et Margeriæ Wadisley uxoris ejus, filiæ et hæredis Johannis Wadisley militis,' in which we may observe that this great heiress retains her maiden name after her marriage.

It is dubious how far this inscription may render it imperative on us to regard this lady as sole daughter

---

[1] Dods. MSS. H. 65 b. Harl. 801. Bradfield.
[2] Harl. MSS. 801. f. 99 a.
[3] Pegge, p. 162.
[4] Dods. MSS. N.N. 24 a. Harl. 801. See also Pegge, p. 146.

[5] Dods. K.K.K. 25. Harl. 801.
[6] Dods. C. 47 a. Harl. 801. Rotherham.
[7] Dods. K.K.K. 76. Harl. 801. from Wortley's Evidences.
[8] Pegge, 112.

and heir. In a collection of Yorkshire genealogy, Lansdowne MSS. in the British Museum[1], she is described as a co-heir, and in another similar collection principally of east riding families made by a judicious and careful hand in the latter end of the reign of Elizabeth[2] it is stated that Sir John Wadsley left by his wife, a daughter and heir of Sir Robert Massey knight,

three daughters his co-heirs, of whom the eldest married Henry Everingham of Stainborough, the second Sir Adam Everingham of Birkin, and the third Waterton of Walton. In both these manuscripts is the same pedigree of six descents of the Wadsleys, which seems hardly reconcileable with the authentic memorials of the family above noticed.

Sir JOHN WADSLEY. ⚭

    THOMAS WADSLEY.⚭ --- dau. of Sir Warin
                 de Bassingbourn.

       WARIN WADSLEY.⚭ --- dau. of Sir John
                    Fillingham of Fillingham.

THOMAS WADSLEY.⚭ --- dau. of Sir John Boys.   LEONARD.   JOHN.

       Sir JOHN WADSLEY.⚭ --- dau. and heir of Sir Robert
                  Massey or Maxett.

Before dismissing the house of De Wadsley we may remark that there is a tradition among the inhabitants of Wadsley, that the ancient owners of the hall were accustomed to entertain twelve men and their horses every Christmas for twelve days; and that at their departure each man was expected to stick a large pin or needle in the mantle-tree[3].

The marriage of the heiress of Wadsley with the house of Everingham was about the time of Richard III., with whom the Everinghams and their neighbour Sir Thomas Wortley were in high favour. It is by no means improbable that Richard visited these two knightly families during his sojourn at Sandal castle. The Everinghams did not desert their hereditary seat at Stainborough, but they for a time at least maintained the house and park at Wadsley. Leland mentions Wadsley as one of the seats of Everingham; and Dodsworth a century later observes of the Don that it goeth by Wortley to Wadsley, ' where in time past Everingham of Stainborough had a park now disparked.'

On inquisition taken at the castle of York after the death of Henry Everingham of Stainborough esquire, before Robert Chambers the king's escheator for the county of York, the jurors delivered in upon oath that the said Henry and Margery late his wife were seised of the manors of Wadsley and Worral in his demesne, as of fee in right of his said wife, and that they had issue Thomas Everingham. Further that the said Henry outlived Margery his wife, and that the premises in Wadsley and Worral aforesaid were held of the Lord Furnival as of his manor of Sheffield[4].

Thomas Everingham of Stainborough esquire, son and successor, married Margaret daughter of Thomas Wentworth of Bretton esquire, and by his will dated the 24th of July 8 Henry VIII. enfeoffed Sir Thomas Wentworth knight, John Wickersley, James Longley, and George Lynacre in his manors, lands, and tenements at Stainborough, Rockley, Wadsley, and Worral to the use of himself for life, and after to the only use of Margaret his wife, until such time as Henry Everingham his son came to the age of twenty-one[5].

Which Henry so succeeding, by Muriel his wife, daughter and at length sole heir of Sir John Burton of Kynsley knight, had issue Henry Everingham his son and heir.

This Henry spent and consumed the greatest part of his estate. In the 31 Henry VIII. he granted the manors of Wadsley and Worral to Sir Thomas Johnson knight, and in the 34th of the same reign made a deed of bargain and sale of the same premises[6]. But he finally parted with the manors to Robert Swyft esquire, to whom he levied a fine of them in Easter term 4 and 5 Philip and Mary[7].

Robert Swyft left only daughters; and on the partition of his estates 22 September 1561 the manors of Wadsley, Worral, and Wickersley were assigned to Sir Francis Leake who married one of them[8].

Leake disposed of the manors of Wadsley and Worral to George earl of Shrewsbury, who died seised of them in 1590[9]; as did his son Gilbert the seventh earl in 1616[10]. They are enumerated among the possessions of the family in the great entail of the third of Charles I.; and among the manors of this family for some time sequestered by parliament.

When or how the manor of Wadsley became alienated from the possessions of the house of Howard does not now appear. But Mr. Wilson notices that in 1741 it was the property of William Burton of Royds-mill esquire, in right of his wife the sister and heir of Mr. Bamforth. In the year 1784 it was the joint property of William and Michael Burton, sons of the said William Burton, who had allotments of land assigned them by the commissioners under the inclosure act of that year, in respect of their manorial rights. The manor is now divided between Lady Burgoyne and George Bustard Greaves of Page-hall, esquire. At the house still called the hall, the courts for the manor have been usually held.

STANNINGTON.

This is the name of an extensive tract of high ground declining on the north to the Loxley, and on the south to the Riveling, by which it is separated from the town-

---

[1] No. 957.
[2] This manuscript was formerly in the library of John Laughton of Eastfield near Tickhill esquire. I had the opportunity of consulting it at the house of the late Mr. Robert Wylde Moult of Wickersly, a name with which I have many pleasing recollections connected with the subjects of many of these pages.
[3] See Beckwith's edition of Blount's Ancient Tenures, 4to edit. p. 532.

[4] Dods. MSS. K. 23 a.   Harl. 801.   Wadsley.
[4] Dods. MSS. K. 24 a.   Harl. 801.   Wadsley.
[5] Norfolk Evidences.   Yorkshire bundle l.
[7] Dods. MSS. K. 23 b.   Harl. 801.   Wadsley.
[8] See p. 211.
[9] Inq. p. m. Blore's Winfield, p. 98.
[10] Inq. p. m. recited in Brooke's MS. collections for this manor.

ship of Upper-Hallam in the parish of Sheffield. It was here that the Roman tables were discovered, and a part of the south exposure of the hill bears the name of Haugh Park. Part of the shaft of an old stone cross is remaining. A considerable population of small agriculturists and still smaller manufacturers is scattered over this hill. There is, properly speaking, no village of Stannington, the principal collections of houses being known as Upper-Gate and Nether-Gate. As late as the reign of Edward III. surnames were not in common use in this district, for in a deed of 1361 in possession of the church-burgesses of Sheffield we find a woman described as widow of Adam del Nethergate in Stannington.

At Revel-grange resided from an early period a family of the name of Revel, whom we often meet in the old genealogies as connected by marriage with the superior gentry of the county of Derby. The attachment of this family to the old profession of religion exposed them to much injurious treatment in the time of the civil wars and commonwealth. From the effect of the severe and heavy fines which were levied upon them at a time when the name of Recusant was supposed to place a man out of the pale of civil protection, the family seems scarcely now to have recovered itself. Mr. Richard Broomhead of this place married the heiress of the Revels about the year 1740.

The inhabitants of this part of the chapelry must have been prevented from attending with any regularity the services in their chapel. The distance was four or five miles; the roads in the best of times scarcely passable for carriages of any description, and in the winter season not at all. This moved one Richard Spoone of Stannington to attempt the establishment of a place of worship nearer home, which he accomplished in 1652 or 1653, building a small chapel, and endowing it with a piece of ground towards the support of the officiating minister.

MINISTERS of the CHAPEL of STANNINGTON.

1652—1655. Ralph Wood.
1655—1657. Robert Matthewman.
1657—1662. Isaac Darwent. His name occurs in Calamy's List of the ejected and silenced ministers; but he was preaching here after the act of Uniformity began to operate, and was tenant of the chapel lands till 1665.
1663—1665. — Hopwood.
1665—1667. Joseph Bacon.
    1668. — Revel.
1668—1671. Timothy Dighton.
1673—1674. Thomas Mellor.
1674—1676. William Walker.
1676—1679. John Marsden.
1679—1683. William Walker.
1684—1689. George Crosland.
1689—1696. Abraham Dawson. In his time the book of common prayer ceased to be used in the chapel.

1696—1713. William Bagshaw. Died here.
1713—1761. Samuel Smith. Died here.
1761—1780. John Hall. Removed to Rotterdam in Holland.
1780—1785. Josiah Rhodes.
1785—1794. Edward Gibson. Removed to Stockport.
1794—1814. Astley Meanley. Died minister of Stannington.
1814— Peter Wright.

The old chapel was taken down in 1742, and a new one erected near the site of the former by Mr. Thomas Marriott of Ughill, assisted by other neighbouring dissenters. At a little distance from the chapel is a comfortable house for the minister's residence, with a spacious garden adjoining, which were much improved by the late inhabitant Mr. Meanley, whose name and that of his amiable and excellent consort (who went hand in hand with him in every work of mercy to the poor around them) will be long venerated by those who knew them, and mentioned with respect in distant times even when all that tasted of their bounty shall have passed from off the stage.

The chapel, like all dissenting meeting-houses, is a plain building. On the communion-table lies the Book of Martyrs, the gift of some unknown hand, intended, I hope, not to create or foster among the simple inhabitants of this district unchristian and inhuman prejudices, but an honest detestation for religious persecution whatever shape it may assume. There have been a few interments at the chapel; and at no great distance, on the brow of the hill opposite to Brookside, was a small and decent inclosure in which were deposited the remains of about ten or twelve persons of the family of Shaw of Brookside. There were several grave-stones, which were taken up, and the ground ploughed, about fifteen years ago.

There is a school in this hamlet which was endowed by William Ronksley in 1723 with forty pounds, for which five children were to be taught, to be chosen by Francis Ronksley of Riveling-side.

The ministers of Stannington have belonged to that class of dissenters called Presbyterian.

There is another dissenting chapel on the hill of Loxley opposite to Stannington. It was built about the year 1789, principally by the exertions of a clergyman of evangelical sentiments, the Reverend A. B. Greaves, minister of Saint Martin's chapel Stony Middleton.

MOREWOOD.

A hamlet of the chapelry mentioned in the *Membra castri de Sheffield*. This, like its neighbour Dungworth, and indeed all the little hamlets throughout Hallamshire, had its resident family of its own name. The Dungworths removed from the neighbourhood about the time of James I. The Morewoods continued much longer, and were indeed for a time among the principal gentry of Hallamshire.

PEDIGREE of MOREWOOD of the OAKS in BRADFIELD.

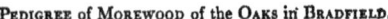

ARMS.—Vert, an oak tree coupé en base argent fructed or.
CREST.—On a torce argent and vert, two arms embowed armed proper, supporting a chaplet of oak-branches vert, fructed or.

WILLIAM MOREWOOD,
Plaintiff respecting lands in Bradfield
10 Hen. VI. Dods. MSS. xxx. 20 b.
Harl. 801. Bradfield.

JOHN MOREWOOD of the Oaks,
temp. Hen. VII. and VIII.

GILBERT MOREWOOD of the Oaks,
11 Eliz.

JOHN MOREWOOD of the Oaks,
15 Eliz.

ROWLAND MOREWOOD of the Oaks, gent. Will dated 19 Feb. 1618, and proved at York 30 Sept. 1619 by John Morewood his son and executor. He directed that his body should be buried in the chancel or quire of Bradfield-church, where he was interred 1 July 1619. A benefactor to the poor of Bradfield and other places.
= CATHERINE, dau. and co-heir of Humphry Stafford of Eyam co. Derb., gent., by Lucy his wife, dau. of Edward Eyre of Holmehall co. Derb. esquire. Buried at Bradfield 16 July 1595.

ANDREW MOREWOOD of Stadon co. Derb. Named an executor in the will of his brother Rowland Morewood. Had a son named Rowland.

———— ——— wife of wife of Richard Row- Goodwin, land. by whom Swane. a son named Joseph Goodwin.

WILLIAM MOREWOOD. Had a son ThomasMorewood, who is mentioned in the will of Rowland Morewood.

ELIZABETH MOREWOOD, mar. at Bradfield 31 Aug. 1590 to Richard Wainwright of Dungworth, lord of the manor of Darnall.

BEATRICE MOREWOOD, mar. at Bradfield 22 Sept. 1591 to George Shaw.

JOHN MOREWOOD of the Oaks, gent. son and heir. Died 23 Nov. 1647, and was buried in the church of Bradfield. Will dated 11 Oct. 1647. Proved at York 20 June 1648.
= GRACE HURST of London, merchant. of the county of York. Died 13 July 1647, and was buried in the church of Bradfield.

GILBERT MOREWOOD Dec. 1586. He acquired large property, which he divided by will bearing date 11 May 1650 among his three daughters and co-heirs[1]. Bap. at Bradfield 21

ANTHONY MOREWOOD, one of the supervisors of his father's will. Living at Hemsworth in Norton co. Derb. 1615. Purchased an estate at Alfreton in 1629, where he died 29 June 1636[2].

HUMPHY, FRANCIS, ANDREW, ROWLAND, of whom the last two were living 1619.

GERTRUDE, wife of Jeffery Roberts. ANNE, wife of James Bullock of Green-hill in Norton, gent.

ALICE, wife of John Bamford of Pule-hill in the parish of Alfreton, esq., a justice of the peace and treasurer for the lame soldiers.

ELIZABETH, wife of Ralph Greaves. FAITH, wife of Reginald Eyre of Maltby co. York.

MARY, living 1619. ELLEN, JOAN, both died in infancy.

ROWLAND MOREWOOD of the Oaks, and also of Norton, esq. A justice of the peace, son and heir. Died at Norton 28 Aug. 1658, and was buried at Bradfield. Will dated 24 March 1657.
= MARY, dau. of Leonard Gill of Norton, gent. Died 25 Mar. 1652, and was bur. in the church of Bradfield.

ANDREW MOREWOOD of the Hallows in the parish of Dronfield gent., and lead-merchant. He was the principal purchaser of the lead on the demolition of Sheffield-castle. Died 17 Oct. 1700.

= MARY, dau. of William Spencer of Attercliffe, gent. Mar. at Sheffield 21 Feb. 1655. Died 30 Apr. 1682.

GILBERT MOREWOOD of Dronfield, gent. Mar. Martha dau. of Nicholas Saunderson of Sheffield, gent. Died in Feb. 1666.

JOHN, FRANCIS, BENJA- MIN, JOSEPH, ANTHO- NY, WIL- LIAM.

ANNE, wife of William Pickford, gent. — Fox of Smallfield, and secondly of Henry Balguy of the Hagg in Hope, gent.

GRACE, wife of James Pickford, gent. — SUSAN, wife of Thomas Jackson gent. — MARY, wife of William Smyth, gent.

SARAH, wife of --- Hillary. — PRISCILLA, wife of --- — ELIZABETH, wife of Jas. Stopford, gent.

SARAH MOREWOOD, aged 4, 1662. Mar. John Cart of Manchester, M B. of the University of Cambridge, son of John Cart rector of Hansworth.

HEPHZIBAH MOREWOOD, wife of Robert Wood of Monk-Bretton co. York, gent.

ELIZABETH MOREWOOD, wife of John Oldfield of Manchester.

HANNAH MOREWOOD, wife of John Latham of Ounston in Dronfield, gent.

RUTH MOREWOOD, died an infant.

BETHIA MOREWOOD, wife of Edw. Greenwood of Lees-hall in Norton, gent.

ELIZABETH, first wife, dau. of Edward Gill of Carhouse, esq., sometime member of parliament for the west riding. Mar. at Rotherham 3 Feb. 1668. Had a dau. Mary, who died an infant.
= JOHN MOREWOOD of Alfreton, esq., to which estate he succeeded on the death of his cousins the granddaughters of Anthony Morewood. Bap. at Norton 5 May 1642. Sheriff of Derbyshire 1677, when he obtained a grant of arms to himself and all the descendants of his grandfather. C. 34, f. 75 b. in Col. Arm. Died 2 Feb. 1680.
= BARBARA, 2d wife, dau. of Arch. Palmer of Wanlip co. Leic. esq., relict of Samuel Sleigh esq. son of Sir Samuel Sleigh.

LEONARD MOREWOOD and GILBERT MOREWOOD, both died in their infancy.

SAMUEL MOREWOOD of the Oaks, 4th, but second surviving son. Bap. at Bradfield 2 Apr. 1648. Bur. there 25 May 1715, and his will was proved at York 20 June following.
= ELIZABETH, dau. and co-heir of John Greaves of Hallfield in the parish of Ecclesfield. Mar. at Bradfield 13 July 1675. Buried there 2 July 1727.

JOSEPH MOREWOOD of Hemsworth in the parish of Norton, gent., youngest son. Baptized at Bradfield 25 Sep. 1649. Died 28 Mar. 1714, and was buried in the church of Norton.
= ANNE, dau. of ----- ----- Thornton.

ROWLAND MOREWOOD of Alfreton, esq. High-sheriff of the county of Derby 1707.
= MARY WIGLEY of Mansfield.

MARTHA and MARY, both living 1708.

MARTHA, first wife, dau. of Edw. Kenyon of Haldworthbank, and sister of Adamson Kenyon of Wickersley, clerk.
= JOHN MOREWOOD of the Oaks, gent., only son and heir. Born 7 March 1689. Sold the Oaks to Robert Newton of Nortonhouse, esq., and died 7 March 1771, aged 83.
= MARTHA, second wife, dau. of Edmund Hancock. Married at Dam chapel in Peakforest 1744. Bur. at Bradfield 28 July 1764.

ELIZABETH, wife of Rev. George Staniland of Worsbro'.

HANNAH, wife of Jonathan Seaton of the parish of Ackworth, gent.

MARIA, wife of Joseph Steer of Sheffield, mercer.

SARAH, wife of Gervas Seaton of Pontefract, gent.

MARTHA, wife of William Scriven of the Herdings in Norton, gent.

MARY, died an infant. ANNE.

JOHN MOREWOOD. Died unmar. 1758.

GEORGE MOREWOOD of Alfreton, esquire. High-sheriff of the county of Derby 1762. Died without issue 1 Jan. 1792, aged 72.
= HELEN, dau. of Richard Goodwin of Ashburn.

= HENRY CASE, second husband, rector of Ladbrooke co. Warw. Married 7 Feb. 1793, when he assumed the surname of MOREWOOD.

SAMUEL MOREWOOD, ROWLAND MOREWOOD, and others.

John Morewood who sold the Oaks had by both his wives a numerous issue, who having lost the estate of their forefathers have sunk into the mass of the population. Mr. Newton took down the house at the Oaks, and erected on its site an ordinary farm-house.

SPOUT-HOUSE.

At this place resided many generations of the family of Morton. Francis Morton of this place and his son Dr. Thomas Morton of Sheffield appeared at Sir William Dugdale's visitation, and delivered in a pedigree of many descents which was duly registered[3]. The arms to which they made pretensions were also allowed them, viz. Or, three ravens sable and a border azure. Dr. Morton married Dorothy daughter of Thomas Wright of Unthank in the parish of Dronfield gentleman, by his wife, a daughter of the family of Shiercliffe of Whitley-hall. He died in 1625 at the age of 36, leaving an only daughter who carried this estate to her husband John Wingfield of Wirksworth gentleman. Her posterity became extinct in her grandson William Wingfield who died in 1736, when Francis Ronksley of Riveling-side, heir general of the Mortons, attempted to establish a claim to the ancient inheritance of the family; but failing, it passed to the representatives of the Wingfields. Dr. Thomas Morton left a dole, as in our northern language it is called, of ten shillings a year to the poor of Westnal Byerlow, a part of Bradfield in which Spout-house is situated, to be paid to ten poor persons sixpence each on Good Friday and Saint Thomas's day for ever.

On the 13th of May 1504 John Morton of Bradfield made his will, in which he directed that his body should be buried in the church of Saint Nicholas.

ONESACRE.

This place, Anesacre, together with Sceuelt now of uncertain appropriation, was a manor of one carucate before the Conquest. It is remarkable that these two places were left out of the grant which conveyed so much territory on every side of them to Roger de Busli. They are surveyed in Domesday as Terra Regis, and in the soke of Wakefield. Godric was the last Saxon proprietor. I am not aware that in later times this has been accounted as a distinct manor. The family of Steade had an ancient freehold of inheritance at this place, a branch no doubt of the family of Stead of Stead in the parish of Wath, which appears in deeds of the reign of Edward III. The present representative is Broughton Benjamin Steade esquire, who resides at Beauchief, and whose father Thomas Steade esquire built the pleasant mansion of Hillsborough, now the residence of John Rimington esquire.

BROOMHEAD-HALL.

The capital mansion called Broomhead-hall in the northern part of this chapelry is about ten miles distant from the town of Sheffield and five from Peniston. It stands at the head of the valley along which flows the Ewden, one of the tributary streams of the Don, and its front windows command a fine view down the valley of the woody steep of Wharncliffe.

It is one of the very few specimens of houses built by the substantial gentry of Hallamshire in the reign of Charles I. In that reign it was built by Christopher Wilson, who was one of those gentlemen in this part of the county of York who were fined for having neglected to appear at the king's coronation to receive the honour of knighthood. He had afterwards a captain's commission in the parliament army.

There had been a house on the same site long before. In it resided the father of Christopher Wilson, of the same name, who took the lead in the opposition which the freeholders of Bradfield made to Gilbert earl of Shrewsbury in the great tythe cause. And on the same estate the ancestors of the said Christopher Wilson had resided from the time of Edward I. In whose reign a grant of lands was made to Adam Wilson his scutiger, by Thomas lord Furnival, at Wightwistle in the neighbourhood of Broomhead, for services in the Scottish wars.

But it appears that before the time of this Adam Wilson there had been of the name residing at or near Broomhead, and that both he and his ancestors married with the families of the best account in this part of Hallamshire.

The estate of Broomhead was till within these few years the last effort of cultivation in that direction. The house stood on the edge of an immense tract of moorland; and it is equally difficult to explain how cultivation should have extended itself so far, and why it should at this point have stopped for a period of six or seven centuries.

This house has a strong claim on the notice and respect of every lover of Hallamshire topography. It was the birth-place and the constant residence of John Wilson esquire, a gentleman to whom we owe the preservation of so much documentary matter, which but for his care it is too probable would have been entirely lost, leaving this district destitute of that evidence by which alone the character of authenticity can be given to the history of many of its institutions, and the account of many of its principal inhabitants. It is to be regretted that no notice was taken of Mr. Wilson at the time of his decease in any of the periodical journals; except that he died 'lamented by a numerous and respectable acquaintance, for in him the gentleman and the christian were happily united.' This is indeed the best of praises; but as he was also the literary man and the antiquary, we cannot but wish that his contemporaries had given us some information respecting his literary habits and pursuits. It is now too late fully to supply the deficiency, but something may be done.

Mr. Wilson was the great grandson of Christopher Wilson the builder of the present house, and was born in it on the 28th of April 1719. He was the eldest

[1] The three daughters of Gilbert Morewood were Barbara, wife of Thomas Rich esquire, afterwards Sir Thomas Rich of Sunning, bart.; Grace, wife of Simon Bennet of Bechampton co. Bucks, esq., to whom she bore three daughters co-heiresses, married into the noble families of Osborne, Cecil, and Bennet; and Frances, who married Sir Thomas Gresley bart. of Drakelow in the county of Derby.

[2] Anthony Morewood of Alfreton by Frances Redhill his wife had two sons twins, Rowland and Anthony, who were baptized at Norton 16 July

1615. Rowland died unmarried in 1647, leaving his brother his heir, who resided at Alfreton and was high-sheriff of the county of Derby in 1649. He had only two daughters, of whom the elder married the honourable Alexander Stanhope, a younger son of the earl of Chesterfield; and the younger, Henry Goring esquire. Both died without issue, when the estate of Alfreton passed to John Morewood the head of the family, son and heir of Rowland Morewood of the Oaks.

[3] C. 40. f. 132 b. in Col. Arm.

son of his father. His education he received at the grammar schools of Sheffield and Chesterfield, and made considerable proficiency in classical studies. His father died about the time when he left school, and he returned to Broomhead to reside with his mother.

Mr. Wilson was not intended for any profession. While the younger children had been sent into the world in different employments and professions, the family estate, neither much increased nor much diminished in the generations through which it had successively passed, had been found sufficient to enable the head of the family to maintain hospitality, and to take a respectable rank among the neighbouring gentry. From the age of sixteen, therefore, Mr. Wilson was never long absent from his hereditary seat.

The very circumstance of birth as the heir of a family which has preserved its estate through a period of five or six centuries, is enough to give a man a taste for that branch of antiquities at least which respects genealogy. But along with the estate had descended an unbroken series of evidences such as is rarely to be found, and which of themselves were sufficient to form the foundation of a collection of charters. The hall too stood in the midst of earth-works of the highest antiquity, and on Mr. Wilson's own estate the plough was every now and then bringing to light relics of the Roman and the Celtic times. How far Mr. Wilson's predilection for these studies might be fostered by his mother's brother the Reverend Dr. Cox Macro, the Suffolk collector and antiquary, does not now appear.

That Mr. Wilson's attention was very early directed to topographical and antiquarian pursuits appears from this—that in 1741, when he was only two-and-twenty, he had completed a topographical survey of Hallamshire, which, while it contains some things which his more matured judgement would have led him to reject, is highly creditable to his industry and spirit of research.

From that time Mr. Wilson seems to have made it the business of his life to collect from all quarters whatever might throw light on the descent of property, on family antiquities, or on the history, manners, and customs of our ancestors. His taste was known, and his knowledge in such matters was properly estimated by many gentlemen in the neighbourhood, who took a pleasure in enriching his collection with charters when they had ceased to be material to the legal security of their estates. Among the principal contributors were Mr. Staniforth of Darnall, Mr. Bosville of Gunthwaite, and Sir Thomas Wentworth of Bretton. The retired life which he led at Broomhead gave him abundant leisure, which he employed principally

in transcribing in a plain and legible hand what he was not allowed to appropriate.

The strength of Mr. Wilson's collection of manuscript matter lay in its charters. But he had formed a curious collection of original letters, of inventories, of old books of accompt, of early and unpublished poetry, and a variety of miscellaneous matter pertaining to our general history, and more especially to the county of York[1]. All these he had carefully perused and sorted, and his finger index appears in all of them pointing to any thing which seemed more peculiarly deserving of notice. Added to these were a transcript of the Domesday book, as far as relates to the county of York, in his own hand; large notices from Torre's manuscripts copied from the extracts made by his friend Dr. Burton of York; copies of the rates for the county of York, of the book of the bridges, and large extracts from many of the parish-registers in his neighbourhood; numerous pedigrees; many valuable church notes in the counties of York and Derby; and memoranda of occurrences in his own time and neighbourhood, or of what he found preserved by tradition among the people around him.

But his attention was not confined to the collecting of charters and other manuscripts. He improved the library which had been collected by his grandfather the vicar of Sheffield, by the addition of many choice printed volumes; he formed a cabinet of coins of considerable value; and he had a little museum consisting of rare prints, a few paintings, and other objects natural and artificial, ancient and modern, of different degrees of curiosity and value.

Frequent attention to the written character in use at different periods gave Mr. Wilson great skill in deciphering ancient records; and I have heard that his numismatical knowledge might justly vindicate for him a claim to the name and character of an antiquary.

As his collection increased, his acquaintance with the antiquaries of his day extended. His correspondence was sought by some of the most eminent among them. He was not a fellow of the Society, but we have seen that his name was coupled in an honourable manner with a communication which in the opinion of the President was one of the most valuable that the Society had ever received. With Bishop Percy Mr. Wilson had a long correspondence on matters connected with his publication of the Reliques of English Poetry, and with the bishop's descent maternally from a family of the name of Wilson. With Mr. Whitaker the historian of Manchester he was in frequent correspondence; as he was also with Mr. Watson the rector of Stockport, and with Brooke, whose untimely death he

[1] Among the manuscript collections made by Mr. Wilson were the following articles:—

An old copy of Kirkby's Inquest for the county of York.

Erdeswick's Staffordshire.

Inventory of the furniture of Sir William Cavendish's house at North Awbrey near Lincoln.

The steward's accompt of the expenses of Sir William Saint Loe's journey from Chatsworth to London, and attendance on the Queen from August to October 1560.

Original manuscript of one of the voyages of a Cavendish in the time of Elizabeth; since published in Purchas's Pilgrims.

Depositions respecting the divorce of Anne of Cleves.

An accompt-book of Richard Bunny of Newland when he was receiver of the northern counties, containing many original letters of Edward VI., Queen Elizabeth, and their councils, with matter pertaining to the life of Bunny.

The accompts of Sir John Travis master of the King's ordnance in Ireland in the reign of Henry VIII.

Sale and Inventory of goods belonging to the priory of Christ Church in Canterbury.

A narrative of the proceedings of the earls of Essex and Southampton, in a contemporary hand.

The Liberties and Customs of the Lead Mines, in verse, by Edward Manlove.

A treatise on Bail and Mainprize by Sir Edward Coke.

The genealogy of the family of Rockley of Rockley in Worsborough-dale, collected by Mr. Robert Rockley, the last of that ancient name.

A book of husbandry in the manner of Tusser, a Fatherly Farewell, and other Poems, by John Kaye of Woodsome esquire, in the time of Elizabeth, with an account of the transactions of that family from 1560 to 1642.

A collection of poetry made in the time of Charles I.

An unpublished descriptive poem entitled 'The Moors,' by Godfrey Boëville of Gunthwaite esquire.

Copy of the Rev. Mr. Garlick's collections for the history of Wakefield.

A Catalogue of the curiosities, manuscripts, early printed books, ancient deeds and writings, collected by Dr. Cox Macro of Norton in Suffolk.

did not live to deplore. He also reckoned among his friends Dr. Pegge the rector of Whittington, and Beckwith, whose edition of Blount's Ancient Tenures owes something to the assistance he received from Mr. Wilson.

But his memory must not be flattered. That he collected some things which were scarcely worth preservation; and that he consumed time in laborious transcription from books which at all times were easily accessible, that might have been much better employed in digesting into some regular and connected form what he had collected, in arranging, for instance, his materials for the history of his own and the neighbouring parishes, it would be wrong to deny. In fact, he arranged and composed nothing, saving his early survey of Hallamshire, and a genealogical account of his own family, which he compiled with great exactness from the body of evidences in his possession, and from such foreign authorities as he was able to procure.

With this aversion to arrangement and composition, it is not surprising that he published scarcely any thing. Indeed nothing is known to be from his pen except a few communications to the *Gentleman's Magazine*: and I much doubt whether he could have been prevailed upon by his friend the Somerset herald to have taken the part assigned him in the scheme which was much canvassed in the year 1775 for dividing the county of York, or at least the west riding, into portions, to be allotted to distinct antiquaries by whose joint labours it was hoped that a general history of the county, on a scale of proper extent, or at least of the riding, might have been accomplished.

The zeal of Mr. Wilson for collecting continued with unabated ardour to the last. He died at the age of sixty-three on the 3d day of March 1783, and was buried with his ancestors in the chancel of the church of Bradfield.—After his decease his coins and library were sold. His manuscript collections remained entire. A room was appropriated to them in the hall at Broomhead, even when the family had ceased to reside there, and it was inhabited by the tenant of the farm. The room was rarely opened; and in 1808, when by the favour of the present possessor I was first allowed to have access to them, I found them nearly in the state in which they had been left by him of whose assiduity and care they are so honourable a memorial.

The engraving of Mr. Wilson which is here given is a faithful copy from a portrait now in the possession of his son Mr. William Wilson of Sheffield.

It remains that we add the pedigree as collected by Mr. Wilson himself with some later additions.

PEDIGREE of WILSON of BROOMHEAD.

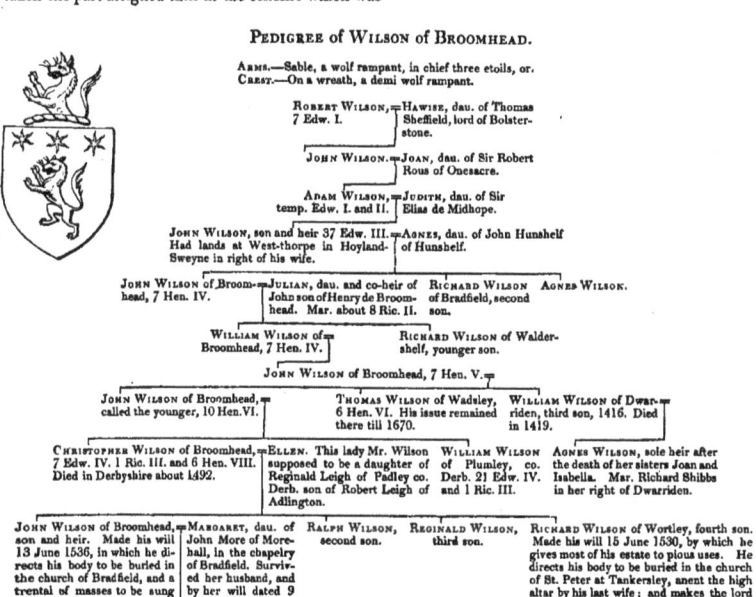

ARMS.—Sable, a wolf rampant, in chief three etoils, or.
CREST.—On a wreath, a demi wolf rampant.

ROBERT WILSON,=HAWISE, dau. of Thomas
7 Edw. I. | Sheffield, lord of Bolsterstone.

JOHN WILSON.=JOAN, dau. of Sir Robert Rous of Onesacre.

ADAM WILSON,=JUDITH, dau. of Sir temp. Edw. I. and II. | Elias de Midhope.

JOHN WILSON, son and heir 37 Edw. III.=AGNES, dau. of John Hunshelf Had lands at West-thorpe in Hoyland- | of Hunshelf. Sweyne in right of his wife.

JOHN WILSON of Broom-=JULIAN, dau. and co-heir of   RICHARD WILSON   AGNES WILSON. head, 7 Hen. IV. | John son of Henry de Broom-   of Bradfield, second head. Mar. about 8 Ric. II.   son.

WILLIAM WILSON of=   RICHARD WILSON of Walder- Broomhead, 7 Hen. IV. | shelf, younger son.

JOHN WILSON of Broomhead, 7 Hen. V.=

JOHN WILSON of Broomhead,=   THOMAS WILSON of Wadsley,   WILLIAM WILSON of Dwar-= called the younger, 10 Hen. VI. | 6 Hen. VI. His issue remained   riden, third son, 1416. Died there till 1670.   in 1419.

CHRISTOPHER WILSON of Broomhead,=ELLEN. This lady Mr. Wilson   WILLIAM WILSON   AGNES WILSON, sole heir after 7 Edw. IV. 1 Ric. III. and 6 Hen. VIII. | supposed to be a daughter of   of Plumley, co.   the death of her sisters Joan and Died in Derbyshire about 1492. | Reginald Leigh of Padley co.   Derb. 21 Edw. IV.   Isabella. Mar. Richard Shibbs Derb. son of Robert Leigh of   and 1 Ric. III.   in her right of Dwarriden. Adlington.

JOHN WILSON of Broomhead,=MARGARET, dau. of   RALPH WILSON,   REGINALD WILSON,   RICHARD WILSON of Wortley, fourth son. son and heir. Made his will | John More of More-   second son.   third son.   Made his will 15 June 1530, by which he 13 June 1536, in which he di- | hall, in the chapelry   gives most of his estate to pious uses. He rects his body to be buried in | of Bradfield. Surviv-   directs his body to be buried in the church the church of Bradfield, and a | ed her husband, and   of St. Peter at Tankersley, anent the high trental of masses to be sung | by her will dated 9   altar by his last wife; and makes the lord for his soul at the altar of St. | Apr. 1553, directed   prior of Burton-abbey supervisor of his John in the said church. | her body to be bur. in   will. No issue. the church of Bradfield.

a

RICHARD WILSON of Broomhead, son and heir-appar. Broomhead and other lands were settled on him, his wife, and their heirs male 14 Henry VIII. Died before his father. = **AGNES**, dau. of Richard Charlesworth of Totties in Holmfirth, to whom George earl of Shrewsbury granted the custody and marriage of her two sons, on his paying to John Wilson the sum of 23l. 6s. 8d.

ARTHUR WILSON of Brookfoot co. Derb. and also of Sheffield. See his will at length p. 60.

CHRISTOPHER WILSON, third son. Living 1557, had two children Christopher and Elizabeth.

GEORGE WILSON, 4th son. Buried in Sheffield church.

JOHN WILSON, 5th son, buried in Sheffield church 1557. Had a son Edward who died young, and one dau. his heir.

ELLEN, wife of John Crosland 1553, by whom Richard, William, Jane, Anne, Grace, John, George, and Raynold.

JANE, wife of Thomas Barber of Welden 1553, had a daughter named Margaret.

ELIZABETH, wife of Edward Greyve 1553. Her Had issue Margaret and other children.

CHRISTOPHER WILSON of Broomhead, heir to his grandfather. Born 1524. Buried in the chancel of Bradfield church 29 Jan. 1591. = **ELIZABETH**, dau. and heir of William Hattersley of Langsett. Buried in the chancel of Bradfield church 4 Feb. 1603.

THOMAS WILSON of Oughtibridge-hall, 2d son.

AGNES. By her will dated 27 May 1564, she directs her body to be buried in the church of Ecclesfield, and it was accordingly interred there 10 June 1564.

GEORGE WILSON, bap. at Bradfield 20 October 1547. Notes by Randal Holme from a register now lost.

JANE. CHARLES. THOMAS. FRANCIS.

REGINALD WILSON of Broomhead, son and heir. Died unmar. Sept. 1594, and was bur. on the 15th in the chancel of Bradfield church.

ELLEN, first wife, dau. of Thos.Bramhall of Storrs in Stannington. Married 3 Feb. 1592. Bur.at Bradfield 21 Oct. 1598. = **CHRISTOPHER WILSON** of Broomhead, second son. Heir to his brother. Made many purchases of lands lying near his house, which he settled by deed dated 3 Jan. 1613 on his five sons Christopher, Reginald, John, Richard, & Ralph. Buried in the chancel of Bradfield church 20 October 1622, aged 67. = **BEATRICE**, second wife, sister of Thomas Cudworth of Eastfield in the parish of Silkston. Took to her second husband Richard Oddy of Hampole, clerk, and was living 1653.

ELLEN, wife of Thomas of Eyre of Greinfoot co. Derb. gent.

JENNET, wife of John Greaves of Windhill.

THOMAS WILSON of Oughtibridge-hall. Had a pardon dated 8 June 6 Eliz. for having killed with a dagger, in his own defence, one Richard Woodhead at Sheffield. His posterity continued for several generations at Oughtibridge-hall.

CHRISTOPHER WILSON of Broomhead, son and heir. Bap. 1 March 1595. A capt. in the parliament army. Will dated 14 Dec.1670.Bur. at Bradfield 21 Mar. 1671. He finished the present house at Broomhead. = **MARY**, dau. and co-heir of John Ibbotson of Wightwistle clerk. Bap 23Dec. 1604. Mar. 29 October 1623. Bur. in the chancel at Bradfield 1662.

ANNE, wife of Thomas Revel of Stannington and of Shiffnal co. Salop, gent.

ELLEN, wife first of John son and heir of Richard Rich of Royd, and secondly of Christopher Marsden of Carlecoats and Peniston.

REGINALD, bap. 13 Dec. 1602. Of Reynar-house 1629. Died unmarried.

RALPH, bap. 18 July1613. Had an estate at Ingburchworth by his father's will 1622.

— **JOHN**, bap. 5 Sept. 1606. Died unmarried.

GEORGE WILSON of the city of Chester, geant., born 21 July 1616. A proctor in the Archbishop's Court, and registrar of theVice-Admiralty Court of Chester, Cheshire, and Lancashire. Living at Nether Rushford 1650. Appeared at the visitation of Cheshire 1664, and entered his coat armour. = **ALICE**, dau.and co-heir of Arthur of Knuts-ford co. Cestr.

RICHARD WILSON son of Hasper Arthur 6 Jan. 1610. = **ELIZABETH**, wife of Ralph Greaves of Yew-trees, and had issue.

CHARLES WILSON, born 26 July 1647. Living unmarried 1670.

ELIZABETH WILSON, eldest dau., wife of Randle Holme of Chester, deputy to Garter-king-at-arms, who entered a pedigree of the Wilsons 1670.

ALICE, wife of Thomas Wasse of Stockport co. Cestr. Living 1670.

MARY, unmarried 1670.

CHRISTOPHER, unmarried 1670.

CHRISTIAN, dead before 1670.

THOMAS WILSON of Broomhead, 1st son.Died unmar. October 1687, aged 61, and was buried in the chancel at Bradfield.

CHARLES WILSON M.A. rector of Babworth co. Notts. and vicar of Sheffield. Bap. 15 June 1631. The estate at Broomhead was settled upon him 1659. In 1695 he resigned the vicarage of Sheffield, and retired to Broomhead, where he died in Sept. 1703, and was buried at Bradfield. = **ANNE**, dau. and co-heir of John Allott B.D. rector of Little-Thurlow and Wratting co. Suff. by Marg.t Wolrich hiswife. Eldest son of Edward Allott, son of John Allott of Chrigleston co. York. Married there about1661.Bur. at Bradfield 22 Feb. 1713.

ROWLAND. — **CHRISTOPHER**, both died infants. **ARTHUR**, of London,merchant. Died unmarried at Bradfield, and was bur. there 24 Jan. 1720.

JOHN WILSON, baptized 4 Feb. 1535,of Bromeley 1659, of Skiers-hall 1684; of Whiston 1688; of Wortley 1698. Died at Babworth aged 84, and was buried there 1720. See below. = **ANNE**, dau. and heir of RichardHey of Bromeley near Wortley. Mar.before Thos. Westby esq. justice of the peace 6Nov.1656. See below.

ZACHARIAH WILSON of Sheffield, seventh son. Bap.13Mar. 1639.One of the churchburgesses of Sheffield 1679. Bur. at Sheffield 1686.

MARY, dau. and heir of Robert Housley of Sheffield. Born 1 May 1639. Mar. 28 April 1662. Bur. 13 March 1702. See below.

REGINALD WILSON, son of Port-Royal in the island of Jamaica. Collector of the customs, naval store officer, and one of the Assembly 1683. Swallowed up with his only son in the earthquake 7 June 1692.

JOHN WILSON of Broomhead,gent., third but eldest surviving son. Born at Kimbolton 13 Sept. 1672. Died Feb. 1735, and was buried on the 27th in the chancel of Bradfield-church. = **MARY**, dau. of Thomas Macro of Bury St. Edmunds esq. by Susan his wife dau. and heir of John Cox rector of Risby. See p. 253. Died at Sheffield 18 June 1761, and was buried in the middle aile of St. Paul's church.

ANNE, CHRISTOPHER, HENRIETTA-MARIA. CHARLES. MARY, CHRISTOPHER, SARAH, MARTHA, all died young between 1662 and 1689.

MARY, wife of Godfrey Crosland of Cartworth in the parish of Kirk-Burton gent. Born 6 June 1670. Mar. 14 July1700. Died Jan. 1,1732, leaving a son Thomas and two daughters.

SUSAN WILSON, born 30 August 1671. Died unmarried at Horbury, and was bur. in the middle aile of the church there 18 Oct. 1736.

ELIZABETH WILSON, born27Mar. 1678. Died unmar. at Huddersfield 21 Jan. 1722, and was buried in the church.

CHRISTOPHER WILSON of Bradfield gent. Born 14 Aug. 1681. Died 2 June1730, and was buried in the church of Bradfield. = **ALICE**, dau. of Richard Bilham of Houlden, born 31 July 1699. Mar. at Barnsley 29 Sept. 1715. Died 5 Jan.1781. Bur. with her husband.

a | b |

JOHN WILSON of Broomhead esq., only surviving son and heir. The collector for Hallamshire. Born 28 April 1719. Bap. at Bradfield 29th. Died at Broomhead-hall 3 Mar. 1783, and was bur. with his ancestors in the chancel of Bradfield church. = SUSANNA, dau. of Joseph Oates of Nether-Denby near Wakefield gent., by Grace his wife dau. of Bartin Allott of Bilham-grange co. York, gent. Born 28 October 1722. Married at Kirk-Heaton 11 Sept. 1746.	THOMAS WILSON, born 23 July 1722. Buried 25 April 1728. — SUSAN WILSON, born 8 Jan. 1712. Mar. at Attercliffe-chapel 13 May 1742 to Gamaliel Milner of Attercliffe, gent.	ISABELLA-MARIA, born 7 Aug. 1729, wife first of Jonathan Ellis of Sheffield attorney, and secondly of Robt. Asline of Sheffield merchant. Died his widow 1805.	RICHARD WILSON of London merchant. Bap. 26 Dec.1716. Died without issue 1 Nov. 1746. = ELIZABETH, dau. of London, capt. of an East-India-man. Survived and re-married John Evans of London.	CHRISTOPHER WILSON of London, merchant. Born at Wightwistle, and bap. at Bradfield 30 Dec. 1726. Died 1811. = HANNAH, dau. of Henry Clarke of King-str. London, whale-bone merchant. Mar. 14 Apr. 1757. See below.	CHRISTOPHER, CHARLES, all died unmar.

JOHN WILSON of London, solicitor, eldest son. Born 1 June 1747. Died in 1810, having bequeathed Broomhead-hall and other estates to his wife Rebecca Wilson. Buried in the burying-ground of St. Andrew Holborn. = REBECCA, sister of General Gent. Sold Broomhead-hall, &c. to her relative Henry Wilson of the city of London merch'.	JOSEPH WILSON, born 22 April 1749. Died unmar. in the Hon. East India Company's service at Boity in Bengal.	THOMAS WILSON of Armley near Leeds, third son. Born 4 Aug. 1652. Died at Sharrow-head in the parish of Sheffield, where he had resided for some years, in August 1817. = SARAH, only dau. of William Wrigglesworth of Armley-ridge. Mar. 5 Apr. 1779.	WILLIAM WILSON of Sheffield, fourth and youngest surviving son. One of the twelve capital burgesses of Sheffield 1818, and owner of the collections made by his father. = SARAH, dau. of John Allen of Chapeltown by Marguerite his wife, dau. of Joseph Scott of Woodsome, by Marguerite his first wife, sister and heir of Robert Rockley of Woodsome-Lees. Died 26 Mar. 1791.	CHARLES WILSON, RICHARD WILSON, in their infancy.

CHARLES WILSON of London, solicitor.	HARRIET WILSON, SUSAN WILSON.	THOMAS WILSON of Armley, only son. Died in his father's life-time 1816. = SARAH, dau. of Thomas Musgrave of Foggathorpe, in the parish of Bubwith co. York.	HANNAH, died unmarried. Buried at Bradfield.	WILLIAM WILSON of High-field near Sheffield, eldest son. = FRANCS, dau. of George Woolhouse of Sheffield. Married 23 May 1812.	JAMES WILSON of Sheffield, solicitor, 2d son.	ROBERT WILSON of Sheffield, third and youngest son. JOHN, CHARLES, both died in infancy.

JOHN WILSON.   THOMAS WILSON.   WILLIAM WILSON.   HANNAH WILSON.   WILLIAM WILSON, born 7 Mar. 1813.   SARAH-ANNE WILSON.   GEORGE WILSON.

CHRISTOPHER WILSON of London, merchant. Born 1726. = HANNAH, dau. of Henry Clarke of London.

HENRY WILSON of the city of London, merchant, eldest son. Purchased the estate of Broomhead of Rebecca Wilson, widow. Living unmarried 1819.	WILLIAM WILSON of London, merchant, 2d son. = ---- dau. of Thomas, Leander of Broxted co. Essex, and formerly of Sheffield, merchant. Mar. 7 July 1800.	MARY-ANNE WILSON, died in Aug. 1760, aged 9 weeks.	MARY WILSON, wife of John Rimington of Sheffield and Hillsborough, esquire, lord of the manor of Bolsterstone. Married 19 June 1784.	HARRIET WILSON, wife of Thomas Newberry of London.

JAMES RIMINGTON esquire, late of Trinity College Camb. and Barrister-at-law. Now residing at Broomhead. Only child. = SARAH, dau. of Samuel Broomhead Ward, of Mount-Pleasant in the township of Ecclesall, esquire. Married at Sheffield 1 Sept. 1817.	CHRISTOPHER WILSON NEWBERRY. Only child.

MARY RIMINGTON.

JOHN WILSON of Wortley, &c. Born 1635. Died 1720. = ANNE, dau. and heir of Richard Hey.

RICHARD WILSON, rector of Babworth, on the resignation of his uncle Charles Wilson. Died unmarried 1727, and was buried at Babworth.	THOMAS WILSON of Povey in the parish of Dronfield. Died unmarried about 1729.	JOHN WILSON, died unmar. 18 Aug. 1688, and was bur. in the church of Whiston.	CHRISTOPHER WILSON, died unmar. 1737, and was buried in the church of Wakefield.	MATTHEW WILSON of Wortley-forge and Dodworth, iron-master. Died unmarried, aged 63, and was buried at Wortley.	ANNE, wife of John Spencer of Cannon-hall, in the parish of Cawthorne, gent., from whom descends the present Walter Spencer Stanhope of Cannon-hall, esq.	SUSANNA, wife of Thos. Cockshutt, minister of Cawthorne. Had issue Thomas, John, Anne, Elizabeth, and Susan.	CATHERINE, wife of James Oates of Dodworth, gent. Left no issue. MARY, died unmar. and was bur. in the chapel at Wortley 1747.

ZACHARIAH WILSON of Sheffield. Born 1639. Died 1702. = MARY, dau. and heir of Robert Housley.

ROBERT WILSON. Died in Jamaica, unmarried, about 1693.	HOUSLEY WILSON, bap. 18 April 1667. Died unmarried.	ZACHARIAH WILSON, born 6 January 1670. Died unmarried at Wells in Norfolk.	MARY, wife of --- Fellow of Wells in Norfolk.	ANNE, wife of Robert Holmes of Alfreton, co. Derb. Woodward to his Grace the Duke of Norfolk.	ELIZABETH, wife of Richard Sherburne of Sheffield gent. An agent of His Grace the Duke of Norfolk. She died without issue 14 Aug. 1732.

BOLSTERSTONE.

This was an ancient estate of inheritance held by the De Sheffields of the Barons Furnival. They gave for arms Argent, a fess between six garbs gules.

'Ralph de Sheffield,' says Dodsworth, 'had two sons by Dyoness his wife, whom afterwards Elias de Midhope took to wife; to wit, Thomas a knight, and William; and of William came John, of John came John and Thomas, and Lucy wife of Thomas Staveley. And the said Thomas hath alienated to Robert de Rockley knight four oxgangs of land by the name of the manor of Bolsterstone[1].'

'Know &c. that I John de Thurgarland have released and quit claimed to John de Shellay the elder and John de Shellay the younger, Isabel that was the wife of William de Scheffeld and John the son of the same William and Isabel, and to either of them, and also to the heirs of the foresaid John, all manner of right or claim which I have or can have in all and singular the lands and tenements which were belonging to Elias de Midhope in Waldershelf, Wytwistle, Midhope, Penyngsale, Swyndin, Bylcliffe, and elsewhere within the metes of the villages of Bradfield and Langside. Witness Nicholas de Wortley knight and others. Dated at Tankersley anno 1329[2].'

The received pedigrees of Rockley represent the Robert de Rockley to whom Dodsworth informs us that the manor of Bolsterstone was conveyed by the Sheffields, as having married Alice sole daughter and heir of Sir Thomas Sheffield[3]. He lived in the time of Richard II. and was the chief of an ancient family residing at Rockley in Worsborough-dale, where they appear to have been seated as early as the reign of Henry. II. It is conjectured that the first settler was of the family of Fitz-William of Sprodborough, whose arms the Rockleys gave, charged with a fess sable.

Respecting the transactions of the Rockleys in respect of their manor of Bolsterstone we have the following notices in the Dodsworth papers.

In the box of entails and feoffments among the charters of Robert de Rockley, William del Hill vicar of Kellington hath given to Sir William Harrington, Sir Thomas Nevil, Robert Waterton esq., and others, one yearly rent of forty shillings, to be received of the manors of Bolsterstone and Penysale, which he had of the gift of Robert de Rockley knight, John son of the said Robert, Robert de Hill chaplain, Robert Moundesere, and Richard de Kerisforth, dated 6 Henry V.[4]

In the same evidences, a covenant between Robert Rockley esquire and Robert Duckenfield esquire, that John son and heir of Robert Rockley shall marry Agnes daughter of the said Robert Duckenfield; and that the said Robert shall make the said John a lease of the manor and demesne of Bolsterstone for four winters[5]. This covenant is on paper.

The Rockleys did not long remain in possession of the manor of Bolsterstone. No evidence that has hitherto presented itself shows however when or how it was alienated. The family continued for many generations at their ancient seat at Rockley. Catherine Rockley sole heiress of the eldest line was married in 1702 to Lewis Westcomb esquire, second son of Sir Martin Westcomb the English consul at Cadiz. She

and her husband resided for a time at Rockley, and Westcomb was much engaged in iron-works and collieries. They sold the manor of Rockley, and in her widowhood Mrs. Westcomb resided in France, where her relation Mr. Robert Rockley visited her at Evreux in Normandy in 1747. She then went by the name of Rockley, which name she also gave to a son whom she bore to Westcomb. In the year 1770 Mr. Robert Rockley of Woodsome-Lees near Huthersfield, the only surviving male descendant of this family, compiled, from collections made by his father and from other materials, an account of his family, being then childless and within three months of seventy years of age. He died not long after, leaving his two sisters (or their posterity) heirs to the name and blood, namely, Mary wife of Benjamin North of Fenay attorney, and Marguerite wife of Joseph Scot of Woodsome-Lees merchant.

Mr. Wilson had observed that in 1442 John earl of Shrewsbury was lord of the manor of Bolsterstone; and in 1573 George the sixth earl. In 1635 it was divided into three parts, one of which belonged to the Countess of Kent, and the other two were in the hands of Philip earl of Pembroke. The manor of Bolsterstone afterwards passed, as did other parts of the Talbot property, to the Saviles, who descended of a sister of Gilbert earl of Shrewsbury, and in 1683 it was part of the possessions of George Savile marquis of Halifax. He left a widow Gertrude marchioness of Halifax, who held this manor in 1698, and on William the second marquis, who died in 1700 leaving three daughters his co-heirs: Anne who married Charles lord Bruce, son and heir of Thomas earl of Ailesbury; Dorothy, who married Richard earl of Burlington; and Mary who became wife of Sackville earl of Thanet. Among these ladies the estates of the Saviles were divided by a partition deed which was confirmed by act of parliament in the 16 George II. Sir Matthew Lambe purchased the manor of the party to whom in the partition it was assigned, whose son Peniston Lambe was created Viscount Melbourne of the kingdom of Ireland in 1780. It has since been purchased of the Melbourne family by John Rimington of Hillsborough esquire.

It was during the time that the Rockleys were in possession of the manor that a chapel was founded at Bolsterstone which was at first nothing more than a private chantry of the family of Rockley, though it came at length to be used as a place of public worship by the inhabitants of the manor living at a great distance from their parish church of Ecclesfield and their parochial chapel of Bradfield. The chapel was founded in 1412 by Sir Robert Rockley, who directed that one perpetual chaplain should therein celebrate masses and other divine services for the good estate of himself and of Robert his son, and for the soul of Elizabeth his wife deceased. And for the sustentation of the said chaplain he obtained the king's license to amortize eight marks annual rent out of the manors of Bolsterstone and Penysale, which he gave and granted to Richard de Westhall chaplain of the chapel of St. Mary in Bolsterstone, and to his successors for ever.

---

[1] Dods. MSS. n. n. 59 b. Extracts from the Rockley Evidences. Harl. 801. Bolsterstone.
[2] Dods. MSS. K. 72 a. Harl. 801. Bradfield.
[3] Duc. Leod. p. 25.
[4] & [5] n. n. 27 b. and 30 a. Harl. 801. Bolsterstone.

Furthermore ordaining that if the chantry should fall vacant, Robert his son and heir after his own death should present a fit chaplain thereunto within fifteen days after such vacation; and if the said Robert should die without heirs of his body, that then the presentation should belong to the Master of the college of St. Trinity at Pontefract. All which was confirmed by Henry Bowet archbishop of York on the 23d of August 1418[1].

Mr. Wilson collected the following Catalogue of Curates of Bolsterstone.

1646. John Thacker.
1653. Thomas Nicholson.
— Dickenson.
1661. — Thorneley.
1665. — Camm.
1667. — Hopwood.
— Mellor, died in December 1673.
1674. William Marsh.
1685. Jeremiah Waterhouse.
1704. John Hoole.
1710. John Pertak. A Bohemian protestant who took refuge in England from persecution on account of his religion. He was patronized by the honourable Thomas Watson-Wentworth, who procured him the presentation to this chapel. He died here, and was buried in the north-east corner of the chapel 2 January 1728.
1728. Francis Haigh.
— Bland, died about 1816.

The honourable Thomas Watson-Wentworth, who had an estate in this manor, gave a library for the use of the minister; and procured an augmentation of 8l. or 10l. a year. In 1714, about sixty acres of common ground were inclosed and annexed to the curacy. The patronage is in the lords of the manor.

In 1688 a school was erected on the green for the use of the poor of Bolsterstone. Before that time the children were taught to read in the chapel.

Mr. Wilson observes, that beside the ordinary courts of the manor, a separate court was held at a place called Townend for lands in this lordship or in other parts of Bradfield, called Lands of Saint John of Jerusalem. These lands belonged to the dissolved priory or hospital of Saint John of Jerusalem. The houses of the people who hold these lands were formerly distinguished by an iron or wooden cross fixed in some conspicuous part. There were about twelve of these houses in 1741. Royds, where a family of the name of South resided in some respectability for several generations, was one of them.

At Bithoms was a deer-park belonging to the earls of Shrewsbury, with a tower in it to overlook the deer. Lead and other minerals have been got in this part of the chapelry.

MORE-HALL.

Trifling circumstances sometimes give circulation to a name which on any other account has but small claims upon public attention. Few of my readers are, it is probable, familiar with the name of Bolsterstone, but who has not heard of More of More-hall?

More-hall is now nothing more than a decent farm-house. But it stands in a charming valley near the Don, and enjoys a luxuriant view of the woods and rocks of Wharncliffe. It is understood that it stands within the manor of Bolsterstone; but the late Godfrey Bosville of Gunthwaite esquire, in some memoirs which he left of his own family, states that it is within his manor of Oxspring and pays to him a rose yearly. There are no remains of the ancient house of the Mores, who may be regarded as a family indigenous to Hallamshire, an unknown but careful and skilful hand having collected their genealogy in the time of Charles I., and shown them resident on this spot in times when in their rank of society the use of hereditary surnames was unknown. I shall present it to the reader as it is found in C. 25, f. 45, in the College of Arms, entered by George More of Burghope in Herefordshire, at the visitation of that county in 1634. The crest was formerly to be seen carved in stone above five feet long at the north-east corner of Bradfield church.

PEDIGREE of MORE of MORE-HALL.

ARMS. MORE.—Paly of six sable and argent, a bend gules; quartering BRIGHTHOLMLEY, azure a chevron between three fleurs de lis argent.
CREST.—In a mural coronet or, a cockatrice sejant vert.
MOTTO.—Nefas flectere.

WALKELINE, temp. Hen. I.

ROBERT FITZ WALKELINE.

WILLIAM DE WALDERSHELF, temp. Ric. I. son of Robert, son of Walkeline, as by several deeds.

RALPH DE MORA of Waldershelf.

GEOFFRY DE MORA, temp. Hen. III. and Edw. I.

ADAM DE MORA, 28 Edw. I.=BREDA.   JOHN DE MORE, 15 Edw. III.
and 5 Edw. III.

JOHN DE MORE of Walder-=EMMA.   CICKLY.   MARGARET.   THOMAS DEL MORE.
shelf, 2 Edw. III.

ADAM DEL MORE,   JOHN,   WILLIAM,   THOMAS DE MORE,=JOAN, dau. of Hugh
2 Edw. III.   16 Edw. III.   16 Edw. III.   41 and 46 Edw. III.   de Brightholmley.

THOMAS DEL MORE,=   ALICE.
40 and 46 Edw. III.

[1] Dr. Burton's Extracts from Torre's MSS.

4 C

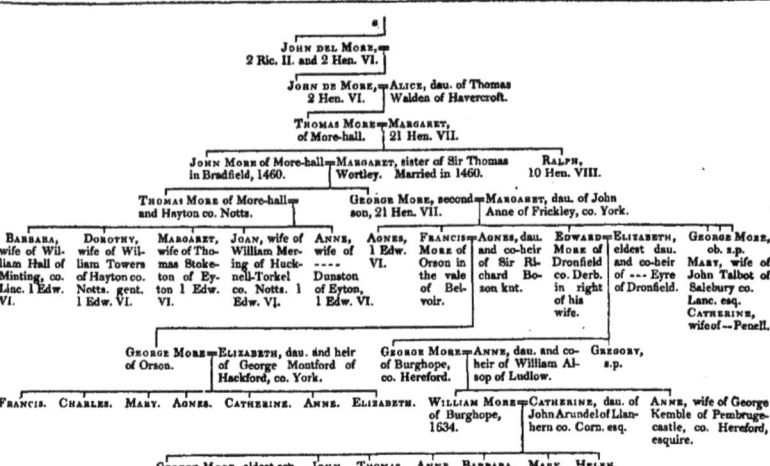

JOHN DEL MORE,
2 Ric. II. and 2 Hen. VI.

JOHN DE MORE,=ALICE, dau. of Thomas
2 Hen. VI. | Walden of Havercroft.

THOMAS MORE=MARGARET,
of More-hall. | 21 Hen. VII.

JOHN MORE of More-hall=MARGARET, sister of Sir Thomas   RALPH,
in Bradfield, 1460. | Wortley. Married in 1460.   10 Hen. VIII.

THOMAS MORE of More-hall=   GEORGE MORE, second=MARGARET, dau. of John
and Hayton co. Notts.   son, 21 Hen. VII. | Anne of Frickley, co. York.

| BARBARA, wife of William Hall of Minting, co. Linc. 1 Edw. VI. | DOROTHY, wife of William Towers of Hayton co. Notts. gent. 1 Edw. VI. | MARGARET, wife of Thomas Stoketon of Eyton 1 Edw. VI. | JOAN, wife of William Mernell-Torkel co. Notts. 1 Edw. VI. | ANNE, wife of ---- Dunston of Eyton, 1 Edw. VI. | AGNES, 1 Edw. VI. | FRANCIS MORE of Orson in the vale of Belvoir. | AGNES, dau. and co-heir of Sir Richard Boson knt. | EDWARD=ELIZABETH, MORE of eldest dau. Dronfield and co-heir co. Derb. of --- Eyre in right of Dronfield. of his wife. | GEORGE MORE, ob. s.p. MARY, wife of John Talbot of Lanc. esq. CATHERINE, wife of --Penell. |

GEORGE MORE=ELIZABETH, dau. and heir   GEORGE MORE=ANNE, dau. and co-   GREGORY,
of Orson. | of George Montford of   of Burghope, | heir of William Al-   s.p.
     Hackford, co. York.   co. Hereford. | sop of Ludlow.

FRANCIS.   CHARLES.   MARY.   AGNES.   CATHERINE.   ANNE.   ELIZABETH.   WILLIAM MORE=CATHERINE, dau. of   ANNE, wife of George
                                            of Burghope, | John Arundel of Llan-   Kemble of Pembruge-
                                            1634.   hern co. Corn. esq.   castle, co. Hereford,
                                                                      esquire.

GEORGE MORE, eldest son,   JOHN.   THOMAS.   ANNE.   BARBARA.   MARY.   HELEN.
aged about 8 years 1634.

On the 23d of January 40 Elizabeth, *anno* 1597, Francis Towers of Hayton in the county of Nottingham gentleman, grandson of William Towers and Dorothy More, one of the six daughters and co-heirs of Thomas More the last of the name who resided here, sold More-hall to George Blount of Eckington esquire for 400*l*. This George Blount was the eldest son of Robert Blount, one of the twenty children of Sir Thomas Blount of Kinlet in the county of Salop knight. How long it remained in that family, and through what other hands it passed, I have not found; but in 1727 Nicholas Steade, son of Thomas Steade of Onesacre, died possessed thereof. From him it passed to his son Thomas Steade who settled his younger son Nicholas Steade on this estate. He was the father of the late Thomas Steade esquire of Burrow-leigh and Hillsborough. About the year 1798 More-hall was sold by the Steade family to Mr. Samuel Deakin of Sheffield merchant.

Dr. Percy had a correspondence with Mr. Wilson respecting the ballad of the Dragon of Wantley, in which More of More-hall cuts so conspicuous a figure. In the later editions of the Reliques may be found the opinion of Mr. Bosville of Gunthwaite on the origin of that extraordinary composition. I have nothing to add to what is said on this subject at page 3 of the present work, except to observe that the pedigree above given shows that if the ballad has an historical basis, it must be in some events which took place before the reign of Edward VI.; since from the first year of that king's reign there has been no More living at More-hall. I know not that the fact of John More having married a sister of Sir Thomas Wortley has been ever brought to bear on this question.

MIDHOPE.

'Midhope a garden in a wilderness!'

Where the manor of Hallam met the manor of Peniston on the north is now a vill of the name of Midhope, with a fertile territory around it, in which manorial rights are exercised by its own lord. This manor is understood to extend over portions both of the chapelry of Bradfield and of the parish of Peniston. The vill and chapel of Midhope are in Bradfield. This manor does not appear in the *Nomina Villarum* 9 Edward II.

The lords of this manor had their residence within it, and were called De Midhope. We find the name in deeds from the reign of John to the time of Edward III., and most of the heads of the family bore the name of Elias. Several of them were knighted; and, we may regard them as standing in the same rank among the ancient families of Hallamshire as the De Sheffields, De Wadsleys, De Ecclesalls, and De Mountenevs. From the De Midhopes the manor passed to the De Barnbys, a family which had great possessions in the wapentake of Staincross, and who had their hereditary surname from their principal seat at Barnby in the parish of Silkston. Edmund de Barnby occurs as lord of Midhope in the time of Edward III., and Thomas Barnby in the 39th year of Elizabeth. Excellent abstracts of the Barnby evidences may be found among Dodsworth's collections; and pedigrees of them in most collections of Yorkshire genealogy. I shall content myself with observing that Sir Charles Barnby knight, son and heir of Thomas, married Hester, a daughter of David Disney of Norton Disney esquire, by whom he had a son Thomas Barnby of Barnby esquire, living in the time of Charles II., the last of his name. This gentleman by Mary his wife, daughter of William Green of Cawthorne gentleman, had two daughters his co-heirs, one of whom married John Allott of Bentley in the parish of Elmley, and Mary who became the wife of Nicholas Bowden of Bowden in the county of Derby esquire.

The arms of Barnby were very peculiar. Or, a lion

rampant sable hung about with escallop shells argent. They appeared in the windows of Silkston church and in other places.

Whether the manor of Midhope remained in possession of the family as long as there were any Barnbys at Barnby-hall I cannot say; but one Henry Hall was in possession in 1690, in which year he sold the manor for 2256*l.* to Godfrey Bosville of Gunthwaite, esquire[1].

Mr. Bosville died without issue in 1714, and left the principal part of his property to his nephew William Bosville, whose son and heir Godfrey Bosville of Gunthwaite esquire was lord of the manor of Midhope in 1741. This gentleman married one of the sisters of Sir Thomas Wentworth of Bretton, (afterwards Blacket) and left a son Colonel William Bosville, on whose decease without issue in 1813 the principal part of the Bosville estates came to his nephew the honourable Mr. Macdonald.

There is an old chapel at Midhope which was probably founded by the De Midhopes or the Barnbys lords of this manor. Its certified value is 7*l.* 13*s.* It is dedicated to Saint James, and the lord of the manor is the patron. The Sequestrators in the time of the Commonwealth ordered 30*l.* a year to be paid out of the estate of Alethea Countess of Arundel to Midhope chapel.

CURATES of MIDHOPE.

1540. Sir John Jackson.
1546. Sir Ralph Roger.
1625. Samuel Newman. He received 5*l.* a year as a free gift from William and Philip earls of Pembroke.
1635. Matthew Booth.
1665. — Camm.
1672. Joshua Wild.
1672. John Garside.
1674. John Marsden.
   William Marsh.
1699. John Aird.
1705. John Hoole.
1710. William Wills. Died in 1723.
   Francis Haigh.

At Midhope is a school founded by the benefactions of various well-disposed persons.

III.

The Parish of Hansworth.

THE church of Hansworth is distant about four miles from Sheffield on the south. It stands in the midst of the village of that name, and on an eminence from which are commanded extensive and beautiful views of the surrounding country. The situation of the village gave occasion to the name. Dean or hen in the Anglo-Saxon signifying high, and the syllable worth which enters into the composition of so many names of places, being nothing more than mansion or dwelling-place. So that Hansworth is the dwelling on the hill.

The church and village are nearly central to the whole parish. The parish consists of about 3400 acres, nearly the whole being inclosed. The parishes on the south are Beighton and Eckington, both of which are in the county of Derby. It has Sheffield, Rotherham, Whiston, Treeton, and Aston on the other sides.

The turnpike-road from Sheffield to Worksop passes through the village of Hansworth.

At a place called the Intake are extensive collieries. These furnish employment to many of the inhabitants; others are engaged in the Sheffield manufactures; but the majority are occupied in the primitive and natural employment of the human race—tilling the ground.

The population in 1811 was found to be 1424. The parish abounds in small freeholders. In 1808 fifty-five of its inhabitants voted for freeholds within the parish. The principal hamlets are Gleadleys, Richmond, Lamb-hill, and Hansworth-Woodhouse.

The earliest notice of this place is in the Domesday survey. It is there described in connexion with Whiston. In Widestan and Handeswrde, Torchil had a manor of five carucates, with seven ploughs. Ricardus Surdus holds one carucate of the earl of Morton, and there are eleven villani, three bordarii, and six sockmen, who have seven carucates and a half. There is a pasturable wood three leuæ in length and one broad. The whole manor is two leuæ and a half in length and two leuæ in breadth. That is of five square leuæ three were woodland, the cultivated carucates being the two which remain. In the time of the Confessor the manor was valued at eight pounds, but at the time of the survey only at forty shillings. This account is not without its difficulties.

Hansworth passed into the hands of the De Lovetots, and from them to the Furnivals and their successors, of whom His Grace the duke of Norfolk is the representative, lord of the manor and patron of the rectory.

In Kirkby's Inquest Thomas de Furnival is returned lord of only a mediety of the manor; and in this point

[1] Memoirs of the Bosvilles by Godfrey Bosville esquire.

the inquest has been followed by Torre in his notice of the rectory. But in the *Nomina Villarum* of a few years later date the same person appears as sole lord.

Sheffield park extended to the very edge of this parish, if part lay not within it. George the sixth earl of Shrewsbury, as we have seen, built a small house for his occasional residence and for the enjoyment of the comforts of quiet and repose, at a little distance from the church. He cut a road through the park from Sheffield Manour to his house. In this house the earl spent much of the last four or five years of his life. It was also for a time inhabited by his son and successor Earl Gilbert, whose second son was born here. This house was lent by Earl Gilbert to his intimate friend, relative and companion Sir Charles Cavendish, whose son William Cavendish, earl, marquis, and duke of Newcastle, here drew his first breath, and was baptized in the church of Hansworth on the 16th of December 1593. This house shared the same fate with the two more extensive mansions, Sheffield Castle and Sheffield Manour. On the death of Gilbert earl of Shrewsbury none of the family were found disposed to inhabit it; and Hansworth-hall has been gradually reduced till it has become a mere farm-house, with nothing but the name to show that it was ever any thing more or better.

The birth of a nobleman who acted so important a part in the transactions of the seventeenth century would have given some celebrity to Hansworth had the fact been noticed in the accounts we possess of that nobleman's life. Dr. Pegge, to whom we owe so much valuable information, was the first to communicate it to the public in his history of the duke's castle of Bolsover.

The monks of Kirkstead had a considerable interest in this parish. That remote house shared in no small degree with Saint Wandrille, Worksop, and Beauchief the favours of the old lords and inhabitants of Hallamshire. Gerard de Furnival gave to it the half of his mill at Woodhouse, and confirmed what Huctred had granted to them at Hansworth, the bovate at Woodhouse which Roger Fitz Arthur had given them, and the half bovate in the same place given by Ralph Blund[1].

The church of Hansworth is an ancient rectory; and out of it Gerard de Furnival gave to the prebend of Laughton-en-le-Morthen in the church of York an annual pension of two marks and a half. Hence it has been reckoned a peculiar belonging to the jurisdiction of the dean and chapter of York by virtue of that prebend. Its value in the time of Elizabeth was 16l. It is a rectory in charge, and its value in the King's books is 12l. 4s. 7d.

A CATALOGUE of the RECTORS of HANSWORTH.

Temp. Instit.	Rectores.	Patroni.
6 Kal. Jan. 1318	Dñs Adam de Brouse	
	Robert Pigot	Dñs Thomas de Furnival.
	John Chamberlayn	
4 Nov. 1368	William Savage, pbr.	William Lord Furnival.
22 Oct. 1369	Robert de Whitewell, cap.	idem
4 April 1377	William de Sauvage, cap.	idem
10 July 1410	William de Newton, cap.	John Talbot, Lord Furnival.
6 May 1413	John de Aston, cap.	idem
24 May 1427	Richard Morteyn, pbr.	idem
	John Barrington	
19 May 1431	Dñs Robert Rasyn, cap.	John Lord Talbot.
15 Dec. 1436	John Doneng, cap.	idem
	Thomas Tylney	
20 August 1469	Mr Henry Kaye, A.M.	Elizabeth countess of Shrewsbury.
23 March 1474	William Otwaye	Guardians of George earl of Shrewsbury.
22 August 1486	John Proctor, decret. b.	George earl of Shrewsbury.
20 September 1486	William Greyburne, S.T.P.	idem
24 Feb. 1501	Dñs Thomas Lowe, pbr.	idem
18 Dec. 1532	Mr John Moreton	idem
19 July 1544	Dñs John Hosyer, cl.	Elizabeth countess of Shrewsbury.
23 August 1554	Mr John Moreton, cl.	eadem.
	Thomas Norborne	
	Thomas Corker	George earl of Shrewsbury.
18 March 1577	Thomas Legge	idem
24 Aug. 1610	Nathaniel Bownde, A.M.	Gilbert earl of Shrewsbury.
3 June 1612	Michael Adams	
6 Jan. 1627	William Cart	William earl of Pembroke.
2 Feb. 1643	John Cart	
1662	Thomas Durant, B.D.	Thomas Danby of Farnley esq. and Sir Richard Onslow of West Clandon by grant for this turn from Henry Lord Howard.
1671	Samuel Drake, D.D.	Walter Laycock gent. by grant for this turn from Henry Lord Howard.
3 April 1679	Cuthbert Browne	Duke of Norfolk.
10 Jan. 1683	Benjamin Adams	The King, per lapsum.
4 Sept. 1693	Francis Lockier, A.M.	The Archbishop, per lapsum.
1740	Charles Steer	
1752	John Griffith, A.M.	
1784	Hon. Philip Howard	
1801	Wilfrid Huddlestone	

[1] *Mon. Ang.* vol. i. p. 807.

The two Carts were father and son. Of the first some interesting particulars may be found in that scarce tract The Ploughman's Vindication, a pamphlet published during the civil wars by Nicholas Ardron, relating to the conduct of Sherland Adams who was removed from the rectory of Treeton. Cart had taken a share in the opposition to Adams, and died pending the consideration of his case by the committee for removing scandalous ministers. Adams had represented the death of Cart as a judgement; which leads Ardron to make the remark, that his death might indeed have been taken as a judgement, 'had he died some sudden or untimely death,' as a brother of Adams had lately died, ' but he died in his bed, and ended his dayes in a most heavenly manner, not ceasing most heavenly exhortation,' p. 30. Ardron then gives some account of the laborjous ministry of Mr. Cart during the sixteen years that he had held the rectory of Hansworth. He died on the 8th of October 1644. His tomb still remains in the church-yard. A rare instance of a sepulchral memorial placed without the walls of a church bearing the name of him whom it was erected to commemorate through the space of one hundred and seventy-five years.—The son John Cart was like minded with the father, a zealous and able puritan divine. But he lived when their star had passed its ascendant, and was ejected by the Act of Uniformity in 1662. In this retired parish Mr. Cart continued to reside, and seems to have met with no molestation. To him Major Taylor of Walling-wells committed the care of his only son, when he was sent to fortify Tangier. On the 8th of September 1674 this ' eminent scholar and great divine,' as he is represented to have been by the historian of the silenced ministers of 1662[1], was laid with his father in the churchyard of Hansworth.

Thomas Stanley, of whom notice has been taken already, was assistant to the Carts in this rectory.

Dr. Samuel Drake was a divine of another school. He was expelled in the time of the civil wars from his fellowship of Saint John's College Cambridge, and went to serve in the royal army. At the Restoration he was made vicar of Pontefract, and died possessed of the rectory of Hansworth on the 3d of April 1679. He published a life of his tutor and friend Cleiveland.

Dr. Lockier, the son of William Lockier of Norwich, was admitted a subsizar of Trinity College Cambridge on the 9th of May 1683, being then fifteen years of age; B.A. 1687, and M.A. 1690. He went over to Hambro' chaplain to the English factory; and while residing there used to pay an annual visit at the court of Hanover. He thus became early in life very well known to George I. who nominated him one of his chaplains in ordinary, and to whose personal regard it seems he owed the deanery of Peterborough, with which he was presented in 1725. Bishop Newton says of Dr. Lockier that ' he was a man of ingenuity and learning, had seen a great deal of the world, and was a most pleasant and agreeable companion.' The reader will recollect what is said of him in Parke's rhyming epistle. He enjoyed this pleasant rectory forty-six years, and for the last nine had also the neighbouring rectory of Aston. When he became dean of Peterborough and could not reside at Hansworth with

the same constancy as before, he was indulged with a clerk in orders, to whom in his absence was intrusted the performance of what is called the occasional duty. The late Reverend Mr. Goodwin of Sheffield used to relate that this person, not content with merely reading the ritual services, would undertake, contrary to an implied engagement, to address the parishioners from the dean's pulpit. The preacher exposed himself, and the rector remonstrated; hinting that, if the new made clergyman thought it necessary to take the chair of instruction, he might have read to the congregation from one of the many volumes of excellent divinity which his library contained. ' What!' replied the chagrined clerk, ' would you have me offer to God that which cost me nothing?' ' Yes, John,' said the Dean,'rather than that which is worth nothing.' Mr. Malone, who has given some further particulars of Dr. Lockier's life and character in his Life of Dryden[2], whom Dr. Lockier knew, has not discovered that he published any thing except a 30th of January sermon in 1726, preached before the House of Commons. Bishop Pearce was his great friend, and to him Dr. Lockier left his valuable library.

Mr. Steer came to this rectory from Bradfield, a change which he would probably much approve. He was one of the six sons of Mr. William Steer of Darnall, and died rector of Hansworth on the 2d of February 1752, aged 54.

Mr. Griffith was one of the sons of Dr. Griffith rector of Eckington, on whose death in 1765 he obtained a dispensation to hold the rectory of Eckington along with Hansworth. He died possessed of both rectories on the 6th of September 1784, aged 67.

The honourable and reverend Philip Howard was of the Suffolk branch of the family, and died rector of Hansworth in July 1801.

THE CHURCH.

The church of Hansworth is a small building. On the tower at the west end is a low pyramid, erected when the more taper spire of former times had been struck down by lightning[3]. The windows of the chancel are of the lancet shape, betokening a high antiquity. Probably this was among the many churches erected in the northern parts of England in the reign of Henry I. It has a north aile. In the windows of the chancel are some small remains of painted glass. We have no early church notes taken at this place, nor indeed does the church appear to have ever contained any thing which might claim the notice of an antiquary.

On a flat stone on the chancel floor is this almost obliterated inscription:

' Here lyeth the body of Thomas Legge, late person ......
preacher of God's word both by his lyfe and doctrine : and
Grysill his wife: Anno Dom. 1610.'

On another stone in the north aile this uncouth inscription:

' Here lyeth the body of John Booth late of Hansworth-
Woodhouse gentleman : sarvant to the right honourable Gilbert earle of Shrewsbury. Hee was ...... in the profession
of the gospel of Jesus Christ, and the same John died in the
same Christian faith, the sixty first yere of his age, the 16 day
of June anno Domini 1613. And Ann his wife.'

[1] Calamy, p. 789.
[2] Dryden's Prose Works, vol. i. p. 481.

[2] The fact is recorded in the parish-register. [3] 1698, July 25. The
steeple was struck down by a ball of fire.

This John Booth was the son of one Oliver Booth of the county of Derby. By his will, which bears date the 12th of June 1613, and was proved at Laughton-en-le-Morthen, he gives something to the poor of Hansworth, Sheffield, Attercliffe, Darnall, Rotherham, Whiston, Treeton, Catcliffe, and Orgrave; and leaves the manor of Worsborough to his son-in-law William Castleford, and after some family remainders to Charles Cavendish esquire, second son of Sir Charles Cavendish knight. He had three daughters his co-heirs, who carried considerable property to the husbands to whom they were married, and the descendants of two of them became persons of principal account in this parish. Anne the eldest married Thomas Stacye of Ballifield; Elizabeth married first William Castleford of Worsborough, and afterwards Gervase Hanson gentleman; and Catherine the third became the wife of John Nodder of Hansworth-Woodhouse. These marriages appear in a pedigree of Booth inserted in Vincent's Shropshire pedigrees, MS. in Col. Arm.

In the church are tablets to the memory of John Smelter of Richmond gentleman, and Mary his wife, a daughter of William Statham gentleman, son of Thomas Statham of Tidswell in the county of Derby, 1777 and 1791 ; of John Parker of Woodthorpe esq. 1794; and of Middlemore, John, and Henrietta Griffith 1763, 1784, 1795.

The churchyard is spacious, retired, and sequestered. The brasses upon the tombs of the family of Cart the rectors have now lain exposed more than a century and half, without having tempted any sacrilegious hand to remove them. There is nothing remarkable in the inscriptions; but they serve to mark the place where the several members of a family respected in its day and generation were returned again to the earth our common mother. The inscriptions on two tombs, of which one is at the east end of the church, are worth preserving.

'M. S.
JOHIS STACYE DE BALLIFIELD,
in com. Ebor. gen. qui obiit
quinto die Augusti anno 1712.
Filius suus maxime natus Thomas
Stacye sacræ ejus cineri hoc æs
grati animi monumentum
merito imposuit, anno 1715.
Omnia Risus, omnia pulvis et omnia nihil
Enim nos omnes morti debemur.'

'Sacred to the memory of
the Hon. JANE HOWARD,
wife of the Hon. and Rev. Philip Howard
rector of this parish,
who died March the 27th 1801, aged 56 years.
And also of
Mrs. BARBARA IDLE,
relict of the late Lord Chief Baron Idle
of the Court of Exchequer
in Scotland, and
mother of the above-named Jane Howard,
who died June the 16th 1801,
aged 83 years.'

Ballifield is at a short distance from the church near the road to Aston. The Stacyes were very ancient at this place, but are now removed. The Reverend Mr. Stacye vicar of Worksop is the representative. Ballifield and Cinderhill (another of their houses) have both been sold. Warburton gave them these arms in his map of Yorkshire: Barry of six argent and gules, a fleur de lis sable. They were converted to quakerism by the preaching of George Fox. While they continued members of that society they had a private cemetery in a very retired corner of their estate at Cinderhill. Several small tombs with inscriptions remain, or at least did within these few years. The Quakers did not then affect to leave unnoticed the place where the remains of their friends and relations were interred.

Fox and some other of the early Quaker preachers were very successful in this little parish. At the village of Woodhouse their converts erected a small meeting-house which is still used. Among the early professors of quakerism in this neighbourhood were the baronet family of Rodes of Barlborough. Sir John Rodes the last baronet, who died unmarried at the age of 73 in 1743, was interred in the Quakers' burying-ground at Woodhouse; as was also his nephew Cornelius Heathcote of Cutthorpe near Chesterfield, M.D. who died before him; and the son of Dr. Heathcote, who was made heir to Sir John Rodes, took his name, and died unmarried in 1768.

Dr. Lockier made some provision for the education of the poor in his parish; and in 1800 a school-room was erected by private subscription, promoted by Mr. Howard and his amiable consort. There are also schools for the poor at Gleadleys and Woodhouse.

The parish-register begins in the first year of Elizabeth, and has been well preserved. It appears from it that George Monke esquire and his wife were residing here from 1707 to 1710. Mrs. Monke was a daughter of the first Lord Molesworth, who spent much of the time which he could spare from the affairs of state at his pleasant seat at Edlington near Doncaster. Mrs. Monke is known as an authoress by a small volume of poems published by the father after her decease.

Richmond is one of the old *Membra castri de Sheffield.* The monks of Beauchief had an interest here. Burroughs Trippett of this place was a disclaimer at the visitation of Sir William Dugdale. He was the principal person in the opposition which was made by the inhabitants of Sheffield to the shutting up of Sheffield park gates by Henry Duke of Norfolk.

Woodthorpe near Richmond was the property of Mr. John Woodruffe; after whom it passed into the name of Cheney, and then into the possession of the Parkers, and is now the pleasant seat of Hugh Parker esquire, one of his majesty's justices of the peace, to whom the inhabitants of Sheffield and the whole vicinity are greatly indebted for a judicious, humane and active exercise of his magisterial authority.

Pedigree of Parker of Woodthorpe.

Arms.—Argent, a chevron pean between three mullets sable, on a chief azure three bucks' heads caboshed or.
Crest.—On a wreath, a talbot's head couped argent, ears and tongue gules, gorged with a collar sable charged with three ermine spots.

Rowland Parker of Norton.

John Parker of Woodthorpe, gent.=Mary, sister of William Staniforth of Mosborough, in the parish of Eckington, gent. Died 5 Jan. 1746. Living there 1731. Afterward of Graystones in the parish of Sheffield. Died 15 April 1779, aged 79, and was buried at Norton.

John Parker of Woodthorpe esquire.=---- dau. and heir of	Sarah Parker, wife	Mary Parker, wife	Elizabeth Parker,
Barrister-at-law. Had the arms in the margin granted 10 Nov. 1775. Died 6 Jan. 1794, aged 66, and was buried in the church of Hansworth. Hugh Marshall of Leeds, merchant, by Elizabeth his wife, dau. of Joseph Oates of Leeds, merchant.	of George Woodhead of Sheffield and High-field, merchant. Died without issue.	of the Rev. Rowland Hodgson rector of Rawmarsh.	Ruth Parker, Samuel Parker, all died young.

John Parker, eldest son and heir-apparent. Died 10 May, aged 7 years. Buried at Hansworth.	Hugh Parker=Mary, dau. of of Woodthorpe, esq., eldest surviving son and heir.	Samuel Walker of Masborough near Rotherham, esquire.	George Parker of---- dau. of George Wilsick-house in the parish of Tickhill esq. second surviving son.	Cooke Yarborough of Campsmount in the parish of Campsall, esquire.	Harriet Parker, wife of John Elli-son of Thorne esq.	Maria Parker, wife of Richard Swallow of Atter-cliffe-forge.

John Parker. Samuel Parker. Hugh Parker.

Gleadleys is a considerable hamlet of this parish, of which I have nothing to observe, but that it was for several generations the residence of a family named Fenton, who had good property in this parish.

IV.

The Parish of Treeton.

THE name of this place is written Trectone in the Domesday survey, which is plainly an error of the transcriber, for in the recapitulation of the York-shire manors, it is written conformably with the pre-sent orthography Treeton. The church and village are about five miles east from the town of Sheffield. The parish is surrounded by Sheffield, Tinsley, Rotherham, Whiston, Aston, and Hansworth. Brampton-en-le-Morthen is a township of this parish; and Catcliffe a hamlet. Part of Ulley is in this parish. The river Rother flows by Treeton, and on it is an ancient mill, without doubt that mentioned in the Domesday sur-vey. The village stands in a retired and pleasant situa-tion, no turnpike road passing through it. The inha-bitants are for the most part employed in agriculture.

The population of the township of Treeton in 1801 was 312, in 1811, 338.

Soon after the Conquest the manor of Treeton was part of the fee of Robert earl of Morton, and is thus described in Domesday book. There were two manors before the Conquest, one of two carucates, the other of one. They were held by Morcar and Ulchil. There might be two ploughs, or perhaps there might be two carucates more. At the time of the survey, Ricardus Surdus held one carucate under the earl of Morton, and there were four villains and thirteen bordarii who had four carucates and a half. There was a mill valued at five shillings and two mill seats, a church and pres-byter. There was a pasturable wood of half a leua in length and one quarenten in breadth. The whole manor is one leua in length and one in breadth. In the time of Edward the Confessor it was valued at forty shillings, now at twenty shillings.

Ulchil was one of the co-lords of Brampton and Tinsley, and had many other estates in the same wa-pentake. Morcar had Wales, Ulley, and part of Bramp-ton in this neighbourhood, and much other property, for he was one of the greatest of the Saxon proprie-tors. He seems to have lost all. It is perhaps to him that the inhabitants of this parish owed the erection among them of a Christian temple. This, as we have already observed, is the only church noticed in the Domesday survey in the district to which the present work relates.

The manor of Treeton passed to the Lovetots and Furnivals, under whom it was held by the Horberys and the Bernaks, and it would seem also by the Pierre-points: for in the 9 Edward II. Robert de Pierrepoint obtained a charter of free warren in all his demesne lands within his lordships of North Anston, South Anston, and Treeton in the county of York; and again in the 6 Henry VIII. Sir William Pierrepoint obtained a confirmation of the grant to his ancestor of free warren in these lordships[1].

In the *Nomina Villarum* 9 Edward II., Thomas

de Furnival is returned as sole lord. Sir Christopher Talbot, a younger son of the second earl of Shrewsbury, is described in various charters as being of Treeton. The Duke of Norfolk is now the sole lord.

The church, says Torre, is an ancient rectory which belonged to the patronage of the lords of the manor, and sometimes to the tenants in fee farm the Horberys and Bernaks. It is dedicated to Saint Helen.

CATALOGUE of the RECTORS of TREETON.

Temp. Inst.	Rectores.	Patroni.
	Mr Wil. or Muschamp	
7 Id. Jan. 1238 . .	Dñs Philip de Heselly	Archbishop by lapse.
3 Id. Mar. 1287 . .	Richard de Tydolfside, subd. . . .	Sir John de Horbery and Richard de Bernak knights.
Kal. Jan. 1293 . . .	John de Duneton vel Lymington, subd.	Sir Richard de Bernak.
9 Kal. Oct. 1307 . .	Thomas de Ebroicis, subd.	. . . . idem . . . .
Id. Oct. 1307 . . .	Richard Bernak, cl.	. . . . idem . . . .
3 Id. Aug. 1318 . .	Richard de Celario, acolitus . . .	Archbishop by lapse.
	Richard de Athelingflete	
4 Id. April 1334 . .	William de Wytherdeley, cler. . .	Sir Thomas de Furnival,
11 Oct. 1364 . . .	William Savage, pbr.	William Lord Furnival.
	John de Wyginstone	
7 May 1398 . . .	Roger Darcy, cap.	Sir Thomas Nevil, Lord Furnival.
8 March 1402 . . .	Thomas de Lowther, pbr.	. . . . idem . . . .
30 Jan. 1412 . . .	William Newton, pbr.	John Lord Talbot.
18 April 1425 . . .	Roger Slideman, pbr.	. . . . idem . . . .
7 April 1442 . . .	Thomas Moore	John Lord Talbot.
6 June 1443 . . .	Nicholas Serle, cap.	John Earl of Shrewsbury.
9 Oct. 1444 . . .	Henry Stafford, cap.	. . . . idem . . . .
17 March 1486 . .	Thomas Thorley, cap.	George Earl of Shrewsbury.
25 Mar. 1513 . . .	Mr Wil. Holme, pbr.	. . . . idem . . . .
20 Dec. 1540 . . .	Edward Hatfield	Francis Earl of Shrewsbury.
27 Nov. 1544 . . .	Thomas Stokes	. . . . idem . . . .
20 Dec. 1556 . . .	John Tyas	. . . . idem . . . .
9 Oct. 1581 . . .	John Johnes, M.D.	George Earl of Shrewsbury.
10 Sept. 1600 . .	Osmond Bourne, B.D.	Gilbert Earl of Shrewsbury.
13 June 1642 . . .	Sherland Adams	Sir Edward Leek of Shipley for Thomas Earl of Arundel.
	Christopher Amgill	
	Sherland Adams	
27 Aug. 1664 . . .	Michael Adams	James Moseley of Sheffield gent. and William Adams of London gent.
21 Feb. 1680 . . .	Cuthbert Browne	Henry Duke of Norfolk.
25 Feb. 1692 . . .	Francis Jessop, A.M.	. . . . idem . . . .
16 Nov. 1728 . . .	Samuel Drake, D.D.	Thomas Lord Malton.
	Middlemore Griffith	
	John Carver . . . . . , . .	
1805 . . .	Thomas Raddish	
	George Chandler	

With several names in the above catalogue we have met before. The first that will now claim our notice is that of Sherland Adams, one of the most zealous and active of the clergy who took the side of the king in the contentions of the seventeeth century, and who suffered in consequence of it a long exclusion from this rectory, as also from his other rectory of Eyam in the county of Derby.

The virulence of party spirit scarcely ever appeared with more of its natural deformity than in a pamphlet published in the year 1646 by Nicholas Ardron, one of Mr. Adams's parishioners at Treeton. It is a small palliation of the violence of Ardron, that political hostility was exasperated in him by a personal injury which he supposed he had received from his pastor, who is

charged with having connived at an attack made upon Ardron's house by some soldiers of the earl of Newcastle, when four mares were forcibly taken from him for the king's service.

The spirit of the pamphlet, of which I know of no other copy than that in the British Museum[2], appears in its title. 'The ploughman's vindication, or a confutation of some passages preached in divers sermons by Sherland Adams, sometime minister of Treeton in the county of Yorke. In which sermons he uttered much bitterness of spirit against all those that sided with the parliament; as also cherishing the malignant party, and much animating them to persist in their bloody designs. Herein also is shewed the lawfulnesse of informing against all such incendiaries; and the

---

[1] Dugd. *Baronage.*

[2] No. 285 of the King's Pamphlets : small 4to.

judgements threatned in holy scripture against such as know and do not reveal their wickednesse. Together with xii. quæries whether the said Adams (or any such ceremonious priest) be a minister of God, yea or no?—Published by Nicholas Ardron at the importunate requests of divers of the inhabitants of the foresaid county.'

It may be collected from this mass of abuse, that Adams had been a chaplain of the earl of Newcastle, and had publicly prayed for him and for the king's army in the north; that he had been in person with Colonel Frescheville in an engagement with the parliament forces near Nottingham; that he had caused the house of Lieutenant-colonel Spencer at Attercliffe to be plundered by the king's party, and Spencer himself to be imprisoned by the earl of Newcastle, and afterwards to pay 350*l.* for his release; that his curate read in the church of Treeton, Adams being present, a proclamation from the king, wherein the earl of Essex and lord Fairfax were declared traitors; that being often sent to by the parliament garrison at Rotherham to lend money on the public faith according to his ability, and having refused to lend any, he had been taken and shut up in the castle of Sheffield, where he paid twenty pounds and was then set at liberty; but when the earl of Newcastle was afterwards master of the country he sent to demand his money again of Robert Stacye, to whom it had been paid. These charges against him were sworn to by Ardron before Henry Westby esquire, a justice of the peace, on the 15th of October 1645. It was further alleged against him, that at the beginning of the troubles, when the cavaliers burned the barns and out-houses of Sir Edward Rodes, and there was a general rising of the country to repel them, the curate of the said Adams with many townsmen of Treeton met the rest of the country on Rotherham-moor, Adams being absent; but when next he met the curate he chid him, and said that he went to countenance a company of rebels to his majesty. This article was attested by Robert Tomson the curate in the presence of Henry Westby. Another charge was that Adams exasperated Lieutenant Appleyard against Mr. Gifforth of Ravenfield, telling the said Appleyard, a cavalier, that Gifforth was an active man against them, and was in the parliament army, and that the said Mr. William Gifforth was at Winfield manor when it was taken by the king's party; this was done when the said Mr. Gifforth was chaplain in Colonel Bright's regiment. This article was attested in the presence of Colonel Bright, one of the committee for the west riding of Yorkshire. William Sechfeld and John Rattlife, inhabitants in Treeton and listed soldiers in the parliament army, affirm that they have frequently heard the inhabitants of Treeton complain, that when the country lay under the command of the earl of Newcastle Mr. Adams did preach and pray against the parliament in his parish church. Sworn before Henry Westby.—Further it is charged against him that he is a man given to much trouble and suits of law, as was well known at Eyam in Derbyshire, where he was rector, where they tasted of this his turbulent spirit; that he gave tythe of lead ore to the king against the parliament, delivered a man and musket against them, and sent a fat ox to the earl of Newcastle as a free gift to maintain the war against the parliament; that the first time he preached after

he was imprisoned by the parliament, as already mentioned, he took his text from the 4th chapter of the Epistle to the Galatians, ' *But as then he that was born after the flesh persecuted him that was born after the spirit, even so it is now;*' and that when Mr. Towlar of Sheffield was put out of his living he said that he was a fool, for before he would have lost his, he would have said the crow was white.

These charges are backed by the following certificates.

' The certificat of 15 godly ministers of Yorkshire.

' Whereas Master Adams, parson of Treeton, was by appointment of the ministers at their meeting at Yorke Feb. 5, 1644, ordered to preach a recantation sermon at Yorke minister upon the first Wednesday of March then immediately following, to give satisfaction to the ministers concerning some things he had delivered in his public sermons against the parliament's proceedings, as was then objected against him: yet when it pleased God to give us that sad blow in raising the siege at Pomfret, March the first, being but four days before Mr. Adams was to preach the abovementioned sermon, the said Mr. Adams being puffed up with the unexpected success of his own party, did not only refuse to preach the sermon as he was appointed, and himself had undertaken, but denied he was to give any such satisfaction, only he would give his lordship, Lord Fairfax, a sermon in the minster; upon which he was unanimously thought fit, in the meeting of ministers, *nemine contradicente*, to be removed from the parsonage of Treeton, though before many inclined to continue him upon satisfaction to be given as abovesaid; the truth of all which we could doe no lesse than certifie under our hands.

Elka. Wales.	Hugh Everard.
Edw. Hill.	Tho. Birkbecke.
Rob. Tod.	Tho. Rawson.
Rog. Atley.	John Shaw.
Tho. Calvert.	John Smith.
Matth. Rowland.	Nicholas Heathcoat.
Josiah Witton.	Stephen Charman.
Dan. Clarke.	

' Another certificat from the best affected and religious people, living near the place where the said Mr. Adams lived.

' Wee whose names are here under-written, doe certifie that Master Adams, parson of Treeton, is a man who hath been a great favourer of the bishops, and their innovations: also malignantly affected to the parliament, and a great friend to the cavaliers; not only an opposer but a persecutor of godly men and the power of godlinesse : upon which ground we humbly recommend it to the honourable Commissioners for the army, seriously to consider of what dangerous consequence it will be to put him in to officiate still at Treeton, where he hath publickly vented his malignity upon pretence of Reformation and compliance with the parliament.

Thomas Birkbeck,	
Thomas Rawson,	
Robert Tomson,	Ministers.
John Hoyland,	
Edward Poole,	
Henry Westby,	Captains.
William Blith,	
John Ellice,	Collectors.
William Staniforth,	
John Dale,	
Edward Sanderson,	
James Creswick,	Sequestrators.
John Crooke,	
John Hoyland,	
Nicholas Ardron,	

Thomas Spademan.	Garvase Lee.
Edward Barlow.	Charles Barlow.
William Starkey.	Edward Creswick.
Nicholas Spademan.	Edward Heape.
John Latham.	Nicholas Hicke.
William Spencer.	John Houker.

4 E

William Bell.
Francis Dalle.
Robert Bot.
John Grant.
George Ardron.
Christopher Birks.
Edward Cuts.
John Bate.
John Couldwell.

Francis Barlow.
Thomas Britland.
George Oxspring.
James Ardron.
John Capper.
Robert Owldalle.
Richard Taylor.
William Shaw.
Clement Rosington.

' I can truly certifie that these parties are religiously disposed and well affected,   John Bright of Carbrook.'

' Master Adams his demeanors are not so well known unto me, as the persons that have subscribed this certificat. That the said persons in number 40 are all of them religiously disposed and well affected is known by me
          ' Edward Gill, Sheffield Castle, Aug. 17, 1645.'

' The copy of a certificat from the Committee for the west riding in Yorkshire, July the 10, 1646.
' These are to certifie your Honors that according to the severall orders made by your Honors the 14th of May and the third of June last, we have examined the witnesses here withall certified, and we do withall certifie your Honours that there hath not been any new charges or points of Delinquency brought in against Sherland Adams, clerk, or charged upon him, other than what was formerly charged upon him, and whereof the said Adams had a copy before any proofe made, and which being reducted into five or six interrogatories, are certified together with the former depositions thereupon: and we do certifie that it is no true surmise by the said Mr. Adams that it was denyed unto him to examine on his part any matter according to your Honours former orders, nor did he offer to except against the testimonie of Nich. Ardron and his wife as he hath suggested, and what is deposed by them is now by Richard Gillat produced by himself, deposed to as concerning his usuall prayer before his sermon, wherein he prayed for the good successe of the Earl of Newcastle's army: in which and in sundry other evidences of malignity it hath been made so notoriously known, as that the Assembly of Divines here, and very many well affected people, as also the Committees employed by the parliament in these parts, did conceive him unworthy and unfit for his calling in the ministry; which neverthelesse we humbly submit to your Honours.
          Robert Barwick.
          John Bright.
          John Farror.'

' I do hereby certifie that I was present at the examinations of Richard Gillat and James Gill, witnesses produced on the behalf of Master Sherland Adams.
          Bryan Stapylton.'

When Adams was deprived of his preferment, he retired to his own estate at Woodlathes near Conisborough. His name appears in the list of noblemen and gentlemen who compounded for their estates when the war was over. The sum he paid was 198*l.* But he lived to see the change of the times, and he was reinstated in his livings, which he held however but a short time, dying on the 11th of April 1664. He was buried in the chancel of the church of Treeton, and in the inscription over his grave his loyalty and sufferings are both commemorated.

' Hic jacet Shoreland Adams, ecclesiæ hujus de Treeton una et de Eyam in Com. Derb. Rector : qui ex ambobus rectoriis vi et armis amotus, et alia multa ob solam erga regem C. I. fidelitatem immobilem perpessus ...... tandemque in pristina jura restaurato jam D. G. Rege C. II. e postliminio rediente anno abhinc iv°, in pace Domini placidè occubuit, Apr. die xi. A.D. m dc lxiv.
          Ps. vii. 11. Deo vindice justi.'

In the same church is also a brass plate on which

is commemorated a son of Nicholas Ardron, the leader of the opposition to Mr. Adams.

' Johan. Ardron sen. vir vere pius, integer, probus; maritus amantissimus; pater optimus; amicus fidelissimus; sub duris ischuriæ cruciatibus duos plus minus annos patientissimus, gravissimo omnium luctu fatis concessit, 3tio die Sept. anno ætatis suæ 56. Annoque Domini 1685.'

When Mr. Adams was put out of this rectory it was given to Christopher Amgill, who held it during the whole period of the Interregnum. Calamy was informed that ' he was one of neat parts, and likely to be very useful,' and that ' he died quickly after he was ejected[1].' The laborious and pious Oliver Heywood in his manuscript diaries states that he died beyond sea.

Michael Adams the son and successor of Sherland Adams has a monument in the chapel of Brassington in the county of Derby, on which it is said that ' forte hinc itinerant. dum rigor foris sæviebat hiemalis, sævior arripuit intus febris calor inextinguibilis et igneo (ad instar Elijæ) vehiculo ad sedes Dñi evexit. Ob. 1680*z.*'

Dr. Samuel Drake was the grandson of the rector of Hansworth of the same name and rank. His father was vicar of Pontefract, and Francis Drake of York the author of the *Eboracum* was his brother. Like all the Drakes he was a man of learning, and like many of them an author. He was a fellow of Saint John's College Cambridge, B.A. 1707, M.A. 1711, B.D. 1718, D.D. 1724. In 1719 he published a *Concio ad clerum* which engaged him in a controversy with Wagstaff the nonjuring clergyman. In 1724 he published another *Concio* on the *Ara ignoto Deo sacra.* He was editor of ' *Balthazaris Castilionis Comitis Libri* iv. *de curiali sive aulico* &c.,' and in 1730 published a beautiful edition of Archbishop Parker's ' *De antiquitate Britannicæ ecclesiæ,* &c.' In 1733 Dr. Drake had a dispensation to hold the vicarage of Holme in Spaldingmore, and dying on the 5th of March 1753 was buried in the church of Treeton. For these particulars I must own myself principally indebted to that rich storehouse of the biography of literary men, the ' Literary Anecdotes of the xviiith century,' a work which contains more original information on the history of English literature than has been brought together since the publication of the *Athenæ Oxonienses.*

The Church.

The church of Treeton, as it is more ancient than that of Hansworth, so had it more to tempt and to gratify antiquarian curiosity. But it seems to have been passed over by the collectors of Yorkshire church notes. None such at least have come under my observation.

On the wood-work of the rector's pew is still to be seen a memorial of one of the earlier pastors of this parish. ' Orate pro anima Magistri Willielmi Holme clerici quondam rectoris ecclesiæ.' This Holme died about 1540. On the floor near this pew is a monumental stone on which is traced the figure of a man, with an inscription, on the verge of which in 1802, when these imperfect church notes were taken, little more was recoverable beside the usual formula of Orate pro anima ..... cujus animæ propicietur Deus, and

---

[1] *Account, &c.* p. 813.

[2] *Lysons's Mag. Brit.* Derbyshire, p. 62.

the date 1486. This date coincides with the time of the death of Henry Stafford a rector of this church; but we should have better reason for ascribing the monument to him, had the armorial insignia which the stone also bears any resemblance to those of the great family of Stafford. The device on one shield appeared to be a fess, and on the other frettée.

In this church is also the effigy of a knight in armour, called by the common people Earl Gilbert; but if it represent any member of the house of Talbot, it is probably Sir Christopher, who fell at Northampton. But still more probably it represents one of the Horberys or Bernaks, who held this manor under the Furnivals.

In the chancel is a stone with arms and effigies covering the remains of William Routh esquire, 1620. He was of Waleswood in this neighbourhood, of a family which appeared at the visitations. His son Sir John Routh was knighted by King Charles I., and his daughter was married into the family of Copley of Sprodborough. The arms on this monument are ROUTH, on a bend cotised .... three mullets .... quartering EYRE .... on a chevron .... three quaterfoils .... impaling .... frettée and a label ....

On another stone in this chancel are the arms of BRADSHAW .... two bends between two martlets .... and the following inscription:

' Hic jacet
EDWARDUS BRADSHAW armiger,
in occiduo cinere
expectans eum
cui nomen est oriens.
Qui XXII. die Decemb.
M.DC.LXV.
occubuit.'

A common opinion at Treeton is, that this stone covers the remains of President John Bradshaw, who is supposed to have retired to this obscure village at the suggestion of William Walker, his accomplice in that deed of guilt and blood, who had found a secure asylum in the neighbouring village of Darnall. Village tradition, fruitful in expedients, assigns as the reason for the name of Edward and not John appearing on the stone, that the true name was suppressed to save the reliques of so obnoxious a man from posthumous indignities. But there was a family of the name of Bradshaw possessing considerable property at Brampton in this parish, of whom there are other memorials in the church of Treeton, to whom doubtless this Edward Bradshaw belonged. Less problematical is it that the person who wrote the inscription had his eye on a passage in Dr. Donne's epitaph. ' Hic licet in occiduo cinere aspicit eum cujus nomen est oriens,' and that there is reference in both to the Vulgate translation of Zech. vi. 12.

The south quire, commonly called the Brampton quire, is paved with monumental stones placed over the remains of the three families of Vescy, Bradshaw, and Lord, who had houses at Brampton, which have long been deserted by their owners. The Vescys were of right ancient extraction, having flourished at this place and at Tickhill for ten or fifteen generations. The persons of this family commemorated here are William Vescy of Brampton gentleman 1605. Elizabeth his wife (daughter of Richard Stevenson of Ounston gentleman) mother of William, Michael, Alexander, and Francis Vescy 1613. Margaret wife of William Vescy of Brampton gentleman, daughter of Robert Buntinge of Rotherham merchant; who had issue four sons, John, Robert, William, and Matthew, and died in 1618.— John the son of William Vescy 1639.—Alice his widow 1658.—Elizabeth the daughter of John Vescy of Brampton gentleman, wife to Francis Bradshaw of Brampton esquire, and in second nuptials to John Bolle esquire, 1676.—Elizabeth the only daughter of Francis Bradshaw of Bradshaw in the county of Derby esquire.—Francis Bradshaw of Brampton esquire in 1659.—John his son who died an infant 1656.— Francis Bradshaw of Brampton esquire 1677.—Mary daughter of John Bolle of Brampton esquire 1673.— Margaret daughter of John Bradshaw esquire 1682. The heiress of this family of Bradshaw married Joshua Galliard of Edmonton esquire.

The sepulchral memorials of the family of Lord are scarcely less numerous. Joan wife of George Lord of Brampton.—Margaret, wife of Thomas Lord, eldest daughter of Ralph Hatfield of Laughton-en-le-Morthen gentleman, 1655.—Thomas Lord 1660.—George Lord his nephew and heir 1699.—William Lord of Worksop attorney, fourth son of George Lord of Brampton gentleman, 1703.—Samuel, Joseph, Anne, Benjamin, Nathaniel, Nicholas, and Henry, children of George Lord who died in their infancy.—George Lord of Rotherham apothecary, second son, 1707. William Alwood Lord esquire of Tupton near Chesterfield is the representative of this family.

In the church of Treeton are also memorials of several of the family of the late Reverend Creed Turner, and of the Pointons of Ulley, of whom Mr. Robert Pointon is said to have attained the age of 100 years, and to have died in 1731.

The old parish-register was burnt in an accidental fire which consumed the house at which it was kept about eighty years ago. The existing register begins about 1680.

Ulley and Brampton were manors distinct from Treeton at the time of the Domesday survey; and also in the 9 Edward II. when the former belonged to the prior of Worksop, and the latter was held jointly by Edmund Wasteneye and James Lyvet. I do not know that they have ever been regarded as falling within the limits of Hallamshire.

V.

The Parish of Whiston.

THE church and village of Whiston are at the distance of seven miles from Sheffield on the south-east. The parish consists of 2448 acres, nearly the whole being in cultivation. The population in 1796 was 612 persons, nearly all agriculturists. The parish is surrounded by Rotherham, Treeton, Aston, and Wickersley. The roads from Sheffield to Tickhill and from Rotherham to Mansfield, which was formerly one of the great highways to the north of England, intersect each other near the village of Whiston.

The Domesday survey of this manor has been already given.

'This town,' says Torre, 'was held by Thomas de Furnival by the fourth part of a knight's fee, of Robert Lutterel, who held it of the king in capite, and paid two shillings to the wapentake. Also William de Councell held in the same town one fee of Thomas de Furnival.

In the 9 Edward II. Thomas de Furnival was returned lord; and the manor of Whiston still belongs to his representative the Duke of Norfolk.

The church is an ancient rectory, having belonged to the Lovetots, and descended from them to the Furnivals, Talbots, and Howards, lords of Sheffield:— 'and although,' says Torre in his collections for this place, ' it has been always a rectory, yet there was sometimes a vicar appointed under the rector, who had for his vicarage the whole church itself with its appurtenances, rendering to the rector ten marks of silver *per annum*, the vicar bearing all the burdens of the church due and accustomed.' On these terms one Robert de Faxterd was instituted to the vicarage in the 13th century.

A CATALOGUE of the RECTORS of WHISTON.

Temp. Instit.	Rectores.	Patroni.
5 Kal. Jul. 1237 . .	Dñs Robertus de Doncaster, cap. . .	Dña Matilda de Lovetot.
14 Kal. Maii 1269 .	Mr Peter de Newark	Sir Thomas de Furnival, knt.
15 Kal. Jan. 1286 . .	Dñs John de Cressel	. . . . idem . . . .
Kal. Jan. 1293 . .	John de Ripon, subd.	. . . . idem . . . .
5 Non. Jul. 1316 . .	John de Bellhouse, acolitus . .	. . . . idem . . . .
Non. Maii 1318 . .	William de Beausey	. . . . idem . . . .
23 Oct. 1349 . . .	John de Ekynton, cap.	Attornat. Dñi Thomæ Furnival.
	John Jurdan, pbr.	. . . .
13 July 1370 . . .	John Dayvil, pbr.	Dña Joan Furnival.
12 May 1379 . . .	Richard Barton, pbr.	eadem.
17 July 1383 . . .	John Wokeedhode, pbr. . . .	eadem.
7 June 1393 . .	Robert de Burton, cap.	eadem.
	Robert de Rossedale	. . . .
29 July 1400 . . .	Mr Robert de Kagenhall, L.B. .	Thomas Nevil Lord Furnival.
2 Sept. 1430 . . .	Dñs Roger Henmer, pbr. . . .	John Talbot Lord Furnival.
26 Aug. 1448 . . .	Mr William Maltester, cl. . . .	John Earl of Shrewsbury.
4 Nov. 1449 . . .	Thomas Moore, decr. b. . . .	. . . . idem . . . .
11 Nov. 1457 . . .	Dñs Henry Stafford, cap. . . .	. . . . idem . . . .
28 April 1487 . . .	Peter Mundevil, cap.	George Earl of Shrewsbury.
23 Jan. 1489 . . .	Thomas Warde, cl.	. . . . idem . . . .
6 July 1528 . . .	William Holme, A.M.	. . . . idem . . . .
8 Nov. 1540 . . .	Dñs Thomas Portington, cl. . . .	Francis Earl of Shrewsbury.
19 April 1550 . . .	Anthony Blake, S.T.B. . . .	. . . . idem . . . .
6 June 1554 . . .	John Atkyn	. . . . idem . . . .
6 Sept. 1570 . . .	Richard Bright, cl.	George Earl of Shrewsbury.
18 Mar. 1578 . . .	Robert Holland	. . . . idem . . . .
9 Oct. 1597 . . .	Osmond Bourne, S.T.B. . . .	Gilbert Earl of Shrewsbury.
	Thomas Rawson	
	— Thelwell	
	Thomas Rawson. Died 1681 . .	
27 Dec. 1681 . . .	William Wagstaff	The King.
	Obadiah Browne. Died 1738.	
	William Steer, junior.	
	John Griffith, D.D. Died.	
	Middlemore Griffith. Died.	
	John Carver. Died 1807.	
1807 . . .	Richard Lacey.	

Few catalogues of incumbents begin earlier than this; and in few rectories has there been a more rapid succession;—thirty-seven in 570 years. Stafford held Treeton along with this living. Holme had at the same time Treeton and Ecclesfield. But this was nothing compared with his successor Anthony Blake B.D. This person held along with Whiston, the vicarage of Doncaster, the livings of Rugby in Warwickshire and Barnet in Middlesex, and was moreover vicar of Saint Dunstan's in the west. The fact is noticed by Strype in his Life of Archbishop Parker, where however the name of the clergyman is written Blage. Atkyns and Holland held Whiston along with the vicarage of Sheffield, and the names of later incumbents are to be found in the lists already given in this work.

The church is a small and low building, containing a few monumental memorials of the names of Brown, Stringer, Bosville, Staniforth, Hebden, Briggs, and Carver. The early registers are lost. That which remains begins in 1653.

Here is a school with a small endowment.

Gilthwaite is a hamlet partly in this parish and partly in that of Rotherham. Here was a mineral spring discovered in 1664 by Mr. George Westby of this place, who made a large bath and built a house over it[1]. The waters had their reputation; but after the death of Mr. Westby, and of Dr. Yarburgh of Newark, who sent many patients to them, they sunk into a state of almost utter neglect.

The family of Stringer was formerly of good account in this parish; descended of Thomas Stringer one of the agents of the Shrewsbury family, several of whose letters are preserved among the Talbot papers. The eldest line removed to Sharlston, and ended in a female heiress married to Thomas earl of Westmorland.

[1] Short's *History of Mineral Waters, &c.* p. 269.

ADDENDA ET CORRIGENDA.

P. 8. c. 1. l. 12. *for* Willughby *read* Willoughby.
P. 9. c. 2. l. 15. The church of Rotherham seems to have better pretensions to be the mother-church of the higher parts of the vale of Don than either of those which are here mentioned. Rotherham, rising like Doncaster out of a station on one of the Roman high-ways, was probably like it a place of considerable comparative consequence before the Conquest. It had a church in the Saxon times. One at least is noticed in Domesday-book : ' *Presbyter et ecclesia.*'
P. 10. c. 2. l. 11. *for* Massam *read* Masham.
———— 12. *for* Massamshire *read* Mashamshire.
P. 11. note 2. *for* Carey *read* Cary.
P. 13. c. 2. last line. In 1818 there were celebrated 662 marriages at the parish-church of Sheffield. There were 2061 baptisms, and 1398 burials, at the three churches and the two rural chapels.
P. 15. c. 1. l. 4. *for* Merseæ *read* Mersee.
P. 26. In the pedigree continue the line from William to Maud.
P. 52. c. 1. l. 13 from bottom, *for* Kinston *read* Kingston.
P. 63. c. 2. l. 10. This was written and printed before the appearance of Mr. Chalmers' work.
P. 71. c. 1. l. 10 from bottom, et al. *for* Beale *read* Beal.
P. 89. c. 2. l 16 from bottom. Supply the blank with ' lot and cope.' They are terms in mining.
P. 94. c. 2. The two letters subscribed *W*. Cavendysshe are from the second son of Elizabeth Countess Dowager of Shrewsbury, Lord Cavendish, and afterwards earl of Devonshire.—His eldest son and heir-apparent, who died in his life-time, had the name of Gilbert, after Gilbert earl of Shrewsbury. This Gilbert lord Cavendish was always supposed to be the author of the ' *Horæ Subsecivæ*: Observations and Discourses,' on the authority of Wood, A. O. ii. 625, till lately that it has been attributed to another noble lord, to whom the initials G. C. are equally appropriate, and who has on the strength of his claim to this volume been admitted into the list of noble authors. The main stress of the objection to Gilbert Cavendish's claim to this work appears to be that ' he died too young to have had the experience which it seems to contain.' See ' *Memoire of the Peers of England*,' p. 385. But this objection is entirely obviated by the testimony of John Hagthorpe, his contemporary, who in his ' *Divine Meditations and Elegies*,' 1622, has an elegiac poem on his death.

———— Let me instance take,
   That Royall hope, whom nature strove to make
The very modell of perfection:
   How soone Fate cut him off! And now is gone
(O word scarce to be named with fewer teares)
   Candishe, the noble, vertuous ; tho' in yeares
Younger than Adon, yet like Nestor wise ;
   Though greene in blooming youth, ripe in advice ;
Whom nature as a cabinet did frame,
   Therin to stow all things that mortals name
Rich, faire, or good, which death by Fate's decree
   Hath broken up, and now quite rob'd we be
Of treasure that enricht this barren time
   And reduct plenty.'—p. 90.

P. 103. c. 1. l. 19 from bottom, *dele* had.
P. 106. note. The same friend to whom I am indebted for a sight of Hagthorpe's most rare volume, has pointed out a passage in Oldys' ' *Dissertation on Pamphlets*,'—' *Phœnix Britannica*,' p. 556, in which this collection of tracts is said to have been made by ' Tomlinson the bookseller.' See also *Lit. Anec.* iv. 102. Tomlinson was an easy blunder for Thomason.

P. 109. c. 1. last line of the note, *for* orignal *read* original.
P. 118. c. 2. l. 5. *for* Henry *read* Richard.
P. 129. c. 1. l. 7 from bottom. The Sheffield canal is now finished ; and the first barge entered the bason on the 22d of February 1819, in the presence of a vast concourse of spectators.
P. 133. c. 1. l. 29 from bottom, *for* Sharpe *read* Sharp.
P. 137. c. 2. The following gentlemen are the present twelve capital burgesses of the town and parish of Sheffield:

Samuel Staniforth.	Samuel Younge.
Gamaliel Milner.	Robert Turner.
John Greaves.	William Wilson.
Robert Wainwright, M.D.	Thomas Watson.
Francis Fenton.	Thomas Newbould.
William Younge, M.D.	Henry L. Toll.

P. 139. c. 2. l. 9. The calling the parish-church of Sheffield the church of the Holy Trinity, probably first began at the Reformation. ' In the reign of King Henry the Eighth,' says Fuller, ' it was enjoined that all churches dedicated to St. Thomas Becket, should be new named, and consigned over to some real saint. Now whilest country people sate in consultation, what new saint such churches should assume, being divided in their opinions, to whome the same should be dedicated, an old man gave this advice, Even dedicate it to the Holy Trinity, which will last and continue, when all other saints may chance to be taken away.' *Church History*, book ix. p. 211. Something like this may have happened at Sheffield when the name of Saint Peter was thought to savour too strongly of the old profession.
P. 141. c. 2. l. 44. The author is sorry to observe that there is an error in these numerals which he has it not now in his power to correct.
P. 158. c. 2. l. 14 from bottom, *for* Cotterell *read* Cotterill.
P. 165. c. 1. l. 5. The ministers by whom Mr. Jollie was ordained were of that class of dissenters called Presbyterian : and the ordination was conducted in the method practised by the Presbyterians, and not according to the method of the Independents. Mr. Timothy Jollie the newly ordained pastor also belonged to the Presbyterian not the Independent denomination. Mr. Oliver Heywood in his private account of the ordination, in which he himself took a part, makes this remark upon it. ' There was more than ordinary mercy in this solemnity and all the transactions : 1. that this church which was always accounted Independent, would admit of a pastor ordained by presbyters; yes, Mr. Durant immediately before that was of another persuasion. I look on this as an olive-branch of peace amongst God's people, &c.'—Those non-conformists in the neighbourhood who were Presbyterians naturally placed themselves under the ministry of the Presbyterian minister Mr. Jollie ; and hence arose the dissentions of the year 1715.
P. 165. c. 2. l. 23. *for* 1665 *read* 1685.
P. 166. c. 1. l. 27. *for* paneygric *read* panegyric.
P. 168. c. 2. note, 5 lines from bottom, *for* even *read* ever.
P. 171. For the information in this page the author is principally indebted to Mr. George Bennet.
P. 180. c. 1. Most if not all the lands settled on the Hospital had been part of the estate of the church ; given on the principle *Bona ecclesiæ sunt bona pauperum.*
P. 205. *for* 1664 *read* 1646 in baptism of Stephen Bright.
P. 231. Pedigree. *Dele* ═ between Robert and John Clay ; and add ═ between George Greaves and Anna-Maria Rooke.
P. 234. c. 2. last line, *for* Staniforth *read* Stainforth.
P. 259. c. 1. line 19 from bottom, *for* Denicourt *read* Deincourt.
P. 268. c. 1. l. 31. *for* sheeep *read* sheep.

INDEX.

THE END.

LONDON:
PRINTED BY RICHARD AND ARTHUR TAYLOR,
1819.

ALERE FLAMMAM.